The Cosmic Informer
An Astrological Guide
to Self-Discovery

The Cosmic Informer
An Astrological Guide to Self-Discovery

by Robert Pelletier
and Leonard Cataldo

Little, Brown and Company • Boston • Toronto

FIRST EDITION

Library of Congress Cataloging in Publication Data

Pelletier, Robert, 1927-
    The cosmic informer.

    1. Astrology.   I. Cataldo, Leonard.   II. Title.
BF1708.1.P42   1984   133.5   83-22247
ISBN 0-316-13198-9

BP
Published simultaneously in Canada
by Little, Brown & Company (Canada) Limited

PRINTED IN THE UNITED STATES OF AMERICA

To my brothers, George and Ray Pelletier,
for the times we shared

To my wife Alice and my daughter Susan
without whose patience and understanding
this book would never have been completed

Contents

The Cosmic Informer
*An Astrological Guide
to Self-Discovery*

CHAPTER **1** **Who Am I?**

The Big Question If you are somebody who wants to know more about yourself; if your love life or marriage could do with some improvements; if you feel lonely and spiritually unfulfilled but don't really know how to change things; if you have a job that is boring and unsatisfying but you are not sure where your potentials lie; if you feel that deep down there is a more capable *you* whose talents and resources have yet to be tapped, then read on. This book can show you the way.

How? Because this book contains the means to answering perhaps the most perplexing question facing each member of the human race since the beginning: *Who am I?*

The question is universal. Each of us has asked it of ourselves. We seek self-knowledge, and yet, as the ancient philosophers have said, self-knowledge is the most difficult to attain.

We are the most difficult people to get to know, and many of us go through life full of defenses and fears. Sometimes we create public images that we are sure are appealing, charming and winning, but sooner or later the mask will fall off and the true self will come through. Whatever the source of our difficulty, we are talking about the lack of self-knowledge. Because of it our potential is limited. The big question, "Who am I?," goes unanswered, yet that answer could make all the difference in the world, for with self-knowledge comes wisdom to live by, as Aristotle said.

What this book will do is help you find the answer to that big question, and find it easily so that you can learn to be true to yourself.

The answer lies in astrology, a science nearly as old as the question "Who am I?," a science that has provided answers to that question for thousands of years. Astrology, unlike the modern sciences of physics, chemistry and astronomy, puts the individual at the center of the universe. It is a science based on the belief that each person's makeup — his or her character — is determined at the moment of birth, and that from an astrological analysis of one's natal or birth chart, it is possible to determine with great accuracy one's purpose in life: one's talents, limitations, assets, shortcomings, responsibilities — in short, the *self.*

Each of us is unique. Even if you are an identical twin, you are different from your sibling inside and out. Nature never duplicates itself exactly. Those fundamental differences can be determined, since each natal chart is, in effect, a map of the individual's personality. Until now the knowledge and ability to draw up such a chart has been limited to professional astrologers and scholars. This book is going to help change that because it will teach you how to draw your own astrological chart or, in fact, one for anybody else whose birthdate falls between January 1, 1920 and December 31, 1985.* In clear, easy language, this book will demonstrate how to decipher the meaning of various configurations of the heavenly bodies that appear in the charts and how to

---

* A chart for any other date can be calculated with use of additional Ephemerides.

apply that knowledge to your own experience. With that knowledge you can begin to fulfill your potential to grow and to avoid conflicts that come from incomplete self-awareness. Within minutes you will be able to draw up your own map and determine how to avoid wasting time in pursuit of uncongenial tasks and meaningless jobs, how to determine the best course of action to take during crises, how to improve relationships with friends and family, and what to do about improving your love life. An astrological evaluation can make all the difference in the world — for yourself or for anyone you know (your children, mate, boss, a political candidate, etc.).

Take, for instance, John and Alice — two real people. From all appearances they are the perfect married couple: married for fourteen years, two beautiful children, a big home in an affluent Boston suburb, summer home in Maine, and both with good, secure positions. To all those who know them they live ideal lives.

Beneath the public exterior John and Alice are two miserable, discontented people. Their inner lives barely touch one another's. They never entertain or attend any social functions. They inhabit the same house, but that's about all. Their marriage continues like a bad habit, with each afraid of divorce and both coping with their own private frustrations, guilt and resentment. There is hardly ever a word about the problem or where they may have gone wrong.

John is a Libra with a Gemini Signature; Alice is a Cancer with a Taurus Signature. John's great need for social activities and conversation is in direct conflict with her desires to stay at home with her family and no desires for any conversations in general. The result is almost a perpetual conflict — anger and resentment continuously for both of them.

It's an old story because there are millions of Johns and Alices in the world, millions of couples made up of two personalities on a collision course. Identities that on the surface seem so well suited are, deep down, incompatible. The sad part is that the basic differences are discovered after too long a time to save the relationship.

What could have saved many of the marriages, or prevented them from taking place, would have been some clear mutual understanding at the beginning of the relationship. Had John and/or Alice drawn a chart on the other or gone to a professional astrologer, they would have recognized the conflicting aspects of their wills and egos along with the conflicting natures from other configurations. John's chart would have revealed his great need for social activities in every sense, while Alice's chart would have shown her to be the quiet, reserved homebody. John would also have learned that regardless of his ability to communicate with reason and clarity it would be worthless against Alice's stubbornness, arising from her "T" Cross and Taurus Signature as well as the malefic Aspect between Mercury and Mars, which all suggest that she is completely intolerant of others' views, is very argumentative, and lacks tact and diplomacy: a complete opposite of John's personality. Another malefic Aspect in Alice's chart between Mars and Uranus would have revealed that she had a revolutionary spirit that gets her uptight at the slightest hurt or provocation and she becomes very argumentative and may even delight in it, while John deeply resents any sort of hostility, verbal or otherwise, though he also can be very vindictive and argumentative when provoked, because of the malefic Aspect between his Sun and Mars.

Alice's refusal to compromise to any extent, along with John's constant verbal attempts, only results in deeper resentment and conflicts. There appears to be no solution for their personal problem. Life for them is one continuous conflict. Had these conditions been known at the beginning, they both would have realized that there would inevitably be serious crises that would most assuredly need to be resolved. Had all the facts been known, there would have been some strong self-sacrifice for both of them. Then again, with the facts known they might have decided against marriage and just remained good friends.

Whatever the course of action had been, had John and Alice begun with an astrological investigation of each other, they would most definitely have avoided all the years of heartache and suffering, let alone the loss of happiness and contentment in their individual ways of life.

How Astrology Can Help

Professional astrologers counsel people on nearly all personal and professional matters. As the above example indicates, one prime concern of astrologers is helping people with problems in love and marriage. You may not be a John or Alice, but there is a good chance that your love life could benefit from astrological analysis.

If, for instance, you are not yet married but are entertaining the prospect with a lover, it might be a good idea to have your and your intended mate's natal charts checked to make absolutely certain that you are fundamentally compatible. If you discover you are not, then, at least, your sources of conflict will be identified so that you can work on them for the sake of making the relationship viable.

Suppose you are happily married. An astrological analysis of your and your spouse's charts could help determine the best time to have children whom you will understand and with whom you will be well integrated. Say, for instance, you are a Libra and your spouse is a Gemini — two signs that are fundamentally quite compatible. If you could possibly conceive a child who would be born a Leo — a sign compatible with both Gemini and Libra — you would increase the chances of having greater family harmony. This is not to say you can have a tailor-made child, nor are we suggesting there would be no parent-child conflicts over the years, but a Leo born of a Gemini and a Libra is a child who would be basically in harmony with his or her mother and father.

Love and marriage are not the only areas where astrology can help. A simple astrological chart may help you get out of an occupational rut. Charts will not spell out suggestions that you should be a secretary instead of a real estate agent or a plumber instead of a teacher or a doctor instead of a lawyer. Charts are not that specific. They characterize, and they tell you about the makeup of your temperament and character. From the charts you can gain insight into your needs and behavior, and they will suggest where your talents lie. If, for example, you are a Leo — one of the "Fire" signs — you have fundamental desires to create and lead. You will probably become very bored and frustrated if you have a job that is predictable or repetitious, such as an assembly-line worker or an accountant. A well-done chart may encourage you to take the chance to hop off an occupational treadmill once you are convinced that your basic abilities could be put to better use in a different job.

In simple day-to-day living, astrological self-analysis can be of tremendous help in avoiding depression, particularly if you have difficulty making decisions. You may, for instance, be a person of great drive and enthusiasm, but you continue to fail in projects you take on. It could be that there are less-than-favorable Aspects from Saturn in your natal chart — a fact that will account for a lack of orderliness and realistic expectations. On the other hand, if you had a grouping of three or four planets in your sign of Pisces, that could indicate you are an ambitious person, but lack the emotional stability to face success. You could be someone whose drive to achieve is countered by a low self-image. "I did not go after it because I would not have liked it anyway" may be the way you habitually rationalize your fear of success. Knowing clearly that these are your traits may in the future encourage you to avoid copping out.

Charts can help you understand other people better, too. Suppose you meet an individual who comes across as standoffish or superior. It could be that that person's chart shows no Aspects to the planet Mercury — the planet of communication. Such a configuration indicates an individual who is untalkative because he or she lacks the ability to communicate, perhaps out of not knowing what to say or how to say it. What you perceive as conceit might actually be a lack of ease with people. With some help, that person may overcome the problem of communication.

The possibilities are endless when it comes to the benefits of astrological analysis. Everybody can benefit in some way from knowing how to do one's own chart and charts of others.

It should be made very clear from the start that whatever the charts indicate, whatever is in the planets, does not destine us to failure or happiness. We all still have free will and may choose to live our lives contrary to the map of the stars. An old dictum in astrology is "the stars impel, they do not compel." This is another way of saying we have the choice to do as we will, and that if we know our deficiencies we may choose to correct them. If we know what our strengths are, we may try to maximize them, or decide otherwise, and the decision is still ours. In any case, it is still better to know ourselves than not.

How to Use This Book

This is a book about doing your own chart, or somebody else's. It is not a general text on the science of astrology or its history. Nor will we bombard you with extraneous information that will do little more than confuse and bore you. What we will do is give you just enough of what you need to know in order to draw astrological charts and to read them.

There are two kinds of astrological charts; for lack of better names, we will call one a simple solar chart and the other a detailed solar chart. The simple solar chart is just what its name implies — a birth chart that is very simple to do, taking only a matter of minutes. Because it is so simple, its astrological results are rather fundamental and give a simple personality portrait of the individual in question. These are the kinds of charts some people do for amusement.

The detailed solar chart goes beyond the simple chart, obviously. It involves additional material and, consequently, its astrological results are more extensive and refined.

In this book we will show you how to do both. We will begin in the next chapter with a demonstration of how to draw a simple solar chart. For those of you who wish to go beyond that, who wish to learn how to do the more refined astrological profiles, and who, in fact, wish to become astrologers in your own right, we will show you exactly how to draw the more detailed solar chart. In simple, nontechnical terms we will explain all the essential concepts involved — Elements, Qualities, Signatures, Planetary Aspects, etc.

Let's begin by putting together a simple solar chart as outlined in chapter 2.

The Simple Chart

To set up a simple chart for a quick analysis, all you need to know is the date of birth of the person whose chart you wish to do. Once you have that information, there are just three simple steps to follow:

1. Look up the date of birth in the Ephemeris in Appendix X.
2. Record the locations of the individual planets in the signs for the date of birth, using a form similar to Figure 2 (page 10).
3. Turn to Appendix I, Planets in Signs, for the astrological interpretation of the planets' positions in the signs.

The result of this procedure is a generalized profile of the individual's chart, a sketch of the basic personality traits of that person.

Here's a sample to show you exactly how it is done. Our subject is Jane Doe, who was born on April 6, 1924.

Step 1 First, look up April 6, 1924 in the Ephemeris in Appendix X (for convenience, we have reproduced the Ephemeris for that month and year in Figure 1). An Ephemeris is a set of tables giving the location of the Sun, Moon and planets by degrees, minutes and seconds in the signs of the Zodiac for any particular date. As we will explain in greater detail later, the degrees, minutes and seconds have to do with the locations of the Sun, Moon and planets within a particular zodiacal sign. It is an indispensable tool for the astrologer, for it gives the important factors required to set up anyone's birth chart. You will notice twelve columns of figures. The first is the month and "day," under which are listed as many as thirty-one days in the month. The next column is "sidereal time," which is a method of reckoning time based upon the Sun's movement in the sky in relation to its high point in the year. This column is not important in doing a simple chart.

The remaining ten columns are important since they give the locations of the Sun, Moon and planets in degrees of arc in the Zodiac. Although the Sun is a star and the Moon a satellite of the Earth, for the sake of convenience and simplicity we refer to all bodies in our solar system as planets.

Let's look at the Sun column. It's astrological symbol, ☉, is given at the top of the column, as are the glyphs for the other planets. If we look across from April 6, we will see that the Sun on that date in 1924 was in the sixteenth degree. In our simple chart, however, we are not interested in anything other than the sign it was in on that day. Once we locate the column for the Sun on the line across from the date in question, we simply glance above the Sun's position to find the symbol for the sign occupied by the Sun (see Figure 1 and the arrow pointing to the symbol for Aries in the Sun's column).

Moving to the right, the next column is for the Moon. On the date in question the Moon's sign position was in Taurus and its symbol, ♉, is on the line for the 6th of April. Continuing to the right for Mercury (☿) we find the sym-

Figure 1. Sample Ephemeris

DAY	TIME (h m s)	SUN ☉ (° ′ ″)	MOON ☽ (° ′)	MERCURY ☿ (°)	VENUS ♀ (°)	MARS ♂ (°)	JUPITER ♃ (°)	SATURN ♄ (°)	URANUS ♅ (°)	NEPTUNE ♆ (°)	PLUTO ♇ (°)
A 1	12 36 18	10♈59 37	2♓35	21♈	25♉	16♑	20♐	0♏R	19♓	18♌R	10♋
P 2	12 40 14	11 58 49	15 24	23	26	16	20	0	19	18	10
R 3	12 44 11	12 57 58	28 2	25	28	17	20	0	19	18	10
I 4	12 48 7	13 57 5	10♈30	27	29	18	20	0	19	18	10
L 5	12 52 4	14 56 10	22 48	29	0♊	18	20	0	19	18	10
6	12 56 1	15 55 13	4♉57	1♉	1	19	20 R	0	19	18	10
7	12 59 57	16 54 14	16 58	2	2	19	20	0	19	18	10
8	13 3 54	17 53 13	28 54	4	3	20	20	0	19	18	10
9	13 7 50	18 52 10	10♊46	6	4	21	20	0	19	18	10
10	13 11 47	19 51 4	22 37	7	5	21	20	0	19	18	10
11	13 15 43	20 49 56	4♋32	9	6	22	20	0	19	18	10
12	13 19 40	21 48 46	16 35	10	7	22	20	0	19	18	10
13	13 23 36	22 47 34	28 50	12	8	23	20	0	19	18	10
14	13 27 33	23 46 20	11♌23	13	9	24	20	29♎	20	18	10
15	13 31 30	24 45 3	24 18	14	10	24	20	29	20	18	10
16	13 35 26	25 43 44	7♍39	15	11	25	20	29	20	18	10
17	13 39 23	26 42 23	21 27	16	12	25	20	29	20	18	10
18	13 43 19	27 40 59	5♎44	17	13	26	20	29	20	18	10
19	13 47 16	28 39 34	20 25	18	14	27	20	29	20	18	10
20	13 51 12	29 38 6	5♏23	19	15	27	20	29	20	18	10
21	13 55 9	0♉36 37	20 30	20	16	28	20	29	20	18	10
22	13 59 5	1 35 6	5♐36	20	17	28	20	29	20	18	10
23	14 3 2	2 33 33	20 30	21	18	29	19	29	20	18	10
24	14 6 59	3 31 59	5♑6	21	19	0♒	19	29	20	18	10
25	14 10 55	4 30 23	19 19	21	20	0	19	29	20	18	10
26	14 14 52	5 28 46	3♒8	21	21	1	19	29	20	18	10
27	14 18 48	6 27 7	16 34	21 R	22	1	19	28	20	18	10
28	14 22 45	7 25 26	29 39	21	23	2	19	28	20	18 D	10
29	14 26 41	8 23 44	12♓27	21	24	3	19	28	20	18	10
30	14 30 38	9 22 0	25 0	21	25	3	19	28	20	18	10

THE SUN ENTERED THE SIGN OF TAURUS AT 8:59 A.M. ON SUN-
DAY, APRIL 20TH.

Aries	Taurus	Gemini	Cancer	Leo	Virgo	Libra	Scorpio	Sagittarius	Capricorn	Aquarius	Pisces
♈	♉	♊	♋	♌	♍	♎	♏	♐	♑	♒	♓

bol ♉ for Taurus located on the line for April 6. Following the same procedure, the next column has Venus in ♊ (Gemini), the next has Mars in ♑ (Capricorn), Jupiter's column shows it is in ♐ (Sagittarius), Saturn is in ♏ (Scorpio), Uranus is in ♓ (Pisces), Neptune is in ♌ (Leo) and Pluto is in ♋ (Cancer). For a simple chart, you do not need the location of the planets by degrees, just the sign in which the planets are located. (For detailed charts, the degrees become important.) Remember, the sign in which a planet is located will be shown by the glyph at the side of or directly above the date in question.

Step 2   Now all you have to do is list these sign locations, as in Figure 2, below.

Figure 2. Jane Doe's Sign Locations

Name	*Jane Doe*
Date	*April 6, 1924*

Planets	in	*Signs*	
(☉) Sun	in	Aries	(♈)
(☽) Moon	in	Taurus	(♉)
(☿) Mercury	in	Taurus	(♉)
(♀) Venus	in	Gemini	(♊)
(♂) Mars	in	Capricorn	(♑)
(♃) Jupiter	in	Sagittarius	(♐)
(♄) Saturn	in	Scorpio	(♏)
(♅) Uranus	in	Pisces	(♓)
(♆) Neptune	in	Leo	(♌)
(♇) Pluto	in	Cancer	(♋)

Step 3   We are now ready for a general profile of our subject based on the above data.

Interpretation. If we turn to Appendix I, Planets in Signs, we will find an interpretation for each of the above planetary locations. Let us see what the analyses have to say for Jane Doe's particular planetary locations.

Sun in Aries: The location of the Sun is the most important of the planetary locations. With her Sun in Aries, Jane Doe is basically a creative, forceful, dynamic and aggressive individual. She is used to having her own way, and becomes more aggressive the more she is challenged. She needs greater moderation in her behavior and must learn to compromise, to be more sensitive to the feelings of others.

Moon in Taurus: Jane Doe is also resourceful, but at times she tends toward selfishness and opportunism. She likes comfort and elegance; she is interested in having money, which is probably a result of her dread of poverty. Her major problem is her fear of taking chances, of gambling on the future, of risking what she has at present. Her major flaw in dealing with people is her insensitivity. On occasion, she uses others to her own advantage.

Special notation on the Moon's position in the signs: Because, in comparison to any other planet in the chart, the Moon travels relatively fast — approximately 13° per day (sometimes more, sometimes less) — it can happen that her location may be in the sign preceding the one in the Ephemeris or in the sign following the one shown on the date in question. This can happen on the day when the Moon changes sign; if you were born early in the day, then her position in the sign will be right for you, but if you were born late in the day, the chances are the Moon had already moved into the next sign. If you know your time of birth, the Moon's position can be calculated without too much difficulty. (See Figure 18, page 60.)

When you read the Moon's position in the sign shown in the Ephemeris on the day when it changes signs, and you feel the interpretation doesn't fit you, we suggest you read the interpretation for the Moon's location in the sign it enters (or leaves) on that day.

Mercury in Taurus: Some consistency in Jane Doe's character is beginning to show. Mercury in Taurus reveals a person who is determined and persistent and who enjoys the comforts of life. She is greatly interested in money and the security that it represents. She is thoughtful about planning things, probably from her fear of taking risks (Moon in Taurus). She is not a particularly generous person, but when she does give, she is sincere. She has a good business sense and can manage her affairs rather expertly. She has a narrow outlook in her domestic and money interests, and is a bit obstinate in her opinions. She needs to develop greater consideration of other people's views.

Venus in Gemini: This planet gives color to the Jane Doe portrait. It shows that Jane is charming and articulate, adapting easily to a variety of people. She is a doer and generally "on the go," for she likes to travel. Refined in her tastes, she is impatient with people who are interested only in mundane matters. Though concerned about the matter of security, which we learned from the placement of her Moon and Mercury, she is not limited by such factors nor is she tolerant of those who are exclusively preoccupied with them. She is not very tolerant of people's feelings, rarely taking them seriously.

Mars in Capricorn: Jane Doe's Mars undescores her ambitious nature, her drive and determination to succeed, established from previous planetary influences. She respects those who exercise common sense and good judgment in planning things, establishing priorities in those matters deserving that kind of attention. It now becomes apparent that Jane Doe is a person with great emotional needs. She needs reassurance from her mate in particular — a kind of guarantee consistent with her need for domestic and financial security. Rather traditional about love and sexual matters, she is not an innovator and, perhaps, is somewhat inhibited. There is that quality of planning and control, for Mars in Capricorn defines a person who needs, above all, to determine what will take place, even in love.

Jupiter in Sagittarius: This configuration confirms some of the basic personality traits previously established in Jane Doe: strong self-assertion, enthusiasm, optimism, restlessness and drive to succeed. She is a visionary who anticipates her goals before they are formalized. What is new, but consistent, is Jane Doe's respect for education and intolerance of ignorance. As defined by Jupiter in Sagittarius, Jane's eagerness is channeled in the direction of knowledge. She values education and has the vision and drive to pursue new intellectual areas. She is someone not intimidated by innovations or new disciplines. She recognizes the value of specialization.

Saturn in Scorpio: This reveals a darker potential for Jane Doe. This placement indicates that she is wary of expressing her opinions and of accepting those of others. She has a naturally suspicious nature that produces caution in making friends. These characteristics do not contradict what preceded. In fact, they suggest some possible depths and potentials that grow out of established traits. For example, we've learned that Jane plans carefully, she is security conscious and has strong emotional needs requiring reassurance from her mate. We also established that she is confident and optimistic about herself. However, being a security-minded person who is sure of herself does not guarantee that she has confidence and trust in others. Jane may be someone whose self-protection and determination to succeed make her a bit uncertain of others and cautious about being too open. Consistent with these traits and with her professional drives, Saturn in Scorpio adds the confirmation of her talents with managing money. She has an analytic mind and a seriousness of purpose that does not allow her to waste time or money on mundane or superficial things. Her concern about constantly receiving approval from her mate (her Mars in Capricorn trait) may make her anxious or, in the extreme, frigid. We also learn that when her trust is violated, Jane Doe is capable of revenge.

Uranus in Pisces: This analysis focuses on something we already know about Jane — her intellectual curiosity. Uranus in Pisces defines one who wants to know more, who questions what she has been taught, who has a fascination about the unknown. In Jane's case, we have a woman whose already established intellectual curiosity and restlessness may lead her to explore matters mysterious and mystical. We already have a consistent picture of a woman who is somewhat visionary, who is not wrapped up in superficial or mundane matters. It is possible that our subject's creative imagination may interest her in areas that most people do not bother with because of their generally forbidden or unknown natures. Uranus in Pisces also suggests a person whose energy, creative talents and higher visions could lead the way to some high social mission in life, perhaps one who takes up social or political causes.

Neptune in Leo: These next two configurations apply to a large number of poeple, since both Neptune and Pluto move so slowly from sign to sign, as you can see from the Ephemeris. What these two planetary locations define are general traits of people from an historical era of social decay and upheaval. Neptune in Leo gives us a picture of individuals whose experience in those troubled times (from 1915 to 1929) made them morally and spiritually responsible for establishing order. For our subject, we add some specific traits nonetheless: a skepticism about social and political leaders; determination to make a success of personal relationships; a strong sense of family responsibility, but not at the expense of self-development, of the exercise of her own creative needs. There is a general confirmation that Jane Doe's sexual nature is conventional, and that her love life may be less than fulfilling.

Pluto in Cancer: Finally, there is Pluto in Cancer, a configuration that is the least specific only because Pluto is the slowest-moving planet. It occupies individual signs for a great number of years. Yet, we can still define some of Jane's characteristics and perhaps add a small dimension to her portrait. She is the product of a time that experienced upheavals and great social anxieties that extended from 1912 to 1938. Like so many, Jane is a child of great changes, particularly in domestic life-style. For her to gain personal fulfillment, she would necessarily have to make considerable adaptations to a constantly changing social scene and to new values. We already learned that hers is a personality that is restless; that Jane likes to do things, to travel, to be on the go. If she is to be a success in life, personally and professionally, then she will necessarily have to be one capable of change, both in the sense of physically relocating from her birthplace and in the sense of abandoning old traditions and attitudes. There is also the emphasis on the need for careful financial planning and the need to maintain a priority of values, to emphasize the essentials.

What do we have now that we have put together a simple solar chart for Jane Doe? Essentially, we have a basic character profile of her, a behavioral framework of her personality. Of course, such a chart can give only fundamental personality traits and this is an incomplete picture, although one that is useful in understanding some of the planetary forces operating on the formation of her being.

As we move on to a discussion of how to do a detailed solar chart, you will discover different ways we can refine our profile of Jane Doe, or anybody else. We will, for instance, go into considerable detail about the zodiacal signs themselves and the effects on human behavior as the result of the planets that "rule" the different signs. With such information you will better understand such astrological interpretations as "Planets in Signs" that appear in Appendix I of this book. In short, you will eventually learn to draw your own astrological conclusions from the principles involved.

For the time being, you have enough to do simple solar charts. You may find that the profile you come up with does not exactly fit the individual in question. If so, remember that you are working only with some basics, and basics of human behavior are often hidden within us. When they are, they will be revealed by more refined analysis. For the most part, what generalized analyses you get from the simple chart will not be inconsistent with the more refined portraits you will get by the time you finish this book. We will demonstrate such consistencies as we return to Jane Doe, for whom we will eventually set up a detailed solar chart.

CHAPTER 3 The Basics of Astrology

To draw a detailed solar chart, there are some basic principles and background information you need to know. As we promised, we will try not to clutter your head with lots of extraneous facts. But you need to know the meaning of some key terms astrologers use. In particular, you must become familiar with the signs of the Zodiac, its structure and organization, with the characteristics of the individual planets that rule the signs and with the way the signs have been subdivided into Elements and Qualities. These and other concepts are crucial to your full understanding of how to set up and interpret a detailed solar chart. Before you become an astrologer in your own right, you have got to know something about the history of the science itself. That is where we begin.

Nobody knows just how long we have been looking to the stars for answers. Probably since our ancestors started walking upright. What we do know is that among the oldest samples of human writing were astrological inscriptions, some appearing on five-thousand-year-old clay tablets excavated from what was once ancient Babylon. There is every indication that even back then astrology was a very old science.

It was also far different from what we practice today. There was no awareness that every person's makeup was determined by the stars, nor was there any concern for individual behavior or affairs, unless the person was a pharaoh or a monarch. Then, of course, the individual's fate was that of a whole people. What the ancients got from studying the stars were clues about major events, such as when to go to war or when to set sail or when to make sacrifices to the gods. The coming of Christ, for instance, was announced by the star of Bethlehem — an occurrence of enormous significance recognized by the three Magi, who, in fact, were astrologers.

The key question is how did the ancients learn to link up events in the heavens with the affairs on Earth? How, in fact, did they realize that the future was "written in the stars"?

The answer lies in the Sun, obviously the most powerful influence in the sky. It rose and set at specific points on the horizon, and in between its path was always the same wide band. Because its motion was cyclic and followed a pattern, the ancients could make definite predictions about the seasons of the year. In fact, it was because of the Sun's position in the sky that the seasons occurred. A brilliant deduction by ancient man, although quite obvious to us from our sophisticated twentieth-century point of view.

How did they know where the Sun was in the sky at any time of the year? Another brilliant deduction made by making reference to the other stars, since the night sky was rigid in its makeup and movement. They converted the otherwise random pinpoints of light into outlines of animals, men and gods, and called these outlines the constellations.

The constellations always held their same shape, since the stars never appeared to move away from each other. They moved in regular paths across the sky throughout the year. By relating the path of the Sun to the movement of the various constellations, the ancients were able to mark off precisely the seasons of the year, which, of course, were observed in nature's patterns. (The

Egyptians' calculations were so accurate that they devised the first 365-day calendar.)

By relating the patterned movements of the Sun to those of the various stars, we had the beginnings of astrology. When the Sun was in that portion of the sky which was the sign of Aries, it was time to plant. When the Sun went into the sign of Libra, it was time to harvest. Without the determination of this cause and effect between patterns in the heavens and events on Earth, mankind would most assuredly never have developed agriculture.

Just how the heavenly bodies affected the affairs of men on Earth was reasoned from the Sun's influence. The Sun obviously radiated mysterious energies in the form of heat and light, which made things grow and change. Surely, the ancients speculated, the Moon, planets and other stars radiated similar energies that mysteriously affected human affairs too. The more they reasoned and observed, the more rigorous became the observation of the various movements and patterns of the skies.

As time passed, the ancients discovered that it was possible to calculate at any specific moment just which bodies were exerting their influences down here. They also learned that by observing which events were taking place on Earth at that moment, they could tell what particular effects those celestial energies were having. One rather obvious example is the correspondence they made between phases of the Moon and the tides of the ocean. Carrying those correspondences over to the stars and various constellations, the ancients developed a very sophisticated system for determining future events. The future was foretold in the stars, and when man began to read them, astrology was born.

Modern Astrology Basics

Modern astrology is about you and me, individual people. It is not the business of foretelling the future or telling monarchs when to go to war. We have read about the people who predicted the deaths of President Kennedy, Martin Luther King and Anwar Sadat. Others have named the day man would land on the moon, years before the actual event. Nostradamus, "the man who saw tomorrow," made thousands of predictions, none of which has been proven wrong.

Modern astrologers will find meaning and purpose in the stars. They recognize the astral influences on historical events, and they have refined their interpretation of individual behavior. Most astrologers do not claim to understand how the energies beamed down to Earth from the planets actually influence human character and behavior. They do recognize the fact that these forces are varied and complex and that they *do* engage in some kind of cyclic correlation with a person's makeup from the moment of birth.

A solar chart is simply a calculation of the positions of particular bodies in the sky on the day of birth of the individual in question, and these are the Sun, Moon and planets in our solar system. These planetary configurations are important because they are central to the study of astrology and form the foundation for the realization that the stars and planets at birth contain the information about the cycles and trends of behavior in that person's life.

The responsibility of the astrologer is to draw charts accurately and to interpret them in terms that are meaningful to the man or woman making the request. The aim is to provide people with answers to modern problems — unfulfilled needs of love and contentment; guidance in avoiding conflicts in personality; direction in making decisions about relationships, finances and careers.

As we stated before, astrology does not predict events in your life. Things are not so predetermined, otherwise there would be no such thing as free will or choice. The stars do not make people do things. They simply reveal tendencies and inclinations.

In this book we intend to demonstrate those tendencies and inclinations as they are reflected in solar charts. We will begin with some basics of astrology, then move through some more technical concepts so that by the end of this book you will have learned how to create your own charts and better understand the persons in question, including yourself. Let us begin with the Zodiac itself.

Signs of the Zodiac

"What's your sign?"

That's a question everyone has heard many times. Of course, what is being asked is the name of the sign of the Zodiac under which you were born. It's also known as your "Sun sign" and refers to the particular portion of the heavens which the Sun occupied on your birthdate.

From a tradition that predates ancient Babylon, the zodiacal signs once referred to twelve specific constellations of stars. These particular twelve were very important to the ancients because they were situated along what is known as the *ecliptic* — that band in the sky through which the Sun moves during the year. Over the twelve months, twelve separate and distinct constellations wheeled slowly through this solar band. Collectively, that stellar dozen was given the name *Zodiac*, meaning "Wheel of Life."

The zodiacal signs bear no relation to the particular constellations sharing the same name, but the traditional names are still used. Today the twelve signs refer to the twelve divisions of the Earth's annual revolution around the Sun. In other words, the zodiacal wheel is a circle of time rather than space. The Zodiac subdivides the solar year rather than the solar path through the heavens. It is, in fact, a kind of calendar (see Figure 3, Zodiacal Wheel and the Twelve Signs).

Each sign occupies exactly 30° of the circle, and collectively these arcs compose a wheel of twelve segments. According to tradition, the wheel begins with Aries, which corresponds to what is known as the vernal equinox — the point where the sun crosses the celestial equator at the beginning of spring. This date is March 21 — a time when the days and nights are of equal length over the whole earth.

Let's get back to the signs. If you were born on, say, August 20, your Sun sign would be Leo. If your were born on August 23, your Sun sign would be Virgo. (For the correct Sun sign of any birthdate, consult the Ephemeris in Appendix X at the back of the book.) There are twelve Sun signs of approximately 30 days each.

In order to draw up an astrological chart for someone, it is essential to know that person's birthdate, since the particular Sun sign can be determined only from that information.

The Sun sign is not the only crucial factor in drawing up a chart. One needs to know the exact astronomical locations of the Moon and planets on the date of the individual's birth. In fact, to get an accurate chart one needs to calculate the precise location of the Sun, Moon and the planets in the signs. These calculations are important factors in the intricate definition of each human personality. Such fine details are in fact what make astrology so complex a study and why modern astrologers now make use of high-speed computers. (The Ephemeris at the back of this book was put together by the computers of Astro Computing Services of San Diego, California.)

**Figure 3.
Zodiacal Wheel
and the Twelve Signs**

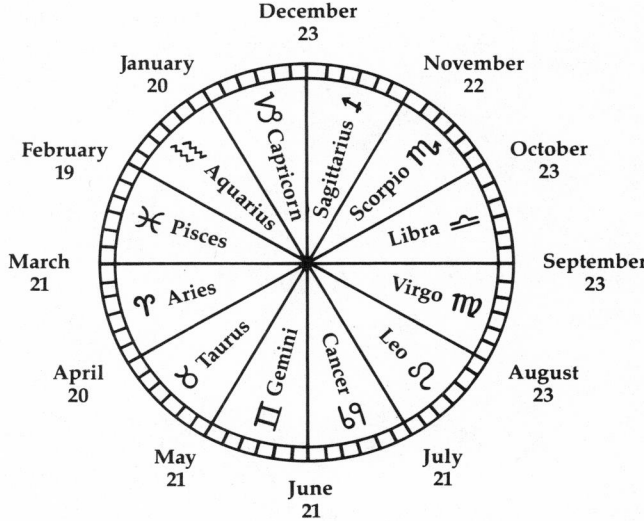

The various locations of the Sun, Moon and planets determine just why two people born under the same Sun sign can be so different. For instance, Bob was born on July 24, 1942, and Mary on August 20 of the same year. Both have Leo Sun signs. On July 24, however, the Sun was early in the sign, according to the Ephemeris. Mary's Sun, on the other hand, was late in the sign, and this difference can easily account for totally different personalities. Similarly, the Moon and planets may occupy significantly different locations within the same Sun sign. They all figure into the makeup of personalities, not just the Sun sign characteristics.

What do the Sun signs mean? What do they indicate about a person's individual nature or temperament?

There are some basic factors about the signs that you must know, for everything else about the signs depends largely on these fundamental principles.

The first principle is called Elements; it refers to the four basic elements by which all things were classified in antiquity, not to the chemical elements such as oxygen, carbon and hydrogen. The Zodiac is divided into the Elements Fire, Earth, Air and Water. These Elements represent the four basic modes of being, and they refer to the methodology that is the foundation for each of the signs of the Zodiac. While they are principally identified with the primary behavioral method in signs of the Zodiac, a closer examination will reveal that they are the connecting tissue that makes every sign dependent upon every other sign to derive its own essence. Because there are four Elements, three signs belong to each Element.

Figure 4. The Signs and Their Elements

FIRE	EARTH	AIR	WATER
Aries	Taurus	Gemini	Cancer
Leo	Virgo	Libra	Scorpio
Sagittarius	Capricorn	Aquarius	Pisces

The Four Elements

A discussion of the Elements and what they mean seems appropriate before we enter into a presentation of each sign of the Zodiac. Once you grasp the significance of the Element each sign belongs to, it will be easier to understand why the signs bear the characteristics for which they are known.

Each of the Elements is symbolic of human attributes with which we are familiar.

Fire: This is the primitive urge to live and the creative inspiration to find a suitable outlet for energy. It represents enthusiasm, spontaneity, faith, intuition and idealism. Aries, Leo and Sagittarius are the Fire signs and they share these qualities, even though their specific natures may differ for other reasons we will discuss later.

Earth: Basic common sense, resourcefulness, management ability, practicality, and skill in any given situation are the building blocks that are the foundation for how this Element succeeds. Taurus, Virgo and Capricorn are the Earth signs and they cling tenaciously to these qualities, but they can be differentiated by using other factors.

Air: This is the world of ideas and how they are communicated. It represents rational judgment, abstract thinking, the intellect, detachment, objectivity and perspective. Clever in various forms of communication, the Air signs — Gemini, Libra and Aquarius — effectively humanize social gatherings. While they share these attributes, they go their separate ways depending on what it is that motivates them.

Water: The world of the intangible, the feelings, anxieties, psychism, sensitivity, self-containment, withdrawal, emotional vulnerability, in-depth perception and mysticism are some of the qualities that identify the signs belonging to this Element. Cancer, Scorpio and Pisces are the Water signs, but even they part company when the urges that provoke them to action are taken into consideration.

The Three Qualities

The second principle you should become familiar with is that of the Qualities of the signs. The signs of the Zodiac are divided into three Qualities of four signs each. The Qualities relate to the basic temperament of the individual belonging to a particular sign so that an identifying characteristic prevails that is rarely ever altered throughout the life, nor does it need to be. The Qualities refer to the basic states of being of the various signs, a posture if you will, or simply the way a sign *is*. The three Qualities are Cardinal, Fixed and Mutable (or Common). Each of these Qualities views the world through a different lens, therefore their perceptions are quite different, their reactions to stimuli vary so that the action they take is quite dissimilar. The pattern of signs belonging to the Qualities is given in the figure below.

Figure 5. The Signs and Their Qualities

CARDINAL	FIXED	MUTABLE
Aries	Taurus	Gemini
Cancer	Leo	Virgo
Libra	Scorpio	Sagittarius
Capricorn	Aquarius	Pisces

We offer a short discussion of each of the Qualities to accompany the information given on each of the Elements. You will find that the signs of the Zodiac will be more meaningful to you with your grasp of these basic principles.

Cardinal: The urge to take action is not easily resisted by this Quality. Impatience, anxiety, eagerness, initiative, reaching out, instigating, manipulating and promoting are some of the characteristics of the Cardinal signs. Though they utilize different techniques to get their jobs done, the underlying principle urging them to action is quite similar.

Fixed: The desires are an important factor sustaining the signs belonging to the Fixed group. These are the signs dealing with the sensory apparatus, so they react strongly to these stimulants that arouse them. Luckily, these signs enjoy a stability that gives them the ability to maintain order in their lives. Stubborn, resistant, reliable, determined, persistent, strong and intense are some of the characteristics of this quality. Taurus, Leo, Scorpio and Aquarius belong to this Quality, but the methods they use will differ depending on the Element identifying them.

Mutable (sometimes known as Common): These signs share a flexibility that is missing in the other two Qualities. These are the problem-solving signs. The Cardinal signs act, the Fixed signs react and the Mutable signs resolve. This is basic, but it's also accurate. Alternating, mediating, resolving, pacifying, modifying, sympathizing, indulging, pardoning, uncertainty, insecurity and anxiety are some of the attributes of these signs. Gemini, Virgo, Sagittarius and Pisces belong to this division of the Qualities, but they can be best understood by observing how they approach and deal with the problems they face as shown by their different Elements.

By studying the foregoing discussions on the Elements and Qualities, you should be able to detect their impact on the various signs and understand how they are as they are and why they perform their tasks as they do.

The circle of the Zodiac symbolically represents altogether the complete range of human experience, that is, the full spectrum of human personality makeup. This does not mean that the whole human race now and forever is made up of a mere twelve personalities. There are over four billion people living today. Each person who has ever breathed is as different and unique as his or her fingerprints. But even fingerprints are classifiable according to basic patterns. Each print, though similar, is yet different and discrete from all the others given the same code. The same is true with astrological signs.

People born under the same zodiacal symbol share fundamental tendencies or behavior traits. These traits may be hidden, or they may be obvious. Just exactly how these traits and tendencies are stimulated depends on the other astrological influences, such as the planets, Moon and the Sun, whose positions at the time of birth can have intensifying or muting effects on the basic Sun sign characteristics.

It is rare that an individual will show pure Sun sign Qualities and nothing else. It is certain though that these Qualities will be there in some form, depending on the effects the other bodies have in the charts. Later on, we will demonstrate just how to calculate the effects of the other heavenly bodies in the charts. Before we get to that, it is important that you know and understand just what the basic zodiacal characteristics are.

The following pages are capsule readings of each of the twelve signs.

CHAPTER 4 Sun Signs

You will now be introduced to the most fascinating and controversial phase of astrology.

In this chapter (in conjunction with the rest of this book), we will show you how you can determine these traits and those particular forces working to repress or distort them.

You must keep in mind that, although your own sign may determine certain facets of your personality, it does not eliminate free will. Certain characteristics listed here may point to unpleasant aspects of your personality. For instance, say your Sun sign is Aries and we say that Ariens are characteristically aggressive and daring. That may not be unknown to you and you may see no harm in these traits. Yet, you may not be aware that with such tendencies you are running the risk of being rude at times, and reckless. The value of knowing your attributes lies in taking advantage of those that work well for you and minimizing those that do not.

Before we get to the individual Sun signs, there are other concepts that must be introduced to enable you to better understand *why* signs have the characteristics they have.

Ruling Planets   Each sign of the Zodiac has a ruling planet. This means that each sign has characteristics that are special to it and that are not duplicated exactly in any other sign. These identifying features emanate from the ruling planet. For example, Ariens have a primitive quality about them. They have a tendency to become easily aroused and will take action at the slightest provocation. Ancient astrologers assigned Mars as the ruler of Aries because Mars influences our aggressive behavior.

We will elaborate on the planets and their natures in the next chapter. For now, we will show you the wheel depicting the signs of the Zodiac and their planetary rulers.

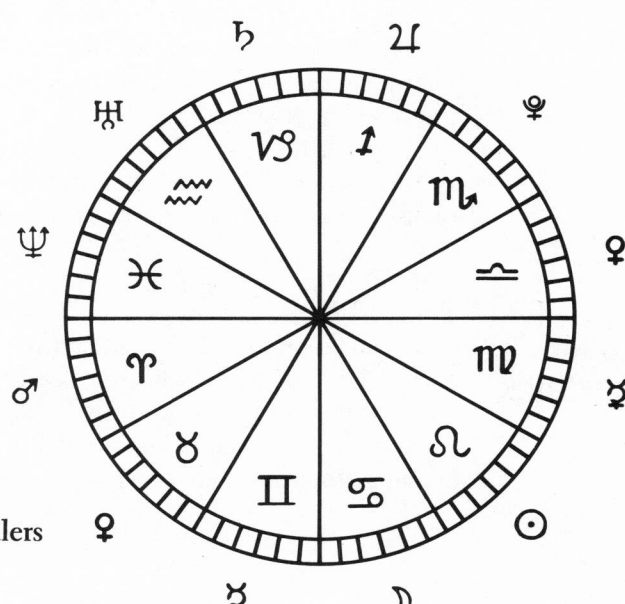

Figure 6.
The Signs and Their Rulers

Let us examine each of the Sun signs, paying attention to the factors put forth in the discussion on the Elements and Qualities.

Aries (♈)
March 20 to April 20
"I am"

The first sign of the Zodiac is Aries, and its symbol or glyph represents the ram, leader of the flock. Aries is also the first sign of spring, the season of beginning and vital energy. It is ruled by the planet Mars, which rules energy, sexual drive, anger, self-assertion and aggression.

As an Aries, you are forceful and possess unequaled energy. When you fail at anything, you simply pick yourself up and start again. With your ability to communicate it is an easy task for you to take over any conversation, especially since your curiosity urges you on. You possess creative ability and have the potential for leadership, so there is no reason why you cannot gain the recognition you seek in a position of authority. One of your negative traits, however, is your impatience when situations and the people involved in them don't proceed as quickly as you wish. Though you seek after positions of leadership, you generally resent those with authority. Though everyone must survive one way or another, you place your survival above everyone else's. More often than not your conversations begin with "I," and that tends to irritate people. Whether you realize it or not, there are other people who are also important.

A few famous people born under this sign are Charlie Chaplin, Harry Houdini, Hugh Hefner, Nikita Khrushchev, and some who are remembered for less-than-honorable deeds.

Taurus (♉)
April 20 to May 21
"I have"

Taurus is the second sign of the Zodiac and its symbol is the bull, a beast of great strength and sometimes fierce determination.

Taurus people have unequaled patience and are most resourceful and acquisitive. Because of your ability to understand your social obligations, you can be more sensitive toward other people's feelings. Organizing finances and business affairs is one of your best traits. With the planet Venus as your ruler, you are possessive, particularly in matters of love, as well as having a great affinity for the beautiful things in life. However, your stubbornness is unmatched anywhere. Your priorities in life are money, food and sex. You are an insecure individual. Though you may not be a great talker, you are inclined to brag about your possessions. You should also learn to curb your tendency to evaluate people by what they have.

Some of the people sharing your sign with you are Harry Truman, Sigmund Freud, Audrey Hepburn and Barbra Streisand. Among the more undesirable people with this Sun sign is Adolf Hitler.

Gemini (♊)
May 21 to June 21
"I think"

Yours is the third sign of the Zodiac. The symbol for Gemini represents the pillars of knowledge, though many people believe it stands for the thinking twins. The ruler of your sign is Mercury, the fleet-footed messenger of the gods, who is always in motion.

As a Gemini, your active mind and insatiable curiosity allow you to be a fine conversationalist. You are enthusiastic and aggressive, with a great capacity for working on many projects at the same time. Because of your quick-witted mental faculties, you are no doubt the life of any party.

As with every other sign, you also have negative tendencies. You tend to talk, talk, talk a lot about nothing that matters to you or anyone. You often ask a lot of meaningless questions, flitting from one subject to another like a graceful and beautiful butterfly. You are here, there, everywhere and never in one place for long.

A few famous people who belong to this sign are Bob Hope, Ralph Waldo Emerson, John F. Kennedy, Judy Garland and Marilyn Monroe.

Cancer (♋) June 21 to July 23 "I feel"

Born a Cancer, you come under the fourth sign of the Zodiac. The symbol is that of the mother's breasts by which she nourishes her young. The home and family are your life, and protecting them is an important consideration for you. The living creature symbolizing your sign is the crab, among whose qualities are self-containment and tenacity. Ruled by the Moon, which also governs the ebb and flow of the tides, she also represents the way your moods change from time to time.

A person of habit and habitat, you are a homebody. Full of warmth, tenderness and sentimentality, a person whose feelings for those you love is never diminished, you go out of your way to protect them. There are times, though, that your excessive caring may alienate those who need to be alone on occasion and may therefore resent your impositions. Don't let love become ownership, for you will surely lose those who need to live their own lives. Let rational judgment enter into the situations that may develop between you and those you love so that a more honest value enters into solving the problems that occur.

Nelson Rockefeller, Calvin Coolidge, Helen Keller, and Anne Morrow Lindbergh were born under the sign of Cancer.

Leo (♌) July 23 to August 23 "I will"

It is the king of beasts, the regal lion, who symbolizes the fifth sign of the Zodiac. It is highly appropriate that its ancient ruler is the Sun. Without a doubt, yours is the most potent and vital sign in the Zodiac, for you were born to lead. Regardless of the project, you seek the highest levels of achievement of which you are capable. Your vitality, like your ambitions, seems as boundless as your pride. You desire the limelight, honors and recognition, and you are optimistic about your abilities to attain them. Your personality can be charming and affable. Like your Sun, you are warm and ardently affectionate, with a strong, commanding personality. In fact, there are times you can be quite dramatic when you want to gain someone's attention. You must, however, guard against your tendency to want to take the helm all the time, because you can make others resentful or envious of you when you can easily avoid this negative effect. You must be careful not to let your desire to lead turn you into a domineering, bossy person or turn natural pride into obnoxious boastfulness. Your urge to rule is coupled with a natural love for luxury.

Some well-known people born with the Sun in Leo are Napoleon, Mussolini, Carl Jung, Jacqueline Onassis, Lucille Ball and Haile Selassie.

Virgo (♍)
August 23 to September 23
"I analyze"

Your sign is symbolized by the virgin, representing purity and freshness. By your very nature you are a clear-eyed person and you tend to view things realistically. You are not swayed by pretense, nor are you susceptible to the prejudices others may have. You are discriminating, conscientious and observant. Your chief talent is your ability to analyze matters and discover things for yourself. This is probably why you never ignore what seems like trivia to everyone else, and you offer your sympathetic understanding of their problems to those requiring it. Because you are something of a perfectionist, you may alienate others with pettiness in what you expect of them.

It is possible, however, for these basic talents to become distorted so that a negative effect results. Fault-finding, carping criticism and telling everyone how to accomplish this or that can only earn their displeasure. Cleanliness may become an exaggerated preoccupation with you and annoy people who resent the implied criticism of theirs. Your nervous system is in constant agitation from your insistence on doing things the only right way — your way. You know you have a problem when and if you develop ulcers (or give them to others). Slow down, ask for advice when you run into problems, and be willing to admit that you have a lot to learn, and always will.

You share this sign with Lyndon Johnson, Leonard Bernstein, Sophia Loren, and Greta Garbo.

Libra (♎)
September 23 to October 23
"I balance"

The scale is the astrological symbol for Libra and it represents balance, harmony and justice. It also symbolizes social exchange and is partly the reason why you need human contact most of the time.

You have all the charm, grace, tact and affable personality anyone could ever want. You dislike coarseness, harshness or vulgarity in any kind of situation. You are fond of the finer things in life and you pursue them for the enrichment and comfort they give you. You are an engaging person who enhances a social function by your presence and articulate manner in conversation.

Your unwillingness to offend anyone is the principal reason you avoid taking sides in a dispute. You never know when you may need someone's support, so you make sure you don't have any unfavorable contacts. Because of your middle-ground position, you are constantly faced with indecision and uncertainty. You are not really as concerned for the other person as you would like people to believe. You use rational explanations rather than extend yourself or feelings toward someone who may be in distress. Being rejected for any reason is a major crisis for you and deeply unsettling. Notice also that the figure holding the scales of justice has a sword in the other hand, and she is blind!

Notables having Libra as their Sun sign are Dwight Eisenhower, Jimmy Carter, Sarah Bernhardt, Eleanor Roosevelt and Lee Harvey Oswald.

Scorpio (♏)
October 23 to November 22
"I desire"

If you were born during these dates you are a Scorpio. Your symbol is the secretive, self-contained creature the scorpion. Ruled by the planet Pluto, Scorpio represents matters of an extreme nature, such as life and death. You are fearless and apparently nerveless in your drive to succeed. Although you are combative, you also have personal magnetism in addition to other facets that show you are intense, dynamic and purposeful. You are intellectually disciplined and, therefore, good at probing ceaselessly until you get at the truth. You are persistent in pursuing your objectives.

Your in-depth perception allows you to provide the understanding and comfort people need in times of difficulty. Once you set your course, it is unlikely that you will deviate from it unless matters beyond your control make it absolutely necessary.

Basically a private person, you rarely violate a confidence once you have made that kind of commitment. A person of intense feelings, when angered you can be most caustic and scornful in response to any provocation. You are very secretive about yourself, with a barrier between you and the people around you. Is this perhaps a defense mechanism to shield your uncertainty about your ability to carry out your plans? Are you perhaps unwilling to let people know how powerful your sex drive is or how difficult it is to apply it in a form that gains greater public approval when you do?

Other Scorpio Sun signs are Pablo Picasso, Teddy Roosevelt, Grace Kelly and Katharine Hepburn.

Sagittarius (♐) November 22 to December 23 "I perceive"

Yours is the ninth sign of the Zodiac, and your symbol is the archer, depicted by a half-man, half-horse creature with a bow and arrow ready and poised to shoot. This symbol represents the struggle between the thinking being and the lower self, the instinctual animal. You take on large-scale tasks with much enthusiam and boundless effort. Often inspired in carrying out you plans, you show great exuberance in facing each step, with your instincts seeming to guide you along the way. Your faith that you will succeed is probably why you take on tasks others shy away from. You reserve the right to pursue your goals without any hindrance or restraints. You are knowledgeable and truly informed on a wide variety of subjects, so you easily formulate plans. There is little wonder then that you really expect the world to make every concession to allow you to do what you want.

Whether consciously or unconsciously, you are, for all practical purposes, the extrovert, the know-it-all who engages in the most exaggerated schemes. Does this dramatic posture really hide the fact that you are not as accomplished as you pretend and that you are afraid someone may successfully challenge your position? Perhaps it bothers you to know that others are also talented and can teach you something. Your glyph shows the arrow pointing at an undefined objective. It is simply aimed out to open space; where, no one knows. Do you really know where your arrow is focused?

Keeping company with you are Mark Twain, Frank Sinatra, Maria Callas and Emily Dickinson.

Capricorn (♑) December 23 to January 20 "I use"

If you were born at this time of the year, you are a Capricorn, whose symbol is the mountain goat, an animal of unsurpassed surefootedness, with the ability to climb precarious ledges to secure a goal. Like this persevering, self-reliant creature, you are able to hurdle all kinds of obstacles. You are an impassive but confident individual who accepts lofty challenges without the need for assistance from anyone. You even take on tasks others turn down as too difficult or demanding.

By your nature, you are eager to learn new things, especially those that can help you reach the highest goals. You are psychologically equipped to overcome reversals and frustrations because you are the supreme realist with a talent to reappraise your position and evaluate what went wrong. Once you've experienced failure, the lesson it teaches you is never forgotten. This is probably why you are disciplined, practical and cautious, and you like to investigate things on your own.

Being almost obsessed with seeking a position of status and honor makes you overly serious and demanding. You go to great lengths to get what you want, even to the extent of using people to your advantage. You show great emotional distress when you are not in control of the people and situations in which you may be involved. Your insensitivity to the feelings of others may result in moral decay, lowered social standards and problems in your relationships and marriage.

Louis Pasteur, Howard Hughes and Albert Schweitzer share your sign, as do Marlene Dietrich and Clara Barton; also Joseph Stalin, Richard Nixon and Hermann Göring.

Aquarius (♒)
January 20 to February 19
"I know"

This is the sign of the water bearer, the humanitarian. The glyph itself represents the free-flowing tides as well as the bolts of lightning. Neither the tides, the lightning nor the Aquarian responds to control.

As an Aquarian, you are, without a doubt, a true individualist with your own ideas. You possess an inventive mentality with talent and skill in thinking for yourself. As a communicator you excel in expressing your views to all who listen (and some who don't) so you can impress them and win their approval. You speak not only for yourself, but for those who are unable to speak for themselves. You ardently uphold the principle of brotherly love and the humanitarian desire to share with those around you.

In spite of all your abilities, you resent and reject any and all authorities out of fear that your freedom to do what you want will be curtailed. You refuse to conform to the accepted standards of society. Brotherly love may be so distorted that complete permissiveness is the order of the day, with negative results. Your engagement in lovemaking is to satisfy the biological necessity and not for the love involved, for love never enters your mind. You resent anyone trying to tell you what to do and you step backward or retreat at the slightest command leveled at you.

Other Aquarians are Ronald Reagan, Abraham Lincoln, Franklin Roosevelt, Mia Farrow and Gypsy Rose Lee.

Pisces (♓)
February 20 to March 21
"I believe"

The symbol for the last sign of the Zodiac is of fish swimming in opposite directions but tied together so that neither can make any progress. Your chief characteristic is your ability to detach yourself from your environment and your own physical needs. Like your natural element, water, you are spiritually accommodating in as much as you can identify with situations outside yourself. It isn't difficult for you to be absorbed into the dilemmas of those around you. You can imagine the needs of people desperately requiring help and you empathize with their suffering. You are finely tuned to human distress, and you usually respond to the need for social responsibility. At times, you may be too self-sacrificing because you feel guilty that those around you who suffer are not being helped.

You must guard against being drawn into situations that can cause you to be victimized by unscrupulous people.

On the negative side, you are the daydreamer who, like the fish that represent you, are always going in different directions at the same time, thereby accomplishing very little. This is probably due to the lack of mental organization. This lack of self-confidence can create such distortions that they become too much to bear. Others criticize you for this and you can barely endure it. You must learn to face up to reality, not escape from it.

Sharing your fantasies with you are Frederic Chopin, Edgar Cayce, Elizabeth Taylor and Jean Harlow. We must also include Adolf Eichmann and Sirhan Sirhan.

As we said earlier, the Sun sign descriptions above represent only capsule summaries of the prime characteristics of the twelve signs. They do not define the whole individual by any means. Nor should you be too hasty to categorize people according to basic sign qualities.

Astrology, like the individual it studies, is far more complex than that, as we shall demonstrate later on. You might have even noticed that some characteristics are not unique to one sign. For instance, Leonians are described as people who strive for high goals in life, but so do Sagittarians and Ariens. They bear a similarity in this respect because they are all Fire signs and their enthusiasm for achievement burns fiercely in each of them.

There is a little bit of every sign in each of us, no matter which particular Sun sign we were born under. Also, each sign is geometrically bound to every other sign. For instance, for every active (positive) sign there is an active (positive) sign directly opposite it in the Zodiac. Because of this, you will inevitably encounter problems in achieving the full identity of your Sun sign. It might be a matter of personal shortcomings that are indicated, but what is more important is seeing yourself in terms of the entire zodiacal circle and in relation to all the Sun signs. From the Elements and Qualities discussion in chapter 3 you noted that there were four signs in each Quality and three signs in each Element. An important point to make here is that *every sign in each Quality is basically hostile to the other three*, while *every sign in each Element is basically harmonious to the other two*.

In other words, the characteristics of the signs belonging to the same Quality as your Sun sign show your shortcomings and indicate those areas needing your attention and development to achieve good relationships and gain a sense of personal well-being.

For instance, an Aries person is, by nature, aggressive, assertive and ardent. But, in the extreme, our Aries can be self-serving and self-righteous. If we look at the complete Zodiac, we see that just opposite Aries is Libra — noted for its compromising and balancing nature. Our Aries person whose problem is too much self-assertion would do himself a big favor if he only took heed of the Libra opportunities by making every effort to develop more awareness of other people's rights and to compromise at times. He would be much more successful with others than the Arien who does not make such concessions.

Of course, it isn't easy to achieve this objective — this opposite nature. The reason is that there are two inhibitors that stand at crossroads to Aries, two signs that are 90° to this sign and that represent adjustments to be made in the impulse-to-action characteristic to all Ariens.

Figure 7. The Inhibiting Factor for Aries

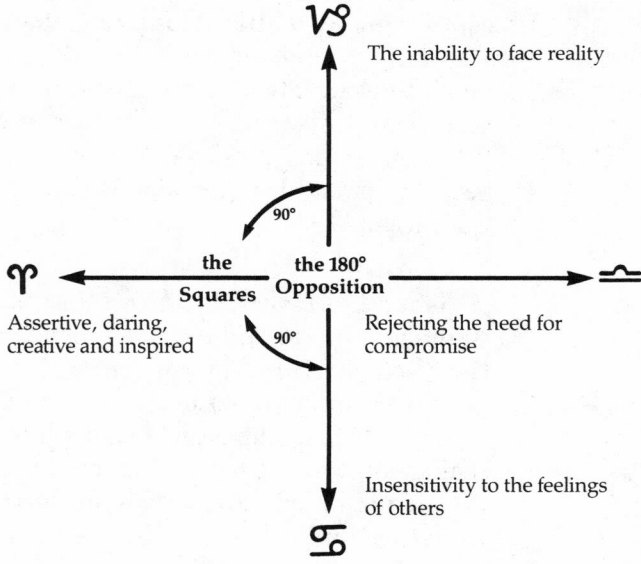

As shown in Figure 7, 90° counterclockwise to Aries is Cancer, a Water sign, which indicates that our Aries person must learn to respect other people's feelings. (Recall that Water signs signify human feelings.) Also, 90° clockwise to Aries is Capricorn, an Earth sign, which indicates that Aries must accept full responsibility for the effects created by his or her behavior. (Earth signs signify responsibility.)

While achieving these tasks might seem arduous, maybe even impossible for our headstrong, proud Arien, there is a way to success. And that too is indicated in the Zodiac.

We have within us natural *resources* from which we can draw strength to achieve those tasks. Resources that, in fact, come from the signs. Not those at 90° — those represent the inhibitors. But from those signs at 60° and 120°. (In chapter 8, on Aspects, these angles we refer to as "sextiles" and "trines.")

If, as Figure 8 shows, we put Aries on the horizontal axis (in fact, its traditional location on the zodiacal circle), we see that 60° clockwise from it is Aquarius, and 60° counterclockwise is Gemini. Also, 120° clockwise from Aries is Sagittarius, and 120° counterclockwise from it is Leo. In Figure 8, Aquarius represents facility in talking, while Gemini signifies communication abilities. Sagittarius characterizes daring, foresight and understanding, while Leo is the sign of authority and creative ability. Drawing from all these resources, our headstrong Arien can avoid his strong impulses and self-righteousness by applying his natural-born foresight and understanding (Sagittarius) with his creative skills (Leo) by opening up lines of communication (Gemini) and talking to others (Aquarius).

Each sign has its natural inhibitors at right angles to it as well as its natural resources at 60° and 120° to it. To make things simple for you, we have put

Figure 8. The Available Resources for Aries

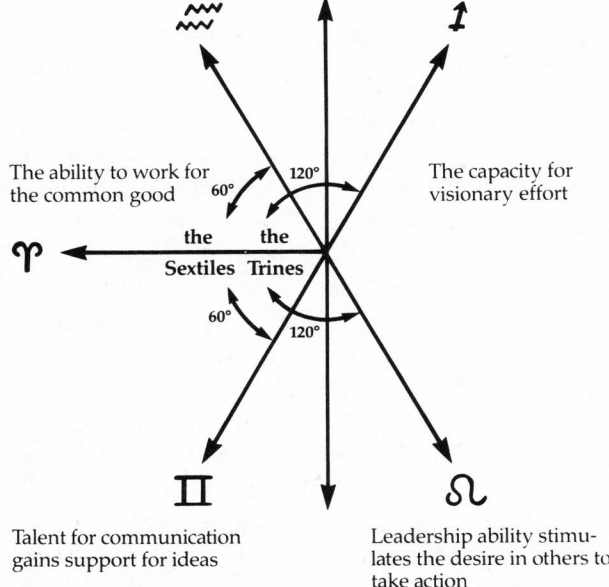

together simple diagrams of all the basic inhibitors and resources for each of the signs, just as we have for Aries in Figures 7 and 8. Use these to help interpret where your difficulties might lay and where your opportunities to overcome them are. By applying these built-in resources to overcome inhibitors, you will allow yourself greater opportunity to enjoy rich and satisfying experiences. Refer to Appendix II, Inhibiting Factors and Available Resources, for completed diagrams for each sign.

CHAPTER 5 The Planets and Their Natures

Back in chapter 3 we made the point that although astrologers do not fully comprehend just *how* the various heavenly bodies affect human character and behavior, they recognize that they do. They also recognize that the various forces beamed down on us by the various planets have particular kinds of effects. To put it another way, astrologers have determined that the different planets "rule" some aspect of the personality. This determination is, in fact, a very important factor of the science of astrology.

A word first about the term *planet*. As we know from our schooldays there are nine planets in our solar system, which are listed from the closest to the most distant from the Sun: Mercury, Venus, Earth, Mars, Jupiter, Saturn, Uranus, Neptune and Pluto. In the science of astronomy these are all the planets in our solar system. In the science of astrology, the term *planets* also refers to the Moon and Sun, even though the Sun is technically a star and the Moon is a satellite. Simply for the sake of convenience, astrology uses the term to cover ten bodies: the Sun, Moon, Mercury, Venus, Mars, Jupiter, Saturn, Uranus, Neptune and Pluto. Of course the Earth is not considered in the list of planets or in the Ephemeris tables or any of the analyses at the back of the book simply because the Earth is not part of our heavens. It beams nothing down on us. If we lived on Mars, then Earth's influence would be considered, not Mars's.

The specific magnitude of the planets' influences upon us depends on the relative position of the planets in the sky at our birth. Later on, when we discuss the concept of Planetary Aspects, we will explain exactly how to determine the angular locations of the planets in the detailed solar chart so as to determine just how the various planetary configurations combine their astral influences to affect different ways we experience life. For the time being, let us just discuss which planets rule which factor or mechanism of our natures.

The most powerful planet in the sky and the most dominant influence on your character is the **Sun**. According to the oldest traditions, the Sun rules your inner self, your will and ego, your personal identity, vitality and creative powers. In other words, the Sun influences the makeup of the real you, that basic temperament which stays the same regardless of the other changes you experience in your lifetime.

The **Moon**, on the other hand, reflects the light of the Sun. It rules your outer personality, how you react to other people and the world around you. It also rules your emotions and their fluctuations, your changing habits and mannerisms, and the various phases of your moods and feelings.

The remaining planets have the names of the Roman gods. The particular influences of these planets on your makeup correspond to the characteristics of the respective gods. The planet Mars, for instance, rules animal instinct and aggressiveness. Mars is also the Roman god of war.

Traditionally, **Mercury** is associated with mental faculties and the ability to interpret and communicate. Mercury was the messenger of the gods, the god of intelligence and eloquence. This planet rules your intellect, particularly your ability to exchange information with other people. Mercury is also the fastest-moving planet except for the Moon, hence the term *mercurial*, which means active, changeable and quick-moving. If your chart indicates a strong Mercury influence, you will display these characteristics. In astrological tradition Mercury influences you primarily through its connections to the other planets and it has a mediating, neutral energy.

Venus signifies love, beauty, peace, magnetic attraction, harmony and the arts. It governs your love nature, as compared to the Mercurial mental nature. It also deals with your personal love relationships. The planet was first associated with the goddess of love by ancient Babylonians. The Greeks and Romans followed the practice centuries later. One theory holds that because Venus appeared just after sunset and at sunrise, it marked off the time for lovemaking. It is interesting to note that recent medical studies have revealed that hormone activity is highest in the evening and early in the morning — the time when Venus appears in the sky. The planet wasn't associated with the goddess of love by accident! She also rules the adjustments and compromises we make to get the things we want.

Mars, as we said, it traditionally associated with belligerence and sexual drive, as well as aggressiveness, physical activity, violent energy, assertion and determination. Just as Mercury rules the mind and Venus rules the love nature, so Mars rules the body. It is Mars that will determine your physical nature, how energetic and active you are. The ancients associated their war gods with the planet Mars because of its red color, the color of fire and blood, both of which symbolize vitality and energy.

Jupiter is astrologically associated with growth, expansion, ennoblement, magnanimity, hope and optimism. It is the ruler of your ability to achieve comfort and wealth. It is also associated with your ability to succeed financially. While it encourages high expectation, in terms of the goals you can reach, it also may cause you to overreach. When positive, Jupiter encourages you to establish and seek new levels of development that qualify you to take on greater responsibility, thereby enriching you with satisfaction in your goals and greater happiness in your personal life.

Saturn is the planet that rules your ability to take on responsibility and to do it dutifully. Saturn is the policeman of the Zodiac, stepping in to demand an accounting of your actions. Saturn is the wisdom that grows when you apply the knowledge you have in useful and meaningful ways. It is the quiet voice within you letting you know that your plans are within the guidelines of legal and social acceptability. Should you decide to challenge the order Saturn requires, the results can be devastating and it is rare when the consequences of your actions don't include repayment. Saturn demands that you are aware of doing what is right by others, and by yourself. Saturn also rules fear, apprehension and depression, but only when you do not play fair and observe the rules of the game.

Uranus is the planet of change, upheaval, detachment, freedom and the unexpected or innovative. It is also the planet of future expectations and of revolution. A strong influence by Uranus will produce a personality characterized by independence, impatience and willfulness. You will be unconventional, unpredictable and likely to say the unexpected at the most inopportune time, sometimes simply to get a reaction from your audience. There may be originality and inventiveness in whatever tasks you perform because you have a highly intuitive mentality. Appropriately, Uranus is the name of the ancient Greek god who was the father and originator of all living things, the god of lightning.

Neptune is the planet of uncertainty and illusion. It shares the name of the Roman god of the sea. Just as water can assume any shape, can flow and shift, so it is with the Neptunian personality. Neptune's influence shows up in your emotional diffusiveness. Anxiety, uncertainty and guilt — these mark the personality influenced by Neptune. If strongly placed in your chart, Neptune indicates a mystic, an idealist, a visionary, one who is vague, dreamy and probably impractical. You might also have a strong interest in music, art and literature because these often require someone with a highly developed emotional nature.

Finally there is **Pluto**, the most recently discovered planet, and the one farthest from the Sun. The planet is commonly associated with regeneration, biosexual drives for reproduction and evolution, both individual and social. Transformation and consciousness development are part of the vocabulary of this powerful planet. When you are influenced by Pluto, you will probably be adept at training the mind or working at scientific and psychic research. As with all the planets, Pluto too has its so-called negative side, and when acting in this less desirable fashion, Pluto is associated with crime, genocide and enforced social changes, usually brought about by those motivated by a form of self-serving madness. Pluto was a strong influence during the rise of Nazism in the thirties and forties. This does not mean that a person strongly influenced by Pluto will follow Hitler's example by any means. You may direct that same energy to finding a cure for cancer or improving the production of food. Pluto also rules psychoanalysis and genetic research.

As the above discussion indicates, the effects of the planets can be either positive or negative, unfavorable or favorable, passive or active. There is a lighter and darker side to each planet. Just how the planets will affect you depends upon the relationships each makes with the other planets in your chart, the "Aspects," or angular distances between them, which is a concept we will discuss more fully in chapter 8. The *potential* effect of the planets — both their active and passive functions — can be codified by some key, handy terms.

What follows are some key words that fit the various planets and will help you to understand quickly their potential influence on your behavior. Most of the words used in the following discussion of planets are simply descriptive of the planets' behavioral dynamics. These nouns and adjectives are basic so that positive does not necessarily mean *good* but simply *active* and negative does not mean *bad* but *passive*. The right or wrong of a word is not intended in these descriptive terms. Take the Moon, for instance. There is nothing particularly wrong with remembering the past, but a problem can certainly result if it represents a resentment for what is taking place today or for the need to make plans for tomorrow. Whether this basic factor the Moon rules (the past) is a problem or not is determined by a process that we will help you with as we proceed.

The basic vocabulary of each planet is at the heart of your understanding of how people behave. When a person's chart shows a particular planet is under stress from other planetary contacts, we can expect a deviation of behavior that emphasizes the darker side of the terms: the "past" becomes confinement, the "ability to make adjustments" becomes someone who can never make a decision without help, "fear" becomes paranoia, "freedom" becomes license, etc. Remember, too, that a planet can incline to the positive so that the "vitality" of the Sun becomes the nourishment that sustains those who need someone strong to help them over a difficult time in life.

Planetary Significance

In the list that follows, we have adhered to the principle of *Planetary Protocol.* This simply means that the speed of a planet in its orbit determines whether it exerts an influence on another planet with whom it forms a relationship by aspect or if it is influenced by that other planet. The faster planet is *always* subjected to the influence of the slower planet with which it is involved. The order followed in the list is with the fastest planet first and the slowest planet last.

MOON	The emotions, the habits, memory, the past, heritage
MERCURY	The interpretive apparatus, mental faculties, the ability to communicate
VENUS	The ability to make adjustments, harmony, love, beauty, the arts
SUN	The will, ego, personal identity, vitality, hope, creativity, authority
MARS	Animal instinct, energy and drive, courage, impulse, sexuality, force
JUPITER	Optimism, ability to grow and expand in consciousness, luck, wealth, hope
SATURN	Wisdom, fear, inhibitions, apprehension, mastery, excellence, status
URANUS	Freedom, detachment, intuition, future expectations, innovation, brotherhood
NEPTUNE	Mysticism, sacrifice, guilt, uncertainty, anxiety, the unknown
PLUTO	The ability to regenerate, transform, evolve, the power to sustain

The above is simply the basic vocabulary of the planets, and there will be instances when these behavioral concepts will be considerably altered, some favorably and other unfavorably. What follows is a list of the favorable and unfavorable characteristics of each of the planets. Refer to the comments following the list that show how the favorable or unfavorable effects take place.

Positive	Negative	Positive	Negative
SUN		**MOON**	
Dignified	Arrogant	Good memory	Remembers
Faithful	Resistant	Imaginative	slights
Gay	Extravagant	Maternal	Faulty reasoning
Powerful	Domineering	Protective	Touchy
Proud	Overbearing	Sensitive	Fussy
			Unreliable
MERCURY		**VENUS**	
Expressive	Slick	Adaptable	Unreliable
Intelligent	Nosy	Peace-loving	Dissatisfied
Clever	Critical	Tactful	Indecisive
Talkative	Chatterbox	Loving	In love with love
Perceptive	Nervous	Graceful	Weak
MARS		**JUPITER**	
Energetic	Restless	Optimistic	Extremist
Impulsive	Foolhardy	Generous	Wasteful
Courageous	Thoughtless	Jovial	Provocative
Passionate	Arrogant	Fond of gambling	Trusting to luck
Direct in speech	Rude	Broad outlook	Nondetailed
SATURN		**URANUS**	
Prudent	Fearful	Inventive	Abnormal
Controlled	Mean	Reformative	Rebellious
Cautious	Limited	Strong-willed	Dangerous
Serious	Uninspired	Outspoken	Eccentric
Practical	Dull	Unconventional	Detached
NEPTUNE		**PLUTO**	
Imaginative	Deceptive	Evolving	Enforced change
Inspirational	Unstable	Eliminative	Eruptive
Sensitive	Subversive	Revealing	Violent
Idealistic	Careless	Regenerative	Crime
Subtle	Perverse	Rebirth	Destruction

Planetary Characteristics

The above characteristics are useful in formulating the resulting effects of planets involved in an aspect or relationship. When the aspect between two planets is a difficult one, the negative tendencies given above will prevail. Conversely, when the aspect or relationship between two planets is a favorable one, the positive indications will result. Be mindful that a negative influence often produces a learning experience indicating a favorable result in the long run, and sometimes a positive influence often causes apathy from which there is little character development.

How are these planetary natures useful to you? There are several ways they can help you. First, knowing the particular planetary influences helps you better to understand the analyses found in Appendix I, Planets in Signs, which you consulted in doing a simple solar chart. From chapter 4 you learned the behavior fundamentals of the twelve signs. By matching the planetary energies with zodiacal character patterns you can better understand how the various planets in the various signs correlate to affect individual behavior. Say, for instance, you did a simple solar chart for someone and there turned out to be a strong Mars influence, that is, Mars appeared in Aries, the sign it rules. You know from chapter 4 that Aries people like to lead, they are strong-willed and aggressive. You now know from the above material on the planets that Mars rules our animal drives. It should make sense, then, that people with their Mars in Aries in their chart would tend to be very aggressive, highly driven, highly assertive individuals. In fact, they would probably be too impulsive. Or, let's take an example of somebody with Mars in Taurus. From chapter 4 we learned that Taureans are determined and resourceful people. Also, they are possessive about money and concerned with their security. Mars, by its very nature, affects our passions, emotions, our physical drives. If we find Mars in the sign of Taurus, we can expect to see in the individual some strong desires to protect his or her belongings and concerns about financial security. This person would also fear being indebted to others. He would be a good planner, a person disciplined and mindful of the dangers of wastefulness.

Let's see what we can learn about our Jane Doe at this point. If you recall, her Mars was in Capricorn. We also know something about what human traits Mars affects: the passions, emotions, physical drives. We also know something about Capricorn: perseverance, self-reliance, confidence, eagerness to learn, ambition, good reasoning ability, caution and a talent for organization. The combination of Mars in Capricorn has the effect of emotionally intensifying these characteristics. The physical energies and drives of Jane Doe are channeled carefully in the direction of accomplishment. Hers is a quality that does not waste time or effort. She feels a physical need to achieve, to assume a position of authority and control. And yet, she is cautious not to allow her aggressiveness to get out of control. She is fundamentally careful not to be reckless in her judgment or actions. She is by nature well-disciplined, and capable of self-control. Because she perseveres, she is physically able to exert herself beyond the point where others may give up.

Knowing the planetary natures will come in handy when we talk about Aspects. For with Aspects we learn to further refine the analyses of the planetary influences since we actually determine the angular locations of the individual planets in the chart and, thus, the particular combinations of the planetary energies, or the Aspects.

Before we go to Aspects, however, there are three more important pieces of our puzzle to consider — the Elements, Qualities and Signatures. These still relate to the zodiacal signs and they are crucial concepts because they explain how the signs are related to each other. Some signs are compatible with each other, some are not. We are not simply talking about different people of different signs. We are referring to which signs have planets in them in the charts we construct. As you may recall, when doing even a simple chart, the first thing we determine is which signs are occupied by the various planets. Up to now, we've only discussed the planets and their influences. We must also consider the natures of the signs in which the planets are located. The signs have natures too, and they have been defined as the Elements and Qualities. From these two characteristics we can determine the Signature — a most important consideration. It should be obvious that having several planets in Aries will produce a different temperament than having them in Leo. This is why in the next chapter we will discuss how astrologers classify the various zodiacal signs according to Elements and Qualities, which in turn allow us to determine a Signature.

CHAPTER **6** Elements, Qualities, and Signatures

Your Sun sign is of great astrological importance because of its dominating influence on your character. In addition to character, personality is also affected by the position of the Moon and the other planets in the Zodiac on your birthdate.

It is an important first step in the construction of a detailed solar chart to determine which planets occupy which signs of the Zodiac. To some extent, we have already talked about the positions of the planets in the signs earlier in the text. Now we must examine the planets from a slightly different angle: the natures (classification) of the signs in which they are located.

As you already know from having looked at Ephemeris tables, each of the ten planets appear someplace in every natal chart. It should be obvious that some signs may not have any planets in them, since there are twelve signs and ten planets! One person's chart may have the ten planets appearing in only four signs. Another person may have planets in seven different signs. Sometimes one sign may be occupied by as many as six different planets. Certain groupings are significant, as are voids that may occur. Different distributions will have different astrological effects on individuals. How do we categorize and interpret different planetary distributions? One way is to interpret the overall spread of the planets in the chart according to the patterns developed by Marc Edmund Jones; they are now simply regarded as the "Jones Patterns" (see Appendix IV). Another way that is both important and precise in its behavioral significance is to classify the signs occupied by the planets according to traditional categories of the Elements and Qualities.

The traditional breakdown is quite simple: there are four Elements consisting of three signs each, and there are three Qualities consisting of four signs each. The Elements relate to the method, strategy or technique the individual uses to handle the affairs and situations in life. The Qualities are associated with the basic temperament and character of the individual. Let us examine the Elements first.

The Elements   The twelve signs are divided into four basic Elements named after the ancient subdivision of all matter.

Element	Sign
FIRE	Aries, Leo, Sagittarius
EARTH	Taurus, Virgo, Capricorn
AIR	Gemini, Libra, Aquarius
WATER	Cancer, Scorpio, Pisces

All matter is, of course, far more complex than these basic "ingredients" imply. Keep in mind that we are not referring to chemical composition, but to *symbolic* subdivisions of matter. These symbolic Elements represent the four outstanding characteristics of the human race, as we say today, the four basic psychological conditions.

Fire represents man's desire and creative energies. *Earth* stands for man's material resources, his environment and his possessions. *Air* symbolizes the intellect, man's ability to reason and communicate. Finally, *Water* relates to human feelings, and, in particular, man's capacity to love and sustain.

These elemental symbols were derived from observing the processes in the natural world. A plant required a suitable environment (earth) in which to grow. Like all life, it displayed the impulse or urge to grow (fire). Essential to its growth is oxygen (air) to allow photosynthesis. The same is true of the need for nourishment (water) in order to sustain life and its regenerative potentials.

Too much or too little of any of these elements can destroy a plant, and the same is true for people. Astrology teaches you how you can examine these elements and the behavior they represent to help you determine the correct balance required so that life may function properly. Your natal chart will reveal how these are structured and what they mean as regards to your personality.

One way to do this is to count the number of planets appearing in each Element. If, for instance, you had most of your planets appearing in *Fire* signs, you would be a person with a fiery temperament, a person capable of much warmth and passion, bright, excitable and aspiring. If the majority of your planets were in *Earth* signs, you would be a solid and dependable person, one who is practical, cautious and quiet. With the majority of planets in *Air* signs, you would be someone who is light and lively by nature, intellectual, idealistic, articulate and with a free-and-easy temperament. When the planets mainly occupy the *Water* signs, it shows that you are a sensitive, almost delicate person, intuitive and secretive. You might appear unstable to some, but this would be mainly because of the uncertainty you have about your emotional life. Your temperament would alternate between moments when you are content and those when you get the impression that your world is falling apart.

Signs falling under the same group of Elements are "in harmony" with each other. People born under signs belonging to the same Element are generally more compatible than those born under signs of different Elements. Virgoans and Capricorns, for instance, relate to each other better than do Virgoans and Sagittarians. Virgo and Capricorn are both Earth, but Virgo and Sagittarius are Earth and Fire.

The Qualities

The twelve signs are divided into three basic Qualities representing different character identities, each with a unique attitude and outlook on life. There are four signs belonging to each Quality.

Quality	Sign
CARDINAL	Aries, Cancer, Libra, Capricorn
FIXED	Taurus, Leo, Scorpio, Aquarius
MUTABLE	Gemini, Virgo, Sagittarius, Pisces

The names of the three Qualities represent basic disposition and character, namely, Cardinal is the *active* disposition, Fixed is the *passive* attitude and Mutable is the *changeable* nature.

Cardinal signs signify the beginning of the seasons of the year. Aries comes on the first day of spring; Cancer on the first day of summer; Libra on the first day of fall; and Capricorn on the first day of winter. Together, the Cardinal signs signify spontaneous transitions, something new about to happen.

If you were born with a majority of your planets in Cardinal signs, you would be a person who is spontaneous, restless, fast-acting and always anxious to be on the move. You would have natural leadership abilities, a person who causes things to happen, to get off the ground. These potentials would show up in the fact that you are an organizer.

The **Fixed** signs mark the midpoints of the seasons. Beginning on April 20, Taurus marks springtime in its fullness. Leo, beginning on July 23, comes when summer is in full swing. Scorpio begins at the center of the fall season, while Aquarius comes in the dead of winter. With the Sun at these seasonal midpoints, nothing much is happening in the way of change.

If you were born with a majority of your planets in Fixed signs, you would be, by comparison to a Cardinal person, a rather stable, established individual. You would be solid and inflexible by nature. You would be suspicious of change, particularly of new ideas and ways of doing things. In behavior and attitude, you would be conservative, not rowdy or faddish, and you would be full of purpose and unswerving in your loyalty to family, friends and causes.

The **Mutable** signs indicate transition. Specifically, the turn of the seasons. Gemini, Virgo, Sagittarius and Pisces all mark the transitional point from the old seasons to the new.

If your chart shows predominance of planets in Mutable signs, you would be given to changes, someone who is adaptable to new people and experiences. You would not go to pieces when procedures on the job change radically or if you were suddenly transferred. You would adjust to these changes. You enjoy being of service to others, because you are characteristically unselfish in your capacity to relinquish the old and accept the new, especially if it's necessary for you to render assistance to someone in need of help.

Signs belonging to the same group of Qualities are "hostile" to each other. In general, people born in signs of the same Quality will be less compatible than with people born in signs of a different Quality. This does not necessarily mean that Ariens and Cancers will hate each other, or not get along. It means that Ariens and Cancers are basically in conflict with each other, a tendency that would have to be watched.

It is important to know both the Element and Quality of each sign so you can round out the portrait of the person you are dealing with. In fact, knowing the Element and Quality of each sign occupied by planets in a person's chart is essential for determining the Signature. This is the next piece of our puzzle.

Signatures

Irrespective of the person's Sun sign, it frequently happens that the Signature has an overriding influence so that the person behaves like, and is motivated by, the sign that is the Signature. For example, the late president John F. Kennedy had his Sun in Gemini, a sign not particularly inclined in the direction of leadership enterprises and certainly not for the awesome demands of the chief executive of the United States. His Signature, however, was Capricorn, a sign especially qualified in character and temperament for the responsibilities of that elected office. The planetary ruler of Capricorn is Saturn and it occupied the most elevated position in Kennedy's chart, the tenth house, the house that relates to, among many other things, the Presidency! We will now show you how to derive the Signature of the people whose charts you want to examine.

Procedure: Once you have determined which signs are occupied by planets, you must then count the number of planets in the individual Qualities and Elements. That is, you simply count the number of planets in the Cardinal, Fixed and Mutable signs, and the number of planets in the Fire, Earth, Air and Water signs. The preponderance of planets in a particular Quality and Element determines the "Signature" of the individual.

Below is a slightly different table from the previous ones for Qualities and Elements. We have combined both so that you can see which signs go with which Quality and Element. The table will help you better understand the concept of Signatures.

	FIRE	WATER	AIR	EARTH
CARDINAL	Aries	Cancer	Libra	Capricorn
FIXED	Leo	Scorpio	Aquarius	Taurus
MUTABLE	Sagittarius	Pisces	Gemini	Virgo

You will notice from the table of Qualities and Elements that there are no duplications, and that no two signs have the same Quality and Element. What does this mean in terms of an individual? It means that this person has a certain *basic temperament* (Quality) for dealing with his or her affairs of life. Remember that the Qualities refer to the basic temperament, character or prevailing attitudes of an individual. The Elements, however, refer to the particular method of technique that person generally uses in dealing with those affairs. Persons with a preponderance of planets in Cardinal signs will have different Signatures depending on the preponderance of planets in the various Elements.

Let us give you an example to show how different combinations of Qualities and Elements give different Signatures. Say we have done a chart for a person who has planets appearing in four Cardinal signs. Fundamentally he is a Cardinal person and is constitutionally impatient with matters, a person who is anxious to get on with the business at hand so he can move on to the next item on his agenda. He responds quickly to stimulating ideas and suggestions. In short, he is a doer. What we have so far is only half the picture — and half the Signature. How he gets his business done is altogether a different matter. He has several strategies or methods he may use in completing the task before him. Just how he usually accomplishes his tasks is determined by the distribution of planets in the Elements.

If, for instance, our Cardinal man's chart shows a majority of planets in Fire signs, let's say four of them, he will handle his problems differently than if he had a majority of planets in Water signs. The Signature for the Cardinal-Fire distribution of planets in his chart is Aries. In fact, this Aries-Signature man solves his problems rather creatively, allowing himself few options to get the results he wants. Recall that a Cardinal person is someone who is anxious to finish his projects, while a Fire person is ardent, creative and imaginative. Aries, his Signature, profiles a person who is energetic and daring and who is innovative in dealing with his affairs. He makes a good statesman or executive.

Let us now return to Jane Doe and see what the planetary distribution in her chart revels for a Signature.

First, let us list her planetary distribution, as we did in chapter 2.

Sun	in	Aries (*Cardinal, Fire*)
Moon	in	Taurus (*Fixed, Earth*)
Mercury	in	Taurus (*Fixed, Earth*)
Venus	in	Gemini (*Mutable, Air*)
Mars	in	Capricorn (*Cardinal, Earth*)
Jupiter	in	Sagittarius (*Mutable, Fire*)
Saturn	in	Scorpio (*Fixed, Water*)
Uranus	in	Pisces (*Mutable, Water*)
Neptune	in	Leo (*Fixed, Fire*)
Pluto	in	Cancer (*Cardinal, Water*)

The next step is to record the number of planets in the signs according to the Qualities and Elements. The distribution for Jane Doe is as follows:

	Cardinal —	3
QUALITIES	Fixed —	4
	Mutable —	3

In similar fashion we record the number of planets in the Elements:

	Fire —	3
ELEMENTS	Earth —	3
	Air —	1
	Water —	3

From the above it should be apparent that, while there is a preponderance of planets in the Qualities (four in Fixed), there is a fairly even distribution among the Elements so that there is no preponderance. Because of this nearly even condition, we cannot seriously establish a Signature in Jane Doe's chart. This kind of situation does occur at times, and what we do in such a case is summarize according to the display of planets as they show a kind of balance in the Elements while showing a slight degree of emphasis in the Qualities, in this case four in Fixed signs.

There is a way to determine which Element has the edge in the case of Jane Doe, and it's this: because the Sun is the identity and forms the nucleus for the development of character, its role in the chart must never be underestimated. By noting the sign occupied by the Sun we can then refer to the planet ruling that sign, and see whether it offers anything in the way of emphasis. The planet that rules Aries is Mars. Now see where Mars is located and the Quality and Element of the sign it occupies. Very often this is enough to give us the emphasis required. In Jane Doe's chart, Mars is in Capricorn, an Earth sign! Because Mars rules the Sun's sign, a most important consideration, we can safely regard its sign position as providing the additional emphasis in the Earth Element. From this we can derive a Signature.* We have already determined that the predominant Quality is Fixed. With the Earth Element gaining additional emphasis as determined in the foregoing discussion, we can now say that there is a Fixed-Earth preponderance in Jane Doe's chart. The effect of this combination is similar to Taurus, the *only* Fixed-Earth sign. The characteristics found in this sign will be strongly evident in the unfolding development of this person and be revealed in her prevailing attitude, behavior and motivation. The overlay of Taurus on the Aries Sun means that she will be ardent, inspired, creative and aggressive (Aries), but also determined, tenacious and resourceful in her endeavors. This is altogether a most productive combination. In fact, one of Aries' lessons in life is to learn responsibility, temperance and persistence.

Refer to Appendix VIII for information on what it means when a Quality or Element is lacking even a single planet. That too is significant.

---

* For you readers who have had a time chart drawn, the ascendant (rising sign) or its ruler will add the necessary emphasis when required.

CHAPTER 7 Individual Sign Divisions

Up to this point we have talked about which planets have which effects upon behavior and makeup. We have also suggested a kind of hierarchy of planetary influences, naming the Sun as the most powerful. And, as a result, we have spent considerable time talking about the Sun signs. But just knowing that the Sun occupies a particular zodiacal sign at your birth is not enough to give a refined picture of your character makeup, your attitudes and your modus operandi. Just *where* the Sun is in that sign is crucial.

Why? Because the mere presence of the Sun in a sign is not the same when the Sun is "early" in the sign as it is when it is "late" in the sign. In other words, the Sun at 10° Aries is not the same as the Sun at 27° Aries. The astrological effect is not the same on the person whose chart is being studied.

But what do we mean by "early" and "late" in a sign? Let's go back to some early discussion of the zodiacal wheel. Recall that the twelve signs describe a perfect circle of 360°. That means each individual sign describes an arc of 30° of the zodiacal wheel.

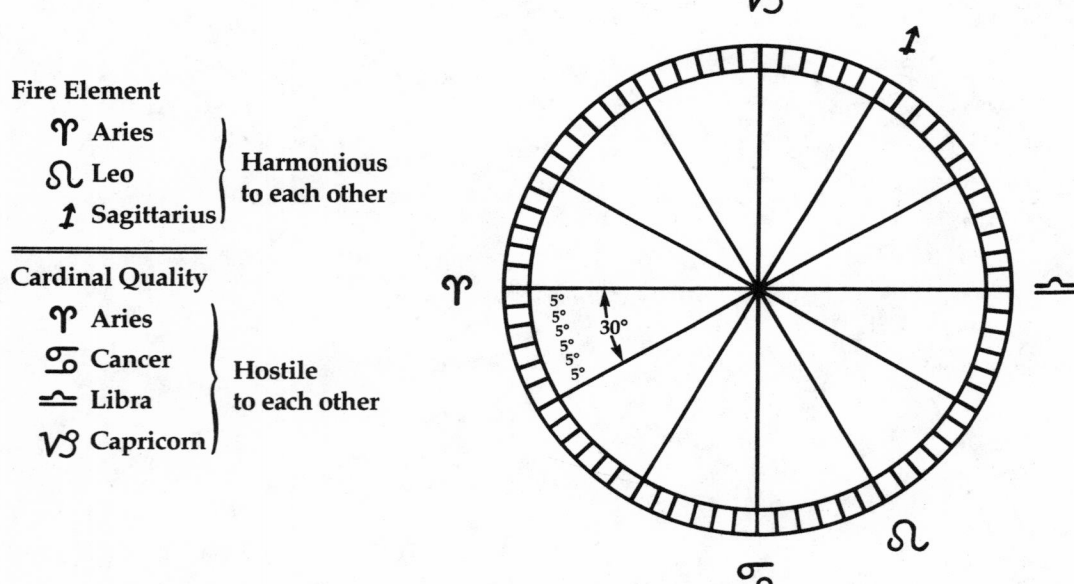

Fire Element

♈ Aries
♌ Leo   } Harmonious to each other
♐ Sagittarius

Cardinal Quality

♈ Aries
♋ Cancer
♎ Libra   } Hostile to each other
♑ Capricorn

To better understand the particular influence of the Sun in a sign, astrologers subdivide each of the signs. Signs of the same Elements (Fire, Earth, Air and Water) are divided into three equal 10° arcs, which are called "Decanates." Signs of the same Quality are divided into four equal 7½° arcs.

Knowing the exact angular location of the Sun in a sign will, according to these subdivisions, determine for us how particular sign principles are enriched or how they are limited by other factors. We will learn what to do about basic behavioral problems.

The Decanates (10°): In any sign there are three decanates. The first is from 0° to 10°, the second from 10° to 20°, and the third from 20° to 30°.

The particular astrological nature of the first decanate is derived from the particular sign under examination. The nature of the second and third decanates is derived from the next two signs of the same Element group moving counterclockwise around the zodiacal chart. Let's consider Aries, for example.

Aries belongs to the Fire Element — it is a Fire sign, in other words. So are Leo and Sagittarius as we read counterclockwise around the zodiacal wheel.

If in a chart the Sun at a person's birth appeared in the first 10° of Aries, the first decanate, we would say that a stronger Aries influence would result — more primitive, Aries derives an eagerness to take action. If the Sun appeared between 10° and 20°, the second decanate, in the same sign of Aries, the influence would take on a subcurrent of Leo, which would modify the potential Aries behavior with more determination. In other words, the Leo influence would be felt on the Aries impulsiveness. The person might manifest restraint because his authority — a Leo characteristic — may be questioned if he or she acted on immediate impulse. If the Sun appeared in the last 10°, the third decanate, there would be a subcurrent of Sagittarius guiding characteristic Aries behavior.

Figure 9. Decanate Lineargraph for Aries

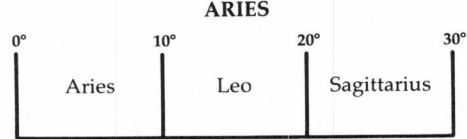

The entire of the Aries sign — all 30° — remains Aries. But the first 10° remains *pure* Aries; the second is Aries with Leo conditioning; the third is Aries with Sagittarius offering wider intellectual perspective upon the basic nature to take action. Three people born with their Suns in the first, second, and third decanates of the same sign will have characteristics in common, but they will operate differently because their perspectives will be different enough to alter the way they pursue their objectives.

These decanate differences among people of the same Sun sign are determined by the different planetary rulers operating within the same sign. Let's go back to our Aries example. Aries itself is ruled by Mars. Yet, if a person is born with his Sun in the second decanate, he will experience influence from Leo which is ruled by the Sun. If a person is born with his Sun in the third decanate of Aries, the Aries-Sagittarius sector (the last 10°), his behavior will manifest some influences of Jupiter which is the ruler of Sagittarius.

The various planetary energies operating in Aries are sufficiently varied so as to differentiate the behaviors of people born with their Sun in the same sign. There is a consistency in this arrangement because all the signs in this example are Fire signs, and there is harmony in the desire for self-expression. If disharmony occurs, it is the result of conflict coming from other factors in the chart. And that is what we want to discuss now.

Quadruplicities (7½°): What we have examined so far are the harmonious forces operating at various planetary positions in a solar chart. Properly understood, these forces can help an individual grow and develop his or her potential. But, unfortunately, life is not all hearts and flowers. Nor are the energies in the signs of the Zodiac. Lurking within the framework of positive forces are patterns that might inhibit growth and development.

These are "hostile" influences that we can locate when we examine the signs and the various planetary positions in them. To do this, we must again subdivide each of the signs. This time into *fourths* — that is, into equal 7½° arcs relating to the three Qualities to which the signs belong: Cardinal, Fixed, and Mutable. This new subdivision helps us determine what stands in the way, or what inhibits, our ability to express ourselves freely. In other words, the four quadruplicity subdivisions relate to the positive sign qualities that we are reluctant to exploit. Knowing these "inhibitors" can only help us make some necessary adjustments for more successful self-expression.

When we subdivide each sign of the Zodiac to four equal 7½° arcs (quadruplicities), we ascribe each to one of the signs of the same Quality group. Let us consider an example of a solar chart with the Sun in Aries. The first quadruplicity corresponds to Aries, the first sign in the Cardinal group; the second, to Cancer; the third to Libra; and the fourth to Capricorn — in that order.

Figure 10. Quadruplicity Lineargraph for Aries

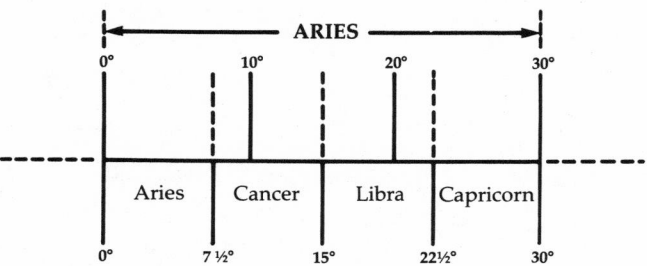

Each of these segments of the sign of Aries has a subruler, that is, the planetary ruler of each of the successive signs of the same Quality moving counterclockwise around the Zodiac. The first segment of Aries is Aries — and a Sun in this position would indicate unmodified Martian energy in the exclusive Aries frame of reference, since Mars is the ruler of this sign. But in the next segment there are inhibiting influences from Cancer's ruling Moon. The same with the successive rulers of Libra and Capricorn as we move along the full 22½° through to the 30° of the complete sign of Aries.

But we must not forget the positive influences coming from the various rulers of the signs of the same Elements. It is quite possible for the Sun, say, to be at 16° Aries, which would be in the second decanate corresponding to Leo, which is ruled by the Sun, yet overlapping the third quadruplicity, Libra, which is ruled by Venus. In fact, to fully understand the distinct kinds of behavior possible by any one planet in any one sign we have to put together the influences of both the Elements and the Qualities.

Putting together the various influences operating in any one sign, we can say that there are *six* distinct kinds of characteristic behaviors possible. Although there are three decanates and four quadruplicities, when graphically laid out straight, we see six possible phases. The illustration below should make this clear.

Figure 11. Decanates and Quadruplicities for Aries

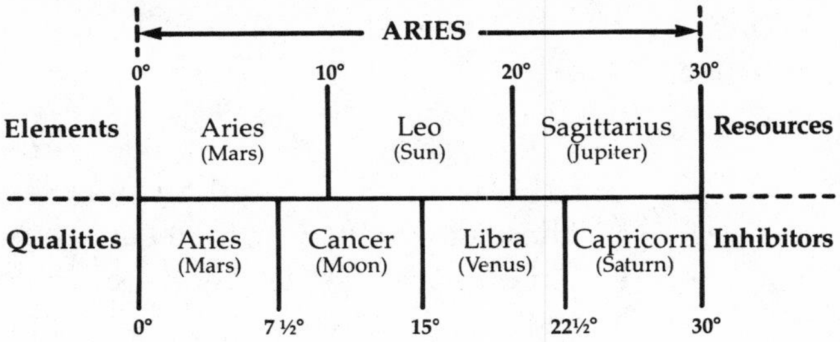

All this might sound quite complicated by now. But you must remember to keep in mind that when doing a chart you are only concerned with that specific degree the Sun occupies on the particular date of birth. If, for instance, at your birth your Sun appeared at 15° Aries, this would mean that you are ardent in expressing yourself — the Aries influence; and you are loyal to those you love — i.e., the Leo influence. But you are inhibited from or reluctant about exploiting some basic Cancer good points, namely a willingness to help others when needed. In other words, you are reluctant to compromise, or you need to be less self-interested, less egocentric.

To illustrate further how the sign divisions work, let's take a look again at our Jane Doe.

Checking the Ephemeris, we learn that Jane Doe, born on April 6, 1924, has her Sun in 15°55′ of Aries. Rounding this off to the nearest degree gives us 16° Aries. Let's see where that puts her Sun on a linear graph: Aries is a Fire Element and a Cardinal Quality:

Figure 12. Decanates and Quadruplicities (Jane Doe Sample)

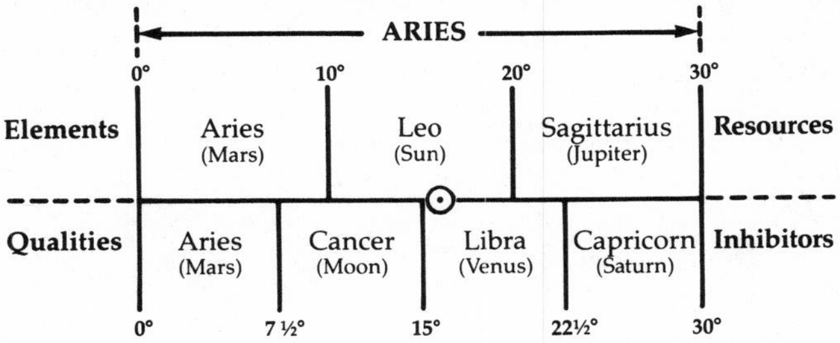

A Sun location of 16° puts Jane Doe in the second decanate and just into the third quadruplicity. What this indicates is that working for her are strong Leonian qualities, that is, her "resources," since her Sun is nearly in the exact middle of the second decanate, which is associated with the second Fire sign, Leo, which in turn is ruled by the Sun. A strong ego drive; enthusiasm; strong self-assertion. But, it also means that working against her are some Libran deficiencies, that is, her "inhibitors," since 16° puts her Sun in the third quadruplicity occupied by the third Cardinal sign, Libra, whose ruler is Venus. What this Libran deficiency translates as is a natural inhibition for Jane Doe to mediate, to weigh her own needs to succeed with the needs of others. She must learn to meet others halfway or she will lose favor of others and perhaps retard achievement of her goals. There will be times when she will need to seek the advice of others, and not operate just on her own motivation.

Sign Divisions and Their Interpretations

The principles operating in making an interpretation of Sun locations is rather simple. First, determine from the Ephemeris the angular location of the sun in the sign. Second, for the sake of convenience draw a simple linear graph as we have done, showing the three decanates above the line and the four quadruplicities below the line. Third, the dominant resources available to the individual are those determined by the characteristics of the sign and its ruler associated with the particular decanate the Sun occupies; likewise, the Quality of the sign below the line determines the individual's inhibitions, those behavioral areas where he is deficient, or where he is reluctant to adjust. These inhibitions can seriously interfere with the successful utilization of one's resources. Therefore, it is important to weigh the positive Element effects against the areas of inhibition or limitation determined by the Quality of the sign below the line.

In Appendix III of this book we have broken down each of the twelve signs into the three decanates and four quadruplicities just as we did in the examples above. And for each of the six behavioral influences operating in any one sign, we have offered simple interpretations.

The next piece of the puzzle follows naturally from what we have just determined. We have just learned about the angular location of the Sun in the zodiacal sign and the significance of the particular occurrence of that planet. But the location of the other planets is also crucial in determining an astrological profile of a person. That brings us to the topic of Planetary Aspects.

CHAPTER **8** Planetary Aspects

As we have been saying all along, the location of the various planets in one's Zodiac are important for the drawing up of a chart, whether simple or detailed. And as we have just shown, the particular angular location of the Sun is crucial — the most important planetary location, since the Sun relates to the formation of the ego. But what about the other planets? Certainly their angular locations are significant.

And they are. But their locations are particularly significant with respect to the locations of the other planets. That is, we are not just concerned with their degree locations within a sign alone; we are concerned here with locations relative to the other planets in the zodiacal wheel. The angular distances *between* the planets which we call Aspects.

Planetary Aspects are crucial because the astrological effect of a planet varies according to how it relates to the other planets in the chart. The angular differences between planets determines a different "aspect" on the kind of influence, say, Mercury exerts on your personality and instincts.

Before we get to the individual aspects, we should familiarize you with the appearance of a detailed solar chart. Astrologers use circular charts. In fact, in shops where astrological books are sold, you can probably buy blank charts without the individual signs written in. Plastic templates for drawing your own charts are also available.

Figure 13. Basic Zodiacal Wheel for Aries

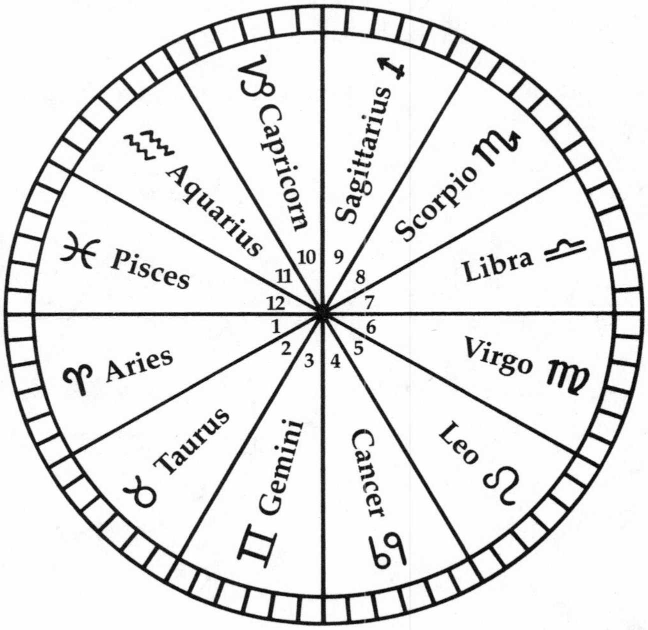

For reasons we will explain later, the Sun sign of the individual being charted corresponds to segment 1 of our circular blank. In other words, for an Aries person such as Jane Doe, the first segment — which, by the way are called "houses," and which we will define later — corresponds to Aries. For a person born with his or her Sun in Taurus, then we would begin with Taurus in the first segment and proceed around the zodiacal wheel, with the remaining signs in their natural order.

Figure 14. Basic Zodiacal Wheel Adapted for a Taurus (♉) Sun Sign

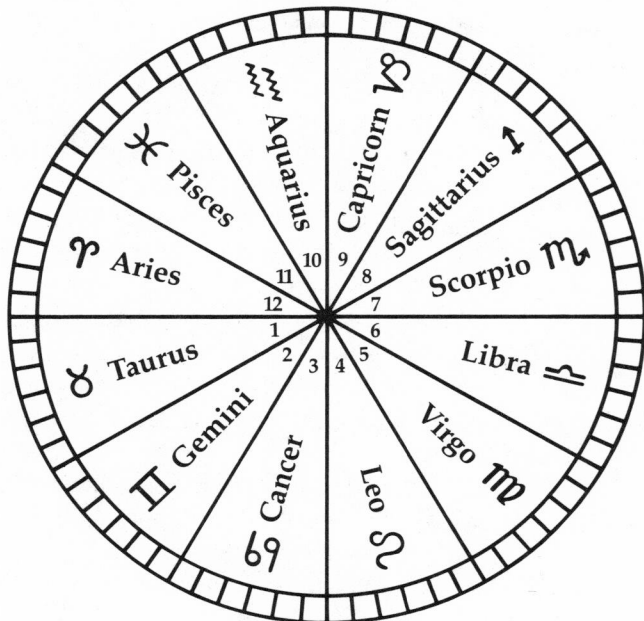

Once we have set up the chart, the next step is to put into the chart the individual planets whose locations we get from the Ephemeris. For Jane Doe, her detailed chart would look like Figure 15.

Figure 15. Jane Doe's Chart (With All Planets Entered)

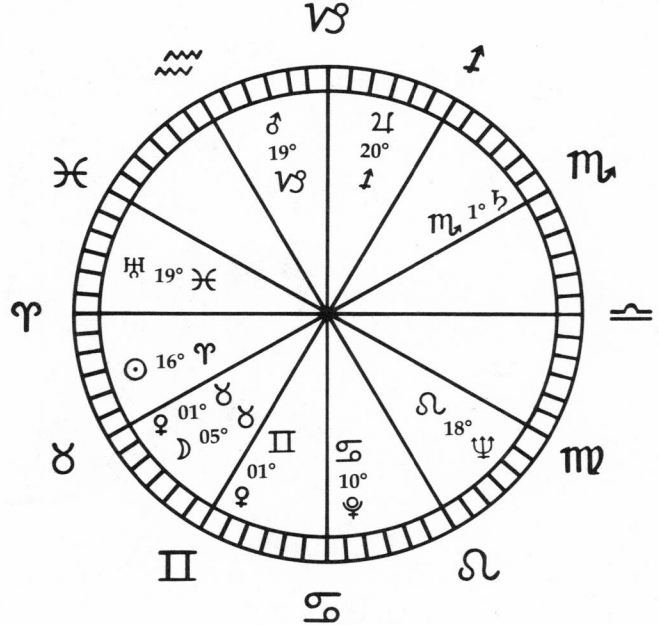

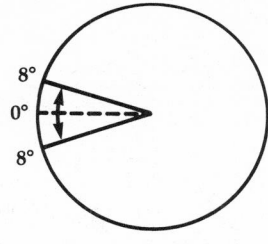

The Conjunction ☌

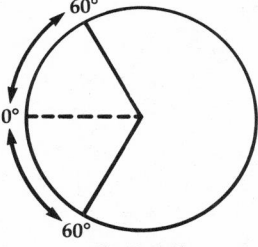

The Sextile ✶

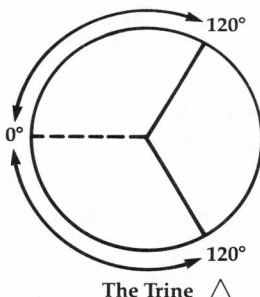

The Square ☐

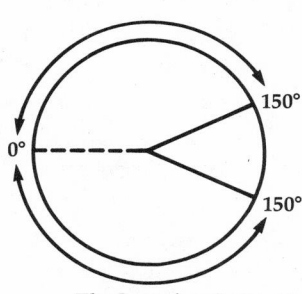

The Trine △

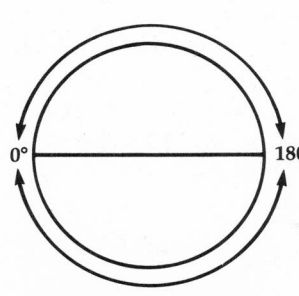

The Inconjunct ⊼

The Opposition ☍

We realize that this may seem confusing at this point. And, yes, we are jumping ahead some, since in later chapters we will go into greater detail on the actual setting up of the chart. But for the time being we want to establish the fact that Planetary Aspects are determined from the relative distances between the planets as they appear on the whole 360° circular chart plan. As you can see from Jane Doe's chart, her Sun at the 16° mark in Aries is not too far from her Mercury (☿) located at 1° in Taurus. In fact, just a matter of 15 degrees. But her Sun is nearly half a circle away from Saturn (♄) located at 0° Scorpio. The distance between them is 166°. There are 30° left in Scorpio plus four entire 30° signs (Sagittarius, Capricorn, Aquarius and Pisces) in addition to 16° of Aries. It is not important at this point to worry about the calculation of the degree locations. What is important is to recognize the fact that the individual planets have varying angular distances between themselves. These distances we call Aspects.

There are six major Aspects we will be dealing with in this book. They are the *conjunction*, the *sextile*, the *square*, the *trine*, the *inconjunct* and the *opposition*. These names refer to the way we divide up in angles the circular distances between them. See Figure 16.

The Conjunction: When there is between 0° and 8° distance between any two planets, they are said to be in conjunction.

The Sextile: This term refers to a division of the circle into 60° arcs. When two planets have 60° between them, plus or minus 6°, they are said to form a sextile.

The Square: As the name suggests, this is a division of the circle into 90° arcs. When any two planets have 90° between them, plus or minus 8°, they are said to be "square" to each other.

The Trine: This term refers to the subdivision of the circle into three 120° arcs. When two planets are separated by 120°, plus or minus 8°, they are said to form a "trine."

The Inconjunct: When there is a 150° distance between any two planets, plus or minus 3°, they are said to be "inconjunct" to each other.

The Opposition: When there is 180° between any two planets, plus or minus 8°, these two planets are in "opposition."

You may find some of the planets are not in Aspect to any other planet. See Appendix VII.

The diagrams to the left are meant only to illustrate the six major Aspects. Since the planets in Aspect can be located anywhere on the chart circle, we are illustrating only the relative degree distance between them. What is important is the angular as well as the shortest distance between them, counting either clockwise or counterclockwise.

Figure 16. Diagrams of Six Major Aspects

In astrology, certain Aspects are benign by nature and are considered as *favorable*. Some planetary Aspects are by nature malefic and are regarded as *unfavorable*.

The favorable Aspects are the sextiles and trines (60° and 120° respectively). The unfavorable Aspects are the squares, inconjuncts and oppositions (90°, 150° and 180° respectively).

Favorable Aspects tend to bring out the positive natures of the planets involved. Unfavorable Aspects tend to activate the negative natures of the planets involved.

But what about two planets that are in conjunction (0°–8°)? When you do a chart and you discover such a conjunction between two planets, in order to understand the astrological effect you have to consider the nature of the planets involved. If only the traditionally benign planets are involved — that is, Sun, Moon, Mercury, Venus and Jupiter — the result is beneficial and helpful. When any planet involved in a conjunction is malefic by nature — that is, Mars, Saturn, Uranus, Neptune or Pluto — then you must regard the effect as stress or strain between the two. In such an unfavorable conjunction, you must take heed of the negative forces of the slower planet working against the positive forces of the faster-moving planet.

A most important point that must also be considered is when three or more planets are involved in a conjunction with each other. When a third planet is within 0°–8° of the second planet, the fourth planet is within 0°–8° of the third planet, and so on. That is the linkage that binds them together and they are to be considered in conjunction with each other. Refer to *Stellium*, Appendix V, Special Planetary Formations and Complexes.

If there is a break in the linkage (more than 8°), then only those planets that are linked together can be considered as being in Aspect. Any other planet that Aspects any single planet in the group must be considered to be in Aspect with each planet in the bind, whether or not they are each in the degree range of the particular Aspect being formed. These type conditions can change the complete nature of the individual.

Refer to chapter 12, Detailed Solar Chart for John Doe. Note the planets Uranus, Moon and Saturn are all in the sign of Gemini and all within 8° of each other. Also note that the planet Uranus is 9° away from Saturn (out of range) but bound by the linkage to the Moon. Now look to the sign of Libra. Here you find the Sun, Mars and Mercury, but only the Sun and Mars are in conjunction. The linkage is broken by Mercury, which is at 26° of Libra, out of range. Therefore the planet Pluto, at 7° of Leo, sextiles each of the planets in Gemini but only sextiles the Sun and Mars in Libra. By coincidence the planet Pluto is within Aspect range to each of the planets in both the conjunctions.

For a second and more involving example, refer to Alice's Adjusted Solar Chart, chapter 11. Note here that by the adjustment of the Moon from 27° Capricorn to 7° Aquarius, it now squares Uranus at 13° of Taurus. But, because Venus conjuncts Uranus, the Moon by linkage also squares Venus even though Venus is out of range individually to the Moon. There also exists a bind between the Venus–Uranus conjunction by the opposition they make to Mars at 20° of Scorpio, which now involves the Moon through its bind to Venus–Uranus. This now creates another special formation, the T-Cross.

How to Interpret Aspects

It is important in the interpretation of detailed solar charts to understand the general significance of the planetary aspects. What follows are some guidelines to aid you with the interpretations of the Aspects.

Conjunctions (☌)
0° to 8°

A conjunction occurs when two planets occupy the same position in a chart, give or take 8°. As we said above, depending on the planets involved, a conjunction can be either favorable or unfavorable. Whatever the case, in a conjunction the two planets' influences are greatly stimulated, greatly concentrated. In fact, all conjunctions acquire a Mars energy force to create strong drives associated with each of the planets involved. Say, for instance, your Sun "conjuncts" Mars, as is said in astrology. We have just learned above that when Mars is in conjunction with another planet, we must consider this Aspect unfavorable. So what does this Aspect mean? It means that the positive natures of the Sun will be in conflict with the negative natures of Mars. If you refer to chapter 5, The Planets and Their Natures, you will recall the positive and negative characteristics of the planets. The Sun, remember, represents the ego, the desire for recognition, self-assertiveness. The positive nature of the Sun has to do with pride, a sense of dignity, the power of your ego. But these are in conjunction with Mars, whose negative natures are arrogance, restlessness, thoughtlessness. Keep in mind that Planetary Protocol means that Mars will overpower the Sun negatively. The combination of the two — the conjunction of the Sun-ego and Mars-drive — creates in you a strong desire to achieve attention, but at the risk of being impulsive and rude. And if you don't learn from these unfavorable potentials, you may offend others and lose their respect and support.

Sextile (✶)
60° plus or minus 6°
(54° through 66°)

According to astrological tradition, the sextile is an aspect of communication. When two planets are sextile, one has the ability to communicate or express the positive natures of each. Let us say, for instance, that in your own chart your Sun sextiles Saturn. From chapter 5 recall that the Sun is representative of your will, your ego striving for recognition. We also recall that Saturn represents control, efficiency, responsibility, practicality. In sextile, the Sun–Saturn Aspect creates in you the tendency to think before you take action in order to achieve the result you desire. In other words, you would be mature and methodical and would know how to promote and how to communicate your ideas effectively.

Square (☐)
90° plus or minus 8°
(82° through 98°)

The square is an Aspect of conflict, fear and inhibitions. The conflict exists in this configuration because your habitual way of doing things runs into reversals or emotional hang-ups. The result is frustration from the way qualities of the two planets in square work at cross purposes to each other. And that happens because the negative natures of one planet override the positive natures of the second planet. But how do we know which planet's natures dominate? We will explain the concept in greater detail shortly, but what determines which planet dominates which in any Aspect is the principle of Planetary Protocol. This concept refers to the relative orbital speeds of the planets around the Earth.

Let it suffice to say for the time being that the following is the order of the planets beginning with the fastest and ending in the slowest: Moon, Mercury, Venus, Sun, Mars, Jupiter, Saturn, Uranus, Neptune, and Pluto. Now let's see how the square works in an example. Let us say that in your chart your Mars squares Saturn. Mars represents your animal aggressiveness, your instinctive self. On the positive side, Mars qualities are energy, courage, directness in speech, sexual passion. Since Saturn is the slower of the two planets from our order above, its *negative* qualities will overrule the positive Mars drive. That is, inhibitions and fears will be a source of constant conflict with the Mars urges to do things. There will be the impulse to achieve things, but habitual hesitation and doubt. Many manic-depressive personalities have Mars square Saturn Aspects in their charts.

Trine (△) 120° plus or minus 8° (112° through 128°)

When two planets are 120° from each other on a chart they form this favorable aspect. The trine is considered an aspect that relates to one's resources. That is, an individual with a trine in his or her chart has as resources the positive — the favorable — natures of the planets involved. And because of Planetary Protocol, the positive nature of the *slower* of the two planets will dominate usually. But generally people with trines in their charts do little about taking advantage of these resources. In other words, more generally than not they sit on their talents, their resources instead of putting them to action, instead of capitalizing on them. Let's give an example. Let us say that in your chart your Sun trines Jupiter. Jupiter is the slower of the planets, so its positive resources will dominate those of the Sun. From chapter 5 we learned that one positive characteristic of Jupiter is optimism. And the Sun, we know, is associated with the drive of your ego, your striving for significance. If your Jupiter trines your Sun, that would indicate that because of your optimism you feel that you can do nearly anything you want or that things will always turn out okay in the end. That is a fine attitude, but sometimes you may not, in your excessive optimism, do anything to bring about those good results. Your own sunny hopefulness may, in fact, make you lazy. Let us consider another example. Say, Mercury trines Mars. Mercury relates to one's communicative powers in general. And Mars, which has protocol over Mercury, relates to one's animal instincts, one's energies and drives. If Mercury trines Mars, the results would be quick-wittedness, a talent for energetic self-expression. But remember, we said that in general people with trines in their charts may not take advantage of their talents so defined by the positive natures of the planets involved. Such powers of forceful, energetic communication may lie dormant.

Inconjunct (⚻) 150° plus or minus 3° (147° through 153°)

When two planets are separated by 150°, plus or minus 3°, they are said to be inconjunct. This aspect brings out the negative characteristics of the two planets involved. An inconjunct in one's chart traditionally is said to signify a condition of self-neglect. Usually, the neglect centers around matters of health. Whatever the specific neglect, a destructive disregard is involved. An inconjunct almost always causes a dilemma, and one that can be understood if we examine the planets involved. If in your chart your Sun inconjuncts Pluto, that would indicate a conflict between Pluto's influences and your ego (your Sun). Since Pluto is associated with social events, regenerations and debts owed, this

Aspect might suggest that your will feels frustrated by the demands upon it to fulfill obligations, to serve others, to be dominated by the needs of others. And any bitterness you would feel would necessarily arise out of the resentment of and intolerance for being controlled by others and social circumstances. Should you yield under pressure to these external demands, then what might result is a specific frustration out of self-denial, or self-neglect. In short, you gave too much of yourself.

Opposition (☍)
180° plus or minus 8°
(172° through 188°)

When two planets are separated by 180° with an 8° margin, they are said to be in opposition to each other. They are, in fact, hostile to each other. Oppositions always involve conflicts, confrontations, differences and separations. But, in general, they are more acutely discernable than the other unfavorable Aspects, squares and inconjuncts, because of the direct "oppositeness" of the planets involved. Two planets in opposition represent two sets of forces tugging in opposite directions. The resulting effect is a difficulty in resolving the conflicts that surface in life situations. There is an inner conflict in you someplace that needs to be worked on. Consider the case where your Mercury is in opposition to your Neptune. As we know, Mercury rules your powers of communication, your effectiveness of communication, your ability to persuade others. But we also know that Neptune is a planet of uncertainties, anxiety and guilt. Because we have an unfavorable Aspect here, the negative natures of Neptune — anxiety, doubt, guilt, uncertainty — will, because of the Principle of Planetary Protocol, distort those positive communicative potentials asserted by Mercury. The result of this Mercury–Neptune opposition is the failure to project yourself with credibility. This might be caused by doubts you have about your own credibility or by conscious deception. In other words, you might deliberately try to mislead or misrepresent yourself. And, more often than not, this opposition will make people question you. Relatively speaking, the opposition Aspect is the least difficult to deal with or to resolve. The square is the most difficult because its contrary forces are deeply seated; they go back to parental conditioning.

To give a complete reading of all possible Aspects would be far too much for the scope of this book. The combinations would go into the hundreds. We have, nonetheless, given in Appendix VI of this book more simplified Aspect interpretations to help you. For more detailed syntheses of the various possible Aspects, we recommend that you consult *Planets in Aspect* by Robert Pelletier. It is also most significant when any planet *is not* in Aspect. For Analyses for unaspected planets refer to Appendix VII in this book.

Planetary Protocol

Earlier in this chapter we introduced you to the concept of Planetary Protocol. The concept is important to the understanding of how Aspects are determined, so we would like to go into more detail about it.

As we said, when two planets are in Aspect to each other, they will not equally affect the individual whose chart is being done. One planet will exert its influences more strongly. In fact, as we said, it is the faster planet that is always subject to the influence of the slower planet. This makes good sense, since the faster planet does not have as much time to affect an individual with its energies as a slower one does.

It is essential that you abide by the Principle of Planetary Protocol before you attempt to determine planetary influences. You should also keep in mind that when planets are in favorable Aspect — sextiles and trines and, depending on the planets involved, conjunctions — the *positive* tendencies of the slower planet prevail. Likewise, when planets are in unfavorable or malefic Aspect — squares, inconjuncts, oppositions and, at times, conjunctions — the *negative* tendencies of the planets prevail, those of the slowest planet dominating the configuration.

Special note: When considering Aspects of any nature, the Aspects that have the closest margin of degrees to being exact will be much more pronounced than those with a wider degree margin. For instance, with Mercury in opposition to Neptune at 172° or 188° they are considered within the orb of the 180° exact degree relationship. An opposition is exactly 180°, but a variance of minus 8° or plus 8° is still considered effective, though the influence would be subtle and perhaps even unnoticed if there are closer Aspects in the chart.

When the Aspect is exact or very close to exact, then the result is much more pronounced. This is true of all Aspects, and when a planet makes more than one Aspect, the Aspect that is closest to the exact degree of perfection is the one having greater priority over all the others.

For the sake of simplicity, we have included some brief comments on effects of the Aspects themselves and suggestions for how to handle them.

ASPECT EFFECTS

CONJUNCTION (♂)	Intense power, desire and energy
SEXTILE (✳)	Mental abilities; the way you think
SQUARE (□)	Inhibiting conditions, hang-ups, fears, obstacles
TRINE (△)	Available resources, creative talent, favorable conditions
INCONJUNCT (⅄)	Obligations to others, or the services you render voluntarily
OPPOSITION (♊)	Conditions that tend to strain relationships, competition, struggle

ASPECT SOLUTIONS

CONJUNCTION (♂)	Direct this energy into creative outlets to derive major benefits.
SEXTILE (✳)	Share what you know that others may enjoy the freedom knowledge brings.
SQUARE (□)	The principles of the planets involved are what you need to learn.
TRINE (△)	Take every chance you can get to develop your creative potentials.
INCONJUNCT (⅄)	Offer your services, but only as much as is absolutely necessary.
OPPOSITION (♊)	Try to think of challenges as opportunities to gain self-mastery.

CHAPTER 9 Using the Ephemeris

Before you can do an Aspect analysis of anybody, including our Jane Doe, you must know exactly how to use the Ephemeris which appears in the back of this book. You cannot set up a chart without the Ephemeris since it is a detailed almanac specifying the zodiacal positions of all the planets from day to day.

Once you are comfortable with the tables you will then be able to draw a detailed solar chart.

What we have called a simple solar chart or detailed solar chart are both *solar* charts. You have heard the term *horoscope,* but it is not the same thing as the solar chart, simple or detailed. A horoscope is a *time* chart that specifies the astrological significance of the planetary locations from hour to hour. The word *horoscope,* in fact, means "view of the hour." The solar chart gives the planets' positions for each day. What are the differences, then?

A *time chart* is a chart that is based on the time of your birth (A.M. or P.M.) and it shows exactly where the nine planets are in the Zodiac and sky when viewed from the particular place of birth. A crucial factor taken into account in setting up a time chart or horoscope is the particular sign that has ascended at the moment of your birth. Just as the Sun rises and sets each day, so does each zodiacal sign. A new sign rises every two hours of the twenty-four-hour day. The particular ascendant sign is important to the meaning of your horoscope, but it can be determined only by knowing the exact time of your birth. The ascendant or rising sign is located in specific degrees from the eastern horizon. For instance, on the hour of your birth you may have had 25° Gemini rising. If the time of birth is known, then your particular planets will be located, not just by angles, but by what astrologers call the "houses" — the abstract twelve-part division of the Earth's daily rotation. The houses refer to the specific departments of your life which the planets will influence.

The solar chart is what this book is preparing you to create on your own. It is the astrological chart that you set up when the time of birth is unknown. The positions of the planets are taken from the Ephemeris for the day you were born, not the exact hour of that day. They are located by degrees in various zodiacal signs. Their relationship to one another is the same as in the time chart (with the exception of the Moon, since it moves so fast), but there is no way of knowing what departments of life they will influence since there is no way of determining what sign was rising without the exact time of birth. The purpose and value of the solar chart is mainly in profiling character and its continued development from the various behavioral dynamics.

How to Use the Ephemeris   In chapter 2 we examined the Ephemeris and learned how to use it when we only needed to known what signs the Sun, Moon and planets were in for the simple chart. In order to set up a detailed chart, we must first learn how to use the Ephemeris with greater attention to the detailed information it provides.

The Sun, Moon and Planets in Zodiacal Degrees: The location of the Sun is given in degrees, minutes and seconds of zodiacal longitude, the Moon's position is given in degrees and minutes, and the planets' position in the signs is given in degrees only. (Minutes and seconds are not necessary in solar charts.) Remember, now, that each sign occupies 30° of the zodiacal circle. Any planet thus enters a sign of 0°00'00" (zero degrees, zero minutes and zero seconds). After traversing 60 minutes of space, it moves to 1° of the sign. It continues at that rate until it has traversed the full 30° of that sign. It then crosses the "cusp" (the boundary between signs) into the next sign, and 30° later it moves to the next sign, and so on all around the 360° of the zodiacal circle.

To help you get familiar with using the tables of the Ephemeris, let us take the sample of Jane Doe, which we used for the simple chart in chapter 2. Her birthdate is April 6, 1924. (See Figure 17, which is a copy from the tables in Appendix X for April 1924.)

As you can see, the Ephemeris shows the locations of the planets at the very beginning of each day during the month. (The day begins at midnight, Greenwich Mean Time.) In the Sun's column you will notice that on the first day of April 1924 the Sun's position is given 10°59'37", which reads 10 degrees, 59 minutes and 37 seconds of Aries. As you go down this column you can trace the Sun's progress in degrees as it traverses this sign of Aries, until on April 6 at midnight it has reached 15°55'13". This we round off to the nearest degree, which is 16°.

As indicated at the top of the table for that month, the Sun then entered the sign of Taurus (shown by the tiny symbol ♉) on April 20 at 8:59 A.M., Greenwich Mean Time, which meant that the Sun at that time was at 0°00'00". By midnight of April 21, the sun had moved to 00°36'37". If we were setting up a chart for somebody born on April 20, 1924, we would record the Sun's position as noted: 29°38'06".

Then we would move to the next column to the right which lists the locations of the Moon for that month. As you can see, this body moves with faster speed through the signs. In fact, from April 1 through April 6, it moves through Pisces, Aries and Taurus. By the end of the month (bottom of the column), the Moon has gone through the entire zodiac and is back to Pisces again. For April 6, the Moon is at 4°57' of Taurus (♉).

In the next column to the right along the April 6 line you will find the positions of Mercury. You will notice that its location — and that of the following planets — is given only in degrees since the movements are slower in contrast to the Moon's. If you look at the April 6 row, you will see that Mercury was at 1° of Taurus. Proceeding right across the April 6 row, you will note the locations of the other planets.

Because Pluto is the planet that is the farthest from the Earth, it moves the slowest through the Zodiac. In fact, Pluto is in 10° of Cancer for the entire month of April.

A few last words about the Ephemeris before we move on to doing an actual sample chart.

There are various Ephemerides (plural of Ephemeris) published that give the locations of planets by sign and degree at either noon or midnight for every

Figure 17. Sample Ephemeris Page (Jane Doe Sample)

DAY	TIME (h m s)	SUN ☉ (° ′ ″)	MOON ☽ (° ′)	MERCURY ☿ (°)	VENUS ♀ (°)	MARS ♂ (°)	JUPITER ♃ (°)	SATURN ♄ (°)	URANUS ♅ (°)	NEPTUNE ♆ (°)	PLUTO ♇ (°)
A 1	12 36 18	10♈59 37	2♓35	21♈	25♉	16♑	20♐	0♏R	19♓	18♌R	10♋
P 2	12 40 14	11 58 49	15 24	23	26	16	20	0	19	18	10
R 3	12 44 11	12 57 58	28 2	25	28	17	20	0	19	18	10
I 4	12 48 7	13 57 5	10♈30	27	29	18	20	0	19	18	10
L 5	12 52 4	14 56 10	22 48	29	0♊	18	20	0	19	18	10
6	12 56 1	15 55 13	4♉57	1♉	1	19	20 R	0	19	18	10
7	12 59 57	16 54 14	16 58	2	2	19	20	0	19	18	10
8	13 3 54	17 53 13	28 54	4	3	20	20	0	19	18	10
9	13 7 50	18 52 10	10♊46	6	4	21	20	0	19	18	10
10	13 11 47	19 51 4	22 37	7	5	21	20	0	19	18	10
11	13 15 43	20 49 56	4♋32	9	6	22	20	0	19	18	10
12	13 19 40	21 48 46	16 35	10	7	22	20	0	19	18	10
13	13 23 36	22 47 34	28 50	12	8	23	20	0	19	18	10
14	13 27 33	23 46 20	11♌23	13	9	24	20	29♎	20	18	10
15	13 31 30	24 45 3	24 18	14	10	24	20	29	20	18	10
16	13 35 26	25 43 44	7♍39	15	11	25	20	29	20	18	10
17	13 39 23	26 42 23	21 27	16	12	25	20	29	20	18	10
18	13 43 19	27 40 59	5♎44	17	13	26	20	29	20	18	10
19	13 47 16	28 39 34	20 25	18	14	27	20	29	20	18	10
20	13 51 12	29 38 6	5♏23	19	15	27	20	29	20	18	10
21	13 55 9	0♉36 37	29 30	20	16	28	20	29	20	18	10
22	13 59 5	1 35 6	5♐36	20	17	28	20	29	20	18	10
23	14 3 2	2 33 33	20 30	21	18	29	19	29	20	18	10
24	14 6 59	3 31 59	5♑ 6	21	19	0♒	19	29	20	18	10
25	14 10 55	4 30 23	19 19	21	20	0	19	29	20	18	10
26	14 14 52	5 28 46	3♒ 8	21	21	1	19	29	20	18	10
27	14 18 48	6 27 7	16 34	21 R	22	1	19	28	20	18	10
28	14 22 45	7 25 26	29 39	21	23	2	19	28	20	18 D	10
29	14 26 41	8 23 44	12♓27	21	24	3	19	28	20	18	10
30	14 30 38	9 22 0	25 0	21	25	3	19	28	20	18	10

THE SUN ENTERED THE SIGN OF TAURUS AT 8:59 A.M. ON SUN-
DAY, APRIL 20TH.

Aries	Taurus	Gemini	Cancer	Leo	Virgo	Libra	Scorpio	Sagittarius	Capricorn	Aquarius	Pisces
♈	♉	♊	♋	♌	♍	♎	♏	♐	♑	♒	♓

day throughout the year, including the Sidereal Time at Greenwich. Few,
however, indicate at what time of day the Sun and the remaining planets
change sign — move out of one and into the next. This occurs every month
with the sun, which moves approximately 1° per day. Knowing *exactly* when
the Sun changs signs is important, especially if you were born on that day. We
have solved that problem by including the exact time of day the Sun changes
sign each month. Without knowing the time of your birth, you would have no

way of knowing which sign your Sun was in — whether the one the Sun was leaving or the one it was moving into. It is not important to know the time when the other planets change signs. The Ephemerides included in this book show the time the sun changes signs at the bottom of each month from January 1, 1920 to December 31, 1985. This crucial information will help settle the problem of two individuals born on the same day but under different signs. The dates when the Sun changes signs are from the 20th through the 24th of the month, depending on the month and sign.

People born on those days are often referred to as being born on the "cusp." If you are one of those people, you were born under one sign or the other. There is little validity to the common belief that people born on the cusp have a little of both signs. People often claim, for example, that they are mostly Taurus, but have a little Gemini in them. Actually, people who make such claims are confused and don't know which sign they were born under. Somebody born on April 20, 1924, could be either an Aries or a Taurus, depending on the time when birth occurred.

The time given on each Ephemeris page is given in GMT (Greenwich Mean Time) and this time must be converted into local mean time of the place of birth. Though the explanation of this conversion procedure may seem complicated and difficult, it is really a very simple calculation as you will see in the forthcoming examples.

The zone standard times are for the sole purpose of maintaining consistent time standards and schedules throughout the world and these are based on Greenwich Mean Time. The local mean time of the various cities within a particular time zone will vary, while the time zone remains the same. If you were born on the East Coast of America, the difference between GMT and Eastern Standard Time would be five hours. As you travel farther west it keeps increasing 1 hour for each time zone until you reach the West Coast where the time difference is eight hours. (This means that when it is noon in Greenwich, it is eight hours earlier in the day on the West Coast.) The same holds true when traveling east from Greenwich, but then the time differences must be added, not subtracted. (It is always later in the day than it is in Greenwich in any location east of Greenwich.)

For an example of the differences of precise time at places of birth against zone standard time we offer the following:

East Coast of America; zone standard difference is 5 hours

City	Longitude	Latitude	Time Difference
BOSTON, MASS.	71°W04′	42°N22′	4:44:16
NEW YORK, N.Y.	74°W00′	40°N43′	4:56:00
MIAMI, FLA.	80°W11′	25°N47′	5:20:44

All the above cities are in the Eastern Standard Time Zone and are therefore five hours earlier than it is in Greenwich at the same time.

Notice that there is quite a difference in the local mean time against the entire time zone. Though this may not make much of a difference for the sake of time itself, it does make a world of difference when considering what your sign is when you were born on the day of the change from one sign to another.

We have included in Appendix XI the longitudes and latitudes of the major cities of the world for your convenience, accuracy and simplicity. Though the longitude and latitude are of no importance to you in determining your Sun sign, the precise time difference for the place of birth is most essential. It is the only method by which you will know exactly what your sign is, if your birth occurred on the day the Sun changed signs. For those of you who don't know your time of birth, it will be difficult to determine it unless you seek the services of those who provide the technique known as "Rectification" to arrive at a time of birth from specific dates of events in your life.

Now for the procedure of calculations from GMT to local mean time.

When you check the Ephemeris pages for April 20, 1924, you will note that the Ephemeris shows that at midnight (the beginning of the day, as previously stated) the Sun was located at 29°38′06″ (29 degrees, 38 minutes and 6 seconds). This would mean that if you looked up this date to find out what sign you were, you would believe you were an Aries (♈), the first sign above the date. You could be right, but you could also be wrong. As we stated, that would depend on what time the birth took place. You will note that on the Ephemeris page for the month of April 1924 it shows that the Sun moved into the sign of Taurus at precisely 8:59 A.M. GMT on Sunday, April 20. As this time is Greenwich Mean Time, it must be converted to local mean time (place and time of birth). In order to do this you now have to look up the precise time difference for the local place of birth in Appendix XI. This precise time difference *must be subtracted* (since the birthplace is *west* of Greenwich) from the GMT of 8:59 A.M. The result will be the local mean time. Now this may all seem confusing and complicated, but it is anything but. Watch how simple a calculation it really is.

For a person born in Boston, Massachusetts on April 20, 1924, look up Boston, Massachusetts in the Longitude and Latitude Appendix and you will note that the time difference between Greenwich, England, and Boston is 4:44:16 (4 hours, 44 minutes, 16 seconds). The Ephemeris shows the Sun entering the sign of Taurus at precisely 8:59 A.M. GMT on that date. Now all you do is subtract 4:44:16 from 8:59:00. The result is 4:14:44 A.M., the local mean time at birthplace. Meaning, if you were born on or before that time you are an Aries, if you were born after that time, you would be a Taurus.

Here's an example of the calculations; remember that you are calculating *time*, not plain digits.

GMT	8:59:00 A.M. =	8:58:60 A.M.	(We borrowed 1 minute — 60 seconds — from the
Time difference	4:44:16	= −4:44:16	59 minutes)
		4:14:44 A.M.	(Local Mean Time)
	(Zone Standard 5 hours)		

When calculations are being made for the position of the Sun or Moon, it is wise to recheck all calculations, for the purpose of insuring that all calculations were made in *time*, and not elementary digits.

To aid you, as well as simplify matters, we offer Figure 18.

Figure 18. Planetary Motion

Planet	Average Daily Motion (Approximate)	Stay in a Sign (Approximate)	Time to Orbit Sun (Approximate)
MOON	13° per day (½° per hour)	2½ days	28 days
MERCURY	1°23″	14–18 days	88 days
VENUS	1°12″	23–24 days	255 days
SUN	59′08″ (2½′ per hour)	30 days	– – – – –
MARS	31′27″	45–47 days	1 year, 325 days
JUPITER	4′59″	1 year	12 years
SATURN	2′01″	2½ years	29½ years
URANUS	42″	7 years	84 years
NEPTUNE	24″	14 years	165 years
PLUTO	15″	20 years	248 years

When calculating Sun or Moon positions to coincide with your birth time, keep in mind that these are GMT positions. You must not forget to add or subtract the distance traveled according to your particular local mean time.

The following example of Jane Doe is offered for those of you who wish to locate the correct position of the Moon at your time of birth.

Jane Doe was born at 5:20 A.M. in the city of Boston, Massachusetts. Boston time is 5:20 A.M. plus the 5 hours Zone standard, or 10:20 A.M. GMT 10:20 A.M. is 10 hours and 20 minutes beyond midnight, GMT. Traveling at 1° of arc every 2 hours of time, or 1′ of arc for every 2 minutes of time, the Moon will move 5°10′ within the 10 hours and 20 minutes that have elapsed since midnight. 5°10′ must now be added to the position of the Moon as taken from the Ephemeris. After this total is obtained, you now *subtract* the distance the Moon will travel in 4 hours and 44 minutes (leave out seconds), which is the local mean time for Boston. This comes to 7°45′. Sounds confusing, but the calculations are much more simple.

1. Moon's position at midnight . . . .   4°57′
                                                                        +

2. Interval from midnight: 10 hours,
        20 minutes   10 hours =   5°
                                                                        +
                                              20 minutes =   0°10′
                    Moon's position at 10:20 A.M. (GMT)   9°67′=10°07′
                                                                        –

3. Time difference between Boston and Greenwich: 4:44:~~16~~
        (Moon travels 2° 22′)   2°22′
4. Position of Moon at 5:20 A.M. Boston, Mass.   7°45′

NOTE: When Daylight Savings Time is in effect, that one hour of time must also be subtracted along with your local mean time.

Notes on Moon Calculations: When making adjustments for the Moon, it may happen that your figures will result in a total that is greater than 30 degrees. When this occurs, it means that the Moon is that many degrees (over 30°) into the next sign and should be entered in that degree of whatever sign it has moved into.

We now move on to the drawing of your detailed chart, and put this puzzle all together.

CHAPTER **10**   Drawing a Detailed Chart

We are now ready to draw a chart, putting together the last pieces of the puzzle. To illustrate the procedure we will use the chart of Jane Doe.

A few words first about the order of the segments of our Figure 19 before we go into any procedures.

Figure 19. Zodiac Chart

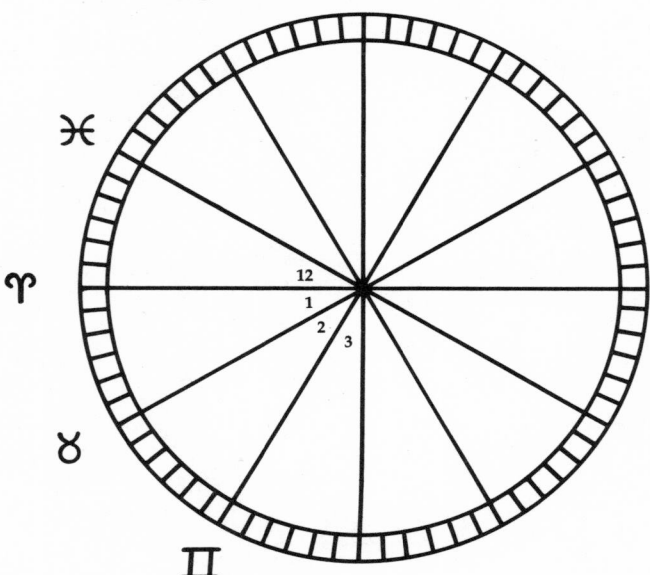

Figure 19 looks very much like the Zodiac, minus the location of the twelve signs. Each spoke of the wheel is called the "cusp," which divides one segment from the next — or one sign from its neighbor. In a chart these pie-shaped segments are called *houses*. Like the signs, there are twelve houses, and they begin where the first sign, Aries, traditionally begins, on the left side of the circle between eight and nine o'clock if you imagine the circle as the face of a clock. The segment where Aries would be is the first house. The second segment, moving counterclockwise, is the second house, or the segment traditionally occupied by Taurus. The third house is next, where Gemini is located, then the fourth, fifth and so on to the twelfth house where Pisces would be, just above the cusp of Aries. Because we are interested in teaching you how to draw a solar chart when the birth time is not known, we will not take into consideration the Ascendent Sign, nor will we make any analyses regarding the affairs of the houses. We are merely using these compartment designations as a format to record the data from the Ephemeris. Should you intend to make a practice of drawing charts, you can purchase blank blocks at most occult bookstores or any astrological society.

Now to the simple procedures of drawing the detailed solar chart.

Step 1   Prior to making any markings or notations of any nature on the blank chart, check the Ephemeris page for the particular date you are going to do. In this case, our fictitious Jane Doe will be used to illustrate how it is done. All we need to know is the birthdate: April 6, 1924. Starting with the Sun, then the Moon followed by Mercury and the remaining planets, observe how many planets are located in any one sign, along with the degrees of each. This procedure will allow you to allot ample space for as many planets as is necessary for any given sign. At times you may find almost any number of planets in one sign.

Starting with the Sun, draw in the glyph of this sign on the cusp of the first house (first segment). For Jane Doe her Sun sign is Aries which, coincidentally, corresponds to the location of the first house. (Should Jane Doe have been born on April 22, then her sun sign would be Taurus which we would place on the first house, followed by Gemini on the second house, Cancer on the third, and so on through the remaining signs.)

The second sign of Jane Doe's chart would be that which follows Aries — Taurus. Then the other signs in the order of the Zodiac. Starting with the sign placed on the first house, the natural order of the Zodiac must always follow. Refer to Figure 20, Completed Zodiac Chart.

Step 2 Considering what we said in step 1, referring to the number of planets in any given sign, proceed as follows. Check the Ephemeris page to see how many planets are in the Sun sign, as well as the degrees of each. In this case, the Sun is the only planet in the sign of Aries. Rounding off the degrees to the nearest degree we find that the Sun is located at 16°. We now enter the symbol of the Sun, with the 16° beside the symbol, along with the glyph of the sign Aries next to the degree notation (☉ 16 ♈). Had there been more than one planet in this sign, we would have drawn in the planet with the fewest degrees first, as you will see with the next notation. Looking at the Ephemeris you will note that two planets occupy the sign of Taurus, the moon at 4°57′ or 5°ounded off), which, in chapter 9, we adjusted to account for the local mean time, or 7°45′, rounded off to 8°, and Mercury at 1°. Draw in the symbol of Mercury with its degree and sign glyph, followed by the Moon and its degree and sign glyph. This procedure is followed for all remaining planets. Upon completion it is wise to count the number of planets drawn into the chart to insure that all planets are accounted for. There should be a total of ten. See Figure 20 for completed Zodiac.

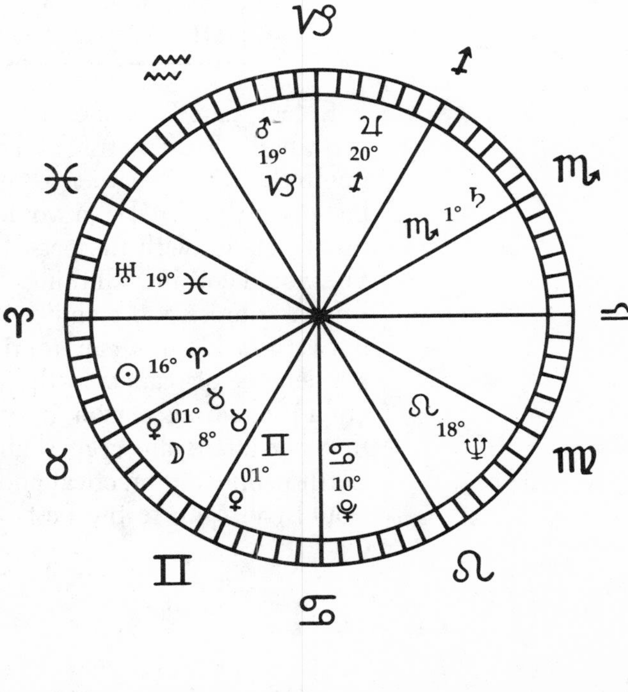

Figure 20.
Completed Zodiac Chart
(Jane Doe Sample)

Step 3   Insuring that all ten planets are accounted for, the next procedure is to count the number of planets in the Elements and Qualities of the signs they occupy. This is to allow the possibility of obtaining the Signature of the individual being charted, in this case our Jane Doe. (You will recall we have done this back in chapter 6.) If you followed the procedure as explained in step 2, marking in the planet's symbol, with the degree and sign glyph beside it, this next procedure is most simple. Starting with the sign Aries, count the number of planets in the Fire signs: Aries, Leo and Sagittarius. Looking at Figure 20 we find one planet in Aries, one planet in Leo and one planet in Sagittarius, for a total of three planets in Fire. This figure is placed on the blank chart beside Fire under the heading of ELEMENTS. We next count the number of planets in the Earth sign by the same method and we find that we have two planets in the sign of Taurus, an Earth sign. There are no planets in Virgo, the next Earth sign, but we do find one planet in the sign of Capricorn, the third sign of the Earth Element. Again, a total of three planets in Earth. This number is now marked into the space beside Earth on the blank chart. This procedure is followed for the Air (Gemini, Libra, and Aquarius) and Water (Cancer, Scorpio and Pisces) signs also. Again these figures should be added together and should total ten if you counted correctly. You now follow the same method for the Qualities, only this time you count the number of planets in the Quality group, Cardinal signs (Aries, Cancer, Libra and Capricorn). Then the Fixed signs (Taurus, Leo, Scorpio and Aquarius), with the Mutable signs next. Again, a total of ten should be the result. In Jane Doe's case, when completed there should be a total of 3 Fire, 3 Earth, 1 Air, 3 Water. Along with a total of 3 Cardinal, 4 Fixed and 3 Mutable.

As we already determined, in Jane Doe's chart there is a fairly equal distribution in the Elements, so no preponderance can be derived from the figures alone. As we explained in chapter 6, there is a method of determining a Signature under the conditions just cited, but, for now, we are keeping matters simple.

	FIRE	WATER	AIR	EARTH
CARDINAL	Aries	Cancer	Libra	Capricorn
FIXED	Leo	Scorpio	Aquarius	Taurus
MUTABLE	Sagittarius	Pisces	Gemini	Virgo

In fact, Jane Doe does have a Taurus Signature, meaning that her temperament had a Fixed nature and her behavior had an Earth methodology, according to the way we earlier defined these concepts. Fixed first: the abundance of planets in the Fixed sign would indicate a basic contentment in matters as they usually stand, with the persistent determination that they remain as they are. She would consider all things for their ultimate value in providing her with the basic resources and stability she needs to feel comfortable. Waste not, want not is probably more appropriate for this Quality than for any other. The preponderance of planets in the Earth Element would have indicated that she is not a pretentious person, but rather an absolute realist, ever watchful for signs that her affairs are even slightly out of order. As we know from chapter 6, Earth people are practical and responsible. Jane Doe would be a woman who would try to make the best of a given situation. She would also use proven methods to get the results she wants rather than take chances or use innovative methods that might actually serve her purposes better. Like the Taurus nature that would be her Signature, each step toward her goal would have to be carefully considered.

Figure 21. Completed Chart showing the Elements and Qualities

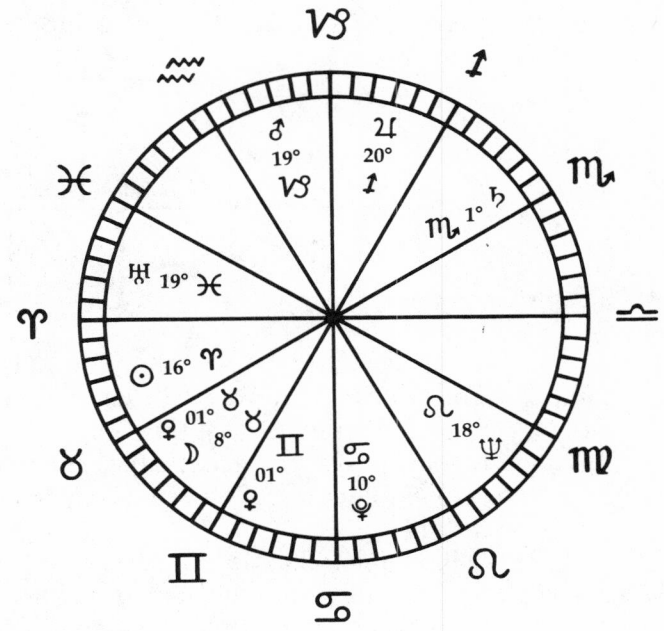

ELEMENTS
Fire 3
Earth 3 + ruling planet in an Earth sign
Air 1
Water 3

QUALITIES
Cardinal 3
Fixed 4
Mutable 3

SIGNATURE
Fixed-Earth, or Taurus

Step 4 We must now determine and interpret the precise location of Jane Doe's Sun in terms of the decanates and quadruplicities. As we calculated in chapter 7, her Sun at 16° of Aries means that it is in the second decanate and third quadruplicity (See Figure 22). The second decanate told us that her resources were her strong Leonian qualities, since the second decanate of Fire-Element Aries was Leo, ruled by the Sun. These Leonian resources are manifested in a strong ego drive, strong self-assertiveness and an enthusiastic temperament. Working against her, however, are her inhibitions to take advantage of the positive qualities of the sign relating to the third quadruplicity — Libra. She is deficient in her desire to be more compromising with others, to temper her own strong will with the will of others. This reference to the inhibitors corroborates what we already hinted at above: that Jane Doe must be more willing to consider the advice and feelings of others. She must restrain the force of her own ego and listen to others if she is going to command respect and achieve success in her goals.

Figure 22. Resources and Inhibitors (Jane Doe Sample)

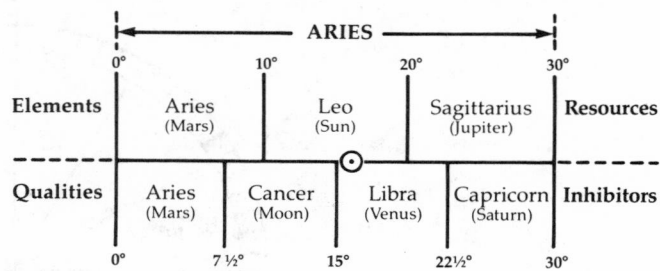

Step 5 The next step is to count the degrees separating the planets from each other so as to determine the Aspects. The method is to take the shortest distance between the planets, going either clockwise or counterclockwise. By using the graph in Figure 23, you will ensure that you have considered all the planets in the chart.

Remember that degree location of any planet in any sign is measured counterclockwise. From the above chart, we can see that the Sun is located at 16° of Aries. Moving counterclockwise, the Sun would have to travel 14° more to reach the cusp of Taurus, plus another 1° to reach Mercury, which is at 1° of Taurus. If we add up the distance, that would put the distance between the Sun and Mercury at exactly 15°:

$$\begin{aligned}
\text{Distance from Sun to cusp of Taurus} &= 14° \\
\text{Location of Mercury in Taurus} &= \underline{\ \ 1°} \\
\text{Total Distance} &= 15°
\end{aligned}$$

The figure 15° we would enter into the appropriate box of the graph.

Venus is listed at 1° Gemini, just barely over the cusp of this sign. Once again, the Sun would have to travel 14° to reach the cusp of Taurus, then the entire 30° of the sign of Taurus, then another 1° to reach Venus.

$$\begin{aligned}
\text{Sun to cusp of Taurus} &= 14° \\
\text{All of Taurus} &= 30° \\
\text{Venus in Gemini} &= \underline{\ \ 1°} \\
\text{Total Distance} &= 45°
\end{aligned}$$

To calculate the distance from the Sun to Mars we would move clockwise because this is the shortest distance between these two planets. Mars is located at 18° of Capricorn. Counting clockwise, the Sun is at 16° Aries, or 16° below the Aries cusp. That distance, plus the full 30° of Pisces, plus the full 30° of Aquarius, plus the 12° left for Mars to travel in Capricorn (or 30° minus 19°) would give us a total distance between the Sun and Mars of 88°.

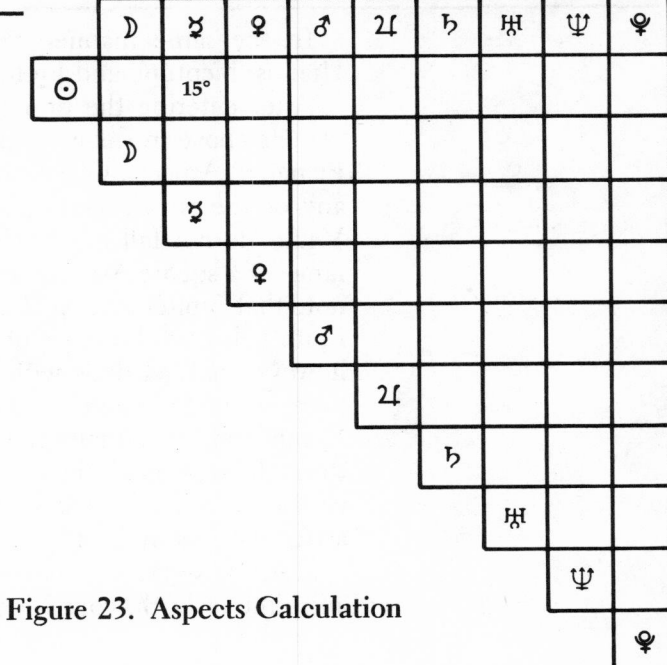

	☽	☿	♀	♂	♃	♄	♅	♆	♇
☉	15°								
☽									
☿									
♀									
♂									
♃									
♄									
♅									
♆									
♇									

Figure 23. Aspects Calculation

Sun's location in Aries   = 16°
All of Pisces   = 30°
All of Aquarius   = 30°
Remaining in Capricorn = 12°
                Total Distance = 88°

To calculate the distance from the Sun to Jupiter, which is located at 20° of Sagittarius, count clockwise (the shortest distance). The Sun is at 16° of Aries, or that distance below the Aries cusp. That distance, plus the full 30° of Pisces, plus the full 30° each of Aquarius and Capricorn, plus the remaining number of degrees remaining in Sagittarius (10°) gives a total of 116°.

Sun's location in Aries =   16°
All of Pisces   =   30°
All of Aquarius   =   30°
All of Capricorn   =   30°
Remaining 10° in
Sagittarius   =   10° (30° minus 20° of Jupiter)
        Total Distance =   116°

To calculate the distance from the Sun to Saturn which is located at 0° Scorpio, barely over the cusp of this sign, we again proceed clockwise, the shortest distance.

Sun's location in Aries   =   16°
All of Pisces   =   30°
All of Aquarius   =   30°
All of Capricorn   =   30°
All of Sagittarius   =   30°
All of Scorpio (Saturn at 0°) =   30°
                Total Distance = 166°

In the same manner we calculate the distances between the Sun and Uranus, Neptune and Pluto.

After entering the number of degrees between the Sun and each of the planets above in the appropriate box of the Aspect graph, refer to chapter 8, Planetary Aspects. Check the distances to see if they fall into the category of any of the six Aspects described. In our example, note that Mercury and Venus do not fall into the range of any Aspect. Mars, however, falls in the range of a square Aspect (from 82° to 98°). Following this procedure you will note that Jupiter and Neptune both fall into the range of a trine Aspect, while Pluto falls into the range of another square Aspect. (See Figure 24.) You are, however, not yet done with Aspects. We must now calculate the Aspects between the Moon and the remaining seven planets, followed by Mercury and Venus and the remaining six planets and so on with the remaining planets through Neptune. When you have completed all calculations for the Aspects, your entry should be as shown in Figure 26. You are now ready to read the astrological analysis of your character as presented in Appendix VI.

SPECIAL NOTE: Unless you have adjusted the Moon's position to the place and time of birth, your Moon's Aspects will not be valid.

Figure 24. The Sun's Aspects (Jane Doe Sample)

	D	☿	♀	♂	♃	♄	♅	♆	♇
☉		15°	45°	87° □	116° △	166°	27°	122° △	84° □
D									
☿									
♀									
♂									
♃									
♄									
♅									
♆									
♇									

Figure 25. All Planets' Aspects (Jane Doe Sample)

	D	☿	♀	♂	♃	♄	♅	♆	♇
☉		15	45	87 □	116 △	166	27	122 △	84 □
D			70 ☌	23	109	138	187 ☍	49	101	62 ✶
☿				30	102	131	180 ☍	42	107	69
♀					132	161	150 ⊼	72	77	39
♂						29	78	60 ✶	151 ⊼	171
♃							49	89 □	122 △	160
♄								138	73	111
♅									149 ⊼	111
♆										38
♇										

Figure 26. Completed Detailed Chart (Jane Doe Sample)

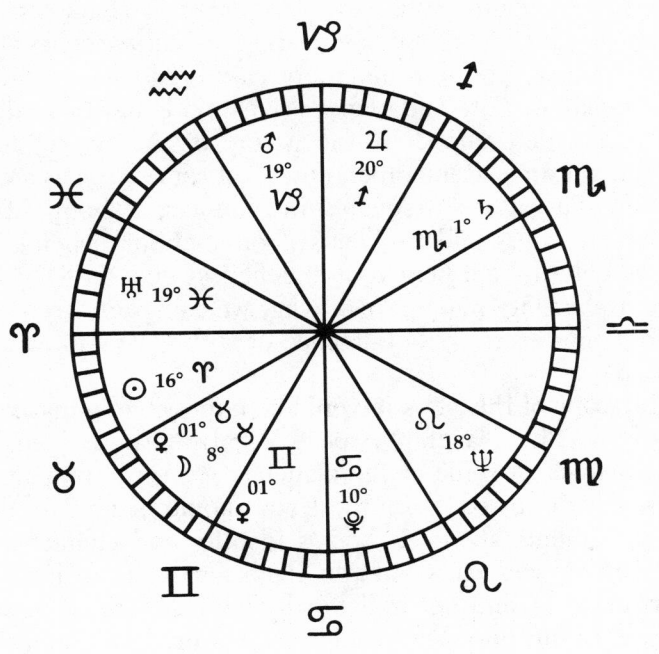

☉	☽	☿	♀	♂	♃	♄	♅	♆	♇
☉	19	15	45	87 □	110 △	166	27	122 △	84 □
	☽	70 ☌	23	109	138	187 ☍	49	101	62 ✳
		☿	30	102	131	180 ☍	42	107	69
			♀	132	161	150 ⊼	72	77	39
				♂	29	78	60 ✳	151 ⊼	171
					♃	49	89 □	122 △	160
						♄	130	73	111
							♅	149 ⊼	111
								♆	38
									♇

ELEMENTS
Fire 3
Earth 3 + ruling planet in Earth sign
Air 1
Water 3

QUALITIES
Cardinal 3
Fixed 4
Mutable 3

SIGNATURE
Fixed-Earth, or Taurus

The significant Aspects are those six we have singled out — the conjunction, sextile, square, trine, inconjunct and the opposition. What we do next is determine the astrological meaning of these different planetary combinations. We do this by relating the particular planetary characteristics to each other. Since each planet represents a dynamic of human behavior, *how* these influences affect us is crucial in the interpretation of an astrological chart. How the planets *relate*, or how one planet's dynamic behavior is altered, positively or negatively, is determined by the nature of the Aspect formed by the two planets in question. Remember, now, that some Aspects are benign — sextiles and trines. The others — squares, inconjuncts, and oppositions — are malefic and produce stress and problems. Conjunctions depend on the planets involved to determine if benign or malefic (see chapter 8). Remember, too, that there is a planetary hierarchy, or what we call Planetary Protocol: the slower-moving planet exerting its influence over the faster-moving planet. (Refer to chapter 6.)

In the scope of this book it would be impossible to make an analysis of each and every possible planetary Aspect. What we can do is make some short, yet precise analyses of some of the planetary Aspects, applying the principles we have already discussed. With these you should be able to make reasonably accurate statements about anybody's identity and character functions from a natal chart. As you can see if you glance at them, we have included only the stressful Aspects, and not individually by degree since, as we said above, the difference for our purposes here is only in a matter of intensity. What we have done is present all the malefic Aspects in a group — the conjunctions, squares, inconjuncts and oppositions. You can determine the intensity of the problems according to the particular Aspects in question when you analyze them.

We have not included the benign Aspects in the Aspect delineations because these "easy" Aspects do not represent personality difficulties that need your attention. Rather, they represent resources, from the planets involved, that can help you solve the problems that are the result of these difficult angles found between planets in malefic Aspect with each other. As we said in the beginning of this book, we want you to learn how to have a more adequately lived life by alleviating stress, blind spots and inhibitors in the makeup of your character. That is why we are more interested in giving you sample interpretations of negative planetary relationships.

Let us now get back to Jane Doe.

If we look to her Aspect Graph we will see the following major planetary Aspects.

Sun square Mars	(*malefic*)
Sun trine Jupiter	(*benign*)
Sun trine Neptune	(*benign*)
Sun square Pluto	(*malefic*)
Moon conjunct Mercury	(*benign*)
Moon opposition Saturn	(*malefic*)
Moon sextile Pluto	(*benign*)
Mercury opposition Saturn	(*malefic*)
Venus inconjunct Saturn	(*malefic*)
Mars sextile Uranus	(*benign*)
Mars inconjunct Neptune	(*malefic*)
Mars opposition Pluto	(*malefic*)

Jupiter square Uranus	(*malefic*)
Jupiter trine Neptune	(*benign*)
Uranus inconjunct Neptune	(*malefic*)

To obtain a brief analysis of these malefic Aspects, what we do next is refer to the Aspect interpretations in Appendix VI. In Jane Doe's case, we have found the following malefic Aspects:

Sun square Mars
Sun square Pluto
Moon opposition Saturn
Mercury opposition Saturn
Venus inconjunct Saturn
Mars inconjunct Neptune
Mars opposition Pluto
Jupiter square Uranus
Uranus inconjunct Neptune

From chapter 8 we get a general interpretation of these Aspects. To simplify matters, we have grouped the problematic Aspects together. That is, the interpretations offered do not break down into individual Aspect angles since the differences in effects between, say, square Aspect and the inconjunct are too fine and the analyses too involved for us to go into, given the range and scope of this book. Nonetheless, we can still put together a fairly accurate analysis of somebody, such as our imaginary subject Jane Doe.

Disregarding the particular angular Aspects of Jane Doe, let us simply list, from the above, those particular problematic planetary relationships we need to look up in our Aspect Analysis:

Sun–Mars
Sun–Pluto
Moon–Saturn
Mercury–Saturn
Venus–Saturn
Mars–Neptune
Mars–Pluto
Jupiter–Uranus
Uranus–Neptune

Now let us turn to the Aspect analyses for the interpretations. (The delineations that follow are offered for the above planetary Aspects.)

Sun–Mars You have a strong desire to control others; when resisted, you have the urge to be vindictive and quarrelsome to the point of physical abuse.

Sun–Pluto You have an obsession with power and the political, social and economic leverage it gives. Sexual needs are a strong factor in your life. Issuing ultimatums is a practice often indulged in for personal gain.

Moon–Saturn You linger in the past and deny yourself the development of new interests and challenges. You rarely let go of romantic ties whose days are numbered. Austerity indicated during the formative years.

Mercury–Saturn You are not a very communicative person, and this unwillingness to talk masks the fact that you enjoy the appearance of having in-depth perception.

Venus–Saturn Early parental conditioning is probably responsible for the guarded concern you have in your romantic interests. It is largely a matter of personal anxiety and doubt that you can live up to the demands of a romantic and/or legal commitment. You may choose to avoid commitments as a way of avoiding risks.

Mars–Neptune Taking definitive actions seems like asking for trouble, since complications usually develop. You tend to dismiss the most pertinent factors as insignificant until you realize too late that you should have paid more attention to them. Physical desires are strong enough to draw you into questionable relationships.

Mars–Pluto You have a powerful urge for exercising control over others in situations that allow you to manipulate them. This drive is so strong that you will eventually enjoy issuing ultimatums to bend people to your desires or to "make them offers they can't refuse."

Jupiter–Uranus You react to those who challenge you by biting off more than you can cope with. You might have impressed them at the time, but they won't be around as you struggle to cope with the problem. You are easily persuaded to put current interests aside so you can indulge in something exciting that just gained your attention.

Uranus–Neptune This is basically a healthy condition even though it often produces negative results and painful repercussions. It is a rebellious attitude you have — one that is usually directed in political enterprises. You may voice displeasure over the state of the country, the city or local community and gain support for your position. You probably lack the continuity to see it through to its successful revision.

If we put together these interpretations of Aspects, we come up with a fairly clear profile of Jane Doe.

The Sun–Mars, Sun–Pluto and Mars–Pluto Aspects in the chart indicate a person who needs to assert power and control over others, one who manipulates others, even threatens them with domination. These planetary contacts form a complex pattern called a T-Cross (see Appendix V), further emphasizing the third quadruplicity, ♎, discussed on page 45. She is also a person who is quarrelsome as well as rebellious (Uranus–Neptune), one whose ego drives her to take up challenges — sometimes overwhelming ones — for the sake of impressing others (Jupiter–Uranus). This urge to control, to dominate, to rebel may take the form of political expression (Uranus–Neptune), or at least the urge may surface in the forceful expression of her opinion. Yet, there is another side of Jane Doe — a secretive self-possessed side that is apparent in the fact that by choice she is not too communicative (Mercury–Saturn). But, in the context of her other traits, one might see this too as a manipulative ploy to appear deep, meditative and, perhaps, mysterious so as to gain admiration. On the more personal side, Jane Doe is also a person who holds on tenaciously to the past (Moon–Saturn). She dwells on the idealized romances of the past (Mars–Neptune), and despite strong physical desires (Sun–Pluto) she grows increasingly guarded about making new romantic commitments (Venus–Saturn). She tends not to follow through with her political convictions (Uranus–Neptune), despite the strength of her feelings in those matters.

As we said, we can offer only brief analyses of the various Aspects, since the scope of this book dose not allow for more elaborate presentations. For more detailed interpretations of planetary Aspects, we recommend *Planets in Aspect* by Robert Pelletier.

CHAPTER 11   Alice's Adjusted Detailed Chart

For those of you who know your time of birth, we now, for the sake of accuracy, offer another example. Though this chart is set up the same as any solar chart, we will adjust the Sun's and the Moon's positions to Alice's time and place of birth. We wish to bring out the importance of what the differences could mean to an individual.

The Sun, though it only moves an average of 59'08" per day, or 2½' per hour of time, may not make much of a difference for some of you. However, for those of you who were born early or very late in the day, it could result in a significant change. When the Sun's midnight position is in the areas of 7½°, 10°, 15°, 20°, 22½° or 30°, the adjustment could change the Sun's position from one sector to another. Being a simple enough procedure, the adjustment is worth making whether any significant change results or not.

The Moon, on the other hand, will more often than not make more than a single change. There are times that the adjustment will change the complete reading of the person. This you will learn from the following adjustments to Alice's chart.

Alice was born in Malden, Massachusetts, at 11:30 P.M. on June 26, 1937. The Ephemeris shows the Sun at 3°57'53", the Moon at 26°56'58". In the adjusted position by motion of the day, the Sun is at 4°48'07" of Cancer, rounded off to 5°. Since no crucial degree shift is involved, there is no change. The Moon's adjusted position changes from 26°56'58" Capricorn to 8°30'58" Aquarius, rounded off to 9°. Notice the difference that the adjustment of the Moon makes.

1. Changes from Capricorn to Aquarius: quite a mental difference (read Appendix I).
2. Changes the Signature and its ruling planet, a very crucial matter.
3. Forms a square Aspect to Uranus and Venus, making the third arm for a T-Cross (see Appendix V).

In the final analysis, an extremely different nature is presented than is if no adjustment is made.

Sample Chart   We offer you this sample chart to help you understand that no two charts are ever exactly alike, although we urge you to follow a systematic plan so that every important factor is considered.

Step 1   Alice was born in June 26, 1937. Refer to the Ephemeris for 1937 and turn to the month of June. List the planets in their respective positions in the Zodiac for the 26th of June.

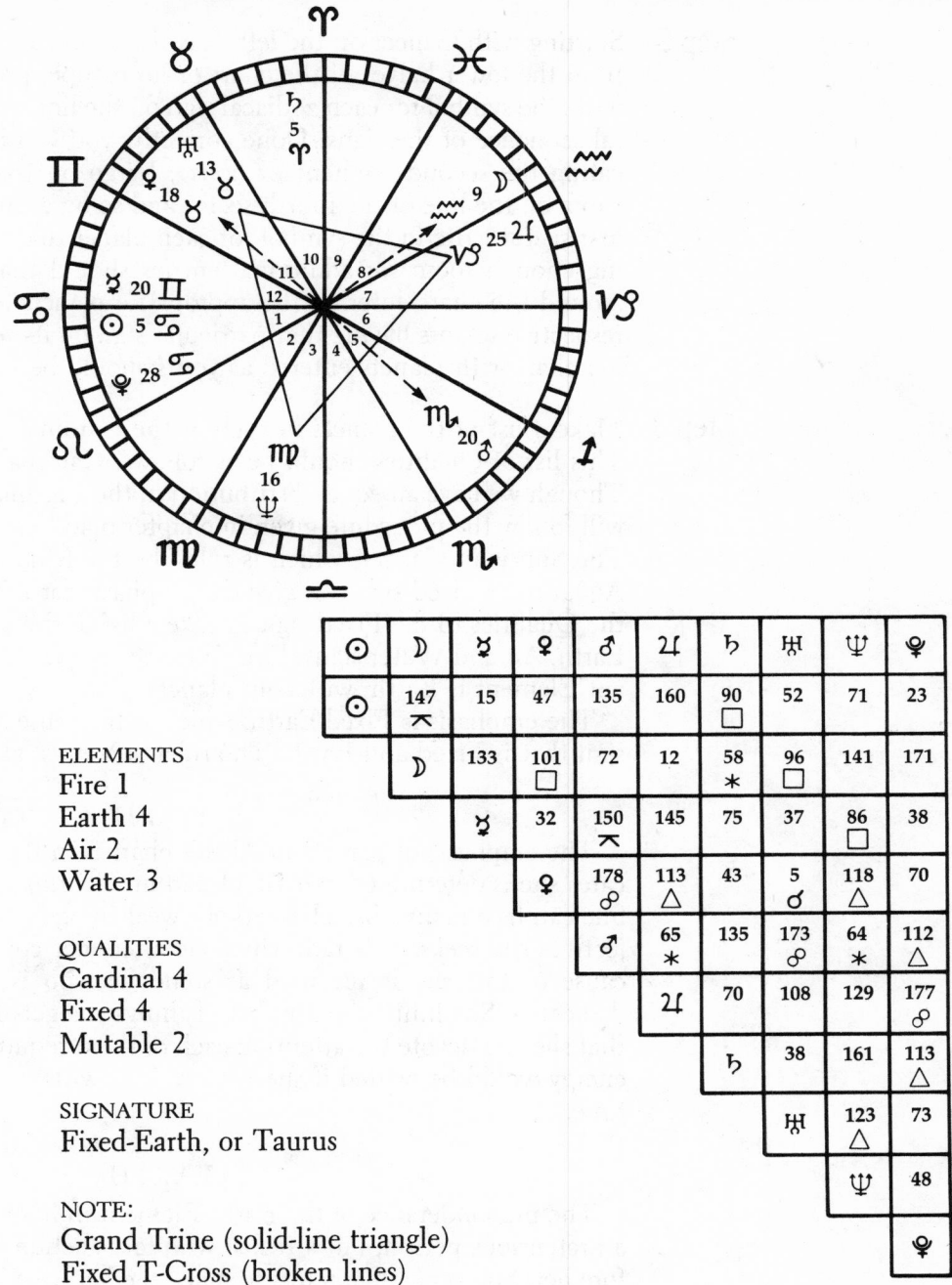

ELEMENTS
Fire 1
Earth 4
Air 2
Water 3

QUALITIES
Cardinal 4
Fixed 4
Mutable 2

SIGNATURE
Fixed-Earth, or Taurus

NOTE:
Grand Trine (solid-line triangle)
Fixed T-Cross (broken lines)

	⊙	☽	☿	♀	♂	♃	♄	♅	♆	♇
⊙	147 ⊼	15	47	135	160	90 □	52	71	23	
☽		133	101 □	72	12	58 ✻	96 □	141	171	
☿			32 ⊼	150	145	75	37	86 □	38	
♀				178 ☍	113 △	43	5 ☌	118 △	70	
♂					65 ✻	135	173 ☍	64 ✻	112 △	
♃						70	108	129	177 ☍	
♄							38	161	113 △	
♅								123 △	73	
♆									48	
♇										

Ephemeris position	Adjusted position	Ephemeris position		
Sun . . . . .3°57′53″ or 4°♋	Sun . . . . . 4°48′07″ or 5°♋	Jupiter	25°	♑
Moon . 26°56′58″ or 27°♑	Moon . . . 8°30′58″ or 9°♒	Saturn	5°	♈
Mercury . . . . 20°♊	Mercury . . . . 20°♊	Uranus	13°	♉
Venus . . . . 18°♉	Venus . . . . 18°♉	Neptune	16°	♍
Mars . . . . .20°♍	Mars . . . . .20°♍	Pluto	28°	♋

Step 2   Starting with Cancer on the left side of the horizontal line dividing the upper from the lower halves of the chart or horoscope, proceed counterclockwise to write the symbol for each zodiacal sign on the line of each segment in the natural sequence of the signs. Done correctly, you will have Leo on the line indicating the second segment or house, Virgo on the line of the third sector, Libra on the line of the fourth sector and so on around the chart. Next, in the first sector write in the symbol for each planet that is in the sign Cancer, leaving enough room for additional entries should that be necessary. Continue around the chart entering the appropriate planets as they are shown in their respective sectors having that particular sign on its sector. See the accompanying chart with planets entered as yours should be.

Step 3   Make a list of the planets in each of the Cardinal, Fixed and Mutable signs. This list of Qualities should be as follows: Cardinal, 4; Fixed, 4; Mutable, 2. Though we have an equal distribution in the Cardinal and Fixed Qualities, we will follow the procedure given in chapter 6 and use the ruler of the Sun sign. The Sun is in Cancer, which is ruled by the Moon. Because the Moon is in Aquarius, a Fixed sign, we give the emphasis for the planetary distribution in the Qualities to the Fixed signs. Make a list of the planets in each of the Fire, Earth, Air and Water signs: Fire, 1; Earth, 4; Air, 2; Water, 3. The preponderant Element is Earth, with four planets.

The emphasis is Fixed-Earth, which is the same as saying Taurus, the *only* sign that is Fixed and Earth. The ruler is Venus, also in Taurus.

FIXED

The emphasis of planets in Alice's chart is in the Fixed Quality. This indicates she is determined, persistent and unrelenting in the pursuit of her goals. She can face many obstacles without weakening in her steadfastness to the objectives she seeks. It is rare when she alters her course once it is set, and because of this she is regarded as someone who is dependable, reliable and dedicated. She limits the number of things she gets involved in at one time so that she can devote the attention each of them requires. She feels that needless energy would be wasted if she got involved with too many things at the same time.

EARTH

The preponderance of the Earth Element in her chart shows that she is not a pretentious person, but a realist who takes action based on the evidence before her. She generally prefers to make the best of a given set of circumstances and she usually gets satisfaction from her ability to succeed even when those conditions provide her with limited resources to work with. She must remember, however, that because her method of solving problems is largely through the physical resources at her disposal, she is somewhat limited in applying other frames of reference to arrive at satisfactory solutions. She prefers to use the tried and true techniques for getting things done rather than take a chance on methods that are untested. She has a basic "nuts and bolts" approach to solving her problems, though at times she may need the services of someone with a more abstract mentality to help her with some of them.

Step 4   Examine the chart for evidence of a Jones Pattern (see Appendix IV). Alice's chart's planetary distribution is a random one and this is called a Splash pattern. This means that she has a universal outlook on life and enjoys a reasonably wide diversity of interests to broaden her field of involvement with the world around her. Sharing her life with others gives her much satisfaction and she is sincere in her willingness to help those less fortunate than she is.

Step 5   From the Ephemeris you have already determined the sign position of each planet in Alice's chart. Refer to Appendix I and read what the Sun, Moon and the other planets mean in the signs. Pay special attention to what the Sun, Moon and Mercury mean, since they represent respectively the ego identity, the personality and the mentality with which she functions. Because her Signature is Taurus, you must also give special attention to Venus, the planet that "rules" Taurus.

Step 6   Examine the chart to determine if there are any special planetary formations or complexes (see Appendix V). Alice has both a Grand Trine and a T-Cross in her chart. These are powerful factors and will significantly influence her life, for they show she must face serious problems that are not easily resolved (T-Cross in Fixed signs), but that she would rise to the occasion is indicated by the many talents she has (Grand Trine in Earth signs).

Step 7   Calculate the Aspects between the planets in Alice's chart. The list should be as follows:

	CONJUNCTIONS	TRINES
	Venus–Uranus	Venus–Jupiter
		Venus–Neptune
	SEXTILES	Jupiter–Neptune
	Moon–Saturn	Uranus–Neptune
	Mars–Jupiter	
	Mars–Neptune	INCONJUNCTS
		Mercury–Mars
	SQUARES	Mercury–Jupiter
These Aspects due	Sun–Saturn	
to Moon's Aspect to {	Moon–Venus	OPPOSITIONS
Uranus (linkage) {	Moon–Mars	Venus–Mars
	Moon–Uranus	Mars–Uranus
	Mercury–Neptune	Jupiter–Pluto

Although there are many Aspects above that are considered favorable, a significant number require special attention because they can be troublesome. Please note that these stress Aspects do not deny her the ability to succeed in her endeavors, but they simply mean that Alice will have to apply herself more diligently to develop the skills from the resources at her disposal. Once she works at them, however, they will always sustain her. Of the foregoing list of Aspects, the ones needing her attention are the squares, inconjuncts and oppositions.

Refer to Appendix VI, Aspect Analyses, and read what each of these problem areas mean.

By the way, the squares almost always relate to problems that developed early in the life and usually involved family contacts in the early domestic environment. The inconjuncts are usually indicative of the complex problems we have in dealing with people who often make demands on us and for whom we extend ourselves, often to our regret. The oppositions always show stress encountered in dealing with people who are largely in the social frame of reference. Included among these are partnership issues and those relating to adversaries in competitive enterprises. Irrespective of the kind of Aspect that you may be working on to derive some positive effect from an otherwise negative energy, there is an unfailing effect that stimulates positive results in the final analysis. You can only do something wrong as long as you can endure the pain and grief it causes, until you eventually realize that there has got to be another way — and there is!

Step 8   With the list of the planets as they appear by degrees and minutes in the various signs of the Zodiac, refer to Appendix III, Sign Divisions, and read the delineations for each of the planets in Alice's chart, making sure that you select the appropriate analysis for each of her planets. For example, you will read the first entry under Cancer of her Sun's position at 5° of that sign. For the Moon, you will read the second entry under the sign Aquarius because her Moon's position is at 9° of that sign. For the planet Mercury, read the fifth paragraph listed under the heading of Gemini at 20°–22½°. Continue with the remaining planets in her chart, paying attention to the fact that each planet relates to a different function of her total being and that what sometimes appear as contradictory indications are simply that incorrect assumptions were made in the judgment of planetary influences. The Sun may show a strong desire for the authority to take charge of things, but her Moon may show she yearns for the person she loves to be strong of character and assertive, but this relates only to matters pertaining to her love affairs and not necessarily to her career and social position.

SUMMARY

From step 3 we determined that Alice is a Fixed-Earth person. This shows that she is determined and persistent in pursuing her goals and she limits them so she can give them her undivided attention. The dominant Earth Element shows that she bases her decisions on the evidence that exists and does nor rely on some untried method to get the same results.

From step 4 we learned that she has a broad and universal outlook on life and that her life is enriched by a wide field of interests. She freely shares her good fortune with those less fortunate than she.

In step 5 the significance of each of her planets in the signs was examined, with special attention given to the Sun, Moon and Mercury because they relate to her identity and character (Sun), the personality derived from the conditioning influence of her early years (Moon) and the nature of her mentality or interpretive apparatus and its rational capability (Mercury). We've given special attention to Venus's influence because it rules the Fixed-Earth, Taurus, Signature.

Step 6 shows that her chart held a Grand Trine and a T-Cross. These are Special Complexes that show serious problems that are difficult to cope with as indicated by the T-Cross in Fixed signs. Luckily, the Grand Trine in Earth provides her with the necessary resourcefulness with which to resolve those problems satisfactorily.

In step 7 we examined the Aspects between the planets in her chart. We gave special attention to the difficult or stress Aspects because they showed what lessons she needed to learn. A quick reference to Appendix VI, Aspect Analyses, will help her understand what these mean and how to deal with them in her continuing development. We gave special attention to the squares, inconjuncts, and oppositions. We noted that Aspects to her Sun will decidedly affect her character and identity fulfillment. Those involving the Moon show how she is still being conditioned through contact with matters pertaining to her emotional affairs. Aspects involving Mercury relate to how her thinking is altered by new experiences and those that involve Venus will profoundly influence her temperament, disposition and general outlook on life.

The suggestions in step 8 will help her understand what she needs to learn from each of her planets' positions in the signs. In general, planets in the early degrees of the signs tend to have a primitive kind of "basic" influence with little or no sophistication. On the other hand, planets in the late degrees indicate some degree of polish in how she handles that particular mechanism of her behavior so that she derives benefits more often than not when she applies the principles they represent.

Detailed Solar Chart for John Doe

We've gone about as far as we can without going beyond the scope of this book. To help you feel even more comfortable with the process of doing a chart, we thought it a good idea to do a final sample for you. Let us consider a male, John Doe, who was born on September 30, 1942.

Step 1 Refer to the Ephemeris for 1942 and turn to the month of September for that year. On a sheet of paper list the positions of all the planets for the 30th day, making sure that you have the correct sign for each planet by checking each column for the sign whose symbol is given in the space above the degree entries. If done correctly you should have the entries as follows (rounded off to the nearest degrees):

SUN	6° ♎	JUPITER	22° ♋
MOON	10° ♊	SATURN	13° ♊
MERCURY	26° ♎	URANUS	4° ♊
VENUS	24° ♍	NEPTUNE	0° ♎
MARS	8° ♎	PLUTO	7° ♌

Step 2 Starting with Libra on the left side of the horizontal line that divides upper from the lower halves of the chart or horoscope, proceed to write the symbol for each zodiacal sign on the line of each segment in the natural sequence of the signs. Done correctly, you will have Scorpio on the line indicating the second segment or house, Sagittarius on the line of the third sector, Capricorn on the line of the fourth sector and so on around the chart. Next, write the symbol for each planet in the first sector (or house) that is in the sign Libra, leaving enough room for additional entries should that be necessary. Continue around the chart entering the appropriate planets as they are shown in their respective sectors.

Step 3 Make a list of the Qualities with the heading for the Cardinal, Fixed and Mutable signs as follows and list the number of planets in each of them: the predominating Quality is Mutable, with five planets.

Make a list of the Elements with headings for the Fire, Earth, Air and Water signs as follows and list the number of planets in each of them: the predominating Element is Air, with six planets.

Refer to Chapter 6, Elements and Qualities, to review information for deriving the Signature. The Signature is Mutable-Air, or Gemini, the Mutable-Air sign.

MUTABLE

Temperamentally, John Doe is versatile in his outlook and utilizes his vast fund of acquired information to sustain him in his pursuits. Ever flexible to the demands of a constantly changing world, he is always timely in his approach to the problems of the day. His is a logical procedure for dealing with the most difficult situations with which he may be confronted, and he always has an alternate plan if his first choice does not work as expected. He never fails to gain significant information from every event in his life and amasses a tremendous collection of valuable material that eventually serves him well in future situations.

AIR

Behaviorally, he is quick to engage in meaningful exchanges with people eager to test him in his facility with words and their impact as he skillfully delivers them to achieve his objective at the moment. He is never at a loss to demonstrate how to lock horns with the most formidable adversary in serious or casual encounter and win hands down. He rarely arouses these antagonists to permanent hostility toward him because he knows how to demonstrate his own vulnerability so that an effective face-saving process takes place to everyone's satisfaction. The art of friendly persuasion has never been used so well as when John Doe applies it.

Step 4 Turn to Appendix I and read the analyses of the planets in the signs. Pay particular attention to the Sun, Moon and Mercury, which, as we stated, represent the ego, the emotions and the mental faculties. Continue examining the remaining planets in signs as listed in the Appendix I.

Step 5 Resources and Inhibitors—Sun Sign Division. John Doe's Sun is located at 6° Libra. Let's do a simple linear graph to determine the decanates and quadruplicities, as presented in chapter 7.

LIBRA

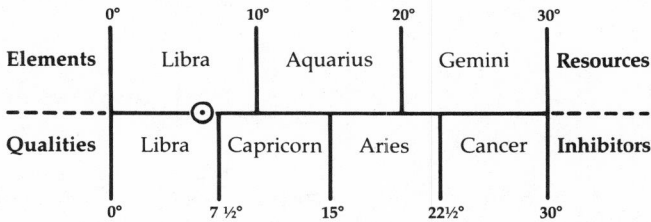

The Sun at 6° Libra would place it in the first decanate and in the first quadruplicity. This means that Libran qualities of conciliation are strongly rooted in John Doe's ego, which would tend to make him very easygoing, affable and eager to please. He would be good at working with different people, weighing carefully the needs and opinions of all, even those whose views oppose each other. His inhibitions are also rooted in his Libran behavior quality. This would mean that his mediating nature would get in its own way. Not wanting to offend or alienate, he may often find himself agreeing with two different points of view for the sake of harmony with each individual.

Step 6: Planetary Aspects. Following the procedure outlined in the last chapter, we calculate the angular distances between the planets. For the sake of space, we will simply list the resulting Aspects.

Moon conjunct Saturn	☽ ☌ ♄	(*malefic*)
Moon conjunct Uranus	☽ ☌ ♅	(*malefic*)
Venus conjunct Neptune	♀ ☌ ♆	(*malefic*)
Sun conjunct Mars	☉ ☌ ♂	(*malefic*)
Saturn conjunct Uranus	♄ ☌ ♅	(*malefic*)
Moon sextile Pluto	☽ ✶ ♇	
Venus sextile Jupiter	♀ ✶ ♃	
Sun sextile Pluto	☉ ✶ ♇	
Mars sextile Neptune	♂ ✶ ♆	
Jupiter sextile Neptune	♃ ✶ ♆	
Saturn sextile Pluto	♄ ✶ ♇	
Uranus sextile Pluto	♅ ✶ ♇	
Mercury square Jupiter	☿ □ ♃	(*malefic*)
Moon trine Sun	☽ △ ☉	
Moon trine Mars	☽ △ ♂	
Sun trine Uranus	☉ △ ♅	
Mars trine Saturn	♂ △ ♄	
Mars trine Uranus	♂ △ ♅	
Sun trine Saturn	☉ △ ♄	

Although *most* of the Aspects listed are favorable in nature, those that are unfavorble deserve special attention because they represent the distorting forces at work in the dynamics of behavior. The unfavorable, malefic Aspects to be concerned about are the following conjunctions and square:

> Moon conjunct Saturn
> Moon conjunct Uranus
> Venus conjunct Neptune
> Sun conjunct Mars
> Saturn conjunct Uranus
> Mercury square Jupiter

What we do now is follow the procedures we used for the last chart — that is, look up the Aspects analyses of these in Appendix VI on planetary Aspects.

Below are the paraphrased interpretations from the Appendix.

Moon conjunct Saturn John Doe is one who lingers in the past, who denies himself the development of new interests and pursuit of new challenges. He does not let go of his romantic ties.

Moon conjunct Uranus John Doe is emotionally impulsive and erratic. Short-lived relationships are a pattern in his life, and although he claims this suits him, he actually longs for an enduring relationship.

Venus conjunct Neptune John Doe's imagination is active, sometimes to excess. He indulges in fantasies and romantic dreams. He idealizes his mate, or a woman he would like as his mate. But he is not a realist. His romantic illusions are largely escapist in nature. He needs to take care that he doesn't misrepresent himself or lose what he has because of self-deception.

Sun conjunct Mars This Aspect tells us something basic about John Doe's personality: a strong desire to control others, as well as being vindictive and combative at times. His Mars drives may overcome his good reason at times.

Saturn conjunct Uranus John Doe, a Libran, has difficulty making decisions. It may arise from not wanting to hurt people's feelings, or, as suggested by this Aspect, it may arise from his lingering ties with the past and the overwhelming demands of the future. He fears the unknown and the untried. He must learn to accept change as an inherent part of the way of the world, of progress and growth.

Mercury square Jupiter These planets both rule some phase of communication. This unfavorable Aspect between them inclines John Doe to take over, to talk too much, or too forcefully. He has a need to be on center stage at times.

Jones Patterns and Planetary Complexes

There is one final step which we have not yet alluded to, yet which may, in some charts, be an important source of information. It is the distribution of the planets in the circular chart.

If you recall, step 4 in constructing the detailed solar chart is the actual drawing of the circular chart with the planets in their proper locations. This distribution of the planets can have astrological significance beyond the particular Aspects that are formed. The overall grouping may conform to a particular pattern in the chart which has been observed to cause definite and distinctive behavior in people.

In Appendix IV we describe seven basic chart patterns, which are called Jones Patterns. The seven kinds of configurations are as follows: the Bundle, Bowl, Bucket, See-saw, Locomotive, Splay and Splash. Turn to the Appendix for more details on each, and on other planetary complexes.

In the case of our John Doe, we find his chart does conform to one such pattern, and it is the Bundle.

Figure 28. The Bundle

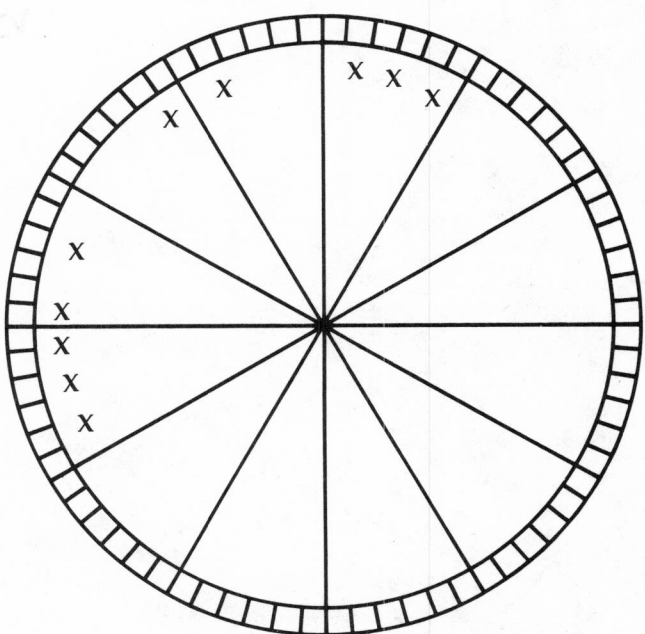

As you can see from the diagram below, John Doe's planets are grouped together in just five signs, and the majority of them are within an angle of 120°. This distribution constitutes the pattern called the Bundle.

For an interpretation we turn to Appendix IV. From it we learn that the intense concentration of planets produces an equally intense and unrelenting behavior in John Doe. Specifically, he is intense in seeking rewards that serve his personal interests. In life, he will pursue things that require deep concentration and full use of his creative potentials. We also find that it is difficult for this man to share his life with anyone else.

Figure 29. The Bundle (John Doe Sample)

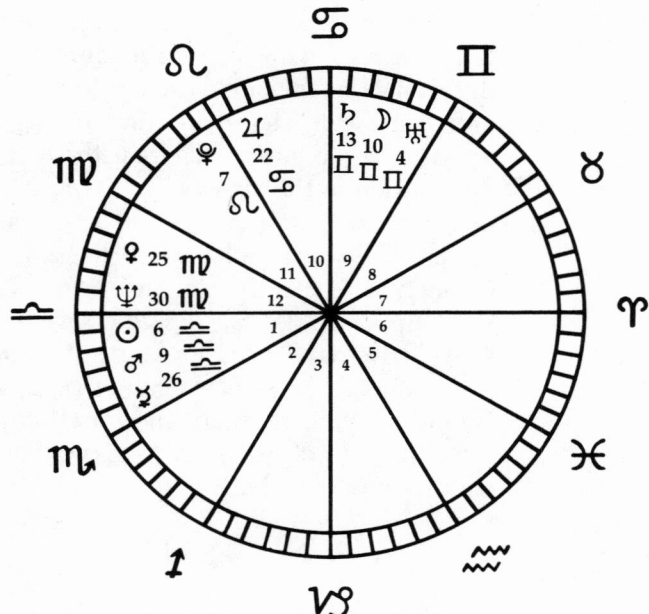

APPENDIX I Planets in Signs

Sun

SUN IN ARIES

You are forceful, dynamic and aggressive. These qualities enable you to have your own way, because you don't stop long enough to determine whether others mind it when you do. Even if they did, however, it wouldn't necessarily stop you. When you are challenged, you become even more demanding and aggressive. You enjoy the attention you get, even if it only boosts your ego for the moment. You pride yourself on your strength and directness, but your closest allies and competitors may resent you for it. You lack moderation in all things, and this can easily lead to serious consequences, such as bitter conflicts with people you have to deal with, and increases your liability to accidents.

Compromise is not one of your strongest points and is probably the most important lesson for you to learn. You tend to ignore reality and to be indifferent to the feelings of others in striving to achieve, and because of this you may not gain their support when you need it to gain your objectives.

You are creative and inspired at times to accomplish goals that are impressive. You don't doubt for a minute that you can succeed because you don't believe anyone with your eagerness and faith can fail. You have a zest for life that never diminishes and you aren't afraid to take chances. Taking chances is a bit risky though, since your judgment needs greater development. Even when you suffer temporary setbacks, you pick yourself up and go on as if you never had them.

You are inclined to come on very strong and you stimulate people to be on the defensive against you. You may be admired and feared, but without greater mutual understanding with people, you will never gain their respect.

SUN IN TAURUS

With your Sun in Taurus, you are determined, forceful, self-indulgent and resistant to change when someone else tries to force it on you. Wanting all the comforts of life, you are willing to apply yourself to get them and you don't allow anyone to stand in your way. Once you acquire the possessions that give you a feeling of security, it is nearly impossible to take them away from you. You are basically quite insecure and much preoccupied with using material acquisition to compensate for this emotional need. You tend to be a taker, not a giver, and for this reason it is essential that you learn to know when giving is as appropriate as receiving. Most people look unfavorably on those who have their hands extended for gifts the greater part of the time.

The one thing you can give that will not appreciably reduce your capital or assets is your time and energy. The investment you will make toward your own future goals cannot be overestimated. You tend to be envious of those who seem to be without any important liability. Were the truth fully known, it might reveal they have as many problems and anxieties as you and are not to be envied at all.

You are enormously resourceful in capitalizing on your creative talents, and instinctively know how to translate your ideas into tangible assets. You need to own things to feel truly comfortable about the future, which you view with some apprehension.

You are reasonably demanding in having your physical appetites satisfied, and you are really offended when your attentions and desires are rejected. You are slow to anger, but devastating when you are pushed beyond your limit.

You strive for a job with a future in it, one where you can gain tenure if possible, which it is if you use your creative potential imaginatively. You need to be more adaptable and utilize your talents more aggressively.

SUN IN GEMINI

Your Sun in Gemini gives you an exciting personality that is the delight of everyone who knows you. Your insatiable curiosity stimulates the development of your mental faculties and allows you to be quite competent in many endeavors. There is little you don't know something about, and you are never without a subject to talk about. You have a breezy outlook on life and are rarely "down in the dumps" about a situation, because you know that conditions will probably change shortly, and things will be looking up again.

You are more concerned about income and financial matters in general than it seems. It takes considerable resources to allow you to indulge in the varieties of interests that attract you. You bore fairly easily, and the novelty of new interests makes life pleasurable. Communication is one of your best assets, and it is quite possible you have some talent for writing and the arts in general. Domestic chores can be boring to you unless you can devise a way to make them more challenging. The choice of career may be somewhat difficult for you because you often don't know what you want. You love people and your career must somehow involve them in a personal way. Hard, physical work you prefer to avoid if you can — you run out of steam early in the game. Though you like the public life, you try to avoid becoming personally involved, so that you can keep your independence. You have a "thing" about making any commitments that would restrict your freedom.

You have to make plans if you hope to realize your goals and objectives, and you have to discipline yourself in your responsibilities in seeing that your plans are carried out.

Your partner or lover must be willing to grant you certain privileges, mainly that freedom to pursue those interests that are fulfilling and enriching to you.

SUN IN CANCER

You are a deep-feeling person with strong family ties and many memories, some of them pleasant and some of them painful, but you wouldn't change them if you could. You may make strong af-

firmations that you want to stand on your own and be reasonably independent, but the situations and events in your life hardly support this claim. Though ego satisfaction may not be an important issue in your life, still it is imperative that you focus your attention on finding ways to achieve some degree of fulfillment in your destiny.

The facts of hard reality are particularly foreign to you and that is the primary source of most of your problems. Being averse to the responsibility for taking action, you tend to withdraw rather than make decisions. It will be difficult for you to reach your goals in life unless you are willing to accept the abrasions and stresses often found in competitive enterprises. It is essential for you to define your career goals and establish a program by which you will attain them. There has to be planning in your affairs if you want to accomplish anything that will be lasting. The feeling of anxiety about gaining financial security should stimulate you to assert yourself to reduce this apprehension.

You need an understanding partner to share your hopes and dreams for the future and to give you a sufficient reason to apply yourself toward an objective. It is also good to have an objective opinion from someone you trust to help you make decisions and stand firm when competition increases and challenges are more difficult to cope with.

Learn to think for yourself and avoid looking for family approval in your actions. A formal education is an absolute necessity to give you the opportunity to reach out beyond the limits of your narrow environmental conditions to a future that is rich with fulfillment and accomplishment.

SUN IN LEO

You are charming, personable and eager to prove your worth to yourself and to others. You have considerable creative potential that must be developed if you hope to gain your goals in life. You demand total freedom to express your desires as you choose without having to explain your actions to anyone, and you understand the rights of others to assert themselves similarly. You are a good conversationalist and are sometimes inspired in how you capture an audience's attention with your flair for dramatics. You genuinely care for people and are at your best when you have a large number gathered around you. You are uncomfortable with people who are weak and unable to stand on their own.

Your focus of attention should be directed to the future and the role you must accept to function in the mainstream of society for a destiny that is truly fulfilling. You often fail to plan for your later years because you are so completely involved with current matters. Your inclination to self-indulgence severely shortchanges you in the achievements that are possible for you.

Your partner must share your enthusiasm for the excitement of every new challenge. He or she must be willing to satisfy your strong sexual needs and leave a powerful legacy of love to nourish those to whom you have given life.

You are rich in creative potential that must be cultivated and developed before it can be rewarding to others and to yourself. You are naturally polished and gracious but you still need the skill that derives from formal training. You cannot afford to be less competent than your competitors, and this you surely understand.

Don't allow the favors bestowed upon you by your parents or guardians to limit your development or you will have to accept the obscurity that results from incompetence.

SUN IN VIRGO

You are a specialist and can excel in many careers requiring attention to detail, persistence in problem-solving and dedication to render an important service to those unable to provide it for themselves. Expecting nothing short of perfection, you are often judgmental in evaluating the tasks performed by others. You aren't always fair in your judgment because you can see only part of the evidence upon which to make a fair decision. You generally avoid what you consider "long-winded" dissertations and prefer to exclude any extraneous considerations that might force you to reconsider your decision. According to you, there is only one way to do things: your way! Still, you have an important role to play in keeping people on their toes and not permitting them to dawdle their time away in nonproductive activity.

Though you are a technician, you may lack the true depth of compassion that is necessary to round you out and make you truly effective in your chosen career. You are very resourceful in capitalizing on your creative potential and it is unlikely that you will ever be unemployed for very long. You have many talents and you will always find a way to convert one of them into cash when conditions require it. Though you may constantly say that you can't wait to retire, the fact is that you will always be active. Inactivity would be lethal to you and cause you painful boredom.

You tend to be traditional about the mutual roles in partnership, and you feel that if it has worked so well in the past, it must be a good way to do things. You are uncomfortable trying to live up to society's expectations, and you resent the artificiality of social pretense.

You like to feel that you are very special to your partner and there may be times when the painful demands of your own children will intrude into the ideal situation that exists between you and your partner.

SUN IN LIBRA

Your Sun in Libra shows that you strive for harmony in your affairs and in your dealings with people. You are generally kind and mild-mannered in disposition and you go out of your way to compromise if it will maintain peace and order. It is difficult for you to make decisions because you aren't usually sufficiently aware of all the pertinent facts and you don't want to offend anyone by what may be a bad judgment.

You are eager to stay in the mainstream of social activity and try to win as many friends as possible and to stay informed on current social events. You will probably be comfortable in a career involving the public where your art of clever communication and dialogue can be demonstrated. You are skilled in saying the right thing at the right time to achieve your objectives. You want constant reassurances that you are effective and competent in your chosen field of work and look for approval at every opportunity. You are basically very insecure about your credibility and need the feedback from appreciative audiences to give you the self-confidence that may be lacking.

Your physical desires are not overly emphasized in your life. What you desire most is a warm, understanding companion who will give you the moral support to help you to succeed.

You are growth oriented and you usually associate with professional people whose positions might prove helpful to you in gaining the recognition you feel your talents deserve. There is little you can accomplish on your own. You identify so much with society that only when you win its admiration do you feel rewarded.

Contributing to the needs of others may be foreign to you, but it is essential for your own growth. The worst thing you can do is make claims that you cannot honestly live up to.

SUN IN SCORPIO

Your Sun in Scorpio shows that you have deep feelings that few people can detect, because you keep them to yourself. You are extremely sensitive and easily disturbed when anyone deals harshly with you. When dealt with this way, you bide your time until you can settle the score, because you never forget and rarely forgive. You have much determination in your endeavors, knowing that persistent effort will yield the results you want. You tend to be self-centered and are usually unwilling to submit to authority unless there is no other alternative. You are an extremist in everything you do, trying desperately to prove your worth to yourself and others.

You will probably enjoy a career where you have the freedom to use your talents in your own way. Not a shirker, you give complete effort in your duties and expect to be well paid for it. Insurance, investment, medicine, research and the occult field in general are fitting to your particular temperament.

Though the word *sex* is associated with this sign, that subject is no more relevant to you than to others. More important, however, is the need to feel you are making substantial contributions to benefit you and your partner in your mutual interests. Giving has got to be an important part of your life, but this can only occur after you have accumulated the evidence of your worth. If you find it difficult to give, the chances are you've become too detached from people and feel they are not deserving of your generosity. Loving others above yourself will go a long way toward making your life richer and more fulfilling.

You tend to be a loner, preferring solitude to the artificial pretensions that many people use in their social activities. You are easily bored with trite, superficial conversation that says even less than the conversationalists intended.

SUN IN SAGITTARIUS

Your Sun in Sagittarius shows that you are flexible when changes occur and willing to adapt so that your life-style will not be too severely curtailed. You are eager to take advantage of any opportunity that allows you to use your wealth of information and creativity for making gains. You rarely look back at what you may have missed, but prefer to look to the future with great anticipation from the lessons learned. Being restless stimulates you to be prepared for any situation you can benefit from. You are morally aware of what is right, though you may

take certain liberties with your ethics to preserve your freedom.

You adapt well to such professional fields as law, politics, education, and spiritual enterprises. Your wheeler-dealer temperament finds easy access to the more gainful types of employment where the growth rate is unlimited. Never content to stand still, you enjoy those careers that give you mobility. You are unhappy with routine occupations and become easily bored with repetitious duties.

You are not the most physically ardent worker, preferring to find a job where this kind of effort is not required. Yet you will thoroughly enjoy yourself in your free time with very physical activities and pleasures. You are self-seeking for the most part and often deny that there are social obligations you could respond to and improve. You make a better leader than a follower, and consider it below your dignity to earn your living as most people do.

You like to think that you are irresistible to the opposite sex because this is an important part of your life. Yet this is the one activity about which you must be extremely cautious because it can undermine all your accomplishments if it isn't kept under control.

You need greater organization in your life to capitalize on your talents more effectively.

SUN IN CAPRICORN

The Sun in Capricorn shows that you are, for the most part, quite realistic in your goals and objectives. You rarely bite off more than you can accomplish, because you know your limits. You know how to mobilize your skills to achieve the greatest results with the least amount of effort. You are basically quite efficient in using your creative potentials to their utmost, willing to make whatever sacrifices are necessary to help you get what you want in life. Beneath that seemingly controlled exterior beats a very sensitive heart, and you are far more vulnerable to criticism than it appears.

You will probably be comfortable working in the competitive fields of business, finance and management where you can excel. You have fairly well defined goals that you are willing to apply yourself to, and you expect your employer to live up to your contractual agreement and offer you any promotion you feel you deserve. You aren't afraid of hard work, provided you are paid accordingly. You are loyal to those you love and faithful to those who employ you. You tend to outgrow the position you hold and need to know there is room at the top for anyone with the ambition and feeling of responsibility that you demonstrate.

You are an avid physical partner and need a mate who is willing to satisfy your strong desire. You don't want complete submission but rather a partner who shares your eagerness and desire, which will provide both of you with much fulfillment.

You are willing to make sacrifices for your children that they may enjoy the benefits and advantages you've worked so hard to give them. Though you are a strict disciplinarian, you are usually fair when exercising your authority. You need to become more detached and learn to let go when matters are out of your hands. Your fear of taking chances unless you are well informed protects you from failure.

SUN IN AQUARIUS

Your Sun in Aquarius shows that you are independent and progressive. You respect only people who are, like yourself, basically honest and sincere. You can detach yourself, however, in situations with people when you don't want to get involved. You are an eager conversationalist and your interests are wide and varied. Though you can relate to all kinds of people regardless of their life direction or interests, you are not likely to be influenced into following in their footsteps. You are so individualistic that you must follow your own instincts and do "your own thing." You reserve the right to choose your friends and, regardless of who or what they are, you will support them in their right to be themselves.

Your career must allow you considerable freedom of choice, which is the reason you prefer jobs where the working hours are flexible and where there is a minimum of routine. You are temperamentally suited to working with the public where your talent for communication is best utilized and where the work environment is stimulating. Public relations, sales, travel and entertainment are some of the fields you would find attractive. A rebel by nature, you find rules and tradition especially uncomfortable since they tend to restrict your creative imagination.

You enjoy a wide circle of friends but you are generally noncommitted to them if it would restrict you in any way. You become uneasy when individuals presume you should be obligated to them, because you want the freedom to come and go as you please. When your trust is violated, you detach yourself and go about your business as though you didn't even know the person.

You are generous and kindly disposed toward others, but you resent it when they assume you can be propositioned casually. Your physical desires are not intense, and you can enjoy people thoroughly without physical contact.

SUN IN PISCES

Your Sun in Pisces shows that you have a deep-feeling nature with compassion for those less fortunate than you. Your extreme sensitivity often causes you to suffer more than others do in the same situations. There is a longing within you for obscure and undefined goals. When you succeed in defining your objectives, you have an abundance of creative imagination and insight to realize them. It is essential that you direct your interests outside you where you can be more effective in serving the needs of others. When you preoccupy yourself with personal matters, you usually have blinders on and fail to see things clearly.

Your career should relate to the affairs of others where you are required to help them when they cannot help themselves. Additionally, you might be fascinated by artistic endeavors as a field of great enrichment and happiness for you, whether as a practitioner or a dealer in the arts. In any capacity, your success can be measured by the formal training you have. An education is absolutely essential for you to derive the most benefit from your creative potential. You must be curious enough to ask questions all through your life and accept the responsibilities the answers suggest. It is not enough to sacrifice your desires for others; you must care enough about people that your efforts in their behalf seem only right and just.

You might have some difficulty relating to people on an individual level because you don't love yourself enough to feel you deserve to be loved in return. This too is an excuse and benefits no one, least of all yourself. On the other hand, there may be times when you engage in extreme self-indulgence, and it is inexcusable for you because you are usually well informed and lack only the ambition to take chances when the competition is keen. Being as sensitive as you are, you can derive the highest aesthetic joy from experiences some people regard as ordinary and commonplace. Don't keep your problems to yourself or you risk illness through the power of autosuggestion.

Moon

MOON IN ARIES

The Moon represents the emotions, and in this sign you react to stimuli through the impressions of your feelings. You tend to jump to premature conclusions on impulse and later discover you made a mistake in judgment. You are extremely restless and eager to form lasting relationships, but you lack staying power to allow an encounter to develop into a permanent one.

You are afraid to fall in love, with its demands and responsibilities, and so you stay uncommitted. You fear rejection from those you care for. You prefer to stay "on the loose" so you always have a reason to justify yourself to yourself. Your reasoning in this matter is more than slightly distorted by emotional considerations. In spite of this, you do have a wide circle of contacts, but few truly intimate ones. It is necessary for the one you love to first make the assertion of caring for you before you admit that you also care.

Although deep within you want to be fair in your dealings with others, you nevertheless assert your feelings whether you are right or wrong. There is little consistency in how you behave since it depends so much on your impressions at any given moment. Should you be on an emotional "high," all will be well, but if you happen to be in the emotional dumps, then others will feel the effects and wonder what is ailing you.

Your sensitivity and feelings could be utilized in expressing your creative potential. You have dramatic flair and should capitalize on it. Perhaps sports, speculation and teaching or writing could help you drain some of your emotional anxieties and direct them into productive channels.

You should maintain a well-balanced diet, and eat only when you are at ease and calm. If you eat when you are upset, you could easily develop headaches and general discomfort. You do have a highly developed imagination which may be creatively expressed, but may also serve to create imagined physical problems. Relaxation is very important for you.

MOON IN TAURUS

You are resourceful in taking advantage of matters that can improve your security, physically and emotionally. Your natural impulse is to take rather than give, although this may not continue throughout your life. This process or attitude has a profound effect on your relationships, since others may find it difficult to be generous with you if you don't reciprocate occasionally.

When you become emotionally involved with anyone, your feelings are stable and consistent. You tend to relate easier to those who have money than to those who don't. Your logic may be that it is just as easy to marry someone with money, easier in fact, than to tie yourself down with someone who would expect you to render assistance if financial conditions became strained. You love beautiful things, a comfortable home, good food (and plenty of it), fine clothes, warm friends and security.

You subconsciously dread poverty and indebtedness or the threat of it when unexpected events drain your resources. Life insurance is high on your list of essentials to avert disaster when unforeseen developments occur. You fear poverty as much as you fear death.

Your major hang-up is your unwillingness to gamble on the future. You are intensely preoccupied with the present and rarely risk losing what you have in taking chances that you feel will put you at a disadvantage at some later date. You are not objective about offering your services to others unless some benefit can be derived for you. Others may respect you, but at the same time they may be secretly envious of you and your self-control in important matters.

You know how to mobilize your talents to capitalize on them. You know how to achieve your goals. You learned from the lessons of your parents or advisers. Your destiny will not be fulfilled, however, until you learn to put a value on the qualities others possess and get away from the physical or material frame of reference.

MOON IN GEMINI

You are a knowledgeable individual, blessed with a sense of humor and the ability to enjoy all kinds of people, no matter who or what they are. You are sufficiently detached not to become unduly impressed by those with whom you communicate. By the same token, people don't take you seriously. You may not show it, but this does bother you. Perhaps this is why you may become interested in writing or teaching. Such a function carries credibility, so you know others will be affected by what you say and do. You need the approval people can give you.

You are extremely restless and need to be constantly on the go. You have nervous irritability when you are forced to stay in one place for very long. There is a conflict between what you know and what you feel, and an intellectual appraisal of a situation you are concerned with may really be an emotional evaluation. It is sometimes difficult for you to make a decision because of this. Logic and feeling make it difficult to find the solution to any problem you have to resolve.

Although you are well informed on many subjects, your lack of follow-through may make it difficult for you to pursue any of them long enough to benefit you. Your mind wanders here and there and everywhere. You are easily distracted by sudden, new fascinations, especially if they are novel or unique.

Your personal relationships may have greater difficulty in becoming established since you seem so disinterested in anything permanent. Perhaps you have a fear of losing your mobility when confined by emotional ties. It is probably better for you to form associations with others in the field of education or communication since they too would be as flexible as you, and good relationships without binding commitments could be established.

You eagerly ask questions of yourself and others, but you must not fail to gain answers. Hard, physical labor is not for you because your constitution, both psychological and physiological, is not geared for that kind of responsibility, and could not resist the deteriorating abuse it would cause you.

MOON IN CANCER

You are emotionally sensitive and easily hurt when others assert themselves arrogantly in their dealings with you. You are a deep, feeling person and appreciate consideration from others in your relationships. You try to understand them and are generally ready to help them when they need it.

You learn fairly well, although you tend to accept information that satisfies your feelings, rather than your intellect. You are tenacious with any knowledge you've gained and rarely forget anything. You may "choose" to forget painful experiences only because you don't want to be reminded of them. You have strong ties to family and home, making it difficult to break away to be on your own. You enjoy the comfort in having someone else take care of the daily necessities, and you would prefer not changing that situation.

You are protective of those you care for, and it isn't easy for you to turn your back on those needing you. Your greatest problem is in letting go when others want to be free and independent. Your feelings are deep and sincere, but your reactions to crit-icism may sometimes border on the neurotic. You have difficulty facing reality and fear the abrasions of competition. It is necessary to be logical in evaluating your problems and to make an effort to render decisions, even if it seems you might be in error. As you learn from your failures your judgment will be refined until you are skilled in applying it.

Your insecurity will be lessened if you participate in social programs for those less fortunate than you. Observing the predicaments of others will focus your attention away from yourself, so that when you are sorry it will be for them and not yourself. Be moderate in eating and drinking. You are prone to add weight. Eat only when you are calm, or distress is sure to follow.

MOON IN LEO

You have strong feelings that you constantly express. You love life and enjoy close relationships with people. You don't wait for others to make gestures of friendship, but eagerly seek to make them feel at ease in your company. You want so much to be liked and loved that you dramatize your feelings toward others so they will respond to you in a similar fashion. In fact, you function best when you know others care for you.

You can easily detach yourself from people who are indifferent or uncaring. Only individuals with depth and substance gain your attention. You are conservative toward people until they demonstrate their worth to you. Once this is done, you will project your feelings with determination, in anticipation of establishing a permanent relationship.

You are proud, sometimes even vain, in seeking the spotlight. Love is very important to you. It rounds out your life with meaning and satisfaction. You tend to exercise a dominant force over those you care for, and you are shattered when they reject you in defiance.

You appreciate fine things. Beautiful people, a comfortable home, good food and warm friends delight your tastes. Even good books, art and the theater give you much enjoyment. However, you may indulge beyond your resources and severely strain your finances. You live for today and try not to look too carefully at tomorrow. You try to avoid the unpleasant — it is so inconsistent with the brighter side of life you expect.

Avoid being too self-centered and acting the "star." Many people are turned off by it.

MOON IN VIRGO

You have a methodical and painstaking nature. You may find it difficult to enjoy casual relationships because you examine people too closely and find what is wrong with them. Your detailed examination too often reveals flaws that you cannot tolerate. If they pass the test you've applied, you enjoy them for what they are and you may fail to appreciate them for who they are. You regard yourself as something of an analyst, and you are. It is also important, however, to be more humane in judging people, realizing that perfection as you expect it is rare. You must be tolerant of human imperfection.

You are especially suited to occupations where detail is important, such as in dietetics, medicine, hygiene and physical therapy. You have the ability to apply yourself toward helping others who cannot help themselves. You innately know how to do the right thing even without being told. You have an appreciation for people who at least try to improve themselves with your assistance.

You don't generally seek the limelight because you are somewhat shy and retiring. In fact, you may show disdain for anyone gaining the spotlight if you know they've done little to deserve it. You expect a lot from others and no less from yourself. In your personal relations, you make demands so that when they are met it will prove how much the other person must really care for you. You don't waste your time on people unless they can establish their worth to you.

You are practical to a fault and always trying to establish your credentials to others. Though you may have deep emotional feelings, you are not regarded as a romantic person. You can best turn people on by turning off the criticism. Accept people with their frailties — it adds dimension and interest to life.

MOON IN LIBRA

You are sociable, refined and sensitive to people's opinions of you. You want to be accepted by those with whom you must deal in your daily life. You try not to antagonize others with your differing views, so you maintain a middle-of-the-road position. You especially avoid argument when you can, since this can really upset you. Harsh language, especially if it is vulgar, disturbs you greatly. If at all possible, you will walk away when a discussion seems headed for bitter display of temper and anger.

You are more sociable than romantic. You can be satisfied with intellectual companions when others could only be comfortable with physical contact. Physical expression is important to you, but not if you cannot relate to an individual in any other way. You are sophisticated and refined and prefer to associate with that element of society if at all possible.

Public relations, artistic enterprises, social organizations and elegant functions are perfectly suited to your temperament. Your charm of manner, attention to proper attire and kindness to others gains their approval of you.

In your desire for cultural surroundings, you may be unrealistic. You may even play-act the part of success while you are under financial stress just so you can keep up with the Joneses. You contrive reasons why you can't attend a particular function if you are financially embarrassed. It would be too shattering to you if the truth were revealed.

Your major problem is being unable to make decisions without getting someone else's approval. You fear being rejected by people if your judgment turns out to be unsatisfactory to them.

MOON IN SCORPIO

You have an intense emotional nature and your feelings are frequently expressed in extreme ways. On the one hand you may become infatuated by the attention you attract from others, and at other times you may enjoy teasing those you entice and nothing more. You attract people with your magnetism because you project desire, and you may not even be aware of it. There is no way you can be sure of the kind of person who will respond to you. The result is that you may have become defensive in your dealings with everyone.

You are possessive with the persons you like and love. Be careful you don't become vindictive because of jealousy. This can cause you endless problems in your relationships. Try to differentiate between people who are sincere in relating to you and those who make no contribution to sustain a genuine relationship. You must also watch that you don't expect a lot from people, since you are inclined to be an opportunist.

You need to avoid indulging in daydreams so that you lose your contact with reality. The present is so important to you that you may not plan for the future by developing your creative potentials. You can easily get into a rut and wonder why you are not progressing. Develop your latent abilities and utilize those talents by applying them efficiently to your goals. You tend to resent suggestions from well-meaning friends as an attempt to discredit you. This is an emotional reaction and not a valid conclusion when you take a realistic view.

When others are honest with you there is nothing you won't do for them and no sacrifice is too great. On the other hand, if anyone undermines you in any way, it's unlikely you will ever forgive them nor forget it.

MOON IN SAGITTARIUS

You have a breezy, freedom-loving kind of personality, constantly on the go, and you enjoy life eagerly. You are optimistic and good-natured on the whole and pessimists really annoy you. You have an insatiable appetite for knowledge and are curious enough to want to know something about a variety of subjects. You are emotionally restless, but at the same time you want to form relationships with people who will accept them even if they are not permanent.

You prefer to associate with persons who are either professionals or who are at least on their way up the ladder of achievement. The common, everyday person does not hold your interest mainly because of the possible lack of variety in his or her life. You find idle chatter boring and a waste of time. You easily adapt to changes of environment. Travel is broadening for you, and though you may not do any, you will travel through the mind in books, theaters and galleries.

Small talk and trivial issues aren't enough to gain your attention, but be careful you don't become intellectually arrogant and become known as the "know-it-all." You would work best in large corporate enterprises, especially if you are assigned tasks that bring you in contact with those in official positions. Education, travel, social functions, political enterprises, campaigns and the like are suitable activities for your temperament.

In your romantic interests, you acquire a taste for individualists who aspire to achieve their goals so they can live the good life in comfort. The "sportin' life" is the life for you. Your mate must accept your inclination to be on the go, because limiting your mobility would destroy your enthusiasm for living.

MOON IN CAPRICORN

Your personality is reserved, cautious and given to moments of incredible loneliness. Your emotions do not permit you to derive any satisfaction without paying some penalty. You are ambitious to achieve the best possible romantic relationship, but you always seem to settle for less than that. You are serious and more concerned with achieving goals and objectives than in having domestic bliss. You have some difficulty in projecting warmth and tenderness; thus you attract those who will accept a contractual relationship with you so that it seems like a business arrangement.

You are intensely emotional and want so much to express your feelings with someone very special. Your judgment is biased by material considerations and security, so that a purely emotional contact is less likely. Your desire for a home and domestic security is shared with your continuing interest in a professional life of your own. You want to be recognized as a very capable, organized individual who doesn't have to depend on anyone, as a person who can succeed on your own merits if you want to.

Parental conditioning may have been the cause of your insecurity, and your father, in particular, may have caused you some bitterness in your youth. Because of this, it might be better for you to accomplish your professional objectives before you turn your attention to marriage. After you've proven yourself to eliminate any self-doubts as to your competence, you may then need to relate in a personal, warm and tender relationship that has all the earmarks of success.

Warm climates are better suited to your physical needs, and above all, try to look at life with optimism.

MOON IN AQUARIUS

From your earliest years you have been extremely curious and eager to know all you could about everything, especially people. Your feelings are combined with intellectuality so that you try to understand those toward whom you have an emotional reaction. It is important that your relationships be a combination of mind and feeling for them to be truly meaningful to you. You are more inclined to pursue interests that pertain to large numbers of people rather than individuals. You are a seeker after truth, and because of this you may be let down by the human frailties you encounter, since truth is sometimes painful.

You are friendly toward everyone, but rarely intimate with anyone unless it satisfies your objectives in life. You often make sacrifices in your emotional enjoyments because you are constantly stimulated by desires to achieve at the level of mass human consciousness with which you easily identify. Learning something philosophically revealing is somewhat like an emotional experience to you, and you enjoy rapture from it. You are very generous with what you acquire in the way of knowledge and you want to share it with everyone within hearing distance.

You demand freedom for yourself and others, and you demonstrated your rebel qualities even as a young person. You feel the pulse of the times and can relate easily to the subtle changes constantly occurring in your environment.

You are somewhat indifferent about money and you resent that freedom is often dependent on it. You are fairly sure about what you know and positive that you owe a part of your future to those who will share it with you.

MOON IN PISCES

With your Moon in Pisces, you are a mass of complex inconsistencies. On the one hand you are enormously aware of the important social obligations you should fulfill and yet are, incredibly, unable to find the means and the conviction to do something about them. Sometimes you are deeply touched by the problems of the unfortunate and yet turn your back if asked to make some commitment toward solving those problems. Perhaps you identify too deeply with those who need sympathetic understanding because you crave sympathy for yourself. Whatever the reason, it still doesn't solve any problems, theirs or yours.

You carry the world's crises on your shoulders so that it is difficult for you to stand under the burden. You are supersensitive to every passing problem, even if it isn't directly related to you. You may not share your concern for these matters with anyone, but you are deeply moved by them just the same.

Generally, you are a loner because most people have to communicate in order to relate to others. You don't communicate too well because your intellect is heavily submerged in emotion. What you say at one time may be vastly different the next time depending on the emotional climate when you say it.

You should occasionally isolate yourself from the mainstream of involvement with people so you can recover the vital forces that seep from you. Rest is very important to you, for without it you are drained of energy.

You don't have the problems you think you have, but your imagination creates them as if you did.

Try to avoid occupations that require you to make contact with the unfortunate element of society. You're not strong enough for it.

Mercury

MERCURY IN ARIES

You are bright, articulate and mentally aggressive, but you are also impatient, unrealistic and sometimes insensitive to the feelings of others. You speak your mind on impulse and you may be totally wrong in your assumptions, but it is difficult for you to admit error and say you're sorry when you should. You have amazing enthusiasm when something gains your interest, though you tend to lose interest as you become more familiar with the subject. You lack staying power to persist with a project to its ultimate conclusion.

Your creative ability is considerable and you will probably use this talent in carving a place for yourself in your career. Greater moderation is indicated when your interest is running high because you often ignore the most obvious facts when your mind is made up. You are like a child with a new toy when a new idea comes to mind, and a team of horses can't hold you back when you decide to put that idea to work. You are fairly well informed, but much of the information you've gained isn't used if it will dampen your enthusiasm with what you are doing. You need to cultivate better judgment in examining the facts before you do anything, and this factor can be very important when, say, you are driving and someone cuts you off. You have a low threshold of tolerance that inclines you to lose your temper when you are provoked.

You enjoy people who are as interested in excitement as you are, people who are ready at a moment's notice to go here and there, wherever the thrills are. There is always someone who will accompany you because you have such a wide circle of friends to pick from. You are ambitious, but not too fond of hard physical labor, especially when it relates to dull, routine tasks.

MERCURY IN TAURUS

You are determined, persistent and enjoy the comforts of life. Good food, interesting friends and a substantial bank account round out your life adequately. You are thoughtful in your decisions because you don't want to waste your time making poor ones. You enjoy the benefits you gain from your efforts because you put a lot of thought and organization into your plans before you take any action. You can be a bit tiring, though, when the subject of your conversations almost invariably ends on the topic of money. You need to vary your interest more and realize there are more interesting subjects that others may prefer to talk about.

Your children occupy much of your attention and you are concerned that they have the opportunity to make their own way that you didn't have. It is important to you that they take advantage of your sound values and use them as a base to establish values they can live by.

You are attracted to a mate or lover who will share your interest in accumulating the assets that will be the security for your later years. You are not a bountiful "giver," but when you do it's given sincerely. You expect your mate to make the necessary sacrifices so that you may both enjoy a long life together, free from the anxieties of insufficient reserves.

You are gifted in occupations requiring some business sense, and your ability in management is considerable. You are a no-nonsense person and appreciate the efforts of those who are organized for action. Take care you aren't obstinate in your opinions and learn to let others make their own decisions. They may learn more when they realize why they failed.

MERCURY IN GEMINI

Your Mercury in Gemini shows that you are mentally alert, versatile in your interests and have a thirst for knowledge that is second to none. There is nothing that doesn't gain your interest, although you are easily distracted when something new attracts your attention. You are easily excited by novelty but your interest diminishes as the newness wears off. You never cease asking questions because you want to know as much as possible about everything. Although you don't appear too concerned about money, the fact is you are very insecure without it. You have a wealth of ideas for making money but you lack the self-discipline to do anything about them. You spend more time talking than actually doing. You are not the most robust person, and your efforts are largely the result of nervous energy.

You devote a lot of time to social relationships and events. It is a pleasure to meet new people and indulge in endless hours of conversation. In keeping with this need to be in communication, your work should bring you into contact with the public. Perhaps teaching or the communications media would serve your purposes and provide you with ample opportunity to do what you do best.

You need greater self-control to gain the full benefit of your active mentality. Perhaps you can team up with someone who has the follow-through you lack and can stabilize you when you feel the inclination to be on the move. Self-discipline is also advised before you express your opinion so you can be sure you have all the facts.

An education is essential to give you polish and refinement so you can take your place comfortably in any social gathering and hold your own in any discussion. With your gifted imagination, writing could enrich your life, if only as an avocation. Invest in a drama course and add to your ability as a persuasive speaker.

MERCURY IN CANCER

Your Mercury in Cancer shows that you have a tenacious memory and never forget anyone who has ever wronged you. You have strong ties to the home and family, and the obligation you feel toward those who cared for you in the past may limit you in becoming completely independent. You are biased in your opinions because your emotions interfere with making logical appraisals. You have a great respect for tradition and you often indulge in nostalgia as you remember the past. You are extremely sensitive to public opinion and when someone is cross in their dealings with you it can be a shattering experience.

Being naturally protective toward those you love, you resent it when anyone expresses a derogatory remark about them and you feel personally challenged. Rather than fight, though, you are more inclined to say very little about it and withdraw to sulk. Though you may have a lot to say when you are provoked, you don't generally seek the platform. There is a shyness in your temperament that makes it difficult for you to stand before a crowd and speak. You have a lot to say, but you don't have the courage and the emotional defenses against those who might disagree with you.

Your imaginative mentality shows that you should write. Your writing would sparkle with humor and tenderness and easily win public attention because of the reader's easy identification with the subject matter.

Your sympathetic nature might also lead into fields dealing with human nature, such as psychology, social welfare, child care or philosophy. A material interest could also draw you to dealing in antiques, conservation of natural resources or real estate. You would probably feel more comfortable working in a familiar environment and with few co-workers, so you might consider conducting your affairs from your own home.

MERCURY IN LEO

With Mercury in Leo you are the supreme optimist. You never really think of defeat because you truly believe in yourself. Your bubbling, articulate mentality sparkles with enthusiasm as you communicate your ideas and opinions with much dramatic persuasion. It is not difficult for you to win friends who will support you in your endeavors. You always seem to know how to say the right thing at the right time to get the results you want. You generally like everyone, and even your competitors admire you for your bright and magnetic personality. While you may not always be as well informed as others, you don't fail to gain the attention you need just the same. Your optimism adds credibility to your statements so that people don't challenge them.

With your creative ability you can direct your energies into various fields of endeavor. You might especially enjoy working with young people, urging them to capitalize on their own resources. They would respond to your influence because you would not challenge their own identities. They would be eager to please you since you seem so eager to please them. The creative arts might also appeal to you, and acting, writing and painting could be marvelous outlets for your need to express yourself.

You might find business or industry a suitable outlet for your energies. You could get a lot done in a position of leadership, but you could function successfully in other capacities as well and command the respect of your co-workers in how you take care of your responsibilities.

You must resist the tendency to be too casual when it is time to be serious. You sometimes don't know when it is time to play and when it is time to work.

MERCURY IN VIRGO

Your Mercury in Virgo shows that although you may be critical of others, you are supercritical of yourself as well. You are mentally versatile, constantly seeking ways to apply your talents to get the best results. Your creative ability is usually directed to activities from which you can derive the most

benefit. Never content to let your achievements remain static, you try to improve on them. Your view is that if anything can be done well, it can very likely be done better. No one can accomplish more with the least to work with than you can. You are efficient in capitalizing on your resources and talents.

Basically honest, it bothers you deeply when those you must deal with are not. It is the slick operator who disturbs you the most, because he or she may not be as capable as you but succeeds by using questionable tactics. You adhere to the principle that if you don't know the answer to a question you will admit it. Later, however, you will inform yourself. You have to be on guard at all times for people who will try to deceive you. It isn't likely they'll succeed, because you are so alert that you can tell if things don't add up as they should. Anyone violating your trust will have a most difficult time trying to regain it from you.

Your interests are so broad and varied that your success can be realized in many ways. You know how to do many things and do them well. You know how to develop your talents so they earn you a comfortable living. You are impatient with people who dawdle their time away in nonproductive interests.

You seek a mate who will be a complement to your resourcefulness. That person must be willing to share the burden for realizing your mutual goals and objectives. He or she must share your desire to work together and play together, and share in the bounty of your combined efforts.

MERCURY IN LIBRA

Mercury in Libra shows that your intellect combines curiosity, creativity and sympathetic understanding with good judgment. You have a well-rounded development that enables you to function well in the broad spectrum of human involvement. It is to your credit that you avoid making decisions until you have all the facts and can make a careful evaluation. You enjoy good relations with people in general because you don't openly challenge them when they are wrong. You quietly present them with the evidence they might have "simply overlooked" and give them the opportunity to revise their opinion. You have a charm in communication that encourages people to think favorably of you. You show refinement and good taste in dealing with people and you are welcome at any social gathering or function.

If you can overcome your indecisiveness you can achieve success in any activity dealing with the general public. Out of a desire to be well liked by everyone you often avoid making judgments that may incur the displeasure of some people. You would function best in a capacity where your skill in bringing people to agreement could be utilized. Marriage counseling, law or an advisory position in politics or business might prove satisfactory vehicles of expression for you.

Your avocational pursuits might include such interests as music, writing, art and public speaking on subjects of current interest. You live a life enriched by many varied activities so that boredom never disturbs the calm and happiness you strive for in all your affairs.

You seek a mate who will be as eager to live a rich, full life as you are. You need a mate with a strong character to complement your inability at times to make decisions. He or she must share your desire to live an active life and compromise to your need for social contact.

MERCURY IN SCORPIO

Your Mercury in Scorpio shows that you are shrewd, clever and have deep perception. Your mind works like that of a detective trying to unravel a mystery, and little escapes your attention. You don't generally reveal what you know unless you are absolutely certain your trust will not be violated. You are naturally suspicious in your dealings because you tend to doubt the truth unless you can see it for yourself. You accept nothing on hearsay since you know how easy it is for people to "doctor" the information they get, if only to make it more interesting or exciting. You can usually spot a phony before he can cause you any difficulty because your sixth sense is always working.

Matters of life and death occupy your attention and this might encourage you to consider occupations that are primarily concerned with them. Insurance, final resting places, investments, legacies, foundations and trusts are areas dealing with the affairs of those who expire. Medicine, medical research, surgery are fields dedicated to the preservation and restoration of the living. Some sacrifice of personal desires is usually required in following these professions but you have the ambition and drive to make this kind of commitment without flinching. There is usually a deep spiritual force that sustains you in your achievements despite the demands made upon you.

When fascinated by the more superficial aspects of life, you might be unduly preoccupied with sex as an outlet for your powerful inner drives. You might dwell excessively so that your other affairs suffer from lack of attention. You can pick likely prospects for your partnership interests out of a crowd, and you are not kindly disposed toward anyone who rejects your advances. When you are angry, you can be vicious and vindictive. When you are pleased, your appreciation is boundless. Try to cultivate a medium course so that your personal and professional affairs get equal time.

MERCURY IN SAGITTARIUS

Your Mercury in Sagittarius shows that you are versatile, restless and extremely curious. Although you are knowledgeable in many subjects, you lack sufficient follow-through to derive full benefit from your potentials. Your curiosity leads you into many areas of interest but you are easily distracted when something new attracts your attention. There are times when you think you don't really need to apply yourself to your goals. Your enthusiasm, while commendable, will never gain the results you want from your creative abilities unless you are willing to work and apply them to the real world. You are not afraid of competition, but you would prefer to "wheel and deal" to attract attention from important people than to work your way up through the ranks. You are a supreme optimist and believing in yourself will carry you far.

Education, law, foreign service, politics and large-scale enterprises are especially suited to your temperament and creative talents. Your work should give you the freedom to function at your own pace. Your judgment is quick and decisive when opportunity knocks and you want the feeling of mobility should a sudden change in tactics seem necessary if you are to take advantage of it.

You relate well to everyone. You have a breezy manner with a fresh outlook at all times that is infectious with those around you. No matter how dismal a situation may be, you just don't believe things won't turn out right in the end.

Your mate must share your enthusiasm and zest for living, and living it up as well. He or she must be willing to live in the mainstream of life where the action is constant and the excitement never diminishes. You want a mate who will stand shoulder to shoulder with you in search for the dreams you share.

MERCURY IN CAPRICORN

Your Mercury in Capricorn shows that you are serious, practical and generally prudent. Even though there are times when you seemingly lack the patience to allow your affairs to mature naturally, you usually get results because you have made a more thorough analysis than it appears. Being basically an efficient person, you rarely do anything without making plans so you can accomplish the most with the least effort. A conservative, you maintain a low profile while building toward your goals and objectives. You will work tirelessly and painstakingly to achieve the goals you've established for yourself. You don't like to be questioned about the methods you use, which may seem primitive to most people, and you simply point to your accomplishments to silence the critics.

On the whole your judgment is finely tuned to take advantage of all the details pertinent to your decisions. You don't like to be pushed to render decisions until you are ready because you want to avoid making mistakes. You want sufficient time to do what is right the first time.

Your realism in dealing with important issues and events gives the impression that you are indifferent in your feelings. You aren't, of course, but you are cautious about expressing your emotions unless you are reasonably certain of a positive response. The fact is, you are very concerned about those close to you and want the best for them that you can provide. As a result, you focus your attention on earning a comfortable income by using your creative talents in the most productive way possible. You generally like whatever work you are doing and are not afraid of responsibilities as long as they serve to benefit you in your ultimate goals.

Even in your avocational pursuits or pleasures, you invest a lot of time and energy to derive all that you can from them.

MERCURY IN AQUARIUS

Your Mercury in Aquarius shows that you have a sharp intellect and are alert, truthful and objective. You are more interested in future developments than you are in the past. You have the mind of a rebel, though, and you can become defiant if anyone tries to control you. You have fixed opinions and only the most convincing argument with substantial evidence can induce you to change your views. You are on friendly terms with everyone, but you can sever relations with anyone who violates your trust, which you consider unforgivable.

You are extremely well read and know something, at least, about everything. You also realize that knowledge for its own sake is wasteful unless it is used to improve the general well-being of society at large. You are not afraid to assert yourself when you know you are right and are willing to admit it when you are wrong.

You function best in the company of large groups of people where you easily relate to them at their level of response. Your tolerance enables you to associate with all kinds of people while still maintaining your own integrity and identity. You are fascinated with variety in human experience and you rarely condemn anyone, no matter what his or her status may be. People are usually receptive to you because you don't establish any rules to which they must adhere. You let everyone do their thing, whatever that might be.

You dislike being cast in a mold with everyone else. The organized structure of society with its "establishment" limits the individual's growth. You insist that no one's freedom should be in the control of another.

You tend to permissiveness in your personal and emotional relationships, and it is difficult for anyone to get really close to you, because you prefer to remain aloof.

MERCURY IN PISCES

You are mentally disorganized and have difficulty keeping your attention on one thing at a time. You enjoy a variety of interests, from the sublime to the ridiculous, and you are fairly well informed on most of them. You lack the self-discipline to apply yourself exclusively to one interest so that you can become reasonably expert in that subject. The truth is, you are inclined to be indifferent to hard, physical application to the task. You are easily distracted by novelty and lose interest in what you were doing before. You will wander aimlessly here and there, accomplishing little, until you exercise greater self-control.

All kinds of people fascinate you, and if there is something mysterious about them you are even more drawn to them. You experience many disappointments in your relationships because you seem unable to accept people for what they are, with all the hang-ups and frailties. You dream of meeting an ideal that somehow never seems to appear. You learn to live with your shattered dreams, however, but your enthusiasm is diminished that the right person will ever come along.

You are gifted in interpreting the most illusive subject matter and yet you are unable to understand the most obvious everyday problems requiring little intellectual skill. You depend on your intuition to see you through difficult periods of your life. You also have a psychic feeling about matters that are sometimes uncomfortable to live with. There may be many "false starts" where you have to do things over again until you develop this psychic ability more. You lose patience when you can't get something done immediately, but the truth is, that is why you have to do things over. You don't take enough time to plan to get it right the first time. Get advice when you aren't sure of yourself. There's no crime in admitting you don't know everything. Who does?

Venus

VENUS IN ARIES

Although you are intense in your love relationships, you sometimes lack the sustained interest necessary for them to endure. It is probably a matter of personal insecurity that causes you to seek temporary encounters that can only satisfy the senses, and you delight in the pleasures these momentary encounters give you. Your main problem is your fear of the responsibility a truly worthwhile relationship requires. You divert your attention from such matters by becoming enthusiastically involved with whatever gains your interest for the moment.

You don't make adjustment easily and prefer that others accommodate you in your desires. You love hard and fiercely, and while the flame of enthusiasm lasts you achieve total satisfaction. There is little communication in your conquests and, therefore, no regrets when they end. You are not really a very emotional person, and you tend to turn your back on reality. This is why you can indulge yourself with reasonable impunity. In time you will become increasingly lonely for companionship, but you will have to compromise with the desires of others to gain it with anyone. Mutual accommodation is essential before an enduring association can be established. You will have to respond emotionally to show you aren't totally indifferent in your feelings toward others. You must also be realistic enough to accept the burdens of any commitment to another that is the basis for mutual trust.

You are creatively inspired to bring great pleasure and enjoyment in your relationships. Give others the opportunity to get close enough to you to show you how much they can enrich your life similarly. You'll never know until you try.

VENUS IN TAURUS

You have an appreciation for beauty and harmony and you try to surround yourself with them whenever you can. You recognize virtue as one of man's important resources that improves human relations. You seek abundance in your life because you enjoy the comforts of a good home, fine furnishings and sincere friends. You are constant in your affections and loyal to your commitments in partnerships. You know your own heart so you are rarely disturbed by emotional insecurity. You jealously protect those you care for, even if the reason is only to protect your "belongings."

Money is important to you because it represents security in those things precious to you. You are not beyond giving, but the reason for generosity must be fully justified. You are reasonably clever in handling money and you might enjoy occupations where its judicious management was required. In business, you are always aware of the money spent and even more concerned with how much is earned from the investment.

Your personal relationships are best served when your partner or mate has the ability to earn a good living. Going without the comforts of life is especially painful to you, and you are prepared to earn your own living rather than make a commitment with someone whose future is, at best, insecure.

You are physically stimulated by persons who seem sure of themselves and who demonstrate strength of character. You are responsive to displays of affection and eagerly contribute to your mutual enjoyment of pleasures. Sex is important to you, but you also enjoy all the pleasures of dining, wining, dancing that you feel should precede that final shared experience.

VENUS IN GEMINI

You are charming and articulate and enjoy many varieties of human experience. You are extremely sociable and find it very difficult to settle down in personal relationships. You adapt easily to different types of people and thoroughly enjoy them because of their distinctive temperaments. You are generally on the go and if you had the means, you would probably spend a great deal of time traveling.

You enjoy life despite any temporary complications you may encounter. You are optimistic by nature and ease out of contact with people who indulge in pessimism. You always have time to communicate with anyone who has something to say, even if it isn't profound. You round out your interesting life-style with art, literature, music and friends, of which you have many.

You are impatient with coarseness of behavior or those with a perverse sense of humor. Your beneficence is improved by your appreciation of nonmaterial interests. You become impatient with persons who are preoccupied with money as the most important element in their lives. You deplore the limitations of such a dimensionless existence.

You would function well in public relations where you could display your affinity for meeting people and making it a pleasurable encounter. There are many avocational pursuits you can follow with remarkable success, since you are a multidimensional person to begin with. You are tolerant of individual failings, but find it difficult to accept failure in anyone, because you know there are many other ways to succeed if one fails.

Your romantic associations may not become permanently established because you don't always take other people's feeling seriously.

VENUS IN CANCER

Your Venus in Cancer shows that you are willing to extend yourself for those you love, even when it means you must get along with less. You have strong sentimental ties with your family so that you could have some difficulty relating to people other than your family in a person-to-person relationship. Your loyalty to people you love is admirable, but it can interfere with forming meaningful outside contacts. You are possessive with the objects of your affections so they may feel unable to do anything without first asking your permission or at least discussing it with you. You don't want to be excluded from any situation your lover may be involved with and you can wear out your welcome unless you change your attitude.

Basically shy, yet susceptible to kindness and flattery, you are uncomfortable with persons who are overly aggressive. You are essentially a dreamer who dwells on romantic imaginings or reveries to satisfy your emotional longings. You are therefore very vulnerable to partners or associates with charming personalities and refinement.

You are unrealistic in facing the harsh realities of life and may postpone taking a partner because you are waiting for the nearly perfect individual to come

into your life. You are inclined to go more than halfway in making concessions if it will produce greater harmony. Be careful you don't allow others to abuse your generosity by making excessive demands on you. Your protective instincts are probably stronger than most and you would defend the one you love in spite of the demands being made.

You can produce many fine works with your creative imagination. Art, literature, music and drama are a marvelous outlet for your romantic disposition.

VENUS IN LEO

Your Venus in Leo shows that you are gracious, well mannered and eager to please. You are generally optimistic about life and enthusiastic in facing each day with whatever incidents or situations it brings. Your warm disposition gains you a wide circle of friends and associates who speak kindly of you. You tend to bring out the best qualities in the people you meet and you are usually remembered long after the initial encounter. You need to be appreciated, though, and when you are ignored when you don't deserve it, you can be vindictive. You sometimes fail to realize that many people have flaws in their makeup that you must tolerate as long as they don't direct them at you. You have to accept the bad with the good and try to focus on the positive traits.

In trying to win friends and influence people, which should take little effort on your part, you may neglect to be honest and sincere. You may judge a person's worth on the basis of his career and elevation, and neglect to make a careful evaluation of worth as a person. You are easily impressed with showy individuals, because appearances mean a great deal to you. You probably spend more time getting ready for a social event than most people do because you are never satisfied with anything less than perfect.

You are attracted to people with "class" and character. Your selection of a lifetime partner is an important step for you because you feel you deserve the very best. Love is too easily used in your conversation for it to have the full meaning that it should. You are capable of a deep love, true and binding, and when a person succeeds in winning that kind of affection from you, you will bring much joy and happiness that will be mutually enriching.

VENUS IN VIRGO

Your Venus in Virgo shows that you tend to be restrained in expressing your feelings. It is painful to discover your emotion is not shared, so you are cautious in revealing how you feel. You are too much of a realist to truly enjoy the full depth of romantic love. You tend to establish too many conditions or prerequisites that frighten even the most ardent lover. There are few people who could possibly fill the mold you want them to fit. While you may be totally rational about every situation in your life that you must deal with, you are completely irrational in your romantic expectations.

If you are already attached, be wary of trying to remake the person you married. The creature you would thus create would no longer resemble the original, and then what would you do? You have got to learn to accept imperfection as par for the course in many of life's situations and encounters. To hold out for nothing less than perfection is the greatest testimony for your lacking it yourself.

You are sensitive and vulnerable. That is why you find it difficult adjusting to people who fall short of your expectations. You don't want to become associated with anyone who isn't at least trying to improve, for fear you will also become indifferent and uncaring about your continued development. On the other hand, you also fear those who are expert and totally competent in what they do since they may cause you to reflect on your own area of incompetence, small though it might be.

Try to direct your attention to the positive qualities people possess and learn to mind your own business where they may lack development. Make a list of the good qualities and the so-called deficiencies in those persons close to you, and you may be surprised to find they are, after all, human and more than tolerable after all.

VENUS IN LIBRA

Your Venus in Libra shows that you seek harmony in all your affairs and in your personal dealings. You generally make concessions to encourage people to be on their best behavior with you. You enjoy the company of friends and associates, and they find you charming and well mannered. You know how to cultivate the best of relations with everyone you come in contact with because it is to your advantage. You want to know there is always someone you can turn to when you need help. With your refinement and poise, people never feel the need to protect themselves in your company, because you don't threaten them or their identities.

You may have incurred the displeasure of your parents or guardians when you indicated a desire to go out on your own. It is essential that you sever some ties at home if you really want to make a life of your own. Don't neglect to assume your obligations to yourself even though it may mean a temporary falling-out with those who may want to protect you from harm or those who will try to take advantage of you. You could easily grow indecisive out of guilt that you owe it to others to yield to them.

You would function well in any occupation requiring you to deal with the public. You consider this kind of contact increases the probability of finding someone to whom you can relate on a person-to-person basis. You want a mate, and if you didn't have one, you would not function as well as you might. You would enjoy someone who was considerate, kind, sociable and respected. You are repelled by vulgarity or coarseness but very much attracted by finesse, social position and financial independence.

More than anything, you want to be wanted and you will use all sorts of enticing tricks to fulfill that desire. You also want all the veneer and show that normally accompanies a sincere relationship. You respond to gifts and social exposure, but don't let that be the only reason for soliciting someone's attention.

VENUS IN SCORPIO

Your Venus in Scorpio shows that you have a deep emotional nature that allows you to experience strong feelings toward those you care for. In fact, you are an extremist in the way you either care strongly for someone or you dislike them. There is rarely a middle ground where you can become truly indifferent about those you deal with. It is difficult for you to make adjustments in your relationships where you will compromise your desires to theirs.

Your ability to meet others halfway depends a lot on what they have to offer in return. You are attracted to persons with substance and value in terms of character development, and you are willing to cultivate those associations that show promise of becoming permanent relationships. You don't like being alone, and this could cause you to lower the requirements you normally would expect in your personal contacts. You might later regret the sacrifices you made to encourage his or her attentions.

Security is quite important to you and is significant enough to influence you in choosing the kind of person with whom you could spend your life. Perhaps it is because you are concerned about the demands that will be made in raising a family and the comfort of financial independence in your later years. In this regard you are willing to share your partner's efforts by helping to supplement the family income. You are quite clever in handling money and show ingenuity in accomplishing a great deal with even a modest income.

Unless you are careful in selecting the persons you can relate to, you can very easily attract questionable types who will try to win your submission by making promises they haven't any intention of keeping.

VENUS IN SAGITTARIUS

Your Venus in Sagittarius shows that you are very sociable and charming for the most part and tend to be overindulgent in your relationships. You cultivate warm, friendly associations by your willingness to concede in your views when others offer convincing evidence for their opinions. You are basically honest in your dealings and respect the rights of others. You appreciate the finer things in life and enjoy good music, art, literature, theater and the company of sincere friends.

You attract people to you in your social activities because of your compromising nature. You are fairly well read and can discuss many topics intelligently. When you don't care for someone you judiciously avoid making any unnecessary contact with them since this makes you uncomfortable. You rarely make promises you can't fulfill and when you chance to, you can usually offer a substantial reason for it.

You are drawn to people who are eager to grow in character and who demonstrate by their actions that life is meaningful to them. You find it especially comfortable to be with professional people and others with cultured tastes. You understand people since you make an effort to listen when they have something to say. Though you have a breezy manner, there is little that escapes your attention and you can usually recount the substance of your conversations with anyone. You are a good conversationalist and you speak with dramatic flair.

You attract people who are active and spirited. Your mate or partner must be mentally agile and interested in a variety of subjects. You want to enjoy the many pleasures that life can offer you with your partner, and you show considerable enthusiasm when you do.

VENUS IN CAPRICORN

Your Venus in Capricorn indicates that you are generally cautious and reserved in your dealings. You carefully examine traits of character and qualities of behavior before you express your feelings toward anyone. Being naturally inhibited, you don't want to form any association that will detract from your own station in life, and you would rather go without personal contacts than have to settle for less.

Security is very important to you, and you try to cultivate relationships with persons who are fairly stable in their careers and established in the direction of their lives. You don't want to risk losing what you may have already acquired merely to satisfy the need for companionship. You are a realist and concerned about having the necessary material acquisitions that will make your life comfortable.

Although you are loyal toward those you love, you will silently endure the pain when your trust is violated rather than have your public image destroyed by revealing it. You are naturally shy and undemonstrative, so it is difficult for people really to know when your private life is in difficulty.

Because of your serene disposition you are attracted to older people with whom you will share your life. You are especially comfortable with mature individuals and will even postpone marrying until the right person comes along who can measure up to your expectations. When that happens, you will fulfill your role in the partnership in traditional style. Since you are more "establishment" than average, you want to do everything according to the rules and play your role to win complete approval of your peer group.

VENUS IN AQUARIUS

You are friendly toward everyone, and because of this people assume you are fickle and undependable in close relationships. This may not be true, but you are an idealist who is constantly looking for the "right" person with whom to identify. Your search takes you into close contact with many varieties of people. You probably look for qualities of intellectual persuasion rather than merely settle for emotional satisfaction in personal relationships. You don't restrict anyone from your careful examination because you realize that you cannot really know anyone from a chance encounter.

The unusual and novel stimulate your interest and you eagerly seek the company of people who are different from the average person. Above all, it is essential that you be permitted complete freedom of mobility. This does not mean that you cannot be faithful to a single individual, but that you are more comfortable knowing that you always have the option to move on if the relationship becomes binding and restricts your development. You are more of a friend than a lover, and your passion is as much of intellectual rapport as it is physical. Among your friends there may be saints or sinners and yet you can remain completely indifferent from becoming either in the association. You respect people's right to "do their thing" whatever it is, and money is rarely an important consideration in the alliances you form.

Your permissiveness may provide you with greater freedom, but it is a liability in acquiring permanent relationships. You could also have difficulty securing some occupations where rules must be observed, both in the function you serve and that restrict fraternization. Your career must enrich your life or you quickly lose interest. You are best fitted to serve the needs of the public, regardless of its social or economic level.

VENUS IN PISCES

The love you have to offer is endowed with compassion and understanding. You seek to identify with individuals who are as sensitive and tender in expressions of love. You have a deep appreciation of beauty and harmony and you try to associate with persons whose ideals match yours. You don't necessarily alienate yourself from those who are unable to respond to your tenderness, but it disturbs you when they appear callous and coarse. You stimulate virtue in those who seem to have none, and you admire those who have.

Music, art, philosophy and literature add to the enrichment in your life. It is probable you have more than average ability in any one of these endeavors, but even if you are not actively involved, they give you much enjoyment.

Your personal relationships may sometimes be painful because you are not prepared for the less desirable qualities some people possess. You look for the sublime and unrealistic kind of encounter and suffer disappointment when it is far less than that. People take advantage of your kindly nature and assume you will put up with all kinds of abusive treatment. This can cause you to withdraw,

unable to endure further suffering. And yet your heart goes out to the suffering and you may offer your services to those unable to help themselves.

You are a sentimentalist and a dreamer who aspires to perfection in all matters. You could become fascinated by organizations whose objectives are to minister to the underdog and find your private life almost nonexistent from the contributions you make in the lives of others. Learn to say no and mean it.

Mars

MARS IN ARIES

With your Mars in Aries, you are inclined to act first and think later, if at all. You are a creature of impulse, and assume that others will understand your behavior, which they won't. You will be criticized for your inability to modify your assertiveness by being more realistic with the facts, and more compassionate with the feelings of others.

You have enormous creative drive and you try to assert yourself whenever you can. Others cannot believe you aren't aware of the chaos you create, because when you are in a rare reflective mood, you react with clarity of thought and you appear to exercise consideration for others. These moments are most often accidental and you should endeavor to develop them with greater consistency.

The foregoing will become revealed to you in specific areas of your life: namely, your domestic scene, partnership interests and most notably in your professional relationships. You can expect resistance in these kinds of circumstances from others who will constantly challenge you until you learn some lessons in self-discipline. Even if you succeed in gaining positions of authority, this problem will still occur and you may experience difficulty in earning respect from those under you.

The primary need for you is to learn to postpone any decision until you have all the facts. Listen to any disagreements with your proposed plan of action and weigh the evidence others put forth. Compromise may well be the obvious way to better achieve your objectives. Try to follow through when you decide on a course of action; you tend to lose interest after your initial effort has been made. Be mindful of others, not headstrong.

MARS IN TAURUS

Your Mars in Taurus shows you are resourceful in the way you assert yourself. You try not to waste effort that is not productive. You are self-disciplined and cautious because you are somewhat fearful of what you would lose if you were not careful. You have strong desires, with the ability to consolidate your potentials so that you can gain them. Your wants outweigh your capacity to respond to other people's needs.

You have powerful biological needs and unless your needs are fulfilled, you exercise pressure and retaliatory resistance to those who frustrate you. You are forceful in projecting your will on others and don't often indicate any willingness to yield when they try to assert theirs.

You are strongly motivated by the desire for financial security and may be envious when others demonstrate they already have it. You are persistent in driving yourself to achieve your goals. You aren't afraid of work but you expect anyone who employs you to fulfill every letter of the contract in paying you precisely what was agreed to. You know how to organize your talents to gain your objectives.

You are uncomfortable with indebtedness. This is why you seek to become financially independent. You never want to be "owned" by anyone and yet you may be forced to take loans, if only to get yourself started. Sometimes it will be the only alternative if you ever expect to exploit your creative potentials. It is very important that you plan for your future, but avoid taking advantage of others who care for you in planning for it. The potential losses you could suffer would hardly be worth the gain.

MARS IN GEMINI

With your Mars in Gemini, communication is your specialty, whether you use if offensively or defensively. Unfortunately, words may not be an adequate substitute for physical action. Your mind is never at rest because questions constantly tantalize you, and you are forever searching for some of the answers. Whatever your Sun sign, you assert yourself through the spoken word or through writing. You are articulate in your delivery, and able to punctuate your remarks with humor so that others are rarely offended even when you criticize them.

You have an insatiable curiosity that can be a liability unless you can consolidate your efforts toward a specific objective. You have an excitable temperament that becomes easily distracted by anything new or novel. In your excitement you tend to speak rapidly and sometimes incoherently. You know what you want to say, but in your haste to say it you may slur or stammer.

In your chosen professional activities you tend to jump to conclusions, so you may waste time doing things over. You usually say what's on your mind out of a compulsion to be forever in motion. You need self-control when someone challenges you, or you may regret what you have said. You love an argument, although you may call it a debate.

You have a wide variety of interests and are reasonably conversant in all of them. You need to define your goals before you mobilize your energy to achieve them. You need direction and purpose in your life so that your efforts are not spilled without achieving results. You are liable to infection settling in the lungs and care should be taken to prevent this.

MARS IN CANCER

Although you want to act when the urge moves you, it isn't easy to do so without some apprehension. You have strong feelings about hurting others, so you may postpone doing what you want out of sympathy for them. You also react emotionally to others, and they may take advantage of your feelings. You are emotionally vulnerable and may take offense at criticism leveled at you.

You are more defensive than offensive. When attacked, you tend to recoil rather than take decisive action to defend yourself. When you were very young you probably ran home crying to your parents when you got the worst end of a fight with your playmates.

You are best suited for self-employment. Occupations such as home building, painting, masonry, plumbing are some at which you can be on your own and not have to submit to authority. Professions dealing with the public would also prove rewarding to you, such as restaurants, fast-food service, gardening.

You want to retain leadership in the home so that you can control the cost of its management. You will resent any neighbors who attempt to intrude in your domestic affairs. It will be difficult for you to permit your parents to live alone when they become elderly. They have probably conditioned you to feel responsible for them when they are unable to function as well without some assistance.

Your home is your castle and the chances are you would like it to be fenced in "to protect it." Eat in moderation; digestion is easier if you eat frequent, small meals. *Never* eat when you are emotionally upset.

MARS IN LEO

With your Mars in Leo you have an abundance of creative energy that you strive to express wherever and whenever you can. You have enormous enthusiasm with which to accomplish many tasks others feel they are unable to do.

You have an ardent love nature and are constantly seeking to have it satisfied. Your eagerness and drive enable you to sustain the pursuit of the one you love, and you don't endure any rejection without flying off the handle. You will go to extreme lengths to secure the affection of those you care for, and you are persistent until you succeed. Sometimes, though, your only motivation may be to satisfy your physical lust, which is considerable.

Pleasure is very important to you and you are generally unrealistic in spending money just to satisfy your desires. You profess love freely even when you don't feel it if it will gain what you want from the individual to whom it is directed.

Young people can relate well to you because there is an element of youthfulness and naïveté in your temperament. You could work well with youngsters because you can arouse their enthusiasm to extend themselves beyond what they normally would.

You are inclined to take risks, and taking chances with your money in games or speculative enterprises could be costly unless you gain the services of an adviser for guidance.

Any occupation in which you could exercise authority would interest you.

MARS IN VIRGO

With your Mars in Virgo, your efforts are more easily directed to working in subordinate capacities, although you have the persistence to become a skilled artisan in your craft. You are generally sought after because it is known you always extend yourself in doing your best. You do not make the best boss since you tend to drive others as you drive yourself.

Your physical needs are often satisfied by the work you do and you may be accused of being "married to the job." Consequently, you are not the most ardent lover, since your energy is usually depleted in other ways, diminishing your love interest. This constant driving yourself toward goals may incline you to suffer intestinal problems such as ulcers and hernia. Even when under a doctor's care, it isn't easy for you to rest as directed. Relaxation is very important for you to maintain good health.

When you marry, you endeavor to support your domestic responsibilities in any way you can, but you overemphasize the importance of material things. You are rarely out of a job, because you are talented in many ways. Any one of these talents can always be converted into cash if it becomes necessary.

In your professional work, you probably encounter more difficulties with co-workers than others do. This is mainly because you are a perfectionist, and you can find fault with their work that others scarcely notice. Yet it may be this quality of concern that gains notice from your superiors so that you can be promoted over others. But nevertheless, you should try to be more tolerant with those who are less talented than you.

MARS IN LIBRA

It may not be obvious to you, but with your Mars in Libra others find you argumentative and openly critical of them. Moderation is not one of your leading qualities. As a result, you will form lasting ties with some people, while others will constantly challenge you whenever they can. The middle ground position is rare with you. Although you can form relations easily, you can just as suddenly break off without a backward glance. It seems important that you always have the upper hand, and, because of this, you encourage others to compete with you by challenging you for superiority.

Permanent relationships are not easy for you to maintain, because you fly off the handle when others disagree with you. Time will alter this somewhat, and you will learn to respect another's opinion. You will become more able to control your impulse to rash judgment and become reflective so you don't lose your temper without good reason. You will also learn to be a good listener.

You will know you're on the right track when you think before you speak so you don't hurt others if they are sensitive. If you can face reality and be compromising in your demands, you will make substantial progress.

Although you enjoy confrontations and turmoil, underneath it all you are really a softy who yearns for peace and quiet. You don't really like violence, but it seems you have to become involved in it before you realize it.

You are demonstrative in love and prefer a partner who continues to show romantic interest. But you also expect a partner who will submit to your needs.

MARS IN SCORPIO

With Mars in Scorpio, you have a powerful and intense physical drive. Your likes and dislikes are extreme; at times you may even appear obsessed with them. Your reactions to situations are emotional, and as a result they may sometimes be unrealistic. You are slow to anger, but once aroused, you don't let up until victory is certain.

You are temperamentally suited to function in the medical field, insurance, corporate finance and research. Each of these fields and others related to them require determination, persistence and an intuitive faculty to anticipate the solutions to problems. You operate largely on the basis of the sensory apparatus, which is highly developed.

Your personal relationships are usually deep ones, since you grow weary of superficial ones. You expect a lot from those you care for and your sexual needs are considerable. Your mate must at least equal you in this area or a growing dissatisfaction will develop that could spell trouble for the relationship. Sex is important to you and you may even be unduly preoccupied with it. You experience deep longings for the highest kind of sexual release so that if you are denied, you may become extremely difficult to live with.

Others sometimes question your motives since you are so noncommittal in revealing what you seek. You don't profess love unless you are extremely certain it is returned. You can be vindictive toward anyone who crosses you. Some difficulty may be experienced in the generative system. Caution advised.

MARS IN SAGITTARIUS

If your friends refer to you as "an eager beaver" it is probably because you have your Mars in Sagittarius. You are restless, sometimes argumentative, but never boring to have around. You are a good story-teller because you are enthusiastic in relating your experiences. You have dramatic flair and are perhaps a bit flashy in your conduct. You are a seeker after dreams that constantly stimulate you. You are thus inclined to take chances and may also gamble, perhaps hoping to realize your dreams this way.

In temperament, you are frank and open. You question the credibility of anyone who is afraid to speak his mind. In this sense then, you are undisciplined, and yet, when future objectives require it, you know how to plan your moves to achieve them.

Your greatest failing is your inclination to do too many things at one time. This deprives you of focus and direction and you waste much energy for nothing. You are extravagant in claiming what you can do, so you may suffer unnecessary disappointments.

Your physical prowess is notable and you burn up energy at a rate that would leave others exhausted. You don't believe in failure because you are ambitious to rise to prominence. You are intolerant of those who are unwilling to extend their full effort in seeking their goals. You are a person on the move and cannot wait for those who can't match your drive to succeed.

You win many victories in your personal relationships because you won't accept defeat. You don't have difficulties with satisfying your sexual needs because you know that there are many who will yield to your demands.

MARS IN CAPRICORN

If anyone can be said to have self-control it would be you who have your Mars in Capricorn. The drive and physical energy you have is always carefully managed to assure success. Conservation of resources and elimination of nonessentials is always characteristic of the way you operate. You are ambitious to achieve a position of authority so you can direct others when they can't manage themselves.

On the surface, it may appear you are all ambition with little else to occupy your attention. The truth is, you are efficient in establishing your priorities and you can take care of all of them when the time comes.

You are patient in encounters with arrogant individuals, knowing they will "spill" their efforts quickly and become defenseless. You have respect for anyone demonstrating common sense and good judgment, if they are unafraid to make decisions after a reasonable examination of the evidence.

Beneath the veneer of your businesslike appearance, you have strong feelings and emotional needs.

You always need the assurance that your mate loves you and constantly satisfies your physical desires, which are probably along traditional lines and methods. In love, you are not an innovator and may be turned off by a partner who is less inhibited than you. Above all, you want to determine what will take place and expect your partner to submit to it.

You are prone to problems affecting the bones and cartilage, probably from accidents, so safety precautions should be adhered to. The knees are especially vulnerable.

MARS IN AQUARIUS

Your Mars in Aquarius signifies the drive and power you have is largely utilized in communication. When you want to you can flex your intellectual muscle where others may only be able to flex their physical energies. It shows you strive to meet others halfway before you assert your position.

You have a wide circle of friends with whom you enjoy mutual understanding. You are comfortable in conversation because you can identify with anyone. Although you are firm in your own convictions, this does not prevent you from appreciating other people's points of view. You also realize you may benefit when exposed to additional information they may provide.

You are primarily concerned that your efforts serve some important social need. You are not selfish with your personal resources, so if someone convinces you of his or her sincere needs, you would share what you have.

You are ingenious and inventive in the way you work. You insist you be given the opportunity to do things your way even if it seems unorthodox by usual standards. You are an opportunist who takes advantage of changes in social structures to benefit yourself. You are sometimes unaware of danger and may take unnecessary risks. This is especially true when driving an automobile. You trust to luck when in fact you should rely on good safety practices instead.

You may not have the strongest physical desires, but when you seek release it isn't usually difficult to locate someone with whom to share a love interest. You are uninhibited, so you can enjoy a variety of physical pleasures.

MARS IN PISCES

With your Mars in Pisces, your efforts to satisfy your ego are characterized by self-doubt, lack of assurance, insufficient energy and lack of follow-through. If this seems harsh, it only means you must plan your efforts with greater care and learn to establish priorities. Try to indulge in only one thing at a time. Consolidate your resources and focus them toward a single objective. You will find you can accomplish what you want in this way.

Once you gain self-confidence by realizing your goals, you will be gratified that very few goals are beyond your reach. Don't let others take advantage of your inability to say no to them when they ask favors of you. If you will let them, they will persecute you. Learn to assert yourself and stop being on the defensive.

On the matter of satisfying your sexual needs, you may indulge in fantasy rather than exploit available sources of physical pleasures. If you are experiencing some frustration, don't compensate with alcohol or drugs! In your case this would only complicate the problem further. You are particularly sensitive to these depressants. You could create a condition that would lead you to suspect you were impotent, and that might not be the case at all.

Your professional interests might require you to work extremely hard to succeed, and the recognition for your efforts may go unnoticed for a long time. It would be better if you chose an occupation where exposure was not required so as to reduce the disappointments when recognition was not achieved. Eat hygienically and nutritiously prepared food to maintain good physical health.

Jupiter

JUPITER IN ARIES

Your Jupiter in Aries shows you have boundless enthusiasm, big ideas and high expectation that you will succeed in whatever you choose to do with your life. You are engaged in striving for nothing less than the best or the most. You have little patience with anyone who lacks drive and ambition.

You are creative, well informed and anxious to prove yourself to yourself and others. The song "Don't Fence Me In" was probably written for someone with your temperament in mind. You react with indignation if anyone says, "You can't do this," and you probably defy them to try and stop you.

You need to be more thoughtful in voicing your opinions, though. Your defiance of restraint does not give you the privilege or freedom to ram your ideas down everybody's throat. You can never justify that abuse by saying you didn't know what you were saying; you *always* know. You may be a prankster, but others may not appreciate it and take you seriously.

Exercise caution in making loans or buying on credit. Your optimism can get you into a lot of hot water when bills come due. You tend to take too much for granted and assume others are as patient as you are not. The road signs that read SLOW were designed for you psychological hot-rodders.

If you apply your talents efficiently and methodically, the sky's the limit in your achievements. Learn to relax and slow down. *Think* before you take on that challenge. Headaches can develop from the pressure of conflict.

JUPITER IN TAURUS

With your Jupiter in Taurus you tend to measure your accomplishments by the money you earn in the process. You understand the value of money and how you can make it grow. At the same time you realize it is necessary to sustain and stabilize yourself in the pursuit of increased security.

In terms of character, you have sound values, firm opinions and the willingness to apply yourself diligently in pursuing your goals. Education means a lot to you — you probably had to work in order to get it. Your focus of attention lies in gaining security for yourself and those who may depend on you. Even if you are temporarily embarrassed by lack of funds, it isn't easy to admit it.

You are optimistic about always being able to earn what you need. Perhaps you are a bit careless in presuming there is always more where that came from. You won't be without too often before you learn to consolidate your efforts to guarantee it won't happen again. You are too generous and vulnerable to sob stories with requests for handouts.

When frustrated, you may eat, and eat so that a weight problem can develop. You should especially cut down on fatty foods that can tax your heart and put a strain on your circulation, particularly in the legs. Moderation in food and drink is essential to your general good health anyway. You may have a sluggish condition that doesn't burn off the food you eat too efficiently.

Your primary interest is in matters that can prove useful when converted into cash. That is what may have decided the education you obtained and the profession you either have or will follow.

JUPITER IN GEMINI

Your Jupiter in Gemini indicates your main interest in gaining an education is the leverage it provides for getting you all the things you want out of life. You talk big, but it is matched with enthusiasm and faith in yourself. You want to know about a lot of things, but you may neglect to know enough about any of them. You give the appearance of being well read and generally well informed and you are welcome in most social gatherings.

Public relations, teaching, writing, law are some of the fields in which your potentials could be easily expressed. In any of these occupations, you must be careful you don't indulge in oratory from the satisfaction you derive from having a captive audience. You *must* have something to say that is meaningful and pertinent. On stage, you are effective because you can dramatize your presentation. Perhaps acting is one of your hidden desires.

Your path to success is in finding a suitable avenue through which to express yourself, such as those mentioned above. Unless you render a service while you exploit your potentials you will not achieve a sense of adequacy and usefulness. You must react responsibly to social needs and strive to accommodate those needs. You tend to turn your back on the ugliness that exists in society, even though you have the talent for helping to change it.

You will undoubtedly choose a partner who is a good listener and who also enjoys social gatherings as you do. Certainly your mate must enjoy being on the move and possibly like to travel.

Try biting off *only* what you can chew. Plan your future within reasonable limits of attainability, and your nerves won't become frayed and jangled.

JUPITER IN CANCER

Your capacity to develop and make progress is strongly conditioned by your emotional sensitivity. You tend to underestimate your potentials because of the overly protective environment in which you were reared. Open hostility in competitive enterprise is abrasive to your docile and gentle nature. You prefer to indulge yourself in private endeavors where you can protect yourself against threats to your security. You only want to meet challenges when you are fairly sure you can meet them successfully. You are defensive rather than offensive in taking on adversaries. You only bet on sure things.

You have an enormous hunger for human companionship and you hope for the human contact that can fulfill all your desires, in a relationship. You lack the courage to assert yourself forcefully to get what you want, but you respond to it when it presents itself.

You may not indulge in social activities that require you elsewhere, but you are always ready to receive company in your own home. You are generous in providing good food and drink and plenty of it, and you are always warm toward your guests so they want to return again. Indeed, this quality would permit you to excel in managing public accommodation enterprises such as hotels, restaurants, clubs, bars and lounges.

You follow traditional lines of behavior in satisfying your social and physical needs. You respect tradition and probably have a secret desire for the life-style that accompanied the "good old days."

You tend to be a loner at heart, even though you can function well with people when you have to. Your success and accomplishment will come later, probably after age thirty-six, and you will be comfortable and secure.

JUPITER IN LEO

Your development and progress will be reasonably fast in comparison to others. You are eager and creative in exploiting your potentials and because of this you have a head start in achieving your goals in life. You have enormous faith in yourself and you use every opportunity to show what you can do. You are inspired in how you creatively promote your capabilities and gain recognition for your efforts. You get the approval of those in authority for putting your ideas to work. You know what your talents are worth, and you expect to be well paid for using them.

You enjoy your leisure time, indulging in recreational activities such as sporting events, theatrical events, working with youth groups and the pleasures of games of chance. In your personal relationships, you enjoy physical expression in love and sex. You live a full life with many rich experiences in relating to people at both the personal and impersonal level. You expect a lot from those close to you, but you are willing to make a substantial contribution to them as well.

You are generous with those you love, and there is almost no one whom you dislike. You have a close contact with your offspring and want to give them the advantages you had. You are on friendly terms with everyone, even your competitors. You respect authority and are authoritative yourself in your accomplishments. You are executive material whether you occupy such a position or not.

You have dramatic ability and you use it convincingly in your dealings. You are persuasive in argument and you are turned off by persons who lack the strength to stand their ground when they know they are right.

JUPITER IN VIRGO

Your planet Jupiter in the sign of Virgo shows that you have the ability to take on large-scale enterprises. You are extremely well informed about many things, which is an asset to you as you strive for your goals. You have a tendency, however, to get bogged down in endless, superficial details that distract you from your main objectives. You are somewhat suspicious that the people with whom you deal, or who are involved in your endeavors, are not sufficiently capable to handle the details of your affairs. In trying to do it all yourself you limit how far and how soon you will reach your goals. You find it difficult to delegate authority to others because you question their competence, and you may be criticized for assuming you alone can cope with major problems and make important decisions. If you can overcome this problem you can devote your energies to planning for the future you've always dreamed about. This is the role in which you function at your very best.

You are very resourceful and capable, and with your wealth of ideas you should go far in terms of achievement. You aren't afraid of work because you know your efforts will yield tangible results. You are an authority in everything you do, but you lack the confidence in other people who may be equally as talented as you in performing their tasks. You are annoyed when anyone questions the way you operate. When competitors succeed, you challenge their competence and question their integrity in how they succeeded. In other words, you tend to "sour grapes" instead of expressing admiration for their achievements.

You are a perfectionist and want the admiration from the people whose opinions you reject. If people don't ask your advice it's because they don't want the riot act read to them about everything they are doing wrong. You know how to do many things well, but you need a few lessons in public relations.

JUPITER IN LIBRA

Your Jupiter in Libra shows that relationships are very important to you and that you are always willing to make concessions to people in order to win their continuing approval of you. You tend to optimism in your dealings and pride yourself on your good judgment in forming the best kind of friendships and associations. It is difficult for you to make quick decisions because you don't want to offend anyone and you try as much as you can to spare people's feelings.

You can achieve great satisfaction by exploiting your talents through public-oriented occupations. Public relations, law, counseling, notary public and similar services are some of the areas in which you could succeed. Meeting people halfway is comparatively easy for you, and you know how to put them at ease and make them feel comfortable. You understand the differences that sometimes cause separation between people and you instinctively know how to resolve the conflict when it develops.

You are eager for close personal relationships, and because of this you have a wide circle of friends. You function best when you can share your life with another, and marriage is more than likely. In addition to romantic love, you also must enjoy intellectual, spiritual and social rapport with your mate so that the life you share will be broad in its perspective and completely fulfilling to both of you.

You are impatient with superficial details and prefer to become involved in large-scale situations where your ease with people can be put to good use. You are always hopeful about the future, although you dislike being tied down by obligations over which you have little control. It is difficult for you to turn down requests for help by others, and even when you can't help you are always willing to listen to their problems.

JUPITER IN SCORPIO

Your Jupiter in Scorpio shows that you have a flair for business and investments in general. You have a strong desire to achieve the freedom from want that only sufficient money will provide you. In your dealings you don't trust anyone and you are always suspicious of others' motives. You are not very

interested in small ventures, preferring to put your efforts into large-scale enterprises where the investment is greater but the returns are also significantly greater.

You make strong demands on those closest to you in your professional activities. You are willing to pay for the services provided, but you expect everyone to fulfill every letter of the contract. You depend heavily on others for financial assistance and you generally get it because you paint glowing pictures of the returns they will get. You need to be careful about legal entanglements in your affairs that could prove costly if you are not completely above-board. It is important for you to have legal counsel in all your dealings in order to protect yourself against unseen legal hazards that may be brewing without your realizing it.

You have strong physical desires and you are easily upset when you are frustrated. You are willing to pay for what you want if that becomes necessary, but you like to believe that it doesn't often come to that. You consider yourself quite desirable and you pride yourself on gaining the satisfaction you need when you desire it.

You are more than casually interested in the unknown and mystery holds a fascination for you. Foreign places and strange names are enticing to you and you will probably travel some day to satisfy your curiosity.

JUPITER IN SAGITTARIUS

Your Jupiter in Sagittarius shows that you love your freedom and defy anyone who tries to restrain you. You want to be free to come and go as you please, and you do whenever you can. You're fairly well informed on many subjects and you can speak intelligently on most of them. You tend to do everything to excess, however, and you need greater self-discipline or your physical resources will be depleted. Your hopefulness knows no bounds and you expect to achieve your objectives. Your optimism is infectious and your associates' hopes are raised in your dealings with them. You are more inspired than most people, and this is the advantage you have over your adversaries. You have vision and can perceive your goals being realized long before it happens.

Not content to stand still for very long, you eagerly assert yourself in your affairs. You are usually well informed on every facet of the enterprises you have so that you are able to successfully manage them. You enjoy competition and the risks associated with challenging situations. You never believe you will not succeed, and this raises the probability of success.

You are thoroughly convinced of the value of education and know that ignorance is unforgivable, especially today when it is so readily available. Because of your interest in the overall aspect of your ventures, you realize the need for special talent to take care of the superficial, yet important, details.

Philosophy adds dimension to your life and you respect learned people for their wisdom. You yearn for the knowledge they possess because you are fascinated by the possibilities for putting it to use in the real world.

JUPITER IN CAPRICORN

You have Jupiter in Capricorn and it indicates you are well informed on many subjects. You appreciate education and training for its value in helping you to achieve your goals and objectives. You know how to organize your knowledge, energy and driving ambition to your dreams so they can be realized. You have the integrity and ethical standards to hold your head up high in your accomplishments knowing that you are in no danger of losing them for having disregarded the law to achieve them. You don't fear the law; you respect it as a necessary part of any civilized culture. You aren't afraid to stick your neck out when opportunity is presented because you know your abilities and limitations. You have good judgment in making decisions, but you generally play by the rules of the game. You accept responsibility as an investment in your future. You fulfill your obligations in the agreements you make, but you insist that others fulfill theirs as well.

Although you have dreams of realizing all your goals, you are not so smug and self-satisfied that you aren't willing to pool all your assets in a planned program to gain them. You are a realist in applying yourself, but you must be careful you don't put all your eggs in one basket. You tend to isolate your interests to exclude other members of your family so that they feel apart from you in your pursuits. This can cause some problems in your home or close partnership interests. Your professional enterprises are likely to be large-scale endeavors because you think big. You understand the details of these activities, so you never lose control of your affairs. You try to manage your time and energy efficiently to get the most results from the least amount of expended energy.

You are essentially business oriented but it would be very easy for you to become involved in the political scene. You don't settle for less than the best and you always strive to improve your business and financial security. You are good to yourself because you feel you deserve any rewards you get.

JUPITER IN AQUARIUS

With your Jupiter in Aquarius you are optimistic about the future because you are completely informed about the past and the lessons you've learned. If you made a bad decision at some time, it is unlikely you will ever make the same mistake again. You are continually refining your skills in judgment and adding to your fund of information. You are authoritative in your professional dealings because you are self-confident about what you know. You are reasonably dedicated to sharing your knowledge with others who show an interest. You communicate freely to help others enjoy the independence that only knowledge can provide.

Your continued growth depends on your willingness to function in the broad context of the public at large. You must operate freely in society, carefully observing what's right with it and, more importantly, what's wrong with it. Communication is your most important product and no one knows more about the truth than you do. Although this is a planetary position that lends itself to the political arena, your best works will be accomplished by remaining on the fringes of politics and stimulating the public from its well-known apathy when it is time for action.

You have a wide circle of friends and you know how to capitalize on their individual talents in order to achieve your goals, and theirs. You would make a good representative for those who have valid disputes but who lack the talent or skill in doing something about them. You would challenge anyone who defends inaction on the basis of lacking the necessary financial leverage. You know that an organized public has enormous leverage to win victories over an unprepared adversary.

You have faith in your ability to succeed and you are impatient with those who fail without trying. Knowing you're properly prepared, you know you will win over any competition.

JUPITER IN PISCES

Your Jupiter in Pisces shows that your enthusiasm about the future often winds down when the going gets rough. You easily slip into a defeatist attitude, which doesn't help matters any. You have a good imagination, and sometimes it works overtime creating problems that don't really exist. Your biggest problem is in defining your objectives and accepting the responsibilities they require. Your guilt is mainly for what you don't do, and there is little defense for this inaction. You tend to waste a lot of time and effort in nonconstructive activities and then you wonder why you aren't getting results. Unless you can define what you want out of life, you will continue to ignore your obligations to society and yourself. Once you focus on a goal, the sky's the limit in what you can accomplish. You will then use your vast resources and dedicate yourself to serving society. You are sympathetic toward the underdog and understand his problems.

There are many fields in which you can find success and contentment. The broad spectrum of human misfortune is an area where you can fill an important role in the lives of other people and be fulfilled at the same time. Teaching is especially appropriate for your talents. The knowledge you possess can be communicated to those in greatest need of it to arouse them to use their own talents and skills to become independently secure through their own efforts. Institutional work could also be attractive to you, and the results of your work would become apparent to you almost from the beginning.

If you are too sensitive to withstand the shock of human suffering or denial, then you could apply yourself to the arts and make your contribution outside the circle of direct involvement with people. Writing could also prove worthwhile as a medium for your creative expression and would be an excellent way to communicate your thoughts about the social conditions you find intolerable and which need to be exposed.

Saturn

SATURN IN ARIES

With your Saturn in Aries you know that if you are to rise above your initial circumstances it will have to come through your own efforts. You are ambitious to succeed, but you are inclined to want to start at the top and avoid all the hard work normally associated with starting at the bottom. You may even assume you have all the talent required to step into ready-made positions. What you don't realize is that you lack the experience from which

your competence develops. You are forceful and demanding of those in positions under you, but you find it difficult to submit to those having authority over you. You establish rules for others separate from those you adhere to yourself because you have a double standard. You are indifferent to the feelings of others on the one hand and totally unrealistic about taking on responsibilities on the other. These two factors will be a constant source of irritation until you learn to compromise your drive to achieve with that of the people you deal with. You *will* learn to refine your judgment eventually, so why not start now? It is no sign of weakness to ask advice, nor is it a crime to be uninformed, but it is unforgivable to remain ignorant.

You have a great advantage over your contemporaries since you have the drive and ambition to rise to prominence. What you may lack is the full awareness of your capabilities and limits. You must establish your own worth in the arena of experience so that you can define your objectives and prepare a plan for realizing them. Stay in communication with people who may prove useful to you at some time in the future. Listen to other people's opinions and learn from them. Be grateful and appreciative for any help you get in your climb to important positions. Modesty and humility have their own way of gaining attention and many are turned on by them, especially today.

SATURN IN TAURUS

Your Saturn in Taurus shows that you know how to capitalize on your talents and resources. You know what you are worth and you expect others to recognize it when they pay for your services. You are determined to fulfill every letter of the contracts you make, and you expect others to do the same. Basically conservative, you generally try to save from your income, no matter how modest it may be. Security is very important to you and you plan for the day when you will no longer be gainfully employed. You expect no gifts from others and you think it over very carefully before making them yourself. You respect people who are mature in their judgments and who are willing to make a heavy investment of their talent to achieve their objectives. You are turned off by people who expect something for nothing or who are too indolent to improve on their circumstances.

You must be careful of expecting too much from people who do not have your sense of values and determination to succeed. You tend to have a one-track mind, and it is aimed primarily toward material affairs. Not everyone is similarly motivated.

You may postpone marriage until you are sufficiently secure. With your children you are a disciplinarian, but you try to be fair in dealing with them. You will assist them to gain the advantages you didn't have, provided they have their objectives fairly well defined and know what they want to do with their lives. You expect them to become gainfully employed when they are old enough, and you probably won't tolerate any freeloading from them.

There is little you won't do for the one you love, so long as you are sure you are loved. You tend to regard your love objects as possessions and that can cause you some problems. Don't be afraid to give. With your talent it is easily replaced.

SATURN IN GEMINI

Your Saturn in Gemini shows that you are serious about everything that gains your attention. You have a contemplative mentality that enables you to solve even the most complex problems. You know exactly where you are with regard to your environment at all times, and you are never without the resourcefulness to capitalize on it, no matter what is available. You are a person of ideas, which you methodically develop so they can be applied constructively to your affairs. Basically honest, you are repelled when anyone is insincere with you. You have a good memory and never forget when someone has been unfair with you. When things don't go your way, however, you tend to get depressed or become vindictive. Your mind works like an adding machine, examining, evaluating and calculating.

There are many professions you could follow that would allow you to use your talents fully. Education, law and accounting are some of the fields you could excel in and earn a substantial income too. You have a low-key sense of humor that may find you getting pleasure out of the macabre or bizarre. The kind of pleasure derived when someone is observed falling or breaks something precious is typical of this position of Saturn.

You abhor ignorance and consider it inexcusable when you are faced with it in the people you deal with. You feel an education is as close as the nearest library and you excuse no one who is uninformed.

Your preoccupation to excel in everything you do was probably fostered by your parents. The chances are they planted the seed which you later cultivated to become as well informed as you are.

You succeed in your goals because you are willing to develop your ideas and you are not afraid to work. Physical labor you avoid when you can — yours is a labor of the mind.

SATURN IN CANCER

Your Saturn in Cancer shows that you feel comfortable in familiar surroundings, with people you've known a long time and in circumstances that are easy for you to identify with. You have a deep loyalty to family concerns and tend to protect them when they are challenged by outsiders. You have a sense of responsibility toward those depending on you and you might carry that feeling of obligation with you throughout your life.

It is difficult for you to establish roots of your own to make a life for yourself. You are somewhat apprehensive about your ability to succeed without the support from someone whom you know you can trust. This feeling of insecurity may cause some delay in your achievements because of complications arising out of your emotional ties to which you give a high priority. Whatever career you choose, you will prefer that it not require you to relocate, since this would be quite painful to you. You might find such fields as real estate, land development, nursing homes, restaurants or building to be suitable occupational interests for you.

You are drawn to people who are conservative in temperament as potential marriage material. Just as you need to feel obligated to others, so should your prospective partner depend on you for support. You need to know that you are the most important person to your mate and that you never need to question his or her loyalty. You will tend to pattern your mate after either or both of your parents and even make comparisons with them, which isn't fair, to be truthful. You will be tenacious with your children, but may find some difficulty in displaying the warmth and affection they need. Try to avoid the tendency to want to live their lives for them, or to deny them the opportunity to develop their own identities. You probably follow lines of behavior that don't violate accepted codes of morality, and you might in fact be somewhat inhibited in expressing yourself romantically and sexually. Learn to unwind and enjoy yourself with greater abandon. You'll learn to love it.

SATURN IN LEO

Your Saturn in Leo indicates you are self-righteous and as demanding of yourself as you are of others. A severe disciplinarian, you give the impression that you expect others to yield to your superior position and that you rarely ever delegate authority to others. The fact is, you are deeply insecure of whatever position you hold and can retain it only by causing others to be on the defensive in their dealings with you. You detach yourself from any personal involvement whenever you can, because you feel that familiarity can reduce your effectiveness.

You feel that a show of affection weakens you in the presence of others, but it rather endears you to them, though you don't know it. To demonstrate your humanness causes people to be won over by you, to let them feel that you are identifying with them. Your career may thrust you into important positions of authority, which you will manage well and with a strong hand. You may be accused of being heartless at times when you dispatch your orders, but you feel that you must make that sacrifice to stay in the good graces of those above you. You observe rules to the letter and you expect others to fall in line. You might find such fields as politics and government, working with young people in a regulatory capacity, industrial management or recreational activities especially suited to your talent and temperament.

You expect your partner to support you in your goals and you truly know that your mutual objectives will one day be realized. You will probably maintain the traditional roles that custom has decreed for males and females to the utter disdain of the more modern exponents of mutual freedom and opportunity for both sexes. Your children may feel somewhat deprived of the warmth and tenderness they feel they deserve from you, but they will probably accept you as you wish, with respect.

Getting what you want may not compensate for the love you may have lost in getting it.

SATURN IN VIRGO

Your Saturn in Virgo indicates that you are basically honest, dutiful, organized and responsible. Unafraid of hard work, there is nothing that can distract you from your goals once you've established them. You are a no-nonsense person who is easily annoyed by people who make claims they can't live up to. Morally upright, you demand that contractual agreements be fulfilled to the letter. You can generally prove what you say because you never make ridiculous statements you can't verify. You work diligently to improve your talents because it is so important that you achieve the highest possible level of competence in your skills.

You could gain considerable recognition for your efforts in many career directions. You would be especially successful in such endeavors as building, farming, conservation, craftwork and most of the trades usually associated with home building. Whatever occupation you decide upon, you will bring much expertise to bear on any of the problems you encounter, and you don't give up until the solution is found.

You tend to follow traditional modes of behavior in your personal relationships. You are drawn to persons who are responsible and who can take care of themselves, but you want to believe that they depend on you for stability and security, which you will certainly provide in abundance. Conservative by nature, you look for a partner who will share your desire to become financially secure and independent in your later years. Though you may say you want to retire early, the fact is you need to be physically active to be content and you might direct your energy to avocational pursuits.

You want a lot for your children and you discipline them to be more self-reliant so they can capitalize on their own talents. You are willing to show them how to make the best of their talents, but the rest is up to them.

SATURN IN LIBRA

Your Saturn in Libra shows that you are motivated by social concerns and that you need the constant feedback you get from your associates to know that your services are still in demand. You consider yourself a good judge of character and you pride yourself on the good judgment you use in your business and social dealings. Your public image is very important to you, and you cultivate the kinds of social contacts that will enhance that image. You are willing to cooperate with others if it will improve the leverage you must have in your business or career. You are an opportunist who can see profit and advantage where others detect nothing. In the spirit of cooperation, however, you are willing to share your good fortune with those who have supported you in the past.

Your career interest might include such professions as law, politics, business management and arbitration. You could also find much fulfillment working with people in social activities as are found in clubs, societies, encounter therapy and counseling. Your mature and polished common sense prevails when there are disagreements in which you are involved.

If you are truly mature and reasonably aware of your own worth, you will find much happiness in marriage and the companionship of someone who shares your enthusiasm with life. If you are unsure of yourself and what you are capable of, you might delay marriage until later in life, after you have made your position secure in the world. You are drawn to older persons, or young people who have achieved some degree of wisdom from their experiences.

Your greatest lessons will come from your relationships and how well you can handle them. Compromise is essential to bring out the very best in you and those you deal with. It is urgent that you give others the same respect you demand from them.

SATURN IN SCORPIO

Your Saturn in Scorpio shows that you are conservative in your opinions and guarded in accepting those of others. Your naturally suspicious nature makes you cautious about making friends, because you have to know everything about them before you let down your barriers. It is difficult for people really to know you for this reason. You are more profound than you appear, with a depth of perception that helps build a truly firm character. You are serious in your endeavors and take great pains to make certain you will succeed in them. You don't waste precious time or money on matters of a superficial nature, reserving your energy for worthwhile activities where you know you derive some residual benefit for your efforts.

You are inclined to professional activities of a large-scale nature where you can devise schemes to achieve your purposes and where there is usually considerable money involved. You have an analytical mind that is best utilized in solving problems as in medicine, research, criminology, politics and any endeavor requiring deductive ability.

Though you have depth of feeling, there may be some anxiety that makes it difficult to express it. Your romantic affairs are so carefully guarded that most people assume you are without emotion. Such is not the case, of course, but there may be times when you are overly apprehensive about your ability to live up to everyone's expectations and a temporary impotence or frigidity may result.

You have a strong will, and when your trust is violated you are unyielding in demanding some kind of retribution. You know you have worked diligently to prove your worth to those close to you, whether in your own family or your associates, and you consider it an affront when there is lack of appreciation for your efforts.

SATURN IN SAGITTARIUS

Your Saturn in Sagittarius shows that you are deeply involved in trying to understand all things. You are hopeful about the future, yet mindful of the lessons of the past. You don't think any problems are unresolvable if you are sufficiently informed, and this guides you in your pursuits. Your greatest worry should be that you may stop asking questions, implying that you know everything that is essential. You are generally uptight about law and order, and you use every opportunity to make your opinions known on the subject. You have high hopes for a better world where individual rights have a high priority and where the laws are only a formality.

You might find great satisfaction in such careers as education, law, travel, writing or the ministry. Any of these would give you the opportunity to speak your mind on the subjects dear to your heart. You want to know that your contribution has made an impact on the thinking of others, and you are concerned that you may always have the noblest of motives in your dedication. You are unhappy when the more precious human qualities are eroded by a preoccupation with material interests. It seems a poor exchange knowing how soon the physical passes on into the past while virtue endures to infinity.

Your mate must have a similar compulsion for knowledge, so that your destinies may be joined in a mutual effort. There must be a firm base of understanding between you and the continuing excitement that stimulates you to ever greater goals and objectives.

Your creative potential is available for you to implement, and only apathy stands in your way. Whether you get a formal education or not does not excuse you from making a valiant contribution from your depth of perception and the spiritual responsibility to make it available to others who can identify with it.

SATURN IN CAPRICORN

Your Saturn in Capricorn indicates you are serious and attentive, with considerable awareness of your own worth, both in your personal life and in your career. Your goals are well defined and you know how to mobilize your talents and resources to achieve them at an early age. You tend to be pessimistic about life in general and you aren't disappointed when your plans don't succeed. Still, you learn so much from your experiences that success becomes fairly common in your affairs as you get older and wiser. You try not to indulge in feeling sorry for yourself, however, because in your opinion, success is the result of doings things right and failure is to be expected if you are doing things wrong or are unqualified. The discipline you got in your early years gave you greater respect for authority and made you willing to persevere until you could become an authority in the field of your choice. Your parents played an important part in your training, and you are indebted to them for cultivating a sense of responsibility in you. You will be repaid many times for what might have seemed a painful frustration when you experienced it.

You might find such endeavors as industrial management, business enterprises, law, politics, engineering or architecture as promising fields for you to follow. Whatever your choice, you will be a credit to your field, with duty beyond call quite normal for you. The specific choice of vocation requires more information from your horoscope than this position of Saturn provides, though it is very important to be sure.

In choosing someone with whom you can enjoy a fulfilling and happy relationship you will have to bend a little. Don't be afraid to admit it when you are emotionally influenced by someone. Your fear of being alone and all the barriers you erect to protect you from being hurt tend to limit the development of a romantic relationship. You tend to put your career above love, and your personal happiness may be delayed by it.

SATURN IN AQUARIUS

Your Saturn in Aquarius shows that your main focus in life is in getting the kind of security that will give you the freedom to do all the things you postponed. It is to your credit that you know how to establish priorities and to apply yourself to your goals with great determination. The efficient management of your talents and resources can help you realize your goals fairly early in life. You know what you want and are willing to accept the responsibilities demanded of you. The fact is, you want security because you don't want to depend on others for anything. You have a hard time letting go of the past and yet your growth and development will be delayed unless you do. As an investment in your future, there are sacrifices you must make in the temporary pleasures you might indulge in. You are only as free as you think you are. With your practical, commonsense attitude you can surely understand this. This is why you use every skill you know to gain complete control in your affairs so that you are sure you will achieve your goals.

You may show interest in such occupations as research and development, science, analytical studies, exploration and law. Whatever field you choose, your efforts will have far-reaching effect on large numbers of people. You need to know that your efforts have been productive contributions for the betterment of man, collectively.

You are mainly interested in a partner who shows some interest in building a better future out of the lessons learned from the past. It is essential that you and your mate have a deep understanding of each other's identity and that your efforts will enhance each of your fields of interest and be mutually beneficial. You are cautious in declaring your love until you've had the chance to examine all of your prospective mate's credentials. The vision you perceive of the future you want to build must be shared by that individual or a binding arrangement cannot be accepted.

SATURN IN PISCES

Your Saturn in Pisces shows that you have a basic fear of subjects you don't understand; and yet you are fascinated by them nonetheless. You are cautious about giving your support to programs or enterprises about which you know little or nothing. You are willing to help those who can't help themselves, but you don't want to feel that you've been used. It is difficult for you to define your goals because you are uncertain about your abilities, but be assured that your cautious nature will prove beneficial in whatever you undertake. If success seems to elude you, it is only temporary because you are overanxious. Your self-sacrificing nature is your subconscious way of saying that perhaps you don't deserve to succeed, at the moment.

It is part of your destiny to use your knowledge for the betterment of man, and there are numerous social uses you can make of your talents. You might apply your skills and creative talents to such fields as medicine, social service, the ministry, institutions for the criminal and for the handicapped. There is abundant need for your kind of self-sacrificing compassion and understanding for the underdog in society.

Ego is not an important issue with you, for you know that only the high side or your true self can be illuminated with wisdom. The work you can accomplish deals mainly with people who have allowed the personality to gain the upper hand in their lives and physical and social decay often results from this manifestation.

Your selection of a life partner must come from the ranks of those who have similar ideals as you. You are willing to apply yourself in any work endeavor that you share, knowing you will both be rewarded highly for your efforts.

Uranus

URANUS IN ARIES

Your Uranus in Aries shows that you are basically a rebel and even though you may not utilize the freedom available to you, when your right to it is challenged, you quickly rise to the occasion. Regardless of your Sun sign, your discomfort with tried-and-true customs allows you to investigate new and more exciting ways to do things. You are fascinated with progress and development no matter how outlandish it is, and your fascination grows as you observe new ideas and methods take shape. It is your responsibility to support change as the necessary ingredient for growth. It should not be difficult for you to see how important it is for you to stay in the mainstream of progress and actively take part in the ever-growing freedom it can provide. In this instance we are referring to progressive change, for without development change is just another word for the same old thing.

You were born at a time when old systems of financial management were breaking down under a laissez-faire attitude of indolent apathy. During the thirties it was essential to reestablish stability in the economy and restore public confidence that it could function vigorously with the proper controls. Your growth during this period was limited by the austerity your parents had to cope with and you might not have had the advantages enjoyed by today's youth. Consequently you were better pre-

pared to take your place with the new methods that made the phenomenal rebirth of industrial solidarity possible. You are more appreciative of the benefits enjoyed today by a free society than those before or after you.

Your aggressive attitude was largely responsible for the greater freedom enjoyed by both sexes today in equal job opportunity, though we realize there is much more that can be done. You demand (though you may not always get) the same considerations given others in seeking opportunity to prove your abilities. You are probably more ardent in your partnership activities and you feel it is only fair that your desires be fulfilled.

URANUS IN TAURUS

Uranus was in Taurus when you were born, showing that your ability to achieve freedom from want depends on how well you can adapt your skills to the marketplace. Your freedom is very important to you as it is to most people, but you have the innovative talent for converting your basic creative potential into tangible assets. You are a product of lean years that saw the world's economy in a state of shambles and you have the talent required to help prevent its repetition. It was this sorry condition that allowed certain individuals to gain control over the destinies of millions of people. You are realistic enough to know that there must be controls if we are to avoid a similar condition developing in the future.

It is unfortunate that too many have equated money with freedom. No amount of money will enable you to love more freely, to speak your mind or to enjoy the beauty around you that can be freely enjoyed. Your career should allow you sufficient mobility and self-determination to be happy in your job. You react disdainfully when superiors try to intimidate you with pressure or ultimatums, but you are realistic enough to know that they are under some pressure too and you can tolerate it for a time. You are easily annoyed when people make demands on you that are unreasonable and, though you maintain a low profile, you figuratively blow up when you are pushed to extremes.

You want security in your relationships, and this is especially true with your partner. You want someone who is stable and who is willing to work with you in planning for the future. You want a mate who will permit you to grow and develop according to your own personal needs, and you would respect his or her desires similarly. You know that if you aren't working together toward a similar objective, then you are straining the relationship. You want your children to admire and respect you for your ability to remain poised under stress and to appreciate your efforts in providing them with a rich and stable heritage with which to seek their own destinies.

URANUS IN GEMINI

With Uranus in Gemini you are known as a person who tells it like it is, but you don't arouse people to anger when you do. You are truthful to a fault, and you consider honesty one of the most important virtues. You especially abhor underhanded dealings or people who indulge in deception. Communication is your best asset and you enjoy a wide circle of friends with your winning personality and willingness to allow others to express their opinions. You enjoy intelligent conversation, for you know it is the basis on which a good working relationship can develop between you and others. You are intensely curious about everything and you are well informed on many subjects. You were born during a period when the world was struggling to preserve the freedom that had been won from the dictators who would have enslaved most of the world. You know how precious your freedom is and you would challenge anyone who would try to take it from you. You know that you must speak out when anyone attempts to undermine it.

Communication is a field you might find attractive and one in which you could succeed. You aren't really that preoccupied with money because you know it's a commodity that can always be replaced. You adapt quite easily to life's situations and you are rarely in a bind for ways to earn a comfortable living. You know that education can improve your earning ability and you take advantage of every opportunity to increase your learning.

You must have open lines of communication with your partner at all times. You know that unless there is dialogue between you, you will drift in separate directions. You are eager to make an important contribution to make life easier for your children and give them the opportunity to develop into happy, contented and successful adults.

You enrich your own life by refusing to get bogged down in tradition or old attitudes. You stay current in your reading and you devise ways to be an active participant in the affairs around you.

URANUS IN CANCER

You were born with the planet Uranus in Cancer at a time when a major thrust was made for greater equality among the sexes. Immediately following the Second World War, it became increasingly evident that both sexes were going to compete in the marketplace for positions of authority and leadership. There was a mass exodus from the limiting confines of the home, and everyone was on the move. Some relocated to new areas, while others demanded greater opportunity to demonstrate their capability to function in peacetime as they had during the recent hostilities. You are among this segment of the population that is unwilling to be limited by traditional roles or confined by custom.

You have probably rebelled against the conservative position of the "establishment," and that might also include the structure of family life as it had been ordained by custom. Luckily, there were many new developments directly resulting from the war effort that found their way into your daily life and you were given more freedom and mobility than had been enjoyed by anyone in times past. A booming economy gave you the funds with which to assert yourself with greater impunity, and you elected to take advantage of it.

There is some liability to the freedom gained, however, and the family was the victim. Too often children were neglected as you insisted that you had the right to a more fulfilling and bountiful lifestyle. It is your responsibility, if a too liberal attitude of laissez-faire resulted in your losing control, to help determine how your children will prosper with proper guidance. You have to judge carefully whether the self-fulfillment you enjoyed was at the risk of eroding the stability essential for the growth and development of your children to mature adults, capable of achieving security in their own identities.

URANUS IN LEO

With Uranus in Leo, you have a basic resentment of authority, especially when it is poorly administered. You demand to be heard when you have something important to say, and you consider your views as valid as those of people in positions of authority, and of course you're right. You feel your freedom is precious enough to raise objections to those who might restrict it in any way. It is your obligation, however, to achieve self-determination knowing there are many responsibilities associated with it. Those of you born between 1955 and 1962 have a tremendous task cut out for you. It isn't enough to revolt against the establishment unless you can offer something that will be an improvement over the "system," no matter what that may be. It is through your combined efforts that honesty, moral responsibility and sincerity are restored to government at all levels.

On the more personal level, you have toppled the social customs that have prevailed in recent times and instituted a more liberal attitude that has found its way into every facet of your everyday living. Love, and its physical expression, has become so liberalized that it barely resembles the binding ties in love relationships of the past. You won't accept someone as a partner unless you are given complete freedom to fulfill your destiny as you see fit. Anything less is unacceptable to you and you will not be intimidated into compromising your position in this matter.

You will probably remain younger than the previous generation because you have great expectations for the future and your interest in current issues is undiminished. It is commendable that you have greater faith in humanity's ability to solve its problems once the deadwood among the leaders is eliminated and replaced by dedicated public servants. You desire strong leaders with character to represent you, and once they are established, you will give them your complete support.

URANUS IN VIRGO

With your Uranus in Virgo, you are clearly unimpressed by pomp and ostentatious display. As a matter of fact, you can be turned off by people who are turned on by that which is dramatic and showy. You are more concerned with honesty in your social encounters and sincerity in your personal relationships. This commendable attitude qualifies you to take issue with the excessive liberties certain political figures take in the official positions they hold. You are especially appalled by the incredible lack of ethics among high government leaders that finally led to the embarrassing Watergate incident in this country and similar problems in other countries throughout the world.

Those of you born between 1962 and 1969 are a new breed of individuals who have the good judgment to resist clever advertising designed to entrap you into using products that are not in your best interests. This is why there will be a reduction in the number of you who will smoke, buy products whose benefits are questionable, or eat foods doctored with the chemical slag from the laboratories. You feel that you can enjoy good health by returning to basic, nutritional habits where you are free from all the artificial additives that perhaps force the body to engage in a kind of chemical warfare.

You demand that you be allowed to question the principles put forth by organized religions, simply because you want answers that don't assail your sensibilities. You want to believe what your own conscience tells you is right and not what someone in some established hierarchy has judged you should believe.

You are deeply concerned about equality in the marketplace for all persons similarly competent no matter what their race, creed or gender.

URANUS IN LIBRA

With Uranus in Libra, you are torn by the need to be true to your own individuality while still remaining loyal to the demands of the society in which you live. Your personal freedom is at stake as you make your position known. You are therefore in a struggle to combine the best of both worlds in a compromise. This is probably why you will develop entirely new attitudes about marriage and other binding contracts between you and those you deal with. You are not entirely against contractual arrangements, but you will insist that you be regarded as an equal member with equal rights. You feel that there must be complete understanding between you and your partner on this issue so that the relationship can endure.

The Uranus in Libra seed was sown between 1969 and 1975. The germinating period is approximately twenty-one years and signifies that you will then become aware of the differences that separate you from the generation that preceded you. You will have devised a new formula by then that will reestablish the necessary sovereignty of the family unit and its value in providing order and guidance in the lives of those being born.

You are convinced of the need for greater law and order and you will urge legislation that will help restore it. You are also deeply concerned about human and natural resources that are being depleted at an alarming rate. You will probably decide to limit the size of your family to insure it will receive the attention it deserves and allow you to enjoy greater freedom to explore ways to achieve personal fulfillment through creative self-expression.

You will never become bored from lack of interesting activity in your life and you will always look forward to every tomorrow and the exciting situations it brings.

URANUS IN SCORPIO

Freedom will mean something quite different for you than it does for others, because you have Uranus in Scorpio. For many, it means escape from responsibility, but to you it means the opportunity to make an important contribution to humanity by exploiting your creative talents for the universal general welfare. You are more "in tune" with higher states of awareness and have the innovative ability to translate what you know from the inner levels so that it becomes a useful tool for social and human improvements.

You are more genuinely honest about such subjects as death, sex and the spiritual continuity of life. You aren't afraid to ask questions, because you aren't fearful of the answers you might receive. The fact is, you are eager to learn all you can about everything, especially if others consider it taboo. In matters of religious teachings, you take a dim view of those who blindly accept anything that has not been carefully scrutinized to determine its validity. You will probably be more aware of your spiritual commitment to others than those who profess but who don't live up to their beliefs in their actions.

You and others born between 1975 and 1982 have an important destiny to fulfill. It is upon you that future generations will depend for the truth and honesty that will allow humanity to progress to new heights in awareness to enjoy a dizzying degree of development through personal and spiritual enlightenment.

Be ready to make whatever contribution you can as your investment in social evolution. With the courage to seek answers and to act upon them, you will, individually and as a group, determine the future role of mankind while he still inhabits the physical Earth and acquires greater freedom from the limiting bondage to it.

URANUS IN SAGITTARIUS

Those of you who have the planet Uranus in Sagittarius are probably more blessed than you know, since this may confer a gift of prophecy. Not that you will necessarily "see" or know all things, but your insight into matters that are difficult to understand is considerable. Sagittarius is the sign of vi-

sions and the ability to know many things before others do. Uranus is the planet of revelation, and the intuitive faculty is highly developed when it is in this sign. Uranus entered this sign for a prolonged stay in November of 1981 and will remain there until early December of 1988. Those of you born during this period will have a disdain for the past and for the leaders who brought the world to the brink of another major catastrophe because of their blunders in international diplomacy.

Communication will develop so rapidly from your efforts that the progress of the past eighty years will seem almost insignificant by comparison. This has already taken place in some respects through the development of space satellites for communication. You have a greater understanding of why a continually shrinking world makes it imperative that some kind of accord be reached for all the principal powers of the world. You may be responsible to devise the kind of dialogue necessary to bring about a lasting peace.

With your ability to know many things before they actually occur and your social awareness, you can promote the kinds of programs to encourage the universal dissemination of knowledge to every nation in the world, that they too may enjoy the freedom that only knowledge can guarantee. If there is anyone who can become a propagandist for the cause of universal understanding and brotherhood, it is you who have Uranus in Sagittarius.

URANUS IN CAPRICORN

Those born between 1988 and 1996 will have Uranus in Capricorn. The matter of preserving and maintaining the freedoms gained in the past will require constant surveillance, or they may be lost in the political maneuvering of special interest groups. The danger is greater than a casual examination will reveal because of the subtle procedures that may be used to undermine or revise the laws as they are written. It is necessary to be especially alert to the widespread use of lobbying tactics that probably need to be investigated for their legality. You will have to stay informed about your elected officials and the integrity with which they perform their duties or you may find they really don't represent you at all.

The permissiveness that developed during the sixties and seventies will probably be seriously reexamined to determine if in the process of the social gains made during those decades, something else might also have been lost. A thoughtful reflection might show that the charm of innocence and naïveté are no longer qualities that can be easily observed, even among the very young. While it is unlikely that you will see any significant effort being made to revert to a slower-paced life-style, still the idea may occupy more than a moment of your attention.

The times in which you live will never cease to astound you for the endless artifacts and wonders of science being constantly brought before you. A nearly computerized way of life will leave you with little privacy, and new laws to protect what little you have might be necessary. Though you may lose some of your privacy, so you will have access to the process of government and how your elected representatives conduct themselves in your behalf. During the early eighties television cameras were permitted in the courtroom to allow the public to observe and vicariously participate in the judicial process. It is quite likely that a similar procedure will be commonplace with respect to the Senate and House of Representatives and how they conduct their business.

Freedom will probably mean a lot to you because you will see how it can be easily lost when the public is ignorant, stupid and indifferent to the process of government. If a watchdog program exists to monitor elected officials, the chances are good that you will belong to it.

URANUS IN AQUARIUS

With Uranus in Aquarius you truly enjoy anything that is new and different. Tradition holds little fascination for you except that it often serves to justify a need for change when it interferes with progress. You are not so shortsighted, however, that you will settle for change unless it improves the quality of life for the individual and the group. You are an advocate of freedom for everyone, although you realize that social order can be maintained only if some discipline accompanies that freedom. It would be especially painful for you if you could not express yourself freely or if your plans for the future were suddenly altered or denied you altogether by some kind of political restraint. You feel that you can make an enormous contribution to society if you are allowed the privilege of self-development through education and/or real-life experience.

You want the same advantages that knowledgeable people enjoy and you urge others to follow your example in securing the best education possible. You know that knowledge is how freedom is won, because it gives you the opportunity to utilize your talents to gain the financial security you need to feel completely independent. This position of Uranus is a good example of one of Norman Rockwell's *Four Freedoms* paintings — *Freedom from Want,* in which a bountiful table is set. You know that when you apply yourself you can succeed in your goals and enjoy prosperity as bounty for your efforts.

You have an understanding of why it is important that you share whatever benefits you enjoy; it is a universal love principle that was generally unknown among people in everyday life until it was proposed by those of you born with Uranus in Aquarius. Your expectations for the future are, for the most part, optimistic. You may not be a traditionally religious person, but you probably have more "religion" because you are a person with deep spiritual convictions that guide you.

URANUS IN PISCES

You have the planet Uranus in Pisces, indicating that there is a constant struggle within you as you try to find logic to explain many of the mysteries you were exposed to during your early years. You were expected to believe as others before you believed and that you should not ask questions or you would be regarded as a maverick or a rebel without a cause. You persist, however, because you feel that ignorance is the prime condition that supports tyranny, and you want some light to eliminate the fear of darkness.

You have a fascination for the unknown, and the more it is forbidden, the more your interest grows. You have an insatiable curiosity for learning about matters mystical in the hope of being able to explain them so you aren't still in the dark about them. You have a rich imagination with which you skillfully exploit the wealth of inspiration that is always available to you. There is a definite asset in the way you blend intuition and psychic sensitivity to produce creative works. Perhaps you feel that this is your mission in life — to make your talents available for the purpose of social evolution.

You are content so long as you know you are free to explore and think for yourself. You hope that others will benefit from your efforts so that they too will be enriched as they seek to fulfill their own destinies.

You must always keep your sights focused on your objectives and be wary of those who would try to entrap you in schemes about which you are insufficiently informed. Learn to listen more intently and confidently to your own inner voice that will keep you advised in your progress.

Neptune

NEPTUNE IN LEO

Your Neptune in Leo shows that you are from the generation that was born between 1915 and 1929 and you are part of the chaotic social decay that prevailed during those years. As a product of those times, it is extremely important that you become morally and spiritually responsible for helping restore some kind of order in the current social environment. You are probably dismayed by the lack of ethics among many of the world's leaders, which has allowed many of the social advantages gained in recent years to be eroded. You tend to view leaders and others in positions of authority with skepticism, and you need continuing evidence of their positive achievements in order to feel comfortable with them. Though it is unsettling, you aren't too surprised when officials turn in disappointing performances.

In your personal affairs, you had to work hard to make a success of your relationships, and if you were unhappy with the way things worked out in marriage, it was probably because you resented the lack of freedom you had. If you succeeded in a permanent relationship, the chances are you accepted the demands on you with resignation. In all probability you found time to exploit your own creative needs in your daily routine so that you don't feel your own drives were sacrificed to the needs of the family, but were included to help enrich and stabilize it instead.

The chances are that there are less intimate ties with your children than you had with your parents when you were growing up, but that was more a product of the times than an indication of neglect. Those times also caused a major upheaval in the sexual attitudes of nearly everyone and the feeling that perhaps something was missing in male-female relationships that would have otherwise produced greater personal fulfillment and happiness.

NEPTUNE IN VIRGO

Your Neptune in Virgo indicates that you experience difficulty trying to do what is right for yourself without hurting others. You are not alone in this dilemma, for everyone born between 1929 and 1943, when Neptune was in Virgo, has this problem. You feel a strong urge to do something worthwhile for others with greater needs than you, and it grieves you that so much suffering and social injustice go unattended. You subconsciously feel that you are somehow partly responsible that such social conditions exist and that perhaps a unified program would be the answer. The need to restore order where chaos seems to prevail occupies much of your attention. Luckily, there are many programs available to you if you are determined and sincere in your concern for others.

The development of a highly mechanized industrial capability has consigned many people to the status of mere numbers in a work force where daily routine tasks tend to frustrate individual creativity. You are among the many thousands who may be a victim in such circumstances, and the only alternative is to acquire the necessary education that will allow you to choose how your talents will be applied. You are probably appalled at the amount of waste that exists, especially when you realize how many could benefit if they only had access to it. You doubtlessly feel that government officials could do more about this type of situation, and you feel powerless that they don't.

In your personal affairs, your children tend to make demands that are very difficult to satisfy and there are times when you question the value of the relationship that you have with your mate. You are a product of the times when there was an attempt to revert morality to pre–Roaring Twenties days, so even today you have residual anxieties in expressing your sexual desires to the fullest.

NEPTUNE IN LIBRA

A product of the Second World War and the postwar period from 1943 to 1957, your social consciousness is vastly different in every respect from the generation that preceded yours. You challenge the idea that either partner in marriage should be dominated by the other or be expected to serve the other's desires without question. Consequently, you and others collectively decided that a major upheaval was due in the institution of marriage, and a movement was started that was to change the concept of binding unions for a long time to come. You feel that the privileges legally sanctioned by marriage are available to those with the courage and daring to assert themselves without legal approval. Sexual permissiveness, you feel, grants greater equality to both sexes, and the male's physical needs are no more significant or demanding than the female's. You realized, of course, that the code of morality had to be rewritten, and it was. In the process, however, the family unit underwent many changes from which it has not yet recovered, and the children resulting from this permissive society suffered greatly from the feeling of not belonging. It caused a massive disorientation among the young that made it painful for them to establish order and direction in their lives; the drug scene, the rising crime rate and the enormous number of runaways attest to the decay that a lack of discipline caused.

There is a thirty percent chance that you are divorced, but if you aren't, you must be commended for having made a wise choice that resulted in a reasonably contented relationship. You realize then that in every human contact there must be compromise. It is urgent that some commitment be made to one another and that both your lives are enriched by the other. You maintain your relationship by choice from the unselfish love for each other and, truly, this is the only valid basis for marriage.

NEPTUNE IN SCORPIO

Between 1955/56 and 1970 Neptune was in Scorpio, indicating that you are part of the generation whose interests in the occult and related fields led you to consider the possibility of dimensional realities other than the purely physical one you live in. Because of this increased interest, a whole new endeavor has crept into your life, and you want answers to questions that previous generations feared to ask. You are dissatisfied with blanket replies by church leaders that don't answer your questions at all. Rather, they cause you to be suspicious of organized religious institutions whose leaders consider themselves privy to that kind of information, and you resent it.

Your general dissatisfaction with the quality of information you received from all segments of the "establishment" forced you to inquire on your own. But there were problems resulting from this misguided effort and the search for nirvana caused the deaths of a large number whose "trips" with drugs were one-way trips to self-destruction. As many people died from drugs as were killed during the Vietnam confrontation, and in the same amount of time! The material and the pseudospiritual endeavors both reaped grim statistics because they were both misguided efforts! It is obvious that only those with the highest motivations were spared, and it is increasingly evident that the search for answers must be continued by those who are prepared to face the dangers involved. There is a need for greater prudence in dealing with the powerful forces that lurk in the domain of Scorpio, and properly equipped teachers should be sought in making this precarious investigation.

Yours is a permissive generation and many have abdicated the responsibility that is inherent in sexual encounters, which also concern Scorpio. You want more out of sex and relationships in general, but are you willing to make the enormous investment required? The fulfillment you crave for the future may well depend on your decision.

NEPTUNE IN SAGITTARIUS

From 1970 to 1984 Neptune is in Sagittarius. Those of you born during this period will have to formulate a new religious philosophy that is consistent with the new awareness that is developing among you. You will experience a visionary insight of an evolving social, political and spiritual concept that must emerge from the chaotic predicament of the past and will unify each of these systems of thought into an appealing structure. A new orderliness will prevail that will see every facet of the human condition spiritually elevated, in which self-awareness and the awareness of others will create greater unity of purpose so that happiness and personal fulfillment will result. This is the awesome responsibility you have in making your contribution, no matter how insignificant you think it is, to help raise the level of consciousness throughout the world.

You will be deeply influenced by lack of direction that characterized those who came before you, especially those born between 1955 and 1970. You will not be allowed to escape from your responsibilities unless you are prepared to face a future without purpose. You will rediscover the truths that were the binding agent in relationships before the concept of permissiveness became popular, and you will rejoice in the greater happiness that results when two people share experiences and are strengthened by the love they share for each other.

It is upon your generation that rests the responsibility for introducing greater spiritual dedication among political leaders, that they may truly represent those who elected them to office. It is also your task to undermine permanently those who have desecrated the official positions they hold by personal greed or any other undesirable motive. You will be especially disturbed by the incredible amount of distortion in the truth that is allowed to infiltrate mass consciousness by those in power. It is your task to restore order and to effect legislation to maintain it.

NEPTUNE IN CAPRICORN

The position of Neptune in Capricorn in your chart shows that you are deeply concerned about making a truly worthwhile contribution that will benefit society at large. You have a political approach to the ever-present problems that continue to plague much of the world's population. You feel that only the combined efforts of the world's more affluent nations can mobilize the programs necessary to relieve hunger, provide medical services, promote employment and minimize the financial anxieties of the elderly.

You realize that there are adequate resources on this planet to satisfy everyone's needs, but that the problem is one of fair and equal distribution. Learning to manage these resources is of deep concern to you, and you may support the kind of leadership that is willing to work at solving this inequity.

You have a pragmatic approach to the whole issue of religion, and you feel that organized groups fail for the most part to deal with the uncertainties that occur when blind faith is the only instrument of control. You can face reality and you are annoyed when those requiring your trust fail to respond to your inquiries on matters of dogma and faith.

You have a kind of doubting Thomas approach to the promises made by political leaders, and your evidence is the past where history records the unfulfilled promises of previous leaders.

You may fight for a return to saner uses for the world's resources, with a strong emphasis on conservation and a reduction of waste, so that the needy may benefit from the greater value of efficient management.

Pluto

PLUTO IN CANCER

You are a product of the years between 1912 and 1938, when Pluto was in Cancer. Notable events during these years were the wars, the Roaring Twenties, and the Great Depression. You grew up in a time when there were devastating social upheavals that seriously intruded on the tranquillity that would have been preferred. You are no stranger to living in extreme situations that force you to rely on your own resources to get by. The changes taking place in the domestic and family institution are phenomena requiring you to adapt or be swept under. The home you make and your relationship with family members make it necessary for you to adopt a whole new attitude, permitting every member to find his or her own way in life and to seek personal fulfillment according to individual destiny. Neither the father nor mother determines the direction the children will take in making their own lives.

The chances are that you either have relocated, or will relocate, away from your place of birth. It is nearly impossible to hold on to old traditions and concepts that are forced by the pressure of daily changes to undergo adaptation. With this in mind, it is easier to make the adjustment to new places and new ideas since the old ones are rapidly disappearing from the scene and you have no alternative but to concede.

You have, in all probability, been forced to limit the size of your family as the density of population becomes increasingly intolerable and the financial means for maintaining it grow oppressingly difficult. This causes some measure of anxiety as it becomes more painful to expect security will be achieved in the immediate future. Careful planning with the emphasis on essentials is imperative or the danger of insolvency will make itself evident. A return to basic family life free from the intrusion of artificiality seems desirable now, and this could be the only alternative to restore reality in daily living.

PLUTO IN LEO

You belong to a generation that has Pluto in Leo, and this was between 1938 and 1957. You are part of an evolutionary process that found it could no longer tolerate absolute authority unless it was given to individuals by popular consent. You demand a say in how you are governed and you will quickly challenge those who would use the power they have for selfish reasons. This same attitude prevails in your relationships, and you insist that your freedom must never be conditional to someone else's whims. It was during the years when Pluto occupied this sign that great strides were made to give the masses greater say in how they would be treated in their place of employment and the wages they would be paid for their services. You feel that no one is so important that he or she can't be replaced. You don't mind playing a role, but you want to determine what that role will be and how you will be rewarded for your efforts.

This newly acquired freedom has strings attached, however — responsibility. It is untenable that you would receive any special favors unless you had made some investment toward that end. Among your generation are some who demanded complete freedom to do "their own thing," but who abdicated when they were asked to demonstrate how they had earned the privilege. The resentment of authority reached disastrous levels during the sixties when there were frightening upheavals around the world, especially in colleges and universities where the students took over administrative offices, caused much destruction, and made unrealistic demands. The rise of rock and roll music was a statement of retaliation against the "establishment" and the customs associated with it. Many positive developments also resulted from these displays, and a new "relevance" emerged in educational institutions.

It is your task to see that the positive results are secured and that continuing refinements in politics, education and social attitudes are maintained.

PLUTO IN VIRGO

You were born between 1957 and 1971, when Pluto was in Virgo. Important developments took place that were urgently needed to improve the quality of life for everyone. Concern for the ecology and the devastating effects of uncontrolled abuse of the natural environment became a high priority. An uphill battle raged between the conservationists and industrialists for control of the planet's resources. As a member of this generation, it is your responsibility to see that further destruction of the Earth's resources is stopped, or at least controlled. It was during this period that tragedy struck in Europe when many children were born deformed because of the use of Thalidomide. This dramatizes the importance for greater control over the unwarranted use of new medicines and drugs until they have been thoroughly tested. It was also during this time that Rachel Carson's *Silent Spring* revealed how seriously man had destroyed the balance in nature and warned that, if it wasn't stopped, that a point of no return would be reached. These are some of the issues prevailing during Pluto's stay in Virgo, and they establish the urgency for reversing the course that was taken in the past.

In all probability, a physician has prescribed for you drugs or other medications that fall in a cate-

gory of suspicion. It is because of the proliferation of such modern substances that nature-food stores have sprung up to counteract the need to rely on artificial additives and substances. While there are admittedly many products that have stood the test of time, the lack of sanitary conditions where food is prepared bears close examination. Botulism and salmonella are frequently reported today, and this seems unforgivable in view of the enormous progress that has been made by science in this regard. It is doubtlessly the lack of responsible leadership that permits these conditions to persist and allows enormous profits to be made at the risk of human life. You should be concerned with these matters; your generation brought them to the world's attention and you will be the catalyst necessary to change them.

PLUTO IN LIBRA

Those of you born between 1971 and 1984 have Pluto in Libra to indicate that you have a completely different outlook on marriage and family life from any of your predecessors. This is really a product of major upheavals that took place during the years 1912 to 1938, when a revision in the male-female status was taking place. A rejection of role-playing was stimulated then and has persisted until the present. Now, however, there is a reexamination of the effects that the original revision had and the lack of unity it spawned between the sexes. The line of demarcation that defines the sexes is hardly discernible, and everywhere there is evidence of this condition — in fashions, in industry, in politics and the language that is heard. More important, though, is the altered state of marriage and the family it was designed to protect. New contractual arrangements are being made prior to marriage that allow each participant to follow his or her destiny and prohibit either from becoming a chattel of the other. Theoretically it sounds ideal, until you examine the offspring in this arrangement. They are the losers in this cold-war situation that often denies them the warmth and close relationship that are the nourishment on which the developing youngster depends. This is a judgment you will have to make for yourself. Selfishness seems to be increasingly promoted in such instances so that one wonders whether a marriage has taken place at all.

The words *fair, honest, individualistic* and *career* seem to have greater importance than *devotion, love, mutuality, unity, respect, cherish* and *harmony.* It's a toss-up which of these classifications gives you a greater feeling of accomplishment and gives you greater happiness.

The preservation of law and order, or its restoration, is a critical priority that you can't ignore in the scramble to achieve public recognition or satisfy your need for attention in the broad arena of social activity, where there is often little room for family concerns.

PLUTO IN SCORPIO

If you were born between November 6, 1983, and November 11, 1985, you have Pluto in Scorpio. Pluto is the co-ruler of Scorpio and is therefore powerful in that sign. Pluto symbolizes the process of evolution that sweeps everyone along toward survival or elimination. This means that to assure your own survival you must offer the world something of great value that somehow enhances its prospects for survival in the midst of evolutionary change. If there is anything to imply a "being born again" process, it is this planetary placement. You are not alone in this awesome task, for many others share your burden.

You may devise new sources of energy or new ways to make use of existing supplies. In any case, you will probably dedicate your life to some important and relevant social effort upon which others depend. It may be in the field of energy itself or in its management as in the geothermal energy resources already being utilized in a comparatively primitive form in various parts of the world.

Your ingenuity may be directed to new forms of financial exchange to replace coinage and folding currency.

Genetic engineering is sure to become a heated issue in the years to come, with fearful cries of "tampering with God's work" and the like becoming common expressions of the traditionalists. Mutations will arouse the public to demand the end to experimentation, with a recommendation that greater effort be given to eliminating the flaws that are currently being transmitted genetically.

There will be reminders that a major tyrant of the 1940s sought to tamper with human genes by a plan to produce a "master race." Near-death experiences will receive considerable attention by educators and the medical profession.

Inhibiting Factors and Available Resources

Aries

THE INHIBITING FACTORS

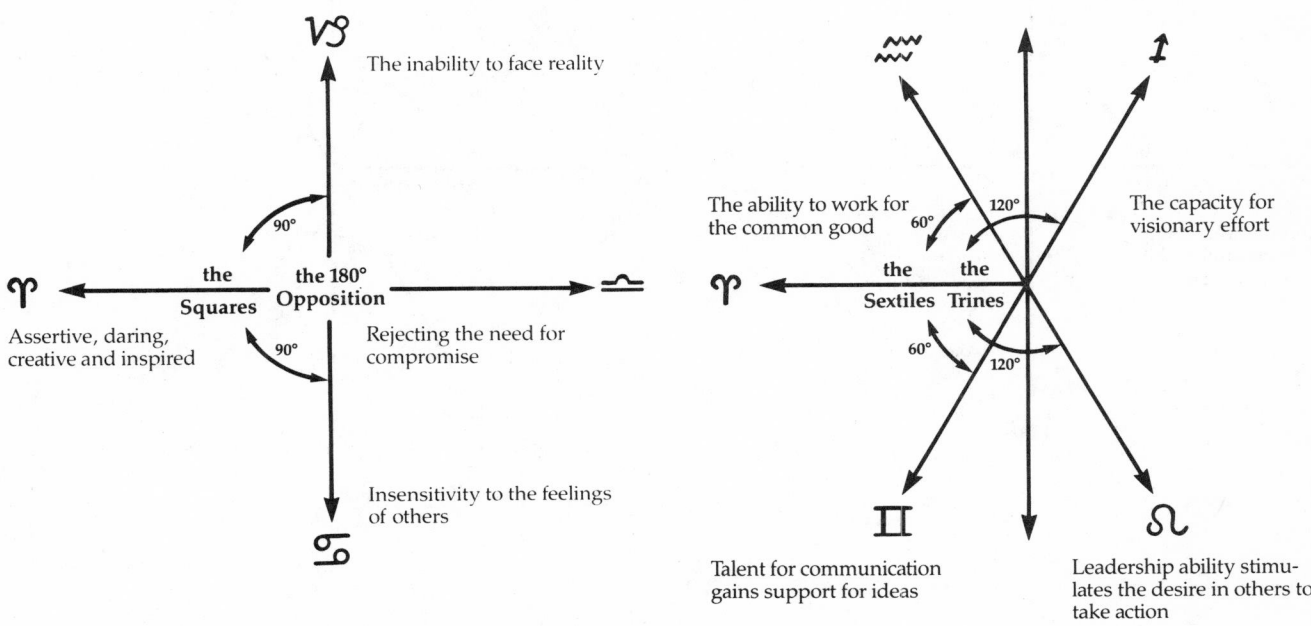

♑

The inability to face reality

90°

♈ ← the Squares | the 180° Opposition → ♎

Assertive, daring, creative and inspired

Rejecting the need for compromise

90°

Insensitivity to the feelings of others

♋

THE AVAILABLE RESOURCES

♒   ♐

The ability to work for the common good   120°   60°

The capacity for visionary effort

♈ ← the Sextiles | the Trines

60°   120°

♊   ♌

Talent for communication gains support for ideas

Leadership ability stimulates the desire in others to take action

Taurus

THE INHIBITING FACTORS

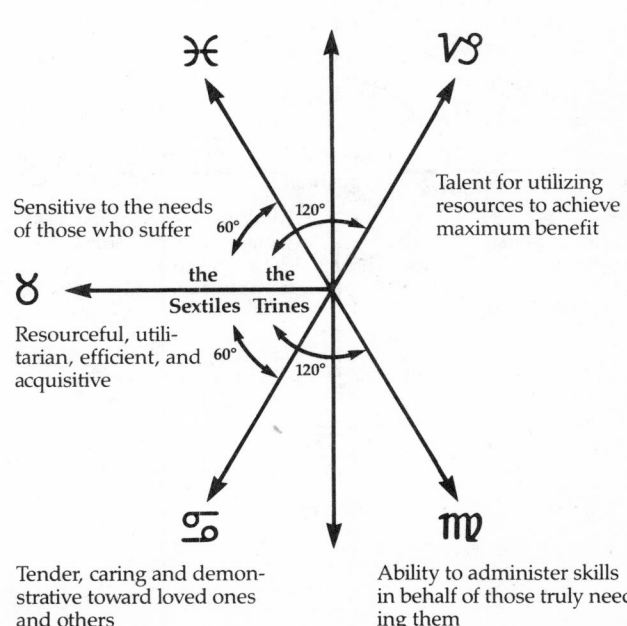

♒

The inability to share

90°

♉ ← the Squares | the 180° Opposition → ♏

Tenacious, demanding, insecure, realistic, sensual, resourceful and patient

Questions the validity of other people's needs

90°

Resists taking the lead and making commitments to others

♌

THE AVAILABLE RESOURCES

♓   ♑

Sensitive to the needs of those who suffer   120°   60°

Talent for utilizing resources to achieve maximum benefit

♉ ← the Sextiles | the Trines

Resourceful, utilitarian, efficient, and acquisitive   60°   120°

♋   ♍

Tender, caring and demonstrative toward loved ones and others

Ability to administer skills in behalf of those truly needing them

Gemini

THE INHIBITING FACTORS

♓

Finds it difficult to accept human failings

90°

Ⅱ ← the Squares · the 180° Opposition → ♐

90°

Insatiable curiosity; communicative, mental agility, interpretive ability; limited perspective

Easily intimidated by truly learned people; denies the need for limiting interests to those that will truly challenge creative inspiration

Avoids the necessity for finding ways to put knowledge to work

♍

THE AVAILABLE RESOURCES

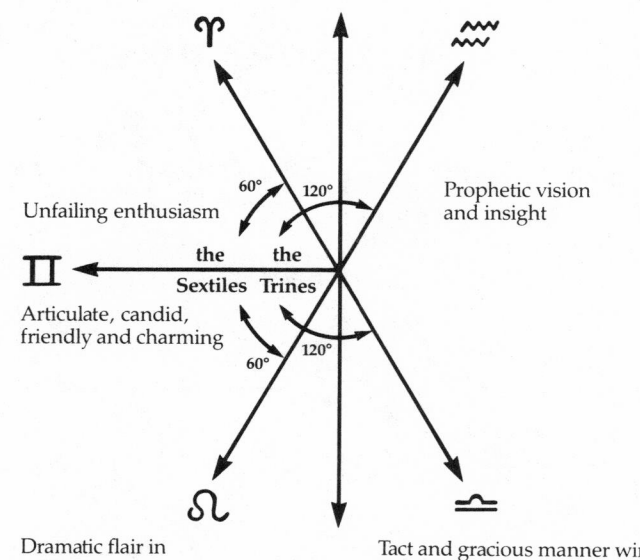

Unfailing enthusiasm

Prophetic vision and insight

Ⅱ ← the Sextiles · the Trines

Articulate, candid, friendly and charming

Dramatic flair in communication

Tact and gracious manner win favorable attention

Cancer

THE INHIBITING FACTORS

♈

Lacks self-assertiveness for fear of rejection

90°

♋ ← the Squares · the 180° Opposition → ♑

90°

Deep feelings, indulgent, caring, sensitive, and protective

Avoids facing reality and its frequent abrasive nature; must learn to make the best of any given situation

Reluctant to make decisions that could hurt anyone

♎

THE AVAILABLE RESOURCES

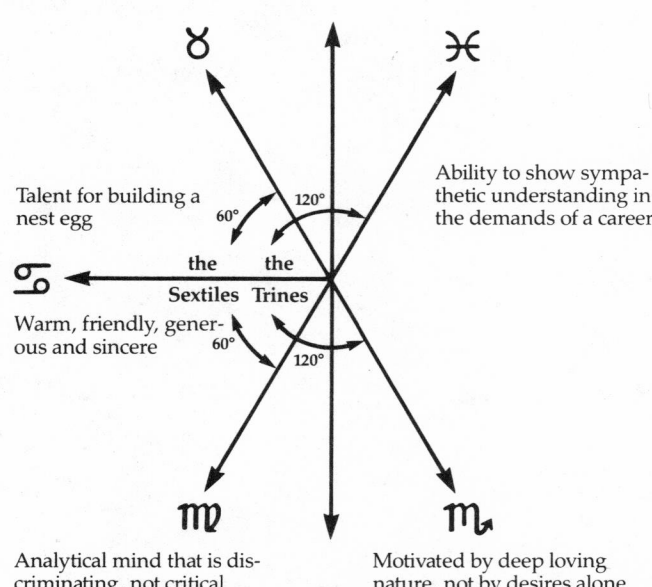

Talent for building a nest egg

Ability to show sympathetic understanding in the demands of a career

♋ ← the Sextiles · the Trines

Warm, friendly, generous and sincere

Analytical mind that is discriminating, not critical

Motivated by deep loving nature, not by desires alone

Leo

THE INHIBITING FACTORS

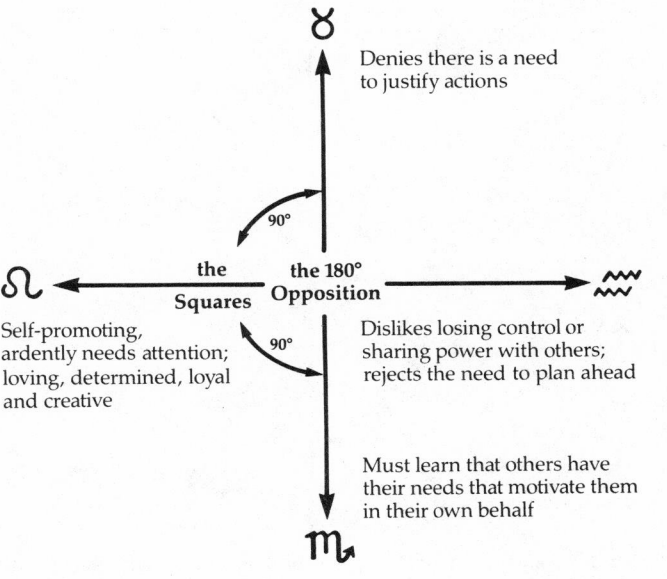

Denies there is a need to justify actions

Self-promoting, ardently needs attention; loving, determined, loyal and creative

Dislikes losing control or sharing power with others; rejects the need to plan ahead

Must learn that others have their needs that motivate them in their own behalf

THE AVAILABLE RESOURCES

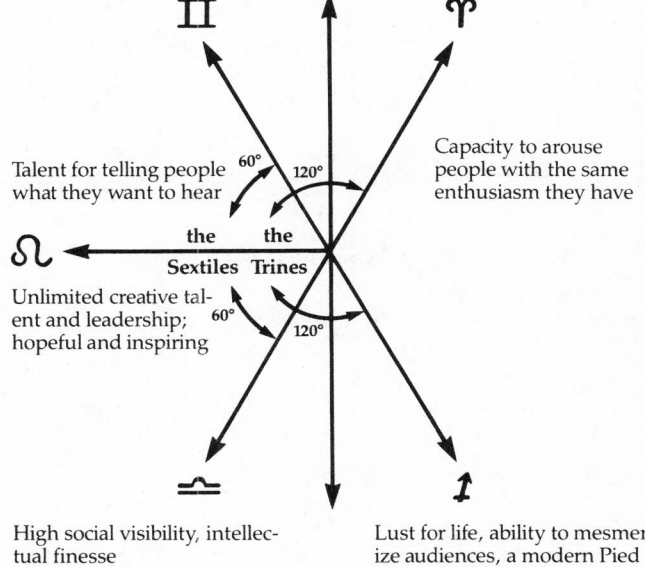

Talent for telling people what they want to hear

Capacity to arouse people with the same enthusiasm they have

Unlimited creative talent and leadership; hopeful and inspiring

High social visibility, intellectual finesse

Lust for life, ability to mesmerize audiences, a modern Pied Piper, talented orator

Virgo

THE INHIBITING FACTORS

Dislikes asking for information — assumes personal view is adequate

A natural critic, many skills, efficient and resourceful

Avoids accepting anything that lacks tangible evidence; rarely displays feelings that can reveal vulnerability

Takes pride in doing things with natural talent — challenges those who lay claim to accomplishments that were not earned

THE AVAILABLE RESOURCES

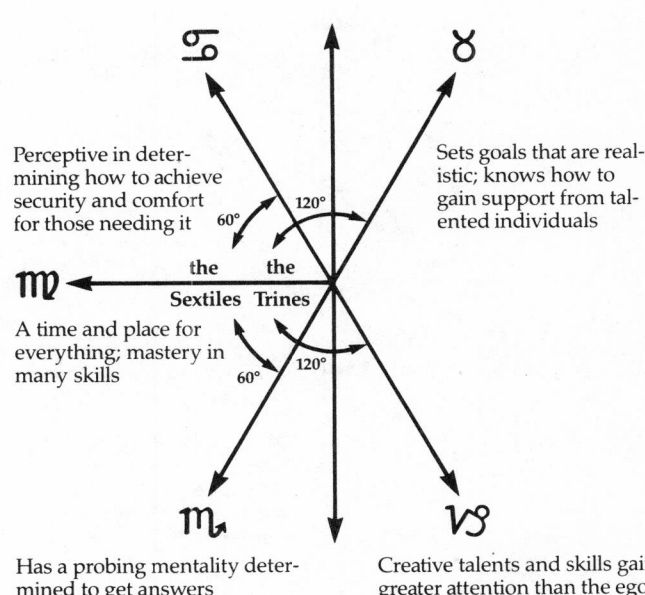

Perceptive in determining how to achieve security and comfort for those needing it

Sets goals that are realistic; knows how to gain support from talented individuals

A time and place for everything; mastery in many skills

Has a probing mentality determined to get answers

Creative talents and skills gain greater attention than the ego or personality

Libra

THE INHIBITING FACTORS

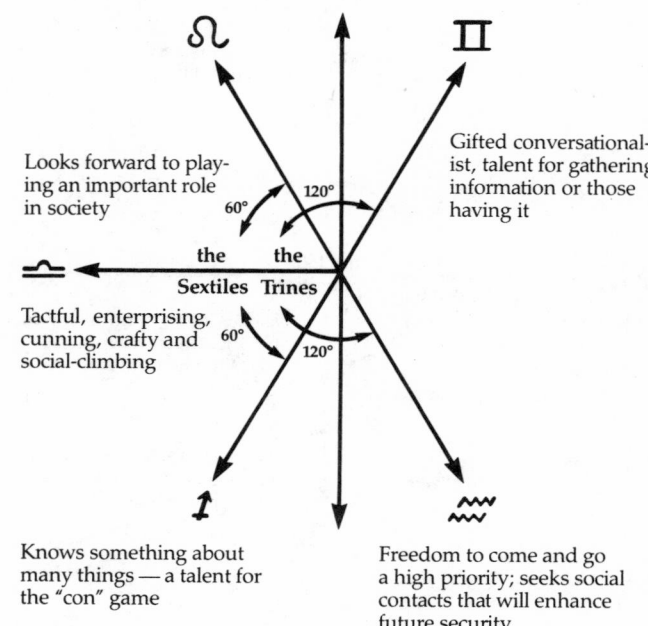

♋

Avoids situations involving the feelings for fear of rejection

90°

♎   the
Squares   the 180°
Opposition   ♈

90°

Moderate, charming, hospitable, communicative and indulgent

Rejects any situation or decision that could cause alienation or isolation; refuses to stand alone or apart

Postpones taking command until there is a guarantee of success and recognition resulting from it

♑

THE AVAILABLE RESOURCES

♌   ♊

Looks forward to playing an important role in society

120°
60°

♎   the   the
Sextiles Trines

60°
120°

Gifted conversationalist, talent for gathering information or those having it

Tactful, enterprising, cunning, crafty and social-climbing

♐   ♒

Knows something about many things — a talent for the "con" game

Freedom to come and go a high priority; seeks social contacts that will enhance future security

Scorpio

THE INHIBITING FACTORS

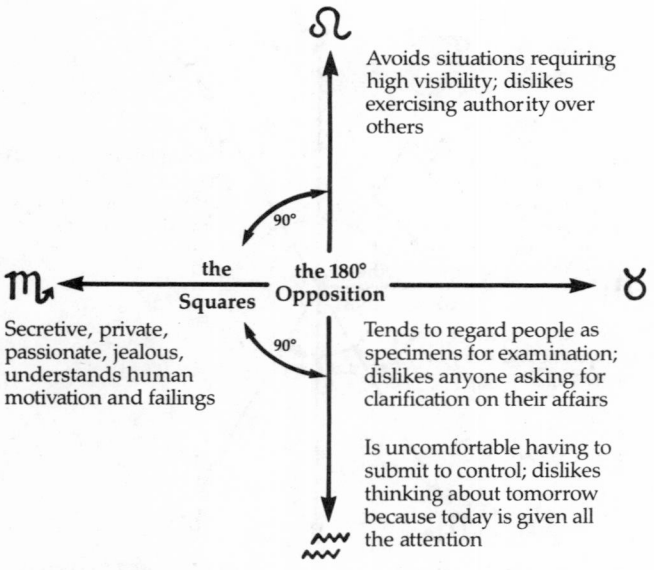

♌

Avoids situations requiring high visibility; dislikes exercising authority over others

90°

♏   the
Squares   the 180°
Opposition   ♉

90°

Secretive, private, passionate, jealous, understands human motivation and failings

Tends to regard people as specimens for examination; dislikes anyone asking for clarification on their affairs

Is uncomfortable having to submit to control; dislikes thinking about tomorrow because today is given all the attention

♒

THE AVAILABLE RESOURCES

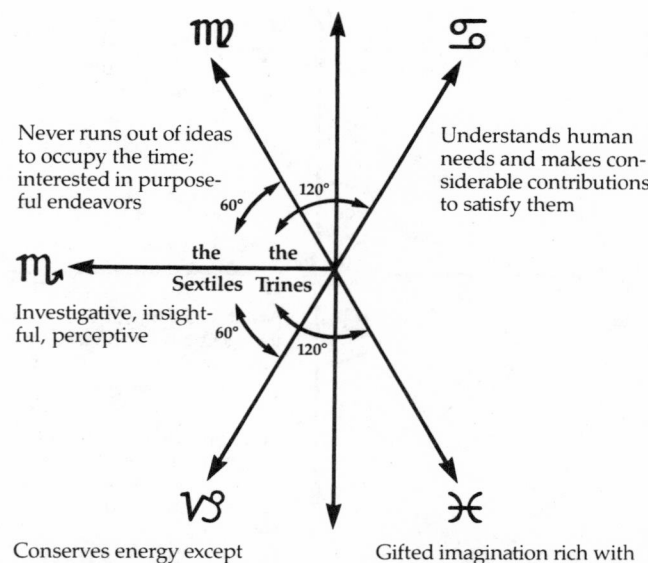

♍   ♋

Never runs out of ideas to occupy the time; interested in purposeful endeavors

120°
60°

♏   the   the
Sextiles Trines

60°
120°

Understands human needs and makes considerable contributions to satisfy them

Investigative, insightful, perceptive

♑   ♓

Conserves energy except when something of true value requires active participation

Gifted imagination rich with inspiration for utilizing it

Sagittarius

THE INHIBITING FACTORS

♍

Lacks the self-application expected of others; unrealistic goals

90°

♐ ← **the Squares** / **the 180° Opposition** → ♊

Wheeler-dealer, extrovert, creative ideas, takes risks, wants to start at the top

90°

On the presumption of already knowing the answers, rarely asks for an opinion

Distaste for anything unpleasant causes problems; doesn't believe anything can stop him

♓

THE AVAILABLE RESOURCES

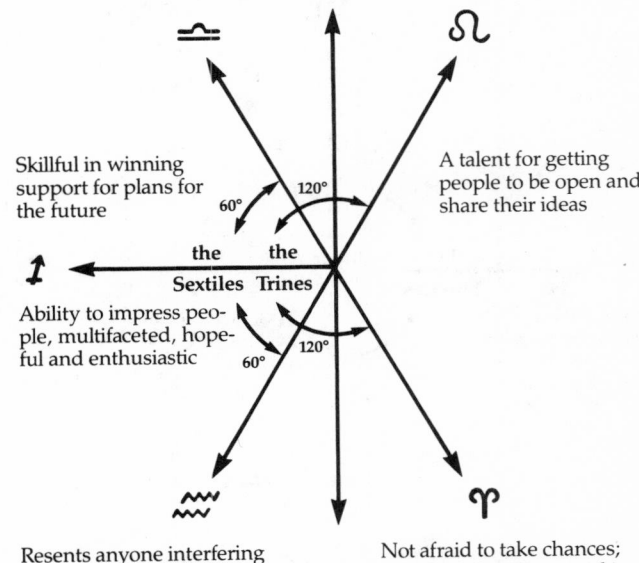

♎

♌

Skillful in winning support for plans for the future

60° 120°

A talent for getting people to be open and share their ideas

♐ ← **the Sextiles** / **the Trines**

Ability to impress people, multifaceted, hopeful and enthusiastic

120°

60°

♒

♈

Resents anyone interfering with freedom-loving ways; intuitive and insightful

Not afraid to take chances; faith in ability to succeed in creative endeavors

Capricorn

THE INHIBITING FACTORS

♎

Difficulty meeting people half way; self-serving manner alienates people

90°

♑ ← **the Squares** / **the 180° Opposition** → ♋

Status-conscious, serious, demanding, resourceful, enterprising and thoughtful

90°

Resists showing emotion for fear it will signify weakness or vulnerability

Prefers organizing to taking personal command of a situation; reluctant to stick neck out where the public will see if things go wrong

♈

THE AVAILABLE RESOURCES

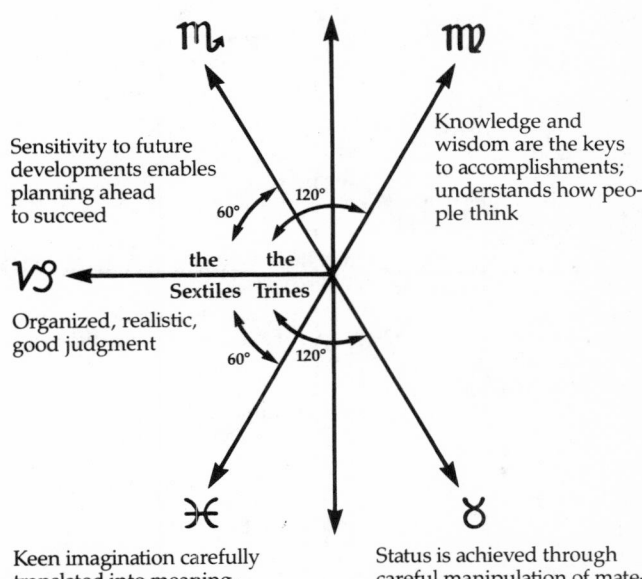

♏

♍

Sensitivity to future developments enables planning ahead to succeed

60° 120°

Knowledge and wisdom are the keys to accomplishments; understands how people think

♑ ← **the Sextiles** / **the Trines**

Organized, realistic, good judgment

60° 120°

♓

♉

Keen imagination carefully translated into meaningful activity

Status is achieved through careful manipulation of material resources

Aquarius

THE INHIBITING FACTORS

♏

Inability to express deepest feelings

90°

the **Squares**   the 180° **Opposition**

♒

Free-thinking, rebel, permissive, sociable, indulging, generous, impersonal love

90°

Lack of sufficient ego results in seeking out those who possess it

♌

Lack of attention to material matters causes delays in accomplishing objectives

♉

THE AVAILABLE RESOURCES

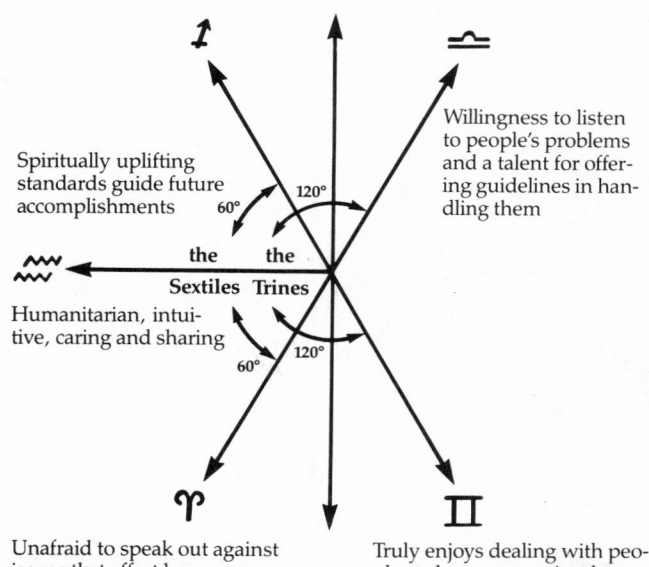

Spiritually uplifting standards guide future accomplishments

60°   120°

Willingness to listen to people's problems and a talent for offering guidelines in handling them

the **Sextiles**   the **Trines**

♒   Humanitarian, intuitive, caring and sharing

60°   120°

Unafraid to speak out against issues that affect large numbers of people

Truly enjoys dealing with people at close range; stimulates people to think for themselves and put their ideas into motion

Pisces

THE INHIBITING FACTORS

♐

Lacks self-confidence and feels the world expects excellence and accomplishments in every endeavor

90°

the **Squares**   the 180° **Opposition**

♓   ♍

The sacrificial lamb who escapes in dreams; carries the world problems on shoulders

90°

Avoids demonstrating talents because of fear of criticism if they are not up to par

Curiosity leads far astray of most urgent priorities; wants freedom to investigate every interest though there is much dawdling with little to show for the effort

♊

THE AVAILABLE RESOURCES

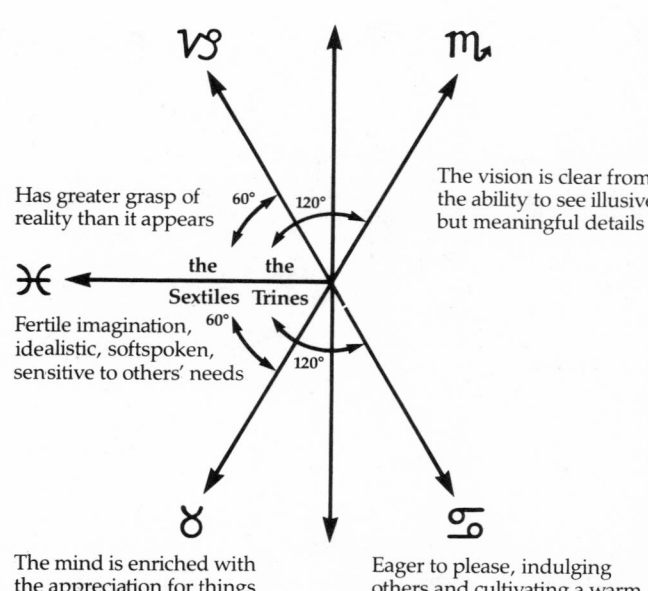

♑   ♏

Has greater grasp of reality than it appears

60°   120°

The vision is clear from the ability to see illusive but meaningful details

the **Sextiles**   the **Trines**

♓   Fertile imagination, idealistic, softspoken, sensitive to others' needs

60°   120°

♉   ♋

The mind is enriched with the appreciation for things of beauty; wide range of ideas that "work" when they are cultivated

Eager to please, indulging others and cultivating a warm response to creative efforts

Aries

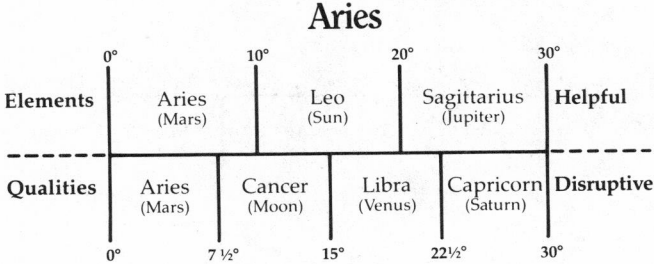

Taurus

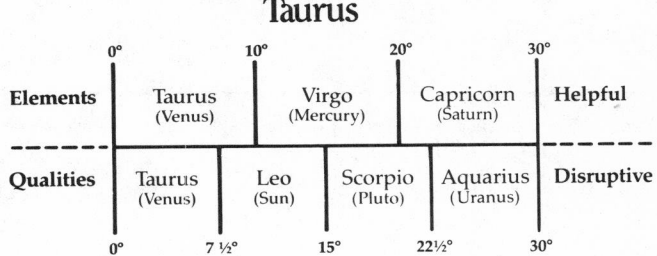

0°–7½°
The instinct to action borders on the primitive, so it is difficult to understand why everyone doesn't behave as you do. Yours is a self-serving procedure that is often alienating with those who could serve you in your ambitions.

7½°–10°
Forceful and energetic in those matters that can help you achieve your goals, you must be considerate of the feelings of those you often intimidate in your pursuits. You usually hurt those closest to you without realizing it. Bend a little.

10°–15°
You generally succeed in winning support in your goal-seeking enterprises because you have a flair for dramatizing your methods, but you fail to notice how much of an effort it is to those you love and who love you. You don't really have to prove yourself to them. Give them the opportunity to turn their attention elsewhere.

15°–20°
Your enthusiasm and drive to succeed are rarely diminished, but your accomplishments will occur much sooner if you learn to seek advice and meet others half way.

20°–22½°
Your ambition and drive to achieve your goals are admirable, though you may overreach yourself at times. Seek wise counsel when facing adversaries, or serious loss can occur.

22½°–30°
In your struggle to distinguish yourself through your accomplishments, your plans are often too adventuresome to be safe; you must learn to be more realistic and gain some of the skills required for sound management in handling your basic resources.

0°–7½°
The need to survive at all costs is so overwhelming a characteristic in you that it restrains, confines and limits you in developing any versatility. Open up, or you will eventually find people will avoid you because you aren't a "giving" person.

7½°–10°
Your persistence and tenacity are admirable when directed to the pursuit of your goals and ambitions. Your unwillingness to yield in the face of those who are recognized authorities sometimes results in unnecessary resistance.

10°–15°
In your desire to gain as much security as you can, you develop the kinds of skills that will offer you the greatest returns for your efforts. Learn to give to those you love and when you do, indulge so that it makes them happy and isn't just "practical."

15°–20°
You exercise practical common sense in your affairs and you expect to be paid well for your services — and you should be. But don't neglect those who may be less fortunate than you. Giving to others in need is an investment in your own security.

20°–22½°
The tenacity with which you conduct your financial affairs is laudable and your resourcefulness unmatched. But the greatest returns can be derived by making an investment in people and their resources. Sharing lightens the burden and doubles the return.

22½°–30°
As you struggle to gain freedom from want, you will enjoy the comforts that financial advantages can provide. You may find that the happiness you expected isn't there unless you've shared some of your good fortune with others. Be a sharing friend to all.

Gemini

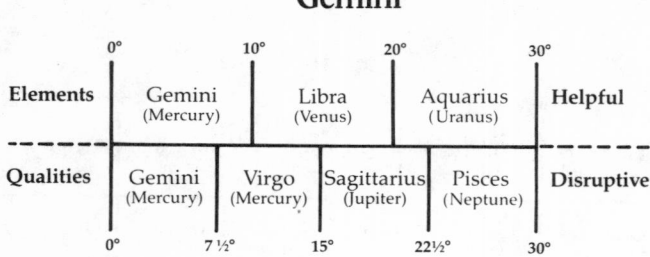

Cancer

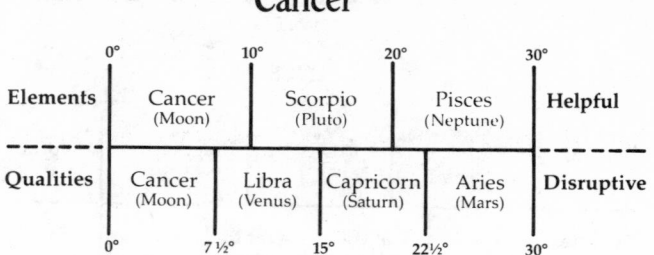

Gemini

0°–7½°
Knowledgeable and articulate about many subjects, you have an insatiable curiosity. You must learn greater continuity in your affairs and direct your efforts into worthwhile endeavors. A breezy personality alone won't carry you to achievements.

7½°–10°
Versatile almost to a fault, you are charming and a delightful conversationalist. What you must develop, however, is a more practical application of your talents.

10°–15°
People love you because you show such warmth and genuine interest in them. Being more selective in forming meaningful relationships would benefit you by helping you consolidate your efforts and direct them into useful channels.

15°–20°
Socializing is enjoyable to you, but you may be avoiding a more critical aspect of your life. You must have a dream that requires dedicated effort from you to give it form, or you face an unfulfilling future.

20°–22½°
You eagerly look to the future with great expectation and you share your enthusiasm with others who have their dreams. Getting the formal or practical training you need is the first step you must take to make it all happen, and it will!

22½°–30°
With your many talents and the ability to make the kinds of social contacts required, it would be to your advantage to devise a plan that allows you to use your skills in applications where human needs are served.

Cancer

0°–7½°
You are warm, tender and affectionate, especially to those closest to you. Basically insecure, you hold those you love close to you and sometimes resent it when they form meaningful ties outside the family. You can only hold them by letting go.

7½°–10°
In your desire to protect your loved ones, you sometimes intrude upon their respective privacies. This is clearly an attempt to win their dependence upon you. You must know that they have to take their place in society on their own terms.

10°–15°
It is important that you slowly include other interests in your life as your family grows and matures, so that you can transfer your attention to personal interests. Avoid issuing ultimatums to loved ones when they indicate the need to be free agents.

15°–20°
Though you are always the confirmed protector and want to indulge others, there is a need to become more practical as time goes on. Realistic application pays off.

20°–22½°
Since you already are an affectionate sentimentalist, why not apply yourself in tasks that can offer relief to those who cannot help themselves? You're tops in this area.

22½°–30°
You usually behave according to society's expectations — sensitive, caring and indulgent to the underdog. It is also necessary that you cultivate a more aggressive attitude about matters that are purely personal. Don't forget to indulge yourself.

Leo

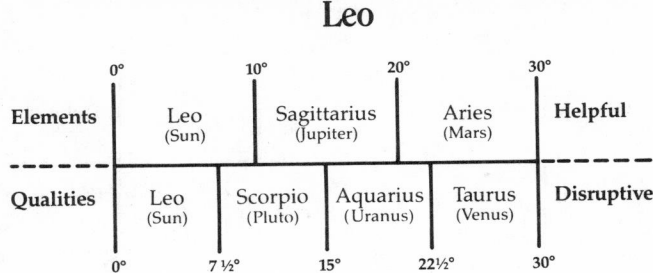

Virgo

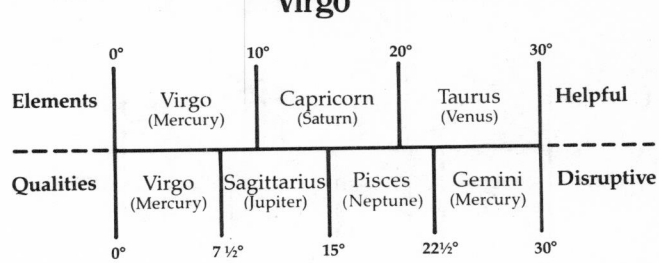

Leo

0°–7½°
Enthusiastic and determined in exploiting your creative talents, your ardor often arouses others to follow your example in their own development. It is urgent that you learn to recognize others' creative efforts as they do yours.

7½°–10°
Your persistent efforts pay off as you reap the benefits from your creative talents, but you need to devise ways to motivate others to enjoy similar rewards for themselves.

10°–15°
You have a talent for promoting enterprises that cannot fail to win the public's attention. When your efforts in these endeavors enrich others as they benefit you, the very best of both worlds is realized. Giving is an investment in receiving.

15°–20°
You tend to get involved in grandoise schemes in which you artfully carry the greater burden of responsibility. If you love others as you would have them love you, you will gladly share your good fortune with them in some way. Have goals that endure.

20°–22½°
Though persistent in your tasks, you also enjoy the advantage of having considerable talent for innovation. When these changes have longlasting benefits that can make life more secure for others, you will have accomplished an important objective.

22½°–30°
You are especially keen in developing the kinds of enterprises that imaginatively arouse the public's interest. It is equally urgent that what you offer the world has something of value that justifies it.

Virgo

0°–7½°
A specialist in everything you do, you tend to be intolerant of those requiring more time and effort to accomplish the tasks you dispose of so easily. When you determine how best to use your skills to relieve human suffering, fulfillment is yours.

7½°–10°
Basically talented in how you apply yourself, with much diversity in expressing yourself, it is to your benefit to get a formal education and the advantages that credentials will provide.

10°–15°
Your ability to solve problems will propel you to significant heights in your professional objectives. When you also seek the support of talented advisers to guide you in your affairs, there is no limit to what you can achieve in the way of success.

15°–20°
Unswerving in your goals and the ability to respond to whatever crises prevail, it would be advantageous to you and especially to those needing your skills if you looked around you and found joy in helping those unable to help themselves.

20°–22½°
Knowing how valuable your skills are to others gives you success in using them, but the satisfaction and fulfillment you derive cannot match what you could have if you used your skills to help others gain greater self-sufficiency.

22½°–30°
Security will be yours fairly early in life and you will pride yourself in the gains you've made while still young. Don't be afraid to share the knowledge and skills you've learned so that others may also achieve early success for themselves.

Libra

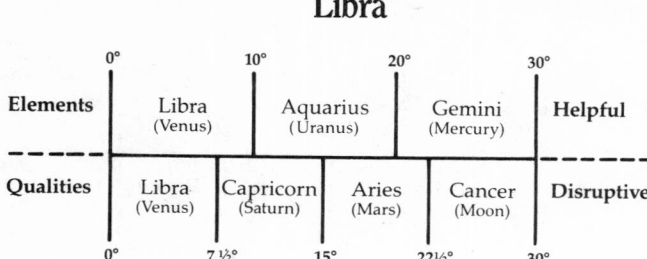

Scorpio

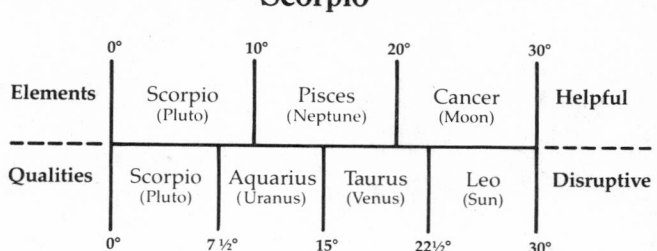

0°–7½°

Easygoing, affable and eager to please in disposition, you are conciliatory to a fault. Not wanting to alienate anyone, you often find you have ageed to two differing points of view because you don't want to offend either party.

7½°–10°

Socially minded, you are often drawn into circles of interest where decisions must be made. You have difficulty making these kinds of decisions because you know that you may incur someone's displeasure. Standing firm in your position is necessary.

10°–15°

You have a talent for winning the kind of support you require in your endeavors by making temporary adjustments in deference to others' needs. Your continuing success demands that you state your position early and develop political finesse in your dealings.

15°–20°

You know that flattery will get you anywhere in your initial dealings with people, but you must be aggressive if you truly want to succeed in your enterprises, whether others go along with you or not. Make the most of what you are — you'll find it's enough.

20°–22½°

You have the articulate skill to say the right thing at the right time to get the job done. You may still deliberate at times trying to decide whether to be forceful or not in a given situation. Don't be afraid to take risks; that's how you develop your skill.

22½°–30°

With the polish and savoire-faire of experience you skillfully wend your way in and out of difficult situations. Your success in this talent may be largely due to an air of detachment. Genuine concern for others must occur for true fulfillment.

0°–7½°

Your in-depth perception of human imperfection qualifies you for a career wherein you face these kinds of problems and strive to correct them where possible. Your sensitivity to human needs suggests that you seek a career that compensates for them.

7½°–10°

In your desire to renovate and overhaul everything and everyone who gains your attention you may occasionally "threaten" those who may be fragile or feel insecure about themselves. You must learn to let people enjoy the freedom to grow at their own pace.

10°–15°

Deeply sensitive to the plight of the underdog, you seek the kinds of skills with which better to make a contribution in their behalf. It is essential that you not forget to plan ahead so that those helped can become self-sufficient.

15°–20°

Dedicated in your calling, you dream of the day when negative elements can be reduced and society can enjoy the longevity that science and medicine have made possible. You must share of your bounty in talent and resources in contributing to that objective.

20°–22½°

Unwavering in your desire to be helpful to everyone in need, but especially those close to you, you are annoyed if your efforts are unappreciated. It distresses you when people you help don't reciprocate. You give nothing if you expect a return!

22½°–30°

You give till it hurts, as they say, and this includes giving of your time, skill and resources when necessary to help someone in need. After the dust clears, so to speak, simply walking away isn't easy for you because you enjoy the attention you get.

Sagittarius

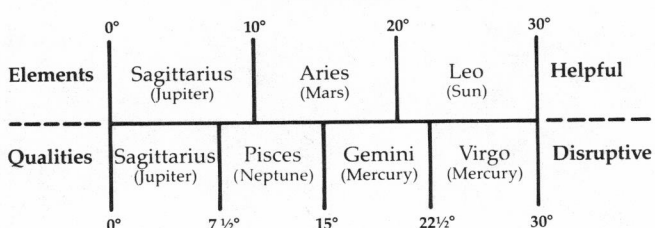

Capricorn

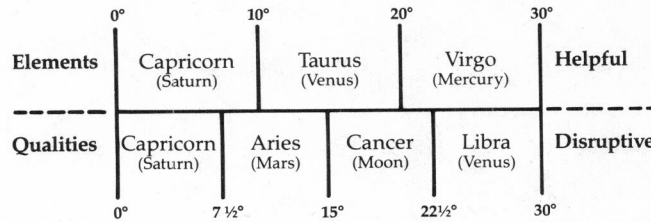

0°–7½°

You have a lusty outlook on life and an unfailing expectation that you will always succeed in whatever you do. You have a high success factor in your favor, but with your rich tastes you have to be more responsible in how to satisfy them.

7½°–10°

You have a wealth of creative potential that merely needs development to make it productive and utilitarian. While serving to satisfy your personal interests primarily, your talents could also give relief to those in need if you aren't afraid to investigate.

10°–15°

Fearless in asserting yourself in your endeavors, you eagerly respond to those depending on your skills to help them through difficult situations. Keep your wits about you, however, or you could be drawn into embarrassing legal difficulties.

15°–20°

Knowledgeable as you are in your many interests, you go forth with undiminished expectations that you will always come out on top of any situation. While that may occur, you would be better advised to realize that there is much you need to learn.

20°–22½°

"Wheeling and dealing" is a way of life for you and you engage in political methods to gain the advantage over your adversaries, although you don't restrict yourself to opponents in a situation. Listen to dissenting opinion before making your decisions.

22½°–30°

Ardent in promoting your ideas and programs, you arouse those around you to support you in them with glowing and dramatic promises. Better that you should test your proposals for enduring feasibility before you involve others in wasted effort.

0°–7½°

Though you are basically a realist and usually resourceful in your endeavors, you often get yourself "locked in" to an enterprise so totally that you fail to consider other matters. Don't neglect those you love and the attention they need from you.

7½°–10°

You are talented in developing your skills and taking advantage of your physical resources. You are "values conscious" and have a knack for deriving the most out of even meager assets. Establish your position early in life and learn to project.

10°–15°

Having considerable insight about your self-worth, you let those around you in your personal and business affairs become aware of it. When you have greater confidence in your ability to succeed, you will go forth with driving ambition in seeking goals.

15°–20°

Resourceful as you are in making full use of your creative skills, you often fail to convince others of the reliability of your enterprises. Not wanting to "let go" of the past and gains already made may result in your missing a golden opportunity.

20°–22½°

You have the creative talent for deriving optimum yield from your resources and assets. You are visionary in your programs and you are realistic in their development. Remain in touch with those close to you or lose them to your career demands.

22½°–30°

You've come a long way, but the road ahead still holds promise of goals to seek. A plan for applying yourself in avocational pursuits should be prepared, so you stay active and productive. Don't be afraid to ask for someone's advice when you need it.

Aquarius

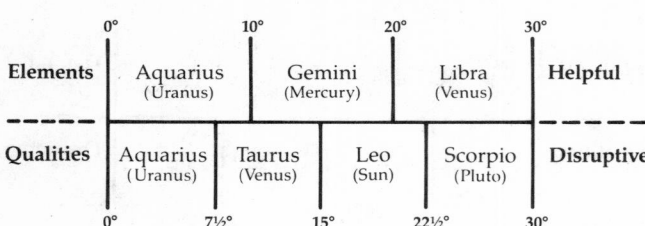

Pisces

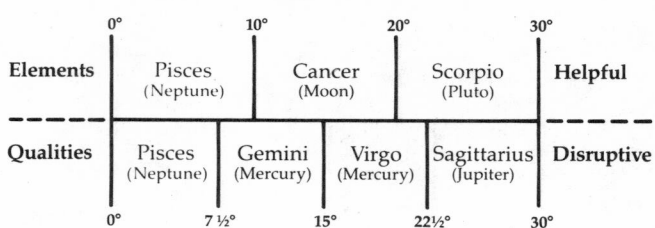

0°–7½°

Mainly a socially inclined individual, you easily relate to all kinds of people regardless of their backgrounds. You favor enterprises that serve the best interests of the masses and you are unshakable in your commitments. Guard against detachment.

7½°–10°

Your quest for social equality is admirable, as is your devotion to those who lack basic human rights. The course of your career should include features leading to improved conditions for everyone. Developing firm roots is an important priority.

10°–15°

You never fail to get people interested in your endeavors because you present them with a high level of value and plausibility in application. What you lack are the basic resources for the implementation. Share that need with those who can help you.

15°–20°

Your talent for gaining sympathy for your causes is matched only by your ability to deal successfully with any opposition you may encounter. You are a skilled rationalist, but you often suffer under the pressure of those in high places you depend on.

20°–22½°

You are probably a master in the art of friendly persuasion and those you've convinced never realize that you have "conned" them. This is not necessarily negative, if you base your efforts on a sincere desire to help because you care about others.

22½°–30°

You are gifted in your ability to win people over when they oppose you and you do it so they never realize it and are therefore not angry about it. On the other side of the coin, don't be "difficult"; learn to yield to other people's opinions.

0°–7½°

You are tuned to the problems of society and the world in general and you are often anxious that you cannot do more to relieve the suffering that prevails in the world. Instead of malingering about it, get involved in programs for dealing with human needs.

7½°–10°

You have a highly developed creative imagination, so you are sensitive to the anxieties of those around you. It is important that you learn to differentiate illusion from the truth. Ask what you can do and be willing to apply yourself to it.

10°–15°

You literally thrive in situations that are often difficult to deal with and you attract people with problems. Your mothering attention is soothing to those in need, but you must let them know they have to stand on their own, too.

15°–20°

You feel cosmic obligation to deal with every problem presented to you for a solution, and you are usually effective in this regard. It is urgent that you learn and gain mastery in the physical sciences to truly succeed.

20°–22½°

Your sense of social dedication is why you feel it is important that you make a commitment to help improve the quality of life for those around you. Your task will be easier if your learn certain skills so that you get personally involved.

22½°–30°

In addition to your sensitivity to social inadequacies and the problems they create, you have the talent for motivating people to engage in programs that will serve in their own best interests. Learn to ask for professional help when that will get results.

APPENDIX IV Jones Patterns

The purpose of this book is to give you as much information as can be derived without erecting a horoscope based on the time you were born. It often happens that the exact time of birth is unknown. When this is the case, you can still gain much insight about yourself by using various techniques to examine the planets in your chart. We have already discussed listing the planets in the various Qualities and Elements from which certain distinguishing features can be determined that set you apart from those whose Sun sign is the same as yours.

Another useful method of determining how you differ from others with your same Sun sign is by observing the way the planets are distributed around the Zodiac on the day of your birth. After you have listed the planets in the signs they occupied on the day you were born and entered them in the basic zodiacal circle, you may observe a pattern of distribution around the chart. This kind of placement has been developed so that definite patterns reveal distinctive behavior. The most basic chart patterns are the following seven: Bundle, Bowl, Bucket, See-saw, Locomotive, Splay, and Splash. Refer to the accompanying illustrations to help you to determine whether or not your chart contains any of these patterns, and the resulting effect in behavior. Be advised that this behavior is mainly of a general type that is nevertheless distinctive enough to be easily recognized apart from that derived from the effect of your Sun sign.

Bundle

In this pattern the planets are grouped together so that they form a "bundle." Ideally, they should be contained within the space of 120°, or the equivalent of the Aspect called a trine. The intense concentration of planets produces a behavior that is equally intense and unrelenting in serving personal interests. The scope of this person's ability to put himself or herself in the other person's shoes is truly limited. Perspective is also diminished and suggests a course in life that allows for entering into those kinds of enterprises that require deep concentration and intense creative utilization of personal potentials. It is difficult for this person to share life with anyone.

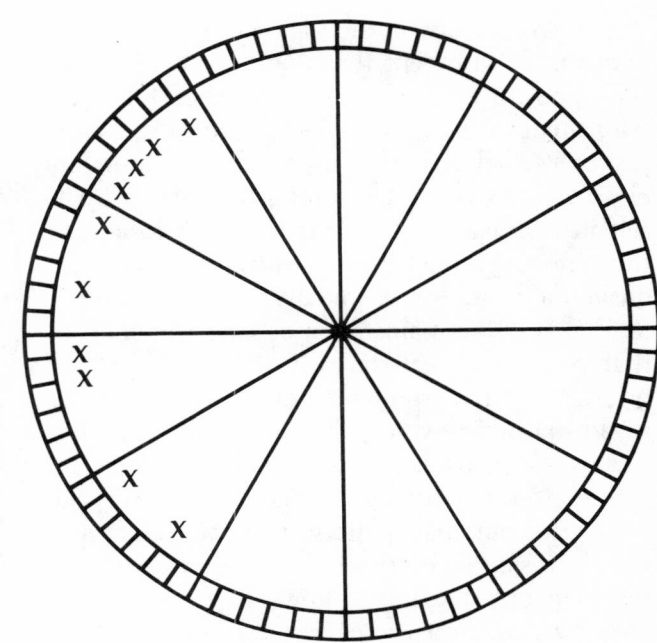

Bowl

If your chart forms a pattern of a bowl, wherein the planets are grouped within one hemisphere (or 180°) of the Zodiac, yours is a life in search of enterprises that are meaningful, fulfilling and relevant to you and those for whom and with whom you engage your efforts. There is a ministerial quality about you that eagerly seeks the right kind of career or avocational pursuit that produces the greatest benefit ultimately, for yourself and those around you. You want so much to be properly polarized (meaningfully exchanged resources and objectives) that you "prowl" the environment to locate a suitable field in which to apply yourself in your creative skills with the opportunity to apply yourself as eagerly as you "need" to.

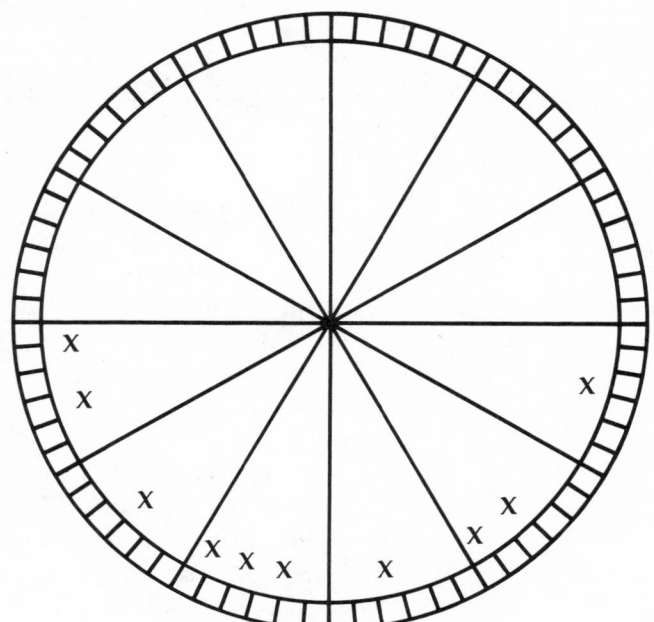

Bucket

This planetary distribution is exactly the same as with the Bowl except that there is one planet in the opposite hemisphere. (Sometimes there are two; this can be allowed if they are in the same degree, called a conjunction, or in reasonably close proximity to each other.) This planet by itself in one-half of the chart serves as a handle, thus creating a bucket form. In this pattern is indicated a desire to become associated with activity that is in the mainstream of social function so that you would feel that you "belonged." Your position is often a unilateral one that expects the world to discover you and what you have to offer (for its own good!). You will probably behave according to the nature of the planet that forms the handle to your chart pattern. Irrespective of what your Sun sign is, there will be strong evidence of this planetary dynamic in how you go about your business and the basic energy you generally use.

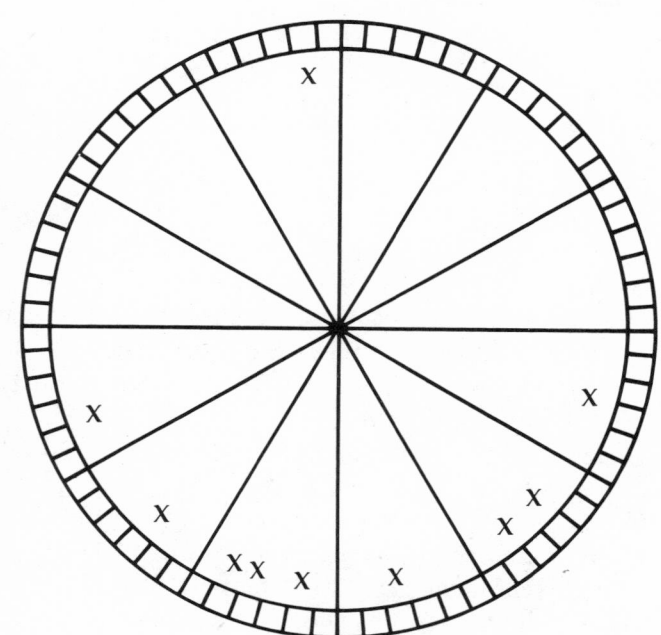

See-Saw

The name of this pattern is self-explanatory in that the planets in your chart are grouped equally on opposite sides of the Zodiac or horoscope. As its name suggests, the life follows a pattern of distinctive alternatives that give sharp contrast to your life endeavors. It is difficult for you to follow a course that is derived from blending the two disparate ends of your world. Competition versus cooperation is always an important consideration. In spite of the stress produced when beset with making the decision about the course you will follow, this pattern increases sophistication through increased awareness of those matters requiring your participation. Eventually, a polished, knowing demeanor grows that allows you to take your place among the more highly evolved types in society. The struggle to achieve poise is not easy, and the tendency to give up the fight is a not uncommon result of this pattern.

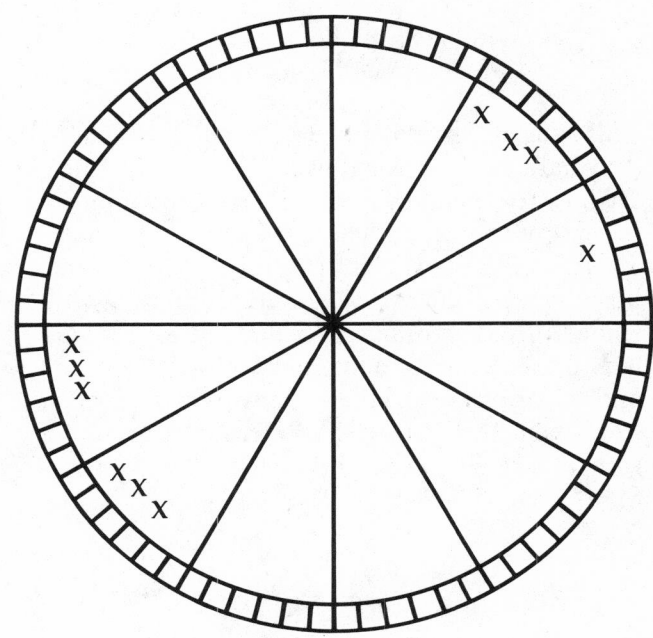

Locomotive

This pattern is produced when all the planets in the horoscope are contained within 240° (equal to two trines of 120°) of the Zodiac so that a 120° segment is completely unoccupied. Pay attention to the planet that rises clockwise following the empty space of the open trine. This planet will significantly influence your life no matter what basic characteristic is indicated by the Sun sign. There will be a self-driving individuality that achieves goals through determined and unrelenting effort. A "loner" in many ways, the public eventually discovers what you have been saying all along when they weren't listening.

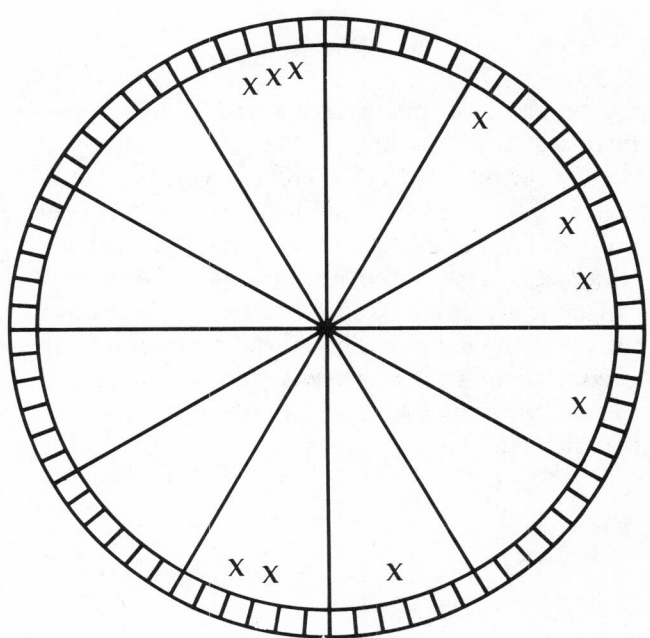

Splay

This type of chart is noteworthy because of the distribution of at least two, but usually three, "pairs" (conjunctions) of planets randomly located around the Zodiac or houses of the chart. There is enormous talent potential that needs deliberate attention to be developed into worthwhile skills. The difficulty is that there is often a lack of relevance among the various skills you might have, so you may not derive the full benefit from them that you could. "Getting your act together" is what you must do to derive every benefit possible.

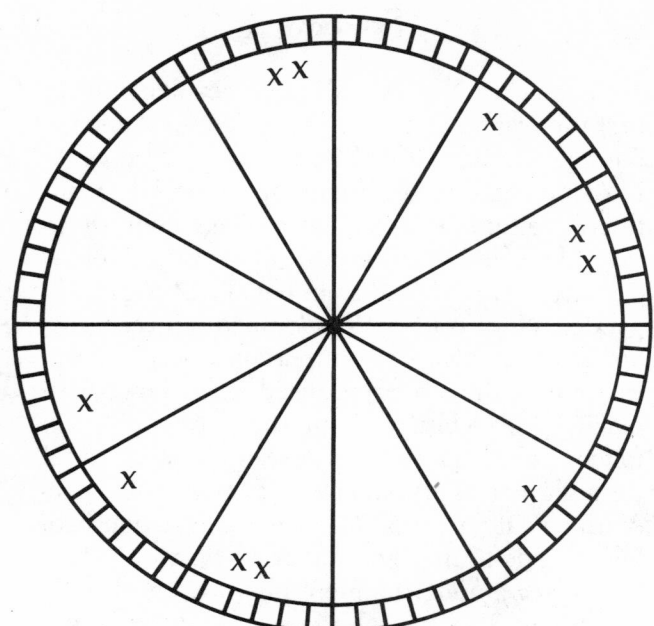

Splash

As the name of this pattern suggests, the planets in this distribution are randomly posited around the Zodiac or houses of the chart with no significant emphasis in evidence. Diversification is your number-one asset, as is your mental outlook, which is an enriching one for its universal approach to those affairs that can be truly meaningful when applied in the broad spectrum of human need. You are truly a messenger of the gods, eager to share your life and resources wherever the need is indicated.

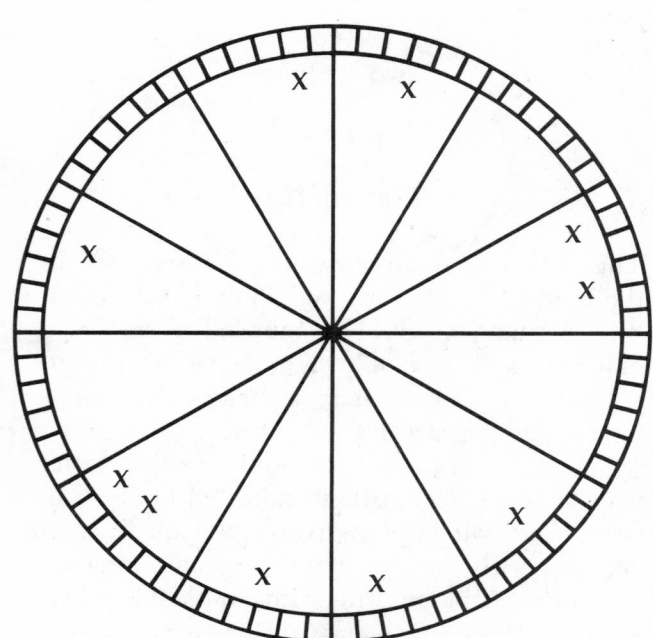

APPENDIX V Special Planetary Formations and Complexes

In addition to the Jones Patterns discussed in Appendix IV, there are often special groupings of planets that form other kinds of complex configurations that require individual attention. These differ from the Jones Patterns in that they are usually made up of a *limited number* of planets in formations that have special meaning, whereas the Jones Patterns are the result of the overall distribution of *all* the planets around the chart in well-defined patterns to which names have been given.

Within the total distribution of planets in the chart, it is frequently found that *some of them* are arranged in groups that represent special talents of liabilities for the individual involved. For the purposes of this presentation we will examine the following formations: Stellium, Grand-Cross, T-Cross, Grand-Trine and Yod (also referred to as the "finger of God" configuration).

The Stellum

This occurs when there are several planets grouped close together in one segment of the Zodiac, usually within the same sign. To be significant, there should be at least four planets forming a continuous relationship within a particular sign (conjunctions 0°–8°). It may sometimes happen that there are instances when they are dispersed throughout the sign so that there is no linkage binding them together. Nevertheless, it will be found that the sign so occupied by that number of planets will strongly influence the life and greatly alter the temperament and character of the person, no matter what the Sun sign may be. Ultimately, the Sun's character will find the opportunity to declare its influence, although with strong conditioning by the effect of the sign in which the Stellium is located. For example, an Aries Sun sign person would normally demonstrate the nature of the ardent ram early in the life, but if there are four or more planets in Pisces it would be nearly impossible to see the driving, aggressive urgency of Aries in the personal normal behavior; rather there would be a kind of "laid back" person cautiously testing for the public's approval for his or her actions. When any sign has a Stellium in a sign that precedes it, mental conflicts will exist in the person's makeup, conditions that are inconsistent with the Sun sign's nature. These types of configurations will seriously alter the individual's natural characteristics, which results in various conditions that should be dealt with. Such conditions will prevail when any Fire Sun sign has a stellium in any Water sign, a Water Sun sign has one in any Air sign, and an Air Sun sign has one in any Earth sign. This is also true for the Earth Sun sign people if they have a stellium in any Fire sign. When these conditions exist in a chart, the individual should seriously consider discussing them with an experienced astrologer. Of course, there are those that could be beneficial, but in any case it would best be served to look into the matter. Tom Jones, the singer, has the Sun in Gemini, which would suggest someone with insatiable curiosity who would have great difficulty developing a course to follow in life.

But Jones has the Moon, Mercury, Venus and Mars in the sign Cancer, giving him an almost desperate need for an emotional relationship with the world at large. This is how he feels enriched and appreciated, and he genuinely cares about the audiences before whom he performs, and he needs that affection returned by them.

The Grand Cross

This planetary configuration is formed when there are at least two planets 180° apart and therefore in an Aspect of opposition and at least two other planets in a similar relationship, but at 90° from the first two. What results is a Cross effect, referred to in astrology as the Grand-Cross. As the name implies, this person does in fact have a cross to carry within his psyche. This kind of complex intensifies the energy with which to take action, but it also inclines the person to make many mistakes so that much of what is ventured must often be repeated. Frequently it happens that the enterprise fails for lack of sufficient planning and training or the unwillingness to be held accountable for whatever results from the action taken. One thing is certain: there is the inability to remain inactive for even short periods of time so that it seems as if the person is under the watchful eye of someone who will be greatly displeased unless results are forthcoming. Unless the person exercises complete control over the stressful conditions in life, something unfortunate usually results. Knowledge and the willingness to apply oneself are essential to minimize the danger of negative effects.

The T-Cross

Though this configuration is similar in some respects to the Grand-Cross, it is the easier of the two to work with. Both are intense in the energies that they give to the person having either of them. The T-Cross is exactly like the Grand-Cross, except one arm of the cross has no planet in it, so it looks like the letter "T". The power of T-Cross dynamic is that the person generally *does not* focus his life to include any activity relative to the nature of the sign on the arm that has no planet in it. As a result, difficulties in relationships usually occur. When a planet passes through this missing arm, a crisis develops. It is as if the person does not realize the missing values in life that need to be developed. What results is that no energy is poured into this area of life and there is a considerable loss of these interests. The individual having this T-Cross should learn to apply himself toward developing the positive natures of the sign on the missing arm.

The Grand Trine

When the Zodiac is divided into three equal portions there has to be 120° separating each of the dividing points. It is the Aspect called a trine and it is a favorable Aspect. If there are at least three planets occupying positions that are 120° from each other, there results a Grand-Trine. A line drawn from each planet to the other around the chart will produce a figure that is a perfect triangle, with all sides of equal length. There is a form of perfection suggested in this kind of planetary arrangement, but in actual practice the result is usually one of apathy, condescension and lassitude. It is similar to the person who was born to great wealth and who can't get too excited at the prospect of having to work hard to earn a living. Money has little meaning to this person since it is always available. The same is true with the person who has a Grand-Trine in his or her chart. It shows enormous creative potential and the ability to take on responsibility without too much effort and be successful in handling it. What is wrong with this complex is that the person rarely ever has the driving ambition to solve the problems that occur in life, out of the sheer apathy that always seems to overwhelm him or her. If the chart has negative conditions elsewhere, then this planetary configuration can be used to deal with them with comparative ease. It is unusual when this person cannot succeed in handling most of the crises that may develop.

The Yod   This is a very special complex and it is more difficult to "locate" in the chart. What it is essentially is a "Y" formation. This occurs when two planets are each 150° from a third planet. Another way to explain it is when a planet inconjuncts two other planets (150° plus or minus 3°) that are sextile to each other (60° plus or minus 6°). An illustration might help to explain what we mean:

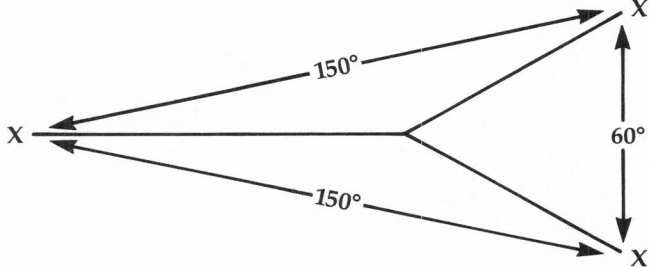

The sextile Aspect is a favorable condition between the planets involved. There is an element of fatality about this condition, so little can be done to dismiss it or its effects. Rest assured there is nothing particularly fatal about the complex, but it does draw you into the lives of others in ways that are difficult to avoid. There are oftentimes major crises that develop periodically, which will test you in your skills and your willingness to respond to someone's urgent need for assistance at the same time you happen to be available. The opportunity to develop mastery in the skills you have is a constant one, as is the chance to volunteer your services in situations where only you understand why you must do something for someone even if you have to do it without their being aware of it.

APPENDIX VI   Aspect Analysis

To help you understand some of the many planetary combinations found in reading a chart, we offer the following examples. Each planet represents a dynamic of behavior, and when they form a relationship through the angle that separates them in the Zodiac, a symbolic "effect" results that has to be analyzed or, in the language of astrology, delineated. We have avoided including the angle of relationships or Aspects that are benign or "easy" because they do not represent problems or stress that needs to be worked out. Rather, they represent assets and resources that can help you solve problems that are the result of the negative or difficult angles that may be found between planets.

In general, the stressful and problem Aspects are those that are formed when two planets are square (90° apart), inconjunct (150° apart) or in opposition (180° apart).

Sun

SUN–MOON: The ego and the personality lack integration, so your will creates conditions that result in problems because of your lack of suitable experience to deal with them. This usually causes problems in relationships, whether in the broad social level or in close, intimate contacts.

SUN–MARS: You have a strong desire to control others, and when you are resisted the urge is to be vindictive and quarrelsome to the point of physical abuse.

SUN–JUPITER: You tend to bite off more than you can chew. Exaggeration is a serious fault that often causes you to disappoint people in their expectations.

SUN–SATURN: You have a strong sense of personal authority that is not easily implemented. Singular views often alienate people with whom you disagree, so you feel rejected.

SUN–URANUS: With complete disregard for law and order, you tend to reserve a special position for yourself; you feel you should not be restrained, making you a rebel without a cause from a distorted sense of self-worth.

SUN–NEPTUNE: Rejection of reality or a revision of the truth is a way to accommodate your inability to deal with it. You are easily drawn into strange alliances or making others captive of your desires: drugs, mysticism, fantasy.

SUN–PLUTO: You are obsessed with power and the political, social and economic leverage it gives. Issuing ultimatums is a practice often indulged in for personal gain. Sexual needs are a strong factor in your life.

Moon

MOON–MERCURY: Conflict arises between the early conditioning factors and the ability to rationalize, or between the head and the heart. Guilt for not living up to parental expectations must be examined and revised with a more personal perspective.

MOON–VENUS: Desire for close personal relationships is in conflict with the fear and anxiety that you may fail in the responsibilities they bring. You tend to avoid contact for fear of the demands created thereby.

MOON–MARS: Serious avoidance factors are used to deny close encounters unless you are given a clear leadership role in them. You prefer that *you* call it all off than have it done to you.

MOON–JUPITER: You are high in response to those who show more than a passing interest in you. You overreact to what may only be a casual desire for your companionship by getting so involved that you make an emotional commitment that may not be mutual.

MOON–SATURN: Ah, yesterday — and how great it was (?). You linger in the past and deny yourself the development of new interests and challenges. You rarely let go of romantic ties whose days are numbered. Austerity is indicated during the formative years.

MOON–URANUS: Emotionally impulsive and erratic, with little continuity. Short-lived relationships seem to be a repetitive phenomenon in your life. You talk as if you really enjoy freedom from any emotional obligation, but the truth is you long for an enduring relationship.

MOON–NEPTUNE: "Faraway places with strange sounding names . . ." How appropriate for the romance in your soul, but disappointing in the realities of life. Few can ever match the qualities you give them. You must allow people to demonstrate their credentials before getting involved with them.

MOON–PLUTO: Your feelings have a depth few can match, but there is danger in cultivating emotional relationships wherein you become victimized. Proceed with extreme caution in romantic alliances in spite of your powerful desire nature.

Mercury

MERCURY–MARS: Argumentative and intolerant of another's views, you tend to let things get out of hand through your lack of tact and diplomacy when the pressure is on. With the proper training, you could be convincing in your efforts.

MERCURY–JUPITER: The only way to shut you up is to put you in the company of those who cannot speak your language. "A little travelin' music" is consistent with your constant need to be on center stage. Politics is suitable for you, since taking liberties with what you say is often condoned.

MERCURY–SATURN: Your gift of gab compares with that of the actor Gary Cooper, who often responded to a lengthy conversation by contributing an occasional "Yep"! Your unwillingness to communicate masks the fact of the deep perception you enjoy.

MERCURY–URANUS: Though you enjoy a highly developed intuition and awareness, your fascination for the unusual robs you of a useful medium in which you could excel. You disagree solely for the effect you create when you do. You tend to be irresponsible in what you say or do. Humility is not your most notable attribute. Arrogant genius.

MERCURY–NEPTUNE: You have difficulty in accepting reality when it imposes unbearable demands on you. Your visionary talents can be wasted in non-

productive enterprises unless you take painstaking care that a useful purpose will be served. Escapism, fanaticism, inconstency, inspiration.

MERCURY–PLUTO: You have considerable psychic ability, with the in-depth perception to persuade people to accomplish tasks they never knew were possible. Curious to a fault, you are critical in the extreme when others can't "see" what is obvious to you.

Venus

VENUS–MARS: The extent of your physical urges and drives tends to cause considerable stress and anxiety in relating to people in general and romantic partners in particular. The peace and calm in harmonious relationships depends entirely on your developing those attitudes with those you love most dearly.

VENUS–JUPITER: Overreaching and overextending lead to problems in management. This applies equally to personal and social affairs and suggests the need for greater self-discipline in personal conduct.

VENUS–SATURN: Early parental conditioning is probably responsible for the guarded concern you have in your romantic interests. It is largely a matter of personal anxiety and doubt that you can live up to the demands of a romantic or legal commitment. You may choose to avoid commitments as a more desirable arrangement than taking risks.

VENUS–URANUS: There is an element of contradiction in the way you seek the company of people who are a bit unusual or generally off the beaten path. Perhaps it is this novelty that gives you the opportunity to dismiss a romantic relationship because "it would never work anyway."

VENUS–NEPTUNE: Your imagination works overtime indulging in romantic fantasy. You idealize the man or woman of your dreams with qualities that are usually inconsistent with basic reality. Take special care that you don't misrepresent yourself or you risk losing what might be the "real thing" because of the deception.

VENUS–PLUTO: It is rare that anyone with this planetary contact (similar to the Moon–Pluto contact) is ever free from the high probability of a painful or distressing emotional affair. It need not occur more than once if it teaches you maturity and cautious reserve in developing new relationships. Oftentimes, your powerful physical drives lead others to assume you aren't too selective.

Mars

MARS–JUPITER: If there is one factor that could cause you endless problems in your life, it would have to be your lack of self-discipline and judicious restraint. Once you develop a sense of follow-through in your objectives and how you handle them, your level of accomplishment will be quite substantial.

MARS–SATURN: This aspect contrasts dramatically with that of Mars–Jupiter and shows a troublesome difficulty getting things going and serious delays once they are under way. The problem is that you are afraid you will fail or . . . succeed!

MARS–URANUS: Quick to respond to any and all stimulation, you get yourself all in a lather at the slightest provocation. Your revolutionary spirit isn't easily restrained, but it had better be or this can result in a lot of unnecessary grief. It is a violent and argumentative position you take and you may even delight in it.

MARS–NEPTUNE: Taking definitive action seems like asking for trouble since complications usually develop. You tend to dismiss the most pertinent factors as insignificant until you realize — too late — that you should have paid more attention to them. Physical desires are strong enough to draw you into questionable relationships.

MARS–PLUTO: You have a powerful urge for exercising control over others in situations that allow you to manipulate them. This drive is so strong that you will eventually enjoy issuing ultimatums to bend people to your desires or "make them offers they can't refuse."

Jupiter

JUPITER–SATURN: Though this represents a reasonably well-developed intellect, there is still a constant gnawing doubt about your ability to succeed in your goals and objectives. Learn your craft well and don't look for others to approve before you start applying yourself.

JUPITER–URANUS: You react to those who challenge you by biting off more than you can truly cope with. You might have impressed them at the time, but they won't be around as you struggle to cope with the problem. You are easily persuaded to put current interests aside so you can indulge in something exciting that just gained your attention.

JUPITER–NEPTUNE: You are a dream merchant who has difficulty realizing your dreams in your own world. If anyone needs an adviser or guidance counselor it is you. Enormously gifted and at times keenly inspired, you need someone to guide you in selecting the best way to apply yourself. Be wary of unscrupulous persons using you for their selfish ends.

JUPITER–PLUTO: It is important that you periodically reexamine the code by which you live. It is so easy to get careless and find yourself only marginally within the law. If "big" deals fascinate you, then get the training that will equip you with a good foundation to sustain you. Take chances if you must, but be sure you understand the odds.

Saturn

SATURN–URANUS: The difficulty you have making decisions comes from the lingering ties with the past and the overwhelming demands of the future. It is largely the fear of the unknown and the untried that may unsettle you temporarily. Saturn represents your comfort with familiar ways of dealing with problems, while Uranus symbolizes the daring chances you take with a new or innovative approach to a solution. You must learn to accept change as an inherent part of progress or the world will simply pass you by.

SATURN–NEPTUNE: It is essential that you get the very best education or training you can because you face the inevitable competition who has. Don't delude yourself that you can succeed without credentials because you can't. Any fear that you may not be as qualified as the next person should itself be a warning to you. If you are willing to measure your progress in small but steady increments, your success will be truly satisfying.

SATURN–PLUTO: The one phrase that seems appropriate in this combination is "sour grapes." What it means is that unless you are winning or have some guarantee that you will, you won't play. There is a militant quality about you that is threatening to those weaker than you, but it is only a matter of time until you tackle someone else who, like yourself, hates to lose. Just be careful your ultimatums don't return to haunt you one day when you least expect it.

Uranus

URANUS–NEPTUNE: This is basically a healthy condition even though it often produces negative results and painful repercussions. It is a rebellious attitude you have that is usually directed in political enterprises. You may voice displeasure over the state of the country, the state or the city and arouse support for your position, but you probably lack the continuity to see things through to a successful revision.

URANUS–PLUTO: The main thrust of this planetary relationship is largely sociological, although this effect is brought about by the interlocking pressures of worldwide geopolitical economics. This influence is so vast that it only involves or affects those with these planets prominent in their charts. Your national loyalty may be tested.

The last two planets, Neptune and Pluto, have not formed a stressful relationship between them since 1825 when the 90° (square) Aspect ended after twelve years! The other two stress relationships, the 150° (inconjunct) and the 180° (opposition), both occurred before 1800.

It should be noted that in the foregoing examples of the significance when two planets form a spatial relationship that is stressful and that symbolically produces behavioral difficulty, we do not consider the signs occupied by the planets involved. This is truly significant in terms of determining the sociological impact and the impression they make on character and its continuing development. In some instances, the "influences" are spread over an extremely large number of people because the planet Uranus spends approximately seven years in a sign, while Neptune spends about fourteen years in a sign and Pluto's stay in a sign is currently a little over eleven years!

You can see, then, that some of the planetary patterns are largely generational in effect, and though an astrologer can easily determine individual reaction to the pressures of these planets, there is a social conditioning or evolutionary effect taking place that involves everyone in one way or another. It isn't possible in a work of this size to include detailed analyses of all the planets in all the signs. What we have included is a short, concise presentation of those planetary positions that should give you a reasonably accurate statement of how your identity and character function from the way early imprinting inclined your response mechanism.

Those of you interested in exploring the foregoing short Aspect examples in greater detail are referred to *Planets in Aspect* by Robert Pelletier, where an extensive presentation of the relations between planets is given. *Planets in Aspect* is published by Para Research, Inc. of Rockport, Massachusetts, and is available in hardcover and paperback editions.

APPENDIX VII   Unaspected Planets

Any kind of activity takes place through the action of the planets as their energies seek expression in the circumstances of the life. When there is contact with another planet in the chart, the resulting display of energy is made more complex, since two different fields or purposes are brought into play. For example, the person with the Sun separated by 90° from the planet Mars will strive to impose his or her will on those around him or her. It will arouse antagonism because the energy is a product of a flaw in the method of utilization (Sun square Mars) and there may well be serious objections expressed when this person becomes unduly forceful in his or her assertions. This is how the planets operate, and when there are benign aspects between them, then the effect is far more harmonious and doesn't incur the displeasure of the negative Aspects. There are instances when a planet has no contact at all with any other planet in the chart and is, therefore, unaspected. This too has significance and it should be noted. Refer to the section dealing with the natures of the planets and the luminaries to get a feel for the behavioral mechanics they represent and to know how this kind of absent factor will make itself evident in the life.

SUN   There is an unwillingness to assert yourself so that people take full advantage of your position. You lack a sense of your own adequacy and have serious doubt that you can ever be effective in achieving goals in the life. But you don't really care if you succeed or not. Your interests will be mainly in the area indicated by the sign your Sun occupies as well as its house position (in a time-of-birth chart).

MOON   This may occur, but owing to the speed at which the Moon travels, we have never seen a chart in which the Moon was unaspected!

MERCURY   The problem with an unaspected Mercury (or because of its proximity to the Sun) is the lack of interest in communication. This then becomes one of the indicators of the so-called silent-type person. It is simply difficult for this person to engage in dialogue or any other form of contact that requires some kind of social exchange.

VENUS   With this planet unaspected there is much stress involved when conditions require some kind of social participation. There is usually an indifferent attitude in situations requiring some kind of compromise, with something like "I don't want to get involved" the only comment, which suggests an uncaring attitude.

MARS   In the struggle to achieve objectives Mars is the symbol of the mobilized physical resources usually brought into play. With an unaspected Mars this person can never find enough energy to handle the simplest kinds of tasks. Though this person may appear indolent or lazy, the fact is that he or she just cannot get excited enough about a situation to do very much about it. Because of this, he or she can be the victim of those who prey on the weak or apathetic.

JUPITER   The world of the person whose Jupiter is unaspected is considerably smaller than it is for others simply because there is resistance to the process of growth, figuratively speaking. There is often reticence about getting involved in matters that allow him or her to expand the consciousness or to explore new worlds of social and intellectual interests. Social withdrawal is not uncommon in this condition.

SATURN   The means by which one establishes his or her credentials is largely diminished in its influence when Saturn is unaspected. Saturn is essential for mobilizing personal resources in a program to fulfill the ambitions. Such a person therefore has great difficulty getting his or her act together through careful planning and methodical implementation. What may develop is a strong defense mechanism to justify the lack of any goals-seeking apparatus.

URANUS   Tradition is a way of life for the person with an unaspected Uranus. There is an inability to see beyond today or to understand why change is simply an indication of a growing process that most frequently improves on conditions it replaces. If most of the world's people had this condition in their charts it would be next to impossible to conduct a revolution, no matter what the provocation. Nostalgia forms a major consideration in the lives of these people and it is often the only one.

NEPTUNE   Neptune unaspected indicates someone who is unable (or unwilling) to respond to the social problems that may prevail in his or her environment. This kind of social indifference is indicative of the subconscious anxiety over conditions that may one day entrap this person and cause him or her to be victimized. This person is commonly heard to say at the time of elections, "It makes no difference whom I vote for because it's always the same types who get elected anyway." A feature of this planetary condition is the way this person is often the victim of the very condition he or she tolerates.

PLUTO   The person with an unaspected Pluto is similar to a particular species of animal that became extinct through a refusal or an inability to adapt to changing circumstances. This means that unless he or she is willing to make the massive adjustments often necessary, survival is virtually impossible. This person fails to notice that there is a kind of commitment everyone has to make in contributing to universal welfare to assure the survival of the many through the contribution of everyone, without exception.

It should be noted that the last three planets, Uranus, Neptune and Pluto, represent the kinds of human attributes that bind the individual to socially relevant conditions and circumstances. Consequently, their effects are far less personal than is the case with the first seven planetary influences. It may be difficult to isolate the particulars if any of these planets is under consideration or examination.

It should be further noted that no one born after September of 1942 has either Neptune and Pluto in an unaspected condition. They formed a sextile Aspect then and will remain in that relationship until the middle of the next century.

APPENDIX VIII Unoccupied Qualities or Elements

LACK OF PLANETS IN:

Cardinal Signs   There is a diminished ability to take advantage of circumstances for personal benefit. Since the Cardinal signs enhance the executive-response mechanism to make the most of a particular situation, this low-key individual fails to take note of the most glaring opportunity.

Fixed Signs   The ability to stay on course is extremely difficult without planets in at least one of the Fixed signs. Consequently, life tends to follow no important direction, and it is painfully difficult to realize any objective without a major struggle.

Mutable Signs   This would indicate someone who was unable to make even the most simplest adjustments to changing circumstances in life. This kind of inflexibility can be troublesome in the pattern of ever-changing conditions that prevails today.

LACK OF PLANETS IN:

Fire   The fires of enthusiasm and creative spirit burn weakly in this individual. This dispirited person can't get too excited over anything, no matter how thrilling it might be to everyone else. Despondency and pessimism are not uncommon, and it would take a very active Sun or Mars in the chart to compensate for this predicament.

Earth   This shows a decided inability to get too excited about life's realities, especially when they make heavy demands in personal accountability and participation. What often happens is that this person feels out of touch with the real world and, as the song suggests, would prefer to "stop the world, I want to get off."

Air	Because this person is so preoccupied with creative functions, emotional involvements or the realities of life, the matters requiring rational or thoughtful consideration are usually given little attention or dismissed entirely. The judgment is that attention is already overburdened with more pressing considerations. This person is often intimidated by contemplative individuals and frequently chastises them "for all your high-falutin intellectual nonsense."
Water	This missing Element can prove deeply troublesome because it denies a suitable platform from which to adequately ventilate the emotional problems the individual may encounter at different times in life. Other people may distrust someone who cannot express any sympathetic understanding for them in their time of distess. This missing element is probably the most difficult one for which to develop some effective kind of suitable compensation through alternative means.

APPENDIX IX   Dynamics of Behavior

The following list of human attributes and principles of behavior is presented with the most likely planetary configurations that relate to them in the individual horoscope. There are often variations that sometimes produce similar types of characteristics, but for the most part these form a reliable guide for you.

ABUSIVENESS The foregoing as it pertains to *anger* will probably be found with the additional interaction from a negative Aspect with Uranus. It is common for this person to function unilaterally and with little regard for the rights of others. And yet they make such a point of exercising "my rights!"

AFFECTION This is found when Venus is well-placed by sign and Aspect so that there is a benign desire to indulge others with acts of kindness and warmth. When there is much Water (many planets in the Water signs), the disposition is to be protective and mothering by nature. When there is much Fire (many planets in Fire signs), the person is usually quite demonstrative.

AMBITION A strong Sun, often in one of the Cardinal signs (Aries, Cancer, Libra or Capricorn) supported by a close Aspect from Saturn (it may be a positive or negative Aspect) usually indicates a power surge that finds fulfillment in careers in management. Theirs is a life wherein the ambitions are best satisfied in dealing with external affairs where the ability to manipulate can be demonstrated.

ANARCHY This "down with the establishment" attitude was a major predicament of the years between 1950 and 1970 and is the result of an intense desire to exercise personal freedom irrespective of the cost to society or to oneself. A powerfully placed Uranus running roughshod over a meekly placed Saturn is usually indicated in the charts of those so inclined. There may be considerable idealism from a prominent Neptune and Pluto. Uranus and Saturn made an important conjunction in the early 1940s, thereby setting the stage for Uranus's takeover twenty-one years later when it made a square Aspect to where the conjunction took place (in Gemini).

ANGER This often results from severe frustration without suitable alternatives. Those with Mars especially active and frustrated by a negative Aspect from Saturn often react angrily when their way is blocked or impeded in any way.

ANXIETY This is commonly found in the chart of those belonging to the Mutable signs (Gemini, Virgo, Sagittarius and Pisces) because they all seem to have "so much on my mind." Sharing this distress are those belonging to the Water signs (Cancer, Scorpio and Pisces). You will notice that Pisces is the one sign belonging to both groups, which is why they can probably claim to be professional worriers.

ARROGANCE Converse to the above, the unfavorable ties between the Sun and Mars, Jupiter or Pluto often produce this characteristic that is usually frowned upon by most people, since it is often so offensive. It shows an exaggerated sense of personal importance that usually exceeds the boundaries of good taste and acceptable social behavior.

ASSERTIVENESS Favorable Aspects of the Sun to Mars, Jupiter or Pluto allow for the development of this useful characteristic. It is the exercise of the will in activity that serves as a useful outlet for the desire to gain significance in the world. It shows vitality and initiative in utilizing the creative potentials.

ASTROLOGY An interest in astrology is indicated by the planet Uranus prominent because of its elevation in the chart and/or its close contact by Aspect (positive or negative) to the Sun, Moon or Mercury. Charles E. O. Carter found that certain degrees of the Zodiac were associated with an interest and proficiency in astrology. He mentions the degrees around 27° Leo–Aquarius and 11° Virgo–Pisces are strong indications for more than a passing interest in astrology.

BENEVOLENCE This is a manifestation of the higher attributes of the planet Jupiter, especially when functioning in a Water environment. When aspected with Saturn, the kindness and generosity will have practical application.

BRAVERY This is a strong Martian attribute but with special qualifications so that it doesn't become rash or foolhardy. True courage and bravery result from a strong Sun in the chart with reasonably good (positive) Aspects from Saturn or Pluto. Sometimes the Aspects from Jupiter can incite to imprudent acts of daring that can prove tragic in the final outcome. With Saturn there are built-in resourcefulness and planning that sustain and support the endeavor. With Jupiter also involved there will often be considerable idealism and vision in the effort.

BRUTALITY This is usually the result of technically "strained" Aspects between Mars and Saturn. Sometimes when the Sun is similarly aspected to Saturn there is a "pushing" quality in the behavior that is often unrelenting for the distress it can cause. The former Premier of Russia, Josef Stalin, had this configuration with his Sun at 11° of Capricorn in close square (90° Aspect) to Saturn at 10° of Aries. (This is one degree short of an exact square!) History records his regime as one of the cruelest in modern times. Hitler had Mars within 3° of an exact square to Saturn in his chart. Be wary of jumping to conclusions simply from this particular configuration in anyone's chart. Other factors must also be present to suggest this characteristic, but it does, admittedly, show an inclination that deserves further examination for other concurring evidence.

CAUTION A cautious nature is bestowed by the benign Aspects of Saturn to the Sun, Moon or Mercury. The methodology of behavior is one of painstaking attention to every detail to make certain that everything is in its proper place at the right time so that an orderly effort can be made. It shows efficiency in managing personal and professional affairs so that an optimum yield is derived from even the most modest investment of time and energy.

CHARITY This is primarily the effect from a well-placed and aspected Sun or Moon with Jupiter. Sometimes the favorable effects from Neptune causes such idealism that sharing is an integral part of the life.

COARSENESS Be it of manner, speech, appearance or temperament, coarseness is largely a product of the signs whose natures have an affinity for the more blatant sensory apparatus. These are principally the Earth and Water signs, Cancer, Scorpio, Pisces and Taurus, Virgo, Capricorn. It is largely from the Water signs that the broad spectrum of human emotion and sensation is derived while the Earth signs offer the means for implementing them physically. The Fire and Air signs are mainly preoccupied with creative inspiration and the rationale for translating it in its social application. Some of the planetary indicators are when Mars is predominantly strong in the chart without the refining influence of Venus or Jupiter or the control factor of Saturn. Under affliction to Saturn there is often a sadistic inclination. An afflicted Sun, say from Nep-

tune, is often unable to correctly determine when indulging oneself leads to a careless disregard for propriety and becomes socially repugnant.

COLDNESS Not to be confused with *frigidity*, coldness is a temperamental aberration resulting from the lack of planets in Fire signs or lack of sufficient Aspects involving the Fire planets — the Sun, Mars or Jupiter. This is usually only the tip of the iceberg and may, upon closer examination, reveal that there has been deep sorrow in the life or emotional repression or denial.

CONCEIT Strange as it may seem, Virgo seems especially qualified for having this characteristic. While a prominent Sun or Jupiter often shows a person who is vain and/or inclined to exaggeration, it is the Earth Element that produces talent in action so that Virgo gains supreme mastery in his or her skills. This conceit as presented here is simply the kind of self-assurance one develops from a job well done. It's an awareness of functional adequacy in performing various tasks.

CUNNING It's another way of saying clever and effective in administering one's talents. When applied in operations where stealth or subterfuge is used, a Mercury–Neptune influence is detected. To be successful there should also be an active Saturn influence associated with this pair.

DECEPTION The retentive nature of this attribute suggests a negative influence. Consequently, the Water Elements are particularly emphasized since they are the experts in the fine art of imitation. Oftentimes it is simply that the observer is unable to determine what this person's frontal approach may be. Double signs (Gemini, Virgo, Sagittarius and Pisces) are quite talented in presenting a variety of sides in any given situation and are accused when all is eventually revealed. There are two ways to accomplish subterfuge — one is positive, in which there is a deliberate plan to deceive; the other is negative, in which a certain amount of information is simply withheld. Maps that have a strong Neptune involved with the Sun, Mercury, Venus or the Moon are inclined this way.

DEPRAVITY This term is falling into disuse because so much of what was formerly regarded as depraved is now accepted between consenting adults. In those instances of a truly depraved nature that are occasionally spotlighted in newspapers, there is a strong influence from the planet Pluto. This is especially true when sexual activity is the focal point of a business enterprise. Those engaging in such activity will have a powerful Aspect, usually a difficult one, involving the

Sun, Jupiter and Saturn from either Neptune or Pluto. In the individual chart, the presence of Jupiter or Neptune in Aspect with the Sun or Mars can precipitate an interest in activity that satisfies the lustful desires.

DESTRUCTIVENESS This is especially relevant to an active relationship between Mars and Uranus. This is the rebel without a cause, and most destructive acts are characterized by lack of motive except the sheer pleasure in destroying property. On occasion you will notice this planetary contact in benign Aspect with the Sun, Jupiter, Saturn or Neptune so that a socially useful effect is the motivating force behind the destructive effort (such as removing an obstruction that is causing floodwaters to back up to threaten a village).

DEVOTION This is commonly found where the Fixed signs prevail (Taurus, Leo, Scorpio and Aquarius). They represent steadfastness in carrying out their affairs.

DIPLOMACY Diplomacy requires a pleasing manner, so a prominent and well-placed Venus is necessary; the Sun enhances the sense of authority one possesses so that one gains the respect from those involved. Mercury in a benign Aspect with Saturn enriches the mental faculties and allows for the penetrating depth of understanding that easily disarms adversaries.

DISHONESTY In a general sense, any disturbing Aspect from Neptune to the personal planets — Sun, Moon, Mercury, Venus and Mars — tends to cause some distortion in how one's concept of right and wrong is established. The comment "What you see is *not* what you get" is appropriate when the planet Neptune participates in planetary configurations. Coincidentally, Neptune is usually active in the charts of writers of fiction, which is, of course, an acceptable outlet for this energy.

ENVY This characteristic seems to be akin to resentment and is therefore related to difficult Sun–Saturn Aspects. Fear is at the root of the problem, so a fairly active Saturn to deny certain advantages is quite evident. It is when denial is viewed against the abundance others seem to enjoy that this attribute becomes active. It is a deep-seated problem, and those with it tell of a heartsick anxiety in the pit of their stomachs whenever it manifests. The stomach is symbolic of the struggle for survival that has endured over the ages and envy may well be the culmination of that anxiety.

EXCESS When Jupiter is involved by Aspect with personal planets, especially the Sun, Venus and Mars,

excesses are almost a certainty. Jupiter is symbolic of abundance and whenever his influence prevails some form of exaggeration is sure to follow. Sagittarius is noted for its excesses.

FANATICISM This characteristic can be associated with a wide variety of "causes." It is primarily found through the effects of the planets in their relationship with each other, rather than through any particular sign of the Zodiac. The three outermost planets, Uranus, Neptune and Pluto, are almost always involved, and this suggests a strong sociological significance with strong political overtones. Mars in a stress Aspect with Uranus is especially notable in providing the energy to carry out these kinds of enterprises, which are often indulged in surreptitiously. Uranus provides a "brave new world" facade, Neptune allows for a search for nirvana, while Pluto instills the desire to replenish the Earth with new blood, with new principles rising out of the ashes of the past.

FATALISM Some signs have a leaning toward fatalism, and Capricorn seems to lead the way in this regard. A strong Saturn making stress Aspects to the Sun, Moon or Mercury sometimes disposes one to a sense of futility.

FEAR This problem is linked to Saturn in the chart. Whenever there are difficult Aspects involving Saturn, especially to the Sun, Moon or Venus, fear prevails. What happens here is that Saturn produces personal anxiety and doubt that one has the resources with which to succeed in one's endeavors and/or relationships. Ignorance is the cause for this dilemma and education the answer for dealing with it.

FRIGIDITY In spite of the changing scenario where sex is concerned today, there still exist numerous instances of frigidity among women and impotence among men. The leading indicator of frigidity among women is the presence of powerful aspects from Saturn to the Moon or Venus. These are usually negative (stress) contacts that seriously undermine the individual's ability to function without first getting approval from some authority figure, usually one (or both) of the parents. It is not uncommon for the Sun to be poorly placed in the chart (in a weak sign and without supportive Aspects from strong planets to give it a more willful disposition) so that the person feels somewhat insignificant or unable to take decisive action. Strong Saturn Aspects to the Moon or Venus increase the fear of pregnancy, while difficult Aspects from Neptune threaten venereal disease. This last contact from Neptune sometimes produces "phantom" distresses that are created as a defense mechanism when fear is overwhelming.

GAMBLING Sagittarius holds the lead among the signs with a desire to gamble. Leo also has a considerable interest in this endeavor. Trusting to luck is a tendency most often indulged in by those with Jupiter prominent in their charts either by Aspect or because it rules Sagittarius.

GREED A strong word to describe many variations of the same principle. A desire for adequacy, for comfort, for a "cushion" or safety margin, whatever terms one may use, survival is at the root. Acquisitiveness is a critical matter for Taurus, Cancer and Capricorn. The interconnecting Aspects involving the Moon, Venus and Saturn are nearly always evident in the charts of those who seem almost desperate to gain the means for survival. So much so that it tends to spill over into other areas of life, so that much criticism is directed toward them.

HATE Scorpio has greater inclination for this trait than do other signs. It must be viewed along with the indications for *envy* to grasp a fuller understanding of why it occurs at all. Mars–Uranus–Saturn contacts are common to allow for acting on the hatred in many instances. Revenge is frequently characteristic of Scorpio. The chart must be carefully studied before arriving at any conclusion relative to this trait.

IMMORALITY The social acceptance of what constitutes morality (or immorality) changes dramatically with the times, so what was unacceptable even as recent as ten years ago is now viewed as normal behavior. Witness the increasing number of people living together without benefit of marriage, a situation that was severely frowned upon a generation ago. Asking a question about sex or how people conduct themselves while indulging in it would have raised a number of eyebrows not long ago; today this same topic is the subject of open forum discussions on television. The astrological indicators for various forms of sexuality and their psychological accompaniment do not change, but what may have previously been indicated by a stressful relationship between Venus–Mars–Uranus because of the way society frowned upon it might now be found as benign relationship between these very same planets, indicating that it no longer produces the anxiety it did yesterday.

IMPOTENCE A fairly common phenomenon in spite of the advances made in matters of a sexual nature. The increased permissiveness as it pertains to both sexes has in fact stimulated an increase in impotence among men. When the male previously set the stage for a sexual encounter it was because of his readiness to perform. Today, it is common for the female to initiate action leading to intercourse, but the timing may not always match the male's preparedness and result in feelings of inadequacy. Once fear is established, nothing can reverse it at the moment and impotence prevails, temporarily at least. Close Aspects from Neptune to the Sun or Mars often cause sufficient distortion of reality that a serious dilemma occurs. Saturn imposing restriction on Mars through difficult Aspects can also temporarily interfere with successful sexual activity. But in the main it is the Aspects to the Sun (leadership, authority, aggressor) that incline to this problem.

INFERIORITY Strong Saturn influences to the Sun especially tend to produce a feeling of inferiority. The prominence of the passive planets arrests the development of aggression and striving for significance. The Sun in the Water signs (Cancer, Scorpio and Pisces) renders it susceptible to the overlay of powerful influences brought about by persons forcing themselves on the susceptible individual. The effect of Water (emotions and feelings) tends to extinguish the ardor of the Sun and weakens it competitively. Not that power and an aggressive display are necessarily indicative of inner strength, since Mahatma Gandhi displayed enormous strength in his passive programs that eventually led India to self-rule after many years of British domination. Even with the Sun in Earth Elements (resourcefulness) can suffer when Saturn imposes its limitations on the will.

REVENGE Deep-seated hatred is commonly found to be the cause for seeking revenge against someone. It is usually associated with persons who have intense, emotional natures that react with deep hurt from the offenses leveled against them, and the desire to retaliate becomes nearly an obsession. Scorpio is high on the list of signs most likely to indulge in this kind of action, but it is mainly the conflict between Mars and Saturn or Uranus in a person's chart that indicates the probability that this vindictive attitude will prevail.

SENSUALITY This is a product of the Earth signs who each have a Fire sign as the eighth sign from their own. Taurus has Sagittarius (exaggeration and taking chances) for its eighth sign; Virgo has Aries (ardent, aggressive desire) for its eighth sign; while Capricorn has Leo (love, romance, pleasure) for its eighth sign. The eighth sign is pertinent to the process of sexual encounter as a primary physical function. Venus and Mars in Aspect to Jupiter increase the desire nature to overflowing. Here we are referring to a purely sensual function without the thinking apparatus or the feeling nature involved in an exchange of love.

SEXUALITY Viewed from the purely biological function, there are some similarities between sexuality and sensuality. The main difference here is that there is usually a strong love relationship that necessarily manifests in a merging of two lovers in the most intimate exchange possible, so that it is the culmination or the extension of blending of lovers in a unified experience. This is then the end result of an intimacy that is already shared on other than the purely biological level. The usual motivating force here is continuing union of separates that culminates oftentimes in reproduction. Venus–Mars contacts are usually active along with a meaningful contact between the Sun, Moon and Mercury. What we have is a broader pattern of involvement the individual needs to share with another. If Saturn or Jupiter is involved, there is a long-range expectation to be derived from whatever follows an interest in someone else.

APPENDIX X   The Ephemeris

SIDEREAL SUN MOON MERCURY VENUS MARS JUPITER SATURN URANUS NEPTUNE PLUTO

DAY	TIME	☉	☽	☿	♀	♂	♃	♄	♅	♆	♇
	h m s	° ' "	° '	°	°	°	°	°	°	°	°
J 1	6 37 25	9♑16 52	2♉ 5	20♐	26♏	17♎	17♌R	12♍R	29♒	11♌R	7♋R
A 2	6 41 22	10 18 1	16 26	21	27	17	17	12	29	11	7
N 3	6 45 18	11 19 10	1♊ 6	22	28	17	17	12	29	11	7
U 4	6 49 15	12 20 18	16 1	24	0♐	18	17	12	29	11	7
A 5	6 53 12	13 21 27	1♋ 3	25	1	18	17	12	29	11	7
R 6	6 57 8	14 22 35	16 4	27	2	19	17	12	29	11	7
Y 7	7 1 5	15 23 43	0♌55	28	3	19	16	11	29	11	7
8	7 5 1	16 24 51	15 27	0♑	4	20	16	11	29	11	7
9	7 8 58	17 25 59	29 33	1	5	20	16	11	29	11	7
10	7 12 54	18 27 7	13♍12	3	7	21	16	11	29	11	6
11	7 16 51	19 28 15	26 21	4	8	21	16	11	29	11	6
12	7 20 47	20 29 23	9♎ 5	6	9	22	16	11	29	11	6
13	7 24 44	21 30 31	21 27	7	10	22	16	11	0♓	11	6
14	7 28 41	22 31 39	3♏31	9	11	23	16	11	0	11	6
15	7 32 37	23 32 47	15 24	10	13	23	16	11	0	11	6
16	7 36 34	24 33 54	27 12	12	14	23	15	11	0	11	6
17	7 40 30	25 35 1	8♐58	13	15	24	15	11	0	11	6
18	7 44 27	26 36 8	20 47	15	16	24	15	11	0	11	6
19	7 48 23	27 37 15	2♑43	16	17	25	15	11	0	11	6
20	7 52 20	28 38 21	14 48	18	19	25	15	11	0	10	6
21	7 56 16	29 39 26	27 5	19	20	26	15	11	0	10	6
22	8 0 13	0♒40 31	9♒33	21	21	26	15	11	0	10	6
23	8 4 10	1 41 35	22 13	23	22	26	15	11	0	10	6
24	8 8 6	2 42 38	5♓ 4	24	23	27	14	11	0	10	6
25	8 12 3	3 43 41	18 8	26	25	27	14	11	0	10	6
26	8 15 59	4 44 42	1♈22	27	26	28	14	11	0	10	6
27	8 19 56	5 45 42	14 48	29	27	28	14	11	0	10	6
28	8 23 52	6 46 41	28 26	1♒	28	28	14	11	0	10	6
29	8 27 49	7 47 39	12♉18	2	29	29	14	11	0	10	6
30	8 31 45	8 48 35	26 23	4	1♑	29	14	10	0	10	6
31	8 35 42	9 49 30	10♊42	6	2	0♏	14	10	0	10	6

THE SUN ENTERS THE SIGN OF AQUARIUS ON JAN 21 AT 08:05.

DAY	TIME	☉	☽	☿	♀	♂	♃	♄	♅	♆	♇
	h m s	° ' "	° '	°	°	°	°	°	°	°	°
F 1	8 39 39	10♒50 24	25♊12	7♒	3♑	0♏	13♌R	10♍R	0♓	10♌R	6♋R
E 2	8 43 35	11 51 17	9♋49	9	4	0	13	10	1	10	6
B 3	8 47 32	12 52 9	24 28	11	5	1	13	10	1	10	6
R 4	8 51 28	13 52 59	9♌ 1	13	7	1	13	10	1	10	6
U 5	8 55 25	14 53 48	23 21	14	8	1	13	10	1	10	6
A 6	8 59 21	15 54 36	7♍22	16	9	2	13	10	1	10	6
R 7	9 3 18	16 55 23	20 59	18	10	2	13	10	1	10	6
Y 8	9 7 14	17 56 8	4♎10	20	12	2	13	10	1	10	6
9	9 11 11	18 56 53	16 57	21	13	3	12	10	1	10	6
10	9 15 8	19 57 36	29 22	23	14	3	12	10	1	10	6
11	9 19 4	20 58 19	11♏30	25	15	3	12	10	1	10	6
12	9 23 1	21 59 1	23 25	27	16	4	12	10	1	10	6
13	9 26 57	22 59 41	5♐14	29	18	4	12	9	1	10	6
14	9 30 54	24 0 20	17 2	0♓	19	4	12	9	1	10	6
15	9 34 50	25 0 58	28 53	2	20	5	12	9	1	10	6
16	9 38 47	26 1 35	10♑54	4	21	5	11	9	1	10	6
17	9 42 43	27 2 11	23 6	6	22	5	11	9	1	10	6
18	9 46 40	28 2 45	5♒34	8	24	5	11	9	1	10	6
19	9 50 37	29 3 18	18 18	10	25	6	11	9	2	10	6
20	9 54 33	0♓ 3 49	1♓17	11	26	6	11	9	2	10	6
21	9 58 30	1 4 18	14 31	13	27	6	11	9	2	10	6
22	10 2 26	2 4 46	27 58	15	29	6	11	9	2	10	6
23	10 6 23	3 5 12	11♈35	17	0♒	7	11	9	2	10	6
24	10 10 19	4 5 36	25 20	19	1	7	11	9	2	10	6
25	10 14 16	5 5 59	9♉12	20	2	7	10	9	2	9	6
26	10 18 12	6 6 19	23 10	22	3	7	10	8	2	9	6
27	10 22 9	7 6 38	7♊12	23	5	7	10	8	2	9	6
28	10 26 6	8 6 54	21 20	25	6	8	10	8	2	9	6
29	10 30 2	9 7 8	5♋31	26	7	8	10	8	2	9	6

THE SUN ENTERS THE SIGN OF PISCES ON FEB 19 AT 22:29.

DAY	TIME	☉	☽	☿	♀	♂	♃	♄	♅	♆	♇
	h m s	° ' "	° '	°	°	°	°	°	°	°	°
M 1	10 33 59	10♓ 7 21	19♋43	28♓	8♒	8♏	10♌R	8♍R	2♓	9♌R	6♋R
A 2	10 37 55	11 7 31	3♌54	29	10	8	10	8	2	9	6
R 3	10 41 52	12 7 39	18 0	0♈	11	8	10	8	2	9	6
C 4	10 45 48	13 7 45	1♍55	1	12	8	10	8	2	9	6
H 5	10 49 45	14 7 50	15 35	2	13	8	10	8	2	9	6
6	10 53 41	15 7 52	28 58	3	14	9	9	8	2	9	6
7	10 57 38	16 7 53	12♎ 0	4	16	9	9	8	2	9	6
8	11 1 35	17 7 51	24 43	4	17	9	9	8	3	9	6
9	11 5 31	18 7 48	7♏ 6	4	18	9	9	8	3	9	6
10	11 9 28	19 7 44	19 15	5 R	19	9	9	7	3	9	6
11	11 13 24	20 7 38	1♐12	5	21	9	9	7	3	9	6
12	11 17 21	21 7 30	13 2	5	22	9	9	7	3	9	6
13	11 21 17	22 7 20	24 51	4	23	9	9	7	3	9	6
14	11 25 14	23 7 9	6♑44	4	24	9	9	7	3	9	6
15	11 29 10	24 6 56	18 47	4	26	9 R	9	7	3	9	6
16	11 33 7	25 6 41	1♒ 3	3	27	9	9	7	3	9	6
17	11 37 4	26 6 24	13 37	2	28	9	9	7	3	9	6
18	11 41 0	27 6 6	26 30	1	29	9	9	7	3	9	6
19	11 44 57	28 5 46	9♓43	1	0♓	9	9	7	3	9	6
20	11 48 53	29 5 23	23 17	0⊙	2	9	8	7	3	9	6 D
21	11 52 50	0♈ 4 59	7♈ 6	29♓	3	9	8	7	3	9	6
22	11 56 46	1 4 33	21 9	28	4	9	8	7	3	9	6
23	12 0 43	2 4 4	5♉21	27	5	9	8	6	3	9	6
24	12 4 39	3 3 34	19 38	26	7	9	8	6	3	9	6
25	12 8 36	4 3 1	3♊55	25	8	8	8	6	3	9	6
26	12 12 32	5 2 26	18 10	25	9	8	8	6	4	9	6
27	12 16 29	6 1 48	2♋20	24	10	8	8	6	4	9	6
28	12 20 26	7 1 9	16 25	23	11	8	8	6	4	9	6
29	12 24 22	8 0 27	0♌23	23	13	8	8	6	4	9	6
30	12 28 19	8 59 42	14 12	22	14	8	8	6	4	9	6
31	12 32 15	9 58 55	27 51	22	15	7	8	6	4	9	6

THE SUN ENTERS THE SIGN OF ARIES ON MAR 20 AT 21:59.

SIDEREAL SUN MOON MERCURY VENUS MARS JUPITER SATURN URANUS NEPTUNE PLUTO

DAY	TIME	☉	☽	☿	♀	♂	♃	♄	♅	♆	♇
	h m s	° ' "	° '	°	°	°	°	°	°	°	°
A 1	12 36 12	10♈58 6	11♍19	22♓R	16♓	7♏R	8♌R	6♍R	4♓	9♌R	6♋
P 2	12 40 8	11 57 14	24 33	22 D	18	7	8	6	4	9	6
R 3	12 44 5	12 56 21	7♎34	22	19	7	8	6	4	9	6
I 4	12 48 1	13 55 25	20 19	22	20	7	8 D	6	4	9	6
L 5	12 51 58	14 54 28	2♏49	22	21	6	8	6	4	9	6
6	12 55 55	15 53 28	15 5	22	23	6	8	6	4	9	6
7	12 59 51	16 52 27	27 9	22	24	6	8	6	4	9	6
8	13 3 48	17 51 24	9♐ 5	23	25	6	8	6	4	9	6
9	13 7 44	18 50 19	20 56	23	26	5	8	5	4	9	6
10	13 11 41	19 49 12	2♑45	24	27	5	8	5	4	9	6
11	13 15 37	20 48 3	14 39	24	29	5	8	5	4	9	6
12	13 19 34	21 46 53	26 41	25	0⊙	4	8	5	4	9	6
13	13 23 30	22 45 41	8♒57	26	1♈	4	8	5	4	9	6
14	13 27 27	23 44 27	21 31	27	2	4	8	5	4	9	6
15	13 31 24	24 43 11	4♓26	27	4	3	8	5	4	9	6
16	13 35 20	25 41 54	17 45	28	5	3	8	5	4	9	6
17	13 39 17	26 40 35	1♈27	29	6	3	8	5	5	9	6
18	13 43 13	27 39 14	15 32	0♈	7	2	8	5	5	9	6
19	13 47 10	28 37 51	29 55	1	8	2	8	5	5	9 D	6
20	13 51 6	29 36 26	14♉31	2	10	1	8	5	5	9	6
21	13 55 3	0♉35 0	29 14	4	11	1	9	5	5	9	6
22	13 58 59	1 33 31	13♊57	5	12	1	9	5	5	9	6
23	14 2 56	2 32 0	28 34	6	13	0	9	5	5	9	6
24	14 6 53	3 30 27	13♋ 0	7	15	0	9	5	5	9	6
25	14 10 49	4 28 52	27 11	8	16	0	9	5	5	9	6
26	14 14 46	5 27 15	11♌ 7	10	17	29♎	9	5	5	9	6
27	14 18 42	6 25 35	24 45	11	18	29	9	5	5	9	6
28	14 22 39	7 23 54	8♍ 7	13	20	28	9	5	5	9	6
29	14 26 35	8 22 10	21 14	14	21	28	9	5	5	9	6
30	14 30 32	9 20 25	4♎ 6	15	22	28	9	5	5	9	6

THE SUN ENTERS THE SIGN OF TAURUS ON APR 20 AT 09:39.

DAY	TIME	☉	☽	☿	♀	♂	♃	♄	♅	♆	♇
	h m s	° ' "	° '	°	°	°	°	°	°	°	°
M 1	14 34 28	10♉18 37	16♎44	17♈	23♈	27♎R	9♌	5♍R	5♓	9♌	6♋
A 2	14 38 25	11 16 47	29 10	18	24	27	9	5	5	9	6
Y 3	14 42 21	12 14 56	11♏25	20	26	27	9	5	5	9	6
4	14 46 18	13 13 3	23 31	22	27	26	9	5	5	9	6
5	14 50 15	14 11 9	5♐29	23	28	26	10	5	5	9	6
6	14 54 11	15 9 13	17 21	25	29	26	10	5	5	9	6
7	14 58 8	16 7 15	29 11	27	1♉	25	10	5 D	5	9	6
8	15 2 4	17 5 16	11♑ 1	28	2	25	10	5	5	9	6
9	15 6 1	18 3 16	22 55	0♉	3	25	10	5	5	9	6
10	15 9 57	19 1 14	4♒58	2	4	24	10	5	5	9	6
11	15 13 54	19 59 11	17 12	4	5	24	10	5	5	9	6
12	15 17 50	20 57 6	29 43	5	7	24	10	5	5	9	6
13	15 21 47	21 55 0	12♓34	7	8	24	10	5	5	9	6
14	15 25 44	22 52 53	25 50	9	9	23	10	5	5	9	6
15	15 29 40	23 50 45	9♈31	11	10	23	11	5	5	9	6
16	15 33 37	24 48 36	23 38	13	12	23	11	5	5	9	6
17	15 37 33	25 46 25	8♉ 9	15	13	23	11	5	5	9	6
18	15 41 30	26 44 13	22 59	17	14	23	11	5	5	9	6
19	15 45 26	27 42 0	8♊ 1	19	15	22	11	5	5	9	6
20	15 49 23	28 39 45	23 6	21	17	22	11	5	5	9	6
21	15 53 19	29 37 29	8♋ 5	23	18	22	11	5	6	9	6
22	15 57 16	0♊35 11	22 51	26	19	22	11	5	6	9	6
23	16 1 13	1 32 52	7♌17	28	20	22	12	5	6	9	6
24	16 5 9	2 30 31	21 19	0♊	21	22	12	5	6	9	6
25	16 9 6	3 28 8	4♍58	2	23	22	12	5	6	9	6
26	16 13 2	4 25 44	18 14	4	24	21	12	5	6	9	6
27	16 16 59	5 23 19	1♎ 9	7	25	21	12	5	6	9	6
28	16 20 55	6 20 52	13 46	9	26	21	12	5	6	9	7
29	16 24 52	7 18 24	26 9	11	28	21	12	5	6	9	7
30	16 28 48	8 15 54	8♏20	13	29	21	13	5	6	9	7
31	16 32 45	9 13 24	20 22	15	0♊	21 D	13	5	6	9	7

THE SUN ENTERS THE SIGN OF GEMINI ON MAY 21 AT 09:22.

DAY	TIME	☉	☽	☿	♀	♂	♃	♄	♅	♆	♇
	h m s	° ' "	° '	°	°	°	°	°	°	°	°
J 1	16 36 42	10♊10 52	2♐19	17♊	1♊	21♎	13♌	5♍	6♓	9♌	7♋
U 2	16 40 38	11 8 19	14 11	20	2	21	13	5	6	9	7
N 3	16 44 35	12 5 45	26 1	22	4	21	13	5	6	9	7
E 4	16 48 31	13 3 11	7♑51	24	5	21	13	5	6	9	7
5	16 52 28	14 0 35	19 44	26	6	21	13	6	6	9	7
6	16 56 24	14 57 59	1♒41	28	7	21	14	6	6	9	7
7	17 0 21	15 55 22	13 45	0♋	9	21	14	6	6	9	7
8	17 4 17	16 52 44	26 1	2	10	22	14	6	6	9	7
9	17 8 14	17 50 6	8♓30	4	11	22	14	6	6	9	7
10	17 12 11	18 47 28	21 18	5	12	22	14	6	6 R	9	7
11	17 16 7	19 44 48	4♈27	7	13	22	14	6	6	9	7
12	17 20 4	20 42 9	18 1	9	15	22	15	6	6	9	7
13	17 24 0	21 39 29	2♉ 1	11	16	22	15	6	6	10	7
14	17 27 57	22 36 48	16 27	12	17	22	15	6	6	10	7
15	17 31 53	23 34 8	1♊17	14	18	22	15	6	6	10	7
16	17 35 50	24 31 26	16 23	16	20	23	15	6	6	10	7
17	17 39 47	25 28 45	1♋38	17	21	23	15	6	6	10	7
18	17 43 43	26 26 2	16 50	19	22	23	16	6	6	10	7
19	17 47 40	27 23 19	1♌51	20	23	23	16	6	6	10	7
20	17 51 36	28 20 36	16 30	22	25	23	16	6	6	10	7
21	17 55 33	29 17 51	0♍44	23	26	24	16	7	6	10	7
22	17 59 29	0♋15 6	14 29	24	27	24	16	7	6	10	7
23	18 3 26	1 12 20	27 47	26	28	24	16	7	6	10	7
24	18 7 22	2 9 34	10♎39	27	29	24	17	7	6	10	7
25	18 11 19	3 6 47	23 10	28	1♋	25	17	7	6	10	7
26	18 15 16	4 4 0	5♏25	29	2	25	17	7	6	10	7
27	18 19 12	5 1 12	17 28	1♌	3	25	17	7	6	10	7
28	18 23 9	5 58 23	29 23	2	4	26	17	7	6	10	7
29	18 27 5	6 55 35	11♐13	3	6	26	18	7	6	10	7
30	18 31 2	7 52 46	23 3	4	7	26	18	7	6	10	7

THE SUN ENTERS THE SIGN OF CANCER ON JUN 21 AT 17:40.

♈ ARIES ♉ TAURUS ♊ GEMINI ♋ CANCER ♌ LEO ♍ VIRGO ♎ LIBRA ♏ SCORPIO ♐ SAGITTARIUS ♑ CAPRICORN ♒ AQUARIUS ♓ PISCES

SIDEREAL SUN MOON MERCURY VENUS MARS JUPITER SATURN URANUS NEPTUNE PLUTO

DAY	TIME	☉	☽	☿	♀	♂	♃	♄	♅	♆	♇
	h m s	° ' "	° '	°	°	°	°	°	°	°	°
J 1	18 34 58	8♋49 57	4♑53	4♌	8♋	26♎	18♌	7♍	6♓R	10♌	7♋
U 2	18 38 55	9 47 7	16 47	5	9	27	18	7	5	10	7
L 3	18 42 51	10 44 18	28 45	6	10	27	18	7	5	10	7
Y 4	18 46 48	11 41 29	10♒49	7	12	27	19	8	5	10	7
5	18 50 45	12 38 40	23 1	7	13	28	19	8	5	10	7
6	18 54 41	13 35 51	5♓22	8	14	28	19	8	5	10	7
7	18 58 38	14 33 2	17 56	9	15	29	19	8	5	10	7
8	19 2 34	15 30 14	0♈44	9	17	29	19	8	5	10	7
9	19 6 31	16 27 26	13 50	9	18	29	20	8	5	10	8
10	19 10 27	17 24 39	27 17	10	19	0♏	20	8	5	10	8
11	19 14 24	18 21 52	11♉ 7	10	20	0	20	8	5	10	8
12	19 18 20	19 19 5	25 22	10	22	0	20	8	5	10	8
13	19 22 17	20 16 20	9♊59	10 R	23	1	20	8	5	10	8
14	19 26 14	21 13 34	24 56	10	24	1	21	8	5	11	8
15	19 30 10	22 10 50	10♋ 4	10	25	2	21	9	5	11	8
16	19 34 7	23 8 5	25 15	10	26	2	21	9	5	11	8
17	19 38 3	24 5 21	10♌18	10	28	3	21	9	5	11	8
18	19 42 0	25 2 38	25 3	10	29	3	21	9	5	11	8
19	19 45 56	25 59 54	9♍23	9	0♌	3	22	9	5	11	8
20	19 49 53	26 57 11	23 14	9	1	4	22	9	5	11	8
21	19 53 49	27 54 28	6♎36	8	3	4	22	9	5	11	8
22	19 57 46	28 51 45	19 31	8	4	5	22	9	5	11	8
23	20 1 43	29 49 3	2♏ 2	7	5	5	22	9	5	11	8
24	20 5 39	0♌46 21	14 16	6	6	6	23	10	5	11	8
25	20 9 36	1 43 39	26 16	6	8	6	23	10	5	11	8
26	20 13 32	2 40 58	8♐ 9	5	9	7	23	10	5	11	8
27	20 17 29	3 38 18	19 58	4	10	7	23	10	5	11	8
28	20 21 25	4 35 38	1♑47	3	11	8	23	10	5	11	8
29	20 25 22	5 32 58	13 41	3	13	8	24	10	5	11	8
30	20 29 18	6 30 20	25 40	2	14	9	24	10	5	11	8
31	20 33 15	7 27 42	7♒47	1	15	9	24	10	5	11	8

THE SUN ENTERS THE SIGN OF LEO ON JUL 23 AT 04:35.

DAY	TIME	☉	☽	☿	♀	♂	♃	♄	♅	♆	♇
	h m s	° ' "	° '	°	°	°	°	°	°	°	°
A 1	20 37 12	8♌25 5	20♒ 2	1♌R	16♌	10♏	24♌	10♍	5♓R	11♌	8♋
U 2	20 41 8	9 22 28	2♓26	0	17	10	25	11	5	11	8
G 3	20 45 5	10 19 53	15 1	0	19	11	25	11	5	11	8
U 4	20 49 1	11 17 19	27 46	0	20	11	25	11	5	11	8
S 5	20 52 58	12 14 46	10♈43	29♋	21	12	25	11	5	11	8
T 6	20 56 54	13 12 14	23 54	29 D	22	12	25	11	5	11	8
7	21 0 51	14 9 44	7♉21	29	24	13	26	11	4	11	8
8	21 4 47	15 7 15	21 6	29	25	13	26	11	4	11	8
9	21 8 44	16 4 47	5♊10	0♌	26	14	26	11	4	11	8
10	21 12 41	17 2 21	19 32	0	27	15	26	11	4	11	8
11	21 16 37	17 59 57	4♋11	0	29	15	26	12	4	12	8
12	21 20 34	18 57 33	19 1	1	0♍	16	27	12	4	12	8
13	21 24 30	19 55 11	3♌55	1	1	16	27	12	4	12	8
14	21 28 27	20 52 51	18 45	2	2	17	27	12	4	12	8
15	21 32 23	21 50 31	3♍21	3	3	17	27	12	4	12	8
16	21 36 20	22 48 13	17 36	4	5	18	28	12	4	12	8
17	21 40 16	23 45 56	1♎26	5	6	19	28	12	4	12	8
18	21 44 13	24 43 40	14 49	6	7	19	28	12	4	12	8
19	21 48 10	25 41 25	27 46	8	8	20	28	13	4	12	8
20	21 52 6	26 39 11	10♏20	9	10	20	28	13	4	12	8
21	21 56 3	27 36 59	22 35	11	11	21	29	13	4	12	8
22	21 59 59	28 34 47	4♐37	12	12	21	29	13	4	12	8
23	22 3 56	29 32 37	16 30	14	13	22	29	13	4	12	8
24	22 7 52	0♍30 28	28 20	15	15	23	29	13	4	12	9
25	22 11 49	1 28 20	10♑12	17	16	23	0♍	13	4	12	9
26	22 15 45	2 26 14	22 9	19	17	24	0	13	4	12	9
27	22 19 42	3 24 9	4♒15	21	18	24	0	14	4	12	9
28	22 23 39	4 22 5	16 31	23	20	25	0	14	4	12	9
29	22 27 35	5 20 3	29 0	25	21	26	0	14	4	12	9
30	22 31 32	6 18 3	11♓40	27	22	26	1	14	4	12	9
31	22 35 28	7 16 4	24 33	28	23	27	1	14	4	12	9

THE SUN ENTERS THE SIGN OF VIRGO ON AUG 23 AT 11:22.

DAY	TIME	☉	☽	☿	♀	♂	♃	♄	♅	♆	♇
	h m s	° ' "	° '	°	°	°	°	°	°	°	°
S 1	22 39 25	8♍14 6	7♈37	0♍	24♍	28♏	1♍	14♍	4♓R	12♌	9♋
E 2	22 43 21	9 12 11	20 53	2	26	28	1	14	3	12	9
P 3	22 47 18	10 10 18	4♉19	4	27	29	1	14	3	12	9
T 4	22 51 14	11 8 26	17 57	6	28	29	2	15	3	12	9
E 5	22 55 11	12 6 36	1♊45	8	29	0♐	2	15	3	12	9
M 6	22 59 7	13 4 49	15 46	10	1♎	1	2	15	3	12	9
B 7	23 3 4	14 3 4	29 58	12	2	1	2	15	3	12	9
E 8	23 7 1	15 1 20	14♋19	14	3	2	3	15	3	13	9
R 9	23 10 57	15 59 39	28 46	16	4	3	3	15	3	13	9
10	23 14 54	16 58 0	13♌15	18	6	3	3	15	3	13	9
11	23 18 50	17 56 23	27 40	20	7	4	3	15	3	13	9
12	23 22 47	18 54 47	11♍54	22	8	5	3	16	3	13	9
13	23 26 43	19 53 14	25 53	23	9	5	4	16	3	13	9
14	23 30 40	20 51 42	9♎32	25	10	6	4	16	3	13	9
15	23 34 36	21 50 12	22 48	27	12	7	4	16	3	13	9
16	23 38 33	22 48 44	5♏42	29	13	7	4	16	3	13	9
17	23 42 30	23 47 18	18 15	0♎	14	8	4	16	3	13	9
18	23 46 26	24 45 53	0♐31	2	15	9	5	16	3	13	9
19	23 50 23	25 44 30	12 34	4	17	9	5	16	3	13	9
20	23 54 19	26 43 9	24 29	6	18	10	5	17	3	13	9
21	23 58 16	27 41 49	6♑21	7	19	11	5	17	3	13	9
22	0 2 12	28 40 31	18 14	9	20	11	6	17	3	13	9
23	0 6 9	29 39 15	0♒14	11	22	12	6	17	3	13	9
24	0 10 5	0♎38 1	12 24	12	23	13	6	17	3	13	9
25	0 14 2	1 36 48	24 47	14	24	13	6	17	3	13	9
26	0 17 59	2 35 37	7♓26	16	25	14	6	17	3	13	9
27	0 21 55	3 34 28	20 21	17	27	15	7	17	3	13	9
28	0 25 52	4 33 21	3♈33	19	28	15	7	18	3	13	9
29	0 29 48	5 32 16	17 0	20	29	16	7	18	2	13	9
30	0 33 45	6 31 13	0♉40	22	0♏	17	7	18	2	13	9

THE SUN ENTERS THE SIGN OF LIBRA ON SEP 23 AT 08:29.

SIDEREAL SUN MOON MERCURY VENUS MARS JUPITER SATURN URANUS NEPTUNE PLUTO

DAY	TIME	☉	☽	☿	♀	♂	♃	♄	♅	♆	♇
	h m s	° ' "	° '	°	°	°	°	°	°	°	°
O 1	0 37 41	7♎30 12	14♉31	23♎	1♏	17♐	7♍	18♍	2♓R	13♌	9♋
C 2	0 41 38	8 29 14	28 31	25	3	18	8	18	2	13	9
T 3	0 45 34	9 28 18	12♊36	26	4	19	8	18	2	13	9
O 4	0 49 31	10 27 24	26 46	28	5	20	8	18	2	13	9
B 5	0 53 27	11 26 32	10♋57	29	6	20	8	18	2	13	9
E 6	0 57 24	12 25 43	25 8	1♏	8	21	8	18	2	13	9
R 7	1 1 21	13 24 56	9♌17	2	9	22	9	19	2	13	9
8	1 5 17	14 24 12	23 22	4	10	22	9	19	2	13	9
9	1 9 14	15 23 30	7♍19	5	11	23	9	19	2	13	9 R
10	1 13 10	16 22 49	21 5	7	13	24	9	19	2	13	9
11	1 17 7	17 22 11	4♎38	8	14	25	9	19	2	13	9
12	1 21 3	18 21 36	17 56	9	15	25	10	19	2	13	9
13	1 25 0	19 21 2	0♏57	11	16	26	10	19	2	13	9
14	1 28 56	20 20 30	13 41	12	17	27	10	19	2	13	9
15	1 32 53	21 20 0	26 9	13	19	27	10	20	2	13	9
16	1 36 50	22 19 33	8♐23	15	20	28	10	20	2	13	9
17	1 40 46	23 19 7	20 25	16	21	29	10	20	2	14	9
18	1 44 43	24 18 42	2♑20	17	22	0♑	11	20	2	14	9
19	1 48 39	25 18 20	14 12	18	24	0	11	20	2	14	9
20	1 52 36	26 17 59	26 5	20	25	1	11	20	2	14	9
21	1 56 32	27 17 40	8♒ 4	21	26	2	11	20	2	14	9
22	2 0 29	28 17 23	20 14	22	27	3	11	20	2	14	9
23	2 4 25	29 17 7	2♓38	23	29	3	12	20	2	14	9
24	2 8 22	0♏16 53	15 21	24	0♐	4	12	20	2	14	9
25	2 12 19	1 16 41	28 25	25	1	5	12	21	2	14	9
26	2 16 15	2 16 31	11♈50	26	2	5	12	21	2	14	9
27	2 20 12	3 16 23	25 36	27	3	6	12	21	2	14	9
28	2 24 8	4 16 16	9♉40	28	5	7	12	21	2	14	9
29	2 28 5	5 16 12	23 59	29	6	8	13	21	2	14	9
30	2 32 1	6 16 9	8♊28	0♐	7	8	13	21	2	14	9
31	2 35 58	7 16 9	23 0	0	8	9	13	21	2	14	9

THE SUN ENTERS THE SIGN OF SCORPIO ON OCT 23 AT 17:13.

DAY	TIME	☉	☽	☿	♀	♂	♃	♄	♅	♆	♇
	h m s	° ' "	° '	°	°	°	°	°	°	°	°
N 1	2 39 54	8♏16 11	7♋30	1♐	10♐	10♑	13♍	21♍	2♓R	14♌	9♋R
O 2	2 43 51	9 16 14	21 54	1	11	11	13	21	2	14	9
V 3	2 47 48	10 16 20	6♌ 8	2	12	11	13	22	2	14	9
E 4	2 51 44	11 16 28	20 10	2	13	12	14	22	2	14	9
M 5	2 55 41	12 16 39	3♍58	2 R	14	13	14	22	2	14	9
B 6	2 59 37	13 16 51	17 33	2	16	14	14	22	2	14	9
E 7	3 3 34	14 17 5	0♎53	2	17	14	14	22	2	14	9
R 8	3 7 30	15 17 21	14 0	2	18	15	14	22	2	14	9
9	3 11 27	16 17 40	26 54	1	19	16	14	22	2	14	9
10	3 15 23	17 18 0	9♏35	1	21	17	15	22	2	14	9
11	3 19 20	18 18 21	22 4	0	22	17	15	22	2 D	14	9
12	3 23 17	19 18 45	4♐22	29♏	23	18	15	22	2	14	9
13	3 27 13	20 19 10	16 30	28	24	19	15	22	2	14	9
14	3 31 10	21 19 37	28 29	27	25	20	15	23	2	14	9
15	3 35 6	22 20 5	10♑23	25	27	20	15	23	2	14	9
16	3 39 3	23 20 34	22 14	24	28	21	15	23	2	14 R	9
17	3 42 59	24 21 5	4♒ 5	23	29	22	15	23	2	14	9
18	3 46 56	25 21 37	16 2	21	0♑	23	16	23	2	14	9
19	3 50 52	26 22 11	28 8	20	2	23	16	23	2	14	9
20	3 54 49	27 22 45	10♓28	19	3	24	16	23	2	14	9
21	3 58 46	28 23 21	23 7	18	4	25	16	23	2	14	9
22	4 2 42	29 23 58	6♈ 9	17	5	26	16	23	2	14	9
23	4 6 39	0♐24 36	19 36	17	6	27	16	23	2	14	9
24	4 10 35	1 25 15	3♉30	16	8	27	16	23	2	14	9
25	4 14 32	2 25 56	17 48	16 D	9	28	16	23	2	14	9
26	4 18 28	3 26 38	2♊28	16	10	29	17	23	2	14	9
27	4 22 25	4 27 21	17 22	16	11	0♒	17	23	2	14	8
28	4 26 21	5 28 6	2♋23	17	12	0	17	24	2	14	8
29	4 30 18	6 28 52	17 20	17	14	1	17	24	2	14	8
30	4 34 15	7 29 39	2♌ 7	18	15	2	17	24	2	14	8

THE SUN ENTERS THE SIGN OF SAGITTARIUS ON NOV 22 AT 14:16.

DAY	TIME	☉	☽	☿	♀	♂	♃	♄	♅	♆	♇
	h m s	° ' "	° '	°	°	°	°	°	°	°	°
D 1	4 38 11	8♐30 28	16♌36	18♏	16♑	3♒	17♍	24♍	2♓	14♌R	8♋R
E 2	4 42 8	9 31 18	0♍44	19	17	3	17	24	2	14	8
C 3	4 46 4	10 32 10	14 29	20	19	4	17	24	2	14	8
E 4	4 50 1	11 33 3	27 53	21	20	5	17	24	2	14	8
M 5	4 53 57	12 33 58	10♎58	22	21	6	18	24	2	14	8
B 6	4 57 54	13 34 53	23 46	23	22	6	18	24	2	14	8
E 7	5 1 50	14 35 50	6♏20	25	23	7	18	24	2	14	8
R 8	5 5 47	15 36 48	18 43	26	25	8	18	24	2	14	8
9	5 9 44	16 37 48	0♐56	27	26	9	18	24	2	14	8
10	5 13 40	17 38 48	13 2	28	27	10	18	24	2	14	8
11	5 17 37	18 39 49	25 2	0♐	28	10	18	24	2	14	8
12	5 21 33	19 40 51	6♑57	1	29	11	18	24	2	14	8
13	5 25 30	20 41 54	18 49	2	1♒	12	18	24	2	14	8
14	5 29 26	21 42 57	0♒40	4	2	13	18	24	2	14	8
15	5 33 23	22 44 1	12 32	5	3	13	18	24	2	14	8
16	5 37 19	23 45 5	24 28	7	4	14	18	24	2	14	8
17	5 41 16	24 46 10	6♓31	8	5	15	18	24	2	14	8
18	5 45 13	25 47 15	18 47	10	7	16	18	25	2	13	8
19	5 49 9	26 48 20	1♈19	11	8	17	19	25	2	13	8
20	5 53 6	27 49 25	14 13	13	9	17	19	25	2	13	8
21	5 57 2	28 50 31	27 32	14	10	18	19	25	2	13	8
22	6 0 59	29 51 37	11♉19	16	11	19	19	25	2	13	8
23	6 4 55	0♑52 44	25 36	17	13	20	19	25	2	13	8
24	6 8 52	1 53 50	10♊19	19	14	20	19	25	3	13	8
25	6 12 48	2 54 57	25 25	20	15	21	19	25	3	13	8
26	6 16 45	3 56 4	10♋42	22	16	22	19	25	3	13	8
27	6 20 42	4 57 12	26 1	23	17	23	19	25	3	13	8
28	6 24 38	5 58 19	11♌10	25	18	24	19	25	3	13	8
29	6 28 35	6 59 28	25 59	26	20	24	19	25	3	13	8
30	6 32 31	8 0 36	10♍22	28	21	25	19	25	3	13	8
31	6 36 28	9 1 45	24 17	29	22	26	19	25	3	13	8

THE SUN ENTERS THE SIGN OF CAPRICORN ON DEC 22 AT 03:18.

♈ ARIES ♉ TAURUS ♊ GEMINI ♋ CANCER ♌ LEO ♍ VIRGO ♎ LIBRA ♏ SCORPIO ♐ SAGITTARIUS ♑ CAPRICORN ♒ AQUARIUS ♓ PISCES

1921

SIDEREAL SUN MOON MERCURY VENUS MARS JUPITER SATURN URANUS NEPTUNE PLUTO

DAY	TIME	☉	☽	☿	♀	♂	♃	♄	♅	♆	♇
	h m s	° ' "	° '	°	°	°	°	°	°	°	°
J 1	6 40 24	10♑ 2 54	7♎44	1♑	23♒	27♒	19♍	25♍	3♓	13♌R	8♋R
A 2	6 44 21	11 4 4	20 45	2	24	27	19	25	3	13	8
N 3	6 48 17	12 5 14	3♏26	4	26	28	19 R	25	3	13	8
U 4	6 52 14	13 6 24	15 49	5	27	29	19	25 R	3	13	8
A 5	6 56 11	14 7 34	28 0	7	28	0♓	19	25	3	13	8
R 6	7 0 7	15 8 45	10♐ 3	9	29	1	19	25	3	13	8
Y 7	7 4 4	16 9 55	21 59	10	0♓	1	19	25	3	13	8
8	7 8 0	17 11 6	3♑53	12	1	2	19	25	3	13	8
9	7 11 57	18 12 16	15 45	13	2	3	19	25	3	13	8
10	7 15 53	19 13 26	27 37	15	4	4	19	25	3	13	8
11	7 19 50	20 14 36	9♒30	17	5	4	19	25	3	13	8
12	7 23 46	21 15 45	21 25	18	6	5	19	25	3	13	8
13	7 27 43	22 16 54	3♓25	20	7	6	19	25	3	13	8
14	7 31 40	23 18 2	15 32	22	8	7	19	25	3	13	8
15	7 35 36	24 19 10	27 48	23	9	8	19	25	3	13	8
16	7 39 33	25 20 17	10♈18	25	10	8	19	25	3	13	8
17	7 43 29	26 21 23	23 6	26	12	9	19	25	4	13	7
18	7 47 26	27 22 28	6♉16	28	13	10	19	25	4	13	7
19	7 51 22	28 23 32	19 51	0♒	14	11	19	25	4	13	7
20	7 55 19	29 24 36	3♊55	2	15	11	18	25	4	13	7
21	7 59 15	0♒25 38	18 27	3	16	12	18	25	4	13	7
22	8 3 12	1 26 40	3♋24	5	17	13	18	25	4	13	7
23	8 7 9	2 27 41	18 38	7	18	14	18	24	4	13	7
24	8 11 5	3 28 41	4♌ 0	8	19	14	18	24	4	13	7
25	8 15 2	4 29 40	19 17	10	21	15	18	24	4	13	7
26	8 18 58	5 30 38	4♍18	12	22	16	18	24	4	13	7
27	8 22 55	6 31 36	18 55	14	23	17	18	24	4	13	7
28	8 26 51	7 32 33	3♎ 2	15	24	18	18	24	4	13	7
29	8 30 48	8 33 29	16 39	17	25	18	18	24	4	12	7
30	8 34 44	9 34 25	29 47	19	26	19	18	24	4	12	7
31	8 38 41	10 35 19	12♏30	21	27	20	18	24	4	12	7

THE SUN ENTERS THE SIGN OF AQUARIUS ON JAN 20 AT 13:55.

DAY	TIME	☉	☽	☿	♀	♂	♃	♄	♅	♆	♇
	h m s	° ' "	° '	°	°	°	°	°	°	°	°
F 1	8 42 38	11♒36 14	24♏53	22♒	28♓	21♓	18♍R	24♍R	4♓	12♌R	7♋R
E 2	8 46 34	12 37 7	7♐ 1	24	29	21	18	24	4	12	7
B 3	8 50 31	13 37 59	19 0	26	0♈	22	17	24	4	12	7
R 4	8 54 27	14 38 51	0♑52	28	1	23	17	24	4	12	7
U 5	8 58 24	15 39 41	12 43	29	2	24	17	24	5	12	7
A 6	9 2 20	16 40 31	24 34	1♓	3	24	17	24	5	12	7
R 7	9 6 17	17 41 19	6♒27	3	4	25	17	24	5	12	7
Y 8	9 10 13	18 42 6	18 25	4	5	26	17	24	5	12	7
9	9 14 10	19 42 52	0♓28	6	6	27	17	24	5	12	7
10	9 18 7	20 43 37	12 38	7	7	28	17	24	5	12	7
11	9 22 3	21 44 20	24 55	9	8	28	17	24	5	12	7
12	9 26 0	22 45 1	7♈21	10	9	29	17	24	5	12	7
13	9 29 56	23 45 41	19 58	12	10	0⊙	16	23	5	12	7
14	9 33 53	24 46 19	2♉50	13	11	1♈	16	23	5	12	7
15	9 37 49	25 46 56	15 59	14	12	1	16	23	5	12	7
16	9 41 46	26 47 31	29 29	15	13	2	16	23	5	12	7
17	9 45 42	27 48 3	13♊21	16	14	3	16	23	5	12	7
18	9 49 39	28 48 35	27 36	16	15	4	16	23	5	12	7
19	9 53 36	29 49 4	12♋14	17	16	4	16	23	5	12	7
20	9 57 32	0♓49 32	27 8	17	17	5	16	23	5	12	7
21	10 1 29	1 49 57	12♌13	18 R	18	6	16	23	5	12	7
22	10 5 25	2 50 21	27 17	18	19	7	15	23	5	12	7
23	10 9 22	3 50 43	12♍12	18	20	7	15	23	6	12	7
24	10 13 18	4 51 4	26 48	17	21	8	15	23	6	12	7
25	10 17 15	5 51 23	10♎59	17	22	9	15	23	6	12	7
26	10 21 11	6 51 40	24 43	16	23	10	15	23	6	12	7
27	10 25 8	7 51 56	7♏59	16	23	10	15	22	6	12	7
28	10 29 5	8 52 11	20 49	15	24	11	15	22	6	12	7

THE SUN ENTERS THE SIGN OF PISCES ON FEB 19 AT 04:20.

DAY	TIME	☉	☽	☿	♀	♂	♃	♄	♅	♆	♇
	h m s	° ' "	° '	°	°	°	°	°	°	°	°
M 1	10 33 1	9♓52 24	3♐17	14♓R	25♈	12♈	15♍R	22♍R	6♓	12♌R	7♋R
A 2	10 36 58	10 52 36	15 29	13	26	13	14	22	6	12	7
R 3	10 40 54	11 52 46	27 29	12	27	13	14	22	6	12	7
C 4	10 44 51	12 52 54	9♑22	11	27	14	14	22	6	12	7
H 5	10 48 47	13 53 1	21 13	10	28	15	14	22	6	12	7
6	10 52 44	14 53 6	3♒ 5	9	29	16	14	22	6	12	7
7	10 56 40	15 53 9	15 2	8	0♉	16	14	22	6	12	7
8	11 0 37	16 53 11	27 6	7	0	17	14	22	6	11	7
9	11 4 34	17 53 11	9♓18	6	1	18	13	22	6	11	7
10	11 8 30	18 53 9	21 40	6	2	19	13	22	6	11	7
11	11 12 27	19 53 5	4♈13	5	2	19	13	22	6	11	7
12	11 16 23	20 52 59	16 57	4	3	20	13	21	6	11	7
13	11 20 20	21 52 51	29 52	4	4	21	13	21	7	11	7
14	11 24 16	22 52 40	13♉ 0	4	4	22	13	21	7	11	7
15	11 28 13	23 52 28	26 21	4	5	22	13	21	7	11	7
16	11 32 9	24 52 14	9♊57	3 D	5	23	13	21	7	11	7
17	11 36 6	25 51 57	23 48	3	6	24	12	21	7	11	7
18	11 40 2	26 51 37	7♋54	4	6	25	12	21	7	11	7
19	11 43 59	27 51 16	22 14	4	7	25	12	21	7	11	7
20	11 47 56	28 50 52	6♌45	4	7	26	12	21	7	11	7
21	11 51 52	29 50 26	21 23	4	8	27	12	21	7	11	7 D
22	11 55 49	0♈49 58	6♍ 1	5	8	28	12	21	7	11	7
23	11 59 45	1 49 27	20 32	5	9	28	12	21	7	11	7
24	12 3 42	2 48 55	4♎51	6	9	29	12	21	7	11	7
25	12 7 38	3 48 20	18 51	7	9	0♉	11	20	7	11	7
26	12 11 35	4 47 43	2♏30	7	9	1	11	20	7	11	7
27	12 15 31	5 47 5	15 45	8	10	1	11	20	7	11	7
28	12 19 28	6 46 24	28 38	9	10	2	11	20	7	11	7
29	12 23 25	7 45 42	11♐11	10	10	3	11	20	7	11	7
30	12 27 21	8 44 58	23 28	11	10	3	11	20	7	11	7
31	12 31 18	9 44 13	5♑31	12	10	4	11	20	8	11	7

THE SUN ENTERS THE SIGN OF ARIES ON MAR 21 AT 03:51.

DAY	TIME	☉	☽	☿	♀	♂	♃	♄	♅	♆	♇
	h m s	° ' "	° '	°	°	°	°	°	°	°	°
A 1	12 35 14	10♈43 25	17♑27	13♓	10♉R	5♉	11♍R	20♍R	8♓	11♌R	7♋
P 2	12 39 11	11 42 36	29 19	14	10	6	11	20	8	11	7
R 3	12 43 7	12 41 45	11♒13	15	10	6	11	20	8	11	7
I 4	12 47 4	13 40 52	23 13	16	10	7	10	20	8	11	7
L 5	12 51 0	14 39 57	5♓21	18	10	8	10	20	8	11	7
6	12 54 57	15 39 0	17 41	19	10	9	10	20	8	11	7
7	12 58 54	16 38 1	0♈15	20	10	9	10	20	8	11	7
8	13 2 50	17 37 1	13 4	21	9	10	10	19	8	11	7
9	13 6 47	18 35 58	26 8	23	9	11	10	19	8	11	7
10	13 10 43	19 34 53	9♉27	24	9	11	10	19	8	11	7
11	13 14 40	20 33 47	23 0	25	8	12	10	19	8	11	7
12	13 18 36	21 32 38	6♊45	27	8	13	10	19	8	11	7
13	13 22 33	22 31 27	20 39	28	8	14	10	19	8	11	7
14	13 26 29	23 30 14	4♋43	0⊙	7	14	10	19	8	11	7
15	13 30 26	24 28 58	18 52	1♈	7	15	10	19	8	11	7
16	13 34 23	25 27 40	3♌ 5	3	6	16	10	19	8	11	7
17	13 38 19	26 26 20	17 20	4	6	16	9	19	8	11	7
18	13 42 16	27 24 58	1♍34	6	5	17	9	19	8	11	7
19	13 46 12	28 23 33	15 44	8	4	18	9	19	8	11	7
20	13 50 9	29 22 6	29 46	9	4	19	9	19	8	11	7
21	13 54 5	0♉20 37	13♎37	11	3	19	9	19	8	11	7
22	13 58 2	1 19 6	27 15	13	2	20	9	19	9	11 D	7
23	14 1 58	2 17 34	10♏37	14	2	21	9	19	9	11	7
24	14 5 55	3 15 59	23 42	16	1	21	9	19	9	11	7
25	14 9 51	4 14 23	6♐30	18	1	22	9	19	9	11	7
26	14 13 48	5 12 45	19 1	20	0	23	9	18	9	11	7
27	14 17 45	6 11 5	1♑17	22	29♈	24	9	18	9	11	7
28	14 21 41	7 9 24	13 22	24	29	24	9	18	9	11	7
29	14 25 38	8 7 41	25 19	26	28	25	9	18	9	11	7
30	14 29 34	9 5 57	7♒13	27	28	26	9	18	9	11	7

THE SUN ENTERS THE SIGN OF TAURUS ON APR 20 AT 15:32.

DAY	TIME	☉	☽	☿	♀	♂	♃	♄	♅	♆	♇
	h m s	° ' "	° '	°	°	°	°	°	°	°	°
M 1	14 33 31	10♉ 4 11	19♒ 7	29♈	27♈R	26♉	9♍R	18♍R	9♓	11♌	7♋
A 2	14 37 27	11 2 23	1♓ 7	1♉	27	27	9	18	9	11	7
Y 3	14 41 24	12 0 34	13 17	3	26	28	9	18	9	11	7
4	14 45 20	12 58 44	25 41	5	26	29	9	18	9	11	7
5	14 49 17	13 56 52	8♈22	8	25	29	9	18	9	11	7
6	14 53 14	14 54 59	21 24	10	25	0♊	9 D	18	9	11	7
7	14 57 10	15 53 4	4♉45	12	25	1	9	18	9	11	7
8	15 1 7	16 51 7	18 27	14	25	1	9	18	9	11	7
9	15 5 3	17 49 9	2♊26	16	24	2	9	18	9	11	7
10	15 9 0	18 47 9	16 39	18	24	3	9	18	9	11	7
11	15 12 56	19 45 8	1♋ 1	20	24	3	9	18	9	11	7
12	15 16 53	20 43 5	15 26	23	24	4	9	18	9	11	7
13	15 20 49	21 41 0	29 50	25	24	5	9	18	9	11	7
14	15 24 46	22 38 53	14♌ 9	27	24 D	6	9	18	9	11	7
15	15 28 43	23 36 44	28 19	29	24	6	9	18	9	11	7
16	15 32 39	24 34 34	12♍19	1♊	24	7	9	18	9	11	7
17	15 36 36	25 32 21	26 8	3	24	8	9	18	9	11	7
18	15 40 32	26 30 8	9♎45	6	24	8	9	18	9	11	7
19	15 44 29	27 27 52	23 10	8	24	9	9	18	9	11	7
20	15 48 25	28 25 35	6♏23	10	25	10	9	18 D	9	11	7
21	15 52 22	29 23 17	19 23	12	25	10	9	18	9	11	7
22	15 56 18	0♊20 57	2♐11	14	25	11	9	18	9	11	7
23	16 0 15	1 18 36	14 46	16	25	12	9	18	9	11	8
24	16 4 12	2 16 13	27 9	18	26	12	9	18	9	11	8
25	16 8 8	3 13 50	9♑21	19	26	13	9	18	9	11	8
26	16 12 5	4 11 26	21 24	21	26	14	10	18	9	11	8
27	16 16 1	5 9 0	3♒20	23	27	15	10	18	10	11	8
28	16 19 58	6 6 34	15 12	25	27	15	10	18	10	11	8
29	16 23 54	7 4 6	27 6	26	28	16	10	18	10	11	8
30	16 27 51	8 1 38	9♓ 4	28	28	17	10	18	10	11	8
31	16 31 47	8 59 9	21 13	0♋	29	17	10	18	10	11	8

THE SUN ENTERS THE SIGN OF GEMINI ON MAY 21 AT 15:17.

DAY	TIME	☉	☽	☿	♀	♂	♃	♄	♅	♆	♇
	h m s	° ' "	° '	°	°	°	°	°	°	°	°
J 1	16 35 44	9♊56 39	3♈36	1♋	29♈	18♊	10♍	18♍	10♓	11♌	8♋
U 2	16 39 41	10 54 9	16 19	3	0♉	19	10	18	10	11	8
N 3	16 43 37	11 51 37	29 25	4	0	19	10	18	10	11	8
E 4	16 47 34	12 49 5	12♉56	6	1	20	10	18	10	11	8
5	16 51 30	13 46 32	26 52	7	2	21	10	18	10	11	8
6	16 55 27	14 43 59	11♊12	8	2	21	10	18	10	11	8
7	16 59 23	15 41 24	25 50	9	3	22	10	18	10	12	8
8	17 3 20	16 38 49	10♋38	11	4	23	11	18	10	12	8
9	17 7 16	17 36 13	25 29	12	4	23	11	18	10	12	8
10	17 11 13	18 33 35	10♌15	13	5	24	11	18	10	12	8
11	17 15 10	19 30 57	24 48	14	6	25	11	18	10	12	8
12	17 19 6	20 28 18	9♍ 5	15	7	25	11	18	10	12	8
13	17 23 3	21 25 37	23 2	16	7	26	11	18	10	12	8
14	17 26 59	22 22 56	6♎42	16	8	27	11	18	10 R	12	8
15	17 30 56	23 20 13	20 3	17	9	27	11	19	10	12	8
16	17 34 52	24 17 30	3♏ 9	18	10	28	11	19	10	12	8
17	17 38 49	25 14 46	16 2	18	11	29	11	19	10	12	8
18	17 42 45	26 12 1	28 42	19	11	29	12	19	10	12	8
19	17 46 42	27 9 16	11♐12	19	12	0♋	12	19	10	12	8
20	17 50 39	28 6 30	23 33	20	13	1	12	19	10	12	8
21	17 54 35	29 3 44	5♑45	20	14	1	12	19	10	12	8
22	17 58 32	0♋ 0 58	17 50	21	15	2	12	19	10	12	8
23	18 2 28	0 58 11	29 48	21	16	3	12	19	10	12	8
24	18 6 25	1 55 23	11♒41	21	17	3	12	19	10	12	8
25	18 10 21	2 52 36	23 33	21 R	17	4	12	19	10	12	8
26	18 14 18	3 49 48	5♓25	21	18	5	13	19	10	12	8
27	18 18 14	4 47 1	17 22	21	19	5	13	19	10	12	8
28	18 22 11	5 44 13	29 28	21	20	6	13	19	10	12	8
29	18 26 8	6 41 26	11♈49	20	21	7	13	19	10	12	8
30	18 30 4	7 38 38	24 29	20	22	7	13	19	10	12	8

THE SUN ENTERS THE SIGN OF CANCER ON JUN 21 AT 23:36.

♈ ARIES ♉ TAURUS ♊ GEMINI ♋ CANCER ♌ LEO ♍ VIRGO ♎ LIBRA ♏ SCORPIO ♐ SAGITTARIUS ♑ CAPRICORN ♒ AQUARIUS ♓ PISCES

SIDEREAL SUN MOON MERCURY VENUS MARS JUPITER SATURN URANUS NEPTUNE PLUTO

DAY	TIME h m s	☉ ° ' "	☽ ° '	☿ °	♀ °	♂ °	♃ °	♄ °	♅ °	♆ °	♇ °
J 1	18 34 1	8♋35 51	7♉33	20♋R	23♉	8♋	13♍	19♍	10♓R	12♌	8♋
U 2	18 37 57	9 33 4	21 4	19	24	9	13	19	10	12	8
L 3	18 41 54	10 30 17	5♊ 5	19	25	9	14	20	10	12	8
Y 4	18 45 50	11 27 31	19 33	18	26	10	14	20	9	12	9
5	18 49 47	12 24 44	4♋25	17	27	11	14	20	9	12	9
6	18 53 43	13 21 58	19 31	17	28	11	14	20	9	12	9
7	18 57 40	14 19 11	4♌42	16	29	12	14	20	9	12	9
8	19 1 37	15 16 25	19 48	16	0♊	13	14	20	9	12	9
9	19 5 33	16 13 38	4♍39	15	1	13	14	20	9	12	9
10	19 9 30	17 10 52	19 8	14	2	14	15	20	9	12	9
11	19 13 26	18 8 5	3♎12	14	3	15	15	20	9	13	9
12	19 17 23	19 5 18	16 52	13	4	15	15	20	9	13	9
13	19 21 19	20 2 31	0♏ 9	13	5	16	15	20	9	13	9
14	19 25 16	20 59 45	13 6	12	6	17	15	20	9	13	9
15	19 29 12	21 56 58	25 47	12	7	17	15	20	9	13	9
16	19 33 9	22 54 11	8♐14	12	8	18	16	21	9	13	9
17	19 37 6	23 51 25	20 31	11	9	19	16	21	9	13	9
18	19 41 2	24 48 39	2♑40	11	10	19	16	21	9	13	9
19	19 44 59	25 45 53	14 42	11 D	11	20	16	21	9	13	9
20	19 48 55	26 43 8	26 40	11	12	21	16	21	9	13	9
21	19 52 52	27 40 23	8♒34	11	13	21	16	21	9	13	9
22	19 56 48	28 37 39	20 25	12	14	22	17	21	9	13	9
23	20 0 45	29 34 55	2♓17	12	15	23	17	21	9	13	9
24	20 4 42	0♌32 12	14 10	12	16	23	17	21	9	13	9
25	20 8 38	1 29 30	26 8	13	17	24	17	21	9	13	9
26	20 12 35	2 26 49	8♈15	13	18	25	17	21	9	13	9
27	20 16 31	3 24 9	20 35	14	19	25	17	22	9	13	9
28	20 20 28	4 21 29	3♉12	15	21	26	18	22	9	13	9
29	20 24 24	5 18 51	16 12	16	22	26	18	22	9	13	9
30	20 28 21	6 16 14	29 39	17	23	27	18	22	9	13	9
31	20 32 17	7 13 38	13♊34	18	24	28	18	22	9	13	9

THE SUN ENTERS THE SIGN OF LEO ON JUL 23 AT 10:31.

DAY	TIME h m s	☉ ° ' "	☽ ° '	☿ °	♀ °	♂ °	♃ °	♄ °	♅ °	♆ °	♇ °
A 1	20 36 14	8♌11 3	27♊59	19♋	25♊	28♋	18♍	22♍	9♓R	13♌	9♋
U 2	20 40 10	9 8 30	12♋49	20	26	29	19	22	9	13	9
G 3	20 44 7	10 5 57	27 58	22	27	0♌	19	22	9	13	9
U 4	20 48 4	11 3 25	13♌17	23	28	0	19	22	9	13	9
S 5	20 52 0	12 0 55	28 32	25	29	1	19	22	9	13	9
T 6	20 55 57	12 58 25	13♍35	26	0♋	2	19	23	9	13	9
7	20 59 53	13 55 56	28 17	28	2	2	20	23	9	14	9
8	21 3 50	14 53 27	12♎32	29	3	3	20	23	9	14	9
9	21 7 46	15 51 0	26 19	1♌	4	4	20	23	9	14	9
10	21 11 43	16 48 33	9♏40	3	5	4	20	23	8	14	9
11	21 15 39	17 46 8	22 36	5	6	5	20	23	8	14	9
12	21 19 36	18 43 43	5♐14	7	7	6	20	23	8	14	9
13	21 23 33	19 41 19	17 35	9	8	6	21	23	8	14	9
14	21 27 29	20 38 56	29 45	11	9	7	21	23	8	14	9
15	21 31 26	21 36 34	11♑46	13	11	7	21	23	8	14	9
16	21 35 22	22 34 14	23 42	15	12	8	21	24	8	14	9
17	21 39 19	23 31 54	5♒36	17	13	9	22	24	8	14	10
18	21 43 15	24 29 36	17 28	19	14	9	22	24	8	14	10
19	21 47 12	25 27 18	29 20	21	15	10	22	24	8	14	10
20	21 51 8	26 25 3	11♓15	23	16	11	22	24	8	14	10
21	21 55 5	27 22 48	23 13	25	17	11	22	24	8	14	10
22	21 59 2	28 20 36	5♈18	27	18	12	23	24	8	14	10
23	22 2 58	29 18 25	17 31	29	20	13	23	24	8	14	10
24	22 6 55	0♍16 15	29 56	1♍	21	13	23	25	8	14	10
25	22 10 51	1 14 7	12♉37	3	22	14	23	25	8	14	10
26	22 14 48	2 12 2	25 36	5	23	14	23	25	8	14	10
27	22 18 44	3 9 57	8♊59	7	24	15	24	25	8	14	10
28	22 22 41	4 7 55	22 46	9	25	16	24	25	8	14	10
29	22 26 37	5 5 55	6♋59	10	27	16	24	25	8	14	10
30	22 30 34	6 3 57	21 37	12	28	17	24	25	8	14	10
31	22 34 31	7 2 0	6♌34	14	29	18	24	25	8	14	10

THE SUN ENTERS THE SIGN OF VIRGO ON AUG 23 AT 17:16.

DAY	TIME h m s	☉ ° ' "	☽ ° '	☿ °	♀ °	♂ °	♃ °	♄ °	♅ °	♆ °	♇ °
S 1	22 38 27	8♍ 0 5	21♌42	16♍	0♌	18♌	25♍	25♍	8♓R	14♌	10♋
E 2	22 42 24	8 58 12	6♍53	18	1	19	25	26	8	14	10
P 3	22 46 20	9 56 21	21 55	20	2	20	25	26	8	15	10
T 4	22 50 17	10 54 31	6♎40	21	4	20	25	26	8	15	10
E 5	22 54 13	11 52 42	21 1	23	5	21	25	26	8	15	10
M 6	22 58 10	12 50 56	4♏56	25	6	21	26	26	7	15	10
B 7	23 2 6	13 49 11	18 23	26	7	22	26	26	7	15	10
E 8	23 6 3	14 47 27	1♐25	28	8	23	26	26	7	15	10
R 9	23 10 0	15 45 45	14 5	0♎	9	23	26	27	7	15	10
10	23 13 56	16 44 4	26 27	1	11	24	27	27	7	15	10
11	23 17 53	17 42 25	8♑35	3	12	25	27	27	7	15	10
12	23 21 49	18 40 48	20 34	5	13	25	27	27	7	15	10
13	23 25 46	19 39 12	2♒28	6	14	26	27	27	7	15	10
14	23 29 42	20 37 38	14 20	8	15	27	27	27	7	15	10
15	23 33 39	21 36 5	26 12	9	17	27	28	27	7	15	10
16	23 37 35	22 34 35	8♓ 8	11	18	28	28	27	7	15	10
17	23 41 32	23 33 6	20 9	12	19	28	28	27	7	15	10
18	23 45 28	24 31 39	2♈18	14	20	29	28	28	7	15	10
19	23 49 25	25 30 13	14 34	15	21	0♍	28	28	7	15	10
20	23 53 22	26 28 50	27 1	17	23	0	29	28	7	15	10
21	23 57 18	27 27 30	9♉40	18	24	1	29	28	7	15	10
22	0 1 15	28 26 11	22 32	20	25	2	29	28	7	15	10
23	0 5 11	29 24 54	5♊40	21	26	2	29	28	7	15	10
24	0 9 8	0♎23 40	19 6	23	27	3	0♎	28	7	15	10
25	0 13 4	1 22 28	2♋50	24	29	3	0	28	7	15	10
26	0 17 1	2 21 19	16 53	25	0♍	4	0	29	7	15	10
27	0 20 57	3 20 11	1♌14	27	1	5	0	29	7	15	10
28	0 24 54	4 19 6	15 50	28	2	5	0	29	7	15	10
29	0 28 51	5 18 3	0♍36	29	3	6	1	29	7	15	10
30	0 32 47	6 17 3	15 26	0♏	5	7	1	29	7	15	10

THE SUN ENTERS THE SIGN OF LIBRA ON SEP 23 AT 14:20.

SIDEREAL SUN MOON MERCURY VENUS MARS JUPITER SATURN URANUS NEPTUNE PLUTO

DAY	TIME h m s	☉ ° ' "	☽ ° '	☿ °	♀ °	♂ °	♃ °	♄ °	♅ °	♆ °	♇ °
O 1	0 36 44	7♎16 4	0♎12	2♏	6♍	7♍	1♎	29♍	7♓R	15♌	10♋
C 2	0 40 40	8 15 7	14 46	3	7	8	1	29	6	15	10
T 3	0 44 37	9 14 13	29 3	4	8	8	2	29	6	15	10
O 4	0 48 33	10 13 20	12♏58	5	9	9	2	0♎	6	15	10
B 5	0 52 30	11 12 30	26 29	6	11	10	2	0	6	15	10
E 6	0 56 26	12 11 41	9♐35	7	12	10	2	0	6	15	10
R 7	1 0 23	13 10 54	22 20	8	13	11	2	0	6	15	10
8	1 4 20	14 10 9	4♑45	9	14	12	3	0	6	15	10
9	1 8 16	15 9 26	16 55	10	16	12	3	0	6	16	10
10	1 12 13	16 8 44	28 54	11	17	13	3	0	6	16	10
11	1 16 9	17 8 4	10♒47	12	18	13	3	0	6	16	10 R
12	1 20 6	18 7 26	22 39	13	19	14	3	1	6	16	10
13	1 24 2	19 6 50	4♓33	14	20	15	4	1	6	16	10
14	1 27 59	20 6 15	16 33	14	22	15	4	1	6	16	10
15	1 31 55	21 5 43	28 41	15	23	16	4	1	6	16	10
16	1 35 52	22 5 12	11♈ 1	15	24	17	4	1	6	16	10
17	1 39 48	23 4 43	23 34	16	25	17	5	1	6	16	10
18	1 43 45	24 4 17	6♉20	16	27	18	5	1	6	16	10
19	1 47 42	25 3 52	19 21	16	28	18	5	1	6	16	10
20	1 51 38	26 3 30	2♊35	16	29	19	5	1	6	16	10
21	1 55 35	27 3 10	16 2	16	0♎	20	5	2	6	16	10
22	1 59 31	28 2 52	29 42	16	2	20	6	2	6	16	10
23	2 3 28	29 2 36	13♋33	16	3	21	6	2	6	16	10
24	2 7 24	0♏ 2 23	27 34	15	4	22	6	2	6	16	10
25	2 11 21	1 2 12	11♌44	15	5	22	6	2	6	16	10
26	2 15 17	2 2 3	26 1	14	7	23	6	2	6	16	10
27	2 19 14	3 1 56	10♍22	13	8	23	7	2	6	16	10
28	2 23 11	4 1 51	24 44	12	9	24	7	2	6	16	10
29	2 27 7	5 1 49	9♎ 3	11	10	25	7	2	6	16	10
30	2 31 4	6 1 49	23 14	9	11	25	7	3	6	16	10
31	2 35 0	7 1 50	7♏13	8	13	26	7	3	6	16	10

THE SUN ENTERS THE SIGN OF SCORPIO ON OCT 23 AT 23:03.

DAY	TIME h m s	☉ ° ' "	☽ ° '	☿ °	♀ °	♂ °	♃ °	♄ °	♅ °	♆ °	♇ °
N 1	2 38 57	8♏ 1 54	20♏57	7♏R	14♎	27♍	8♎	3♎	6♓R	16♌	10♋R
O 2	2 42 53	9 1 59	4♐22	5	15	27	8	3	6	16	10
V 3	2 46 50	10 2 6	17 27	4	16	28	8	3	6	16	10
E 4	2 50 46	11 2 15	0♑12	3	18	28	8	3	6	16	10
M 5	2 54 43	12 2 25	12 38	2	19	29	8	3	6	16	10
B 6	2 58 40	13 2 37	24 50	2	20	0♎	9	3	6	16	10
E 7	3 2 36	14 2 51	6♒50	1	21	0	9	3	6	16	10
R 8	3 6 33	15 3 6	18 43	1	23	1	9	4	6	16	10
9	3 10 29	16 3 22	0♓34	0 D	24	1	9	4	6	16	10
10	3 14 26	17 3 40	12 28	0	25	2	9	4	6	16	10
11	3 18 22	18 3 59	24 29	1	26	3	10	4	6	16	10
12	3 22 19	19 4 20	6♈43	1	28	3	10	4	6	16	10
13	3 26 15	20 4 42	19 12	1	29	4	10	4	6	16	10
14	3 30 12	21 5 6	1♉59	2	0♏	4	10	4	6	16	10
15	3 34 9	22 5 32	15 4	3	1	5	10	4	6 D	16	10
16	3 38 5	23 5 58	28 29	4	3	6	10	4	6	16	10
17	3 42 2	24 6 27	12♊10	5	4	6	11	4	6	16	10
18	3 45 58	25 6 57	26 6	6	5	7	11	5	6	16 R	10
19	3 49 55	26 7 29	10♋10	7	6	8	11	5	6	16	10
20	3 53 51	27 8 3	24 21	8	8	8	11	5	6	16	10
21	3 57 48	28 8 38	8♌34	10	9	9	11	5	6	16	10
22	4 1 44	29 9 15	22 45	11	10	9	12	5	6	16	10
23	4 5 41	0♐ 9 54	6♍54	12	11	10	12	5	6	16	10
24	4 9 38	1 10 35	20 57	14	13	11	12	5	6	16	10
25	4 13 34	2 11 17	4♎55	15	14	11	12	5	6	16	10
26	4 17 31	3 12 0	18 46	16	15	12	12	5	6	16	10
27	4 21 27	4 12 46	2♏29	18	16	12	12	5	6	16	10
28	4 25 24	5 13 33	16 3	19	18	13	13	5	6	16	10
29	4 29 20	6 14 21	29 25	21	19	14	13	6	6	16	10
30	4 33 17	7 15 10	12♐34	22	20	14	13	6	6	16	10

THE SUN ENTERS THE SIGN OF SAGITTARIUS ON NOV 22 AT 20:05.

DAY	TIME h m s	☉ ° ' "	☽ ° '	☿ °	♀ °	♂ °	♃ °	♄ °	♅ °	♆ °	♇ °
D 1	4 37 13	8♐16 1	25♐28	24♏	21♏	15♎	13♎	6♎	6♓	16♌R	10♋R
E 2	4 41 10	9 16 52	8♑ 7	25	23	15	13	6	6	16	10
C 3	4 45 7	10 17 45	20 30	27	24	16	13	6	6	16	10
E 4	4 49 3	11 18 39	2♒40	28	25	17	14	6	6	16	10
M 5	4 53 0	12 19 33	14 39	0♐	26	17	14	6	6	16	10
B 6	4 56 56	13 20 28	26 31	2	28	18	14	6	6	16	10
E 7	5 0 53	14 21 24	8♓21	3	29	18	14	6	6	16	9
R 8	5 4 49	15 22 21	20 13	5	0♐	19	14	6	6	16	9
9	5 8 46	16 23 18	2♈12	6	1	20	14	6	6	16	9
10	5 12 42	17 24 16	14 25	8	3	20	15	6	6	16	9
11	5 16 39	18 25 15	26 56	9	4	21	15	6	6	16	9
12	5 20 36	19 26 14	9♉50	11	5	21	15	6	6	16	9
13	5 24 32	20 27 14	23 7	12	7	22	15	7	6	16	9
14	5 28 29	21 28 15	6♊50	14	8	23	15	7	6	16	9
15	5 32 25	22 29 16	20 55	15	9	23	15	7	6	16	9
16	5 36 22	23 30 18	5♋18	17	10	24	15	7	6	16	9
17	5 40 18	24 31 20	19 53	19	12	24	15	7	6	16	9
18	5 44 15	25 32 24	4♌32	20	13	25	16	7	6	16	9
19	5 48 11	26 33 28	19 7	22	14	26	16	7	6	16	9
20	5 52 8	27 34 33	3♍34	23	15	26	16	7	6	16	9
21	5 56 5	28 35 38	17 49	25	17	27	16	7	6	16	9
22	6 0 1	29 36 45	1♎49	26	18	27	16	7	6	16	9
23	6 3 58	0♑37 52	15 35	28	19	28	16	7	6	16	9
24	6 7 54	1 39 0	29 8	0♑	20	29	16	7	6	16	9
25	6 11 51	2 40 9	12♏29	1	22	29	16	7	6	16	9
26	6 15 47	3 41 18	25 38	3	23	0♏	17	7	6	16	9
27	6 19 44	4 42 28	8♐37	4	24	0	17	7	6	16	9
28	6 23 40	5 43 38	21 25	6	25	1	17	7	6	16	9
29	6 27 37	6 44 48	4♑ 2	8	27	1	17	7	7	16	9
30	6 31 34	7 45 59	16 28	9	28	2	17	7	7	16	9
31	6 35 30	8 47 9	28 43	11	29	3	17	7	7	15	9

THE SUN ENTERS THE SIGN OF CAPRICORN ON DEC 22 AT 09:08.

♈ ARIES ♉ TAURUS ♊ GEMINI ♋ CANCER ♌ LEO ♍ VIRGO ♎ LIBRA ♏ SCORPIO ♐ SAGITTARIUS ♑ CAPRICORN ♒ AQUARIUS ♓ PISCES

164 Appendix X
1922

SIDEREAL SUN MOON MERCURY VENUS MARS JUPITER SATURN URANUS NEPTUNE PLUTO

DAY	TIME	☉	☽	☿	♀	♂	♃	♄	♅	♆	♇
	h m s	° ' "	° '	°	°	°	°	°	°	°	°
J 1	6 39 27	9♑48 20	10♒48	12♑	0♑	3♏	17♎	7♎	7♓	15♌R	9♋R
A 2	6 43 23	10 49 30	22 44	14	2	4	17	7	7	15	9
N 3	6 47 20	11 50 41	4♓33	16	3	4	17	7	7	15	9
U 4	6 51 16	12 51 51	16 21	17	4	5	18	7	7	15	9
A 5	6 55 13	13 53 0	28 10	19	5	6	18	7	7	15	9
R 6	6 59 9	14 54 10	10♈ 7	21	7	6	18	7	7	15	9
Y 7	7 3 6	15 55 19	22 16	22	8	7	18	8	7	15	9
8	7 7 3	16 56 28	4♉43	24	9	7	18	8	7	15	9
9	7 10 59	17 57 36	17 34	25	10	8	18	8	7	15	9
10	7 14 56	18 58 44	0♊52	27	12	8	18	8	7	15	9
11	7 18 52	19 59 51	14 40	29	13	9	18	8	7	15	9
12	7 22 49	21 0 58	28 55	0♒	14	10	18	8	7	15	9
13	7 26 45	22 2 4	13♋35	2	15	10	18	8	7	15	9
14	7 30 42	23 3 10	28 32	4	17	11	18	8	7	15	9
15	7 34 39	24 4 15	13♌36	6	18	11	18	8	7	15	9
16	7 38 35	25 5 20	28 37	7	19	12	18	8	7	15	9
17	7 42 32	26 6 25	13♍27	9	21	12	18	8 R	7	15	9
18	7 46 28	27 7 29	28 0	10	22	13	18	8	7	15	9
19	7 50 25	28 8 33	12♎11	12	23	14	19	8	7	15	9
20	7 54 21	29 9 37	26 1	14	24	14	19	8	7	15	9
21	7 58 18	0♒10 40	9♏30	15	26	15	19	8	7	15	9
22	8 2 14	1 11 43	22 41	17	27	15	19	8	8	15	9
23	8 6 11	2 12 46	5♐36	18	28	16	19	8	8	15	9
24	8 10 8	3 13 48	18 17	20	29	16	19	8	8	15	9
25	8 14 4	4 14 50	0♑47	21	1♒	17	19	8	8	15	9
26	8 18 1	5 15 51	13 8	23	2	17	19	8	8	15	8
27	8 21 57	6 16 51	25 19	24	3	18	19	8	8	15	8
28	8 25 54	7 17 50	7♒23	25	4	19	19	8	8	15	8
29	8 29 50	8 18 48	19 20	27	6	19	19	7	8	15	8
30	8 33 47	9 19 45	1♓12	28	7	20	19	7	8	15	8
31	8 37 43	10 20 42	13 0	29	8	20	19	7	8	15	8

THE SUN ENTERS THE SIGN OF AQUARIUS ON JAN 20 AT 19:48.

DAY	TIME	☉	☽	☿	♀	♂	♃	♄	♅	♆	♇
	h m s	° ' "	° '	°	°	°	°	°	°	°	°
F 1	8 41 40	11♒21 36	24♓47	29♒	9♒	21♏	19♎	7♎R	8♓	15♌R	8♋R
E 2	8 45 37	12 22 30	6♈37	0♓	11	21	19 R	7	8	15	8
B 3	8 49 33	13 23 23	18 33	1	12	22	19	7	8	15	8
R 4	8 53 30	14 24 14	0♉40	1	13	22	19	7	8	15	8
U 5	8 57 26	15 25 3	13 4	1 R	14	23	19	7	8	15	8
A 6	9 1 23	16 25 51	25 49	1	16	23	19	7	8	15	8
R 7	9 5 19	17 26 38	9♊ 0	1	17	24	19	7	8	15	8
Y 8	9 9 16	18 27 23	22 41	1	18	24	19	7	8	14	8
9	9 13 12	19 28 7	6♋51	0	19	25	19	7	8	14	8
10	9 17 9	20 28 49	21 30	29♒	21	26	19	7	9	14	8
11	9 21 6	21 29 30	6♌30	29	22	26	19	7	9	14	8
12	9 25 2	22 30 9	21 44	28	23	27	19	7	9	14	8
13	9 28 59	23 30 47	7♍ 1	27	24	27	19	7	9	14	8
14	9 32 55	24 31 23	22 10	25	26	28	19	7	9	14	8
15	9 36 52	25 31 58	7♎ 2	24	27	28	19	7	9	14	8
16	9 40 48	26 32 32	21 31	23	28	29	19	7	9	14	8
17	9 44 45	27 33 5	5♏35	22	29	29	19	7	9	14	8
18	9 48 41	28 33 36	19 13	21	1♓	0♐	19	7	9	14	8
19	9 52 38	29 34 6	2♐26	20	2	0	18	7	9	14	8
20	9 56 34	0♓34 35	15 18	19	3	1	18	7	9	14	8
21	10 0 31	1 35 3	27 53	18	4	1	18	7	9	14	8
22	10 4 28	2 35 29	10♑13	18	6	2	18	7	9	14	8
23	10 8 24	3 35 54	22 22	17	7	2	18	6	9	14	8
24	10 12 21	4 36 17	4♒23	17	8	3	18	6	9	14	8
25	10 16 17	5 36 39	16 18	16	9	3	18	6	9	14	8
26	10 20 14	6 36 59	28 9	16	11	4	18	6	9	14	8
27	10 24 10	7 37 17	9♓58	16 D	12	4	18	6	9	14	8
28	10 28 7	8 37 34	21 46	16	13	5	18	6	10	14	8

THE SUN ENTERS THE SIGN OF PISCES ON FEB 19 AT 10:16.

DAY	TIME	☉	☽	☿	♀	♂	♃	♄	♅	♆	♇
	h m s	° ' "	° '	°	°	°	°	°	°	°	°
M 1	10 32 3	9♓37 49	3♈37	16♒	14♓	5♐	18♎R	6♎R	10♓	14♌R	8♋R
A 2	10 36 0	10 38 2	15 31	16	16	6	18	6	10	14	8
R 3	10 39 57	11 38 13	27 33	17	17	6	18	6	10	14	8
C 4	10 43 53	12 38 22	9♉45	17	18	7	18	6	10	14	8
H 5	10 47 50	13 38 28	22 11	18	19	7	18	6	10	14	8
6	10 51 46	14 38 33	4♊55	18	21	7	17	6	10	14	8
7	10 55 43	15 38 36	18 1	19	22	8	17	6	10	14	8
8	10 59 39	16 38 37	1♋32	20	23	8	17	6	10	14	8
9	11 3 36	17 38 35	15 30	20	24	9	17	6	10	14	8
10	11 7 32	18 38 31	29 54	21	26	9	17	5	10	14	8
11	11 11 29	19 38 25	14♌41	22	27	10	17	5	10	14	8
12	11 15 26	20 38 17	29 46	23	28	10	17	5	10	14	8
13	11 19 22	21 38 7	14♍59	24	29	11	17	5	10	14	8
14	11 23 19	22 37 55	0♎10	25	1♈	11	17	5	10	14	8
15	11 27 15	23 37 40	15 10	26	2	11	17	5	10	14	8
16	11 31 12	24 37 25	29 52	27	3	12	16	5	10	14	8
17	11 35 8	25 37 7	14♏ 9	28	4	12	16	5	11	14	8
18	11 39 5	26 36 47	27 59	0♓	6	13	16	5	11	14	8
19	11 43 1	27 36 26	11♐22	1	7	13	16	5	11	14	8
20	11 46 58	28 36 3	24 21	2	8	14	16	5	11	14	8
21	11 50 55	29 35 39	6♑57	3	9	14	16	5	11	13	8
22	11 54 51	0♈35 12	19 16	5	11	14	16	5	11	13	8 D
23	11 58 48	1 34 44	1♒21	6	12	15	16	4	11	13	8
24	12 2 44	2 34 14	13 17	7	13	15	15	4	11	13	8
25	12 6 41	3 33 42	25 7	9	14	16	15	4	11	13	8
26	12 10 37	4 33 8	6♓55	10	16	16	15	4	11	13	8
27	12 14 34	5 32 33	18 43	12	17	16	15	4	11	13	8
28	12 18 30	6 31 55	0♈35	13	18	17	15	4	11	13	8
29	12 22 27	7 31 15	12 32	15	19	17	15	4	11	13	8
30	12 26 23	8 30 33	24 36	16	21	17	15	4	11	13	8
31	12 30 20	9 29 50	6♉50	18	22	18	15	4	11	13	8

THE SUN ENTERS THE SIGN OF ARIES ON MAR 21 AT 09:48.

SIDEREAL SUN MOON MERCURY VENUS MARS JUPITER SATURN URANUS NEPTUNE PLUTO

DAY	TIME	☉	☽	☿	♀	♂	♃	♄	♅	♆	♇
	h m s	° ' "	° '	°	°	°	°	°	°	°	°
A 1	12 34 17	10♈29 4	19♉14	19♓	23♈	18♐	14♎R	4♎R	11♓	13♌R	8♋
P 2	12 38 13	11 28 15	1♊52	21	24	18	14	4	11	13	8
R 3	12 42 10	12 27 25	14 44	23	25	19	14	4	11	13	8
I 4	12 46 6	13 26 32	27 54	24	27	19	14	4	11	13	8
L 5	12 50 3	14 25 37	11♋23	26	28	19	14	3	12	13	8
6	12 53 59	15 24 40	25 12	28	29	20	14	3	12	13	8
7	12 57 56	16 23 40	9♌21	29	0♉	20	14	3	12	13	8
8	13 1 52	17 22 38	23 48	1♈	2	20	14	3	12	13	8
9	13 5 49	18 21 34	8♍31	3	3	21	13	3	12	13	8
10	13 9 46	19 20 27	23 24	5	4	21	13	3	12	13	8
11	13 13 42	20 19 18	8♎20	6	5	21	13	3	12	13	8
12	13 17 39	21 18 8	23 11	8	7	21	13	3	12	13	8
13	13 21 35	22 16 55	7♏50	10	8	22	13	3	12	13	8
14	13 25 32	23 15 40	22 9	12	9	22	13	3	12	13	8
15	13 29 28	24 14 24	6♐ 5	14	10	22	13	3	12	13	8
16	13 33 25	25 13 5	19 36	16	12	22	13	3	12	13	8
17	13 37 21	26 11 46	2♑41	18	13	23	12	3	12	13	8
18	13 41 18	27 10 24	15 22	20	14	23	12	3	12	13	8
19	13 45 15	28 9 1	27 44	22	15	23	12	2	12	13	8
20	13 49 11	29 7 36	9♒50	24	16	23	12	2	12	13	8
21	13 53 8	0♉ 6 9	21 45	26	18	24	12	2	12	13	8
22	13 57 4	1 4 41	3♓34	28	19	24	12	2	12	13	8
23	14 1 1	2 3 10	15 22	0♉	20	24	12	2	12	13	8
24	14 4 57	3 1 39	27 13	2	21	24	12	2	12	13 D	8
25	14 8 54	4 0 5	9♈ 9	4	23	24	12	2	12	13	8
26	14 12 50	4 58 30	21 15	6	24	24	11	2	12	13	8
27	14 16 47	5 56 53	3♉32	9	25	25	11	2	13	13	8
28	14 20 43	6 55 14	16 2	11	26	25	11	2	13	13	8
29	14 24 40	7 53 34	28 45	13	27	25	11	2	13	13	8
30	14 28 37	8 51 51	11♊42	15	29	25	11	2	13	13	8

THE SUN ENTERS THE SIGN OF TAURUS ON APR 20 AT 21:29.

DAY	TIME	☉	☽	☿	♀	♂	♃	♄	♅	♆	♇
	h m s	° ' "	° '	°	°	°	°	°	°	°	°
M 1	14 32 33	9♉50 7	24♊53	17♉	0♊	25♐	11♎R	2♎R	13♓	13♌	8♋
A 2	14 36 30	10 48 21	8♋17	19	1	25	11	2	13	13	8
Y 3	14 40 26	11 46 32	21 54	21	2	25	11	2	13	13	8
4	14 44 23	12 44 42	5♌44	23	4	25	11	2	13	13	8
5	14 48 19	13 42 50	19 46	25	5	25	10	2	13	13	8
6	14 52 16	14 40 55	3♍58	27	6	25	10	1	13	13	8
7	14 56 12	15 38 59	18 20	29	7	25	10	1	13	13	8
8	15 0 9	16 37 0	2♎48	1♊	8	25 R	10	1	13	13	8
9	15 4 6	17 35 0	17 19	3	10	25	10	1	13	13	8
10	15 8 2	18 32 58	1♏48	5	11	25	10	1	13	13	8
11	15 11 59	19 30 55	16 9	7	12	25	10	1	13	13	8
12	15 15 55	20 28 50	0♐16	9	13	25	10	1	13	13	8
13	15 19 52	21 26 43	14 5	10	15	25	10	1	13	13	8
14	15 23 48	22 24 35	27 34	12	16	25	10	1	13	13	8
15	15 27 45	23 22 26	10♑39	13	17	25	10	1	13	13	8
16	15 31 41	24 20 16	23 22	15	18	25	10	1	13	13	8
17	15 35 38	25 18 4	5♒46	16	19	25	10	1	13	13	9
18	15 39 35	26 15 51	17 53	18	21	25	10	1	13	13	9
19	15 43 31	27 13 37	29 50	19	22	25	9	1	13	13	9
20	15 47 28	28 11 22	11♓40	20	23	24	9	1	13	13	9
21	15 51 24	29 9 5	23 28	21	24	24	9	1	13	13	9
22	15 55 21	0♊ 6 48	5♈21	23	26	24	9	1	13	13	9
23	15 59 17	1 4 29	17 22	24	27	24	9	1	13	13	9
24	16 3 14	2 2 9	29 36	25	28	24	9	1	13	13	9
25	16 7 10	2 59 49	12♉ 6	25	29	24	9	1	13	13	9
26	16 11 7	3 57 27	24 52	26	0♋	23	9	1	13	13	9
27	16 15 4	4 55 4	7♊56	27	2	23	9	1	13	13	9
28	16 19 0	5 52 40	21 17	28	3	23	9	1	13	13	9
29	16 22 57	6 50 15	4♋52	28	4	23	9	1	13	13	9
30	16 26 53	7 47 48	18 39	29	5	22	9	1	13	14	9
31	16 30 50	8 45 20	2♌35	0♋	6	22	9	1	13	14	9

THE SUN ENTERS THE SIGN OF GEMINI ON MAY 21 AT 21:10.

DAY	TIME	☉	☽	☿	♀	♂	♃	♄	♅	♆	♇
	h m s	° ' "	° '	°	°	°	°	°	°	°	°
J 1	16 34 46	9♊42 51	16♌37	0♋	8♋	22♐R	9♎R	1♎R	13♓	14♌	9♋
U 2	16 38 43	10 40 20	0♍42	0	9	22	9	1	13	14	9
N 3	16 42 39	11 37 48	14 50	1	10	21	9	1 D	13	14	9
E 4	16 46 36	12 35 15	28 59	1	11	21	9	1	14	14	9
5	16 50 33	13 32 41	13♎ 8	1 R	12	21	9	1	14	14	9
6	16 54 29	14 30 5	27 14	1	14	20	9 D	1	14	14	9
7	16 58 26	15 27 28	11♏17	1	15	20	9	1	14	14	9
8	17 2 22	16 24 51	25 13	1	16	20	9	1	14	14	9
9	17 6 19	17 22 12	8♐59	1	17	19	9	1	14	14	9
10	17 10 15	18 19 33	22 30	0	18	19	9	1	14	14	9
11	17 14 12	19 16 53	5♑45	0	20	19	9	1	14	14	9
12	17 18 8	20 14 12	18 42	0	21	18	9	1	14	14	9
13	17 22 5	21 11 30	1♒21	29♊	22	18	9	1	14	14	9
14	17 26 2	22 8 48	13 42	29	23	18	9	1	14	14	9
15	17 29 58	23 6 6	25 48	28	24	17	9	1	14	14	9
16	17 33 55	24 3 23	7♓44	28	26	17	9	1	14	14	9
17	17 37 51	25 0 40	19 34	27	27	17	9	1	14	14	9
18	17 41 48	25 57 56	1♈23	27	28	16	9	1	14 R	14	9
19	17 45 44	26 55 13	13 16	26	29	16	9	1	14	14	9
20	17 49 41	27 52 29	25 20	25	0♌	16	9	1	14	14	9
21	17 53 37	28 49 44	7♉39	25	2	16	9	1	14	14	9
22	17 57 34	29 47 0	20 17	24	3	15	9	1	14	14	9
23	18 1 31	0♋44 15	3♊16	24	4	15	9	1	14	14	9
24	18 5 27	1 41 31	16 37	23	5	15	9	1	14	14	9
25	18 9 24	2 38 46	0♋19	23	6	14	9	1	14	14	9
26	18 13 20	3 36 0	14 19	23	8	14	10	1	14	14	9
27	18 17 17	4 33 15	28 32	22	9	14	10	1	14	14	9
28	18 21 13	5 30 29	12♌52	22	10	14	10	1	14	14	9
29	18 25 10	6 27 42	27 14	22 D	11	13	10	1	14	14	9
30	18 29 7	7 24 55	11♍35	22	12	13	10	1	14	14	10

THE SUN ENTERS THE SIGN OF CANCER ON JUN 22 AT 05:27.

♈ ARIES ♉ TAURUS ♊ GEMINI ♋ CANCER ♌ LEO ♍ VIRGO ♎ LIBRA ♏ SCORPIO ♐ SAGITTARIUS ♑ CAPRICORN ♒ AQUARIUS ♓ PISCES

1922

SIDEREAL SUN MOON MERCURY VENUS MARS JUPITER SATURN URANUS NEPTUNE PLUTO

SIDEREAL SUN MOON MERCURY VENUS MARS JUPITER SATURN URANUS NEPTUNE PLUTO

DAY	TIME	☉	☽	☿	♀	♂	♃	♄	♅	♆	♇
	h m s	° ' "	° '	°	°	°	°	°	°	°	°
J 1	18 33 3	8♋22 8	25♍49	22♊	13♌	13♐R	10♎	1♎	14♓R	14♌	10♋
U 2	18 37 0	9 19 20	9♎57	22	15	13	10	1	14	14	10
L 3	18 40 56	10 16 32	23 56	22	16	12	10	2	14	14	10
Y 4	18 44 53	11 13 44	7♏46	23	17	12	10	2	14	14	10
5	18 48 49	12 10 55	21 28	23	18	12	10	2	13	14	10
6	18 52 46	13 8 6	5♐ 0	24	19	12	10	2	13	14	10
7	18 56 42	14 5 17	18 22	24	20	12	10	2	13	15	10
8	19 0 39	15 2 28	1♑31	25	22	12	10	2	13	15	10
9	19 4 36	15 59 39	14 27	25	23	12	11	2	13	15	10
10	19 8 32	16 56 51	27 9	26	24	11	11	2	13	15	10
11	19 12 29	17 54 2	9♒36	27	25	11	11	2	13	15	10
12	19 16 25	18 51 14	21 50	28	26	11	11	2	13	15	10
13	19 20 22	19 48 26	3♓51	29	28	11	11	2	13	15	10
14	19 24 18	20 45 38	15 44	0♋	29	11	11	2	13	15	10
15	19 28 15	21 42 51	27 33	1	0♍	11	11	2	13	15	10
16	19 32 11	22 40 5	9♈21	3	1	11	11	2	13	15	10
17	19 36 8	23 37 19	21 14	4	2	11 D	11	2	13	15	10
18	19 40 5	24 34 34	3♉18	5	3	11	11	2	13	15	10
19	19 44 1	25 31 49	15 38	7	4	11	12	2	13	15	10
20	19 47 58	26 29 6	28 18	8	6	11	12	3	13	15	10
21	19 51 54	27 26 23	11♊22	10	7	11	12	3	13	15	10
22	19 55 51	28 23 41	24 52	12	8	11	12	3	13	15	10
23	19 59 47	29 20 59	8♋47	13	9	11	12	3	13	15	10
24	20 3 44	0♌18 19	23 5	15	10	11	12	3	13	15	10
25	20 7 40	1 15 39	7♌39	17	11	12	12	3	13	15	10
26	20 11 37	2 12 59	22 23	19	13	12	12	3	13	15	10
27	20 15 34	3 10 20	7♍10	21	14	12	13	3	13	15	10
28	20 19 30	4 7 42	21 51	23	15	12	13	3	13	15	10
29	20 23 27	5 5 4	6♎21	25	16	12	13	3	13	15	10
30	20 27 23	6 2 27	20 38	27	17	12	13	3	13	15	10
31	20 31 20	6 59 50	4♏39	29	18	12	13	3	13	15	10

THE SUN ENTERS THE SIGN OF LEO ON JUL 23 AT 16:20.

DAY	TIME	☉	☽	☿	♀	♂	♃	♄	♅	♆	♇
	h m s	° ' "	° '	°	°	°	°	°	°	°	°
A 1	20 35 16	7♌57 14	18♏24	1♌	19♍	13♐	13♎	4♎	13♓R	15♌	10♋
U 2	20 39 13	8 54 38	1♐54	3	21	13	13	4	13	15	10
G 3	20 43 9	9 52 3	15 10	5	22	13	14	4	13	15	10
U 4	20 47 6	10 49 29	28 11	7	23	13	14	4	13	16	10
S 5	20 51 3	11 46 55	11♑ 0	9	24	13	14	4	13	16	10
T 6	20 54 59	12 44 23	23 36	11	25	14	14	4	13	16	10
7	20 58 56	13 41 51	6♒ 1	13	26	14	14	4	13	16	10
8	21 2 52	14 39 20	18 15	15	27	14	14	4	13	16	10
9	21 6 49	15 36 50	0♓18	17	28	15	14	4	13	16	10
10	21 10 45	16 34 22	12 14	20	0♎	15	15	4	13	16	10
11	21 14 42	17 31 54	24 4	22	1	15	15	4	13	16	11
12	21 18 38	18 29 28	5♈50	23	2	15	15	5	13	16	11
13	21 22 35	19 27 4	17 38	25	3	16	15	5	13	16	11
14	21 26 31	20 24 40	29 31	27	4	16	15	5	12	16	11
15	21 30 28	21 22 19	11♉35	29	5	16	15	5	12	16	11
16	21 34 25	22 19 58	23 53	1♍	6	17	16	5	12	16	11
17	21 38 21	23 17 40	6♊31	3	7	17	16	5	12	16	11
18	21 42 18	24 15 23	19 33	5	8	18	16	5	12	16	11
19	21 46 14	25 13 7	3♋ 2	7	10	18	16	5	12	16	11
20	21 50 11	26 10 54	16 59	8	11	18	16	5	12	16	11
21	21 54 7	27 8 41	1♌22	10	12	19	16	5	12	16	11
22	21 58 4	28 6 31	16 6	12	13	19	17	6	12	16	11
23	22 2 0	29 4 21	1♍ 5	14	14	20	17	6	12	16	11
24	22 5 57	0♍ 2 14	16 10	15	15	20	17	6	12	16	11
25	22 9 54	1 0 7	1♎12	17	16	20	17	6	12	16	11
26	22 13 50	1 58 2	16 2	19	17	21	17	6	12	16	11
27	22 17 47	2 55 58	0♏35	20	18	21	17	6	12	16	11
28	22 21 43	3 53 56	14 47	22	19	22	18	6	12	16	11
29	22 25 40	4 51 55	28 37	24	20	22	18	6	12	16	11
30	22 29 36	5 49 55	12♐ 5	25	21	23	18	6	12	16	11
31	22 33 33	6 47 56	25 13	27	22	23	18	7	12	16	11

THE SUN ENTERS THE SIGN OF VIRGO ON AUG 23 AT 23:05.

DAY	TIME	☉	☽	☿	♀	♂	♃	♄	♅	♆	♇
	h m s	° ' "	° '	°	°	°	°	°	°	°	°
S 1	22 37 29	7♍45 59	8♑ 3	28♍	23♎	24♐	18♎	7♎	12♓R	17♌	11♋
E 2	22 41 26	8 44 3	20 37	0♎	25	24	19	7	12	17	11
P 3	22 45 23	9 42 9	2♒58	1	26	25	19	7	12	17	11
T 4	22 49 19	10 40 16	15 8	3	27	25	19	7	12	17	11
E 5	22 53 16	11 38 25	27 10	4	28	25	19	7	12	17	11
M 6	22 57 12	12 36 36	9♓ 5	6	29	26	19	7	12	17	11
B 7	23 1 9	13 34 48	20 55	7	0♏	27	20	7	12	17	11
E 8	23 5 5	14 33 2	2♈42	8	1	27	20	7	11	17	11
R 9	23 9 2	15 31 17	14 30	10	2	28	20	8	11	17	11
10	23 12 58	16 29 35	26 20	11	3	28	20	8	11	17	11
11	23 16 55	17 27 55	8♉16	12	4	29	20	8	11	17	11
12	23 20 52	18 26 17	20 21	14	5	29	21	8	11	17	11
13	23 24 48	19 24 41	2♊40	15	6	0♑	21	8	11	17	11
14	23 28 45	20 23 7	15 16	16	7	0	21	8	11	17	11
15	23 32 41	21 21 35	28 14	17	8	1	21	8	11	17	11
16	23 36 38	22 20 5	11♋36	18	9	1	21	8	11	17	11
17	23 40 34	23 18 38	25 25	19	10	2	22	9	11	17	11
18	23 44 31	24 17 13	9♌40	20	11	2	22	9	11	17	11
19	23 48 27	25 15 49	24 20	22	12	3	22	9	11	17	11
20	23 52 24	26 14 28	9♍18	23	12	4	22	9	11	17	11
21	23 56 20	27 13 9	24 28	24	13	4	22	9	11	17	11
22	0 0 17	28 11 52	9♎40	24	14	5	23	9	11	17	11
23	0 4 14	29 10 37	24 45	25	15	5	23	9	11	17	11
24	0 8 10	0♎ 9 23	9♏33	26	16	6	23	9	11	17	11
25	0 12 7	1 8 12	24 0	27	17	7	23	9	11	17	11
26	0 16 3	2 7 2	8♐ 1	28	18	7	23	10	11	17	11
27	0 20 0	3 5 54	21 35	28	19	8	24	10	11	17	11
28	0 23 56	4 4 48	4♑45	29	20	8	24	10	11	17	11
29	0 27 53	5 3 43	17 31	29	21	9	24	10	11	17	11
30	0 31 49	6 2 41	29 59	0♏	21	10	24	10	11	17	11

THE SUN ENTERS THE SIGN OF LIBRA ON SEP 23 AT 20:10.

DAY	TIME	☉	☽	☿	♀	♂	♃	♄	♅	♆	♇
	h m s	° ' "	° '	°	°	°	°	°	°	°	°
O 1	0 35 46	7♎ 1 39	12♒11	0♏	22♏	10♑	24♎	10♎	11♓R	17♌	11♋
C 2	0 39 43	8 0 40	24 12	0	23	11	25	10	11	17	11
T 3	0 43 39	8 59 43	6♓ 6	0 R	24	12	25	10	11	18	11
O 4	0 47 36	9 58 47	17 55	0	25	12	25	11	11	18	11
B 5	0 51 32	10 57 53	29 42	0	26	13	25	11	10	18	11
E 6	0 55 29	11 57 2	11♈31	0	26	13	25	11	10	18	11
R 7	0 59 25	12 56 12	23 22	29♎	27	14	26	11	10	18	11
8	1 3 22	13 55 25	5♉19	29	28	15	26	11	10	18	11
9	1 7 18	14 54 39	17 24	28	29	15	26	11	10	18	11
10	1 11 15	15 53 56	29 37	27	29	16	26	11	10	18	11
11	1 15 12	16 53 15	12♊ 3	26	0♐	17	27	11	10	18	11
12	1 19 8	17 52 37	24 43	25	1	17	27	12	10	18	11 R
13	1 23 5	18 52 0	7♋40	24	1	18	27	12	10	18	11
14	1 27 1	19 51 27	20 56	23	2	19	27	12	10	18	11
15	1 30 58	20 50 55	4♌34	22	3	19	27	12	10	18	11
16	1 34 54	21 50 26	18 35	21	3	20	28	12	10	18	11
17	1 38 51	22 49 59	2♍59	19	4	21	28	12	10	18	11
18	1 42 47	23 49 34	17 43	18	4	21	28	12	10	18	11
19	1 46 44	24 49 11	2♎41	17	5	22	28	12	10	18	11
20	1 50 40	25 48 51	17 47	16	6	23	29	13	10	18	11
21	1 54 37	26 48 32	2♏51	16	6	23	29	13	10	18	11
22	1 58 34	27 48 16	17 45	15	6	24	29	13	10	18	11
23	2 2 30	28 48 1	2♐21	15	7	25	29	13	10	18	11
24	2 6 27	29 47 49	16 32	15 D	7	25	29	13	10	18	11
25	2 10 23	0♏47 38	0♑15	15	8	26	0♏	13	10	18	11
26	2 14 20	1 47 29	13 30	15	8	27	0	13	10	18	11
27	2 18 16	2 47 21	26 20	15	8	27	0	13	10	18	11
28	2 22 13	3 47 16	8♒47	16	9	28	0	14	10	18	11
29	2 26 9	4 47 11	20 57	17	9	29	0	14	10	18	11
30	2 30 6	5 47 9	2♓55	17	9	29	1	14	10	18	11
31	2 34 3	6 47 8	14 45	18	9	0♒	1	14	10	18	11

THE SUN ENTERS THE SIGN OF SCORPIO ON OCT 24 AT 04:54.

DAY	TIME	☉	☽	☿	♀	♂	♃	♄	♅	♆	♇
	h m s	° ' "	° '	°	°	°	°	°	°	°	°
N 1	2 37 59	7♏47 8	26♓32	19♎	10♐	1♒	1♏	14♎	10♓R	18♌	11♋R
O 2	2 41 56	8 47 11	8♈19	20	10	2	1	14	10	18	11
V 3	2 45 52	9 47 15	20 11	22	10	2	2	14	10	18	11
E 4	2 49 49	10 47 21	2♉10	23	10 R	3	2	14	10	18	11
M 5	2 53 45	11 47 28	14 18	24	10	4	2	14	10	18	11
B 6	2 57 42	12 47 38	26 36	26	10	4	2	15	10	18	11
E 7	3 1 38	13 47 50	9♊ 5	27	10	5	2	15	10	18	11
R 8	3 5 35	14 48 3	21 46	29	10	6	3	15	10	18	11
9	3 9 32	15 48 18	4♋39	0♏	9	6	3	15	10	18	11
10	3 13 28	16 48 35	17 44	2	9	7	3	15	10	18	11
11	3 17 25	17 48 55	1♌ 4	3	9	8	3	15	10	18	11
12	3 21 21	18 49 16	14 38	5	9	9	4	15	10	18	11
13	3 25 18	19 49 39	28 29	6	8	9	4	15	10	18	11
14	3 29 14	20 50 4	12♍35	8	8	10	4	15	10	18	11
15	3 33 11	21 50 31	26 58	9	8	11	4	16	10	18	11
16	3 37 7	22 51 0	11♎34	11	7	11	4	16	10	18	11
17	3 41 4	23 51 30	26 19	13	7	12	5	16	10	18	11
18	3 45 1	24 52 3	11♏ 6	14	6	13	5	16	10	18	11
19	3 48 57	25 52 37	25 49	16	6	14	5	16	10 D	18	11
20	3 52 54	26 53 12	10♐19	17	5	14	5	16	10	18	11
21	3 56 50	27 53 50	24 29	19	5	15	5	16	10	18 R	11
22	4 0 47	28 54 28	8♑15	21	4	16	6	16	10	18	11
23	4 4 43	29 55 8	21 34	22	4	16	6	16	10	18	11
24	4 8 40	0♐55 48	4♒28	24	3	17	6	16	10	18	11
25	4 12 36	1 56 30	16 58	25	2	18	6	17	10	18	11
26	4 16 33	2 57 13	29 10	27	2	19	6	17	10	18	11
27	4 20 30	3 57 57	11♓ 8	28	1	19	7	17	10	18	11
28	4 24 26	4 58 42	22 58	0♐	1	20	7	17	10	18	11
29	4 28 23	5 59 28	4♈44	2	0	21	7	17	10	18	11
30	4 32 19	7 0 15	16 34	3	29♏	22	7	17	10	18	11

THE SUN ENTERS THE SIGN OF SAGITTARIUS ON NOV 23 AT 01:56.

DAY	TIME	☉	☽	☿	♀	♂	♃	♄	♅	♆	♇
	h m s	° ' "	° '	°	°	°	°	°	°	°	°
D 1	4 36 16	8♐ 1 3	28♈30	5♐	29♏R	22♒	7♏	17♎	10♓	18♌R	11♋R
E 2	4 40 12	9 1 52	10♉36	6	28	23	8	17	10	18	11
C 3	4 44 9	10 2 42	22 56	8	28	24	8	17	10	18	11
E 4	4 48 5	11 3 33	5♊29	10	27	24	8	17	10	18	11
M 5	4 52 2	12 4 25	18 18	11	27	25	8	17	10	18	11
B 6	4 55 59	13 5 19	1♋20	13	26	26	8	18	10	18	11
E 7	4 59 55	14 6 13	14 35	14	26	27	9	18	10	18	11
R 8	5 3 52	15 7 9	28 0	16	26	27	9	18	10	18	11
9	5 7 48	16 8 5	11♌35	17	25	28	9	18	10	18	11
10	5 11 45	17 9 3	25 18	19	25	29	9	18	10	18	11
11	5 15 41	18 10 2	9♍10	21	25	0♓	9	18	10	18	11
12	5 19 38	19 11 2	23 9	22	25	0	10	18	10	18	11
13	5 23 34	20 12 4	7♎17	24	25	1	10	18	10	18	11
14	5 27 31	21 13 6	21 31	25	25	2	10	18	10	18	11
15	5 31 28	22 14 9	5♏50	27	25 D	3	10	18	10	18	11
16	5 35 24	23 15 14	20 11	28	25	3	10	18	10	18	10
17	5 39 21	24 16 19	4♐29	0♑	25	4	11	18	10	18	10
18	5 43 17	25 17 25	18 38	2	25	5	11	19	10	18	10
19	5 47 14	26 18 31	2♑32	3	25	5	11	19	10	18	10
20	5 51 10	27 19 39	16 8	5	25	6	11	19	10	18	10
21	5 55 7	28 20 46	29 23	6	25	7	11	19	10	18	10
22	5 59 4	29 21 54	12♒15	8	25	8	12	19	10	18	10
23	6 3 0	0♑23 2	24 46	10	26	8	12	19	10	18	10
24	6 6 57	1 24 11	6♓58	11	26	9	12	19	10	18	10
25	6 10 53	2 25 19	18 57	13	26	10	12	19	10	18	10
26	6 14 50	3 26 27	0♈48	14	27	11	12	19	10	18	10
27	6 18 46	4 27 36	12 35	16	27	11	12	19	10	18	10
28	6 22 43	5 28 44	24 26	17	27	12	13	19	10	18	10
29	6 26 39	6 29 53	6♉24	19	28	13	13	19	10	18	10
30	6 30 36	7 31 1	18 34	21	28	14	13	19	10	18	10
31	6 34 32	8 32 10	1♊ 1	22	29	14	13	19	10	18	10

THE SUN ENTERS THE SIGN OF CAPRICORN ON DEC 22 AT 14:57.

♈ ARIES ♉ TAURUS ♊ GEMINI ♋ CANCER ♌ LEO ♍ VIRGO ♎ LIBRA ♏ SCORPIO ♐ SAGITTARIUS ♑ CAPRICORN ♒ AQUARIUS ♓ PISCES

1923

SIDEREAL SUN MOON MERCURY VENUS MARS JUPITER SATURN URANUS NEPTUNE PLUTO

DAY	TIME	☉	☽	☿	♀	♂	♃	♄	♅	♆	♇
	h m s	° ' "	° '	°	°	°	°	°	°	°	°
J 1	6 38 29	9♑33 18	13♊47	24♑	29♏	15♓	13♏	19♎	10♓	18♌R	10♋R
A 2	6 42 26	10 34 27	26 52	25	0♐	16	13	19	10	18	10
N 3	6 46 22	11 35 35	10♋15	27	0	16	14	19	10	18	10
U 4	6 50 19	12 36 44	23 55	29	1	17	14	20	11	18	10
A 5	6 54 15	13 37 52	7♌47	0♒	2	18	14	20	11	18	10
R 6	6 58 12	14 39 0	21 47	2	2	19	14	20	11	18	10
Y 7	7 2 8	15 40 9	5♍53	3	3	19	14	20	11	18	10
8	7 6 5	16 41 17	20 0	4	4	20	14	20	11	18	10
9	7 10 2	17 42 26	4♎ 8	6	4	21	14	20	11	18	10
10	7 13 58	18 43 35	18 14	7	5	22	15	20	11	18	10
11	7 17 55	19 44 43	2♏18	8	6	22	15	20	11	18	10
12	7 21 51	20 45 52	16 19	10	7	23	15	20	11	17	10
13	7 25 48	21 47 1	0♐15	11	7	24	15	20	11	17	10
14	7 29 44	22 48 9	14 5	12	8	25	15	20	11	17	10
15	7 33 41	23 49 18	27 46	13	9	25	15	20	11	17	10
16	7 37 37	24 50 26	11♑16	13	10	26	15	20	11	17	10
17	7 41 34	25 51 34	24 30	14	11	27	16	20	11	17	10
18	7 45 31	26 52 41	7♒29	15	11	27	16	20	11	17	10
19	7 49 27	27 53 47	20 10	15	12	28	16	20	11	17	10
20	7 53 24	28 54 53	2♓35	15 R	13	29	16	20	11	17	10
21	7 57 20	29 55 58	14 45	15	14	0☉	16	20	11	17	10
22	8 1 17	0♒57 2	26 43	15	15	0♈	16	20	11	17	10
23	8 5 13	1 58 5	8♈34	14	16	1	16	20	11	17	10
24	8 9 10	2 59 7	20 22	14	17	2	16	20	11	17	10
25	8 13 6	4 0 8	2♉12	13	18	3	17	20	11	17	10
26	8 17 3	5 1 8	14 9	12	19	3	17	20	11	17	10
27	8 21 0	6 2 7	26 20	11	20	4	17	20	12	17	10
28	8 24 56	7 3 5	8♊48	10	20	5	17	20	12	17	10
29	8 28 53	8 4 1	21 37	8	21	6	17	20 R	12	17	10
30	8 32 49	9 4 57	4♋49	7	22	6	17	20	12	17	10
31	8 36 46	10 5 51	18 25	6	23	7	17	20	12	17	10

THE SUN ENTERS THE SIGN OF AQUARIUS ON JAN 21 AT 01:35.

DAY	TIME	☉	☽	☿	♀	♂	♃	♄	♅	♆	♇
	h m s	° ' "	° '	°	°	°	°	°	°	°	°
F 1	8 40 42	11♒ 6 44	2♌23	5♒R	24♐	8♈	17♏	20♎R	12♓	17♌R	10♋R
E 2	8 44 39	12 7 37	16 38	4	25	8	17	20	12	17	10
B 3	8 48 35	13 8 28	1♍ 5	3	26	9	17	20	12	17	10
R 4	8 52 32	14 9 17	15 39	2	27	10	18	20	12	17	10
U 5	8 56 29	15 10 6	0♎13	1	28	11	18	20	12	17	9
A 6	9 0 25	16 10 54	14 42	0	29	11	18	20	12	17	9
R 7	9 4 22	17 11 41	29 2	0	0♑	12	18	20	12	17	9
Y 8	9 8 18	18 12 28	13♏11	29♑	1	13	18	20	12	17	9
9	9 12 15	19 13 13	27 8	29	2	14	18	20	12	17	9
10	9 16 11	20 13 57	10♐51	29 D	4	14	18	20	12	17	9
11	9 20 8	21 14 40	24 22	29	5	15	18	20	12	17	9
12	9 24 4	22 15 23	7♑39	29	6	16	18	20	12	17	9
13	9 28 1	23 16 3	20 43	0♒	7	16	18	20	12	17	9
14	9 31 58	24 16 43	3♒33	0	8	17	18	20	12	17	9
15	9 35 54	25 17 21	16 11	0	9	18	18	20	13	17	9
16	9 39 51	26 17 58	28 36	1	10	19	18	20	13	17	9
17	9 43 47	27 18 34	10♓49	2	11	19	19	20	13	17	9
18	9 47 44	28 19 7	22 52	2	12	20	19	20	13	16	9
19	9 51 40	29 19 39	4♈47	3	13	21	19	20	13	16	9
20	9 55 37	0♓20 10	16 36	4	14	21	19	20	13	16	9
21	9 59 33	1 20 38	28 24	5	15	22	19	20	13	16	9
22	10 3 30	2 21 5	10♉14	6	16	23	19	20	13	16	9
23	10 7 26	3 21 30	22 11	7	17	24	19	20	13	16	9
24	10 11 23	4 21 53	4♊19	8	19	24	19	20	13	16	9
25	10 15 20	5 22 14	16 44	9	20	25	19	20	13	16	9
26	10 19 16	6 22 33	29 29	10	21	26	19	19	13	16	9
27	10 23 13	7 22 50	12♋38	11	22	26	19	19	13	16	9
28	10 27 9	8 23 6	26 14	12	23	27	19	19	13	16	9

THE SUN ENTERS THE SIGN OF PISCES ON FEB 19 AT 15:60.

DAY	TIME	☉	☽	☿	♀	♂	♃	♄	♅	♆	♇
	h m s	° ' "	° '	°	°	°	°	°	°	°	°
M 1	10 31 6	9♓23 19	10♌16	13♒	24♑	28♈	19♏	19♎R	13♓	16♌R	9♋R
A 2	10 35 2	10 23 30	24 42	15	25	29	19	19	13	16	9
R 3	10 38 59	11 23 39	9♍26	16	26	29	19	19	13	16	9
C 4	10 42 55	12 23 47	24 22	17	27	0♉	19	19	13	16	9
H 5	10 46 52	13 23 53	9♎22	18	29	1	19 R	19	14	16	9
6	10 50 49	14 23 56	24 17	20	0♒	1	19	19	14	16	9
7	10 54 45	15 23 59	9♏ 0	21	1	2	19	19	14	16	9
8	10 58 42	16 24 0	23 27	23	2	3	19	19	14	16	9
9	11 2 38	17 23 59	7♐32	24	3	4	19	19	14	16	9
10	11 6 35	18 23 57	21 17	25	4	4	19	19	14	16	9
11	11 10 31	19 23 53	4♑40	27	5	5	19	19	14	16	9
12	11 14 28	20 23 47	17 44	28	7	6	19	19	14	16	9
13	11 18 24	21 23 40	0♒30	0♓	8	6	19	19	14	16	9
14	11 22 21	22 23 31	13 2	1	9	7	19	19	14	16	9
15	11 26 18	23 23 20	25 21	3	10	8	19	19	14	16	9
16	11 30 14	24 23 7	7♓31	4	11	8	19	18	14	16	9
17	11 34 11	25 22 52	19 31	6	12	9	19	18	14	16	9
18	11 38 7	26 22 36	1♈26	8	13	10	19	18	14	16	9
19	11 42 4	27 22 17	13 16	9	15	11	19	18	14	16	9
20	11 46 0	28 21 56	25 5	11	16	11	19	18	14	16	9
21	11 49 57	29 21 33	6♉54	13	17	12	19	18	14	16	9
22	11 53 53	0♈21 8	18 45	14	18	13	19	18	15	16	9
23	11 57 50	1 20 41	0♊44	16	19	13	18	18	15	16	9
24	12 1 46	2 20 12	12 52	18	20	14	18	18	15	16	9 D
25	12 5 43	3 19 40	25 14	19	22	15	18	18	15	16	9
26	12 9 40	4 19 6	7♋55	21	23	15	18	18	15	16	9
27	12 13 36	5 18 30	20 57	23	24	16	18	18	15	16	9
28	12 17 33	6 17 51	4♌24	25	25	17	18	18	15	16	9
29	12 21 29	7 17 10	18 19	27	26	18	18	18	15	16	9
30	12 25 26	8 16 27	2♍39	29	27	18	18	17	15	16	9
31	12 29 22	9 15 41	17 24	0♈	29	19	18	17	15	16	9

THE SUN ENTERS THE SIGN OF ARIES ON MAR 21 AT 15:29.

DAY	TIME	☉	☽	☿	♀	♂	♃	♄	♅	♆	♇
	h m s	° ' "	° '	°	°	°	°	°	°	°	°
A 1	12 33 19	10♈14 53	2♎27	2♈	0♓	20♉	18♏R	17♎R	15♓	16♌R	9♋
P 2	12 37 15	11 14 3	17 40	4	1	20	18	17	15	16	9
R 3	12 41 12	12 13 11	2♏53	6	2	21	18	17	15	16	9
I 4	12 45 9	13 12 18	17 57	8	3	22	18	17	15	16	9
L 5	12 49 5	14 11 22	2♐42	10	4	22	18	17	15	16	9
6	12 53 2	15 10 25	17 3	12	6	23	17	17	15	16	9
7	12 56 58	16 9 26	0♑57	14	7	24	17	17	15	15	9
8	13 0 55	17 8 25	14 24	16	8	24	17	17	15	15	9
9	13 4 51	18 7 22	27 26	18	9	25	17	17	15	15	9
10	13 8 48	19 6 18	10♒ 6	20	10	26	17	17	16	15	9
11	13 12 44	20 5 12	22 28	23	12	26	17	17	16	15	9
12	13 16 41	21 4 4	4♓36	25	13	27	17	16	16	15	9
13	13 20 38	22 2 54	16 35	27	14	28	17	16	16	15	9
14	13 24 34	23 1 42	28 27	29	15	29	17	16	16	15	9
15	13 28 31	24 0 29	10♈16	1♉	16	29	17	16	16	15	9
16	13 32 27	24 59 13	22 4	3	17	0♊	16	16	16	15	9
17	13 36 24	25 57 56	3♉53	5	19	1	16	16	16	15	9
18	13 40 20	26 56 37	15 46	7	20	1	16	16	16	15	9
19	13 44 17	27 55 15	27 43	9	21	2	16	16	16	15	9
20	13 48 13	28 53 52	9♊48	11	22	3	16	16	16	15	9
21	13 52 10	29 52 27	22 1	13	23	3	16	16	16	15	9
22	13 56 7	0♉50 59	4♋27	15	25	4	16	16	16	15	9
23	14 0 3	1 49 29	17 7	17	26	5	16	16	16	15	9
24	14 4 0	2 47 57	0♌ 5	19	27	5	16	16	16	15	9
25	14 7 56	3 46 23	13 24	20	28	6	15	15	16	15	9
26	14 11 53	4 44 47	27 7	22	29	7	15	15	16	15	9
27	14 15 49	5 43 9	11♍16	24	1♈	7	15	15	16	15 D	9
28	14 19 46	6 41 28	25 48	25	2	8	15	15	16	15	9
29	14 23 42	7 39 46	10♎42	27	3	9	15	15	16	15	9
30	14 27 39	8 38 1	25 51	28	4	9	15	15	16	15	9

THE SUN ENTERS THE SIGN OF TAURUS ON APR 21 AT 03:05.

DAY	TIME	☉	☽	☿	♀	♂	♃	♄	♅	♆	♇
	h m s	° ' "	° '	°	°	°	°	°	°	°	°
M 1	14 31 35	9♉36 15	11♏ 5	0♊	5♈	10♊	15♏R	15♎R	16♓	15♌	9♋
A 2	14 35 32	10 34 27	26 15	1	6	11	15	15	16	15	9
Y 3	14 39 29	11 32 37	11♐10	2	8	11	14	15	17	15	9
4	14 43 25	12 30 46	25 42	3	9	12	14	15	17	15	9
5	14 47 22	13 28 53	9♑46	4	10	13	14	15	17	15	9
6	14 51 18	14 26 59	23 21	5	11	13	14	15	17	15	9
7	14 55 15	15 25 4	6♒27	6	12	14	14	15	17	15	9
8	14 59 11	16 23 7	19 8	7	14	15	14	15	17	15	9
9	15 3 8	17 21 8	1♓28	8	15	15	14	15	17	15	9
10	15 7 4	18 19 9	13 33	9	16	16	14	14	17	15	9
11	15 11 1	19 17 8	25 28	9	17	17	13	14	17	15	10
12	15 14 58	20 15 5	7♈16	10	18	17	13	14	17	15	10
13	15 18 54	21 13 1	19 3	10	20	18	13	14	17	15	10
14	15 22 51	22 10 56	0♉52	10	21	19	13	14	17	15	10
15	15 26 47	23 8 49	12 45	11	22	19	13	14	17	15	10
16	15 30 44	24 6 41	24 44	11	23	20	13	14	17	15	10
17	15 34 40	25 4 32	6♊51	11 R	24	21	13	14	17	15	10
18	15 38 37	26 2 21	19 7	11	26	21	13	14	17	16	10
19	15 42 33	27 0 9	1♋32	11	27	22	12	14	17	16	10
20	15 46 30	27 57 55	14 8	11	28	23	12	14	17	16	10
21	15 50 27	28 55 39	26 56	10	29	23	12	14	17	16	10
22	15 54 23	29 53 22	9♌59	10	0♉	24	12	14	17	16	10
23	15 58 20	0♊51 3	23 17	10	2	25	12	14	17	16	10
24	16 2 16	1 48 43	6♍54	9	3	25	12	14	17	16	10
25	16 6 13	2 46 21	20 51	9	4	26	12	14	17	16	10
26	16 10 9	3 43 57	5♎ 9	8	5	27	12	14	17	16	10
27	16 14 6	4 41 32	19 45	8	6	27	11	14	17	16	10
28	16 18 2	5 39 6	4♏37	7	8	28	11	14	17	16	10
29	16 21 59	6 36 39	19 36	7	9	29	11	14	17	16	10
30	16 25 56	7 34 10	4♐36	6	10	29	11	14	17	16	10
31	16 29 52	8 31 40	19 25	6	11	0♋	11	14	17	16	10

THE SUN ENTERS THE SIGN OF GEMINI ON MAY 22 AT 02:45.

DAY	TIME	☉	☽	☿	♀	♂	♃	♄	♅	♆	♇
	h m s	° ' "	° '	°	°	°	°	°	°	°	°
J 1	16 33 49	9♊29 9	3♑55	5♊R	12♉	1♋	11♏R	14♎R	17♓	16♌	10♋
U 2	16 37 45	10 26 37	18 1	5	14	1	11	14	17	16	10
N 3	16 41 42	11 24 4	1♒38	4	15	2	11	14	17	16	10
E 4	16 45 38	12 21 31	14 48	4	16	3	11	13	17	16	10
5	16 49 35	13 18 57	27 32	3	17	3	11	13	17	16	10
6	16 53 31	14 16 22	9♓55	3	19	4	10	13	17	16	10
7	16 57 28	15 13 46	22 1	3	20	5	10	13	17	16	10
8	17 1 25	16 11 10	3♈56	3	21	5	10	13	17	16	10
9	17 5 21	17 8 33	15 45	2	22	6	10	13	17	16	10
10	17 9 18	18 5 56	27 34	2 D	23	7	10	13	17	16	10
11	17 13 14	19 3 18	9♉25	2	25	7	10	13	17	16	10
12	17 17 11	20 0 40	21 24	2	26	8	10	13	18	16	10
13	17 21 7	20 58 0	3♊32	3	27	9	10	13	18	16	10
14	17 25 4	21 55 21	15 50	3	28	9	10	13	18	16	10
15	17 29 0	22 52 41	28 20	3	29	10	10	13	18	16	10
16	17 32 57	23 50 0	11♋ 2	3	1♊	11	10	13 D	18	16	10
17	17 36 54	24 47 18	23 55	4	2	11	10	13	18	16	10
18	17 40 50	25 44 36	7♌ 0	4	3	12	10	13	18	16	10
19	17 44 47	26 41 53	20 16	5	4	13	10	13	18	16	10
20	17 48 43	27 39 9	3♍44	6	5	13	10	13	18	16	10
21	17 52 40	28 36 24	17 25	7	7	14	9	13	18	16	10
22	17 56 36	29 33 39	1♎19	7	8	14	9	13	18	16	10
23	18 0 33	0♋30 53	15 27	8	9	15	9	13	18 R	16	10
24	18 4 29	1 28 6	29 48	9	10	16	9	13	18	16	10
25	18 8 26	2 25 19	14♏18	10	12	16	9	13	18	16	11
26	18 12 23	3 22 31	28 55	11	13	17	9	13	18	16	11
27	18 16 19	4 19 43	13♐31	12	14	18	9	13	18	16	11
28	18 20 16	5 16 54	28 0	14	15	18	9	13	18	16	11
29	18 24 12	6 14 5	12♑15	15	16	19	9	13	18	16	11
30	18 28 9	7 11 16	26 10	16	18	20	9	13	18	16	11

THE SUN ENTERS THE SIGN OF CANCER ON JUN 22 AT 11:03.

♈ ARIES ♉ TAURUS ♊ GEMINI ♋ CANCER ♌ LEO ♍ VIRGO ♎ LIBRA ♏ SCORPIO ♐ SAGITTARIUS ♑ CAPRICORN ♒ AQUARIUS ♓ PISCES

SIDEREAL · SUN · MOON · MERCURY · VENUS · MARS · JUPITER · SATURN · URANUS · NEPTUNE · PLUTO

DAY	TIME	☉	☽	☿	♀	♂	♃	♄	♅	♆	♇
	h m s	° ' "	° '	°	°	°	°	°	°	°	°
J 1	18 32 5	8♋ 8 27	9♒41	18♊	19♊	20♋	9♏R	14♎	18♓R	16♌	11♋
U 2	18 36 2	9 5 38	22 49	19	20	21	9	14	18	16	11
L 3	18 39 59	10 2 49	5♓33	21	21	22	9	14	18	17	11
Y 4	18 43 55	11 0 0	17 56	22	22	22	9	14	18	17	11
5	18 47 52	11 57 11	0♈ 4	24	24	23	9	14	17	17	11
6	18 51 48	12 54 23	12 1	25	25	24	9	14	17	17	11
7	18 55 45	13 51 34	23 52	27	26	24	9 D	14	17	17	11
8	18 59 41	14 48 47	5♉43	29	27	25	9	14	17	17	11
9	19 3 38	15 45 59	17 38	1♋	29	25	9	14	17	17	11
10	19 7 34	16 43 12	29 41	3	0♋	26	9	14	17	17	11
11	19 11 31	17 40 26	11♊56	5	1	27	9	14	17	17	11
12	19 15 28	18 37 39	24 25	7	2	27	9	14	17	17	11
13	19 19 24	19 34 53	7♋10	9	3	28	9	14	17	17	11
14	19 23 21	20 32 8	20 9	11	5	29	9	14	17	17	11
15	19 27 17	21 29 23	3♌23	13	6	29	9	14	17	17	11
16	19 31 14	22 26 38	16 50	15	7	0♌	9	14	17	17	11
17	19 35 10	23 23 53	0♍28	17	8	1	9	14	17	17	11
18	19 39 7	24 21 8	14 16	19	10	1	9	14	17	17	11
19	19 43 3	25 18 23	28 12	21	11	2	9	14	17	17	11
20	19 47 0	26 15 39	12♎14	23	12	3	9	14	17	17	11
21	19 50 57	27 12 55	26 22	26	13	3	9	14	17	17	11
22	19 54 53	28 10 11	10♏35	28	14	4	9	14	17	17	11
23	19 58 50	29 7 28	24 49	0♌	16	4	9	14	17	17	11
24	20 2 46	0♌ 4 44	9♐ 4	2	17	5	9	14	17	17	11
25	20 6 43	1 2 2	23 14	4	18	6	10	15	17	17	11
26	20 10 39	1 59 19	7♑16	6	19	6	10	15	17	17	11
27	20 14 36	2 56 37	21 5	8	21	7	10	15	17	17	11
28	20 18 32	3 53 56	4♒39	10	22	8	10	15	17	17	11
29	20 22 29	4 51 16	17 55	12	23	8	10	15	17	17	11
30	20 26 26	5 48 36	0♓52	14	24	9	10	15	17	17	11
31	20 30 22	6 45 57	13 29	16	25	10	10	15	17	17	11

THE SUN ENTERS THE SIGN OF LEO ON JUL 23 AT 22:01.

DAY	TIME	☉	☽	☿	♀	♂	♃	♄	♅	♆	♇
	h m s	° ' "	° '	°	°	°	°	°	°	°	°
A 1	20 34 19	7♌43 19	25♓50	18♌	27♋	10♌	10♏	15♎	17♓R	18♌	11♋
U 2	20 38 15	8 40 43	7♈58	20	28	11	10	15	17	18	11
G 3	20 42 12	9 38 7	19 55	22	29	11	10	15	17	18	11
U 4	20 46 8	10 35 32	1♉47	24	0♌	12	10	15	17	18	11
S 5	20 50 5	11 32 59	13 39	25	2	13	10	15	17	18	12
T 6	20 54 1	12 30 27	25 36	27	3	13	10	15	17	18	12
7	20 57 58	13 27 56	7♊41	29	4	14	10	15	17	18	12
8	21 1 55	14 25 27	19 59	1♍	5	15	11	16	17	18	12
9	21 5 51	15 22 59	2♋35	2	7	15	11	16	17	18	12
10	21 9 48	16 20 32	15 29	4	8	16	11	16	17	18	12
11	21 13 44	17 18 6	28 42	6	9	17	11	16	17	18	12
12	21 17 41	18 15 42	12♌15	7	10	17	11	16	17	18	12
13	21 21 37	19 13 19	26 5	9	11	18	11	16	17	18	12
14	21 25 34	20 10 57	10♍ 8	11	13	19	11	16	17	18	12
15	21 29 30	21 8 36	24 22	12	14	19	11	16	17	18	12
16	21 33 27	22 6 16	8♎41	14	15	20	11	16	17	18	12
17	21 37 24	23 3 57	23 3	15	16	20	11	16	16	18	12
18	21 41 20	24 1 39	7♏22	17	18	21	12	16	16	18	12
19	21 45 17	24 59 23	21 37	18	19	22	12	16	16	18	12
20	21 49 13	25 57 7	5♐45	20	20	22	12	17	16	18	12
21	21 53 10	26 54 53	19 44	21	21	23	12	17	16	18	12
22	21 57 6	27 52 39	3♑32	22	23	24	12	17	16	18	12
23	22 1 3	28 50 27	17 8	24	24	24	12	17	16	18	12
24	22 4 59	29 48 16	0♒31	25	25	25	12	17	16	18	12
25	22 8 56	0♍46 6	13 41	26	26	26	12	17	16	18	12
26	22 12 53	1 43 58	26 35	28	28	26	13	17	16	18	12
27	22 16 49	2 41 51	9♓15	29	29	27	13	17	16	18	12
28	22 20 46	3 39 46	21 42	0♎	0♍	27	13	17	16	19	12
29	22 24 42	4 37 42	3♈56	1	1	28	13	17	16	19	12
30	22 28 39	5 35 40	15 59	2	2	29	13	17	16	19	12
31	22 32 35	6 33 40	27 55	3	4	29	13	18	16	19	12

THE SUN ENTERS THE SIGN OF VIRGO ON AUG 24 AT 04:53.

DAY	TIME	☉	☽	☿	♀	♂	♃	♄	♅	♆	♇
	h m s	° ' "	° '	°	°	°	°	°	°	°	°
S 1	22 36 32	7♍31 42	9♉47	5♎	5♍	0♍	13♏	18♎	16♓R	19♌	12♋
E 2	22 40 28	8 29 45	21 39	6	6	1	13	18	16	19	12
P 3	22 44 25	9 27 51	3♊34	7	7	1	14	18	16	19	12
T 4	22 48 21	10 25 59	15 38	7	9	2	14	18	16	19	12
E 5	22 52 18	11 24 8	27 56	8	10	3	14	18	16	19	12
M 6	22 56 15	12 22 20	10♋31	9	11	3	14	18	16	19	12
B 7	23 0 11	13 20 33	23 27	10	12	4	14	18	16	19	12
E 8	23 4 8	14 18 49	6♌46	11	14	4	14	18	16	19	12
R 9	23 8 4	15 17 6	20 29	11	15	5	15	19	16	19	12
10	23 12 1	16 15 25	4♍34	12	16	6	15	19	16	19	12
11	23 15 57	17 13 47	19 0	12	17	6	15	19	16	19	12
12	23 19 54	18 12 9	3♎39	13	19	7	15	19	15	19	12
13	23 23 50	19 10 34	18 26	13	20	8	15	19	15	19	12
14	23 27 47	20 9 1	3♏12	14	21	8	15	19	15	19	12
15	23 31 44	21 7 29	17 52	14	22	9	16	19	15	19	12
16	23 35 40	22 5 59	2♐20	14 R	24	10	16	19	15	19	12
17	23 39 37	23 4 30	16 32	14	25	10	16	19	15	19	12
18	23 43 33	24 3 3	0♑26	14	26	11	16	20	15	19	12
19	23 47 30	25 1 38	14 2	13	27	11	16	20	15	19	12
20	23 51 26	26 0 14	27 20	13	29	12	16	20	15	19	12
21	23 55 23	26 58 52	10♒21	13	0♎	13	17	20	15	19	12
22	23 59 19	27 57 32	23 8	12	1	13	17	20	15	19	12
23	0 3 16	28 56 13	5♓43	11	2	14	17	20	15	19	12
24	0 7 13	29 54 57	18 5	10	4	15	17	20	15	19	12
25	0 11 9	0♎53 42	0♈18	9	5	15	17	20	15	19	12
26	0 15 6	1 52 29	12 23	8	6	16	17	20	15	19	12
27	0 19 2	2 51 18	24 21	7	7	17	18	21	15	19	12
28	0 22 59	3 50 10	6♉15	6	9	17	18	21	15	20	12
29	0 26 55	4 49 3	18 6	5	10	18	18	21	15	20	12
30	0 30 52	5 47 59	29 57	4	11	18	18	21	15	20	12

THE SUN ENTERS THE SIGN OF LIBRA ON SEP 24 AT 02:05.

SIDEREAL · SUN · MOON · MERCURY · VENUS · MARS · JUPITER · SATURN · URANUS · NEPTUNE · PLUTO

DAY	TIME	☉	☽	☿	♀	♂	♃	♄	♅	♆	♇
	h m s	° ' "	° '	°	°	°	°	°	°	°	°
O 1	0 34 48	6♎46 57	11♊52	3♎R	12♎	19♍	18♏	21♎	15♓R	20♌	12♋
C 2	0 38 45	7 45 58	23 54	2	14	20	19	21	15	20	12
T 3	0 42 41	8 45 0	6♋ 8	1	15	20	19	21	15	20	12
O 4	0 46 38	9 44 5	18 39	0	16	21	19	21	15	20	12
B 5	0 50 35	10 43 13	1♌30	0	17	22	19	22	15	20	12
E 6	0 54 31	11 42 22	14 45	29♍	19	22	19	22	15	20	12
R 7	0 58 28	12 41 34	28 26	29	20	23	20	22	15	20	12
8	1 2 24	13 40 48	12♍36	29 D	21	24	20	22	14	20	12
9	1 6 21	14 40 5	27 10	29	22	24	20	22	14	20	12
10	1 10 17	15 39 23	12♎ 5	29	24	25	20	22	14	20	12
11	1 14 14	16 38 44	27 12	29	25	25	20	22	14	20	12
12	1 18 10	17 38 6	12♏22	0♎	26	26	21	22	14	20	12
13	1 22 7	18 37 31	27 25	1	27	27	21	23	14	20	12 R
14	1 26 4	19 36 57	12♐13	2	29	27	21	23	14	20	12
15	1 30 0	20 36 25	26 38	3	0♏	28	21	23	14	20	12
16	1 33 57	21 35 55	10♑37	4	1	29	21	23	14	20	12
17	1 37 53	22 35 27	24 12	5	2	29	22	23	14	20	12
18	1 41 50	23 35 1	7♒22	6	3	0♎	22	23	14	20	12
19	1 45 46	24 34 36	20 12	7	5	1	22	23	14	20	12
20	1 49 43	25 34 13	2♓44	9	6	1	22	23	14	20	12
21	1 53 39	26 33 51	15 3	10	7	2	22	23	14	20	12
22	1 57 36	27 33 32	27 12	12	8	2	23	24	14	20	12
23	2 1 33	28 33 14	9♈14	13	10	3	23	24	14	20	12
24	2 5 29	29 32 58	21 11	15	11	4	23	24	14	20	12
25	2 9 26	0♏32 44	3♉ 4	17	12	4	23	24	14	20	12
26	2 13 22	1 32 33	14 56	18	13	5	23	24	14	20	12
27	2 17 19	2 32 23	26 48	20	15	6	24	24	14	20	12
28	2 21 15	3 32 15	8♊41	22	16	6	24	24	14	20	12
29	2 25 12	4 32 10	20 38	23	17	7	24	24	14	20	12
30	2 29 8	5 32 6	2♋42	25	18	8	24	25	14	20	12
31	2 33 5	6 32 5	14 55	26	20	8	25	25	14	20	12

THE SUN ENTERS THE SIGN OF SCORPIO ON OCT 24 AT 10:52.

DAY	TIME	☉	☽	☿	♀	♂	♃	♄	♅	♆	♇
	h m s	° ' "	° '	°	°	°	°	°	°	°	°
N 1	2 37 1	7♏32 6	27♋22	28♎	21♏	9♎	25♏	25♎	14♓R	20♌	12♋R
O 2	2 40 58	8 32 9	10♌ 7	0♏	22	9	25	25	14	20	12
V 3	2 44 55	9 32 14	23 13	1	23	10	25	25	14	20	12
E 4	2 48 51	10 32 21	6♍46	3	25	11	25	25	14	20	12
M 5	2 52 48	11 32 30	20 46	5	26	11	26	25	14	20	12
B 6	2 56 44	12 32 42	5♎14	6	27	12	26	25	14	20	12
E 7	3 0 41	13 32 55	20 8	8	28	13	26	26	14	20	12
R 8	3 4 37	14 33 11	5♏20	10	0♐	13	26	26	14	20	12
9	3 8 34	15 33 28	20 40	11	1	14	27	26	14	20	12
10	3 12 30	16 33 47	5♐57	13	2	15	27	26	14	20	12
11	3 16 27	17 34 7	21 1	15	3	15	27	26	14	20	12
12	3 20 24	18 34 29	5♑41	16	5	16	27	26	14	20	12
13	3 24 20	19 34 53	19 52	18	6	16	27	26	14	20	12
14	3 28 17	20 35 18	3♒34	19	7	17	28	26	14	20	12
15	3 32 13	21 35 44	16 47	21	8	18	28	26	14	20	12
16	3 36 10	22 36 12	29 36	23	10	18	28	27	14	20	12
17	3 40 6	23 36 41	12♓ 3	24	11	19	28	27	14	20	12
18	3 44 3	24 37 11	24 16	26	12	20	29	27	14	20	12
19	3 47 59	25 37 43	6♈17	27	13	20	29	27	14	20	12
20	3 51 56	26 38 16	18 12	29	15	21	29	27	14	20	12
21	3 55 53	27 38 50	0♉ 3	0♐	16	22	29	27	14	20	12
22	3 59 49	28 39 25	11 54	2	17	22	29	27	14	20	12
23	4 3 46	29 40 2	23 47	4	18	23	0♐	27	14 D	20 R	12
24	4 7 42	0♐40 41	5♊42	5	20	24	0	27	14	20	12
25	4 11 39	1 41 20	17 41	7	21	24	0	28	14	20	12
26	4 15 35	2 42 2	29 46	8	22	25	0	28	14	20	12
27	4 19 32	3 42 45	11♋57	10	23	25	1	28	14	20	12
28	4 23 28	4 43 29	24 17	11	25	26	1	28	14	20	12
29	4 27 25	5 44 14	6♌47	13	26	27	1	28	14	20	12
30	4 31 22	6 45 2	19 32	15	27	27	1	28	14	20	12

THE SUN ENTERS THE SIGN OF SAGITTARIUS ON NOV 23 AT 07:54.

DAY	TIME	☉	☽	☿	♀	♂	♃	♄	♅	♆	♇
	h m s	° ' "	° '	°	°	°	°	°	°	°	°
D 1	4 35 18	7♐45 50	2♍34	16♐	28♐	28♎	1♐	28♎	14♓	20♌R	12♋R
E 2	4 39 15	8 46 40	15 58	18	0♑	29	2	28	14	20	12
C 3	4 43 11	9 47 32	29 46	19	1	29	2	28	14	20	12
E 4	4 47 8	10 48 25	13♎59	21	2	0♏	2	29	14	20	12
M 5	4 51 4	11 49 19	28 37	22	3	1	2	29	14	20	12
B 6	4 55 1	12 50 15	13♏35	24	5	1	3	29	14	20	12
E 7	4 58 57	13 51 12	28 46	25	6	2	3	29	14	20	12
R 8	5 2 54	14 52 10	13♐59	27	7	3	3	29	14	20	12
9	5 6 51	15 53 9	29 3	28	8	3	3	29	14	20	12
10	5 10 47	16 54 9	13♑49	0♑	10	4	3	29	14	20	12
11	5 14 44	17 55 9	28 9	2	11	4	4	29	14	20	12
12	5 18 40	18 56 11	11♒59	3	12	5	4	29	14	20	12
13	5 22 37	19 57 12	25 20	5	13	6	4	29	14	20	12
14	5 26 33	20 58 15	8♓14	6	15	6	4	29	14	20	12
15	5 30 30	21 59 17	20 45	8	16	7	4	0♏	14	20	12
16	5 34 27	23 0 21	2♈58	9	17	8	5	0	14	20	12
17	5 38 23	24 1 24	14 58	11	18	8	5	0	14	20	12
18	5 42 20	25 2 28	26 52	12	20	9	5	0	14	20	12
19	5 46 16	26 3 33	8♉42	13	21	10	5	0	14	20	12
20	5 50 13	27 4 37	20 33	15	22	10	6	0	14	20	12
21	5 54 9	28 5 43	2♊28	16	23	11	6	0	14	20	12
22	5 58 6	29 6 48	14 28	18	25	11	6	0	14	20	12
23	6 2 2	0♑ 7 54	26 36	19	26	12	6	0	14	20	12
24	6 5 59	1 9 1	8♋52	20	27	13	6	0	14	20	12
25	6 9 56	2 10 8	21 17	22	28	13	7	0	14	20	12
26	6 13 52	3 11 15	3♌51	23	0♒	14	7	0	14	20	11
27	6 17 49	4 12 23	16 36	24	1	15	7	1	14	20	11
28	6 21 45	5 13 31	29 32	25	2	15	7	1	14	20	11
29	6 25 42	6 14 40	12♍42	26	3	16	7	1	14	20	11
30	6 29 38	7 15 49	26 7	27	5	17	8	1	14	20	11
31	6 33 35	8 16 58	9♎49	27	6	17	8	1	14	20	11

THE SUN ENTERS THE SIGN OF CAPRICORN ON DEC 22 AT 20:54.

♈ ARIES ♉ TAURUS ♊ GEMINI ♋ CANCER ♌ LEO ♍ VIRGO ♎ LIBRA ♏ SCORPIO ♐ SAGITTARIUS ♑ CAPRICORN ♒ AQUARIUS ♓ PISCES

SIDEREAL SUN MOON MERCURY VENUS MARS JUPITER SATURN URANUS NEPTUNE PLUTO

DAY	TIME	☉	☽	☿	♀	♂	♃	♄	♅	♆	♇
	h m s	° ' "	° '	°	°	°	°	°	°	°	°
J 1	6 37 31	9♑18 8	23♎50	28♑	7♒	18♏	8♐	1♏	14♓	20♌R	11♋R
A 2	6 41 28	10 19 19	8♏10	29	8	19	8	1	14	20	11
N 3	6 45 25	11 20 29	22 45	29	10	19	9	1	14	20	11
U 4	6 49 21	12 21 40	7♐32	29 R	11	20	9	1	14	20	11
A 5	6 53 18	13 22 52	22 22	29	12	20	9	1	14	20	11
R 6	6 57 14	14 24 3	7♑ 9	29	13	21	9	1	14	20	11
Y 7	7 1 11	15 25 14	21 42	28	14	22	9	1	14	20	11
8	7 5 7	16 26 25	5♒57	27	16	22	10	1	14	20	11
9	7 9 4	17 27 36	19 47	27	17	23	10	1	15	20	11
10	7 13 0	18 28 46	3♓11	26	18	24	10	1	15	20	11
11	7 16 57	19 29 56	16 10	25	19	24	10	1	15	20	11
12	7 20 54	20 31 5	28 46	23	21	25	10	2	15	20	11
13	7 24 50	21 32 14	11♈ 4	22	22	26	11	2	15	20	11
14	7 28 47	22 33 22	23 8	21	23	26	11	2	15	20	11
15	7 32 43	23 34 29	5♉ 3	19	24	27	11	2	15	20	11
16	7 36 40	24 35 36	16 54	18	26	28	11	2	15	20	11
17	7 40 36	25 36 42	28 47	17	27	28	11	2	15	20	11
18	7 44 33	26 37 47	10♊44	16	28	29	11	2	15	20	11
19	7 48 29	27 38 52	22 49	15	29	29	12	2	15	20	11
20	7 52 26	28 39 55	5♋ 5	14	1♓	0♐	12	2	15	20	11
21	7 56 23	29 40 58	17 33	14	2	1	12	2	15	20	11
22	8 0 19	0♒42 1	0♌14	13	3	1	12	2	15	20	11
23	8 4 16	1 43 2	13 8	13	4	2	12	2	15	19	11
24	8 8 12	2 44 3	26 14	13 D	5	3	13	2	15	19	11
25	8 12 9	3 45 3	9♍33	13	7	3	13	2	15	19	11
26	8 16 5	4 46 3	23 3	13	8	4	13	2	15	19	11
27	8 20 2	5 47 2	6♎44	13	9	5	13	2	15	19	11
28	8 23 58	6 48 0	20 35	14	10	5	13	2	15	19	11
29	8 27 55	7 48 58	4♏36	14	12	6	13	2	15	19	11
30	8 31 52	8 49 55	18 46	15	13	7	14	2	15	19	11
31	8 35 48	9 50 51	3♐ 3	15	14	7	14	2	15	19	11

THE SUN ENTERS THE SIGN OF AQUARIUS ON JAN 21 AT 07:29.

DAY	TIME	☉	☽	☿	♀	♂	♃	♄	♅	♆	♇
	h m s	° ' "	° '	°	°	°	°	°	°	°	°
F 1	8 39 45	10♒51 47	17♐24	16♑	15♓	8♐	14♐	2♏	16♓	19♌R	11♋R
E 2	8 43 41	11 52 42	1♑46	17	16	8	14	2	16	19	11
B 3	8 47 38	12 53 36	16 2	18	18	9	14	2	16	19	11
R 4	8 51 34	13 54 29	0♒10	18	19	10	14	2	16	19	11
U 5	8 55 31	14 55 21	14 3	19	20	10	15	2	16	19	11
A 6	8 59 27	15 56 12	27 39	20	21	11	15	2	16	19	11
R 7	9 3 24	16 57 1	10♓55	22	23	12	15	2	16	19	11
Y 8	9 7 21	17 57 49	23 51	23	24	12	15	2	16	19	11
9	9 11 17	18 58 36	6♈28	24	25	13	15	2	16	19	11
10	9 15 14	19 59 21	18 49	25	26	14	15	2	16	19	11
11	9 19 10	21 0 5	0♉55	26	27	14	16	2 R	16	19	11
12	9 23 7	22 0 47	12 53	27	29	15	16	2	16	19	11
13	9 27 3	23 1 27	24 46	29	0☉	16	16	2	16	19	11
14	9 31 0	24 2 6	6♊39	0♒	1♈	16	16	2	16	19	11
15	9 34 56	25 2 43	18 37	1	2	17	16	2	16	19	11
16	9 38 53	26 3 19	0♋44	2	3	17	16	2	16	19	11
17	9 42 50	27 3 52	13 4	4	5	18	16	2	16	19	10
18	9 46 46	28 4 24	25 39	5	6	19	17	2	16	19	10
19	9 50 43	29 4 55	8♌33	7	7	19	17	2	16	19	10
20	9 54 39	0♓ 5 23	21 44	8	8	20	17	2	17	19	10
21	9 58 36	1 5 50	5♍13	9	9	21	17	2	17	19	10
22	10 2 32	2 6 15	18 59	11	11	21	17	2	17	19	10
23	10 6 29	3 6. 39	2♎57	12	12	22	17	2	17	19	10
24	10 10 25	4 7 1	17 5	14	13	23	17	2	17	19	10
25	10 14 22	5 7 22	1♏19	15	14	23	17	2	17	19	10
26	10 18 19	6 7 42	15 35	17	15	24	18	2	17	19	10
27	10 22 15	7 8 0	29 50	18	17	24	18	2	17	19	10
28	10 26 12	8 8 16	14♐ 2	20	18	25	18	2	17	18	10
29	10 30 8	9 8 32	28 7	21	19	26	18	2	17	18	10

THE SUN ENTERS THE SIGN OF PISCES ON FEB 19 AT 21:52.

DAY	TIME	☉	☽	☿	♀	♂	♃	♄	♅	♆	♇
	h m s	° ' "	° '	°	°	°	°	°	°	°	°
M 1	10 34 5	10♓ 8 45	12♑ 5	23♒	20♈	26♐	18♐	2♏R	17♓	18♌R	10♋R
A 2	10 38 1	11 8 58	25 54	25	21	27	18	2	17	18	10
R 3	10 41 58	12 9 8	9♒32	26	22	28	18	2	17	18	10
C 4	10 45 54	13 9 17	22 57	28	24	28	18	2	17	18	10
H 5	10 49 51	14 9 24	6♓10	0♓	25	29	18	2	17	18	10
6	10 53 47	15 9 29	19 8	1	26	29	18	2	17	18	10
7	10 57 44	16 9 33	1♈52	3	27	0♑	19	2	17	18	10
8	11 1 41	17 9 34	14 22	5	28	1	19	2	17	18	10
9	11 5 37	18 9 33	26 39	6	29	1	19	2	18	18	10
10	11 9 34	19 9 30	8♉45	8	1♉	2	19	2	18	18	10
11	11 13 30	20 9 26	20 43	10	2	3	19	2	18	18	10
12	11 17 27	21 9 19	2♊36	12	3	3	19	2	18	18	10
13	11 21 23	22 9 9	14 29	14	4	4	19	2	18	18	10
14	11 25 20	23 8 58	26 25	15	5	5	19	1	18	18	10
15	11 29 16	24 8 44	8♋31	17	6	5	19	1	18	18	10
16	11 33 13	25 8 29	20 50	19	7	6	19	1	18	18	10
17	11 37 10	26 8 10	3♌26	21	9	6	19	1	18	18	10
18	11 41 6	27 7 50	16 24	23	10	7	19	1	18	18	10
19	11 45 3	28 7 27	29 45	25	11	8	19	1	18	18	10
20	11 48 59	29 7 3	13♍30	27	12	8	19	1	18	18	10
21	11 52 56	0♈ 6 36	27 37	29	13	9	19	1	18	18	10
22	11 56 52	1 6 7	12♎ 2	1♈	14	10	20	1	18	18	10
23	12 0 49	2 5 36	26 39	3	15	10	20	1	18	18	10
24	12 4 45	3 5 3	11♏22	5	17	11	20	1	18	18	10 D
25	12 8 42	4 4 29	26 3	7	18	11	20	1	18	18	10
26	12 12 39	5 3 52	10♐36	9	19	12	20	1	19	18	10
27	12 16 35	6 3 14	24 55	11	20	13	20	1	19	18	10
28	12 20 32	7 2 34	8♑59	13	21	13	20	1	19	18	10
29	12 24 28	8 1 53	22 46	15	22	14	20	1	19	18	10
30	12 28 25	9 1 10	6♒17	17	23	15	20	1	19	18	10
31	12 32 21	10 0 24	19 33	19	24	15	20	0	19	18	10

THE SUN ENTERS THE SIGN OF ARIES ON MAR 20 AT 21:20.

SIDEREAL SUN MOON MERCURY VENUS MARS JUPITER SATURN URANUS NEPTUNE PLUTO

DAY	TIME	☉	☽	☿	♀	♂	♃	♄	♅	♆	♇
	h m s	° ' "	° '	°	°	°	°	°	°	°	°
A 1	12 36 18	10♈59 37	2♓35	21♈	25♉	16♑	20♐	0♏R	19♓	18♌R	10♋
P 2	12 40 14	11 58 49	15 24	23	26	16	20	0	19	18	10
R 3	12 44 11	12 57 58	28 2	25	28	17	20	0	19	18	10
I 4	12 48 7	13 57 5	10♈30	27	29	18	20	0	19	18	10
L 5	12 52 4	14 56 10	22 48	29	0♊	18	20	0	19	18	10
6	12 56 1	15 55 13	4♉57	1♉	1	19	20 R	0	19	18	10
7	12 59 57	16 54 14	16 58	2	2	19	20	0	19	18	10
8	13 3 54	17 53 13	28 54	4	3	20	20	0	19	18	10
9	13 7 50	18 52 10	10♊46	6	4	21	20	0	19	18	10
10	13 11 47	19 51 4	22 37	7	5	21	20	0	19	18	10
11	13 15 43	20 49 56	4♋32	9	6	22	20	0	19	18	10
12	13 19 40	21 48 46	16 35	10	7	22	20	0	19	18	10
13	13 23 36	22 47 34	28 50	12	8	23	20	0	19	18	10
14	13 27 33	23 46 20	11♌23	13	9	24	20	29♎	20	18	10
15	13 31 30	24 45 3	24 18	14	10	24	20	29	20	18	10
16	13 35 26	25 43 44	7♍39	15	11	25	20	29	20	18	10
17	13 39 23	26 42 23	21 27	16	12	25	20	29	20	18	10
18	13 43 19	27 40 59	5♎44	17	13	26	20	29	20	18	10
19	13 47 16	28 39 34	20 25	18	14	27	20	29	20	18	10
20	13 51 12	29 38 6	5♏23	19	15	27	20	29	20	18	10
21	13 55 9	0♉36 37	20 30	20	16	28	20	29	20	18	10
22	13 59 5	1 35 6	5♐36	20	17	28	20	29	20	18	10
23	14 3 2	2 33 33	20 30	21	18	29	19	29	20	18	10
24	14 6 59	3 31 59	5♑ 6	21	19	0♒	19	29	20	18	10
25	14 10 55	4 30 23	19 19	21	20	0	19	29	20	18	10
26	14 14 52	5 28 46	3♒ 8	21	21	1	19	29	20	18	10
27	14 18 48	6 27 7	16 34	21 R	22	1	19	28	20	18	10
28	14 22 45	7 25 26	29 39	21	23	2	19	28	20	18 D	10
29	14 26 41	8 23 44	12♓27	21	24	3	19	28	20	18	10
30	14 30 38	9 22 0	25 0	21	25	3	19	28	20	18	10

THE SUN ENTERS THE SIGN OF TAURUS ON APR 20 AT 08:58.

DAY	TIME	☉	☽	☿	♀	♂	♃	♄	♅	♆	♇
	h m s	° ' "	° '	°	°	°	°	°	°	°	°
M 1	14 34 34	10♉20 15	7♈22	21♉R	26♊	4♒	19♐R	28♎R	20♓	18♌	11♋
A 2	14 38 31	11 18 28	19 36	20	26	4	19	28	20	18	11
Y 3	14 42 28	12 16 39	1♉42	20	27	5	19	28	20	18	11
4	14 46 24	13 14 49	13 42	20	28	5	19	28	20	18	11
5	14 50 21	14 12 57	25 38	19	29	6	19	28	20	18	11
6	14 54 17	15 11 3	7♊31	18	0♋	7	19	28	20	18	11
7	14 58 14	16 9 8	19 22	18	1	7	18	28	21	18	11
8	15 2 10	17 7 11	1♋14	17	2	8	18	28	21	18	11
9	15 6 7	18 5 12	13 9	17	2	8	18	28	21	18	11
10	15 10 3	19 3 11	25 11	16	3	9	18	28	21	18	11
11	15 14 0	20 1 9	7♌25	15	4	9	18	27	21	18	11
12	15 17 57	20 59 4	19 54	15	5	10	18	27	21	18	11
13	15 21 53	21 56 58	2♍44	14	6	10	18	27	21	18	11
14	15 25 50	22 54 50	15 59	14	6	11	18	27	21	18	11
15	15 29 46	23 52 40	29 43	13	7	12	18	27	21	18	11
16	15 33 43	24 50 29	13♎57	13	8	12	18	27	21	18	11
17	15 37 39	25 48 16	28 39	13	8	13	17	27	21	18	11
18	15 41 36	26 46 1	13♏43	12	9	13	17	27	21	18	11
19	15 45 32	27 43 45	29 0	12	10	14	17	27	21	18	11
20	15 49 29	28 41 27	14♐19	12	10	14	17	27	21	18	11
21	15 53 26	29 39 9	29 29	12 D	11	15	17	27	21	18	11
22	15 57 22	0♊36 49	14♑21	12	12	15	17	27	21	18	11
23	16 1 19	1 34 28	28 46	12	12	16	17	27	21	18	11
24	16 5 15	2 32 6	12♒44	12	13	16	17	27	21	18	11
25	16 9 12	3 29 43	26 14	13	13	17	17	27	21	18	11
26	16 13 8	4 27 19	9♓19	13	14	17	16	27	21	18	11
27	16 17 5	5 24 54	22 3	13	14	18	16	26	21	18	11
28	16 21 1	6 22 29	4♈30	14	15	18	16	26	21	18	11
29	16 24 58	7 20 2	16 44	14	15	19	16	26	21	18	11
30	16 28 55	8 17 34	28 48	15	15	19	16	26	21	18	11
31	16 32 51	9 15 6	10♉47	16	16	20	16	26	21	18	11

THE SUN ENTERS THE SIGN OF GEMINI ON MAY 21 AT 08:40.

DAY	TIME	☉	☽	☿	♀	♂	♃	♄	♅	♆	♇
	h m s	° ' "	° '	°	°	°	°	°	°	°	°
J 1	16 36 48	10♊12 37	22♉41	16♉	16♋	20♒	16♐R	26♎R	21♓	18♌	11♋
U 2	16 40 44	11 10 6	4♊33	17	16	21	16	26	21	18	11
N 3	16 44 41	12 7 35	16 25	18	17	21	15	26	21	18	11
E 4	16 48 37	13 5 3	28 17	19	17	22	15	26	21	18	11
5	16 52 34	14 2 30	10♋12	20	17	22	15	26	21	18	11
6	16 56 30	14 59 56	22 12	21	17	23	15	26	21	18	11
7	17 0 27	15 57 20	4♌19	22	17	23	15	26	21	18	11
8	17 4 24	16 54 44	16 36	23	18	23	15	26	21	18	11
9	17 8 20	17 52 7	29 7	25	18	24	15	26	21	18	11
10	17 12 17	18 49 28	11♍56	26	18 R	24	15	26	21	18	11
11	17 16 13	19 46 49	25 7	27	18	25	14	26	21	18	11
12	17 20 10	20 44 8	8♎44	28	18	25	14	26	21	18	11
13	17 24 6	21 41 26	22 49	0♊	17	26	14	26	21	18	11
14	17 28 3	22 38 44	7♏21	1	17	26	14	26	21	18	11
15	17 31 59	23 36 1	22 15	3	17	26	14	26	21	18	11
16	17 35 56	24 33 17	7♐26	4	17	27	14	26	21	18	11
17	17 39 53	25 30 32	22 43	6	17	27	14	26	21	18	11
18	17 43 49	26 27 47	7♑54	8	16	28	14	26	21	18	11
19	17 47 46	27 25 1	22 51	9	16	28	13	26	21	18	12
20	17 51 42	28 22 15	7♒24	11	16	28	13	26	21	18	12
21	17 55 39	29 19 29	21 30	13	15	29	13	26	22	18	12
22	17 59 35	0♋16 42	5♓ 8	15	15	29	13	26	22	18	12
23	18 3 32	1 13 56	18 18	17	14	29	13	26	22	18	12
24	18 7 28	2 11 9	1♈ 5	19	14	0♓	13	26	22	18	12
25	18 11 25	3 8 22	13 32	21	13	0	13	26	22	18	12
26	18 15 22	4 5 35	25 45	23	13	0	13	26	22 R	18	12
27	18 19 18	5 2 48	7♉46	25	12	1	12	26	22	19	12
28	18 23 15	6 0 1	19 41	27	12	1	12	26	22	19	12
29	18 27 11	6 57 15	1♊33	29	11	1	12	26 D	22	19	12
30	18 31 8	7 54 28	13 24	1♋	10	2	12	26	22	19	12

THE SUN ENTERS THE SIGN OF CANCER ON JUN 21 AT 16:60.

♈ ARIES ♉ TAURUS ♊ GEMINI ♋ CANCER ♌ LEO ♍ VIRGO ♎ LIBRA ♏ SCORPIO ♐ SAGITTARIUS ♑ CAPRICORN ♒ AQUARIUS ♓ PISCES

SIDEREAL SUN MOON MERCURY VENUS MARS JUPITER SATURN URANUS NEPTUNE PLUTO

DAY	TIME	☉	☽	☿	♀	♂	♃	♄	♅	♆	♇
	h m s	° ' "	° '	°	°	°	°	°	°	°	°
J 1	18 35 4	8♋51 41	25♊18	3♋	10♋R	2♓	12♐R	26♎	22♓R	19♌	12♋
U 2	18 39 1	9 48 54	7♋15	5	9	2	12	26	22	19	12
L 3	18 42 57	10 46 7	19 17	7	8	2	12	26	21	19	12
Y 4	18 46 54	11 43 20	1♌26	10	8	3	12	26	21	19	12
5	18 50 51	12 40 33	13 43	12	7	3	12	26	21	19	12
6	18 54 47	13 37 46	26 11	14	7	3	12	26	21	19	12
7	18 58 44	14 34 59	8♍52	16	6	3	11	26	21	19	12
8	19 2 40	15 32 11	21 48	18	5	4	11	26	21	19	12
9	19 6 37	16 29 24	5♎ 3	20	5	4	11	26	21	19	12
10	19 10 33	17 26 36	18 38	22	4	4	11	26	21	19	12
11	19 14 30	18 23 48	2♏35	25	4	4	11	26	21	19	12
12	19 18 26	19 21 0	16 53	27	4	4	11	26	21	19	12
13	19 22 23	20 18 12	1♐31	29	3	4	11	26	21	19	12
14	19 26 20	21 15 24	16 23	1♌	3	5	11	26	21	19	12
15	19 30 16	22 12 37	1♑22	3	2	5	11	26	21	19	12
16	19 34 13	23 9 49	16 19	5	2	5	11	26	21	19	12
17	19 38 9	24 7 2	1♒ 6	7	2	5	11	26	21	19	12
18	19 42 6	25 4 16	15 36	8	2	5	11	26	21	19	12
19	19 46 2	26 1 30	29 42	10	1	5	11	26	21	19	12
20	19 49 59	26 58 44	13♓23	12	1	5	11	26	21	19	12
21	19 53 55	27 55 59	26 38	14	1	5	11	26	21	19	12
22	19 57 52	28 53 15	9♈30	16	1	5	10	26	21	19	12
23	20 1 49	29 50 32	22 1	18	1 D	5	10	26	21	19	12
24	20 5 45	0♌47 50	4♉15	19	1	5 R	10	26	21	19	12
25	20 9 42	1 45 9	16 18	21	1	5	10	26	21	19	12
26	20 13 38	2 42 28	28 13	23	1	5	10	26	21	19	12
27	20 17 35	3 39 49	10♊ 5	24	1	5	10	26	21	20	12
28	20 21 31	4 37 10	21 57	26	2	5	10	26	21	20	12
29	20 25 28	5 34 33	3♋54	27	2	5	10	26	21	20	13
30	20 29 24	6 31 56	15 57	29	2	5	10	26	21	20	13
31	20 33 21	7 29 21	28 8	0♍	2	5	10	26	21	20	13

THE SUN ENTERS THE SIGN OF LEO ON JUL 23 AT 03:58.

DAY	TIME	☉	☽	☿	♀	♂	♃	♄	♅	♆	♇
	h m s	° ' "	° '	°	°	°	°	°	°	°	°
A 1	20 37 18	8♌26 46	10♌30	2♍	2♋	5♓R	10♐R	26♎	21♓R	20♌	13♋
U 2	20 41 14	9 24 12	23 4	3	3	5	10	27	21	20	13
G 3	20 45 11	10 21 39	5♍50	5	3	5	10	27	21	20	13
U 4	20 49 7	11 19 6	18 49	6	4	5	10	27	21	20	13
S 5	20 53 4	12 16 35	2♎ 2	8	4	4	10	27	21	20	13
T 6	20 57 0	13 14 4	15 30	9	4	4	10	27	21	20	13
7	21 0 57	14 11 34	29 12	10	5	4	10 D	27	21	20	13
8	21 4 53	15 9 5	13♏ 8	11	5	4	10	27	21	20	13
9	21 8 50	16 6 38	27 18	13	6	4	10	27	21	20	13
10	21 12 47	17 4 9	11♐39	14	6	4	10	27	21	20	13
11	21 16 43	18 1 42	26 9	15	7	3	10	27	21	20	13
12	21 20 40	18 59 16	10♑43	16	8	3	10	27	21	20	13
13	21 24 36	19 56 52	25 15	17	8	3	10	27	21	20	13
14	21 28 33	20 54 28	9♒40	18	9	3	10	27	21	20	13
15	21 32 29	21 52 5	23 53	19	9	2	10	27	21	20	13
16	21 36 26	22 49 44	7♓48	20	10	2	10	27	21	20	13
17	21 40 22	23 47 24	21 24	21	11	2	10	28	21	20	13
18	21 44 19	24 45 6	4♈37	22	11	2	10	28	21	20	13
19	21 48 16	25 42 49	17 30	23	12	1	10	28	20	20	13
20	21 52 12	26 40 33	0♉ 3	23	13	1	10	28	20	20	13
21	21 56 9	27 38 20	12 20	24	14	1	10	28	20	20	13
22	22 0 5	28 36 8	24 24	25	14	1	10	28	20	20	13
23	22 4 2	29 33 57	6♊20	25	15	0	10	28	20	20	13
24	22 7 58	0♍31 49	18 12	26	16	0	10	28	20	21	13
25	22 11 55	1 29 42	0♋ 6	26	17	0	11	28	20	21	13
26	22 15 51	2 27 37	12 5	26	18	0	11	28	20	21	13
27	22 19 48	3 25 34	24 13	27	18	29♒	11	28	20	21	13
28	22 23 45	4 23 32	6♌33	27	19	29	11	28	20	21	13
29	22 27 41	5 21 32	19 8	27 R	20	29	11	28	20	21	13
30	22 31 38	6 19 34	1♍59	27	21	29	11	29	20	21	13
31	22 35 34	7 17 37	15 7	27	22	28	11	29	20	21	13

THE SUN ENTERS THE SIGN OF VIRGO ON AUG 23 AT 10:49.

DAY	TIME	☉	☽	☿	♀	♂	♃	♄	♅	♆	♇
	h m s	° ' "	° '	°	°	°	°	°	°	°	°
S 1	22 39 31	8♍15 42	28♍31	26♍R	23♋	28♒R	11♐	29♎	20♓R	21♌	13♋
E 2	22 43 27	9 13 49	12♎ 9	26	24	28	11	29	20	21	13
P 3	22 47 24	10 11 57	25 59	26	24	28	11	29	20	21	13
T 4	22 51 20	11 10 6	9♏59	25	25	27	11	29	20	21	13
E 5	22 55 17	12 8 17	24 6	24	26	27	11	29	20	21	13
M 6	22 59 14	13 6 30	8♐16	24	27	27	11	29	20	21	13
B 7	23 3 10	14 4 44	22 29	23	28	27	11	29	20	21	13
E 8	23 7 7	15 3 0	6♑42	22	29	27	12	29	20	21	13
R 9	23 11 3	16 1 17	20 52	21	0♌	26	12	0♏	20	21	13
10	23 15 0	16 59 35	4♒57	20	1	26	12	0	20	21	13
11	23 18 56	17 57 55	18 54	19	2	26	12	0	20	21	13
12	23 22 53	18 56 17	2♓42	18	3	26	12	0	20	21	13
13	23 26 49	19 54 41	16 17	17	4	26	12	0	20	21	13
14	23 30 46	20 53 6	29 37	16	5	26	12	0	19	21	13
15	23 34 42	21 51 33	12♈41	15	6	26	12	0	19	21	13
16	23 38 39	22 50 2	25 28	14	7	26	12	0	19	21	13
17	23 42 36	23 48 34	7♉58	14	8	26	13	0	19	21	13
18	23 46 32	24 47 7	20 14	13	9	25	13	0	19	21	13
19	23 50 29	25 45 43	2♊18	13	10	25	13	1	19	21	13
20	23 54 25	26 44 21	14 14	13 D	11	25	13	1	19	21	13
21	23 58 22	27 43 1	26 5	13	12	25	13	1	19	21	13
22	0 2 18	28 41 43	7♋58	13	13	25 D	13	1	19	22	13
23	0 6 15	29 40 28	19 57	13	14	25	13	1	19	22	13
24	0 10 11	0♎39 14	2♌ 6	14	15	25	13	1	19	22	13
25	0 14 8	1 38 4	14 31	14	16	25	14	1	19	22	13
26	0 18 5	2 36 55	27 15	15	17	25	14	1	19	22	13
27	0 22 1	3 35 48	10♍20	16	18	25	14	1	19	22	13
28	0 25 58	4 34 43	23 47	17	19	26	14	2	19	22	14
29	0 29 54	5 33 41	7♎35	18	21	26	14	2	19	22	14
30	0 33 51	6 32 40	21 40	19	22	26	14	2	19	22	14

THE SUN ENTERS THE SIGN OF LIBRA ON SEP 23 AT 07:59.

DAY	TIME	☉	☽	☿	♀	♂	♃	♄	♅	♆	♇
	h m s	° ' "	° '	°	°	°	°	°	°	°	°
O 1	0 37 47	7♎31 42	5♏59	20♍	23♌	26♒	14♐	2♏	19♓R	22♌	14♋
C 2	0 41 44	8 30 45	20 25	22	24	26	14	2	19	22	14
T 3	0 45 40	9 29 51	4♐52	23	25	26	15	2	19	22	14
O 4	0 49 37	10 28 58	19 16	25	26	26	15	2	19	22	14
B 5	0 53 34	11 28 7	3♑31	26	27	26	15	2	19	22	14
E 6	0 57 30	12 27 17	17 37	28	28	27	15	2	19	22	14
R 7	1 1 27	13 26 30	1♒32	0♎	29	27	15	3	19	22	14
8	1 5 23	14 25 44	15 16	1	0♍	27	15	3	19	22	14
9	1 9 20	15 25 0	28 49	3	2	27	16	3	19	22	14
10	1 13 16	16 24 17	12♓11	5	3	27	16	3	18	22	14
11	1 17 13	17 23 37	25 22	7	4	28	16	3	18	22	14
12	1 21 9	18 22 58	8♈22	8	5	28	16	3	18	22	14
13	1 25 6	19 22 22	21 9	10	6	28	16	3	18	22	14
14	1 29 2	20 21 47	3♉44	12	7	28	16	3	18	22	14 R
15	1 32 59	21 21 15	16 7	14	8	29	17	3	18	22	14
16	1 36 56	22 20 45	28 18	15	9	29	17	4	18	22	14
17	1 40 52	23 20 17	10♊19	17	11	29	17	4	18	22	14
18	1 44 49	24 19 51	22 12	19	12	29	17	4	18	22	14
19	1 48 45	25 19 28	4♋ 2	20	13	0♓	17	4	18	22	14
20	1 52 42	26 19 7	15 53	22	14	0	17	4	18	22	14
21	1 56 38	27 18 48	27 49	24	15	0	18	4	18	22	14
22	2 0 35	28 18 31	9♌56	26	16	1	18	4	18	22	14
23	2 4 31	29 18 17	22 19	27	18	1	18	4	18	22	14
24	2 8 28	0♏18 4	5♍ 4	29	19	1	18	5	18	22	14
25	2 12 25	1 17 54	18 13	1♏	20	2	18	5	18	22	14
26	2 16 21	2 17 46	1♎50	2	21	2	19	5	18	22	14
27	2 20 18	3 17 41	15 53	4	22	3	19	5	18	22	14
28	2 24 14	4 17 37	0♏20	6	23	3	19	5	18	22	14
29	2 28 11	5 17 35	15 5	7	25	3	19	5	18	22	14
30	2 32 7	6 17 35	29 58	9	26	4	19	5	18	22	14
31	2 36 4	7 17 37	14♐51	10	27	4	20	5	18	22	14

THE SUN ENTERS THE SIGN OF SCORPIO ON OCT 23 AT 16:45.

DAY	TIME	☉	☽	☿	♀	♂	♃	♄	♅	♆	♇
	h m s	° ' "	° '	°	°	°	°	°	°	°	°
N 1	2 40 0	8♏17 41	29♐36	12♏	28♍	5♓	20♐	6♏	18♓R	22♌	13♋R
O 2	2 43 57	9 17 46	14♑ 6	14	29	5	20	6	18	22	13
V 3	2 47 54	10 17 53	28 19	15	0♎	5	20	6	18	22	13
E 4	2 51 50	11 18 2	12♒12	17	2	6	20	6	18	22	13
M 5	2 55 47	12 18 12	25 46	18	3	6	21	6	18	22	13
B 6	2 59 43	13 18 23	9♓ 4	20	4	7	21	6	18	22	13
E 7	3 3 40	14 18 36	22 8	21	5	7	21	6	18	22	13
R 8	3 7 36	15 18 50	4♈59	23	6	8	21	6	18	23	13
9	3 11 33	16 19 6	17 38	25	8	8	21	6	18	23	13
10	3 15 29	17 19 24	0♉ 8	26	9	8	22	7	18	23	13
11	3 19 26	18 19 43	12 29	28	10	9	22	7	18	23	13
12	3 23 23	19 20 4	24 40	29	11	9	22	7	18	23	13
13	3 27 19	20 20 27	6♊44	1♐	12	10	22	7	18	23	13
14	3 31 16	21 20 51	18 40	2	14	10	22	7	18	23	13
15	3 35 12	22 21 17	0♋31	4	15	11	23	7	18	23	13
16	3 39 9	23 21 45	12 19	5	16	11	23	7	18	23	13
17	3 43 5	24 22 15	24 8	7	17	12	23	7	18	23	13
18	3 47 2	25 22 46	6♌ 2	8	18	12	23	8	18	23	13
19	3 50 58	26 23 20	18 6	10	20	13	23	8	18	23	13
20	3 54 55	27 23 55	0♍25	11	21	13	24	8	18	23	13
21	3 58 52	28 24 32	13 5	13	22	14	24	8	18	23	13
22	4 2 48	29 25 10	26 10	14	23	14	24	8	18	23	13
23	4 6 45	0♐25 50	9♎44	16	25	15	24	8	18	23	13
24	4 10 41	1 26 32	23 49	17	26	16	25	8	18	23	13
25	4 14 38	2 27 15	8♏22	19	27	16	25	8	18	23 R	13
26	4 18 34	3 28 0	23 18	20	28	17	25	8	18	23	13
27	4 22 31	4 28 47	8♐28	22	29	17	25	9	18 D	23	13
28	4 26 27	5 29 34	23 42	23	1♏	18	25	9	18	23	13
29	4 30 24	6 30 23	8♑49	25	2	18	26	9	18	23	13
30	4 34 21	7 31 13	23 40	26	3	19	26	9	18	23	13

THE SUN ENTERS THE SIGN OF SAGITTARIUS ON NOV 22 AT 13:47.

DAY	TIME	☉	☽	☿	♀	♂	♃	♄	♅	♆	♇
	h m s	° ' "	° '	°	°	°	°	°	°	°	°
D 1	4 38 17	8♐32 4	8♒ 8	27♐	4♏	19♓	26♐	9♏	18♓	23♌R	13♋R
E 2	4 42 14	9 32 55	22 12	29	6	20	26	9	18	23	13
C 3	4 46 10	10 33 48	5♓50	0♑	7	20	27	9	18	23	13
E 4	4 50 7	11 34 41	19 6	1	8	21	27	9	18	23	13
M 5	4 54 3	12 35 35	2♈ 2	3	9	22	27	9	18	23	13
B 6	4 58 0	13 36 30	14 42	4	10	22	27	10	18	23	13
E 7	5 1 56	14 37 25	27 9	5	12	23	27	10	18	23	13
R 8	5 5 53	15 38 22	9♉25	6	13	23	28	10	18	23	13
9	5 9 50	16 39 19	21 32	7	14	24	28	10	18	23	13
10	5 13 46	17 40 17	3♊33	8	15	24	28	10	18	23	13
11	5 17 43	18 41 16	15 29	9	17	25	28	10	18	23	13
12	5 21 39	19 42 15	27 21	10	18	26	29	10	18	23	13
13	5 25 36	20 43 16	9♋11	11	19	26	29	10	18	23	13
14	5 29 32	21 44 17	21 1	12	20	27	29	10	18	22	13
15	5 33 29	22 45 19	2♌52	12	22	27	29	11	18	22	13
16	5 37 25	23 46 22	14 48	13	23	28	29	11	18	22	13
17	5 41 22	24 47 26	26 53	13	24	29	0♑	11	18	22	13
18	5 45 19	25 48 31	9♍12	13 R	25	29	0	11	18	22	13
19	5 49 15	26 49 36	21 48	13	26	0⊙	0	11	18	22	13
20	5 53 12	27 50 42	4♎47	13	28	0♈	0	11	18	22	13
21	5 57 8	28 51 49	18 12	12	29	1	1	11	18	22	13
22	6 1 5	29 52 57	2♏ 6	12	0♐	2	1	11	18	22	13
23	6 5 1	0♑54 6	16 29	11	1	2	1	11	18	22	13
24	6 8 58	1 55 15	1♐18	10	3	3	1	11	18	22	13
25	6 12 54	2 56 25	16 26	9	4	3	2	11	18	22	13
26	6 16 51	3 57 36	1♑43	7	5	4	2	12	18	22	13
27	6 20 48	4 58 46	16 59	6	6	5	2	12	18	22	13
28	6 24 44	5 59 57	2♒ 4	5	8	5	2	12	18	22	13
29	6 28 41	7 1 8	16 48	3	9	6	2	12	18	22	13
30	6 32 37	8 2 19	1♓ 7	2	10	6	3	12	18	22	13
31	6 36 34	9 3 29	14 58	1	11	7	3	12	18	22	13

THE SUN ENTERS THE SIGN OF CAPRICORN ON DEC 22 AT 02:46.

♈ ARIES ♉ TAURUS ♊ GEMINI ♋ CANCER ♌ LEO ♍ VIRGO ♎ LIBRA ♏ SCORPIO ♐ SAGITTARIUS ♑ CAPRICORN ♒ AQUARIUS ♓ PISCES

1925

SIDEREAL SUN MOON MERCURY VENUS MARS JUPITER SATURN URANUS NEPTUNE PLUTO

DAY	TIME	☉	☽	☿	♀	♂	♃	♄	♅	♆	♇
	h m s	° ' "	° '	°	°	°	°	°	°	°	°
J 1	6 40 30	10♑ 4 39	28♓23	0♑R	13♐	8♈	3♑	12♏	18♓	22♌R	13♋R
A 2	6 44 27	11 5 50	11♈23	29♐	14	8	3	12	18	22	13
N 3	6 48 24	12 6 59	24 2	28	15	9	4	12	18	22	12
U 4	6 52 20	13 8 9	6♉24	27	16	9	4	12	18	22	12
A 5	6 56 17	14 9 18	18 33	27	18	10	4	12	18	22	12
R 6	7 0 13	15 10 27	0♊33	27 D	19	11	4	12	18	22	12
Y 7	7 4 10	16 11 36	12 28	27	20	11	5	13	18	22	12
8	7 8 6	17 12 44	24 18	27	21	12	5	13	18	22	12
9	7 12 3	18 13 53	6♋ 8	27	23	13	5	13	18	22	12
10	7 15 59	19 15 0	17 59	27	24	13	5	13	18	22	12
11	7 19 56	20 16 8	29 53	28	25	14	5	13	18	22	12
12	7 23 53	21 17 15	11♌51	28	26	14	6	13	18	22	12
13	7 27 49	22 18 22	23 57	29	28	15	6	13	19	22	12
14	7 31 46	23 19 28	6♍11	0♑	29	16	6	13	19	22	12
15	7 35 42	24 20 35	18 37	1	0♑	16	6	13	19	22	12
16	7 39 39	25 21 41	1♎19	1	1	17	7	13	19	22	12
17	7 43 35	26 22 47	14 18	2	3	18	7	13	19	22	12
18	7 47 32	27 23 52	27 38	3	4	18	7	13	19	22	12
19	7 51 28	28 24 57	11♏21	4	5	19	7	13	19	22	12
20	7 55 25	29 26 3	25 28	5	6	20	7	13	19	22	12
21	7 59 22	0♒27 7	9♐58	7	8	20	8	13	19	22	12
22	8 3 18	1 28 11	24 46	8	9	21	8	13	19	22	12
23	8 7 15	2 29 15	9♑48	9	10	21	8	14	19	22	12
24	8 11 11	3 30 18	24 53	10	11	22	8	14	19	22	12
25	8 15 8	4 31 21	9♒54	11	13	23	9	14	19	22	12
26	8 19 4	5 32 22	24 41	13	14	23	9	14	19	22	12
27	8 23 1	6 33 22	9♓ 8	14	15	24	9	14	19	22	12
28	8 26 57	7 34 22	23 9	15	16	25	9	14	19	22	12
29	8 30 54	8 35 20	6♈44	17	18	25	9	14	19	22	12
30	8 34 51	9 36 17	19 53	18	19	26	10	14	19	22	12
31	8 38 47	10 37 12	2♉39	19	20	27	10	14	19	22	12

THE SUN ENTERS THE SIGN OF AQUARIUS ON JAN 20 AT 13:21.

DAY	TIME	☉	☽	☿	♀	♂	♃	♄	♅	♆	♇
	h m s	° ' "	° '	°	°	°	°	°	°	°	°
F 1	8 42 44	11♒38 6	15♉ 4	21♑	21♑	27♈	10♑	14♏	19♓	21♌R	12♋R
E 2	8 46 40	12 38 59	27 13	22	23	28	10	14	19	21	12
B 3	8 50 37	13 39 51	9♊11	24	24	28	10	14	19	21	12
R 4	8 54 33	14 40 41	21 3	25	25	29	11	14	19	21	12
U 5	8 58 30	15 41 30	2♋52	27	26	0♉	11	14	20	21	12
A 6	9 2 26	16 42 18	14 42	28	28	0	11	14	20	21	12
R 7	9 6 23	17 43 4	26 36	29	29	1	11	14	20	21	12
Y 8	9 10 20	18 43 49	8♌36	1♒	0♒	2	12	14	20	21	12
9	9 14 16	19 44 32	20 46	3	1	2	12	14	20	21	12
10	9 18 13	20 45 14	3♍ 5	4	3	3	12	14	20	21	12
11	9 22 9	21 45 55	15 36	6	4	4	12	14	20	21	12
12	9 26 6	22 46 34	28 20	7	5	4	12	14	20	21	12
13	9 30 2	23 47 12	11♎17	9	6	5	13	14	20	21	12
14	9 33 59	24 47 49	24 29	10	8	6	13	14	20	21	12
15	9 37 55	25 48 25	7♏55	12	9	6	13	14	20	21	12
16	9 41 52	26 49 0	21 37	14	10	7	13	14	20	21	12
17	9 45 49	27 49 33	5♐35	15	11	7	13	14	20	21	12
18	9 49 45	28 50 6	19 47	17	13	8	14	14	20	21	12
19	9 53 42	29 50 37	4♑12	18	14	9	14	14	20	21	12
20	9 57 38	0♓51 7	18 47	20	15	9	14	14	20	21	12
21	10 1 35	1 51 35	3♒27	22	16	10	14	14	20	21	12
22	10 5 31	2 52 2	18 7	24	18	11	14	14 R	20	21	12
23	10 9 28	3 52 27	2♓39	25	19	11	14	14	20	21	12
24	10 13 24	4 52 50	16 57	27	20	12	15	14	21	21	12
25	10 17 21	5 53 12	0♈57	29	21	13	15	14	21	21	12
26	10 21 17	6 53 32	14 34	1♓	23	13	15	14	21	21	12
27	10 25 14	7 53 50	27 48	2	24	14	15	14	21	21	12
28	10 29 11	8 54 6	10♉38	4	25	15	15	14	21	21	12

THE SUN ENTERS THE SIGN OF PISCES ON FEB 19 AT 03:43.

DAY	TIME	☉	☽	☿	♀	♂	♃	♄	♅	♆	♇
	h m s	° ' "	° '	°	°	°	°	°	°	°	°
M 1	10 33 7	9♓54 20	23♉ 8	6♓	26♒	15♉	16♑	14♏R	21♓	21♌R	12♋R
A 2	10 37 4	10 54 32	5♊20	8	27	16	16	14	21	21	12
R 3	10 41 0	11 54 42	17 20	10	29	16	16	14	21	21	12
C 4	10 44 57	12 54 50	29 12	12	0♓	17	16	14	21	21	12
H 5	10 48 53	13 54 55	11♋ 1	13	1	18	16	14	21	21	11
6	10 52 50	14 54 59	22 51	15	2	18	16	14	21	21	11
7	10 56 46	15 55 1	4♌49	17	4	19	17	14	21	21	11
8	11 0 43	16 55 0	16 56	19	5	20	17	14	21	21	11
9	11 4 40	17 54 58	29 16	21	6	20	17	14	21	20	11
10	11 8 36	18 54 53	11♍51	23	7	21	17	14	21	20	11
11	11 12 33	19 54 46	24 43	25	9	22	17	14	21	20	11
12	11 16 29	20 54 38	7♎50	27	10	22	17	14	21	20	11
13	11 20 26	21 54 27	21 11	29	11	23	18	14	21	20	11
14	11 24 22	22 54 15	4♏45	1♈	12	24	18	14	22	20	11
15	11 28 19	23 54 1	18 30	3	14	24	18	14	22	20	11
16	11 32 15	24 53 46	2♐24	5	15	25	18	14	22	20	11
17	11 36 12	25 53 28	16 25	7	16	25	18	14	22	20	11
18	11 40 9	26 53 9	0♑31	9	17	26	18	14	22	20	11
19	11 44 5	27 52 49	14 41	11	19	27	18	14	22	20	11
20	11 48 2	28 52 26	28 54	12	20	27	19	14	22	20	11
21	11 51 58	29 52 2	13♒ 7	14	21	28	19	14	22	20	11
22	11 55 55	0♈51 36	27 19	16	22	29	19	14	22	20	11
23	11 59 51	1 51 8	11♓25	18	24	29	19	14	22	20	11
24	12 3 48	2 50 38	25 21	19	25	0♊	19	14	22	20	11
25	12 7 44	3 50 6	9♈ 5	21	26	1	19	14	22	20	11 D
26	12 11 41	4 49 33	22 32	22	27	1	19	13	22	20	11
27	12 15 38	5 48 57	5♉40	24	29	2	20	13	22	20	11
28	12 19 34	6 48 18	18 28	25	0☉	3	20	13	22	20	11
29	12 23 31	7 47 38	0♊58	26	1♈	3	20	13	22	20	11
30	12 27 27	8 46 55	13 11	28	2	4	20	13	22	20	11
31	12 31 24	9 46 10	25 11	29	4	4	20	13	23	20	11

THE SUN ENTERS THE SIGN OF ARIES ON MAR 21 AT 03:12.

SIDEREAL SUN MOON MERCURY VENUS MARS JUPITER SATURN URANUS NEPTUNE PLUTO

DAY	TIME	☉	☽	☿	♀	♂	♃	♄	♅	♆	♇
	h m s	° ' "	° '	°	°	°	°	°	°	°	°
A 1	12 35 20	10♈45 23	7♋ 3	29♈	5♈	5♊	20♑	13♏R	23♓	20♌R	11♋
P 2	12 39 17	11 44 33	18 52	0♉	6	6	20	13	23	20	11
R 3	12 43 13	12 43 41	0♌43	1	7	6	20	13	23	20	11
I 4	12 47 10	13 42 47	12 42	2	9	7	20	13	23	20	11
L 5	12 51 6	14 41 51	24 53	2	10	8	21	13	23	20	11
6	12 55 3	15 40 52	7♍21	2	11	8	21	13	23	20	11
7	12 59 0	16 39 51	20 8	3	12	9	21	13	23	20	11
8	13 2 56	17 38 48	3♎16	3 R	13	10	21	13	23	20	11
9	13 6 53	18 37 42	16 45	3	15	10	21	13	23	20	11
10	13 10 49	19 36 35	0♏32	3	16	11	21	13	23	20	11
11	13 14 46	20 35 26	14 34	2	17	12	21	13	23	20	11
12	13 18 42	21 34 15	28 46	2	18	12	21	12	23	20	11
13	13 22 39	22 33 2	13♐ 2	2	20	13	21	12	23	20	11
14	13 26 35	23 31 48	27 18	1	21	13	21	12	23	20	11
15	13 30 32	24 30 31	11♑32	1	22	14	22	12	23	20	11
16	13 34 29	25 29 13	25 40	0	23	15	22	12	23	20	11
17	13 38 25	26 27 54	9♒42	29♈	25	15	22	12	23	20	12
18	13 42 22	27 26 33	23 38	29	26	16	22	12	23	20	12
19	13 46 18	28 25 10	7♓26	28	27	17	22	12	24	20	12
20	13 50 15	29 23 45	21 7	27	28	17	22	12	24	20	12
21	13 54 11	0♉22 18	4♈38	27	0♉	18	22	12	24	20	12
22	13 58 8	1 20 50	17 58	26	1	19	22	12	24	20	12
23	14 2 4	2 19 20	1♉ 5	25	2	19	22	12	24	20	12
24	14 6 1	3 17 48	13 58	25	3	20	22	12	24	20	12
25	14 9 58	4 16 14	26 36	24	5	20	22	12	24	20	12
26	14 13 54	5 14 39	8♊59	24	6	21	22	11	24	20	12
27	14 17 51	6 13 1	21 8	23	7	22	22	11	24	20	12
28	14 21 47	7 11 21	3♋ 6	23	8	22	22	11	24	20	12
29	14 25 44	8 9 39	14 57	22	9	23	22	11	24	20	12
30	14 29 40	9 7 56	26 45	22	11	24	22	11	24	20	12

THE SUN ENTERS THE SIGN OF TAURUS ON APR 20 AT 14:51.

DAY	TIME	☉	☽	☿	♀	♂	♃	♄	♅	♆	♇
	h m s	° ' "	° '	°	°	°	°	°	°	°	°
M 1	14 33 37	10♉ 6 10	8♌35	22♈R	12♉	24♊	22♑	11♏R	24♓	20♌D	12♋
A 2	14 37 33	11 4 22	20 33	22 D	13	25	22	11	24	20	12
Y 3	14 41 30	12 2 32	2♍45	22	14	26	22	11	24	20	12
4	14 45 27	13 0 40	15 15	22	16	26	22	11	24	20	12
5	14 49 23	13 58 47	28 7	22	17	27	22	11	24	20	12
6	14 53 20	14 56 51	11♎25	23	18	27	22	11	24	20	12
7	14 57 16	15 54 53	25 7	23	19	28	22	11	24	20	12
8	15 1 13	16 52 54	9♏14	23	21	29	23	11	24	20	12
9	15 5 9	17 50 53	23 39	24	22	29	23	10	24	20	12
10	15 9 6	18 48 51	8♐16	24	23	0♋	23 R	10	24	20	12
11	15 13 2	19 46 47	22 58	25	24	1	23	10	24	20	12
12	15 16 59	20 44 42	7♑37	26	25	1	23	10	25	20	12
13	15 20 56	21 42 35	22 8	26	27	2	23	10	25	20	12
14	15 24 52	22 40 28	6♒27	27	28	3	23	10	25	20	12
15	15 28 49	23 38 19	20 31	28	29	3	22	10	25	20	12
16	15 32 45	24 36 9	4♓22	29	0♊	4	22	10	25	20	12
17	15 36 42	25 33 57	17 58	0♉	2	4	22	10	25	20	12
18	15 40 38	26 31 45	1♈21	1	3	5	22	10	25	20	12
19	15 44 35	27 29 31	14 31	2	4	6	22	10	25	20	12
20	15 48 31	28 27 16	27 29	3	5	6	22	10	25	20	12
21	15 52 28	29 25 0	10♉16	4	7	7	22	10	25	20	12
22	15 56 25	0♊22 43	22 50	6	8	8	22	10	25	20	12
23	16 0 21	1 20 24	5♊13	7	9	8	22	9	25	20	12
24	16 4 18	2 18 5	17 25	8	10	9	22	9	25	20	12
25	16 8 14	3 15 44	29 26	9	11	10	22	9	25	20	12
26	16 12 11	4 13 21	11♋20	11	13	10	22	9	25	20	12
27	16 16 7	5 10 57	23 8	12	14	11	22	9	25	20	12
28	16 20 4	6 8 32	4♌55	14	15	11	22	9	25	20	12
29	16 24 0	7 6 6	16 44	15	16	12	22	9	25	20	12
30	16 27 57	8 3 38	28 42	17	18	13	22	9	25	20	12
31	16 31 54	9 1 9	10♍52	18	19	13	22	9	25	20	12

THE SUN ENTERS THE SIGN OF GEMINI ON MAY 21 AT 14:33.

DAY	TIME	☉	☽	☿	♀	♂	♃	♄	♅	♆	♇
	h m s	° ' "	° '	°	°	°	°	°	°	°	°
J 1	16 35 50	9♊58 38	23♍21	20♉	20♊	14♋	22♑R	9♏R	25♓	20♌	12♋
U 2	16 39 47	10 56 6	6♎12	22	21	15	22	9	25	20	12
N 3	16 43 43	11 53 33	19 30	23	23	15	22	9	25	20	12
E 4	16 47 40	12 50 59	3♏17	25	24	16	22	9	25	20	12
5	16 51 36	13 48 23	17 30	27	25	17	22	9	25	20	12
6	16 55 33	14 45 47	2♐ 7	29	26	17	21	9	25	20	12
7	16 59 29	15 43 10	17 0	1♊	27	18	21	9	25	20	12
8	17 3 26	16 40 32	2♑ 2	3	29	18	21	9	25	20	12
9	17 7 23	17 37 53	17 3	5	0♋	19	21	8	25	20	12
10	17 11 19	18 35 13	1♒54	7	1	20	21	8	25	20	12
11	17 15 16	19 32 33	16 30	9	2	20	21	8	25	20	12
12	17 19 12	20 29 53	0♓47	11	4	21	21	8	25	20	12
13	17 23 9	21 27 12	14 43	13	5	22	21	8	25	20	13
14	17 27 5	22 24 30	28 18	15	6	22	21	8	25	20	13
15	17 31 2	23 21 48	11♈33	17	7	23	21	8	25	20	13
16	17 34 58	24 19 6	24 32	19	8	23	21	8	25	20	13
17	17 38 55	25 16 24	7♉15	21	10	24	20	8	25	20	13
18	17 42 52	26 13 41	19 45	23	11	25	20	8	25	20	13
19	17 46 48	27 10 58	2♊ 4	26	12	25	20	8	25	20	13
20	17 50 45	28 8 14	14 13	28	13	26	20	8	25	20	13
21	17 54 41	29 5 31	26 13	0♋	15	27	20	8	25	20	13
22	17 58 38	0♋ 2 46	8♋ 7	2	16	27	20	8	25	20	13
23	18 2 34	1 0 2	19 56	4	17	28	20	8	25	21	13
24	18 6 31	1 57 17	1♌43	7	18	28	20	8	25	21	13
25	18 10 27	2 54 31	13 30	9	19	29	20	8	25	21	13
26	18 14 24	3 51 45	25 21	11	21	0♌	19	8	25	21	13
27	18 18 21	4 48 58	7♍19	13	22	0	19	8	25	21	13
28	18 22 17	5 46 11	19 30	15	23	1	19	8	25	21	13
29	18 26 14	6 43 24	1♎58	17	24	2	19	8	25	21	13
30	18 30 10	7 40 36	14 47	19	26	2	19	8	25 R	21	13

THE SUN ENTERS THE SIGN OF CANCER ON JUN 21 AT 22:50.

♈ ARIES ♉ TAURUS ♊ GEMINI ♋ CANCER ♌ LEO ♍ VIRGO ♎ LIBRA ♏ SCORPIO ♐ SAGITTARIUS ♑ CAPRICORN ♒ AQUARIUS ♓ PISCES

SIDEREAL SUN MOON MERCURY VENUS MARS JUPITER SATURN URANUS NEPTUNE PLUTO

DAY	TIME	☉	☽	☿	♀	♂	♃	♄	♅	♆	♇
	h m s	° ' "	° '	°	°	°	°	°	°	°	°
J 1	18 34 7	8♋37 48	28♎ 0	21♋	27♋	3♌	19♑R	8♏R	25♓R	21♌	13♋
U 2	18 38 3	9 34 59	11♏41	23	28	4	19	8	25	21	13
L 3	18 42 0	10 32 10	25 50	25	29	4	19	8	25	21	13
Y 4	18 45 56	11 29 21	10♐25	27	0♌	5	18	8	25	21	13
5	18 49 53	12 26 31	25 21	29	2	5	18	8	25	21	13
6	18 53 50	13 23 42	10♑29	0♌	3	6	18	8	25	21	13
7	18 57 46	14 20 53	25 41	2	4	7	18	8	25	21	13
8	19 1 43	15 18 3	10♒48	4	5	7	18	8	25	21	13
9	19 5 39	16 15 14	25 40	6	7	8	18	8	25	21	13
10	19 9 36	17 12 26	10♓11	7	8	9	18	8	25	21	13
11	19 13 32	18 9 37	24 18	9	9	9	18	8 D	25	21	13
12	19 17 29	19 6 50	8♈ 0	11	10	10	17	8	25	21	13
13	19 21 25	20 4 2	21 18	12	11	10	17	8	25	21	13
14	19 25 22	21 1 16	4♉13	14	13	11	17	8	25	21	13
15	19 29 19	21 58 30	16 50	15	14	12	17	8	25	21	13
16	19 33 15	22 55 44	29 10	17	15	12	17	8	25	21	13
17	19 37 12	23 52 59	11♊18	18	16	13	17	8	25	21	13
18	19 41 8	24 50 15	23 17	20	18	14	17	8	25	21	13
19	19 45 5	25 47 31	5♋10	21	19	14	17	8	25	21	13
20	19 49 1	26 44 48	16 58	22	20	15	16	8	25	21	13
21	19 52 58	27 42 6	28 45	24	21	16	16	8	25	21	13
22	19 56 54	28 39 24	10♌33	25	22	16	16	8	25	21	13
23	20 0 51	29 36 42	22 24	26	24	17	16	8	25	21	14
24	20 4 48	0♌34 1	4♍21	27	25	17	16	8	25	21	14
25	20 8 44	1 31 21	16 26	28	26	18	16	8	25	22	14
26	20 12 41	2 28 41	28 42	29	27	19	16	8	25	22	14
27	20 16 37	3 26 1	11♎13	1♍	29	19	16	8	25	22	14
28	20 20 34	4 23 22	24 3	2	0♍	20	15	8	25	22	14
29	20 24 30	5 20 43	7♏13	2	1	21	15	8	25	22	14
30	20 28 27	6 18 5	20 46	3	2	21	15	8	25	22	14
31	20 32 23	7 15 27	4♐44	4	3	22	15	8	25	22	14

THE SUN ENTERS THE SIGN OF LEO ON JUL 23 AT 09:45.

DAY	TIME	☉	☽	☿	♀	♂	♃	♄	♅	♆	♇
	h m s	° ' "	° '	°	°	°	°	°	°	°	°
A 1	20 36 20	8♌12 50	19♐ 7	5♍	5♍	22♌	15♑R	8♏	25♓R	22♌	14♋
U 2	20 40 17	9 10 14	3♑51	6	6	23	15	8	25	22	14
G 3	20 44 13	10 7 39	18 51	6	7	24	15	8	25	22	14
U 4	20 48 10	11 5 4	4♒ 0	7	8	24	15	8	25	22	14
S 5	20 52 6	12 2 30	19 8	8	9	25	15	8	25	22	14
T 6	20 56 3	12 59 57	4♓ 6	8	11	26	14	8	25	22	14
7	20 59 59	13 57 25	18 47	9	12	26	14	8	25	22	14
8	21 3 56	14 54 54	3♈ 5	9	13	27	14	8	25	22	14
9	21 7 52	15 52 25	16 56	9	14	28	14	8	25	22	14
10	21 11 49	16 49 57	0♉20	9	15	28	14	8	25	22	14
11	21 15 46	17 47 31	13 18	9 R	17	29	14	8	25	22	14
12	21 19 42	18 45 5	25 54	9	18	29	14	8	25	22	14
13	21 23 39	19 42 42	8♊11	9	19	0♍	14	8	25	22	14
14	21 27 35	20 40 20	20 15	9	20	1	14	9	25	22	14
15	21 31 32	21 37 59	2♋ 9	9	22	1	14	9	25	22	14
16	21 35 28	22 35 40	13 57	9	23	2	14	9	25	22	14
17	21 39 25	23 33 22	25 44	8	24	3	14	9	25	22	14
18	21 43 21	24 31 6	7♌32	8	25	3	13	9	25	22	14
19	21 47 18	25 28 51	19 25	7	26	4	13	9	25	22	14
20	21 51 15	26 26 37	1♍24	6	28	5	13	9	25	22	14
21	21 55 11	27 24 25	13 31	5	29	5	13	9	25	23	14
22	21 59 8	28 22 14	25 49	5	0♎	6	13	9	24	23	14
23	22 3 4	29 20 5	8♎18	4	1	6	13	9	24	23	14
24	22 7 1	0♍17 56	21 0	3	2	7	13	9	24	23	14
25	22 10 57	1 15 49	3♏57	2	4	8	13	9	24	23	14
26	22 14 54	2 13 44	17 9	1	5	8	13	9	24	23	14
27	22 18 50	3 11 39	0♐40	0	6	9	13	9	24	23	14
28	22 22 47	4 9 36	14 29	29♌	7	10	13	9	24	23	14
29	22 26 44	5 7 34	28 37	29	8	10	13	9	24	23	14
30	22 30 40	6 5 34	13♑ 3	28	10	11	13	10	24	23	14
31	22 34 37	7 3 34	27 44	27	11	12	13	10	24	23	14

THE SUN ENTERS THE SIGN OF VIRGO ON AUG 23 AT 16:34.

DAY	TIME	☉	☽	☿	♀	♂	♃	♄	♅	♆	♇
	h m s	° ' "	° '	°	°	°	°	°	°	°	°
S 1	22 38 33	8♍ 1 37	12♒35	27♌R	12♎	12♍	13♑R	10♏	24♓R	23♌	14♋
E 2	22 42 30	8 59 40	27 29	27	13	13	13	10	24	23	14
P 3	22 46 26	9 57 46	12♓20	26	14	13	13	10	24	23	14
T 4	22 50 23	10 55 53	26 58	26 D	16	14	13	10	24	23	14
E 5	22 54 19	11 54 1	11♈17	26	17	15	13	10	24	23	14
M 6	22 58 16	12 52 12	25 12	27	18	15	13	10	24	23	14
B 7	23 2 13	13 50 24	8♉40	27	19	16	13	10	24	23	14
E 8	23 6 9	14 48 39	21 43	27	20	17	13	10	24	23	14
R 9	23 10 6	15 46 56	4♊21	28	22	17	13 D	10	24	23	14
10	23 14 2	16 45 14	16 40	29	23	18	13	10	24	23	14
11	23 17 59	17 43 35	28 43	0♍	24	19	13	10	24	23	15
12	23 21 55	18 41 58	10♋36	1	25	19	13	11	24	23	15
13	23 25 52	19 40 23	22 23	2	26	20	13	11	24	23	15
14	23 29 48	20 38 50	4♌11	3	28	20	13	11	24	23	15
15	23 33 45	21 37 20	16 2	5	29	21	13	11	24	23	15
16	23 37 42	22 35 51	28 1	6	0♏	22	13	11	24	23	15
17	23 41 38	23 34 24	10♍10	8	1	22	13	11	23	23	15
18	23 45 35	24 32 59	22 32	9	2	23	13	11	23	24	15
19	23 49 31	25 31 36	5♎ 7	11	3	24	13	11	23	24	15
20	23 53 28	26 30 15	17 55	12	5	24	13	11	23	24	15
21	23 57 24	27 28 56	0♏56	14	6	25	13	11	23	24	15
22	0 1 21	28 27 38	14 9	16	7	26	13	12	23	24	15
23	0 5 17	29 26 23	27 35	18	8	26	13	12	23	24	15
24	0 9 14	0♎25 9	11♐12	20	9	27	13	12	23	24	15
25	0 13 10	1 23 57	25 0	21	11	28	13	12	23	24	15
26	0 17 7	2 22 46	8♑59	23	12	28	13	12	23	24	15
27	0 21 4	3 21 38	23 10	25	13	29	13	12	23	24	15
28	0 25 0	4 20 31	7♒29	27	14	29	13	12	23	24	15
29	0 28 57	5 19 25	21 57	29	15	0♎	13	12	23	24	15
30	0 32 53	6 18 22	6♓28	0♎	16	1	13	12	23	24	15

THE SUN ENTERS THE SIGN OF LIBRA ON SEP 23 AT 13:44.

DAY	TIME	☉	☽	☿	♀	♂	♃	♄	♅	♆	♇
	h m s	° ' "	° '	°	°	°	°	°	°	°	°
O 1	0 36 50	7♎17 20	20♓57	2♎	18♏	1♎	13♑	12♏	23♓R	24♌	15♋
C 2	0 40 46	8 16 20	5♈18	4	19	2	13	13	23	24	15
T 3	0 44 43	9 15 23	19 25	6	20	3	14	13	23	24	15
O 4	0 48 39	10 14 27	3♉14	8	21	3	14	13	23	24	15
B 5	0 52 36	11 13 34	16 39	9	22	4	14	13	23	24	15
E 6	0 56 33	12 12 42	29 41	11	23	5	14	13	23	24	15
R 7	1 0 29	13 11 54	12♊21	13	25	5	14	13	23	24	15
8	1 4 26	14 11 7	24 40	15	26	6	14	13	23	24	15
9	1 8 22	15 10 23	6♋44	16	27	7	14	13	23	24	15
10	1 12 19	16 9 41	18 37	18	28	7	14	13	23	24	15
11	1 16 15	17 9 1	0♌25	20	29	8	14	14	23	24	15
12	1 20 12	18 8 24	12 13	21	0♐	9	14	14	23	24	15
13	1 24 8	19 7 48	24 8	23	2	9	14	14	22	24	15
14	1 28 5	20 7 16	6♍12	25	3	10	15	14	22	24	15
15	1 32 2	21 6 45	18 30	26	4	11	15	14	22	24	15 R
16	1 35 58	22 6 16	1♎ 5	28	5	11	15	14	22	24	15
17	1 39 55	23 5 50	13 57	0♏	6	12	15	14	22	24	15
18	1 43 51	24 5 25	27 6	1	7	12	15	14	22	24	15
19	1 47 48	25 5 3	10♏31	3	9	13	15	14	22	24	15
20	1 51 44	26 4 43	24 9	5	10	14	15	15	22	24	15
21	1 55 41	27 4 25	7♐57	6	11	14	15	15	22	24	15
22	1 59 37	28 4 8	21 52	8	12	15	15	15	22	24	15
23	2 3 34	29 3 53	5♑52	9	13	16	16	15	22	24	15
24	2 7 31	0♏ 3 40	19 54	11	14	16	16	15	22	24	15
25	2 11 27	1 3 29	3♒59	12	15	17	16	15	22	24	15
26	2 15 24	2 3 19	18 6	14	17	18	16	15	22	24	15
27	2 19 20	3 3 11	2♓13	15	18	18	16	15	22	25	15
28	2 23 17	4 3 4	16 19	17	19	19	16	15	22	25	15
29	2 27 13	5 2 59	0♈21	19	20	20	16	16	22	25	15
30	2 31 10	6 2 56	14 17	20	21	20	17	16	22	25	15
31	2 35 6	7 2 55	28 1	22	22	21	17	16	22	25	15

THE SUN ENTERS THE SIGN OF SCORPIO ON OCT 23 AT 22:32.

DAY	TIME	☉	☽	☿	♀	♂	♃	♄	♅	♆	♇
	h m s	° ' "	° '	°	°	°	°	°	°	°	°
N 1	2 39 3	8♏ 2 55	11♉31	23♏	23♐	22♎	17♑	16♏	22♓R	25♌	15♋R
O 2	2 42 59	9 2 57	24 44	24	24	22	17	16	22	25	15
V 3	2 46 56	10 3 2	7♊37	26	26	23	17	16	22	25	15
E 4	2 50 53	11 3 8	20 12	27	27	24	17	16	22	25	15
M 5	2 54 49	12 3 17	2♋29	29	28	24	17	16	22	25	15
B 6	2 58 46	13 3 27	14 32	0♐	29	25	18	17	22	25	15
E 7	3 2 42	14 3 40	26 25	2	0♑	26	18	17	22	25	15
R 8	3 6 39	15 3 54	8♌13	3	1	26	18	17	22	25	15
9	3 10 35	16 4 11	20 2	5	2	27	18	17	22	25	15
10	3 14 32	17 4 29	1♍56	6	3	28	18	17	22	25	15
11	3 18 28	18 4 49	14 2	7	4	28	18	17	22	25	15
12	3 22 25	19 5 12	26 24	9	6	29	19	17	22	25	15
13	3 26 22	20 5 36	9♎ 6	10	7	0♏	19	17	22	25	15
14	3 30 18	21 6 2	22 9	11	8	0	19	17	22	25	15
15	3 34 15	22 6 30	5♏35	13	9	1	19	18	22	25	15
16	3 38 11	23 6 59	19 21	14	10	2	19	18	22	25	15
17	3 42 8	24 7 31	3♐24	15	11	2	19	18	22	25	15
18	3 46 4	25 8 3	17 39	17	12	3	20	18	22	25	15
19	3 50 1	26 8 38	2♑ 1	18	13	4	20	18	22	25	15
20	3 53 57	27 9 13	16 23	19	14	4	20	18	22	25	15
21	3 57 54	28 9 50	0♒43	20	15	5	20	18	22	25	14
22	4 1 51	29 10 28	14 57	21	16	6	20	18	22	25	14
23	4 5 47	0♐11 7	29 3	22	17	6	21	19	22	25	14
24	4 9 44	1 11 47	13♓ 1	23	18	7	21	19	22	25	14
25	4 13 40	2 12 28	26 50	24	19	8	21	19	22	25	14
26	4 17 37	3 13 11	10♈30	25	20	8	21	19	22	25	14
27	4 21 33	4 13 54	24 0	25	21	9	21	19	22	25 R	14
28	4 25 30	5 14 38	7♉19	26	22	10	22	19	22	25	14
29	4 29 26	6 15 24	20 25	27	23	10	22	19	22	25	14
30	4 33 23	7 16 11	3♊17	27	24	11	22	19	22	25	14

THE SUN ENTERS THE SIGN OF SAGITTARIUS ON NOV 22 AT 19:36.

DAY	TIME	☉	☽	☿	♀	♂	♃	♄	♅	♆	♇
	h m s	° ' "	° '	°	°	°	°	°	°	°	°
D 1	4 37 20	8♐16 59	15♊55	27♐R	25♑	12♏	22♑	20♏	22♓D	25♌R	14♋R
E 2	4 41 16	9 17 48	28 18	27	26	12	22	20	22	25	14
C 3	4 45 13	10 18 39	10♋29	27	27	13	23	20	22	25	14
E 4	4 49 9	11 19 30	22 28	27	28	14	23	20	22	25	14
M 5	4 53 6	12 20 23	4♌20	26	29	14	23	20	22	25	14
B 6	4 57 2	13 21 17	16 7	26	0♒	15	23	20	22	25	14
E 7	5 0 59	14 22 13	27 55	25	1	16	23	20	22	25	14
R 8	5 4 56	15 23 9	9♍48	24	2	16	24	20	22	25	14
9	5 8 52	16 24 7	21 52	23	3	17	24	20	22	25	14
10	5 12 49	17 25 6	4♎13	21	4	18	24	21	22	25	14
11	5 16 45	18 26 6	16 53	20	5	18	24	21	22	25	14
12	5 20 42	19 27 8	29 58	19	6	19	24	21	22	25	14
13	5 24 38	20 28 10	13♏28	17	7	20	25	21	22	25	14
14	5 28 35	21 29 13	27 24	16	8	20	25	21	22	25	14
15	5 32 31	22 30 18	11♐43	15	9	21	25	21	22	25	14
16	5 36 28	23 31 23	26 19	14	9	22	25	21	22	25	14
17	5 40 25	24 32 28	11♑ 6	13	10	22	25	21	22	25	14
18	5 44 21	25 33 35	25 56	12	11	23	26	21	22	25	14
19	5 48 18	26 34 41	10♒41	12	12	24	26	22	22	25	14
20	5 52 14	27 35 48	25 16	11	13	25	26	22	22	25	14
21	5 56 11	28 36 55	9♓37	11 D	13	25	26	22	22	25	14
22	6 0 7	29 38 3	23 41	11	14	26	27	22	22	25	14
23	6 4 4	0♑39 10	7♈27	11	15	27	27	22	22	25	14
24	6 8 0	1 40 18	20 56	11	16	27	27	22	22	25	14
25	6 11 57	2 41 25	4♉ 9	12	16	28	27	22	22	25	14
26	6 15 54	3 42 33	17 6	12	17	29	27	22	22	25	14
27	6 19 50	4 43 41	29 50	13	18	29	28	22	22	25	14
28	6 23 47	5 44 49	12♊21	14	19	0♐	28	22	22	25	14
29	6 27 43	6 45 57	24 41	14	19	1	28	23	22	25	14
30	6 31 40	7 47 5	6♋51	15	20	1	28	23	22	25	14
31	6 35 36	8 48 14	18 52	16	20	2	29	23	22	24	14

THE SUN ENTERS THE SIGN OF CAPRICORN ON DEC 22 AT 08:37.

♈ ARIES ♉ TAURUS ♊ GEMINI ♋ CANCER ♌ LEO ♍ VIRGO ♎ LIBRA ♏ SCORPIO ♐ SAGITTARIUS ♑ CAPRICORN ♒ AQUARIUS ♓ PISCES

SIDEREAL TIME, SUN, MOON, MERCURY, VENUS, MARS, JUPITER, SATURN, URANUS, NEPTUNE, PLUTO

DAY	TIME h m s	☉ ° ' "	☽ ° '	☿ °	♀ °	♂ °	♃ °	♄ °	♅ °	♆ °	♇ °
J 1	6 39 33	9♑49 22	0♌46	17♐	21♒	3♐	29♑	23♏	22♓	24♌R	14♋R
A 2	6 43 29	10 50 31	12 35	18	21	3	29	23	22	24	14
N 3	6 47 26	11 51 40	24 23	19	22	4	29	23	22	24	14
U 4	6 51 23	12 52 49	6♍11	21	22	5	0♒	23	22	24	14
A 5	6 55 19	13 53 58	18 5	22	23	5	0	23	22	24	14
R 6	6 59 16	14 55 7	0♎ 8	23	23	6	0	23	22	24	14
Y 7	7 3 12	15 56 17	12 25	24	24	7	0	23	22	24	14
8	7 7 9	16 57 26	25 1	26	24	8	0	23	22	24	14
9	7 11 5	17 58 36	7♏59	27	25	8	1	24	22	24	14
10	7 15 2	18 59 46	21 23	28	25	9	1	24	22	24	14
11	7 18 58	20 0 55	5♐14	0♑	25	10	1	24	22	24	14
12	7 22 55	21 2 5	19 32	1	25	10	1	24	22	24	14
13	7 26 52	22 3 15	4♑14	2	26	11	2	24	22	24	13
14	7 30 48	23 4 24	19 13	4	26	12	2	24	22	24	13
15	7 34 45	24 5 33	4♒21	5	26	12	2	24	22	24	13
16	7 38 41	25 6 41	19 29	7	26	13	2	24	22	24	13
17	7 42 38	26 7 49	4♓28	8	26 R	14	3	24	22	24	13
18	7 46 34	27 8 55	19 10	9	26	14	3	24	22	24	13
19	7 50 31	28 10 1	3♈31	11	26	15	3	24	23	24	13
20	7 54 27	29 11 6	17 27	12	26	16	3	24	23	24	13
21	7 58 24	0♒12 10	0♉58	14	26	17	4	24	23	24	13
22	8 2 21	1 13 13	14 6	15	26	17	4	25	23	24	13
23	8 6 17	2 14 16	26 53	17	26	18	4	25	23	24	13
24	8 10 14	3 15 17	9♊24	18	25	19	4	25	23	24	13
25	8 14 10	4 16 17	21 40	20	25	19	4	25	23	24	13
26	8 18 7	5 17 16	3♋46	21	25	20	5	25	23	24	13
27	8 22 3	6 18 14	15 43	23	24	21	5	25	23	24	13
28	8 26 0	7 19 11	27 36	25	24	21	5	25	23	24	13
29	8 29 56	8 20 8	9♌25	26	24	22	5	25	23	24	13
30	8 33 53	9 21 3	21 13	28	23	23	6	25	23	24	13
31	8 37 50	10 21 57	3♍ 3	29	23	24	6	25	23	24	13

THE SUN ENTERS THE SIGN OF AQUARIUS ON JAN 20 AT 19:13.

DAY	TIME h m s	☉ ° ' "	☽ ° '	☿ °	♀ °	♂ °	♃ °	♄ °	♅ °	♆ °	♇ °
F 1	8 41 46	11♒22 50	14♍55	1♒	22♒R	24♐	6♒	25♏	23♓	24♌R	13♋R
E 2	8 45 43	12 23 43	26 54	3	21	25	6	25	23	24	13
B 3	8 49 39	13 24 34	9♎ 1	4	21	26	7	25	23	24	13
R 4	8 53 36	14 25 25	21 19	6	20	26	7	25	23	24	13
U 5	8 57 32	15 26 14	3♏52	7	20	27	7	25	23	24	13
A 6	9 1 29	16 27 3	16 44	9	19	28	7	25	23	24	13
R 7	9 5 25	17 27 51	29 59	11	18	28	8	25	23	24	13
Y 8	9 9 22	18 28 38	13♐38	13	18	29	8	25	23	24	13
9	9 13 19	19 29 24	27 43	14	17	0♑	8	26	23	24	13
10	9 17 15	20 30 9	12♑13	16	17	1	8	26	24	23	13
11	9 21 12	21 30 53	27 6	18	16	1	8	26	24	23	13
12	9 25 8	22 31 36	12♒14	19	15	2	9	26	24	23	13
13	9 29 5	23 32 17	27 29	21	15	3	9	26	24	23	13
14	9 33 1	24 32 57	12♓41	23	14	3	9	26	24	23	13
15	9 36 58	25 33 35	27 40	25	14	4	9	26	24	23	13
16	9 40 54	26 34 11	12♈17	27	13	5	10	26	24	23	13
17	9 44 51	27 34 46	26 27	28	13	6	10	26	24	23	13
18	9 48 48	28 35 19	10♉ 8	0♓	12	6	10	26	24	23	13
19	9 52 44	29 35 50	23 21	2	12	7	10	26	24	23	13
20	9 56 41	0♓36 19	6♊ 9	4	12	8	11	26	24	23	13
21	10 0 37	1 36 47	18 36	6	11	8	11	26	24	23	13
22	10 4 34	2 37 13	0♋46	8	11	9	11	26	24	23	13
23	10 8 30	3 37 36	12 44	10	11	10	11	26	24	23	13
24	10 12 27	4 37 58	24 35	11	11	11	11	26	24	23	13
25	10 16 23	5 38 18	6♌23	13	11	11	12	26	24	23	13
26	10 20 20	6 38 36	18 10	15	10	12	12	26	24	23	13
27	10 24 17	7 38 53	0♍ 0	17	10	12	12	26	24	23	13
28	10 28 13	8 39 7	11 55	19	10 D	13	12	26	24	23	13

THE SUN ENTERS THE SIGN OF PISCES ON FEB 19 AT 09:35.

DAY	TIME h m s	☉ ° ' "	☽ ° '	☿ °	♀ °	♂ °	♃ °	♄ °	♅ °	♆ °	♇ °
M 1	10 32 10	9♓39 20	23♍55	21♓	10♒	14♑	13♒	26♏	25♓	23♌R	13♋R
A 2	10 36 6	10 39 31	6♎ 3	23	10	15	13	26	25	23	13
R 3	10 40 3	11 39 40	18 20	25	10	16	13	26	25	23	13
C 4	10 43 59	12 39 48	0♏48	26	11	16	13	26	25	23	13
H 5	10 47 56	13 39 54	13 28	28	11	17	13	26	25	23	13
6	10 51 52	14 39 59	26 22	0☉	11	18	14	26 R	25	23	13
7	10 55 49	15 40 2	9♐33	1♈	11	18	14	26	25	23	13
8	10 59 46	16 40 3	23 3	3	12	19	14	26	25	23	13
9	11 3 42	17 40 3	6♑54	5	12	20	14	26	25	23	13
10	11 7 39	18 40 1	21 8	6	12	21	15	26	25	23	13
11	11 11 35	19 39 58	5♒42	7	13	21	15	26	25	23	13
12	11 15 32	20 39 53	20 34	9	13	22	15	26	25	23	13
13	11 19 28	21 39 46	5♓37	10	13	23	15	26	25	23	13
14	11 23 25	22 39 37	20 42	11	14	23	15	26	25	23	13
15	11 27 21	23 39 26	5♈40	12	14	24	16	26	25	23	13
16	11 31 18	24 39 13	20 22	13	15	25	16	26	25	23	13
17	11 35 15	25 38 58	4♉39	13	15	26	16	26	25	23	13
18	11 39 11	26 38 41	18 28	14	16	26	16	26	26	23	13
19	11 43 8	27 38 21	1♊48	14	16	27	16	26	26	23	13
20	11 47 4	28 38 0	14 41	15	17	28	17	26	26	22	13
21	11 51 1	29 37 36	27 11	15 R	18	28	17	26	26	22	13
22	11 54 57	0♈37 10	9♋22	15	18	29	17	26	26	22	13
23	11 58 54	1 36 41	21 19	15	19	0♒	17	26	26	22	13
24	12 2 50	2 36 10	3♌ 9	14	20	1	17	26	26	22	13
25	12 6 47	3 35 37	14 56	14	20	1	18	26	26	22	13
26	12 10 43	4 35 2	26 44	14	21	2	18	26	26	22	13
27	12 14 40	5 34 24	8♍38	13	22	3	18	26	26	22	13 D
28	12 18 37	6 33 44	20 39	12	23	3	18	26	26	22	13
29	12 22 33	7 33 2	2♎50	12	23	4	18	26	26	22	13
30	12 26 30	8 32 18	15 12	11	24	5	19	26	26	22	13
31	12 30 26	9 31 33	27 44	10	25	6	19	26	26	22	13

THE SUN ENTERS THE SIGN OF ARIES ON MAR 21 AT 09:01.

DAY	TIME h m s	☉ ° ' "	☽ ° '	☿ °	♀ °	♂ °	♃ °	♄ °	♅ °	♆ °	♇ °
A 1	12 34 23	10♈30 45	10♏28	9♈R	26♒	6♒	19♒	26♏R	26♓	22♌R	13♋
P 2	12 38 19	11 29 55	23 24	8	26	7	19	25	26	22	13
R 3	12 42 16	12 29 3	6♐30	8	27	8	19	25	26	22	13
I 4	12 46 12	13 28 10	19 49	7	28	9	20	25	26	22	13
L 5	12 50 9	14 27 15	3♑22	6	29	9	20	25	27	22	13
6	12 54 6	15 26 18	17 8	5	0♓	10	20	25	27	22	13
7	12 58 2	16 25 19	1♒10	5	1	11	20	25	27	22	13
8	13 1 59	17 24 19	15 27	4	2	11	20	25	27	22	13
9	13 5 55	18 23 17	29 58	4	3	12	21	25	27	22	13
10	13 9 52	19 22 13	14♓38	3	3	13	21	25	27	22	13
11	13 13 48	20 21 7	29 21	3	4	14	21	25	27	22	13
12	13 17 45	21 19 59	14♈ 1	3	5	14	21	25	27	22	13
13	13 21 41	22 18 49	28 30	3 D	6	15	21	25	27	22	13
14	13 25 38	23 17 38	12♉40	3	7	16	21	25	27	22	13
15	13 29 35	24 16 24	26 26	3	8	16	22	25	27	22	13
16	13 33 31	25 15 8	9♊46	3	9	17	22	25	27	22	13
17	13 37 28	26 13 50	22 41	3	10	18	22	25	27	22	13
18	13 41 24	27 12 30	5♋13	3	11	19	22	25	27	22	13
19	13 45 21	28 11 8	17 27	4	12	19	22	25	27	22	13
20	13 49 17	29 9 43	29 27	4	13	20	22	25	27	22	13
21	13 53 14	0♉ 8 16	11♌18	5	14	21	22	24	27	22	13
22	13 57 10	1 6 48	23 6	5	15	22	23	24	27	22	13
23	14 1 7	2 5 16	4♍57	6	16	22	23	24	27	22	13
24	14 5 4	3 3 43	16 55	7	17	23	23	24	28	22	13
25	14 9 0	4 2 8	29 3	7	18	24	23	24	28	22	13
26	14 12 57	5 0 30	11♎24	8	19	24	23	24	28	22	13
27	14 16 53	5 58 51	23 59	9	20	25	23	24	28	22	13
28	14 20 50	6 57 10	6♏49	10	21	26	24	24	28	22	13
29	14 24 46	7 55 27	19 53	11	22	27	24	24	28	22	13
30	14 28 43	8 53 42	3♐10	12	23	27	24	24	28	22	13

THE SUN ENTERS THE SIGN OF TAURUS ON APR 20 AT 20:36.

DAY	TIME h m s	☉ ° ' "	☽ ° '	☿ °	♀ °	♂ °	♃ °	♄ °	♅ °	♆ °	♇ °
M 1	14 32 39	9♉51 56	16♐38	13♈	24♓	28♒	24♒	24♏R	28♓	22♌R	13♋
A 2	14 36 36	10 50 8	0♑16	14	25	29	24	24	28	22	13
Y 3	14 40 33	11 48 19	14 2	15	26	29	24	24	28	22 D	13
4	14 44 29	12 46 28	27 57	17	27	0♓	24	24	28	22	13
5	14 48 26	13 44 36	11♒59	18	28	1	24	23	28	22	13
6	14 52 22	14 42 42	26 8	19	29	2	25	23	28	22	13
7	14 56 19	15 40 47	10♓23	21	0♈	2	25	23	28	22	13
8	15 0 15	16 38 51	24 41	22	1	3	25	23	28	22	13
9	15 4 12	17 36 53	8♈59	23	3	4	25	23	28	22	13
10	15 8 8	18 34 54	23 12	25	4	5	25	23	28	22	13
11	15 12 5	19 32 53	7♉16	26	5	5	25	23	28	22	13
12	15 16 1	20 30 51	21 5	28	6	6	25	23	28	22	13
13	15 19 58	21 28 47	4♊36	29	7	7	25	23	28	22	13
14	15 23 55	22 26 42	17 46	1♉	8	7	25	23	28	22	13
15	15 27 51	23 24 35	0♋35	2	9	8	25	23	28	22	13
16	15 31 48	24 22 27	13 5	4	10	9	26	23	28	22	13
17	15 35 44	25 20 17	25 18	6	11	10	26	23	28	22	13
18	15 39 41	26 18 5	7♌19	8	12	10	26	23	29	22	13
19	15 43 37	27 15 52	19 12	9	13	11	26	22	29	22	13
20	15 47 34	28 13 36	1♍ 2	11	15	12	26	22	29	22	13
21	15 51 31	29 11 20	12 55	13	16	12	26	22	29	22	13
22	15 55 27	0♊ 9 1	24 55	15	17	13	26	22	29	22	13
23	15 59 24	1 6 41	7♎ 6	17	18	14	26	22	29	22	13
24	16 3 20	2 4 20	19 34	19	19	15	26	22	29	22	13
25	16 7 17	3 1 57	2♏18	21	20	15	26	22	29	22	13
26	16 11 13	3 59 33	15 22	23	21	16	26	22	29	22	13
27	16 15 10	4 57 7	28 44	25	22	17	27	22	29	22	13
28	16 19 6	5 54 41	12♐23	27	23	17	27	22	29	22	13
29	16 23 3	6 52 13	26 16	29	25	18	27	22	29	22	13
30	16 27 0	7 49 44	10♑19	1♊	26	19	27	22	29	22	13
31	16 30 56	8 47 15	24 29	3	27	20	27	22	29	22	13

THE SUN ENTERS THE SIGN OF GEMINI ON MAY 21 AT 20:15.

DAY	TIME h m s	☉ ° ' "	☽ ° '	☿ °	♀ °	♂ °	♃ °	♄ °	♅ °	♆ °	♇ °
J 1	16 34 53	9♊44 44	8♒43	5♊	28♈	20♓	27♒	21♏R	29♓	22♌	13♋
U 2	16 38 49	10 42 13	22 57	7	29	21	27	21	29	22	13
N 3	16 42 46	11 39 41	7♓10	10	0♉	22	27	21	29	22	13
E 4	16 46 42	12 37 8	21 20	12	1	22	27	21	29	22	13
5	16 50 39	13 34 35	5♈24	14	2	23	27	21	29	22	13
6	16 54 35	14 32 0	19 22	16	4	24	27	21	29	22	13
7	16 58 32	15 29 26	3♉10	18	5	24	27	21	29	22	14
8	17 2 29	16 26 50	16 46	21	6	25	27	21	29	22	14
9	17 6 25	17 24 14	0♊ 9	23	7	26	27	21	29	22	14
10	17 10 22	18 21 38	13 18	25	8	27	27	21	29	22	14
11	17 14 18	19 19 0	26 10	27	9	27	27	21	29	22	14
12	17 18 15	20 16 22	8♋46	29	10	28	27	21	29	22	14
13	17 22 11	21 13 43	21 8	1♋	12	29	27	21	29	22	14
14	17 26 8	22 11 3	3♌17	3	13	29	27	21	29	22	14
15	17 30 4	23 8 23	15 15	5	14	0☉	27	21	29	22	14
16	17 34 1	24 5 41	27 8	7	15	1♈	27 R	21	29	22	14
17	17 37 58	25 2 59	8♍58	9	16	1	27	20	29	23	14
18	17 41 54	26 0 16	20 51	11	17	2	27	20	29	23	14
19	17 45 51	26 57 32	2♎51	13	19	3	27	20	29	23	14
20	17 49 47	27 54 47	15 4	15	20	3	27	20	29	23	14
21	17 53 44	28 52 1	27 32	17	21	4	27	20	29	23	14
22	17 57 40	29 49 15	10♏20	18	22	5	27	20	29	23	14
23	18 1 37	0♋46 29	23 30	20	23	5	27	20	29	23	14
24	18 5 33	1 43 41	7♐ 3	22	24	6	27	20	29	23	14
25	18 9 30	2 40 54	20 58	23	25	7	27	20	29	23	14
26	18 13 27	3 38 6	5♑11	25	27	7	27	20	29	23	14
27	18 17 23	4 35 18	19 39	27	28	8	27	20	29	23	14
28	18 21 20	5 32 29	4♒16	28	29	9	27	20	29	23	14
29	18 25 16	6 29 41	18 54	0♌	0♊	9	27	20	29	23	14
30	18 29 13	7 26 52	3♓30	1	1	10	27	20	29	23	14

THE SUN ENTERS THE SIGN OF CANCER ON JUN 22 AT 04:30.

♈ ARIES ♉ TAURUS ♊ GEMINI ♋ CANCER ♌ LEO ♍ VIRGO ♎ LIBRA ♏ SCORPIO ♐ SAGITTARIUS ♑ CAPRICORN ♒ AQUARIUS ♓ PISCES

SIDEREAL SUN MOON MERCURY VENUS MARS JUPITER SATURN URANUS NEPTUNE PLUTO

DAY	TIME	☉	☽	☿	♀	♂	♃	♄	♅	♆	♇
	h m s	° ' "	° '	°	°	°	°	°	°	°	°
J 1	18 33 9	8♋24 4	17♓58	3♌	2♊	11♈	27♒R	20♏R	29♓	23♌	14♋
U 2	18 37 6	9 21 16	2♈13	4	4	11	27	20	29	23	14
L 3	18 41 2	10 18 28	16 15	5	5	12	27	20	29	23	14
Y 4	18 44 59	11 15 40	0♉ 0	7	6	13	27	20	29	23	14
5	18 48 56	12 12 52	13 31	8	7	13	27	20	29 R	23	14
6	18 52 52	13 10 5	26 45	9	8	14	27	20	29	23	14
7	18 56 49	14 7 18	9♊45	10	10	15	26	20	29	23	14
8	19 0 45	15 4 32	22 31	11	11	15	26	20	29	23	14
9	19 4 42	16 1 45	5♋ 3	12	12	16	26	20	29	23	14
10	19 8 38	16 58 59	17 24	13	13	17	26	20	29	23	14
11	19 12 35	17 56 13	29 34	14	14	17	26	20	29	23	14
12	19 16 31	18 53 27	11♌36	15	15	18	26	20	29	23	14
13	19 20 28	19 50 42	23 31	16	17	18	26	20	29	23	14
14	19 24 25	20 47 56	5♍22	17	18	19	26	20	29	23	14
15	19 28 21	21 45 10	17 12	18	19	20	26	19	29	23	14
16	19 32 18	22 42 25	29 4	18	20	20	26	19	29	23	14
17	19 36 14	23 39 39	11♎ 4	19	21	21	26	19	29	23	15
18	19 40 11	24 36 54	23 14	19	23	22	26	19	29	23	15
19	19 44 7	25 34 9	5♏40	20	24	22	26	19	29	23	15
20	19 48 4	26 31 24	18 25	20	25	23	25	19	29	23	15
21	19 52 0	27 28 40	1♐34	21	26	23	25	19	29	23	15
22	19 55 57	28 25 56	15 8	21	27	24	25	19	29	24	15
23	19 59 54	29 23 12	29 8	21	28	25	25	19	29	24	15
24	20 3 50	0♌20 29	13♑32	21 R	0♋	25	25	19 D	29	24	15
25	20 7 47	1 17 46	28 16	21	1	26	25	19	29	24	15
26	20 11 43	2 15 4	13♒13	21	2	26	25	19	29	24	15
27	20 15 40	3 12 22	28 16	21	3	27	25	19	29	24	15
28	20 19 36	4 9 41	13♓15	21	4	28	25	19	29	24	15
29	20 23 33	5 7 2	28 2	20	6	28	24	19	29	24	15
30	20 27 29	6 4 23	12♈32	20	7	29	24	19	29	24	15
31	20 31 26	7 1 45	26 39	20	8	29	24	19	29	24	15

THE SUN ENTERS THE SIGN OF LEO ON JUL 23 AT 15:25.

DAY	TIME	☉	☽	☿	♀	♂	♃	♄	♅	♆	♇
	h m s	° ' "	° '	°	°	°	°	°	°	°	°
A 1	20 35 23	7♌59 8	10♉24	19♌R	9♋	0♉	24♒R	19♏	29♓R	24♌	15♋
U 2	20 39 19	8 56 33	23 46	18	10	0	24	19	29	24	15
G 3	20 43 16	9 53 59	6♊47	18	12	1	24	19	29	24	15
U 4	20 47 12	10 51 26	19 31	17	13	1	24	20	29	24	15
S 5	20 51 9	11 48 54	2♋ 0	16	14	2	24	20	29	24	15
T 6	20 55 5	12 46 24	14 16	16	15	3	23	20	29	24	15
7	20 59 2	13 43 54	26 23	15	16	3	23	20	29	24	15
8	21 2 59	14 41 26	8♌23	14	18	4	23	20	29	24	15
9	21 6 55	15 38 59	20 17	13	19	4	23	20	29	24	15
10	21 10 52	16 36 32	2♍ 9	12	20	5	23	20	29	24	15
11	21 14 48	17 34 7	13 59	12	21	5	23	20	29	24	15
12	21 18 45	18 31 43	25 49	11	22	6	23	20	29	24	15
13	21 22 41	19 29 20	7♎43	11	24	6	23	20	29	24	15
14	21 26 38	20 26 57	19 43	10	25	7	22	20	29	24	15
15	21 30 34	21 24 36	1♏53	10	26	7	22	20	29	24	15
16	21 34 31	22 22 16	14 17	10	27	8	22	20	29	24	15
17	21 38 27	23 19 57	26 57	9 D	29	8	22	20	29	24	15
18	21 42 24	24 17 39	10♐ 0	9	0♌	8	22	20	29	25	15
19	21 46 21	25 15 22	23 27	9	1	9	22	20	29	25	15
20	21 50 17	26 13 6	7♑22	10	2	9	22	20	29	25	15
21	21 54 14	27 10 51	21 43	10	3	10	22	20	29	25	15
22	21 58 10	28 8 37	6♒30	11	5	10	21	20	29	25	15
23	22 2 7	29 6 25	21 35	11	6	11	21	20	29	25	15
24	22 6 3	0♍ 4 14	6♓51	12	7	11	21	20	29	25	15
25	22 10 0	1 2 5	22 7	13	8	12	21	20	28	25	15
26	22 13 56	1 59 57	7♈11	14	10	12	21	20	28	25	15
27	22 17 53	2 57 51	21 56	15	11	12	21	20	28	25	15
28	22 21 50	3 55 46	6♉16	16	12	13	21	20	28	25	15
29	22 25 46	4 53 44	20 7	17	13	13	21	20	28	25	15
30	22 29 43	5 51 43	3♊30	19	14	13	20	20	28	25	15
31	22 33 39	6 49 45	16 27	20	16	14	20	21	28	25	16

THE SUN ENTERS THE SIGN OF VIRGO ON AUG 23 AT 22:14.

DAY	TIME	☉	☽	☿	♀	♂	♃	♄	♅	♆	♇
	h m s	° ' "	° '	°	°	°	°	°	°	°	°
S 1	22 37 36	7♍47 48	29♊ 4	22♌	17♌	14♉	20♒R	21♏	28♓R	25♌	16♋
E 2	22 41 32	8 45 53	11♋23	23	18	15	20	21	28	25	16
P 3	22 45 29	9 44 0	23 30	25	19	15	20	21	28	25	16
T 4	22 49 25	10 42 9	5♌28	27	21	15	20	21	28	25	16
E 5	22 53 22	11 40 20	17 20	28	22	15	20	21	28	25	16
M 6	22 57 19	12 38 33	29 10	0♍	23	16	20	21	28	25	16
B 7	23 1 15	13 36 47	11♍ 0	2	24	16	19	21	28	25	16
E 8	23 5 12	14 35 3	22 52	4	25	16	19	21	28	25	16
R 9	23 9 8	15 33 21	4♎47	6	27	17	19	21	28	25	16
10	23 13 5	16 31 40	16 46	8	28	17	19	21	28	25	16
11	23 17 1	17 30 1	28 51	10	29	17	19	21	28	25	16
12	23 20 58	18 28 24	11♏ 5	12	0♍	17	19	21	28	25	16
13	23 24 54	19 26 49	23 31	13	2	18	19	21	28	25	16
14	23 28 51	20 25 15	6♐10	15	3	18	19	21	28	25	16
15	23 32 48	21 23 43	19 8	17	4	18	19	22	28	26	16
16	23 36 44	22 22 12	2♑28	19	5	18	19	22	28	26	16
17	23 40 41	23 20 43	16 12	21	7	18	19	22	28	26	16
18	23 44 37	24 19 16	0♒22	23	8	19	18	22	28	26	16
19	23 48 34	25 17 50	14 58	25	9	19	18	22	28	26	16
20	23 52 30	26 16 26	29 56	27	10	19	18	22	28	26	16
21	23 56 27	27 15 3	15♓ 8	28	12	19	18	22	27	26	16
22	0 0 23	28 13 43	0♈25	0♎	13	19	18	22	27	26	16
23	0 4 20	29 12 24	15 36	2	14	19	18	22	27	26	16
24	0 8 16	0♎11 8	0♉29	4	15	19	18	22	27	26	16
25	0 12 13	1 9 54	14 58	6	16	19	18	22	27	26	16
26	0 16 10	2 8 41	28 57	7	18	19	18	22	27	26	16
27	0 20 6	3 7 32	12♊26	9	19	19	18	23	27	26	16
28	0 24 3	4 6 24	25 27	11	20	19	18	23	27	26	16
29	0 27 59	5 5 19	8♋ 4	12	21	19 R	18	23	27	26	16
30	0 31 56	6 4 16	20 21	14	23	19	18	23	27	26	16

THE SUN ENTERS THE SIGN OF LIBRA ON SEP 23 AT 19:27.

SIDEREAL SUN MOON MERCURY VENUS MARS JUPITER SATURN URANUS NEPTUNE PLUTO

DAY	TIME	☉	☽	☿	♀	♂	♃	♄	♅	♆	♇
	h m s	° ' "	° '	°	°	°	°	°	°	°	°
O 1	0 35 52	7♎ 3 16	2♌25	16♎	24♍	19♉R	18♒R	23♏	27♓R	26♌	16♋
C 2	0 39 49	8 2 17	14 19	17	25	19	18	23	27	26	16
T 3	0 43 45	9 1 21	26 9	19	26	19	18	23	27	26	16
O 4	0 47 42	10 0 27	7♍58	21	28	19	17	23	27	26	16
B 5	0 51 39	10 59 35	19 50	22	29	19	17	23	27	26	16
E 6	0 55 35	11 58 46	1♎45	24	0♎	19	17	23	27	26	16
R 7	0 59 32	12 57 58	13 47	25	1	19	17	24	27	26	16
8	1 3 28	13 57 12	25 56	27	3	19	17	24	27	26	16
9	1 7 25	14 56 29	8♏12	29	4	19	17	24	27	26	16
10	1 11 21	15 55 47	20 38	0♏	5	19	17	24	27	26	16
11	1 15 18	16 55 8	3♐13	2	6	18	17	24	27	26	16
12	1 19 14	17 54 30	16 0	3	8	18	17	24	27	26	16
13	1 23 11	18 53 54	29 1	5	9	18	17	24	27	26	16
14	1 27 8	19 53 20	12♑19	6	10	18	17 D	24	27	26	16
15	1 31 4	20 52 47	25 56	8	11	18	17	24	27	26	16
16	1 35 1	21 52 17	9♒54	9	13	17	17	24	27	26	16
17	1 38 57	22 51 47	24 14	11	14	17	17	25	26	26	16 R
18	1 42 54	23 51 20	8♓53	12	15	17	17	25	26	26	16
19	1 46 50	24 50 54	23 47	13	16	17	17	25	26	27	16
20	1 50 47	25 50 31	8♈49	15	18	16	17	25	26	27	16
21	1 54 43	26 50 9	23 48	16	19	16	17	25	26	27	16
22	1 58 40	27 49 49	8♉35	18	20	16	17	25	26	27	16
23	2 2 37	28 49 31	23 2	19	21	15	17	25	26	27	16
24	2 6 33	29 49 16	7♊ 3	20	23	15	17	25	26	27	16
25	2 10 30	0♏49 2	20 36	22	24	15	18	25	26	27	16
26	2 14 26	1 48 51	3♋42	23	25	14	18	26	26	27	16
27	2 18 23	2 48 42	16 23	24	26	14	18	26	26	27	16
28	2 22 19	3 48 35	28 43	26	28	14	18	26	26	27	16
29	2 26 16	4 48 30	10♌49	27	29	13	18	26	26	27	16
30	2 30 12	5 48 28	22 44	28	0♏	13	18	26	26	27	16
31	2 34 9	6 48 28	4♍34	29	1	13	18	26	26	27	16

THE SUN ENTERS THE SIGN OF SCORPIO ON OCT 24 AT 04:19.

DAY	TIME	☉	☽	☿	♀	♂	♃	♄	♅	♆	♇
	h m s	° ' "	° '	°	°	°	°	°	°	°	°
N 1	2 38 6	7♏48 29	16♍25	1♐	3♏	12♉R	18♒	26♏	26♓R	27♌	16♋R
O 2	2 42 2	8 48 33	28 19	2	4	12	18	26	26	27	16
V 3	2 45 59	9 48 39	10♎20	3	5	12	18	26	26	27	16
E 4	2 49 55	10 48 47	22 30	4	6	11	18	27	26	27	16
M 5	2 53 52	11 48 56	4♏50	5	8	11	18	27	26	27	16
B 6	2 57 48	12 49 8	17 22	6	9	11	18	27	26	27	16
E 7	3 1 45	13 49 21	0♐ 4	7	10	10	18	27	26	27	16
R 8	3 5 41	14 49 36	12 58	8	11	10	18	27	26	27	16
9	3 9 38	15 49 53	26 3	9	13	10	18	27	26	27	16
10	3 13 35	16 50 12	9♑19	9	14	9	18	27	26	27	16
11	3 17 31	17 50 31	22 47	10	15	9	19	27	26	27	16
12	3 21 28	18 50 53	6♒28	10	16	9	19	28	26	27	16
13	3 25 24	19 51 15	20 23	11	18	8	19	28	26	27	16
14	3 29 21	20 51 39	4♓31	11	19	8	19	28	26	27	16
15	3 33 17	21 52 5	18 51	11 R	20	8	19	28	26	27	16
16	3 37 14	22 52 31	3♈21	11	22	8	19	28	26	27	16
17	3 41 10	23 52 59	17 56	11	23	7	19	28	26	27	16
18	3 45 7	24 53 28	2♉29	11	24	7	19	28	26	27	16
19	3 49 4	25 53 59	16 54	10	25	7	19	28	26	27	16
20	3 53 0	26 54 31	1♊ 4	10	27	7	19	28	26	27	16
21	3 56 57	27 55 5	14 55	9	28	6	20	29	26	27	16
22	4 0 53	28 55 40	28 24	8	29	6	20	29	26	27	16
23	4 4 50	29 56 17	11♋29	7	0♐	6	20	29	26	27	16
24	4 8 46	0♐56 56	24 12	6	2	6	20	29	26	27	16
25	4 12 43	1 57 36	6♌35	4	3	6	20	29	26	27	16
26	4 16 39	2 58 18	18 44	3	4	5	20	29	26	27	16
27	4 20 36	3 59 1	0♍42	2	5	5	20	29	26	27	16
28	4 24 33	4 59 46	12 34	0	7	5	20	29	26	27	16
29	4 28 29	6 0 32	24 26	29♏	8	5	21	0♐	26	27 R	16
30	4 32 26	7 1 20	6♎22	28	9	5	21	0	26	27	16

THE SUN ENTERS THE SIGN OF SAGITTARIUS ON NOV 23 AT 01:29.

DAY	TIME	☉	☽	☿	♀	♂	♃	♄	♅	♆	♇
	h m s	° ' "	° '	°	°	°	°	°	°	°	°
D 1	4 36 22	8♐ 2 9	18♎26	27♏R	10♐	5♉R	21♒	0♐	26♓R	27♌R	16♋R
E 2	4 40 19	9 3 0	0♏41	26	12	5	21	0	26	27	16
C 3	4 44 15	10 3 52	13 11	26	13	5	21	0	26	27	16
E 4	4 48 12	11 4 45	25 56	25	14	5	21	0	26	27	16
M 5	4 52 8	12 5 40	8♐57	25 D	15	5	21	0	26 D	27	15
B 6	4 56 5	13 6 36	22 13	25	17	5	22	0	26	27	15
E 7	5 0 2	14 7 32	5♑43	25	18	5 D	22	0	26	27	15
R 8	5 3 58	15 8 30	19 25	26	19	5	22	1	26	27	15
9	5 7 55	16 9 28	3♒16	26	20	5	22	1	26	27	15
10	5 11 51	17 10 27	17 15	27	22	5	22	1	26	27	15
11	5 15 48	18 11 27	1♓20	27	23	5	22	1	26	27	15
12	5 19 44	19 12 27	15 29	28	24	5	23	1	26	27	15
13	5 23 41	20 13 27	29 40	29	25	5	23	1	26	27	15
14	5 27 37	21 14 28	13♈52	0♐	27	5	23	1	26	27	15
15	5 31 34	22 15 30	28 0	1	28	5	23	1	26	27	15
16	5 35 31	23 16 32	12♉ 4	2	29	5	23	2	26	27	15
17	5 39 27	24 17 34	25 59	3	0♑	5	23	2	26	27	15
18	5 43 24	25 18 37	9♊42	5	2	5	24	2	26	27	15
19	5 47 20	26 19 41	23 11	6	3	5	24	2	26	27	15
20	5 51 17	27 20 45	6♋23	7	4	6	24	2	26	27	15
21	5 55 13	28 21 50	19 18	8	6	6	24	2	26	27	15
22	5 59 10	29 22 55	1♌56	10	7	6	24	2	26	27	15
23	6 3 6	0♑24 1	14 19	11	8	6	25	2	26	27	15
24	6 7 3	1 25 8	26 28	12	9	6	25	2	26	27	15
25	6 11 0	2 26 15	8♍27	14	11	6	25	3	26	27	15
26	6 14 56	3 27 23	20 21	15	12	7	25	3	26	27	15
27	6 18 53	4 28 31	2♎13	17	13	7	25	3	26	27	15
28	6 22 49	5 29 39	14 9	18	14	7	26	3	26	27	15
29	6 26 46	6 30 49	26 12	20	16	7	26	3	26	27	15
30	6 30 42	7 31 58	8♏28	21	17	8	26	3	26	27	15
31	6 34 39	8 33 9	21 1	22	18	8	26	3	26	27	15

THE SUN ENTERS THE SIGN OF CAPRICORN ON DEC 22 AT 14:34.

♈ ARIES ♉ TAURUS ♊ GEMINI ♋ CANCER ♌ LEO ♍ VIRGO ♎ LIBRA ♏ SCORPIO ♐ SAGITTARIUS ♑ CAPRICORN ♒ AQUARIUS ♓ PISCES

1927

174 Appendix X

SIDEREAL SUN MOON MERCURY VENUS MARS JUPITER SATURN URANUS NEPTUNE PLUTO

DAY	TIME	☉	☽	☿	♀	♂	♃	♄	♅	♆	♇
	h m s	° ' "	° '	°	°	°	°	°	°	°	°
J 1	6 38 35	9♑34 19	3♐52	24♐	19♑	8♉	26♒	3♐	26♓	27♌R	15♋R
A 2	6 42 32	10 35 30	17 5	25	21	8	26	3	26	27	15
N 3	6 46 29	11 36 41	0♑39	27	22	9	27	3	26	27	15
U 4	6 50 25	12 37 52	14 33	28	23	9	27	4	26	27	15
A 5	6 54 22	13 39 3	28 42	0♑	24	9	27	4	26	27	15
R 6	6 58 18	14 40 14	13♒ 4	1	26	10	27	4	26	27	15
Y 7	7 2 15	15 41 25	27 32	3	27	10	28	4	26	27	15
8	7 6 11	16 42 35	12♓ 0	4	28	10	28	4	26	27	15
9	7 10 8	17 43 44	26 25	6	29	11	28	4	26	27	15
10	7 14 5	18 44 54	10♈42	8	1♒	11	28	4	26	27	15
11	7 18 1	19 46 2	24 48	9	2	11	28	4	26	27	15
12	7 21 58	20 47 10	8♉42	11	3	12	29	4	26	26	15
13	7 25 54	21 48 18	22 23	12	4	12	29	4	26	26	15
14	7 29 51	22 49 25	5♊52	14	6	12	29	5	26	26	15
15	7 33 47	23 50 31	19 7	15	7	13	29	5	26	26	15
16	7 37 44	24 51 36	2♋10	17	8	13	29	5	26	26	15
17	7 41 40	25 52 42	15 0	18	9	13	0♓	5	26	26	15
18	7 45 37	26 53 46	27 38	20	11	14	0	5	26	26	15
19	7 49 34	27 54 50	10♌ 5	22	12	14	0	5	26	26	15
20	7 53 30	28 55 53	22 20	23	13	15	0	5	26	26	15
21	7 57 27	29 56 56	4♍26	25	14	15	1	5	26	26	15
22	8 1 23	0♒57 58	16 24	27	16	15	1	5	26	26	15
23	8 5 20	1 59 0	28 18	28	17	16	1	5	26	26	15
24	8 9 16	3 0 1	10♎ 9	0♒	18	16	1	5	27	26	14
25	8 13 13	4 1 2	22 3	2	19	17	1	5	27	26	14
26	8 17 9	5 2 2	4♏ 4	3	21	17	2	6	27	26	14
27	8 21 6	6 3 1	16 17	5	22	18	2	6	27	26	14
28	8 25 3	7 4 0	28 45	7	23	18	2	6	27	26	14
29	8 28 59	8 4 59	11♐35	8	24	18	2	6	27	26	14
30	8 32 56	9 5 56	24 49	10	26	19	3	6	27	26	14
31	8 36 52	10 6 53	8♑29	12	27	19	3	6	27	26	14

THE SUN ENTERS THE SIGN OF AQUARIUS ON JAN 21 AT 01:12.

DAY	TIME	☉	☽	☿	♀	♂	♃	♄	♅	♆	♇
	h m s	° ' "	° '	°	°	°	°	°	°	°	°
F 1	8 40 49	11♒ 7 49	22♑35	14♒	28♒	20♉	3♓	6♐	27♓	26♌R	14♋R
E 2	8 44 45	12 8 45	7♒ 4	15	29	20	3	6	27	26	14
B 3	8 48 42	13 9 39	21 51	17	1♓	21	4	6	27	26	14
R 4	8 52 38	14 10 31	6♓47	19	2	21	4	6	27	26	14
U 5	8 56 35	15 11 23	21 45	21	3	22	4	6	27	26	14
A 6	9 0 32	16 12 13	6♈34	22	4	22	4	6	27	26	14
R 7	9 4 28	17 13 2	21 9	24	6	23	4	6	27	26	14
Y 8	9 8 25	18 13 49	5♉24	26	7	23	5	6	27	26	14
9	9 12 21	19 14 35	19 18	28	8	24	5	7	27	26	14
10	9 16 18	20 15 19	2♊51	0♓	9	24	5	7	27	26	14
11	9 20 14	21 16 1	16 4	1	11	24	5	7	27	26	14
12	9 24 11	22 16 42	29 1	3	12	25	6	7	27	26	14
13	9 28 7	23 17 22	11♋43	5	13	25	6	7	27	26	14
14	9 32 4	24 17 59	24 13	7	14	26	6	7	27	26	14
15	9 36 1	25 18 35	6♌34	9	16	26	6	7	28	26	14
16	9 39 57	26 19 10	18 47	10	17	27	7	7	28	26	14
17	9 43 54	27 19 43	0♍52	12	18	27	7	7	28	26	14
18	9 47 50	28 20 14	12 52	14	19	28	7	7	28	26	14
19	9 51 47	29 20 44	24 47	15	21	28	7	7	28	26	14
20	9 55 43	0♓21 13	6♎40	17	22	29	8	7	28	25	14
21	9 59 40	1 21 40	18 32	18	23	29	8	7	28	25	14
22	10 3 36	2 22 6	0♏25	20	24	0♊	8	7	28	25	14
23	10 7 33	3 22 30	12 25	21	26	0	8	7	28	25	14
24	10 11 30	4 22 53	24 34	22	27	1	9	7	28	25	14
25	10 15 26	5 23 15	6♐58	23	28	2	9	7	28	25	14
26	10 19 23	6 23 35	19 41	24	29	2	9	7	28	25	14
27	10 23 19	7 23 54	2♑48	25	1♈	3	9	7	28	25	14
28	10 27 16	8 24 11	16 23	26	2	3	10	7	28	25	14

THE SUN ENTERS THE SIGN OF PISCES ON FEB 19 AT 15:35.

DAY	TIME	☉	☽	☿	♀	♂	♃	♄	♅	♆	♇
	h m s	° ' "	° '	°	°	°	°	°	°	°	°
M 1	10 31 12	9♓24 27	0♒27	27♓	3♈	4♊	10♓	7♐	28♓	25♌R	14♋R
A 2	10 35 9	10 24 41	15 0	27	4	4	10	7	28	25	14
R 3	10 39 5	11 24 54	29 56	27	5	5	10	7	28	25	14
C 4	10 43 2	12 25 4	15♓ 9	28 R	7	5	10	8	28	25	14
H 5	10 46 59	13 25 13	0♈26	27	8	6	11	8	28	25	14
6	10 50 55	14 25 20	15 37	27	9	6	11	8	29	25	14
7	10 54 52	15 25 25	0♉32	27	10	7	11	8	29	25	14
8	10 58 48	16 25 28	15 4	27	12	7	11	8	29	25	14
9	11 2 45	17 25 28	29 8	26	13	8	12	8	29	25	14
10	11 6 41	18 25 27	12♊46	25	14	8	12	8	29	25	14
11	11 10 38	19 25 23	25 57	24	15	9	12	8	29	25	14
12	11 14 34	20 25 17	8♋47	24	17	10	12	8	29	25	14
13	11 18 31	21 25 9	21 20	23	18	10	13	8	29	25	14
14	11 22 28	22 24 59	3♌38	22	19	11	13	8	29	25	14
15	11 26 24	23 24 47	15 47	21	20	11	13	8	29	25	14
16	11 30 21	24 24 32	27 49	20	21	12	13	8	29	25	14
17	11 34 17	25 24 15	9♍46	19	23	12	14	8	29	25	14
18	11 38 14	26 23 56	21 41	18	24	13	14	8 R	29	25	14
19	11 42 10	27 23 35	3♎34	17	25	13	14	8	29	25	14
20	11 46 7	28 23 13	15 26	16	26	14	14	8	29	25	14
21	11 50 3	29 22 48	27 20	16	28	15	15	8	29	25	14
22	11 54 0	0♈22 21	9♏17	15	29	15	15	8	29	25	14
23	11 57 56	1 21 53	21 20	15	0♉	16	15	8	0⊙	25	14
24	12 1 53	2 21 22	3♐31	14	1	16	15	8	0	25	14
25	12 5 50	3 20 50	15 54	14	2	17	16	8	0	25	14
26	12 9 46	4 20 17	28 35	14	4	17	16	8	0	25	14
27	12 13 43	5 19 41	11♑36	14 D	5	18	16	8	0	25	14
28	12 17 39	6 19 4	25 2	14	6	18	16	8	0	25	14 D
29	12 21 36	7 18 25	8♒57	14	7	19	16	8	0	25	14
30	12 25 32	8 17 44	23 20	14	9	20	17	8	0	25	14
31	12 29 29	9 17 1	8♓ 9	15	10	20	17	8	0	25	14

THE SUN ENTERS THE SIGN OF ARIES ON MAR 21 AT 14:59.

SIDEREAL SUN MOON MERCURY VENUS MARS JUPITER SATURN URANUS NEPTUNE PLUTO

DAY	TIME	☉	☽	☿	♀	♂	♃	♄	♅	♆	♇
	h m s	° ' "	° '	°	°	°	°	°	°	°	°
A 1	12 33 25	10♈16 16	23♓18	15♓	11♉	21♊	17♓	8♐R	0♈	25♌R	14♋
P 2	12 37 22	11 15 30	8♈37	15	12	21	17	7	0	24	14
R 3	12 41 19	12 14 41	23 55	16	13	22	18	7	0	24	14
I 4	12 45 15	13 13 50	9♉ 1	17	15	22	18	7	0	24	14
L 5	12 49 12	14 12 57	23 45	17	16	23	18	7	0	24	14
6	12 53 8	15 12 2	8♊ 1	18	17	24	18	7	0	24	14
7	12 57 5	16 11 5	21 48	19	18	24	19	7	0	24	14
8	13 1 1	17 10 5	5♋ 6	20	19	25	19	7	0	24	14
9	13 4 58	18 9 3	17 59	21	21	25	19	7	0	24	14
10	13 8 54	19 7 59	0♌31	21	22	26	19	7	1	24	14
11	13 12 51	20 6 53	12 47	22	23	26	19	7	1	24	14
12	13 16 48	21 5 44	24 51	24	24	27	20	7	1	24	14
13	13 20 44	22 4 33	6♍48	25	25	28	20	7	1	24	14
14	13 24 41	23 3 19	18 41	26	27	28	20	7	1	24	14
15	13 28 37	24 2 4	0♎33	27	28	29	20	7	1	24	14
16	13 32 34	25 0 46	12 25	28	29	29	21	7	1	24	14
17	13 36 30	25 59 26	24 21	29	0♊	0♋	21	7	1	24	14
18	13 40 27	26 58 5	6♏20	1♈	1	1	21	7	1	24	14
19	13 44 23	27 56 42	18 25	2	3	1	21	7	1	24	14
20	13 48 20	28 55 16	0♐36	3	4	2	21	7	1	24	14
21	13 52 16	29 53 49	12 56	5	5	2	22	7	1	24	14
22	13 56 13	0♉52 21	25 28	6	6	3	22	7	1	24	14
23	14 0 10	1 50 50	8♑13	8	7	3	22	7	1	24	14
24	14 4 6	2 49 18	21 16	9	9	4	22	7	1	24	14
25	14 8 3	3 47 45	4♒40	11	10	5	22	7	1	24	14
26	14 11 59	4 46 10	18 26	12	11	5	23	6	1	24	14
27	14 15 56	5 44 33	2♓37	14	12	6	23	6	1	24	14
28	14 19 52	6 42 55	17 10	15	13	6	23	6	1	24	14
29	14 23 49	7 41 15	2♈ 2	17	14	7	23	6	2	24	14
30	14 27 45	8 39 33	17 6	19	16	8	23	6	2	24	14

THE SUN ENTERS THE SIGN OF TAURUS ON APR 21 AT 02:31.

DAY	TIME	☉	☽	☿	♀	♂	♃	♄	♅	♆	♇
	h m s	° ' "	° '	°	°	°	°	°	°	°	°
M 1	14 31 42	9♉37 50	2♉13	20♈	17♊	8♋	24♓	6♐R	2♈	24♌R	14♋
A 2	14 35 39	10 36 5	17 11	22	18	9	24	6	2	24	14
Y 3	14 39 35	11 34 18	1♊54	24	19	9	24	6	2	24	14
4	14 43 32	12 32 30	16 13	25	20	10	24	6	2	24	14
5	14 47 28	13 30 40	0♋ 5	27	21	11	24	6	2	24	14
6	14 51 25	14 28 47	13 29	29	23	11	25	6	2	24 D	14
7	14 55 21	15 26 53	26 28	1♉	24	12	25	6	2	24	14
8	14 59 18	16 24 57	9♌ 5	3	25	12	25	6	2	24	14
9	15 3 15	17 22 59	21 24	5	26	13	25	6	2	24	14
10	15 7 11	18 20 59	3♍29	7	27	14	25	6	2	24	14
11	15 11 8	19 18 57	15 26	9	28	14	26	6	2	24	14
12	15 15 4	20 16 54	27 18	11	0♋	15	26	5	2	24	14
13	15 19 1	21 14 48	9♎10	13	1	15	26	5	2	24	14
14	15 22 57	22 12 41	21 5	15	2	16	26	5	2	24	14
15	15 26 54	23 10 32	3♏ 4	17	3	16	26	5	2	24	14
16	15 30 50	24 8 22	15 11	19	4	17	27	5	2	24	14
17	15 34 47	25 6 10	27 27	21	5	18	27	5	2	24	14
18	15 38 43	26 3 57	9♐52	23	6	18	27	5	2	24	14
19	15 42 40	27 1 43	22 28	26	8	19	27	5	2	24	14
20	15 46 37	27 59 27	5♑15	28	9	19	27	5	2	24	14
21	15 50 33	28 57 10	18 16	0♊	10	20	27	5	2	24	14
22	15 54 30	29 54 52	1♒31	2	11	21	28	5	2	24	14
23	15 58 26	0♊52 33	15 2	4	12	21	28	5	3	24	14
24	16 2 23	1 50 13	28 49	7	13	22	28	5	3	24	14
25	16 6 19	2 47 51	12♓53	9	14	22	28	4	3	24	14
26	16 10 16	3 45 29	27 13	11	16	23	28	4	3	24	14
27	16 14 13	4 43 6	11♈45	13	17	24	28	4	3	24	14
28	16 18 9	5 40 42	26 25	15	18	24	29	4	3	24	14
29	16 22 6	6 38 17	11♉ 7	17	19	25	29	4	3	24	14
30	16 26 2	7 35 51	25 45	19	20	25	29	4	3	24	14
31	16 29 59	8 33 25	10♊10	21	21	26	29	4	3	24	15

THE SUN ENTERS THE SIGN OF GEMINI ON MAY 22 AT 02:08.

DAY	TIME	☉	☽	☿	♀	♂	♃	♄	♅	♆	♇
	h m s	° ' "	° '	°	°	°	°	°	°	°	°
J 1	16 33 55	9♊30 57	24♊18	23♊	22♋	27♋	29♓	4♐R	3♈	24♌	15♋
U 2	16 37 52	10 28 28	8♋ 5	25	23	27	29	4	3	24	15
N 3	16 41 48	11 25 57	21 29	27	24	28	0⊙	4	3	24	15
E 4	16 45 45	12 23 26	4♌30	29	26	28	0	4	3	24	15
5	16 49 42	13 20 53	17 10	1♋	27	29	0	4	3	24	15
6	16 53 38	14 18 20	29 32	3	28	0♌	0	4	3	24	15
7	16 57 35	15 15 44	11♍40	4	29	0	0♈	4	3	24	15
8	17 1 31	16 13 8	23 38	6	0♌	1	0	3	3	24	15
9	17 5 28	17 10 31	5♎32	8	1	2	0	3	3	25	15
10	17 9 24	18 7 53	17 25	9	2	2	0	3	3	25	15
11	17 13 21	19 5 13	29 22	11	3	3	1	3	3	25	15
12	17 17 17	20 2 33	11♏26	12	4	3	1	3	3	25	15
13	17 21 14	20 59 52	23 40	14	5	4	1	3	3	25	15
14	17 25 11	21 57 10	6♐ 7	15	6	5	1	3	3	25	15
15	17 29 7	22 54 27	18 47	16	7	5	1	3	3	25	15
16	17 33 4	23 51 44	1♑42	18	8	6	1	3	3	25	15
17	17 37 0	24 49 0	14 52	19	9	6	1	3	3	25	15
18	17 40 57	25 46 16	28 16	20	11	7	1	3	3	25	15
19	17 44 53	26 43 31	11♒53	21	12	8	2	3	3	25	15
20	17 48 50	27 40 46	25 41	23	13	8	2	3	3	25	15
21	17 52 46	28 38 1	9♓40	24	14	9	2	3	3	25	15
22	17 56 43	29 35 15	23 48	25	15	9	2	3	3	25	15
23	18 0 40	0♋32 30	8♈ 1	26	16	10	2	2	3	25	15
24	18 4 36	1 29 44	22 19	27	17	11	2	2	3	25	15
25	18 8 33	2 26 58	6♉37	27	18	11	2	2	3	25	15
26	18 12 29	3 24 13	20 52	28	19	12	2	2	3	25	15
27	18 16 26	4 21 27	5♊ 2	29	20	12	2	2	3	25	15
28	18 20 22	5 18 41	19 2	0♌	21	13	2	2	3	25	15
29	18 24 19	6 15 55	2♋49	0	22	14	2	2	3	25	15
30	18 28 15	7 13 9	16 20	1	23	14	3	2	3	25	15

THE SUN ENTERS THE SIGN OF CANCER ON JUN 22 AT 10:22.

♈ ARIES ♉ TAURUS ♊ GEMINI ♋ CANCER ♌ LEO ♍ VIRGO ♎ LIBRA ♏ SCORPIO ♐ SAGITTARIUS ♑ CAPRICORN ♒ AQUARIUS ♓ PISCES

SIDEREAL SUN MOON MERCURY VENUS MARS JUPITER SATURN URANUS NEPTUNE PLUTO

DAY	TIME	☉	☽	☿	♀	♂	♃	♄	♅	♆	♇
	h m s	° ' "	° '	°	°	°	°	°	°	°	°
J 1	18 32 12	8♋10 23	29♋33	1♌	24♌	15♌	3♈	2♐R	3♈	25♌	15♋
U 2	18 36 9	9 7 36	12♌29	1	25	16	3	2	3	25	15
L 3	18 40 5	10 4 49	25 6	2	26	16	3	2	3	25	15
Y 4	18 44 2	11 2 2	7♍28	2	26	17	3	2	3	25	15
5	18 47 58	11 59 15	19 36	2	27	17	3	2	3	25	15
6	18 51 55	12 56 27	1♎36	2 R	28	18	3	2	3	25	15
7	18 55 51	13 53 39	13 30	2	29	19	3	2	3	25	15
8	18 59 48	14 50 51	25 23	2	0♍	19	3	2	3	25	15
9	19 3 44	15 48 3	7♏20	2	1	20	3	2	3 R	25	15
10	19 7 41	16 45 14	19 26	2	2	20	3	2	3	25	15
11	19 11 38	17 42 26	1♐45	1	3	21	3	2	3	25	16
12	19 15 34	18 39 38	14 20	1	4	22	3	2	3	25	16
13	19 19 31	19 36 50	27 13	1	5	22	3	1	3	25	16
14	19 23 27	20 34 2	10♑26	0	6	23	3	1	3	25	16
15	19 27 24	21 31 14	23 58	0	6	24	3	1	3	25	16
16	19 31 20	22 28 27	7♒48	29♋	7	24	3	1	3	25	16
17	19 35 17	23 25 39	21 52	28	8	25	3	1	3	25	16
18	19 39 14	24 22 53	6♓ 7	28	9	25	3	1	3	26	16
19	19 43 10	25 20 7	20 27	27	10	26	3	1	3	26	16
20	19 47 7	26 17 22	4♈48	26	10	27	3	1	3	26	16
21	19 51 3	27 14 37	19 6	26	11	27	3	1	3	26	16
22	19 55 0	28 11 54	3♉18	25	12	28	4	1	3	26	16
23	19 58 56	29 9 11	17 22	24	13	29	4	1	3	26	16
24	20 2 53	0♌ 6 29	1♊17	24	13	29	4 R	1	3	26	16
25	20 6 49	1 3 48	15 2	23	14	0♍	4	1	3	26	16
26	20 10 46	2 1 8	28 35	23	15	0	4	1	3	26	16
27	20 14 43	2 58 29	11♋57	22	16	1	4	1	3	26	16
28	20 18 39	3 55 50	25 7	22	16	2	4	1	3	26	16
29	20 22 36	4 53 13	8♌ 3	22	17	2	3	1	3	26	16
30	20 26 32	5 50 36	20 46	22 D	18	3	3	1	3	26	16
31	20 30 29	6 48 0	3♍15	22	18	4	3	1	3	26	16

THE SUN ENTERS THE SIGN OF LEO ON JUL 23 AT 21:17.

DAY	TIME	☉	☽	☿	♀	♂	♃	♄	♅	♆	♇
	h m s	° ' "	° '	°	°	°	°	°	°	°	°
A 1	20 34 25	7♌45 24	15♍32	22♋	19♍	4♍	3♈R	1♐R	3♈R	26♌	16♋
U 2	20 38 22	8 42 49	27 38	22	19	5	3	1	3	26	16
G 3	20 42 18	9 40 15	9♎35	22	20	5	3	1	3	26	16
U 4	20 46 15	10 37 41	21 28	23	20	6	3	1	3	26	16
S 5	20 50 11	11 35 9	3♏20	23	21	7	3	1 D	3	26	16
T 6	20 54 8	12 32 36	15 15	24	21	7	3	1	3	26	16
7	20 58 5	13 30 5	27 20	25	22	8	3	1	3	26	16
8	21 2 1	14 27 35	9♐39	25	22	9	3	1	3	26	16
9	21 5 58	15 25 5	22 16	26	23	9	3	1	3	26	16
10	21 9 54	16 22 36	5♑15	27	23	10	3	1	3	26	16
11	21 13 51	17 20 8	18 39	29	23	10	3	1	3	26	16
12	21 17 47	18 17 42	2♒28	0♌	24	11	3	1	3	26	16
13	21 21 44	19 15 16	16 40	1	24	12	3	1	3	26	16
14	21 25 41	20 12 51	1♓10	3	24	12	3	1	3	26	16
15	21 29 37	21 10 28	15 52	4	24	13	3	1	3	27	16
16	21 33 34	22 8 6	0♈38	6	25	14	3	1	3	27	16
17	21 37 30	23 5 45	15 21	7	25	14	3	1	3	27	16
18	21 41 27	24 3 26	29 53	9	25	15	3	1	3	27	16
19	21 45 23	25 1 8	14♉10	11	25	16	2	1	3	27	16
20	21 49 20	25 58 53	28 11	13	25 R	16	2	1	3	27	16
21	21 53 16	26 56 39	11♊55	14	25	17	2	1	3	27	17
22	21 57 13	27 54 27	25 23	16	25	17	2	1	3	27	17
23	22 1 10	28 52 16	8♋37	18	25	18	2	1	3	27	17
24	22 5 6	29 50 7	21 37	20	25	19	2	1	3	27	17
25	22 9 3	0♍48 0	4♌26	22	25	19	2	1	3	27	17
26	22 12 59	1 45 54	17 4	24	24	20	2	1	3	27	17
27	22 16 56	2 43 50	29 31	26	24	21	2	1	3	27	17
28	22 20 52	3 41 47	11♍49	28	24	21	2	1	3	27	17
29	22 24 49	4 39 46	23 58	0♍	24	22	2	1	2	27	17
30	22 28 45	5 37 46	5♎58	2	23	23	1	1	2	27	17
31	22 32 42	6 35 48	17 52	4	23	23	1	2	2	27	17

THE SUN ENTERS THE SIGN OF VIRGO ON AUG 24 AT 04:06.

DAY	TIME	☉	☽	☿	♀	♂	♃	♄	♅	♆	♇
	h m s	° ' "	° '	°	°	°	°	°	°	°	°
S 1	22 36 38	7♍33 51	29♎42	6♍	22♍R	24♍	1♈R	2♐	2♈R	27♌	17♋
E 2	22 40 35	8 31 56	11♏32	8	22	24	1	2	2	27	17
P 3	22 44 32	9 30 2	23 25	10	21	25	1	2	2	27	17
T 4	22 48 28	10 28 10	5♐27	12	21	26	1	2	2	27	17
E 5	22 52 25	11 26 19	17 42	14	20	26	1	2	2	27	17
M 6	22 56 21	12 24 30	0♑17	16	20	27	1	2	2	27	17
B 7	23 0 18	13 22 42	13 15	17	19	28	1	2	2	27	17
E 8	23 4 14	14 20 55	26 40	19	19	28	0	2	2	27	17
R 9	23 8 11	15 19 11	10♒34	21	18	29	0	2	2	27	17
10	23 12 7	16 17 27	24 57	23	17	0♎	0	2	2	27	17
11	23 16 4	17 15 46	9♓43	25	17	0	0	2	2	27	17
12	23 20 1	18 14 6	24 46	26	16	1	0⊙	2	2	28	17
13	23 23 57	19 12 28	9♈55	28	16	2	0	2	2	28	17
14	23 27 54	20 10 52	24 59	0♎	15	2	0	2	2	28	17
15	23 31 50	21 9 18	9♉50	2	14	3	0	2	2	28	17
16	23 35 47	22 7 46	24 22	3	14	4	29♓	2	2	28	17
17	23 39 43	23 6 16	8♊30	5	13	4	29	2	2	28	17
18	23 43 40	24 4 49	22 15	7	13	5	29	2	2	28	17
19	23 47 36	25 3 24	5♋38	8	12	5	29	3	2	28	17
20	23 51 33	26 2 1	18 41	10	12	6	29	3	2	28	17
21	23 55 30	27 0 40	1♌28	11	11	7	29	3	2	28	17
22	23 59 26	27 59 21	14 2	13	11	7	29	3	2	28	17
23	0 3 23	28 58 5	26 24	15	11	8	28	3	2	28	17
24	0 7 19	29 56 50	8♍38	16	10	9	28	3	1	28	17
25	0 11 16	0♎55 38	20 44	18	10	9	28	3	1	28	17
26	0 15 12	1 54 28	2♎44	19	10	10	28	3	1	28	17
27	0 19 9	2 53 19	14 39	21	9	11	28	3	1	28	17
28	0 23 5	3 52 13	26 30	22	9	11	28	3	1	28	17
29	0 27 2	4 51 8	8♏19	24	9	12	28	3	1	28	17
30	0 30 59	5 50 6	20 9	25	9	13	28	3	1	28	17

THE SUN ENTERS THE SIGN OF LIBRA ON SEP 24 AT 01:18.

DAY	TIME	☉	☽	☿	♀	♂	♃	♄	♅	♆	♇
	h m s	° ' "	° '	°	°	°	°	°	°	°	°
O 1	0 34 55	6♎49 5	2♐ 2	27♎	9♍R	13♎	27♓R	3♐	1♈R	28♌	17♋
C 2	0 38 52	7 48 6	14 3	28	9 D	14	27	4	1	28	17
T 3	0 42 48	8 47 9	26 16	29	9	15	27	4	1	28	17
O 4	0 46 45	9 46 14	8♑47	1♏	9	15	27	4	1	28	17
B 5	0 50 41	10 45 21	21 40	2	9	16	27	4	1	28	17
E 6	0 54 38	11 44 29	4♒59	4	9	17	27	4	1	28	17
R 7	0 58 34	12 43 39	18 48	5	9	17	27	4	1	28	17
8	1 2 31	13 42 51	3♓ 7	6	10	18	26	4	1	28	17
9	1 6 28	14 42 4	17 54	8	10	19	26	4	1	28	17
10	1 10 24	15 41 20	3♈ 1	9	10	19	26	4	1	28	17
11	1 14 21	16 40 37	18 19	10	10	20	26	4	1	28	17
12	1 18 17	17 39 57	3♉38	11	11	21	26	4	1	28	17
13	1 22 14	18 39 19	18 45	13	11	21	26	5	1	28	17
14	1 26 10	19 38 42	3♊32	14	11	22	26	5	1	29	17
15	1 30 7	20 38 9	17 54	15	12	23	26	5	1	29	17
16	1 34 3	21 37 37	1♋48	16	12	23	26	5	1	29	17
17	1 38 0	22 37 8	15 16	17	13	24	25	5	1	29	17
18	1 41 56	23 36 41	28 20	18	13	25	25	5	1	29	17 R
19	1 45 53	24 36 17	11♌ 3	19	14	25	25	5	1	29	17
20	1 49 50	25 35 54	23 30	20	14	26	25	5	0	29	17
21	1 53 46	26 35 34	5♍44	21	15	27	25	5	0	29	17
22	1 57 43	27 35 17	17 48	22	16	27	25	5	0	29	17
23	2 1 39	28 35 1	29 46	23	16	28	25	5	0	29	17
24	2 5 36	29 34 47	11♎40	23	17	29	25	6	0	29	17
25	2 9 32	0♏34 36	23 31	24	18	29	25	6	0	29	17
26	2 13 29	1 34 26	5♏21	24	18	0♏	25	6	0	29	17
27	2 17 25	2 34 18	17 12	25	19	1	25	6	0	29	17
28	2 21 22	3 34 13	29 6	25	20	1	24	6	0	29	17
29	2 25 19	4 34 9	11♐ 5	25	20	2	24	6	0	29	17
30	2 29 15	5 34 7	23 11	26 R	21	3	24	6	0	29	17
31	2 33 12	6 34 7	5♑28	26	22	3	24	6	0	29	17

THE SUN ENTERS THE SIGN OF SCORPIO ON OCT 24 AT 10:08.

DAY	TIME	☉	☽	☿	♀	♂	♃	♄	♅	♆	♇
	h m s	° ' "	° '	°	°	°	°	°	°	°	°
N 1	2 37 8	7♏34 8	18♑ 0	25♏R	23♍	4♏	24♓R	6♐	0♈R	29♌	17♋R
O 2	2 41 5	8 34 11	0♒51	25	24	5	24	7	0	29	17
V 3	2 45 1	9 34 15	14 4	24	24	5	24	7	0	29	17
E 4	2 48 58	10 34 21	27 43	24	25	6	24	7	0	29	17
M 5	2 52 54	11 34 29	11♓50	23	26	7	24	7	0⊙	29	17
B 6	2 56 51	12 34 38	26 22	22	27	7	24	7	0	29	17
E 7	3 0 48	13 34 48	11♈17	21	28	8	24	7	0	29	17
R 8	3 4 44	14 35 1	26 26	20	29	9	24	7	0	29	17
9	3 8 41	15 35 15	11♉41	18	29	10	24	7	0	29	17
10	3 12 37	16 35 30	26 50	17	0♎	10	24	7	0	29	17
11	3 16 34	17 35 48	11♊44	16	1	11	24	8	0	29	17
12	3 20 30	18 36 7	26 17	15	2	12	24	8	0	29	17
13	3 24 27	19 36 29	10♋22	13	3	12	24	8	0	29	17
14	3 28 23	20 36 52	24 0	12	4	13	24	8	0	29	17
15	3 32 20	21 37 17	7♌12	11	5	14	24	8	0	29	17
16	3 36 17	22 37 44	19 59	11	6	14	24	8	0	29	17
17	3 40 13	23 38 12	2♍27	10	7	15	24	8	0	29	17
18	3 44 10	24 38 43	14 39	10	8	16	24	8	0	29	17
19	3 48 6	25 39 15	26 41	10 D	9	16	24 D	8	0	29	17
20	3 52 3	26 39 49	8♎35	10	10	17	24	9	0	29	17
21	3 55 59	27 40 25	20 25	10	11	18	24	9	0	29	17
22	3 59 56	28 41 3	2♏15	10	12	18	24	9	0	29	17
23	4 3 52	29 41 42	14 7	11	13	19	24	9	0	29	17
24	4 7 49	0♐42 22	26 3	11	14	20	24	9	0	29	17
25	4 11 46	1 43 4	8♐ 5	12	15	21	24	9	0	29	17
26	4 15 42	2 43 48	20 15	13	16	21	24	9	0	29	17
27	4 19 39	3 44 32	2♑34	14	17	22	24	9	0	29	17
28	4 23 35	4 45 18	15 4	15	18	23	24	10	0	29	17
29	4 27 32	5 46 5	27 48	16	19	23	24	10	0	29	17
30	4 31 28	6 46 53	10♒46	17	20	24	24	10	0	29	17

THE SUN ENTERS THE SIGN OF SAGITTARIUS ON NOV 23 AT 07:15.

DAY	TIME	☉	☽	☿	♀	♂	♃	♄	♅	♆	♇
	h m s	° ' "	° '	°	°	°	°	°	°	°	°
D 1	4 35 25	7♐47 42	24♒ 2	18♏	21♎	25♏	24♓	10♐	0⊙R	29♌	17♋R
E 2	4 39 21	8 48 32	7♓37	20	22	25	24	10	0	29 R	17
C 3	4 43 18	9 49 22	21 32	21	24	26	24	10	0	29	17
E 4	4 47 15	10 50 13	5♈46	22	25	27	24	10	0	29	17
M 5	4 51 11	11 51 5	20 19	24	26	28	24	10	0	29	17
B 6	4 55 8	12 51 58	5♉ 4	25	27	28	24	10	29♓	29	17
E 7	4 59 4	13 52 52	19 58	27	28	29	24	11	29	29	17
R 8	5 3 1	14 53 47	4♊51	28	29	0♐	24	11	29	29	17
9	5 6 57	15 54 43	19 35	29	0♏	0	24	11	29 D	29	17
10	5 10 54	16 55 40	4♋ 5	1♐	1	1	24	11	29	29	17
11	5 14 51	17 56 37	18 13	2	2	2	24	11	29	29	17
12	5 18 47	18 57 36	1♌58	4	3	3	24	11	29	29	17
13	5 22 44	19 58 36	15 17	5	5	3	25	11	29	29	17
14	5 26 40	20 59 36	28 11	7	6	4	25	11	0⊙	29	17
15	5 30 37	22 0 38	10♍44	8	7	5	25	12	0	29	17
16	5 34 33	23 1 41	23 0	10	8	5	25	12	0	29	17
17	5 38 30	24 2 44	5♎ 2	11	9	6	25	12	0	29	17
18	5 42 26	25 3 49	16 56	13	10	7	25	12	0	29	17
19	5 46 23	26 4 54	28 45	14	11	7	25	12	0	29	16
20	5 50 20	27 6 0	10♏36	16	13	8	25	12	0	29	16
21	5 54 16	28 7 7	22 30	17	14	9	25	12	0	29	16
22	5 58 13	29 8 15	4♐32	19	15	10	25	12	0	29	16
23	6 2 9	0♑ 9 23	16 45	21	16	10	25	12	0	29	16
24	6 6 6	1 10 32	29 9	22	17	11	26	13	0	29	16
25	6 10 2	2 11 41	11♑46	24	18	12	26	13	0	29	16
26	6 13 59	3 12 51	24 38	25	19	12	26	13	0	29	16
27	6 17 55	4 14 0	7♒42	27	21	13	26	13	0	29	16
28	6 21 52	5 15 10	21 1	28	22	14	26	13	0	29	16
29	6 25 49	6 16 20	4♓31	0♑	23	15	26	13	0	29	16
30	6 29 45	7 17 30	18 14	1	24	15	26	13	0	29	16
31	6 33 42	8 18 39	2♈ 9	3	25	16	26	13	0	29	16

THE SUN ENTERS THE SIGN OF CAPRICORN ON DEC 22 AT 20:19.

♈ ARIES ♉ TAURUS ♊ GEMINI ♋ CANCER ♌ LEO ♍ VIRGO ♎ LIBRA ♏ SCORPIO ♐ SAGITTARIUS ♑ CAPRICORN ♒ AQUARIUS ♓ PISCES

SIDEREAL SUN MOON MERCURY VENUS MARS JUPITER SATURN URANUS NEPTUNE PLUTO

DAY	TIME	☉	☽	☿	♀	♂	♃	♄	♅	♆	♇
	h m s	° ' "	° '	°	°	°	°	°	°	°	°
J 1	6 37 38	9♑19 48	16♈13	5♑	26♏	17♐	27♓	13♐	0♈	29♌R	16♋R
A 2	6 41 35	10 20 57	0♉27	6	28	18	27	14	0	29	16
N 3	6 45 31	11 22 6	14 47	8	29	18	27	14	0	29	16
U 4	6 49 28	12 23 15	29 12	9	0♐	19	27	14	0	29	16
A 5	6 53 24	13 24 24	13♊36	11	1	20	27	14	0	29	16
R 6	6 57 21	14 25 32	27 56	13	2	20	27	14	0	29	16
Y 7	7 1 18	15 26 40	12♋ 7	14	4	21	27	14	0	29	16
8	7 5 14	16 27 48	26 4	16	5	22	28	14	0	29	16
9	7 9 11	17 28 56	9♌42	17	6	23	28	14	0	29	16
10	7 13 7	18 30 4	23 0	19	7	23	28	14	0	29	16
11	7 17 4	19 31 11	5♍57	21	8	24	28	15	0	29	16
12	7 21 0	20 32 19	18 33	22	9	25	28	15	0	29	16
13	7 24 57	21 33 26	0♎52	24	11	26	28	15	0	29	16
14	7 28 53	22 34 33	12 56	26	12	26	28	15	0♈	29	16
15	7 32 50	23 35 41	24 51	27	13	27	29	15	0	29	16
16	7 36 47	24 36 48	6♏41	29	14	28	29	15	0	29	16
17	7 40 43	25 37 54	18 31	1♒	15	28	29	15	0	29	16
18	7 44 40	26 39 1	0♐27	2	17	29	29	15	0	29	16
19	7 48 36	27 40 7	12 33	4	18	0♑	29	15	0	29	16
20	7 52 33	28 41 13	24 52	6	19	1	29	15	0	29	16
21	7 56 29	29 42 18	7♑29	8	20	1	0♈	16	0	29	16
22	8 0 26	0♒43 23	20 24	9	21	2	0	16	0	29	16
23	8 4 23	1 44 27	3♒38	11	23	3	0	16	0	28	16
24	8 8 19	2 45 31	17 9	13	24	4	0♈	16	0	28	16
25	8 12 16	3 46 33	0♓55	14	25	4	0	16	0	28	16
26	8 16 12	4 47 35	14 52	16	26	5	1	16	0	28	16
27	8 20 9	5 48 35	28 56	18	28	6	1	16	0	28	16
28	8 24 5	6 49 35	13♈ 4	20	29	7	1	16	0	28	16
29	8 28 2	7 50 33	27 13	21	0♑	7	1	16	1	28	16
30	8 31 58	8 51 30	11♉21	23	1	8	1	16	1	28	16
31	8 35 55	9 52 26	25 26	25	2	9	1	16	1	28	16

THE SUN ENTERS THE SIGN OF AQUARIUS ON JAN 21 AT 06:57.

DAY	TIME	☉	☽	☿	♀	♂	♃	♄	♅	♆	♇
	h m s	° ' "	° '	°	°	°	°	°	°	°	°
F 1	8 39 52	10♒53 20	9♊28	26♒	4♑	10♑	2♈	17♐	1♈	28♌R	16♋R
E 2	8 43 48	11 54 13	23 26	28	5	10	2	17	1	28	16
B 3	8 47 45	12 55 5	7♋17	29	6	11	2	17	1	28	16
R 4	8 51 41	13 55 56	21 0	1♓	7	12	2	17	1	28	16
U 5	8 55 38	14 56 45	4♌34	2	8	13	2	17	1	28	16
A 6	8 59 34	15 57 33	17 54	4	10	13	3	17	1	28	15
R 7	9 3 31	16 58 20	1♍ 0	5	11	14	3	17	1	28	15
Y 8	9 7 27	17 59 6	13 49	6	12	15	3	17	1	28	15
9	9 11 24	18 59 50	26 22	7	13	16	3	17	1	28	15
10	9 15 21	20 0 34	8♎39	8	15	16	3	17	1	28	15
11	9 19 17	21 1 16	20 43	9	16	17	4	17	1	28	15
12	9 23 14	22 1 57	2♏37	10	17	18	4	17	1	28	15
13	9 27 10	23 2 37	14 27	10	18	18	4	18	1	28	15
14	9 31 7	24 3 16	26 16	11	19	19	4	18	1	28	15
15	9 35 3	25 3 54	8♐11	11 R	21	20	5	18	1	28	15
16	9 39 0	26 4 30	20 17	11	22	21	5	18	1	28	15
17	9 42 56	27 5 6	2♑39	11	23	21	5	18	1	28	15
18	9 46 53	28 5 40	15 22	10	24	22	5	18	1	28	15
19	9 50 50	29 6 13	28 27	10	26	23	5	18	1	28	15
20	9 54 46	0♓ 6 44	11♒57	9	27	24	6	18	2	28	15
21	9 58 43	1 7 14	25 50	8	28	25	6	18	2	28	15
22	10 2 39	2 7 42	10♓ 2	7	29	25	6	18	2	28	15
23	10 6 36	3 8 9	24 28	7	0♒	26	6	18	2	28	15
24	10 10 32	4 8 34	9♈ 0	5	2	27	6	18	2	28	15
25	10 14 29	5 8 56	23 32	4	3	28	7	18	2	28	15
26	10 18 25	6 9 17	7♉59	3	4	28	7	18	2	28	15
27	10 22 22	7 9 37	22 16	2	5	29	7	18	2	28	15
28	10 26 18	8 9 54	6♊21	1	7	0♒	7	18	2	28	15
29	10 30 15	9 10 9	20 14	0	8	1	8	18	2	27	15

THE SUN ENTERS THE SIGN OF PISCES ON FEB 19 AT 21:20.

DAY	TIME	☉	☽	☿	♀	♂	♃	♄	♅	♆	♇
	h m s	° ' "	° '	°	°	°	°	°	°	°	°
M 1	10 34 12	10♓10 22	3♋56	29♒R	9♒	1♒	8♈	18♐	2♈	27♌R	15♋R
A 2	10 38 8	11 10 33	17 26	29	10	2	8	19	2	27	15
R 3	10 42 5	12 10 42	0♌45	28	11	3	8	19	2	27	15
C 4	10 46 1	13 10 48	13 54	27	13	4	9	19	2	27	15
H 5	10 49 58	14 10 53	26 52	27	14	4	9	19	2	27	15
6	10 53 54	15 10 56	9♍38	26	15	5	9	19	2	27	15
7	10 57 51	16 10 57	22 12	26	16	6	9	19	2	27	15
8	11 1 47	17 10 56	4♎34	26 D	18	7	9	19	2	27	15
9	11 5 44	18 10 53	16 45	26	19	7	10	19	2	27	15
10	11 9 41	19 10 49	28 45	26	20	8	10	19	3	27	15
11	11 13 37	20 10 42	10♏37	26	21	9	10	19	3	27	15
12	11 17 34	21 10 34	22 25	27	22	10	10	19	3	27	15
13	11 21 30	22 10 25	4♐14	27	24	10	11	19	3	27	15
14	11 25 27	23 10 13	16 7	27	25	11	11	19	3	27	15
15	11 29 23	24 10 0	28 11	28	26	12	11	19	3	27	15
16	11 33 20	25 9 46	10♑31	29	27	13	11	19	3	27	15
17	11 37 16	26 9 29	23 13	29	29	13	12	19	3	27	15
18	11 41 13	27 9 11	6♒20	0♓	0♓	14	12	19	3	27	15
19	11 45 10	28 8 51	19 54	1	1	15	12	19	3	27	15
20	11 49 6	29 8 29	3♓56	2	2	16	12	19	3	27	15
21	11 53 3	0♈ 8 5	18 24	2	4	17	13	19	3	27	15
22	11 56 59	1 7 39	3♈ 9	3	5	17	13	19	3	27	15
23	12 0 56	2 7 11	18 5	4	6	18	13	19	3	27	15
24	12 4 52	3 6 41	3♉ 3	5	7	19	13	19	3	27	15
25	12 8 49	4 6 9	17 53	6	8	20	14	19	3	27	15
26	12 12 45	5 5 35	2♊29	8	10	20	14	19	3	27	15
27	12 16 42	6 4 59	16 47	9	11	21	14	19	4	27	15
28	12 20 39	7 4 20	0♋45	10	12	22	14	19 R	4	27	15 D
29	12 24 35	8 3 38	14 24	11	13	23	14	19	4	27	15
30	12 28 32	9 2 55	27 45	12	15	23	15	19	4	27	15
31	12 32 28	10 2 9	10♌51	14	16	24	15	19	4	27	15

THE SUN ENTERS THE SIGN OF ARIES ON MAR 20 AT 20:45.

DAY	TIME	☉	☽	☿	♀	♂	♃	♄	♅	♆	♇
	h m s	° ' "	° '	°	°	°	°	°	°	°	°
A 1	12 36 25	11♈ 1 21	23♌42	15♓	17♓	25♒	15♈	19♐R	4♈	27♌R	15♋
P 2	12 40 21	12 0 30	6♍21	16	18	26	15	19	4	27	15
R 3	12 44 18	12 59 37	18 50	18	19	26	16	19	4	27	15
I 4	12 48 14	13 58 42	1♎ 8	19	21	27	16	19	4	27	15
L 5	12 52 11	14 57 45	13 17	21	22	28	16	19	4	27	15
6	12 56 8	15 56 46	25 18	22	23	29	16	19	4	27	15
7	13 0 4	16 55 45	7♏12	24	24	0♓	17	19	4	27	15
8	13 4 1	17 54 42	19 2	25	26	0	17	19	4	27	15
9	13 7 57	18 53 37	0♐49	27	27	1	17	19	4	27	15
10	13 11 54	19 52 30	12 38	28	28	2	17	19	4	27	15
11	13 15 50	20 51 22	24 32	0♈	29	3	18	19	4	27	15
12	13 19 47	21 50 11	6♑35	1♈	1♈	3	18	19	4	27	15
13	13 23 43	22 48 59	18 54	3	2	4	18	19	4	27	15
14	13 27 40	23 47 46	1♒32	5	3	5	18	19	5	27	15
15	13 31 37	24 46 30	14 35	7	4	6	19	19	5	27	15
16	13 35 33	25 45 13	28 5	8	5	6	19	19	5	27	15
17	13 39 30	26 43 54	12♓ 5	10	7	7	19	19	5	27	15
18	13 43 26	27 42 34	26 32	12	8	8	19	19	5	26	15
19	13 47 23	28 41 11	11♈22	14	9	9	20	19	5	26	15
20	13 51 19	29 39 47	26 27	15	10	9	20	19	5	26	15
21	13 55 16	0♉38 21	11♉39	17	12	10	20	19	5	26	15
22	13 59 12	1 36 53	26 47	19	13	11	20	19	5	26	15
23	14 3 9	2 35 23	11♊41	21	14	12	20	19	5	26	15
24	14 7 5	3 33 51	26 16	23	15	13	21	19	5	26	15
25	14 11 2	4 32 17	10♋28	25	16	13	21	19	5	26	15
26	14 14 59	5 30 40	24 16	27	18	14	21	18	5	26	15
27	14 18 55	6 29 2	7♌40	29	19	15	21	18	5	26	15
28	14 22 52	7 27 21	20 42	1♉	20	16	22	18	5	26	15
29	14 26 48	8 25 38	3♍26	3	21	16	22	18	5	26	15
30	14 30 45	9 23 54	15 54	5	23	17	22	18	5	26	15

THE SUN ENTERS THE SIGN OF TAURUS ON APR 20 AT 08:17.

DAY	TIME	☉	☽	☿	♀	♂	♃	♄	♅	♆	♇
	h m s	° ' "	° '	°	°	°	°	°	°	°	°
M 1	14 34 41	10♉22 7	28♍10	7♉	24♈	18♓	22♈	18♐R	5♈	26♌R	15♋
A 2	14 38 38	11 20 18	10♎16	10	25	19	23	18	5	26	15
Y 3	14 42 34	12 18 27	22 15	12	26	19	23	18	6	26	15
4	14 46 31	13 16 35	4♏ 8	14	28	20	23	18	6	26	15
5	14 50 28	14 14 41	15 58	16	29	21	23	18	6	26	15
6	14 54 24	15 12 45	27 46	18	0♉	22	24	18	6	26	15
7	14 58 21	16 10 48	9♐35	20	1	22	24	18	6	26 D	15
8	15 2 17	17 8 49	21 27	23	2	23	24	18	6	26	15
9	15 6 14	18 6 48	3♑26	25	4	24	24	18	6	26	15
10	15 10 10	19 4 47	15 34	27	5	25	24	18	6	26	15
11	15 14 7	20 2 43	27 56	29	6	26	25	18	6	26	15
12	15 18 3	21 0 39	10♒35	1♊	7	26	25	18	6	26	15
13	15 22 0	21 58 33	23 35	3	9	27	25	18	6	26	15
14	15 25 57	22 56 26	6♓59	5	10	28	25	18	6	26	15
15	15 29 53	23 54 18	20 49	7	11	29	26	17	6	26	15
16	15 33 50	24 52 9	5♈ 6	9	12	29	26	17	6	26	15
17	15 37 46	25 49 58	19 46	11	13	0♈	26	17	6	26	15
18	15 41 43	26 47 46	4♉45	13	15	1	26	17	6	26	15
19	15 45 39	27 45 33	19 55	15	16	2	27	17	6	26	15
20	15 49 36	28 43 19	5♊ 5	16	17	2	27	17	6	26	15
21	15 53 32	29 41 3	20 8	18	18	3	27	17	6	26	16
22	15 57 29	0♊38 46	4♋55	20	20	4	27	17	6	26	16
23	16 1 26	1 36 27	19 19	21	21	5	27	17	6	26	16
24	16 5 22	2 34 7	3♌17	23	22	5	28	17	6	26	16
25	16 9 19	3 31 46	16 49	25	23	6	28	17	6	26	16
26	16 13 15	4 29 23	29 56	26	25	7	28	17	6	26	16
27	16 17 12	5 26 58	12♍40	27	26	8	28	17	7	26	16
28	16 21 8	6 24 32	25 6	29	27	8	28	17	7	27	16
29	16 25 5	7 22 4	7♎17	0♋	28	9	29	16	7	27	16
30	16 29 2	8 19 35	19 16	1	29	10	29	16	7	27	16
31	16 32 58	9 17 5	1♏ 9	2	1♊	11	29	16	7	27	16

THE SUN ENTERS THE SIGN OF GEMINI ON MAY 21 AT 07:52.

DAY	TIME	☉	☽	☿	♀	♂	♃	♄	♅	♆	♇
	h m s	° ' "	° '	°	°	°	°	°	°	°	°
J 1	16 36 55	10♊14 34	12♏58	4♋	2♊	11♈	29♈	16♐R	7♈	27♌	16♋
U 2	16 40 51	11 12 1	24 46	5	3	12	0♉	16	7	27	16
N 3	16 44 48	12 9 28	6♐36	6	4	13	0	16	7	27	16
E 4	16 48 44	13 6 53	18 30	7	6	14	0	16	7	27	16
5	16 52 41	14 4 18	0♑30	7	7	14	0	16	7	27	16
6	16 56 37	15 1 42	12 39	8	8	15	0	16	7	27	16
7	17 0 34	15 59 5	24 58	9	9	16	1	16	7	27	16
8	17 4 31	16 56 27	7♒30	10	10	17	1	16	7	27	16
9	17 8 27	17 53 49	20 17	10	12	17	1	16	7	27	16
10	17 12 24	18 51 10	3♓21	11	13	18	1	16	7	27	16
11	17 16 20	19 48 30	16 44	11	14	19	1	16	7	27	16
12	17 20 17	20 45 50	0♈27	12	15	20	2	15	7	27	16
13	17 24 13	21 43 10	14 31	12	17	20	2	15	7	27	16
14	17 28 10	22 40 29	28 56	12	18	21	2	15	7	27	16
15	17 32 6	23 37 48	13♉37	12	19	22	2	15	7	27	16
16	17 36 3	24 35 7	28 30	12 R	20	22	2	15	7	27	16
17	17 40 0	25 32 25	13♊29	12	22	23	3	15	7	27	16
18	17 43 56	26 29 43	28 24	12	23	24	3	15	7	27	16
19	17 47 53	27 27 1	13♋ 9	12	24	25	3	15	7	27	16
20	17 51 49	28 24 17	27 36	12	25	25	3	15	7	27	16
21	17 55 46	29 21 33	11♌40	12	26	26	3	15	7	27	16
22	17 59 42	0♋18 49	25 18	11	28	27	3	15	7	27	16
23	18 3 39	1 16 4	8♍30	11	29	28	4	15	7	27	16
24	18 7 35	2 13 18	21 18	11	0♋	28	4	15	7	27	16
25	18 11 32	3 10 31	3♎45	10	1	29	4	15	7	27	16
26	18 15 29	4 7 44	15 55	10	3	0♉	4	14	7	27	16
27	18 19 25	5 4 56	27 53	9	4	0	4	14	7	27	16
28	18 23 22	6 2 8	9♏43	8	5	1	4	14	7	27	16
29	18 27 18	6 59 20	21 31	8	6	2	5	14	7	27	16
30	18 31 15	7 56 31	3♐20	7	7	3	5	14	7	27	16

THE SUN ENTERS THE SIGN OF CANCER ON JUN 21 AT 16:07.

♈ ARIES ♉ TAURUS ♊ GEMINI ♋ CANCER ♌ LEO ♍ VIRGO ♎ LIBRA ♏ SCORPIO ♐ SAGITTARIUS ♑ CAPRICORN ♒ AQUARIUS ♓ PISCES

1928

SIDEREAL · SUN · MOON · MERCURY · VENUS · MARS · JUPITER · SATURN · URANUS · NEPTUNE · PLUTO

DAY	TIME h m s	☉ ° ' "	☽ ° '	☿ °	♀ °	♂ °	♃ °	♄ °	♅ °	♆ °	♇ °
J 1	18 35 11	8♋53 42	15♐14	7♋R	9♋	3♉	5♉	14♐R	7♈	27♌	16♋
U 2	18 39 8	9 50 53	27 16	6	10	4	5	14	7	27	16
L 3	18 43 4	10 48 4	9♑28	6	11	5	5	14	7	27	17
Y 4	18 47 1	11 45 14	21 52	5	12	5	5	14	7	27	17
5	18 50 58	12 42 25	4♒28	5	14	6	6	14	7	27	17
6	18 54 54	13 39 36	17 17	4	15	7	6	14	7	27	17
7	18 58 51	14 36 47	0♓20	4	16	8	6	14	7	27	17
8	19 2 47	15 33 58	13 37	4	17	8	6	14	7	27	17
9	19 6 44	16 31 10	27 7	3	19	9	6	14	7	27	17
10	19 10 40	17 28 22	10♈51	3 D	20	10	6	14	7	27	17
11	19 14 37	18 25 34	24 49	3	21	10	7	14	7	27	17
12	19 18 33	19 22 47	8♉59	3	22	11	7	13	7 R	27	17
13	19 22 30	20 20 1	23 22	3	23	12	7	13	7	28	17
14	19 26 27	21 17 15	7♊53	4	25	12	7	13	7	28	17
15	19 30 23	22 14 30	22 29	4	26	13	7	13	7	28	17
16	19 34 20	23 11 46	7♋ 5	4	27	14	7	13	7	28	17
17	19 38 16	24 9 1	21 35	5	28	15	7	13	7	28	17
18	19 42 13	25 6 18	5♌51	6	0♌	15	7	13	7	28	17
19	19 46 9	26 3 34	19 50	6	1	16	8	13	7	28	17
20	19 50 6	27 0 51	3♍26	7	2	17	8	13	7	28	17
21	19 54 3	27 58 8	16 38	8	3	17	8	13	7	28	17
22	19 57 59	28 55 26	29 27	9	5	18	8	13	7	28	17
23	20 1 56	29 52 44	11♎55	10	6	19	8	13	7	28	17
24	20 5 52	0♌50 2	24 6	11	7	19	8	13	7	28	17
25	20 9 49	1 47 21	6♏ 4	12	8	20	8	13	7	28	17
26	20 13 45	2 44 40	17 54	14	9	21	8	13	7	28	17
27	20 17 42	3 41 59	29 43	15	11	21	9	13	7	28	17
28	20 21 38	4 39 19	11♐34	16	12	22	9	13	7	28	17
29	20 25 35	5 36 40	23 33	18	13	23	9	13	7	28	17
30	20 29 32	6 34 1	5♑43	20	14	23	9	13	7	28	17
31	20 33 28	7 31 23	18 6	21	16	24	9	13	7	28	17

THE SUN ENTERS THE SIGN OF LEO ON JUL 23 AT 03:03.

DAY	TIME h m s	☉ ° ' "	☽ ° '	☿ °	♀ °	♂ °	♃ °	♄ °	♅ °	♆ °	♇ °
A 1	20 37 25	8♌28 46	0♒46	23♋	17♌	25♉	9♉	13♐R	7♈R	28♌	17♋
U 2	20 41 21	9 26 9	13 42	25	18	25	9	13	7	28	17
G 3	20 45 18	10 23 33	26 54	27	19	26	9	13	7	28	17
U 4	20 49 14	11 20 59	10♓20	28	21	27	9	13	7	28	17
S 5	20 53 11	12 18 25	23 57	0♌	22	27	9	13	7	28	17
T 6	20 57 7	13 15 53	7♈44	2	23	28	9	13	7	28	17
7	21 1 4	14 13 22	21 39	4	24	29	10	13	7	28	17
8	21 5 1	15 10 52	5♉40	6	26	29	10	13	7	28	17
9	21 8 57	16 8 24	19 45	8	27	0♊	10	13	7	28	17
10	21 12 54	17 5 57	3♊55	10	28	1	10	13	7	28	17
11	21 16 50	18 3 31	18 7	12	29	1	10	13	7	28	17
12	21 20 47	19 1 8	2♋20	14	0♍	2	10	13	7	29	18
13	21 24 43	19 58 45	16 31	17	2	2	10	13	7	29	18
14	21 28 40	20 56 24	0♌37	19	3	3	10	13	7	29	18
15	21 32 36	21 54 4	14 32	21	4	4	10	13	7	29	18
16	21 36 33	22 51 45	28 14	23	5	4	10	12	7	29	18
17	21 40 30	23 49 28	11♍38	25	7	5	10	12 D	7	29	18
18	21 44 26	24 47 12	24 43	27	8	6	10	12	7	29	18
19	21 48 23	25 44 57	7♎27	29	9	6	10	13	7	29	18
20	21 52 19	26 42 43	19 53	1♍	10	7	10	13	7	29	18
21	21 56 16	27 40 31	2♏ 2	3	12	7	10	13	7	29	18
22	22 0 12	28 38 19	13 59	4	13	8	10	13	7	29	18
23	22 4 9	29 36 9	25 50	6	14	9	10	13	7	29	18
24	22 8 5	0♍34 0	7♐38	8	15	9	10	13	7	29	18
25	22 12 2	1 31 53	19 30	10	16	10	10	13	7	29	18
26	22 15 59	2 29 46	1♑31	12	18	10	10	13	7	29	18
27	22 19 55	3 27 41	13 46	14	19	11	10	13	7	29	18
28	22 23 52	4 25 38	26 18	15	20	12	10	13	7	29	18
29	22 27 48	5 23 35	9♒11	17	21	12	10	13	7	29	18
30	22 31 45	6 21 34	22 24	19	23	13	10 R	13	7	29	18
31	22 35 41	7 19 35	5♓58	21	24	13	10	13	7	29	18

THE SUN ENTERS THE SIGN OF VIRGO ON AUG 23 AT 09:54.

DAY	TIME h m s	☉ ° ' "	☽ ° '	☿ °	♀ °	♂ °	♃ °	♄ °	♅ °	♆ °	♇ °
S 1	22 39 38	8♍17 37	19♓48	22♍	25♍	14♊	10♉R	13♐	6♈R	29♌	18♋
E 2	22 43 34	9 15 41	3♈51	24	26	14	10	13	6	29	18
P 3	22 47 31	10 13 47	18 3	26	28	15	10	13	6	29	18
T 4	22 51 27	11 11 55	2♉18	27	29	16	10	13	6	29	18
E 5	22 55 24	12 10 4	16 33	29	0♎	16	10	13	6	29	18
M 6	22 59 21	13 8 16	0♊45	1♎	1	17	10	13	6	29	18
B 7	23 3 17	14 6 30	14 53	2	3	17	10	13	6	29	18
E 8	23 7 14	15 4 46	28 55	4	4	18	10	13	6	0♍	18
R 9	23 11 10	16 3 4	12♋51	5	5	18	10	13	6	0	18
10	23 15 7	17 1 24	26 40	7	6	19	10	13	6	0	18
11	23 19 3	17 59 46	10♌21	8	7	19	10	13	6	0	18
12	23 23 0	18 58 10	23 51	10	9	20	10	13	6	0	18
13	23 26 57	19 56 36	7♍10	11	10	20	10	13	6	0	18
14	23 30 53	20 55 4	20 15	13	11	21	10	13	6	0	18
15	23 34 50	21 53 34	3♎ 4	14	12	22	10	13	6	0	18
16	23 38 46	22 52 6	15 38	15	14	22	10	13	6	0	18
17	23 42 43	23 50 39	27 56	17	15	23	10	13	6	0	18
18	23 46 39	24 49 14	10♏ 1	18	16	23	10	13	6	0	18
19	23 50 36	25 47 51	21 56	19	17	24	10	13	6	0	18
20	23 54 32	26 46 30	3♐44	21	19	24	10	13	6	0	18
21	23 58 29	27 45 11	15 32	22	20	25	10	13	6	0	18
22	0 2 25	28 43 53	27 23	23	21	25	10	14	6	0	18
23	0 6 22	29 42 37	9♑23	25	22	25	10	14	6	0	18
24	0 10 19	0♎41 23	21 39	26	23	26	9	14	6	0	18
25	0 14 15	1 40 10	4♒13	27	25	26	9	14	6	0	18
26	0 18 12	2 38 59	17 11	28	26	27	9	14	6	0	18
27	0 22 8	3 37 50	0♓33	29	27	27	9	14	5	0	18
28	0 26 5	4 36 43	14 20	0♏	28	28	9	14	5	0	18
29	0 30 1	5 35 38	28 30	1	0♏	28	9	14	5	0	18
30	0 33 58	6 34 34	12♈56	2	1	29	9	14	5	0	18

THE SUN ENTERS THE SIGN OF LIBRA ON SEP 23 AT 07:06.

DAY	TIME h m s	☉ ° ' "	☽ ° '	☿ °	♀ °	♂ °	♃ °	♄ °	♅ °	♆ °	♇ °
O 1	0 37 54	7♎33 33	27♈33	3♏	2♏	29♊	9♉R	14♐	5♈R	0♍	18♋
C 2	0 41 51	8 32 34	12♉14	4	3	0♋	9	14	5	0	18
T 3	0 45 48	9 31 37	26 52	5	5	0	9	14	5	0	18
O 4	0 49 44	10 30 42	11♊22	6	6	0	8	14	5	0	18
B 5	0 53 41	11 29 50	25 40	7	7	1	8	14	5	0	18
E 6	0 57 37	12 29 0	9♋44	7	8	1	8	14	5	0	18
R 7	1 1 34	13 28 13	23 34	8	9	2	8	15	5	0	18
8	1 5 30	14 27 28	7♌10	8	11	2	8	15	5	1	18
9	1 9 27	15 26 45	20 32	9	12	2	8	15	5	1	18
10	1 13 23	16 26 4	3♍41	9	13	3	8	15	5	1	18
11	1 17 20	17 25 26	16 37	9	14	3	8	15	5	1	18
12	1 21 17	18 24 50	29 21	10 R	16	3	8	15	5	1	18
13	1 25 13	19 24 15	11♎52	10	17	4	7	15	5	1	18
14	1 29 10	20 23 43	24 11	9	18	4	7	15	5	1	18
15	1 33 6	21 23 13	6♏18	9	19	4	7	15	5	1	18
16	1 37 3	22 22 45	18 17	9	21	5	7	15	5	1	18
17	1 40 59	23 22 19	0♐ 8	9	22	5	7	15	5	1	18
18	1 44 56	24 21 55	11 54	8	23	5	7	15	5	1	18
19	1 48 52	25 21 33	23 41	7	24	6	7	16	5	1	18 R
20	1 52 49	26 21 12	5♑31	6	25	6	7	16	5	1	18
21	1 56 46	27 20 54	17 30	5	27	6	6	16	5	1	18
22	2 0 42	28 20 37	29 43	4	28	6	6	16	5	1	18
23	2 4 39	29 20 21	12♒14	2	29	7	6	16	4	1	18
24	2 8 35	0♏20 8	25 8	1	0♐	7	6	16	4	1	18
25	2 12 32	1 19 56	8♓29	0	2	7	6	16	4	1	18
26	2 16 28	2 19 46	22 17	29♎	3	7	6	16	4	1	18
27	2 20 25	3 19 37	6♈32	28	4	8	6	16	4	1	18
28	2 24 21	4 19 30	21 10	26	5	8	5	16	4	1	18
29	2 28 18	5 19 25	6♉ 4	26	6	8	5	16	4	1	18
30	2 32 14	6 19 23	21 6	25	8	8	5	17	4	1	18
31	2 36 11	7 19 22	6♊ 8	24	9	8	5	17	4	1	18

THE SUN ENTERS THE SIGN OF SCORPIO ON OCT 23 AT 15:55.

DAY	TIME h m s	☉ ° ' "	☽ ° '	☿ °	♀ °	♂ °	♃ °	♄ °	♅ °	♆ °	♇ °
N 1	2 40 8	8♏19 23	21♊ 1	24♎R	10♐	8♋	5♉R	17♐	4♈R	1♍	18♋R
O 2	2 44 4	9 19 26	5♋39	24 D	11	9	5	17	4	1	18
V 3	2 48 1	10 19 32	19 57	24	13	9	5	17	4	1	18
E 4	2 51 57	11 19 40	3♌53	24	14	9	5	17	4	1	18
M 5	2 55 54	12 19 49	17 28	24	15	9	4	17	4	1	18
B 6	2 59 50	13 20 1	0♍43	25	16	9	4	17	4	1	18
E 7	3 3 47	14 20 15	13 39	26	17	9	4	17	4	1	18
R 8	3 7 44	15 20 30	26 18	26	19	9	4	17	4	1	18
9	3 11 40	16 20 48	8♎44	27	20	9	4	18	4	1	18
10	3 15 37	17 21 8	20 59	28	21	9	4	18	4	1	18
11	3 19 33	18 21 29	3♏ 4	0♏	22	9	4	18	4	1	18
12	3 23 30	19 21 52	15 1	1	24	9 R	4	18	4	1	18
13	3 27 26	20 22 17	26 53	2	25	9	3	18	4	1	18
14	3 31 23	21 22 44	8♐41	3	26	9	3	18	4	1	18
15	3 35 19	22 23 12	20 27	5	27	9	3	18	4	1	18
16	3 39 16	23 23 42	2♑15	6	28	9	3	18	4	1	18
17	3 43 13	24 24 13	14 7	7	0♑	9	3	18	4	1	18
18	3 47 9	25 24 45	26 8	9	1	9	3	19	4	1	18
19	3 51 6	26 25 19	8♒20	10	2	9	3	19	4	1	18
20	3 55 2	27 25 54	20 48	12	3	9	3	19	4	1	18
21	3 58 59	28 26 30	3♓36	13	5	9	2	19	4	1	18
22	4 2 55	29 27 7	16 48	15	6	9	2	19	4	1	18
23	4 6 52	0♐27 46	0♈26	16	7	8	2	19	4	1	18
24	4 10 48	1 28 25	14 32	18	8	8	2	19	4	1	18
25	4 14 45	2 29 6	29 4	20	9	8	2	19	4	1	18
26	4 18 42	3 29 48	13♉58	21	11	8	2	19	4	1	18
27	4 22 38	4 30 31	29 7	23	12	8	2	20	4	1	18
28	4 26 35	5 31 15	14♊22	24	13	7	2	20	4	1	18
29	4 30 31	6 32 1	29 33	26	14	7	2	20	4	1	18
30	4 34 28	7 32 48	14♋30	27	15	7	2	20	4	1	18

THE SUN ENTERS THE SIGN OF SAGITTARIUS ON NOV 22 AT 13:01.

DAY	TIME h m s	☉ ° ' "	☽ ° '	☿ °	♀ °	♂ °	♃ °	♄ °	♅ °	♆ °	♇ °
D 1	4 38 24	8♐33 36	29♋ 7	29♏	17♑	7♋R	1♉R	20♐	4♈R	1♍	18♋R
E 2	4 42 21	9 34 26	13♌18	0♐	18	6	1	20	4	1	18
C 3	4 46 17	10 35 18	27 2	2	19	6	1	20	4	1 R	18
E 4	4 50 14	11 36 10	10♍20	4	20	6	1	20	4	1	18
M 5	4 54 11	12 37 4	23 14	5	22	6	1	21	3	1	18
B 6	4 58 7	13 37 59	5♎47	7	23	5	1	21	3	1	18
E 7	5 2 4	14 38 56	18 3	8	24	5	1	21	3	1	18
R 8	5 6 0	15 39 53	0♏ 7	10	25	5	1	21	3	1	18
9	5 9 57	16 40 52	12 2	11	26	4	1	21	3	1	18
10	5 13 53	17 41 52	23 52	13	28	4	1	21	3	1	18
11	5 17 50	18 42 53	5♐39	15	29	4	1	21	3	1	18
12	5 21 46	19 43 55	17 26	16	0♒	3	1	21	3 D	1	18
13	5 25 43	20 44 57	29 16	18	1	3	1	21	3	1	18
14	5 29 40	21 46 1	11♑ 9	19	2	2	1	22	3	1	18
15	5 33 36	22 47 5	23 9	21	4	2	1	22	3	1	18
16	5 37 33	23 48 9	5♒17	22	5	2	1	22	3	1	18
17	5 41 29	24 49 14	17 35	24	6	1	1	22	3	1	18
18	5 45 26	25 50 20	0♓ 6	26	7	1	1	22	3	1	18
19	5 49 22	26 51 25	12 52	27	8	0	1	22	3	1	18
20	5 53 19	27 52 31	25 58	29	9	0	0	22	3	1	18
21	5 57 15	28 53 37	9♈25	0♑	11	0	0	22	3	1	18
22	6 1 12	29 54 44	23 16	2	12	29♊	0	23	4	1	18
23	6 5 9	0♑55 50	7♉31	3	13	29	0	23	4	1	18
24	6 9 5	1 56 57	22 9	5	14	29	0	23	4	1	18
25	6 13 2	2 58 4	7♊ 5	7	15	28	0 D	23	4	1	18
26	6 16 58	3 59 11	22 13	8	17	28	0	23	4	1	18
27	6 20 55	5 0 18	7♋25	10	18	27	0	23	4	1	18
28	6 24 51	6 1 26	22 29	11	19	27	0	23	4	1	18
29	6 28 48	7 2 34	7♌17	13	20	27	0	23	4	1	18
30	6 32 45	8 3 42	21 41	15	21	26	0	23	4	1	17
31	6 36 41	9 4 50	5♍37	16	22	26	0	24	4	1	17

THE SUN ENTERS THE SIGN OF CAPRICORN ON DEC 22 AT 02:04.

♈ ARIES ♉ TAURUS ♊ GEMINI ♋ CANCER ♌ LEO ♍ VIRGO ♎ LIBRA ♏ SCORPIO ♐ SAGITTARIUS ♑ CAPRICORN ♒ AQUARIUS ♓ PISCES

SIDEREAL SUN MOON MERCURY VENUS MARS JUPITER SATURN URANUS NEPTUNE PLUTO

DAY	TIME	☉	☽	☿	♀	♂	♃	♄	♅	♆	♇
	h m s	° ' "	° '	°	°	°	°	°	°	°	°
J 1	6 40 38	10♑ 5 59	19♍ 4	18♑	24♒	26♊R	0♉	24♐	4♈	1♍R	17♋R
A 2	6 44 34	11 7 8	2♎ 4	20	25	25	1	24	4	1	17
N 3	6 48 31	12 8 18	14 38	21	26	25	1	24	4	1	17
U 4	6 52 27	13 9 27	26 54	23	27	25	1	24	4	1	17
A 5	6 56 24	14 10 37	8♏54	25	28	24	1	24	4	1	17
R 6	7 0 20	15 11 47	20 45	26	29	24	1	24	4	1	17
Y 7	7 4 17	16 12 57	2♐32	28	1♓	24	1	24	4	1	17
8	7 8 14	17 14 7	14 18	29	2	24	1	24	4	1	17
9	7 12 10	18 15 18	26 7	1♒	3	23	1	25	4	1	17
10	7 16 7	19 16 28	8♑ 2	3	4	23	1	25	4	1	17
11	7 20 3	20 17 37	20 4	4	5	23	1	25	4	1	17
12	7 24 0	21 18 47	2♒16	6	6	23	1	25	4	1	17
13	7 27 56	22 19 56	14 38	8	7	22	1	25	4	1	17
14	7 31 53	23 21 4	27 10	9	9	22	1	25	4	1	17
15	7 35 49	24 22 12	9♓54	11	10	22	1	25	4	1	17
16	7 39 46	25 23 19	22 50	12	11	22	1	25	4	1	17
17	7 43 43	26 24 26	6♈ 0	14	12	22	1	25	4	1	17
18	7 47 39	27 25 31	19 24	15	13	22	1	26	4	1	17
19	7 51 36	28 26 36	3♉ 6	16	14	21	1	26	4	1	17
20	7 55 32	29 27 40	17 5	18	15	21	1	26	4	1	17
21	7 59 29	0♒28 43	1♊22	19	16	21	2	26	4	1	17
22	8 3 25	1 29 45	15 55	20	18	21	2	26	4	1	17
23	8 7 22	2 30 46	0♋42	21	19	21	2	26	4	1	17
24	8 11 18	3 31 46	15 35	22	20	21	2	26	4	1	17
25	8 15 15	4 32 45	0♌27	23	21	21	2	26	4	1	17
26	8 19 12	5 33 43	15 8	23	22	21	2	26	4	1	17
27	8 23 8	6 34 41	29 32	24	23	21 D	2	27	4	1	17
28	8 27 5	7 35 37	13♍31	24	24	21	2	27	4	1	17
29	8 31 1	8 36 33	27 4	24 R	25	21	2	27	4	1	17
30	8 34 58	9 37 28	10♎ 9	24	26	21	2	27	4	1	17
31	8 38 54	10 38 22	22 48	24	27	21	3	27	4	1	17

THE SUN ENTERS THE SIGN OF AQUARIUS ON JAN 20 AT 12:43.

DAY	TIME	☉	☽	☿	♀	♂	♃	♄	♅	♆	♇
	h m s	° ' "	° '	°	°	°	°	°	°	°	°
F 1	8 42 51	11♒39 16	5♏ 7	24♒R	28♓	21♊	3♉	27♐	5♈	1♍R	17♋R
E 2	8 46 47	12 40 9	17 9	23	29	21	3	27	5	0	17
B 3	8 50 44	13 41 1	29 1	22	0♈	21	3	27	5	0	17
R 4	8 54 41	14 41 52	10♐48	21	1	21	3	27	5	0	17
U 5	8 58 37	15 42 42	22 35	20	2	21	3	27	5	0	17
A 6	9 2 34	16 43 31	4♑28	19	4	22	3	27	5	0	17
R 7	9 6 30	17 44 20	16 28	18	5	22	3	28	5	0	17
Y 8	9 10 27	18 45 7	28 41	17	6	22	4	28	5	0	17
9	9 14 23	19 45 53	11♒ 6	16	7	22	4	28	5	0	17
10	9 18 20	20 46 37	23 45	15	8	22	4	28	5	0	17
11	9 22 16	21 47 20	6♓37	13	9	22	4	28	5	0	17
12	9 26 13	22 48 2	19 41	12	10	22	4	28	5	0	17
13	9 30 10	23 48 42	2♈57	12	10	23	4	28	5	0	17
14	9 34 6	24 49 21	16 23	11	11	23	4	28	5	0	17
15	9 38 3	25 49 58	29 59	10	12	23	5	28	5	0	17
16	9 41 59	26 50 33	13♉44	10	13	23	5	28	5	0	17
17	9 45 56	27 51 6	27 39	9	14	23	5	28	5	0	17
18	9 49 52	28 51 38	11♊44	9	15	24	5	28	5	0	17
19	9 53 49	29 52 8	25 58	9 D	16	24	5	29	5	0	17
20	9 57 45	0♓52 36	10♋20	9	17	24	5	29	5	0	16
21	10 1 42	1 53 2	24 46	9	18	24	6	29	5	0	16
22	10 5 39	2 53 26	9♌12	9	19	25	6	29	5	0	16
23	10 9 35	3 53 49	23 31	10	20	25	6	29	6	0	16
24	10 13 32	4 54 9	7♍37	10	21	25	6	29	6	0	16
25	10 17 28	5 54 28	21 25	10	21	25	6	29	6	0	16
26	10 21 25	6 54 46	4♎51	11	22	26	6	29	6	0	16
27	10 25 21	7 55 1	17 54	12	23	26	7	29	6	0	16
28	10 29 18	8 55 16	0♏34	12	24	26	7	29	6	0	16

THE SUN ENTERS THE SIGN OF PISCES ON FEB 19 AT 03:07.

DAY	TIME	☉	☽	☿	♀	♂	♃	♄	♅	♆	♇
	h m s	° ' "	° '	°	°	°	°	°	°	°	°
M 1	10 33 14	9♓55 28	12♏55	13♒	25♈	27♊	7♉	29♐	6♈	0♍R	16♋R
A 2	10 37 11	10 55 39	25 0	14	25	27	7	29	6	0	16
R 3	10 41 8	11 55 49	6♐54	15	26	27	7	29	6	0	16
C 4	10 45 4	12 55 57	18 43	16	27	28	7	29	6	0	16
H 5	10 49 1	13 56 4	0♑32	17	28	28	8	29	6	0	16
6	10 52 57	14 56 9	12 26	18	28	28	8	0♑	6	0	16
7	10 56 54	15 56 12	24 31	19	29	29	8	0	6	0	16
8	11 0 50	16 56 14	6♒50	20	0♉	29	8	0	6	0	16
9	11 4 47	17 56 14	19 25	21	0	29	8	0	6	0	16
10	11 8 43	18 56 12	2♓19	22	1	0♋	9	0	6	29♌	16
11	11 12 40	19 56 8	15 30	23	2	0	9	0	6	29	16
12	11 16 37	20 56 2	28 57	25	2	0	9	0	6	29	16
13	11 20 33	21 55 54	12♈37	26	3	1	9	0	6	29	16
14	11 24 30	22 55 45	26 28	27	3	1	9	0	7	29	16
15	11 28 26	23 55 33	10♉26	29	4	2	10	0	7	29	16
16	11 32 23	24 55 19	24 29	0♓	4	2	10	0	7	29	16
17	11 36 19	25 55 3	8♊35	1	5	2	10	0	7	29	16
18	11 40 16	26 54 44	22 42	3	5	3	10	0	7	29	16
19	11 44 12	27 54 23	6♋50	4	6	3	10	0	7	29	16
20	11 48 9	28 54 0	20 56	6	6	4	11	0	7	29	16
21	11 52 6	29 53 35	5♌ 0	7	6	4	11	0	7	29	16
22	11 56 2	0♈53 7	18 59	9	7	4	11	0	7	29	16
23	11 59 59	1 52 37	2♍49	10	7	5	11	0	7	29	16
24	12 3 55	2 52 5	16 29	12	7	5	11	0	7	29	16
25	12 7 52	3 51 30	29 53	13	8	6	12	0	7	29	16
26	12 11 48	4 50 54	13♎ 2	15	8	6	12	0	7	29	16
27	12 15 45	5 50 16	25 52	16	8	7	12	0	7	29	16
28	12 19 41	6 49 35	8♏26	18	8	7	12	0	7	29	16
29	12 23 38	7 48 53	20 43	20	8	7	13	0	7	29	16
30	12 27 35	8 48 9	2♐47	21	8 R	8	13	0	7	29	16 D
31	12 31 31	9 47 23	14 42	23	8	8	13	0	7	29	16

THE SUN ENTERS THE SIGN OF ARIES ON MAR 21 AT 02:34.

DAY	TIME	☉	☽	☿	♀	♂	♃	♄	♅	♆	♇
	h m s	° ' "	° '	°	°	°	°	°	°	°	°
A 1	12 35 28	10♈46 35	26♐32	25♓	8♉R	9♋	13♉	0♑	8♈	29♌R	16♋
P 2	12 39 24	11 45 46	8♑22	27	8	9	13	0	8	29	16
R 3	12 43 21	12 44 55	20 17	28	8	10	14	0	8	29	16
I 4	12 47 17	13 44 2	2♒23	0♈	8	10	14	0	8	29	16
L 5	12 51 14	14 43 7	14 44	2	7	11	14	1	8	29	16
6	12 55 10	15 42 10	27 23	4	7	11	14	1	8	29	16
7	12 59 7	16 41 12	10♓24	6	7	12	14	1	8	29	16
8	13 3 4	17 40 11	23 46	8	6	12	15	1	8	29	16
9	13 7 0	18 39 9	7♈30	10	6	12	15	1 R	8	29	16
10	13 10 57	19 38 5	21 32	12	6	13	15	1	8	29	16
11	13 14 53	20 36 59	5♉48	13	5	13	15	1	8	29	16
12	13 18 50	21 35 50	20 13	15	5	14	16	1	8	29	16
13	13 22 46	22 34 40	4♊42	17	4	14	16	1	8	29	16
14	13 26 43	23 33 28	19 10	20	4	15	16	1	8	29	16
15	13 30 39	24 32 13	3♋32	22	3	15	16	0	8	29	16
16	13 34 36	25 30 56	17 46	24	3	16	17	0	8	29	16
17	13 38 33	26 29 37	1♌50	26	2	16	17	0	8	29	16
18	13 42 29	27 28 15	15 43	28	1	17	17	0	8	29	16
19	13 46 26	28 26 51	29 23	0♉	1	17	17	0	9	29	16
20	13 50 22	29 25 25	12♍50	2	0	18	17	0	9	29	16
21	13 54 19	0♉23 57	26 4	4	29♈	18	18	0	9	29	16
22	13 58 15	1 22 27	9♎ 4	6	29	19	18	0	9	29	16
23	14 2 12	2 20 54	21 50	8	28	19	18	0	9	29	16
24	14 6 8	3 19 20	4♏23	11	28	20	18	0	9	29	16
25	14 10 5	4 17 44	16 43	13	27	20	19	0	9	29	16
26	14 14 1	5 16 6	28 52	15	26	21	19	0	9	29	16
27	14 17 58	6 14 27	10♐51	17	26	21	19	0	9	29	16
28	14 21 55	7 12 46	22 44	19	25	22	19	0	9	29	16
29	14 25 51	8 11 3	4♑34	21	25	22	20	0	9	29	16
30	14 29 48	9 9 19	16 25	23	24	23	20	0	9	29	16

THE SUN ENTERS THE SIGN OF TAURUS ON APR 20 AT 14:10.

DAY	TIME	☉	☽	☿	♀	♂	♃	♄	♅	♆	♇
	h m s	° ' "	° '	°	°	°	°	°	°	°	°
M 1	14 33 44	10♉ 7 33	28♑20	25♉	24♈R	24♋	20♉	0♑R	9♈	29♌R	16♋
A 2	14 37 41	11 5 46	10♒26	27	23	24	20	0	9	29	16
Y 3	14 41 37	12 3 57	22 45	28	23	25	20	0	9	29	16
4	14 45 34	13 2 7	5♓23	0♊	23	25	21	0	9	29	16
5	14 49 30	14 0 15	18 23	2	23	26	21	0	9	29	16
6	14 53 27	14 58 22	1♈47	4	22	26	21	0	9	29	16
7	14 57 24	15 56 27	15 36	5	22	27	21	0	9	29	16
8	15 1 20	16 54 31	29 49	7	22	27	22	0	10	29	16
9	15 5 17	17 52 33	14♉22	8	22	28	22	0	10	29 D	17
10	15 9 13	18 50 34	29 9	9	22	28	22	0	10	29	17
11	15 13 10	19 48 33	14♊ 3	11	22 D	29	22	0	10	29	17
12	15 17 6	20 46 31	28 55	12	22	29	23	0	10	29	17
13	15 21 3	21 44 27	13♋40	13	22	0♌	23	0	10	29	17
14	15 25 0	22 42 21	28 10	14	22	0	23	0	10	29	17
15	15 28 56	23 40 13	12♌23	15	22	1	23	0	10	29	17
16	15 32 53	24 38 3	26 16	16	22	2	24	29♐	10	29	17
17	15 36 49	25 35 52	9♍48	17	22	2	24	29	10	29	17
18	15 40 46	26 33 39	23 2	18	22	3	24	29	10	29	17
19	15 44 42	27 31 24	5♎57	19	23	3	24	29	10	29	17
20	15 48 39	28 29 8	18 38	20	23	4	25	29	10	29	17
21	15 52 35	29 26 50	1♏ 5	20	23	4	25	29	10	29	17
22	15 56 32	0♊24 31	13 21	21	24	5	25	29	10	29	17
23	16 0 28	1 22 10	25 28	21	24	5	25	29	10	29	17
24	16 4 25	2 19 48	7♐27	22	24	6	25	29	10	29	17
25	16 8 22	3 17 25	19 21	22	25	7	26	29	10	29	17
26	16 12 18	4 15 1	1♑12	22	25	7	26	29	10	29	17
27	16 16 15	5 12 36	13 2	22	26	8	26	29	10	29	17
28	16 20 11	6 10 10	24 53	22 R	26	8	26	29	10	29	17
29	16 24 8	7 7 42	6♒50	22	27	9	27	29	10	29	17
30	16 28 4	8 5 14	18 56	22	27	9	27	29	10	29	17
31	16 32 1	9 2 45	1♓14	22	28	10	27	29	11	29	17

THE SUN ENTERS THE SIGN OF GEMINI ON MAY 21 AT 13:48.

DAY	TIME	☉	☽	☿	♀	♂	♃	♄	♅	♆	♇
	h m s	° ' "	° '	°	°	°	°	°	°	°	°
J 1	16 35 58	10♊ 0 15	13♓48	22♊R	28♈	11♌	27♉	29♐R	11♈	29♌	17♋
U 2	16 39 54	10 57 45	26 43	22	29	11	28	28	11	29	17
N 3	16 43 51	11 55 13	10♈ 3	21	0♉	12	28	28	11	29	17
E 4	16 47 47	12 52 41	23 48	21	0	12	28	28	11	29	17
5	16 51 44	13 50 9	7♉59	20	1	13	28	28	11	29	17
6	16 55 40	14 47 35	22 36	20	2	13	29	28	11	29	17
7	16 59 37	15 45 1	7♊32	19	2	14	29	28	11	29	17
8	17 3 33	16 42 26	22 40	19	3	14	29	28	11	29	17
9	17 7 30	17 39 51	7♋51	18	4	15	29	28	11	29	17
10	17 11 27	18 37 14	22 55	18	5	16	29	28	11	29	17
11	17 15 23	19 34 37	7♌43	17	5	16	0♊	28	11	29	17
12	17 19 20	20 31 58	22 10	17	6	17	0	28	11	29	17
13	17 23 16	21 29 18	6♍10	16	7	17	0	28	11	29	17
14	17 27 13	22 26 38	19 45	16	8	18	0	28	11	29	17
15	17 31 9	23 23 56	2♎54	15	9	19	1	28	11	29	17
16	17 35 6	24 21 13	15 42	15	9	19	1	27	11	29	17
17	17 39 2	25 18 30	28 11	15	10	20	1	27	11	29	17
18	17 42 59	26 15 46	10♏26	14	11	20	1	27	11	29	17
19	17 46 56	27 13 1	22 30	14	12	21	1	27	11	29	17
20	17 50 52	28 10 16	4♐26	14	13	21	2	27	11	29	17
21	17 54 49	29 7 30	16 19	14 D	14	22	2	27	11	29	17
22	17 58 45	0♋ 4 44	28 9	14	15	23	2	27	11	29	17
23	18 2 42	1 1 57	9♑59	14	16	23	2	27	11	29	17
24	18 6 38	1 59 10	21 51	14	16	24	3	27	11	29	17
25	18 10 35	2 56 23	3♒47	14	17	24	3	27	11	29	18
26	18 14 31	3 53 35	15 48	15	18	25	3	27	11	29	18
27	18 18 28	4 50 47	27 58	15	19	26	3	27	11	29	18
28	18 22 25	5 48 0	10♓18	16	20	26	3	27	11	29	18
29	18 26 21	6 45 12	22 53	16	21	27	4	26	11	29	18
30	18 30 18	7 42 24	5♈44	17	22	27	4	26	11	29	18

THE SUN ENTERS THE SIGN OF CANCER ON JUN 21 AT 22:01.

♈ ARIES ♉ TAURUS ♊ GEMINI ♋ CANCER ♌ LEO ♍ VIRGO ♎ LIBRA ♏ SCORPIO ♐ SAGITTARIUS ♑ CAPRICORN ♒ AQUARIUS ♓ PISCES

1929

SIDEREAL SUN MOON MERCURY VENUS MARS JUPITER SATURN URANUS NEPTUNE PLUTO

DAY	TIME	☉	☽	☿	♀	♂	♃	♄	♅	♆	♇
	h m s	° ' "	° '	°	°	°	°	°	°	°	°
J 1	18 34 14	8♋39 37	18♈57	18♊	23♉	28♌	4♊	26♐R	11♈	29♌	18♋
U 2	18 38 11	9 36 50	2♉34	18	24	29	4	26	11	29	18
L 3	18 42 7	10 34 3	16 37	19	25	29	5	26	11	29	18
Y 4	18 46 4	11 31 16	1♊ 5	20	26	0♍	5	26	11	29	18
5	18 50 0	12 28 30	15 55	21	27	0	5	26	11	29	18
6	18 53 57	13 25 43	1♋ 3	22	28	1	5	26	11	29	18
7	18 57 54	14 22 57	16 18	23	29	2	5	26	11	29	18
8	19 1 50	15 20 11	1♌30	25	0♊	2	6	26	11	29	18
9	19 5 47	16 17 25	16 29	26	1	3	6	26	11	0♍	18
10	19 9 43	17 14 39	1♍ 6	27	2	3	6	26	11	0	18
11	19 13 40	18 11 53	15 16	29	3	4	6	26	11	0	18
12	19 17 36	19 9 6	28 56	0♋	4	5	6	26	11	0	18
13	19 21 33	20 6 20	12♎ 8	2	5	5	7	26	11	0	18
14	19 25 30	21 3 34	24 55	3	6	6	7	25	11	0	18
15	19 29 26	22 0 47	7♏21	5	7	6	7	25	11	0	18
16	19 33 23	22 58 1	19 31	7	8	7	7	25	11	0	18
17	19 37 19	23 55 15	1♐29	9	9	8	7	25	11 R	0	18
18	19 41 16	24 52 29	13 21	10	10	8	8	25	11	0	18
19	19 45 12	25 49 44	25 10	12	11	9	8	25	11	0	18
20	19 49 9	26 46 59	7♑ 0	14	12	9	8	25	11	0	18
21	19 53 5	27 44 14	18 53	16	13	10	8	25	11	0	18
22	19 57 2	28 41 30	0♒50	18	14	11	8	25	11	0	18
23	20 0 59	29 38 46	12 53	20	16	11	9	25	11	0	18
24	20 4 55	0♌36 3	25 4	22	17	12	9	25	11	0	18
25	20 8 52	1 33 21	7♓23	24	18	12	9	25	11	0	18
26	20 12 48	2 30 39	19 52	27	19	13	9	25	11	0	18
27	20 16 45	3 27 58	2♈33	29	20	14	9	25	11	0	18
28	20 20 41	4 25 19	15 27	1♌	21	14	9	25	11	0	18
29	20 24 38	5 22 40	28 39	3	22	15	10	25	11	0	18
30	20 28 34	6 20 2	12♉10	5	23	16	10	25	11	0	18
31	20 32 31	7 17 26	26 3	7	24	16	10	25	11	0	18

THE SUN ENTERS THE SIGN OF LEO ON JUL 23 AT 08:54.

DAY	TIME	☉	☽	☿	♀	♂	♃	♄	♅	♆	♇
	h m s	° ' "	° '	°	°	°	°	°	°	°	°
A 1	20 36 28	8♌14 51	10♊18	9♌	25♊	17♍	10♊	25♐R	11♈R	0♍	18♋
U 2	20 40 24	9 12 17	24 54	11	26	17	10	24	11	0	18
G 3	20 44 21	10 9 44	9♋47	13	28	18	10	24	11	0	19
U 4	20 48 17	11 7 12	24 51	15	29	19	11	24	11	0	19
S 5	20 52 14	12 4 41	9♌56	17	0♋	19	11	24	11	0	19
T 6	20 56 10	13 2 11	24 51	19	1	20	11	24	11	0	19
7	21 0 7	13 59 42	9♍28	21	2	21	11	24	11	0	19
8	21 4 3	14 57 14	23 41	23	3	21	11	24	11	0	19
9	21 8 0	15 54 47	7♎25	25	4	22	11	24	11	1	19
10	21 11 57	16 52 20	20 41	27	5	22	12	24	11	1	19
11	21 15 53	17 49 55	3♏30	29	6	23	12	24	11	1	19
12	21 19 50	18 47 30	15 57	1♍	8	24	12	24	11	1	19
13	21 23 46	19 45 7	28 7	3	9	24	12	24	11	1	19
14	21 27 43	20 42 44	10♐ 5	4	10	25	12	24	11	1	19
15	21 31 39	21 40 22	21 57	6	11	26	12	24	11	1	19
16	21 35 36	22 38 2	3♑46	8	12	26	13	24	11	1	19
17	21 39 32	23 35 42	15 38	10	13	27	13	24	11	1	19
18	21 43 29	24 33 24	27 35	11	14	28	13	24	11	1	19
19	21 47 26	25 31 6	9♒39	13	16	28	13	24	11	1	19
20	21 51 22	26 28 51	21 53	15	17	29	13	24	11	1	19
21	21 55 19	27 26 36	4♓16	16	18	29	13	24	11	1	19
22	21 59 15	28 24 23	16 50	18	19	0♎	13	24	11	1	19
23	22 3 12	29 22 11	29 35	19	20	1	13	24	11	1	19
24	22 7 8	0♍20 1	12♈30	21	21	1	14	24	11	1	19
25	22 11 5	1 17 52	25 37	22	22	2	14	24	11	1	19
26	22 15 1	2 15 46	8♉57	24	24	3	14	24	11	1	19
27	22 18 58	3 13 41	22 31	25	25	3	14	24	11	1	19
28	22 22 55	4 11 38	6♊20	27	26	4	14	24	11	1	19
29	22 26 51	5 9 37	20 25	28	27	5	14	24 D	11	1	19
30	22 30 48	6 7 38	4♋46	0♎	28	5	14	24	11	1	19
31	22 34 44	7 5 41	19 19	1	29	6	14	24	11	1	19

THE SUN ENTERS THE SIGN OF VIRGO ON AUG 23 AT 15:42.

DAY	TIME	☉	☽	☿	♀	♂	♃	♄	♅	♆	♇
	h m s	° ' "	° '	°	°	°	°	°	°	°	°
S 1	22 38 41	8♍ 3 45	4♌ 1	2♎	1♌	6♎	15♊	24♐	11♈R	1♍	19♋
E 2	22 42 37	9 1 52	18 45	4	2	7	15	24	11	1	19
P 3	22 46 34	10 0 0	3♍22	5	3	8	15	24	11	1	19
T 4	22 50 30	10 58 10	17 46	6	4	8	15	24	10	1	19
E 5	22 54 27	11 56 21	1♎49	8	5	9	15	24	10	2	19
M 6	22 58 24	12 54 34	15 29	9	6	10	15	24	10	2	19
B 7	23 2 20	13 52 49	28 44	10	8	10	15	24	10	2	19
E 8	23 6 17	14 51 5	11♏34	11	9	11	15	24	10	2	19
R 9	23 10 13	15 49 23	24 3	12	10	12	15	24	10	2	19
10	23 14 10	16 47 43	6♐15	13	11	12	15	24	10	2	19
11	23 18 6	17 46 4	18 15	14	12	13	15	24	10	2	19
12	23 22 3	18 44 26	0♑ 7	15	14	14	16	24	10	2	19
13	23 25 59	19 42 51	11 58	16	15	14	16	24	10	2	19
14	23 29 56	20 41 16	23 52	17	16	15	16	24	10	2	19
15	23 33 53	21 39 44	5♒53	18	17	16	16	24	10	2	19
16	23 37 49	22 38 13	18 4	19	18	16	16	24	10	2	19
17	23 41 46	23 36 44	0♓27	20	20	17	16	24	10	2	19
18	23 45 42	24 35 16	13 5	20	21	18	16	24	10	2	19
19	23 49 39	25 33 51	25 56	21	22	18	16	24	10	2	19
20	23 53 35	26 32 27	9♈ 1	22	23	19	16	24	10	2	19
21	23 57 32	27 31 5	22 18	22	24	20	16	24	10	2	19
22	0 1 28	28 29 46	5♉46	23	26	20	16	24	10	2	19
23	0 5 25	29 28 29	19 25	23	27	21	16	24	10	2	19
24	0 9 21	0♎27 14	3♊13	23	28	22	16	24	10	2	19
25	0 13 18	1 26 1	17 10	23 R	29	22	16	24	10	2	19
26	0 17 15	2 24 50	1♋15	23	0♍	23	16	25	10	2	20
27	0 21 11	3 23 42	15 27	23	2	24	16	25	10	2	20
28	0 25 8	4 22 36	29 43	23	3	24	16	25	10	2	20
29	0 29 4	5 21 33	14♌ 2	23	4	25	16	25	10	2	20
30	0 33 1	6 20 31	28 18	22	5	26	16	25	10	2	20

THE SUN ENTERS THE SIGN OF LIBRA ON SEP 23 AT 12:53.

DAY	TIME	☉	☽	☿	♀	♂	♃	♄	♅	♆	♇
	h m s	° ' "	° '	°	°	°	°	°	°	°	°
O 1	0 36 57	7♎19 32	12♍28	22♎R	6♍	26♎	16♊	25♐	9♈R	2♍	20♋
C 2	0 40 54	8 18 35	26 27	21	8	27	16	25	9	2	20
T 3	0 44 50	9 17 40	10♎10	20	9	28	16	25	9	2	20
O 4	0 48 47	10 16 47	23 36	19	10	28	16	25	9	3	20
B 5	0 52 44	11 15 56	6♏41	18	11	29	16 R	25	9	3	20
E 6	0 56 40	12 15 7	19 26	17	13	0♏	16	25	9	3	20
R 7	1 0 37	13 14 20	1♐54	16	14	0	16	25	9	3	20
8	1 4 33	14 13 35	14 6	15	15	1	16	25	9	3	20
9	1 8 30	15 12 52	26 7	14	16	2	16	25	9	3	20
10	1 12 26	16 12 10	8♑ 0	12	17	2	16	25	9	3	20
11	1 16 23	17 11 30	19 52	11	19	3	16	25	9	3	20
12	1 20 19	18 10 52	1♒47	10	20	4	16	25	9	3	20
13	1 24 16	19 10 16	13 49	10	21	4	16	25	9	3	20
14	1 28 13	20 9 42	26 2	9	22	5	16	26	9	3	20
15	1 32 9	21 9 9	8♓31	8	24	6	16	26	9	3	20
16	1 36 6	22 8 38	21 17	8	25	6	16	26	9	3	20
17	1 40 2	23 8 9	4♈22	8 D	26	7	16	26	9	3	20
18	1 43 59	24 7 42	17 46	8	27	8	16	26	9	3	20
19	1 47 55	25 7 17	1♉27	8	28	9	16	26	9	3	20
20	1 51 52	26 6 54	15 22	9	0♎	9	16	26	9	3	20
21	1 55 48	27 6 33	29 28	9	1	10	16	26	9	3	20 R
22	1 59 45	28 6 14	13♊41	10	2	11	16	26	9	3	20
23	2 3 42	29 5 58	27 58	11	3	11	16	26	9	3	20
24	2 7 38	0♏ 5 44	12♋15	12	5	12	16	26	9	3	20
25	2 11 35	1 5 32	26 30	13	6	13	16	26	9	3	20
26	2 15 31	2 5 22	10♌39	14	7	13	16	26	9	3	20
27	2 19 28	3 5 15	24 41	15	8	14	16	27	8	3	20
28	2 23 24	4 5 10	8♍34	17	10	15	16	27	8	3	20
29	2 27 21	5 5 7	22 17	18	11	15	15	27	8	3	20
30	2 31 17	6 5 6	5♎48	19	12	16	15	27	8	3	20
31	2 35 14	7 5 7	19 5	21	13	17	15	27	8	3	20

THE SUN ENTERS THE SIGN OF SCORPIO ON OCT 23 AT 21:42.

DAY	TIME	☉	☽	☿	♀	♂	♃	♄	♅	♆	♇
	h m s	° ' "	° '	°	°	°	°	°	°	°	°
N 1	2 39 11	8♏ 5 10	2♏ 8	22♎	15♎	18♏	15♊R	27♐	8♈R	3♍	20♋R
O 2	2 43 7	9 5 15	14 57	24	16	18	15	27	8	3	20
V 3	2 47 4	10 5 22	27 31	26	17	19	15	27	8	3	20
E 4	2 51 0	11 5 30	9♐52	27	18	20	15	27	8	3	20
M 5	2 54 57	12 5 41	22 1	29	20	20	15	27	8	3	20
B 6	2 58 53	13 5 53	4♑ 0	0♏	21	21	15	27	8	3	20
E 7	3 2 50	14 6 6	15 54	2	22	22	15	28	8	3	20
R 8	3 6 46	15 6 21	27 45	4	23	22	15	28	8	3	20
9	3 10 43	16 6 38	9♒38	5	25	23	14	28	8	3	20
10	3 14 40	17 6 56	21 38	7	26	24	14	28	8	3	20
11	3 18 36	18 7 16	3♓50	8	27	25	14	28	8	3	20
12	3 22 33	19 7 37	16 17	10	28	25	14	28	8	3	20
13	3 26 29	20 7 59	29 4	12	0♏	26	14	28	8	3	20
14	3 30 26	21 8 22	12♈14	13	1	27	14	28	8	3	20
15	3 34 22	22 8 48	25 47	15	2	27	14	28	8	3	20
16	3 38 19	23 9 14	9♉44	16	3	28	14	28	8	3	19
17	3 42 15	24 9 43	24 2	18	5	29	14	29	8	3	19
18	3 46 12	25 10 12	8♊35	20	6	0♐	13	29	8	3	19
19	3 50 9	26 10 44	23 18	21	7	0	13	29	8	4	19
20	3 54 5	27 11 17	8♋ 4	23	8	1	13	29	8	4	19
21	3 58 2	28 11 52	22 44	24	10	2	13	29	8	4	19
22	4 1 58	29 12 29	7♌15	26	11	2	13	29	8	4	19
23	4 5 55	0♐13 7	21 30	28	12	3	13	29	8	4	19
24	4 9 51	1 13 47	5♍29	29	13	4	13	29	8	4	19
25	4 13 48	2 14 28	19 9	1♐	15	5	13	29	8	4	19
26	4 17 44	3 15 11	2♎33	2	16	5	12	0♑	8	4	19
27	4 21 41	4 15 56	15 41	4	17	6	12	0	8	4	19
28	4 25 38	5 16 42	28 35	6	18	7	12	0	8	4	19
29	4 29 34	6 17 30	11♏15	7	20	8	12	0	8	4	19
30	4 33 31	7 18 19	23 45	9	21	8	12	0	8	4	19

THE SUN ENTERS THE SIGN OF SAGITTARIUS ON NOV 22 AT 18:49.

DAY	TIME	☉	☽	☿	♀	♂	♃	♄	♅	♆	♇
	h m s	° ' "	° '	°	°	°	°	°	°	°	°
D 1	4 37 27	8♐19 10	6♐ 4	10♐	22♏	9♐	12♊R	0♑	8♈R	4♍	19♋R
E 2	4 41 24	9 20 1	18 15	12	23	10	12	0	8	4	19
C 3	4 45 20	10 20 54	0♑17	13	25	10	11	0	8	4	19
E 4	4 49 17	11 21 48	12 14	15	26	11	11	0	8	4	19
M 5	4 53 14	12 22 42	24 6	16	27	12	11	1	8	4	19
B 6	4 57 10	13 23 38	5♒56	18	28	13	11	1	8	4 R	19
E 7	5 1 7	14 24 34	17 49	20	0♐	13	11	1	7	4	19
R 8	5 5 3	15 25 31	29 46	21	1	14	11	1	7	4	19
9	5 9 0	16 26 29	11♓53	23	2	15	11	1	7	4	19
10	5 12 56	17 27 27	24 15	24	3	16	11	1	7	4	19
11	5 16 53	18 28 26	6♈56	26	5	16	10	1	7	4	19
12	5 20 49	19 29 26	20 0	27	6	17	10	1	7	4	19
13	5 24 46	20 30 26	3♉31	29	7	18	10	1	7	4	19
14	5 28 43	21 31 26	17 30	1♑	8	19	10	2	7	4	19
15	5 32 39	22 32 28	1♊56	2	10	19	10	2	7	4	19
16	5 36 36	23 33 29	16 46	4	11	20	10	2	7	4	19
17	5 40 32	24 34 32	1♋51	5	12	21	10	2	7 D	4	19
18	5 44 29	25 35 35	17 2	7	13	21	9	2	7	4	19
19	5 48 25	26 36 39	2♌ 9	8	15	22	9	2	7	4	19
20	5 52 22	27 37 44	17 2	10	16	23	9	2	7	4	19
21	5 56 18	28 38 49	1♍35	12	17	24	9	2	7	4	19
22	6 0 15	29 39 55	15 42	13	18	24	9	3	7	4	19
23	6 4 12	0♑41 2	29 24	15	20	25	9	3	7	4	19
24	6 8 8	1 42 9	12♎42	16	21	26	9	3	7	3	19
25	6 12 5	2 43 17	25 39	18	22	27	9	3	7	3	19
26	6 16 1	3 44 26	8♏18	19	24	27	9	3	7	3	19
27	6 19 58	4 45 35	20 43	21	25	28	8	3	7	3	19
28	6 23 54	5 46 45	2♐57	22	26	29	8	3	8	3	19
29	6 27 51	6 47 55	15 2	24	27	0♑	8	3	8	3	19
30	6 31 47	7 49 6	27 3	25	29	0	8	3	8	3	19
31	6 35 44	8 50 16	8♑58	27	0♑	1	8	4	8	3	19

THE SUN ENTERS THE SIGN OF CAPRICORN ON DEC 22 AT 07:53.

♈ ARIES ♉ TAURUS ♊ GEMINI ♋ CANCER ♌ LEO ♍ VIRGO ♎ LIBRA ♏ SCORPIO ♐ SAGITTARIUS ♑ CAPRICORN ♒ AQUARIUS ♓ PISCES

1930

SIDEREAL SUN MOON MERCURY VENUS MARS JUPITER SATURN URANUS NEPTUNE PLUTO

DAY	TIME	☉	☽	☿	♀	♂	♃	♄	♅	♆	♇
	h m s	° ' "	° '	°	°	°	°	°	°	°	°
J 1	6 39 41	9♑51 27	20♑52	28♑	1♑	2♑	8♊R	4♑	8♈	3♍R	19♋R
A 2	6 43 37	10 52 38	2♒43	29	2	3	8	4	8	3	19
N 3	6 47 34	11 53 49	14 35	1♒	4	3	8	4	8	3	19
U 4	6 51 30	12 54 59	26 29	2	5	4	8	4	8	3	19
A 5	6 55 27	13 56 9	8♓27	3	6	5	8	4	8	3	19
R 6	6 59 23	14 57 19	20 33	4	7	6	7	4	8	3	19
Y 7	7 3 20	15 58 29	2♈52	5	9	6	7	4	8	3	19
8	7 7 16	16 59 38	15 26	6	10	7	7	5	8	3	19
9	7 11 13	18 0 46	28 22	7	11	8	7	5	8	3	19
10	7 15 10	19 1 54	11♉42	7	12	9	7	5	8	3	19
11	7 19 6	20 3 2	25 32	8	14	9	7	5	8	3	19
12	7 23 3	21 4 9	9♊51	8	15	10	7	5	8	3	18
13	7 26 59	22 5 15	24 37	8 R	16	11	7	5	8	3	18
14	7 30 56	23 6 21	9♋46	8	17	12	7	5	8	3	18
15	7 34 52	24 7 27	25 7	8	19	13	7	5	8	3	18
16	7 38 49	25 8 32	10♌29	7	20	13	7	5	8	3	18
17	7 42 46	26 9 37	25 40	7	21	14	7	6	8	3	18
18	7 46 42	27 10 41	10♍30	6	22	15	7	6	8	3	18
19	7 50 39	28 11 44	24 53	5	24	16	7	6	8	3	18
20	7 54 35	29 12 48	8♎46	4	25	16	7	6	8	3	18
21	7 58 32	0♒13 51	22 10	3	26	17	7	6	8	3	18
22	8 2 28	1 14 53	5♏ 7	1	27	18	7	6	8	3	18
23	8 6 25	2 15 55	17 43	0	29	19	6	6	8	3	18
24	8 10 21	3 16 57	0♐ 2	29♑	0♒	19	6	6	8	3	18
25	8 14 18	4 17 58	12 8	28	1	20	6	6	8	3	18
26	8 18 15	5 18 59	24 6	26	2	21	6	7	8	3	18
27	8 22 11	6 19 59	6♑ 0	25	4	22	6	7	8	3	18
28	8 26 8	7 20 58	17 51	25	5	22	6	7	8	3	18
29	8 30 4	8 21 57	29 42	24	6	23	6	7	8	3	18
30	8 34 1	9 22 54	11♒35	23	8	24	6	7	8	3	18
31	8 37 57	10 23 50	23 31	23	9	25	6 D	7	8	3	18

THE SUN ENTERS THE SIGN OF AQUARIUS ON JAN 20 AT 18:33.

DAY	TIME	☉	☽	☿	♀	♂	♃	♄	♅	♆	♇
	h m s	° ' "	° '	°	°	°	°	°	°	°	°
F 1	8 41 54	11♒24 46	5♓31	22♑R	10♒	26♑	6♊	7♑	8♈	3♍R	18♋R
E 2	8 45 50	12 25 40	17 36	22 D	11	26	6	7	8	3	18
B 3	8 49 47	13 26 32	29 48	22	13	27	6	7	8	3	18
R 4	8 53 44	14 27 24	12♈11	22	14	28	6	8	8	3	18
U 5	8 57 40	15 28 14	24 46	23	15	29	6	8	8	3	18
A 6	9 1 37	16 29 3	7♉39	23	16	29	6	8	9	3	18
R 7	9 5 33	17 29 50	20 53	23	18	0♒	6	8	9	3	18
Y 8	9 9 30	18 30 35	4♊31	24	19	1	6	8	9	3	18
9	9 13 26	19 31 20	18 35	24	20	2	6	8	9	3	18
10	9 17 23	20 32 2	3♋ 6	25	21	3	7	8	9	3	18
11	9 21 19	21 32 43	18 0	26	23	3	7	8	9	3	18
12	9 25 16	22 33 23	3♌10	27	24	4	7	8	9	2	18
13	9 29 13	23 34 1	18 26	27	25	5	7	8	9	2	18
14	9 33 9	24 34 37	3♍38	28	26	6	7	8	9	2	18
15	9 37 6	25 35 12	18 33	29	28	6	7	9	9	2	18
16	9 41 2	26 35 46	3♎ 5	0♒	29	7	7	9	9	2	18
17	9 44 59	27 36 18	17 8	1	0♓	8	7	9	9	2	18
18	9 48 55	28 36 49	0♏42	3	1	9	7	9	9	2	18
19	9 52 52	29 37 19	13 47	4	3	9	7	9	9	2	18
20	9 56 48	0♓37 47	26 28	5	4	10	7	9	9	2	18
21	10 0 45	1 38 14	8♐49	6	5	11	7	9	9	2	18
22	10 4 42	2 38 40	20 55	7	6	12	7	9	9	2	18
23	10 8 38	3 39 5	2♑52	9	8	13	7	9	9	2	18
24	10 12 35	4 39 28	14 44	10	9	13	7	9	9	2	18
25	10 16 31	5 39 50	26 34	11	10	14	7	9	9	2	18
26	10 20 28	6 40 10	8♒26	12	11	15	7	10	9	2	18
27	10 24 24	7 40 28	20 22	14	13	16	8	10	9	2	18
28	10 28 21	8 40 45	2♓24	15	14	17	8	10	10	2	18

THE SUN ENTERS THE SIGN OF PISCES ON FEB 19 AT 08:60.

DAY	TIME	☉	☽	☿	♀	♂	♃	♄	♅	♆	♇
	h m s	° ' "	° '	°	°	°	°	°	°	°	°
M 1	10 32 17	9♓41 0	14♓33	17♒	15♓	17♒	8♊	10♑	10♈	2♍R	18♋R
A 2	10 36 14	10 41 13	26 50	18	16	18	8	10	10	2	18
R 3	10 40 11	11 41 24	9♈16	19	18	19	8	10	10	2	18
C 4	10 44 7	12 41 34	21 52	21	19	20	8	10	10	2	18
H 5	10 48 4	13 41 41	4♉39	22	20	20	8	10	10	2	18
6	10 52 0	14 41 46	17 41	24	21	21	8	10	10	2	18
7	10 55 57	15 41 49	0♊58	25	23	22	8	10	10	2	18
8	10 59 53	16 41 51	14 34	27	24	23	8	10	10	2	18
9	11 3 50	17 41 50	28 29	29	25	24	9	10	10	2	18
10	11 7 46	18 41 46	12♋44	0♓	26	24	9	10	10	2	18
11	11 11 43	19 41 41	27 17	2	28	25	9	10	10	2	18
12	11 15 40	20 41 33	12♌ 4	3	29	26	9	11	10	2	18
13	11 19 36	21 41 23	26 57	5	0♈	27	9	11	10	2	18
14	11 23 33	22 41 11	11♍50	7	1	27	9	11	10	2	18
15	11 27 29	23 40 57	26 32	8	3	28	9	11	10	2	17
16	11 31 26	24 40 41	10♎57	10	4	29	9	11	10	2	17
17	11 35 22	25 40 23	24 59	12	5	0♓	9	11	10	2	17
18	11 39 19	26 40 4	8♏35	13	6	1	10	11	10	2	17
19	11 43 15	27 39 42	21 46	15	8	1	10	11	11	2	17
20	11 47 12	28 39 19	4♐32	17	9	2	10	11	11	2	17
21	11 51 8	29 38 54	16 59	19	10	3	10	11	11	1	17
22	11 55 5	0♈38 27	29 10	21	11	4	10	11	11	1	17
23	11 59 2	1 37 59	11♑ 9	22	13	5	10	11	11	1	17
24	12 2 58	2 37 29	23 2	24	14	5	10	11	11	1	17
25	12 6 55	3 36 57	4♒54	26	15	6	11	11	11	1	17
26	12 10 51	4 36 23	16 48	28	16	7	11	11	11	1	17
27	12 14 48	5 35 47	28 48	0♈	17	8	11	11	11	1	17
28	12 18 44	6 35 10	10♓56	2	19	8	11	11	11	1	17
29	12 22 41	7 34 30	23 15	4	20	9	11	11	11	1	17
30	12 26 37	8 33 48	5♈46	6	21	10	11	11	11	1	17
31	12 30 34	9 33 5	18 29	8	22	11	12	12	11	1	17 D

THE SUN ENTERS THE SIGN OF ARIES ON MAR 21 AT 08:30.

SIDEREAL SUN MOON MERCURY VENUS MARS JUPITER SATURN URANUS NEPTUNE PLUTO

DAY	TIME	☉	☽	☿	♀	♂	♃	♄	♅	♆	♇
	h m s	° ' "	° '	°	°	°	°	°	°	°	°
A 1	12 34 31	10♈32 19	1♉25	10♈	24♈	12♓	12♊	12♑	11♈	1♍R	17♋
P 2	12 38 27	11 31 32	14 34	12	25	12	12	12	11	1	17
R 3	12 42 24	12 30 42	27 55	14	26	13	12	12	11	1	17
I 4	12 46 20	13 29 49	11♊29	16	27	14	12	12	11	1	17
L 5	12 50 17	14 28 55	25 15	18	29	15	12	12	12	1	17
6	12 54 13	15 27 59	9♋13	20	0♉	15	13	12	12	1	17
7	12 58 10	16 26 59	23 22	22	1	16	13	12	12	1	17
8	13 2 6	17 25 58	7♌40	24	2	17	13	12	12	1	17
9	13 6 3	18 24 54	22 4	26	4	18	13	12	12	1	17
10	13 10 0	19 23 48	6♍30	29	5	19	13	12	12	1	17
11	13 13 56	20 22 40	20 54	1♉	6	19	13	12	12	1	17
12	13 17 53	21 21 29	5♎10	3	7	20	14	12	12	1	17
13	13 21 49	22 20 17	19 13	5	8	21	14	12	12	1	17
14	13 25 46	23 19 2	2♏59	7	10	22	14	12	12	1	17
15	13 29 42	24 17 46	16 26	8	11	22	14	12	12	1	17
16	13 33 39	25 16 28	29 33	10	12	23	14	12	12	1	17
17	13 37 35	26 15 8	12♐20	12	13	24	15	12	12	1	17
18	13 41 32	27 13 46	24 49	14	15	25	15	12	12	1	17
19	13 45 29	28 12 23	7♑ 2	15	16	26	15	12	12	1	18
20	13 49 25	29 10 57	19 5	17	17	26	15	12	12	1	18
21	13 53 22	0♉ 9 31	1♒ 0	19	18	27	15	12 R	12	1	18
22	13 57 18	1 8 2	12 53	20	20	28	16	12	12	1	18
23	14 1 15	2 6 32	24 48	22	21	29	16	12	13	1	18
24	14 5 11	3 5 0	6♓50	23	22	29	16	12	13	1	18
25	14 9 8	4 3 27	19 3	24	23	0♈	16	12	13	1	18
26	14 13 4	5 1 52	1♈29	25	24	1	16	12	13	1	18
27	14 17 1	6 0 15	14 11	26	26	2	17	12	13	1	18
28	14 20 58	6 58 36	27 11	27	27	3	17	12	13	1	18
29	14 24 54	7 56 56	10♉28	28	28	3	17	12	13	1	18
30	14 28 51	8 55 14	24 1	29	29	4	17	12	13	1	18

THE SUN ENTERS THE SIGN OF TAURUS ON APR 20 AT 20:06.

DAY	TIME	☉	☽	☿	♀	♂	♃	♄	♅	♆	♇
	h m s	° ' "	° '	°	°	°	°	°	°	°	°
M 1	14 32 47	9♉53 30	7♊50	0♊	1♊	5♈	17♊	12♑R	13♈	1♍R	18♋
A 2	14 36 44	10 51 45	21 49	0	2	6	18	12	13	1	18
Y 3	14 40 40	11 49 57	5♋58	1	3	6	18	12	13	1	18
4	14 44 37	12 48 8	20 11	2	4	7	18	12	13	1	18
5	14 48 33	13 46 16	4♌26	2	5	8	18	12	13	1	18
6	14 52 30	14 44 22	18 40	2	7	9	18	12	13	1	18
7	14 56 27	15 42 27	2♍50	2	8	9	19	12	13	1	18
8	15 0 23	16 40 29	16 55	3 R	9	10	19	12	13	1	18
9	15 4 20	17 38 30	0♎52	3	10	11	19	12	13	1	18
10	15 8 16	18 36 28	14 39	3	12	12	19	12	13	1	18
11	15 12 13	19 34 25	28 15	2	13	13	19	12	13	1	18
12	15 16 9	20 32 21	11♏38	2	14	13	20	12	14	1 D	18
13	15 20 6	21 30 15	24 47	2	15	14	20	12	14	1	18
14	15 24 2	22 28 7	7♐41	2	16	15	20	11	14	1	18
15	15 27 59	23 25 58	20 20	1	18	16	20	11	14	1	18
16	15 31 56	24 23 47	2♑44	1	19	16	21	11	14	1	18
17	15 35 52	25 21 36	14 57	0	20	17	21	11	14	1	18
18	15 39 49	26 19 23	26 59	0	21	18	21	11	14	1	18
19	15 43 45	27 17 9	8♒54	29♉	23	19	21	11	14	1	18
20	15 47 42	28 14 53	20 47	29	24	19	21	11	14	1	18
21	15 51 38	29 12 37	2♓42	28	25	20	22	11	14	1	18
22	15 55 35	0♊10 20	14 44	27	26	21	22	11	14	1	18
23	15 59 31	1 8 1	26 57	27	27	22	22	11	14	1	18
24	16 3 28	2 5 41	9♈25	26	29	22	22	11	14	1	18
25	16 7 25	3 3 21	22 13	26	0♋	23	22	11	14	1	18
26	16 11 21	4 0 59	5♉23	25	1	24	23	11	14	1	18
27	16 15 18	4 58 37	18 56	25	2	25	23	11	14	1	18
28	16 19 14	5 56 13	2♊51	25	3	25	23	11	14	1	18
29	16 23 11	6 53 48	17 5	24	5	26	23	11	14	1	18
30	16 27 7	7 51 22	1♋33	24	6	27	24	11	14	1	18
31	16 31 4	8 48 55	16 9	24	7	28	24	11	14	1	18

THE SUN ENTERS THE SIGN OF GEMINI ON MAY 21 AT 19:42.

DAY	TIME	☉	☽	☿	♀	♂	♃	♄	♅	♆	♇
	h m s	° ' "	° '	°	°	°	°	°	°	°	°
J 1	16 35 1	9♊46 27	0♌45	24♉D	8♋	28♈	24♊	11♑R	14♈	1♍	18♋
U 2	16 38 57	10 43 57	15 17	24	9	29	24	11	14	1	18
N 3	16 42 54	11 41 26	29 38	24	11	0♉	25	11	14	1	18
E 4	16 46 50	12 38 54	13♍46	24	12	1	25	10	14	1	18
5	16 50 47	13 36 20	27 40	24	13	1	25	10	15	1	18
6	16 54 43	14 33 45	11♎19	24	14	2	25	10	15	1	18
7	16 58 40	15 31 9	24 45	25	15	3	25	10	15	1	18
8	17 2 36	16 28 32	7♏57	25	17	4	26	10	15	1	18
9	17 6 33	17 25 54	20 57	26	18	4	26	10	15	1	18
10	17 10 30	18 23 15	3♐45	26	19	5	26	10	15	1	18
11	17 14 26	19 20 35	16 22	27	20	6	26	10	15	1	18
12	17 18 23	20 17 55	28 48	28	21	7	27	10	15	1	18
13	17 22 19	21 15 14	11♑ 4	28	23	7	27	10	15	1	18
14	17 26 16	22 12 32	23 10	29	24	8	27	10	15	1	18
15	17 30 12	23 9 50	5♒ 9	0♊	25	9	27	10	15	1	18
16	17 34 9	24 7 7	17 3	1	26	10	27	10	15	1	18
17	17 38 5	25 4 24	28 55	2	27	10	28	10	15	1	19
18	17 42 2	26 1 40	10♓48	3	29	11	28	10	15	1	19
19	17 45 59	26 58 57	22 48	4	0♌	12	28	9	15	1	19
20	17 49 55	27 56 12	4♈58	6	1	12	28	9	15	1	19
21	17 53 52	28 53 28	17 25	7	2	13	29	9	15	1	19
22	17 57 48	29 50 44	0♉13	8	3	14	29	9	15	1	19
23	18 1 45	0♋47 59	13 26	10	5	15	29	9	15	1	19
24	18 5 41	1 45 15	27 5	11	6	15	29	9	15	1	19
25	18 9 38	2 42 30	11♊12	12	7	16	0♋	9	15	1	19
26	18 13 34	3 39 45	25 43	14	8	17	0	9	15	1	19
27	18 17 31	4 37 0	10♋33	16	9	18	0	9	15	1	19
28	18 21 28	5 34 15	25 33	17	10	18	0	9	15	1	19
29	18 25 24	6 31 29	10♌33	19	12	19	0	9	15	1	19
30	18 29 21	7 28 43	25 25	21	13	20	1	9	15	1	19

THE SUN ENTERS THE SIGN OF CANCER ON JUN 22 AT 03:53.

♈ ARIES ♉ TAURUS ♊ GEMINI ♋ CANCER ♌ LEO ♍ VIRGO ♎ LIBRA ♏ SCORPIO ♐ SAGITTARIUS ♑ CAPRICORN ♒ AQUARIUS ♓ PISCES

SIDEREAL SUN MOON MERCURY VENUS MARS JUPITER SATURN URANUS NEPTUNE PLUTO

DAY	TIME	☉	☽	☿	♀	♂	♃	♄	♅	♆	♇
	h m s	° ' "	° '	°	°	°	°	°	°	°	°
J 1	18 33 17	8♋25 56	10♍ 1	22♊	14♌	20♉	1♋	9♑R	15♈	1♍	19♋
U 2	18 37 14	9 23 9	24 17	24	15	21	1	9	15	1	19
L 3	18 41 10	10 20 22	8♎11	26	16	22	1	8	15	1	19
Y 4	18 45 7	11 17 34	21 44	28	18	23	2	8	15	2	19
5	18 49 3	12 14 46	4♏58	0♋	19	23	2	8	15	2	19
6	18 53 0	13 11 58	17 54	2	20	24	2	8	15	2	19
7	18 56 57	14 9 9	0♐37	4	21	25	2	8	15	2	19
8	19 0 53	15 6 21	13 8	6	22	25	3	8	15	2	19
9	19 4 50	16 3 33	25 29	8	23	26	3	8	15	2	19
10	19 8 46	17 0 44	7♑42	11	25	27	3	8	15	2	19
11	19 12 43	17 57 56	19 48	13	26	28	3	8	15	2	19
12	19 16 39	18 55 8	1♒48	15	27	28	3	8	15	2	19
13	19 20 36	19 52 20	13 43	17	28	29	4	8	15	2	19
14	19 24 33	20 49 33	25 35	19	29	0♊	4	8	15	2	19
15	19 28 29	21 46 45	7♓26	21	0♍	0	4	8	15	2	19
16	19 32 26	22 43 59	19 18	23	2	1	4	8	15	2	19
17	19 36 22	23 41 13	1♈17	26	3	2	5	7	15	2	19
18	19 40 19	24 38 28	13 26	28	4	2	5	7	15	2	19
19	19 44 15	25 35 43	25 50	0♌	5	3	5	7	15	2	19
20	19 48 12	26 32 59	8♉35	2	6	4	5	7	15	2	19
21	19 52 8	27 30 16	21 44	4	7	4	5	7	15 R	2	19
22	19 56 5	28 27 34	5♊22	6	8	5	6	7	15	2	19
23	20 0 2	29 24 52	19 29	8	10	6	6	7	15	2	19
24	20 3 58	0♌22 12	4♋ 4	10	11	7	6	7	15	2	19
25	20 7 55	1 19 32	19 2	12	12	7	6	7	15	2	19
26	20 11 51	2 16 53	4♌15	14	13	8	7	7	15	2	20
27	20 15 48	3 14 15	19 31	16	14	9	7	7	15	2	20
28	20 19 44	4 11 37	4♍40	18	15	9	7	7	15	2	20
29	20 23 41	5 8 59	19 31	19	16	10	7	7	15	2	20
30	20 27 37	6 6 23	4♎ 0	21	18	11	7	7	15	2	20
31	20 31 34	7 3 46	18 2	23	19	11	8	7	15	2	20

THE SUN ENTERS THE SIGN OF LEO ON JUL 23 AT 14:42.

DAY	TIME	☉	☽	☿	♀	♂	♃	♄	♅	♆	♇
	h m s	° ' "	° '	°	°	°	°	°	°	°	°
A 1	20 35 31	8♌ 1 11	1♏38	25♌	20♍	12♊	8♋	6♑R	15♈R	2♍	20♋
U 2	20 39 27	8 58 35	14 49	26	21	13	8	6	15	2	20
G 3	20 43 24	9 56 1	27 40	28	22	13	8	6	15	2	20
U 4	20 47 20	10 53 27	10♐14	0♍	23	14	8	6	15	2	20
S 5	20 51 17	11 50 54	22 35	1	24	15	9	6	15	3	20
T 6	20 55 13	12 48 22	4♑46	3	25	15	9	6	15	3	20
7	20 59 10	13 45 50	16 49	5	27	16	9	6	15	3	20
8	21 3 6	14 43 20	28 47	6	28	17	9	6	15	3	20
9	21 7 3	15 40 50	10♒42	8	29	17	9	6	15	3	20
10	21 11 0	16 38 22	22 34	9	0♎	18	10	6	15	3	20
11	21 14 56	17 35 54	4♓25	11	1	19	10	6	15	3	20
12	21 18 53	18 33 28	16 18	12	2	19	10	6	15	3	20
13	21 22 49	19 31 3	28 14	14	3	20	10	6	15	3	20
14	21 26 46	20 28 39	10♈16	15	4	21	10	6	15	3	20
15	21 30 42	21 26 17	22 27	16	5	21	11	6	15	3	20
16	21 34 39	22 23 56	4♉53	18	7	22	11	6	15	3	20
17	21 38 35	23 21 37	17 36	19	8	23	11	6	15	3	20
18	21 42 32	24 19 20	0♊41	20	9	23	11	6	15	3	20
19	21 46 29	25 17 4	14 12	22	10	24	11	6	15	3	20
20	21 50 25	26 14 50	28 12	23	11	25	12	6	15	3	20
21	21 54 22	27 12 37	12♋39	24	12	25	12	6	15	3	20
22	21 58 18	28 10 27	27 31	25	13	26	12	6	15	3	20
23	22 2 15	29 8 17	12♌40	26	14	27	12	6	15	3	20
24	22 6 11	0♍ 6 9	27 57	27	15	27	12	5	15	3	20
25	22 10 8	1 4 3	13♍10	28	16	28	13	5	15	3	20
26	22 14 4	2 1 58	28 10	29	17	28	13	5	15	3	20
27	22 18 1	2 59 54	12♎48	0♎	18	29	13	5	15	3	20
28	22 21 58	3 57 52	27 0	1	19	0♋	13	5	15	3	20
29	22 25 54	4 55 51	10♏43	2	21	0	13	5	15	3	20
30	22 29 51	5 53 51	24 0	3	22	1	13	5	15	3	20
31	22 33 47	6 51 53	6♐53	3	23	2	14	5	15	3	20

THE SUN ENTERS THE SIGN OF VIRGO ON AUG 23 AT 21:27.

DAY	TIME	☉	☽	☿	♀	♂	♃	♄	♅	♆	♇
	h m s	° ' "	° '	°	°	°	°	°	°	°	°
S 1	22 37 44	7♍49 56	19♐26	4♎	24♎	2♋	14♋	5♑R	15♈R	3♍	20♋
E 2	22 41 40	8 48 1	1♑44	5	25	3	14	5	15	4	20
P 3	22 45 37	9 46 7	13 50	5	26	3	14	5	15	4	20
T 4	22 49 33	10 44 14	25 48	6	27	4	14	5	15	4	20
E 5	22 53 30	11 42 23	7♒42	6	28	5	15	5	15	4	20
M 6	22 57 27	12 40 34	19 34	6	29	5	15	5	15	4	20
B 7	23 1 23	13 38 46	1♓26	7	0♏	6	15	5	15	4	20
E 8	23 5 20	14 36 59	13 20	7 R	1	6	15	5	15	4	20
R 9	23 9 16	15 35 15	25 18	7	2	7	15	5 D	14	4	21
10	23 13 13	16 33 32	7♈22	7	3	8	15	5	14	4	21
11	23 17 9	17 31 51	19 34	7	4	8	16	5	14	4	21
12	23 21 6	18 30 12	1♉55	6	5	9	16	5	14	4	21
13	23 25 2	19 28 35	14 28	6	6	10	16	5	14	4	21
14	23 28 59	20 27 1	27 17	5	7	10	16	5	14	4	21
15	23 32 55	21 25 28	10♊24	5	8	11	16	5	14	4	21
16	23 36 52	22 23 58	23 52	4	9	11	16	5	14	4	21
17	23 40 49	23 22 30	7♋43	3	10	12	16	5	14	4	21
18	23 44 45	24 21 4	21 57	2	11	12	17	5	14	4	21
19	23 48 42	25 19 40	6♌32	1	11	13	17	5	14	4	21
20	23 52 38	26 18 19	21 24	0	12	14	17	5	14	4	21
21	23 56 35	27 16 59	6♍25	29♍	13	14	17	5	14	4	21
22	0 0 31	28 15 42	21 27	28	14	15	17	5	14	4	21
23	0 4 28	29 14 26	6♎21	27	15	15	17	5	14	4	21
24	0 8 24	0♎13 13	20 58	26	16	16	17	5	14	4	21
25	0 12 21	1 12 1	5♏13	25	17	17	18	5	14	4	21
26	0 16 18	2 10 51	19 3	24	18	17	18	5	14	4	21
27	0 20 14	3 9 43	2♐26	23	19	18	18	5	14	4	21
28	0 24 11	4 8 37	15 25	23	19	18	18	6	14	4	21
29	0 28 7	5 7 32	28 2	22	20	19	18	6	14	4	21
30	0 32 4	6 6 30	10♑21	22 D	21	19	18	6	14	5	21

THE SUN ENTERS THE SIGN OF LIBRA ON SEP 23 AT 18:37.

DAY	TIME	☉	☽	☿	♀	♂	♃	♄	♅	♆	♇
	h m s	° ' "	° '	°	°	°	°	°	°	°	°
O 1	0 36 0	7♎ 5 29	22♑26	22♍	22♏	20♋	18♋	6♑	14♈R	5♍	21♋
C 2	0 39 57	8 4 29	4♒23	22	23	20	18	6	14	5	21
T 3	0 43 53	9 3 32	16 16	22	24	21	18	6	14	5	21
O 4	0 47 50	10 2 36	28 7	23	24	22	19	6	14	5	21
B 5	0 51 47	11 1 42	10♓ 1	23	25	22	19	6	13	5	21
E 6	0 55 43	12 0 50	22 0	24	26	23	19	6	13	5	21
R 7	0 59 40	13 0 0	4♈ 7	25	27	23	19	6	13	5	21
8	1 3 36	13 59 12	16 23	26	27	24	19	6	13	5	21
9	1 7 33	14 58 26	28 50	27	28	24	19	6	13	5	21
10	1 11 29	15 57 42	11♉28	28	29	25	19	6	13	5	21
11	1 15 26	16 57 1	24 19	0♎	29	25	19	6	13	5	21
12	1 19 22	17 56 21	7♊23	1	0♐	26	19	6	13	5	21
13	1 23 19	18 55 44	20 42	3	1	26	19	6	13	5	21
14	1 27 16	19 55 10	4♋16	4	1	27	19	6	13	5	21
15	1 31 12	20 54 37	18 6	6	2	27	20	6	13	5	21
16	1 35 9	21 54 7	2♌10	7	2	28	20	6	13	5	21
17	1 39 5	22 53 39	16 28	9	3	28	20	6	13	5	21
18	1 43 2	23 53 14	0♍57	10	3	29	20	6	13	5	21
19	1 46 58	24 52 50	15 33	12	4	29	20	6	13	5	21
20	1 50 55	25 52 29	0♎10	14	4	0♌	20	7	13	5	21
21	1 54 51	26 52 10	14 43	15	5	0	20	7	13	5	21
22	1 58 48	27 51 53	29 5	17	5	1	20	7	13	5	21 R
23	2 2 45	28 51 38	13♏11	19	5	1	20	7	13	5	21
24	2 6 41	29 51 25	26 57	21	6	2	20	7	13	5	21
25	2 10 38	0♏51 14	10♐21	22	6	2	20	7	13	5	21
26	2 14 34	1 51 5	23 23	24	6	3	20	7	13	5	21
27	2 18 31	2 50 58	6♑ 3	26	7	3	20	7	13	5	21
28	2 22 27	3 50 52	18 26	27	7	3	20	7	13	5	21
29	2 26 24	4 50 48	0♒33	29	7	4	20	7	13	5	21
30	2 30 20	5 50 45	12 31	1♏	7	4	20	7	13	5	21
31	2 34 17	6 50 44	24 23	2	7	5	20	7	12	5	21

THE SUN ENTERS THE SIGN OF SCORPIO ON OCT 24 AT 03:27.

DAY	TIME	☉	☽	☿	♀	♂	♃	♄	♅	♆	♇
	h m s	° ' "	° '	°	°	°	°	°	°	°	°
N 1	2 38 14	7♏50 45	6♓14	4♏	7♐	5♌	20♋	7♑	12♈R	5♍	21♋R
O 2	2 42 10	8 50 47	18 10	6	7 R	6	20	7	12	5	21
V 3	2 46 7	9 50 51	0♈13	7	7	6	20	8	12	5	21
E 4	2 50 3	10 50 56	12 27	9	7	6	20	8	12	5	21
M 5	2 54 0	11 51 4	24 55	11	7	7	20	8	12	5	21
B 6	2 57 56	12 51 13	7♉39	12	7	7	21	8	12	6	21
E 7	3 1 53	13 51 23	20 39	14	7	8	21	8	12	6	21
R 8	3 5 49	14 51 36	3♊54	15	7	8	21 R	8	12	6	21
9	3 9 46	15 51 51	17 24	17	6	8	21	8	12	6	21
10	3 13 43	16 52 7	1♋ 6	19	6	9	21	8	12	6	21
11	3 17 39	17 52 26	14 58	20	6	9	21	8	12	6	21
12	3 21 36	18 52 46	28 58	22	5	9	20	8	12	6	21
13	3 25 32	19 53 9	13♌ 4	23	5	10	20	8	12	6	21
14	3 29 29	20 53 33	27 13	25	5	10	20	8	12	6	21
15	3 33 25	21 53 59	11♍25	27	4	11	20	9	12	6	21
16	3 37 22	22 54 27	25 36	28	4	11	20	9	12	6	21
17	3 41 18	23 54 57	9♎45	0♐	3	11	20	9	12	6	21
18	3 45 15	24 55 29	23 49	1	3	12	20	9	12	6	21
19	3 49 12	25 56 2	7♏45	3	2	12	20	9	12	6	21
20	3 53 8	26 56 37	21 31	4	1	12	20	9	12	6	21
21	3 57 5	27 57 14	5♐ 2	6	1	12	20	9	12	6	21
22	4 1 1	28 57 52	18 17	7	0	13	20	9	12	6	21
23	4 4 58	29 58 31	1♑14	9	0	13	20	9	12	6	21
24	4 8 54	0♐59 12	13 52	10	29♏	13	20	9	12	6	21
25	4 12 51	1 59 54	26 15	12	28	14	20	10	12	6	21
26	4 16 47	3 0 37	8♒23	14	28	14	20	10	12	6	21
27	4 20 44	4 1 21	20 20	15	27	14	20	10	12	6	21
28	4 24 41	5 2 6	2♓12	17	27	14	20	10	12	6	21
29	4 28 37	6 2 53	14 2	18	26	15	20	10	12	6	21
30	4 32 34	7 3 40	25 57	20	26	15	20	10	12	6	21

THE SUN ENTERS THE SIGN OF SAGITTARIUS ON NOV 23 AT 00:35.

DAY	TIME	☉	☽	☿	♀	♂	♃	♄	♅	♆	♇
	h m s	° ' "	° '	°	°	°	°	°	°	°	°
D 1	4 36 30	8♐ 4 28	8♈ 0	21♐	25♏R	15♌	20♋R	10♑	12♈R	6♍	21♋R
E 2	4 40 27	9 5 17	20 18	23	25	15	20	10	12	6	21
C 3	4 44 23	10 6 7	2♉54	24	24	15	19	10	12	6	21
E 4	4 48 20	11 6 57	15 50	26	24	15	19	11	12	6	21
M 5	4 52 16	12 7 49	29 8	27	23	16	19	11	12	6	21
B 6	4 56 13	13 8 42	12♊47	29	23	16	19	11	12	6	21
E 7	5 0 10	14 9 36	26 45	0♑	23	16	19	11	12	6	20
R 8	5 4 6	15 10 32	10♋57	2	23	16	19	11	12	6 R	20
9	5 8 3	16 11 28	25 17	3	22	16	19	11	12	6	20
10	5 11 59	17 12 25	9♌40	5	22	16	19	11	11	6	20
11	5 15 56	18 13 24	24 0	6	22	16	19	11	11	6	20
12	5 19 52	19 14 23	8♍15	7	22	17	19	11	11	6	20
13	5 23 49	20 15 24	22 22	9	22 D	17	19	11	11	6	20
14	5 27 46	21 16 25	6♎20	10	22	17	18	12	11	6	20
15	5 31 42	22 17 28	20 8	12	22	17	18	12	11	6	20
16	5 35 39	23 18 32	3♏47	13	22	17	18	12	11	6	20
17	5 39 35	24 19 36	17 16	14	22	17	18	12	11	6	20
18	5 43 32	25 20 42	0♐36	15	22	17 R	18	12	11	6	20
19	5 47 28	26 21 48	13 45	16	23	17	18	12	11	6	20
20	5 51 25	27 22 55	26 42	17	23	17	18	12	11	6	20
21	5 55 21	28 24 3	9♑25	19	23	17	18	12	11 D	6	20
22	5 59 18	29 25 11	21 56	19	24	17	18	12	11	6	20
23	6 3 15	0♑26 19	4♒13	20	24	17	17	13	11	6	20
24	6 7 11	1 27 28	16 18	21	24	17	17	13	11	6	20
25	6 11 8	2 28 36	28 13	21	25	17	17	13	11	6	20
26	6 15 4	3 29 45	10♓ 3	22	25	16	17	13	11	6	20
27	6 19 1	4 30 54	21 51	22 R	26	16	17	13	11	6	20
28	6 22 57	5 32 3	3♈43	22	26	16	17	13	11	6	20
29	6 26 54	6 33 12	15 44	22	27	16	17	13	11	6	20
30	6 30 50	7 34 21	28 0	22	27	16	17	13	11	6	20
31	6 34 47	8 35 29	10♉35	21	28	16	16	14	11	6	20

THE SUN ENTERS THE SIGN OF CAPRICORN ON DEC 22 AT 13:40.

♈ ARIES ♉ TAURUS ♊ GEMINI ♋ CANCER ♌ LEO ♍ VIRGO ♎ LIBRA ♏ SCORPIO ♐ SAGITTARIUS ♑ CAPRICORN ♒ AQUARIUS ♓ PISCES

SIDEREAL SUN MOON MERCURY VENUS MARS JUPITER SATURN URANUS NEPTUNE PLUTO

DAY	TIME	☉	☽	☿	♀	♂	♃	♄	♅	♆	♇
	h m s	° ' "	° '	°	°	°	°	°	°	°	°
J 1	6 38 44	9♑36 38	23♉35	21♑R	28♏	16♌R	16♋R	14♑	11♈	6♍R	20♋R
A 2	6 42 40	10 37 46	7♊ 1	20	29	15	16	14	11	6	20
N 3	6 46 37	11 38 55	20 54	19	29	15	16	14	12	6	20
U 4	6 50 33	12 40 3	5♋12	18	0♐	15	16	14	12	6	20
A 5	6 54 30	13 41 12	19 48	16	1	15	16	14	12	6	20
R 6	6 58 26	14 42 20	4♌37	15	1	15	16	14	12	6	20
Y 7	7 2 23	15 43 28	19 28	14	2	14	15	14	12	6	20
8	7 6 20	16 44 36	4♍13	12	3	14	15	15	12	6	20
9	7 10 16	17 45 45	18 47	11	4	14	15	15	12	6	20
10	7 14 13	18 46 53	3♎ 4	10	4	13	15	15	12	6	20
11	7 18 9	19 48 1	17 3	9	5	13	15	15	12	5	20
12	7 22 6	20 49 9	0♏45	8	6	13	15	15	12	5	20
13	7 26 2	21 50 18	14 10	7	7	12	15	15	12	5	20
14	7 29 59	22 51 26	27 22	7	8	12	14	15	12	5	20
15	7 33 55	23 52 34	10♐20	6	8	12	14	15	12	5	20
16	7 37 52	24 53 42	23 8	6	9	11	14	15	12	5	20
17	7 41 49	25 54 49	5♑45	6 D	10	11	14	16	12	5	20
18	7 45 45	26 55 56	18 11	6	11	11	14	16	12	5	20
19	7 49 42	27 57 3	0♒28	6	12	10	14	16	12	5	20
20	7 53 38	28 58 9	12 36	7	13	10	14	16	12	5	20
21	7 57 35	29 59 14	24 35	7	14	10	14	16	12	5	20
22	8 1 31	1♒ 0 19	6♓27	8	15	9	13	16	12	5	20
23	8 5 28	2 1 22	18 15	8	16	9	13	16	12	5	20
24	8 9 24	3 2 25	0♈ 2	9	17	8	13	16	12	5	20
25	8 13 21	4 3 26	11 53	10	18	8	13	17	12	5	20
26	8 17 18	5 4 27	23 51	10	18	8	13	17	12	5	19
27	8 21 14	6 5 26	6♉ 3	11	19	7	13	17	12	5	19
28	8 25 11	7 6 24	18 33	12	20	7	13	17	12	5	19
29	8 29 7	8 7 21	1♊28	13	21	6	13	17	12	5	19
30	8 33 4	9 8 17	14 51	14	22	6	13	17	12	5	19
31	8 37 0	10 9 12	28 44	15	23	6	12	17	12	5	19

THE SUN ENTERS THE SIGN OF AQUARIUS ON JAN 21 AT 00:18.

DAY	TIME	☉	☽	☿	♀	♂	♃	♄	♅	♆	♇
	h m s	° ' "	° '	°	°	°	°	°	°	°	°
F 1	8 40 57	11♒10 6	13♋ 5	16♑	24♐	5♌R	12♋R	17♑	12♈	5♍R	19♋R
E 2	8 44 53	12 10 58	27 52	18	25	5	12	17	12	5	19
B 3	8 48 50	13 11 49	12♌56	19	26	4	12	18	12	5	19
R 4	8 52 47	14 12 39	28 8	20	27	4	12	18	12	5	19
U 5	8 56 43	15 13 28	13♍17	21	28	4	12	18	12	5	19
A 6	9 0 40	16 14 16	28 12	23	29	3	12	18	12	5	19
R 7	9 4 36	17 15 2	12♎49	24	1♑	3	12	18	12	5	19
Y 8	9 8 33	18 15 48	27 3	25	2	3	12	18	12	5	19
9	9 12 29	19 16 33	10♏52	27	3	2	12	18	12	5	19
10	9 16 26	20 17 17	24 18	28	4	2	11	18	13	5	19
11	9 20 22	21 18 0	7♐24	29	5	2	11	18	13	5	19
12	9 24 19	22 18 42	20 13	1♒	6	1	11	19	13	5	19
13	9 28 16	23 19 23	2♑47	2	7	1	11	19	13	5	19
14	9 32 12	24 20 2	15 9	4	8	1	11	19	13	5	19
15	9 36 9	25 20 41	27 21	5	9	0	11	19	13	5	19
16	9 40 5	26 21 18	9♒25	6	10	0	11	19	13	5	19
17	9 44 2	27 21 53	21 23	8	11	0	11	19	13	5	19
18	9 47 58	28 22 27	3♓16	9	12	0	11	19	13	5	19
19	9 51 55	29 22 59	15 5	11	13	29♋	11	19	13	5	19
20	9 55 51	0♓23 30	26 53	13	14	29	11	19	13	5	19
21	9 59 48	1 23 59	8♈41	14	16	29	11	19	13	4	19
22	10 3 45	2 24 26	20 34	16	17	29	11	20	13	4	19
23	10 7 41	3 24 52	2♉34	17	18	29	11	20	13	4	19
24	10 11 38	4 25 15	14 46	19	19	28	11	20	13	4	19
25	10 15 34	5 25 37	27 14	20	20	28	11	20	13	4	19
26	10 19 31	6 25 56	10♊ 4	22	21	28	11	20	13	4	19
27	10 23 27	7 26 14	23 19	24	22	28	11	20	13	4	19
28	10 27 24	8 26 30	7♋ 2	25	23	28	11	20	13	4	19

THE SUN ENTERS THE SIGN OF PISCES ON FEB 19 AT 14:41.

DAY	TIME	☉	☽	☿	♀	♂	♃	♄	♅	♆	♇
	h m s	° ' "	° '	°	°	°	°	°	°	°	°
M 1	10 31 20	9♓26 44	21♋15	27♒	24♑	28♋R	11♋R	20♑	13♈	4♍R	19♋R
A 2	10 35 17	10 26 55	5♌54	29	26	28	10	20	13	4	19
R 3	10 39 14	11 27 5	20 54	0♓	27	28	10	20	13	4	19
C 4	10 43 10	12 27 13	6♍ 8	2	28	28	10	20	14	4	19
H 5	10 47 7	13 27 18	21 25	4	29	28	10	21	14	4	19
6	10 51 3	14 27 22	6♎35	6	0♒	27	10	21	14	4	19
7	10 55 0	15 27 25	21 28	8	1	27	10 D	21	14	4	19
8	10 58 56	16 27 25	5♏58	9	2	27 D	10	21	14	4	19
9	11 2 53	17 27 24	20 2	11	4	27	10	21	14	4	19
10	11 6 49	18 27 21	3♐38	13	5	27	10	21	14	4	19
11	11 10 46	19 27 17	16 50	15	6	27	10	21	14	4	19
12	11 14 43	20 27 11	29 39	17	7	28	10	21	14	4	19
13	11 18 39	21 27 4	12♑10	19	8	28	11	21	14	4	19
14	11 22 36	22 26 55	24 25	21	9	28	11	21	14	4	19
15	11 26 32	23 26 44	6♒29	22	10	28	11	21	14	4	19
16	11 30 29	24 26 31	18 25	24	12	28	11	21	14	4	19
17	11 34 25	25 26 16	0♓16	26	13	28	11	21	14	4	19
18	11 38 22	26 25 59	12 5	28	14	28	11	22	14	4	19
19	11 42 18	27 25 41	23 53	0♈	15	28	11	22	14	4	19
20	11 46 15	28 25 20	5♈43	2	16	28	11	22	14	4	19
21	11 50 12	29 24 58	17 37	4	17	28	11	22	14	4	19
22	11 54 8	0♈24 33	29 38	6	19	28	11	22	14	4	19
23	11 58 5	1 24 6	11♉46	8	20	29	11	22	15	4	19
24	12 2 1	2 23 37	24 6	10	21	29	11	22	15	4	19
25	12 5 58	3 23 6	6♊40	12	22	29	11	22	15	4	19
26	12 9 54	4 22 33	19 32	14	23	29	11	22	15	4	19
27	12 13 51	5 21 57	2♋44	16	24	29	11	22	15	4	19
28	12 17 47	6 21 19	16 19	18	26	0♌	11	22	15	4	19
29	12 21 44	7 20 38	0♌18	20	27	0	11	22	15	4	19
30	12 25 41	8 19 56	14 41	22	28	0	11	22	15	4	19
31	12 29 37	9 19 10	29 24	24	29	0	11	22	15	4	19

THE SUN ENTERS THE SIGN OF ARIES ON MAR 21 AT 14:06.

SIDEREAL SUN MOON MERCURY VENUS MARS JUPITER SATURN URANUS NEPTUNE PLUTO

DAY	TIME	☉	☽	☿	♀	♂	♃	♄	♅	♆	♇
	h m s	° ' "	° '	°	°	°	°	°	°	°	°
A 1	12 33 34	10♈18 23	14♍23	26♈	0♓	0♌	11♋	22♑	15♈	3♍R	19♋R
P 2	12 37 30	11 17 33	29 29	27	1	1	11	22	15	3	19 D
R 3	12 41 27	12 16 42	14♎34	29	3	1	12	23	15	3	19
I 4	12 45 23	13 15 48	29 29	1♉	4	1	12	23	15	3	19
L 5	12 49 20	14 14 52	14♏ 6	2	5	1	12	23	15	3	19
6	12 53 16	15 13 55	28 20	4	6	2	12	23	15	3	19
7	12 57 13	16 12 55	12♐ 7	5	7	2	12	23	15	3	19
8	13 1 9	17 11 54	25 28	6	8	2	12	23	15	3	19
9	13 5 6	18 10 51	8♑23	7	10	3	12	23	15	3	19
10	13 9 3	19 9 47	20 57	8	11	3	12	23	16	3	19
11	13 12 59	20 8 40	3♒13	9	12	3	12	23	16	3	19
12	13 16 56	21 7 32	15 15	10	13	3	12	23	16	3	19
13	13 20 52	22 6 22	27 8	11	14	4	13	23	16	3	19
14	13 24 49	23 5 11	8♓56	12	16	4	13	23	16	3	19
15	13 28 45	24 3 57	20 44	12	17	4	13	23	16	3	19
16	13 32 42	25 2 42	2♈34	13	18	5	13	23	16	3	19
17	13 36 38	26 1 24	14 29	13	19	5	13	23	16	3	19
18	13 40 35	27 0 5	26 32	13	20	6	13	23	16	3	19
19	13 44 32	27 58 44	8♉45	13 R	22	6	13	23	16	3	19
20	13 48 28	28 57 21	21 8	13	23	6	13	23	16	3	19
21	13 52 25	29 55 56	3♊44	13	24	7	13	23	16	3	19
22	13 56 21	0♉54 29	16 33	13	25	7	14	23	16	3	19
23	14 0 18	1 53 0	29 37	13	26	7	14	23	16	3	19
24	14 4 14	2 51 29	12♋56	13	28	8	14	23	16	3	19
25	14 8 11	3 49 55	26 31	12	29	8	14	23	16	3	19
26	14 12 7	4 48 19	10♌23	12	0♈	8	14	23	16	3	19
27	14 16 4	5 46 42	24 32	11	1♈	9	14	23	17	3	19
28	14 20 1	6 45 2	8♍55	11	2	9	14	23	17	3	19
29	14 23 57	7 43 20	23 31	10	3	10	15	23	17	3	19
30	14 27 54	8 41 36	8♎14	9	5	10	15	23	17	3	19

THE SUN ENTERS THE SIGN OF TAURUS ON APR 21 AT 01:39.

DAY	TIME	☉	☽	☿	♀	♂	♃	♄	♅	♆	♇
	h m s	° ' "	° '	°	°	°	°	°	°	°	°
M 1	14 31 50	9♉39 49	22♎59	9♉R	6♈	11♌	15♋	23♑	17♈	3♍R	19♋
A 2	14 35 47	10 38 2	7♏40	8	7	11	15	23	17	3	19
Y 3	14 39 43	11 36 12	22 8	7	8	11	15	23 R	17	3	19
4	14 43 40	12 34 21	6♐19	7	9	12	15	23	17	3	19
5	14 47 36	13 32 28	20 8	6	11	12	15	23	17	3	19
6	14 51 33	14 30 34	3♑32	6	12	13	16	23	17	3	19
7	14 55 30	15 28 38	16 32	5	13	13	16	23	17	3	19
8	14 59 26	16 26 41	29 10	5	14	13	16	23	17	3	19
9	15 3 23	17 24 43	11♒28	4	15	14	16	23	17	3	19
10	15 7 19	18 22 43	23 32	4	17	14	16	23	17	3	19
11	15 11 16	19 20 41	5♓25	4	18	15	16	23	17	3	19
12	15 15 12	20 18 39	17 14	4	19	15	17	23	17	3	19
13	15 19 9	21 16 35	29 2	4 D	20	16	17	23	17	3	19
14	15 23 5	22 14 29	10♈55	4	21	16	17	23	17	3	19
15	15 27 2	23 12 23	22 57	4	23	17	17	23	17	3 D	19
16	15 30 59	24 10 15	5♉10	4	24	17	17	23	17	3	19
17	15 34 55	25 8 6	17 36	4	25	18	17	23	18	3	19
18	15 38 52	26 5 55	0♊18	4	26	18	18	23	18	3	19
19	15 42 48	27 3 43	13 14	5	27	19	18	23	18	3	19
20	15 46 45	28 1 29	26 25	5	29	19	18	23	18	3	19
21	15 50 41	28 59 14	9♋50	6	0♉	20	18	23	18	3	19
22	15 54 38	29 56 58	23 26	6	1	20	18	23	18	3	19
23	15 58 35	0♊54 40	7♌13	7	2	20	19	23	18	3	19
24	16 2 31	1 52 20	21 9	8	3	21	19	23	18	3	19
25	16 6 28	2 49 59	5♍13	8	5	21	19	23	18	3	19
26	16 10 24	3 47 36	19 24	9	6	22	19	23	18	3	19
27	16 14 21	4 45 12	3♎40	10	7	22	19	23	18	3	19
28	16 18 17	5 42 46	17 59	11	8	23	19	23	18	3	19
29	16 22 14	6 40 19	2♏18	12	10	23	20	23	18	3	19
30	16 26 10	7 37 50	16 34	13	11	24	20	23	18	3	19
31	16 30 7	8 35 21	0♐42	14	12	24	20	23	18	3	19

THE SUN ENTERS THE SIGN OF GEMINI ON MAY 22 AT 01:15.

DAY	TIME	☉	☽	☿	♀	♂	♃	♄	♅	♆	♇
	h m s	° ' "	° '	°	°	°	°	°	°	°	°
J 1	16 34 4	9♊32 50	14♐37	15♉	13♉	25♌	20♋	23♑R	18♈	3♍	19♋
U 2	16 38 0	10 30 19	28 15	17	14	25	20	23	18	3	19
N 3	16 41 57	11 27 46	11♑33	18	16	26	21	23	18	3	19
E 4	16 45 53	12 25 12	24 30	19	17	27	21	23	18	3	19
5	16 49 50	13 22 38	7♒ 7	20	18	27	21	22	18	3	19
6	16 53 46	14 20 3	19 25	22	19	28	21	22	18	3	19
7	16 57 43	15 17 28	1♓29	23	20	28	21	22	18	3	19
8	17 1 39	16 14 51	13 23	25	22	29	22	22	18	3	20
9	17 5 36	17 12 14	25 12	26	23	29	22	22	19	3	20
10	17 9 33	18 9 37	7♈ 2	28	24	0♍	22	22	19	3	20
11	17 13 29	19 6 59	18 58	29	25	0	22	22	19	3	20
12	17 17 26	20 4 20	1♉ 4	1♊	26	1	22	22	19	3	20
13	17 21 22	21 1 41	13 25	3	28	1	23	22	19	3	20
14	17 25 19	21 59 2	26 3	5	29	2	23	22	19	3	20
15	17 29 15	22 56 22	9♊ 1	6	0♊	2	23	22	19	3	20
16	17 33 12	23 53 41	22 19	8	1	3	23	22	19	3	20
17	17 37 8	24 51 0	5♋54	10	2	3	23	22	19	3	20
18	17 41 5	25 48 18	19 44	12	4	4	24	22	19	3	20
19	17 45 2	26 45 36	3♌45	14	5	5	24	22	19	3	20
20	17 48 58	27 42 53	17 52	16	6	5	24	22	19	3	20
21	17 52 55	28 40 9	2♍ 2	18	7	6	24	22	19	3	20
22	17 56 51	29 37 24	16 13	20	9	6	24	21	19	3	20
23	18 0 48	0♋34 39	0♎22	22	10	7	25	21	19	3	20
24	18 4 44	1 31 53	14 28	24	11	7	25	21	19	3	20
25	18 8 41	2 29 6	28 30	27	12	8	25	21	19	3	20
26	18 12 37	3 26 19	12♏27	29	13	8	25	21	19	3	20
27	18 16 34	4 23 31	26 18	1♋	15	9	26	21	19	3	20
28	18 20 31	5 20 43	10♐ 1	3	16	10	26	21	19	4	20
29	18 24 27	6 17 55	23 33	5	17	10	26	21	19	4	20
30	18 28 24	7 15 6	6♑51	7	18	11	26	21	19	4	20

THE SUN ENTERS THE SIGN OF CANCER ON JUN 22 AT 09:28.

♈ ARIES ♉ TAURUS ♊ GEMINI ♋ CANCER ♌ LEO ♍ VIRGO ♎ LIBRA ♏ SCORPIO ♐ SAGITTARIUS ♑ CAPRICORN ♒ AQUARIUS ♓ PISCES

SIDEREAL SUN MOON MERCURY VENUS MARS JUPITER SATURN URANUS NEPTUNE PLUTO

DAY	TIME	☉	☽	☿	♀	♂	♃	♄	♅	♆	♇
	h m s	° ' "	° '	°	°	°	°	°	°	°	°
J 1	18 32 20	8♋12 17	19♑54	10♋	19♊	11♍	26♋	21♑R	19♈	4♍	20♋
U 2	18 36 17	9 9 28	2♒40	12	21	12	27	21	19	4	20
L 3	18 40 13	10 6 39	15 10	14	22	12	27	21	19	4	20
Y 4	18 44 10	11 3 51	27 24	16	23	13	27	21	19	4	20
5	18 48 7	12 1 2	9♓25	18	24	14	27	21	19	4	20
6	18 52 3	12 58 13	21 18	20	26	14	28	21	19	4	20
7	18 56 0	13 55 25	3♈ 7	22	27	15	28	20	19	4	20
8	18 59 56	14 52 37	14 56	24	28	15	28	20	19	4	20
9	19 3 53	15 49 49	26 52	26	29	16	28	20	19	4	20
10	19 7 49	16 47 2	9♉ 0	28	0♋	16	28	20	19	4	20
11	19 11 46	17 44 16	21 25	0♌	2	17	29	20	19	4	20
12	19 15 42	18 41 29	4♊10	2	3	18	29	20	19	4	20
13	19 19 39	19 38 44	17 19	4	4	18	29	20	19	4	20
14	19 23 36	20 35 58	0♋51	6	5	19	29	20	19	4	20
15	19 27 32	21 33 13	14 46	8	7	19	29	20	19	4	20
16	19 31 29	22 30 29	28 59	10	8	20	0♌	20	19	4	20
17	19 35 25	23 27 45	13♌25	11	9	21	0	20	19	4	21
18	19 39 22	24 25 1	27 57	13	10	21	0	20	19	4	21
19	19 43 18	25 22 17	12♍30	15	11	22	0	20	19	4	21
20	19 47 15	26 19 33	26 57	16	13	22	1	19	19	4	21
21	19 51 11	27 16 50	11♎15	18	14	23	1	19	19	4	21
22	19 55 8	28 14 7	25 22	20	15	24	1	19	19	4	21
23	19 59 5	29 11 24	9♏18	21	16	24	1	19	19	4	21
24	20 3 1	0♌ 8 41	23 2	23	18	25	1	19	19	4	21
25	20 6 58	1 5 59	6♐34	24	19	25	2	19	19	4	21
26	20 10 54	2 3 17	19 55	26	20	26	2	19	19 R	4	21
27	20 14 51	3 0 36	3♑ 4	27	21	27	2	19	19	4	21
28	20 18 47	3 57 55	16 0	29	22	27	2	19	19	4	21
29	20 22 44	4 55 15	28 44	0♍	24	28	3	19	19	4	21
30	20 26 40	5 52 36	11♒15	1	25	28	3	19	19	4	21
31	20 30 37	6 49 57	23 32	3	26	29	3	19	19	4	21

THE SUN ENTERS THE SIGN OF LEO ON JUL 23 AT 20:22.

DAY	TIME	☉	☽	☿	♀	♂	♃	♄	♅	♆	♇
	h m s	° ' "	° '	°	°	°	°	°	°	°	°
A 1	20 34 34	7♌47 19	5♓39	4♍	27♋	0♎	3♌	19♑R	19♈R	4♍	21♋
U 2	20 38 30	8 44 42	17 35	5	29	0	3	19	19	5	21
G 3	20 42 27	9 42 7	29 25	6	0♌	1	4	18	19	5	21
U 4	20 46 23	10 39 32	11♈13	8	1	1	4	18	19	5	21
S 5	20 50 20	11 36 59	23 1	9	2	2	4	18	19	5	21
T 6	20 54 16	12 34 26	4♉57	10	4	3	4	18	19	5	21
7	20 58 13	13 31 55	17 4	11	5	3	5	18	19	5	21
8	21 2 9	14 29 26	29 28	12	6	4	5	18	19	5	21
9	21 6 6	15 26 58	12♊13	13	7	5	5	18	19	5	21
10	21 10 3	16 24 31	25 24	14	8	5	5	18	19	5	21
11	21 13 59	17 22 5	9♋ 2	15	10	6	5	18	19	5	21
12	21 17 56	18 19 41	23 6	15	11	6	6	18	19	5	21
13	21 21 52	19 17 18	7♌33	16	12	7	6	18	19	5	21
14	21 25 49	20 14 56	22 18	17	13	8	6	18	19	5	21
15	21 29 45	21 12 36	7♍12	17	15	8	6	18	19	5	21
16	21 33 42	22 10 16	22 7	18	16	9	7	18	19	5	21
17	21 37 38	23 7 58	6♎55	18	17	10	7	18	19	5	21
18	21 41 35	24 5 41	21 30	19	18	10	7	18	19	5	21
19	21 45 32	25 3 24	5♏49	19	20	11	7	18	19	5	21
20	21 49 28	26 1 9	19 49	19	21	11	7	17	19	5	21
21	21 53 25	26 58 55	3♐31	20	22	12	8	17	19	5	21
22	21 57 21	27 56 43	16 54	20 R	23	13	8	17	19	5	21
23	22 1 18	28 54 31	0♑ 1	20	24	13	8	17	19	5	21
24	22 5 14	29 52 20	12 52	20	26	14	8	17	19	5	21
25	22 9 11	0♍50 11	25 30	19	27	15	9	17	19	5	21
26	22 13 7	1 48 3	7♒56	19	28	15	9	17	19	5	21
27	22 17 4	2 45 57	20 11	19	29	16	9	17	19	5	22
28	22 21 1	3 43 52	2♓17	18	1♍	17	9	17	19	5	22
29	22 24 57	4 41 48	14 14	18	2	17	9	17	19	5	22
30	22 28 54	5 39 46	26 5	17	3	18	10	17	19	6	22
31	22 32 50	6 37 46	7♈53	16	4	19	10	17	19	6	22

THE SUN ENTERS THE SIGN OF VIRGO ON AUG 24 AT 03:11.

DAY	TIME	☉	☽	☿	♀	♂	♃	♄	♅	♆	♇
	h m s	° ' "	° '	°	°	°	°	°	°	°	°
S 1	22 36 47	7♍35 47	19♈40	15♍R	6♍	19♎	10♌	17♑R	19♈R	6♍	22♋
E 2	22 40 43	8 33 50	1♉29	14	7	20	10	17	19	6	22
P 3	22 44 40	9 31 55	13 25	13	8	20	10	17	19	6	22
T 4	22 48 36	10 30 3	25 32	12	9	21	11	17	19	6	22
E 5	22 52 33	11 28 12	7♊55	11	11	22	11	17	19	6	22
M 6	22 56 30	12 26 23	20 37	11	12	22	11	17	19	6	22
B 7	23 0 26	13 24 36	3♋44	10	13	23	11	17	19	6	22
E 8	23 4 23	14 22 51	17 17	9	14	24	11	17	19	6	22
R 9	23 8 19	15 21 9	1♌18	8	16	24	12	17	19	6	22
10	23 12 16	16 19 28	15 46	7	17	25	12	17	19	6	22
11	23 16 12	17 17 49	0♍35	7	18	26	12	17	19	6	22
12	23 20 9	18 16 12	15 39	6	19	26	12	17	19	6	22
13	23 24 5	19 14 37	0♎48	6	21	27	12	17	18	6	22
14	23 28 2	20 13 3	15 55	6 D	22	28	13	17	18	6	22
15	23 31 59	21 11 31	0♏49	6	23	28	13	17	18	6	22
16	23 35 55	22 10 2	15 24	6	24	29	13	17	18	6	22
17	23 39 52	23 8 33	29 37	6	26	0♏	13	17	18	6	22
18	23 43 48	24 7 7	13♐25	7	27	0	13	17	18	6	22
19	23 47 45	25 5 42	26 49	8	28	1	14	17	18	6	22
20	23 51 41	26 4 18	9♑51	8	29	2	14	17	18	6	22
21	23 55 38	27 2 57	22 34	9	1♎	2	14	17 D	18	6	22
22	23 59 34	28 1 37	5♒ 0	10	2	3	14	17	18	6	22
23	0 3 31	29 0 18	17 13	11	3	4	14	17	18	6	22
24	0 7 28	29 59 2	29 16	13	4	4	15	17	18	6	22
25	0 11 24	0♎57 47	11♓11	14	5	5	15	17	18	6	22
26	0 15 21	1 56 34	23 2	15	7	6	15	17	18	7	22
27	0 19 17	2 55 23	4♈50	17	8	7	15	17	18	7	22
28	0 23 14	3 54 14	16 38	18	9	7	15	17	18	7	22
29	0 27 10	4 53 7	28 28	20	10	8	15	17	18	7	22
30	0 31 7	5 52 3	10♉21	22	12	9	16	17	18	7	22

THE SUN ENTERS THE SIGN OF LIBRA ON SEP 24 AT 00:25.

DAY	TIME	☉	☽	☿	♀	♂	♃	♄	♅	♆	♇
	h m s	° ' "	° '	°	°	°	°	°	°	°	°
O 1	0 35 3	6♎51 0	22♉23	23♍	13♎	9♏	16♌	17♑	18♈R	7♍	22♋
C 2	0 39 0	7 50 0	4♊34	25	14	10	16	17	18	7	22
T 3	0 42 57	8 49 2	16 58	27	15	11	16	17	18	7	22
O 4	0 46 53	9 48 7	29 40	29	17	11	16	17	18	7	22
B 5	0 50 50	10 47 13	12♋41	0♎	18	12	16	17	18	7	22
E 6	0 54 46	11 46 22	26 6	2	19	13	17	17	18	7	22
R 7	0 58 43	12 45 34	9♌57	4	20	13	17	17	18	7	22
8	1 2 39	13 44 47	24 12	6	22	14	17	17	18	7	22
9	1 6 36	14 44 3	8♍51	8	23	15	17	17	17	7	22
10	1 10 32	15 43 21	23 48	9	24	15	17	17	17	7	22
11	1 14 29	16 42 41	8♎57	11	25	16	17	17	17	7	22
12	1 18 25	17 42 4	24 9	13	27	17	18	17	17	7	22
13	1 22 22	18 41 28	9♏13	15	28	18	18	17	17	7	22
14	1 26 19	19 40 54	24 1	16	29	18	18	17	17	7	22
15	1 30 15	20 40 22	8♐27	18	0♏	19	18	17	17	7	22
16	1 34 12	21 39 53	22 27	20	2	20	18	17	17	7	22
17	1 38 8	22 39 24	5♑58	21	3	20	18	17	17	7	22
18	1 42 5	23 38 58	19 3	23	4	21	19	17	17	7	22
19	1 46 1	24 38 33	1♒45	25	5	22	19	17	17	7	22
20	1 49 58	25 38 10	14 7	27	7	22	19	17	17	7	22
21	1 53 55	26 37 49	26 14	28	8	23	19	17	17	7	22
22	1 57 51	27 37 30	8♓10	0♏	9	24	19	17	17	7	22
23	2 1 48	28 37 12	20 0	1	10	25	19	17	17	7	22
24	2 5 44	29 36 56	1♈47	3	12	25	19	17	17	7	22 R
25	2 9 41	0♏36 42	13 35	5	13	26	19	18	17	7	22
26	2 13 37	1 36 29	25 26	6	14	27	20	18	17	7	22
27	2 17 34	2 36 19	7♉22	8	15	27	20	18	17	7	22
28	2 21 30	3 36 11	19 26	10	17	28	20	18	17	7	22
29	2 25 27	4 36 5	1♊38	11	18	29	20	18	17	7	22
30	2 29 23	5 36 0	14 1	13	19	0♐	20	18	17	7	22
31	2 33 20	6 35 58	26 35	14	20	0	20	18	17	8	22

THE SUN ENTERS THE SIGN OF SCORPIO ON OCT 24 AT 09:16.

DAY	TIME	☉	☽	☿	♀	♂	♃	♄	♅	♆	♇
	h m s	° ' "	° '	°	°	°	°	°	°	°	°
N 1	2 37 17	7♏35 58	9♋23	16♏	22♏	1♐	20♌	18♑	17♈R	8♍	22♋R
O 2	2 41 13	8 36 1	22 26	17	23	2	20	18	17	8	22
V 3	2 45 10	9 36 5	5♌47	19	24	2	21	18	17	8	22
E 4	2 49 6	10 36 11	19 27	21	25	3	21	18	16	8	22
M 5	2 53 3	11 36 20	3♍27	22	27	4	21	18	16	8	22
B 6	2 56 59	12 36 31	17 47	24	28	5	21	18	16	8	22
E 7	3 0 56	13 36 43	2♎26	25	29	5	21	18	16	8	22
R 8	3 4 52	14 36 58	17 18	27	0♐	6	21	18	16	8	22
9	3 8 49	15 37 15	2♏17	28	2	7	21	18	16	8	22
10	3 12 46	16 37 33	17 15	0♐	3	8	21	19	16	8	22
11	3 16 42	17 37 53	2♐ 3	1	4	8	21	19	16	8	22
12	3 20 39	18 38 15	16 33	3	5	9	21	19	16	8	22
13	3 24 35	19 38 39	0♑39	4	7	10	22	19	16	8	22
14	3 28 32	20 39 4	14 18	6	8	11	22	19	16	8	22
15	3 32 28	21 39 30	27 29	7	9	11	22	19	16	8	22
16	3 36 25	22 39 58	10♒14	9	10	12	22	19	16	8	22
17	3 40 22	23 40 27	22 38	10	12	13	22	19	16	8	22
18	3 44 18	24 40 57	4♓44	12	13	13	22	19	16	8	22
19	3 48 15	25 41 28	16 39	13	14	14	22	19	16	8	22
20	3 52 11	26 42 1	28 27	14	15	15	22	19	16	8	22
21	3 56 8	27 42 35	10♈14	16	17	16	22	19	16	8	22
22	4 0 4	28 43 10	22 4	17	18	16	22	20	16	8	22
23	4 4 1	29 43 47	3♉59	19	19	17	22	20	16	8	22
24	4 7 57	0♐44 25	16 5	20	20	18	22	20	16	8	22
25	4 11 54	1 45 4	28 21	21	22	19	22	20	16	8	22
26	4 15 51	2 45 45	10♊49	23	23	19	22	20	16	8	22
27	4 19 47	3 46 27	23 30	24	24	20	22	20	16	8	22
28	4 23 44	4 47 11	6♋23	25	25	21	22	20	16	8	22
29	4 27 40	5 47 56	19 27	27	27	22	22	20	16	8	22
30	4 31 37	6 48 42	2♌43	28	28	22	22	20	16	8	22

THE SUN ENTERS THE SIGN OF SAGITTARIUS ON NOV 23 AT 06:26.

DAY	TIME	☉	☽	☿	♀	♂	♃	♄	♅	♆	♇
	h m s	° ' "	° '	°	°	°	°	°	°	°	°
D 1	4 35 33	7♐49 30	16♌11	29♐	29♐	23♐	23♌	20♑	16♈R	8♍	22♋R
E 2	4 39 30	8 50 19	29 50	0♑	0♑	24	23	20	16	8	22
C 3	4 43 26	9 51 10	13♍42	1	2	25	23	21	16	8	22
E 4	4 47 23	10 52 2	27 47	2	3	25	23	21	16	8	22
M 5	4 51 20	11 52 55	12♎ 4	3	4	26	23	21	16	8	22
B 6	4 55 16	12 53 50	26 32	4	5	27	23	21	16	8	22
E 7	4 59 13	13 54 47	11♏ 6	5	7	28	23	21	16	8	22
R 8	5 3 9	14 55 44	25 43	5	8	28	23	21	16	8	22
9	5 7 6	15 56 43	10♐13	6	9	29	23 R	21	16	8	22
10	5 11 2	16 57 42	24 32	6	10	0♑	23	21	16	8	22
11	5 14 59	17 58 42	8♑32	6 R	12	1	23	21	16	8 R	22
12	5 18 55	18 59 44	22 9	6	13	1	23	22	16	8	22
13	5 22 52	20 0 46	5♒22	6	14	2	23	22	16	8	22
14	5 26 49	21 1 48	18 9	6	15	3	23	22	15	8	22
15	5 30 45	22 2 51	0♓36	6	17	4	23	22	15	8	22
16	5 34 42	23 3 54	12 44	5	18	4	23	22	15	8	22
17	5 38 38	24 4 58	24 40	4	19	5	23	22	15	8	22
18	5 42 35	25 6 2	6♈28	3	20	6	23	22	15	8	22
19	5 46 31	26 7 6	18 16	2	22	7	22	22	15	8	22
20	5 50 28	27 8 11	0♉ 7	0	23	8	22	22	15	8	22
21	5 54 24	28 9 16	12 7	29♐	24	8	22	22	15	8	22
22	5 58 21	29 10 21	24 20	28	25	9	22	23	15	8	22
23	6 2 18	0♑11 27	6♊47	26	26	10	22	23	15	8	21
24	6 6 14	1 12 33	19 31	25	28	11	22	23	15	8	21
25	6 10 11	2 13 40	2♋32	24	29	11	22	23	15 D	8	21
26	6 14 7	3 14 47	15 48	23	0♒	12	22	23	15	8	21
27	6 18 4	4 15 54	29 17	22	1	13	22	23	15	8	21
28	6 22 0	5 17 2	12♌56	21	3	14	22	23	15	8	21
29	6 25 57	6 18 10	26 43	21	4	14	22	23	15	8	21
30	6 29 54	7 19 18	10♍36	20	5	15	22	24	15	8	21
31	6 33 50	8 20 27	24 34	20 D	6	16	22	24	15	8	21

THE SUN ENTERS THE SIGN OF CAPRICORN ON DEC 22 AT 19:30.

♈ ARIES ♉ TAURUS ♊ GEMINI ♋ CANCER ♌ LEO ♍ VIRGO ♎ LIBRA ♏ SCORPIO ♐ SAGITTARIUS ♑ CAPRICORN ♒ AQUARIUS ♓ PISCES

SIDEREAL SUN MOON MERCURY VENUS MARS JUPITER SATURN URANUS NEPTUNE PLUTO

DAY	TIME	☉	☽	☿	♀	♂	♃	♄	♅	♆	♇
	h m s	° ' "	° '	°	°	°	°	°	°	°	°
J 1	6 37 47	9♑21 36	8♎36	20♐	8♒	17♑	22♌R	24♑	15♈	8♍R	21♋R
A 2	6 41 43	10 22 46	22 42	20	9	18	22	24	15	8	21
N 3	6 45 40	11 23 56	6♏50	20	10	18	22	24	15	8	21
U 4	6 49 36	12 25 7	21 0	21	11	19	22	24	15	8	21
A 5	6 53 33	13 26 17	5♐ 9	21	13	20	22	24	15	8	21
R 6	6 57 29	14 27 28	19 12	22	14	21	21	24	15	8	21
Y 7	7 1 26	15 28 39	3♑ 6	23	15	21	21	24	16	8	21
8	7 5 23	16 29 50	16 46	23	16	22	21	25	16	8	21
9	7 9 19	17 31 1	0♒ 9	24	18	23	21	25	16	8	21
10	7 13 16	18 32 11	13 12	25	19	24	21	25	16	8	21
11	7 17 12	19 33 21	25 55	26	20	25	21	25	16	8	21
12	7 21 9	20 34 30	8♓20	27	21	25	21	25	16	8	21
13	7 25 5	21 35 39	20 28	28	23	26	21	25	16	8	21
14	7 29 2	22 36 48	2♈25	29	24	27	21	25	16	8	21
15	7 32 58	23 37 55	14 14	1♑	25	28	21	25	16	8	21
16	7 36 55	24 39 2	26 2	2	26	28	20	26	16	8	21
17	7 40 52	25 40 8	7♉54	3	27	29	20	26	16	8	21
18	7 44 48	26 41 14	19 55	4	29	0♒	20	26	16	8	21
19	7 48 45	27 42 19	2♊10	5	0♓	1	20	26	16	8	21
20	7 52 41	28 43 23	14 43	7	1	2	20	26	16	8	21
21	7 56 38	29 44 26	27 37	8	2	2	20	26	16	8	21
22	8 0 34	0♒45 28	10♋51	9	4	3	20	26	16	8	21
23	8 4 31	1 46 30	24 27	11	5	4	20	26	16	7	21
24	8 8 27	2 47 30	8♌19	12	6	5	20	26	16	7	21
25	8 12 24	3 48 30	22 26	14	7	5	19	27	16	7	21
26	8 16 21	4 49 30	6♍40	15	8	6	19	27	16	7	21
27	8 20 17	5 50 28	20 59	16	10	7	19	27	16	7	21
28	8 24 14	6 51 26	5♎17	18	11	8	19	27	16	7	21
29	8 28 10	7 52 23	19 32	19	12	9	19	27	16	7	21
30	8 32 7	8 53 20	3♏42	21	13	9	19	27	16	7	21
31	8 36 3	9 54 16	17 45	22	15	10	19	27	16	7	21

THE SUN ENTERS THE SIGN OF AQUARIUS ON JAN 21 AT 06:07.

DAY	TIME	☉	☽	☿	♀	♂	♃	♄	♅	♆	♇
	h m s	° ' "	° '	°	°	°	°	°	°	°	°
F 1	8 40 0	10♒55 11	1♐40	24♑	16♓	11♒	19♌R	27♑	16♈	7♍R	21♋R
E 2	8 43 56	11 56 6	15 27	25	17	12	18	28	16	7	21
B 3	8 47 53	12 56 59	29 4	27	18	13	18	28	16	7	21
R 4	8 51 50	13 57 52	12♑31	28	19	13	18	28	16	7	21
U 5	8 55 46	14 58 44	25 45	0♒	21	14	18	28	16	7	21
A 6	8 59 43	15 59 35	8♒45	1	22	15	18	28	16	7	21
R 7	9 3 39	17 0 25	21 30	3	23	16	18	28	16	7	21
Y 8	9 7 36	18 1 13	4♓ 1	5	24	16	18	28	16	7	21
9	9 11 32	19 2 0	16 17	6	26	17	17	28	16	7	21
10	9 15 29	20 2 46	28 21	8	27	18	17	28	16	7	20
11	9 19 26	21 3 30	10♈16	9	28	19	17	29	16	7	20
12	9 23 22	22 4 12	22 6	11	29	20	17	29	16	7	20
13	9 27 19	23 4 53	3♉53	13	0♈	20	17	29	16	7	20
14	9 31 15	24 5 32	15 45	14	2	21	17	29	16	7	20
15	9 35 12	25 6 10	27 45	16	3	22	17	29	17	7	20
16	9 39 8	26 6 46	9♊58	18	4	23	17	29	17	7	20
17	9 43 5	27 7 20	22 30	19	5	24	16	29	17	7	20
18	9 47 1	28 7 52	5♋24	21	6	24	16	29	17	7	20
19	9 50 58	29 8 23	18 42	23	8	25	16	29	17	7	20
20	9 54 55	0♓ 8 52	2♌25	25	9	26	16	0♒	17	7	20
21	9 58 51	1 9 19	16 32	26	10	27	16	0	17	7	20
22	10 2 48	2 9 45	0♍58	28	11	28	16	0	17	7	20
23	10 6 44	3 10 8	15 37	0♓	12	28	16	0	17	7	20
24	10 10 41	4 10 31	0♎23	2	13	29	16	0	17	7	20
25	10 14 37	5 10 51	15 9	4	15	0♓	15	0	17	7	20
26	10 18 34	6 11 10	29 48	5	16	1	15	0	17	7	20
27	10 22 30	7 11 28	14♏15	7	17	1	15	0	17	7	20
28	10 26 27	8 11 45	28 27	9	18	2	15	0	17	7	20
29	10 30 23	9 12 0	12♐22	11	19	3	15	1	17	7	20

THE SUN ENTERS THE SIGN OF PISCES ON FEB 19 AT 20:29.

DAY	TIME	☉	☽	☿	♀	♂	♃	♄	♅	♆	♇
	h m s	° ' "	° '	°	°	°	°	°	°	°	°
M 1	10 34 20	10♓12 13	26♐ 1	13♓	21♈	4♓	15♌R	1♒	17♈	7♍R	20♋R
A 2	10 38 17	11 12 25	9♑22	15	22	5	15	1	17	6	20
R 3	10 42 13	12 12 35	22 28	17	23	5	15	1	17	6	20
C 4	10 46 10	13 12 44	5♒19	19	24	6	15	1	17	6	20
H 5	10 50 6	14 12 51	17 57	21	25	7	14	1	17	6	20
6	10 54 3	15 12 57	0♓23	23	26	8	14	1	17	6	20
7	10 57 59	16 13 0	12 37	25	28	9	14	1	17	6	20
8	11 1 56	17 13 2	24 43	26	29	9	14	1	18	6	20
9	11 5 52	18 13 1	6♈40	28	0♉	10	14	1	18	6	20
10	11 9 49	19 12 59	18 31	0♈	1	11	14	1	18	6	20
11	11 13 46	20 12 55	0♉20	2	2	12	14	2	18	6	20
12	11 17 42	21 12 48	12 8	4	3	13	14	2	18	6	20
13	11 21 39	22 12 39	24 0	6	5	13	14	2	18	6	20
14	11 25 35	23 12 29	5♊59	8	6	14	14	2	18	6	20
15	11 29 32	24 12 16	18 11	9	7	15	14	2	18	6	20
16	11 33 28	25 12 1	0♋39	11	8	16	13	2	18	6	20
17	11 37 25	26 11 43	13 27	13	9	16	13	2	18	6	20
18	11 41 21	27 11 24	26 40	14	10	17	13	2	18	6	20
19	11 45 18	28 11 1	10♌19	16	11	18	13	2	18	6	20
20	11 49 15	29 10 37	24 25	17	12	19	13	2	18	6	20
21	11 53 11	0♈10 10	8♍56	18	14	20	13	2	18	6	20
22	11 57 8	1 9 42	23 47	20	15	20	13	3	18	6	20
23	12 1 4	2 9 11	8♎50	21	16	21	13	3	18	6	20
24	12 5 1	3 8 38	23 58	22	17	22	13	3	18	6	20
25	12 8 57	4 8 3	9♏ 1	22	18	23	13	3	18	6	20
26	12 12 54	5 7 27	23 51	23	19	24	13	3	19	6	20
27	12 16 50	6 6 49	8♐21	24	20	24	13	3	19	6	20
28	12 20 47	7 6 9	22 27	24	21	25	13	3	19	6	20
29	12 24 44	8 5 27	6♑ 9	25	22	26	13	3	19	6	20
30	12 28 40	9 4 43	19 27	25	24	27	13	3	19	6	20
31	12 32 37	10 3 58	2♒24	25 R	25	27	13	3	19	6	20

THE SUN ENTERS THE SIGN OF ARIES ON MAR 20 AT 19:54.

DAY	TIME	☉	☽	☿	♀	♂	♃	♄	♅	♆	♇
	h m s	° ' "	° '	°	°	°	°	°	°	°	°
A 1	12 36 33	11♈ 3 11	15♒ 2	25♈R	26♉	28♓	13♌R	3♒	19♈	6♍R	20♋R
P 2	12 40 30	12 2 22	27 24	25	27	29	13	3	19	6	20 D
R 3	12 44 26	13 1 31	9♓35	25	28	0⊙	13	3	19	6	20
I 4	12 48 23	14 0 38	21 36	24	29	1♈	13	3	19	6	20
L 5	12 52 19	14 59 44	3♈31	24	0♊	1	13	4	19	6	20
6	12 56 16	15 58 47	15 22	23	1	2	13	4	19	6	20
7	13 0 13	16 57 48	27 11	23	2	3	13	4	19	6	20
8	13 4 9	17 56 47	9♉ 0	22	3	4	13 D	4	19	6	20
9	13 8 6	18 55 44	20 50	21	4	4	13	4	19	6	20
10	13 12 2	19 54 40	2♊46	21	5	5	13	4	19	6	20
11	13 15 59	20 53 32	14 48	20	6	6	13	4	19	6	20
12	13 19 55	21 52 23	27 1	19	7	7	13	4	19	6	20
13	13 23 52	22 51 11	9♋28	18	8	8	13	4	20	5	20
14	13 27 48	23 49 58	22 12	18	9	8	13	4	20	5	20
15	13 31 45	24 48 41	5♌18	17	10	9	13	4	20	5	20
16	13 35 42	25 47 23	18 48	16	11	10	13	4	20	5	20
17	13 39 38	26 46 2	2♍44	16	12	11	13	4	20	5	20
18	13 43 35	27 44 39	17 6	15	13	11	13	4	20	5	20
19	13 47 31	28 43 14	1♎52	15	14	12	13	4	20	5	20
20	13 51 28	29 41 47	16 56	14	15	13	13	4	20	5	20
21	13 55 24	0♉40 18	2♏11	14	16	14	13	4	20	5	20
22	13 59 21	1 38 47	17 26	14	17	14	13	4	20	5	20
23	14 3 17	2 37 14	2♐31	14	18	15	13	4	20	5	20
24	14 7 14	3 35 39	17 17	14 D	19	16	13	4	20	5	20
25	14 11 11	4 34 3	1♑37	14	20	17	13	4	20	5	20
26	14 15 7	5 32 26	15 29	14	21	18	13	4	20	5	20
27	14 19 4	6 30 46	28 52	14	22	18	13	5	20	5	20
28	14 23 0	7 29 6	11♒49	14	23	19	13	5	20	5	20
29	14 26 57	8 27 23	24 23	15	24	20	13	5	20	5	20
30	14 30 53	9 25 39	6♓39	15	25	21	13	5	20	5	20

THE SUN ENTERS THE SIGN OF TAURUS ON APR 20 AT 07:28.

DAY	TIME	☉	☽	☿	♀	♂	♃	♄	♅	♆	♇
	h m s	° ' "	° '	°	°	°	°	°	°	°	°
M 1	14 34 50	10♉23 54	18♓42	16♈	25♊	21♈	13♌	5♒	21♈	5♍R	20♋
A 2	14 38 46	11 22 7	0♈36	16	26	22	13	5	21	5	20
Y 3	14 42 43	12 20 18	12 25	17	27	23	14	5	21	5	20
4	14 46 40	13 18 28	24 13	18	28	24	14	5	21	5	20
5	14 50 36	14 16 36	6♉ 1	18	29	24	14	5	21	5	20
6	14 54 33	15 14 43	17 53	19	0♋	25	14	5	21	5	20
7	14 58 29	16 12 48	29 50	20	1	26	14	5	21	5	20
8	15 2 26	17 10 51	11♊53	21	1	27	14	5	21	5	20
9	15 6 22	18 8 53	24 4	22	2	27	14	5	21	5	20
10	15 10 19	19 6 52	6♋25	23	3	28	14	5	21	5	20
11	15 14 15	20 4 50	18 57	24	4	29	14	5	21	5	20
12	15 18 12	21 2 47	1♌44	25	4	0♉	14	5	21	5	20
13	15 22 9	22 0 41	14 47	26	5	0	14	5	21	5	20
14	15 26 5	22 58 34	28 10	28	6	1	14	5 R	21	5	20
15	15 30 2	23 56 24	11♍56	29	6	2	15	5	21	5	20
16	15 33 58	24 54 13	26 5	0♉	7	3	15	5	21	5 D	20
17	15 37 55	25 52 1	10♎36	1	8	3	15	5	21	5	20
18	15 41 51	26 49 46	25 28	3	8	4	15	5	21	5	20
19	15 45 48	27 47 30	10♏33	4	9	5	15	5	21	5	20
20	15 49 44	28 45 13	25 43	6	10	6	15	5	22	5	20
21	15 53 41	29 42 54	10♐47	7	10	6	15	5	22	5	20
22	15 57 38	0♊40 35	25 37	9	11	7	15	5	22	5	20
23	16 1 34	1 38 14	10♑ 3	10	11	8	15	5	22	5	20
24	16 5 31	2 35 51	24 2	12	12	9	16	5	22	5	20
25	16 9 27	3 33 28	7♒31	14	12	9	16	5	22	5	20
26	16 13 24	4 31 4	20 32	15	13	10	16	5	22	5	21
27	16 17 20	5 28 39	3♓ 8	17	13	11	16	5	22	5	21
28	16 21 17	6 26 13	15 25	19	13	12	16	5	22	5	21
29	16 25 13	7 23 46	27 26	21	14	12	16	5	22	5	21
30	16 29 10	8 21 18	9♈19	22	14	13	16	5	22	5	21
31	16 33 7	9 18 50	21 7	24	14	14	17	5	22	5	21

THE SUN ENTERS THE SIGN OF GEMINI ON MAY 21 AT 07:06.

DAY	TIME	☉	☽	☿	♀	♂	♃	♄	♅	♆	♇
	h m s	° ' "	° '	°	°	°	°	°	°	°	°
J 1	16 37 3	10♊16 20	2♉55	26♉	15♋	15♉	17♌	5♒R	22♈	5♍	21♋
U 2	16 41 0	11 13 50	14 46	28	15	15	17	4	22	5	21
N 3	16 44 56	12 11 19	26 43	0♊	15	16	17	4	22	5	21
E 4	16 48 53	13 8 47	8♊48	2	15	17	17	4	22	5	21
5	16 52 49	14 6 14	21 3	4	15	17	17	4	22	5	21
6	16 56 46	15 3 40	3♋27	6	15	18	17	4	22	5	21
7	17 0 42	16 1 5	16 2	8	15 R	19	18	4	22	5	21
8	17 4 39	16 58 30	28 48	10	15	20	18	4	22	5	21
9	17 8 36	17 55 53	11♌45	13	15	20	18	4	22	5	21
10	17 12 32	18 53 15	24 56	15	15	21	18	4	22	5	21
11	17 16 29	19 50 36	8♍21	17	15	22	18	4	22	5	21
12	17 20 25	20 47 56	22 3	19	15	23	18	4	23	5	21
13	17 24 22	21 45 15	6♎ 2	21	15	23	18	4	23	5	21
14	17 28 18	22 42 33	20 19	24	15	24	19	4	23	5	21
15	17 32 15	23 39 50	4♏53	26	14	25	19	4	23	5	21
16	17 36 11	24 37 6	19 38	28	14	25	19	4	23	5	21
17	17 40 8	25 34 22	4♐29	0♋	14	26	19	4	23	5	21
18	17 44 5	26 31 37	19 18	2	13	27	19	4	23	5	21
19	17 48 1	27 28 52	3♑55	4	13	28	19	4	23	5	21
20	17 51 58	28 26 6	18 15	7	12	28	20	4	23	6	21
21	17 55 54	29 23 20	2♒10	9	12	29	20	4	23	6	21
22	17 59 51	0♋20 33	15 40	11	11	0♊	20	4	23	6	21
23	18 3 47	1 17 46	28 42	13	11	0	20	4	23	6	21
24	18 7 44	2 14 59	11♓21	15	10	1	20	4	23	6	21
25	18 11 41	3 12 12	23 39	17	10	2	21	3	23	6	21
26	18 15 37	4 9 25	5♈43	19	9	3	21	3	23	6	21
27	18 19 34	5 6 38	17 37	20	9	3	21	3	23	6	21
28	18 23 30	6 3 51	29 26	22	8	4	21	3	23	6	21
29	18 27 27	7 1 4	11♉17	24	7	5	21	3	23	6	21
30	18 31 23	7 58 17	23 12	26	7	5	21	3	23	6	21

THE SUN ENTERS THE SIGN OF CANCER ON JUN 21 AT 15:23.

♈ ARIES ♉ TAURUS ♊ GEMINI ♋ CANCER ♌ LEO ♍ VIRGO ♎ LIBRA ♏ SCORPIO ♐ SAGITTARIUS ♑ CAPRICORN ♒ AQUARIUS ♓ PISCES

SIDEREAL SUN MOON MERCURY VENUS MARS JUPITER SATURN URANUS NEPTUNE PLUTO

DAY	TIME	☉	☽	☿	♀	♂	♃	♄	♅	♆	♇
	h m s	° ' "	° '	°	°	°	°	°	°	°	°
J 1	18 35 20	8♋55 30	5♊15	28♋	6♋R	6♊	22♌	3♒R	23♈	6♍	21♋
U 2	18 39 16	9 52 43	17 29	29	5	7	22	3	23	6	21
L 3	18 43 13	10 49 57	29 56	1♌	5	8	22	3	23	6	21
Y 4	18 47 10	11 47 10	12♋36	3	4	8	22	3	23	6	21
5	18 51 6	12 44 24	25 29	4	4	9	22	3	23	6	21
6	18 55 3	13 41 37	8♌35	6	3	10	23	3	23	6	21
7	18 58 59	14 38 50	21 51	7	3	10	23	3	23	6	22
8	19 2 56	15 36 3	5♍19	9	2	11	23	3	23	6	22
9	19 6 52	16 33 16	18 57	10	2	12	23	3	23	6	22
10	19 10 49	17 30 29	2♎46	12	1	12	23	2	23	6	22
11	19 14 45	18 27 42	16 45	13	1	13	24	2	23	6	22
12	19 18 42	19 24 55	0♏55	15	0	14	24	2	23	6	22
13	19 22 39	20 22 7	15 13	16	0	14	24	2	23	6	22
14	19 26 35	21 19 20	29 37	17	0	15	24	2	23	6	22
15	19 30 32	22 16 33	14♐ 4	18	0	16	24	2	23	6	22
16	19 34 28	23 13 46	28 27	20	29♊	17	24	2	23	6	22
17	19 38 25	24 11 0	12♑42	21	29	17	25	2	23	6	22
18	19 42 21	25 8 13	26 42	22	29	18	25	2	23	6	22
19	19 46 18	26 5 27	10♒23	23	29	19	25	2	23	6	22
20	19 50 15	27 2 42	23 42	24	29 D	19	25	2	23	6	22
21	19 54 11	27 59 57	6♓40	25	29	20	26	2	23	6	22
22	19 58 8	28 57 13	19 17	26	29	21	26	2	23	6	22
23	20 2 4	29 54 30	1♈35	27	29	21	26	2	23	6	22
24	20 6 1	0♌51 47	13 40	27	29	22	26	1	23	6	22
25	20 9 57	1 49 6	25 36	28	29	23	26	1	23	6	22
26	20 13 54	2 46 25	7♉27	29	29	23	27	1	23	6	22
27	20 17 50	3 43 46	19 19	0♍	0♋	24	27	1	23	6	22
28	20 21 47	4 41 7	1♊17	0	0	25	27	1	23	7	22
29	20 25 44	5 38 29	13 25	1	0	25	27	1	23 R	7	22
30	20 29 40	6 35 53	25 46	1	0	26	27	1	23	7	22
31	20 33 37	7 33 17	8♋22	1	1	27	28	1	23	7	22

THE SUN ENTERS THE SIGN OF LEO ON JUL 23 AT 02:19.

DAY	TIME	☉	☽	☿	♀	♂	♃	♄	♅	♆	♇
	h m s	° ' "	° '	°	°	°	°	°	°	°	°
A 1	20 37 33	8♌30 43	21♋16	2♍	1♋	27♊	28♌	1♒R	23♈R	7♍	22♋
U 2	20 41 30	9 28 9	4♌27	2	2	28	28	1	23	7	22
G 3	20 45 26	10 25 37	17 54	2 R	2	29	28	1	23	7	22
U 4	20 49 23	11 23 5	1♍34	2	2	29	28	1	23	7	22
S 5	20 53 19	12 20 34	15 26	2	3	0♋	29	1	23	7	22
T 6	20 57 16	13 18 4	29 27	2	3	1	29	1	23	7	22
7	21 1 13	14 15 34	13♎34	1	4	1	29	0	23	7	22
8	21 5 9	15 13 6	27 44	1	4	2	29	0	23	7	22
9	21 9 6	16 10 38	11♏56	1	5	3	0♍	0	23	7	22
10	21 13 2	17 8 11	26 8	0	6	3	0	0	23	7	22
11	21 16 59	18 5 45	10♐18	0	6	4	0	0	23	7	22
12	21 20 55	19 3 20	24 23	29♌	7	5	0	0	23	7	22
13	21 24 52	20 0 56	8♑20	28	7	5	0	0	23	7	22
14	21 28 48	20 58 33	22 7	27	8	6	1	0	23	7	22
15	21 32 45	21 56 11	5♒41	27	9	7	1	0	23	7	23
16	21 36 42	22 53 50	19 0	26	10	7	1	0	23	7	23
17	21 40 38	23 51 30	2♓ 2	25	10	8	1	0	23	7	23
18	21 44 35	24 49 12	14 47	24	11	9	1	0	23	7	23
19	21 48 31	25 46 55	27 16	23	12	9	2	0	23	7	23
20	21 52 28	26 44 39	9♈31	22	12	10	2	0	23	7	23
21	21 56 24	27 42 25	21 35	22	13	11	2	0	23	7	23
22	22 0 21	28 40 13	3♉30	21	14	11	2	29♑	23	7	23
23	22 4 17	29 38 3	15 22	20	15	12	3	29	23	7	23
24	22 8 14	0♍35 54	27 14	20	16	13	3	29	23	7	23
25	22 12 11	1 33 47	9♊12	20	17	13	3	29	23	7	23
26	22 16 7	2 31 42	21 21	19	17	14	3	29	23	8	23
27	22 20 4	3 29 38	3♋43	19 D	18	15	3	29	23	8	23
28	22 24 0	4 27 37	16 24	19	19	15	4	29	23	8	23
29	22 27 57	5 25 37	29 25	19	20	16	4	29	23	8	23
30	22 31 53	6 23 39	12♌48	20	21	16	4	29	23	8	23
31	22 35 50	7 21 43	26 32	20	22	17	4	29	23	8	23

THE SUN ENTERS THE SIGN OF VIRGO ON AUG 23 AT 09:07.

DAY	TIME	☉	☽	☿	♀	♂	♃	♄	♅	♆	♇
	h m s	° ' "	° '	°	°	°	°	°	°	°	°
S 1	22 39 46	8♍19 48	10♍35	21♌	23♋	18♋	4♍	29♑R	23♈R	8♍	23♋
E 2	22 43 43	9 17 55	24 52	21	24	18	5	29	23	8	23
P 3	22 47 40	10 16 3	9♎20	22	24	19	5	29	23	8	23
T 4	22 51 36	11 14 13	23 53	23	25	20	5	29	23	8	23
E 5	22 55 33	12 12 25	8♏24	24	26	20	5	29	23	8	23
M 6	22 59 29	13 10 38	22 50	25	27	21	6	29	23	8	23
B 7	23 3 26	14 8 53	7♐ 7	27	28	21	6	29	23	8	23
E 8	23 7 22	15 7 9	21 12	28	29	22	6	29	23	8	23
R 9	23 11 19	16 5 27	5♑ 4	0♍	0♌	23	6	29	23	8	23
10	23 15 15	17 3 46	18 41	1	1	23	6	29	23	8	23
11	23 19 12	18 2 6	2♒ 4	3	2	24	7	28	23	8	23
12	23 23 9	19 0 29	15 13	4	3	25	7	28	23	8	23
13	23 27 5	19 58 53	28 8	6	4	25	7	28	23	8	23
14	23 31 2	20 57 18	10♓49	8	5	26	7	28	23	8	23
15	23 34 58	21 55 46	23 18	10	6	26	8	28	23	8	23
16	23 38 55	22 54 15	5♈36	11	7	27	8	28	23	8	23
17	23 42 51	23 52 46	17 44	13	8	28	8	28	22	8	23
18	23 46 48	24 51 19	29 43	15	9	28	8	28	22	8	23
19	23 50 44	25 49 55	11♉37	17	10	29	8	28	22	8	23
20	23 54 41	26 48 33	23 28	19	11	0♌	9	28	22	8	23
21	23 58 37	27 47 12	5♊20	21	12	0	9	28	22	8	23
22	0 2 34	28 45 54	17 17	23	13	1	9	28	22	9	23
23	0 6 31	29 44 39	29 23	24	14	1	9	28	22	9	23
24	0 10 27	0♎43 25	11♋42	26	16	2	9	28	22	9	23
25	0 14 24	1 42 14	24 20	28	17	3	10	28	22	9	23
26	0 18 20	2 41 5	7♌20	0♎	18	3	10	28	22	9	23
27	0 22 17	3 39 58	20 45	2	19	4	10	28	22	9	23
28	0 26 13	4 38 53	4♍36	4	20	4	10	28	22	9	23
29	0 30 10	5 37 51	18 51	5	21	5	10	28	22	9	23
30	0 34 6	6 36 51	3♎27	7	22	6	11	28	22	9	23

THE SUN ENTERS THE SIGN OF LIBRA ON SEP 23 AT 06:17.

DAY	TIME	☉	☽	☿	♀	♂	♃	♄	♅	♆	♇
	h m s	° ' "	° '	°	°	°	°	°	°	°	°
O 1	0 38 3	7♎35 52	18♎19	9♎	23♌	6♌	11♍	28♑R	22♈R	9♍	23♋
C 2	0 42 0	8 34 56	3♏17	11	24	7	11	28 D	22	9	23
T 3	0 45 56	9 34 1	18 15	12	25	7	11	28	22	9	23
O 4	0 49 53	10 33 9	3♐ 2	14	26	8	11	28	22	9	23
B 5	0 53 49	11 32 18	17 34	16	28	8	12	28	22	9	23
E 6	0 57 46	12 31 29	1♑45	17	29	9	12	28	22	9	23
R 7	1 1 42	13 30 42	15 35	19	0♍	10	12	28	22	9	23
8	1 5 39	14 29 57	29 2	21	1	10	12	28	22	9	23
9	1 9 35	15 29 13	12♒10	22	2	11	12	28	22	9	23
10	1 13 32	16 28 31	25 1	24	3	11	13	28	22	9	23
11	1 17 29	17 27 51	7♓37	26	4	12	13	28	22	9	23
12	1 21 25	18 27 13	20 0	27	5	12	13	28	22	9	23
13	1 25 22	19 26 36	2♈14	29	7	13	13	28	21	9	23
14	1 29 18	20 26 2	14 20	1♏	8	14	13	28	21	9	23
15	1 33 15	21 25 29	26 19	2	9	14	14	28	21	9	23
16	1 37 11	22 24 59	8♉14	4	10	15	14	28	21	9	23
17	1 41 8	23 24 30	20 6	5	11	15	14	28	21	9	23
18	1 45 4	24 24 4	1♊57	7	12	16	14	28	21	9	23
19	1 49 1	25 23 40	13 50	8	13	16	14	28	21	9	23
20	1 52 58	26 23 19	25 46	10	15	17	15	28	21	9	23
21	1 56 54	27 22 59	7♋51	11	16	18	15	28	21	9	23
22	2 0 51	28 22 42	20 7	13	17	18	15	28	21	9	23
23	2 4 47	29 22 27	2♌40	14	18	19	15	28	21	9	23
24	2 8 44	0♏22 15	15 33	16	19	19	15	28	21	10	23 R
25	2 12 40	1 22 4	28 50	17	20	20	16	29	21	10	23
26	2 16 37	2 21 56	12♍36	19	22	20	16	29	21	10	23
27	2 20 33	3 21 50	26 49	20	23	21	16	29	21	10	23
28	2 24 30	4 21 45	11♎29	22	24	21	16	29	21	10	23
29	2 28 27	5 21 44	26 31	23	25	22	16	29	21	10	23
30	2 32 23	6 21 44	11♏45	25	26	22	16	29	21	10	23
31	2 36 20	7 21 46	27 2	26	27	23	17	29	21	10	23

THE SUN ENTERS THE SIGN OF SCORPIO ON OCT 23 AT 15:05.

DAY	TIME	☉	☽	☿	♀	♂	♃	♄	♅	♆	♇
	h m s	° ' "	° '	°	°	°	°	°	°	°	°
N 1	2 40 16	8♏21 49	12♐11	27♏	29♍	23♌	17♍	29♑	21♈R	10♍	23♋R
O 2	2 44 13	9 21 55	27 1	29	0♎	24	17	29	21	10	23
V 3	2 48 9	10 22 2	11♑26	0♐	1	25	17	29	21	10	23
E 4	2 52 6	11 22 11	25 24	2	2	25	17	29	21	10	23
M 5	2 56 2	12 22 21	8♒53	3	3	26	17	29	21	10	23
B 6	2 59 59	13 22 33	21 58	4	5	26	18	29	21	10	23
E 7	3 3 56	14 22 46	4♓40	6	6	27	18	29	20	10	23
R 8	3 7 52	15 23 0	17 5	7	7	27	18	29	20	10	23
9	3 11 49	16 23 16	29 17	8	8	28	18	29	20	10	23
10	3 15 45	17 23 34	11♈20	9	9	28	18	29	20	10	23
11	3 19 42	18 23 53	23 17	10	11	29	18	29	20	10	23
12	3 23 38	19 24 13	5♉10	12	12	29	19	29	20	10	23
13	3 27 35	20 24 36	17 2	13	13	0♍	19	0♒	20	10	23
14	3 31 31	21 25 0	28 54	14	14	0	19	0	20	10	23
15	3 35 28	22 25 26	10♊47	15	15	1	19	0	20	10	23
16	3 39 25	23 25 53	22 44	16	17	1	19	0	20	10	23
17	3 43 21	24 26 22	4♋45	17	18	1	19	0	20	10	23
18	3 47 18	25 26 53	16 53	18	19	2	19	0	20	10	23
19	3 51 14	26 27 26	29 11	18	20	2	20	0	20	10	23
20	3 55 11	27 28 0	11♌41	19	21	3	20	0	20	10	23
21	3 59 7	28 28 36	24 29	20	23	3	20	0	20	10	23
22	4 3 4	29 29 14	7♍38	20	24	4	20	0	20	10	23
23	4 7 0	0♐29 53	21 12	20	25	4	20	0	20	10	23
24	4 10 57	1 30 34	5♎14	21 R	26	5	20	0	20	10	23
25	4 14 54	2 31 17	19 43	21	28	5	20	0	20	10	23
26	4 18 50	3 32 1	4♏36	20	29	6	20	0	20	10	23
27	4 22 47	4 32 47	19 48	20	0♏	6	21	1	20	10	23
28	4 26 43	5 33 34	5♐ 8	20	1	7	21	1	20	10	23
29	4 30 40	6 34 23	20 24	19	2	7	21	1	20	10	23
30	4 34 36	7 35 13	5♑25	18	4	7	21	1	20	10	23

THE SUN ENTERS THE SIGN OF SAGITTARIUS ON NOV 22 AT 12:11.

DAY	TIME	☉	☽	☿	♀	♂	♃	♄	♅	♆	♇
	h m s	° ' "	° '	°	°	°	°	°	°	°	°
D 1	4 38 33	8♐36 4	20♑ 3	17♐R	5♏	8♍	21♍	1♒	20♈R	10♍	23♋R
E 2	4 42 29	9 36 55	4♒12	16	6	8	21	1	20	10	23
C 3	4 46 26	10 37 48	17 51	15	7	9	21	1	20	10	23
E 4	4 50 23	11 38 41	1♓ 0	13	9	9	21	1	20	10	23
M 5	4 54 19	12 39 35	13 45	12	10	9	21	1	20	10	23
B 6	4 58 16	13 40 30	26 8	11	11	10	22	1	20	10	23
E 7	5 2 12	14 41 26	8♈17	9	12	10	22	1	20	10	23
R 8	5 6 9	15 42 22	20 15	8	14	11	22	2	20	10	23
9	5 10 5	16 43 19	2♉ 8	7	15	11	22	2	20	10	23
10	5 14 2	17 44 17	13 58	6	16	11	22	2	20	10	23
11	5 17 58	18 45 15	25 49	5	17	12	22	2	20	10	23
12	5 21 55	19 46 14	7♊44	5	18	12	22	2	20	10 R	23
13	5 25 52	20 47 14	19 42	5	20	12	22	2	20	10	23
14	5 29 48	21 48 15	1♋47	4 D	21	13	22	2	20	10	23
15	5 33 45	22 49 17	13 58	4	22	13	22	2	20	10	23
16	5 37 41	23 50 19	26 16	5	23	14	22	2	20	10	23
17	5 41 38	24 51 22	8♌44	5	25	14	22	2	20	10	23
18	5 45 34	25 52 26	21 22	5	26	14	23	3	19	10	23
19	5 49 31	26 53 31	4♍14	6	27	14	23	3	19	10	23
20	5 53 28	27 54 36	17 22	7	28	15	23	3	19	10	23
21	5 57 24	28 55 43	0♎50	7	0♐	15	23	3	19	10	23
22	6 1 21	29 56 50	14 40	8	1	15	23	3	19	10	23
23	6 5 17	0♑57 58	28 52	9	2	16	23	3	19	10	23
24	6 9 14	1 59 6	13♏26	10	3	16	23	3	19	10	23
25	6 13 10	3 0 15	28 18	11	5	16	23	3	19	10	23
26	6 17 7	4 1 25	13♐21	12	6	17	23	3	19	10	23
27	6 21 3	5 2 35	28 25	13	7	17	23	3	19	10	23
28	6 25 0	6 3 46	13♑21	15	8	17	23	4	19 D	10	23
29	6 28 57	7 4 57	27 58	16	10	17	23	4	19	10	23
30	6 32 53	8 6 7	12♒11	17	11	18	23	4	19	10	23
31	6 36 50	9 7 18	25 56	18	12	18	23	4	19	10	23

THE SUN ENTERS THE SIGN OF CAPRICORN ON DEC 22 AT 01:15.

♈ ARIES ♉ TAURUS ♊ GEMINI ♋ CANCER ♌ LEO ♍ VIRGO ♎ LIBRA ♏ SCORPIO ♐ SAGITTARIUS ♑ CAPRICORN ♒ AQUARIUS ♓ PISCES

1933

SIDEREAL SUN MOON MERCURY VENUS MARS JUPITER SATURN URANUS NEPTUNE PLUTO

DAY	TIME h m s	☉ ° ' "	☽ ° '	☿ °	♀ °	♂ °	♃ °	♄ °	♅ °	♆ °	♇ °
J 1	6 40 46	10♑ 8 28	9♓12	20♐	13♐	18♍	23♍	4♒	19♈	10♍R	23♋R
A 2	6 44 43	11 9 38	22 3	21	15	18	23	4	19	10	23
N 3	6 48 39	12 10 48	4♈31	22	16	18	23	4	19	10	23
U 4	6 52 36	13 11 58	16 43	24	17	19	23	4	19	10	23
A 5	6 56 32	14 13 7	28 42	25	18	19	23	4	19	10	23
R 6	7 0 29	15 14 16	10♉35	27	20	19	23	5	19	10	23
Y 7	7 4 26	16 15 25	22 25	28	21	19	23	5	19	10	22
8	7 8 22	17 16 33	4♊18	29	22	19	23 R	5	19	10	22
9	7 12 19	18 17 41	16 15	1♑	23	19	23	5	19	10	22
10	7 16 15	19 18 49	28 20	2	24	20	23	5	20	10	22
11	7 20 12	20 19 56	10♋34	4	26	20	23	5	20	10	22
12	7 24 8	21 21 3	22 58	5	27	20	23	5	20	10	22
13	7 28 5	22 22 9	5♌33	7	28	20	23	5	20	10	22
14	7 32 2	23 23 16	18 18	8	29	20	23	6	20	10	22
15	7 35 58	24 24 21	1♍15	10	1♑	20	23	6	20	10	22
16	7 39 55	25 25 27	14 23	11	2	20	23	6	20	10	22
17	7 43 51	26 26 32	27 44	13	3	20	23	6	20	10	22
18	7 47 48	27 27 37	11♎18	14	4	20	23	6	20	10	22
19	7 51 44	28 28 41	25 6	16	6	20	23	6	20	10	22
20	7 55 41	29 29 45	9♏ 9	17	7	20	23	6	20	10	22
21	7 59 37	0♒30 49	23 26	19	8	20 R	23	6	20	10	22
22	8 3 34	1 31 53	7♐55	20	9	20	23	6	20	10	22
23	8 7 31	2 32 56	22 30	22	11	20	23	7	20	10	22
24	8 11 27	3 33 59	7♑ 7	24	12	20	23	7	20	10	22
25	8 15 24	4 35 1	21 39	25	13	20	23	7	20	10	22
26	8 19 20	5 36 2	5♒58	27	14	20	23	7	20	10	22
27	8 23 17	6 37 3	19 59	28	16	20	23	7	20	10	22
28	8 27 13	7 38 2	3♓39	0♒	17	20	23	7	20	10	22
29	8 31 10	8 39 0	16 55	2	18	20	23	7	20	10	22
30	8 35 6	9 39 57	29 49	3	19	20	23	7	20	10	22
31	8 39 3	10 40 53	12♈22	5	21	20	22	8	20	10	22

THE SUN ENTERS THE SIGN OF AQUARIUS ON JAN 20 AT 11:53.

DAY	TIME h m s	☉ ° ' "	☽ ° '	☿ °	♀ °	♂ °	♃ °	♄ °	♅ °	♆ °	♇ °
F 1	8 43 0	11♒41 47	24♈37	7♒	22♑	20♍R	22♍R	8♒	20♈	10♍R	22♋R
E 2	8 46 56	12 42 40	6♉40	8	23	19	22	8	20	10	22
B 3	8 50 53	13 43 32	18 35	10	24	19	22	8	20	9	22
R 4	8 54 49	14 44 23	0♊27	12	26	19	22	8	20	9	22
U 5	8 58 46	15 45 12	12 21	14	27	19	22	8	20	9	22
A 6	9 2 42	16 46 0	24 20	15	28	19	22	8	20	9	22
R 7	9 6 39	17 46 46	6♋29	17	29	18	22	8	20	9	22
Y 8	9 10 35	18 47 31	18 51	19	1♒	18	22	8	20	9	22
9	9 14 32	19 48 14	1♌27	21	2	18	22	9	20	9	22
10	9 18 29	20 48 56	14 17	22	3	18	22	9	20	9	22
11	9 22 25	21 49 37	27 24	24	4	17	21	9	20	9	22
12	9 26 22	22 50 16	10♍44	26	6	17	21	9	20	9	22
13	9 30 18	23 50 54	24 18	28	7	17	21	9	20	9	22
14	9 34 15	24 51 30	8♎ 3	0♓	8	17	21	9	20	9	22
15	9 38 11	25 52 6	21 57	1	9	16	21	9	20	9	22
16	9 42 8	26 52 40	6♏ 0	3	11	16	21	9	20	9	22
17	9 46 4	27 53 13	20 7	5	12	16	21	10	20	9	22
18	9 50 1	28 53 45	4♐19	7	13	15	21	10	21	9	22
19	9 53 58	29 54 16	18 32	9	14	15	21	10	21	9	22
20	9 57 54	0♓54 45	2♑44	11	16	15	21	10	21	9	22
21	10 1 51	1 55 13	16 52	13	17	14	20	10	21	9	22
22	10 5 47	2 55 40	0♒53	14	18	14	20	10	21	9	22
23	10 9 44	3 56 5	14 44	16	19	13	20	10	21	9	22
24	10 13 40	4 56 28	28 21	18	21	13	20	10	21	9	22
25	10 17 37	5 56 50	11♓43	20	22	13	20	10	21	9	22
26	10 21 33	6 57 10	24 48	22	23	12	20	11	21	9	22
27	10 25 30	7 57 28	7♈35	23	24	12	20	11	21	9	21
28	10 29 27	8 57 44	20 6	25	26	12	20	11	21	9	21

THE SUN ENTERS THE SIGN OF PISCES ON FEB 19 AT 02:16.

DAY	TIME h m s	☉ ° ' "	☽ ° '	☿ °	♀ °	♂ °	♃ °	♄ °	♅ °	♆ °	♇ °
M 1	10 33 23	9♓57 59	2♉22	26♓	27♒	11♍R	19♍R	11♒	21♈	9♍R	21♋R
A 2	10 37 20	10 58 11	14 27	28	28	11	19	11	21	9	21
R 3	10 41 16	11 58 21	26 23	29	29	10	19	11	21	9	21
C 4	10 45 13	12 58 30	8♊16	1♈	1♓	10	19	11	21	9	21
H 5	10 49 9	13 58 36	20 10	2	2	10	19	11	21	9	21
6	10 53 6	14 58 40	2♋ 9	3	3	9	19	11	21	9	21
7	10 57 2	15 58 42	14 18	4	4	9	19	12	21	9	21
8	11 0 59	16 58 42	26 42	5	6	8	19	12	21	9	21
9	11 4 56	17 58 40	9♌23	6	7	8	18	12	21	9	21
10	11 8 52	18 58 36	22 25	6	8	8	18	12	21	9	21
11	11 12 49	19 58 29	5♍47	7	9	7	18	12	21	9	21
12	11 16 45	20 58 21	19 29	7	11	7	18	12	22	8	21
13	11 20 42	21 58 10	3♎30	7 R	12	7	18	12	22	8	21
14	11 24 38	22 57 58	17 44	7	13	6	18	12	22	8	21
15	11 28 35	23 57 44	2♏ 8	7	14	6	18	12	22	8	21
16	11 32 31	24 57 28	16 35	7	16	6	17	12	22	8	21
17	11 36 28	25 57 10	1♐ 1	7	17	5	17	13	22	8	21
18	11 40 25	26 56 51	15 21	6	18	5	17	13	22	8	21
19	11 44 21	27 56 30	29 32	6	19	5	17	13	22	8	21
20	11 48 18	28 56 8	13♑33	5	21	4	17	13	22	8	21
21	11 52 14	29 55 43	27 21	4	22	4	17	13	22	8	21
22	11 56 11	0♈55 17	10♒57	3	23	4	17	13	22	8	21
23	12 0 7	1 54 49	24 20	3	24	3	17	13	22	8	21
24	12 4 4	2 54 19	7♓31	2	26	3	16	13	22	8	21
25	12 8 0	3 53 47	20 30	1	27	3	16	13	22	8	21
26	12 11 57	4 53 13	3♈16	0♈	28	3	16	13	22	8	21
27	12 15 53	5 52 38	15 50	29♓	29	3	16	14	22	8	21
28	12 19 50	6 52 0	28 12	28	1♈	2	16	14	22	8	21
29	12 23 47	7 51 20	10♉23	28	2	2	16	14	22	8	21
30	12 27 43	8 50 37	22 25	27	3	2	16	14	23	8	21
31	12 31 40	9 49 53	4♊21	26	4	2	16	14	23	8	21

THE SUN ENTERS THE SIGN OF ARIES ON MAR 21 AT 01:43.

SIDEREAL SUN MOON MERCURY VENUS MARS JUPITER SATURN URANUS NEPTUNE PLUTO

DAY	TIME h m s	☉ ° ' "	☽ ° '	☿ °	♀ °	♂ °	♃ °	♄ °	♅ °	♆ °	♇ °
A 1	12 35 36	10♈49 6	16♊13	26♓R	5♈	2♍R	16♍R	14♒	23♈	8♍R	21♋R
P 2	12 39 33	11 48 17	28 6	25	7	2	15	14	23	8	21
R 3	12 43 29	12 47 26	10♋ 3	25	8	1	15	14	23	8	21
I 4	12 47 26	13 46 33	22 10	25	9	1	15	14	23	8	21 D
L 5	12 51 22	14 45 37	4♌31	25 D	10	1	15	14	23	8	21
6	12 55 19	15 44 39	17 12	25	12	1	15	14	23	8	21
7	12 59 16	16 43 38	0♍15	25	13	1	15	14	23	8	21
8	13 3 12	17 42 35	13 43	25	14	1	15	14	23	8	21
9	13 7 9	18 41 30	27 38	25	15	1	15	14	23	8	21
10	13 11 5	19 40 23	11♎57	25	17	1	15	15	23	8	21
11	13 15 2	20 39 14	26 35	26	18	1	15	15	23	8	21
12	13 18 58	21 38 3	11♏26	26	19	1 D	15	15	23	8	21
13	13 22 55	22 36 50	26 21	27	20	1	14	15	23	8	21
14	13 26 51	23 35 35	11♐12	27	22	1	14	15	23	8	21
15	13 30 48	24 34 19	25 51	28	23	1	14	15	23	8	21
16	13 34 45	25 33 1	10♑12	29	24	1	14	15	23	8	21
17	13 38 41	26 31 41	24 14	29	25	1	14	15	24	8	21
18	13 42 38	27 30 20	7♒55	0♈	27	1	14	15	24	8	21
19	13 46 34	28 28 56	21 18	1	28	1	14	15	24	8	21
20	13 50 31	29 27 32	4♓23	2	29	1	14	15	24	8	21
21	13 54 27	0♉26 5	17 14	3	0♉	1	14	15	24	8	21
22	13 58 24	1 24 37	29 52	4	1	1	14	15	24	8	21
23	14 2 20	2 23 6	12♈20	5	3	2	14	15	24	8	21
24	14 6 17	3 21 35	24 39	6	4	2	14	15	24	8	21
25	14 10 14	4 20 1	6♉49	8	5	2	14	16	24	8	21
26	14 14 10	5 18 26	18 53	9	6	2	14	16	24	8	21
27	14 18 7	6 16 48	0♊50	10	8	2	14	16	24	8	21
28	14 22 3	7 15 9	12 44	11	9	2	14	16	24	8	21
29	14 26 0	8 13 28	24 35	13	10	2	13	16	24	8	21
30	14 29 56	9 11 45	6♋27	14	11	3	13	16	24	7	21

THE SUN ENTERS THE SIGN OF TAURUS ON APR 20 AT 13:18.

DAY	TIME h m s	☉ ° ' "	☽ ° '	☿ °	♀ °	♂ °	♃ °	♄ °	♅ °	♆ °	♇ °
M 1	14 33 53	10♉ 9 59	18♋23	15♈	13♉	3♍	13♍R	16♒	24♈	7♍R	21♋
A 2	14 37 49	11 8 12	0♌27	17	14	3	13	16	24	7	21
Y 3	14 41 46	12 6 23	12 45	18	15	3	13	16	24	7	21
4	14 45 43	13 4 32	25 21	20	16	4	13	16	24	7	21
5	14 49 39	14 2 39	8♍20	21	18	4	13	16	25	7	21
6	14 53 36	15 0 43	21 46	23	19	4	13	16	25	7	21
7	14 57 32	15 58 46	5♎41	24	20	4	13	16	25	7	21
8	15 1 29	16 56 47	20 5	26	21	5	13	16	25	7	21
9	15 5 25	17 54 47	4♏54	28	22	5	13	16	25	7	21
10	15 9 22	18 52 44	20 1	29	24	5	13 D	16	25	7	21
11	15 13 18	19 50 40	5♐16	1♉	25	5	13	16	25	7	22
12	15 17 15	20 48 35	20 27	3	26	6	13	16	25	7	22
13	15 21 12	21 46 29	5♑25	5	27	6	13	16	25	7	22
14	15 25 8	22 44 21	20 2	7	29	6	13	16	25	7	22
15	15 29 5	23 42 12	4♒14	8	0♊	7	13	16	25	7	22
16	15 33 1	24 40 1	18 0	10	1	7	13	16	25	7	22
17	15 36 58	25 37 50	1♓20	12	2	7	13	16	25	7	22
18	15 40 54	26 35 37	14 19	14	4	7	13	16	25	7	22
19	15 44 51	27 33 23	27 0	16	5	8	13	16	25	7 D	22
20	15 48 47	28 31 8	9♈26	18	6	8	13	16	25	7	22
21	15 52 44	29 28 51	21 41	20	7	9	13	16	25	7	22
22	15 56 41	0♊26 34	3♉48	22	8	9	13	16	25	7	22
23	16 0 37	1 24 16	15 49	24	10	9	14	16	25	7	22
24	16 4 34	2 21 56	27 45	27	11	10	14	16	26	7	22
25	16 8 30	3 19 35	9♊38	29	12	10	14	16	26	7	22
26	16 12 27	4 17 13	21 30	1♊	13	10	14	16	26	7	22
27	16 16 23	5 14 50	3♋22	3	15	11	14	16 R	26	7	22
28	16 20 20	6 12 25	15 15	5	16	11	14	16	26	7	22
29	16 24 17	7 9 59	27 13	7	17	12	14	16	26	7	22
30	16 28 13	8 7 32	9♌18	10	18	12	14	16	26	7	22
31	16 32 10	9 5 3	21 36	12	20	12	14	16	26	7	22

THE SUN ENTERS THE SIGN OF GEMINI ON MAY 21 AT 12:57.

DAY	TIME h m s	☉ ° ' "	☽ ° '	☿ °	♀ °	♂ °	♃ °	♄ °	♅ °	♆ °	♇ °
J 1	16 36 6	10♊ 2 33	4♍10	14♊	21♊	13♍	14♍	16♒R	26♈	7♍	22♋
U 2	16 40 3	11 0 2	17 5	16	22	13	14	16	26	7	22
N 3	16 43 59	11 57 29	0♎25	18	23	14	14	16	26	7	22
E 4	16 47 56	12 54 55	14 14	21	24	14	14	16	26	7	22
5	16 51 52	13 52 20	28 32	23	26	14	14	16	26	7	22
6	16 55 49	14 49 44	13♏17	25	27	15	14	16	26	7	22
7	16 59 46	15 47 7	28 23	27	28	15	14	16	26	7	22
8	17 3 42	16 44 29	13♐42	29	29	16	14	16	26	8	22
9	17 7 39	17 41 50	29 1	1♋	1♋	16	15	16	26	8	22
10	17 11 35	18 39 10	14♑10	3	2	17	15	16	26	8	22
11	17 15 32	19 36 30	28 58	5	3	17	15	16	26	8	22
12	17 19 28	20 33 49	13♒21	7	4	18	15	16	26	8	22
13	17 23 25	21 31 8	27 16	8	5	18	15	16	26	8	22
14	17 27 21	22 28 26	10♓42	10	7	18	15	16	26	8	22
15	17 31 18	23 25 44	23 43	12	8	19	15	16	26	8	22
16	17 35 15	24 23 2	6♈22	14	9	19	15	16	27	8	22
17	17 39 11	25 20 19	18 45	15	10	20	15	16	27	8	22
18	17 43 8	26 17 36	0♉54	17	12	20	15	16	27	8	22
19	17 47 4	27 14 52	12 55	19	13	21	16	16	27	8	22
20	17 51 1	28 12 9	24 50	20	14	21	16	16	27	8	22
21	17 54 57	29 9 25	6♊42	22	15	22	16	16	27	8	22
22	17 58 54	0♋ 6 41	18 34	23	16	22	16	16	27	8	22
23	18 2 50	1 3 56	0♋26	25	18	23	16	16	27	8	22
24	18 6 47	2 1 11	12 21	26	19	23	16	16	27	8	22
25	18 10 44	2 58 26	24 20	27	20	24	16	16	27	8	22
26	18 14 40	3 55 40	6♌25	29	21	24	16	16	27	8	22
27	18 18 37	4 52 54	18 38	0♌	23	25	16	16	27	8	22
28	18 22 33	5 50 8	1♍ 2	1	24	25	17	16	27	8	23
29	18 26 30	6 47 21	13 40	2	25	26	17	16	27	8	23
30	18 30 26	7 44 33	26 37	3	26	26	17	15	27	8	23

THE SUN ENTERS THE SIGN OF CANCER ON JUN 21 AT 21:12.

♈ ARIES ♉ TAURUS ♊ GEMINI ♋ CANCER ♌ LEO ♍ VIRGO ♎ LIBRA ♏ SCORPIO ♐ SAGITTARIUS ♑ CAPRICORN ♒ AQUARIUS ♓ PISCES

SIDEREAL SUN MOON MERCURY VENUS MARS JUPITER SATURN URANUS NEPTUNE PLUTO

DAY	TIME	☉	☽	☿	♀	♂	♃	♄	♅	♆	♇
	h m s	° ' "	° '	°	°	°	°	°	°	°	°
J 1	18 34 23	8♋41 45	9♎54	4♌	27♋	27♍	17♍	15♒R	27♈	8♍	23♋
U 2	18 38 19	9 38 57	23 36	6	29	27	17	15	27	8	23
L 3	18 42 16	10 36 8	7♏44	6	0♌	28	17	15	27	8	23
Y 4	18 46 13	11 33 20	22 16	7	1	28	17	15	27	8	23
5	18 50 9	12 30 31	7♐ 9	8	2	29	18	15	27	8	23
6	18 54 6	13 27 41	22 15	9	4	0♎	18	15	27	8	23
7	18 58 2	14 24 52	7♑25	10	5	0	18	15	27	8	23
8	19 1 59	15 22 3	22 30	10	6	1	18	15	27	8	23
9	19 5 55	16 19 14	7♒19	11	7	1	18	15	27	8	23
10	19 9 52	17 16 25	21 46	12	8	2	18	15	27	8	23
11	19 13 49	18 13 37	5♓46	12	10	2	18	15	27	8	23
12	19 17 45	19 10 49	19 18	12	11	3	19	15	27	8	23
13	19 21 42	20 8 1	2♈25	13	12	3	19	15	27	8	23
14	19 25 38	21 5 14	15 8	13	13	4	19	15	27	8	23
15	19 29 35	22 2 28	27 32	13	15	4	19	15	27	8	23
16	19 33 31	22 59 42	9♉42	13 R	16	5	19	15	27	8	23
17	19 37 28	23 56 57	21 42	13	17	6	19	14	27	8	23
18	19 41 24	24 54 12	3♊35	13	18	6	20	14	27	8	23
19	19 45 21	25 51 28	15 27	13	19	7	20	14	27	8	23
20	19 49 18	26 48 45	27 19	13	21	7	20	14	27	8	23
21	19 53 14	27 46 3	9♋14	13	22	8	20	14	27	8	23
22	19 57 11	28 43 21	21 15	12	23	8	20	14	27	8	23
23	20 1 7	29 40 40	3♌24	12	24	9	20	14	27	8	23
24	20 5 4	0♌37 59	15 40	11	26	10	21	14	27	8	23
25	20 9 0	1 35 19	28 7	11	27	10	21	14	27	9	23
26	20 12 57	2 32 39	10♍45	10	28	11	21	14	27	9	23
27	20 16 53	3 30 0	23 37	9	29	11	21	14	27	9	23
28	20 20 50	4 27 21	6♎44	9	0♍	12	21	14	27	9	23
29	20 24 47	5 24 43	20 7	8	2	13	21	14	27	9	23
30	20 28 43	6 22 6	3♏49	7	3	13	22	14	27	9	23
31	20 32 40	7 19 29	17 50	6	4	14	22	13	27	9	23

THE SUN ENTERS THE SIGN OF LEO ON JUL 23 AT 08:06.

DAY	TIME	☉	☽	☿	♀	♂	♃	♄	♅	♆	♇
	h m s	° ' "	° '	°	°	°	°	°	°	°	°
A 1	20 36 36	8♌16 52	2♐ 8	6♌R	5♍	14♎	22♍	13♒R	27♈	9♍	23♋
U 2	20 40 33	9 14 16	16 42	5	6	15	22	13	27 R	9	23
G 3	20 44 29	10 11 41	1♑26	4	8	15	22	13	27	9	23
U 4	20 48 26	11 9 7	16 14	4	9	16	22	13	27	9	23
S 5	20 52 22	12 6 33	1♒ 0	3	10	17	23	13	27	9	24
T 6	20 56 19	13 4 0	15 35	3	11	17	23	13	27	9	24
7	21 0 16	14 1 29	29 54	3	12	18	23	13	27	9	24
8	21 4 12	14 58 58	13♓51	2	14	19	23	13	27	9	24
9	21 8 9	15 56 28	27 24	2 D	15	19	23	13	27	9	24
10	21 12 5	16 54 0	10♈34	2	16	20	24	13	27	9	24
11	21 16 2	17 51 33	23 21	2	17	20	24	13	27	9	24
12	21 19 58	18 49 8	5♉48	2	19	21	24	13	27	9	24
13	21 23 55	19 46 44	18 0	3	20	22	24	13	27	9	24
14	21 27 51	20 44 22	0♊ 1	3	21	22	24	12	27	9	24
15	21 31 48	21 42 1	11 55	4	22	23	25	12	27	9	24
16	21 35 45	22 39 41	23 47	4	23	23	25	12	27	9	24
17	21 39 41	23 37 24	5♋41	5	25	24	25	12	27	9	24
18	21 43 38	24 35 7	17 40	6	26	25	25	12	27	9	24
19	21 47 34	25 32 53	29 48	7	27	25	25	12	27	9	24
20	21 51 31	26 30 39	12♌ 7	8	28	26	26	12	27	9	24
21	21 55 27	27 28 27	24 39	9	29	27	26	12	27	9	24
22	21 59 24	28 26 17	7♍24	11	1♎	27	26	12	27	9	24
23	22 3 20	29 24 7	20 23	12	2	28	26	12	27	10	24
24	22 7 17	0♍22 0	3♎36	14	3	29	26	12	27	10	24
25	22 11 14	1 19 53	17 3	15	4	29	27	12	27	10	24
26	22 15 10	2 17 48	0♏43	17	5	0♏	27	12	27	10	24
27	22 19 7	3 15 44	14 35	18	7	0	27	12	27	10	24
28	22 23 3	4 13 42	28 37	20	8	1	27	11	27	10	24
29	22 27 0	5 11 40	12♐48	22	9	2	27	11	27	10	24
30	22 30 56	6 9 40	27 5	24	10	2	28	11	27	10	24
31	22 34 53	7 7 42	11♑27	26	11	3	28	11	27	10	24

THE SUN ENTERS THE SIGN OF VIRGO ON AUG 23 AT 14:53.

DAY	TIME	☉	☽	☿	♀	♂	♃	♄	♅	♆	♇
	h m s	° ' "	° '	°	°	°	°	°	°	°	°
S 1	22 38 49	8♍ 5 45	25♑49	28♌	13♎	4♏	28♍	11♒R	27♈R	10♍	24♋
E 2	22 42 46	9 3 49	10♒ 8	0♍	14	4	28	11	27	10	24
P 3	22 46 43	10 1 54	24 18	1	15	5	28	11	27	10	24
T 4	22 50 39	11 0 2	8♓17	3	16	6	29	11	27	10	24
E 5	22 54 36	11 58 10	22 0	5	17	6	29	11	27	10	24
M 6	22 58 32	12 56 21	5♈25	7	19	7	29	11	27	10	24
B 7	23 2 29	13 54 34	18 30	9	20	8	29	11	27	10	24
E 8	23 6 25	14 52 48	1♉16	11	21	8	0♎	11	27	10	24
R 9	23 10 22	15 51 5	13 45	13	22	9	0	11	27	10	24
10	23 14 18	16 49 23	25 58	15	23	10	0	11	27	10	24
11	23 18 15	17 47 44	8♊ 0	17	25	10	0	11	27	10	24
12	23 22 12	18 46 7	19 54	19	26	11	0	11	27	10	24
13	23 26 8	19 44 31	1♋46	21	27	12	1	11	27	10	24
14	23 30 5	20 42 58	13 40	22	28	12	1	10	27	10	24
15	23 34 1	21 41 28	25 42	24	29	13	1	10	27	10	24
16	23 37 58	22 39 59	7♌54	26	0♏	14	1	10	27	10	24
17	23 41 54	23 38 32	20 21	28	2	14	1	10	27	10	24
18	23 45 51	24 37 7	3♍ 6	0♎	3	15	2	10	27	10	24
19	23 49 47	25 35 44	16 9	1	4	16	2	10	27	11	24
20	23 53 44	26 34 24	29 31	3	5	16	2	10	27	11	24
21	23 57 40	27 33 5	13♎10	5	6	17	2	10	27	11	25
22	0 1 37	28 31 48	27 5	7	8	18	3	10	26	11	25
23	0 5 34	29 30 33	11♏10	8	9	18	3	10	26	11	25
24	0 9 30	0♎29 20	25 22	10	10	19	3	10	26	11	25
25	0 13 27	1 28 8	9♐37	12	11	20	3	10	26	11	25
26	0 17 23	2 26 58	23 51	13	12	21	3	10	26	11	25
27	0 21 20	3 25 50	8♑ 2	15	13	21	4	10	26	11	25
28	0 25 16	4 24 44	22 9	17	15	22	4	10	26	11	25
29	0 29 13	5 23 40	6♒ 8	18	16	23	4	10	26	11	25
30	0 33 10	6 22 37	20 0	20	17	23	4	10	26	11	25

THE SUN ENTERS THE SIGN OF LIBRA ON SEP 23 AT 12:02.

SIDEREAL SUN MOON MERCURY VENUS MARS JUPITER SATURN URANUS NEPTUNE PLUTO

DAY	TIME	☉	☽	☿	♀	♂	♃	♄	♅	♆	♇
	h m s	° ' "	° '	°	°	°	°	°	°	°	°
O 1	0 37 6	7♎21 35	3♓44	21♎	18♏	24♏	4♎	10♒R	26♈R	11♍	25♋
C 2	0 41 3	8 20 36	17 17	23	19	25	5	10	26	11	25
T 3	0 44 59	9 19 39	0♈38	25	20	25	5	10	26	11	25
O 4	0 48 56	10 18 43	13 46	26	22	26	5	10	26	11	25
B 5	0 52 52	11 17 50	26 39	28	23	27	5	10	26	11	25
E 6	0 56 49	12 16 58	9♉18	29	24	28	6	10	26	11	25
R 7	1 0 45	13 16 9	21 42	1♏	25	28	6	10	26	11	25
8	1 4 42	14 15 23	3♊53	2	26	29	6	10	26	11	25
9	1 8 38	15 14 38	15 54	3	27	0♐	6	10	26	11	25
10	1 12 35	16 13 56	27 47	5	29	0	6	10	26	11	25
11	1 16 32	17 13 16	9♋38	6	0♐	1	7	10	26	11	25
12	1 20 28	18 12 38	21 30	8	1	2	7	10	26	11	25
13	1 24 25	19 12 3	3♌30	9	2	3	7	10	26	11	25
14	1 28 21	20 11 30	15 42	11	3	3	7	10 D	26	11	25
15	1 32 18	21 10 59	28 12	12	4	4	7	10	26	11	25
16	1 36 14	22 10 31	11♍ 2	13	6	5	8	10	26	11	25
17	1 40 11	23 10 4	24 17	15	7	5	8	10	26	11	25
18	1 44 7	24 9 40	7♎56	16	8	6	8	10	25	11	25
19	1 48 4	25 9 18	21 59	17	9	7	8	10	25	12	25
20	1 52 1	26 8 58	6♏20	19	10	8	9	10	25	12	25
21	1 55 57	27 8 40	20 54	20	11	8	9	10	25	12	25
22	1 59 54	28 8 24	5♐33	21	12	9	9	10	25	12	25
23	2 3 50	29 8 9	20 11	22	14	10	9	10	25	12	25
24	2 7 47	0♏ 7 57	4♑40	24	15	10	9	10	25	12	25
25	2 11 43	1 7 46	18 58	25	16	11	10	10	25	12	25
26	2 15 40	2 7 37	3♒ 1	26	17	12	10	10	25	12	25 R
27	2 19 36	3 7 29	16 49	27	18	13	10	10	25	12	25
28	2 23 33	4 7 23	0♓24	28	19	13	10	10	25	12	25
29	2 27 30	5 7 19	13 45	29	20	14	10	10	25	12	25
30	2 31 26	6 7 16	26 55	0♐	21	15	11	10	25	12	25
31	2 35 23	7 7 15	9♈53	1	23	16	11	10	25	12	25

THE SUN ENTERS THE SIGN OF SCORPIO ON OCT 23 AT 20:49.

DAY	TIME	☉	☽	☿	♀	♂	♃	♄	♅	♆	♇
	h m s	° ' "	° '	°	°	°	°	°	°	°	°
N 1	2 39 19	8♏ 7 15	22♈41	2♐	24♐	16♐	11♎	10♒	25♈R	12♍	25♋R
O 2	2 43 16	9 7 18	5♉18	2	25	17	11	10	25	12	25
V 3	2 47 12	10 7 22	17 44	3	26	18	11	10	25	12	25
E 4	2 51 9	11 7 28	29 59	4	27	19	12	10	25	12	25
M 5	2 55 5	12 7 37	12♊ 4	4	28	19	12	10	25	12	25
B 6	2 59 2	13 7 47	24 1	4	29	20	12	10	25	12	25
E 7	3 2 59	14 7 59	5♋52	5	0♑	21	12	10	25	12	25
R 8	3 6 55	15 8 13	17 41	5 R	1	22	12	10	25	12	25
9	3 10 52	16 8 29	29 31	5	3	22	13	10	25	12	25
10	3 14 48	17 8 47	11♌28	5	4	23	13	10	25	12	25
11	3 18 45	18 9 7	23 37	4	5	24	13	10	25	12	25
12	3 22 41	19 9 29	6♍ 3	4	6	24	13	10	24	12	25
13	3 26 38	20 9 53	18 52	3	7	25	13	10	24	12	25
14	3 30 34	21 10 19	2♎ 7	2	8	26	14	10	24	12	25
15	3 34 31	22 10 46	15 52	1	9	27	14	11	24	12	25
16	3 38 28	23 11 16	0♏ 5	0	10	28	14	11	24	12	25
17	3 42 24	24 11 47	14 42	29♏	11	28	14	11	24	12	25
18	3 46 21	25 12 20	29 38	28	12	29	14	11	24	12	25
19	3 50 17	26 12 54	14♐42	26	13	0♑	15	11	24	12	25
20	3 54 14	27 13 30	29 45	25	14	1	15	11	24	12	25
21	3 58 10	28 14 7	14♑37	24	15	1	15	11	24	12	25
22	4 2 7	29 14 46	29 11	22	16	2	15	11	24	12	25
23	4 6 3	0♐15 25	13♒24	21	17	3	15	11	24	12	25
24	4 10 0	1 16 6	27 15	20	18	4	15	11	24	12	25
25	4 13 57	2 16 47	10♓45	20	19	4	16	11	24	12	25
26	4 17 53	3 17 30	23 56	19	20	5	16	11	24	12	25
27	4 21 50	4 18 13	6♈51	19	22	6	16	11	24	12	25
28	4 25 46	5 18 58	19 32	19 D	23	7	16	11	24	12	25
29	4 29 43	6 19 43	2♉ 3	19	24	7	16	11	24	12	25
30	4 33 39	7 20 30	14 23	19	24	8	17	11	24	12	25

THE SUN ENTERS THE SIGN OF SAGITTARIUS ON NOV 22 AT 17:54.

DAY	TIME	☉	☽	☿	♀	♂	♃	♄	♅	♆	♇
	h m s	° ' "	° '	°	°	°	°	°	°	°	°
D 1	4 37 36	8♐21 18	26♉35	19♏	25♑	9♑	17♎	12♒	24♈R	12♍	25♋R
E 2	4 41 32	9 22 7	8♊40	20	26	10	17	12	24	12	24
C 3	4 45 29	10 22 58	20 39	20	27	10	17	12	24	12	24
E 4	4 49 26	11 23 49	2♋32	21	28	11	17	12	24	12	24
M 5	4 53 22	12 24 42	14 21	22	29	12	17	12	24	12	24
B 6	4 57 19	13 25 35	26 9	23	0♒	13	18	12	24	12	24
E 7	5 1 15	14 26 30	7♌59	24	1	14	18	12	24	12	24
R 8	5 5 12	15 27 26	19 55	25	2	14	18	12	24	12	24
9	5 9 8	16 28 23	2♍ 2	26	3	15	18	12	24	12	24
10	5 13 5	17 29 22	14 24	27	4	16	18	12	24	12	24
11	5 17 2	18 30 21	27 8	29	5	17	18	12	24	12	24
12	5 20 58	19 31 22	10♎16	0♐	6	17	18	12	24	12	24
13	5 24 55	20 32 24	23 54	1	6	18	19	13	24	12	24
14	5 28 51	21 33 26	8♏ 3	2	7	19	19	13	24	12	24
15	5 32 48	22 34 30	22 39	4	8	20	19	13	24	12 R	24
16	5 36 44	23 35 35	7♐39	5	9	21	19	13	24	12	24
17	5 40 41	24 36 41	22 54	7	10	21	19	13	24	12	24
18	5 44 37	25 37 47	8♑12	8	11	22	19	13	24	12	24
19	5 48 34	26 38 53	23 22	9	11	23	19	13	24	12	24
20	5 52 31	27 40 0	8♒15	11	12	24	20	13	24	12	24
21	5 56 27	28 41 8	22 46	12	13	24	20	13	24	12	24
22	6 0 24	29 42 15	6♓50	14	14	25	20	13	24	12	24
23	6 4 20	0♑43 23	20 27	15	14	26	20	13	24	12	24
24	6 8 17	1 44 30	3♈40	17	15	27	20	14	23	12	24
25	6 12 13	2 45 38	16 32	18	16	28	20	14	23	12	24
26	6 16 10	3 46 46	29 7	20	16	28	20	14	23	12	24
27	6 20 6	4 47 54	11♉27	21	17	29	21	14	23	12	24
28	6 24 3	5 49 2	23 37	23	18	0♒	21	14	23	12	24
29	6 28 0	6 50 10	5♊38	24	18	1	21	14	23	12	24
30	6 31 56	7 51 18	17 35	26	19	1	21	14	23	12	24
31	6 35 53	8 52 26	29 27	27	19	2	21	14	23	12	24

THE SUN ENTERS THE SIGN OF CAPRICORN ON DEC 22 AT 06:58.

♈ ARIES ♉ TAURUS ♊ GEMINI ♋ CANCER ♌ LEO ♍ VIRGO ♎ LIBRA ♏ SCORPIO ♐ SAGITTARIUS ♑ CAPRICORN ♒ AQUARIUS ♓ PISCES

SIDEREAL SUN MOON MERCURY VENUS MARS JUPITER SATURN URANUS NEPTUNE PLUTO

DAY	TIME	☉	☽	☿	♀	♂	♃	♄	♅	♆	♇
	h m s	° ' "	° '	°	°	°	°	°	°	°	°
J 1	6 39 49	9♑53 35	11♋17	29♐	20♒	3♒	21♎	14♒	23♈R	12♍R	24♋R
A 2	6 43 46	10 54 43	23 7	0♑	20	4	21	14	23 D	12	24
N 3	6 47 42	11 55 51	4♌58	2	21	5	21	15	23	12	24
U 4	6 51 39	12 57 0	16 53	3	21	5	21	15	23	12	24
A 5	6 55 36	13 58 8	28 55	5	22	6	22	15	23	12	24
R 6	6 59 32	14 59 17	11♍ 6	7	22	7	22	15	23	12	24
Y 7	7 3 29	16 0 25	23 30	8	22	8	22	15	23	12	24
8	7 7 25	17 1 34	6♎12	10	23	9	22	15	23	12	24
9	7 11 22	18 2 43	19 16	11	23	9	22	15	23	12	24
10	7 15 18	19 3 52	2♏44	13	23	10	22	15	23	12	24
11	7 19 15	20 5 1	16 40	14	23	11	22	15	23	12	24
12	7 23 11	21 6 10	1♐ 2	16	23	12	22	16	24	12	24
13	7 27 8	22 7 19	15 48	18	24	12	22	16	24	12	24
14	7 31 5	23 8 28	0♑52	19	24	13	22	16	24	12	24
15	7 35 1	24 9 36	16 6	21	24 R	14	22	16	24	12	24
16	7 38 58	25 10 44	1♒18	23	24	15	22	16	24	12	24
17	7 42 54	26 11 52	16 20	24	24	16	22	16	24	12	24
18	7 46 51	27 12 58	1♓ 2	26	24	16	23	16	24	12	24
19	7 50 47	28 14 4	15 20	28	23	17	23	16	24	12	24
20	7 54 44	29 15 9	29 10	29	23	18	23	17	24	12	24
21	7 58 40	0♒16 13	12♈33	1♒	23	19	23	17	24	12	24
22	8 2 37	1 17 17	25 32	3	23	20	23	17	24	12	23
23	8 6 34	2 18 19	8♉ 8	4	22	20	23	17	24	12	23
24	8 10 30	3 19 20	20 27	6	22	21	23	17	24	12	23
25	8 14 27	4 20 20	2♊33	8	22	22	23	17	24	12	23
26	8 18 23	5 21 20	14 30	9	21	23	23	17	24	12	23
27	8 22 20	6 22 18	26 21	11	21	24	23	17	24	12	23
28	8 26 16	7 23 15	8♋10	13	20	24	23	17	24	12	23
29	8 30 13	8 24 11	20 0	15	20	25	23	18	24	12	23
30	8 34 9	9 25 6	1♌53	16	19	26	23	18	24	12	23
31	8 38 6	10 26 0	13 51	18	19	27	23	18	24	12	23

THE SUN ENTERS THE SIGN OF AQUARIUS ON JAN 20 AT 17:37.

DAY	TIME	☉	☽	☿	♀	♂	♃	♄	♅	♆	♇
	h m s	° ' "	° '	°	°	°	°	°	°	°	°
F 1	8 42 3	11♒26 53	25♌56	20♒	18♒R	27♒	23♎	18♒	24♈	12♍R	23♋R
E 2	8 45 59	12 27 44	8♍10	22	18	28	23	18	24	12	23
B 3	8 49 56	13 28 35	20 34	23	17	29	23	18	24	12	23
R 4	8 53 52	14 29 25	3♎10	25	16	0♓	23	18	24	12	23
U 5	8 57 49	15 30 14	16 2	27	16	1	23	18	24	12	23
A 6	9 1 45	16 31 2	29 9	29	15	1	23	19	24	12	23
R 7	9 5 42	17 31 49	12♏36	0♓	15	2	23 R	19	24	12	23
Y 8	9 9 38	18 32 35	26 22	2	14	3	23	19	24	12	23
9	9 13 35	19 33 21	10♐28	4	13	4	23	19	24	12	23
10	9 17 32	20 34 5	24 53	6	13	5	23	19	24	12	23
11	9 21 28	21 34 49	9♑34	7	12	5	23	19	24	12	23
12	9 25 25	22 35 31	24 26	9	12	6	23	19	24	12	23
13	9 29 21	23 36 12	9♒21	10	11	7	23	19	24	11	23
14	9 33 18	24 36 51	24 12	12	11	8	23	20	24	11	23
15	9 37 14	25 37 29	8♓50	13	10	9	23	20	24	11	23
16	9 41 11	26 38 6	23 10	14	10	9	23	20	24	11	23
17	9 45 7	27 38 40	7♈ 7	16	9	10	23	20	24	11	23
18	9 49 4	28 39 13	20 39	17	9	11	23	20	24	11	23
19	9 53 1	29 39 45	3♉45	18	9	12	23	20	24	11	23
20	9 56 57	0♓40 14	16 28	19	9	12	23	20	24	11	23
21	10 0 54	1 40 42	28 50	19	8	13	23	20	24	11	23
22	10 4 50	2 41 8	10♊58	20	8	14	23	20	25	11	23
23	10 8 47	3 41 32	22 54	20	8	15	23	21	25	11	23
24	10 12 43	4 41 54	4♋44	20 R	8	16	23	21	25	11	23
25	10 16 40	5 42 14	16 33	20	8 D	16	23	21	25	11	23
26	10 20 36	6 42 32	28 24	20	8	17	23	21	25	11	23
27	10 24 33	7 42 49	10♌21	20	8	18	23	21	25	11	23
28	10 28 30	8 43 3	22 27	20	8	19	23	21	25	11	23

THE SUN ENTERS THE SIGN OF PISCES ON FEB 19 AT 08:02.

DAY	TIME	☉	☽	☿	♀	♂	♃	♄	♅	♆	♇
	h m s	° ' "	° '	°	°	°	°	°	°	°	°
M 1	10 32 26	9♓43 16	4♍45	19♓R	8♒	20♓	22♎R	21♒	25♈	11♍R	23♋R
A 2	10 36 23	10 43 27	17 15	18	8	20	22	21	25	11	23
R 3	10 40 19	11 43 36	29 59	18	8	21	22	22	25	11	23
C 4	10 44 16	12 43 43	12♎56	17	9	22	22	22	25	11	23
H 5	10 48 12	13 43 48	26 7	16	9	23	22	22	25	11	23
6	10 52 9	14 43 52	9♏31	15	9	23	22	22	25	11	23
7	10 56 5	15 43 55	23 8	14	10	24	22	22	25	11	23
8	11 0 2	16 43 56	6♐57	13	10	25	22	22	25	11	23
9	11 3 59	17 43 55	20 57	12	10	26	22	22	25	11	23
10	11 7 55	18 43 53	5♑ 7	11	11	27	22	22	25	11	23
11	11 11 52	19 43 49	19 26	10	11	27	22	22	25	11	23
12	11 15 48	20 43 44	3♒51	9	12	28	22	23	25	11	23
13	11 19 45	21 43 36	18 19	8	12	29	21	23	25	11	23
14	11 23 41	22 43 27	2♓45	8	13	0⊙	21	23	25	11	23
15	11 27 38	23 43 16	17 3	7	13	0♈	21	23	25	11	23
16	11 31 34	24 43 3	1♈10	7	14	1	21	23	26	11	23
17	11 35 31	25 42 48	14 59	7	14	2	21	23	26	11	23
18	11 39 28	26 42 31	28 28	6	15	3	21	23	26	11	23
19	11 43 24	27 42 12	11♉35	6 D	16	4	21	23	26	11	23
20	11 47 21	28 41 51	24 20	6	16	4	21	23	26	11	23
21	11 51 17	29 41 27	6♊46	6	17	5	21	24	26	11	23
22	11 55 14	0♈41 1	18 55	7	18	6	21	24	26	10	23
23	11 59 10	1 40 33	0♋53	7	18	7	20	24	26	10	23
24	12 3 7	2 40 3	12 44	7	19	7	20	24	26	10	23
25	12 7 3	3 39 30	24 33	8	20	8	20	24	26	10	23
26	12 11 0	4 38 55	6♌25	8	20	9	20	24	26	10	23
27	12 14 57	5 38 18	18 26	9	21	10	20	24	26	10	23
28	12 18 53	6 37 39	0♍39	10	22	11	20	24	26	10	23
29	12 22 50	7 36 57	13 7	10	23	11	20	24	26	10	23
30	12 26 46	8 36 13	25 53	11	24	12	20	24	26	10	23
31	12 30 43	9 35 27	8♎57	12	24	13	19	25	26	10	23

THE SUN ENTERS THE SIGN OF ARIES ON MAR 21 AT 07:28.

SIDEREAL SUN MOON MERCURY VENUS MARS JUPITER SATURN URANUS NEPTUNE PLUTO

DAY	TIME	☉	☽	☿	♀	♂	♃	♄	♅	♆	♇
	h m s	° ' "	° '	°	°	°	°	°	°	°	°
A 1	12 34 39	10♈34 39	22♎19	13♓	25♒	14♈	19♎R	25♒	26♈	10♍R	23♋R
P 2	12 38 36	11 33 49	5♏56	14	26	14	19	25	26	10	23
R 3	12 42 32	12 32 57	19 45	15	27	15	19	25	27	10	23
I 4	12 46 29	13 32 3	3♐44	16	28	16	19	25	27	10	23
L 5	12 50 25	14 31 8	17 48	17	29	17	19	25	27	10	23 D
6	12 54 22	15 30 11	1♑55	18	0♓	17	19	25	27	10	23
7	12 58 19	16 29 12	16 2	19	1	18	19	25	27	10	23
8	13 2 15	17 28 11	0♒10	20	1	19	18	25	27	10	23
9	13 6 12	18 27 9	14 16	22	2	20	18	25	27	10	23
10	13 10 8	19 26 5	28 19	23	3	20	18	25	27	10	23
11	13 14 5	20 24 59	12♓18	24	4	21	18	26	27	10	23
12	13 18 1	21 23 51	26 10	26	5	22	18	26	27	10	23
13	13 21 58	22 22 41	9♈53	27	6	23	18	26	27	10	23
14	13 25 54	23 21 29	23 23	28	7	23	18	26	27	10	23
15	13 29 51	24 20 16	6♉38	0⊙	8	24	18	26	27	10	23
16	13 33 48	25 19 0	19 35	1♈	9	25	17	26	27	10	23
17	13 37 44	26 17 43	2♊15	3	10	26	17	26	27	10	23
18	13 41 41	27 16 23	14 38	4	11	27	17	26	27	10	23
19	13 45 37	28 15 1	26 46	6	12	27	17	26	27	10	23
20	13 49 34	29 13 37	8♋44	7	13	28	17	26	27	10	23
21	13 53 30	0♉12 11	20 34	9	14	29	17	26	28	10	23
22	13 57 27	1 10 42	2♌23	11	15	0♉	17	26	28	10	23
23	14 1 23	2 9 12	14 15	12	16	0	17	26	28	10	23
24	14 5 20	3 7 39	26 17	14	17	1	16	27	28	10	23
25	14 9 17	4 6 4	8♍33	16	18	2	16	27	28	10	23
26	14 13 13	5 4 27	21 7	17	19	3	16	27	28	10	23
27	14 17 10	6 2 48	4♎ 4	19	20	3	16	27	28	10	23
28	14 21 6	7 1 7	17 23	21	21	4	16	27	28	10	23
29	14 25 3	7 59 24	1♏ 5	23	22	5	16	27	28	10	23
30	14 28 59	8 57 40	15 7	25	23	5	16	27	28	10	23

THE SUN ENTERS THE SIGN OF TAURUS ON APR 20 AT 19:00.

DAY	TIME	☉	☽	☿	♀	♂	♃	♄	♅	♆	♇
	h m s	° ' "	° '	°	°	°	°	°	°	°	°
M 1	14 32 56	9♉55 54	29♏23	27♈	24♓	6♉	16♎R	27♒	28♈	10♍R	23♋
A 2	14 36 52	10 54 6	13♐48	28	25	7	16	27	28	10	23
Y 3	14 40 49	11 52 16	28 15	0♉	26	8	15	27	28	10	23
4	14 44 46	12 50 25	12♑40	2	27	8	15	27	28	10	23
5	14 48 42	13 48 33	26 59	4	29	9	15	27	28	10	23
6	14 52 39	14 46 39	11♒ 8	6	0⊙	10	15	27	28	10	23
7	14 56 35	15 44 44	25 7	9	1♈	11	15	27	28	10	23
8	15 0 32	16 42 47	8♓56	11	2	11	15	27	29	10	23
9	15 4 28	17 40 49	22 36	13	3	12	15	27	29	10	23
10	15 8 25	18 38 49	6♈ 5	15	4	13	15	27	29	10	23
11	15 12 21	19 36 49	19 23	17	5	14	15	28	29	10	23
12	15 16 18	20 34 46	2♉30	19	6	14	15	28	29	10	23
13	15 20 15	21 32 43	15 24	21	7	15	14	28	29	10	23
14	15 24 11	22 30 38	28 6	23	8	16	14	28	29	10	23
15	15 28 8	23 28 31	10♊33	26	9	17	14	28	29	10	23
16	15 32 4	24 26 23	22 48	28	10	17	14	28	29	10	23
17	15 36 1	25 24 14	4♋51	0♊	12	18	14	28	29	10	23
18	15 39 57	26 22 2	16 45	2	13	19	14	28	29	10	23
19	15 43 54	27 19 49	28 34	4	14	19	14	28	29	10	23
20	15 47 50	28 17 35	10♌22	6	15	20	14	28	29	10	23
21	15 51 47	29 15 19	22 13	9	16	21	14	28	29	10 D	23
22	15 55 44	0♊13 1	4♍14	11	17	22	14	28	29	10	23
23	15 59 40	1 10 42	16 29	13	18	22	14	28	29	10	23
24	16 3 37	2 8 20	29 5	15	19	23	14	28	29	10	23
25	16 7 33	3 5 58	12♎ 4	17	20	24	14	28	29	10	23
26	16 11 30	4 3 34	25 30	19	22	24	14	28	29	10	23
27	16 15 26	5 1 9	9♏22	21	23	25	14	28	0♉	10	23
28	16 19 23	5 58 42	23 39	22	24	26	14	28	0	10	23
29	16 23 19	6 56 15	8♐16	24	25	27	14	28	0	10	23
30	16 27 16	7 53 46	23 4	26	26	27	13	28	0	10	23
31	16 31 13	8 51 16	7♑55	28	27	28	13	28	0	10	23

THE SUN ENTERS THE SIGN OF GEMINI ON MAY 21 AT 18:35.

DAY	TIME	☉	☽	☿	♀	♂	♃	♄	♅	♆	♇
	h m s	° ' "	° '	°	°	°	°	°	°	°	°
J 1	16 35 9	9♊48 46	22♑43	29♊	28♈	29♉	13♎R	28♒	0♉	10♍	23♋
U 2	16 39 6	10 46 14	7♒20	1♋	0♉	0♊	13	28	0	10	23
N 3	16 43 2	11 43 42	21 41	3	1	0	13	28	0	10	23
E 4	16 46 59	12 41 9	5♓46	4	2	1	13	28	0	10	23
5	16 50 55	13 38 35	19 33	6	3	2	13	28	0	10	23
6	16 54 52	14 36 1	3♈ 3	7	4	2	13	28	0	10	23
7	16 58 48	15 33 26	16 18	8	5	3	13	28	0	10	23
8	17 2 45	16 30 50	29 19	10	6	4	13	28 R	0	10	23
9	17 6 42	17 28 14	12♉ 6	11	8	4	13	28	0	10	23
10	17 10 38	18 25 37	24 41	12	9	5	13 D	28	0	10	23
11	17 14 35	19 23 0	7♊ 5	13	10	6	13	28	0	10	23
12	17 18 31	20 20 22	19 19	15	11	7	13	28	0	10	23
13	17 22 28	21 17 43	1♋23	16	12	7	13	28	0	10	23
14	17 26 24	22 15 3	13 19	17	13	8	13	28	0	10	23
15	17 30 21	23 12 23	25 9	18	14	9	13	28	0	10	23
16	17 34 18	24 9 42	6♌56	19	16	9	13	28	0	10	23
17	17 38 14	25 7 0	18 43	19	17	10	13	28	0	10	24
18	17 42 11	26 4 17	0♍34	20	18	11	13	28	0	10	24
19	17 46 7	27 1 34	12 34	21	19	12	13	28	1	10	24
20	17 50 4	27 58 50	24 49	21	20	12	13	28	1	10	24
21	17 54 0	28 56 5	7♎22	22	21	13	13	28	1	10	24
22	17 57 57	29 53 19	20 19	23	23	14	13	28	1	10	24
23	18 1 53	0♋50 33	3♏43	23	24	14	14	28	1	10	24
24	18 5 50	1 47 46	17 35	23	25	15	14	28	1	10	24
25	18 9 47	2 44 58	1♐55	24	26	16	14	28	1	10	24
26	18 13 43	3 42 10	16 38	24	27	16	14	28	1	10	24
27	18 17 40	4 39 22	1♑38	24	28	17	14	28	1	10	24
28	18 21 36	5 36 34	16 45	24 R	0♊	18	14	28	1	10	24
29	18 25 33	6 33 45	1♒51	24	1	18	14	28	1	10	24
30	18 29 29	7 30 57	16 47	24	2	19	14	28	1	10	24

THE SUN ENTERS THE SIGN OF CANCER ON JUN 22 AT 02:48.

♈ ARIES ♉ TAURUS ♊ GEMINI ♋ CANCER ♌ LEO ♍ VIRGO ♎ LIBRA ♏ SCORPIO ♐ SAGITTARIUS ♑ CAPRICORN ♒ AQUARIUS ♓ PISCES

1934

SIDEREAL SUN MOON MERCURY VENUS MARS JUPITER SATURN URANUS NEPTUNE PLUTO

DAY	TIME h m s	☉ ° ' "	☽ ° '	☿ °	♀ °	♂ °	♃ °	♄ °	♅ °	♆ °	♇ °
J 1	18 33 26	8♋28 8	1♓26	24♋R	3♊	20♊	14♎	28♒R	1♉	10♍	24♋
U 2	18 37 22	9 25 19	15 43	23	4	21	14	28	1	10	24
L 3	18 41 19	10 22 31	29 38	23	5	21	14	28	1	10	24
Y 4	18 45 16	11 19 43	13♈ 9	23	7	22	14	28	1	10	24
5	18 49 12	12 16 55	26 20	22	8	23	14	28	1	10	24
6	18 53 9	13 14 7	9♉11	22	9	23	14	28	1	10	24
7	18 57 5	14 11 20	21 46	21	10	24	14	28	1	10	24
8	19 1 2	15 8 33	4♊ 8	21	11	25	14	28	1	10	24
9	19 4 58	16 5 47	16 19	20	12	25	14	27	1	10	24
10	19 8 55	17 3 0	28 20	19	14	26	15	27	1	10	24
11	19 12 51	18 0 14	10♋15	19	15	27	15	27	1	10	24
12	19 16 48	18 57 28	22 5	18	16	27	15	27	1	10	24
13	19 20 45	19 54 43	3♌52	18	17	28	15	27	1	10	24
14	19 24 41	20 51 57	15 39	17	18	29	15	27	1	10	24
15	19 28 38	21 49 12	27 28	16	20	29	15	27	1	10	24
16	19 32 34	22 46 27	9♍23	16	21	0♋	15	27	1	10	24
17	19 36 31	23 43 42	21 26	15	22	1	15	27	1	10	24
18	19 40 27	24 40 57	3♎43	15	23	1	15	27	1	10	24
19	19 44 24	25 38 13	16 16	15	24	2	15	27	1	10	24
20	19 48 20	26 35 28	29 10	14	26	3	15	27	1	11	24
21	19 52 17	27 32 44	12♏28	14	27	3	16	27	1	11	24
22	19 56 14	28 30 0	26 13	14 D	28	4	16	27	1	11	24
23	20 0 10	29 27 17	10♐25	14	29	5	16	27	1	11	24
24	20 4 7	0♌24 34	25 1	14	0♋	5	16	27	1	11	24
25	20 8 3	1 21 51	9♑57	14	1	6	16	27	1	11	25
26	20 12 0	2 19 9	25 6	15	3	7	16	27	1	11	25
27	20 15 56	3 16 27	10♒19	15	4	7	16	26	1	11	25
28	20 19 53	4 13 47	25 25	16	5	8	16	26	1	11	25
29	20 23 50	5 11 6	10♓17	16	6	9	17	26	1	11	25
30	20 27 46	6 8 27	24 48	17	7	9	17	26	1	11	25
31	20 31 43	7 5 49	8♈54	18	9	10	17	26	1	11	25

THE SUN ENTERS THE SIGN OF LEO ON JUL 23 AT 13:43.

DAY	TIME h m s	☉ ° ' "	☽ ° '	☿ °	♀ °	♂ °	♃ °	♄ °	♅ °	♆ °	♇ °
A 1	20 35 39	8♌ 3 12	22♈33	19♋	10♋	11♋	17♎	26♒R	1♉	11♍	25♋
U 2	20 39 36	9 0 36	5♉47	20	11	11	17	26	1	11	25
G 3	20 43 32	9 58 2	18 37	21	12	12	17	26	1	11	25
U 4	20 47 29	10 55 28	1♊ 8	22	13	13	17	26	1	11	25
S 5	20 51 25	11 52 56	13 22	23	15	13	17	26	1	11	25
T 6	20 55 22	12 50 25	25 25	25	16	14	18	26	1	11	25
7	20 59 19	13 47 56	7♋19	26	17	15	18	26	1 R	11	25
8	21 3 15	14 45 27	19 8	27	18	15	18	26	1	11	25
9	21 7 12	15 43 0	0♌55	29	20	16	18	26	1	11	25
10	21 11 8	16 40 34	12 43	1♌	21	17	18	25	1	11	25
11	21 15 5	17 38 8	24 33	2	22	17	18	25	1	11	25
12	21 19 1	18 35 44	6♍29	4	23	18	19	25	1	11	25
13	21 22 58	19 33 21	18 32	6	24	19	19	25	1	11	25
14	21 26 54	20 30 59	0♎44	8	26	19	19	25	1	11	25
15	21 30 51	21 28 39	13 9	10	27	20	19	25	1	11	25
16	21 34 48	22 26 19	25 48	12	28	21	19	25	1	11	25
17	21 38 44	23 24 0	8♏44	14	29	21	19	25	1	11	25
18	21 42 41	24 21 42	21 59	16	0♌	22	19	25	1	11	25
19	21 46 37	25 19 26	5♐36	18	2	23	20	25	1	11	25
20	21 50 34	26 17 10	19 36	20	3	23	20	25	1	12	25
21	21 54 30	27 14 56	3♑57	22	4	24	20	25	1	12	25
22	21 58 27	28 12 43	18 38	24	5	24	20	25	1	12	25
23	22 2 23	29 10 31	3♒33	26	7	25	20	24	1	12	25
24	22 6 20	0♍ 8 20	18 37	28	8	26	20	24	1	12	25
25	22 10 17	1 6 11	3♓40	0♍	9	26	21	24	1	12	25
26	22 14 13	2 4 3	18 34	2	10	27	21	24	1	12	25
27	22 18 10	3 1 56	3♈11	4	11	28	21	24	1	12	25
28	22 22 6	3 59 52	17 24	6	13	28	21	24	1	12	25
29	22 26 3	4 57 49	1♉11	8	14	29	21	24	1	12	25
30	22 29 59	5 55 48	14 30	10	15	0♌	22	24	1	12	25
31	22 33 56	6 53 49	27 24	11	16	0	22	24	1	12	25

THE SUN ENTERS THE SIGN OF VIRGO ON AUG 23 AT 20:33.

DAY	TIME h m s	☉ ° ' "	☽ ° '	☿ °	♀ °	♂ °	♃ °	♄ °	♅ °	♆ °	♇ °
S 1	22 37 52	7♍51 52	9♊55	13♍	18♌	1♌	22♎	24♒R	1♉R	12♍	25♋
E 2	22 41 49	8 49 56	22 9	15	19	2	22	24	1	12	25
P 3	22 45 46	9 48 3	4♋ 8	17	20	2	22	24	1	12	25
T 4	22 49 42	10 46 12	15 59	19	21	3	22	24	1	12	25
E 5	22 53 39	11 44 22	27 46	21	22	3	23	24	1	12	26
M 6	22 57 35	12 42 35	9♌34	22	24	4	23	23	1	12	26
B 7	23 1 32	13 40 49	21 24	24	25	5	23	23	1	12	26
E 8	23 5 28	14 39 5	3♍22	26	26	5	23	23	1	12	26
R 9	23 9 25	15 37 23	15 28	28	27	6	23	23	1	12	26
10	23 13 21	16 35 43	27 44	29	29	7	24	23	1	12	26
11	23 17 18	17 34 4	10♎12	1♎	0♍	7	24	23	1	12	26
12	23 21 14	18 32 28	22 52	3	1	8	24	23	1	12	26
13	23 25 11	19 30 52	5♏45	4	2	8	24	23	1	12	26
14	23 29 8	20 29 19	18 52	6	4	9	24	23	1	12	26
15	23 33 4	21 27 47	2♐12	7	5	10	25	23	1	12	26
16	23 37 1	22 26 17	15 48	9	6	10	25	23	1	13	26
17	23 40 57	23 24 49	29 39	11	7	11	25	23	1	13	26
18	23 44 54	24 23 22	13♑46	12	8	12	25	23	1	13	26
19	23 48 50	25 21 57	28 7	14	10	12	25	23	1	13	26
20	23 52 47	26 20 33	12♒41	15	11	13	26	23	1	13	26
21	23 56 43	27 19 11	27 24	17	12	13	26	23	1	13	26
22	0 0 40	28 17 51	12♓ 9	18	13	14	26	22	1	13	26
23	0 4 37	29 16 33	26 50	20	15	15	26	22	1	13	26
24	0 8 33	0♎15 16	11♈19	21	16	15	26	22	1	13	26
25	0 12 30	1 14 2	25 29	22	17	16	27	22	1	13	26
26	0 16 26	2 12 50	9♉16	24	18	17	27	22	1	13	26
27	0 20 23	3 11 40	22 38	25	20	17	27	22	0	13	26
28	0 24 19	4 10 32	5♊35	27	21	18	27	22	0	13	26
29	0 28 16	5 9 27	18 8	28	22	18	27	22	0	13	26
30	0 32 12	6 8 23	0♋23	29	23	19	28	22	0	13	26

THE SUN ENTERS THE SIGN OF LIBRA ON SEP 23 AT 17:46.

SIDEREAL SUN MOON MERCURY VENUS MARS JUPITER SATURN URANUS NEPTUNE PLUTO

DAY	TIME h m s	☉ ° ' "	☽ ° '	☿ °	♀ °	♂ °	♃ °	♄ °	♅ °	♆ °	♇ °
O 1	0 36 9	7♎ 7 23	12♋23	0♏	25♍	20♌	28♎	22♒R	0♉R	13♍	26♋
C 2	0 40 6	8 6 24	24 14	2	26	20	28	22	0	13	26
T 3	0 44 2	9 5 28	6♌ 1	3	27	21	28	22	0	13	26
O 4	0 47 59	10 4 34	17 50	4	28	21	28	22	0	13	26
B 5	0 51 55	11 3 42	29 45	5	0♎	22	29	22	0	13	26
E 6	0 55 52	12 2 52	11♍49	7	1	23	29	22	0	13	26
R 7	0 59 48	13 2 4	24 6	8	2	23	29	22	0	13	26
8	1 3 45	14 1 19	6♎38	9	3	24	29	22	0	13	26
9	1 7 41	15 0 36	19 25	10	5	24	0♏	22	0	13	26
10	1 11 38	15 59 55	2♏27	11	6	25	0	22	0	13	26
11	1 15 35	16 59 15	15 41	12	7	26	0	22	0	13	26
12	1 19 31	17 58 38	29 8	13	8	26	0	22	0	13	26
13	1 23 28	18 58 3	12♐45	14	10	27	0	22	0	13	26
14	1 27 24	19 57 29	26 30	15	11	27	1	22	0	13	26
15	1 31 21	20 56 57	10♑23	16	12	28	1	22	0	14	26
16	1 35 17	21 56 27	24 24	16	13	29	1	22	0	14	26
17	1 39 14	22 55 59	8♒32	17	15	29	1	22	0	14	26
18	1 43 10	23 55 32	22 45	18	16	0♍	1	22	0	14	26
19	1 47 7	24 55 7	7♓ 4	18	17	0	2	22	0	14	26
20	1 51 4	25 54 44	21 23	18	18	1	2	22	0	14	26
21	1 55 0	26 54 22	5♈39	19	20	2	2	22	0	14	26
22	1 58 57	27 54 3	19 47	19 R	21	2	2	22	0	14	26
23	2 2 53	28 53 45	3♉42	19	22	3	3	22	29♈	14	26
24	2 6 50	29 53 30	17 18	19	23	3	3	22	29	14	26
25	2 10 46	0♏53 16	0♊34	19	25	4	3	22	29	14	26
26	2 14 43	1 53 5	13 28	18	26	5	3	21 D	29	14	26
27	2 18 39	2 52 56	26 0	18	27	5	3	21	29	14	26
28	2 22 36	3 52 49	8♋15	17	28	6	4	21	29	14	26 R
29	2 26 33	4 52 44	20 15	16	0♏	6	4	22	29	14	26
30	2 30 29	5 52 41	2♌ 7	15	1	7	4	22	29	14	26
31	2 34 26	6 52 41	13 54	14	2	7	4	22	29	14	26

THE SUN ENTERS THE SIGN OF SCORPIO ON OCT 24 AT 02:37.

DAY	TIME h m s	☉ ° ' "	☽ ° '	☿ °	♀ °	♂ °	♃ °	♄ °	♅ °	♆ °	♇ °
N 1	2 38 22	7♏52 42	25♌44	13♏R	3♏	8♍	5♏	22♒	29♈R	14♍	26♋R
O 2	2 42 19	8 52 46	7♍41	12	5	9	5	22	29	14	26
V 3	2 46 15	9 52 52	19 50	10	6	9	5	22	29	14	26
E 4	2 50 12	10 52 59	2♎15	9	7	10	5	22	29	14	26
M 5	2 54 8	11 53 9	14 59	8	8	10	5	22	29	14	26
B 6	2 58 5	12 53 21	28 3	7	10	11	6	22	29	14	26
E 7	3 2 2	13 53 35	11♏25	6	11	11	6	22	29	14	26
R 8	3 5 58	14 53 50	25 5	5	12	12	6	22	29	14	26
9	3 9 55	15 54 7	8♐57	4	13	13	6	22	29	14	26
10	3 13 51	16 54 26	22 59	3	15	13	6	22	29	14	26
11	3 17 48	17 54 47	7♑ 6	3	16	14	7	22	29	14	26
12	3 21 44	18 55 9	21 14	3 D	17	14	7	22	29	14	26
13	3 25 41	19 55 32	5♒23	3	18	15	7	22	29	14	26
14	3 29 37	20 55 57	19 29	3	20	15	7	22	29	14	26
15	3 33 34	21 56 23	3♓33	4	21	16	8	22	29	14	26
16	3 37 31	22 56 50	17 33	4	22	17	8	22	29	14	26
17	3 41 27	23 57 18	1♈29	5	23	17	8	22	28	14	26
18	3 45 24	24 57 48	15 18	6	25	18	8	22	28	14	26
19	3 49 20	25 58 19	29 0	7	26	18	8	22	28	14	26
20	3 53 17	26 58 52	12♉29	8	27	19	9	22	28	14	26
21	3 57 13	27 59 26	25 45	9	28	19	9	22	28	14	26
22	4 1 10	29 0 1	8♊45	10	0♐	20	9	22	28	14	26
23	4 5 6	0♐ 0 38	21 28	11	1	20	9	22	28	14	26
24	4 9 3	1 1 17	3♋54	12	2	21	9	22	28	14	26
25	4 13 0	2 1 57	16 5	14	4	21	10	22	28	14	26
26	4 16 56	3 2 38	28 4	15	5	22	10	22	28	14	26
27	4 20 53	4 3 21	9♌55	16	6	23	10	22	28	14	26
28	4 24 49	5 4 6	21 42	18	7	23	10	22	28	14	26
29	4 28 46	6 4 52	3♍31	19	9	24	11	22	28	14	26
30	4 32 42	7 5 40	15 28	21	10	24	11	22	28	14	26

THE SUN ENTERS THE SIGN OF SAGITTARIUS ON NOV 22 AT 23:45.

DAY	TIME h m s	☉ ° ' "	☽ ° '	☿ °	♀ °	♂ °	♃ °	♄ °	♅ °	♆ °	♇ °
D 1	4 36 39	8♐ 6 29	27♍37	22♏	11♐	25♍	11♏	23♒	28♈R	15♍	26♋R
E 2	4 40 35	9 7 19	10♎ 3	24	12	25	11	23	28	15	26
C 3	4 44 32	10 8 11	22 51	25	14	26	11	23	28	15	26
E 4	4 48 29	11 9 4	6♏ 2	27	15	26	12	23	28	15	26
M 5	4 52 25	12 9 59	19 38	28	16	27	12	23	28	15	26
B 6	4 56 22	13 10 55	3♐35	0♐	17	27	12	23	28	15	26
E 7	5 0 18	14 11 52	17 51	1	19	28	12	23	28	15	26
R 8	5 4 15	15 12 50	2♑20	3	20	28	12	23	28	15	26
9	5 8 11	16 13 48	16 54	4	21	29	13	23	28	15	26
10	5 12 8	17 14 48	1♒28	6	22	29	13	23	28	15	26
11	5 16 4	18 15 48	15 57	7	24	0♎	13	23	28	15	26
12	5 20 1	19 16 48	0♓17	9	25	0	13	23	28	15	26
13	5 23 58	20 17 50	14 26	10	26	1	13	23	28	15	26
14	5 27 54	21 18 51	28 21	12	27	1	14	23	28	15	26
15	5 31 51	22 19 53	12♈ 4	13	29	2	14	24	28	15	26
16	5 35 47	23 20 55	25 35	15	0♑	2	14	24	28	15	26
17	5 39 44	24 21 58	8♉52	17	1	3	14	24	28	15 R	26
18	5 43 40	25 23 2	21 57	18	2	3	14	24	28	15	26
19	5 47 37	26 24 6	4♊49	20	4	4	15	24	28	15	26
20	5 51 33	27 25 10	17 28	21	5	4	15	24	28	15	26
21	5 55 30	28 26 15	29 54	23	6	5	15	24	28	15	26
22	5 59 27	29 27 20	12♋ 9	24	7	5	15	24	28	15	25
23	6 3 23	0♑28 26	24 13	26	9	6	15	24	28	15	25
24	6 7 20	1 29 32	6♌ 8	27	10	6	15	24	28	15	25
25	6 11 16	2 30 39	17 57	29	11	7	16	24	28	15	25
26	6 15 13	3 31 46	29 44	1♑	12	7	16	24	28	15	25
27	6 19 9	4 32 54	11♍33	2	14	7	16	25	28	15	25
28	6 23 6	5 34 2	23 28	4	15	8	16	25	28	15	25
29	6 27 3	6 35 11	5♎35	5	16	8	16	25	28	15	25
30	6 30 59	7 36 20	17 58	7	18	9	17	25	28	15	25
31	6 34 56	8 37 30	0♏42	9	19	9	17	25	28	15	25

THE SUN ENTERS THE SIGN OF CAPRICORN ON DEC 22 AT 12:50.

♈ ARIES ♉ TAURUS ♊ GEMINI ♋ CANCER ♌ LEO ♍ VIRGO ♎ LIBRA ♏ SCORPIO ♐ SAGITTARIUS ♑ CAPRICORN ♒ AQUARIUS ♓ PISCES

1935

SIDEREAL · SUN · MOON · MERCURY · VENUS · MARS · JUPITER · SATURN · URANUS · NEPTUNE · PLUTO

DAY	TIME	☉	☽	☿	♀	♂	♃	♄	♅	♆	♇
	h m s	° ' "	° '	°	°	°	°	°	°	°	°
J 1	6 38 52	9♑38 40	13♏51	10♑	20♑	10♎	17♏	25♒	28♈R	15♍R	25♋R
A 2	6 42 49	10 39 51	27 26	12	21	10	17	25	28	15	25
N 3	6 46 45	11 41 2	11♐27	13	23	11	17	25	28	15	25
U 4	6 50 42	12 42 13	25 53	15	24	11	17	25	27	14	25
A 5	6 54 38	13 43 24	10♑38	17	25	11	18	25	27	14	25
R 6	6 58 35	14 44 35	25 35	18	26	12	18	25	27 D	14	25
Y 7	7 2 32	15 45 46	10♒35	20	28	12	18	26	27	14	25
8	7 6 28	16 46 56	25 30	22	29	13	18	26	27	14	25
9	7 10 25	17 48 6	10♓13	23	0♒	13	18	26	28	14	25
10	7 14 21	18 49 16	24 39	25	1	13	18	26	28	14	25
11	7 18 18	19 50 25	8♈44	27	3	14	18	26	28	14	25
12	7 22 14	20 51 33	22 28	28	4	14	19	26	28	14	25
13	7 26 11	21 52 41	5♉52	0♒	5	15	19	26	28	14	25
14	7 30 7	22 53 48	18 56	2	6	15	19	26	28	14	25
15	7 34 4	23 54 54	1♊44	3	8	15	19	26	28	14	25
16	7 38 1	24 56 0	14 17	5	9	16	19	27	28	14	25
17	7 41 57	25 57 5	26 37	7	10	16	19	27	28	14	25
18	7 45 54	26 58 10	8♋48	8	11	16	19	27	28	14	25
19	7 49 50	27 59 14	20 49	10	13	17	20	27	28	14	25
20	7 53 47	29 0 17	2♌45	12	14	17	20	27	28	14	25
21	7 57 43	0♒ 1 19	14 36	13	15	18	20	27	28	14	25
22	8 1 40	1 2 21	26 24	15	16	18	20	27	28	14	25
23	8 5 36	2 3 22	8♍12	17	18	18	20	27	28	14	25
24	8 9 33	3 4 23	20 3	18	19	19	20	27	28	14	25
25	8 13 30	4 5 23	2♎ 0	20	20	19	20	28	28	14	25
26	8 17 26	5 6 23	14 7	21	21	19	21	28	28	14	25
27	8 21 23	6 7 22	26 28	23	23	19	21	28	28	14	25
28	8 25 19	7 8 20	9♏ 7	24	24	20	21	28	28	14	25
29	8 29 16	8 9 18	22 7	26	25	20	21	28	28	14	25
30	8 33 12	9 10 15	5♐33	27	26	20	21	28	28	14	25
31	8 37 9	10 11 11	19 25	28	28	21	21	28	28	14	25

THE SUN ENTERS THE SIGN OF AQUARIUS ON JAN 20 AT 23:29.

DAY	TIME	☉	☽	☿	♀	♂	♃	♄	♅	♆	♇
	h m s	° ' "	° '	°	°	°	°	°	°	°	°
F 1	8 41 5	11♒12 7	3♑45	29♒	29♒	21♎	21♏	28♒	28♈	14♍R	25♋R
E 2	8 45 2	12 13 2	18 28	1♓	0♓	21	21	28	28	14	25
B 3	8 48 59	13 13 56	3♒30	1	1	21	21	29	28	14	25
R 4	8 52 55	14 14 49	18 43	2	3	22	22	29	28	14	25
U 5	8 56 52	15 15 40	3♓56	3	4	22	22	29	28	14	25
A 6	9 0 48	16 16 30	19 0	3	5	22	22	29	28	14	25
R 7	9 4 45	17 17 19	3♈46	4	6	22	22	29	28	14	25
Y 8	9 8 41	18 18 7	18 9	4 R	8	22	22	29	28	14	24
9	9 12 38	19 18 52	2♉ 5	4	9	23	22	29	28	14	24
10	9 16 34	20 19 37	15 33	4	10	23	22	29	28	14	24
11	9 20 31	21 20 20	28 37	3	11	23	22	0♓	28	14	24
12	9 24 28	22 21 1	11♊18	3	13	23	22	0	28	14	24
13	9 28 24	23 21 40	23 41	2	14	23	22	0	28	14	24
14	9 32 21	24 22 18	5♋51	1	15	23	22	0	28	14	24
15	9 36 17	25 22 54	17 50	0	16	24	22	0	28	14	24
16	9 40 14	26 23 29	29 43	29♒	18	24	22	0	28	14	24
17	9 44 10	27 24 2	11♌32	28	19	24	23	0	28	14	24
18	9 48 7	28 24 33	23 20	27	20	24	23	0	28	14	24
19	9 52 3	29 25 3	5♍ 9	26	21	24	23	1	28	14	24
20	9 56 0	0♓25 31	17 1	25	23	24	23	1	28	14	24
21	9 59 57	1 25 57	28 59	24	24	24	23	1	28	14	24
22	10 3 53	2 26 22	11♎ 3	23	25	24	23	1	28	14	24
23	10 7 50	3 26 46	23 16	22	26	24	23	1	28	13	24
24	10 11 46	4 27 8	5♏41	21	27	25	23	1	28	13	24
25	10 15 43	5 27 29	18 20	21	29	25	23	1	29	13	24
26	10 19 39	6 27 49	1♐16	20	0♈	25	23	1	29	13	24
27	10 23 36	7 28 7	14 33	19	1♈	25 R	23	2	29	13	24
28	10 27 32	8 28 24	28 13	19	2	25	23	2	29	13	24

THE SUN ENTERS THE SIGN OF PISCES ON FEB 19 AT 13:52.

DAY	TIME	☉	☽	☿	♀	♂	♃	♄	♅	♆	♇
	h m s	° ' "	° '	°	°	°	°	°	°	°	°
M 1	10 31 29	9♓28 39	12♑17	19♒R	4♈	25♎R	23♏	2♓	29♈	13♍R	24♋R
A 2	10 35 26	10 28 53	26 46	19 D	5	25	23	2	29	13	24
R 3	10 39 22	11 29 5	11♒36	19	6	25	23	2	29	13	24
C 4	10 43 19	12 29 15	26 42	19	7	24	23	2	29	13	24
H 5	10 47 15	13 29 24	11♓54	19	9	24	23	2	29	13	24
6	10 51 12	14 29 31	27 4	20	10	24	23	2	29	13	24
7	10 55 8	15 29 36	12♈ 0	20	11	24	23	2	29	13	24
8	10 59 5	16 29 39	26 35	21	12	24	23	3	29	13	24
9	11 3 1	17 29 39	10♉43	21	14	24	23	3	29	13	24
10	11 6 58	18 29 38	24 21	22	15	24	23 R	3	29	13	24
11	11 10 55	19 29 35	7♊31	22	16	24	23	3	29	13	24
12	11 14 51	20 29 29	20 15	23	17	24	23	3	29	13	24
13	11 18 48	21 29 21	2♋37	24	18	23	23	3	29	13	24
14	11 22 44	22 29 11	14 44	25	20	23	23	3	29	13	24
15	11 26 41	23 28 59	26 39	26	21	23	23	3	29	13	24
16	11 30 37	24 28 44	8♌27	27	22	23	23	4	29	13	24
17	11 34 34	25 28 28	20 14	28	23	23	23	4	29	13	24
18	11 38 30	26 28 9	2♍ 2	29	25	22	23	4	29	13	24
19	11 42 27	27 27 48	13 55	0♓	26	22	23	4	0♉	13	24
20	11 46 24	28 27 25	25 54	1	27	22	23	4	0	13	24
21	11 50 20	29 27 0	8♎ 2	2	28	22	23	4	0	13	24
22	11 54 17	0♈26 33	20 18	4	29	21	23	4	0	13	24
23	11 58 13	1 26 4	2♏44	5	1♉	21	23	4	0	13	24
24	12 2 10	2 25 33	15 21	6	2	21	23	4	0	13	24
25	12 6 6	3 25 0	28 10	7	3	21	23	5	0	13	24
26	12 10 3	4 24 26	11♐12	9	4	20	23	5	0	13	24
27	12 13 59	5 23 50	24 29	10	6	20	23	5	0	13	24
28	12 17 56	6 23 12	8♑ 3	12	7	20	23	5	0	13	24
29	12 21 53	7 22 32	21 56	13	8	19	23	5	0	13	24
30	12 25 49	8 21 51	6♒ 8	14	9	19	23	5	0	13	24
31	12 29 46	9 21 8	20 39	16	10	19	23	5	0	13	24

THE SUN ENTERS THE SIGN OF ARIES ON MAR 21 AT 13:18.

DAY	TIME	☉	☽	☿	♀	♂	♃	♄	♅	♆	♇
	h m s	° ' "	° '	°	°	°	°	°	°	°	°
A 1	12 33 42	10♈20 23	5♓24	17♓	12♉	18♎R	23♏R	5♓	0♉	12♍R	24♋R
P 2	12 37 39	11 19 36	20 20	19	13	18	22	5	0	12	24
R 3	12 41 35	12 18 47	5♈16	21	14	17	22	6	0	12	24
I 4	12 45 32	13 17 56	20 5	22	15	17	22	6	0	12	24
L 5	12 49 28	14 17 3	4♉37	24	16	17	22	6	0	12	24
6	12 53 25	15 16 8	18 47	25	18	16	22	6	0	12	24
7	12 57 22	16 15 11	2♊29	27	19	16	22	6	1	12	24 D
8	13 1 18	17 14 12	15 43	29	20	16	22	6	1	12	24
9	13 5 15	18 13 10	28 31	0♈	21	15	22	6	1	12	24
10	13 9 11	19 12 6	10♋57	2	22	15	22	6	1	12	24
11	13 13 8	20 11 0	23 5	4	24	14	22	6	1	12	24
12	13 17 4	21 9 51	5♌ 1	6	25	14	22	6	1	12	24
13	13 21 1	22 8 41	16 50	7	26	14	22	7	1	12	24
14	13 24 57	23 7 27	28 38	9	27	13	21	7	1	12	24
15	13 28 54	24 6 12	10♍29	11	28	13	21	7	1	12	24
16	13 32 50	25 4 55	22 26	13	0♊	12	21	7	1	12	24
17	13 36 47	26 3 35	4♎33	15	1	12	21	7	1	12	24
18	13 40 44	27 2 14	16 52	17	2	12	21	7	1	12	24
19	13 44 40	28 0 50	29 23	19	3	11	21	7	1	12	24
20	13 48 37	28 59 25	12♏ 7	21	4	11	21	7	1	12	24
21	13 52 33	29 57 57	25 3	23	6	11	21	7	1	12	24
22	13 56 30	0♉56 28	8♐10	25	7	10	21	7	1	12	24
23	14 0 26	1 54 58	21 28	27	8	10	21	7	1	12	24
24	14 4 23	2 53 25	4♑57	29	9	10	20	8	2	12	24
25	14 8 19	3 51 51	18 37	1♉	10	9	20	8	2	12	24
26	14 12 16	4 50 16	2♒29	3	11	9	20	8	2	12	24
27	14 16 13	5 48 38	16 33	5	13	9	20	8	2	12	24
28	14 20 9	6 47 0	0♓48	7	14	9	20	8	2	12	24
29	14 24 6	7 45 19	15 13	10	15	8	20	8	2	12	24
30	14 28 2	8 43 38	29 44	12	16	8	20	8	2	12	24

THE SUN ENTERS THE SIGN OF TAURUS ON APR 21 AT 00:50.

DAY	TIME	☉	☽	☿	♀	♂	♃	♄	♅	♆	♇
	h m s	° ' "	° '	°	°	°	°	°	°	°	°
M 1	14 31 59	9♉41 54	14♈16	14♉	17♊	8♎R	20♏R	8♓	2♉	12♍R	24♋
A 2	14 35 55	10 40 9	28 42	16	19	8	19	8	2	12	24
Y 3	14 39 52	11 38 22	12♉57	18	20	8	19	8	2	12	24
4	14 43 48	12 36 34	26 53	20	21	7	19	8	2	12	24
5	14 47 45	13 34 44	10♊28	22	22	7	19	8	2	12	24
6	14 51 42	14 32 52	23 39	24	23	7	19	8	2	12	24
7	14 55 38	15 30 58	6♋26	27	24	7	19	9	2	12	24
8	14 59 35	16 29 3	18 53	29	25	7	19	9	2	12	24
9	15 3 31	17 27 5	1♌ 3	1♊	27	7	19	9	2	12	24
10	15 7 28	18 25 6	13 0	3	28	6	18	9	2	12	24
11	15 11 24	19 23 4	24 52	4	29	6	18	9	2	12	24
12	15 15 21	20 21 1	6♍41	6	0♋	6	18	9	2	12	24
13	15 19 17	21 18 56	18 35	8	1	6	18	9	3	12	24
14	15 23 14	22 16 49	0♎36	10	2	6	18	9	3	12	24
15	15 27 11	23 14 41	12 50	12	4	6	18	9	3	12	24
16	15 31 7	24 12 31	25 18	13	5	6	18	9	3	12	24
17	15 35 4	25 10 19	8♏ 3	15	6	6 D	18	9	3	12	24
18	15 39 0	26 8 6	21 3	16	7	6	17	9	3	12	24
19	15 42 57	27 5 51	4♐20	18	8	6	17	9	3	12	24
20	15 46 53	28 3 35	17 50	19	9	6	17	9	3	12	24
21	15 50 50	29 1 18	1♑31	21	10	6	17	9	3	12	24
22	15 54 46	29 59 0	15 22	22	11	6	17	9	3	12	24
23	15 58 43	0♊56 40	29 20	23	13	6	17	10	3	12	24
24	16 2 40	1 54 20	13♒23	24	14	6	17	10	3	12 D	24
25	16 6 36	2 51 58	27 30	26	15	6	17	10	3	12	24
26	16 10 33	3 49 36	11♓41	27	16	6	16	10	3	12	24
27	16 14 29	4 47 12	25 52	28	17	7	16	10	3	12	24
28	16 18 26	5 44 48	10♈ 3	28	18	7	16	10	3	12	24
29	16 22 22	6 42 23	24 10	29	19	7	16	10	3	12	24
30	16 26 19	7 39 57	8♉ 9	0♋	20	7	16	10	3	12	24
31	16 30 15	8 37 30	21 57	1	22	7	16	10	4	12	24

THE SUN ENTERS THE SIGN OF GEMINI ON MAY 22 AT 00:25.

DAY	TIME	☉	☽	☿	♀	♂	♃	♄	♅	♆	♇
	h m s	° ' "	° '	°	°	°	°	°	°	°	°
J 1	16 34 12	9♊35 2	5♊31	2♋	23♋	7♎	16♏R	10♓	4♉	12♍	24♋
U 2	16 38 9	10 32 33	18 47	2	24	7	16	10	4	12	24
N 3	16 42 5	11 30 3	1♋45	3	25	8	15	10	4	12	24
E 4	16 46 2	12 27 32	14 24	3	26	8	15	10	4	12	24
5	16 49 58	13 25 0	26 47	3	27	8	15	10	4	12	25
6	16 53 55	14 22 26	8♌55	4	28	8	15	10	4	12	25
7	16 57 51	15 19 52	20 53	4	29	8	15	10	4	12	25
8	17 1 48	16 17 16	2♍45	4	0♌	9	15	10	4	12	25
9	17 5 45	17 14 39	14 36	4 R	1	9	15	10	4	12	25
10	17 9 41	18 12 1	26 30	4	2	9	15	10	4	12	25
11	17 13 38	19 9 22	8♎33	4	3	9	15	10	4	12	25
12	17 17 34	20 6 42	20 50	4	4	10	15	10	4	12	25
13	17 21 31	21 4 2	3♏23	4	6	10	15	10	4	12	25
14	17 25 27	22 1 20	16 15	3	7	10	15	10	4	12	25
15	17 29 24	22 58 37	29 28	3	8	11	14	10	4	12	25
16	17 33 20	23 55 54	13♐ 1	2	9	11	14	10	4	12	25
17	17 37 17	24 53 10	26 52	2	10	11	14	10	4	12	25
18	17 41 14	25 50 26	10♑58	2	11	11	14	10	4	12	25
19	17 45 10	26 47 41	25 15	1	12	12	14	10	4	12	25
20	17 49 7	27 44 56	9♒38	0	13	12	14	10	4	12	25
21	17 53 3	28 42 10	24 3	0	14	12	14	10 R	4	12	25
22	17 57 0	29 39 24	8♓25	29♊	15	13	14	10	5	12	25
23	18 0 56	0♋36 38	22 42	29	16	13	14	10	5	12	25
24	18 4 53	1 33 52	6♈51	28	17	13	14	10	5	12	25
25	18 8 49	2 31 6	20 50	28	18	14	14	10	5	12	25
26	18 12 46	3 28 20	4♉38	27	19	14	14	10	5	12	25
27	18 16 43	4 25 34	18 14	27	20	15	14	10	5	12	25
28	18 20 39	5 22 48	1♊36	26	21	15	14	10	5	12	25
29	18 24 36	6 20 2	14 44	26	22	15	14	10	5	12	25
30	18 28 32	7 17 16	27 38	26	23	16	14	10	5	12	25

THE SUN ENTERS THE SIGN OF CANCER ON JUN 22 AT 08:38.

♈ ARIES ♉ TAURUS ♊ GEMINI ♋ CANCER ♌ LEO ♍ VIRGO ♎ LIBRA ♏ SCORPIO ♐ SAGITTARIUS ♑ CAPRICORN ♒ AQUARIUS ♓ PISCES

1935

SIDEREAL SUN MOON MERCURY VENUS MARS JUPITER SATURN URANUS NEPTUNE PLUTO

DAY	TIME	☉	☽	☿	♀	♂	♃	♄	♅	♆	♇
	h m s	° ' "	° '	°	°	°	°	°	°	°	°
J 1	18 32 29	8♋14 29	10♋18	25♊R	24♌	16♎	14♏R	10♓R	5♉	12♍	25♋
U 2	18 36 25	9 11 43	22 44	25	25	17	14	10	5	12	25
L 3	18 40 22	10 8 56	4♌58	25 D	26	17	14	10	5	12	25
Y 4	18 44 18	11 6 9	17 1	25	26	17	14	10	5	12	25
5	18 48 15	12 3 22	28 56	25	27	18	13	10	5	12	25
6	18 52 12	13 0 35	10♍47	26	28	18	13	10	5	12	25
7	18 56 8	13 57 48	22 38	26	29	19	13	10	5	12	25
8	19 0 5	14 55 0	4♎32	26	0♍	19	13	10	5	12	25
9	19 4 1	15 52 12	16 35	27	1	20	13	10	5	12	25
10	19 7 58	16 49 24	28 50	27	2	20	13	10	5	12	25
11	19 11 54	17 46 36	11♏23	28	3	21	13 D	10	5	12	25
12	19 15 51	18 43 48	24 16	28	4	21	13	10	5	12	25
13	19 19 47	19 41 0	7♐32	29	4	21	13	10	5	12	25
14	19 23 44	20 38 12	21 13	0♋	5	22	13	10	5	12	25
15	19 27 41	21 35 25	5♑17	1	6	22	13	10	5	12	26
16	19 31 37	22 32 37	19 42	2	7	23	13	10	5	13	26
17	19 35 34	23 29 50	4♒22	3	8	23	13	10	5	13	26
18	19 39 30	24 27 3	19 10	4	9	24	13	10	5	13	26
19	19 43 27	25 24 17	4♓ 0	6	9	24	14	10	5	13	26
20	19 47 23	26 21 31	18 44	7	10	25	14	10	5	13	26
21	19 51 20	27 18 46	3♈17	8	11	25	14	10	5	13	26
22	19 55 17	28 16 2	17 33	10	12	26	14	9	5	13	26
23	19 59 13	29 13 19	1♉32	11	12	26	14	9	5	13	26
24	20 3 10	0♌10 37	15 11	13	13	27	14	9	5	13	26
25	20 7 6	1 7 55	28 31	15	14	27	14	9	5	13	26
26	20 11 3	2 5 15	11♊34	16	14	28	14	9	5	13	26
27	20 14 59	3 2 36	24 22	18	15	29	14	9	5	13	26
28	20 18 56	3 59 57	6♋55	20	16	29	14	9	5	13	26
29	20 22 52	4 57 19	19 17	22	16	0♏	14	9	5	13	26
30	20 26 49	5 54 42	1♌29	24	17	0	14	9	5	13	26
31	20 30 46	6 52 6	13 32	26	17	1	14	9	5	13	26

THE SUN ENTERS THE SIGN OF LEO ON JUL 23 AT 19:33.

DAY	TIME	☉	☽	☿	♀	♂	♃	♄	♅	♆	♇
	h m s	° ' "	° '	°	°	°	°	°	°	°	°
A 1	20 34 42	7♌49 30	25♌29	28♋	18♍	1♏	14♏	9♓R	5♉	13♍	26♋
U 2	20 38 39	8 46 56	7♍21	0♌	18	2	14	9	5	13	26
G 3	20 42 35	9 44 22	19 11	2	19	2	14	9	5	13	26
U 4	20 46 32	10 41 48	1♎ 2	4	19	3	14	9	5	13	26
S 5	20 50 28	11 39 16	12 56	6	20	3	14	9	5	13	26
T 6	20 54 25	12 36 44	24 58	8	20	4	14	9	6	13	26
7	20 58 21	13 34 13	7♏11	10	21	5	14	9	6	13	26
8	21 2 18	14 31 43	19 40	12	21	5	15	9	6	13	26
9	21 6 15	15 29 14	2♐28	14	21	6	15	8	6	13	26
10	21 10 11	16 26 45	15 41	16	22	6	15	8	6	13	26
11	21 14 8	17 24 17	29 19	18	22	7	15	8	6 R	13	26
12	21 18 4	18 21 51	13♑25	20	22	7	15	8	6	13	26
13	21 22 1	19 19 25	27 56	22	22	8	15	8	6	13	26
14	21 25 57	20 17 0	12♒48	24	22	9	15	8	6	13	26
15	21 29 54	21 14 37	27 54	26	23	9	15	8	6	13	26
16	21 33 50	22 12 14	13♓ 5	28	23	10	15	8	6	13	26
17	21 37 47	23 9 53	28 11	0♍	23	10	15	8	6	14	26
18	21 41 44	24 7 34	13♈ 2	2	23 R	11	15	8	5	14	26
19	21 45 40	25 5 16	27 33	4	23	12	16	8	5	14	26
20	21 49 37	26 3 0	11♉38	6	23	12	16	8	5	14	26
21	21 53 33	27 0 45	25 18	8	23	13	16	8	5	14	26
22	21 57 30	27 58 32	8♊33	10	22	14	16	8	5	14	27
23	22 1 26	28 56 21	21 26	11	22	14	16	7	5	14	27
24	22 5 23	29 54 12	4♋ 1	13	22	15	16	7	5	14	27
25	22 9 19	0♍52 4	16 21	15	22	15	16	7	5	14	27
26	22 13 16	1 49 58	28 29	16	22	16	16	7	5	14	27
27	22 17 13	2 47 54	10♌30	18	21	17	16	7	5	14	27
28	22 21 9	3 45 51	22 25	20	21	17	17	7	5	14	27
29	22 25 6	4 43 50	4♍16	21	20	18	17	7	5	14	27
30	22 29 2	5 41 50	16 7	23	20	19	17	7	5	14	27
31	22 32 59	6 39 52	27 57	25	20	19	17	7	5	14	27

THE SUN ENTERS THE SIGN OF VIRGO ON AUG 24 AT 02:25.

DAY	TIME	☉	☽	☿	♀	♂	♃	♄	♅	♆	♇
	h m s	° ' "	° '	°	°	°	°	°	°	°	°
S 1	22 36 55	7♍37 55	9♎50	26♍	19♍R	20♏	17♏	7♓R	5♉R	14♍	27♋
E 2	22 40 52	8 36 0	21 47	28	19	20	17	7	5	14	27
P 3	22 44 48	9 34 7	3♏51	29	18	21	17	7	5	14	27
T 4	22 48 45	10 32 15	16 5	1♎	17	22	18	7	5	14	27
E 5	22 52 41	11 30 24	28 32	2	17	22	18	6	5	14	27
M 6	22 56 38	12 28 35	11♐16	4	16	23	18	6	5	14	27
B 7	23 0 35	13 26 48	24 21	5	16	24	18	6	5	14	27
E 8	23 4 31	14 25 1	7♑51	7	15	24	18	6	5	14	27
R 9	23 8 28	15 23 17	21 48	8	14	25	18	6	5	14	27
10	23 12 24	16 21 34	6♒13	10	14	26	18	6	5	14	27
11	23 16 21	17 19 52	21 2	11	13	26	19	6	5	14	27
12	23 20 17	18 18 12	6♓11	12	13	27	19	6	5	14	27
13	23 24 14	19 16 34	21 29	14	12	28	19	6	5	15	27
14	23 28 10	20 14 58	6♈46	15	11	28	19	6	5	15	27
15	23 32 7	21 13 23	21 52	16	11	29	19	6	5	15	27
16	23 36 4	22 11 51	6♉36	17	10	0♐	19	6	5	15	27
17	23 40 0	23 10 21	20 52	19	10	0	20	6	5	15	27
18	23 43 57	24 8 53	4♊39	20	9	1	20	6	5	15	27
19	23 47 53	25 7 27	17 57	21	9	2	20	5	5	15	27
20	23 51 50	26 6 4	0♋49	22	8	2	20	5	5	15	27
21	23 55 46	27 4 43	13 19	23	8	3	20	5	5	15	27
22	23 59 43	28 3 24	25 33	24	8	4	20	5	5	15	27
23	0 3 39	29 2 7	7♌35	25	8	4	21	5	5	15	27
24	0 7 36	0♎ 0 52	19 29	26	7	5	21	5	5	15	27
25	0 11 33	0 59 40	1♍19	27	7	6	21	5	5	15	27
26	0 15 29	1 58 29	13 9	28	7	6	21	5	5	15	27
27	0 19 26	2 57 21	25 0	29	7	7	21	5	5	15	27
28	0 23 22	3 56 15	6♎54	0♏	7	8	21	5	5	15	27
29	0 27 19	4 55 10	18 53	0	7 D	9	22	5	5	15	27
30	0 31 15	5 54 8	0♏57	1	7	9	22	5	5	15	27

THE SUN ENTERS THE SIGN OF LIBRA ON SEP 23 AT 23:39.

SIDEREAL SUN MOON MERCURY VENUS MARS JUPITER SATURN URANUS NEPTUNE PLUTO

DAY	TIME	☉	☽	☿	♀	♂	♃	♄	♅	♆	♇
	h m s	° ' "	° '	°	°	°	°	°	°	°	°
O 1	0 35 12	6♎53 7	13♏ 9	1♏	7♍	10♐	22♏	5♓R	5♉R	15♍	27♋
C 2	0 39 8	7 52 9	25 29	2	7	11	22	5	5	15	27
T 3	0 43 5	8 51 12	8♐ 1	2	7	11	22	5	4	15	27
O 4	0 47 2	9 50 18	20 46	3	7	12	23	5	4	15	27
B 5	0 50 58	10 49 25	3♑49	3	7	13	23	4	4	15	27
E 6	0 54 55	11 48 33	17 12	3 R	7	13	23	4	4	15	27
R 7	0 58 51	12 47 44	0♒58	3	8	14	23	4	4	15	27
8	1 2 48	13 46 56	15 9	3	8	15	23	4	4	15	27
9	1 6 44	14 46 10	29 43	2	8	16	23	4	4	15	27
10	1 10 41	15 45 26	14♓39	2	9	16	24	4	4	15	27
11	1 14 37	16 44 43	29 47	1	9	17	24	4	4	16	27
12	1 18 34	17 44 3	14♈59	1	9	18	24	4	4	16	27
13	1 22 31	18 43 24	0♉ 4	0	10	18	24	4	4	16	27
14	1 26 27	19 42 48	14 52	29♎	10	19	24	4	4	16	27
15	1 30 24	20 42 14	29 14	28	11	20	25	4	4	16	27
16	1 34 20	21 41 42	13♊ 8	27	11	21	25	4	4	16	27
17	1 38 17	22 41 13	26 32	25	12	21	25	4	4	16	27
18	1 42 13	23 40 46	9♋28	24	12	22	25	4	4	16	27
19	1 46 10	24 40 21	22 1	23	13	23	25	4	4	16	27
20	1 50 6	25 39 58	4♌15	22	14	24	26	4	4	16	27
21	1 54 3	26 39 38	16 16	21	14	24	26	4	4	16	27
22	1 58 0	27 39 20	28 9	20	15	25	26	4	4	16	27
23	2 1 56	28 39 4	9♍59	19	15	26	26	4	4	16	27
24	2 5 53	29 38 50	21 49	18	16	26	27	4	4	16	27
25	2 9 49	0♏38 38	3♎43	18	17	27	27	4	4	16	27
26	2 13 46	1 38 29	15 43	17	18	28	27	4	4	16	27
27	2 17 42	2 38 22	27 50	17 D	18	29	27	4	4	16	27
28	2 21 39	3 38 16	10♏ 6	17	19	29	27	4	4	16	27
29	2 25 35	4 38 13	22 32	18	20	0♑	28	4	3	16	27 R
30	2 29 32	5 38 11	5♐ 6	18	21	1	28	4	3	16	27
31	2 33 28	6 38 11	17 52	19	22	2	28	4	3	16	27

THE SUN ENTERS THE SIGN OF SCORPIO ON OCT 24 AT 08:30.

DAY	TIME	☉	☽	☿	♀	♂	♃	♄	♅	♆	♇
	h m s	° ' "	° '	°	°	°	°	°	°	°	°
N 1	2 37 25	7♏38 13	0♑48	19♎	22♍	2♑	28♏	4♓R	3♉R	16♍	27♋R
O 2	2 41 22	8 38 17	13 58	20	23	3	28	4	3	16	27
V 3	2 45 18	9 38 22	27 22	21	24	4	29	4	3	16	27
E 4	2 49 15	10 38 28	11♒ 4	22	25	5	29	4	3	16	27
M 5	2 53 11	11 38 37	25 4	23	26	5	29	4	3	16	27
B 6	2 57 8	12 38 46	9♓22	24	27	6	29	4	3	16	27
E 7	3 1 4	13 38 57	23 56	26	28	7	0♐	4 D	3	16	27
R 8	3 5 1	14 39 10	8♈41	27	28	8	0	4	3	16	27
9	3 8 57	15 39 24	23 32	28	29	8	0	4	3	16	27
10	3 12 54	16 39 40	8♉19	0♏	0♎	9	0	4	3	16	27
11	3 16 51	17 39 58	22 54	1	1	10	0	4	3	16	27
12	3 20 47	18 40 17	7♊10	3	2	11	1	4	3	16	27
13	3 24 44	19 40 39	21 2	4	3	11	1	4	3	16	27
14	3 28 40	20 41 2	4♋28	6	4	12	1	4	3	16	27
15	3 32 37	21 41 27	17 28	7	5	13	1	4	3	16	27
16	3 36 33	22 41 54	0♌ 5	9	6	14	2	4	3	16	27
17	3 40 30	23 42 22	12 23	11	7	14	2	4	3	16	27
18	3 44 27	24 42 52	24 26	12	8	15	2	4	3	16	27
19	3 48 23	25 43 25	6♍21	14	9	16	2	4	3	17	27
20	3 52 20	26 43 59	18 12	15	10	17	2	4	3	17	27
21	3 56 16	27 44 34	0♎ 4	17	11	18	3	4	3	17	27
22	4 0 13	28 45 12	12 0	18	12	18	3	4	3	17	27
23	4 4 9	29 45 51	24 6	20	13	19	3	4	2	17	27
24	4 8 6	0♐46 32	6♏22	22	14	20	3	4	2	17	27
25	4 12 2	1 47 14	18 50	23	15	21	4	4	2	17	27
26	4 15 59	2 47 57	1♐31	25	16	21	4	4	2	17	27
27	4 19 56	3 48 43	14 25	26	17	22	4	4	2	17	27
28	4 23 52	4 49 29	27 32	28	18	23	4	4	2	17	27
29	4 27 49	5 50 17	10♑50	0♐	19	24	4	4	2	17	27
30	4 31 45	6 51 5	24 20	1	21	24	5	4	2	17	27

THE SUN ENTERS THE SIGN OF SAGITTARIUS ON NOV 23 AT 05:36.

DAY	TIME	☉	☽	☿	♀	♂	♃	♄	♅	♆	♇
	h m s	° ' "	° '	°	°	°	°	°	°	°	°
D 1	4 35 42	7♐51 55	7♒59	3♐	22♎	25♑	5♐	4♓	2♉R	17♍	27♋R
E 2	4 39 38	8 52 45	21 49	4	23	26	5	4	2	17	27
C 3	4 43 35	9 53 36	5♓49	6	24	27	5	4	2	17	27
E 4	4 47 31	10 54 29	19 58	7	25	28	6	4	2	17	27
M 5	4 51 28	11 55 21	4♈14	9	26	28	6	4	2	17	27
B 6	4 55 25	12 56 15	18 35	11	27	29	6	4	2	17	27
E 7	4 59 21	13 57 9	2♉57	12	28	0♒	6	4	2	17	27
R 8	5 3 18	14 58 5	17 15	14	29	1	6	4	2	17	27
9	5 7 14	15 59 1	1♊24	15	0♏	1	7	4	2	17	27
10	5 11 11	16 59 58	15 19	17	2	2	7	4	2	17	27
11	5 15 7	18 0 56	28 56	18	3	3	7	4	2	17	27
12	5 19 4	19 1 55	12♋13	20	4	4	7	5	2	17	27
13	5 23 0	20 2 55	25 10	22	5	5	8	5	2	17	27
14	5 26 57	21 3 55	7♌47	23	6	5	8	5	2	17	27
15	5 30 54	22 4 57	20 7	25	7	6	8	5	2	17	27
16	5 34 50	23 5 59	2♍14	26	8	7	8	5	2	17	27
17	5 38 47	24 7 3	14 11	28	9	8	8	5	2	17	27
18	5 42 43	25 8 7	26 3	29	11	8	9	5	2	17	27
19	5 46 40	26 9 12	7♎56	1♑	12	9	9	5	2	17 R	27
20	5 50 36	27 10 18	19 54	3	13	10	9	5	2	17	27
21	5 54 33	28 11 25	2♏ 0	4	14	11	9	5	2	17	27
22	5 58 29	29 12 33	14 20	6	15	12	10	5	2	17	27
23	6 2 26	0♑13 41	26 56	7	16	12	10	5	2	17	27
24	6 6 23	1 14 50	9♐50	9	18	13	10	5	2	17	27
25	6 10 19	2 16 0	23 2	11	19	14	10	5	2	17	27
26	6 14 16	3 17 10	6♑31	12	20	15	10	5	2	17	27
27	6 18 12	4 18 20	20 16	14	21	15	11	6	2	17	27
28	6 22 9	5 19 30	4♒13	15	22	16	11	6	2	17	27
29	6 26 5	6 20 41	18 20	17	23	17	11	6	2	17	27
30	6 30 2	7 21 51	2♓33	19	25	18	11	6	2	17	27
31	6 33 58	8 23 1	16 48	20	26	19	11	6	2	17	27

THE SUN ENTERS THE SIGN OF CAPRICORN ON DEC 22 AT 18:38.

♈ ARIES ♉ TAURUS ♊ GEMINI ♋ CANCER ♌ LEO ♍ VIRGO ♎ LIBRA ♏ SCORPIO ♐ SAGITTARIUS ♑ CAPRICORN ♒ AQUARIUS ♓ PISCES

SIDEREAL SUN MOON MERCURY VENUS MARS JUPITER SATURN URANUS NEPTUNE PLUTO

DAY	TIME	☉	☽	☿	♀	♂	♃	♄	♅	♆	♇
	h m s	° ' "	° '	°	°	°	°	°	°	°	°
J 1	6 37 55	9♑24 12	1♈ 2	22♑	27♏	19♒	12♐	6♓	2♉R	17♍R	27♋R
A 2	6 41 52	10 25 21	15 13	23	28	20	12	6	2	17	27
N 3	6 45 48	11 26 31	29 18	25	29	21	12	6	2	17	27
U 4	6 49 45	12 27 40	13♉17	27	0♐	22	12	6	2	17	27
A 5	6 53 41	13 28 50	27 6	28	2	22	12	6	2	17	27
R 6	6 57 38	14 29 58	10♊45	0♒	3	23	13	6	2	17	27
Y 7	7 1 34	15 31 7	24 12	1	4	24	13	6	2	17	27
8	7 5 31	16 32 15	7♋25	3	5	25	13	7	2	17	27
9	7 9 28	17 33 23	20 24	4	6	26	13	7	2	17	26
10	7 13 24	18 34 31	3♌ 9	6	8	26	14	7	2 D	17	26
11	7 17 21	19 35 39	15 39	7	9	27	14	7	2	17	26
12	7 21 17	20 36 46	27 56	9	10	28	14	7	2	17	26
13	7 25 14	21 37 54	10♍ 2	10	11	29	14	7	2	17	26
14	7 29 10	22 39 1	21 59	11	12	0♓	14	7	2	17	26
15	7 33 7	23 40 8	3♎52	12	14	0	15	7	2	17	26
16	7 37 3	24 41 14	15 44	14	15	1	15	7	2	17	26
17	7 41 0	25 42 21	27 41	15	16	2	15	7	2	17	26
18	7 44 57	26 43 27	9♏45	15	17	3	15	8	2	17	26
19	7 48 53	27 44 33	22 4	16	18	3	15	8	2	17	26
20	7 52 50	28 45 39	4♐40	17	20	4	15	8	2	17	26
21	7 56 46	29 46 44	17 37	17	21	5	16	8	2	16	26
22	8 0 43	0♒47 49	0♑57	18	22	6	16	8	2	16	26
23	8 4 39	1 48 53	14 41	18 R	23	7	16	8	2	16	26
24	8 8 36	2 49 57	28 47	18	24	7	16	8	2	16	26
25	8 12 32	3 51 0	13♒11	17	26	8	16	8	2	16	26
26	8 16 29	4 52 2	27 48	17	27	9	17	8	2	16	26
27	8 20 26	5 53 3	12♓31	16	28	10	17	8	2	16	26
28	8 24 22	6 54 3	27 12	15	29	10	17	9	2	16	26
29	8 28 19	7 55 1	11♈45	14	1♑	11	17	9	2	16	26
30	8 32 15	8 55 59	26 5	13	2	12	17	9	2	16	26
31	8 36 12	9 56 55	10♉10	12	3	13	18	9	2	16	26

THE SUN ENTERS THE SIGN OF AQUARIUS ON JAN 21 AT 05:13.

DAY	TIME	☉	☽	☿	♀	♂	♃	♄	♅	♆	♇
	h m s	° ' "	° '	°	°	°	°	°	°	°	°
F 1	8 40 8	10♒57 50	23♉58	11♒R	4♑	14♓	18♐	9♓	2♉	16♍R	26♋R
E 2	8 44 5	11 58 44	7♊29	10	5	14	18	9	2	16	26
B 3	8 48 1	12 59 36	20 46	8	7	15	18	9	2	16	26
R 4	8 51 58	14 0 27	3♋48	7	8	16	18	9	2	16	26
U 5	8 55 55	15 1 17	16 37	6	9	17	18	10	2	16	26
A 6	8 59 51	16 2 5	29 15	5	10	17	19	10	2	16	26
R 7	9 3 48	17 2 52	11♌42	4	11	18	19	10	2	16	26
Y 8	9 7 44	18 3 38	24 0	4	13	19	19	10	2	16	26
9	9 11 41	19 4 22	6♍ 9	3	14	20	19	10	2	16	26
10	9 15 37	20 5 5	18 11	2	15	21	19	10	2	16	26
11	9 19 34	21 5 47	0♎ 7	2	16	21	19	10	2	16	26
12	9 23 30	22 6 28	11 59	2	18	22	20	10	2	16	26
13	9 27 27	23 7 8	23 51	2 D	19	23	20	10	2	16	26
14	9 31 24	24 7 46	5♏46	2	20	24	20	11	2	16	26
15	9 35 20	25 8 23	17 48	2	21	24	20	11	2	16	26
16	9 39 17	26 9 0	0♐ 2	2	22	25	20	11	2	16	26
17	9 43 13	27 9 35	12 33	3	24	26	20	11	2	16	26
18	9 47 10	28 10 8	25 25	3	25	27	20	11	2	16	26
19	9 51 6	29 10 41	8♑43	4	26	28	21	11	2	16	26
20	9 55 3	0♓11 12	22 29	4	27	28	21	11	2	16	26
21	9 58 59	1 11 42	6♒42	5	29	29	21	11	2	16	26
22	10 2 56	2 12 10	21 21	6	0♒	0⊙	21	12	2	16	26
23	10 6 53	3 12 37	6♓18	7	1	1♈	21	12	2	16	26
24	10 10 49	4 13 2	21 26	7	2	1	21	12	2	16	26
25	10 14 46	5 13 25	6♈33	8	3	2	21	12	2	16	26
26	10 18 42	6 13 46	21 30	9	5	3	21	12	2	16	26
27	10 22 39	7 14 5	6♉ 9	10	6	4	22	12	2	16	25
28	10 26 35	8 14 23	20 25	11	7	4	22	12	3	16	25
29	10 30 32	9 14 38	4♊17	13	8	5	22	12	3	16	25

THE SUN ENTERS THE SIGN OF PISCES ON FEB 19 AT 19:33.

DAY	TIME	☉	☽	☿	♀	♂	♃	♄	♅	♆	♇
	h m s	° ' "	° '	°	°	°	°	°	°	°	°
M 1	10 34 28	10♓14 51	17♊45	14♒	10♒	6♈	22♐	13♓	3♉	16♍R	25♋R
A 2	10 38 25	11 15 3	0♋51	15	11	7	22	13	3	16	25
R 3	10 42 22	12 15 12	13 39	16	12	8	22	13	3	15	25
C 4	10 46 18	13 15 19	26 12	17	13	8	22	13	3	15	25
H 5	10 50 15	14 15 24	8♌34	19	14	9	22	13	3	15	25
6	10 54 11	15 15 27	20 46	20	16	10	23	13	3	15	25
7	10 58 8	16 15 28	2♍52	21	17	11	23	13	3	15	25
8	11 2 4	17 15 27	14 52	23	18	11	23	13	3	15	25
9	11 6 1	18 15 24	26 48	24	19	12	23	13	3	15	25
10	11 9 57	19 15 19	8♎42	25	21	13	23	14	3	15	25
11	11 13 54	20 15 12	20 34	27	22	14	23	14	3	15	25
12	11 17 50	21 15 3	2♏27	28	23	14	23	14	3	15	25
13	11 21 47	22 14 53	14 23	0♓	24	15	23	14	3	15	25
14	11 25 44	23 14 41	26 25	1	26	16	23	14	3	15	25
15	11 29 40	24 14 28	8♐37	3	27	17	23	14	3	15	25
16	11 33 37	25 14 12	21 4	4	28	17	23	14	3	15	25
17	11 37 33	26 13 55	3♑50	6	29	18	23	14	3	15	25
18	11 41 30	27 13 36	17 1	7	0♓	19	24	15	3	15	25
19	11 45 26	28 13 16	0♒39	9	2	20	24	15	3	15	25
20	11 49 23	29 12 54	14 47	10	3	20	24	15	3	15	25
21	11 53 19	0♈12 29	29 23	12	4	21	24	15	4	15	25
22	11 57 16	1 12 3	14♓24	14	5	22	24	15	4	15	25
23	12 1 13	2 11 35	29 40	15	7	23	24	15	4	15	25
24	12 5 9	3 11 5	15♈ 0	17	8	23	24	15	4	15	25
25	12 9 6	4 10 33	0♉14	19	9	24	24	15	4	15	25
26	12 13 2	5 9 59	15 10	21	10	25	24	16	4	15	25
27	12 16 59	6 9 22	29 41	22	12	26	24	16	4	15	25
28	12 20 55	7 8 44	13♊44	24	13	26	24	16	4	15	25
29	12 24 52	8 8 3	27 18	26	14	27	24	16	4	15	25
30	12 28 48	9 7 19	10♋26	28	15	28	24	16	4	15	25
31	12 32 45	10 6 34	23 11	0⊙	16	29	24	16	4	15	25

THE SUN ENTERS THE SIGN OF ARIES ON MAR 20 AT 18:58.

SIDEREAL SUN MOON MERCURY VENUS MARS JUPITER SATURN URANUS NEPTUNE PLUTO

DAY	TIME	☉	☽	☿	♀	♂	♃	♄	♅	♆	♇
	h m s	° ' "	° '	°	°	°	°	°	°	°	°
A 1	12 36 42	11♈ 5 46	5♌39	1♈	18♓	29♈	24♐	16♓	4♉	15♍R	25♋R
P 2	12 40 38	12 4 55	17 52	3	19	0♉	24	16	4	15	25
R 3	12 44 35	13 4 2	29 56	5	20	1	24	16	4	15	25
I 4	12 48 31	14 3 7	11♍54	7	21	2	24	17	4	15	25
L 5	12 52 28	15 2 10	23 48	9	23	2	24	17	4	15	25
6	12 56 24	16 1 11	5♎41	11	24	3	24	17	4	15	25
7	13 0 21	17 0 10	17 33	13	25	4	24	17	4	15	25 D
8	13 4 17	17 59 6	29 28	15	26	5	24	17	4	15	25
9	13 8 14	18 58 1	11♏24	17	28	5	24	17	5	15	25
10	13 12 11	19 56 54	23 25	19	29	6	24 R	17	5	15	25
11	13 16 7	20 55 45	5♐33	21	0⊙	7	24	17	5	14	25
12	13 20 4	21 54 34	17 50	24	1♈	7	24	17	5	14	25
13	13 24 0	22 53 21	0♑19	26	2	8	24	18	5	14	25
14	13 27 57	23 52 7	13 5	28	4	9	24	18	5	14	25
15	13 31 53	24 50 51	26 12	0♉	5	10	24	18	5	14	25
16	13 35 50	25 49 33	9♒43	2	6	10	24	18	5	14	25
17	13 39 46	26 48 14	23 40	4	7	11	24	18	5	14	25
18	13 43 43	27 46 52	8♓ 5	6	9	12	24	18	5	14	25
19	13 47 40	28 45 30	22 53	8	10	13	24	18	5	14	25
20	13 51 36	29 44 5	8♈ 0	10	11	13	24	18	5	14	25
21	13 55 33	0♉42 39	23 15	12	12	14	24	18	5	14	25
22	13 59 29	1 41 10	8♉28	14	13	15	24	19	5	14	25
23	14 3 26	2 39 40	23 28	16	15	15	24	19	5	14	25
24	14 7 22	3 38 8	8♊ 6	18	16	16	24	19	5	14	25
25	14 11 19	4 36 34	22 18	20	17	17	24	19	5	14	25
26	14 15 15	5 34 58	6♋ 0	22	18	18	24	19	5	14	25
27	14 19 12	6 33 20	19 15	24	20	18	24	19	6	14	25
28	14 23 9	7 31 39	2♌ 5	25	21	19	24	19	6	14	25
29	14 27 5	8 29 57	14 34	27	22	20	24	19	6	14	25
30	14 31 2	9 28 12	26 47	28	23	20	24	19	6	14	25

THE SUN ENTERS THE SIGN OF TAURUS ON APR 20 AT 06:31.

DAY	TIME	☉	☽	☿	♀	♂	♃	♄	♅	♆	♇
	h m s	° ' "	° '	°	°	°	°	°	°	°	°
M 1	14 34 58	10♉26 26	8♍49	0♊	25♈	21♉	24♐R	19♓	6♉	14♍R	25♋
A 2	14 38 55	11 24 37	20 45	1	26	22	24	19	6	14	25
Y 3	14 42 51	12 22 47	2♎37	3	27	23	24	20	6	14	25
4	14 46 48	13 20 54	14 28	4	28	23	24	20	6	14	25
5	14 50 44	14 19 0	26 23	5	29	24	24	20	6	14	25
6	14 54 41	15 17 4	8♏21	6	1♉	25	23	20	6	14	25
7	14 58 37	16 15 6	20 25	7	2	25	23	20	6	14	25
8	15 2 34	17 13 7	2♐36	8	3	26	23	20	6	14	25
9	15 6 31	18 11 6	14 55	9	4	27	23	20	6	14	25
10	15 10 27	19 9 4	27 24	10	6	28	23	20	6	14	25
11	15 14 24	20 7 0	10♑ 5	11	7	28	23	20	6	14	25
12	15 18 20	21 4 55	23 0	12	8	29	23	20	6	14	25
13	15 22 17	22 2 49	6♒12	12	9	0♊	23	20	6	14	25
14	15 26 13	23 0 42	19 43	13	10	0	23	20	7	14	25
15	15 30 10	23 58 33	3♓34	13	12	1	23	21	7	14	25
16	15 34 7	24 56 23	17 46	13	13	2	23	21	7	14	25
17	15 38 3	25 54 12	2♈18	14	14	3	22	21	7	14	25
18	15 42 0	26 52 0	17 4	14	15	3	22	21	7	14	25
19	15 45 56	27 49 46	2♉ 0	14 R	17	4	22	21	7	14	26
20	15 49 53	28 47 32	16 55	14	18	5	22	21	7	14	26
21	15 53 49	29 45 16	1♊43	14	19	5	22	21	7	14	26
22	15 57 46	0♊42 59	16 14	14	20	6	22	21	7	14	26
23	16 1 42	1 40 40	0♋24	14	22	7	22	21	7	14	26
24	16 5 39	2 38 20	14 8	13	23	7	22	21	7	14	26
25	16 9 36	3 35 59	27 27	13	24	8	22	21	7	14 D	26
26	16 13 32	4 33 36	10♌21	13	25	9	21	21	7	14	26
27	16 17 29	5 31 12	22 55	12	26	10	21	21	7	14	26
28	16 21 25	6 28 46	5♍11	12	28	10	21	21	7	14	26
29	16 25 22	7 26 19	17 15	11	29	11	21	21	7	14	26
30	16 29 18	8 23 50	29 11	11	0♊	12	21	22	7	14	26
31	16 33 15	9 21 20	11♎ 4	10	1	12	21	22	7	14	26

THE SUN ENTERS THE SIGN OF GEMINI ON MAY 21 AT 06:07.

DAY	TIME	☉	☽	☿	♀	♂	♃	♄	♅	♆	♇
	h m s	° ' "	° '	°	°	°	°	°	°	°	°
J 1	16 37 11	10♊18 49	22♎57	10♊R	3♊	13♊	21♐R	22♓	7♉	14♍	26♋
U 2	16 41 8	11 16 16	4♏54	9	4	14	21	22	8	14	26
N 3	16 45 5	12 13 43	16 57	8	5	14	21	22	8	14	26
E 4	16 49 1	13 11 8	29 10	8	6	15	20	22	8	14	26
5	16 52 58	14 8 33	11♐33	7	7	16	20	22	8	14	26
6	16 56 54	15 5 56	24 8	7	9	16	20	22	8	14	26
7	17 0 51	16 3 19	6♑56	7	10	17	20	22	8	14	26
8	17 4 47	17 0 41	19 56	6	11	18	20	22	8	14	26
9	17 8 44	17 58 2	3♒10	6	12	19	20	22	8	14	26
10	17 12 40	18 55 23	16 37	6	14	19	20	22	8	14	26
11	17 16 37	19 52 43	0♓19	6	15	20	20	22	8	14	26
12	17 20 34	20 50 3	14 14	6 D	16	21	19	22	8	14	26
13	17 24 30	21 47 22	28 21	5	17	21	19	22	8	14	26
14	17 28 27	22 44 41	12♈39	6	19	22	19	22	8	14	26
15	17 32 23	23 42 0	27 6	6	20	23	19	22	8	14	26
16	17 36 20	24 39 18	11♉36	6	21	23	19	22	8	14	26
17	17 40 16	25 36 36	26 6	6	22	24	19	22	8	14	26
18	17 44 13	26 33 53	10♊28	7	23	25	19	22	8	14	26
19	17 48 9	27 31 11	24 40	7	25	25	19	22	8	14	26
20	17 52 6	28 28 27	8♋35	8	26	26	18	22	8	14	26
21	17 56 3	29 25 44	22 10	8	27	27	18	22	8	14	26
22	17 59 59	0♋22 59	5♌25	9	28	27	18	22	8	14	26
23	18 3 56	1 20 14	18 19	10	0♋	28	18	22	8	14	26
24	18 7 52	2 17 29	0♍54	10	1	29	18	22	9	14	26
25	18 11 49	3 14 42	13 13	11	2	29	18	22	9	14	26
26	18 15 45	4 11 56	25 18	12	3	0♋	18	22	9	14	26
27	18 19 42	5 9 8	7♎16	13	4	1	18	22	9	14	26
28	18 23 38	6 6 21	19 9	14	6	1	17	23	9	14	26
29	18 27 35	7 3 33	1♏ 3	15	7	2	17	23	9	14	26
30	18 31 32	8 0 44	13 2	17	8	3	17	23	9	14	26

THE SUN ENTERS THE SIGN OF CANCER ON JUN 21 AT 14:22.

♈ ARIES ♉ TAURUS ♊ GEMINI ♋ CANCER ♌ LEO ♍ VIRGO ♎ LIBRA ♏ SCORPIO ♐ SAGITTARIUS ♑ CAPRICORN ♒ AQUARIUS ♓ PISCES

SIDEREAL SUN MOON MERCURY VENUS MARS JUPITER SATURN URANUS NEPTUNE PLUTO

DAY	TIME h m s	☉ ° ' "	☽ ° '	☿ °	♀ °	♂ °	♃ °	♄ °	♅ °	♆ °	♇ °
J 1	18 35 28	8♋57 55	25♍10	18♊	9♋	3♋	17♐R	23♓	9♉	14♍	26♋
U 2	18 39 25	9 55 6	7♐30	19	11	4	17	23	9	14	26
L 3	18 43 21	10 52 17	20 5	21	12	5	17	23 R	9	14	27
Y 4	18 47 18	11 49 28	2♑56	22	13	5	17	23	9	14	27
5	18 51 14	12 46 38	16 4	24	14	6	17	23	9	14	27
6	18 55 11	13 43 49	29 28	25	16	7	17	23	9	14	27
7	18 59 8	14 41 0	13♒ 7	27	17	7	16	23	9	14	27
8	19 3 4	15 38 11	26 59	28	18	8	16	23	9	14	27
9	19 7 1	16 35 22	11♓ 1	0♋	19	8	16	23	9	15	27
10	19 10 57	17 32 33	25 10	2	20	9	16	22	9	15	27
11	19 14 54	18 29 45	9♈23	4	22	10	16	22	9	15	27
12	19 18 50	19 26 58	23 37	6	23	11	16	22	9	15	27
13	19 22 47	20 24 11	7♉50	8	24	11	16	22	9	15	27
14	19 26 43	21 21 25	21 59	10	25	12	16	22	9	15	27
15	19 30 40	22 18 39	6♊ 3	12	27	13	16	22	9	15	27
16	19 34 37	23 15 55	19 58	14	28	13	16	22	9	15	27
17	19 38 33	24 13 10	3♋43	16	29	14	16	22	9	15	27
18	19 42 30	25 10 26	17 16	18	0♌	15	16	22	9	15	27
19	19 46 26	26 7 43	0♌34	20	2	15	15	22	9	15	27
20	19 50 23	27 5 0	13 36	22	3	16	15	22	9	15	27
21	19 54 19	28 2 17	26 23	24	4	17	15	22	9	15	27
22	19 58 16	28 59 35	8♍53	26	5	17	15	22	9	15	27
23	20 2 12	29 56 53	21 10	29	6	18	15	22	9	15	27
24	20 6 9	0♌54 12	3♎15	1♌	8	19	15	22	9	15	27
25	20 10 6	1 51 31	15 12	3	9	19	15	22	9	15	27
26	20 14 2	2 48 50	27 5	5	10	20	15	22	9	15	27
27	20 17 59	3 46 10	8♏58	7	11	21	15	22	9	15	27
28	20 21 55	4 43 30	20 57	9	13	21	15	22	9	15	27
29	20 25 52	5 40 51	3♐ 5	11	14	22	15	22	9	15	27
30	20 29 48	6 38 13	15 29	13	15	23	15	22	9	15	27
31	20 33 45	7 35 35	28 10	15	16	23	15	22	9	15	27

THE SUN ENTERS THE SIGN OF LEO ON JUL 23 AT 01:18.

DAY	TIME h m s	☉ ° ' "	☽ ° '	☿ °	♀ °	♂ °	♃ °	♄ °	♅ °	♆ °	♇ °
A 1	20 37 41	8♌32 57	11♑13	17♌	18♌	24♋	15♐R	22♓R	10♉	15♍	27♋
U 2	20 41 38	9 30 21	24 38	19	19	25	15	22	10	15	27
G 3	20 45 35	10 27 45	8♒24	21	20	25	15	22	10	15	27
U 4	20 49 31	11 25 10	22 30	23	21	26	15	22	10	15	27
S 5	20 53 28	12 22 37	6♓50	25	22	26	15	22	10	15	27
T 6	20 57 24	13 20 4	21 19	26	24	27	15	22	10	15	27
7	21 1 21	14 17 32	5♈50	28	25	28	15	22	10	15	27
8	21 5 17	15 15 2	20 18	0♍	26	28	15	22	10	15	28
9	21 9 14	16 12 33	4♉39	2	27	29	15	21	10	15	28
10	21 13 10	17 10 6	18 49	4	29	0♌	15	21	10	15	28
11	21 17 7	18 7 40	2♊47	5	0♍	0	15 D	21	10	15	28
12	21 21 4	19 5 15	16 32	7	1	1	15	21	10	15	28
13	21 25 0	20 2 53	0♋ 4	9	2	2	15	21	10	16	28
14	21 28 57	21 0 31	13 25	10	4	2	15	21	10	16	28
15	21 32 53	21 58 11	26 34	12	5	3	15	21	10 R	16	28
16	21 36 50	22 55 52	9♌31	13	6	4	15	21	10	16	28
17	21 40 46	23 53 35	22 16	15	7	4	15	21	10	16	28
18	21 44 43	24 51 18	4♍49	16	9	5	15	21	10	16	28
19	21 48 39	25 49 4	17 11	18	10	6	15	21	10	16	28
20	21 52 36	26 46 50	29 21	19	11	6	15	21	10	16	28
21	21 56 33	27 44 38	11♎22	21	12	7	15	21	10	16	28
22	22 0 29	28 42 26	23 17	22	13	7	15	21	10	16	28
23	22 4 26	29 40 17	5♏ 8	24	15	8	15	21	10	16	28
24	22 8 22	0♍38 8	16 59	25	16	9	15	21	10	16	28
25	22 12 19	1 36 1	28 55	26	17	9	15	20	10	16	28
26	22 16 15	2 33 55	11♐ 1	28	18	10	15	20	10	16	28
27	22 20 12	3 31 50	23 23	29	20	11	15	20	10	16	28
28	22 24 8	4 29 46	6♑ 5	0♎	21	11	15	20	10	16	28
29	22 28 5	5 27 44	19 11	2	22	12	15	20	10	16	28
30	22 32 2	6 25 43	2♒44	3	23	13	15	20	10	16	28
31	22 35 58	7 23 44	16 45	4	25	13	15	20	9	16	28

THE SUN ENTERS THE SIGN OF VIRGO ON AUG 23 AT 08:11.

DAY	TIME h m s	☉ ° ' "	☽ ° '	☿ °	♀ °	♂ °	♃ °	♄ °	♅ °	♆ °	♇ °
S 1	22 39 55	8♍21 46	1♓ 9	5♎	26♍	14♌	15♐	20♓R	9♉R	16♍	28♋
E 2	22 43 51	9 19 50	15 53	6	27	14	15	20	9	16	28
P 3	22 47 48	10 17 55	0♈48	7	28	15	15	20	9	16	28
T 4	22 51 44	11 16 3	15 44	8	29	16	15	20	9	16	28
E 5	22 55 41	12 14 12	0♉34	9	1♎	16	15	20	9	16	28
M 6	22 59 37	13 12 23	15 10	10	2	17	16	20	9	16	28
B 7	23 3 34	14 10 36	29 28	11	3	18	16	20	9	16	28
E 8	23 7 30	15 8 52	13♊25	12	4	18	16	19	9	16	28
R 9	23 11 27	16 7 9	27 3	13	6	19	16	19	9	16	28
10	23 15 24	17 5 29	10♋23	13	7	20	16	19	9	17	28
11	23 19 20	18 3 50	23 26	14	8	20	16	19	9	17	28
12	23 23 17	19 2 14	6♌16	15	9	21	16	19	9	17	28
13	23 27 13	20 0 40	18 55	15	11	21	16	19	9	17	28
14	23 31 10	20 59 7	1♍23	16	12	22	16	19	9	17	28
15	23 35 6	21 57 37	13 42	16	13	23	16	19	9	17	28
16	23 39 3	22 56 8	25 52	16	14	23	16	19	9	17	28
17	23 42 59	23 54 42	7♎55	16	16	24	17	19	9	17	28
18	23 46 56	24 53 17	19 51	16 R	17	25	17	19	9	17	28
19	23 50 53	25 51 54	1♏42	16	18	25	17	19	9	17	28
20	23 54 49	26 50 33	13 31	16	19	26	17	18	9	17	28
21	23 58 46	27 49 14	25 21	16	20	26	17	18	9	17	28
22	0 2 42	28 47 56	7♐15	16	22	27	17	18	9	17	28
23	0 6 39	29 46 41	19 19	15	23	28	17	18	9	17	28
24	0 10 35	0♎45 27	1♑37	15	24	28	17	18	9	17	28
25	0 14 32	1 44 15	14 15	14	25	29	17	18	9	17	29
26	0 18 28	2 43 4	27 17	13	27	0♍	18	18	9	17	29
27	0 22 25	3 41 55	10♒48	12	28	0	18	18	9	17	29
28	0 26 22	4 40 48	24 49	11	29	1	18	18	9	17	29
29	0 30 18	5 39 43	9♓19	10	0♏	1	18	18	9	17	29
30	0 34 15	6 38 39	24 14	9	2	2	18	18	9	17	29

THE SUN ENTERS THE SIGN OF LIBRA ON SEP 23 AT 05:27.

DAY	TIME h m s	☉ ° ' "	☽ ° '	☿ °	♀ °	♂ °	♃ °	♄ °	♅ °	♆ °	♇ °
O 1	0 38 11	7♎37 37	9♈24	8♎R	3♏	3♍	18♐	18♓R	9♉R	17♍	29♋
C 2	0 42 8	8 36 38	24 39	7	4	3	18	18	9	17	29
T 3	0 46 4	9 35 41	9♉49	5	5	4	19	18	9	17	29
O 4	0 50 1	10 34 46	24 44	4	6	5	19	18	9	17	29
B 5	0 53 57	11 33 53	9♊16	4	8	5	19	17	9	17	29
E 6	0 57 54	12 33 3	23 24	3	9	6	19	17	9	17	29
R 7	1 1 51	13 32 14	7♋ 5	2	10	6	19	17	9	18	29
8	1 5 47	14 31 29	20 23	2	11	7	19	17	9	18	29
9	1 9 44	15 30 45	3♌21	1	13	8	19	17	8	18	29
10	1 13 40	16 30 4	16 1	1 D	14	8	20	17	8	18	29
11	1 17 37	17 29 25	28 27	1	15	9	20	17	8	18	29
12	1 21 33	18 28 49	10♍42	2	16	10	20	17	8	18	29
13	1 25 30	19 28 14	22 49	2	17	10	20	17	8	18	29
14	1 29 26	20 27 42	4♎50	3	19	11	20	17	8	18	29
15	1 33 23	21 27 12	16 46	3	20	11	20	17	8	18	29
16	1 37 19	22 26 44	28 38	4	21	12	21	17	8	18	29
17	1 41 16	23 26 18	10♏28	5	22	13	21	17	8	18	29
18	1 45 13	24 25 54	22 17	6	24	13	21	17	8	18	29
19	1 49 9	25 25 32	4♐ 8	8	25	14	21	17	8	18	29
20	1 53 6	26 25 11	16 5	9	26	14	21	17	8	18	29
21	1 57 2	27 24 53	28 9	10	27	15	21	17	8	18	29
22	2 0 59	28 24 36	10♑27	12	29	16	22	16	8	18	29
23	2 4 55	29 24 22	23 2	13	0♐	16	22	16	8	18	29
24	2 8 52	0♏24 8	5♒59	15	1	17	22	16	8	18	29
25	2 12 48	1 23 57	19 22	16	2	18	22	16	8	18	29
26	2 16 45	2 23 47	3♓14	18	3	18	22	16	8	18	29
27	2 20 42	3 23 38	17 36	19	5	19	22	16	8	18	29
28	2 24 38	4 23 32	2♈23	21	6	19	23	16	8	18	29
29	2 28 35	5 23 27	17 31	23	7	20	23	16	8	18	29
30	2 32 31	6 23 24	2♉50	24	8	21	23	16	8	18	29 R
31	2 36 28	7 23 23	18 8	26	10	21	23	16	8	18	29

THE SUN ENTERS THE SIGN OF SCORPIO ON OCT 23 AT 14:19.

DAY	TIME h m s	☉ ° ' "	☽ ° '	☿ °	♀ °	♂ °	♃ °	♄ °	♅ °	♆ °	♇ °
N 1	2 40 24	8♏23 24	3♊14	28♎	11♐	22♍	23♐	16♓R	8♉R	18♍	29♋R
O 2	2 44 21	9 23 27	18 1	29	12	22	24	16	8	18	29
V 3	2 48 17	10 23 32	2♋21	1♏	13	23	24	16	7	18	29
E 4	2 52 14	11 23 39	16 14	3	14	24	24	16	7	18	29
M 5	2 56 11	12 23 48	29 40	4	16	24	24	16	7	18	29
B 6	3 0 7	13 24 0	12♌40	6	17	25	24	16	7	18	29
E 7	3 4 4	14 24 13	25 20	7	18	25	25	16	7	18	29
R 8	3 8 0	15 24 28	7♍42	9	19	26	25	16	7	18	29
9	3 11 57	16 24 46	19 52	11	21	27	25	16	7	18	29
10	3 15 53	17 25 5	1♎52	12	22	27	25	16	7	19	29
11	3 19 50	18 25 26	13 46	14	23	28	25	16	7	19	29
12	3 23 46	19 25 49	25 38	16	24	28	26	16	7	19	29
13	3 27 43	20 26 14	7♏28	17	25	29	26	16	7	19	29
14	3 31 40	21 26 41	19 19	19	27	0♎	26	16	7	19	29
15	3 35 36	22 27 9	1♐13	20	28	0	26	16	7	19	29
16	3 39 33	23 27 39	13 11	22	29	1	26	16	7	19	29
17	3 43 29	24 28 11	25 16	24	0♑	1	27	16	7	19	29
18	3 47 26	25 28 43	7♑29	25	1	2	27	16	7	19	29
19	3 51 22	26 29 18	19 54	27	3	3	27	16 D	7	19	29
20	3 55 19	27 29 53	2♒34	28	4	3	27	16	7	19	29
21	3 59 15	28 30 30	15 31	0♐	5	4	28	16	7	19	29
22	4 3 12	29 31 7	28 50	2	6	4	28	16	7	19	29
23	4 7 9	0♐31 46	12♓32	3	8	5	28	16	7	19	29
24	4 11 5	1 32 26	26 38	5	9	6	28	16	7	19	29
25	4 15 2	2 33 7	11♈ 8	6	10	6	28	16	7	19	29
26	4 18 58	3 33 50	25 57	8	11	7	29	16	7	19	29
27	4 22 55	4 34 33	10♉59	9	12	7	29	16	7	19	29
28	4 26 51	5 35 18	26 6	11	14	8	29	16	6	19	29
29	4 30 48	6 36 4	11♊ 8	12	15	9	29	16	6	19	29
30	4 34 44	7 36 51	25 57	14	16	9	29	16	6	19	29

THE SUN ENTERS THE SIGN OF SAGITTARIUS ON NOV 22 AT 11:26.

DAY	TIME h m s	☉ ° ' "	☽ ° '	☿ °	♀ °	♂ °	♃ °	♄ °	♅ °	♆ °	♇ °
D 1	4 38 41	8♐37 39	10♋24	16♐	17♑	10♎	0♑	16♓	6♉R	19♍	29♋R
E 2	4 42 38	9 38 29	24 26	17	18	10	0	16	6	19	29
C 3	4 46 34	10 39 20	8♌ 2	19	20	11	0	16	6	19	29
E 4	4 50 31	11 40 12	21 11	20	21	11	0	16	6	19	29
M 5	4 54 27	12 41 6	3♍56	22	22	12	1	16	6	19	28
B 6	4 58 24	13 42 1	16 22	23	23	13	1	16	6	19	28
E 7	5 2 20	14 42 57	28 32	25	24	13	1	16	6	19	28
R 8	5 6 17	15 43 55	10♎31	26	26	14	1	16	6	19	28
9	5 10 14	16 44 53	22 23	28	27	14	1	16	6	19	28
10	5 14 10	17 45 53	4♏12	0♑	28	15	2	16	6	19	28
11	5 18 7	18 46 54	16 2	1	29	16	2	16	6	19	28
12	5 22 3	19 47 56	27 57	3	0♒	16	2	16	6	19	28
13	5 26 0	20 48 59	9♐57	4	2	17	2	16	6	19	28
14	5 29 56	21 50 2	22 6	6	3	17	3	16	6	19	28
15	5 33 53	22 51 7	4♑25	7	4	18	3	16	6	19	28
16	5 37 49	23 52 12	16 55	9	5	18	3	16	6	19	28
17	5 41 46	24 53 18	29 37	10	6	19	3	16	6	19	28
18	5 45 43	25 54 24	12♒33	12	8	20	4	17	6	19	28
19	5 49 39	26 55 30	25 42	13	9	20	4	17	6	19	28
20	5 53 36	27 56 37	9♓ 7	15	10	21	4	17	6	19	28
21	5 57 32	28 57 44	22 48	16	11	21	4	17	6	19 R	28
22	6 1 29	29 58 51	6♈45	18	12	22	4	17	6	19	28
23	6 5 25	0♑59 58	20 57	19	14	22	5	17	6	19	28
24	6 9 22	2 1 5	5♉22	20	15	23	5	17	6	19	28
25	6 13 18	3 2 13	19 58	22	16	23	5	17	6	19	28
26	6 17 15	4 3 20	4♊39	23	17	24	5	17	6	19	28
27	6 21 12	5 4 28	19 19	24	18	25	6	17	6	19	28
28	6 25 8	6 5 36	3♋51	26	19	25	6	17	6	19	28
29	6 29 5	7 6 44	18 10	27	21	26	6	17	6	19	28
30	6 33 1	8 7 53	2♌10	28	22	26	6	17	6	19	28
31	6 36 58	9 9 1	15 48	29	23	27	7	17	6	19	28

THE SUN ENTERS THE SIGN OF CAPRICORN ON DEC 22 AT 00:27.

♈ ARIES ♉ TAURUS ♊ GEMINI ♋ CANCER ♌ LEO ♍ VIRGO ♎ LIBRA ♏ SCORPIO ♐ SAGITTARIUS ♑ CAPRICORN ♒ AQUARIUS ♓ PISCES

1937

SIDEREAL SUN MOON MERCURY VENUS MARS JUPITER SATURN URANUS NEPTUNE PLUTO

DAY	TIME	☉	☽	☿	♀	♂	♃	♄	♅	♆	♇
	h m s	° ' "	° '	°	°	°	°	°	°	°	°
J 1	6 40 54	10♑10 10	29♌ 3	29♑	24♒	27♎	7♑	17♓	6♉R	19♍R	28♋R
A 2	6 44 51	11 11 19	11♍54	0♒	25	28	7	17	6	19	28
N 3	6 48 47	12 12 28	24 24	1	26	28	7	17	6	19	28
U 4	6 52 44	13 13 38	6♎38	1	28	29	7	18	6	19	28
A 5	6 56 41	14 14 48	18 38	1 R	29	0♏	8	18	6	19	28
R 6	7 0 37	15 15 58	0♏30	2	0♓	0	8	18	6	19	28
Y 7	7 4 34	16 17 8	12 20	1	1	1	8	18	6	19	28
8	7 8 30	17 18 18	24 11	1	2	1	8	18	6	19	28
9	7 12 27	18 19 28	6♐ 8	1	3	2	9	18	6	19	28
10	7 16 23	19 20 38	18 15	0	4	2	9	18	6	19	28
11	7 20 20	20 21 48	0♑34	29♑	6	3	9	18	6	19	28
12	7 24 16	21 22 58	13 9	28	7	3	9	18	6	19	28
13	7 28 13	22 24 8	25 59	27	8	4	10	18	6 D	19	28
14	7 32 10	23 25 17	9♒ 4	26	9	4	10	18	6	19	28
15	7 36 6	24 26 25	22 25	24	10	5	10	18	6	19	28
16	7 40 3	25 27 33	5♓58	23	11	5	10	19	6	19	28
17	7 43 59	26 28 40	19 42	22	12	6	10	19	6	19	28
18	7 47 56	27 29 47	3♈36	20	13	6	11	19	6	19	28
19	7 51 52	28 30 52	17 36	19	15	7	11	19	6	19	28
20	7 55 49	29 31 57	1♉42	18	16	7	11	19	6	19	28
21	7 59 45	0♒33 0	15 51	17	17	8	11	19	6	19	28
22	8 3 42	1 34 3	0♊ 4	17	18	9	12	19	6	19	28
23	8 7 39	2 35 5	14 16	16	19	9	12	19	6	19	28
24	8 11 35	3 36 6	28 27	16	20	10	12	19	6	19	28
25	8 15 32	4 37 5	12♋32	16	21	10	12	19	6	19	27
26	8 19 28	5 38 4	26 28	15 D	22	11	12	20	6	19	27
27	8 23 25	6 39 2	10♌12	15	23	11	13	20	6	19	27
28	8 27 21	7 39 59	23 39	16	24	12	13	20	6	19	27
29	8 31 18	8 40 55	6♍48	16	25	12	13	20	6	19	27
30	8 35 15	9 41 50	19 38	16	26	13	13	20	6	19	27
31	8 39 11	10 42 44	2♎ 9	17	27	13	14	20	6	19	27

THE SUN ENTERS THE SIGN OF AQUARIUS ON JAN 20 AT 11:01.

DAY	TIME	☉	☽	☿	♀	♂	♃	♄	♅	♆	♇
	h m s	° ' "	° '	°	°	°	°	°	°	°	°
F 1	8 43 8	11♒43 38	14♎24	17♑	29♓	14♏	14♑	20♓	6♉	19♍R	27♋R
E 2	8 47 4	12 44 31	26 26	18	0☉	14	14	20	6	18	27
B 3	8 51 1	13 45 23	8♏19	19	1♈	14	14	20	6	18	27
R 4	8 54 57	14 46 13	20 8	19	2	15	14	20	6	18	27
U 5	8 58 54	15 47 4	1♐59	20	3	15	15	21	6	18	27
A 6	9 2 50	16 47 53	13 57	21	4	16	15	21	6	18	27
R 7	9 6 47	17 48 41	26 7	22	5	16	15	21	6	18	27
Y 8	9 10 44	18 49 28	8♑33	23	6	17	15	21	6	18	27
9	9 14 40	19 50 15	21 18	24	7	17	15	21	6	18	27
10	9 18 37	20 50 59	4♒24	25	8	18	16	21	6	18	27
11	9 22 33	21 51 43	17 52	26	9	18	16	21	6	18	27
12	9 26 30	22 52 25	1♓38	28	10	19	16	21	6	18	27
13	9 30 26	23 53 6	15 40	29	10	19	16	21	6	18	27
14	9 34 23	24 53 45	29 53	0♒	11	20	17	22	6	18	27
15	9 38 19	25 54 23	14♈10	1	12	20	17	22	6	18	27
16	9 42 16	26 54 59	28 28	3	13	20	17	22	6	18	27
17	9 46 12	27 55 33	12♉42	4	14	21	17	22	6	18	27
18	9 50 9	28 56 5	26 51	5	15	21	17	22	6	18	27
19	9 54 6	29 56 35	10♊53	6	16	22	18	22	6	18	27
20	9 58 2	0♓57 4	24 47	8	17	22	18	22	6	18	27
21	10 1 59	1 57 31	8♋33	9	18	23	18	22	6	18	27
22	10 5 55	2 57 56	22 12	11	19	23	18	23	6	18	27
23	10 9 52	3 58 19	5♌41	12	19	23	18	23	6	18	27
24	10 13 48	4 58 40	19 0	14	20	24	18	23	6	18	27
25	10 17 45	5 58 59	2♍ 8	15	21	24	19	23	6	18	27
26	10 21 41	6 59 16	15 2	16	22	25	19	23	6	18	27
27	10 25 38	7 59 32	27 41	18	23	25	19	23	6	18	27
28	10 29 35	8 59 46	10♎ 6	20	23	25	19	23	6	18	27

THE SUN ENTERS THE SIGN OF PISCES ON FEB 19 AT 01:20.

DAY	TIME	☉	☽	☿	♀	♂	♃	♄	♅	♆	♇
	h m s	° ' "	° '	°	°	°	°	°	°	°	°
M 1	10 33 31	9♓59 59	22♎17	21♒	24♈	26♏	19♑	23♓	7♉	18♍R	27♋R
A 2	10 37 28	11 0 10	4♏17	23	25	26	20	23	7	18	27
R 3	10 41 24	12 0 19	16 9	24	26	27	20	24	7	18	27
C 4	10 45 21	13 0 27	27 58	26	26	27	20	24	7	18	27
H 5	10 49 17	14 0 33	9♐48	27	27	27	20	24	7	18	27
6	10 53 14	15 0 38	21 44	29	28	28	20	24	7	18	27
7	10 57 10	16 0 41	3♑53	1♓	28	28	21	24	7	18	27
8	11 1 7	17 0 43	16 19	2	29	28	21	24	7	18	27
9	11 5 4	18 0 42	29 8	4	0♉	29	21	24	7	18	27
10	11 9 0	19 0 41	12♒22	6	0	29	21	24	7	18	27
11	11 12 57	20 0 37	26 2	7	1	29	21	25	7	18	27
12	11 16 53	21 0 31	10♓ 6	9	1	0♐	21	25	7	18	27
13	11 20 50	22 0 24	24 32	11	2	0	22	25	7	17	27
14	11 24 46	23 0 14	9♈10	13	2	0	22	25	7	17	27
15	11 28 43	24 0 3	23 55	15	3	1	22	25	7	17	27
16	11 32 39	24 59 49	8♉38	16	3	1	22	25	7	17	27
17	11 36 36	25 59 33	23 12	18	4	1	22	25	7	17	27
18	11 40 33	26 59 15	7♊33	20	4	1	22	25	7	17	27
19	11 44 29	27 58 55	21 39	22	4	2	23	26	7	17	27
20	11 48 26	28 58 32	5♋29	24	5	2	23	26	7	17	27
21	11 52 22	29 58 7	19 5	26	5	2	23	26	7	17	27
22	11 56 19	0♈57 40	2♌26	28	5	2	23	26	7	17	27
23	12 0 15	1 57 10	15 35	0☉	5	3	23	26	7	17	27
24	12 4 12	2 56 38	28 32	2♈	6	3	23	26	8	17	27
25	12 8 8	3 56 4	11♍18	4	6	3	23	26	8	17	27
26	12 12 5	4 55 28	23 53	6	6	3	24	26	8	17	27
27	12 16 2	5 54 49	6♎17	8	6 R	4	24	27	8	17	27
28	12 19 58	6 54 9	18 31	10	6	4	24	27	8	17	27
29	12 23 55	7 53 27	0♏34	12	6	4	24	27	8	17	27
30	12 27 51	8 52 42	12 30	14	6	4	24	27	8	17	27
31	12 31 48	9 51 56	24 20	16	6	4	24	27	8	17	27

THE SUN ENTERS THE SIGN OF ARIES ON MAR 21 AT 00:45.

SIDEREAL SUN MOON MERCURY VENUS MARS JUPITER SATURN URANUS NEPTUNE PLUTO

DAY	TIME	☉	☽	☿	♀	♂	♃	♄	♅	♆	♇
	h m s	° ' "	° '	°	°	°	°	°	°	°	°
A 1	12 35 44	10♈51 8	6♐ 7	18♈	5♉R	4♐	24♑	27♓	8♉	17♍R	27♋R
P 2	12 39 41	11 50 18	17 56	20	5	5	24	27	8	17	27
R 3	12 43 37	12 49 26	29 52	22	5	5	25	27	8	17	27
I 4	12 47 34	13 48 33	11♑59	24	5	5	25	28	8	17	27
L 5	12 51 30	14 47 38	24 23	26	4	5	25	28	8	17	26
6	12 55 27	15 46 41	7♒ 9	28	4	5	25	28	8	17	26
7	12 59 24	16 45 42	20 22	0♉	4	5	25	28	8	17	26
8	13 3 20	17 44 41	4♓ 3	2	3	5	25	28	8	17	26
9	13 7 17	18 43 39	18 12	4	3	5	25	28	8	17	26 D
10	13 11 13	19 42 34	2♈46	5	2	5	25	28	8	17	26
11	13 15 10	20 41 28	17 40	7	2	5	25	28	8	17	26
12	13 19 6	21 40 20	2♉44	9	1	5	26	28	9	17	26
13	13 23 3	22 39 9	17 48	10	1	6	26	29	9	17	26
14	13 26 59	23 37 57	2♊44	12	0	6 R	26	29	9	17	26
15	13 30 56	24 36 42	17 24	13	0	6	26	29	9	17	27
16	13 34 53	25 35 26	1♋45	15	29♈	6	26	29	9	17	27
17	13 38 49	26 34 7	15 43	16	28	5	26	29	9	17	27
18	13 42 46	27 32 46	29 20	17	28	5	26	29	9	17	27
19	13 46 42	28 31 22	12♌37	18	27	5	26	29	9	17	27
20	13 50 39	29 29 56	25 35	19	26	5	26	29	9	17	27
21	13 54 35	0♉28 28	8♍19	20	26	5	26	0☉	9	17	27
22	13 58 32	1 26 58	20 49	21	25	5	26	0	9	17	27
23	14 2 28	2 25 26	3♎ 8	22	25	5	27	0	9	16	27
24	14 6 25	3 23 52	15 18	23	24	5	27	0	9	16	27
25	14 10 22	4 22 16	27 20	23	23	5	27	0	9	16	27
26	14 14 18	5 20 38	9♏16	24	23	5	27	0♈	9	16	27
27	14 18 15	6 18 58	21 6	24	22	5	27	0	9	16	27
28	14 22 11	7 17 16	2♐54	24	22	4	27	0	9	16	27
29	14 26 8	8 15 33	14 42	24	22	4	27	0	10	16	27
30	14 30 4	9 13 48	26 33	24 R	21	4	27	1	10	16	27

THE SUN ENTERS THE SIGN OF TAURUS ON APR 20 AT 12:19.

DAY	TIME	☉	☽	☿	♀	♂	♃	♄	♅	♆	♇
	h m s	° ' "	° '	°	°	°	°	°	°	°	°
M 1	14 34 1	10♉12 2	8♑31	24♉R	21♈R	4♐R	27♑	1♈	10♉	16♍R	27♋
A 2	14 37 57	11 10 14	20 39	24	20	4	27	1	10	16	27
Y 3	14 41 54	12 8 24	3♒ 3	24	20	3	27	1	10	16	27
4	14 45 51	13 6 34	15 47	24	20	3	27	1	10	16	27
5	14 49 47	14 4 41	28 55	24	20	3	27	1	10	16	27
6	14 53 44	15 2 47	12♓29	23	20	3	27	1	10	16	27
7	14 57 40	16 0 52	26 32	23	20	2	27	1	10	16	27
8	15 1 37	16 58 56	11♈ 2	22	19	2	27	1	10	16	27
9	15 5 33	17 56 58	25 54	22	19 D	2	27	1	10	16	27
10	15 9 30	18 54 58	11♉ 1	21	19	2	27	2	10	16	27
11	15 13 26	19 52 57	26 14	21	19	1	27	2	10	16	27
12	15 17 23	20 50 55	11♊23	20	20	1	27	2	10	16	27
13	15 21 20	21 48 51	26 19	19	20	1	27	2	10	16	27
14	15 25 16	22 46 45	10♋54	19	20	0	27	2	10	16	27
15	15 29 13	23 44 38	25 6	18	20	0	27 R	2	10	16	27
16	15 33 9	24 42 28	8♌52	18	20	0	27	2	10	16	27
17	15 37 6	25 40 17	22 13	17	21	29♏	27	2	11	16	27
18	15 41 2	26 38 4	5♍12	17	21	29	27	2	11	16	27
19	15 44 59	27 35 50	17 50	16	21	29	27	2	11	16	27
20	15 48 55	28 33 33	0♎13	16	22	28	27	2	11	16	27
21	15 52 52	29 31 16	12 23	16	22	28	27	3	11	16	27
22	15 56 49	0♊28 56	24 23	15	22	28	27	3	11	16	27
23	16 0 45	1 26 36	6♏17	15	23	27	27	3	11	16	27
24	16 4 42	2 24 14	18 7	15 D	23	27	27	3	11	16	27
25	16 8 38	3 21 50	29 55	15	24	27	27	3	11	16	27
26	16 12 35	4 19 26	11♐44	15	24	26	27	3	11	16	27
27	16 16 31	5 17 0	23 36	16	25	26	27	3	11	16 D	27
28	16 20 28	6 14 34	5♑33	16	25	25	27	3	11	16	27
29	16 24 24	7 12 6	17 38	16	26	25	27	3	11	16	27
30	16 28 21	8 9 37	29 53	17	27	25	27	3	11	16	27
31	16 32 18	9 7 7	12♒22	17	27	24	27	3	11	16	27

THE SUN ENTERS THE SIGN OF GEMINI ON MAY 21 AT 11:57.

DAY	TIME	☉	☽	☿	♀	♂	♃	♄	♅	♆	♇
	h m s	° ' "	° '	°	°	°	°	°	°	°	°
J 1	16 36 14	10♊ 4 37	25♒ 9	18♉	28♈	24♏R	27♑R	3♈	11♉	16♍	27♋
U 2	16 40 11	11 2 6	8♓15	18	28	24	27	3	11	16	27
N 3	16 44 7	11 59 34	21 44	19	29	24	27	4	11	16	27
E 4	16 48 4	12 57 1	5♈37	20	0♉	23	27	4	12	16	27
5	16 52 0	13 54 28	19 54	20	1	23	27	4	12	16	27
6	16 55 57	14 51 54	4♉33	21	1	23	27	4	12	16	27
7	16 59 53	15 49 20	19 28	22	2	22	27	4	12	16	27
8	17 3 50	16 46 44	4♊33	23	3	22	26	4	12	16	27
9	17 7 47	17 44 8	19 40	24	4	22	26	4	12	16	27
10	17 11 43	18 41 32	4♋39	25	4	22	26	4	12	16	27
11	17 15 40	19 38 54	19 21	26	5	21	26	4	12	16	27
12	17 19 36	20 36 16	3♌42	28	6	21	26	4	12	16	27
13	17 23 33	21 33 36	17 37	29	7	21	26	4	12	16	27
14	17 27 29	22 30 56	1♍ 6	0♊	8	21	26	4	12	16	27
15	17 31 26	23 28 14	14 9	1	8	21	26	4	12	16	27
16	17 35 22	24 25 32	26 49	3	9	20	26	4	12	16	27
17	17 39 19	25 22 49	9♎10	4	10	20	26	4	12	16	27
18	17 43 16	26 20 5	21 16	6	11	20	26	4	12	16	27
19	17 47 12	27 17 21	3♏13	7	12	20	26	4	12	16	27
20	17 51 9	28 14 35	15 3	9	13	20	25	5	12	16	27
21	17 55 5	29 11 49	26 50	11	14	20	25	5	12	16	27
22	17 59 2	0♋ 9 3	8♐39	12	15	20	25	5	12	16	28
23	18 2 58	1 6 16	20 32	14	15	20	25	5	12	16	28
24	18 6 55	2 3 29	2♑31	16	16	20	25	5	12	16	28
25	18 10 51	3 0 41	14 39	18	17	20	25	5	12	16	28
26	18 14 48	3 57 53	26 57	20	18	20	25	5	13	16	28
27	18 18 45	4 55 5	9♒26	22	19	20 D	25	5	13	16	28
28	18 22 41	5 52 17	22 9	24	20	20	25	5	13	16	28
29	18 26 38	6 49 29	5♓ 6	26	21	20	24	5	13	16	28
30	18 30 34	7 46 41	18 18	28	22	20	24	5	13	16	28

THE SUN ENTERS THE SIGN OF CANCER ON JUN 21 AT 20:12.

♈ ARIES ♉ TAURUS ♊ GEMINI ♋ CANCER ♌ LEO ♍ VIRGO ♎ LIBRA ♏ SCORPIO ♐ SAGITTARIUS ♑ CAPRICORN ♒ AQUARIUS ♓ PISCES

SIDEREAL SUN MOON MERCURY VENUS MARS JUPITER SATURN URANUS NEPTUNE PLUTO

DAY	TIME	☉	☽	☿	♀	♂	♃	♄	♅	♆	♇
	h m s	° ' "	° '	°	°	°	°	°	°	°	°
J 1	18 34 31	8♋43 52	1♈47	0♋	23♉	20♏	24♑R	5♈	13♉	16♍	28♋
U 2	18 38 27	9 41 5	15 35	2	24	20	24	5	13	17	28
L 3	18 42 24	10 38 17	29 39	4	25	20	24	5	13	17	28
Y 4	18 46 20	11 35 30	14♉ 1	6	26	20	24	5	13	17	28
5	18 50 17	12 32 43	28 37	8	27	20	24	5	13	17	28
6	18 54 14	13 29 56	13♊23	11	28	20	24	5	13	17	28
7	18 58 10	14 27 10	28 13	13	29	20	23	5	13	17	28
8	19 2 7	15 24 23	13♋ 0	15	0♊	20	23	5	13	17	28
9	19 6 3	16 21 37	27 36	17	1	20	23	5	13	17	28
10	19 10 0	17 18 51	11♌55	19	2	21	23	5	13	17	28
11	19 13 56	18 16 5	25 52	21	3	21	23	5	13	17	28
12	19 17 53	19 13 19	9♍24	23	4	21	23	5	13	17	28
13	19 21 50	20 10 33	22 30	26	5	21	23	5	13	17	28
14	19 25 46	21 7 47	5♎13	28	6	21	23	5	13	17	28
15	19 29 43	22 5 1	17 35	0♌	7	22	22	5	13	17	28
16	19 33 39	23 2 15	29 42	2	8	22	22	5	13	17	28
17	19 37 36	23 59 29	11♏37	4	9	22	22	5 R	13	17	28
18	19 41 32	24 56 43	23 27	6	11	22	22	5	13	17	28
19	19 45 29	25 53 58	5♐15	8	12	23	22	5	13	17	28
20	19 49 25	26 51 13	17 6	9	13	23	22	5	13	17	28
21	19 53 22	27 48 28	29 4	11	14	23	22	5	13	17	28
22	19 57 19	28 45 44	11♑13	13	15	23	22	5	13	17	28
23	20 1 15	29 43 0	23 34	15	16	24	21	5	13	17	28
24	20 5 12	0♌40 17	6♒ 8	17	17	24	21	5	13	17	28
25	20 9 8	1 37 34	18 57	19	18	24	21	5	13	17	28
26	20 13 5	2 34 52	2♓ 0	20	19	25	21	5	13	17	28
27	20 17 1	3 32 11	15 15	22	20	25	21	5	13	17	28
28	20 20 58	4 29 31	28 43	24	21	25	21	5	13	17	28
29	20 24 54	5 26 52	12♈23	25	22	26	21	5	13	17	29
30	20 28 51	6 24 13	26 13	27	24	26	21	5	14	17	29
31	20 32 48	7 21 37	10♉13	29	25	26	20	5	14	17	29

THE SUN ENTERS THE SIGN OF LEO ON JUL 23 AT 07:07.

DAY	TIME	☉	☽	☿	♀	♂	♃	♄	♅	♆	♇
	h m s	° ' "	° '	°	°	°	°	°	°	°	°
A 1	20 36 44	8♌19 1	24♉22	0♍	26♊	27♏	20♑R	5♈R	14♉	17♍	29♋
U 2	20 40 41	9 16 26	8♊39	2	27	27	20	5	14	17	29
G 3	20 44 37	10 13 53	23 3	3	28	28	20	5	14	17	29
U 4	20 48 34	11 11 20	7♋29	5	29	28	20	5	14	17	29
S 5	20 52 30	12 8 49	21 53	6	0♋	28	20	5	14	17	29
T 6	20 56 27	13 6 19	6♌10	8	1	29	20	5	14	17	29
7	21 0 23	14 3 50	20 15	9	2	29	20	5	14	17	29
8	21 4 20	15 1 22	4♍ 3	10	4	0♐	20	5	14	17	29
9	21 8 17	15 58 55	17 29	12	5	0	19	5	14	17	29
10	21 12 13	16 56 29	0♎33	13	6	0	19	5	14	18	29
11	21 16 10	17 54 3	13 15	14	7	1	19	5	14	18	29
12	21 20 6	18 51 39	25 38	15	8	1	19	5	14	18	29
13	21 24 3	19 49 15	7♏44	17	9	2	19	5	14	18	29
14	21 27 59	20 46 53	19 40	18	10	2	19	4	14	18	29
15	21 31 56	21 44 32	1♐29	19	11	3	19	4	14	18	29
16	21 35 52	22 42 11	13 18	20	13	3	19	4	14	18	29
17	21 39 49	23 39 52	25 11	21	14	4	19	4	14	18	29
18	21 43 46	24 37 34	7♑14	22	15	4	19	4	14	18	29
19	21 47 42	25 35 17	19 31	23	16	5	19	4	14 R	18	29
20	21 51 39	26 33 1	2♒ 4	24	17	5	18	4	14	18	29
21	21 55 35	27 30 46	14 55	25	18	6	18	4	14	18	29
22	21 59 32	28 28 32	28 4	25	20	6	18	4	14	18	29
23	22 3 28	29 26 20	11♓30	26	21	7	18	4	14	18	29
24	22 7 25	0♍24 10	25 10	27	22	7	18	4	14	18	29
25	22 11 21	1 22 1	9♈ 2	28	23	8	18	4	14	18	29
26	22 15 18	2 19 54	23 0	28	24	8	18	4	14	18	29
27	22 19 14	3 17 48	7♉ 4	29	25	9	18	4	14	18	29
28	22 23 11	4 15 45	21 10	29	26	10	18	4	14	18	29
29	22 27 8	5 13 43	5♊17	29	28	10	18	4	14	18	29
30	22 31 4	6 11 44	19 23	29	29	11	18	4	14	18	29
31	22 35 1	7 9 46	3♋29	0♎	0♌	11	18	4	14	18	29

THE SUN ENTERS THE SIGN OF VIRGO ON AUG 23 AT 13:58.

DAY	TIME	☉	☽	☿	♀	♂	♃	♄	♅	♆	♇
	h m s	° ' "	° '	°	°	°	°	°	°	°	°
S 1	22 38 57	8♍ 7 50	17♋33	0♎R	1♌	12♐	18♑R	3♈R	14♉R	18♍	29♋
E 2	22 42 54	9 5 56	1♌32	0	2	12	18	3	14	18	29
P 3	22 46 50	10 4 4	15 24	29♍	4	13	18	3	14	18	29
T 4	22 50 47	11 2 13	29 6	29	5	13	18	3	14	18	29
E 5	22 54 43	12 0 25	12♍35	29	6	14	18	3	14	18	29
M 6	22 58 40	12 58 38	25 46	28	7	15	18	3	14	18	29
B 7	23 2 37	13 56 52	8♎40	28	8	15	18	3	14	19	0♌
E 8	23 6 33	14 55 9	21 15	27	9	16	18	3	14	19	0
R 9	23 10 30	15 53 27	3♏34	26	11	16	18	3	14	19	0
10	23 14 26	16 51 46	15 38	26	12	17	18	3	14	19	0
11	23 18 23	17 50 8	27 32	25	13	18	17	3	13	19	0
12	23 22 19	18 48 31	9♐21	24	14	18	17	3	13	19	0
13	23 26 16	19 46 55	21 10	23	15	19	17 D	3	13	19	0
14	23 30 12	20 45 21	3♑ 3	22	17	19	17	3	13	19	0
15	23 34 9	21 43 49	15 8	21	18	20	17	2	13	19	0
16	23 38 6	22 42 18	27 28	20	19	21	17	2	13	19	0
17	23 42 2	23 40 49	10♒ 8	19	20	21	17	2	13	19	0
18	23 45 59	24 39 21	23 10	18	21	22	18	2	13	19	0
19	23 49 55	25 37 56	6♓34	17	23	23	18	2	13	19	0
20	23 53 52	26 36 32	20 21	16	24	23	18	2	13	19	0
21	23 57 48	27 35 10	4♈25	16	25	24	18	2	13	19	0
22	0 1 45	28 33 50	18 42	16	26	25	18	2	13	19	0
23	0 5 41	29 32 32	3♉ 7	15 D	27	25	18	2	13	19	0
24	0 9 38	0♎31 17	17 33	15	29	26	18	2	13	19	0
25	0 13 35	1 30 3	1♊56	15	0♍	26	18	2	13	19	0
26	0 17 31	2 28 52	16 12	16	1	27	18	2	13	19	0
27	0 21 28	3 27 43	0♋21	16	2	28	18	2	13	19	0
28	0 25 24	4 26 37	14 20	17	3	28	18	1	13	19	0
29	0 29 21	5 25 33	28 9	18	5	29	18	1	13	19	0
30	0 33 17	6 24 31	11♌48	19	6	0♑	18	1	13	19	0

THE SUN ENTERS THE SIGN OF LIBRA ON SEP 23 AT 11:14.

SIDEREAL SUN MOON MERCURY VENUS MARS JUPITER SATURN URANUS NEPTUNE PLUTO

DAY	TIME	☉	☽	☿	♀	♂	♃	♄	♅	♆	♇
	h m s	° ' "	° '	°	°	°	°	°	°	°	°
O 1	0 37 14	7♎23 31	25♌17	20♍	7♍	0♑	18♑	1♈R	13♉R	19♍	0♌
C 2	0 41 10	8 22 34	8♍34	21	8	1	18	1	13	19	0
T 3	0 45 7	9 21 38	21 39	22	10	2	18	1	13	19	0
O 4	0 49 4	10 20 45	4♎31	23	11	2	18	1	13	20	0
B 5	0 53 0	11 19 54	17 8	25	12	3	18	1	13	20	0
E 6	0 56 57	12 19 5	29 32	26	13	4	18	1	13	20	0
R 7	1 0 53	13 18 18	11♏42	28	14	4	18	1	13	20	0
8	1 4 50	14 17 33	23 42	29	16	5	18	1	13	20	0
9	1 8 46	15 16 49	5♐33	1♎	17	6	18	1	13	20	0
10	1 12 43	16 16 8	17 20	3	18	7	19	1	13	20	0
11	1 16 39	17 15 28	29 7	4	19	7	19	1	13	20	0
12	1 20 36	18 14 51	11♑ 0	6	21	8	19	0	13	20	0
13	1 24 32	19 14 15	23 3	8	22	9	19	0	13	20	0
14	1 28 29	20 13 40	5♒22	9	23	9	19	0	13	20	0
15	1 32 26	21 13 8	18 1	11	24	10	19	0	13	20	0
16	1 36 22	22 12 37	1♓ 4	13	25	11	19	0	12	20	0
17	1 40 19	23 12 8	14 34	15	27	11	19	0	12	20	0
18	1 44 15	24 11 41	28 30	16	28	12	19	0	12	20	0
19	1 48 12	25 11 16	12♈49	18	29	13	19	0⊙	12	20	0
20	1 52 8	26 10 52	27 27	20	0♎	14	19	0	12	20	0
21	1 56 5	27 10 31	12♉15	21	2	14	20	0	12	20	0
22	2 0 1	28 10 12	27 7	23	3	15	20	0	12	20	0
23	2 3 58	29 9 55	11♊54	25	4	16	20	0	12	20	0
24	2 7 55	0♏ 9 40	26 31	27	5	16	20	0	12	20	0
25	2 11 51	1 9 28	10♋53	28	7	17	20	0	12	20	0
26	2 15 48	2 9 17	24 58	0♏	8	18	20	0	12	20	0
27	2 19 44	3 9 10	8♌45	2	9	19	20	29♓	12	20	0
28	2 23 41	4 9 4	22 14	3	10	19	20	29	12	20	0
29	2 27 37	5 9 0	5♍28	5	12	20	21	29	12	20	0
30	2 31 34	6 8 58	18 26	7	13	21	21	29	12	20	0
31	2 35 30	7 8 59	1♎10	8	14	21	21	29	12	20	0 R

THE SUN ENTERS THE SIGN OF SCORPIO ON OCT 23 AT 20:07.

DAY	TIME	☉	☽	☿	♀	♂	♃	♄	♅	♆	♇
	h m s	° ' "	° '	°	°	°	°	°	°	°	°
N 1	2 39 27	8♏ 9 2	13♎41	10♏	15♎	22♑	21♑	29♓R	12♉R	20♍	0♌R
O 2	2 43 24	9 9 6	26 1	11	17	23	21	29	12	20	0
V 3	2 47 20	10 9 13	8♏11	13	18	24	21	29	12	20	0
E 4	2 51 17	11 9 22	20 12	15	19	24	21	29	12	20	0
M 5	2 55 13	12 9 32	2♐ 5	16	20	25	22	29	12	20	0
B 6	2 59 10	13 9 44	13 54	18	21	26	22	29	12	21	0
E 7	3 3 6	14 9 58	25 40	19	23	26	22	29	12	21	0
R 8	3 7 3	15 10 13	7♑27	21	24	27	22	29	12	21	0
9	3 10 59	16 10 30	19 19	23	25	28	22	29	11	21	0
10	3 14 56	17 10 48	1♒21	24	26	29	22	29	11	21	0
11	3 18 53	18 11 8	13 37	26	28	29	22	29	11	21	0
12	3 22 49	19 11 29	26 12	27	29	0♒	23	29	11	21	0
13	3 26 46	20 11 52	9♓ 9	29	0♏	1	23	29	11	21	0
14	3 30 42	21 12 16	22 33	0♐	1	2	23	29	11	21	0
15	3 34 39	22 12 41	6♈25	2	3	2	23	29	11	21	0
16	3 38 35	23 13 8	20 43	3	4	3	23	29	11	21	0
17	3 42 32	24 13 36	5♉26	5	5	4	23	29	11	21	0
18	3 46 28	25 14 6	20 26	6	6	5	24	29	11	21	0
19	3 50 25	26 14 37	5♊35	8	8	5	24	29	11	21	0
20	3 54 22	27 15 10	20 44	9	9	6	24	28	11	21	0
21	3 58 18	28 15 44	5♋44	11	10	7	24	28	11	21	0
22	4 2 15	29 16 20	20 26	12	11	8	24	28	11	21	0
23	4 6 11	0♐16 58	4♌47	14	13	8	25	28	11	21	0
24	4 10 8	1 17 38	18 44	15	14	9	25	28	11	21	0
25	4 14 4	2 18 19	2♍16	17	15	10	25	28	11	21	0
26	4 18 1	3 19 1	15 25	18	16	11	25	28	11	21	0
27	4 21 57	4 19 45	28 14	20	18	11	25	28	11	21	0
28	4 25 54	5 20 31	10♎45	21	19	12	25	28	11	21	0
29	4 29 51	6 21 19	23 2	23	20	13	26	28	11	21	0
30	4 33 47	7 22 7	5♏ 8	24	22	14	26	28	11	21	0

THE SUN ENTERS THE SIGN OF SAGITTARIUS ON NOV 22 AT 17:17.

DAY	TIME	☉	☽	☿	♀	♂	♃	♄	♅	♆	♇
	h m s	° ' "	° '	°	°	°	°	°	°	°	°
D 1	4 37 44	8♐22 58	17♏ 6	26♐	23♏	14♒	26♑	28♓D	11♉R	21♍	0♌R
E 2	4 41 40	9 23 49	28 58	27	24	15	26	28	11	21	0
C 3	4 45 37	10 24 42	10♐47	29	25	16	26	28	11	21	0
E 4	4 49 33	11 25 36	22 34	0♑	27	17	27	28	11	21	0
M 5	4 53 30	12 26 31	4♑22	1	28	17	27	28	11	21	0
B 6	4 57 26	13 27 26	16 13	3	29	18	27	28	10	21	0
E 7	5 1 23	14 28 23	28 10	4	0♐	19	27	28	10	21	0
R 8	5 5 20	15 29 20	10♒15	5	2	20	27	28	10	21	0
9	5 9 16	16 30 19	22 32	7	3	20	28	28	10	21	0
10	5 13 13	17 31 17	5♓ 4	8	4	21	28	28	10	21	0
11	5 17 9	18 32 17	17 56	9	5	22	28	28	10	21	0
12	5 21 6	19 33 17	1♈10	10	7	23	28	28	10	21	0
13	5 25 2	20 34 17	14 49	11	8	23	28	28	10	21	0
14	5 28 59	21 35 18	28 54	12	9	24	29	28	10	21	0
15	5 32 55	22 36 20	13♉25	13	10	25	29	29	10	21	0
16	5 36 52	23 37 22	28 18	14	12	26	29	29	10	21	0
17	5 40 49	24 38 24	13♊26	14	13	26	29	29	10	21	0
18	5 44 45	25 39 28	28 42	15	14	27	0♒	29	10	21	0
19	5 48 42	26 40 32	13♋54	15	15	28	0	29	10	21	0
20	5 52 38	27 41 36	28 53	16 R	17	29	0	29	10	21	0
21	5 56 35	28 42 41	13♌31	16	18	29	0	29	10	21	0
22	6 0 31	29 43 47	27 42	15	19	0♓	0	29	10	21	0
23	6 4 28	0♑44 53	11♍25	15	20	1	1	29	10	21 R	0
24	6 8 25	1 46 1	24 40	15	22	2	1	29	10	21	0
25	6 12 21	2 47 8	7♎30	14	23	2	1	29	10	21	0
26	6 16 18	3 48 17	19 57	13	24	3	1	29	10	21	0
27	6 20 14	4 49 26	2♏ 8	12	25	4	2	29	10	21	0
28	6 24 11	5 50 35	14 7	11	27	5	2	29	10	21	29♋
29	6 28 7	6 51 45	25 58	10	28	5	2	29	10	21	29
30	6 32 4	7 52 56	7♐45	8	29	6	2	29	10	21	29
31	6 36 0	8 54 7	19 32	7	0♑	7	2	29	10	21	29

THE SUN ENTERS THE SIGN OF CAPRICORN ON DEC 22 AT 06:22.

♈ ARIES ♉ TAURUS ♊ GEMINI ♋ CANCER ♌ LEO ♍ VIRGO ♎ LIBRA ♏ SCORPIO ♐ SAGITTARIUS ♑ CAPRICORN ♒ AQUARIUS ♓ PISCES

1938

SIDEREAL SUN MOON MERCURY VENUS MARS JUPITER SATURN URANUS NEPTUNE PLUTO

DAY	TIME	☉	☽	☿	♀	♂	♃	♄	♅	♆	♇
	h m s	° ' "	° '	°	°	°	°	°	°	°	°
J 1	6 39 57	9♑55 18	1♑20	5♑R	2♑	8♓	3♒	29♓	10♉R	21♍R	29♋R
A 2	6 43 54	10 56 29	13 13	4	3	9	3	29	10	21	29
N 3	6 47 50	11 57 40	25 13	3	4	9	3	29	10	21	29
U 4	6 51 47	12 58 51	7♒19	2	6	10	3	29	10	21	29
A 5	6 55 43	14 0 1	19 35	1	7	11	4	29	10	21	29
R 6	6 59 40	15 1 12	2♓ 2	0	8	12	4	29	10	21	29
Y 7	7 3 36	16 2 22	14 40	0	9	12	4	29	10	21	29
8	7 7 33	17 3 32	27 34	0	11	13	4	0⊙	10	21	29
9	7 11 29	18 4 41	10♈44	29♐D	12	14	4	0	10	21	29
10	7 15 26	19 5 50	24 13	29	13	15	5	0	10	21	29
11	7 19 23	20 6 58	8♉ 3	29	14	15	5	0	10	21	29
12	7 23 19	21 8 6	22 15	0♑	16	16	5	0	10	21	29
13	7 27 16	22 9 13	6♊48	0	17	17	5	0	10	21	29
14	7 31 12	23 10 20	21 39	0	18	18	6	0	10	21	29
15	7 35 9	24 11 26	6♋41	1	19	18	6	0♈	10	21	29
16	7 39 5	25 12 31	21 46	2	21	19	6	0	10	21	29
17	7 43 2	26 13 36	6♌45	2	22	20	6	0	10	21	29
18	7 46 58	27 14 40	21 28	3	23	21	7	0	10 D	21	29
19	7 50 55	28 15 44	5♍47	4	24	21	7	0	10	21	29
20	7 54 52	29 16 47	19 40	5	26	22	7	0	10	21	29
21	7 58 48	0♒17 50	3♎ 3	6	27	23	7	1	10	21	29
22	8 2 45	1 18 53	15 59	7	28	24	8	1	10	21	29
23	8 6 41	2 19 55	28 30	8	29	24	8	1	10	21	29
24	8 10 38	3 20 57	10♏42	9	1♒	25	8	1	10	21	29
25	8 14 34	4 21 58	22 40	10	2	26	8	1	10	21	29
26	8 18 31	5 22 58	4♐29	12	3	27	8	1	10	21	29
27	8 22 27	6 23 58	16 15	13	4	27	9	1	10	21	29
28	8 26 24	7 24 58	28 3	14	6	28	9	1	10	21	29
29	8 30 21	8 25 56	9♑55	15	7	29	9	1	10	21	29
30	8 34 17	9 26 54	21 55	17	8	0⊙	9	1	10	21	29
31	8 38 14	10 27 51	4♒ 4	18	9	0♈	10	1	10	21	29

THE SUN ENTERS THE SIGN OF AQUARIUS ON JAN 20 AT 16:59.

DAY	TIME	☉	☽	☿	♀	♂	♃	♄	♅	♆	♇
	h m s	° ' "	° '	°	°	°	°	°	°	°	°
F 1	8 42 10	11♒28 47	16♒25	19♑	11♒	1♈	10♒	1♈	10♉	21♍R	29♋R
E 2	8 46 7	12 29 42	28 57	21	12	2	10	2	10	21	29
B 3	8 50 3	13 30 35	11♓41	22	13	3	10	2	10	21	29
R 4	8 54 0	14 31 27	24 37	23	14	3	11	2	10	21	29
U 5	8 57 56	15 32 18	7♈43	25	16	4	11	2	10	21	29
A 6	9 1 53	16 33 8	21 2	26	17	5	11	2	10	21	29
R 7	9 5 50	17 33 56	4♉33	28	18	6	11	2	10	21	29
Y 8	9 9 46	18 34 42	18 17	29	20	6	12	2	10	21	29
9	9 13 43	19 35 27	2♊16	1♒	21	7	12	2	10	21	29
10	9 17 39	20 36 11	16 30	2	22	8	12	2	10	21	29
11	9 21 36	21 36 52	0♋57	4	23	9	12	2	10	21	29
12	9 25 32	22 37 33	15 34	5	25	9	13	3	10	20	28
13	9 29 29	23 38 11	0♌16	7	26	10	13	3	10	20	28
14	9 33 25	24 38 48	14 56	8	27	11	13	3	10	20	28
15	9 37 22	25 39 24	29 26	10	28	11	13	3	10	20	28
16	9 41 19	26 39 58	13♍38	11	0♓	12	13	3	10	20	28
17	9 45 15	27 40 30	27 28	13	1	13	14	3	10	20	28
18	9 49 12	28 41 1	10♎53	15	2	14	14	3	10	20	28
19	9 53 8	29 41 31	23 52	16	3	14	14	3	10	20	28
20	9 57 5	0♓42 0	6♏27	18	5	15	14	3	10	20	28
21	10 1 1	1 42 27	18 42	20	6	16	15	4	10	20	28
22	10 4 58	2 42 53	0♐43	21	7	17	15	4	10	20	28
23	10 8 54	3 43 17	12 34	23	8	17	15	4	10	20	28
24	10 12 51	4 43 41	24 22	25	10	18	15	4	10	20	28
25	10 16 48	5 44 2	6♑11	26	11	19	16	4	10	20	28
26	10 20 44	6 44 22	18 6	28	12	20	16	4	10	20	28
27	10 24 41	7 44 41	0♒12	0♓	13	20	16	4	10	20	28
28	10 28 37	8 44 58	12 31	2	15	21	16	4	10	20	28

THE SUN ENTERS THE SIGN OF PISCES ON FEB 19 AT 07:20.

DAY	TIME	☉	☽	☿	♀	♂	♃	♄	♅	♆	♇
	h m s	° ' "	° '	°	°	°	°	°	°	°	°
M 1	10 32 34	9♓45 14	25♒ 6	3♓	16♓	22♈	16♒	4♈	10♉	20♍R	28♋R
A 2	10 36 30	10 45 27	7♓56	5	17	23	17	5	10	20	28
R 3	10 40 27	11 45 39	21 0	7	18	23	17	5	11	20	28
C 4	10 44 23	12 45 49	4♈18	9	20	24	17	5	11	20	28
H 5	10 48 20	13 45 57	17 47	11	21	25	17	5	11	20	28
6	10 52 16	14 46 3	1♉26	13	22	25	18	5	11	20	28
7	10 56 13	15 46 7	15 12	14	23	26	18	5	11	20	28
8	11 0 10	16 46 9	29 6	16	25	27	18	5	11	20	28
9	11 4 6	17 46 9	13♊ 5	18	26	28	18	5	11	20	28
10	11 8 3	18 46 7	27 11	20	27	28	18	6	11	20	28
11	11 11 59	19 46 2	11♋22	22	28	29	19	6	11	20	28
12	11 15 56	20 45 55	25 37	24	0⊙	0♉	19	6	11	20	28
13	11 19 52	21 45 46	9♌52	26	1♈	0	19	6	11	20	28
14	11 23 49	22 45 35	24 4	28	2	1	19	6	11	20	28
15	11 27 45	23 45 21	8♍ 8	0⊙	3	2	20	6	11	20	28
16	11 31 42	24 45 6	21 58	2♈	4	3	20	6	11	20	28
17	11 35 39	25 44 48	5♎32	4	6	3	20	6	11	20	28
18	11 39 35	26 44 28	18 46	6	7	4	20	7	11	20	28
19	11 43 32	27 44 7	1♏39	8	8	5	20	7	11	20	28
20	11 47 28	28 43 44	14 12	10	9	6	21	7	11	20	28
21	11 51 25	29 43 19	26 28	12	11	6	21	7	11	20	28
22	11 55 21	0♈42 52	8♐30	14	12	7	21	7	11	19	28
23	11 59 18	1 42 24	20 23	16	13	8	21	7	11	19	28
24	12 3 14	2 41 53	2♑12	17	14	8	21	7	11	19	28
25	12 7 11	3 41 21	14 3	19	16	9	22	7	11	19	28
26	12 11 8	4 40 47	26 0	21	17	10	22	8	12	19	28
27	12 15 4	5 40 12	8♒ 9	22	18	11	22	8	12	19	28
28	12 19 1	6 39 34	20 34	24	19	11	22	8	12	19	28
29	12 22 57	7 38 55	3♓17	25	21	12	23	8	12	19	28
30	12 26 54	8 38 13	16 19	27	22	13	23	8	12	19	28
31	12 30 50	9 37 30	29 41	28	23	13	23	8	12	19	28

THE SUN ENTERS THE SIGN OF ARIES ON MAR 21 AT 06:43.

SIDEREAL SUN MOON MERCURY VENUS MARS JUPITER SATURN URANUS NEPTUNE PLUTO

DAY	TIME	☉	☽	☿	♀	♂	♃	♄	♅	♆	♇
	h m s	° ' "	° '	°	°	°	°	°	°	°	°
A 1	12 34 47	10♈36 45	13♈21	29♈	24♈	14♉	23♒	8♈	12♉	19♍R	28♋R
P 2	12 38 43	11 35 57	27 15	0♉	26	15	23	8	12	19	28
R 3	12 42 40	12 35 8	11♉19	1	27	15	23	9	12	19	28
I 4	12 46 37	13 34 16	25 31	2	28	16	24	9	12	19	28
L 5	12 50 33	14 33 22	9♊45	3	29	17	24	9	12	19	28
6	12 54 30	15 32 26	24 0	4	1♉	18	24	9	12	19	28
7	12 58 26	16 31 28	8♋12	4	2	18	24	9	12	19	28
8	13 2 23	17 30 27	22 20	5	3	19	24	9	12	19	28
9	13 6 19	18 29 24	6♌23	5	4	20	25	9	12	19	28
10	13 10 16	19 28 19	20 18	5	5	20	25	9	12	19	28
11	13 14 12	20 27 11	4♍ 5	6 R	7	21	25	10	12	19	28 D
12	13 18 9	21 26 1	17 41	6	8	22	25	10	12	19	28
13	13 22 5	22 24 49	1♎ 5	6	9	23	25	10	12	19	28
14	13 26 2	23 23 34	14 15	5	10	23	26	10	13	19	28
15	13 29 59	24 22 18	27 9	5	12	24	26	10	13	19	28
16	13 33 55	25 21 0	9♏48	5	13	25	26	10	13	19	28
17	13 37 52	26 19 40	22 12	4	14	25	26	10	13	19	28
18	13 41 48	27 18 18	4♐23	4	15	26	26	10	13	19	28
19	13 45 45	28 16 54	16 23	3	17	27	26	11	13	19	28
20	13 49 41	29 15 29	28 16	2	18	27	27	11	13	19	28
21	13 53 38	0♉14 2	10♑ 6	2	19	28	27	11	13	19	28
22	13 57 34	1 12 33	21 57	1	20	29	27	11	13	19	28
23	14 1 31	2 11 2	3♒55	0	21	29	27	11	13	19	28
24	14 5 28	3 9 30	16 4	0	23	0♊	27	11	13	19	28
25	14 9 24	4 7 56	28 29	29♈	24	1	27	11	13	19	28
26	14 13 21	5 6 21	11♓13	28	25	2	28	11	13	19	28
27	14 17 17	6 4 44	24 20	28	26	2	28	11	13	19	28
28	14 21 14	7 3 5	7♈51	27	28	3	28	12	13	19	28
29	14 25 10	8 1 25	21 44	27	29	4	28	12	13	19	28
30	14 29 7	8 59 43	5♉56	26	0♊	4	28	12	13	19	28

THE SUN ENTERS THE SIGN OF TAURUS ON APR 20 AT 18:15.

DAY	TIME	☉	☽	☿	♀	♂	♃	♄	♅	♆	♇
	h m s	° ' "	° '	°	°	°	°	°	°	°	°
M 1	14 33 3	9♉57 59	20♉25	26♈R	1♊	5♊	28♒	12♈	13♉	19♍R	28♋
A 2	14 37 0	10 56 14	5♊ 2	26	2	6	28	12	14	19	28
Y 3	14 40 57	11 54 27	19 43	25	4	6	29	12	14	19	28
4	14 44 53	12 52 37	4♋21	25	5	7	29	12	14	19	28
5	14 48 50	13 50 46	18 51	25 D	6	8	29	12	14	19	28
6	14 52 46	14 48 53	3♌ 8	25	7	8	29	13	14	19	28
7	14 56 43	15 46 58	17 11	25	9	9	29	13	14	19	28
8	15 0 39	16 45 1	0♍59	25	10	10	29	13	14	18	28
9	15 4 36	17 43 2	14 30	26	11	10	29	13	14	18	28
10	15 8 32	18 41 1	27 46	26	12	11	29	13	14	18	28
11	15 12 29	19 38 58	10♎46	26	13	12	0♓	13	14	18	28
12	15 16 26	20 36 53	23 33	27	15	12	0	13	14	18	28
13	15 20 22	21 34 47	6♏ 7	27	16	13	0	13	14	18	28
14	15 24 19	22 32 39	18 29	28	17	14	0	13	14	18	28
15	15 28 15	23 30 30	0♐40	29	18	15	0	14	14	18	28
16	15 32 12	24 28 19	12 42	29	20	15	0	14	14	18	28
17	15 36 8	25 26 7	24 38	0♉	21	16	0	14	14	18	28
18	15 40 5	26 23 54	6♑29	1	22	17	0	14	14	18	28
19	15 44 1	27 21 39	18 19	2	23	17	1	14	15	18	28
20	15 47 58	28 19 23	0♒11	3	24	18	1	14	15	18	28
21	15 51 55	29 17 6	12 9	4	26	19	1	14	15	18	28
22	15 55 51	0♊14 48	24 17	5	27	19	1	14	15	18	28
23	15 59 48	1 12 29	6♓40	6	28	20	1	14	15	18	28
24	16 3 44	2 10 9	19 22	7	29	21	1	14	15	18	28
25	16 7 41	3 7 48	2♈26	8	0♋	21	1	15	15	18	28
26	16 11 37	4 5 26	15 55	10	2	22	1	15	15	18	28
27	16 15 34	5 3 3	29 50	11	3	23	1	15	15	18	28
28	16 19 30	6 0 39	14♉10	12	4	23	1	15	15	18	28
29	16 23 27	6 58 14	28 51	14	5	24	1	15	15	18	28
30	16 27 24	7 55 48	13♊46	15	6	25	1	15	15	18 D	28
31	16 31 20	8 53 21	28 49	17	8	25	2	15	15	18	28

THE SUN ENTERS THE SIGN OF GEMINI ON MAY 21 AT 17:50.

DAY	TIME	☉	☽	☿	♀	♂	♃	♄	♅	♆	♇
	h m s	° ' "	° '	°	°	°	°	°	°	°	°
J 1	16 35 17	9♊50 52	13♋50	18♉	9♋	26♊	2♓	15♈	15♉	18♍	28♋
U 2	16 39 13	10 48 23	28 41	20	10	27	2	15	15	18	28
N 3	16 43 10	11 45 52	13♌15	21	11	27	2	15	15	18	28
E 4	16 47 6	12 43 20	27 28	23	12	28	2	15	15	18	28
5	16 51 3	13 40 46	11♍17	25	14	29	2	16	15	18	28
6	16 54 59	14 38 12	24 44	26	15	29	2	16	15	18	28
7	16 58 56	15 35 36	7♎49	28	16	0♋	2	16	16	18	28
8	17 2 53	16 32 59	20 35	0♊	17	1	2	16	16	18	29
9	17 6 49	17 30 21	3♏ 6	2	18	1	2	16	16	18	29
10	17 10 46	18 27 42	15 23	4	20	2	2	16	16	18	29
11	17 14 42	19 25 2	27 31	6	21	3	2	16	16	18	29
12	17 18 39	20 22 21	9♐31	8	22	3	2	16	16	18	29
13	17 22 35	21 19 40	21 25	10	23	4	2	16	16	18	29
14	17 26 32	22 16 58	3♑17	12	24	5	2	16	16	18	29
15	17 30 28	23 14 15	15 7	14	26	5	2	16	16	18	29
16	17 34 25	24 11 32	26 58	16	27	6	2	16	16	18	29
17	17 38 22	25 8 48	8♒52	18	28	7	2	16	16	18	29
18	17 42 18	26 6 4	20 53	20	29	7	2	17	16	18	29
19	17 46 15	27 3 19	3♓ 2	22	0♌	8	2	17	16	18	29
20	17 50 11	28 0 35	15 24	24	2	9	2	17	16	18	29
21	17 54 8	28 57 50	28 2	27	3	9	2 R	17	16	18	29
22	17 58 4	29 55 5	11♈ 1	29	4	10	2	17	16	18	29
23	18 2 1	0♋52 19	24 24	1♋	5	11	2	17	16	19	29
24	18 5 57	1 49 34	8♉12	3	6	11	2	17	16	19	29
25	18 9 54	2 46 49	22 27	5	7	12	2	17	16	19	29
26	18 13 51	3 44 3	7♊ 7	8	9	12	2	17	16	19	29
27	18 17 47	4 41 18	22 7	10	10	13	2	17	16	19	29
28	18 21 44	5 38 32	7♋20	12	11	14	2	17	17	19	29
29	18 25 40	6 35 47	22 34	14	12	14	2	17	17	19	29
30	18 29 37	7 33 0	7♌41	16	13	15	2	17	17	19	29

THE SUN ENTERS THE SIGN OF CANCER ON JUN 22 AT 02:04.

♈ ARIES ♉ TAURUS ♊ GEMINI ♋ CANCER ♌ LEO ♍ VIRGO ♎ LIBRA ♏ SCORPIO ♐ SAGITTARIUS ♑ CAPRICORN ♒ AQUARIUS ♓ PISCES

SIDEREAL SUN MOON MERCURY VENUS MARS JUPITER SATURN URANUS NEPTUNE PLUTO

DAY	TIME	☉	☽	☿	♀	♂	♃	♄	♅	♆	♇
	h m s	° ' "	° '	°	°	°	°	°	°	°	°
J 1	18 33 33	8♋30 14	22♌30	18♋	15♌	16♋	2♓R	17♈	17♉	19♍	29♋
U 2	18 37 30	9 27 27	6♍55	20	16	16	2	17	17	19	29
L 3	18 41 27	10 24 40	20 52	22	17	17	2	17	17	19	29
Y 4	18 45 23	11 21 52	4♎22	24	18	18	2	17	17	19	29
5	18 49 20	12 19 4	17 25	26	19	18	2	17	17	19	29
6	18 53 16	13 16 16	0♏ 6	28	20	19	2	18	17	19	29
7	18 57 13	14 13 28	12 28	0♌	22	20	2	18	17	19	29
8	19 1 9	15 10 39	24 37	2	23	20	2	18	17	19	29
9	19 5 6	16 7 51	6♐36	3	24	21	2	18	17	19	29
10	19 9 2	17 5 2	18 29	5	25	22	2	18	17	19	29
11	19 12 59	18 2 14	0♑19	7	26	22	2	18	17	19	29
12	19 16 56	18 59 25	12 9	9	27	23	2	18	17	19	29
13	19 20 52	19 56 37	24 0	10	29	24	2	18	17	19	29
14	19 24 49	20 53 49	5♒55	12	0♍	24	1	18	17	19	29
15	19 28 45	21 51 2	17 55	13	1	25	1	18	17	19	29
16	19 32 42	22 48 15	0♓ 2	15	2	26	1	18	17	19	29
17	19 36 38	23 45 28	12 17	17	3	26	1	18	17	19	0♌
18	19 40 35	24 42 42	24 44	18	4	27	1	18	17	19	0
19	19 44 31	25 39 57	7♈24	20	5	27	1	18	17	19	0
20	19 48 28	26 37 12	20 20	21	7	28	1	18	17	19	0
21	19 52 25	27 34 28	3♉37	22	8	29	1	18	17	19	0
22	19 56 21	28 31 46	17 17	24	9	29	1	18	17	19	0
23	20 0 18	29 29 4	1♊21	25	10	0♌	1	18	17	19	0
24	20 4 14	0♌26 22	15 50	26	11	1	1	18	17	19	0
25	20 8 11	1 23 42	0♋41	28	12	1	1	18	17	19	0
26	20 12 7	2 21 3	15 47	29	14	2	0	18	17	19	0
27	20 16 4	3 18 24	1♌ 0	0♍	15	3	0	18	17	19	0
28	20 20 0	4 15 46	16 9	1	16	3	0	18	18	19	0
29	20 23 57	5 13 9	1♍ 3	2	17	4	0	18	18	19	0
30	20 27 54	6 10 32	15 35	3	18	5	0	18 R	18	19	0
31	20 31 50	7 7 56	29 40	4	19	5	0	18	18	19	0

THE SUN ENTERS THE SIGN OF LEO ON JUL 23 AT 12:58.

DAY	TIME	☉	☽	☿	♀	♂	♃	♄	♅	♆	♇
	h m s	° ' "	° '	°	°	°	°	°	°	°	°
A 1	20 35 47	8♌ 5 20	13♎15	5♍	20♍	6♌	0♓R	18♈R	18♉	19♍	0♌
U 2	20 39 43	9 2 45	26 21	6	21	6	0	18	18	19	0
G 3	20 43 40	10 0 11	9♏ 2	7	23	7	0	18	18	19	0
U 4	20 47 36	10 57 37	21 24	8	24	8	29♒	18	18	19	0
S 5	20 51 33	11 55 4	3♐29	9	25	8	29	18	18	19	0
T 6	20 55 29	12 52 32	15 25	9	26	9	29	18	18	20	0
7	20 59 26	13 50 0	27 16	10	27	10	29	18	18	20	0
8	21 3 23	14 47 30	9♑ 5	11	28	10	29	18	18	20	0
9	21 7 19	15 45 0	20 56	11	29	11	29	18	18	20	0
10	21 11 16	16 42 31	2♒52	11	0♎	12	29	18	18	20	0
11	21 15 12	17 40 4	14 54	12	1	12	29	18	18	20	0
12	21 19 9	18 37 37	27 4	12	3	13	28	18	18	20	0
13	21 23 5	19 35 12	9♓22	12	4	14	28	18	18	20	0
14	21 27 2	20 32 48	21 50	12 R	5	14	28	18	18	20	0
15	21 30 58	21 30 25	4♈27	12	6	15	28	18	18	20	0
16	21 34 55	22 28 4	17 16	12	7	15	28	18	18	20	0
17	21 38 51	23 25 44	0♉19	12	8	16	28	18	18	20	0
18	21 42 48	24 23 26	13 37	12	9	17	28	18	18	20	0
19	21 46 45	25 21 9	27 13	11	10	17	28	18	18	20	0
20	21 50 41	26 18 54	11♊ 8	11	11	18	27	18	18	20	0
21	21 54 38	27 16 41	25 23	10	12	19	27	18	18	20	0
22	21 58 34	28 14 30	9♋57	10	13	19	27	18	18	20	0
23	22 2 31	29 12 20	24 45	9	14	20	27	18	18	20	1
24	22 6 27	0♍10 12	9♌41	8	16	21	27	18	18 R	20	1
25	22 10 24	1 8 5	24 37	7	17	21	27	18	18	20	1
26	22 14 21	2 6 0	9♍22	7	18	22	27	17	18	20	1
27	22 18 17	3 3 56	23 50	6	19	22	27	17	18	20	1
28	22 22 14	4 1 54	7♎53	5	20	23	26	17	18	20	1
29	22 26 10	4 59 53	21 30	4	21	24	26	17	18	20	1
30	22 30 7	5 57 54	4♏38	3	22	24	26	17	18	20	1
31	22 34 3	6 55 56	17 22	2	23	25	26	17	18	20	1

THE SUN ENTERS THE SIGN OF VIRGO ON AUG 23 AT 19:46.

DAY	TIME	☉	☽	☿	♀	♂	♃	♄	♅	♆	♇
	h m s	° ' "	° '	°	°	°	°	°	°	°	°
S 1	22 38 0	7♍53 59	29♏46	1♍R	24♎	26♌	26♒R	17♈R	18♉R	20♍	1♌
E 2	22 41 56	8 52 4	11♐53	1	25	26	26	17	18	20	1
P 3	22 45 53	9 50 10	23 49	0	26	27	26	17	18	20	1
T 4	22 49 49	10 48 18	5♑40	0	27	28	25	17	18	21	1
E 5	22 53 46	11 46 27	17 31	29♌	28	28	25	17	18	21	1
M 6	22 57 43	12 44 37	29 25	29 D	29	29	25	17	18	21	1
B 7	23 1 39	13 42 49	11♒26	29	0♏	29	25	17	18	21	1
E 8	23 5 36	14 41 3	23 36	29	1	0♍	25	17	18	21	1
R 9	23 9 32	15 39 18	5♓57	29	2	1	25	17	18	21	1
10	23 13 29	16 37 35	18 30	0♍	3	1	25	17	18	21	1
11	23 17 25	17 35 54	1♈15	0	4	2	25	17	18	21	1
12	23 21 22	18 34 14	14 11	1	5	3	25	17	18	21	1
13	23 25 18	19 32 37	27 18	2	6	3	24	16	18	21	1
14	23 29 15	20 31 2	10♉36	3	7	4	24	16	18	21	1
15	23 33 12	21 29 29	24 6	4	8	5	24	16	18	21	1
16	23 37 8	22 27 58	7♊48	5	9	5	24	16	18	21	1
17	23 41 5	23 26 29	21 42	6	10	6	24	16	18	21	1
18	23 45 1	24 25 3	5♋49	7	10	6	24	16	18	21	1
19	23 48 58	25 23 38	20 7	9	11	7	24	16	18	21	1
20	23 52 54	26 22 16	4♌34	10	12	8	24	16	18	21	1
21	23 56 51	27 20 56	19 6	12	13	8	24	16	18	21	1
22	0 0 47	28 19 38	3♍36	14	14	9	24	16	17	21	1
23	0 4 44	29 18 22	18 0	15	15	10	24	16	17	21	1
24	0 8 41	0♎17 9	2♎ 9	17	16	10	23	16	17	21	1
25	0 12 37	1 15 57	16 0	19	17	11	23	16	17	21	1
26	0 16 34	2 14 47	29 29	21	17	12	23	16	17	21	1
27	0 20 30	3 13 39	12♏34	22	18	12	23	15	17	21	1
28	0 24 27	4 12 33	25 18	24	19	13	23	15	17	21	1
29	0 28 23	5 11 29	7♐42	26	20	13	23	15	17	21	1
30	0 32 20	6 10 26	19 51	28	21	14	23	15	17	21	1

THE SUN ENTERS THE SIGN OF LIBRA ON SEP 23 AT 17:00.

SIDEREAL SUN MOON MERCURY VENUS MARS JUPITER SATURN URANUS NEPTUNE PLUTO

DAY	TIME	☉	☽	☿	♀	♂	♃	♄	♅	♆	♇
	h m s	° ' "	° '	°	°	°	°	°	°	°	°
O 1	0 36 16	7♎ 9 25	1♑49	0♎	22♏	15♍	23♒R	15♈R	17♉R	21♍	1♌
C 2	0 40 13	8 8 26	13 41	1	22	15	23	15	17	22	1
T 3	0 44 9	9 7 29	25 33	3	23	16	23	15	17	22	1
O 4	0 48 6	10 6 34	7♒29	5	24	17	23	15	17	22	1
B 5	0 52 3	11 5 40	19 33	7	24	17	23	15	17	22	1
E 6	0 55 59	12 4 48	1♓50	9	25	18	23	15	17	22	1
R 7	0 59 56	13 3 58	14 20	10	26	18	23	15	17	22	1
8	1 3 52	14 3 10	27 6	12	27	19	23	15	17	22	1
9	1 7 49	15 2 23	10♈ 8	14	27	20	23	15	17	22	1
10	1 11 45	16 1 39	23 26	16	28	20	23	14	17	22	1
11	1 15 42	17 0 57	6♉57	17	28	21	23	14	17	22	1
12	1 19 38	18 0 17	20 40	19	29	22	22	14	17	22	1
13	1 23 35	18 59 40	4♊32	21	0♐	22	22	14	17	22	1
14	1 27 32	19 59 4	18 33	22	0	23	22	14	17	22	1
15	1 31 28	20 58 31	2♋38	24	1	24	22	14	17	22	1
16	1 35 25	21 58 0	16 48	26	1	24	22	14	17	22	1
17	1 39 21	22 57 32	0♌59	27	2	25	22	14	17	22	1
18	1 43 18	23 57 6	15 11	29	2	25	22	14	17	22	1
19	1 47 14	24 56 42	29 19	1♏	2	26	22 D	14	17	22	1
20	1 51 11	25 56 20	13♍23	2	3	27	22	14	17	22	1
21	1 55 7	26 56 1	27 17	4	3	27	22	14	17	22	1
22	1 59 4	27 55 44	11♎ 0	6	4	28	22	14	17	22	1
23	2 3 1	28 55 28	24 28	7	4	29	22	13	16	22	1
24	2 6 57	29 55 15	7♏40	9	4	29	22	13	16	22	1
25	2 10 54	0♏55 4	20 34	10	4	0♎	22	13	16	22	1
26	2 14 50	1 54 55	3♐11	12	5	0	22	13	16	22	1
27	2 18 47	2 54 47	15 32	13	5	1	22	13	16	22	2
28	2 22 43	3 54 42	27 40	15	5	2	23	13	16	22	2
29	2 26 40	4 54 38	9♑39	17	5	2	23	13	16	22	2
30	2 30 36	5 54 35	21 32	18	5 R	3	23	13	16	22	2
31	2 34 33	6 54 35	3♒23	20	5	4	23	13	16	22	2

THE SUN ENTERS THE SIGN OF SCORPIO ON OCT 24 AT 01:55.

DAY	TIME,	☉	☽	☿	♀	♂	♃	♄	♅	♆	♇
	h m s	° ' "	° '	°	°	°	°	°	°	°	°
N 1	2 38 30	7♏54 35	15♒19	21♏	5♐R	4♎	23♒	13♈R	16♉R	23♍	2♌
O 2	2 42 26	8 54 38	27 23	23	5	5	23	13	16	23	2 R
V 3	2 46 23	9 54 42	9♓40	24	5	6	23	13	16	23	2
E 4	2 50 19	10 54 48	22 13	26	5	6	23	13	16	23	2
M 5	2 54 16	11 54 55	5♈ 6	27	4	7	23	13	16	23	2
B 6	2 58 12	12 55 4	18 19	29	4	7	23	13	16	23	2
E 7	3 2 9	13 55 14	1♉54	0♐	4	8	23	12	16	23	2
R 8	3 6 5	14 55 27	15 48	1	4	9	23	12	16	23	2
9	3 10 2	15 55 41	29 58	3	3	9	23	12	16	23	2
10	3 13 59	16 55 57	14♊20	4	3	10	23	12	16	23	1
11	3 17 55	17 56 15	28 48	6	2	11	23	12	16	23	1
12	3 21 52	18 56 35	13♋17	7	2	11	23	12	16	23	1
13	3 25 48	19 56 57	27 42	9	1	12	23	12	16	23	1
14	3 29 45	20 57 20	12♌ 0	10	1	12	23	12	16	23	1
15	3 33 41	21 57 46	26 8	11	0	13	24	12	16	23	1
16	3 37 38	22 58 13	10♍ 3	13	0	14	24	12	16	23	1
17	3 41 34	23 58 43	23 46	14	29♏	14	24	12	15	23	1
18	3 45 31	24 59 14	7♎15	15	29	15	24	12	15	23	1
19	3 49 28	25 59 47	20 30	17	28	16	24	12	15	23	1
20	3 53 24	27 0 21	3♏33	18	27	16	24	12	15	23	1
21	3 57 21	28 0 58	16 22	19	27	17	24	12	15	23	1
22	4 1 17	29 1 36	28 59	20	26	17	24	12	15	23	1
23	4 5 14	0♐ 2 15	11♐24	22	26	18	24	12	15	23	1
24	4 9 10	1 2 56	23 38	23	25	19	24	12	15	23	1
25	4 13 7	2 3 38	5♑42	24	24	19	25	12	15	23	1
26	4 17 3	3 4 21	17 39	25	24	20	25	12	15	23	1
27	4 21 0	4 5 5	29 31	26	23	21	25	12	15	23	1
28	4 24 57	5 5 51	11♒22	27	23	21	25	11	15	23	1
29	4 28 53	6 6 37	23 16	27	22	22	25	11	15	23	1
30	4 32 50	7 7 24	5♓16	28	22	22	25	11	15	23	1

THE SUN ENTERS THE SIGN OF SAGITTARIUS ON NOV 22 AT 23:07.

DAY	TIME	☉	☽	☿	♀	♂	♃	♄	♅	♆	♇
	h m s	° ' "	° '	°	°	°	°	°	°	°	°
D 1	4 36 46	8♐ 8 13	17♓29	29♐	22♏R	23♎	25♒	11♈R	15♉R	23♍	1♌R
E 2	4 40 43	9 9 2	29 59	29	21	24	25	11	15	23	1
C 3	4 44 39	10 9 52	12♈49	0♑	21	24	26	11	15	23	1
E 4	4 48 36	11 10 43	26 3	0 R	21	25	26	11	15	23	1
M 5	4 52 32	12 11 35	9♉43	0	20	26	26	11	15	23	1
B 6	4 56 29	13 12 28	23 49	0	20	26	26	11	15	23	1
E 7	5 0 26	14 13 22	8♊18	29♐	20	27	26	11	15	23	1
R 8	5 4 22	15 14 17	23 5	29	20	28	26	11	15	23	1
9	5 8 19	16 15 12	8♋ 2	28	20	28	26	11	15	23	1
10	5 12 15	17 16 9	23 0	27	20 D	29	27	11	15	23	1
11	5 16 12	18 17 7	7♌50	26	20	29	27	11	15	23	1
12	5 20 8	19 18 6	22 26	25	20	0♏	27	11	15	23	1
13	5 24 5	20 19 6	6♍44	24	20	1	27	11	15	23	1
14	5 28 1	21 20 8	20 39	22	20	1	27	11 D	14	23	1
15	5 31 58	22 21 10	4♎14	21	20	2	27	11	14	23	1
16	5 35 55	23 22 13	17 28	20	20	3	28	11	14	23	1
17	5 39 51	24 23 17	0♏25	18	20	3	28	11	14	23	1
18	5 43 48	25 24 22	13 7	17	21	4	28	11	14	23	1
19	5 47 44	26 25 28	25 36	16	21	4	28	11	14	23	1
20	5 51 41	27 26 35	7♐56	15	21	5	28	11	14	23	1
21	5 55 37	28 27 42	20 7	14	22	6	28	11	14	23	1
22	5 59 34	29 28 50	2♑11	14	22	6	29	11	14	23	1
23	6 3 30	0♑29 59	14 9	14	22	7	29	11	14	23	1
24	6 7 27	1 31 7	26 3	13 D	23	8	29	11	14	23	1
25	6 11 24	2 32 16	7♒54	13	23	8	29	11	14	23	1
26	6 15 20	3 33 26	19 45	14	24	9	29	11	14	23 R	1
27	6 19 17	4 34 35	1♓39	14	24	9	29	11	14	23	1
28	6 23 13	5 35 44	13 38	14	25	10	0♓	11	14	23	1
29	6 27 10	6 36 53	25 47	15	25	11	0	11	14	23	1
30	6 31 6	7 38 3	8♈10	16	26	11	0	11	14	23	1
31	6 35 3	8 39 12	20 52	16	27	12	0	11	14	23	1

THE SUN ENTERS THE SIGN OF CAPRICORN ON DEC 22 AT 12:14.

♈ ARIES ♉ TAURUS ♊ GEMINI ♋ CANCER ♌ LEO ♍ VIRGO ♎ LIBRA ♏ SCORPIO ♐ SAGITTARIUS ♑ CAPRICORN ♒ AQUARIUS ♓ PISCES

SIDEREAL SUN MOON MERCURY VENUS MARS JUPITER SATURN URANUS NEPTUNE PLUTO

DAY	TIME	☉	☽	☿	♀	♂	♃	♄	♅	♆	♇
	h m s	° ' "	° '	°	°	°	°	°	°	°	°
J 1	6 38 59	9♑40 21	3♉59	17♐	27♏	12♏	0♓	11♈	14♉R	23♍R	1♌R
A 2	6 42 56	10 41 29	17 32	18	28	13	1	12	14	23	1
N 3	6 46 53	11 42 38	1♊35	19	29	14	1	12	14	23	1
U 4	6 50 49	12 43 47	16 7	20	29	14	1	12	14	23	1
A 5	6 54 46	13 44 55	1♋ 3	21	0♐	15	1	12	14	23	1
R 6	6 58 42	14 46 3	16 15	22	1	16	1	12	14	23	1
Y 7	7 2 39	15 47 12	1♌34	23	2	16	2	12	14	23	1
8	7 6 35	16 48 20	16 48	25	2	17	2	12	14	23	1
9	7 10 32	17 49 27	1♍46	26	3	17	2	12	14	23	1
10	7 14 28	18 50 35	16 21	27	4	18	2	12	14	23	1
11	7 18 25	19 51 43	0♎28	28	5	19	2	12	14	23	1
12	7 22 22	20 52 51	14 8	0♑	6	19	3	12	14	23	1
13	7 26 18	21 53 59	27 21	1	6	20	3	12	14	23	1
14	7 30 15	22 55 7	10♏11	2	7	21	3	12	14	23	1
15	7 34 11	23 56 15	22 43	4	8	21	3	12	14	23	1
16	7 38 8	24 57 23	5♐ 1	5	9	22	3	12	14	23	0
17	7 42 4	25 58 30	17 8	6	10	22	4	12	14	23	0
18	7 46 1	26 59 37	29 8	8	11	23	4	12	14	23	0
19	7 49 57	28 0 44	11♑ 4	9	12	24	4	12	14	23	0
20	7 53 54	29 1 50	22 57	11	13	24	4	12	14	23	0
21	7 57 51	0♒ 2 55	4♒49	12	14	25	5	12	14	23	0
22	8 1 47	1 4 0	16 41	14	15	25	5	13	14 D	23	0
23	8 5 44	2 5 4	28 35	15	15	26	5	13	14	23	0
24	8 9 40	3 6 7	10♓32	17	16	27	5	13	14	23	0
25	8 13 37	4 7 9	22 34	18	17	27	5	13	14	23	0
26	8 17 33	5 8 10	4♈44	20	18	28	6	13	14	23	0
27	8 21 30	6 9 10	17 6	21	19	29	6	13	14	23	0
28	8 25 26	7 10 9	29 44	23	20	29	6	13	14	23	0
29	8 29 23	8 11 7	12♉43	24	21	0♐	6	13	14	23	0
30	8 33 20	9 12 3	26 6	26	22	0	7	13	14	23	0
31	8 37 16	10 12 59	9♊57	27	23	1	7	13	14	23	0

THE SUN ENTERS THE SIGN OF AQUARIUS ON JAN 20 AT 22:51.

DAY	TIME	☉	☽	☿	♀	♂	♃	♄	♅	♆	♇
	h m s	° ' "	° '	°	°	°	°	°	°	°	°
F 1	8 41 13	11♒13 53	24♊17	29♑	24♐	2♐	7♓	13♈	14♉	23♍R	0♌R
E 2	8 45 9	12 14 46	9♋ 4	0♒	25	2	7	13	14	23	0
B 3	8 49 6	13 15 37	24 12	2	26	3	8	13	14	23	0
R 4	8 53 2	14 16 27	9♌32	4	28	3	8	14	14	23	0
U 5	8 56 59	15 17 16	24 53	5	29	4	8	14	14	23	0
A 6	9 0 56	16 18 4	10♍ 3	7	0♑	5	8	14	14	23	0
R 7	9 4 52	17 18 51	24 52	9	1	5	8	14	14	23	0
Y 8	9 8 49	18 19 37	9♎13	10	2	6	9	14	14	23	0
9	9 12 45	19 20 22	23 4	12	3	6	9	14	14	23	0
10	9 16 42	20 21 5	6♏25	14	4	7	9	14	14	23	0
11	9 20 38	21 21 48	19 19	15	5	8	9	14	14	23	0
12	9 24 35	22 22 30	1♐52	17	6	8	10	14	14	23	0
13	9 28 31	23 23 11	14 7	19	7	9	10	14	14	23	0
14	9 32 28	24 23 50	26 10	20	8	9	10	14	14	23	0
15	9 36 24	25 24 29	8♑ 5	22	9	10	10	14	14	23	0
16	9 40 21	26 25 6	19 57	24	10	11	11	15	14	23	0
17	9 44 18	27 25 41	1♒48	26	11	11	11	15	14	23	0
18	9 48 14	28 26 16	13 40	28	13	12	11	15	14	23	0
19	9 52 11	29 26 48	25 35	29	14	12	11	15	14	23	0
20	9 56 7	0♓27 20	7♓34	1♓	15	13	12	15	14	23	0
21	10 0 4	1 27 49	19 39	3	16	14	12	15	14	23	0
22	10 4 0	2 28 17	1♈50	5	17	14	12	15	14	22	0
23	10 7 57	3 28 43	14 10	7	18	15	12	15	14	22	0
24	10 11 53	4 29 7	26 40	9	19	15	12	15	14	22	0
25	10 15 50	5 29 30	9♉24	11	20	16	13	16	14	22	0
26	10 19 47	6 29 51	22 23	12	21	17	13	16	14	22	0
27	10 23 43	7 30 9	5♊42	14	23	17	13	16	14	22	0
28	10 27 40	8 30 26	19 24	16	24	18	13	16	14	22	0

THE SUN ENTERS THE SIGN OF PISCES ON FEB 19 AT 13:10.

DAY	TIME	☉	☽	☿	♀	♂	♃	♄	♅	♆	♇
	h m s	° ' "	° '	°	°	°	°	°	°	°	°
M 1	10 31 36	9♓30 40	3♋30	18♓	25♑	18♐	14♓	16♈	14♉	22♍R	0♌R
A 2	10 35 33	10 30 53	17 59	20	26	19	14	16	14	22	0
R 3	10 39 29	11 31 3	2♌48	22	27	20	14	16	15	22	0
C 4	10 43 26	12 31 11	17 51	24	28	20	14	16	15	22	0
H 5	10 47 22	13 31 18	2♍58	26	29	21	15	16	15	22	0
6	10 51 19	14 31 22	18 0	28	1♒	21	15	17	15	22	0
7	10 55 16	15 31 25	2♎47	29	2	22	15	17	15	22	29♋
8	10 59 12	16 31 25	17 12	1♈	3	22	15	17	15	22	29
9	11 3 9	17 31 24	1♏ 9	3	4	23	16	17	15	22	29
10	11 7 5	18 31 22	14 38	4	5	24	16	17	15	22	29
11	11 11 2	19 31 18	27 40	6	6	24	16	17	15	22	29
12	11 14 58	20 31 12	10♐18	8	7	25	16	17	15	22	29
13	11 18 55	21 31 4	22 38	9	9	25	17	17	15	22	29
14	11 22 51	22 30 55	4♑43	10	10	26	17	17	15	22	29
15	11 26 48	23 30 44	16 39	12	11	26	17	18	15	22	29
16	11 30 45	24 30 31	28 30	13	12	27	17	18	15	22	29
17	11 34 41	25 30 17	10♒21	14	13	28	18	18	15	22	29
18	11 38 38	26 30 1	22 15	15	14	28	18	18	15	22	29
19	11 42 34	27 29 42	4♓15	16	16	29	18	18	15	22	29
20	11 46 31	28 29 22	16 21	16	17	29	18	18	15	22	29
21	11 50 27	29 29 0	28 37	17	18	0♑	19	18	15	22	29
22	11 54 24	0♈28 36	11♈ 3	17	19	0	19	18	15	22	29
23	11 58 20	1 28 10	23 39	17	20	1	19	19	15	22	29
24	12 2 17	2 27 42	6♉26	18 R	21	1	19	19	15	22	29
25	12 6 13	3 27 11	19 25	18	23	2	19	19	15	22	29
26	12 10 10	4 26 39	2♊38	17	24	3	20	19	15	22	29
27	12 14 7	5 26 4	16 6	17	25	3	20	19	15	22	29
28	12 18 3	6 25 27	29 49	17	26	4	20	19	16	22	29
29	12 22 0	7 24 47	13♋48	16	27	4	20	19	16	22	29
30	12 25 56	8 24 5	28 3	16	28	5	21	19	16	22	29
31	12 29 53	9 23 21	12♌31	15	0♓	5	21	20	16	21	29

THE SUN ENTERS THE SIGN OF ARIES ON MAR 21 AT 12:28.

SIDEREAL SUN MOON MERCURY VENUS MARS JUPITER SATURN URANUS NEPTUNE PLUTO

DAY	TIME	☉	☽	☿	♀	♂	♃	♄	♅	♆	♇
	h m s	° ' "	° '	°	°	°	°	°	°	°	°
A 1	12 33 49	10♈22 34	27♌ 9	15♈R	1♓	6♑	21♓	20♈	16♉	21♍R	29♋R
P 2	12 37 46	11 21 45	11♍50	14	2	6	21	20	16	21	29
R 3	12 41 42	12 20 54	26 29	13	3	7	22	20	16	21	29
I 4	12 45 39	13 20 1	10♎56	12	4	7	22	20	16	21	29
L 5	12 49 36	14 19 5	25 8	11	5	8	22	20	16	21	29
6	12 53 32	15 18 8	8♏59	11	7	9	22	20	16	21	29
7	12 57 29	16 17 9	22 26	10	8	9	23	20	16	21	29
8	13 1 25	17 16 8	5♐31	9	9	10	23	21	16	21	29
9	13 5 22	18 15 5	18 13	8	10	10	23	21	16	21	29
10	13 9 18	19 14 0	0♑37	8	11	11	23	21	16	21	29
11	13 13 15	20 12 54	12 47	7	13	11	23	21	16	21	29
12	13 17 11	21 11 46	24 46	7	14	12	24	21	16	21	29 D
13	13 21 8	22 10 36	6♒39	6	15	12	24	21	16	21	29
14	13 25 5	23 9 24	18 32	6	16	13	24	21	16	21	29
15	13 29 1	24 8 10	0♓28	6	17	13	24	21	16	21	29
16	13 32 58	25 6 55	12 31	6 D	19	14	25	22	16	21	29
17	13 36 54	26 5 38	24 44	6	20	14	25	22	17	21	29
18	13 40 51	27 4 19	7♈10	6	21	15	25	22	17	21	29
19	13 44 47	28 2 58	19 50	6	22	15	25	22	17	21	29
20	13 48 44	29 1 36	2♉44	6	23	16	25	22	17	21	29
21	13 52 40	0♉ 0 11	15 54	6	25	16	26	22	17	21	29
22	13 56 37	0 58 45	29 17	7	26	17	26	22	17	21	29
23	14 0 33	1 57 16	12♊53	7	27	17	26	22	17	21	29
24	14 4 30	2 55 46	26 41	8	28	18	26	23	17	21	29
25	14 8 27	3 54 13	10♋38	8	29	18	27	23	17	21	29
26	14 12 23	4 52 38	24 44	9	0♈	19	27	23	17	21	29
27	14 16 20	5 51 1	8♌56	10	2	19	27	23	17	21	29
28	14 20 16	6 49 22	23 11	10	3	19	27	23	17	21	29
29	14 24 13	7 47 40	7♍28	11	4	20	27	23	17	21	29
30	14 28 9	8 45 57	21 43	12	5	20	28	23	17	21	29

THE SUN ENTERS THE SIGN OF TAURUS ON APR 20 AT 23:55.

DAY	TIME	☉	☽	☿	♀	♂	♃	♄	♅	♆	♇
	h m s	° ' "	° '	°	°	°	°	°	°	°	°
M 1	14 32 6	9♉44 11	5♎52	13♈	6♈	21♑	28♓	23♈	17♉	21♍R	29♋
A 2	14 36 2	10 42 24	19 52	14	8	21	28	24	17	21	29
Y 3	14 39 59	11 40 35	3♏39	15	9	22	28	24	17	21	29
4	14 43 56	12 38 43	17 11	16	10	22	28	24	18	21	29
5	14 47 52	13 36 51	0♐27	17	11	23	29	24	18	21	29
6	14 51 49	14 34 57	13 24	18	12	23	29	24	18	21	29
7	14 55 45	15 33 1	26 4	20	14	23	29	24	18	21	29
8	14 59 42	16 31 3	8♑28	21	15	24	29	24	18	21	29
9	15 3 38	17 29 5	20 38	22	16	24	29	24	18	21	29
10	15 7 35	18 27 4	2♒39	23	17	25	0☉	25	18	21	29
11	15 11 31	19 25 3	14 34	25	18	25	0	25	18	21	29
12	15 15 28	20 23 0	26 27	26	20	25	0♈	25	18	21	29
13	15 19 25	21 20 56	8♓23	28	21	26	0	25	18	21	29
14	15 23 21	22 18 50	20 28	29	22	26	0	25	18	21	29
15	15 27 18	23 16 44	2♈44	1♉	23	27	1	25	18	21	29
16	15 31 14	24 14 35	15 16	2	24	27	1	25	18	21	29
17	15 35 11	25 12 26	28 7	4	26	27	1	25	18	21	29
18	15 39 7	26 10 15	11♉17	5	27	28	1	25	18	21	29
19	15 43 4	27 8 4	24 47	7	28	28	1	26	18	21	29
20	15 47 0	28 5 50	8♊36	9	29	28	2	26	18	21	0♌
21	15 50 57	29 3 36	22 40	11	0♉	29	2	26	19	21	0
22	15 54 54	0♊ 1 20	6♋55	12	2	29	2	26	19	21	0
23	15 58 50	0 59 2	21 16	14	3	29	2	26	19	21	0
24	16 2 47	1 56 43	5♌39	16	4	0♒	2	26	19	21	0
25	16 6 43	2 54 22	20 0	18	5	0	2	26	19	21	0
26	16 10 40	3 51 59	4♍14	20	7	0	3	26	19	21	0
27	16 14 36	4 49 35	18 19	22	8	1	3	26	19	21	0
28	16 18 33	5 47 10	2♎15	24	9	1	3	27	19	21	0
29	16 22 29	6 44 43	16 0	26	10	1	3	27	19	21	0
30	16 26 26	7 42 15	29 33	28	11	1	3	27	19	21	0
31	16 30 23	8 39 46	12♏55	0♊	13	2	3	27	19	21	0

THE SUN ENTERS THE SIGN OF GEMINI ON MAY 21 AT 23:27.

DAY	TIME	☉	☽	☿	♀	♂	♃	♄	♅	♆	♇
	h m s	° ' "	° '	°	°	°	°	°	°	°	°
J 1	16 34 19	9♊37 15	26♏ 4	2♊	14♉	2♒	4♈	27♈	19♉	21♍D	0♌
U 2	16 38 16	10 34 43	9♐ 0	4	15	2	4	27	19	21	0
N 3	16 42 12	11 32 10	21 43	6	16	2	4	27	19	21	0
E 4	16 46 9	12 29 37	4♑14	8	17	3	4	27	19	21	0
5	16 50 5	13 27 2	16 32	10	19	3	4	27	19	21	0
6	16 54 2	14 24 27	28 39	13	20	3	4	27	19	21	0
7	16 57 58	15 21 51	10♒39	15	21	3	5	28	19	21	0
8	17 1 55	16 19 14	22 32	17	22	3	5	28	19	21	0
9	17 5 52	17 16 36	4♓25	19	23	4	5	28	20	21	0
10	17 9 48	18 13 58	16 20	21	25	4	5	28	20	21	0
11	17 13 45	19 11 20	28 23	24	26	4	5	28	20	21	0
12	17 17 41	20 8 41	10♈39	26	27	4	5	28	20	21	0
13	17 21 38	21 6 1	23 12	28	28	4	5	28	20	21	0
14	17 25 34	22 3 21	6♉ 7	0♋	29	4	6	28	20	21	0
15	17 29 31	23 0 41	19 26	2	1♊	4	6	28	20	21	0
16	17 33 27	23 58 0	3♊10	4	2	4	6	28	20	21	0
17	17 37 24	24 55 19	17 17	6	3	4	6	29	20	21	0
18	17 41 21	25 52 37	1♋45	8	4	5	6	29	20	21	0
19	17 45 17	26 49 55	16 27	10	6	5	6	29	20	21	0
20	17 49 14	27 47 11	1♌15	12	7	5	6	29	20	21	0
21	17 53 10	28 44 28	16 1	14	8	5	6	29	20	21	0
22	17 57 7	29 41 43	0♍38	16	9	5 R	7	29	20	21	0
23	18 1 3	0♋38 58	15 1	18	10	5	7	29	20	21	0
24	18 5 0	1 36 12	29 7	20	12	5	7	29	20	21	0
25	18 8 57	2 33 26	12♎55	21	13	5	7	29	20	21	0
26	18 12 53	3 30 39	26 26	23	14	5	7	29	20	21	0
27	18 16 50	4 27 51	9♏41	25	15	5	7	29	20	21	0
28	18 20 46	5 25 3	22 41	26	16	5	7	29	20	21	0
29	18 24 43	6 22 14	5♐30	28	18	4	7	0♉	21	21	0
30	18 28 39	7 19 26	18 7	0♌	19	4	7	0	21	21	0

THE SUN ENTERS THE SIGN OF CANCER ON JUN 22 AT 07:40.

♈ ARIES ♉ TAURUS ♊ GEMINI ♋ CANCER ♌ LEO ♍ VIRGO ♎ LIBRA ♏ SCORPIO ♐ SAGITTARIUS ♑ CAPRICORN ♒ AQUARIUS ♓ PISCES

SIDEREAL SUN MOON MERCURY VENUS MARS JUPITER SATURN URANUS NEPTUNE PLUTO

DAY	TIME	☉	☽	☿	♀	♂	♃	♄	♅	♆	♇
	h m s	° ' "	° '	°	°	°	°	°	°	°	°
J 1	18 32 36	8♋16 37	0♑34	1♌	20♊	4♒R	7♈	0♉	21♉	21♍	0♌
U 2	18 36 32	9 13 47	12 52	3	21	4	8	0	21	21	0
L 3	18 40 29	10 10 58	25 1	4	23	4	8	0	21	21	0
Y 4	18 44 26	11 8 9	7♒ 3	5	24	4	8	0	21	21	0
5	18 48 22	12 5 19	18 59	7	25	4	8	0	21	21	1
6	18 52 19	13 2 30	0♓51	8	26	4	8	0	21	21	1
7	18 56 15	13 59 41	12 42	9	27	3	8	0	21	21	1
8	19 0 12	14 56 53	24 36	11	29	3	8	0	21	21	1
9	19 4 8	15 54 4	6♈37	12	0♋	3	8	0	21	21	1
10	19 8 5	16 51 16	18 50	13	1	3	8	0	21	21	1
11	19 12 1	17 48 29	1♉21	14	2	3	8	0	21	21	1
12	19 15 58	18 45 42	14 13	15	4	2	8	0	21	21	1
13	19 19 55	19 42 55	27 32	16	5	2	8	0	21	21	1
14	19 23 51	20 40 10	11♊20	17	6	2	8	0	21	21	1
15	19 27 48	21 37 24	25 36	18	7	2	8	0	21	21	1
16	19 31 44	22 34 39	10♋17	19	8	2	8	1	21	21	1
17	19 35 41	23 31 55	25 16	20	10	1	9	1	21	21	1
18	19 39 37	24 29 11	10♌25	21	11	1	9	1	21	21	1
19	19 43 34	25 26 27	25 32	21	12	1	9	1	21	21	1
20	19 47 30	26 23 43	10♍28	22	13	0	9	1	21	21	1
21	19 51 27	27 21 0	25 6	22	15	0	9	1	21	21	1
22	19 55 24	28 18 16	9♎21	23	16	0	9	1	21	21	1
23	19 59 20	29 15 34	23 11	23	17	0	9	1	21	21	1
24	20 3 17	0♌12 51	6♏38	24	18	29♑	9	1	21	21	1
25	20 7 13	1 10 9	19 45	24	19	29	9	1	21	21	1
26	20 11 10	2 7 27	2♐34	24	21	29	9	1	22	21	1
27	20 15 6	3 4 46	15 8	24 R	22	29	9	1	22	21	1
28	20 19 3	4 2 5	27 31	24	23	28	9	1	22	21	1
29	20 22 59	4 59 25	9♑45	24	24	28	9 R	1	22	21	1
30	20 26 56	5 56 45	21 51	24	26	28	9	1	22	21	1
31	20 30 53	6 54 6	3♒52	24	27	27	9	1	22	21	1

THE SUN ENTERS THE SIGN OF LEO ON JUL 23 AT 18:37.

DAY	TIME	☉	☽	☿	♀	♂	♃	♄	♅	♆	♇
	h m s	° ' "	° '	°	°	°	°	°	°	°	°
A 1	20 34 49	7♌51 28	15♒48	23♌R	28♋	27♑R	9♈R	1♉	22♉	21♍	1♌
U 2	20 38 46	8 48 51	27 41	23	29	27	9	1	22	21	1
G 3	20 42 42	9 46 14	9♓32	23	1♌	27	9	1	22	22	1
U 4	20 46 39	10 43 39	21 23	22	2	26	9	1	22	22	1
S 5	20 50 35	11 41 5	3♈18	21	3	26	9	1	22	22	1
T 6	20 54 32	12 38 32	15 19	21	4	26	9	1	22	22	1
7	20 58 28	13 36 0	27 32	20	5	26	9	1	22	22	1
8	21 2 25	14 33 29	10♉ 0	19	7	26	9	1	22	22	1
9	21 6 22	15 31 0	22 50	18	8	25	9	1	22	22	1
10	21 10 18	16 28 33	6♊ 4	18	9	25	9	1	22	22	2
11	21 14 15	17 26 6	19 47	17	10	25	9	1	22	22	2
12	21 18 11	18 23 41	3♋59	16	12	25	9	1	22	22	2
13	21 22 8	19 21 18	18 39	15	13	25	8	1	22	22	2
14	21 26 4	20 18 56	3♌41	15	14	25	8	1 R	22	22	2
15	21 30 1	21 16 35	18 57	14	15	24	8	1	22	22	2
16	21 33 57	22 14 15	4♍15	13	17	24	8	1	22	22	2
17	21 37 54	23 11 57	19 24	13	18	24	8	1	22	22	2
18	21 41 51	24 9 39	4♎15	13	19	24	8	1	22	22	2
19	21 45 47	25 7 23	18 42	12	20	24	8	1	22	22	2
20	21 49 44	26 5 8	2♏41	12 D	21	24	8	1	22	22	2
21	21 53 40	27 2 54	16 13	12	23	24	8	1	22	22	2
22	21 57 37	28 0 41	29 20	12	24	24	8	1	22	22	2
23	22 1 33	28 58 30	12♐ 6	12	25	24	8	1	22	22	2
24	22 5 30	29 56 19	24 35	13	26	24 D	8	1	22	22	2
25	22 9 26	0♍54 10	6♑50	13	28	24	8	1	22	22	2
26	22 13 23	1 52 2	18 56	14	29	24	8	1	22	22	2
27	22 17 20	2 49 55	0♒55	15	0♍	24	8	1	22	22	2
28	22 21 16	3 47 50	12 50	16	1	24	7	1	22 R	22	2
29	22 25 13	4 45 46	24 42	17	3	24	7	1	22	22	2
30	22 29 9	5 43 44	6♓34	18	4	24	7	1	22	22	2
31	22 33 6	6 41 43	18 27	19	5	24	7	1	22	22	2

THE SUN ENTERS THE SIGN OF VIRGO ON AUG 24 AT 01:32.

DAY	TIME	☉	☽	☿	♀	♂	♃	♄	♅	♆	♇
	h m s	° ' "	° '	°	°	°	°	°	°	°	°
S 1	22 37 2	7♍39 44	0♈22	20♌	6♍	24♑	7♈R	1♉R	22♉R	22♍	2♌
E 2	22 40 59	8 37 47	12 22	22	8	24	7	1	22	23	2
P 3	22 44 55	9 35 51	24 30	23	9	25	7	1	22	23	2
T 4	22 48 52	10 33 58	6♉47	25	10	25	7	1	22	23	2
E 5	22 52 48	11 32 6	19 19	26	11	25	7	1	22	23	2
M 6	22 56 45	12 30 16	2♊ 8	28	13	25	7	1	22	23	2
B 7	23 0 42	13 28 29	15 20	0♍	14	25	6	1	22	23	2
E 8	23 4 38	14 26 43	28 55	1	15	25	6	1	22	23	2
R 9	23 8 35	15 25 0	12♋58	3	16	26	6	1	22	23	2
10	23 12 31	16 23 18	27 26	5	18	26	6	1	22	23	2
11	23 16 28	17 21 39	12♌16	7	19	26	6	1	22	23	2
12	23 20 24	18 20 1	27 22	9	20	26	6	1	22	23	2
13	23 24 21	19 18 26	12♍34	11	21	27	6	1	22	23	2
14	23 28 17	20 16 52	27 43	13	22	27	6	0	22	23	2
15	23 32 14	21 15 20	12♎38	15	24	27	5	0	22	23	2
16	23 36 11	22 13 50	27 11	16	25	27	5	0	22	23	2
17	23 40 7	23 12 22	11♏18	18	26	28	5	0	22	23	2
18	23 44 4	24 10 56	24 58	20	27	28	5	0	22	23	2
19	23 48 0	25 9 31	8♐12	22	29	28	5	0	22	23	2
20	23 51 57	26 8 8	21 1	24	0♎	29	5	0	22	23	2
21	23 55 53	27 6 46	3♑31	26	1	29	5	0	22	23	2
22	23 59 50	28 5 26	15 45	28	2	29	5	0	22	23	3
23	0 3 46	29 4 8	27 48	29	4	0♒	4	0	22	23	3
24	0 7 43	0♎ 2 51	9♒44	1♎	5	0	4	0	22	23	3
25	0 11 40	1 1 37	21 36	3	6	0	4	0	22	23	3
26	0 15 36	2 0 24	3♓28	5	7	1	4	0	22	23	3
27	0 19 33	2 59 13	15 21	7	9	1	4	0	22	23	3
28	0 23 29	3 58 4	27 19	8	10	2	4	0	22	23	3
29	0 27 26	4 56 56	9♈22	10	11	2	4	0	22	24	3
30	0 31 22	5 55 51	21 33	12	12	2	3	29♈	22	24	3

THE SUN ENTERS THE SIGN OF LIBRA ON SEP 23 AT 22:50.

SIDEREAL SUN MOON MERCURY VENUS MARS JUPITER SATURN URANUS NEPTUNE PLUTO

DAY	TIME	☉	☽	☿	♀	♂	♃	♄	♅	♆	♇
	h m s	° ' "	° '	°	°	°	°	°	°	°	°
O 1	0 35 19	6♎54 48	3♉53	13♎	14♎	3♒	3♈R	29♈R	22♉R	24♍	3♌
C 2	0 39 15	7 53 48	16 24	15	15	3	3	29	21	24	3
T 3	0 43 12	8 52 49	29 7	17	16	4	3	29	21	24	3
O 4	0 47 8	9 51 53	12♊ 6	18	17	4	3	29	21	24	3
B 5	0 51 5	10 50 59	25 21	20	19	4	3	29	21	24	3
E 6	0 55 2	11 50 7	8♋55	22	20	5	3	29	21	24	3
R 7	0 58 58	12 49 18	22 50	23	21	5	3	29	21	24	3
8	1 2 55	13 48 31	7♌ 3	25	22	6	2	29	21	24	3
9	1 6 51	14 47 46	21 34	27	24	6	2	29	21	24	3
10	1 10 48	15 47 4	6♍18	28	25	7	2	29	21	24	3
11	1 14 44	16 46 24	21 10	0♏	26	7	2	29	21	24	3
12	1 18 41	17 45 45	6♎ 1	1	27	8	2	29	21	24	3
13	1 22 37	18 45 10	20 44	3	29	8	2	29	21	24	3
14	1 26 34	19 44 36	5♏12	4	0♏	9	2	28	21	24	3
15	1 30 31	20 44 4	19 20	6	1	9	2	28	21	24	3
16	1 34 27	21 43 34	3♐ 3	7	2	10	1	28	21	24	3
17	1 38 24	22 43 6	16 22	9	4	10	1	28	21	24	3
18	1 42 20	23 42 40	29 16	10	5	11	1	28	21	24	3
19	1 46 17	24 42 15	11♑50	12	6	11	1	28	21	24	3
20	1 50 13	25 41 53	24 7	13	7	12	1	28	21	24	3
21	1 54 10	26 41 32	6♒11	15	9	12	1	28	21	24	3
22	1 58 6	27 41 12	18 6	16	10	13	1	28	21	24	3
23	2 2 3	28 40 55	29 57	18	11	14	1	28	21	24	3
24	2 6 0	29 40 39	11♓49	19	12	14	1	28	21	24	3
25	2 9 56	0♏40 25	23 45	20	14	15	0	28	21	24	3
26	2 13 53	1 40 12	5♈48	22	15	15	0	27	21	24	3
27	2 17 49	2 40 2	18 2	23	16	16	0	27	21	24	3
28	2 21 46	3 39 53	0♉26	24	17	16	0	27	21	25	3
29	2 25 42	4 39 47	13 4	26	19	17	0	27	21	25	3
30	2 29 39	5 39 42	25 55	27	20	17	0	27	21	25	3
31	2 33 35	6 39 40	9♊ 0	28	21	18	0⊙	27	20	25	3

THE SUN ENTERS THE SIGN OF SCORPIO ON OCT 24 AT 07:47.

DAY	TIME	☉	☽	☿	♀	♂	♃	♄	♅	♆	♇
	h m s	° ' "	° '	°	°	°	°	°	°	°	°
N 1	2 37 32	7♏39 39	22♊19	0♐	22♏	19♒	0⊙R	27♈R	20♉R	25♍	3♌
O 2	2 41 29	8 39 41	5♋50	1	24	19	0	27	20	25	3
V 3	2 45 25	9 39 45	19 34	2	25	20	0	27	20	25	3 R
E 4	2 49 22	10 39 51	3♌29	3	26	20	0	27	20	25	3
M 5	2 53 18	11 39 58	17 35	4	27	21	0	27	20	25	3
B 6	2 57 15	12 40 9	1♍49	6	29	22	29♓	27	20	25	3
E 7	3 1 11	13 40 21	16 10	7	0♐	22	29	27	20	25	3
R 8	3 5 8	14 40 35	0♎34	8	1	23	29	26	20	25	3
9	3 9 4	15 40 51	14 58	9	2	23	29	26	20	25	3
10	3 13 1	16 41 9	29 16	10	4	24	29	26	20	25	3
11	3 16 57	17 41 29	13♏25	10	5	25	29	26	20	25	3
12	3 20 54	18 41 51	27 19	11	6	25	29	26	20	25	3
13	3 24 51	19 42 14	10♐55	12	7	26	29	26	20	25	3
14	3 28 47	20 42 39	24 11	13	9	26	29	26	20	25	3
15	3 32 44	21 43 6	7♑ 7	13	10	27	29	26	20	25	3
16	3 36 40	22 43 34	19 43	14	11	28	29	26	20	25	3
17	3 40 37	23 44 3	2♒ 2	14	12	28	29	26	20	25	3
18	3 44 33	24 44 33	14 7	14 R	14	29	29	26	20	25	3
19	3 48 30	25 45 5	26 3	14	15	0♓	29	26	20	25	3
20	3 52 26	26 45 38	7♓54	14	16	0	29	26	20	25	3
21	3 56 23	27 46 12	19 45	13	17	1	29	26	20	25	3
22	4 0 20	28 46 48	1♈42	13	19	1	29	26	20	25	3
23	4 4 16	29 47 25	13 49	12	20	2	29	25	20	25	3
24	4 8 13	0♐48 2	26 9	11	21	3	29 D	25	20	25	3
25	4 12 9	1 48 42	8♉46	10	22	3	29	25	19	25	3
26	4 16 6	2 49 22	21 41	9	24	4	29	25	19	25	3
27	4 20 2	3 50 4	4♊55	8	25	5	29	25	19	25	3
28	4 23 59	4 50 47	18 26	7	26	5	29	25	19	25	3
29	4 27 55	5 51 32	2♋12	5	27	6	29	25	19	25	3
30	4 31 52	6 52 18	16 10	4	29	7	29	25	19	25	3

THE SUN ENTERS THE SIGN OF SAGITTARIUS ON NOV 23 AT 04:59.

DAY	TIME	☉	☽	☿	♀	♂	♃	♄	♅	♆	♇
	h m s	° ' "	° '	°	°	°	°	°	°	°	°
D 1	4 35 49	7♐53 5	0♌15	3♐R	0♑	7♓	29♓	25♈R	19♉R	25♍	3♌R
E 2	4 39 45	8 53 54	14 25	1	1	8	29	25	19	25	3
C 3	4 43 42	9 54 44	28 35	0	2	9	29	25	19	25	3
E 4	4 47 38	10 55 36	12♍45	29♏	3	9	29	25	19	25	3
M 5	4 51 35	11 56 29	26 51	29	5	10	29	25	19	25	3
B 6	4 55 31	12 57 23	10♎53	28	6	11	29	25	19	25	3
E 7	4 59 28	13 58 18	24 49	28	7	11	29	25	19	25	3
R 8	5 3 24	14 59 15	8♏39	28 D	8	12	29	25	19	25	3
9	5 7 21	16 0 14	22 21	28	10	13	29	25	19	25	3
10	5 11 18	17 1 13	5♐52	28	11	13	29	25	19	25	3
11	5 15 14	18 2 13	19 10	28	12	14	29	25	19	25	3
12	5 19 11	19 3 14	2♑14	29	13	15	29	25	19	25	3
13	5 23 7	20 4 16	15 2	29	15	15	29	25	19	25	3
14	5 27 4	21 5 18	27 34	0♐	16	16	29	25	19	25	3
15	5 31 0	22 6 21	9♒51	1	17	17	0⊙	25	19	25	3
16	5 34 57	23 7 25	21 55	2	18	17	0	25	19	25	3
17	5 38 54	24 8 29	3♓50	3	20	18	0	25	19	25	3
18	5 42 50	25 9 33	15 40	4	21	19	0	25	19	25	3
19	5 46 47	26 10 38	27 30	5	22	19	0	24	19	25	3
20	5 50 43	27 11 43	9♈25	6	23	20	0	24	19	25	2
21	5 54 40	28 12 48	21 31	7	25	21	0♈	24	19	26	2
22	5 58 36	29 13 54	3♉53	9	26	21	0	24	19	26	2
23	6 2 33	0♑15 0	16 34	10	27	22	0	24	18	26	2
24	6 6 29	1 16 6	29 39	11	28	23	0	24	18	26	2
25	6 10 26	2 17 13	13♊ 9	12	0♒	23	0	24	18	26	2
26	6 14 23	3 18 19	27 2	14	1	24	0	24	18	26	2
27	6 18 19	4 19 26	11♋15	15	2	25	1	24	18	26	2
28	6 22 16	5 20 34	25 42	16	3	25	1	24 D	18	26 R	2
29	6 26 12	6 21 41	10♌17	18	5	26	1	24	18	26	2
30	6 30 9	7 22 49	24 52	19	6	27	1	24	18	26	2
31	6 34 5	8 23 58	9♍21	21	7	27	1	24	18	26	2

THE SUN ENTERS THE SIGN OF CAPRICORN ON DEC 22 AT 18:07.

♈ ARIES ♉ TAURUS ♊ GEMINI ♋ CANCER ♌ LEO ♍ VIRGO ♎ LIBRA ♏ SCORPIO ♐ SAGITTARIUS ♑ CAPRICORN ♒ AQUARIUS ♓ PISCES

SIDEREAL SUN MOON MERCURY VENUS MARS JUPITER SATURN URANUS NEPTUNE PLUTO

DAY	TIME	☉	☽	☿	♀	♂	♃	♄	♅	♆	♇
	h m s	° ' "	° '	°	°	°	°	°	°	°	°
J 1	6 38 2	9♑25 7	23♍40	22♐	8♒	28♓	1♈	24♈	18♉R	26♍R	2♌R
A 2	6 41 58	10 26 16	7♎46	24	10	29	1	24	18	26	2
N 3	6 45 55	11 27 25	21 39	25	11	29	1	24	18	26	2
U 4	6 49 52	12 28 35	5♏20	27	12	0♈	2	24	18	26	2
A 5	6 53 48	13 29 46	18 48	28	13	1♈	2	24	18	26	2
R 6	6 57 45	14 30 56	2♐ 5	0♑	14	1	2	24	18	25	2
Y 7	7 1 41	15 32 7	15 12	1	16	2	2	25	18	25	2
8	7 5 38	16 33 17	28 8	3	17	3	2	25	18	25	2
9	7 9 34	17 34 28	10♑53	4	18	3	2	25	18	25	2
10	7 13 31	18 35 38	23 26	6	19	4	2	25	18	25	2
11	7 17 27	19 36 48	5♒48	7	21	5	2	25	18	25	2
12	7 21 24	20 37 58	17 58	9	22	5	3	25	18	25	2
13	7 25 21	21 39 7	29 58	10	23	6	3	25	18	25	2
14	7 29 17	22 40 15	11♓51	12	24	7	3	25	18	25	2
15	7 33 14	23 41 23	23 39	13	26	7	3	25	18	25	2
16	7 37 10	24 42 31	5♈27	15	27	8	3	25	18	25	2
17	7 41 7	25 43 37	17 19	16	28	9	3	25	18	25	2
18	7 45 3	26 44 43	29 22	18	29	10	4	25	18	25	2
19	7 49 0	27 45 48	11♉40	20	1♓	10	4	25	18	25	2
20	7 52 56	28 46 53	24 19	21	2	11	4	25	18	25	2
21	7 56 53	29 47 56	7♊24	23	3	12	4	25	18	25	2
22	8 0 50	0♒48 59	20 56	24	4	12	4	25	18	25	2
23	8 4 46	1 50 0	4♋58	26	5	13	4	25	18	25	2
24	8 8 43	2 51 1	19 26	28	7	14	5	25	18	25	2
25	8 12 39	3 52 1	4♌14	29	8	14	5	25	18	25	2
26	8 16 36	4 53 0	19 13	1♒	9	15	5	25	18 D	25	2
27	8 20 32	5 53 59	4♍15	3	10	16	5	25	18	25	2
28	8 24 29	6 54 56	19 9	4	12	16	5	25	18	25	2
29	8 28 25	7 55 53	3♎48	6	13	17	5	25	18	25	2
30	8 32 22	8 56 49	18 9	8	14	18	6	25	18	25	2
31	8 36 19	9 57 45	2♏ 8	9	15	18	6	25	18	25	2

THE SUN ENTERS THE SIGN OF AQUARIUS ON JAN 21 AT 04:44.

DAY	TIME	☉	☽	☿	♀	♂	♃	♄	♅	♆	♇
	h m s	° ' "	° '	°	°	°	°	°	°	°	°
F 1	8 40 15	10♒58 40	15♏47	11♒	16♓	19♈	6♈	26♈	18♉	25♍R	2♌R
E 2	8 44 12	11 59 34	29 7	13	18	20	6	26	18	25	2
B 3	8 48 8	13 0 27	12♐11	15	19	20	6	26	18	25	2
R 4	8 52 5	14 1 20	25 0	16	20	21	7	26	18	25	2
U 5	8 56 1	15 2 12	7♑38	18	21	22	7	26	18	25	1
A 6	8 59 58	16 3 2	20 4	20	22	22	7	26	18	25	1
R 7	9 3 54	17 3 52	2♒22	22	24	23	7	26	18	25	1
Y 8	9 7 51	18 4 41	14 31	24	25	24	7	26	18	25	1
9	9 11 48	19 5 28	26 32	25	26	25	7	26	18	25	1
10	9 15 44	20 6 14	8♓26	27	27	25	8	26	18	25	1
11	9 19 41	21 6 58	20 16	29	29	26	8	26	18	25	1
12	9 23 37	22 7 41	2♈ 3	1♓	0♈	27	8	26	18	25	1
13	9 27 34	23 8 22	13 51	3	1♈	27	8	26	18	25	1
14	9 31 30	24 9 2	25 43	4	2	28	9	26	18	25	1
15	9 35 27	25 9 40	7♉44	6	3	29	9	27	18	25	1
16	9 39 23	26 10 17	19 59	8	5	29	9	27	18	25	1
17	9 43 20	27 10 52	2♊34	10	6	0♉	9	27	18	25	1
18	9 47 17	28 11 25	15 32	12	7	1	9	27	18	25	1
19	9 51 13	29 11 56	28 59	13	8	1	10	27	18	25	1
20	9 55 10	0♓12 25	12♋56	15	9	2	10	27	18	25	1
21	9 59 6	1 12 53	27 21	17	10	3	10	27	18	25	1
22	10 3 3	2 13 19	12♌12	18	12	3	10	27	18	25	1
23	10 6 59	3 13 43	27 20	20	13	4	10	27	18	25	1
24	10 10 56	4 14 5	12♍36	21	14	5	11	27	18	25	1
25	10 14 52	5 14 26	27 48	23	15	5	11	27	18	25	1
26	10 18 49	6 14 45	12♎48	24	16	6	11	28	18	25	1
27	10 22 46	7 15 3	27 27	25	18	7	11	28	18	25	1
28	10 26 42	8 15 19	11♏43	26	19	7	12	28	18	25	1
29	10 30 39	9 15 34	25 32	27	20	8	12	28	18	25	1

THE SUN ENTERS THE SIGN OF PISCES ON FEB 19 AT 19:04.

DAY	TIME	☉	☽	☿	♀	♂	♃	♄	♅	♆	♇
	h m s	° ' "	° '	°	°	°	°	°	°	°	°
M 1	10 34 35	10♓15 47	8♐57	28♓	21♈	9♉	12♈	28♈	18♉	25♍R	1♌R
A 2	10 38 32	11 15 59	21 59	29	22	9	12	28	19	25	1
R 3	10 42 28	12 16 9	4♑43	29	23	10	12	28	19	24	1
C 4	10 46 25	13 16 18	17 11	0♈	25	11	13	28	19	24	1
H 5	10 50 21	14 16 25	29 26	0♈	26	11	13	28	19	24	1
6	10 54 18	15 16 30	11♒31	0 R	27	12	13	28	19	24	1
7	10 58 15	16 16 34	23 30	0	28	13	13	29	19	24	1
8	11 2 11	17 16 36	5♓23	0	29	13	14	29	19	24	1
9	11 6 8	18 16 36	17 12	0♈	0♉	14	14	29	19	24	1
10	11 10 4	19 16 34	29 0	29♓	2	15	14	29	19	24	1
11	11 14 1	20 16 30	10♈49	29	3	15	14	29	19	24	1
12	11 17 57	21 16 24	22 40	28	4	16	14	29	19	24	1
13	11 21 54	22 16 16	4♉37	27	5	17	15	29	19	24	1
14	11 25 50	23 16 6	16 43	26	6	17	15	29	19	24	1
15	11 29 47	24 15 54	29 1	25	7	18	15	29	19	24	1
16	11 33 43	25 15 40	11♊36	24	8	19	15	29	19	24	1
17	11 37 40	26 15 23	24 31	24	9	19	16	0♉	19	24	1
18	11 41 37	27 15 4	7♋51	23	11	20	16	0	19	24	1
19	11 45 33	28 14 43	21 37	22	12	21	16	0	19	24	1
20	11 49 30	29 14 19	5♌50	21	13	21	16	0	19	24	1
21	11 53 26	0♈13 53	20 27	20	14	22	17	0	19	24	1
22	11 57 23	1 13 25	5♍26	19	15	23	17	0	19	24	1
23	12 1 19	2 12 55	20 36	19	16	23	17	0	19	24	1
24	12 5 16	3 12 23	5♎50	18	17	24	17	0	19	24	1
25	12 9 12	4 11 48	20 57	18	18	25	18	1	19	24	1
26	12 13 9	5 11 12	5♏48	17	20	25	18	1	19	24	1
27	12 17 6	6 10 34	20 17	17	21	26	18	1	19	24	1
28	12 21 2	7 9 54	4♐20	17	22	27	18	1	20	24	1
29	12 24 59	8 9 12	17 55	17 D	23	27	18	1	20	24	1
30	12 28 55	9 8 29	1♑ 5	17	24	28	19	1	20	24	1
31	12 32 52	10 7 43	13 51	17	25	29	19	1	20	24	1

THE SUN ENTERS THE SIGN OF ARIES ON MAR 20 AT 18:24.

SIDEREAL SUN MOON MERCURY VENUS MARS JUPITER SATURN URANUS NEPTUNE PLUTO

DAY	TIME	☉	☽	☿	♀	♂	♃	♄	♅	♆	♇
	h m s	° ' "	° '	°	°	°	°	°	°	°	°
A 1	12 36 48	11♈ 6 56	26♑18	17♓	26♉	29♉	19♈	1♉	20♉	24♍R	1♌R
P 2	12 40 45	12 6 7	8♒30	18	27	0♊	19	2	20	24	1
R 3	12 44 41	13 5 17	20 30	18	28	1	20	2	20	24	1
I 4	12 48 38	14 4 24	2♓22	18	29	1	20	2	20	24	1
L 5	12 52 35	15 3 29	14 11	19	0♊	2	20	2	20	24	1
6	12 56 31	16 2 33	25 59	19	1	3	20	2	20	24	1
7	13 0 28	17 1 35	7♈48	20	2	3	21	2	20	24	1
8	13 4 24	18 0 34	19 41	21	3	4	21	2	20	24	1
9	13 8 21	18 59 32	1♉41	22	4	5	21	2	20	23	1
10	13 12 17	19 58 28	13 48	23	5	5	21	3	20	23	1
11	13 16 14	20 57 21	26 6	23	6	6	22	3	20	23	1
12	13 20 10	21 56 13	8♊35	24	7	7	22	3	20	23	1
13	13 24 7	22 55 2	21 19	25	8	7	22	3	20	23	1 D
14	13 28 3	23 53 49	4♋20	26	9	8	22	3	20	23	1
15	13 32 0	24 52 34	17 39	27	10	9	23	3	20	23	1
16	13 35 57	25 51 16	1♌18	29	11	9	23	3	20	23	1
17	13 39 53	26 49 56	15 18	0♈	12	10	23	3	21	23	1
18	13 43 50	27 48 34	29 39	1♈	13	11	23	4	21	23	1
19	13 47 46	28 47 10	14♍17	2	14	11	24	4	21	23	1
20	13 51 43	29 45 43	29 8	3	15	12	24	4	21	23	1
21	13 55 39	0♉44 15	14♎ 6	5	16	13	24	4	21	23	1
22	13 59 36	1 42 44	29 2	6	17	13	24	4	21	23	1
23	14 3 32	2 41 12	13♏49	8	18	14	25	4	21	23	1
24	14 7 29	3 39 38	28 20	9	19	15	25	4	21	23	1
25	14 11 26	4 38 2	12♐28	10	20	15	25	4	21	23	1
26	14 15 22	5 36 24	26 11	12	21	16	25	5	21	23	1
27	14 19 19	6 34 45	9♑27	13	22	17	25	5	21	23	1
28	14 23 15	7 33 4	22 19	15	23	17	26	5	21	23	1
29	14 27 12	8 31 22	4♒50	17	24	18	26	5	21	23	1
30	14 31 8	9 29 38	17 3	18	24	19	26	5	21	23	1

THE SUN ENTERS THE SIGN OF TAURUS ON APR 20 AT 05:51.

DAY	TIME	☉	☽	☿	♀	♂	♃	♄	♅	♆	♇
	h m s	° ' "	° '	°	°	°	°	°	°	°	°
M 1	14 35 5	10♉27 52	29♒ 2	20♈	25♊	19♊	26♈	5♉	21♉	23♍R	1♌
A 2	14 39 1	11 26 5	10♓54	21	26	20	27	5	21	23	1
Y 3	14 42 58	12 24 17	22 41	23	27	21	27	5	21	23	1
4	14 46 55	13 22 27	4♈30	25	28	21	27	6	21	23	1
5	14 50 51	14 20 35	16 23	27	29	22	27	6	22	23	1
6	14 54 48	15 18 42	28 23	28	29	22	28	6	22	23	1
7	14 58 44	16 16 47	10♉33	0♉	0♋	23	28	6	22	23	1
8	15 2 41	17 14 51	22 55	2	1	24	28	6	22	23	1
9	15 6 37	18 12 53	5♊30	4	2	24	28	6	22	23	1
10	15 10 34	19 10 54	18 18	6	2	25	29	6	22	23	1
11	15 14 30	20 8 52	1♋20	8	3	26	29	6	22	23	1
12	15 18 27	21 6 49	14 36	10	4	26	29	7	22	23	1
13	15 22 24	22 4 45	28 5	12	4	27	29	7	22	23	1
14	15 26 20	23 2 38	11♌48	14	5	28	29	7	22	23	1
15	15 30 17	24 0 30	25 43	16	6	28	0♉	7	22	23	1
16	15 34 13	24 58 19	9♍51	18	6	29	0	7	22	23	1
17	15 38 10	25 56 7	24 11	20	7	0♋	0	7	22	23	1
18	15 42 6	26 53 53	8♎39	22	8	0	0	7	22	23	1
19	15 46 3	27 51 38	23 12	24	8	1	1	7	22	23	1
20	15 49 59	28 49 21	7♏46	27	9	2	1	8	22	23	1
21	15 53 56	29 47 3	22 14	29	9	2	1	8	22	23	1
22	15 57 53	0♊44 43	6♐31	1♊	10	3	1	8	23	23	1
23	16 1 49	1 42 22	20 31	3	10	3	2	8	23	23	1
24	16 5 46	2 40 0	4♑11	5	11	4	2	8	23	23	1
25	16 9 42	3 37 37	17 28	7	11	5	2	8	23	23	1
26	16 13 39	4 35 13	0♒22	10	11	5	2	8	23	23	1
27	16 17 35	5 32 48	12 54	12	12	6	2	8	23	23	1
28	16 21 32	6 30 22	25 9	14	12	7	3	9	23	23	1
29	16 25 28	7 27 55	7♓ 9	16	12	7	3	9	23	23	1
30	16 29 25	8 25 27	19 1	18	13	8	3	9	23	23	1
31	16 33 22	9 22 58	0♈50	20	13	9	3	9	23	23	1

THE SUN ENTERS THE SIGN OF GEMINI ON MAY 21 AT 05:23.

DAY	TIME	☉	☽	☿	♀	♂	♃	♄	♅	♆	♇
	h m s	° ' "	° '	°	°	°	°	°	°	°	°
J 1	16 37 18	10♊20 28	12♈40	22♊	13♋	9♋	3♉	9♉	23♉	23♍R	1♌
U 2	16 41 15	11 17 58	24 36	24	13	10	4	9	23	23	1
N 3	16 45 11	12 15 27	6♉43	26	13	11	4	9	23	23 D	1
E 4	16 49 8	13 12 55	19 4	28	13	11	4	9	23	23	1
5	16 53 4	14 10 22	1♊41	0♋	13 R	12	4	9	23	23	1
6	16 57 1	15 7 48	14 35	2	13	12	5	10	23	23	1
7	17 0 57	16 5 14	27 45	4	13	13	5	10	23	23	1
8	17 4 54	17 2 38	11♋11	6	13	14	5	10	23	23	1
9	17 8 51	18 0 2	24 50	7	13	14	5	10	24	23	1
10	17 12 47	18 57 25	8♌39	9	13	15	5	10	24	23	1
11	17 16 44	19 54 46	22 35	11	13	16	6	10	24	23	1
12	17 20 40	20 52 7	6♍38	12	12	16	6	10	24	23	1
13	17 24 37	21 49 26	20 44	14	12	17	6	10	24	23	1
14	17 28 33	22 46 45	4♎53	15	12	18	6	10	24	23	1
15	17 32 30	23 44 2	19 3	17	11	18	6	11	24	23	1
16	17 36 26	24 41 19	3♏14	18	11	19	7	11	24	23	1
17	17 40 23	25 38 35	17 22	19	11	20	7	11	24	23	1
18	17 44 20	26 35 50	1♐25	21	10	20	7	11	24	23	1
19	17 48 16	27 33 5	15 19	22	10	21	7	11	24	23	1
20	17 52 13	28 30 19	29 1	23	9	21	7	11	24	23	2
21	17 56 9	29 27 33	12♑26	24	9	22	8	11	24	23	2
22	18 0 6	0♋24 46	25 34	26	8	23	8	11	24	23	2
23	18 4 2	1 21 59	8♒22	27	7	23	8	11	24	23	2
24	18 7 59	2 19 12	20 51	28	7	24	8	11	24	23	2
25	18 11 55	3 16 24	3♓ 4	29	6	25	8	12	24	23	2
26	18 15 52	4 13 37	15 4	29	6	25	8	12	24	23	2
27	18 19 49	5 10 49	26 56	0♌	5	26	9	12	24	23	2
28	18 23 45	6 8 2	8♈45	1	4	27	9	12	24	23	2
29	18 27 42	7 5 14	20 36	2	4	27	9	12	25	23	2
30	18 31 38	8 2 27	2♉34	3	3	28	9	12	25	23	2

THE SUN ENTERS THE SIGN OF CANCER ON JUN 21 AT 13:37.

♈ ARIES ♉ TAURUS ♊ GEMINI ♋ CANCER ♌ LEO ♍ VIRGO ♎ LIBRA ♏ SCORPIO ♐ SAGITTARIUS ♑ CAPRICORN ♒ AQUARIUS ♓ PISCES

SIDEREAL SUN MOON MERCURY VENUS MARS JUPITER SATURN URANUS NEPTUNE PLUTO

DAY	TIME	☉	☽	☿	♀	♂	♃	♄	♅	♆	♇
	h m s	° ' "	° '	°	°	°	°	°	°	°	°
J 1	18 35 35	8♋59 39	14♉45	3♌	3♋R	28♋	9♉	12♉	25♉	23♍	2♌
U 2	18 39 31	9 56 52	27 13	4	2	29	10	12	25	23	2
L 3	18 43 28	10 54 5	10♊ 2	4	1	0♌	10	12	25	23	2
Y 4	18 47 24	11 51 19	23 11	4	1	0	10	12	25	23	2
5	18 51 21	12 48 32	6♋42	5	0	1	10	12	25	23	2
6	18 55 18	13 45 45	20 31	5	0	2	10	13	25	23	2
7	18 59 14	14 42 59	4♌35	5	29♊	2	10	13	25	23	2
8	19 3 11	15 40 12	18 50	5 R	29	3	11	13	25	23	2
9	19 7 7	16 37 25	3♍ 8	5	29	4	11	13	25	23	2
10	19 11 4	17 34 38	17 27	5	28	4	11	13	25	23	2
11	19 15 0	18 31 51	1♎43	5	28	5	11	13	25	23	2
12	19 18 57	19 29 4	15 52	5	28	5	11	13	25	23	2
13	19 22 53	20 26 17	29 56	5	27	6	11	13	25	23	2
14	19 26 50	21 23 30	13♏52	4	27	7	11	13	25	23	2
15	19 30 47	22 20 43	27 40	4	27	7	12	13	25	23	2
16	19 34 43	23 17 56	11♐20	3	27	8	12	13	25	23	2
17	19 38 40	24 15 9	24 49	3	27	9	12	13	25	23	2
18	19 42 36	25 12 23	8♑ 8	2	27 D	9	12	13	25	23	2
19	19 46 33	26 9 37	21 13	1	27	10	12	13	25	23	2
20	19 50 29	27 6 51	4♒ 3	1	27	11	12	14	25	23	2
21	19 54 26	28 4 6	16 39	0	27	11	12	14	25	23	2
22	19 58 22	29 1 22	29 0	29♋	27	12	13	14	25	23	2
23	20 2 19	29 58 38	11♓ 7	29	27	12	13	14	25	23	2
24	20 6 16	0♌55 55	23 4	28	27	13	13	14	26	23	2
25	20 10 12	1 53 13	4♈54	27	28	14	13	14	26	23	2
26	20 14 9	2 50 31	16 42	27	28	14	13	14	26	23	2
27	20 18 5	3 47 51	28 33	26	28	15	13	14	26	23	3
28	20 22 2	4 45 11	10♉31	26	28	16	13	14	26	23	3
29	20 25 58	5 42 33	22 43	25	29	16	13	14	26	24	3
30	20 29 55	6 39 56	5♊13	25	29	17	14	14	26	24	3
31	20 33 51	7 37 20	18 5	25	0♋	18	14	14	26	24	3

THE SUN ENTERS THE SIGN OF LEO ON JUL 23 AT 00:35.

DAY	TIME	☉	☽	☿	♀	♂	♃	♄	♅	♆	♇
	h m s	° ' "	° '	°	°	°	°	°	°	°	°
A 1	20 37 48	8♌34 45	1♋23	25♋D	0♋	18♌	14♉	14♉	26♉	24♍	3♌
U 2	20 41 45	9 32 11	15 6	25	0	19	14	14	26	24	3
G 3	20 45 41	10 29 38	29 12	25	1	19	14	14	26	24	3
U 4	20 49 38	11 27 5	13♌37	25	1	20	14	14	26	24	3
S 5	20 53 34	12 24 34	28 15	25	2	21	14	14	26	24	3
T 6	20 57 31	13 22 4	12♍59	26	2	21	14	14	26	24	3
7	21 1 27	14 19 35	27 40	26	3	22	14	14	26	24	3
8	21 5 24	15 17 6	12♎13	27	4	23	14	14	26	24	3
9	21 9 20	16 14 38	26 35	27	4	23	15	14	26	24	3
10	21 13 17	17 12 11	10♏42	28	5	24	15	15	26	24	3
11	21 17 14	18 9 45	24 35	29	6	24	15	15	26	24	3
12	21 21 10	19 7 20	8♐13	0♌	6	25	15	15	26	24	3
13	21 25 7	20 4 56	21 36	1	7	26	15	15	26	24	3
14	21 29 3	21 2 33	4♑46	3	8	26	15	15	26	24	3
15	21 33 0	22 0 10	17 43	4	8	27	15	15	26	24	3
16	21 36 56	22 57 49	0♒28	5	9	28	15	15	26	24	3
17	21 40 53	23 55 29	13 0	7	10	28	15	15	26	24	3
18	21 44 49	24 53 11	25 20	9	11	29	15	15	26	24	3
19	21 48 46	25 50 53	7♓29	10	11	0♍	15	15	26	24	3
20	21 52 43	26 48 37	19 29	12	12	0	15	15	26	24	3
21	21 56 39	27 46 23	1♈22	14	13	1	15	15	26	24	3
22	22 0 36	28 44 10	13 10	16	14	1	15	15	26	24	3
23	22 4 32	29 41 58	24 56	17	15	2	15	15	26	24	3
24	22 8 29	0♍39 49	6♉46	19	15	3	15	15	26	24	3
25	22 12 25	1 37 41	18 44	21	16	3	15	15	26	24	3
26	22 16 22	2 35 35	0♊55	23	17	4	16	15	26	24	3
27	22 20 18	3 33 30	13 23	25	18	5	16	15 R	26	24	3
28	22 24 15	4 31 28	26 14	27	19	5	16	15	26	24	3
29	22 28 12	5 29 27	9♋30	29	20	6	16	15	26	25	3
30	22 32 8	6 27 29	23 14	1♍	21	7	16	15	26	25	3
31	22 36 5	7 25 32	7♌26	3	22	7	16	15	26	25	3

THE SUN ENTERS THE SIGN OF VIRGO ON AUG 23 AT 07:29.

DAY	TIME	☉	☽	☿	♀	♂	♃	♄	♅	♆	♇
	h m s	° ' "	° '	°	°	°	°	°	°	°	°
S 1	22 40 1	8♍23 37	22♌ 0	5♍	23♋	8♍	16♉	15♉R	26♉R	25♍	3♌
E 2	22 43 58	9 21 43	6♍53	7	24	8	16	15	26	25	4
P 3	22 47 54	10 19 51	21 54	9	24	9	16	15	26	25	4
T 4	22 51 51	11 18 1	6♎57	11	25	10	16 R	15	26	25	4
E 5	22 55 47	12 16 13	21 51	13	26	10	16	15	26	25	4
M 6	22 59 44	13 14 26	6♏31	15	27	11	16	15	26	25	4
B 7	23 3 40	14 12 40	20 52	17	28	12	16	15	26	25	4
E 8	23 7 37	15 10 56	4♐51	18	29	12	16	15	26	25	4
R 9	23 11 34	16 9 14	18 29	20	0♌	13	16	15	26	25	4
10	23 15 30	17 7 33	1♑46	22	1	14	16	15	26	25	4
11	23 19 27	18 5 54	14 45	24	2	14	16	15	26	25	4
12	23 23 23	19 4 16	27 27	26	3	15	16	15	26	25	4
13	23 27 20	20 2 40	9♒56	27	4	16	16	15	26	25	4
14	23 31 16	21 1 5	22 12	29	5	16	16	15	26	25	4
15	23 35 13	21 59 32	4♓19	1♎	6	17	15	14	26	25	4
16	23 39 9	22 58 1	16 17	3	7	17	15	14	26	25	4
17	23 43 6	23 56 32	28 10	4	8	18	15	14	26	25	4
18	23 47 3	24 55 5	9♈59	6	9	19	15	14	26	25	4
19	23 50 59	25 53 39	21 46	8	11	19	15	14	26	25	4
20	23 54 56	26 52 16	3♉34	9	12	20	15	14	26	25	4
21	23 58 52	27 50 55	15 26	11	13	21	15	14	26	25	4
22	0 2 49	28 49 36	27 26	13	14	21	15	14	26	25	4
23	0 6 45	29 48 20	9♊37	14	15	22	15	14	26	25	4
24	0 10 42	0♎47 5	22 4	16	16	23	15	14	26	25	4
25	0 14 38	1 45 53	4♋51	17	17	23	15	14	26	25	4
26	0 18 35	2 44 44	18 2	19	18	24	15	14	26	26	4
27	0 22 32	3 43 36	1♌38	20	19	24	15	14	26	26	4
28	0 26 28	4 42 31	15 42	22	20	25	15	14	26	26	4
29	0 30 25	5 41 28	0♍11	23	21	26	15	14	26	26	4
30	0 34 21	6 40 27	15 2	25	22	26	15	14	26	26	4

THE SUN ENTERS THE SIGN OF LIBRA ON SEP 23 AT 04:47.

DAY	TIME	☉	☽	☿	♀	♂	♃	♄	♅	♆	♇
	h m s	° ' "	° '	°	°	°	°	°	°	°	°
O 1	0 38 18	7♎39 28	0♎ 8	26♎	23♌	27♍	15♉R	14♉R	26♉R	26♍	4♌
C 2	0 42 14	8 38 32	15 21	28	25	28	14	14	26	26	4
T 3	0 46 11	9 37 37	0♏30	29	26	28	14	14	26	26	4
O 4	0 50 7	10 36 44	15 27	1♏	27	29	14	14	26	26	4
B 5	0 54 4	11 35 54	0♐ 3	2	28	0♎	14	14	26	26	4
E 6	0 58 0	12 35 5	14 16	4	29	0	14	13	26	26	4
R 7	1 1 57	13 34 18	28 2	5	0♍	1	14	13	26	26	4
8	1 5 54	14 33 32	11♑23	6	1	2	14	13	26	26	4
9	1 9 50	15 32 49	24 19	8	2	2	14	13	26	26	4
10	1 13 47	16 32 7	6♒56	9	4	3	14	13	26	26	4
11	1 17 43	17 31 27	19 15	10	5	3	14	13	26	26	4
12	1 21 40	18 30 48	1♓21	12	6	4	13	13	25	26	4
13	1 25 36	19 30 12	13 18	13	7	5	13	13	25	26	4
14	1 29 33	20 29 37	25 9	14	8	5	13	13	25	26	4
15	1 33 29	21 29 5	6♈58	15	9	6	13	13	25	26	4
16	1 37 26	22 28 34	18 45	16	10	7	13	13	25	26	4
17	1 41 23	23 28 5	0♉35	18	12	7	13	13	25	26	4
18	1 45 19	24 27 39	12 28	19	13	8	13	13	25	26	4
19	1 49 16	25 27 14	24 28	20	14	9	13	13	25	26	4
20	1 53 12	26 26 52	6♊35	21	15	9	12	12	25	26	4
21	1 57 9	27 26 32	18 54	22	16	10	12	12	25	26	4
22	2 1 5	28 26 14	1♋25	23	17	11	12	12	25	26	4
23	2 5 2	29 25 58	14 12	24	19	11	12	12	25	26	4
24	2 8 58	0♏25 45	27 19	24	20	12	12	12	25	27	4
25	2 12 55	1 25 34	10♌46	25	21	13	12	12	25	27	4
26	2 16 52	2 25 25	24 37	26	22	13	12	12	25	27	4
27	2 20 48	3 25 18	8♍51	27	23	14	12	12	25	27	4
28	2 24 45	4 25 14	23 26	27	24	14	11	12	25	27	4
29	2 28 41	5 25 11	8♎20	28	26	15	11	12	25	27	4
30	2 32 38	6 25 11	23 26	28	27	16	11	12	25	27	4
31	2 36 34	7 25 13	8♏34	28	28	16	11	12	25	27	4

THE SUN ENTERS THE SIGN OF SCORPIO ON OCT 23 AT 13:40.

DAY	TIME	☉	☽	☿	♀	♂	♃	♄	♅	♆	♇
	h m s	° ' "	° '	°	°	°	°	°	°	°	°
N 1	2 40 31	8♏25 16	23♏35	28♏R	29♍	17♎	11♉R	12♉R	25♉R	27♍	4♌
O 2	2 44 27	9 25 22	8♐22	28	0♎	18	11	11	25	27	4
V 3	2 48 24	10 25 29	22 45	28	2	18	11	11	25	27	4
E 4	2 52 21	11 25 38	6♑42	27	3	19	10	11	25	27	4
M 5	2 56 17	12 25 48	20 10	27	4	20	10	11	25	27	4 R
B 6	3 0 14	13 26 0	3♒11	26	5	20	10	11	25	27	4
E 7	3 4 10	14 26 13	15 48	25	6	21	10	11	25	27	4
R 8	3 8 7	15 26 28	28 6	24	8	22	10	11	24	27	4
9	3 12 3	16 26 44	10♓ 8	23	9	22	10	11	24	27	4
10	3 16 0	17 27 2	22 1	22	10	23	10	11	24	27	4
11	3 19 56	18 27 22	3♈49	21	11	24	10	11	24	27	4
12	3 23 53	19 27 42	15 36	19	12	24	9	11	24	27	4
13	3 27 50	20 28 5	27 25	18	14	25	9	11	24	27	4
14	3 31 46	21 28 28	9♉20	17	15	26	9	10	24	27	4
15	3 35 43	22 28 54	21 22	16	16	26	9	10	24	27	4
16	3 39 39	23 29 21	3♊34	15	17	27	9	10	24	27	4
17	3 43 36	24 29 50	15 56	14	18	28	9	10	24	27	4
18	3 47 32	25 30 20	28 29	13	20	28	9	10	24	27	4
19	3 51 29	26 30 52	11♋14	12	21	29	9	10	24	27	4
20	3 55 25	27 31 26	24 11	12	22	0♏	8	10	24	27	4
21	3 59 22	28 32 2	7♌22	12 D	23	0	8	10	24	27	4
22	4 3 19	29 32 39	20 48	12	24	1	8	10	24	27	4
23	4 7 15	0♐33 18	4♍30	12	26	2	8	10	24	27	4
24	4 11 12	1 33 58	18 29	13	27	2	8	10	24	27	4
25	4 15 8	2 34 41	2♎45	13	28	3	8	10	24	27	4
26	4 19 5	3 35 25	17 17	14	29	3	8	10	24	27	4
27	4 23 1	4 36 10	2♏ 0	15	1♏	4	8	10	24	27	4
28	4 26 58	5 36 57	16 50	16	2	5	7	9	24	27	4
29	4 30 54	6 37 45	1♐39	17	3	5	7	9	24	27	4
30	4 34 51	7 38 35	16 19	18	4	6	7	9	24	27	4

THE SUN ENTERS THE SIGN OF SAGITTARIUS ON NOV 22 AT 10:50.

DAY	TIME	☉	☽	☿	♀	♂	♃	♄	♅	♆	♇
	h m s	° ' "	° '	°	°	°	°	°	°	°	°
D 1	4 38 48	8♐39 26	0♑41	19♏	5♏	7♏	7♉R	9♉R	24♉R	27♍	4♌R
E 2	4 42 44	9 40 18	14 40	20	7	7	7	9	24	27	4
C 3	4 46 41	10 41 10	28 13	21	8	8	7	9	23	27	4
E 4	4 50 37	11 42 4	11♒19	22	9	9	7	9	23	28	4
M 5	4 54 34	12 42 59	24 0	24	10	9	7	9	23	28	4
B 6	4 58 30	13 43 54	6♓20	25	12	10	7	9	23	28	4
E 7	5 2 27	14 44 50	18 24	26	13	11	7	9	23	28	4
R 8	5 6 23	15 45 46	0♈16	28	14	11	7	9	23	28	4
9	5 10 20	16 46 44	12 4	29	15	12	7	9	23	28	4
10	5 14 17	17 47 42	23 51	1♐	17	13	6	9	23	28	4
11	5 18 13	18 48 40	5♉43	2	18	13	6	9	23	28	4
12	5 22 10	19 49 40	17 44	4	19	14	6	9	23	28	4
13	5 26 6	20 50 40	29 56	5	20	15	6	9	23	28	4
14	5 30 3	21 51 40	12♊21	7	22	15	6	9	23	28	4
15	5 33 59	22 52 42	25 1	8	23	16	6	8	23	28	4
16	5 37 56	23 53 44	7♋54	9	24	17	6	8	23	28	4
17	5 41 52	24 54 47	21 0	11	25	17	6	8	23	28	4
18	5 45 49	25 55 50	4♌18	12	27	18	6	8	23	28	4
19	5 49 46	26 56 55	17 46	14	28	19	6	8	23	28	4
20	5 53 42	27 58 0	1♍23	16	29	19	6	8	23	28	4
21	5 57 39	28 59 5	15 9	17	0♐	20	6	8	23	28	4
22	6 1 35	0♑ 0 12	29 3	19	1	21	6	8	23	28	4
23	6 5 32	1 1 20	13♎ 7	20	3	21	6	8	23	28	4
24	6 9 28	2 2 28	27 19	22	4	22	6	8	23	28	4
25	6 13 25	3 3 36	11♏39	23	5	23	6	8	23	28	4
26	6 17 21	4 4 46	26 2	25	6	23	6	8	23	28	4
27	6 21 18	5 5 56	10♐25	26	8	24	6	8	23	28	4
28	6 25 15	6 7 6	24 42	28	9	25	6	8	23	28	4
29	6 29 11	7 8 16	8♑47	29	10	25	6	8	23	28 R	4
30	6 33 8	8 9 27	22 35	1♑	11	26	6	8	23	28	4
31	6 37 4	9 10 38	6♒ 2	3	13	27	6 D	8	23	28	4

THE SUN ENTERS THE SIGN OF CAPRICORN ON DEC 21 AT 23:55.

♈ ARIES ♉ TAURUS ♊ GEMINI ♋ CANCER ♌ LEO ♍ VIRGO ♎ LIBRA ♏ SCORPIO ♐ SAGITTARIUS ♑ CAPRICORN ♒ AQUARIUS ♓ PISCES

1941

SIDEREAL SUN MOON MERCURY VENUS MARS JUPITER SATURN URANUS NEPTUNE PLUTO

DAY	TIME	☉	☽	☿	♀	♂	♃	♄	♅	♆	♇
	h m s	° ' "	° '	°	°	°	°	°	°	°	°
J 1	6 41 1	10♑11 49	19♒ 6	4♑	14♐	27♏	6♉	8♉R	23♉R	28♍R	4♌R
A 2	6 44 57	11 12 59	1♓47	6	15	28	6	8	22	28	4
N 3	6 48 54	12 14 10	14 8	7	16	29	6	8	22	28	4
U 4	6 52 50	13 15 20	26 14	9	18	29	6	8	22	28	4
A 5	6 56 47	14 16 29	8♈ 8	10	19	0♐	6	8	22	28	4
R 6	7 0 44	15 17 39	19 56	12	20	1	6	8	22	28	4
Y 7	7 4 40	16 18 48	1♉44	14	21	1	6	8	22	28	4
8	7 8 37	17 19 56	13 38	15	23	2	6	8	22	28	4
9	7 12 33	18 21 5	25 42	17	24	3	6	8 D	22	28	4
10	7 16 30	19 22 12	8♊ 0	18	25	3	6	8	22	28	4
11	7 20 26	20 23 20	20 35	20	26	4	6	8	22	28	3
12	7 24 23	21 24 26	3♋30	22	28	5	6	8	22	28	3
13	7 28 19	22 25 33	16 42	23	29	6	6	8	22	28	3
14	7 32 16	23 26 39	0♌12	25	0♑	6	6	8	22	28	3
15	7 36 13	24 27 44	13 55	27	1	7	6	8	22	28	3
16	7 40 9	25 28 50	27 49	28	3	8	6	8	22	28	3
17	7 44 6	26 29 54	11♍49	0♒	4	8	6	8	22	28	3
18	7 48 2	27 30 59	25 53	2	5	9	6	8	22	28	3
19	7 51 59	28 32 3	9♎59	3	6	10	6	8	22	28	3
20	7 55 55	29 33 7	24 5	5	8	10	6	8	22	28	3
21	7 59 52	0♒34 10	8♏11	7	9	11	6	8	22	28	3
22	8 3 48	1 35 13	22 14	9	10	12	6	8	22	28	3
23	8 7 45	2 36 16	6♐15	10	11	12	7	8	22	28	3
24	8 11 42	3 37 19	20 11	12	13	13	7	8	22	28	3
25	8 15 38	4 38 20	4♑ 0	14	14	14	7	8	22	28	3
26	8 19 35	5 39 21	17 38	16	15	14	7	8	22	27	3
27	8 23 31	6 40 21	1♒ 3	17	16	15	7	8	22	27	3
28	8 27 28	7 41 21	14 12	19	18	16	7	8	22	27	3
29	8 31 24	8 42 19	27 3	21	19	16	7	8	22	27	3
30	8 35 21	9 43 16	9♓37	22	20	17	7	8	22 D	27	3
31	8 39 17	10 44 13	21 55	24	21	18	7	8	22	27	3

THE SUN ENTERS THE SIGN OF AQUARIUS ON JAN 20 AT 10:34.

DAY	TIME	☉	☽	☿	♀	♂	♃	♄	♅	♆	♇
	h m s	° ' "	° '	°	°	°	°	°	°	°	°
F 1	8 43 14	11♒45 7	3♈59	26♒	23♑	18♐	7♉	8♉	22♉	27♍R	3♌R
E 2	8 47 11	12 46 1	15 53	27	24	19	7	8	22	27	3
B 3	8 51 7	13 46 53	27 42	29	25	20	8	8	22	27	3
R 4	8 55 4	14 47 44	9♉30	1♓	26	20	8	8	22	27	3
U 5	8 59 0	15 48 34	21 24	2	28	21	8	9	22	27	3
A 6	9 2 57	16 49 22	3♊28	4	29	22	8	9	22	27	3
R 7	9 6 53	17 50 9	15 47	5	0♒	22	8	9	22	27	3
Y 8	9 10 50	18 50 54	28 25	7	1	23	8	9	22	27	3
9	9 14 46	19 51 37	11♋25	8	3	24	8	9	22	27	3
10	9 18 43	20 52 20	24 49	9	4	25	8	9	22	27	3
11	9 22 40	21 53 0	8♌34	10	5	25	9	9	22	27	3
12	9 26 36	22 53 39	22 39	11	6	26	9	9	22	27	3
13	9 30 33	23 54 17	6♍58	12	8	27	9	9	22	27	3
14	9 34 29	24 54 54	21 27	12	9	27	9	9	22	27	3
15	9 38 26	25 55 29	5♎59	13	10	28	9	9	22	27	3
16	9 42 22	26 56 3	20 28	13	11	29	9	9	22	27	3
17	9 46 19	27 56 35	4♏51	13 R	13	29	9	9	22	27	3
18	9 50 15	28 57 7	19 5	13	14	0♑	10	9	22	27	3
19	9 54 12	29 57 37	3♐ 8	13	15	1	10	9	22	27	3
20	9 58 9	0♓58 6	16 59	13	16	1	10	9	22	27	3
21	10 2 5	1 58 34	0♑37	12	18	2	10	10	22	27	3
22	10 6 2	2 59 0	14 3	12	19	3	10	10	22	27	3
23	10 9 58	3 59 25	27 15	11	20	3	10	10	22	27	3
24	10 13 55	4 59 48	10♒15	10	21	4	10	10	22	27	3
25	10 17 51	6 0 10	23 1	9	23	5	11	10	22	27	3
26	10 21 48	7 0 30	5♓34	8	24	6	11	10	22	27	2
27	10 25 44	8 0 49	17 54	7	25	6	11	10	22	27	2
28	10 29 41	9 1 5	0♈ 3	6	26	7	11	10	23	27	2

THE SUN ENTERS THE SIGN OF PISCES ON FEB 19 AT 00:56.

DAY	TIME	☉	☽	☿	♀	♂	♃	♄	♅	♆	♇
	h m s	° ' "	° '	°	°	°	°	°	°	°	°
M 1	10 33 38	10♓ 1 20	12♈ 2	5♓R	28♒	8♑	11♉	10♉	23♉	27♍R	2♌R
A 2	10 37 34	11 1 33	23 54	4	29	8	11	10	23	27	2
R 3	10 41 31	12 1 43	5♉42	3	0♓	9	12	10	23	27	2
C 4	10 45 27	13 1 52	17 31	2	1	10	12	10	23	27	2
H 5	10 49 24	14 1 59	29 24	1	3	10	12	10	23	27	2
6	10 53 20	15 2 4	11♊26	1	4	11	12	11	23	27	2
7	10 57 17	16 2 6	23 43	0	5	12	12	11	23	27	2
8	11 1 13	17 2 7	6♋18	0	6	12	12	11	23	27	2
9	11 5 10	18 2 5	19 16	29♒	8	13	13	11	23	27	2
10	11 9 7	19 2 1	2♌39	29	9	14	13	11	23	27	2
11	11 13 3	20 1 55	16 27	29 D	10	14	13	11	23	27	2
12	11 17 0	21 1 47	0♍41	29	11	15	13	11	23	26	2
13	11 20 56	22 1 37	15 16	29	13	16	13	11	23	26	2
14	11 24 53	23 1 25	0♎ 5	29	14	17	14	11	23	26	2
15	11 28 49	24 1 10	15 2	29	15	17	14	11	23	26	2
16	11 32 46	25 0 54	29 58	0♓	16	18	14	12	23	26	2
17	11 36 42	26 0 37	14♏46	0	18	19	14	12	23	26	2
18	11 40 39	27 0 17	29 19	1	19	19	14	12	23	26	2
19	11 44 35	27 59 56	13♐34	1	20	20	15	12	23	26	2
20	11 48 32	28 59 33	27 29	2	21	21	15	12	23	26	2
21	11 52 29	29 59 9	11♑ 2	3	22	21	15	12	23	26	2
22	11 56 25	0♈58 42	24 16	4	24	22	15	12	23	26	2
23	12 0 22	1 58 14	7♒12	4	25	23	15	12	23	26	2
24	12 4 18	2 57 44	19 52	5	26	23	16	12	23	26	2
25	12 8 15	3 57 12	2♓19	6	27	24	16	13	23	26	2
26	12 12 11	4 56 39	14 34	7	29	25	16	13	23	26	2
27	12 16 8	5 56 3	26 40	8	0⊙	26	16	13	23	26	2
28	12 20 4	6 55 25	8♈38	9	1♈	26	16	13	23	26	2
29	12 24 1	7 54 46	20 31	10	2	27	17	13	24	26	2
30	12 27 58	8 54 4	2♉21	12	4	28	17	13	24	26	2
31	12 31 54	9 53 20	14 9	13	5	28	17	13	24	26	2

THE SUN ENTERS THE SIGN OF ARIES ON MAR 21 AT 00:20.

SIDEREAL SUN MOON MERCURY VENUS MARS JUPITER SATURN URANUS NEPTUNE PLUTO

DAY	TIME	☉	☽	☿	♀	♂	♃	♄	♅	♆	♇
	h m s	° ' "	° '	°	°	°	°	°	°	°	°
A 1	12 35 51	10♈52 34	25♉59	14♓	6♈	29♑	17♉	13♉	24♉	26♍R	2♌R
P 2	12 39 47	11 51 46	7♊54	15	7	0♒	17	13	24	26	2
R 3	12 43 44	12 50 55	19 57	17	9	0	18	14	24	26	2
I 4	12 47 40	13 50 2	2♋12	18	10	1	18	14	24	26	2
L 5	12 51 37	14 49 7	14 43	19	11	2	18	14	24	26	2
6	12 55 33	15 48 10	27 35	21	12	2	18	14	24	26	2
7	12 59 30	16 47 10	10♌50	22	14	3	19	14	24	26	2
8	13 3 27	17 46 8	24 32	23	15	4	19	14	24	26	2
9	13 7 23	18 45 3	8♍41	25	16	4	19	14	24	26	2
10	13 11 20	19 43 57	23 15	26	17	5	19	14	24	26	2
11	13 15 16	20 42 48	8♎10	28	19	6	19	14	24	26	2
12	13 19 13	21 41 37	23 19	0⊙	20	7	20	15	24	26	2
13	13 23 9	22 40 24	8♏33	1♈	21	7	20	15	24	26	2
14	13 27 6	23 39 10	23 41	3	22	8	20	15	24	26	2 D
15	13 31 2	24 37 53	8♐34	4	24	9	20	15	24	26	2
16	13 34 59	25 36 35	23 6	6	25	9	21	15	24	26	2
17	13 38 55	26 35 15	7♑12	8	26	10	21	15	24	26	2
18	13 42 52	27 33 54	20 51	9	27	11	21	15	25	26	2
19	13 46 49	28 32 31	4♒ 5	11	28	11	21	15	25	25	2
20	13 50 45	29 31 6	16 55	13	0♉	12	21	16	25	25	2
21	13 54 42	0♉29 39	29 25	15	1	13	22	16	25	25	2
22	13 58 38	1 28 11	11♓41	17	2	13	22	16	25	25	2
23	14 2 35	2 26 41	23 44	18	3	14	22	16	25	25	2
24	14 6 31	3 25 9	5♈40	20	5	15	22	16	25	25	2
25	14 10 28	4 23 36	17 31	22	6	16	23	16	25	25	2
26	14 14 24	5 22 1	29 19	24	7	16	23	16	25	25	2
27	14 18 21	6 20 24	11♉ 8	26	8	17	23	16	25	25	2
28	14 22 18	7 18 45	22 58	28	10	18	23	17	25	25	2
29	14 26 14	8 17 4	4♊53	0♉	11	18	24	17	25	25	2
30	14 30 11	9 15 22	16 53	2	12	19	24	17	25	25	2

THE SUN ENTERS THE SIGN OF TAURUS ON APR 20 AT 11:50.

DAY	TIME	☉	☽	☿	♀	♂	♃	♄	♅	♆	♇
	h m s	° ' "	° '	°	°	°	°	°	°	°	°
M 1	14 34 7	10♉13 37	29♊ 1	4♉	13♉	20♒	24♉	17♉	25♉	25♍R	2♌
A 2	14 38 4	11 11 51	11♋19	6	15	20	24	17	25	25	2
Y 3	14 42 0	12 10 3	23 52	8	16	21	24	17	25	25	2
4	14 45 57	13 8 12	6♌41	10	17	22	25	17	25	25	2
5	14 49 53	14 6 20	19 50	13	18	22	25	18	25	25	2
6	14 53 50	15 4 26	3♍22	15	19	23	25	18	26	25	2
7	14 57 47	16 2 29	17 19	17	21	24	25	18	26	25	2
8	15 1 43	17 0 31	1♎42	19	22	24	26	18	26	25	2
9	15 5 40	17 58 31	16 28	21	23	25	26	18	26	25	2
10	15 9 36	18 56 29	1♏32	23	24	26	26	18	26	25	2
11	15 13 33	19 54 26	16 46	26	26	26	26	18	26	25	2
12	15 17 29	20 52 21	2♐ 0	28	27	27	27	18	26	25	2
13	15 21 26	21 50 14	17 3	0♊	28	28	27	19	26	25	2
14	15 25 22	22 48 6	1♑47	2	29	29	27	19	26	25	2
15	15 29 19	23 45 57	16 4	4	1♊	29	27	19	26	25	2
16	15 33 16	24 43 47	29 51	6	2	0♓	28	19	26	25	2
17	15 37 12	25 41 35	13♒10	8	3	1	28	19	26	25	2
18	15 41 9	26 39 22	26 2	10	4	1	28	19	26	25	2
19	15 45 5	27 37 9	8♓31	12	5	2	28	19	26	25	2
20	15 49 2	28 34 53	20 43	14	7	3	28	19	26	25	2
21	15 52 58	29 32 37	2♈42	16	8	3	29	20	26	25	2
22	15 56 55	0♊30 20	14 33	18	9	4	29	20	26	25	2
23	16 0 51	1 28 2	26 21	19	10	5	29	20	27	25	2
24	16 4 48	2 25 42	8♉ 8	21	12	5	29	20	27	25	2
25	16 8 45	3 23 22	19 59	23	13	6	0♊	20	27	25	2
26	16 12 41	4 21 0	1♊55	24	14	7	0	20	27	25	2
27	16 16 38	5 18 37	13 57	26	15	7	0	20	27	25	2
28	16 20 34	6 16 13	26 7	28	17	8	0	20	27	25	2
29	16 24 31	7 13 47	8♋25	29	18	9	1	21	27	25	2
30	16 28 27	8 11 21	20 54	0♋	19	9	1	21	27	25	2
31	16 32 24	9 8 53	3♌35	2	20	10	1	21	27	25	2

THE SUN ENTERS THE SIGN OF GEMINI ON MAY 21 AT 11:23.

DAY	TIME	☉	☽	☿	♀	♂	♃	♄	♅	♆	♇
	h m s	° ' "	° '	°	°	°	°	°	°	°	°
J 1	16 36 20	10♊ 6 24	16♌29	3♋	21♊	11♓	1♊	21♉	27♉	25♍R	2♌
U 2	16 40 17	11 3 53	29 39	4	23	11	2	21	27	25	3
N 3	16 44 14	12 1 22	13♍ 6	5	24	12	2	21	27	25	3
E 4	16 48 10	12 58 48	26 55	7	25	12	2	21	27	25	3
5	16 52 7	13 56 14	11♎ 4	8	26	13	2	21	27	25 D	3
6	16 56 3	14 53 38	25 34	9	28	14	2	22	27	25	3
7	17 0 0	15 51 2	10♏22	10	29	14	3	22	27	25	3
8	17 3 56	16 48 24	25 22	10	0♋	15	3	22	27	25	3
9	17 7 53	17 45 46	10♐25	11	1	16	3	22	27	25	3
10	17 11 49	18 43 6	25 21	12	2	16	3	22	28	25	3
11	17 15 46	19 40 26	10♑ 3	13	4	17	4	22	28	25	3
12	17 19 43	20 37 45	24 21	13	5	18	4	22	28	25	3
13	17 23 39	21 35 4	8♒12	14	6	18	4	22	28	25	3
14	17 27 36	22 32 22	21 34	14	7	19	4	23	28	25	3
15	17 31 32	23 29 40	4♓30	15	9	20	5	23	28	25	3
16	17 35 29	24 26 57	17 1	15	10	20	5	23	28	25	3
17	17 39 25	25 24 14	29 14	15	11	21	5	23	28	25	3
18	17 43 22	26 21 31	11♈14	16	12	21	5	23	28	25	3
19	17 47 18	27 18 48	23 5	16 R	13	22	5	23	28	25	3
20	17 51 15	28 16 4	4♉54	16	15	23	6	23	28	25	3
21	17 55 12	29 13 20	16 43	16	16	23	6	23	28	25	3
22	17 59 8	0♋10 36	28 38	16	17	24	6	23	28	25	3
23	18 3 5	1 7 51	10♊40	15	18	25	6	24	28	25	3
24	18 7 1	2 5 6	22 52	15	20	25	7	24	28	25	3
25	18 10 58	3 2 22	5♋15	15	21	26	7	24	28	25	3
26	18 14 54	3 59 36	17 49	14	22	26	7	24	28	25	3
27	18 18 51	4 56 51	0♌35	14	23	27	7	24	28	25	3
28	18 22 47	5 54 4	13 31	13	24	28	7	24	28	25	3
29	18 26 44	6 51 18	26 39	13	26	28	8	24	29	25	3
30	18 30 41	7 48 31	10♍ 0	12	27	29	8	24	29	25	3

THE SUN ENTERS THE SIGN OF CANCER ON JUN 21 AT 19:34.

♈ ARIES ♉ TAURUS ♊ GEMINI ♋ CANCER ♌ LEO ♍ VIRGO ♎ LIBRA ♏ SCORPIO ♐ SAGITTARIUS ♑ CAPRICORN ♒ AQUARIUS ♓ PISCES

SIDEREAL SUN MOON MERCURY VENUS MARS JUPITER SATURN URANUS NEPTUNE PLUTO

DAY	TIME	☉	☽	☿	♀	♂	♃	♄	♅	♆	♇
	h m s	° ' "	° '	°	°	°	°	°	°	°	°
J 1	18 34 37	8♋45 44	23♍33	12♋R	28♋	29♓	8♊	24♉	29♉	25♍	3♌
U 2	18 38 34	9 42 56	7♎20	11	29	0⊙	8	25	29	25	3
L 3	18 42 30	10 40 8	21 22	10	1♌	0♈	9	25	29	25	3
Y 4	18 46 27	11 37 20	5♏38	10	2	1	9	25	29	25	3
5	18 50 23	12 34 31	20 7	9	3	2	9	25	29	25	3
6	18 54 20	13 31 42	4♐45	9	4	2	9	25	29	25	3
7	18 58 16	14 28 53	19 26	8	5	3	9	25	29	25	3
8	19 2 13	15 26 4	4♑ 2	8	7	3	10	25	29	25	3
9	19 6 10	16 23 15	18 27	7	8	4	10	25	29	25	3
10	19 10 6	17 20 27	2♒34	7	9	4	10	25	29	25	3
11	19 14 3	18 17 38	16 18	7	10	5	10	25	29	25	3
12	19 17 59	19 14 50	29 37	6	12	5	10	25	29	25	3
13	19 21 56	20 12 2	12♓32	6	13	6	11	26	29	25	4
14	19 25 52	21 9 14	25 5	6 D	14	7	11	26	29	25	4
15	19 29 49	22 6 28	7♈19	6	15	7	11	26	29	25	4
16	19 33 45	23 3 41	19 21	6	16	8	11	26	29	25	4
17	19 37 42	24 0 56	1♉14	7	18	8	11	26	29	25	4
18	19 41 39	24 58 11	13 4	7	19	9	12	26	29	25	4
19	19 45 35	25 55 27	24 57	7	20	9	12	26	29	25	4
20	19 49 32	26 52 43	6♊55	8	21	10	12	26	29	25	4
21	19 53 28	27 50 0	19 4	8	23	10	12	26	29	25	4
22	19 57 25	28 47 18	1♋25	9	24	11	12	26	0♊	25	4
23	20 1 21	29 44 37	14 1	10	25	11	13	26	0	25	4
24	20 5 18	0♌41 56	26 52	11	26	12	13	27	0	26	4
25	20 9 14	1 39 16	9♌56	12	27	12	13	27	0	26	4
26	20 13 11	2 36 37	23 14	13	29	13	13	27	0	26	4
27	20 17 8	3 33 58	6♍44	14	0♍	13	13	27	0	26	4
28	20 21 4	4 31 19	20 24	15	1	13	14	27	0	26	4
29	20 25 1	5 28 41	4♎14	16	2	14	14	27	0	26	4
30	20 28 57	6 26 4	18 11	18	3	14	14	27	0	26	4
31	20 32 54	7 23 27	2♏16	19	5	15	14	27	0	26	4

THE SUN ENTERS THE SIGN OF LEO ON JUL 23 AT 06:27.

DAY	TIME	☉	☽	☿	♀	♂	♃	♄	♅	♆	♇
	h m s	° ' "	° '	°	°	°	°	°	°	°	°
A 1	20 36 50	8♌20 51	16♏27	21♋	6♍	15♈	14♊	27♉	0♊	26♍	4♌
U 2	20 40 47	9 18 15	0♐42	22	7	16	15	27	0	26	4
G 3	20 44 43	10 15 40	14 59	24	8	16	15	27	0	26	4
U 4	20 48 40	11 13 6	29 14	26	9	16	15	27	0	26	4
S 5	20 52 37	12 10 32	13♑24	28	11	17	15	27	0	26	4
T 6	20 56 33	13 7 59	27 23	0♌	12	17	15	27	0	26	4
7	21 0 30	14 5 27	11♒ 7	1	13	18	15	27	0	26	4
8	21 4 26	15 2 56	24 34	3	14	18	16	28	0	26	4
9	21 8 23	16 0 27	7♓42	5	16	18	16	28	0	26	4
10	21 12 19	16 57 58	20 30	7	17	19	16	28	0	26	4
11	21 16 16	17 55 31	2♈59	9	18	19	16	28	0	26	4
12	21 20 12	18 53 5	15 13	11	19	19	16	28	0	26	4
13	21 24 9	19 50 40	27 15	13	20	20	16	28	0	26	4
14	21 28 6	20 48 17	9♉ 9	15	22	20	17	28	0	26	4
15	21 32 2	21 45 55	21 0	17	23	20	17	28	0	26	4
16	21 35 59	22 43 35	2♊54	20	24	21	17	28	0	26	4
17	21 39 55	23 41 16	14 55	22	25	21	17	28	0	26	4
18	21 43 52	24 38 59	27 6	24	26	21	17	28	0	26	5
19	21 47 48	25 36 44	9♋33	26	28	21	17	28	0	26	5
20	21 51 45	26 34 30	22 17	28	29	22	17	28	0	26	5
21	21 55 41	27 32 18	5♌20	0♍	0♎	22	18	28	0	26	5
22	21 59 38	28 30 7	18 42	2	1	22	18	28	0	26	5
23	22 3 35	29 27 58	2♍22	3	2	22	18	28	0	26	5
24	22 7 31	0♍25 50	16 16	5	4	22	18	28	0	26	5
25	22 11 28	1 23 43	0♎23	7	5	23	18	28	0	26	5
26	22 15 24	2 21 38	14 37	9	6	23	18	28	0	26	5
27	22 19 21	3 19 34	28 55	11	7	23	18	28	0	27	5
28	22 23 17	4 17 31	13♏14	13	8	23	19	28	0	27	5
29	22 27 14	5 15 30	27 30	15	10	23	19	28	0	27	5
30	22 31 10	6 13 30	11♐41	16	11	23	19	28	0	27	5
31	22 35 7	7 11 31	25 45	18	12	23	19	28	0	27	5

THE SUN ENTERS THE SIGN OF VIRGO ON AUG 23 AT 13:18.

DAY	TIME	☉	☽	☿	♀	♂	♃	♄	♅	♆	♇
	h m s	° ' "	° '	°	°	°	°	°	°	°	°
S 1	22 39 4	8♍ 9 34	9♑40	20♍	13♎	23♈	19♊	28♉	0♊	27♍	5♌
E 2	22 43 0	9 7 38	23 24	22	14	24	19	28	0	27	5
P 3	22 46 57	10 5 44	6♒56	23	16	24	19	28	0	27	5
T 4	22 50 53	11 3 51	20 15	25	17	24	19	29	0	27	5
E 5	22 54 50	12 1 59	3♓19	27	18	24	19	29	0 R	27	5
M 6	22 58 46	13 0 10	16 8	28	19	24 R	20	29	0	27	5
B 7	23 2 43	13 58 21	28 43	0♎	20	24	20	29	0	27	5
E 8	23 6 39	14 56 35	11♈ 4	2	21	24	20	29	0	27	5
R 9	23 10 36	15 54 51	23 13	3	23	24	20	29	0	27	5
10	23 14 32	16 53 9	5♉13	5	24	24	20	29 R	0	27	5
11	23 18 29	17 51 28	17 6	6	25	24	20	29	0	27	5
12	23 22 26	18 49 50	28 58	8	26	24	20	29	0	27	5
13	23 26 22	19 48 14	10♊51	9	27	23	20	29	0	27	5
14	23 30 19	20 46 40	22 51	11	29	23	20	29	0	27	5
15	23 34 15	21 45 8	5♋ 1	12	0♏	23	20	29	0	27	5
16	23 38 12	22 43 39	17 27	14	1	23	20	29	0	27	5
17	23 42 8	23 42 11	0♌13	15	2	23	21	29	0	27	5
18	23 46 5	24 40 46	13 20	17	3	23	21	29	0	27	5
19	23 50 1	25 39 22	26 51	18	5	23	21	28	0	27	5
20	23 53 58	26 38 1	10♍45	19	6	22	21	28	0	27	5
21	23 57 55	27 36 42	25 0	21	7	22	21	28	0	27	5
22	0 1 51	28 35 25	9♎32	22	8	22	21	28	0	27	5
23	0 5 48	29 34 9	24 13	23	9	22	21	28	0	28	5
24	0 9 44	0♎32 56	8♏58	25	10	22	21	28	0	28	5
25	0 13 41	1 31 44	23 40	26	12	21	21	28	0	28	5
26	0 17 37	2 30 34	8♐12	27	13	21	21	28	0	28	5
27	0 21 34	3 29 26	22 31	28	14	21	21	28	0	28	5
28	0 25 30	4 28 20	6♑33	0♏	15	21	21	28	0	28	5
29	0 29 27	5 27 15	20 17	1	16	20	21	28	0	28	5
30	0 33 24	6 26 12	3♒44	2	17	20	21	28	0	28	5

THE SUN ENTERS THE SIGN OF LIBRA ON SEP 23 AT 10:34.

SIDEREAL SUN MOON MERCURY VENUS MARS JUPITER SATURN URANUS NEPTUNE PLUTO

DAY	TIME	☉	☽	☿	♀	♂	♃	♄	♅	♆	♇
	h m s	° ' "	° '	°	°	°	°	°	°	°	°
O 1	0 37 20	7♎25 11	16♒55	3♏	19♏	20♈R	21♊	28♉R	0♊R	28♍	5♌
C 2	0 41 17	8 24 11	29 50	4	20	19	21	28	0	28	6
T 3	0 45 13	9 23 13	12♓32	5	21	19	21	28	0	28	6
O 4	0 49 10	10 22 18	25 2	6	22	19	21	28	0	28	6
B 5	0 53 6	11 21 24	7♈22	7	23	19	21	28	0	28	6
E 6	0 57 3	12 20 32	19 32	8	24	18	21	28	0	28	6
R 7	1 0 59	13 19 42	1♉34	8	26	18	21	28	0	28	6
8	1 4 56	14 18 55	13 30	9	27	18	21	28	0	28	6
9	1 8 52	15 18 9	25 22	10	28	17	21	28	0	28	6
10	1 12 49	16 17 26	7♊13	11	29	17	21 R	28	0	28	6
11	1 16 46	17 16 45	19 6	11	0♐	17	21	28	0	28	6
12	1 20 42	18 16 7	1♋ 4	11	1	16	21	28	0	28	6
13	1 24 39	19 15 31	13 11	12	3	16	21	28	0	28	6
14	1 28 35	20 14 57	25 33	12	4	16	21	28	0	28	6
15	1 32 32	21 14 25	8♌14	12 R	5	15	21	28	0	28	6
16	1 36 28	22 13 56	21 17	12	6	15	21	27	0	28	6
17	1 40 25	23 13 28	4♍46	12	7	15	21	27	0	28	6
18	1 44 21	24 13 4	18 42	12	8	15	21	27	0	28	6
19	1 48 18	25 12 41	3♎ 5	11	9	14	21	27	0	28	6
20	1 52 15	26 12 20	17 51	11	11	14	21	27	0	28	6
21	1 56 11	27 12 2	2♏53	10	12	14	21	27	0	29	6
22	2 0 8	28 11 45	18 2	9	13	14	21	27	0	29	6
23	2 4 4	29 11 31	3♐ 8	8	14	13	21	27	29♉	29	6
24	2 8 1	0♏11 18	18 2	7	15	13	21	27	29	29	6
25	2 11 57	1 11 7	2♑36	6	16	13	21	27	29	29	6
26	2 15 54	2 10 58	16 47	5	17	13	21	27	29	29	6
27	2 19 50	3 10 50	0♒32	3	18	12	21	27	29	29	6
28	2 23 47	4 10 44	13 53	2	20	12	21	27	29	29	6
29	2 27 44	5 10 40	26 53	1	21	12	21	27	29	29	6
30	2 31 40	6 10 37	9♓34	0	22	12	21	27	29	29	6
31	2 35 37	7 10 36	22 0	29♎	23	12	21	26	29	29	6

THE SUN ENTERS THE SIGN OF SCORPIO ON OCT 23 AT 19:28.

DAY	TIME	☉	☽	☿	♀	♂	♃	♄	♅	♆	♇
	h m s	° ' "	° '	°	°	°	°	°	°	°	°
N 1	2 39 33	8♏10 37	4♈15	28♎R	24♐	12♈R	21♊R	26♉R	29♉R	29♍	6♌
O 2	2 43 30	9 10 39	16 21	27	25	12	21	26	29	29	6
V 3	2 47 26	10 10 43	28 21	27	26	11	21	26	29	29	6
E 4	2 51 23	11 10 49	10♉16	26	27	11	20	26	29	29	6
M 5	2 55 19	12 10 57	22 9	26 D	28	11	20	26	29	29	6
B 6	2 59 16	13 11 6	4♊ 1	26	0♑	11	20	26	29	29	6 R
E 7	3 3 13	14 11 18	15 53	27	1	11	20	26	29	29	6
R 8	3 7 9	15 11 31	27 48	27	2	11	20	26	29	29	6
9	3 11 6	16 11 46	9♋47	28	3	11	20	26	29	29	6
10	3 15 2	17 12 4	21 54	28	4	11 D	20	26	29	29	6
11	3 18 59	18 12 23	4♌14	29	5	11	20	26	29	29	6
12	3 22 55	19 12 44	16 49	0♏	6	11	20	26	29	29	6
13	3 26 52	20 13 7	29 44	1	7	11	20	25	29	29	6
14	3 30 48	21 13 32	13♍ 4	2	8	11	20	25	29	29	6
15	3 34 45	22 13 59	26 51	4	9	11	19	25	29	29	6
16	3 38 42	23 14 28	11♎ 7	5	10	11	19	25	29	29	6
17	3 42 38	24 14 59	25 50	6	11	11	19	25	29	29	6
18	3 46 35	25 15 31	10♏55	7	12	11	19	25	28	29	6
19	3 50 31	26 16 5	26 14	9	13	12	19	25	28	29	6
20	3 54 28	27 16 41	11♐34	10	14	12	19	25	28	29	6
21	3 58 24	28 17 18	26 45	12	15	12	19	25	28	29	6
22	4 2 21	29 17 57	11♑36	13	16	12	19	25	28	29	6
23	4 6 17	0♐18 36	26 1	15	17	12	18	25	28	29	6
24	4 10 14	1 19 17	9♒56	16	19	12	18	25	28	29	6
25	4 14 11	2 19 59	23 22	18	20	12	18	24	28	29	6
26	4 18 7	3 20 41	6♓22	19	21	13	18	24	28	0♎	6
27	4 22 4	4 21 25	18 59	21	21	13	18	24	28	0	6
28	4 26 0	5 22 10	1♈18	22	22	13	18	24	28	0	6
29	4 29 57	6 22 56	13 25	24	23	13	18	24	28	0	6
30	4 33 53	7 23 43	25 23	25	24	13	18	24	28	0	6

THE SUN ENTERS THE SIGN OF SAGITTARIUS ON NOV 22 AT 16:39.

DAY	TIME	☉	☽	☿	♀	♂	♃	♄	♅	♆	♇
	h m s	° ' "	° '	°	°	°	°	°	°	°	°
D 1	4 37 50	8♐24 31	7♉16	27♏	25♑	14♈	17♊R	24♉R	28♉R	0♎	6♌R
E 2	4 41 46	9 25 20	19 8	28	26	14	17	24	28	0	6
C 3	4 45 43	10 26 10	0♊59	0♐	27	14	17	24	28	0	6
E 4	4 49 40	11 27 1	12 53	2	28	14	17	24	28	0	6
M 5	4 53 36	12 27 53	24 49	3	29	15	17	24	28	0	6
B 6	4 57 33	13 28 47	6♋50	5	0♒	15	17	24	28	0	6
E 7	5 1 29	14 29 41	18 56	6	1	15	17	24	28	0	6
R 8	5 5 26	15 30 37	1♌10	8	2	16	16	23	28	0	6
9	5 9 22	16 31 33	13 34	9	3	16	16	23	28	0	6
10	5 13 19	17 32 31	26 10	11	4	16	16	23	28	0	6
11	5 17 15	18 33 30	9♍ 2	12	4	17	16	23	28	0	6
12	5 21 12	19 34 30	22 15	14	5	17	16	23	27	0	6
13	5 25 9	20 35 32	5♎51	16	6	17	16	23	27	0	6
14	5 29 5	21 36 34	19 53	17	7	18	16	23	27	0	5
15	5 33 2	22 37 37	4♏21	19	8	18	16	23	27	0	5
16	5 36 58	23 38 41	19 12	20	9	18	15	23	27	0	5
17	5 40 55	24 39 47	4♐19	22	9	19	15	23	27	0	5
18	5 44 51	25 40 53	19 35	23	10	19	15	23	27	0	5
19	5 48 48	26 41 59	4♑46	25	11	19	15	23	27	0	5
20	5 52 44	27 43 7	19 42	27	11	20	15	23	27	0	5
21	5 56 41	28 44 14	4♒16	28	12	20	15	23	27	0	5
22	6 0 38	29 45 22	18 21	0♑	13	21	15	23	27	0	5
23	6 4 34	0♑46 30	1♓55	1	14	21	14	23	27	0	5
24	6 8 31	1 47 38	15 1	3	14	21	14	22	27	0	5
25	6 12 27	2 48 46	27 43	5	15	22	14	22	27	0	5
26	6 16 24	3 49 54	10♈ 4	6	15	22	14	22	27	0	5
27	6 20 20	4 51 3	22 10	8	16	23	14	22	27	0	5
28	6 24 17	5 52 11	4♉ 6	9	17	23	14	22	27	0	5
29	6 28 13	6 53 19	15 58	11	17	24	14	22	27	0	5
30	6 32 10	7 54 27	27 48	13	18	24	14	22	27	0	5
31	6 36 7	8 55 36	9♊40	14	18	24	14	22	27	0	5

THE SUN ENTERS THE SIGN OF CAPRICORN ON DEC 22 AT 05:45.

♈ ARIES ♉ TAURUS ♊ GEMINI ♋ CANCER ♌ LEO ♍ VIRGO ♎ LIBRA ♏ SCORPIO ♐ SAGITTARIUS ♑ CAPRICORN ♒ AQUARIUS ♓ PISCES

1942

SIDEREAL SUN MOON MERCURY VENUS MARS JUPITER SATURN URANUS NEPTUNE PLUTO

DAY	TIME	☉	☽	☿	♀	♂	♃	♄	♅	♆	♇
	h m s	° ' "	° '	°	°	°	°	°	°	°	°
J 1	6 40 3	9♑56 44	21♊37	16♑	18♒	25♈	13♊R	22♉R	27♉R	0♎R	5♌R
A 2	6 44 0	10 57 52	3♋41	17	19	25	13	22	27	0	5
N 3	6 47 56	11 59 1	15 51	19	19	26	13	22	27	0	5
U 4	6 51 53	13 0 9	28 10	21	20	26	13	22	27	0	5
A 5	6 55 49	14 1 17	10♌38	22	20	27	13	22	27	0	5
R 6	6 59 46	15 2 26	23 15	24	20	27	13	22	27	0	5
Y 7	7 3 42	16 3 34	6♍ 3	26	20	28	13	22	27	0	5
8	7 7 39	17 4 42	19 4	27	21	28	13	22	27	0	5
9	7 11 36	18 5 51	2♎20	29	21	29	13	22	27	0	5
10	7 15 32	19 6 59	15 53	1♒	21	29	13	22	27	0	5
11	7 19 29	20 8 8	29 46	2	21	0♉	12	22	27	0	5
12	7 23 25	21 9 16	13♏57	4	21	0	12	22	27	0	5
13	7 27 22	22 10 25	28 27	6	21 R	1	12	22	27	0	5
14	7 31 18	23 11 33	13♐12	7	21	1	12	22	27	0	5
15	7 35 15	24 12 42	28 4	9	21	2	12	22	27	0	5
16	7 39 11	25 13 49	12♑56	10	21	2	12	22	26	0	5
17	7 43 8	26 14 57	27 39	12	21	3	12	22	26	0	5
18	7 47 5	27 16 4	12♒ 5	13	21	3	12	22	26	0	5
19	7 51 1	28 17 10	26 8	15	20	4	12	22	26	0	5
20	7 54 58	29 18 16	9♓46	16	20	4	12	22	26	0	5
21	7 58 54	0♒19 20	22 57	18	20	5	12	22	26	0	5
22	8 2 51	1 20 24	5♈44	19	20	5	12	22	26	0	5
23	8 6 47	2 21 27	18 11	21	19	6	12	22 D	26	0	5
24	8 10 44	3 22 28	0♉21	22	19	6	12	22	26	0	5
25	8 14 40	4 23 29	12 20	23	18	7	12	22	26	0	5
26	8 18 37	5 24 28	24 12	24	18	7	12	22	26	0	5
27	8 22 34	6 25 27	6♊ 4	25	17	8	12	22	26	0	5
28	8 26 30	7 26 24	17 58	26	17	8	12	22	26	0	5
29	8 30 27	8 27 21	29 58	26	16	9	11	22	26	0	5
30	8 34 23	9 28 16	12♋ 8	27	16	9	11	22	26	0	5
31	8 38 20	10 29 10	24 28	27	15	10	11	22	26	0	5

THE SUN ENTERS THE SIGN OF AQUARIUS ON JAN 20 AT 16:24.

DAY	TIME	☉	☽	☿	♀	♂	♃	♄	♅	♆	♇
	h m s	° ' "	° '	°	°	°	°	°	°	°	°
F 1	8 42 16	11♒30 3	7♌ 1	27♒R	14♒R	10♉	11♊R	22♉	26♉R	0♎R	4♌R
E 2	8 46 13	12 30 55	19 46	27	14	11	11	22	26	0	4
B 3	8 50 9	13 31 46	2♍44	27	13	12	11	22	26 D	0	4
R 4	8 54 6	14 32 35	15 54	26	12	12	11	22	26	0	4
U 5	8 58 3	15 33 24	29 16	26	12	13	11 D	22	26	0	4
A 6	9 1 59	16 34 12	12♎50	25	11	13	11	22	26	0	4
R 7	9 5 56	17 34 58	26 34	24	11	14	11	22	26	0	4
Y 8	9 9 52	18 35 44	10♏30	23	10	14	11	22	26	29♍	4
9	9 13 49	19 36 29	24 36	22	10	15	11	22	26	29	4
10	9 17 45	20 37 13	8♐51	21	9	15	11	22	26	29	4
11	9 21 42	21 37 56	23 13	19	9	16	11	22	26	29	4
12	9 25 38	22 38 38	7♑37	18	8	17	11	22	26	29	4
13	9 29 35	23 39 19	21 59	17	8	17	11	22	26	29	4
14	9 33 32	24 39 58	6♒14	16	7	18	12	22	26	29	4
15	9 37 28	25 40 36	20 18	15	7	18	12	22	26	29	4
16	9 41 25	26 41 13	4♓ 5	14	7	19	12	22	26	29	4
17	9 45 21	27 41 48	17 32	13	6	19	12	22	26	29	4
18	9 49 18	28 42 21	0♈40	13	6	20	12	22	26	29	4
19	9 53 14	29 42 53	13 27	12	6	21	12	22	26	29	4
20	9 57 11	0♓43 23	25 55	12	6	21	12	22	26	29	4
21	10 1 7	1 43 51	8♉ 8	12	6	22	12	22	26	29	4
22	10 5 4	2 44 18	20 10	12 D	6	22	12	22	26	29	4
23	10 9 1	3 44 42	2♊ 5	12	6 D	23	12	23	27	29	4
24	10 12 57	4 45 5	13 58	12	6	23	12	23	27	29	4
25	10 16 54	5 45 25	25 52	12	6	24	12	23	27	29	4
26	10 20 50	6 45 44	7♋54	12	6	25	12	23	27	29	4
27	10 24 47	7 46 1	20 7	13	6	25	12	23	27	29	4
28	10 28 43	8 46 16	2♌34	13	6	26	12	23	27	29	4

THE SUN ENTERS THE SIGN OF PISCES ON FEB 19 AT 06:47.

DAY	TIME	☉	☽	☿	♀	♂	♃	♄	♅	♆	♇
	h m s	° ' "	° '	°	°	°	°	°	°	°	°
M 1	10 32 40	9♓46 29	15♌17	14♒	6♒	26♉	12♊	23♉	27♉	29♍R	4♌R
A 2	10 36 36	10 46 40	28 18	14	6	27	12	23	27	29	4
R 3	10 40 33	11 46 49	11♍36	15	7	27	12	23	27	29	4
C 4	10 44 30	12 46 56	25 12	16	7	28	13	23	27	29	4
H 5	10 48 26	13 47 1	9♎ 1	17	7	29	13	23	27	29	4
6	10 52 23	14 47 5	23 2	18	8	29	13	23	27	29	4
7	10 56 19	15 47 7	7♏11	18	8	0♊	13	23	27	29	4
8	11 0 16	16 47 8	21 24	19	8	0	13	23	27	29	4
9	11 4 12	17 47 7	5♐39	20	9	1	13	23	27	29	4
10	11 8 9	18 47 4	19 53	22	9	2	13	24	27	29	4
11	11 12 5	19 47 0	4♑ 2	23	10	2	13	24	27	29	4
12	11 16 2	20 46 54	18 5	24	10	3	13	24	27	29	4
13	11 19 59	21 46 47	2♒ 1	25	11	3	13	24	27	29	4
14	11 23 55	22 46 37	15 47	26	12	4	14	24	27	29	4
15	11 27 52	23 46 26	29 21	27	12	5	14	24	27	29	4
16	11 31 48	24 46 14	12♓43	29	13	5	14	24	27	29	4
17	11 35 45	25 45 59	25 51	0♓	13	6	14	24	27	29	4
18	11 39 41	26 45 42	8♈44	1	14	6	14	24	27	29	4
19	11 43 38	27 45 23	21 22	3	15	7	14	24	27	29	4
20	11 47 34	28 45 2	3♉47	4	15	8	14	24	27	29	4
21	11 51 31	29 44 39	15 58	5	16	8	14	24	27	28	4
22	11 55 27	0♈44 14	28 0	7	17	9	15	25	27	28	4
23	11 59 24	1 43 46	9♊55	8	18	9	15	25	27	28	4
24	12 3 21	2 43 16	21 48	10	18	10	15	25	27	28	4
25	12 7 17	3 42 44	3♋42	11	19	10	15	25	27	28	4
26	12 11 14	4 42 10	15 43	13	20	11	15	25	27	28	4
27	12 15 10	5 41 33	27 54	14	21	12	15	25	27	28	4
28	12 19 7	6 40 54	10♌22	16	22	12	15	25	28	28	4
29	12 23 3	7 40 13	23 8	18	22	13	15	25	28	28	4
30	12 27 0	8 39 29	6♍17	19	23	13	16	25	28	28	4
31	12 30 56	9 38 44	19 49	21	24	14	16	25	28	28	4

THE SUN ENTERS THE SIGN OF ARIES ON MAR 21 AT 06:10.

SIDEREAL SUN MOON MERCURY VENUS MARS JUPITER SATURN URANUS NEPTUNE PLUTO

DAY	TIME	☉	☽	☿	♀	♂	♃	♄	♅	♆	♇
	h m s	° ' "	° '	°	°	°	°	°	°	°	°
A 1	12 34 53	10♈37 56	3♎44	23♓	25♒	15♊	16♊	26♉	28♉	28♍R	4♌R
P 2	12 38 50	11 37 6	17 59	24	26	15	16	26	28	28	4
R 3	12 42 46	12 36 14	2♏29	26	27	16	16	26	28	28	4
I 4	12 46 43	13 35 20	17 7	28	28	16	16	26	28	28	3
L 5	12 50 39	14 34 24	1♐47	29	29	17	17	26	28	28	3
6	12 54 36	15 33 27	16 22	1♈	29	18	17	26	28	28	3
7	12 58 32	16 32 28	0♑47	3	0♓	18	17	26	28	28	3
8	13 2 29	17 31 27	14 57	5	1	19	17	26	28	28	3
9	13 6 25	18 30 24	28 53	7	2	20	17	26	28	28	3
10	13 10 22	19 29 20	12♒33	9	3	20	17	27	28	28	3
11	13 14 19	20 28 14	25 57	11	4	21	18	27	28	28	3
12	13 18 15	21 27 6	9♓ 8	13	5	21	18	27	28	28	3
13	13 22 12	22 25 56	22 6	14	6	22	18	27	28	28	3
14	13 26 8	23 24 45	4♈51	16	7	23	18	27	28	28	3
15	13 30 5	24 23 31	17 26	18	8	23	18	27	28	28	3
16	13 34 1	25 22 16	29 51	20	9	24	18	27	28	28	3 D
17	13 37 58	26 20 58	12♉ 5	23	10	24	19	27	28	28	3
18	13 41 54	27 19 39	24 11	25	11	25	19	27	28	28	3
19	13 45 51	28 18 18	6♊10	27	12	26	19	28	29	28	3
20	13 49 47	29 16 54	18 4	29	13	26	19	28	29	28	3
21	13 53 44	0♉15 29	29 55	1♉	14	27	19	28	29	28	3
22	13 57 41	1 14 1	11♋48	3	15	27	20	28	29	28	3
23	14 1 37	2 12 31	23 46	5	16	28	20	28	29	28	3
24	14 5 34	3 10 59	5♌55	7	17	29	20	28	29	28	3
25	14 9 30	4 9 25	18 19	9	18	29	20	28	29	28	3
26	14 13 27	5 7 49	1♍ 3	12	19	0♋	20	28	29	28	3
27	14 17 23	6 6 10	14 11	14	20	0	20	29	29	28	3
28	14 21 20	7 4 30	27 47	16	21	1	21	29	29	28	3
29	14 25 16	8 2 47	11♎50	18	22	2	21	29	29	28	3
30	14 29 13	9 1 3	26 20	20	23	2	21	29	29	27	4

THE SUN ENTERS THE SIGN OF TAURUS ON APR 20 AT 17:39.

DAY	TIME	☉	☽	☿	♀	♂	♃	♄	♅	♆	♇
	h m s	° ' "	° '	°	°	°	°	°	°	°	°
M 1	14 33 10	9♉59 17	11♏ 9	22♉	25♓	3♋	21♊	29♉	29♉	27♍R	4♌
A 2	14 37 6	10 57 29	26 12	24	26	3	21	29	29	27	4
Y 3	14 41 3	11 55 39	11♐17	26	27	4	22	29	29	27	4
4	14 44 59	12 53 48	26 15	28	28	5	22	29	29	27	4
5	14 48 56	13 51 56	10♑58	0♊	29	5	22	0♊	29	27	4
6	14 52 52	14 50 2	25 20	1	0⊙	6	22	0	29	27	4
7	14 56 49	15 48 7	9♒19	3	1♈	7	22	0	0♊	27	4
8	15 0 45	16 46 10	22 56	5	2	7	23	0	0	27	4
9	15 4 42	17 44 12	6♓11	7	3	8	23	0	0	27	4
10	15 8 39	18 42 12	19 8	8	4	8	23	0	0	27	4
11	15 12 35	19 40 11	1♈49	10	5	9	23	0	0	27	4
12	15 16 32	20 38 9	14 18	11	6	10	24	0	0	27	4
13	15 20 28	21 36 6	26 38	12	8	10	24	1	0	27	4
14	15 24 25	22 34 1	8♉49	14	9	11	24	1	0	27	4
15	15 28 21	23 31 54	20 53	15	10	11	24	1	0	27	4
16	15 32 18	24 29 47	2♊52	16	11	12	24	1	0	27	4
17	15 36 14	25 27 37	14 46	17	12	13	25	1	0	27	4
18	15 40 11	26 25 27	26 38	18	13	13	25	1	0	27	4
19	15 44 8	27 23 14	8♋29	19	14	14	25	1	0	27	4
20	15 48 4	28 21 1	20 22	20	15	15	25	1	0	27	4
21	15 52 1	29 18 45	2♌19	21	16	15	25	2	0	27	4
22	15 55 57	0♊16 28	14 27	22	18	16	26	2	0	27	4
23	15 59 54	1 14 10	26 48	23	19	16	26	2	0	27	4
24	16 3 50	2 11 50	9♍28	23	20	17	26	2	1	27	4
25	16 7 47	3 9 28	22 32	24	21	18	26	2	1	27	4
26	16 11 43	4 7 5	6♎ 3	24	22	18	27	2	1	27	4
27	16 15 40	5 4 40	20 4	25	23	19	27	2	1	27	4
28	16 19 37	6 2 14	4♏33	25	24	19	27	2	1	27	4
29	16 23 33	6 59 47	19 28	25	25	20	27	3	1	27	4
30	16 27 30	7 57 18	4♐40	26	27	21	27	3	1	27	4
31	16 31 26	8 54 49	20 0	26 R	28	21	28	3	1	27	4

THE SUN ENTERS THE SIGN OF GEMINI ON MAY 21 AT 17:09.

DAY	TIME	☉	☽	☿	♀	♂	♃	♄	♅	♆	♇
	h m s	° ' "	° '	°	°	°	°	°	°	°	°
J 1	16 35 23	9♊52 18	5♑14	26♊R	29♈	22♋	28♊	3♊	1♊	27♍R	4♌
U 2	16 39 19	10 49 47	20 13	26	0♉	23	28	3	1	27	4
N 3	16 43 16	11 47 14	4♒50	25	1	23	28	3	1	27	4
E 4	16 47 12	12 44 41	18 59	25	2	24	29	3	1	27	4
5	16 51 9	13 42 8	2♓41	25	3	24	29	4	1	27	4
6	16 55 6	14 39 33	15 57	25	5	25	29	4	1	27	4
7	16 59 2	15 36 58	28 51	24	6	26	29	4	1	27	4
8	17 2 59	16 34 22	11♈25	24	7	26	29	4	1	27 D	4
9	17 6 55	17 31 46	23 46	23	8	27	0♋	4	1	27	4
10	17 10 52	18 29 9	5♉55	23	9	27	0	4	1	27	4
11	17 14 48	19 26 32	17 57	22	10	28	0	4	2	27	4
12	17 18 45	20 23 54	29 54	22	11	29	0	4	2	27	4
13	17 22 41	21 21 15	11♊48	21	13	29	1	5	2	27	4
14	17 26 38	22 18 36	23 39	21	14	0♌	1	5	2	27	4
15	17 30 35	23 15 56	5♋31	20	15	1	1	5	2	27	4
16	17 34 31	24 13 16	17 24	20	16	1	1	5	2	27	4
17	17 38 28	25 10 35	29 20	19	17	2	1	5	2	27	4
18	17 42 24	26 7 53	11♌22	19	18	2	2	5	2	27	4
19	17 46 21	27 5 10	23 33	18	20	3	2	5	2	27	4
20	17 50 17	28 2 26	5♍56	18	21	4	2	5	2	27	4
21	17 54 14	28 59 42	18 36	18	22	4	2	6	2	27	4
22	17 58 10	29 56 57	1♎36	17	23	5	3	6	2	27	4
23	18 2 7	0♋54 12	15 2	17	24	5	3	6	2	27	4
24	18 6 4	1 51 25	28 55	17 D	25	6	3	6	2	27	4
25	18 10 0	2 48 39	13♏16	17	27	7	3	6	2	27	4
26	18 13 57	3 45 51	28 2	17	28	7	4	6	2	27	4
27	18 17 53	4 43 3	13♐ 8	17	29	8	4	6	2	27	4
28	18 21 50	5 40 15	28 24	17	0♊	9	4	6	2	27	5
29	18 25 46	6 37 27	13♑40	18	1	9	4	6	3	27	5
30	18 29 43	7 34 38	28 45	18	2	10	4	7	3	27	5

THE SUN ENTERS THE SIGN OF CANCER ON JUN 22 AT 01:16.

♈ ARIES ♉ TAURUS ♊ GEMINI ♋ CANCER ♌ LEO ♍ VIRGO ♎ LIBRA ♏ SCORPIO ♐ SAGITTARIUS ♑ CAPRICORN ♒ AQUARIUS ♓ PISCES

1942

SIDEREAL SUN MOON MERCURY VENUS MARS JUPITER SATURN URANUS NEPTUNE PLUTO

DAY	TIME	☉	☽	☿	♀	♂	♃	♄	♅	♆	♇
	h m s	° ' "	° '	°	°	°	°	°	°	°	°
J 1	18 33 40	8♋31 50	13♒29	19♊	4♊	10♌	5♋	7♊	3♊	27♍	5♌
U 2	18 37 36	9 29 1	27 48	19	5	11	5	7	3	27	5
L 3	18 41 33	10 26 13	11♓38	20	6	12	5	7	3	27	5
Y 4	18 45 29	11 23 24	25 0	20	7	12	5	7	3	27	5
5	18 49 26	12 20 36	7♈57	21	8	13	6	7	3	27	5
6	18 53 22	13 17 49	20 33	22	9	14	6	7	3	27	5
7	18 57 19	14 15 1	2♉52	23	11	14	6	7	3	27	5
8	19 1 15	15 12 14	14 58	24	12	15	6	8	3	27	5
9	19 5 12	16 9 27	26 56	25	13	15	7	8	3	27	5
10	19 9 8	17 6 41	8♊49	26	14	16	7	8	3	27	5
11	19 13 5	18 3 55	20 41	28	15	17	7	8	3	27	5
12	19 17 2	19 1 9	2♋33	29	17	17	7	8	3	27	5
13	19 20 58	19 58 24	14 27	0♋	18	18	7	8	3	27	5
14	19 24 55	20 55 39	26 25	2	19	19	8	8	3	27	5
15	19 28 51	21 52 54	8♌29	3	20	19	8	8	3	27	5
16	19 32 48	22 50 9	20 41	5	21	20	8	8	3	27	5
17	19 36 44	23 47 25	3♍ 2	6	23	20	8	8	3	27	5
18	19 40 41	24 44 41	15 34	8	24	21	9	9	3	28	5
19	19 44 38	25 41 57	28 22	10	25	22	9	9	3	28	5
20	19 48 34	26 39 13	11♎26	12	26	22	9	9	3	28	5
21	19 52 31	27 36 29	24 51	13	27	23	9	9	4	28	5
22	19 56 27	28 33 46	8♏38	15	28	24	9	9	4	28	5
23	20 0 24	29 31 3	22 48	17	0♋	24	10	9	4	28	5
24	20 4 20	0♌28 20	7♐19	19	1	25	10	9	4	28	5
25	20 8 17	1 25 38	22 7	21	2	25	10	9	4	28	5
26	20 12 13	2 22 56	7♑ 6	23	3	26	10	9	4	28	5
27	20 16 10	3 20 14	22 8	25	4	27	11	9	4	28	5
28	20 20 7	4 17 34	7♒ 3	28	6	27	11	10	4	28	5
29	20 24 3	5 14 54	21 43	0♌	7	28	11	10	4	28	5
30	20 28 0	6 12 15	6♓ 1	2	8	29	11	10	4	28	5
31	20 31 56	7 9 36	19 55	4	9	29	11	10	4	28	5

THE SUN ENTERS THE SIGN OF LEO ON JUL 23 AT 12:08.

DAY	TIME	☉	☽	☿	♀	♂	♃	♄	♅	♆	♇
	h m s	° ' "	° '	°	°	°	°	°	°	°	°
A 1	20 35 53	8♌ 6 59	3♈22	6♌	10♋	0♍	12♋	10♊	4♊	28♍	5♌
U 2	20 39 49	9 4 23	16 24	8	12	0	12	10	4	28	5
G 3	20 43 46	10 1 48	29 4	10	13	1	12	10	4	28	6
U 4	20 47 42	10 59 14	11♉25	12	14	2	12	10	4	28	6
S 5	20 51 39	11 56 41	23 33	14	15	2	12	10	4	28	6
T 6	20 55 35	12 54 10	5♊31	16	17	3	13	10	4	28	6
7	20 59 32	13 51 40	17 24	18	18	4	13	10	4	28	6
8	21 3 29	14 49 11	29 15	20	19	4	13	11	4	28	6
9	21 7 25	15 46 43	11♋ 9	22	20	5	13	11	4	28	6
10	21 11 22	16 44 17	23 8	24	21	5	13	11	4	28	6
11	21 15 18	17 41 52	5♌14	26	23	6	14	11	4	28	6
12	21 19 15	18 39 28	17 29	28	24	7	14	11	4	28	6
13	21 23 11	19 37 5	29 55	0♍	25	7	14	11	4	28	6
14	21 27 8	20 34 43	12♍33	2	26	8	14	11	4	28	6
15	21 31 4	21 32 23	25 23	4	27	9	15	11	4	28	6
16	21 35 1	22 30 3	8♎27	5	29	9	15	11	4	28	6
17	21 38 58	23 27 45	21 46	7	0♌	10	15	11	4	28	6
18	21 42 54	24 25 27	5♏19	9	1	11	15	11	4	28	6
19	21 46 51	25 23 11	19 8	11	2	11	15	11	4	28	6
20	21 50 47	26 20 56	3♐12	12	3	12	16	11	4	28	6
21	21 54 44	27 18 42	17 29	14	5	12	16	11	4	28	6
22	21 58 40	28 16 28	1♑57	16	6	13	16	11	4	28	6
23	22 2 37	29 14 17	16 32	17	7	14	16	12	4	28	6
24	22 6 33	0♍12 6	1♒ 8	19	8	14	16	12	4	29	6
25	22 10 30	1 9 57	15 41	20	10	15	16	12	4	29	6
26	22 14 27	2 7 49	0♓ 3	22	11	16	17	12	4	29	6
27	22 18 23	3 5 42	14 9	24	12	16	17	12	4	29	6
28	22 22 20	4 3 37	27 56	25	13	17	17	12	5	29	6
29	22 26 16	5 1 34	11♈21	27	14	18	17	12	5	29	6
30	22 30 13	5 59 32	24 24	28	16	18	17	12	5	29	6
31	22 34 9	6 57 32	7♉ 7	29	17	19	18	12	5	29	6

THE SUN ENTERS THE SIGN OF VIRGO ON AUG 23 AT 18:59.

DAY	TIME	☉	☽	☿	♀	♂	♃	♄	♅	♆	♇
	h m s	° ' "	° '	°	°	°	°	°	°	°	°
S 1	22 38 6	7♍55 34	19♉31	1♎	18♌	19♍	18♋	12♊	5♊	29♍	6♌
E 2	22 42 2	8 53 38	1♊40	2	19	20	18	12	5	29	6
P 3	22 45 59	9 51 45	13 39	4	21	21	18	12	5	29	6
T 4	22 49 56	10 49 53	25 33	5	22	21	18	12	5	29	6
E 5	22 53 52	11 48 2	7♋25	6	23	22	18	12	5	29	6
M 6	22 57 49	12 46 14	19 20	8	24	23	19	12	5	29	6
B 7	23 1 45	13 44 28	1♌23	9	26	23	19	12	5	29	6
E 8	23 5 42	14 42 44	13 36	10	27	24	19	12	5	29	6
R 9	23 9 38	15 41 1	26 3	11	28	25	19	12	5	29	6
10	23 13 35	16 39 21	8♍45	13	29	25	19	12	5 R	29	7
11	23 17 31	17 37 42	21 43	14	0♍	26	20	12	5	29	7
12	23 21 28	18 36 5	4♎57	15	2	26	20	12	5	29	7
13	23 25 25	19 34 30	18 25	16	3	27	20	12	5	29	7
14	23 29 21	20 32 57	2♏ 7	17	4	28	20	12	5	29	7
15	23 33 18	21 31 25	16 0	18	5	28	20	12	5	29	7
16	23 37 14	22 29 55	0♐ 1	19	7	29	20	12	5	29	7
17	23 41 11	23 28 26	14 9	20	8	0♎	20	12	5	29	7
18	23 45 7	24 26 59	28 20	21	9	0	21	12	5	29	7
19	23 49 4	25 25 34	12♑34	22	10	1	21	12	5	29	7
20	23 53 0	26 24 10	26 46	22	12	2	21	12	5	29	7
21	23 56 57	27 22 49	10♒56	23	13	2	21	13	5	0♎	7
22	0 0 53	28 21 28	25 1	24	14	3	21	13	5	0	7
23	0 4 50	29 20 10	8♓56	24	15	4	21	13	5	0	7
24	0 8 47	0♎18 53	22 41	25	17	4	22	13	5	0	7
25	0 12 43	1 17 38	6♈11	25	18	5	22	13 R	4	0	7
26	0 16 40	2 16 25	19 25	26	19	6	22	13	4	0	7
27	0 20 36	3 15 15	2♉22	26	20	6	22	13	4	0	7
28	0 24 33	4 14 6	15 1	26 R	22	7	22	13	4	0	7
29	0 28 29	5 13 0	27 24	26	23	8	22	13	4	0	7
30	0 32 26	6 11 56	9♊34	26	24	8	22	13	4	0	7

THE SUN ENTERS THE SIGN OF LIBRA ON SEP 23 AT 16:17.

DAY	TIME	☉	☽	☿	♀	♂	♃	♄	♅	♆	♇
	h m s	° ' "	° '	°	°	°	°	°	°	°	°
O 1	0 36 22	7♎10 54	21♊33	26♎R	25♍	9♎	22♋	12♊R	4♊R	0♎	7♌
C 2	0 40 19	8 9 55	3♋26	25	27	9	23	12	4	0	7
T 3	0 44 16	9 8 57	15 17	25	28	10	23	12	4	0	7
O 4	0 48 12	10 8 2	27 12	24	29	11	23	12	4	0	7
B 5	0 52 9	11 7 10	9♌16	24	0♎	11	23	12	4	0	7
E 6	0 56 5	12 6 19	21 32	23	2	12	23	12	4	0	7
R 7	1 0 2	13 5 31	4♍ 6	22	3	13	23	12	4	0	7
8	1 3 58	14 4 45	17 0	21	4	13	23	12	4	0	7
9	1 7 55	15 4 1	0♎15	20	5	14	23	12	4	0	7
10	1 11 51	16 3 20	13 52	18	7	15	23	12	4	0	7
11	1 15 48	17 2 40	27 47	17	8	15	24	12	4	0	7
12	1 19 45	18 2 2	11♏57	16	9	16	24	12	4	0	7
13	1 23 41	19 1 27	26 18	15	10	17	24	12	4	0	7
14	1 27 38	20 0 53	10♐42	14	11	17	24	12	4	0	7
15	1 31 34	21 0 21	25 5	13	13	18	24	12	4	0	7
16	1 35 31	21 59 51	9♑23	12	14	19	24	12	4	0	7
17	1 39 27	22 59 22	23 33	11	15	19	24	12	4	0	7
18	1 43 24	23 58 56	7♒33	11	17	20	24	12	4	1	7
19	1 47 20	24 58 30	21 23	11	18	21	24	12	4	1	7
20	1 51 17	25 58 7	5♓ 3	11 D	19	21	24	12	4	1	7
21	1 55 14	26 57 45	18 33	11	20	22	24	12	4	1	7
22	1 59 10	27 57 25	1♈52	11	22	23	24	12	4	1	7
23	2 3 7	28 57 7	15 0	11	23	23	25	12	4	1	7
24	2 7 3	29 56 51	27 56	12	24	24	25	12	4	1	7
25	2 11 0	0♏56 37	10♉39	13	25	25	25	12	4	1	7
26	2 14 56	1 56 25	23 9	14	27	25	25	12	4	1	7
27	2 18 53	2 56 15	5♊27	15	28	26	25	12	4	1	7
28	2 22 49	3 56 7	17 33	16	29	27	25	12	4	1	7
29	2 26 46	4 56 2	29 30	17	0♏	27	25	12	4	1	7
30	2 30 42	5 55 58	11♋21	18	2	28	25	11	4	1	7
31	2 34 39	6 55 57	23 11	19	3	29	25	11	4	1	7

THE SUN ENTERS THE SIGN OF SCORPIO ON OCT 24 AT 01:17.

DAY	TIME	☉	☽	☿	♀	♂	♃	♄	♅	♆	♇
	h m s	° ' "	° '	°	°	°	°	°	°	°	°
N 1	2 38 36	7♏55 57	5♌ 3	21♎	4♏	29♎	25♋	11♊R	4♊R	1♎	7♌
O 2	2 42 32	8 56 0	17 4	22	5	0♏	25	11	4	1	7
V 3	2 46 29	9 56 5	29 19	24	7	1	25	11	3	1	7
E 4	2 50 25	10 56 12	11♍53	25	8	1	25	11	3	1	7
M 5	2 54 22	11 56 21	24 50	27	9	2	25	11	3	1	7
B 6	2 58 18	12 56 32	8♎13	28	10	3	25	11	3	1	7
E 7	3 2 15	13 56 45	22 3	0♏	12	3	25	11	3	1	7
R 8	3 6 11	14 57 0	6♏19	1	13	4	25	11	3	1	7 R
9	3 10 8	15 57 17	20 54	3	14	5	25	11	3	1	7
10	3 14 5	16 57 35	5♐42	5	15	5	25	11	3	1	7
11	3 18 1	17 57 55	20 33	6	17	6	25	11	3	1	7
12	3 21 58	18 58 17	5♑21	8	18	7	25 R	11	3	1	7
13	3 25 54	19 58 41	19 56	9	19	7	25	11	3	1	7
14	3 29 51	20 59 5	4♒16	11	20	8	25	10	3	1	7
15	3 33 47	21 59 31	18 17	13	22	9	25	10	3	1	7
16	3 37 44	22 59 58	2♓ 0	14	23	10	25	10	3	1	7
17	3 41 40	24 0 27	15 26	16	24	10	25	10	3	1	7
18	3 45 37	25 0 56	28 38	18	25	11	25	10	3	1	7
19	3 49 34	26 1 27	11♈36	19	27	12	25	10	3	1	7
20	3 53 30	27 2 0	24 24	21	28	12	25	10	3	2	7
21	3 57 27	28 2 33	7♉ 0	22	29	13	25	10	3	2	7
22	4 1 23	29 3 8	19 27	24	0♐	14	25	10	3	2	7
23	4 5 20	0♐ 3 45	1♊44	25	2	14	25	10	3	2	7
24	4 9 16	1 4 23	13 53	27	3	15	25	10	3	2	7
25	4 13 13	2 5 2	25 53	29	4	16	25	10	3	2	7
26	4 17 9	3 5 43	7♋47	0♐	5	16	25	10	3	2	7
27	4 21 6	4 6 26	19 36	2	7	17	25	9	3	2	7
28	4 25 3	5 7 9	1♌24	3	8	18	25	9	2	2	7
29	4 28 59	6 7 55	13 14	5	9	18	25	9	2	2	7
30	4 32 56	7 8 42	25 13	7	10	19	25	9	2	2	7

THE SUN ENTERS THE SIGN OF SAGITTARIUS ON NOV 22 AT 22:31.

DAY	TIME	☉	☽	☿	♀	♂	♃	♄	♅	♆	♇
	h m s	° ' "	° '	°	°	°	°	°	°	°	°
D 1	4 36 52	8♐ 9 30	7♍24	8♐	12♐	20♏	25♋R	9♊R	2♊R	2♎	7♌R
E 2	4 40 49	9 10 20	19 53	10	13	20	25	9	2	2	7
C 3	4 44 45	10 11 11	2♎46	11	14	21	25	9	2	2	7
E 4	4 48 42	11 12 3	16 6	13	15	22	24	9	2	2	7
M 5	4 52 38	12 12 57	29 56	14	17	23	24	9	2	2	7
B 6	4 56 35	13 13 52	14♏16	16	18	23	24	9	2	2	7
E 7	5 0 32	14 14 49	29 1	18	19	24	24	9	2	2	7
R 8	5 4 28	15 15 46	14♐ 5	19	21	25	24	9	2	2	7
9	5 8 25	16 16 45	29 18	21	22	25	24	8	2	2	7
10	5 12 21	17 17 45	14♑27	22	23	26	24	8	2	2	7
11	5 16 18	18 18 45	29 25	24	24	27	24	8	2	2	7
12	5 20 14	19 19 45	14♒ 3	25	26	27	24	8	2	2	7
13	5 24 11	20 20 47	28 17	27	27	28	24	8	2	2	7
14	5 28 7	21 21 49	12♓ 7	29	28	29	24	8	2	2	7
15	5 32 4	22 22 51	25 33	0♑	29	0♐	24	8	2	2	7
16	5 36 1	23 23 53	8♈39	2	1♑	0	23	8	2	2	7
17	5 39 57	24 24 56	21 27	3	2	1	23	8	2	2	7
18	5 43 54	25 26 0	4♉ 1	5	3	2	23	8	2	2	7
19	5 47 50	26 27 4	16 23	6	4	2	23	8	2	2	7
20	5 51 47	27 28 8	28 36	8	6	3	23	8	2	2	7
21	5 55 43	28 29 13	10♊41	10	7	4	23	8	2	2	7
22	5 59 40	29 30 18	22 40	11	8	4	23	7	2	2	7
23	6 3 37	0♑31 23	4♋34	13	9	5	23	7	1	2	7
24	6 7 33	1 32 29	16 25	14	11	6	23	7	1	2	7
25	6 11 30	2 33 36	28 14	16	12	7	22	7	1	2	7
26	6 15 26	3 34 43	10♌ 3	17	13	7	22	7	1	2	7
27	6 19 23	4 35 50	21 56	19	14	8	22	7	1	2	7
28	6 23 19	5 36 58	3♍56	21	16	9	22	7	1	2	7
29	6 27 16	6 38 6	16 7	22	17	9	22	7	1	2	7
30	6 31 12	7 39 15	28 33	24	18	10	22	7	1	2	7
31	6 35 9	8 40 24	11♎21	25	19	11	22	7	1	2	7

THE SUN ENTERS THE SIGN OF CAPRICORN ON DEC 22 AT 11:40.

♈ ARIES ♉ TAURUS ♊ GEMINI ♋ CANCER ♌ LEO ♍ VIRGO ♎ LIBRA ♏ SCORPIO ♐ SAGITTARIUS ♑ CAPRICORN ♒ AQUARIUS ♓ PISCES

SIDEREAL SUN MOON MERCURY VENUS MARS JUPITER SATURN URANUS NEPTUNE PLUTO

DAY	TIME	☉	☽	☿	♀	♂	♃	♄	♅	♆	♇
	h m s	° ' "	° '	°	°	°	°	°	°	°	°
J 1	6 39 6	9♑41 34	24♎33	27♑	21♑	11♐	22♋R	7♊R	1♊R	2♎	7♌R
A 2	6 43 2	10 42 44	8♏14	28	22	12	21	7	1	2	7
N 3	6 46 59	11 43 54	22 24	0♒	23	13	21	7	1	2 R	7
U 4	6 50 55	12 45 5	7♐ 1	1	24	14	21	7	1	2	7
A 5	6 54 52	13 46 16	22 2	2	26	14	21	7	1	2	7
R 6	6 58 48	14 47 27	7♑16	4	27	15	21	6	1	2	7
Y 7	7 2 45	15 48 38	22 34	5	28	16	21	6	1	2	7
8	7 6 41	16 49 48	7♒45	6	29	16	21	6	1	2	7
9	7 10 38	17 50 59	22 39	7	1♒	17	21	6	1	2	7
10	7 14 35	18 52 9	7♓10	8	2	18	20	6	1	2	6
11	7 18 31	19 53 18	21 15	9	3	19	20	6	1	2	6
12	7 22 28	20 54 27	4♈51	10	4	19	20	6	1	2	6
13	7 26 24	21 55 35	18 3	10	6	20	20	6	1	2	6
14	7 30 21	22 56 42	0♉52	11	7	21	20	6	1	2	6
15	7 34 17	23 57 49	13 22	11 R	8	21	20	6	1	2	6
16	7 38 14	24 58 55	25 38	11	10	22	20	6	1	2	6
17	7 42 10	26 0 1	7♊42	11	11	23	19	6	1	2	6
18	7 46 7	27 1 6	19 40	10	12	24	19	6	1	2	6
19	7 50 4	28 2 10	1♋32	10	13	24	19	6	1	2	6
20	7 54 0	29 3 13	13 22	9	15	25	19	6	1	2	6
21	7 57 57	0♒ 4 16	25 12	8	16	26	19	6	1	2	6
22	8 1 53	1 5 18	7♌ 3	7	17	27	19	6	1	2	6
23	8 5 50	2 6 19	18 58	6	18	27	19	6	1	2	6
24	8 9 46	3 7 19	0♍59	5	20	28	19	6	1	2	6
25	8 13 43	4 8 19	13 7	4	21	29	18	6	1	2	6
26	8 17 39	5 9 19	25 26	2	22	29	18	6	1	2	6
27	8 21 36	6 10 17	7♎59	1	23	0♒	18	6	1	2	6
28	8 25 33	7 11 15	20 48	0	25	1	18	6	1	2	6
29	8 29 29	8 12 13	3♏57	29♑	26	2	18	6	1	2	6
30	8 33 26	9 13 9	17 30	28	27	2	18	6	1	2	6
31	8 37 22	10 14 5	1♐26	27	28	3	18	6	1	2	6

THE SUN ENTERS THE SIGN OF AQUARIUS ON JAN 20 AT 22:19.

DAY	TIME	☉	☽	☿	♀	♂	♃	♄	♅	♆	♇
	h m s	° ' "	° '	°	°	°	°	°	°	°	°
F 1	8 41 19	11♒15 1	15♐46	26♑R	0♓	4♑	18♋R	6♊R	1♊R	2♎R	6♌R
E 2	8 45 15	12 15 56	0♑27	26	1	5	17	6	1	2	6
B 3	8 49 12	13 16 50	15 25	25	2	5	17	6	1	2	6
R 4	8 53 8	14 17 42	0♒31	25	3	6	17	6	1	2	6
U 5	8 57 5	15 18 34	15 36	25 D	5	7	17	6	1	2	6
A 6	9 1 2	16 19 25	0♓32	25	6	7	17	6 D	1	2	6
R 7	9 4 58	17 20 14	15 10	25	7	8	17	6	1	2	6
Y 8	9 8 55	18 21 2	29 25	25	8	9	17	6	1 D	2	6
9	9 12 51	19 21 48	13♈13	26	10	10	17	6	1	2	6
10	9 16 48	20 22 33	26 34	26	11	10	17	6	1	2	6
11	9 20 44	21 23 16	9♉31	27	12	11	17	6	1	2	6
12	9 24 41	22 23 58	22 5	27	13	12	16	6	1	2	6
13	9 28 37	23 24 38	4♊21	28	14	13	16	6	1	2	6
14	9 32 34	24 25 16	16 25	29	16	13	16	6	1	2	6
15	9 36 31	25 25 53	28 19	29	17	14	16	6	1	2	6
16	9 40 27	26 26 28	10♋ 8	0♒	18	15	16	6	1	2	6
17	9 44 24	27 27 1	21 57	1	19	16	16	6	1	2	6
18	9 48 20	28 27 33	3♌48	2	21	16	16	6	1	2	6
19	9 52 17	29 28 3	15 45	3	22	17	16	6	1	2	6
20	9 56 13	0♓28 31	27 48	4	23	18	16	6	1	1	6
21	10 0 10	1 28 58	10♍ 1	5	24	18	16	6	1	1	6
22	10 4 6	2 29 23	22 25	6	26	19	16	6	1	1	6
23	10 8 3	3 29 47	5♎ 1	8	27	20	16	6	1	1	6
24	10 11 59	4 30 9	17 49	9	28	21	16	6	1	1	5
25	10 15 56	5 30 30	0♏52	10	29	21	16	6	1	1	5
26	10 19 53	6 30 49	14 10	11	1♈	22	15	6	1	1	5
27	10 23 49	7 31 7	27 43	12	2	23	15	6	1	1	5
28	10 27 46	8 31 23	11♐33	14	3	24	15	6	1	1	5

THE SUN ENTERS THE SIGN OF PISCES ON FEB 19 AT 12:41.

DAY	TIME	☉	☽	☿	♀	♂	♃	♄	♅	♆	♇
	h m s	° ' "	° '	°	°	°	°	°	°	°	°
M 1	10 31 42	9♓31 38	25♐39	15♒	4♈	24♑	15♋R	6♊	1♊	1♎R	5♌R
A 2	10 35 39	10 31 52	10♑ 0	16	6	25	15	6	1	1	5
R 3	10 39 35	11 32 4	24 32	18	7	26	15	6	1	1	5
C 4	10 43 32	12 32 14	9♒13	19	8	27	15	6	1	1	5
H 5	10 47 28	13 32 23	23 56	21	9	27	15	6	1	1	5
6	10 51 25	14 32 30	8♓35	22	10	28	15	6	1	1	5
7	10 55 22	15 32 35	23 3	24	12	29	15	6	1	1	5
8	10 59 18	16 32 38	7♈14	25	13	0♒	15	6	1	1	5
9	11 3 15	17 32 40	21 4	27	14	0	15	6	1	1	5
10	11 7 11	18 32 39	4♉29	28	15	1	15	7	1	1	5
11	11 11 8	19 32 36	17 31	0♓	17	2	15	7	1	1	5
12	11 15 4	20 32 31	0♊11	1	18	3	15 D	7	1	1	5
13	11 19 1	21 32 23	12 31	3	19	3	15	7	1	1	5
14	11 22 57	22 32 14	24 36	4	20	4	15	7	1	1	5
15	11 26 54	23 32 2	6♋31	6	22	5	15	7	1	1	5
16	11 30 51	24 31 48	18 20	8	23	6	15	7	1	1	5
17	11 34 47	25 31 32	0♌ 9	9	24	6	15	7	1	1	5
18	11 38 44	26 31 14	12 2	11	25	7	15	7	1	1	5
19	11 42 40	27 30 53	24 4	13	26	8	15	7	1	1	5
20	11 46 37	28 30 31	6♍16	15	28	9	15	7	1	1	5
21	11 50 33	29 30 6	18 43	16	29	9	15	7	1	1	5
22	11 54 30	0♈29 39	1♎25	18	0♉	10	15	7	1	1	5
23	11 58 26	1 29 10	14 22	20	1	11	15	7	1	1	5
24	12 2 23	2 28 39	27 34	22	3	12	15	7	1	1	5
25	12 6 20	3 28 6	10♏59	23	4	12	15	8	1	1	5
26	12 10 16	4 27 32	24 37	25	5	13	15	8	1	1	5
27	12 14 13	5 26 55	8♐25	27	6	14	16	8	2	1	5
28	12 18 9	6 26 17	22 21	29	7	15	16	8	2	1	5
29	12 22 6	7 25 37	6♑24	1♈	9	15	16	8	2	1	5
30	12 26 2	8 24 56	20 33	3	10	16	16	8	2	0	5
31	12 29 59	9 24 12	4♒46	5	11	17	16	8	2	0	5

THE SUN ENTERS THE SIGN OF ARIES ON MAR 21 AT 12:03.

DAY	TIME	☉	☽	☿	♀	♂	♃	♄	♅	♆	♇
	h m s	° ' "	° '	°	°	°	°	°	°	°	°
A 1	12 33 55	10♈23 27	19♒ 2	7♈	12♉	18♒	16♋	8♊	2♊	0♎R	5♌R
P 2	12 37 52	11 22 40	3♓18	9	13	18	16	8	2	0	5
R 3	12 41 48	12 21 51	17 30	11	15	19	16	8	2	0	5
I 4	12 45 45	13 21 1	1♈35	13	16	20	16	8	2	0	5
L 5	12 49 42	14 20 8	15 28	15	17	21	16	8	2	0	5
6	12 53 38	15 19 13	29 5	17	18	21	16	9	2	0	5
7	12 57 35	16 18 16	12♉24	19	19	22	16	9	2	0	5
8	13 1 31	17 17 17	25 23	21	21	23	16	9	2	0	5
9	13 5 28	18 16 16	8♊ 2	23	22	24	16	9	2	0	5
10	13 9 24	19 15 13	20 23	25	23	24	16	9	2	0	5
11	13 13 21	20 14 7	2♋29	28	24	25	17	9	2	0	5
12	13 17 17	21 12 59	14 24	0♉	25	26	17	9	2	0	5
13	13 21 14	22 11 49	26 14	2	27	27	17	9	2	0	5
14	13 25 11	23 10 37	8♌ 3	4	28	27	17	9	2	0	5
15	13 29 7	24 9 22	19 57	6	29	28	17	9	2	0	5
16	13 33 4	25 8 5	2♍ 2	8	0♊	29	17	10	2	0	5
17	13 37 0	26 6 46	14 21	10	1	0♓	17	10	2	0	5
18	13 40 57	27 5 25	26 58	11	3	0	17	10	2	0	5 D
19	13 44 53	28 4 1	9♎55	13	4	1	17	10	3	0	5
20	13 48 50	29 2 36	23 12	15	5	2	17	10	3	0	5
21	13 52 46	0♉ 1 9	6♏48	17	6	3	18	10	3	0	5
22	13 56 43	0 59 40	20 40	19	7	3	18	10	3	0	5
23	14 0 40	1 58 9	4♐44	20	8	4	18	10	3	0	5
24	14 4 36	2 56 36	18 56	22	10	5	18	10	3	0	5
25	14 8 33	3 55 2	3♑10	23	11	6	18	11	3	0	5
26	14 12 29	4 53 26	17 23	25	12	6	18	11	3	0	5
27	14 16 26	5 51 49	1♒33	26	13	7	18	11	3	0	5
28	14 20 22	6 50 10	15 39	27	14	8	18	11	3	0	5
29	14 24 19	7 48 30	29 39	28	16	9	19	11	3	0	5
30	14 28 15	8 46 48	13♓33	29	17	9	19	11	3	0	5

THE SUN ENTERS THE SIGN OF TAURUS ON APR 20 AT 23:32.

DAY	TIME	☉	☽	☿	♀	♂	♃	♄	♅	♆	♇
	h m s	° ' "	° '	°	°	°	°	°	°	°	°
M 1	14 32 12	9♉45 4	27♓20	0♊	18♊	10♓	19♋	11♊	3♊	0♎R	5♌
A 2	14 36 9	10 43 19	10♈59	1	19	11	19	11	3	0	5
Y 3	14 40 5	11 41 32	24 28	2	20	12	19	11	3	0	5
4	14 44 2	12 39 44	7♉44	3	21	12	19	12	3	0	5
5	14 47 58	13 37 54	20 47	3	23	13	19	12	3	0	5
6	14 51 55	14 36 2	3♊33	4	24	14	20	12	3	0	5
7	14 55 51	15 34 9	16 4	5	25	15	20	12	4	0	5
8	14 59 48	16 32 14	28 20	5	26	16	20	12	4	0	5
9	15 3 44	17 30 17	10♋24	5	27	16	20	12	4	0	5
10	15 7 41	18 28 18	22 18	6	28	17	20	12	4	0	5
11	15 11 38	19 26 17	4♌ 6	6	29	18	20	12	4	0	5
12	15 15 34	20 24 15	15 55	6 R	1♋	19	20	13	4	0	5
13	15 19 31	21 22 10	27 49	6	2	19	21	13	4	29♍	5
14	15 23 27	22 20 4	9♍54	6	3	20	21	13	4	29	5
15	15 27 24	23 17 56	22 15	5	4	21	21	13	4	29	5
16	15 31 20	24 15 47	4♎56	5	5	22	21	13	4	29	5
17	15 35 17	25 13 35	18 1	5	6	22	21	13	4	29	5
18	15 39 13	26 11 22	1♏31	4	7	23	21	13	4	29	5
19	15 43 10	27 9 8	15 25	4	9	24	22	13	4	29	5
20	15 47 6	28 6 52	29 40	4	10	24	22	14	4	29	5
21	15 51 3	29 4 35	14♐ 9	3	11	25	22	14	4	29	5
22	15 55 0	0♊ 2 17	28 47	2	12	26	22	14	4	29	5
23	15 58 56	0 59 57	13♑25	2	13	27	22	14	4	29	5
24	16 2 53	1 57 37	27 57	1	14	27	22	14	4	29	5
25	16 6 49	2 55 15	12♒20	1	15	28	23	14	5	29	5
26	16 10 46	3 52 52	26 31	0	16	29	23	14	5	29	5
27	16 14 42	4 50 29	10♓28	0	17	0☉	23	14	5	29	5
28	16 18 39	5 48 4	24 11	29♉	19	0♈	23	15	5	29	5
29	16 22 36	6 45 39	7♈42	29	20	1	23	15	5	29	5
30	16 26 32	7 43 13	21 1	28	21	2	24	15	5	29	5
31	16 30 29	8 40 46	4♉ 7	28	22	3	24	15	5	29	5

THE SUN ENTERS THE SIGN OF GEMINI ON MAY 21 AT 23:03.

DAY	TIME	☉	☽	☿	♀	♂	♃	♄	♅	♆	♇
	h m s	° ' "	° '	°	°	°	°	°	°	°	°
J 1	16 34 25	9♊38 18	17♉ 2	28♉R	23♋	3♈	24♋	15♊	5♊	29♍R	5♌
U 2	16 38 22	10 35 49	29 44	27	24	4	24	15	5	29	5
N 3	16 42 18	11 33 19	12♊15	27	25	5	24	15	5	29	5
E 4	16 46 15	12 30 48	24 33	27	26	6	25	16	5	29	5
5	16 50 11	13 28 16	6♋40	27 D	27	6	25	16	5	29	5
6	16 54 8	14 25 43	18 37	27	28	7	25	16	5	29	5
7	16 58 5	15 23 10	0♌28	27	29	8	25	16	5	29	5
8	17 2 1	16 20 35	12 15	27	1♌	9	25	16	5	29	5
9	17 5 58	17 17 59	24 3	28	2	9	25	16	5	29	5
10	17 9 54	18 15 21	5♍56	28	3	10	26	16	5	29 D	6
11	17 13 51	19 12 43	18 0	28	4	11	26	16	6	29	6
12	17 17 47	20 10 4	0♎20	29	5	11	26	17	6	29	6
13	17 21 44	21 7 24	13 0	29	6	12	26	17	6	29	6
14	17 25 40	22 4 42	26 6	0♊	7	13	26	17	6	29	6
15	17 29 37	23 2 0	9♏39	1	8	14	27	17	6	29	6
16	17 33 34	23 59 17	23 40	1	9	14	27	17	6	29	6
17	17 37 30	24 56 34	8♐ 6	2	10	15	27	17	6	29	6
18	17 41 27	25 53 50	22 51	3	11	16	27	17	6	29	6
19	17 45 23	26 51 5	7♑48	4	12	17	28	17	6	29	6
20	17 49 20	27 48 20	22 48	5	13	17	28	18	6	29	6
21	17 53 16	28 45 34	7♒42	6	14	18	28	18	6	29	6
22	17 57 13	29 42 48	22 24	7	15	19	28	18	6	29	6
23	18 1 9	0♋40 2	6♓48	9	16	19	28	18	6	29	6
24	18 5 6	1 37 16	20 52	10	17	20	29	18	6	29	6
25	18 9 3	2 34 30	4♈37	11	18	21	29	18	6	29	6
26	18 12 59	3 31 44	18 2	12	19	22	29	18	6	29	6
27	18 16 56	4 28 57	1♉ 9	14	20	22	29	18	6	29	6
28	18 20 52	5 26 11	14 1	15	21	23	29	19	6	29	6
29	18 24 49	6 23 25	26 38	17	22	24	0♌	19	7	29	6
30	18 28 45	7 20 39	9♊ 4	19	23	24	0	19	7	29	6

THE SUN ENTERS THE SIGN OF CANCER ON JUN 22 AT 07:13.

♈ ARIES ♉ TAURUS ♊ GEMINI ♋ CANCER ♌ LEO ♍ VIRGO ♎ LIBRA ♏ SCORPIO ♐ SAGITTARIUS ♑ CAPRICORN ♒ AQUARIUS ♓ PISCES

1943

SIDEREAL SUN MOON MERCURY VENUS MARS JUPITER SATURN URANUS NEPTUNE PLUTO

DAY	TIME	☉	☽	☿	♀	♂	♃	♄	♅	♆	♇
	h m s	° ' "	° '	°	°	°	°	°	°	°	°
J 1	18 32 42	8♋17 52	21♊19	20♊	24♌	25♈	0♌	19♊	7♊	29♍	6♌
U 2	18 36 38	9 15 6	3♋24	22	25	26	0	19	7	29	6
L 3	18 40 35	10 12 20	15 21	24	26	27	0	19	7	29	6
Y 4	18 44 32	11 9 33	27 13	25	26	27	1	19	7	29	6
5	18 48 28	12 6 47	9♌ 0	27	27	28	1	19	7	29	6
6	18 52 25	13 4 0	20 47	29	28	29	1	20	7	29	6
7	18 56 21	14 1 14	2♍35	1♋	29	29	1	20	7	29	6
8	19 0 18	14 58 26	14 30	3	0♍	0♉	2	20	7	29	6
9	19 4 14	15 55 39	26 34	5	1	1	2	20	7	29	6
10	19 8 11	16 52 52	8♎53	7	2	1	2	20	7	0♎	6
11	19 12 7	17 50 5	21 32	9	3	2	2	20	7	0	6
12	19 16 4	18 47 17	4♏34	11	3	3	2	20	7	0	6
13	19 20 1	19 44 30	18 3	14	4	3	3	20	7	0	6
14	19 23 57	20 41 43	2♐ 0	16	5	4	3	21	7	0	6
15	19 27 54	21 38 55	16 23	18	6	5	3	21	7	0	6
16	19 31 50	22 36 8	1♑10	20	7	6	3	21	7	0	6
17	19 35 47	23 33 21	16 14	22	7	6	3	21	7	0	6
18	19 39 43	24 30 35	1♒25	24	8	7	4	21	7	0	6
19	19 43 40	25 27 49	16 34	26	9	8	4	21	8	0	6
20	19 47 36	26 25 3	1♓32	29	10	8	4	21	8	0	7
21	19 51 33	27 22 18	16 13	1♌	10	9	4	21	8	0	7
22	19 55 30	28 19 34	0♈30	3	11	10	5	22	8	0	7
23	19 59 26	29 16 50	14 23	5	12	10	5	22	8	0	7
24	20 3 23	0♌14 8	27 51	7	12	11	5	22	8	0	7
25	20 7 19	1 11 26	10♉57	9	13	12	5	22	8	0	7
26	20 11 16	2 8 45	23 42	11	14	12	5	22	8	0	7
27	20 15 12	3 6 6	6♊10	13	14	13	6	22	8	0	7
28	20 19 9	4 3 27	18 24	15	15	14	6	22	8	0	7
29	20 23 5	5 0 49	0♋28	17	15	14	6	22	8	0	7
30	20 27 2	5 58 12	12 24	19	16	15	6	22	8	0	7
31	20 30 59	6 55 36	24 14	20	16	15	7	22	8	0	7

THE SUN ENTERS THE SIGN OF LEO ON JUL 23 AT 18:05.

DAY	TIME	☉	☽	☿	♀	♂	♃	♄	♅	♆	♇
	h m s	° ' "	° '	°	°	°	°	°	°	°	°
A 1	20 34 55	7♌53 1	6♌ 2	22♌	17♍	16♉	7♌	23♊	8♊	0♎	7♌
U 2	20 38 52	8 50 26	17 49	24	17	17	7	23	8	0	7
G 3	20 42 48	9 47 53	29 38	26	18	17	7	23	8	0	7
U 4	20 46 45	10 45 20	11♍30	28	18	18	7	23	8	0	7
S 5	20 50 41	11 42 48	23 30	29	18	19	8	23	8	0	7
T 6	20 54 38	12 40 17	5♎40	1♍	19	19	8	23	8	0	7
7	20 58 34	13 37 46	18 3	3	19	20	8	23	8	0	7
8	21 2 31	14 35 17	0♏43	4	19	21	8	23	8	0	7
9	21 6 28	15 32 48	13 42	6	20	21	9	23	8	0	7
10	21 10 24	16 30 20	27 5	7	20	22	9	23	8	0	7
11	21 14 21	17 27 53	10♐52	9	20	22	9	24	8	0	7
12	21 18 17	18 25 26	25 5	11	20	23	9	24	8	0	7
13	21 22 14	19 23 1	9♑41	12	20	24	9	24	8	0	7
14	21 26 10	20 20 37	24 35	13	20	24	10	24	8	0	7
15	21 30 7	21 18 13	9♒42	15	21 R	25	10	24	8	0	7
16	21 34 3	22 15 51	24 53	16	21	25	10	24	8	0	7
17	21 38 0	23 13 30	9♓58	18	21	26	10	24	8	0	7
18	21 41 57	24 11 11	24 48	19	20	27	11	24	9	0	7
19	21 45 53	25 8 52	9♈17	20	20	27	11	24	9	0	7
20	21 49 50	26 6 36	23 20	22	20	28	11	24	9	0	7
21	21 53 46	27 4 21	6♉56	23	20	28	11	24	9	1	7
22	21 57 43	28 2 8	20 5	24	20	29	11	25	9	1	7
23	22 1 39	28 59 56	2♊51	25	20	29	12	25	9	1	7
24	22 5 36	29 57 46	15 17	27	19	0♊	12	25	9	1	8
25	22 9 32	0♍55 38	27 26	28	19	1	12	25	9	1	8
26	22 13 29	1 53 32	9♋24	29	18	1	12	25	9	1	8
27	22 17 26	2 51 27	21 15	0♎	18	2	12	25	9	1	8
28	22 21 22	3 49 24	3♌ 2	1	18	2	13	25	9	1	8
29	22 25 19	4 47 23	14 49	2	17	3	13	25	9	1	8
30	22 29 15	5 45 24	26 38	3	17	3	13	25	9	1	8
31	22 33 12	6 43 26	8♍33	4	16	4	13	25	9	1	8

THE SUN ENTERS THE SIGN OF VIRGO ON AUG 24 AT 00:56.

DAY	TIME	☉	☽	☿	♀	♂	♃	♄	♅	♆	♇
	h m s	° ' "	° '	°	°	°	°	°	°	°	°
S 1	22 37 8	7♍41 29	20♍36	5♎	16♍R	4♊	14♌	25♊	9♊	1♎	8♌
E 2	22 41 5	8 39 34	2♎47	5	15	5	14	25	9	1	8
P 3	22 45 1	9 37 41	15 8	6	14	5	14	25	9	1	8
T 4	22 48 58	10 35 49	27 42	7	14	6	14	25	9	1	8
E 5	22 52 55	11 33 59	10♏30	7	13	6	14	26	9	1	8
M 6	22 56 51	12 32 10	23 34	8	13	7	15	26	9	1	8
B 7	23 0 48	13 30 23	6♐55	8	12	7	15	26	9	1	8
E 8	23 4 44	14 28 37	20 34	9	11	8	15	26	9	1	8
R 9	23 8 41	15 26 53	4♑34	9	11	8	15	26	9	1	8
10	23 12 37	16 25 10	18 53	9	10	9	15	26	9	1	8
11	23 16 34	17 23 29	3♒29	9 R	10	9	16	26	9	1	8
12	23 20 30	18 21 49	18 19	9	9	10	16	26	9	1	8
13	23 24 27	19 20 11	3♓15	9	8	10	16	26	9	1	8
14	23 28 23	20 18 35	18 11	9	8	11	16	26	9 R	1	8
15	23 32 20	21 17 0	2♈58	9	7	11	16	26	9	1	8
16	23 36 17	22 15 27	17 28	8	7	12	17	26	9	1	8
17	23 40 13	23 13 57	1♉36	8	7	12	17	26	9	1	8
18	23 44 10	24 12 28	15 18	7	6	13	17	26	9	2	8
19	23 48 6	25 11 2	28 32	7	6	13	17	26	9	2	8
20	23 52 3	26 9 38	11♊21	6	5	13	17	26	9	2	8
21	23 55 59	27 8 16	23 48	5	5	14	18	26	9	2	8
22	23 59 56	28 6 56	5♋57	4	5	14	18	26	9	2	8
23	0 3 52	29 5 39	17 54	3	5	15	18	26	9	2	8
24	0 7 49	0♎ 4 24	29 43	2	5	15	18	26	9	2	8
25	0 11 46	1 3 11	11♌30	0	4	15	18	26	9	2	8
26	0 15 42	2 2 0	23 19	29♍	4	16	19	26	9	2	8
27	0 19 39	3 0 51	5♍13	28	4 D	16	19	26	9	2	8
28	0 23 35	3 59 45	17 16	27	4	16	19	27	9	2	8
29	0 27 32	4 58 40	29 31	27	4	17	19	27	9	2	8
30	0 31 28	5 57 37	11♎58	26	4	17	19	27	9	2	8

THE SUN ENTERS THE SIGN OF LIBRA ON SEP 23 AT 22:12.

SIDEREAL SUN MOON MERCURY VENUS MARS JUPITER SATURN URANUS NEPTUNE PLUTO

DAY	TIME	☉	☽	☿	♀	♂	♃	♄	♅	♆	♇
	h m s	° ' "	° '	°	°	°	°	°	°	°	°
O 1	0 35 25	6♎56 37	24♎37	25♍R	5♍	17♊	19♌	27♊	9♊R	2♎	8♌
C 2	0 39 21	7 55 38	7♏30	25	5	18	20	27	9	2	8
T 3	0 43 18	8 54 42	20 35	25 D	5	18	20	27	9	2	8
O 4	0 47 15	9 53 47	3♐52	25	5	18	20	27	9	2	8
B 5	0 51 11	10 52 54	17 21	25	5	19	20	27	9	2	8
E 6	0 55 8	11 52 3	1♑ 2	25	6	19	20	27	9	2	8
R 7	0 59 4	12 51 14	14 56	26	6	19	21	27	9	2	8
8	1 3 1	13 50 26	29 1	26	6	20	21	27	9	2	9
9	1 6 57	14 49 40	13♒18	27	7	20	21	27 R	9	2	9
10	1 10 54	15 48 56	27 44	28	7	20	21	27	9	2	9
11	1 14 50	16 48 13	12♓17	29	8	20	21	27	9	2	9
12	1 18 47	17 47 33	26 51	0♎	8	20	21	27	9	2	9
13	1 22 43	18 46 54	11♈20	1	9	21	22	27	9	2	9
14	1 26 40	19 46 17	25 38	3	9	21	22	27	8	2	9
15	1 30 37	20 45 43	9♉38	4	10	21	22	27	8	3	9
16	1 34 33	21 45 10	23 16	5	10	21	22	27	8	3	9
17	1 38 30	22 44 40	6♊30	7	11	21	22	27	8	3	9
18	1 42 26	23 44 12	19 20	8	11	21	22	27	8	3	9
19	1 46 23	24 43 46	1♋49	10	12	22	22	27	8	3	9
20	1 50 19	25 43 23	13 59	12	13	22	23	27	8	3	9
21	1 54 16	26 43 2	25 57	13	13	22	23	27	8	3	9
22	1 58 12	27 42 43	7♌46	15	14	22	23	26	8	3	9
23	2 2 9	28 42 26	19 34	17	15	22	23	26	8	3	9
24	2 6 6	29 42 12	1♍24	18	16	22	23	26	8	3	9
25	2 10 2	0♏41 59	13 23	20	16	22	23	26	8	3	9
26	2 13 59	1 41 49	25 33	22	17	22	23	26	8	3	9
27	2 17 55	2 41 41	7♎59	23	18	22	24	26	8	3	9
28	2 21 52	3 41 35	20 42	25	19	22 R	24	26	8	3	9
29	2 25 48	4 41 31	3♏41	27	20	22	24	26	8	3	9
30	2 29 45	5 41 29	16 56	28	20	22	24	26	8	3	9
31	2 33 41	6 41 29	0♐26	0♏	21	22	24	26	8	3	9

THE SUN ENTERS THE SIGN OF SCORPIO ON OCT 24 AT 07:09.

DAY	TIME	☉	☽	☿	♀	♂	♃	♄	♅	♆	♇
	h m s	° ' "	° '	°	°	°	°	°	°	°	°
N 1	2 37 38	7♏41 31	14♐ 6	2♏	22♍	22♊R	24♌	26♊R	8♊R	3♎	9♌
O 2	2 41 35	8 41 34	27 55	3	23	22	24	26	8	3	9
V 3	2 45 31	9 41 39	11♑49	5	24	22	24	26	8	3	9
E 4	2 49 28	10 41 46	25 49	7	25	22	25	26	8	3	9
M 5	2 53 24	11 41 54	9♒52	8	26	22	25	26	8	3	9
B 6	2 57 21	12 42 4	23 57	10	26	22	25	26	8	3	9
E 7	3 1 17	13 42 15	8♓ 5	12	27	22	25	26	8	3	9
R 8	3 5 14	14 42 28	22 14	13	28	21	25	26	8	3	9
9	3 9 10	15 42 42	6♈22	15	29	21	25	26	8	3	9
10	3 13 7	16 42 57	20 24	16	0♎	21	25	26	8	3	9 R
11	3 17 4	17 43 14	4♉18	18	1	21	25	26	8	3	9
12	3 21 0	18 43 33	17 58	20	2	21	25	26	8	3	9
13	3 24 57	19 43 54	1♊22	21	3	20	26	26	8	3	9
14	3 28 53	20 44 16	14 26	23	4	20	26	26	7	3	9
15	3 32 50	21 44 41	27 11	24	5	20	26	25	7	3	9
16	3 36 46	22 45 6	9♋37	26	6	20	26	25	7	4	9
17	3 40 43	23 45 34	21 47	28	7	19	26	25	7	4	9
18	3 44 39	24 46 4	3♌44	29	8	19	26	25	7	4	9
19	3 48 36	25 46 35	15 34	1♐	9	19	26	25	7	4	9
20	3 52 33	26 47 8	27 22	2	10	19	26	25	7	4	9
21	3 56 29	27 47 43	9♍13	4	11	18	26	25	7	4	9
22	4 0 26	28 48 20	21 12	5	12	18	26	25	7	4	9
23	4 4 22	29 48 58	3♎26	7	13	18	26	25	7	4	9
24	4 8 19	0♐49 38	15 57	8	14	17	26	25	7	4	9
25	4 12 15	1 50 19	28 50	10	15	17	26	25	7	4	9
26	4 16 12	2 51 2	12♏ 4	12	16	16	27	25	7	4	9
27	4 20 8	3 51 47	25 38	13	18	16	27	25	7	4	9
28	4 24 5	4 52 33	9♐32	15	19	16	27	25	7	4	9
29	4 28 2	5 53 20	23 38	16	20	15	27	25	7	4	9
30	4 31 58	6 54 8	7♑54	18	21	15	27	24	7	4	9

THE SUN ENTERS THE SIGN OF SAGITTARIUS ON NOV 23 AT 04:23.

DAY	TIME	☉	☽	☿	♀	♂	♃	♄	♅	♆	♇
	h m s	° ' "	° '	°	°	°	°	°	°	°	°
D 1	4 35 55	7♐54 58	22♑14	19♐	22♎	15♊R	27♌	24♊R	7♊R	4♎	9♌R
E 2	4 39 51	8 55 48	6♒32	21	23	14	27	24	7	4	9
C 3	4 43 48	9 56 39	20 47	22	24	14	27	24	7	4	9
E 4	4 47 44	10 57 31	4♓56	24	25	13	27	24	7	4	9
M 5	4 51 41	11 58 24	18 59	25	26	13	27	24	7	4	9
B 6	4 55 37	12 59 18	2♈53	27	27	13	27	24	7	4	9
E 7	4 59 34	14 0 12	16 40	28	29	12	27	24	7	4	9
R 8	5 3 31	15 1 7	0♉17	0♑	0♏	12	27	24	6	4	9
9	5 7 27	16 2 3	13 43	1	1	12	27	24	6	4	9
10	5 11 24	17 3 0	26 58	3	2	11	27	24	6	4	9
11	5 15 20	18 3 57	10♊ 0	4	3	11	27	24	6	4	9
12	5 19 17	19 4 56	22 46	6	4	10	27	23	6	4	9
13	5 23 13	20 5 55	5♋18	7	5	10	27 R	23	6	4	9
14	5 27 10	21 6 55	17 36	9	6	10	27	23	6	4	9
15	5 31 6	22 7 56	29 42	10	8	9	27	23	6	4	8
16	5 35 3	23 8 58	11♌37	12	9	9	27	23	6	4	8
17	5 39 0	24 10 1	23 26	13	10	9	27	23	6	4	8
18	5 42 56	25 11 4	5♍13	14	11	8	27	23	6	4	8
19	5 46 53	26 12 9	17 3	16	12	8	27	23	6	4	8
20	5 50 49	27 13 14	29 2	17	13	8	27	23	6	4	8
21	5 54 46	28 14 20	11♎14	18	14	8	27	23	6	4	8
22	5 58 42	29 15 27	23 44	19	16	7	27	23	6	4	8
23	6 2 39	0♑16 34	6♏37	20	17	7	27	23	6	4	8
24	6 6 35	1 17 43	19 54	21	18	7	27	22	6	4	8
25	6 10 32	2 18 52	3♐37	22	19	7	27	22	6	4	8
26	6 14 29	3 20 1	17 44	23	20	6	27	22	6	4	8
27	6 18 25	4 21 11	2♑11	24	21	6	27	22	6	4	8
28	6 22 22	5 22 21	16 51	24	23	6	27	22	6	4	8
29	6 26 18	6 23 32	1♒38	25	24	6	27	22	6	4	8
30	6 30 15	7 24 42	16 24	25 R	25	6	27	22	6	4	8
31	6 34 11	8 25 52	1♓ 2	25	26	6	27	22	6	4	8

THE SUN ENTERS THE SIGN OF CAPRICORN ON DEC 22 AT 17:30.

♈ ARIES ♉ TAURUS ♊ GEMINI ♋ CANCER ♌ LEO ♍ VIRGO ♎ LIBRA ♏ SCORPIO ♐ SAGITTARIUS ♑ CAPRICORN ♒ AQUARIUS ♓ PISCES

SIDEREAL SUN MOON MERCURY VENUS MARS JUPITER SATURN URANUS NEPTUNE PLUTO

DAY	TIME	☉	☽	☿	♀	♂	♃	♄	♅	♆	♇
	h m s	° ' "	° '	°	°	°	°	°	°	°	°
J 1	6 38 8	9♑27 3	15♓29	25♑R	27♏	5♊R	27♌R	22♊R	6♊R	4♎	8♌R
A 2	6 42 5	10 28 13	29 40	24	29	5	26	22	6	4	8
N 3	6 46 1	11 29 22	13♈35	24	0♐	5	26	22	6	4	8
U 4	6 49 58	12 30 32	27 12	23	1	5	26	22	5	4	8
A 5	6 53 54	13 31 41	10♉34	22	2	5	26	22	5	4	8
R 6	6 57 51	14 32 50	23 40	21	3	5	26	21	5	4 R	8
Y 7	7 1 47	15 33 58	6♊33	20	5	5	26	21	5	4	8
8	7 5 44	16 35 7	19 12	19	6	5	26	21	5	4	8
9	7 9 40	17 36 15	1♋39	17	7	5	26	21	5	4	8
10	7 13 37	18 37 22	13 55	16	8	5 D	26	21	5	4	8
11	7 17 34	19 38 30	26 1	15	9	5	26	21	5	4	8
12	7 21 30	20 39 37	7♌59	13	11	5	26	21	5	4	8
13	7 25 27	21 40 44	19 51	12	12	5	26	21	5	4	8
14	7 29 23	22 41 51	1♍39	11	13	5	26	21	5	4	8
15	7 33 20	23 42 57	13 27	11	14	5	25	21	5	4	8
16	7 37 16	24 44 3	25 17	10	15	5	25	21	5	4	8
17	7 41 13	25 45 9	7♎15	9	17	5	25	21	5	4	8
18	7 45 9	26 46 15	19 25	9	18	5	25	21	5	4	8
19	7 49 6	27 47 20	1♏51	9 D	19	5	25	21	5	4	8
20	7 53 3	28 48 25	14 38	9	20	5	25	21	5	4	8
21	7 56 59	29 49 30	27 49	9	21	6	25	21	5	4	8
22	8 0 56	0♒50 34	11♐27	9	23	6	25	20	5	4	8
23	8 4 52	1 51 38	25 32	9	24	6	25	20	5	4	8
24	8 8 49	2 52 42	10♑ 3	10	25	6	24	20	5	4	8
25	8 12 45	3 53 45	24 54	10	26	6	24	20	5	4	8
26	8 16 42	4 54 47	9♒57	11	27	6	24	20	5	4	8
27	8 20 38	5 55 48	25 6	11	29	7	24	20	5	4	8
28	8 24 35	6 56 48	10♓ 9	12	0♑	7	24	20	5	4	8
29	8 28 32	7 57 47	24 58	13	1	7	24	20	5	4	8
30	8 32 28	8 58 45	9♈29	14	2	7	24	20	5	4	8
31	8 36 25	9 59 41	23 36	15	3	7	24	20	5	4	8

THE SUN ENTERS THE SIGN OF AQUARIUS ON JAN 21 AT 04:07.

DAY	TIME	☉	☽	☿	♀	♂	♃	♄	♅	♆	♇
	h m s	° ' "	° '	°	°	°	°	°	°	°	°
F 1	8 40 21	11♒ 0 37	7♉19	16♑	5♑	8♊	24♌R	20♊R	5♊R	4♎R	8♌R
E 2	8 44 18	12 1 31	20 38	17	6	8	23	20	5	4	7
B 3	8 48 14	13 2 23	3♊35	18	7	8	23	20	5	4	7
R 4	8 52 11	14 3 15	16 14	19	8	8	23	20	5	4	7
U 5	8 56 7	15 4 5	28 38	20	10	9	23	20	5	4	7
A 6	9 0 4	16 4 53	10♋50	21	11	9	23	20	5	4	7
R 7	9 4 1	17 5 40	22 52	23	12	9	23	20	5	4	7
Y 8	9 7 57	18 6 26	4♌47	24	13	9	23	20	5	4	7
9	9 11 54	19 7 11	16 39	25	14	10	22	20	5	4	7
10	9 15 50	20 7 54	28 27	27	16	10	22	20	5	4	7
11	9 19 47	21 8 36	10♍16	28	17	10	22	20	5	4	7
12	9 23 43	22 9 17	22 7	29	18	11	22	20	5 D	4	7
13	9 27 40	23 9 56	4♎ 2	1♒	19	11	22	20	5	4	7
14	9 31 36	24 10 34	16 3	2	21	11	22	20	5	4	7
15	9 35 33	25 11 11	28 15	3	22	12	22	20	5	4	7
16	9 39 30	26 11 47	10♏40	5	23	12	22	20	5	4	7
17	9 43 26	27 12 21	23 23	6	24	12	21	20	5	4	7
18	9 47 23	28 12 55	6♐26	8	25	13	21	20	5	4	7
19	9 51 19	29 13 27	19 53	9	27	13	21	20	5	4	7
20	9 55 16	0♓13 58	3♑46	11	28	13	21	20 D	5	4	7
21	9 59 12	1 14 28	18 6	12	29	14	21	20	5	4	7
22	10 3 9	2 14 56	2♒49	14	0♒	14	21	20	5	4	7
23	10 7 5	3 15 23	17 51	15	2	15	21	20	5	4	7
24	10 11 2	4 15 48	3♓ 5	17	3	15	21	20	5	4	7
25	10 14 59	5 16 11	18 20	18	4	15	20	20	5	4	7
26	10 18 55	6 16 33	3♈26	20	5	16	20	20	5	4	7
27	10 22 52	7 16 53	18 13	22	7	16	20	20	5	4	7
28	10 26 48	8 17 11	2♉36	23	8	17	20	20	5	4	7
29	10 30 45	9 17 26	16 31	25	9	17	20	20	5	4	7

THE SUN ENTERS THE SIGN OF PISCES ON FEB 19 AT 18:28.

DAY	TIME	☉	☽	☿	♀	♂	♃	♄	♅	♆	♇
	h m s	° ' "	° '	°	°	°	°	°	°	°	°
M 1	10 34 41	10♓17 40	29♉57	26♒	10♒	17♊	20♌R	20♊	5♊	3♎R	7♌R
A 2	10 38 38	11 17 52	12♊56	28	11	18	20	20	5	3	7
R 3	10 42 34	12 18 2	25 32	0♓	13	18	20	20	5	3	7
C 4	10 46 31	13 18 10	7♋50	2	14	19	19	20	5	3	7
H 5	10 50 27	14 18 15	19 54	3	15	19	19	20	5	3	7
6	10 54 24	15 18 19	1♌49	5	16	19	19	20	5	3	7
7	10 58 21	16 18 20	13 38	7	18	20	19	20	5	3	7
8	11 2 17	17 18 19	25 25	9	19	20	19	20	5	3	7
9	11 6 14	18 18 17	7♍14	10	20	21	19	20	5	3	7
10	11 10 10	19 18 12	19 5	12	21	21	19	20	5	3	7
11	11 14 7	20 18 5	1♎ 2	14	22	22	19	20	5	3	7
12	11 18 3	21 17 57	13 6	16	24	22	19	20	5	3	7
13	11 22 0	22 17 46	25 17	18	25	23	19	20	5	3	7
14	11 25 56	23 17 34	7♏38	20	26	23	18	20	5	3	7
15	11 29 53	24 17 20	20 10	22	27	24	18	20	5	3	7
16	11 33 50	25 17 5	2♐56	23	29	24	18	20	5	3	7
17	11 37 46	26 16 47	15 58	25	0♓	24	18	20	5	3	7
18	11 41 43	27 16 28	29 19	27	1	25	18	20	5	3	7
19	11 45 39	28 16 8	13♑ 0	29	2	25	18	20	5	3	7
20	11 49 36	29 15 45	27 4	1♈	4	26	18	20	5	3	7
21	11 53 32	0♈15 21	11♒30	3	5	26	18	20	5	3	7
22	11 57 29	1 14 55	26 17	5	6	27	18	21	5	3	7
23	12 1 25	2 14 27	11♓17	7	7	27	18	21	5	3	7
24	12 5 22	3 13 58	26 24	9	8	28	18	21	6	3	7
25	12 9 19	4 13 26	11♈29	11	10	28	18	21	6	3	7
26	12 13 15	5 12 52	26 20	13	11	29	18	21	6	3	7
27	12 17 12	6 12 16	10♉49	15	12	29	17	21	6	3	7
28	12 21 8	7 11 37	24 52	17	13	0♋	17	21	6	3	7
29	12 25 5	8 10 57	8♊26	19	15	0	17	21	6	3	6
30	12 29 1	9 10 14	21 31	21	16	1	17	21	6	3	6
31	12 32 58	10 9 29	4♋11	23	17	1	17	21	6	3	6

THE SUN ENTERS THE SIGN OF ARIES ON MAR 20 AT 17:49.

SIDEREAL SUN MOON MERCURY VENUS MARS JUPITER SATURN URANUS NEPTUNE PLUTO

DAY	TIME	☉	☽	☿	♀	♂	♃	♄	♅	♆	♇
	h m s	° ' "	° '	°	°	°	°	°	°	°	°
A 1	12 36 54	11♈ 8 42	16♋30	25♈	18♓	2♋	17♌R	21♊	6♊	3♎R	6♌R
P 2	12 40 51	12 7 52	28 33	27	20	2	17	21	6	3	6
R 3	12 44 48	13 7 0	10♌26	29	21	3	17	21	6	3	6
I 4	12 48 44	14 6 6	22 14	0♉	22	3	17	21	6	3	6
L 5	12 52 41	15 5 9	4♍ 1	2	23	4	17	21	6	3	6
6	12 56 37	16 4 10	15 52	4	24	4	17	22	6	3	6
7	13 0 34	17 3 9	27 49	5	26	5	17	22	6	2	6
8	13 4 30	18 2 6	9♎54	7	27	5	17	22	6	2	6
9	13 8 27	19 1 1	22 9	8	28	6	17	22	6	2	6
10	13 12 23	19 59 53	4♏35	9	29	6	17	22	6	2	6
11	13 16 20	20 58 44	17 11	10	1♈	7	17	22	6	2	6
12	13 20 16	21 57 33	29 59	11	2	8	17	22	6	2	6
13	13 24 13	22 56 21	12♐58	12	3	8	17 D	22	6	2	6
14	13 28 10	23 55 6	26 9	13	4	9	17	22	6	2	6
15	13 32 6	24 53 50	9♑33	14	6	9	17	22	6	2	6
16	13 36 3	25 52 32	23 13	15	7	10	17	22	6	2	6
17	13 39 59	26 51 13	7♒ 8	15	8	10	17	22	7	2	6
18	13 43 56	27 49 51	21 19	16	9	11	17	23	7	2	6 D
19	13 47 52	28 48 28	5♓46	16	10	11	17	23	7	2	6
20	13 51 49	29 47 4	20 25	16	12	12	17	23	7	2	6
21	13 55 45	0♉45 37	5♈11	16	13	12	17	23	7	2	6
22	13 59 42	1 44 9	19 56	16 R	14	13	17	23	7	2	6
23	14 3 39	2 42 39	4♉33	16	15	13	17	23	7	2	6
24	14 7 35	3 41 7	18 54	16	17	14	17	23	7	2	6
25	14 11 32	4 39 34	2♊53	16	18	14	17	23	7	2	6
26	14 15 28	5 37 58	16 27	16	19	15	17	23	7	2	6
27	14 19 25	6 36 20	29 34	15	20	16	17	23	7	2	6
28	14 23 21	7 34 41	12♋16	15	22	16	17	24	7	2	6
29	14 27 18	8 32 59	24 38	14	23	17	17	24	7	2	6
30	14 31 14	9 31 15	6♌43	14	24	17	17	24	7	2	6

THE SUN ENTERS THE SIGN OF TAURUS ON APR 20 AT 05:18.

DAY	TIME	☉	☽	☿	♀	♂	♃	♄	♅	♆	♇
	h m s	° ' "	° '	°	°	°	°	°	°	°	°
M 1	14 35 11	10♉29 29	18♌38	13♉R	25♈	18♋	18♌	24♊	7♊	2♎R	6♌
A 2	14 39 8	11 27 41	0♍27	13	26	18	18	24	7	2	6
Y 3	14 43 4	12 25 51	12 16	12	28	19	18	24	7	2	6
4	14 47 1	13 23 59	24 10	11	29	19	18	24	7	2	6
5	14 50 57	14 22 5	6♎12	11	0♉	20	18	24	7	2	6
6	14 54 54	15 20 10	18 26	10	1	21	18	24	8	2	6
7	14 58 50	16 18 12	0♏53	10	3	21	18	25	8	2	6
8	15 2 47	17 16 13	13 34	9	4	22	18	25	8	2	6
9	15 6 43	18 14 12	26 29	8	5	22	18	25	8	2	6
10	15 10 40	19 12 10	9♐37	8	6	23	18	25	8	2	7
11	15 14 37	20 10 6	22 57	8	7	23	18	25	8	2	7
12	15 18 33	21 8 1	6♑28	7	9	24	18	25	8	2	7
13	15 22 30	22 5 55	20 8	7	10	25	18	25	8	2	7
14	15 26 26	23 3 47	3♒57	7	11	25	18	25	8	2	7
15	15 30 23	24 1 38	17 55	7 D	12	26	19	25	8	2	7
16	15 34 19	24 59 28	2♓ 1	7	14	26	19	26	8	2	7
17	15 38 16	25 57 17	16 14	7	15	27	19	26	8	2	7
18	15 42 12	26 55 4	0♈34	7	16	27	19	26	8	2	7
19	15 46 9	27 52 51	14 55	7	17	28	19	26	8	2	7
20	15 50 6	28 50 36	29 15	7	19	29	19	26	8	2	7
21	15 54 2	29 48 20	13♉27	8	20	29	19	26	8	2	7
22	15 57 59	0♊46 3	27 26	8	21	0♌	19	26	8	2	7
23	16 1 55	1 43 44	11♊ 8	9	22	0	19	26	8	2	7
24	16 5 52	2 41 25	24 30	9	23	1	19	27	9	2	7
25	16 9 48	3 39 4	7♋30	10	25	1	20	27	9	2	7
26	16 13 45	4 36 42	20 10	11	26	2	20	27	9	2	7
27	16 17 41	5 34 18	2♌31	11	27	3	20	27	9	2	7
28	16 21 38	6 31 53	14 37	12	28	3	20	27	9	2	7
29	16 25 35	7 29 26	26 33	13	0♊	4	20	27	9	2	7
30	16 29 31	8 26 58	8♍24	14	1	4	20	27	9	2	7
31	16 33 28	9 24 29	20 15	15	2	5	20	27	9	2	7

THE SUN ENTERS THE SIGN OF GEMINI ON MAY 21 AT 04:51.

DAY	TIME	☉	☽	☿	♀	♂	♃	♄	♅	♆	♇
	h m s	° ' "	° '	°	°	°	°	°	°	°	°
J 1	16 37 24	10♊21 58	2♎11	16♉	3♊	5♌	20♌	28♊	9♊	1♎R	7♌
U 2	16 41 21	11 19 26	14 17	17	4	6	21	28	9	1	7
N 3	16 45 17	12 16 53	26 36	18	6	7	21	28	9	1	7
E 4	16 49 14	13 14 19	9♏12	19	7	7	21	28	9	1	7
5	16 53 10	14 11 43	22 5	21	8	8	21	28	9	1	7
6	16 57 7	15 9 7	5♐17	22	9	8	21	28	9	1	7
7	17 1 4	16 6 30	18 45	23	11	9	21	28	9	1	7
8	17 5 0	17 3 52	2♑29	25	12	10	21	28	9	1	7
9	17 8 57	18 1 13	16 24	26	13	10	22	29	9	1	7
10	17 12 53	18 58 34	0♒28	28	14	11	22	29	10	1	7
11	17 16 50	19 55 54	14 37	29	16	11	22	29	10	1	7
12	17 20 46	20 53 13	28 50	1♊	17	12	22	29	10	1 D	7
13	17 24 43	21 50 32	13♓ 3	2	18	12	22	29	10	1	7
14	17 28 39	22 47 51	27 14	4	19	13	22	29	10	1	7
15	17 32 36	23 45 9	11♈22	6	20	14	22	29	10	1	7
16	17 36 33	24 42 27	25 25	8	22	14	23	29	10	1	7
17	17 40 29	25 39 45	9♉20	9	23	15	23	0♋	10	1	7
18	17 44 26	26 37 2	23 6	11	24	15	23	0	10	1	7
19	17 48 22	27 34 19	6♊38	13	25	16	23	0	10	1	7
20	17 52 19	28 31 36	19 56	15	27	17	23	0	10	1	7
21	17 56 15	29 28 53	2♋59	17	28	17	23	0	10	1	7
22	18 0 12	0♋26 8	15 44	19	29	18	24	0	10	1	7
23	18 4 8	1 23 24	28 14	21	0♋	18	24	0	10	1	7
24	18 8 5	2 20 39	10♌29	23	1	19	24	0	10	2	7
25	18 12 2	3 17 53	22 33	25	3	20	24	1	10	2	7
26	18 15 58	4 15 7	4♍28	28	4	20	24	1	10	2	7
27	18 19 55	5 12 21	16 20	0♋	5	21	24	1	11	2	7
28	18 23 51	6 9 34	28 11	2	6	21	25	1	11	2	7
29	18 27 48	7 6 46	10♎ 7	4	8	22	25	1	11	2	7
30	18 31 44	8 3 58	22 14	6	9	23	25	1	11	2	7

THE SUN ENTERS THE SIGN OF CANCER ON JUN 21 AT 13:03.

♈ ARIES ♉ TAURUS ♊ GEMINI ♋ CANCER ♌ LEO ♍ VIRGO ♎ LIBRA ♏ SCORPIO ♐ SAGITTARIUS ♑ CAPRICORN ♒ AQUARIUS ♓ PISCES

1944

SIDEREAL TIME · SUN · MOON · MERCURY · VENUS · MARS · JUPITER · SATURN · URANUS · NEPTUNE · PLUTO

DAY	TIME	☉	☽	☿	♀	♂	♃	♄	♅	♆	♇
	h m s	° ' "	° '	°	°	°	°	°	°	°	°
J 1	18 35 41	9♋ 1 10	4♏34	8♋	10♋	23♌	25♌	1♋	11♊	2♎	7♌
U 2	18 39 37	9 58 21	17 13	11	11	24	25	2	11	2	8
L 3	18 43 34	10 55 32	0♐12	13	13	24	26	2	11	2	8
Y 4	18 47 31	11 52 43	13 33	15	14	25	26	2	11	2	8
5	18 51 27	12 49 54	27 16	17	15	26	26	2	11	2	8
6	18 55 24	13 47 5	11♑19	19	16	26	26	2	11	2	8
7	18 59 20	14 44 15	25 39	21	17	27	26	2	11	2	8
8	19 3 17	15 41 26	10♒ 9	23	19	27	26	2	11	2	8
9	19 7 13	16 38 38	24 44	25	20	28	27	2	11	2	8
10	19 11 10	17 35 49	9♓19	27	21	29	27	3	11	2	8
11	19 15 7	18 33 1	23 49	29	22	29	27	3	11	2	8
12	19 19 3	19 30 13	8♈ 9	1♌	24	0♍	27	3	11	2	8
13	19 23 0	20 27 26	22 17	3	25	1	27	3	11	2	8
14	19 26 56	21 24 40	6♉11	5	26	1	28	3	11	2	8
15	19 30 53	22 21 54	19 49	7	27	2	28	3	11	2	8
16	19 34 49	23 19 9	3♊13	9	29	2	28	3	11	2	8
17	19 38 46	24 16 24	16 22	11	0♌	3	28	3	12	2	8
18	19 42 42	25 13 40	29 16	12	1	4	28	4	12	2	8
19	19 46 39	26 10 57	11♋57	14	2	4	29	4	12	2	8
20	19 50 36	27 8 14	24 26	16	3	5	29	4	12	2	8
21	19 54 32	28 5 32	6♌42	18	5	5	29	4	12	2	8
22	19 58 29	29 2 50	18 49	19	6	6	29	4	12	2	8
23	20 2 25	0♌ 0 9	0♍47	21	7	7	29	4	12	2	8
24	20 6 22	0 57 28	12 40	23	8	7	0♍	4	12	2	8
25	20 10 18	1 54 47	24 30	24	10	8	0	4	12	2	8
26	20 14 15	2 52 7	6♎21	26	11	9	0	5	12	2	8
27	20 18 11	3 49 28	18 17	27	12	9	0	5	12	2	8
28	20 22 8	4 46 49	0♏22	29	13	10	0	5	12	2	8
29	20 26 5	5 44 10	12 40	0♍	15	10	1	5	12	2	8
30	20 30 1	6 41 32	25 16	1	16	11	1	5	12	2	8
31	20 33 58	7 38 55	8♐14	3	17	12	1	5	12	2	8

THE SUN ENTERS THE SIGN OF LEO ON JUL 22 AT 23:56.

DAY	TIME	☉	☽	☿	♀	♂	♃	♄	♅	♆	♇
	h m s	° ' "	° '	°	°	°	°	°	°	°	°
A 1	20 37 54	8♌36 18	21♐36	4♍	18♌	12♍	1♍	5♋	12♊	2♎	8♌
U 2	20 41 51	9 33 42	5♑23	5	19	13	1	5	12	2	8
G 3	20 45 47	10 31 7	19 36	7	21	14	2	5	12	2	8
U 4	20 49 44	11 28 32	4♒11	8	22	14	2	6	12	2	8
S 5	20 53 40	12 25 58	19 1	9	23	15	2	6	12	2	8
T 6	20 57 37	13 23 26	4♓ 1	10	24	15	2	6	12	2	8
7	21 1 34	14 20 54	19 0	11	26	16	2	6	12	2	9
8	21 5 30	15 18 24	3♈52	13	27	17	3	6	12	2	9
9	21 9 27	16 15 55	18 28	14	28	17	3	6	12	2	9
10	21 13 23	17 13 27	2♉45	15	29	18	3	6	12	2	9
11	21 17 20	18 11 1	16 40	16	1♍	19	3	6	13	2	9
12	21 21 16	19 8 36	0♊12	16	2	19	4	6	13	2	9
13	21 25 13	20 6 13	13 23	17	3	20	4	7	13	2	9
14	21 29 9	21 3 51	26 16	18	4	20	4	7	13	2	9
15	21 33 6	22 1 31	8♋52	19	5	21	4	7	13	2	9
16	21 37 3	22 59 12	21 16	20	7	22	4	7	13	2	9
17	21 40 59	23 56 55	3♌28	20	8	22	5	7	13	3	9
18	21 44 56	24 54 39	15 33	21	9	23	5	7	13	3	9
19	21 48 52	25 52 24	27 31	21	10	24	5	7	13	3	9
20	21 52 49	26 50 11	9♍24	22	12	24	5	7	13	3	9
21	21 56 45	27 47 59	21 15	22	13	25	5	7	13	3	9
22	22 0 42	28 45 48	3♎ 5	22	14	26	6	7	13	3	9
23	22 4 38	29 43 39	14 57	22	15	26	6	8	13	3	9
24	22 8 35	0♍41 31	26 53	22 R	17	27	6	8	13	3	9
25	22 12 31	1 39 24	8♏57	22	18	27	6	8	13	3	9
26	22 16 28	2 37 19	21 14	22	19	28	7	8	13	3	9
27	22 20 25	3 35 14	3♐45	22	20	29	7	8	13	3	9
28	22 24 21	4 33 11	16 37	22	22	29	7	8	13	3	9
29	22 28 18	5 31 10	29 53	21	23	0♎	7	8	13	3	9
30	22 32 14	6 29 10	13♑35	21	24	1	7	8	13	3	9
31	22 36 11	7 27 11	27 45	20	25	1	8	8	13	3	9

THE SUN ENTERS THE SIGN OF VIRGO ON AUG 23 AT 06:47.

DAY	TIME	☉	☽	☿	♀	♂	♃	♄	♅	♆	♇
	h m s	° ' "	° '	°	°	°	°	°	°	°	°
S 1	22 40 7	8♍25 13	12♒21	20♍R	26♍	2♎	8♍	8♋	13♊	3♎	9♌
E 2	22 44 4	9 23 17	27 19	19	28	3	8	8	13	3	9
P 3	22 48 0	10 21 23	12♓32	18	29	3	8	9	13	3	9
T 4	22 51 57	11 19 30	27 48	17	0♎	4	9	9	13	3	9
E 5	22 55 54	12 17 39	12♈58	16	1	5	9	9	13	3	9
M 6	22 59 50	13 15 50	27 52	15	3	5	9	9	13	3	9
B 7	23 3 47	14 14 3	12♉23	14	4	6	9	9	13	3	9
E 8	23 7 43	15 12 18	26 26	13	5	6	9	9	13	3	9
R 9	23 11 40	16 10 35	10♊ 1	12	6	7	10	9	13	3	9
10	23 15 36	17 8 54	23 9	11	8	8	10	9	13	3	9
11	23 19 33	18 7 16	5♋55	11	9	8	10	9	13	3	9
12	23 23 29	19 5 39	18 22	10	10	9	10	9	13	3	9
13	23 27 26	20 4 5	0♌35	9	11	10	10	9	13	3	10
14	23 31 23	21 2 32	12 37	9	12	10	11	9	13	3	10
15	23 35 19	22 1 2	24 33	9	14	11	11	9	13	4	10
16	23 39 16	22 59 33	6♍25	9 D	15	12	11	10	13	4	10
17	23 43 12	23 58 7	18 15	9	16	12	11	10	13	4	10
18	23 47 9	24 56 42	0♎ 6	9	17	13	12	10	13 R	4	10
19	23 51 5	25 55 19	11 58	9	19	14	12	10	13	4	10
20	23 55 2	26 53 58	23 54	10	20	14	12	10	13	4	10
21	23 58 58	27 52 40	5♏56	10	21	15	12	10	13	4	10
22	0 2 55	28 51 22	18 4	11	22	16	12	10	13	4	10
23	0 6 52	29 50 7	0♐22	12	24	16	13	10	13	4	10
24	0 10 48	0♎48 53	12 54	13	25	17	13	10	13	4	10
25	0 14 45	1 47 42	25 42	14	26	18	13	10	13	4	10
26	0 18 41	2 46 31	8♑50	15	27	18	13	10	13	4	10
27	0 22 38	3 45 23	22 23	17	28	19	13	10	13	4	10
28	0 26 34	4 44 16	6♒22	18	0♏	20	14	10	13	4	10
29	0 30 31	5 43 11	20 47	20	1	20	14	10	13	4	10
30	0 34 27	6 42 8	5♓37	21	2	21	14	10	13	4	10

THE SUN ENTERS THE SIGN OF LIBRA ON SEP 23 AT 04:03.

DAY	TIME	☉	☽	☿	♀	♂	♃	♄	♅	♆	♇
	h m s	° ' "	° '	°	°	°	°	°	°	°	°
O 1	0 38 24	7♎41 7	20♓46	23♍	3♏	22♎	14♍	10♋	13♊R	4♎	10♌
C 2	0 42 20	8 40 7	6♈ 4	25	5	22	14	10	13	4	10
T 3	0 46 17	9 39 10	21 20	26	6	23	15	10	13	4	10
O 4	0 50 14	10 38 14	6♉23	28	7	24	15	10	13	4	10
B 5	0 54 10	11 37 21	21 4	0♎	8	24	15	10	13	4	10
E 6	0 58 7	12 36 30	5♊16	2	10	25	15	10	13	4	10
R 7	1 2 3	13 35 42	18 59	3	11	26	16	11	13	4	10
8	1 6 0	14 34 56	2♋12	5	12	26	16	11	13	4	10
9	1 9 56	15 34 12	14 59	7	13	27	16	11	13	4	10
10	1 13 53	16 33 30	27 25	9	14	28	16	11	13	4	10
11	1 17 49	17 32 51	9♌35	10	16	28	16	11	13	4	10
12	1 21 46	18 32 14	21 33	12	17	29	17	11	13	5	10
13	1 25 43	19 31 39	3♍25	14	18	0♏	17	11	13	5	10
14	1 29 39	20 31 6	15 14	16	19	0	17	11	13	5	10
15	1 33 36	21 30 36	27 4	17	21	1	17	11	13	5	10
16	1 37 32	22 30 8	8♎58	19	22	2	17	11	13	5	10
17	1 41 29	23 29 42	20 56	21	23	2	18	11	13	5	10
18	1 45 25	24 29 17	3♏ 0	22	24	3	18	11	13	5	10
19	1 49 22	25 28 55	15 11	24	25	4	18	11	13	5	10
20	1 53 18	26 28 35	27 30	26	27	4	18	11	13	5	10
21	1 57 15	27 28 17	9♐58	28	28	5	18	11	13	5	10
22	2 1 12	28 28 0	22 37	29	29	6	18	11	13	5	10
23	2 5 8	29 27 46	5♑30	1♏	0♐	6	19	11 R	13	5	10
24	2 9 5	0♏27 33	18 38	3	2	7	19	11	13	5	10
25	2 13 1	1 27 21	2♒ 5	4	3	8	19	11	13	5	10
26	2 16 58	2 27 12	15 53	6	4	9	19	11	13	5	10
27	2 20 54	3 27 4	0♓ 4	7	5	9	19	11	13	5	10
28	2 24 51	4 26 57	14 36	9	6	10	20	11	13	5	10
29	2 28 47	5 26 52	29 26	11	8	11	20	11	12	5	10
30	2 32 44	6 26 49	14♈28	12	9	11	20	11	12	5	10
31	2 36 41	7 26 48	29 32	14	10	12	20	11	12	5	10

THE SUN ENTERS THE SIGN OF SCORPIO ON OCT 23 AT 12:57.

DAY	TIME	☉	☽	☿	♀	♂	♃	♄	♅	♆	♇
	h m s	° ' "	° '	°	°	°	°	°	°	°	°
N 1	2 40 37	8♏26 49	14♉28	15♏	11♐	13♏	20♍	11♋R	12♊R	5♎	10♌
O 2	2 44 34	9 26 51	29 7	17	13	13	20	11	12	5	10
V 3	2 48 30	10 26 56	13♊22	19	14	14	21	11	12	5	10
E 4	2 52 27	11 27 2	27 9	20	15	15	21	11	12	5	10
M 5	2 56 23	12 27 11	10♋27	22	16	15	21	11	12	5	10
B 6	3 0 20	13 27 21	23 20	23	17	16	21	11	12	5	10
E 7	3 4 16	14 27 34	5♌49	25	19	17	21	11	12	5	10
R 8	3 8 13	15 27 49	18 1	26	20	18	21	11	12	5	10
9	3 12 10	16 28 5	0♍ 0	28	21	18	22	11	12	5	10
10	3 16 6	17 28 24	11 53	29	22	19	22	10	12	6	10
11	3 20 3	18 28 45	23 42	1♐	24	20	22	10	12	6	10 R
12	3 23 59	19 29 7	5♎34	2	25	20	22	10	12	6	10
13	3 27 56	20 29 31	17 31	4	26	21	22	10	12	6	10
14	3 31 52	21 29 57	29 36	5	27	22	22	10	12	6	10
15	3 35 49	22 30 25	11♏50	7	28	22	23	10	12	6	10
16	3 39 45	23 30 55	24 14	8	0♑	23	23	10	12	6	10
17	3 43 42	24 31 26	6♐49	10	1	24	23	10	12	6	10
18	3 47 39	25 31 59	19 35	11	2	25	23	10	12	6	10
19	3 51 35	26 32 33	2♑32	13	3	25	23	10	12	6	10
20	3 55 32	27 33 8	15 40	14	4	26	23	10	12	6	10
21	3 59 28	28 33 45	29 0	16	6	27	23	10	12	6	10
22	4 3 25	29 34 23	12♒33	17	7	27	24	10	12	6	10
23	4 7 21	0♐35 2	26 20	18	8	28	24	10	12	6	10
24	4 11 18	1 35 42	10♓22	20	9	29	24	10	12	6	10
25	4 15 14	2 36 23	24 37	21	11	0♐	24	10	11	6	10
26	4 19 11	3 37 5	9♈ 5	23	12	0	24	10	11	6	10
27	4 23 8	4 37 49	23 40	24	13	1	24	10	11	6	10
28	4 27 4	5 38 33	8♉18	25	14	2	24	10	11	6	10
29	4 31 1	6 39 18	22 51	27	15	2	25	10	11	6	10
30	4 34 57	7 40 5	7♊11	28	17	3	25	10	11	6	10

THE SUN ENTERS THE SIGN OF SAGITTARIUS ON NOV 22 AT 10:08.

DAY	TIME	☉	☽	☿	♀	♂	♃	♄	♅	♆	♇
	h m s	° ' "	° '	°	°	°	°	°	°	°	°
D 1	4 38 54	8♐40 53	21♊14	29♐	18♑	4♐	25♍	9♋R	11♊R	6♎	10♌R
E 2	4 42 50	9 41 42	4♋56	0♑	19	5	25	9	11	6	10
C 3	4 46 47	10 42 32	18 13	2	20	5	25	9	11	6	10
E 4	4 50 43	11 43 24	1♌ 7	3	21	6	25	9	11	6	10
M 5	4 54 40	12 44 17	13 40	4	23	7	25	9	11	6	10
B 6	4 58 37	13 45 11	25 56	5	24	7	25	9	11	6	10
E 7	5 2 33	14 46 6	7♍58	6	25	8	25	9	11	6	10
R 8	5 6 30	15 47 3	19 53	7	26	9	26	9	11	6	10
9	5 10 26	16 48 1	1♎44	7	27	10	26	9	11	6	10
10	5 14 23	17 49 0	13 37	8	29	10	26	9	11	6	10
11	5 18 19	18 50 0	25 37	8	0♒	11	26	9	11	6	10
12	5 22 16	19 51 1	7♏46	9	1	12	26	9	11	6	10
13	5 26 12	20 52 3	20 8	9 R	2	12	26	9	11	6	10
14	5 30 9	21 53 6	2♐44	9	3	13	26	9	11	6	10
15	5 34 6	22 54 10	15 35	9	5	14	26	8	11	6	10
16	5 38 2	23 55 15	28 42	8	6	15	26	8	11	6	10
17	5 41 59	24 56 21	12♑ 2	8	7	15	26	8	11	6	10
18	5 45 55	25 57 26	25 35	7	8	16	27	8	11	6	10
19	5 49 52	26 58 33	9♒19	6	9	17	27	8	10	6	10
20	5 53 48	27 59 40	23 13	5	10	18	27	8	10	6	10
21	5 57 45	29 0 46	7♓13	4	12	18	27	8	10	6	10
22	6 1 41	0♑ 1 53	21 19	3	13	19	27	8	10	6	10
23	6 5 38	1 3 1	5♈29	1	14	20	27	8	10	6	10
24	6 9 35	2 4 8	19 42	0	15	21	27	8	10	6	10
25	6 13 31	3 5 15	3♉54	29♐	16	21	27	8	10	6	10
26	6 17 28	4 6 23	18 2	27	18	22	27	8	10	6	10
27	6 21 24	5 7 30	2♊ 4	26	19	23	27	7	10	6	10
28	6 25 21	6 8 38	15 56	25	20	23	27	7	10	6	10
29	6 29 17	7 9 46	29 35	24	21	24	27	7	10	6	10
30	6 33 14	8 10 54	12♋58	24	22	25	27	7	10	6	10
31	6 37 11	9 12 2	26 4	23	23	26	27	7	10	6	10

THE SUN ENTERS THE SIGN OF CAPRICORN ON DEC 21 AT 23:15.

♈ ARIES ♉ TAURUS ♊ GEMINI ♋ CANCER ♌ LEO ♍ VIRGO ♎ LIBRA ♏ SCORPIO ♐ SAGITTARIUS ♑ CAPRICORN ♒ AQUARIUS ♓ PISCES

1945

SIDEREAL SUN MOON MERCURY VENUS MARS JUPITER SATURN URANUS NEPTUNE PLUTO

DAY	TIME	☉	☽	☿	♀	♂	♃	♄	♅	♆	♇
	h m s	° ' "	° '	°	°	°	°	°	°	°	°
J 1	6 41 7	10♑13 10	8♌52	23♐R	24♒	26♐	27♍	7♋R	10♊R	6♎	10♌R
A 2	6 45 4	11 14 18	21 23	23 D	26	27	27	7	10	6	10
N 3	6 49 0	12 15 27	3♍39	23	27	28	27	7	10	6	10
U 4	6 52 57	13 16 36	15 43	23	28	29	27	7	10	6	10
A 5	6 56 53	14 17 45	27 39	23	29	29	27	7	10	6	10
R 6	7 0 50	15 18 54	9♎32	23	0♓	0♑	27	7	10	6	10
Y 7	7 4 46	16 20 3	21 25	24	1	1	27	7	10	6 R	10
8	7 8 43	17 21 12	3♏24	25	3	2	27	7	10	6	10
9	7 12 40	18 22 22	15 33	25	4	2	27	6	10	6	10
10	7 16 36	19 23 31	27 57	26	5	3	27	6	10	6	10
11	7 20 33	20 24 41	10♐38	27	6	4	27	6	10	6	10
12	7 24 29	21 25 50	23 39	28	7	5	27 R	6	10	6	9
13	7 28 26	22 26 59	7♑ 1	29	8	5	27	6	10	6	9
14	7 32 22	23 28 8	20 44	0♑	9	6	27	6	10	6	9
15	7 36 19	24 29 16	4♒43	1	10	7	27	6	10	6	9
16	7 40 15	25 30 24	18 57	2	11	8	27	6	10	6	9
17	7 44 12	26 31 31	3♓20	3	13	8	27	6	9	6	9
18	7 48 9	27 32 38	17 46	4	14	9	27	6	9	6	9
19	7 52 5	28 33 43	2♈11	6	15	10	27	6	9	6	9
20	7 56 2	29 34 48	16 31	7	16	11	27	6	9	6	9
21	7 59 58	0♒35 52	0♉42	8	17	11	27	6	9	6	9
22	8 3 55	1 36 54	14 43	9	18	12	27	5	9	6	9
23	8 7 51	2 37 56	28 32	11	19	13	27	5	9	6	9
24	8 11 48	3 38 57	12♊ 8	12	20	14	27	5	9	6	9
25	8 15 44	4 39 57	25 32	13	21	14	27	5	9	6	9
26	8 19 41	5 40 56	8♋43	15	22	15	27	5	9	6	9
27	8 23 38	6 41 53	21 42	16	23	16	27	5	9	6	9
28	8 27 34	7 42 50	4♌28	18	24	17	27	5	9	6	9
29	8 31 31	8 43 46	17 2	19	26	17	27	5	9	6	9
30	8 35 27	9 44 41	29 25	20	27	18	27	5	9	6	9
31	8 39 24	10 45 35	11♍36	22	28	19	27	5	9	6	9

THE SUN ENTERS THE SIGN OF AQUARIUS ON JAN 20 AT 09:54.

DAY	TIME	☉	☽	☿	♀	♂	♃	♄	♅	♆	♇
	h m s	° ' "	° '	°	°	°	°	°	°	°	°
F 1	8 43 20	11♒46 28	23♍39	23♑	29♓	20♑	27♍R	5♋R	9♊R	6♎R	9♌R
E 2	8 47 17	12 47 20	5♎34	25	0O	20	27	5	9	6	9
B 3	8 51 13	13 48 11	17 27	26	1♈	21	27	5	9	6	9
R 4	8 55 10	14 49 1	29 19	28	2	22	27	5	9	6	9
U 5	8 59 7	15 49 51	11♏16	29	3	23	27	5	9	6	9
A 6	9 3 3	16 50 39	23 22	1♒	4	24	27	5	9	6	9
R 7	9 7 0	17 51 27	5♐42	2	5	24	26	4	9	6	9
Y 8	9 10 56	18 52 14	18 21	4	6	25	26	4	9	6	9
9	9 14 53	19 52 59	1♑23	6	7	26	26	4	9	6	9
10	9 18 49	20 53 44	14 49	7	8	27	26	4	9	6	9
11	9 22 46	21 54 27	28 42	9	9	27	26	4	9	6	9
12	9 26 42	22 55 10	12♒59	10	9	28	26	4	9	6	9
13	9 30 39	23 55 50	27 37	12	10	29	26	4	9	6	9
14	9 34 36	24 56 30	12♓27	14	11	0♒	26	4	9	6	9
15	9 38 32	25 57 7	27 23	15	12	0	26	4	9 D	6	9
16	9 42 29	26 57 43	12♈15	17	13	1	26	4	9	6	9
17	9 46 25	27 58 18	26 55	19	14	2	26	4	9	6	9
18	9 50 22	28 58 50	11♉19	20	15	3	25	4	9	6	9
19	9 54 18	29 59 21	25 23	22	16	4	25	4	9	6	9
20	9 58 15	0♓59 50	9♊ 6	24	17	4	25	4	9	6	9
21	10 2 11	2 0 17	22 29	26	17	5	25	4	9	6	9
22	10 6 8	3 0 42	5♋35	27	18	6	25	4	9	6	9
23	10 10 5	4 1 6	18 25	29	19	7	25	4	9	6	9
24	10 14 1	5 1 27	1♌ 3	1♓	20	7	25	4	9	6	9
25	10 17 58	6 1 47	13 31	3	21	8	25	4	9	6	9
26	10 21 54	7 2 4	25 49	5	21	9	25	4	9	6	8
27	10 25 51	8 2 20	7♍59	6	22	10	24	4	9	6	8
28	10 29 47	9 2 34	20 3	8	23	10	24	4	9	6	8

THE SUN ENTERS THE SIGN OF PISCES ON FEB 19 AT 00:15.

DAY	TIME	☉	☽	☿	♀	♂	♃	♄	♅	♆	♇
	h m s	° ' "	° '	°	°	°	°	°	°	°	°
M 1	10 33 44	10♓ 2 47	2♎ 1	10♓	24♈	11♒	24♍R	4♋R	9♊	6♎R	8♌R
A 2	10 37 40	11 2 57	13 55	12	24	12	24	4	9	6	8
R 3	10 41 37	12 3 6	25 47	14	25	13	24	4	9	6	8
C 4	10 45 33	13 3 14	7♏39	16	26	14	24	4	9	6	8
H 5	10 49 30	14 3 20	19 35	18	26	14	24	4 D	9	6	8
6	10 53 27	15 3 24	1♐39	20	27	15	24	4	9	6	8
7	10 57 23	16 3 27	13 55	22	28	16	23	4	9	6	8
8	11 1 20	17 3 28	26 28	24	28	17	23	4	9	6	8
9	11 5 16	18 3 27	9♑24	26	29	17	23	4	9	6	8
10	11 9 13	19 3 25	22 45	28	29	18	23	4	9	6	8
11	11 13 9	20 3 22	6♒36	29	0♉	19	23	4	9	5	8
12	11 17 6	21 3 16	20 55	1♈	0	20	23	4	9	5	8
13	11 21 2	22 3 9	5♓41	3	1	21	23	4	9	5	8
14	11 24 59	23 2 59	20 46	5	1	21	23	4	9	5	8
15	11 28 56	24 2 48	6♈ 1	7	2	22	22	4	9	5	8
16	11 32 52	25 2 35	21 15	9	2	23	22	4	9	5	8
17	11 36 49	26 2 19	6♉17	11	2	24	22	4	9	5	8
18	11 40 45	27 2 2	20 59	12	3	24	22	4	9	5	8
19	11 44 42	28 1 42	5♊15	14	3	25	22	4	10	5	8
20	11 48 38	29 1 20	19 4	16	3	26	22	4	10	5	8
21	11 52 35	0♈ 0 55	2♋28	17	3	27	22	4	10	5	8
22	11 56 31	1 0 29	15 28	19	3	28	21	4	10	5	8
23	12 0 28	2 0 0	28 9	20	3	28	21	4	10	5	8
24	12 4 25	2 59 28	10♌35	21	4	29	21	4	10	5	8
25	12 8 21	3 58 55	22 50	23	4 R	0♓	21	4	10	5	8
26	12 12 18	4 58 19	4♍56	24	4	1	21	4	10	5	8
27	12 16 14	5 57 41	16 56	25	4	1	21	4	10	5	8
28	12 20 11	6 57 1	28 53	25	3	2	21	4	10	5	8
29	12 24 7	7 56 19	10♎47	26	3	3	21	4	10	5	8
30	12 28 4	8 55 34	22 39	27	3	4	20	4	10	5	8
31	12 32 0	9 54 48	4♏32	27	3	5	20	4	10	5	8

THE SUN ENTERS THE SIGN OF ARIES ON MAR 20 AT 23:38.

SIDEREAL SUN MOON MERCURY VENUS MARS JUPITER SATURN URANUS NEPTUNE PLUTO

DAY	TIME	☉	☽	☿	♀	♂	♃	♄	♅	♆	♇
	h m s	° ' "	° '	°	°	°	°	°	°	°	°
A 1	12 35 57	10♈54 0	16♏27	28♈	3♉R	5♓	20♍R	4♋	10♊	5♎R	8♌R
P 2	12 39 54	11 53 10	28 26	28	2	6	20	5	10	5	8
R 3	12 43 50	12 52 18	10♐32	28 R	2	7	20	5	10	5	8
I 4	12 47 47	13 51 24	22 48	28	2	8	20	5	10	5	8
L 5	12 51 43	14 50 29	5♑19	28	1	8	20	5	10	5	8
6	12 55 40	15 49 31	18 10	28	1	9	20	5	10	5	8
7	12 59 36	16 48 33	1♒25	27	0	10	20	5	10	5	8
8	13 3 33	17 47 32	15 7	27	0	11	20	5	10	5	8
9	13 7 29	18 46 29	29 18	26	29♈	12	19	5	10	5	8
10	13 11 26	19 45 25	13♓56	26	29	12	19	5	10	5	8
11	13 15 22	20 44 19	28 58	25	28	13	19	5	10	5	8
12	13 19 19	21 43 11	14♈14	24	28	14	19	5	10	5	8
13	13 23 16	22 42 1	29 34	24	27	15	19	5	10	5	8
14	13 27 12	23 40 49	14♉47	23	26	15	19	5	10	5	8
15	13 31 9	24 39 35	29 41	22	26	16	19	5	11	5	8
16	13 35 5	25 38 19	14♊ 9	22	25	17	19	5	11	5	8
17	13 39 2	26 37 0	28 9	21	25	18	19	5	11	4	8
18	13 42 58	27 35 40	11♋40	20	24	19	19	5	11	4	8
19	13 46 55	28 34 17	24 44	19	23	19	19	6	11	4	8
20	13 50 51	29 32 52	7♌26	19	23	20	18	6	11	4	8 D
21	13 54 48	0♉31 25	19 49	18	22	21	18	6	11	4	8
22	13 58 45	1 29 55	1♍59	18	22	22	18	6	11	4	8
23	14 2 41	2 28 24	14 0	18	21	22	18	6	11	4	8
24	14 6 38	3 26 50	25 55	17	20	23	18	6	11	4	8
25	14 10 34	4 25 14	7♎47	17	20	24	18	6	11	4	8
26	14 14 31	5 23 37	19 39	17	20	25	18	6	11	4	8
27	14 18 27	6 21 57	1♏33	17 D	19	25	18	6	11	4	8
28	14 22 24	7 20 16	13 29	17	19	26	18	6	11	4	8
29	14 26 20	8 18 32	25 30	17	18	27	18	6	11	4	8
30	14 30 17	9 16 48	7♐37	17	18	28	18	6	11	4	8

THE SUN ENTERS THE SIGN OF TAURUS ON APR 20 AT 11:07.

DAY	TIME	☉	☽	☿	♀	♂	♃	♄	♅	♆	♇
	h m s	° ' "	° '	°	°	°	°	°	°	°	°
M 1	14 34 14	10♉15 1	19♐51	17♈	18♈R	29♓	18♍R	7♋	11♊	4♎R	8♌
A 2	14 38 10	11 13 13	2♑15	18	18	29	18	7	11	4	8
Y 3	14 42 7	12 11 24	14 52	18	17	0♈	18	7	11	4	8
4	14 46 3	13 9 33	27 46	19	17	1	18	7	11	4	8
5	14 50 0	14 7 40	10♒59	19	17	2	18	7	11	4	8
6	14 53 56	15 5 46	24 35	20	17 D	2	18	7	12	4	8
7	14 57 53	16 3 51	8♓36	21	17	3	18	7	12	4	8
8	15 1 49	17 1 54	23 1	21	17	4	18	7	12	4	8
9	15 5 46	17 59 56	7♈47	22	17	5	18	7	12	4	8
10	15 9 43	18 57 57	22 48	23	17	5	18	7	12	4	8
11	15 13 39	19 55 56	7♉57	24	18	6	18	8	12	4	8
12	15 17 36	20 53 54	23 2	25	18	7	18	8	12	4	8
13	15 21 32	21 51 50	7♊53	26	18	8	18	8	12	4	8
14	15 25 29	22 49 45	22 24	27	18	9	18 D	8	12	4	8
15	15 29 25	23 47 38	6♋29	28	18	9	18	8	12	4	8
16	15 33 22	24 45 29	20 6	29	19	10	18	8	12	4	8
17	15 37 18	25 43 19	3♌17	0♉	19	11	18	8	12	4	8
18	15 41 15	26 41 6	16 3	2	19	12	18	8	12	4	8
19	15 45 12	27 38 53	28 30	3	20	12	18	8	12	4	8
20	15 49 8	28 36 37	10♍41	4	20	13	18	8	12	4	8
21	15 53 5	29 34 20	22 41	6	21	14	18	9	12	4	8
22	15 57 1	0♊32 1	4♎36	7	21	15	18	9	12	4	8
23	16 0 58	1 29 41	16 27	9	22	15	18	9	13	4	8
24	16 4 54	2 27 19	28 20	10	22	16	18	9	13	4	8
25	16 8 51	3 24 56	10♏17	12	23	17	18	9	13	4	8
26	16 12 47	4 22 32	22 19	13	23	18	18	9	13	4	8
27	16 16 44	5 20 7	4♐29	15	24	18	18	9	13	4	8
28	16 20 41	6 17 40	16 47	16	25	19	18	9	13	4	8
29	16 24 37	7 15 12	29 16	18	25	20	18	9	13	4	8
30	16 28 34	8 12 43	11♑55	20	26	21	18	10	13	4	8
31	16 32 30	9 10 14	24 48	22	26	21	18	10	13	4	8

THE SUN ENTERS THE SIGN OF GEMINI ON MAY 21 AT 10:40.

DAY	TIME	☉	☽	☿	♀	♂	♃	♄	♅	♆	♇
	h m s	° ' "	° '	°	°	°	°	°	°	°	°
J 1	16 36 27	10♊ 7 43	7♒54	23♉	27♈	22♈	18♍	10♋	13♊	4♎R	8♌
U 2	16 40 23	11 5 12	21 16	25	28	23	18	10	13	4	8
N 3	16 44 20	12 2 40	4♓55	27	29	24	18	10	13	4	8
E 4	16 48 16	13 0 7	18 51	29	29	24	18	10	13	4	8
5	16 52 13	13 57 33	3♈ 5	1♊	0♉	25	18	10	13	4	8
6	16 56 10	14 54 59	17 33	3	1	26	18	10	13	4	8
7	17 0 6	15 52 24	2♉13	5	2	27	18	11	13	4	8
8	17 4 3	16 49 49	16 58	7	2	27	18	11	13	4	8
9	17 7 59	17 47 13	1♊41	9	3	28	18	11	14	4	8
10	17 11 56	18 44 37	16 15	11	4	29	19	11	14	4	8
11	17 15 52	19 41 59	0♋34	14	5	0♉	19	11	14	4	8
12	17 19 49	20 39 21	14 33	16	6	0	19	11	14	4	8
13	17 23 46	21 36 42	28 8	18	6	1	19	11	14	4	9
14	17 27 42	22 34 2	11♌20	20	7	2	19	11	14	4 D	9
15	17 31 39	23 31 22	24 10	22	8	3	19	12	14	4	9
16	17 35 35	24 28 40	6♍40	24	9	3	19	12	14	4	9
17	17 39 32	25 25 57	18 54	27	10	4	19	12	14	4	9
18	17 43 28	26 23 14	0♎57	29	11	5	19	12	14	4	9
19	17 47 25	27 20 30	12 52	1♋	12	6	19	12	14	4	9
20	17 51 21	28 17 45	24 45	3	13	6	19	12	14	4	9
21	17 55 18	29 15 0	6♏39	5	14	7	20	12	14	4	9
22	17 59 15	0♋12 13	18 39	7	15	8	20	12	14	4	9
23	18 3 11	1 9 27	0♐47	10	15	8	20	13	14	4	9
24	18 7 8	2 6 40	13 6	12	16	9	20	13	14	4	9
25	18 11 4	3 3 52	25 38	14	17	10	20	13	14	4	9
26	18 15 1	4 1 4	8♑24	16	18	11	20	13	14	4	9
27	18 18 57	4 58 16	21 25	18	19	11	20	13	15	4	9
28	18 22 54	5 55 28	4♒39	20	20	12	20	13	15	4	9
29	18 26 50	6 52 40	18 7	22	21	13	20	13	15	4	9
30	18 30 47	7 49 51	1♓48	23	22	14	21	13	15	4	9

THE SUN ENTERS THE SIGN OF CANCER ON JUN 21 AT 18:52.

♈ ARIES ♉ TAURUS ♊ GEMINI ♋ CANCER ♌ LEO ♍ VIRGO ♎ LIBRA ♏ SCORPIO ♐ SAGITTARIUS ♑ CAPRICORN ♒ AQUARIUS ♓ PISCES

SIDEREAL SUN MOON MERCURY VENUS MARS JUPITER SATURN URANUS NEPTUNE PLUTO

DAY	TIME	☉	☽	☿	♀	♂	♃	♄	♅	♆	♇
	h m s	° ' "	° '	°	°	°	°	°	°	°	°
J 1	18 34 44	8♋47 3	15♓40	25♋	23♉	14♉	21♍	14♋	15♊	4♎	9♌
U 2	18 38 40	9 44 15	29 43	27	24	15	21	14	15	4	9
L 3	18 42 37	10 41 27	13♈53	29	25	16	21	14	15	4	9
Y 4	18 46 33	11 38 39	28 10	1♌	26	16	21	14	15	4	9
5	18 50 30	12 35 52	12♉30	2	27	17	21	14	15	4	9
6	18 54 26	13 33 5	26 49	4	28	18	21	14	15	4	9
7	18 58 23	14 30 18	11♊ 5	6	29	19	21	14	15	4	9
8	19 2 19	15 27 32	25 13	7	0♊	19	22	15	15	4	9
9	19 6 16	16 24 46	9♋10	9	1	20	22	15	15	4	9
10	19 10 13	17 22 0	22 51	10	2	21	22	15	15	4	9
11	19 14 9	18 19 14	6♌15	12	3	21	22	15	15	4	9
12	19 18 6	19 16 29	19 21	13	4	22	22	15	15	4	9
13	19 22 2	20 13 43	2♍ 8	15	6	23	22	15	15	4	9
14	19 25 59	21 10 57	14 37	16	7	23	22	15	15	4	9
15	19 29 55	22 8 12	26 52	17	8	24	23	15	16	4	9
16	19 33 52	23 5 26	8♎55	19	9	25	23	16	16	4	9
17	19 37 48	24 2 41	20 51	20	10	26	23	16	16	4	9
18	19 41 45	24 59 56	2♏44	21	11	26	23	16	16	4	9
19	19 45 42	25 57 11	14 39	22	12	27	23	16	16	4	9
20	19 49 38	26 54 26	26 40	24	13	28	23	16	16	4	9
21	19 53 35	27 51 42	8♐52	25	14	28	24	16	16	4	9
22	19 57 31	28 48 58	21 18	26	15	29	24	16	16	4	10
23	20 1 28	29 46 14	4♑ 1	27	16	0♊	24	16	16	4	10
24	20 5 24	0♌43 31	17 3	28	17	0	24	17	16	4	10
25	20 9 21	1 40 49	0♒24	29	18	1	24	17	16	4	10
26	20 13 17	2 38 7	14 4	29	20	2	24	17	16	4	10
27	20 17 14	3 35 26	27 59	0♍	21	2	25	17	16	4	10
28	20 21 11	4 32 45	12♓ 6	1	22	3	25	17	16	4	10
29	20 25 7	5 30 6	26 21	2	23	4	25	17	16	4	10
30	20 29 4	6 27 28	10♈39	2	24	5	25	17	16	4	10
31	20 33 0	7 24 50	24 57	3	25	5	25	17	16	4	10

THE SUN ENTERS THE SIGN OF LEO ON JUL 23 AT 05:46.

DAY	TIME	☉	☽	☿	♀	♂	♃	♄	♅	♆	♇
	h m s	° ' "	° '	°	°	°	°	°	°	°	°
A 1	20 36 57	8♌22 14	9♉12	3♍	26♊	6♊	25♍	18♋	16♊	4♎	10♌
U 2	20 40 53	9 19 39	23 20	4	27	7	26	18	16	4	10
G 3	20 44 50	10 17 5	7♊21	4	28	7	26	18	16	4	10
U 4	20 48 46	11 14 33	21 12	4	29	8	26	18	16	4	10
S 5	20 52 43	12 12 1	4♋54	5	1♋	9	26	18	16	4	10
T 6	20 56 40	13 9 31	18 24	5 R	2	9	26	18	16	4	10
7	21 0 36	14 7 2	1♌43	5	3	10	26	18	17	4	10
8	21 4 33	15 4 34	14 48	5	4	11	27	18	17	4	10
9	21 8 29	16 2 7	27 40	5	5	11	27	19	17	4	10
10	21 12 26	16 59 41	10♍17	4	6	12	27	19	17	4	10
11	21 16 22	17 57 17	22 41	4	7	13	27	19	17	4	10
12	21 20 19	18 54 53	4♎53	4	9	13	27	19	17	5	10
13	21 24 15	19 52 30	16 54	3	10	14	28	19	17	5	10
14	21 28 12	20 50 8	28 48	2	11	14	28	19	17	5	10
15	21 32 9	21 47 47	10♏40	2	12	15	28	19	17	5	10
16	21 36 5	22 45 27	22 33	1	13	16	28	19	17	5	10
17	21 40 2	23 43 8	4♐33	0	14	16	28	20	17	5	10
18	21 43 58	24 40 50	16 44	29♌	15	17	29	20	17	5	10
19	21 47 55	25 38 34	29 12	29	17	18	29	20	17	5	10
20	21 51 51	26 36 18	12♑ 0	28	18	18	29	20	17	5	10
21	21 55 48	27 34 4	25 12	27	19	19	29	20	17	5	10
22	21 59 44	28 31 51	8♒49	26	20	20	29	20	17	5	10
23	22 3 41	29 29 39	22 49	25	21	20	0♎	20	17	5	10
24	22 7 38	0♍27 29	7♓ 9	24	22	21	0	20	17	5	10
25	22 11 34	1 25 20	21 44	24	24	22	0	20	17	5	11
26	22 15 31	2 23 12	6♈26	23	25	22	0	21	17	5	11
27	22 19 27	3 21 7	21 8	23	26	23	0	21	17	5	11
28	22 23 24	4 19 3	5♉43	22	27	23	1	21	17	5	11
29	22 27 20	5 17 1	20 5	22	28	24	1	21	17	5	11
30	22 31 17	6 15 1	4♊13	22 D	29	25	1	21	17	5	11
31	22 35 13	7 13 3	18 5	22	1♌	25	1	21	17	5	11

THE SUN ENTERS THE SIGN OF VIRGO ON AUG 23 AT 12:36.

DAY	TIME	☉	☽	☿	♀	♂	♃	♄	♅	♆	♇
	h m s	° ' "	° '	°	°	°	°	°	°	°	°
S 1	22 39 10	8♍11 7	1♋41	22♌	2♌	26♊	1♎	21♋	17♊	5♎	11♌
E 2	22 43 7	9 9 13	15 3	22	3	26	2	21	17	5	11
P 3	22 47 3	10 7 20	28 11	23	4	27	2	21	17	5	11
T 4	22 51 0	11 5 30	11♌ 8	23	5	28	2	21	17	5	11
E 5	22 54 56	12 3 41	23 53	24	6	28	2	22	17	5	11
M 6	22 58 53	13 1 54	6♍28	25	8	29	2	22	17	5	11
B 7	23 2 49	14 0 9	18 52	26	9	29	3	22	17	5	11
E 8	23 6 46	14 58 26	1♎ 7	27	10	0♋	3	22	17	5	11
R 9	23 10 42	15 56 44	13 12	28	11	1	3	22	17	5	11
10	23 14 39	16 55 4	25 9	0♍	12	1	3	22	17	5	11
11	23 18 36	17 53 26	7♏ 1	1	14	2	3	22	17	5	11
12	23 22 32	18 51 49	18 50	2	15	2	4	22	17	6	11
13	23 26 29	19 50 14	0♐41	4	16	3	4	22	17	6	11
14	23 30 25	20 48 41	12 38	6	17	4	4	22	17	6	11
15	23 34 22	21 47 9	24 46	7	18	4	4	22	17	6	11
16	23 38 18	22 45 39	7♑11	9	20	5	5	23	17	6	11
17	23 42 15	23 44 11	19 57	11	21	5	5	23	17	6	11
18	23 46 11	24 42 44	3♒10	13	22	6	5	23	17	6	11
19	23 50 8	25 41 18	16 51	14	23	6	5	23	17	6	11
20	23 54 4	26 39 55	1♓ 0	16	24	7	5	23	17	6	11
21	23 58 1	27 38 33	15 36	18	26	8	6	23	17	6	11
22	0 1 58	28 37 13	0♈31	20	27	8	6	23	17	6	11
23	0 5 54	29 35 56	15 36	22	28	9	6	23	17 R	6	11
24	0 9 51	0♎34 40	0♉42	24	29	9	6	23	17	6	11
25	0 13 47	1 33 26	15 38	25	0♍	10	6	23	17	6	11
26	0 17 44	2 32 15	0♊17	27	2	10	7	23	17	6	11
27	0 21 40	3 31 6	14 35	29	3	11	7	23	17	6	11
28	0 25 37	4 29 59	28 29	1♎	4	11	7	23	17	6	11
29	0 29 33	5 28 55	12♋ 2	3	5	12	7	24	17	6	11
30	0 33 30	6 27 52	25 14	5	6	12	8	24	17	6	11

THE SUN ENTERS THE SIGN OF LIBRA ON SEP 23 AT 09:51.

SIDEREAL SUN MOON MERCURY VENUS MARS JUPITER SATURN URANUS NEPTUNE PLUTO

DAY	TIME	☉	☽	☿	♀	♂	♃	♄	♅	♆	♇
	h m s	° ' "	° '	°	°	°	°	°	°	°	°
O 1	0 37 27	7♎26 53	8♌10	6♎	8♍	13♋	8♎	24♋	17♊R	6♎	11♌
C 2	0 41 23	8 25 55	20 51	8	9	13	8	24	17	6	11
T 3	0 45 20	9 25 0	3♍20	10	10	14	8	24	17	6	11
O 4	0 49 16	10 24 6	15 39	12	11	14	8	24	17	6	11
B 5	0 53 13	11 23 15	27 50	13	13	15	9	24	17	6	11
E 6	0 57 9	12 22 26	9♎54	15	14	15	9	24	17	6	11
R 7	1 1 6	13 21 39	21 52	17	15	16	9	24	17	6	11
8	1 5 2	14 20 54	3♏45	18	16	16	9	24	17	6	12
9	1 8 59	15 20 11	15 35	20	17	17	9	24	17	7	12
10	1 12 56	16 19 30	27 23	22	19	17	10	24	17	7	12
11	1 16 52	17 18 51	9♐14	23	20	18	10	24	17	7	12
12	1 20 49	18 18 14	21 10	25	21	18	10	24	17	7	12
13	1 24 45	19 17 38	3♑16	27	22	19	10	24	17	7	12
14	1 28 42	20 17 5	15 38	28	24	19	11	24	17	7	12
15	1 32 38	21 16 33	28 19	0♏	25	20	11	24	17	7	12
16	1 36 35	22 16 3	11♒26	2	26	20	11	24	17	7	12
17	1 40 31	23 15 34	25 1	3	27	21	11	25	17	7	12
18	1 44 28	24 15 7	9♓ 7	5	29	21	11	25	17	7	12
19	1 48 25	25 14 42	23 42	6	0♎	22	12	25	17	7	12
20	1 52 21	26 14 19	8♈41	8	1	22	12	25	17	7	12
21	1 56 18	27 13 58	23 56	9	2	22	12	25	17	7	12
22	2 0 14	28 13 39	9♉15	11	3	23	12	25	17	7	12
23	2 4 11	29 13 21	24 28	12	5	23	12	25	17	7	12
24	2 8 7	0♏13 6	9♊24	14	6	24	13	25	17	7	12
25	2 12 4	1 12 54	23 57	16	7	24	13	25	17	7	12
26	2 16 0	2 12 43	8♋ 4	17	8	24	13	25	17	7	12
27	2 19 57	3 12 35	21 43	18	10	25	13	25	17	7	12
28	2 23 54	4 12 29	4♌58	20	11	25	14	25	17	7	12
29	2 27 50	5 12 25	17 50	21	12	26	14	25	17	7	12
30	2 31 47	6 12 23	0♍25	23	13	26	14	25	17	7	12
31	2 35 43	7 12 23	12 45	24	15	26	14	25	17	7	12

THE SUN ENTERS THE SIGN OF SCORPIO ON OCT 23 AT 18:44.

DAY	TIME	☉	☽	☿	♀	♂	♃	♄	♅	♆	♇
	h m s	° ' "	° '	°	°	°	°	°	°	°	°
N 1	2 39 40	8♏12 25	24♍54	26♏	16♎	27♋	14♎	25♋	17♊R	7♎	12♌
O 2	2 43 36	9 12 30	6♎56	27	17	27	15	25	17	7	12
V 3	2 47 33	10 12 36	18 52	29	18	27	15	25	17	7	12
E 4	2 51 29	11 12 45	0♏45	0♐	20	28	15	25	17	7	12
M 5	2 55 26	12 12 55	12 35	1	21	28	15	25	17	7	12
B 6	2 59 22	13 13 7	24 25	3	22	28	15	25 R	17	7	12
E 7	3 3 19	14 13 21	6♐16	4	23	29	16	25	17	8	12
R 8	3 7 16	15 13 37	18 11	6	25	29	16	25	17	8	12
9	3 11 12	16 13 54	0♑12	7	26	29	16	25	17	8	12
10	3 15 9	17 14 12	12 23	8	27	29	16	25	17	8	12
11	3 19 5	18 14 33	24 46	9	28	0♌	16	25	17	8	12
12	3 23 2	19 14 54	7♒26	11	0♏	0	17	25	16	8	12
13	3 26 58	20 15 17	20 28	12	1	0	17	25	16	8	12 R
14	3 30 55	21 15 42	3♓55	13	2	1	17	25	16	8	12
15	3 34 52	22 16 7	17 49	14	3	1	17	25	16	8	12
16	3 38 48	23 16 34	2♈10	15	5	1	17	25	16	8	12
17	3 42 45	24 17 3	16 57	17	6	1	18	25	16	8	12
18	3 46 41	25 17 32	2♉ 1	18	7	1	18	25	16	8	12
19	3 50 38	26 18 3	17 16	19	8	2	18	25	16	8	12
20	3 54 34	27 18 36	2♊30	19	10	2	18	25	16	8	12
21	3 58 31	28 19 10	17 33	20	11	2	18	25	16	8	12
22	4 2 27	29 19 46	2♋17	21	12	2	19	25	16	8	12
23	4 6 24	0♐20 23	16 36	22	13	2	19	25	16	8	12
24	4 10 21	1 21 2	0♌27	22	15	2	19	25	16	8	12
25	4 14 17	2 21 43	13 51	23	16	3	19	25	16	8	12
26	4 18 14	3 22 25	26 49	23	17	3	19	25	16	8	12
27	4 22 10	4 23 9	9♍26	23 R	18	3	19	25	16	8	12
28	4 26 7	5 23 54	21 45	23	20	3	20	24	16	8	12
29	4 30 3	6 24 41	3♎51	23	21	3	20	24	16	8	12
30	4 34 0	7 25 29	15 48	23	22	3	20	24	16	8	12

THE SUN ENTERS THE SIGN OF SAGITTARIUS ON NOV 22 AT 15:56.

DAY	TIME	☉	☽	☿	♀	♂	♃	♄	♅	♆	♇
	h m s	° ' "	° '	°	°	°	°	°	°	°	°
D 1	4 37 56	8♐26 18	27♎40	22♐R	23♏	3♌	20♎	24♋R	16♊R	8♎	12♌R
E 2	4 41 53	9 27 9	9♏30	21	25	3	20	24	16	8	12
C 3	4 45 50	10 28 2	21 20	20	26	3	21	24	16	8	12
E 4	4 49 46	11 28 55	3♐13	19	27	3 R	21	24	16	8	12
M 5	4 53 43	12 29 50	15 11	18	28	3	21	24	16	8	12
B 6	4 57 39	13 30 46	27 16	17	0♐	3	21	24	16	8	12
E 7	5 1 36	14 31 43	9♑29	16	1	3	21	24	15	8	12
R 8	5 5 32	15 32 40	21 52	14	2	3	21	24	15	8	12
9	5 9 29	16 33 38	4♒27	13	3	3	22	24	15	8	12
10	5 13 25	17 34 37	17 16	12	5	3	22	24	15	8	12
11	5 17 22	18 35 37	0♓22	10	6	3	22	24	15	8	12
12	5 21 19	19 36 37	13 46	9	7	3	22	24	15	8	12
13	5 25 15	20 37 38	27 31	8	9	3	22	24	15	8	12
14	5 29 12	21 38 39	11♈37	8	10	3	22	24	15	8	12
15	5 33 8	22 39 40	26 3	7	11	3	22	24	15	8	12
16	5 37 5	23 40 42	10♉44	7	12	2	23	24	15	8	12
17	5 41 1	24 41 45	25 37	7 D	14	2	23	23	15	8	12
18	5 44 58	25 42 48	10♊33	7	15	2	23	23	15	8	12
19	5 48 54	26 43 51	25 25	7	16	2	23	23	15	8	12
20	5 52 51	27 44 56	10♋ 4	7	17	2	23	23	15	8	12
21	5 56 48	28 46 0	24 25	8	19	1	23	23	15	9	11
22	6 0 44	29 47 6	8♌22	8	20	1	24	23	15	9	11
23	6 4 41	0♑48 11	21 54	9	21	1	24	23	15	9	11
24	6 8 37	1 49 18	5♍ 1	10	22	1	24	23	15	9	11
25	6 12 34	2 50 25	17 44	11	24	0	24	23	15	9	11
26	6 16 30	3 51 33	0♎ 7	12	25	0	24	23	15	9	11
27	6 20 27	4 52 41	12 15	13	26	0	24	23	15	9	11
28	6 24 23	5 53 50	24 12	14	27	0	24	23	15	9	11
29	6 28 20	6 54 59	6♏ 3	15	29	29♋	24	23	15	9	11
30	6 32 17	7 56 9	17 52	16	0♑	29	25	23	15	9	11
31	6 36 13	8 57 19	29 44	17	1	29	25	22	14	9	11

THE SUN ENTERS THE SIGN OF CAPRICORN ON DEC 22 AT 05:04.

♈ ARIES ♉ TAURUS ♊ GEMINI ♋ CANCER ♌ LEO ♍ VIRGO ♎ LIBRA ♏ SCORPIO ♐ SAGITTARIUS ♑ CAPRICORN ♒ AQUARIUS ♓ PISCES

1946

SIDEREAL SUN MOON MERCURY VENUS MARS JUPITER SATURN URANUS NEPTUNE PLUTO

DAY	TIME	☉	☽	☿	♀	♂	♃	♄	♅	♆	♇
	h m s	° ' "	° '	°	°	°	°	°	°	°	°
J 1	6 40 10	9♑58 29	11♐41	18♐	2♑	28♋R	25♎	22♋R	14♊R	9♎	11♌R
A 2	6 44 6	10 59 40	23 47	20	4	28	25	22	14	9	11
N 3	6 48 3	12 0 51	6♑ 4	21	5	28	25	22	14	9	11
U 4	6 51 59	13 2 1	18 33	22	6	27	25	22	14	9	11
A 5	6 55 56	14 3 12	1♒16	24	7	27	25	22	14	9	11
R 6	6 59 53	15 4 23	14 12	25	9	26	25	22	14	9	11
Y 7	7 3 49	16 5 33	27 21	26	10	26	25	22	14	9	11
8	7 7 46	17 6 43	10♓44	28	11	26	26	22	14	9	11
9	7 11 42	18 7 52	24 19	29	12	25	26	22	14	9	11
10	7 15 39	19 9 1	8♈ 7	1♑	14	25	26	22	14	9 R	11
11	7 19 35	20 10 9	22 6	2	15	24	26	22	14	9	11
12	7 23 32	21 11 17	6♉16	3	16	24	26	21	14	9	11
13	7 27 28	22 12 24	20 34	5	18	24	26	21	14	9	11
14	7 31 25	23 13 30	4♊59	6	19	23	26	21	14	9	11
15	7 35 22	24 14 36	19 27	8	20	23	26	21	14	9	11
16	7 39 18	25 15 41	3♋52	9	21	22	26	21	14	9	11
17	7 43 15	26 16 46	18 11	11	23	22	26	21	14	9	11
18	7 47 11	27 17 50	2♌18	12	24	22	26	21	14	9	11
19	7 51 8	28 18 53	16 8	14	25	21	27	21	14	9	11
20	7 55 4	29 19 56	29 37	15	26	21	27	21	14	9	11
21	7 59 1	0♒20 58	12♍46	17	28	21	27	21	14	9	11
22	8 2 57	1 22 0	25 32	18	29	20	27	21	14	9	11
23	8 6 54	2 23 1	7♎59	20	0♒	20	27	21	14	9	11
24	8 10 51	3 24 2	20 10	22	1	19	27	20	14	9	11
25	8 14 47	4 25 2	2♏ 9	23	3	19	27	20	14	9	11
26	8 18 44	5 26 2	14 0	25	4	19	27	20	14	9	11
27	8 22 40	6 27 1	25 50	26	5	18	27	20	14	9	11
28	8 26 37	7 28 0	7♐42	28	6	18	27	20	14	9	11
29	8 30 33	8 28 58	19 42	0♒	8	18	27	20	14	9	11
30	8 34 30	9 29 55	1♑54	1	9	18	27	20	14	9	11
31	8 38 26	10 30 52	14 21	3	10	17	27	20	14	8	11

THE SUN ENTERS THE SIGN OF AQUARIUS ON JAN 20 AT 15:45.

DAY	TIME	☉	☽	☿	♀	♂	♃	♄	♅	♆	♇
	h m s	° ' "	° '	°	°	°	°	°	°	°	°
F 1	8 42 23	11♒31 47	27♑ 5	4♒	11♒	17♋R	27♎	20♋R	14♊R	8♎R	11♌R
E 2	8 46 20	12 32 42	10♒ 8	6	13	17	27	20	14	8	11
B 3	8 50 16	13 33 35	23 29	8	14	16	27	20	14	8	11
R 4	8 54 13	14 34 27	7♓ 5	9	15	16	27	20	14	8	11
U 5	8 58 9	15 35 18	20 54	11	16	16	27	20	14	8	11
A 6	9 2 6	16 36 8	4♈53	13	18	16	27	20	14	8	10
R 7	9 6 2	17 36 56	18 57	15	19	16	27	19	13	8	10
Y 8	9 9 59	18 37 42	3♉ 4	16	20	15	27	19	13	8	10
9	9 13 55	19 38 27	17 12	18	21	15	27	19	13	8	10
10	9 17 52	20 39 11	1♊19	20	23	15	27	19	13	8	10
11	9 21 49	21 39 52	15 24	22	24	15	27 R	19	13	8	10
12	9 25 45	22 40 33	29 26	23	25	15	27	19	13	8	10
13	9 29 42	23 41 11	13♋23	25	26	15	27	19	13	8	10
14	9 33 38	24 41 48	27 13	27	28	15	27	19	13	8	10
15	9 37 35	25 42 24	10♌55	29	29	14	27	19	13	8	10
16	9 41 31	26 42 58	24 25	1♓	0♓	14	27	19	13	8	10
17	9 45 28	27 43 30	7♍40	2	1	14	27	19	13	8	10
18	9 49 24	28 44 1	20 39	4	3	14	27	19	13	8	10
19	9 53 21	29 44 30	3♎21	6	4	14	27	19	13	8	10
20	9 57 18	0♓44 58	15 46	8	5	14	27	19	13 D	8	10
21	10 1 14	1 45 24	27 57	10	6	14 D	27	19	13	8	10
22	10 5 11	2 45 50	9♏56	12	8	14	27	19	13	8	10
23	10 9 7	3 46 13	21 47	14	9	14	27	19	13	8	10
24	10 13 4	4 46 36	3♐36	16	10	14	27	18	13	8	10
25	10 17 0	5 46 57	15 28	17	11	14	27	18	13	8	10
26	10 20 57	6 47 17	27 28	19	13	14	27	18	13	8	10
27	10 24 53	7 47 35	9♑41	21	14	14	27	18	13	8	10
28	10 28 50	8 47 52	22 13	23	15	14	27	18	13	8	10

THE SUN ENTERS THE SIGN OF PISCES ON FEB 19 AT 06:09.

DAY	TIME	☉	☽	☿	♀	♂	♃	♄	♅	♆	♇
	h m s	° ' "	° '	°	°	°	°	°	°	°	°
M 1	10 32 47	9♓48 7	5♒ 6	25♓	16♓	14♋	27♎R	18♋R	13♊	8♎R	10♌R
A 2	10 36 43	10 48 20	18 23	26	18	15	27	18	13	8	10
R 3	10 40 40	11 48 32	2♓ 4	28	19	15	27	18	13	8	10
C 4	10 44 36	12 48 42	16 5	29	20	15	27	18	13	8	10
H 5	10 48 33	13 48 50	0♈22	1♈	21	15	27	18	13	8	10
6	10 52 29	14 48 56	14 49	2	23	15	27	18	13	8	10
7	10 56 26	15 49 0	29 19	4	24	15	26	18	14	8	10
8	11 0 22	16 49 2	13♉46	5	25	15	26	18	14	8	10
9	11 4 19	17 49 3	28 6	6	26	15	26	18	14	8	10
10	11 8 15	18 49 0	12♊16	7	28	16	26	18	14	8	10
11	11 12 12	19 48 56	26 15	8	29	16	26	18	14	8	10
12	11 16 9	20 48 49	10♋ 3	9	0♈	16	26	18	14	8	10
13	11 20 5	21 48 41	23 41	9	1	16	26	18	14	8	10
14	11 24 2	22 48 30	7♌ 8	10	3	16	26	18	14	8	10
15	11 27 58	23 48 16	20 24	10	4	17	26	18	14	8	10
16	11 31 55	24 48 1	3♍30	10 R	5	17	26	18	14	8	10
17	11 35 51	25 47 43	16 25	10	6	17	26	18	14	8	10
18	11 39 48	26 47 24	29 7	10	8	17	26	18	14	8	10
19	11 43 44	27 47 2	11♎37	10	9	18	25	18	14	8	10
20	11 47 41	28 46 39	23 54	10	10	18	25	18 D	14	7	10
21	11 51 38	29 46 13	5♏59	9	11	18	25	18	14	7	10
22	11 55 34	0♈45 46	17 55	8	13	18	25	18	14	7	10
23	11 59 31	1 45 17	29 45	8	14	19	25	18	14	7	10
24	12 3 27	2 44 46	11♐33	7	15	19	25	18	14	7	10
25	12 7 24	3 44 14	23 23	6	16	19	25	18	14	7	10
26	12 11 20	4 43 40	5♑22	5	18	19	25	18	14	7	10
27	12 15 17	5 43 4	17 34	5	19	20	25	18	14	7	10
28	12 19 13	6 42 26	0♒ 5	4	20	20	24	18	14	7	10
29	12 23 10	7 41 46	12 59	3	21	20	24	18	14	7	10
30	12 27 7	8 41 5	26 20	2	23	21	24	18	14	7	10
31	12 31 3	9 40 21	10♓ 9	1	24	21	24	18	14	7	10

THE SUN ENTERS THE SIGN OF ARIES ON MAR 21 AT 05:33.

SIDEREAL SUN MOON MERCURY VENUS MARS JUPITER SATURN URANUS NEPTUNE PLUTO

DAY	TIME	☉	☽	☿	♀	♂	♃	♄	♅	♆	♇
	h m s	° ' "	° '	°	°	°	°	°	°	°	°
A 1	12 35 0	10♈39 36	24♓24	1♈R	25♈	21♋	24♎R	18♋	14♊	7♎R	10♌R
P 2	12 38 56	11 38 49	8♈59	0☉	26	22	24	18	14	7	10
R 3	12 42 53	12 37 59	23 49	29♓	27	22	24	18	14	7	10
I 4	12 46 49	13 37 8	8♉44	29	29	22	24	18	14	7	10
L 5	12 50 46	14 36 15	23 36	28	0♉	23	24	18	14	7	9
6	12 54 42	15 35 19	8♊17	28	1	23	23	18	14	7	9
7	12 58 39	16 34 21	22 42	28	2	24	23	18	14	7	9
8	13 2 36	17 33 21	6♋49	28	4	24	23	18	14	7	9
9	13 6 32	18 32 18	20 37	28 D	5	24	23	18	14	7	9
10	13 10 29	19 31 14	4♌ 7	28	6	25	23	18	14	7	9
11	13 14 25	20 30 6	17 21	28	7	25	23	18	14	7	9
12	13 18 22	21 28 57	0♍21	28	9	25	23	18	14	7	9
13	13 22 18	22 27 45	13 8	28	10	26	22	18	15	7	9
14	13 26 15	23 26 31	25 44	29	11	26	22	19	15	7	9
15	13 30 11	24 25 15	8♎ 8	29	12	27	22	19	15	7	9
16	13 34 8	25 23 57	20 23	0☉	14	27	22	19	15	7	9
17	13 38 5	26 22 37	2♏29	0♈	15	28	22	19	15	7	9
18	13 42 1	27 21 15	14 27	1	16	28	22	19	15	7	9
19	13 45 58	28 19 51	26 18	2	17	28	22	19	15	7	9
20	13 49 54	29 18 26	8♐ 6	2	18	29	22	19	15	7	9
21	13 53 51	0♉16 58	19 54	3	20	29	21	19	15	7	9
22	13 57 47	1 15 29	1♑45	4	21	0♌	21	19	15	7	9 D
23	14 1 44	2 13 59	13 43	5	22	0	21	19	15	7	9
24	14 5 40	3 12 26	25 54	6	23	1	21	19	15	7	9
25	14 9 37	4 10 52	8♒23	7	25	1	21	19	15	7	9
26	14 13 34	5 9 17	21 14	8	26	1	21	19	15	7	9
27	14 17 30	6 7 40	4♓32	9	27	2	21	19	15	6	9
28	14 21 27	7 6 1	18 18	10	28	2	21	19	15	6	9
29	14 25 23	8 4 21	2♈33	12	29	3	20	19	15	6	9
30	14 29 20	9 2 39	17 13	13	1♊	3	20	19	15	6	9

THE SUN ENTERS THE SIGN OF TAURUS ON APR 20 AT 17:02.

DAY	TIME	☉	☽	☿	♀	♂	♃	♄	♅	♆	♇
	h m s	° ' "	° '	°	°	°	°	°	°	°	°
M 1	14 33 16	10♉ 0 55	2♉11	14♈	2♊	4♌	20♎R	19♋	15♊	6♎R	9♌
A 2	14 37 13	10 59 10	17 20	16	3	4	20	20	15	6	9
Y 3	14 41 9	11 57 23	2♊29	17	4	5	20	20	15	6	9
4	14 45 6	12 55 34	17 29	18	6	5	20	20	16	6	9
5	14 49 2	13 53 44	2♋12	20	7	6	20	20	16	6	9
6	14 52 59	14 51 51	16 34	21	8	6	20	20	16	6	9
7	14 56 56	15 49 57	0♌32	23	9	7	20	20	16	6	9
8	15 0 52	16 48 0	14 6	24	10	7	20	20	16	6	9
9	15 4 49	17 46 2	27 19	26	12	8	19	20	16	6	9
10	15 8 45	18 44 1	10♍12	27	13	8	19	20	16	6	10
11	15 12 42	19 41 59	22 48	29	14	8	19	20	16	6	10
12	15 16 38	20 39 55	5♎11	1♉	15	9	19	20	16	6	10
13	15 20 35	21 37 49	17 23	2	16	9	19	20	16	6	10
14	15 24 31	22 35 42	29 26	4	18	10	19	21	16	6	10
15	15 28 28	23 33 33	11♏22	6	19	10	19	21	16	6	10
16	15 32 25	24 31 22	23 13	8	20	11	19	21	16	6	10
17	15 36 21	25 29 10	5♐ 2	10	21	11	19	21	16	6	10
18	15 40 18	26 26 57	16 50	11	23	12	19	21	16	6	10
19	15 44 14	27 24 42	28 40	13	24	13	19	21	16	6	10
20	15 48 11	28 22 27	10♑34	15	25	13	18	21	16	6	10
21	15 52 7	29 20 10	22 37	17	26	14	18	21	16	6	10
22	15 56 4	0♊17 51	4♒51	19	27	14	18	21	17	6	10
23	16 0 1	1 15 32	17 22	21	29	15	18	21	17	6	10
24	16 3 57	2 13 12	0♓11	23	0♋	15	18	21	17	6	10
25	16 7 54	3 10 51	13 24	25	1	16	18	22	17	6	10
26	16 11 50	4 8 28	27 3	27	2	16	18	22	17	6	10
27	16 15 47	5 6 5	11♈ 9	0♊	3	17	18	22	17	6	10
28	16 19 43	6 3 41	25 39	2	5	17	18	22	17	6	10
29	16 23 40	7 1 16	10♉31	4	6	18	18	22	17	6	10
30	16 27 36	7 58 50	25 37	6	7	18	18	22	17	6	10
31	16 31 33	8 56 23	10♊49	8	8	19	18	22	17	6	10

THE SUN ENTERS THE SIGN OF GEMINI ON MAY 21 AT 16:34.

DAY	TIME	☉	☽	☿	♀	♂	♃	♄	♅	♆	♇
	h m s	° ' "	° '	°	°	°	°	°	°	°	°
J 1	16 35 30	9♊53 55	25♊57	11♊	9♋	19♌	18♎R	22♋	17♊	6♎R	10♌
U 2	16 39 26	10 51 26	10♋51	13	11	20	18	22	17	6	10
N 3	16 43 23	11 48 56	25 26	15	12	20	18	22	17	6	10
E 4	16 47 19	12 46 24	9♌36	17	13	21	18	23	17	6	10
5	16 51 16	13 43 52	23 20	19	14	21	18	23	17	6	10
6	16 55 12	14 41 18	6♍37	21	15	22	18	23	17	6	10
7	16 59 9	15 38 42	19 32	24	17	23	18	23	17	6	10
8	17 3 5	16 36 6	2♎ 6	26	18	23	18	23	18	6	10
9	17 7 2	17 33 29	14 23	28	19	24	18	23	18	6	10
10	17 10 59	18 30 50	26 28	0♋	20	24	17	23	18	6	10
11	17 14 55	19 28 10	8♏24	2	21	25	17	23	18	6	10
12	17 18 52	20 25 30	20 14	4	23	25	17	24	18	6	10
13	17 22 48	21 22 49	2♐ 2	6	24	26	17	24	18	6	10
14	17 26 45	22 20 7	13 51	8	25	26	17 D	24	18	6	10
15	17 30 41	23 17 24	25 42	10	26	27	17	24	18	6	10
16	17 34 38	24 14 41	7♑38	11	27	28	17	24	18	6	10
17	17 38 34	25 11 58	19 42	13	29	28	17	24	18	6 D	10
18	17 42 31	26 9 13	1♒55	15	0♌	29	17	24	18	6	10
19	17 46 28	27 6 29	14 19	17	1	29	17	24	18	6	10
20	17 50 24	28 3 44	26 57	18	2	0♍	17	24	18	6	10
21	17 54 21	29 0 59	9♓51	20	3	0	18	25	18	6	10
22	17 58 17	29 58 13	23 5	22	4	1	18	25	18	6	10
23	18 2 14	0♋55 28	6♈38	23	6	2	18	25	18	6	10
24	18 6 10	1 52 42	20 34	25	7	2	18	25	18	6	10
25	18 10 7	2 49 57	4♉50	26	8	3	18	25	19	6	10
26	18 14 3	3 47 11	19 26	28	9	3	18	25	19	6	10
27	18 18 0	4 44 26	4♊16	29	10	4	18	25	19	6	10
28	18 21 57	5 41 40	19 15	0♌	12	4	18	25	19	6	10
29	18 25 53	6 38 54	4♋15	2	13	5	18	26	19	6	10
30	18 29 50	7 36 8	19 8	3	14	6	18	26	19	6	10

THE SUN ENTERS THE SIGN OF CANCER ON JUN 22 AT 00:45.

♈ ARIES ♉ TAURUS ♊ GEMINI ♋ CANCER ♌ LEO ♍ VIRGO ♎ LIBRA ♏ SCORPIO ♐ SAGITTARIUS ♑ CAPRICORN ♒ AQUARIUS ♓ PISCES

SIDEREAL SUN MOON MERCURY VENUS MARS JUPITER SATURN URANUS NEPTUNE PLUTO

DAY	TIME	☉	☽	☿	♀	♂	♃	♄	♅	♆	♇
	h m s	° ' "	° '	°	°	°	°	°	°	°	°
J 1	18 33 46	8♋33 22	3♌45	4♌	15♌	6♍	18♎	26♋	19♊	6♎	10♌
U 2	18 37 43	9 30 36	18 0	5	16	7	18	26	19	6	10
L 3	18 41 39	10 27 49	1♍51	6	17	7	18	26	19	6	10
Y 4	18 45 36	11 25 2	15 15	7	19	8	18	26	19	6	11
5	18 49 32	12 22 15	28 13	8	20	8	18	26	19	6	11
6	18 53 29	13 19 27	10♎49	9	21	9	18	26	19	6	11
7	18 57 26	14 16 39	23 6	10	22	10	18	27	19	6	11
8	19 1 22	15 13 51	5♏9	11	23	10	18	27	19	6	11
9	19 5 19	16 11 3	17 2	12	24	11	18	27	19	6	11
10	19 9 15	17 8 15	28 51	13	26	11	18	27	19	6	11
11	19 13 12	18 5 27	10♐39	13	27	12	18	27	19	6	11
12	19 17 8	19 2 38	22 30	14	28	13	19	27	19	6	11
13	19 21 5	19 59 51	4♑27	15	29	13	19	27	20	6	11
14	19 25 2	20 57 3	16 33	15	0♍	14	19	27	20	6	11
15	19 28 58	21 54 15	28 49	15	1	14	19	28	20	6	11
16	19 32 55	22 51 28	11♒17	16	3	15	19	28	20	6	11
17	19 36 51	23 48 41	23 58	16	4	16	19	28	20	6	11
18	19 40 48	24 45 55	6♓53	16	5	16	19	28	20	6	11
19	19 44 44	25 43 10	20 0	16 R	6	17	19	28	20	6	11
20	19 48 41	26 40 25	3♈22	16	7	17	19	28	20	6	11
21	19 52 37	27 37 41	16 58	16	8	18	19	28	20	6	11
22	19 56 34	28 34 57	0♉49	16	9	19	19	29	20	6	11
23	20 0 31	29 32 15	14 54	16	11	19	20	29	20	6	11
24	20 4 27	0♌29 33	29 13	16	12	20	20	29	20	6	11
25	20 8 24	1 26 53	13♊42	15	13	20	20	29	20	6	11
26	20 12 20	2 24 13	28 20	15	14	21	20	29	20	6	11
27	20 16 17	3 21 34	13♋0	14	15	22	20	29	20	6	11
28	20 20 13	4 18 56	27 36	14	16	22	20	29	20	6	11
29	20 24 10	5 16 19	12♌2	13	17	23	20	29	20	6	11
30	20 28 6	6 13 42	26 12	12	18	23	20	0♌	20	6	11
31	20 32 3	7 11 7	10♍0	12	20	24	20	0	20	6	11

THE SUN ENTERS THE SIGN OF LEO ON JUL 23 AT 11:38.

DAY	TIME	☉	☽	☿	♀	♂	♃	♄	♅	♆	♇
	h m s	° ' "	° '	°	°	°	°	°	°	°	°
A 1	20 36 0	8♌8 31	23♍24	11♌R	21♍	25♍	21♎	0♌	20♊	6♎	11♌
U 2	20 39 56	9 5 57	6♎24	10	22	25	21	0	20	6	11
G 3	20 43 53	10 3 23	19 2	9	23	26	21	0	21	6	11
U 4	20 47 49	11 0 49	1♏20	9	24	27	21	0	21	6	11
S 5	20 51 46	11 58 17	13 23	8	25	27	21	0	21	6	11
T 6	20 55 42	12 55 45	25 16	7	26	28	21	0	21	6	11
7	20 59 39	13 53 14	7♐5	7	27	28	21	1	21	7	11
8	21 3 35	14 50 44	18 54	6	29	29	21	1	21	7	12
9	21 7 32	15 48 14	0♑48	6	0♎	0♎	22	1	21	7	12
10	21 11 29	16 45 46	12 52	5	1	0	22	1	21	7	12
11	21 15 25	17 43 18	25 8	5	2	1	22	1	21	7	12
12	21 19 22	18 40 52	7♒39	5 D	3	2	22	1	21	7	12
13	21 23 18	19 38 27	20 25	5	4	2	22	1	21	7	12
14	21 27 15	20 36 2	3♓27	5	5	3	22	1	21	7	12
15	21 31 11	21 33 40	16 44	5	6	3	23	2	21	7	12
16	21 35 8	22 31 18	0♈13	5	7	4	23	2	21	7	12
17	21 39 4	23 28 58	13 53	6	8	5	23	2	21	7	12
18	21 43 1	24 26 39	27 41	6	9	5	23	2	21	7	12
19	21 46 58	25 24 22	11♉37	7	10	6	23	2	21	7	12
20	21 50 54	26 22 7	25 40	8	12	7	23	2	21	7	12
21	21 54 51	27 19 53	9♊48	9	13	7	23	2	21	7	12
22	21 58 47	28 17 42	24 0	10	14	8	24	2	21	7	12
23	22 2 44	29 15 32	8♋15	11	15	9	24	3	21	7	12
24	22 6 40	0♍13 23	22 31	12	16	9	24	3	21	7	12
25	22 10 37	1 11 16	6♌43	14	17	10	24	3	21	7	12
26	22 14 33	2 9 11	20 47	15	18	10	24	3	21	7	12
27	22 18 30	3 7 8	4♍39	16	19	11	24	3	21	7	12
28	22 22 27	4 5 6	18 14	18	20	12	25	3	21	7	12
29	22 26 23	5 3 5	1♎30	20	21	12	25	3	21	7	12
30	22 30 20	6 1 6	14 25	21	22	13	25	3	21	7	12
31	22 34 16	6 59 8	27 0	23	23	14	25	3	21	7	12

THE SUN ENTERS THE SIGN OF VIRGO ON AUG 23 AT 18:27.

DAY	TIME	☉	☽	☿	♀	♂	♃	♄	♅	♆	♇
	h m s	° ' "	° '	°	°	°	°	°	°	°	°
S 1	22 38 13	7♍57 12	9♏16	25♌	24♎	14♎	25♎	4♌	21♊	7♎	12♌
E 2	22 42 9	8 55 17	21 19	27	25	15	25	4	22	7	12
P 3	22 46 6	9 53 23	3♐12	29	26	16	26	4	22	7	12
T 4	22 50 2	10 51 31	15 0	1♍	27	16	26	4	22	7	12
E 5	22 53 59	11 49 41	26 50	3	28	17	26	4	22	7	12
M 6	22 57 55	12 47 52	8♑46	4	29	18	26	4	22	7	12
B 7	23 1 52	13 46 4	20 54	6	0♏	18	26	4	22	7	12
E 8	23 5 49	14 44 18	3♒17	8	1	19	27	4	22	7	12
R 9	23 9 45	15 42 34	15 59	10	2	20	27	4	22	8	12
10	23 13 42	16 40 51	29 1	12	3	20	27	5	22	8	12
11	23 17 38	17 39 10	12♓24	14	4	21	27	5	22	8	12
12	23 21 35	18 37 30	26 4	16	5	22	27	5	22	8	12
13	23 25 31	19 35 53	9♈59	18	6	22	28	5	22	8	13
14	23 29 28	20 34 17	24 4	20	7	23	28	5	22	8	13
15	23 33 24	21 32 44	8♉14	22	8	24	28	5	22	8	13
16	23 37 21	22 31 12	22 27	23	8	24	28	5	22	8	13
17	23 41 18	23 29 43	6♊38	25	9	25	28	5	22	8	13
18	23 45 14	24 28 17	20 47	27	10	26	29	5	22	8	13
19	23 49 11	25 26 52	4♋51	29	11	26	29	6	22	8	13
20	23 53 7	26 25 30	18 51	1♎	12	27	29	6	22	8	13
21	23 57 4	27 24 9	2♌46	2	13	28	29	6	22	8	13
22	0 1 0	28 22 51	16 33	4	14	28	29	6	22	8	13
23	0 4 57	29 21 35	0♍12	6	15	29	0♏	6	22	8	13
24	0 8 53	0♎20 22	13 40	8	15	0♏	0	6	22	8	13
25	0 12 50	1 19 10	26 54	9	16	0	0	6	22	8	13
26	0 16 47	2 18 0	9♎53	11	17	1	0	6	22	8	13
27	0 20 43	3 16 52	22 36	13	18	2	0	6	22 R	8	13
28	0 24 40	4 15 46	5♏3	14	19	2	1	6	22	8	13
29	0 28 36	5 14 42	17 14	16	19	3	1	6	22	8	13
30	0 32 33	6 13 40	29 14	18	20	4	1	7	22	8	13

THE SUN ENTERS THE SIGN OF LIBRA ON SEP 23 AT 15:41.

SIDEREAL SUN MOON MERCURY VENUS MARS JUPITER SATURN URANUS NEPTUNE PLUTO

DAY	TIME	☉	☽	☿	♀	♂	♃	♄	♅	♆	♇
	h m s	° ' "	° '	°	°	°	°	°	°	°	°
O 1	0 36 29	7♎12 40	11♐5	19♎	21♏	4♏	1♏	7♌	22♊R	8♎	13♌
C 2	0 40 26	8 11 41	22 53	21	22	5	1	7	22	8	13
T 3	0 44 22	9 10 45	4♑41	22	22	6	2	7	22	8	13
O 4	0 48 19	10 9 50	16 37	24	23	6	2	7	22	8	13
B 5	0 52 16	11 8 57	28 45	26	24	7	2	7	22	8	13
E 6	0 56 12	12 8 5	11♒10	27	24	8	2	7	22	9	13
R 7	1 0 9	13 7 16	23 56	29	25	8	2	7	22	9	13
8	1 4 5	14 6 28	7♓6	0♏	26	9	3	7	22	9	13
9	1 8 2	15 5 42	20 41	2	26	10	3	7	22	9	13
10	1 11 58	16 4 58	4♈39	3	27	10	3	7	22	9	13
11	1 15 55	17 4 16	18 56	5	27	11	3	7	22	9	13
12	1 19 51	18 3 36	3♉26	6	28	12	3	7	22	9	13
13	1 23 48	19 2 58	18 3	8	28	13	4	8	22	9	13
14	1 27 44	20 2 22	2♊40	9	29	13	4	8	22	9	13
15	1 31 41	21 1 49	17 11	10	29	14	4	8	22	9	13
16	1 35 38	22 1 18	1♋33	12	0♐	15	4	8	22	9	13
17	1 39 34	23 0 50	15 43	13	0	15	5	8	22	9	13
18	1 43 31	24 0 23	29 40	15	1	16	5	8	22	9	13
19	1 47 27	24 59 59	13♌23	16	1	17	5	8	22	9	13
20	1 51 24	25 59 37	26 53	17	1	17	5	8	22	9	13
21	1 55 20	26 59 18	10♍10	19	2	18	5	8	22	9	13
22	1 59 17	27 59 0	23 15	20	2	19	6	8	22	9	13
23	2 3 13	28 58 45	6♎6	21	2	20	6	8	22	9	13
24	2 7 10	29 58 32	18 45	22	2	20	6	8	22	9	13
25	2 11 7	0♏58 21	1♏11	24	2	21	6	8	21	9	13
26	2 15 3	1 58 12	13 26	25	2	22	7	8	21	9	13
27	2 19 0	2 58 4	25 29	26	2	22	7	8	21	9	13
28	2 22 56	3 57 59	7♐24	27	2 R	23	7	8	21	9	13
29	2 26 53	4 57 56	19 13	28	2	24	7	8	21	9	13
30	2 30 49	5 57 54	0♑59	0♐	2	24	7	8	21	9	13
31	2 34 46	6 57 54	12 47	1	2	25	8	8	21	9	13

THE SUN ENTERS THE SIGN OF SCORPIO ON OCT 24 AT 00:36.

DAY	TIME	☉	☽	☿	♀	♂	♃	♄	♅	♆	♇
	h m s	° ' "	° '	°	°	°	°	°	°	°	°
N 1	2 38 42	7♏57 55	24♑41	2♐	2♐R	26♏	8♏	9♌	21♊R	9♎	13♌
O 2	2 42 39	8 57 59	6♒46	2	2	27	8	9	21	9	13
V 3	2 46 36	9 58 3	19 8	3	2	27	8	9	21	10	13
E 4	2 50 32	10 58 10	1♓52	4	2	28	8	9	21	10	13
M 5	2 54 29	11 58 17	14 59	5	1	29	9	9	21	10	13
B 6	2 58 25	12 58 27	28 34	6	1	29	9	9	21	10	13
E 7	3 2 22	13 58 38	12♈37	6	1	0♐	9	9	21	10	13
R 8	3 6 18	14 58 50	27 3	7	0	1	9	9	21	10	13
9	3 10 15	15 59 4	11♉49	7	0	2	10	9	21	10	13
10	3 14 11	16 59 20	26 47	7	29♏	2	10	9	21	10	13
11	3 18 8	17 59 38	11♊49	7 R	29	3	10	9	21	10	13
12	3 22 5	18 59 58	26 45	7	28	4	10	9	21	10	13
13	3 26 1	20 0 20	11♋29	7	28	4	10	9	21	10	13
14	3 29 58	21 0 43	25 55	7	27	5	11	9	21	10	13
15	3 33 54	22 1 9	10♌1	6	27	6	11	9	21	10	13 R
16	3 37 51	23 1 36	23 46	5	26	7	11	9	21	10	13
17	3 41 47	24 2 5	7♍10	5	25	7	11	9	21	10	13
18	3 45 44	25 2 36	20 16	4	25	8	12	9	21	10	13
19	3 49 41	26 3 9	3♎4	2	24	9	12	9	21	10	13
20	3 53 37	27 3 43	15 37	1	24	10	12	9 R	21	10	13
21	3 57 34	28 4 19	27 58	0	23	10	12	9	21	10	13
22	4 1 30	29 4 57	10♏9	28♏	22	11	12	9	21	10	13
23	4 5 27	0♐5 36	22 11	27	22	12	13	9	21	10	13
24	4 9 23	1 6 17	4♐6	26	21	13	13	9	21	10	13
25	4 13 20	2 6 59	15 55	25	21	13	13	9	20	10	13
26	4 17 16	3 7 43	27 43	24	20	14	13	9	20	10	13
27	4 21 13	4 8 28	9♑29	23	20	15	13	9	20	10	13
28	4 25 10	5 9 14	21 19	22	19	15	14	9	20	10	13
29	4 29 6	6 10 1	3♒15	22	19	16	14	9	20	10	13
30	4 33 3	7 10 49	15 20	21	19	17	14	9	20	10	13

THE SUN ENTERS THE SIGN OF SAGITTARIUS ON NOV 22 AT 21:47.

DAY	TIME	☉	☽	☿	♀	♂	♃	♄	♅	♆	♇
	h m s	° ' "	° '	°	°	°	°	°	°	°	°
D 1	4 36 59	8♐11 38	27♒39	21♏D	18♏R	18♐	14♏	9♌R	20♊R	10♎	13♌R
E 2	4 40 56	9 12 27	10♓17	21	18	18	15	9	20	10	13
C 3	4 44 52	10 13 18	23 17	21	18	19	15	9	20	10	13
E 4	4 48 49	11 14 9	6♈43	22	18	20	15	9	20	10	13
M 5	4 52 45	12 15 2	20 36	22	17	21	15	9	20	10	13
B 6	4 56 42	13 15 55	4♉56	23	17	21	15	9	20	10	13
E 7	5 0 39	14 16 49	19 41	24	17	22	16	9	20	10	13
R 8	5 4 35	15 17 44	4♊44	25	17 D	23	16	9	20	10	13
9	5 8 32	16 18 40	19 57	26	17	24	16	9	20	10	13
10	5 12 28	17 19 37	5♋10	27	17	24	16	9	20	10	13
11	5 16 25	18 20 35	20 15	28	17	25	16	9	20	11	13
12	5 20 21	19 21 33	5♌1	29	17	26	17	8	20	11	13
13	5 24 18	20 22 33	19 25	0♐	18	27	17	8	20	11	13
14	5 28 14	21 23 34	3♍21	1	18	27	17	8	20	11	13
15	5 32 11	22 24 36	16 51	2	18	28	17	8	20	11	13
16	5 36 8	23 25 39	29 56	4	18	29	17	8	20	11	13
17	5 40 4	24 26 42	12♎38	5	19	0♑	18	8	20	11	13
18	5 44 1	25 27 47	25 3	6	19	0	18	8	20	11	13
19	5 47 57	26 28 53	7♏13	8	19	1	18	8	19	11	13
20	5 51 54	27 29 59	19 12	9	20	2	18	8	19	11	13
21	5 55 50	28 31 6	1♐5	11	20	3	18	8	19	11	13
22	5 59 47	29 32 14	12 53	12	21	3	19	8	19	11	13
23	6 3 43	0♑33 22	24 40	14	21	4	19	8	19	11	13
24	6 7 40	1 34 31	6♑28	15	22	5	19	8	19	11	13
25	6 11 37	2 35 40	18 19	16	22	6	19	8	19	11	13
26	6 15 33	3 36 50	0♒15	18	23	6	19	8	19	11	13
27	6 19 30	4 37 59	12 18	19	23	7	19	8	19	11	13
28	6 23 26	5 39 9	24 29	21	24	8	20	8	19	11	13
29	6 27 23	6 40 19	6♓53	22	24	9	20	8	19	11	13
30	6 31 19	7 41 28	19 31	24	25	10	20	8	19	11	13
31	6 35 16	8 42 38	2♈26	25	26	10	20	7	19	11	13

THE SUN ENTERS THE SIGN OF CAPRICORN ON DEC 22 AT 10:54.

♈ ARIES ♉ TAURUS ♊ GEMINI ♋ CANCER ♌ LEO ♍ VIRGO ♎ LIBRA ♏ SCORPIO ♐ SAGITTARIUS ♑ CAPRICORN ♒ AQUARIUS ♓ PISCES

1947

SIDEREAL SUN MOON MERCURY VENUS MARS JUPITER SATURN URANUS NEPTUNE PLUTO

DAY	TIME	☉	☽	☿	♀	♂	♃	♄	♅	♆	♇
	h m s	° ' "	° '	°	°	°	°	°	°	°	°
J 1	6 39 12	9♑43 47	15♈42	27♐	27♏	11♑	20♏	7♌R	19♊R	11♎	13♌R
A 2	6 43 9	10 44 56	29 22	28	27	12	21	7	19	11	13
N 3	6 47 6	11 46 5	13♉26	0♑	28	13	21	7	19	11	13
U 4	6 51 2	12 47 14	27 54	1	29	13	21	7	19	11	13
A 5	6 54 59	13 48 22	12♊43	3	29	14	21	7	19	11	13
R 6	6 58 55	14 49 31	27 48	4	0♐	15	21	7	19	11	13
Y 7	7 2 52	15 50 39	13♋ 1	6	1	16	21	7	19	11	13
8	7 6 48	16 51 47	28 11	8	2	16	22	7	19	11	13
9	7 10 45	17 52 55	13♌ 9	9	3	17	22	7	19	11	13
10	7 14 42	18 54 2	27 45	11	4	18	22	7	19	11	13
11	7 18 38	19 55 10	11♍55	12	4	19	22	7	19	11	13
12	7 22 35	20 56 17	25 36	14	5	20	22	7	19	11 R	13
13	7 26 31	21 57 24	8♎48	15	6	20	22	7	19	11	13
14	7 30 28	22 58 32	21 34	17	7	21	23	6	18	11	13
15	7 34 24	23 59 39	3♏58	19	8	22	23	6	18	11	13
16	7 38 21	25 0 46	16 5	20	9	23	23	6	18	11	13
17	7 42 17	26 1 53	28 0	22	10	23	23	6	18	11	13
18	7 46 14	27 2 59	9♐48	24	11	24	23	6	18	11	13
19	7 50 11	28 4 5	21 34	25	12	25	23	6	18	11	13
20	7 54 7	29 5 11	3♑21	27	13	26	23	6	18	11	12
21	7 58 4	0♒ 6 16	15 13	29	13	27	24	6	18	11	12
22	8 2 0	1 7 21	27 11	0♒	14	27	24	6	18	11	12
23	8 5 57	2 8 25	9♒17	2	15	28	24	6	18	11	12
24	8 9 53	3 9 28	21 32	4	16	29	24	6	18	11	12
25	8 13 50	4 10 30	3♓58	5	17	0♒	24	6	18	11	12
26	8 17 46	5 11 31	16 34	7	18	0	24	5	18	11	12
27	8 21 43	6 12 32	29 22	9	19	1	24	5	18	11	12
28	8 25 40	7 13 31	12♈23	10	20	2	25	5	18	11	12
29	8 29 36	8 14 29	25 39	12	21	3	25	5	18	11	12
30	8 33 33	9 15 25	9♉12	14	22	4	25	5	18	11	12
31	8 37 29	10 16 21	23 2	16	23	4	25	5	18	11	12

THE SUN ENTERS THE SIGN OF AQUARIUS ON JAN 20 AT 21:32.

DAY	TIME	☉	☽	☿	♀	♂	♃	♄	♅	♆	♇
	h m s	° ' "	° '	°	°	°	°	°	°	°	°
F 1	8 41 26	11♒17 15	7♊12	17♒	24♐	5♒	25♏	5♌R	18♊R	11♎R	12♌R
E 2	8 45 22	12 18 8	21 39	19	26	6	25	5	18	11	12
B 3	8 49 19	13 19 0	6♋23	21	27	7	25	5	18	11	12
R 4	8 53 15	14 19 50	21 16	23	28	7	25	5	18	11	12
U 5	8 57 12	15 20 39	6♌12	25	29	8	25	5	18	11	12
A 6	9 1 9	16 21 27	21 2	26	0♑	9	26	5	18	11	12
R 7	9 5 5	17 22 13	5♍37	28	1	10	26	4	18	11	12
Y 8	9 9 2	18 22 58	19 49	0♓	2	11	26	4	18	11	12
9	9 12 58	19 23 43	3♎35	2	3	11	26	4	18	11	12
10	9 16 55	20 24 26	16 54	3	4	12	26	4	18	11	12
11	9 20 51	21 25 8	29 45	5	5	13	26	4	18	11	12
12	9 24 48	22 25 49	12♏13	7	6	14	26	4	18	11	12
13	9 28 44	23 26 29	24 22	8	7	14	26	4	18	11	12
14	9 32 41	24 27 8	6♐19	10	8	15	26	4	18	11	12
15	9 36 38	25 27 45	18 7	12	9	16	26	4	18	11	12
16	9 40 34	26 28 22	29 54	13	11	17	26	4	18	10	12
17	9 44 31	27 28 57	11♑43	15	12	18	27	4	18	10	12
18	9 48 27	28 29 31	23 39	16	13	18	27	4	18	10	12
19	9 52 24	29 30 3	5♒45	17	14	19	27	4	18	10	12
20	9 56 20	0♓30 34	18 2	19	15	20	27	4	18	10	12
21	10 0 17	1 31 4	0♓33	20	16	21	27	3	18	10	12
22	10 4 13	2 31 32	13 16	21	17	22	27	3	18	10	12
23	10 8 10	3 31 58	26 13	21	18	22	27	3	18	10	12
24	10 12 7	4 32 22	9♈20	22	20	23	27	3	18	10	12
25	10 16 3	5 32 44	22 39	23	21	24	27	3	18 D	10	12
26	10 20 0	6 33 5	6♉ 7	23	22	25	27	3	18	10	12
27	10 23 56	7 33 24	19 46	23 R	23	26	27	3	18	10	12
28	10 27 53	8 33 41	3♊36	23	24	26	27	3	18	10	12

THE SUN ENTERS THE SIGN OF PISCES ON FEB 19 AT 11:52.

DAY	TIME	☉	☽	☿	♀	♂	♃	♄	♅	♆	♇
	h m s	° ' "	° '	°	°	°	°	°	°	°	°
M 1	10 31 49	9♓33 55	17♊36	23♓R	25♑	27♒	27♏	3♌R	18♊	10♎R	12♌R
A 2	10 35 46	10 34 8	1♋48	23	26	28	27	3	18	10	12
R 3	10 39 42	11 34 18	16 8	22	27	29	27	3	18	10	12
C 4	10 43 39	12 34 27	0♌36	22	29	29	27	3	18	10	12
H 5	10 47 36	13 34 33	15 6	21	0♒	0♓	27	3	18	10	12
6	10 51 32	14 34 38	29 32	20	1	1	27	3	18	10	11
7	10 55 29	15 34 40	13♍48	19	2	2	27	3	18	10	11
8	10 59 25	16 34 40	27 47	18	3	3	27	3	18	10	11
9	11 3 22	17 34 39	11♎26	17	4	3	28	3	18	10	11
10	11 7 18	18 34 36	24 41	16	6	4	28	3	18	10	11
11	11 11 15	19 34 31	7♏32	15	7	5	28	2	18	10	11
12	11 15 11	20 34 24	20 2	14	8	6	28	2	18	10	11
13	11 19 8	21 34 16	2♐14	14	9	7	28	2	18	10	11
14	11 23 5	22 34 6	14 13	13	10	7	28 R	2	18	10	11
15	11 27 1	23 33 55	26 4	12	11	8	28	2	18	10	11
16	11 30 58	24 33 41	7♑52	11	12	9	28	2	18	10	11
17	11 34 54	25 33 26	19 43	11	14	10	28	2	18	10	11
18	11 38 51	26 33 10	1♒43	10	15	10	28	2	18	10	11
19	11 42 47	27 32 51	13 54	10	16	11	28	2	18	10	11
20	11 46 44	28 32 31	26 20	9	17	12	28	2	18	10	11
21	11 50 40	29 32 8	9♓ 4	9	18	13	27	2	18	10	11
22	11 54 37	0♈31 44	22 4	9 D	19	14	27	2	18	10	11
23	11 58 33	1 31 18	5♈21	9	21	14	27	2	18	10	11
24	12 2 30	2 30 50	18 52	9	22	15	27	2	18	10	11
25	12 6 27	3 30 19	2♉35	10	23	16	27	2	18	10	11
26	12 10 23	4 29 47	16 27	10	24	17	27	2	18	10	11
27	12 14 20	5 29 12	0♊26	10	25	18	27	2	18	10	11
28	12 18 16	6 28 35	14 28	11	27	18	27	2	18	10	11
29	12 22 13	7 27 56	28 34	11	28	19	27	2	18	9	11
30	12 26 9	8 27 14	12♋42	12	29	20	27	2	18	9	11
31	12 30 6	9 26 30	26 50	12	0♓	21	27	2	18	9	11

THE SUN ENTERS THE SIGN OF ARIES ON MAR 21 AT 11:13.

SIDEREAL SUN MOON MERCURY VENUS MARS JUPITER SATURN URANUS NEPTUNE PLUTO

DAY	TIME	☉	☽	☿	♀	♂	♃	♄	♅	♆	♇
	h m s	° ' "	° '	°	°	°	°	°	°	°	°
A 1	12 34 2	10♈25 44	10♌58	13♓	1♓	21♓	27♏R	2♌R	18♊	9♎R	11♌R
P 2	12 37 59	11 24 55	25 2	14	2	22	27	2	18	9	11
R 3	12 41 56	12 24 4	9♍ 0	15	4	23	27	2 D	18	9	11
I 4	12 45 52	13 23 11	22 48	16	5	24	27	2	18	9	11
L 5	12 49 49	14 22 15	6♎23	17	6	25	27	2	18	9	11
6	12 53 45	15 21 18	19 42	18	7	25	27	2	18	9	11
7	12 57 42	16 20 18	2♏43	19	8	26	27	2	18	9	11
8	13 1 38	17 19 17	15 25	20	10	27	27	2	19	9	11
9	13 5 35	18 18 13	27 51	21	11	28	27	2	19	9	11
10	13 9 31	19 17 8	10♐ 1	22	12	28	26	2	19	9	11
11	13 13 28	20 16 1	22 0	23	13	29	26	2	19	9	11
12	13 17 25	21 14 53	3♑52	24	14	0♈	26	2	19	9	11
13	13 21 21	22 13 42	15 42	26	16	1	26	2	19	9	11
14	13 25 18	23 12 30	27 35	27	17	2	26	2	19	9	11
15	13 29 14	24 11 16	9♒35	28	18	2	26	2	19	9	11
16	13 33 11	25 10 1	21 49	0☉	19	3	26	2	19	9	11
17	13 37 7	26 8 43	4♓19	1♈	20	4	26	2	19	9	11
18	13 41 4	27 7 24	17 8	3	21	5	26	2	19	9	11
19	13 45 0	28 6 3	0♈19	4	23	5	26	2	19	9	11
20	13 48 57	29 4 40	13 51	6	24	6	26	2	19	9	11
21	13 52 54	0♉ 3 16	27 42	7	25	7	25	2	19	9	11
22	13 56 50	1 1 49	11♉49	9	26	8	25	2	19	9	11
23	14 0 47	2 0 21	26 7	10	27	9	25	2	19	9	11 D
24	14 4 43	2 58 51	10♊32	12	29	9	25	2	19	9	11
25	14 8 40	3 57 19	24 58	13	0☉	10	25	2	19	9	11
26	14 12 36	4 55 44	9♋22	15	1♈	11	25	2	19	9	11
27	14 16 33	5 54 7	23 39	17	2	12	25	2	19	9	11
28	14 20 29	6 52 29	7♌48	19	3	12	25	2	19	9	11
29	14 24 26	7 50 48	21 47	20	5	13	25	3	19	9	11
30	14 28 23	8 49 5	5♍35	22	6	14	24	3	19	9	11

THE SUN ENTERS THE SIGN OF TAURUS ON APR 20 AT 22:40.

DAY	TIME	☉	☽	☿	♀	♂	♃	♄	♅	♆	♇
	h m s	° ' "	° '	°	°	°	°	°	°	°	°
M 1	14 32 19	9♉47 20	19♍10	24♈	7♈	15♈	24♏R	3♌	19♊	9♎R	11♌
A 2	14 36 16	10 45 32	2♎33	26	8	15	24	3	20	9	11
Y 3	14 40 12	11 43 43	15 42	28	9	16	24	3	20	9	11
4	14 44 9	12 41 52	28 37	0♉	11	17	24	3	20	9	11
5	14 48 5	13 40 0	11♏18	1	12	18	24	3	20	9	11
6	14 52 2	14 38 5	23 46	3	13	19	24	3	20	9	11
7	14 55 58	15 36 9	6♐ 1	5	14	19	24	3	20	9	11
8	14 59 55	16 34 12	18 6	7	15	20	24	3	20	8	11
9	15 3 52	17 32 13	0♑ 2	9	17	21	23	3	20	8	11
10	15 7 48	18 30 13	11 54	12	18	22	23	3	20	8	11
11	15 11 45	19 28 11	23 44	14	19	22	23	3	20	8	11
12	15 15 41	20 26 8	5♒37	16	20	23	23	3	20	8	11
13	15 19 38	21 24 3	17 37	18	21	24	23	3	20	8	11
14	15 23 34	22 21 57	29 49	20	23	25	23	3	20	8	11
15	15 27 31	23 19 50	12♓18	22	24	25	23	3	20	8	11
16	15 31 27	24 17 42	25 7	24	25	26	22	4	20	8	11
17	15 35 24	25 15 32	8♈20	27	26	27	22	4	20	8	11
18	15 39 21	26 13 22	21 57	29	27	28	22	4	20	8	11
19	15 43 17	27 11 10	5♉58	1♊	29	28	22	4	20	8	11
20	15 47 14	28 8 56	20 21	3	0♉	29	22	4	20	8	11
21	15 51 10	29 6 42	5♊ 0	5	1	0♉	22	4	21	8	11
22	15 55 7	0♊ 4 26	19 49	7	2	1	22	4	21	8	11
23	15 59 3	1 2 9	4♋40	10	4	1	22	4	21	8	11
24	16 3 0	1 59 50	19 27	12	5	2	21	4	21	8	11
25	16 6 56	2 57 30	4♌ 3	14	6	3	21	4	21	8	11
26	16 10 53	3 55 8	18 23	16	7	4	21	4	21	8	11
27	16 14 50	4 52 45	2♍25	18	8	4	21	4	21	8	11
28	16 18 46	5 50 20	16 7	20	10	5	21	4	21	8	11
29	16 22 43	6 47 54	29 30	22	11	6	21	5	21	8	11
30	16 26 39	7 45 26	12♎35	24	12	7	21	5	21	8	11
31	16 30 36	8 42 57	25 24	25	13	7	21	5	21	8	11

THE SUN ENTERS THE SIGN OF GEMINI ON MAY 21 AT 22:09.

DAY	TIME	☉	☽	☿	♀	♂	♃	♄	♅	♆	♇
	h m s	° ' "	° '	°	°	°	°	°	°	°	°
J 1	16 34 32	9♊40 27	7♏59	27♊	14♉	8♉	21♏R	5♌	21♊	8♎R	11♌
U 2	16 38 29	10 37 55	20 22	29	16	9	20	5	21	8	11
N 3	16 42 25	11 35 22	2♐35	1♋	17	10	20	5	21	8	11
E 4	16 46 22	12 32 49	14 39	2	18	10	20	5	21	8	11
5	16 50 19	13 30 14	26 36	4	19	11	20	5	21	8	11
6	16 54 15	14 27 39	8♑28	6	20	12	20	5	21	8	11
7	16 58 12	15 25 3	20 19	7	22	13	20	5	22	8	11
8	17 2 8	16 22 26	2♒ 9	9	23	13	20	5	22	8	11
9	17 6 5	17 19 48	14 3	10	24	14	20	6	22	8	11
10	17 10 1	18 17 10	26 4	11	25	15	20	6	22	8	11
11	17 13 58	19 14 31	8♓15	13	26	15	19	6	22	8	11
12	17 17 54	20 11 52	20 42	14	28	16	19	6	22	8	12
13	17 21 51	21 9 12	3♈27	15	29	17	19	6	22	8	12
14	17 25 48	22 6 32	16 35	16	0♊	18	19	6	22	8	12
15	17 29 44	23 3 51	0♉ 8	18	1	18	19	6	22	8	12
16	17 33 41	24 1 10	14 8	19	3	19	19	6	22	8	12
17	17 37 37	24 58 29	28 33	20	4	20	19	6	22	8	12
18	17 41 34	25 55 47	13♊21	21	5	21	19	7	22	8	12
19	17 45 30	26 53 5	28 24	21	6	21	19	7	22	8 D	12
20	17 49 27	27 50 22	13♋34	22	7	22	19	7	22	8	12
21	17 53 24	28 47 39	28 41	23	9	23	19	7	22	8	12
22	17 57 20	29 44 55	13♌36	24	10	23	19	7	22	8	12
23	18 1 17	0♋42 11	28 11	24	11	24	18	7	22	8	12
24	18 5 13	1 39 25	12♍23	25	12	25	18	7	23	8	12
25	18 9 10	2 36 39	26 9	26	13	26	18	7	23	8	12
26	18 13 6	3 33 53	9♎29	26	15	26	18	7	23	8	12
27	18 17 3	4 31 6	22 27	26	16	27	18	8	23	8	12
28	18 20 59	5 28 18	5♏ 5	27	17	28	18	8	23	8	12
29	18 24 56	6 25 30	17 27	27	18	28	18	8	23	8	12
30	18 28 53	7 22 41	29 37	27	20	29	18	8	23	8	12

THE SUN ENTERS THE SIGN OF CANCER ON JUN 22 AT 06:19.

♈ ARIES ♉ TAURUS ♊ GEMINI ♋ CANCER ♌ LEO ♍ VIRGO ♎ LIBRA ♏ SCORPIO ♐ SAGITTARIUS ♑ CAPRICORN ♒ AQUARIUS ♓ PISCES

SIDEREAL SUN MOON MERCURY VENUS MARS JUPITER SATURN URANUS NEPTUNE PLUTO

DAY	TIME	☉	☽	☿	♀	♂	♃	♄	♅	♆	♇
	h m s	° ' "	° '	°	°	°	°	°	°	°	°
J 1	18 32 49	8♋19 53	11♐38	27♋R	21♊	0♊	18♏R	8♌	23♊	8♎	12♌
U 2	18 36 46	9 17 4	23 33	27	22	1	18	8	23	8	12
L 3	18 40 42	10 14 14	5♑24	27	23	1	18	8	23	8	12
Y 4	18 44 39	11 11 25	17 15	27	24	2	18	8	23	8	12
5	18 48 35	12 8 36	29 6	27	26	3	18	8	23	8	12
6	18 52 32	13 5 47	10♒59	26	27	3	18	9	23	8	12
7	18 56 28	14 2 58	22 57	26	28	4	18	9	23	8	12
8	19 0 25	15 0 9	5♓ 1	26	29	5	18	9	23	8	12
9	19 4 22	15 57 20	17 15	25	1♋	6	18	9	23	8	12
10	19 8 18	16 54 32	29 42	24	2	6	18	9	23	8	12
11	19 12 15	17 51 44	12♈25	24	3	7	18	9	24	8	12
12	19 16 11	18 48 57	25 27	23	4	8	18	9	24	8	12
13	19 20 8	19 46 10	8♉53	23	5	8	18	9	24	8	12
14	19 24 4	20 43 24	22 44	22	7	9	18	10	24	8	12
15	19 28 1	21 40 38	7♊ 2	21	8	10	18 D	10	24	8	12
16	19 31 57	22 37 53	21 44	21	9	10	18	10	24	8	12
17	19 35 54	23 35 9	6♋46	20	10	11	18	10	24	8	12
18	19 39 51	24 32 25	22 0	19	12	12	18	10	24	8	12
19	19 43 47	25 29 41	7♌15	19	13	13	18	10	24	8	12
20	19 47 44	26 26 58	22 21	18	14	13	18	10	24	8	12
21	19 51 40	27 24 15	7♍ 9	18	15	14	18	10	24	8	12
22	19 55 37	28 21 32	21 31	18	16	15	18	11	24	8	13
23	19 59 33	29 18 50	5♎24	17	18	15	18	11	24	8	13
24	20 3 30	0♌16 8	18 48	17	19	16	18	11	24	8	13
25	20 7 26	1 13 26	1♏46	17 D	20	17	18	11	24	8	13
26	20 11 23	2 10 45	14 21	17	21	17	18	11	24	8	13
27	20 15 20	3 8 4	26 38	17	23	18	18	11	24	8	13
28	20 19 16	4 5 23	8♐41	17	24	19	18	11	24	8	13
29	20 23 13	5 2 43	20 36	18	25	19	18	11	24	8	13
30	20 27 9	6 0 4	2♑27	18	26	20	18	12	24	8	13
31	20 31 6	6 57 25	14 16	18	27	21	18	12	25	8	13

THE SUN ENTERS THE SIGN OF LEO ON JUL 23 AT 17:15.

DAY	TIME	☉	☽	☿	♀	♂	♃	♄	♅	♆	♇
	h m s	° ' "	° '	°	°	°	°	°	°	°	°
A 1	20 35 2	7♌54 47	26♑ 7	19♋	29♋	21♊	18♏	12♌	25♊	8♎	13♌
U 2	20 38 59	8 52 10	8♒ 2	20	0♌	22	18	12	25	9	13
G 3	20 42 55	9 49 34	20 1	21	1	23	18	12	25	9	13
U 4	20 46 52	10 46 58	2♓ 7	21	2	23	18	12	25	9	13
S 5	20 50 49	11 44 24	14 20	22	4	24	18	12	25	9	13
T 6	20 54 45	12 41 50	26 42	24	5	25	18	12	25	9	13
7	20 58 42	13 39 18	9♈16	25	6	25	18	13	25	9	13
8	21 2 38	14 36 47	22 2	26	7	26	18	13	25	9	13
9	21 6 35	15 34 18	5♉ 4	27	9	27	19	13	25	9	13
10	21 10 31	16 31 49	18 26	29	10	27	19	13	25	9	13
11	21 14 28	17 29 23	2♊ 8	0♌	11	28	19	13	25	9	13
12	21 18 24	18 26 58	16 14	2	12	29	19	13	25	9	13
13	21 22 21	19 24 34	0♋43	4	13	29	19	13	25	9	13
14	21 26 18	20 22 11	15 31	5	15	0♋	19	13	25	9	13
15	21 30 14	21 19 51	0♌34	7	16	1	19	14	25	9	13
16	21 34 11	22 17 31	15 41	9	17	1	19	14	25	9	13
17	21 38 7	23 15 13	0♍44	11	18	2	19	14	25	9	13
18	21 42 4	24 12 55	15 32	13	20	3	19	14	25	9	13
19	21 46 0	25 10 39	29 57	15	21	3	19	14	25	9	13
20	21 49 57	26 8 25	13♎55	17	22	4	19	14	25	9	13
21	21 53 53	27 6 11	27 23	19	23	5	20	14	25	9	13
22	21 57 50	28 3 58	10♏24	21	25	5	20	15	25	9	13
23	22 1 47	29 1 47	23 1	23	26	6	20	15	25	9	13
24	22 5 43	29 59 37	5♐18	25	27	7	20	15	26	9	14
25	22 9 40	0♍57 28	17 21	27	28	7	20	15	26	9	14
26	22 13 36	1 55 21	29 15	29	0♍	8	20	15	26	9	14
27	22 17 33	2 53 14	11♑ 5	1♍	1	9	20	15	26	9	14
28	22 21 29	3 51 9	22 55	3	2	9	20	15	26	9	14
29	22 25 26	4 49 6	4♒49	5	3	10	20	15	26	9	14
30	22 29 22	5 47 3	16 49	7	5	10	21	16	26	9	14
31	22 33 19	6 45 3	28 57	9	6	11	21	16	26	9	14

THE SUN ENTERS THE SIGN OF VIRGO ON AUG 24 AT 00:10.

DAY	TIME	☉	☽	☿	♀	♂	♃	♄	♅	♆	♇
	h m s	° ' "	° '	°	°	°	°	°	°	°	°
S 1	22 37 16	7♍43 3	11♓14	10♍	7♍	12♋	21♏	16♌	26♊	9♎	14♌
E 2	22 41 12	8 41 6	23 41	12	8	12	21	16	26	9	14
P 3	22 45 9	9 39 10	6♈18	14	9	13	21	16	26	9	14
T 4	22 49 5	10 37 16	19 6	16	11	14	21	16	26	9	14
E 5	22 53 2	11 35 24	2♉ 5	18	12	14	21	16	26	9	14
M 6	22 56 58	12 33 34	15 16	20	13	15	21	16	26	10	14
B 7	23 0 55	13 31 46	28 42	22	14	15	22	16	26	10	14
E 8	23 4 51	14 30 0	12♊23	23	16	16	22	17	26	10	14
R 9	23 8 48	15 28 16	26 21	25	17	17	22	17	26	10	14
10	23 12 45	16 26 34	10♋35	27	18	17	22	17	26	10	14
11	23 16 41	17 24 54	25 5	29	19	18	22	17	26	10	14
12	23 20 38	18 23 17	9♌47	0♎	21	19	22	17	26	10	14
13	23 24 34	19 21 41	24 33	2	22	19	23	17	26	10	14
14	23 28 31	20 20 7	9♍17	4	23	20	23	17	26	10	14
15	23 32 27	21 18 35	23 51	5	24	20	23	17	26	10	14
16	23 36 24	22 17 5	8♎ 7	7	26	21	23	18	26	10	14
17	23 40 20	23 15 37	22 0	8	27	22	23	18	26	10	14
18	23 44 17	24 14 11	5♏27	10	28	22	23	18	26	10	14
19	23 48 14	25 12 46	18 29	12	29	23	23	18	26	10	14
20	23 52 10	26 11 23	1♐ 8	13	1♎	23	24	18	26	10	14
21	23 56 7	27 10 2	13 27	15	2	24	24	18	26	10	14
22	0 0 3	28 8 43	25 32	16	3	25	24	18	26	10	14
23	0 4 0	29 7 25	7♑27	18	4	25	24	18	26	10	14
24	0 7 56	0♎ 6 9	19 18	19	6	26	24	18	26	10	14
25	0 11 53	1 4 55	1♒10	21	7	26	24	19	26	10	14
26	0 15 49	2 3 42	13 7	22	8	27	25	19	26	10	14
27	0 19 46	3 2 31	25 13	24	9	28	25	19	26	10	14
28	0 23 43	4 1 22	7♓29	25	11	28	25	19	26	10	14
29	0 27 39	5 0 15	19 58	26	12	29	25	19	26	10	14
30	0 31 36	5 59 10	2♈41	28	13	29	25	19	26	10	14

THE SUN ENTERS THE SIGN OF LIBRA ON SEP 23 AT 21:29.

SIDEREAL SUN MOON MERCURY VENUS MARS JUPITER SATURN URANUS NEPTUNE PLUTO

DAY	TIME	☉	☽	☿	♀	♂	♃	♄	♅	♆	♇
	h m s	° ' "	° '	°	°	°	°	°	°	°	°
O 1	0 35 32	6♎58 7	15♈37	29♎	14♎	0♌	25♏	19♌	26♊	10♎	14♌
C 2	0 39 29	7 57 6	28 45	0♏	16	1	26	19	26 R	10	14
T 3	0 43 25	8 56 7	12♉ 5	2	17	1	26	19	26	10	15
O 4	0 47 22	9 55 10	25 36	3	18	2	26	19	26	11	15
B 5	0 51 18	10 54 16	9♊18	4	19	2	26	20	26	11	15
E 6	0 55 15	11 53 24	23 8	6	21	3	26	20	26	11	15
R 7	0 59 12	12 52 34	7♋ 8	7	22	3	27	20	26	11	15
8	1 3 8	13 51 47	21 17	8	23	4	27	20	26	11	15
9	1 7 5	14 51 2	5♌32	9	24	5	27	20	26	11	15
10	1 11 1	15 50 19	19 52	10	26	5	27	20	26	11	15
11	1 14 58	16 49 39	4♍12	12	27	6	27	20	26	11	15
12	1 18 54	17 49 0	18 29	13	28	6	28	20	26	11	15
13	1 22 51	18 48 24	2♎37	14	29	7	28	20	26	11	15
14	1 26 47	19 47 51	16 31	15	1♏	7	28	20	26	11	15
15	1 30 44	20 47 19	0♏ 8	16	2	8	28	20	26	11	15
16	1 34 40	21 46 49	13 25	17	3	8	28	21	26	11	15
17	1 38 37	22 46 21	26 21	17	4	9	29	21	26	11	15
18	1 42 34	23 45 55	8♐58	18	6	9	29	21	26	11	15
19	1 46 30	24 45 31	21 17	19	7	10	29	21	26	11	15
20	1 50 27	25 45 9	3♑23	20	8	11	29	21	26	11	15
21	1 54 23	26 44 49	15 20	20	9	11	29	21	26	11	15
22	1 58 20	27 44 30	27 12	21	11	12	0♐	21	26	11	15
23	2 2 16	28 44 13	9♒ 5	21	12	12	0	21	26	11	15
24	2 6 13	29 43 57	21 3	21	13	13	0	21	26	11	15
25	2 10 9	0♏43 44	3♓10	21 R	14	13	0	21	26	11	15
26	2 14 6	1 43 32	15 31	21	15	14	0	21	26	11	15
27	2 18 3	2 43 22	28 8	21	17	14	1	21	26	11	15
28	2 21 59	3 43 13	11♈ 2	21	18	15	1	21	26	11	15
29	2 25 56	4 43 7	24 15	21	19	15	1	21	26	11	15
30	2 29 52	5 43 2	7♉45	20	20	16	1	22	26	11	15
31	2 33 49	6 43 0	21 31	19	22	16	1	22	26	12	15

THE SUN ENTERS THE SIGN OF SCORPIO ON OCT 24 AT 06:27.

DAY	TIME	☉	☽	☿	♀	♂	♃	♄	♅	♆	♇
	h m s	° ' "	° '	°	°	°	°	°	°	°	°
N 1	2 37 45	7♏42 59	5♊30	19♏R	23♏	17♌	2♐	22♌	26♊R	12♎	15♌
O 2	2 41 42	8 43 0	19 37	18	24	17	2	22	26	12	15
V 3	2 45 38	9 43 4	3♋50	16	25	18	2	22	26	12	15
E 4	2 49 35	10 43 10	18 5	15	27	18	2	22	26	12	15
M 5	2 53 32	11 43 18	2♌20	14	28	19	3	22	26	12	15
B 6	2 57 28	12 43 27	16 32	13	29	19	3	22	26	12	15
E 7	3 1 25	13 43 39	0♍38	11	0♐	20	3	22	26	12	15
R 8	3 5 21	14 43 53	14 37	10	2	20	3	22	26	12	15
9	3 9 18	15 44 9	28 27	9	3	21	3	22	26	12	15
10	3 13 14	16 44 27	12♎ 6	8	4	21	4	22	26	12	15
11	3 17 11	17 44 47	25 33	7	5	22	4	22	26	12	15
12	3 21 7	18 45 9	8♏45	6	7	22	4	22	25	12	15
13	3 25 4	19 45 32	21 43	6	8	22	4	22	25	12	15
14	3 29 1	20 45 58	4♐27	6	9	23	4	22	25	12	15
15	3 32 57	21 46 24	16 55	5 D	10	23	5	22	25	12	15
16	3 36 54	22 46 53	29 11	6	12	24	5	22	25	12	15 R
17	3 40 50	23 47 23	11♑15	6	13	24	5	22	25	12	15
18	3 44 47	24 47 54	23 12	6	14	25	5	22	25	12	15
19	3 48 43	25 48 26	5♒ 4	7	15	25	6	22	25	12	15
20	3 52 40	26 49 0	16 55	8	17	26	6	22	25	12	15
21	3 56 36	27 49 35	28 52	8	18	26	6	23	25	12	15
22	4 0 33	28 50 11	10♓57	9	19	26	6	23	25	12	15
23	4 4 30	29 50 48	23 16	10	20	27	6	23	25	12	15
24	4 8 26	0♐51 27	5♈53	11	22	27	7	23	25	12	15
25	4 12 23	1 52 6	18 51	13	23	28	7	23	25	12	15
26	4 16 19	2 52 47	2♉12	14	24	28	7	23	25	12	15
27	4 20 16	3 53 29	15 56	15	25	28	7	23	25	12	15
28	4 24 12	4 54 13	0♊ 3	16	27	29	8	23	25	12	15
29	4 28 9	5 54 57	14 27	18	28	29	8	23	25	12	15
30	4 32 5	6 55 43	29 4	19	29	29	8	23	25	12	15

THE SUN ENTERS THE SIGN OF SAGITTARIUS ON NOV 23 AT 03:39.

DAY	TIME	☉	☽	☿	♀	♂	♃	♄	♅	♆	♇
	h m s	° ' "	° '	°	°	°	°	°	°	°	°
D 1	4 36 2	7♐56 31	13♋47	20♏	0♑	0♍	8♐	23♌	25♊R	12♎	15♌R
E 2	4 39 59	8 57 20	28 28	22	2	0	8	23	25	12	15
C 3	4 43 55	9 58 10	13♌ 2	23	3	1	9	23	25	12	15
E 4	4 47 52	10 59 1	27 24	25	4	1	9	23 R	25	12	15
M 5	4 51 48	11 59 54	11♍30	26	5	1	9	23	25	13	15
B 6	4 55 45	13 0 48	25 19	28	7	2	9	23	25	13	15
E 7	4 59 41	14 1 44	8♎52	29	8	2	10	23	25	13	15
R 8	5 3 38	15 2 40	22 9	1♐	9	2	10	23	25	13	15
9	5 7 35	16 3 38	5♏11	2	10	2	10	23	24	13	15
10	5 11 31	17 4 37	18 0	4	12	3	10	23	24	13	15
11	5 15 28	18 5 38	0♐37	5	13	3	11	23	24	13	15
12	5 19 24	19 6 39	13 3	7	14	3	11	23	24	13	15
13	5 23 21	20 7 41	25 19	8	15	4	11	23	24	13	15
14	5 27 17	21 8 44	7♑26	10	17	4	11	23	24	13	15
15	5 31 14	22 9 48	19 27	11	18	4	11	23	24	13	15
16	5 35 10	23 10 52	1♒21	13	19	4	12	23	24	13	15
17	5 39 7	24 11 56	13 12	14	20	5	12	23	24	13	15
18	5 43 4	25 13 2	25 3	16	22	5	12	23	24	13	15
19	5 47 0	26 14 7	6♓58	18	23	5	12	22	24	13	15
20	5 50 57	27 15 13	18 59	19	24	5	13	22	24	13	15
21	5 54 53	28 16 19	1♈13	21	25	6	13	22	24	13	15
22	5 58 50	29 17 25	13 44	22	27	6	13	22	24	13	15
23	6 2 46	0♑18 31	26 37	24	28	6	13	22	24	13	15
24	6 6 43	1 19 38	9♉54	25	29	6	13	22	24	13	15
25	6 10 39	2 20 45	23 40	27	0♒	6	14	22	24	13	15
26	6 14 36	3 21 52	7♊53	28	1	7	14	22	24	13	15
27	6 18 33	4 23 0	22 31	0♑	3	7	14	22	24	13	15
28	6 22 29	5 24 7	7♋29	2	4	7	14	22	24	13	15
29	6 26 26	6 25 15	22 37	3	5	7	14	22	24	13	15
30	6 30 22	7 26 23	7♌45	5	6	7	15	22	24	13	15
31	6 34 19	8 27 32	22 44	6	8	7	15	22	24	13	15

THE SUN ENTERS THE SIGN OF CAPRICORN ON DEC 22 AT 16:44.

♈ ARIES ♉ TAURUS ♊ GEMINI ♋ CANCER ♌ LEO ♍ VIRGO ♎ LIBRA ♏ SCORPIO ♐ SAGITTARIUS ♑ CAPRICORN ♒ AQUARIUS ♓ PISCES

SIDEREAL SUN MOON MERCURY VENUS MARS JUPITER SATURN URANUS NEPTUNE PLUTO

DAY	TIME	☉	☽	☿	♀	♂	♃	♄	♅	♆	♇
	h m s	° ' "	° '	°	°	°	°	°	°	°	°
J 1	6 38 15	9♑28 40	7♍26	8♑	9♒	7♍	15♐	22♌R	24♊R	13♎	15♌R
A 2	6 42 12	10 29 49	21 45	10	10	7	15	22	23	13	14
N 3	6 46 9	11 30 59	5♎38	11	11	7	16	22	23	13	14
U 4	6 50 5	12 32 8	19 8	13	13	7	16	22	23	13	14
A 5	6 54 2	13 33 18	2♏14	14	14	8	16	22	23	13	14
R 6	6 57 58	14 34 28	15 2	16	15	8	16	22	23	13	14
Y 7	7 1 55	15 35 39	27 35	18	16	8	16	22	23	13	14
8	7 5 51	16 36 49	9♐55	19	18	8 R	17	22	23	13	14
9	7 9 48	17 38 0	22 6	21	19	8	17	22	23	13	14
10	7 13 44	18 39 10	4♑10	23	20	8	17	21	23	13	14
11	7 17 41	19 40 21	16 9	24	21	8	17	21	23	13	14
12	7 21 38	20 41 30	28 4	26	23	8	17	21	23	13	14
13	7 25 34	21 42 40	9♒56	28	24	7	18	21	23	13	14
14	7 29 31	22 43 49	21 48	29	25	7	18	21	23	13 R	14
15	7 33 27	23 44 58	3♓40	1♒	26	7	18	21	23	13	14
16	7 37 24	24 46 6	15 35	3	27	7	18	21	23	13	14
17	7 41 20	25 47 13	27 37	4	29	7	18	21	23	13	14
18	7 45 17	26 48 19	9♈48	6	0♓	7	19	21	23	13	14
19	7 49 13	27 49 25	22 14	8	1	7	19	21	23	13	14
20	7 53 10	28 50 30	4♉58	9	2	7	19	21	23	13	14
21	7 57 7	29 51 34	18 7	11	4	7	19	21	23	13	14
22	8 1 3	0♒52 37	1♊43	13	5	6	19	21	23	13	14
23	8 5 0	1 53 39	15 48	15	6	6	20	21	23	13	14
24	8 8 56	2 54 40	0♋22	16	7	6	20	21	23	13	14
25	8 12 53	3 55 40	15 22	18	8	6	20	20	23	13	14
26	8 16 49	4 56 39	0♌38	20	10	6	20	20	23	13	14
27	8 20 46	5 57 38	16 1	21	11	5	20	20	23	13	14
28	8 24 42	6 58 35	1♍18	23	12	5	21	20	23	13	14
29	8 28 39	7 59 32	16 19	24	13	5	21	20	23	13	14
30	8 32 36	9 0 28	0♎54	26	15	5	21	20	23	13	14
31	8 36 32	10 1 23	15 1	27	16	4	21	20	22	13	14

THE SUN ENTERS THE SIGN OF AQUARIUS ON JAN 21 AT 03:19.

DAY	TIME	☉	☽	☿	♀	♂	♃	♄	♅	♆	♇
	h m s	° ' "	° '	°	°	°	°	°	°	°	°
F 1	8 40 29	11♒ 2 18	28♎38	29♒	17♓	4♍R	21♐	20♌R	22♊R	13♎R	14♌R
E 2	8 44 25	12 3 12	11♏47	0♓	18	4	22	20	22	13	14
B 3	8 48 22	13 4 5	24 33	1	19	3	22	20	22	13	14
R 4	8 52 18	14 4 57	7♐ 0	2	21	3	22	20	22	13	14
U 5	8 56 15	15 5 48	19 12	3	22	3	22	20	22	13	14
A 6	9 0 11	16 6 39	1♑15	4	23	2	22	19	22	13	14
R 7	9 4 8	17 7 28	13 11	5	24	2	22	19	22	13	14
Y 8	9 8 5	18 8 17	25 4	6	25	2	23	19	22	13	14
9	9 12 1	19 9 4	6♒55	6	27	1	23	19	22	13	14
10	9 15 58	20 9 50	18 47	6	28	1	23	19	22	13	14
11	9 19 54	21 10 34	0♓41	7 R	29	1	23	19	22	13	14
12	9 23 51	22 11 17	12 38	6	0♈	0	23	19	22	13	14
13	9 27 47	23 11 59	24 39	6	1	0	23	19	22	13	14
14	9 31 44	24 12 39	6♈46	6	3	29♌	24	19	22	13	14
15	9 35 40	25 13 18	19 2	5	4	29	24	19	22	13	14
16	9 39 37	26 13 55	1♉30	4	5	29	24	19	22	13	13
17	9 43 34	27 14 30	14 13	4	6	28	24	19	22	13	13
18	9 47 30	28 15 3	27 16	3	7	28	24	19	22	13	13
19	9 51 27	29 15 35	10♊43	2	9	27	24	18	22	13	13
20	9 55 23	0♓16 4	24 35	1	10	27	25	18	22	13	13
21	9 59 20	1 16 32	8♋55	29♒	11	27	25	18	22	13	13
22	10 3 16	2 16 59	23 40	28	12	26	25	18	22	13	13
23	10 7 13	3 17 23	8♌45	27	13	26	25	18	22	13	13
24	10 11 9	4 17 45	24 1	26	15	25	25	18	22	13	13
25	10 15 6	5 18 6	9♍17	25	16	25	25	18	22	13	13
26	10 19 3	6 18 25	24 22	24	17	25	25	18	22	13	13
27	10 22 59	7 18 42	9♎ 6	24	18	24	26	18	22	13	13
28	10 26 56	8 18 58	23 23	23	19	24	26	18	22	12	13
29	10 30 52	9 19 12	7♏11	22	20	24	26	18	22 D	12	13

THE SUN ENTERS THE SIGN OF PISCES ON FEB 19 AT 17:37.

DAY	TIME	☉	☽	☿	♀	♂	♃	♄	♅	♆	♇
	h m s	° ' "	° '	°	°	°	°	°	°	°	°
M 1	10 34 49	10♓19 25	20♏29	22♒R	22♈	23♌R	26♐	18♌R	22♊	12♎R	13♌R
A 2	10 38 45	11 19 36	3♐21	22	23	23	26	18	22	12	13
R 3	10 42 42	12 19 46	15 51	22	24	23	26	17	22	12	13
C 4	10 46 38	13 19 54	28 4	22 D	25	22	26	17	22	12	13
H 5	10 50 35	14 20 0	10♑ 5	22	26	22	26	17	22	12	13
6	10 54 32	15 20 5	21 59	22	27	22	27	17	22	12	13
7	10 58 28	16 20 9	3♒50	22	29	21	27	17	22	12	13
8	11 2 25	17 20 10	15 40	22	0♉	21	27	17	22	12	13
9	11 6 21	18 20 10	27 34	23	1	21	27	17	22	12	13
10	11 10 18	19 20 8	9♓32	23	2	21	27	17	22	12	13
11	11 14 14	20 20 4	21 36	24	3	20	27	17	22	12	13
12	11 18 11	21 19 58	3♈48	25	4	20	27	17	22	12	13
13	11 22 7	22 19 50	16 7	25	5	20	27	17	22	12	13
14	11 26 4	23 19 40	28 36	26	7	20	27	17	22	12	13
15	11 30 1	24 19 28	11♉16	27	8	19	27	17	22	12	13
16	11 33 57	25 19 14	24 9	28	9	19	28	17	22	12	13
17	11 37 54	26 18 57	7♊17	29	10	19	28	17	22	12	13
18	11 41 50	27 18 39	20 43	0♓	11	19	28	17	22	12	13
19	11 45 47	28 18 18	4♋29	1	12	19	28	17	22	12	13
20	11 49 43	29 17 55	18 36	2	13	19	28	16	22	12	13
21	11 53 40	0♈17 29	3♌ 3	3	14	19	28	16	22	12	13
22	11 57 36	1 17 1	17 46	4	15	18	28	16	22	12	13
23	12 1 33	2 16 31	2♍40	5	17	18	28	16	22	12	13
24	12 5 30	3 15 58	17 36	6	18	18	28	16	22	12	13
25	12 9 26	4 15 24	2♎26	8	19	18	28	16	22	12	13
26	12 13 23	5 14 47	17 2	9	20	18	28	16	22	12	13
27	12 17 19	6 14 8	1♏16	10	21	18	28	16	22	12	13
28	12 21 16	7 13 28	15 6	12	22	18	28	16	22	12	13
29	12 25 12	8 12 45	28 29	13	23	18 D	28	16	22	12	13
30	12 29 9	9 12 1	11♐27	14	24	18	29	16	22	12	13
31	12 33 5	10 11 15	24 2	16	25	18	29	16	23	12	13

THE SUN ENTERS THE SIGN OF ARIES ON MAR 20 AT 16:57.

SIDEREAL SUN MOON MERCURY VENUS MARS JUPITER SATURN URANUS NEPTUNE PLUTO

DAY	TIME	☉	☽	☿	♀	♂	♃	♄	♅	♆	♇
	h m s	° ' "	° '	°	°	°	°	°	°	°	°
A 1	12 37 2	11♈10 28	6♑20	17♓	26♉	18♌	29♐	16♌R	23♊	12♎R	13♌R
P 2	12 40 58	12 9 38	18 25	19	27	18	29	16	23	12	13
R 3	12 44 55	13 8 47	0♒20	20	28	18	29	16	23	12	13
I 4	12 48 52	14 7 54	12 12	22	29	18	29	16	23	12	13
L 5	12 52 48	15 6 59	24 4	23	0♊	18	29	16	23	12	13
6	12 56 45	16 6 2	6♓ 1	25	2	18	29	16	23	12	13
7	13 0 41	17 5 3	18 4	27	3	19	29	16	23	11	13
8	13 4 38	18 4 3	0♈16	28	4	19	29	16	23	11	13
9	13 8 34	19 3 0	12 39	0☉	5	19	29	16	23	11	13
10	13 12 31	20 1 56	25 14	2♈	6	19	29	16	23	11	13
11	13 16 27	21 0 49	8♉ 2	3	7	19	29	16	23	11	13
12	13 20 24	21 59 41	21 2	5	8	19	29	16	23	11	13
13	13 24 21	22 58 30	4♊15	7	9	19	29	16	23	11	13
14	13 28 17	23 57 17	17 40	9	10	19	29	16	23	11	13
15	13 32 14	24 56 2	1♋19	10	11	20	29 R	16	23	11	13
16	13 36 10	25 54 45	15 11	12	12	20	29	16	23	11	13
17	13 40 7	26 53 25	29 15	14	13	20	29	16 D	23	11	13
18	13 44 3	27 52 3	13♌30	16	13	20	29	16	23	11	13
19	13 48 0	28 50 39	27 53	18	14	20	29	16	23	11	13
20	13 51 56	29 49 13	12♍21	20	15	21	29	16	23	11	13
21	13 55 53	0♉47 44	26 50	22	16	21	29	16	23	11	13
22	13 59 50	1 46 14	11♎13	24	17	21	29	16	23	11	13
23	14 3 46	2 44 41	25 25	26	18	21	29	16	23	11	13
24	14 7 43	3 43 7	9♏22	28	19	22	29	16	23	11	13 D
25	14 11 39	4 41 30	23 1	0♉	20	22	29	16	23	11	13
26	14 15 36	5 39 52	6♐19	2	21	22	29	16	23	11	13
27	14 19 32	6 38 12	19 16	4	22	22	29	16	23	11	13
28	14 23 29	7 36 31	1♑54	6	23	23	29	16	24	11	13
29	14 27 25	8 34 48	14 14	8	23	23	29	16	24	11	13
30	14 31 22	9 33 4	26 22	10	24	23	29	16	24	11	13

THE SUN ENTERS THE SIGN OF TAURUS ON APR 20 AT 04:25.

DAY	TIME	☉	☽	☿	♀	♂	♃	♄	♅	♆	♇
	h m s	° ' "	° '	°	°	°	°	°	°	°	°
M 1	14 35 19	10♉31 18	8♒20	13♉	25♊	24♌	29♐R	16♌	24♊	11♎R	13♌
A 2	14 39 15	11 29 30	20 13	15	26	24	29	16	24	11	13
Y 3	14 43 12	12 27 41	2♓ 7	17	27	24	28	16	24	11	13
4	14 47 8	13 25 51	14 5	19	27	25	28	16	24	11	13
5	14 51 5	14 23 59	26 11	21	28	25	28	16	24	11	13
6	14 55 1	15 22 5	8♈30	23	29	25	28	16	24	11	13
7	14 58 58	16 20 10	21 3	25	0♋	26	28	16	24	11	13
8	15 2 54	17 18 14	3♉52	28	0	26	28	16	24	11	13
9	15 6 51	18 16 16	16 59	0♊	1	26	28	16	24	11	13
10	15 10 48	19 14 16	0♊22	2	2	27	28	16	24	11	13
11	15 14 44	20 12 15	14 1	4	3	27	28	16	24	11	13
12	15 18 41	21 10 12	27 53	6	3	27	28	16	24	11	13
13	15 22 37	22 8 8	11♋55	7	4	28	28	16	24	11	13
14	15 26 34	23 6 1	26 4	9	4	28	28	16	24	11	13
15	15 30 30	24 3 53	10♌17	11	5	28	28	16	24	11	13
16	15 34 27	25 1 43	24 31	13	6	29	28	16	24	11	13
17	15 38 23	25 59 32	8♍44	15	6	29	27	17	24	11	13
18	15 42 20	26 57 18	22 53	16	7	0♍	27	17	25	11	13
19	15 46 17	27 55 3	6♎56	18	7	0	27	17	25	10	13
20	15 50 13	28 52 46	20 51	19	8	0	27	17	25	10	13
21	15 54 10	29 50 28	4♏36	21	8	1	27	17	25	10	13
22	15 58 6	0♊48 8	18 8	22	9	1	27	17	25	10	13
23	16 2 3	1 45 47	1♐27	24	9	2	27	17	25	10	13
24	16 5 59	2 43 25	14 30	25	9	2	27	17	25	10	13
25	16 9 56	3 41 2	27 18	26	10	3	27	17	25	10	13
26	16 13 52	4 38 37	9♑50	27	10	3	27	17	25	10	13
27	16 17 49	5 36 12	22 9	28	10	3	26	17	25	10	13
28	16 21 46	6 33 45	4♒16	0♋	10	4	26	17	25	10	13
29	16 25 42	7 31 18	16 14	1	11	4	26	17	25	10	13
30	16 29 39	8 28 49	28 8	1	11	5	26	17	25	10	13
31	16 33 35	9 26 20	10♓ 1	2	11	5	26	17	25	10	13

THE SUN ENTERS THE SIGN OF GEMINI ON MAY 21 AT 03:58.

DAY	TIME	☉	☽	☿	♀	♂	♃	♄	♅	♆	♇
	h m s	° ' "	° '	°	°	°	°	°	°	°	°
J 1	16 37 32	10♊23 50	21♓59	3♋	11♋	6♍	26♐R	17♌	25♊	10♎R	13♌
U 2	16 41 28	11 21 19	4♈ 6	4	11	6	26	18	25	10	13
N 3	16 45 25	12 18 47	16 26	5	11 R	7	26	18	25	10	13
E 4	16 49 21	13 16 15	29 5	5	11	7	25	18	26	10	13
5	16 53 18	14 13 42	12♉ 3	6	11	8	25	18	26	10	13
6	16 57 15	15 11 8	25 24	6	11	8	25	18	26	10	13
7	17 1 11	16 8 34	9♊ 7	7	11	9	25	18	26	10	13
8	17 5 8	17 5 59	23 11	7	11	9	25	18	26	10	13
9	17 9 4	18 3 23	7♋30	7	10	9	25	18	26	10	13
10	17 13 1	19 0 46	22 0	7	10	10	25	18	26	10	13
11	17 16 57	19 58 7	6♌33	7 R	10	10	25	18	26	10	13
12	17 20 54	20 55 28	21 5	7	10	11	24	18	26	10	13
13	17 24 51	21 52 48	5♍30	7	9	11	24	18	26	10	13
14	17 28 47	22 50 8	19 43	7	9	12	24	19	26	10	13
15	17 32 44	23 47 25	3♎44	7	8	12	24	19	26	10	13
16	17 36 40	24 44 42	17 32	7	8	13	24	19	26	10	13
17	17 40 37	25 41 59	1♏ 5	6	7	13	24	19	26	10	13
18	17 44 33	26 39 14	14 26	6	7	14	24	19	26	10	13
19	17 48 30	27 36 29	27 34	5	6	14	24	19	26	10	13
20	17 52 26	28 33 43	10♐31	5	6	15	23	19	26	10	13
21	17 56 23	29 30 57	23 15	4	5	16	23	19	27	10 D	13
22	18 0 20	0♋28 10	5♑48	4	5	16	23	19	27	10	13
23	18 4 16	1 25 23	18 11	3	4	17	23	19	27	10	13
24	18 8 13	2 22 36	0♒22	3	3	17	23	19	27	10	13
25	18 12 9	3 19 48	12 25	2	3	18	23	20	27	10	13
26	18 16 6	4 17 0	24 22	1	2	18	23	20	27	10	13
27	18 20 2	5 14 13	6♓14	1	1	19	23	20	27	10	13
28	18 23 59	6 11 25	18 6	0	1	19	22	20	27	10	13
29	18 27 55	7 8 37	0♈ 2	0	0	20	22	20	27	10	13
30	18 31 52	8 5 49	12 7	29♊	0	20	22	20	27	10	13

THE SUN ENTERS THE SIGN OF CANCER ON JUN 21 AT 12:11.

♈ ARIES ♉ TAURUS ♊ GEMINI ♋ CANCER ♌ LEO ♍ VIRGO ♎ LIBRA ♏ SCORPIO ♐ SAGITTARIUS ♑ CAPRICORN ♒ AQUARIUS ♓ PISCES

SIDEREAL SUN MOON MERCURY VENUS MARS JUPITER SATURN URANUS NEPTUNE PLUTO

DAY	TIME	☉	☽	☿	♀	♂	♃	♄	♅	♆	♇
	h m s	° ' "	° '	°	°	°	°	°	°	°	°
J 1	18 35 49	9♋ 3 1	24♈26	29♊R	29♊R	21♍	22♐R	20♌	27♊	10♎	14♌
U 2	18 39 45	10 0 14	7♉ 3	29	29	21	22	20	27	10	14
L 3	18 43 42	10 57 27	20 4	29	28	22	22	20	27	10	14
Y 4	18 47 38	11 54 40	3♊31	28	28	23	22	21	27	10	14
5	18 51 35	12 51 53	17 25	28 D	27	23	22	21	27	10	14
6	18 55 31	13 49 6	1♋44	28	27	24	22	21	27	10	14
7	18 59 28	14 46 20	16 25	28	26	24	21	21	27	10	14
8	19 3 24	15 43 33	1♌19	29	26	25	21	21	28	10	14
9	19 7 21	16 40 47	16 18	29	26	25	21	21	28	10	14
10	19 11 18	17 38 1	1♍12	29	25	26	21	21	28	10	14
11	19 15 14	18 35 14	15 53	0♋	25	26	21	21	28	10	14
12	19 19 11	19 32 27	0♎17	0	25	27	21	21	28	10	14
13	19 23 7	20 29 41	14 20	1	25	28	21	22	28	10	14
14	19 27 4	21 26 54	28 3	1	25	28	21	22	28	10	14
15	19 31 0	22 24 7	11♏26	2	25	29	21	22	28	10	14
16	19 34 57	23 21 21	24 31	3	25 D	29	21	22	28	10	14
17	19 38 54	24 18 35	7♐22	4	25	0♎	20	22	28	10	14
18	19 42 50	25 15 49	20 0	5	25	0	20	22	28	10	14
19	19 46 47	26 13 3	2♑28	6	25	1	20	22	28	10	14
20	19 50 43	27 10 17	14 47	7	25	2	20	22	28	10	14
21	19 54 40	28 7 32	26 57	8	25	2	20	22	28	10	14
22	19 58 36	29 4 48	9♒ 1	10	25	3	20	23	28	10	14
23	20 2 33	0♌ 2 4	20 58	11	25	3	20	23	28	10	14
24	20 6 29	0 59 21	2♓51	13	26	4	20	23	28	10	14
25	20 10 26	1 56 38	14 42	14	26	5	20	23	28	11	14
26	20 14 23	2 53 57	26 33	16	26	5	20	23	28	11	14
27	20 18 19	3 51 16	8♈28	18	27	6	20	23	29	11	14
28	20 22 16	4 48 36	20 32	19	27	6	20	23	29	11	14
29	20 26 12	5 45 57	2♉48	21	28	7	20	23	29	11	14
30	20 30 9	6 43 20	15 22	23	28	8	20	24	29	11	14
31	20 34 5	7 40 43	28 20	25	28	8	19	24	29	11	14

THE SUN ENTERS THE SIGN OF LEO ON JUL 22 AT 23:08.

DAY	TIME	☉	☽	☿	♀	♂	♃	♄	♅	♆	♇
	h m s	° ' "	° '	°	°	°	°	°	°	°	°
A 1	20 38 2	8♌38 8	11♊45	27♋	29♊	9♎	19♐R	24♌	29♊	11♎	14♌
U 2	20 41 58	9 35 33	25 39	29	29	9	19	24	29	11	14
G 3	20 45 55	10 33 0	10♋ 2	1♌	0♋	10	19	24	29	11	14
U 4	20 49 52	11 30 28	24 51	3	1	11	19	24	29	11	14
S 5	20 53 48	12 27 57	9♌57	5	1	11	19	24	29	11	15
T 6	20 57 45	13 25 27	25 12	7	2	12	19	24	29	11	15
7	21 1 41	14 22 58	10♍24	9	2	12	19	25	29	11	15
8	21 5 38	15 20 30	25 23	11	3	13	19	25	29	11	15
9	21 9 34	16 18 3	10♎ 1	13	4	14	19	25	29	11	15
10	21 13 31	17 15 36	24 14	15	4	14	19	25	29	11	15
11	21 17 27	18 13 10	8♏ 1	17	5	15	19	25	29	11	15
12	21 21 24	19 10 46	21 23	19	6	16	19	25	29	11	15
13	21 25 21	20 8 22	4♐24	21	6	16	19	25	29	11	15
14	21 29 17	21 5 59	17 6	23	7	17	19	25	29	11	15
15	21 33 14	22 3 37	29 33	25	8	17	19	26	29	11	15
16	21 37 10	23 1 16	11♑50	27	9	18	19 D	26	29	11	15
17	21 41 7	23 58 57	23 57	29	9	19	19	26	0♋	11	15
18	21 45 3	24 56 38	5♒58	1♍	10	19	19	26	0	11	15
19	21 49 0	25 54 21	17 55	3	11	20	19	26	0	11	15
20	21 52 56	26 52 5	29 48	5	12	21	19	26	0	11	15
21	21 56 53	27 49 50	11♓40	7	13	21	19	26	0	11	15
22	22 0 50	28 47 37	23 31	9	14	22	19	26	0	11	15
23	22 4 46	29 45 25	5♈24	11	14	22	19	27	0	11	15
24	22 8 43	0♍43 15	17 22	12	15	23	19	27	0	11	15
25	22 12 39	1 41 7	29 28	14	16	24	19	27	0	11	15
26	22 16 36	2 39 0	11♉45	16	17	24	19	27	0	11	15
27	22 20 32	3 36 56	24 19	18	18	25	19	27	0	11	15
28	22 24 29	4 34 53	7♊13	19	19	26	19	27	0	11	15
29	22 28 25	5 32 52	20 32	21	20	26	19	27	0	11	15
30	22 32 22	6 30 53	4♋19	23	21	27	19	28	0	11	15
31	22 36 19	7 28 56	18 35	24	22	28	19	28	0	11	15

THE SUN ENTERS THE SIGN OF VIRGO ON AUG 23 AT 06:04.

DAY	TIME	☉	☽	☿	♀	♂	♃	♄	♅	♆	♇
	h m s	° ' "	° '	°	°	°	°	°	°	°	°
S 1	22 40 15	8♍27 0	3♌17	26♍	23♋	28♎	19♐	28♌	0♋	11♎	15♌
E 2	22 44 12	9 25 7	18 21	27	24	29	20	28	0	12	15
P 3	22 48 8	10 23 15	3♍36	29	25	0♏	20	28	0	12	15
T 4	22 52 5	11 21 25	18 53	1♎	25	0	20	28	0	12	15
E 5	22 56 1	12 19 36	4♎ 1	2	26	1	20	28	0	12	15
M 6	22 59 58	13 17 50	18 49	4	27	2	20	28	0	12	15
B 7	23 3 54	14 16 4	3♏13	5	28	2	20	29	0	12	15
E 8	23 7 51	15 14 21	17 9	7	29	3	20	29	0	12	15
R 9	23 11 48	16 12 38	0♐38	8	0♌	4	20	29	0	12	16
10	23 15 44	17 10 58	13 41	9	1	4	20	29	0	12	16
11	23 19 41	18 9 19	26 23	11	2	5	20	29	0	12	16
12	23 23 37	19 7 42	8♑47	12	3	6	20	29	0	12	16
13	23 27 34	20 6 6	20 59	14	4	6	20	29	0	12	16
14	23 31 30	21 4 32	3♒ 0	15	6	7	20	29	0	12	16
15	23 35 27	22 2 59	14 56	16	7	8	20	29	0	12	16
16	23 39 23	23 1 28	26 49	18	8	8	21	0♍	0	12	16
17	23 43 20	23 59 59	8♓40	19	9	9	21	0	0	12	16
18	23 47 16	24 58 32	20 33	20	10	10	21	0	0	12	16
19	23 51 13	25 57 6	2♈28	21	11	10	21	0	0	12	16
20	23 55 10	26 55 43	14 28	22	12	11	21	0	0	12	16
21	23 59 6	27 54 21	26 34	24	13	12	21	0	0	12	16
22	0 3 3	28 53 2	8♉48	25	14	12	21	0	0	12	16
23	0 6 59	29 51 45	21 14	26	15	13	21	0	1	12	16
24	0 10 56	0♎50 30	3♊54	27	16	14	21	1	1	12	16
25	0 14 52	1 49 18	16 50	28	17	14	21	1	1	12	16
26	0 18 49	2 48 7	0♋ 8	29	18	15	22	1	1	12	16
27	0 22 45	3 46 59	13 48	0♏	19	16	22	1	1	12	16
28	0 26 42	4 45 54	27 52	1	20	16	22	1	1	12	16
29	0 30 39	5 44 50	12♌19	1	22	17	22	1	1	12	16
30	0 34 35	6 43 49	27 5	2	23	18	22	1	1	13	16

THE SUN ENTERS THE SIGN OF LIBRA ON SEP 23 AT 03:23.

SIDEREAL SUN MOON MERCURY VENUS MARS JUPITER SATURN URANUS NEPTUNE PLUTO

DAY	TIME	☉	☽	☿	♀	♂	♃	♄	♅	♆	♇
	h m s	° ' "	° '	°	°	°	°	°	°	°	°
O 1	0 38 32	7♎42 50	12♍ 5	3♏	24♌	19♏	22♐	1♍	1♋	13♎	16♌
C 2	0 42 28	8 41 53	27 10	3	25	19	22	1	1	13	16
T 3	0 46 25	9 40 59	12♎11	4	26	20	22	2	1	13	16
O 4	0 50 21	10 40 6	26 58	5	27	21	23	2	1	13	16
B 5	0 54 18	11 39 15	11♏25	5	28	21	23	2	1	13	16
E 6	0 58 14	12 38 26	25 28	5	29	22	23	2	1 R	13	16
R 7	1 2 11	13 37 40	9♐ 4	5	1♍	23	23	2	1	13	16
8	1 6 8	14 36 55	22 14	5 R	2	23	23	2	1	13	16
9	1 10 4	15 36 11	5♑ 0	5	3	24	23	2	1	13	16
10	1 14 1	16 35 30	17 27	5	4	25	23	2	1	13	16
11	1 17 57	17 34 50	29 39	5	5	26	24	2	1	13	16
12	1 21 54	18 34 12	11♒39	4	6	26	24	3	1	13	16
13	1 25 50	19 33 36	23 33	4	7	27	24	3	1	13	16
14	1 29 47	20 33 2	5♓24	3	9	28	24	3	1	13	16
15	1 33 43	21 32 29	17 16	2	10	28	24	3	1	13	16
16	1 37 40	22 31 58	29 12	1	11	29	24	3	1	13	16
17	1 41 37	23 31 30	11♈14	0	12	0♐	25	3	1	13	16
18	1 45 33	24 31 3	23 24	29♎	13	1	25	3	1	13	16
19	1 49 30	25 30 38	5♉43	28	14	1	25	3	1	13	16
20	1 53 26	26 30 16	18 14	27	15	2	25	3	0	13	16
21	1 57 23	27 29 55	0♊56	25	17	3	25	3	0	13	16
22	2 1 19	28 29 37	13 52	24	18	3	25	3	0	13	16
23	2 5 16	29 29 21	27 1	23	19	4	26	4	0	13	16
24	2 9 12	0♏29 7	10♋26	22	20	5	26	4	0	13	16
25	2 13 9	1 28 55	24 7	21	21	6	26	4	0	13	16
26	2 17 6	2 28 46	8♌ 4	21	23	6	26	4	0	13	16
27	2 21 2	3 28 39	22 16	20	24	7	26	4	0	13	16
28	2 24 59	4 28 34	6♍42	20 D	25	8	26	4	0	14	16
29	2 28 55	5 28 31	21 17	20	26	8	27	4	0	14	16
30	2 32 52	6 28 31	5♎57	20	27	9	27	4	0	14	16
31	2 36 48	7 28 32	20 35	20	28	10	27	4	0	14	16

THE SUN ENTERS THE SIGN OF SCORPIO ON OCT 23 AT 12:19.

DAY	TIME	☉	☽	☿	♀	♂	♃	♄	♅	♆	♇
	h m s	° ' "	° '	°	°	°	°	°	°	°	°
N 1	2 40 45	8♏28 36	5♏ 6	21♎	0♎	11♐	27♐	4♍	0♋R	14♎	16♌
O 2	2 44 41	9 28 41	19 23	21	1	11	27	4	0	14	17
V 3	2 48 38	10 28 48	3♐21	22	2	12	28	4	0	14	17
E 4	2 52 35	11 28 57	16 58	23	3	13	28	5	0	14	17
M 5	2 56 31	12 29 8	0♑11	24	4	14	28	5	0	14	17
B 6	3 0 28	13 29 20	13 2	25	6	14	28	5	0	14	17
E 7	3 4 24	14 29 34	25 32	26	7	15	28	5	0	14	17
R 8	3 8 21	15 29 50	7♒46	27	8	16	29	5	0	14	17
9	3 12 17	16 30 6	19 48	29	9	17	29	5	0	14	17
10	3 16 14	17 30 25	1♓42	0♏	10	17	29	5	0	14	17
11	3 20 10	18 30 44	13 33	1	12	18	29	5	0	14	17
12	3 24 7	19 31 5	25 25	3	13	19	29	5	0	14	17
13	3 28 4	20 31 28	7♈24	4	14	20	0♑	5	0	14	17
14	3 32 0	21 31 52	19 31	6	15	20	0	5	0	14	17
15	3 35 57	22 32 17	1♉52	7	17	21	0	5	0	14	17
16	3 39 53	23 32 44	14 26	9	18	22	0	5	0	14	17
17	3 43 50	24 33 13	27 16	10	19	23	0	5	0	14	17 R
18	3 47 46	25 33 43	10♊22	12	20	23	1	5	0	14	17
19	3 51 43	26 34 15	23 42	13	21	24	1	5	0	14	17
20	3 55 39	27 34 49	7♋16	15	23	25	1	6	0	14	17
21	3 59 36	28 35 24	21 1	16	24	26	1	6	0	14	17
22	4 3 33	29 36 1	4♌55	18	25	26	1	6	0	14	17
23	4 7 29	0♐36 40	18 56	20	26	27	2	6	0	14	17
24	4 11 26	1 37 20	3♍ 3	21	28	28	2	6	0	14	17
25	4 15 22	2 38 2	17 14	23	29	29	2	6	0	14	17
26	4 19 19	3 38 45	1♎27	24	0♏	29	2	6	0	14	17
27	4 23 15	4 39 31	15 39	26	1	0♑	2	6	0	14	17
28	4 27 12	5 40 17	29 49	27	2	1	3	6	29♊	15	17
29	4 31 8	6 41 6	13♏52	29	4	2	3	6	29	15	17
30	4 35 5	7 41 55	27 47	1♐	5	2	3	6	29	15	17

THE SUN ENTERS THE SIGN OF SAGITTARIUS ON NOV 22 AT 09:30.

DAY	TIME	☉	☽	☿	♀	♂	♃	♄	♅	♆	♇
	h m s	° ' "	° '	°	°	°	°	°	°	°	°
D 1	4 39 2	8♐42 46	11♐28	2♐	6♏	3♑	3♑	6♍	29♊R	15♎	17♌R
E 2	4 42 58	9 43 38	24 53	4	7	4	4	6	29	15	17
C 3	4 46 55	10 44 31	8♑ 1	5	9	5	4	6	29	15	17
E 4	4 50 51	11 45 26	20 50	7	10	5	4	6	29	15	17
M 5	4 54 48	12 46 21	3♒21	8	11	6	4	6	29	15	16
B 6	4 58 44	13 47 16	15 35	10	12	7	4	6	29	15	16
E 7	5 2 41	14 48 13	27 38	12	14	8	5	6	29	15	16
R 8	5 6 38	15 49 10	9♓31	13	15	8	5	6	29	15	16
9	5 10 34	16 50 8	21 21	15	16	9	5	6	29	15	16
10	5 14 31	17 51 7	3♈13	16	17	10	5	6	29	15	16
11	5 18 27	18 52 6	15 11	18	18	11	6	6	29	15	16
12	5 22 24	19 53 5	27 21	19	20	12	6	6	29	15	16
13	5 26 20	20 54 6	9♉47	21	21	12	6	6	29	15	16
14	5 30 17	21 55 7	22 32	23	22	13	6	6	29	15	16
15	5 34 13	22 56 9	5♊39	24	23	14	6	6	29	15	16
16	5 38 10	23 57 11	19 6	26	25	15	7	6	29	15	16
17	5 42 7	24 58 14	2♋53	27	26	15	7	6 R	29	15	16
18	5 46 3	25 59 18	16 56	29	27	16	7	6	29	15	16
19	5 50 0	27 0 22	1♌ 9	0♑	28	17	7	6	29	15	16
20	5 53 56	28 1 27	15 29	2	0♐	18	8	6	29	15	16
21	5 57 53	29 2 33	29 48	4	1	18	8	6	29	15	16
22	6 1 49	0♑ 3 39	14♍ 5	5	2	19	8	6	28	15	16
23	6 5 46	1 4 46	28 15	7	3	20	8	6	28	15	16
24	6 9 42	2 5 54	12♎17	8	5	21	9	6	28	15	16
25	6 13 39	3 7 3	26 10	10	6	22	9	6	28	15	16
26	6 17 36	4 8 12	9♏56	12	7	22	9	6	28	15	16
27	6 21 32	5 9 22	23 32	13	8	23	9	6	28	15	16
28	6 25 29	6 10 32	7♐ 0	15	10	24	9	6	28	15	16
29	6 29 25	7 11 43	20 17	17	11	25	10	6	28	15	16
30	6 33 22	8 12 54	3♑22	18	12	26	10	6	28	15	16
31	6 37 18	9 14 5	16 15	20	13	26	10	6	28	15	16

THE SUN ENTERS THE SIGN OF CAPRICORN ON DEC 21 AT 22:34.

♈ ARIES ♉ TAURUS ♊ GEMINI ♋ CANCER ♌ LEO ♍ VIRGO ♎ LIBRA ♏ SCORPIO ♐ SAGITTARIUS ♑ CAPRICORN ♒ AQUARIUS ♓ PISCES

1949

SIDEREAL SUN MOON MERCURY VENUS MARS JUPITER SATURN URANUS NEPTUNE PLUTO

SIDEREAL SUN MOON MERCURY VENUS MARS JUPITER SATURN URANUS NEPTUNE PLUTO

DAY	TIME	☉	☽	☿	♀	♂	♃	♄	♅	♆	♇
	h m s	° ' "	° '	°	°	°	°	°	°	°	°
J 1	6 41 15	10♑15 16	28♑53	21♑	15♐	27♑	10♑	6♍R	28♊R	15♎	16♌R
A 2	6 45 11	11 16 27	11♒18	23	16	28	11	6	28	15	16
N 3	6 49 8	12 17 38	23 29	25	17	29	11	6	28	15	16
U 4	6 53 5	13 18 49	5♓30	26	18	29	11	6	28	15	16
A 5	6 57 1	14 19 59	17 22	28	20	0♒	11	6	28	15	16
R 6	7 0 58	15 21 9	29 10	29	21	1	12	6	28	15	16
Y 7	7 4 54	16 22 19	11♈ 0	1♒	22	2	12	6	28	15	16
8	7 8 51	17 23 28	22 56	3	23	3	12	6	28	15	16
9	7 12 47	18 24 37	5♉ 3	4	25	3	12	6	28	15	16
10	7 16 44	19 25 46	17 29	6	26	4	12	6	28	15	16
11	7 20 40	20 26 54	0♊16	7	27	5	13	6	28	15	16
12	7 24 37	21 28 1	13 28	9	28	6	13	6	28	15	16
13	7 28 34	22 29 8	27 8	10	0♑	6	13	6	28	15	16
14	7 32 30	23 30 14	11♋13	11	1	7	13	5	28	15	16
15	7 36 27	24 31 20	25 39	13	2	8	14	5	27	15	16
16	7 40 23	25 32 26	10♌21	14	3	9	14	5	27	15 R	16
17	7 44 20	26 33 31	25 9	15	5	10	14	5	27	15	16
18	7 48 16	27 34 35	9♍55	16	6	10	14	5	27	15	16
19	7 52 13	28 35 39	24 32	17	7	11	15	5	27	15	16
20	7 56 10	29 36 43	8♎56	18	8	12	15	5	27	15	16
21	8 0 6	0♒37 46	23 3	19	10	13	15	5	27	15	16
22	8 4 3	1 38 49	6♏53	19	11	14	15	5	27	15	16
23	8 7 59	2 39 52	20 27	20	12	14	15	5	27	15	16
24	8 11 56	3 40 54	3♐47	20 R	13	15	16	5	27	15	16
25	8 15 52	4 41 56	16 53	20	15	16	16	5	27	15	16
26	8 19 49	5 42 57	29 48	20	16	17	16	5	27	15	16
27	8 23 45	6 43 57	12♑32	20	17	18	16	5	27	15	16
28	8 27 42	7 44 57	25 6	19	18	18	17	5	27	15	16
29	8 31 39	8 45 55	7♒30	19	20	19	17	5	27	15	16
30	8 35 35	9 46 53	19 43	18	21	20	17	5	27	15	16
31	8 39 32	10 47 50	1♓47	17	22	21	17	4	27	15	15

THE SUN ENTERS THE SIGN OF AQUARIUS ON JAN 20 AT 09:09.

DAY	TIME	☉	☽	☿	♀	♂	♃	♄	♅	♆	♇
	h m s	° ' "	° '	°	°	°	°	°	°	°	°
F 1	8 43 28	11♒48 45	13♓43	16♒R	23♑	21♒	17♑	4♍R	27♊R	15♎R	15♌R
E 2	8 47 25	12 49 39	25 32	14	25	22	18	4	27	15	15
B 3	8 51 21	13 50 32	7♈19	13	26	23	18	4	27	15	15
R 4	8 55 18	14 51 24	19 7	12	27	24	18	4	27	15	15
U 5	8 59 14	15 52 14	1♉ 1	11	28	25	18	4	27	15	15
A 6	9 3 11	16 53 3	13 6	10	0♒	25	19	4	27	15	15
R 7	9 7 8	17 53 50	25 27	9	1	26	19	4	27	15	15
Y 8	9 11 4	18 54 36	8♊10	8	2	27	19	4	27	15	15
9	9 15 1	19 55 21	21 19	7	3	28	19	4	27	15	15
10	9 18 57	20 56 3	4♋57	6	5	29	19	4	27	15	15
11	9 22 54	21 56 45	19 5	6	6	29	20	4	27	15	15
12	9 26 50	22 57 24	3♌40	5	7	0♓	20	4	27	15	15
13	9 30 47	23 58 2	18 36	5	8	1	20	3	27	15	15
14	9 34 43	24 58 39	3♍44	5 D	10	2	20	3	27	15	15
15	9 38 40	25 59 14	18 53	5	11	3	20	3	27	15	15
16	9 42 37	26 59 48	3♎54	5	12	3	21	3	27	15	15
17	9 46 33	28 0 20	18 39	5	13	4	21	3	27	15	15
18	9 50 30	29 0 52	3♏ 2	5	15	5	21	3	27	15	15
19	9 54 26	0♓ 1 22	17 2	5	16	6	21	3	27	15	15
20	9 58 23	1 1 50	0♐39	6	17	7	22	3	27	15	15
21	10 2 19	2 2 18	13 56	6	18	7	22	3	27	15	15
22	10 6 16	3 2 44	26 53	7	20	8	22	3	27	15	15
23	10 10 12	4 3 9	9♑35	8	21	9	22	3	27	15	15
24	10 14 9	5 3 32	22 4	9	22	10	22	3	27	15	15
25	10 18 6	6 3 54	4♒22	9	23	10	23	3	27	15	15
26	10 22 2	7 4 14	16 31	10	25	11	23	2	27	15	15
27	10 25 59	8 4 33	28 33	11	26	12	23	2	27	15	15
28	10 29 55	9 4 50	10♓29	12	27	13	23	2	27	15	15

THE SUN ENTERS THE SIGN OF PISCES ON FEB 18 AT 23:28.

DAY	TIME	☉	☽	☿	♀	♂	♃	♄	♅	♆	♇
	h m s	° ' "	° '	°	°	°	°	°	°	°	°
M 1	10 33 52	10♓ 5 5	22♓20	13♒	28♒	14♓	23♑	2♍R	27♊R	15♎R	15♌R
A 2	10 37 48	11 5 18	4♈ 8	14	29	14	24	2	27	15	15
R 3	10 41 45	12 5 29	15 55	15	1♓	15	24	2	27	15	15
C 4	10 45 41	13 5 38	27 45	16	2	16	24	2	27	15	15
H 5	10 49 38	14 5 46	9♉40	18	3	17	24	2	27 D	15	15
6	10 53 35	15 5 51	21 46	19	4	18	24	2	27	15	15
7	10 57 31	16 5 54	4♊ 6	20	6	18	24	2	27	15	15
8	11 1 28	17 5 55	16 45	21	7	19	25	2	27	15	15
9	11 5 24	18 5 54	29 48	23	8	20	25	2	27	14	15
10	11 9 21	19 5 51	13♋18	24	9	21	25	2	27	14	15
11	11 13 17	20 5 45	27 17	25	11	21	25	1	27	14	15
12	11 17 14	21 5 37	11♌45	27	12	22	25	1	27	14	15
13	11 21 10	22 5 27	26 36	28	13	23	26	1	27	14	15
14	11 25 7	23 5 15	11♍45	29	14	24	26	1	27	14	15
15	11 29 4	24 5 1	27 2	1♓	16	25	26	1	27	14	15
16	11 33 0	25 4 45	12♎15	2	17	25	26	1	27	14	15
17	11 36 57	26 4 27	27 16	4	18	26	26	1	27	14	15
18	11 40 53	27 4 7	11♏57	5	19	27	26	1	27	14	14
19	11 44 50	28 3 46	26 12	7	21	28	27	1	27	14	14
20	11 48 46	29 3 22	10♐ 1	8	22	29	27	1	27	14	14
21	11 52 43	0♈ 2 57	23 25	10	23	29	27	1	27	14	14
22	11 56 39	1 2 31	6♑24	12	24	0♈	27	1	27	14	14
23	12 0 36	2 2 2	19 4	13	26	1	27	1	27	14	14
24	12 4 33	3 1 32	1♒27	15	27	2	27	1	27	14	14
25	12 8 29	4 1 0	13 36	17	28	2	28	0	27	14	14
26	12 12 26	5 0 26	25 37	18	29	3	28	0	27	14	14
27	12 16 22	5 59 50	7♓30	20	1♈	4	28	0	27	14	14
28	12 20 19	6 59 12	19 20	22	2	5	28	0	27	14	14
29	12 24 15	7 58 33	1♈ 8	23	3	5	28	0	27	14	14
30	12 28 12	8 57 51	12 57	25	4	6	28	0	27	14	14
31	12 32 8	9 57 7	24 48	27	6	7	28	0	27	14	14

THE SUN ENTERS THE SIGN OF ARIES ON MAR 20 AT 22:49.

DAY	TIME	☉	☽	☿	♀	♂	♃	♄	♅	♆	♇
	h m s	° ' "	° '	°	°	°	°	°	°	°	°
A 1	12 36 5	10♈56 21	6♉44	29♓	7♈	8♈	29♑	0♍R	27♊	14♎R	14♌R
P 2	12 40 1	11 55 33	18 47	1♈	8	9	29	0	27	14	14
R 3	12 43 58	12 54 43	1♊ 0	2	9	9	29	0	27	14	14
I 4	12 47 55	13 53 50	13 26	4	11	10	29	0	27	14	14
L 5	12 51 51	14 52 56	26 8	6	12	11	29	0	27	14	14
6	12 55 48	15 51 59	9♋10	8	13	12	29	0	27	14	14
7	12 59 44	16 50 59	22 35	10	14	12	29	0	27	14	14
8	13 3 41	17 49 57	6♌23	12	16	13	29	0	27	14	14
9	13 7 37	18 48 53	20 36	14	17	14	0♒	0	27	14	14
10	13 11 34	19 47 47	5♍11	16	18	15	0	0	27	14	14
11	13 15 30	20 46 38	20 5	18	19	16	0	0	27	14	14
12	13 19 27	21 45 27	5♎10	20	20	16	0	0	27	14	14
13	13 23 24	22 44 15	20 18	22	22	17	0	0	27	14	14
14	13 27 20	23 43 0	5♏19	24	23	18	0	0	27	14	14
15	13 31 17	24 41 43	20 6	27	24	19	0	0	27	14	14
16	13 35 13	25 40 24	4♐32	29	25	19	0	0	27	13	14
17	13 39 10	26 39 4	18 32	1♉	27	20	0	29♌	27	13	14
18	13 43 6	27 37 42	2♑ 5	3	28	21	1	29	27	13	14
19	13 47 3	28 36 18	15 12	5	29	22	1	29	27	13	14
20	13 50 59	29 34 53	27 55	7	0♉	22	1	29	27	13	14
21	13 54 56	0♉33 26	10♒19	9	2	23	1	29	27	13	14
22	13 58 53	1 31 57	22 27	11	3	24	1	29	27	13	14
23	14 2 49	2 30 27	4♓24	13	4	25	1	29	28	13	14
24	14 6 46	3 28 55	16 14	15	5	25	1	29	28	13	14
25	14 10 42	4 27 21	28 2	17	7	26	1	29	28	13	14
26	14 14 39	5 25 45	9♈50	19	8	27	1	29	28	13	14 D
27	14 18 35	6 24 8	21 42	21	9	28	1	29	28	13	14
28	14 22 32	7 22 29	3♉40	23	10	28	1	29	28	13	14
29	14 26 28	8 20 48	15 46	25	11	29	1	29	28	13	14
30	14 30 25	9 19 6	28 2	27	13	0♉	2	29	28	13	14

THE SUN ENTERS THE SIGN OF TAURUS ON APR 20 AT 10:17.

DAY	TIME	☉	☽	☿	♀	♂	♃	♄	♅	♆	♇
	h m s	° ' "	° '	°	°	°	°	°	°	°	°
M 1	14 34 22	10♉17 22	10♊30	28♉	14♉	1♉	2♒	29♌D	28♊	13♎R	14♌
A 2	14 38 18	11 15 35	23 11	0♊	15	1	2	29	28	13	14
Y 3	14 42 15	12 13 47	6♋ 6	1	16	2	2	29	28	13	14
4	14 46 11	13 11 57	19 16	3	18	3	2	29	28	13	14
5	14 50 8	14 10 5	2♌43	4	19	4	2	29	28	13	14
6	14 54 4	15 8 11	16 27	6	20	4	2	29	28	13	14
7	14 58 1	16 6 15	0♍28	7	21	5	2	29	28	13	14
8	15 1 57	17 4 17	14 47	8	23	6	2	29	28	13	14
9	15 5 54	18 2 17	29 19	9	24	7	2	29	28	13	14
10	15 9 51	19 0 15	14♎ 2	10	25	7	2	29	28	13	14
11	15 13 47	19 58 12	28 50	11	26	8	2	29	28	13	14
12	15 17 44	20 56 6	13♏36	12	28	9	2	29	28	13	14
13	15 21 40	21 54 0	28 13	13	29	10	2	29	28	13	14
14	15 25 37	22 51 52	12♐34	14	0♊	10	2	29	28	13	14
15	15 29 33	23 49 42	26 35	15	1	11	2	29	29	13	14
16	15 33 30	24 47 31	10♑12	15	2	12	2	0♍	29	13	14
17	15 37 26	25 45 19	23 23	16	4	13	2	0	29	13	14
18	15 41 23	26 43 6	6♒11	16	5	13	2	0	29	13	14
19	15 45 20	27 40 51	18 37	17	6	14	2	0	29	13	14
20	15 49 16	28 38 36	0♓47	17	7	15	2 R	0	29	13	14
21	15 53 13	29 36 19	12 44	17	9	15	2	0	29	13	14
22	15 57 9	0♊34 1	24 35	17	10	16	2	0	29	13	14
23	16 1 6	1 31 42	6♈22	17 R	11	17	2	0	29	13	14
24	16 5 2	2 29 22	18 12	17	12	18	2	0	29	13	14
25	16 8 59	3 27 1	0♉ 9	17	13	18	2	0	29	13	14
26	16 12 55	4 24 39	12 15	17	15	19	2	0	29	13	14
27	16 16 52	5 22 16	24 34	17	16	20	2	0	29	13	14
28	16 20 49	6 19 52	7♊ 7	16	17	21	2	0	29	13	14
29	16 24 45	7 17 26	19 54	16	18	21	2	0	29	13	14
30	16 28 42	8 15 0	2♋56	16	20	22	2	0	29	13	14
31	16 32 38	9 12 32	16 11	15	21	23	2	0	29	13	14

THE SUN ENTERS THE SIGN OF GEMINI ON MAY 21 AT 09:51.

DAY	TIME	☉	☽	☿	♀	♂	♃	♄	♅	♆	♇
	h m s	° ' "	° '	°	°	°	°	°	°	°	°
J 1	16 36 35	10♊10 3	29♋39	15♊R	22♊	24♉	2♒R	0♍	29♊	13♎R	14♌
U 2	16 40 31	11 7 33	13♌19	14	23	24	2	0	0♋	13	14
N 3	16 44 28	12 5 1	27 9	14	25	25	2	0	0	13	14
E 4	16 48 25	13 2 29	11♍ 9	13	26	26	2	0	0	12	14
5	16 52 21	13 59 54	25 17	12	27	26	2	0	0	12	14
6	16 56 18	14 57 19	9♎32	12	28	27	2	0	0	12	15
7	17 0 14	15 54 42	23 52	11	29	28	2	0	0	12	15
8	17 4 11	16 52 5	8♏15	11	1♋	29	2	1	0	12	15
9	17 8 7	17 49 26	22 37	10	2	29	2	1	0	12	15
10	17 12 4	18 46 47	6♐52	10	3	0♊	2	1	0	12	15
11	17 16 0	19 44 7	20 57	10	4	1	1	1	0	12	15
12	17 19 57	20 41 26	4♑46	9	6	1	1	1	0	12	15
13	17 23 54	21 38 44	18 15	9	7	2	1	1	0	12	15
14	17 27 50	22 36 2	1♒23	9	8	3	1	1	0	12	15
15	17 31 47	23 33 19	14 9	9	9	4	1	1	0	12	15
16	17 35 43	24 30 36	26 36	9 D	10	4	1	1	0	12	15
17	17 39 40	25 27 53	8♓46	9	12	5	1	1	0	12	15
18	17 43 36	26 25 9	20 44	9	13	6	1	1	0	12	15
19	17 47 33	27 22 25	2♈35	9	14	6	1	1	1	12	15
20	17 51 29	28 19 41	14 24	9	15	7	1	1	1	12	15
21	17 55 26	29 16 56	26 16	10	17	8	1	1	1	12	15
22	17 59 23	0♋14 11	8♉16	10	18	8	1	2	1	12	15
23	18 3 19	1 11 26	20 29	11	19	9	0	2	1	12 D	15
24	18 7 16	2 8 42	2♊58	11	20	10	0	2	1	12	15
25	18 11 12	3 5 56	15 46	12	21	11	0	2	1	12	15
26	18 15 9	4 3 11	28 53	12	23	11	0	2	1	12	15
27	18 19 5	5 0 25	12♋17	13	24	12	0	2	1	12	15
28	18 23 2	5 57 40	25 58	14	25	13	0	2	1	12	15
29	18 26 58	6 54 53	9♌50	15	26	13	0	2	1	12	15
30	18 30 55	7 52 7	23 52	16	28	14	0	2	1	12	15

THE SUN ENTERS THE SIGN OF CANCER ON JUN 21 AT 18:03.

♈ ARIES ♉ TAURUS ♊ GEMINI ♋ CANCER ♌ LEO ♍ VIRGO ♎ LIBRA ♏ SCORPIO ♐ SAGITTARIUS ♑ CAPRICORN ♒ AQUARIUS ♓ PISCES

1949

SIDEREAL SUN MOON MERCURY VENUS MARS JUPITER SATURN URANUS NEPTUNE PLUTO

DAY	TIME	☉	☽	☿	♀	♂	♃	♄	♅	♆	♇
	h m s	° ' "	° '	°	°	°	°	°	°	°	°
J 1	18 34 52	8♋49 20	7♍58	17♊	29♋	15♊	0♒R	2♍	1♋	12♎	15♌
U 2	18 38 48	9 46 33	22 7	18	0♌	15	0	2	1	12	15
L 3	18 42 45	10 43 45	6♎16	20	1	16	29♑	2	1	12	15
Y 4	18 46 41	11 40 57	20 23	21	2	17	29	3	1	12	15
5	18 50 38	12 38 8	4♏28	22	4	18	29	3	1	12	15
6	18 54 34	13 35 20	18 30	24	5	18	29	3	2	12	15
7	18 58 31	14 32 31	2♐28	25	6	19	29	3	2	12	15
8	19 2 27	15 29 42	16 18	27	7	20	29	3	2	12	15
9	19 6 24	16 26 53	29 58	28	9	20	29	3	2	12	15
10	19 10 21	17 24 4	13♑26	0♋	10	21	29	3	2	12	15
11	19 14 17	18 21 16	26 39	1	11	22	28	3	2	12	15
12	19 18 14	19 18 27	9♒35	3	12	22	28	3	2	12	15
13	19 22 10	20 15 39	22 14	5	13	23	28	3	2	12	15
14	19 26 7	21 12 52	4♓35	7	15	24	28	4	2	13	15
15	19 30 3	22 10 4	16 43	9	16	24	28	4	2	13	15
16	19 34 0	23 7 18	28 39	11	17	25	28	4	2	13	15
17	19 37 57	24 4 32	10♈29	13	18	26	28	4	2	13	15
18	19 41 53	25 1 46	22 18	15	19	26	28	4	2	13	16
19	19 45 50	25 59 1	4♉10	17	21	27	27	4	2	13	16
20	19 49 46	26 56 17	16 12	19	22	28	27	4	2	13	16
21	19 53 43	27 53 34	28 28	21	23	28	27	4	2	13	16
22	19 57 39	28 50 52	11♊ 3	23	24	29	27	4	2	13	16
23	20 1 36	29 48 10	24 0	25	26	0♋	27	5	3	13	16
24	20 5 32	0♌45 30	7♋21	27	27	1	27	5	3	13	16
25	20 9 29	1 42 49	21 4	0♌	28	1	27	5	3	13	16
26	20 13 26	2 40 10	5♌ 7	2	29	2	27	5	3	13	16
27	20 17 22	3 37 31	19 25	4	0♍	3	26	5	3	13	16
28	20 21 19	4 34 53	3♍52	6	2	3	26	5	3	13	16
29	20 25 15	5 32 16	18 21	8	3	4	26	5	3	13	16
30	20 29 12	6 29 39	2♎48	10	4	5	26	5	3	13	16
31	20 33 8	7 27 2	17 8	12	5	5	26	5	3	13	16

THE SUN ENTERS THE SIGN OF LEO ON JUL 23 AT 04:57.

DAY	TIME	☉	☽	☿	♀	♂	♃	♄	♅	♆	♇
	h m s	° ' "	° '	°	°	°	°	°	°	°	°
A 1	20 37 5	8♌24 26	1♏20	14♌	6♍	6♋	26♑R	6♍	3♋	13♎	16♌
U 2	20 41 1	9 21 51	15 21	16	8	7	26	6	3	13	16
G 3	20 44 58	10 19 16	29 11	18	9	7	26	6	3	13	16
U 4	20 48 55	11 16 42	12♐51	20	10	8	25	6	3	13	16
S 5	20 52 51	12 14 9	26 19	22	11	9	25	6	3	13	16
T 6	20 56 48	13 11 36	9♑37	24	13	9	25	6	3	13	16
7	21 0 44	14 9 5	22 42	26	14	10	25	6	3	13	16
8	21 4 41	15 6 34	5♒34	28	15	11	25	6	3	13	16
9	21 8 37	16 4 4	18 13	29	16	11	25	7	3	13	16
10	21 12 34	17 1 35	0♓38	1♍	17	12	25	7	3	13	16
11	21 16 30	17 59 8	12 51	3	19	12	25	7	3	13	16
12	21 20 27	18 56 42	24 52	5	20	13	25	7	4	13	16
13	21 24 24	19 54 17	6♈45	6	21	14	24	7	4	13	16
14	21 28 20	20 51 53	18 33	8	22	14	24	7	4	13	16
15	21 32 17	21 49 31	0♉21	10	23	15	24	7	4	13	16
16	21 36 13	22 47 10	12 12	11	25	16	24	7	4	13	16
17	21 40 10	23 44 51	24 13	13	26	16	24	8	4	13	16
18	21 44 6	24 42 34	6♊29	15	27	17	24	8	4	13	16
19	21 48 3	25 40 18	19 4	16	28	18	24	8	4	13	16
20	21 51 59	26 38 4	2♋ 3	18	29	18	24	8	4	13	17
21	21 55 56	27 35 51	15 28	19	1♎	19	24	8	4	13	17
22	21 59 53	28 33 40	29 20	21	2	20	24	8	4	13	17
23	22 3 49	29 31 31	13♌36	22	3	20	23	8	4	13	17
24	22 7 46	0♍29 23	28 12	24	4	21	23	8	4	13	17
25	22 11 42	1 27 17	13♍ 0	25	5	22	23	9	4	13	17
26	22 15 39	2 25 12	27 53	26	7	22	23	9	4	13	17
27	22 19 35	3 23 8	12♎43	28	8	23	23	9	4	13	17
28	22 23 32	4 21 6	27 23	29	9	24	23	9	4	13	17
29	22 27 28	5 19 5	11♏48	0♎	10	24	23	9	4	13	17
30	22 31 25	6 17 5	25 56	2	11	25	23	9	4	14	17
31	22 35 22	7 15 7	9♐45	3	13	25	23	9	4	14	17

THE SUN ENTERS THE SIGN OF VIRGO ON AUG 23 AT 11:49.

DAY	TIME	☉	☽	☿	♀	♂	♃	♄	♅	♆	♇
	h m s	° ' "	° '	°	°	°	°	°	°	°	°
S 1	22 39 18	8♍13 10	23♐17	4♎	14♎	26♋	23♑R	9♍	4♋	14♎	17♌
E 2	22 43 15	9 11 14	6♑33	5	15	27	23	10	4	14	17
P 3	22 47 11	10 9 20	19 33	7	16	27	23	10	4	14	17
T 4	22 51 8	11 7 28	2♒19	8	17	28	23	10	4	14	17
E 5	22 55 4	12 5 37	14 52	9	18	29	23	10	4	14	17
M 6	22 59 1	13 3 47	27 13	10	20	29	23	10	4	14	17
B 7	23 2 57	14 1 59	9♓24	11	21	0♌	23	10	5	14	17
E 8	23 6 54	15 0 13	21 26	12	22	1	23	10	5	14	17
R 9	23 10 51	15 58 28	3♈21	13	23	1	22	10	5	14	17
10	23 14 47	16 56 45	15 10	14	24	2	22	11	5	14	17
11	23 18 44	17 55 5	26 57	15	26	2	22	11	5	14	17
12	23 22 40	18 53 26	8♉45	15	27	3	22	11	5	14	17
13	23 26 37	19 51 50	20 37	16	28	4	22	11	5	14	17
14	23 30 33	20 50 15	2♊38	17	29	4	22	11	5	14	17
15	23 34 30	21 48 43	14 52	17	0♏	5	22	11	5	14	17
16	23 38 26	22 47 13	27 25	18	2	6	22	11	5	14	17
17	23 42 23	23 45 45	10♋20	18	3	6	22	11	5	14	17
18	23 46 20	24 44 19	23 41	19	4	7	22 D	12	5	14	17
19	23 50 16	25 42 56	7♌29	19	5	7	22	12	5	14	17
20	23 54 13	26 41 34	21 45	19	6	8	22	12	5	14	17
21	23 58 9	27 40 15	6♍25	19 R	7	9	22	12	5	14	17
22	0 2 6	28 38 57	21 23	19	9	9	22	12	5	14	17
23	0 6 2	29 37 42	6♎30	19	10	10	22	12	5	14	17
24	0 9 59	0♎36 28	21 38	19	11	10	22	12	5	14	17
25	0 13 55	1 35 17	6♏38	18	12	11	22	12	5	14	18
26	0 17 52	2 34 7	21 21	18	13	12	22	13	5	14	18
27	0 21 48	3 32 59	5♐44	17	14	12	22	13	5	14	18
28	0 25 45	4 31 53	19 43	16	16	13	22	13	5	15	18
29	0 29 42	5 30 49	3♑17	16	17	13	23	13	5	15	18
30	0 33 38	6 29 46	16 29	15	18	14	23	13	5	15	18

THE SUN ENTERS THE SIGN OF LIBRA ON SEP 23 AT 09:07.

DAY	TIME	☉	☽	☿	♀	♂	♃	♄	♅	♆	♇
	h m s	° ' "	° '	°	°	°	°	°	°	°	°
O 1	0 37 35	7♎28 45	29♑21	13♎R	19♏	15♌	23♑	13♍	5♋	15♎	18♌
C 2	0 41 31	8 27 46	11♒55	12	20	15	23	13	5	15	18
T 3	0 45 28	9 26 49	24 15	11	21	16	23	13	5	15	18
O 4	0 49 24	10 25 53	6♓23	10	23	17	23	13	5	15	18
B 5	0 53 21	11 24 59	18 23	9	24	17	23	14	5	15	18
E 6	0 57 17	12 24 8	0♈16	8	25	18	23	14	5	15	18
R 7	1 1 14	13 23 18	12 5	7	26	18	23	14	5	15	18
8	1 5 11	14 22 30	23 53	6	27	19	23	14	5	15	18
9	1 9 7	15 21 44	5♉41	5	28	20	23	14	5	15	18
10	1 13 4	16 21 1	17 32	5	0♐	20	23	14	5	15	18
11	1 17 0	17 20 19	29 29	4	1	21	23	14	5 R	15	18
12	1 20 57	18 19 40	11♊34	4 D	2	21	23	14	5	15	18
13	1 24 53	19 19 4	23 51	4	3	22	23	14	5	15	18
14	1 28 50	20 18 29	6♋23	4	4	22	23	15	5	15	18
15	1 32 46	21 17 57	19 14	4	5	23	23	15	5	15	18
16	1 36 43	22 17 27	2♌28	5	6	24	24	15	5	15	18
17	1 40 40	23 17 0	16 6	5	8	24	24	15	5	15	18
18	1 44 36	24 16 34	0♍10	6	9	25	24	15	5	15	18
19	1 48 33	25 16 11	14 39	7	10	25	24	15	5	15	18
20	1 52 29	26 15 50	29 30	8	11	26	24	15	5	15	18
21	1 56 26	27 15 32	14♎36	9	12	27	24	15	5	15	18
22	2 0 22	28 15 15	29 48	10	13	27	24	15	5	15	18
23	2 4 19	29 15 0	14♏58	12	14	28	24	16	5	15	18
24	2 8 15	0♏14 48	29 55	13	15	28	24	16	5	15	18
25	2 12 12	1 14 37	14♐32	15	17	29	24	16	5	16	18
26	2 16 9	2 14 28	28 44	16	18	29	25	16	5	16	18
27	2 20 5	3 14 21	12♑28	18	19	0♍	25	16	5	16	18
28	2 24 2	4 14 15	25 45	19	20	1	25	16	5	16	18
29	2 27 58	5 14 11	8♒37	21	21	1	25	16	5	16	18
30	2 31 55	6 14 9	21 8	22	22	2	25	16	5	16	18
31	2 35 51	7 14 8	3♓21	24	23	2	25	16	5	16	18

THE SUN ENTERS THE SIGN OF SCORPIO ON OCT 23 AT 18:04.

DAY	TIME	☉	☽	☿	♀	♂	♃	♄	♅	♆	♇
	h m s	° ' "	° '	°	°	°	°	°	°	°	°
N 1	2 39 48	8♏14 9	15♓22	25♎	24♐	3♍	25♑	16♍	5♋R	16♎	18♌
O 2	2 43 44	9 14 11	27 15	27	25	3	25	17	5	16	18
V 3	2 47 41	10 14 15	9♈ 3	29	27	4	25	17	5	16	18
E 4	2 51 38	11 14 21	20 50	0♏	28	4	26	17	5	16	18
M 5	2 55 34	12 14 28	2♉39	2	29	5	26	17	5	16	18
B 6	2 59 31	13 14 38	14 32	4	0♑	6	26	17	5	16	18
E 7	3 3 27	14 14 49	26 31	5	1	6	26	17	5	16	18
R 8	3 7 24	15 15 2	8♊38	7	2	7	26	17	5	16	18
9	3 11 20	16 15 17	20 54	9	3	7	26	17	5	16	18
10	3 15 17	17 15 34	3♋21	10	4	8	26	17	5	16	18
11	3 19 13	18 15 53	16 0	12	5	8	27	17	5	16	18
12	3 23 10	19 16 14	28 54	13	6	9	27	17	5	16	18
13	3 27 7	20 16 36	12♌ 5	15	7	9	27	17	5	16	18
14	3 31 3	21 17 1	25 35	17	8	10	27	18	5	16	18
15	3 35 0	22 17 27	9♍26	18	9	10	27	18	5	16	18
16	3 38 56	23 17 56	23 37	20	10	11	27	18	4	16	18
17	3 42 53	24 18 26	8♎ 9	21	11	12	28	18	4	16	18
18	3 46 49	25 18 58	22 57	23	12	12	28	18	4	16	18
19	3 50 46	26 19 32	7♏56	25	13	13	28	18	4	16	18 R
20	3 54 42	27 20 7	22 58	26	15	13	28	18	4	16	18
21	3 58 39	28 20 44	7♐54	28	16	14	28	18	4	16	18
22	4 2 36	29 21 23	22 36	29	17	14	28	18	4	16	18
23	4 6 32	0♐22 3	6♑55	1♐	18	15	29	18	4	16	18
24	4 10 29	1 22 44	20 47	3	19	15	29	18	4	17	18
25	4 14 25	2 23 26	4♒11	4	20	16	29	18	4	17	18
26	4 18 22	3 24 9	17 8	6	20	16	29	18	4	17	18
27	4 22 18	4 24 53	29 42	7	21	17	29	18	4	17	18
28	4 26 15	5 25 39	11♓55	9	22	17	29	19	4	17	18
29	4 30 12	6 26 25	23 55	10	23	18	0♒	19	4	17	18
30	4 34 8	7 27 12	5♈45	12	24	18	0	19	4	17	18

THE SUN ENTERS THE SIGN OF SAGITTARIUS ON NOV 22 AT 15:17.

DAY	TIME	☉	☽	☿	♀	♂	♃	♄	♅	♆	♇
	h m s	° ' "	° '	°	°	°	°	°	°	°	°
D 1	4 38 5	8♐28 0	17♈32	14♐	25♑	19♍	0♒	19♍	4♋R	17♎	18♌R
E 2	4 42 1	9 28 49	29 20	15	26	19	0	19	4	17	18
C 3	4 45 58	10 29 39	11♉12	17	27	20	0	19	4	17	18
E 4	4 49 54	11 30 30	23 11	18	28	20	1	19	4	17	18
M 5	4 53 51	12 31 23	5♊21	20	29	21	1	19	4	17	18
B 6	4 57 47	13 32 16	17 42	21	0♒	21	1	19	4	17	18
E 7	5 1 44	14 33 10	0♋15	23	1	22	1	19	4	17	18
R 8	5 5 41	15 34 6	13 0	24	2	22	1	19	4	17	18
9	5 9 37	16 35 2	25 56	26	2	23	2	19	4	17	18
10	5 13 34	17 36 0	9♌ 4	28	3	23	2	19	4	17	18
11	5 17 30	18 36 58	22 24	29	4	23	2	19	4	17	18
12	5 21 27	19 37 58	5♍56	1♑	5	24	2	19	4	17	18
13	5 25 23	20 38 59	19 41	2	6	24	2	19	3	17	18
14	5 29 20	21 40 1	3♎39	4	6	25	3	19	3	17	18
15	5 33 16	22 41 4	17 52	5	7	25	3	19	3	17	18
16	5 37 13	23 42 8	2♏17	7	8	26	3	19	3	17	18
17	5 41 10	24 43 13	16 51	8	9	26	3	19	3	17	18
18	5 45 6	25 44 18	1♐30	10	9	27	3	19	3	17	18
19	5 49 3	26 45 25	16 8	12	10	27	4	19	3	17	18
20	5 52 59	27 46 32	0♑36	13	11	27	4	19	3	17	18
21	5 56 56	28 47 40	14 48	15	11	28	4	19	3	17	18
22	6 0 52	29 48 48	28 38	16	12	28	4	19	3	17	18
23	6 4 49	0♑49 57	12♒ 3	18	13	29	5	19	3	17	18
24	6 8 45	1 51 5	25 3	19	13	29	5	19	3	17	18
25	6 12 42	2 52 14	7♓39	20	14	0♎	5	19	3	17	18
26	6 16 39	3 53 23	19 56	22	14	0	5	19	3	17	18
27	6 20 35	4 54 32	1♈57	23	15	0	5	19	3	17	18
28	6 24 32	5 55 41	13 48	25	15	1	6	19	3	17	18
29	6 28 28	6 56 49	25 35	26	16	1	6	19	3	17	18
30	6 32 25	7 57 58	7♉24	27	16	1	6	19 R	3	17	18
31	6 36 21	8 59 7	19 19	28	17	2	6	19	3	17	18

THE SUN ENTERS THE SIGN OF CAPRICORN ON DEC 22 AT 04:24.

♈ ARIES ♉ TAURUS ♊ GEMINI ♋ CANCER ♌ LEO ♍ VIRGO ♎ LIBRA ♏ SCORPIO ♐ SAGITTARIUS ♑ CAPRICORN ♒ AQUARIUS ♓ PISCES

SIDEREAL SUN MOON MERCURY VENUS MARS JUPITER SATURN URANUS NEPTUNE PLUTO

DAY	TIME	☉	☽	☿	♀	♂	♃	♄	♅	♆	♇
	h m s	° ' "	° '	°	°	°	°	°	°	°	°
J 1	6 40 18	10♑ 0 15	1♊25	29♑	17♒	2♎	7♒	19♍R	3♋R	17♎	18♌R
A 2	6 44 14	11 1 24	13 44	0♒	17	3	7	19	3	17	18
N 3	6 48 11	12 2 33	26 19	1	18	3	7	19	3	17	18
U 4	6 52 8	13 3 41	9♋10	2	18	3	7	19	3	17	18
A 5	6 56 4	14 4 50	22 16	3	18	4	7	19	3	17	18
R 6	7 0 1	15 5 58	5♌36	3	18	4	8	19	2	17	18
Y 7	7 3 57	16 7 6	19 7	4	18	4	8	19	2	17	18
8	7 7 54	17 8 15	2♍48	4 R	19	5	8	19	2	17	18
9	7 11 50	18 9 23	16 36	4	19	5	3	19	2	17	18
10	7 15 47	19 10 31	0♎30	4	19 R	5	9	19	2	17	18
11	7 19 44	20 11 39	14 29	4	19	6	9	19	2	17	18
12	7 23 40	21 12 48	28 33	3	19	6	9	19	2	17	18
13	7 27 37	22 13 56	12♏41	2	19	6	9	19	2	17	18
14	7 31 33	23 15 5	26 53	1	18	6	9	19	2	17	18
15	7 35 30	24 16 13	11♐ 5	0	18	7	10	19	2	17	18
16	7 39 26	25 17 21	25 14	29♑	18	7	10	19	2	17	17
17	7 43 23	26 18 28	9♑16	28	18	7	10	19	2	17	17
18	7 47 19	27 19 36	23 7	27	18	8	10	19	2	17 R	17
19	7 51 16	28 20 42	6♒41	25	17	8	11	19	2	17	17
20	7 55 13	29 21 48	19 55	24	17	8	11	19	2	17	17
21	7 59 9	0♒22 53	2♓49	23	17	8	11	19	2	17	17
22	8 3 6	1 23 58	15 23	22	16	9	11	19	2	17	17
23	8 7 2	2 25 1	27 40	21	16	9	12	19	2	17	17
24	8 10 59	3 26 4	9♈42	20	15	9	12	19	2	17	17
25	8 14 55	4 27 5	21 34	19	15	9	12	19	2	17	17
26	8 18 52	5 28 5	3♉22	19	14	9	12	19	2	17	17
27	8 22 48	6 29 5	15 12	18	13	10	13	19	2	17	17
28	8 26 45	7 30 3	27 8	18	13	10	13	19	2	17	17
29	8 30 42	8 31 0	9♊15	18 D	12	10	13	19	2	17	17
30	8 34 38	9 31 56	21 39	18	12	10	13	19	2	17	17
31	8 38 35	10 32 50	4♋22	18	11	10	14	19	2	17	17

THE SUN ENTERS THE SIGN OF AQUARIUS ON JAN 20 AT 15:00.

DAY	TIME	☉	☽	☿	♀	♂	♃	♄	♅	♆	♇
	h m s	° ' "	° '	°	°	°	°	°	°	°	°
F 1	8 42 31	11♒33 44	17♋25	19♑	10♒R	10♎	14♒	18♍R	2♋R	17♎R	17♌R
E 2	8 46 28	12 34 36	0♌49	19	10	10	14	18	1	17	17
B 3	8 50 24	13 35 27	14 31	19	9	11	14	18	1	17	17
R 4	8 54 21	14 36 17	28 28	20	9	11	14	18	1	17	17
U 5	8 58 17	15 37 6	12♍36	21	8	11	15	18	1	17	17
A 6	9 2 14	16 37 54	26 50	21	7	11	15	18	1	17	17
R 7	9 6 11	17 38 41	11♎ 6	22	7	11	15	18	1	17	17
Y 8	9 10 7	18 39 26	25 21	23	6	11	15	18	1	17	17
9	9 14 4	19 40 11	9♏33	24	6	11	16	18	1	17	17
10	9 18 0	20 40 55	23 39	25	5	11	16	18	1	17	17
11	9 21 57	21 41 38	7♐39	26	5	11	16	18	1	17	17
12	9 25 53	22 42 20	21 32	27	5	11 R	16	18	1	17	17
13	9 29 50	23 43 1	5♑17	28	4	11	17	18	1	17	17
14	9 33 46	24 43 41	18 51	29	4	11	17	18	1	17	17
15	9 37 43	25 44 19	2♒14	0♒	4	11	17	18	1	17	17
16	9 41 40	26 44 56	15 24	1	4	11	17	18	1	17	17
17	9 45 36	27 45 31	28 18	3	3	11	18	17	1	17	17
18	9 49 33	28 46 5	10♓58	4	3	11	18	17	1	17	17
19	9 53 29	29 46 38	23 22	5	3	11	18	17	1	17	17
20	9 57 26	0♓47 8	5♈33	6	3 D	11	18	17	1	17	17
21	10 1 22	1 47 37	17 33	8	3	11	19	17	1	17	17
22	10 5 19	2 48 4	29 25	9	3	10	19	17	1	17	17
23	10 9 15	3 48 30	11♉13	11	3	10	19	17	1	17	17
24	10 13 12	4 48 53	23 2	12	3	10	19	17	1	17	17
25	10 17 9	5 49 14	4♊58	13	3	10	19	17	1	17	17
26	10 21 5	6 49 34	17 4	15	4	10	20	17	1	17	17
27	10 25 2	7 49 52	29 27	16	4	10	20	17	1	17	17
28	10 28 58	8 50 7	12♋10	18	4	9	20	17	1	17	16

THE SUN ENTERS THE SIGN OF PISCES ON FEB 19 AT 05:18.

DAY	TIME	☉	☽	☿	♀	♂	♃	♄	♅	♆	♇
	h m s	° ' "	° '	°	°	°	°	°	°	°	°
M 1	10 32 55	9♓50 21	25♋15	19♒	4♒	9♎R	20♒	17♍R	1♋R	17♎R	16♌R
A 2	10 36 51	10 50 33	8♌46	21	5	9	21	16	1	17	16
R 3	10 40 48	11 50 42	22 40	22	5	9	21	16	1	17	16
C 4	10 44 44	12 50 50	6♍55	24	5	9	21	16	1	17	16
H 5	10 48 41	13 50 56	21 26	25	6	8	21	16	1	17	16
6	10 52 38	14 50 59	6♎ 8	27	6	8	22	16	1	17	16
7	10 56 34	15 51 2	20 52	29	7	8	22	16	1	17	16
8	11 0 31	16 51 2	5♏32	0♓	7	7	22	16	1	17	16
9	11 4 27	17 51 1	20 4	2	8	7	22	16	1 D	17	16
10	11 8 24	18 50 59	4♐22	3	8	7	22	16	1	17	16
11	11 12 20	19 50 54	18 26	5	9	7	23	16	1	17	16
12	11 16 17	20 50 49	2♑13	7	9	6	23	16	1	17	16
13	11 20 13	21 50 41	15 43	9	10	6	23	16	1	17	16
14	11 24 10	22 50 32	28 58	10	11	6	23	16	1	17	16
15	11 28 7	23 50 21	11♒59	12	11	5	24	15	1	17	16
16	11 32 3	24 50 8	24 45	14	12	5	24	15	1	17	16
17	11 36 0	25 49 54	7♓18	16	13	4	24	15	1	17	16
18	11 39 56	26 49 37	19 39	17	13	4	24	15	1	17	16
19	11 43 53	27 49 19	1♈50	19	14	4	24	15	1	16	16
20	11 47 49	28 48 58	13 52	21	15	3	25	15	1	16	16
21	11 51 46	29 48 35	25 47	23	16	3	25	15	1	16	16
22	11 55 42	0♈48 11	7♉37	25	16	3	25	15	1	16	16
23	11 59 39	1 47 44	19 25	27	17	2	25	15	1	16	16
24	12 3 36	2 47 15	1♊15	29	18	2	26	15	1	16	16
25	12 7 32	3 46 43	13 10	1♈	19	1	26	15	1	16	16
26	12 11 29	4 46 10	25 16	3	20	1	26	15	1	16	16
27	12 15 25	5 45 34	7♋35	5	20	1	26	15	1	16	16
28	12 19 22	6 44 56	20 14	7	21	0	26	14	1	16	16
29	12 23 18	7 44 15	3♌15	9	22	0	27	14	1	16	16
30	12 27 15	8 43 32	16 41	11	23	29♍	27	14	1	16	16
31	12 31 11	9 42 47	0♍35	13	24	29	27	14	1	16	16

THE SUN ENTERS THE SIGN OF ARIES ON MAR 21 AT 04:35.

SIDEREAL SUN MOON MERCURY VENUS MARS JUPITER SATURN URANUS NEPTUNE PLUTO

DAY	TIME	☉	☽	☿	♀	♂	♃	♄	♅	♆	♇
	h m s	° ' "	° '	°	°	°	°	°	°	°	°
A 1	12 35 8	10♈42 0	14♍53	15♈	25♒	29♍R	27♒	14♍R	1♋	16♎R	16♌R
P 2	12 39 5	11 41 10	29 35	17	26	28	27	14	1	16	16
R 3	12 43 1	12 40 18	14♎32	19	27	28	28	14	1	16	16
I 4	12 46 58	13 39 24	29 37	21	28	28	28	14	1	16	16
L 5	12 50 54	14 38 28	14♏42	23	28	27	28	14	1	16	16
6	12 54 51	15 37 31	29 37	25	29	27	28	14	1	16	16
7	12 58 47	16 36 32	14♐15	27	0♓	27	28	14	1	16	16
8	13 2 44	17 35 31	28 32	29	1	26	29	14	1	16	16
9	13 6 40	18 34 28	12♑25	1♉	2	26	29	14	1	16	16
10	13 10 37	19 33 23	25 55	3	3	26	29	14	1	16	16
11	13 14 34	20 32 17	9♒ 2	5	4	25	29	14	1	16	16
12	13 18 30	21 31 9	21 49	7	5	25	29	14	1	16	16
13	13 22 27	22 29 59	4♓20	8	6	25	0♓	13	1	16	16
14	13 26 23	23 28 47	16 37	10	7	25	0	13	1	16	16
15	13 30 20	24 27 34	28 44	12	8	24	0	13	2	16	16
16	13 34 16	25 26 18	10♈43	13	9	24	0	13	2	16	16
17	13 38 13	26 25 1	22 36	15	10	24	0	13	2	16	16
18	13 42 9	27 23 42	4♉26	16	11	24	0	13	2	16	16
19	13 46 6	28 22 21	16 15	18	12	23	1	13	2	16	16
20	13 50 2	29 20 58	28 4	19	13	23	1	13	2	16	16
21	13 53 59	0♉19 32	9♊57	20	14	23	1	13	2	16	16
22	13 57 56	1 18 5	21 55	21	15	23	1	13	2	16	16
23	14 1 52	2 16 36	4♋ 2	22	16	23	1	13	2	16	16
24	14 5 49	3 15 5	16 22	23	17	23	2	13	2	16	16
25	14 9 45	4 13 31	28 57	24	18	22	2	13	2	15	16
26	14 13 42	5 11 55	11♌53	25	19	22	2	13	2	15	16
27	14 17 38	6 10 17	25 11	25	21	22	2	13	2	15	16
28	14 21 35	7 8 37	8♍55	26	22	22	2	13	2	15	16 D
29	14 25 31	8 6 55	23 6	27	23	22	2	13	2	15	16
30	14 29 28	9 5 11	7♎42	27	24	22	3	13	2	15	16

THE SUN ENTERS THE SIGN OF TAURUS ON APR 20 AT 15:59.

DAY	TIME	☉	☽	☿	♀	♂	♃	♄	♅	♆	♇
	h m s	° ' "	° '	°	°	°	°	°	°	°	°
M 1	14 33 25	10♉ 3 25	22♎39	27♉	25♓	22♍R	3♓	13♍R	2♋	15♎R	16♌
A 2	14 37 21	11 1 37	7♏51	27	26	22	3	13	2	15	16
Y 3	14 41 18	11 59 47	23 7	28 R	27	22 D	3	13	2	15	16
4	14 45 14	12 57 56	8♐18	28	28	22	3	13	2	15	16
5	14 49 11	13 56 3	23 12	27	29	22	3	13	2	15	16
6	14 53 7	14 54 9	7♑44	27	0♈	22	3	13	2	15	16
7	14 57 4	15 52 13	21 48	27	1	22	4	13	2	15	16
8	15 1 1	16 50 16	5♒24	27	2	22	4	13	2	15	16
9	15 4 57	17 48 18	18 32	26	3	22	4	13	2	15	16
10	15 8 54	18 46 18	1♓16	26	5	22	4	13	2	15	16
11	15 12 50	19 44 16	13 41	25	6	22	4	13	3	15	16
12	15 16 47	20 42 14	25 50	25	7	22	4	13	3	15	16
13	15 20 43	21 40 10	7♈49	24	8	23	4	13	3	15	16
14	15 24 40	22 38 4	19 40	24	9	23	5	13	3	15	16
15	15 28 36	23 35 58	1♉29	23	10	23	5	13 D	3	15	16
16	15 32 33	24 33 50	13 17	23	11	23	5	13	3	15	16
17	15 36 29	25 31 41	25 7	22	12	23	5	13	3	15	16
18	15 40 26	26 29 30	7♊ 0	21	13	23	5	13	3	15	16
19	15 44 23	27 27 18	18 59	21	15	23	5	13	3	15	16
20	15 48 19	28 25 4	1♋ 5	20	16	24	5	13	3	15	16
21	15 52 16	29 22 49	13 20	20	17	24	5	13	3	15	16
22	15 56 12	0♊20 32	25 45	20	18	24	5	13	3	15	16
23	16 0 9	1 18 14	8♌24	19	19	24	6	13	3	15	16
24	16 4 5	2 15 54	21 18	19	20	24	6	13	3	15	16
25	16 8 2	3 13 33	4♍32	19	21	25	6	13	3	15	16
26	16 11 59	4 11 10	18 7	19	22	25	6	13	3	15	16
27	16 15 55	5 8 45	2♎ 6	19 D	24	25	6	13	3	15	16
28	16 19 52	6 6 19	16 29	19	25	25	6	13	3	15	16
29	16 23 48	7 3 52	1♏14	19	26	26	6	13	3	15	16
30	16 27 45	8 1 23	16 15	19	27	26	6	13	4	15	16
31	16 31 41	8 58 54	1♐26	19	28	26	6	13	4	15	16

THE SUN ENTERS THE SIGN OF GEMINI ON MAY 21 AT 15:27.

DAY	TIME	☉	☽	☿	♀	♂	♃	♄	♅	♆	♇
	h m s	° ' "	° '	°	°	°	°	°	°	°	°
J 1	16 35 38	9♊56 23	16♐36	19♉	29♈	26♍	6♓	13♍	4♋	15♎R	16♌
U 2	16 39 34	10 53 51	1♑35	20	0♉	27	6	13	4	15	16
N 3	16 43 31	11 51 19	16 13	20	2	27	7	13	4	15	16
E 4	16 47 28	12 48 45	0♒24	21	3	27	7	13	4	15	16
5	16 51 24	13 46 11	14 6	21	4	28	7	13	4	15	16
6	16 55 21	14 43 36	27 20	22	5	28	7	13	4	15	16
7	16 59 17	15 41 0	10♓ 6	23	6	28	7	13	4	15	16
8	17 3 14	16 38 24	22 31	23	7	29	7	13	4	15	16
9	17 7 10	17 35 47	4♈39	24	9	29	7	13	4	15	16
10	17 11 7	18 33 10	16 36	25	10	29	7	13	4	15	16
11	17 15 3	19 30 32	28 25	26	11	0♎	7	13	4	15	16
12	17 19 0	20 27 53	10♉13	27	12	0	7	13	4	15	16
13	17 22 57	21 25 14	22 2	28	13	0	7	13	4	15	16
14	17 26 53	22 22 35	3♊56	29	14	1	7	13	4	15	16
15	17 30 50	23 19 54	15 56	0♊	15	1	7	13	4	15	16
16	17 34 46	24 17 14	28 5	2	17	2	7	13	5	15	16
17	17 38 43	25 14 33	10♋23	3	18	2	7	13	5	15	16
18	17 42 39	26 11 51	22 51	4	19	2	7	14	5	15	16
19	17 46 36	27 9 8	5♌29	6	20	3	7	14	5	15	16
20	17 50 32	28 6 25	18 19	7	21	3	7	14	5	15	16
21	17 54 29	29 3 41	1♍21	9	22	4	7	14	5	15	16
22	17 58 26	0♋ 0 56	14 38	10	24	4	7	14	5	15	16
23	18 2 22	0 58 11	28 11	12	25	4	7	14	5	15	16
24	18 6 19	1 55 24	12♎ 3	14	26	5	7	14	5	15	16
25	18 10 15	2 52 38	26 13	15	27	5	7	14	5	15	16
26	18 14 12	3 49 50	10♏41	17	28	6	7	14	5	15 D	17
27	18 18 8	4 47 3	25 24	19	29	6	7 R	14	5	15	17
28	18 22 5	5 44 14	10♐16	21	1♊	7	7	14	5	15	17
29	18 26 2	6 41 26	25 10	23	2	7	7	14	5	15	17
30	18 29 58	7 38 37	9♑57	25	3	8	7	14	5	15	17

THE SUN ENTERS THE SIGN OF CANCER ON JUN 21 AT 23:37.

♈ ARIES ♉ TAURUS ♊ GEMINI ♋ CANCER ♌ LEO ♍ VIRGO ♎ LIBRA ♏ SCORPIO ♐ SAGITTARIUS ♑ CAPRICORN ♒ AQUARIUS ♓ PISCES

SIDEREAL SUN MOON MERCURY VENUS MARS JUPITER SATURN URANUS NEPTUNE PLUTO

DAY	TIME	☉	☽	☿	♀	♂	♃	♄	♅	♆	♇
	h m s	° ' "	° '	°	°	°	°	°	°	°	°
J 1	18 33 55	8♋35 48	24♑27	27♊	4♊	8♎	7♓R	14♍	5♋	15♎	17♌
U 2	18 37 51	9 32 59	8♒36	29	5	8	7	14	5	15	17
L 3	18 41 48	10 30 10	22 18	1♋	7	9	7	15	6	15	17
Y 4	18 45 44	11 27 22	5♓32	3	8	9	7	15	6	15	17
5	18 49 41	12 24 33	18 22	5	9	10	7	15	6	15	17
6	18 53 37	13 21 44	0♈49	7	10	10	7	15	6	15	17
7	18 57 34	14 18 56	12 59	9	11	11	7	15	6	15	17
8	19 1 31	15 16 8	24 56	11	12	11	7	15	6	15	17
9	19 5 27	16 13 21	6♉47	14	14	12	7	15	6	15	17
10	19 9 24	17 10 34	18 37	16	15	12	7	15	6	15	17
11	19 13 20	18 7 47	0♊29	18	16	13	7	15	6	15	17
12	19 17 17	19 5 1	12 28	20	17	13	7	15	6	15	17
13	19 21 13	20 2 16	24 36	22	18	14	7	15	6	15	17
14	19 25 10	20 59 30	6♋55	24	20	14	7	15	6	15	17
15	19 29 6	21 56 45	19 28	26	21	15	7	16	6	15	17
16	19 33 3	22 54 1	2♌12	29	22	15	7	16	6	15	17
17	19 37 0	23 51 16	15 9	1♌	23	16	7	16	6	15	17
18	19 40 56	24 48 32	28 17	3	24	17	7	16	6	15	17
19	19 44 53	25 45 48	11♍37	5	26	17	7	16	6	15	17
20	19 48 49	26 43 5	25 8	7	27	18	7	16	7	15	17
21	19 52 46	27 40 21	8♎50	9	28	18	7	16	7	15	17
22	19 56 42	28 37 38	22 43	11	29	19	6	16	7	15	17
23	20 0 39	29 34 55	6♏48	12	0♋	19	6	16	7	15	17
24	20 4 35	0♌32 12	21 3	14	2	20	6	16	7	15	17
25	20 8 32	1 29 30	5♐27	16	3	20	6	16	7	15	17
26	20 12 29	2 26 49	19 56	18	4	21	6	17	7	15	17
27	20 16 25	3 24 7	4♑25	20	5	21	6	17	7	15	17
28	20 20 22	4 21 27	18 48	21	6	22	6	17	7	15	17
29	20 24 18	5 18 47	2♒58	23	8	23	6	17	7	15	17
30	20 28 15	6 16 7	16 51	25	9	23	6	17	7	15	17
31	20 32 11	7 13 29	0♓23	27	10	24	6	17	7	15	17

THE SUN ENTERS THE SIGN OF LEO ON JUL 23 AT 10:31.

DAY	TIME	☉	☽	☿	♀	♂	♃	♄	♅	♆	♇
	h m s	° ' "	° '	°	°	°	°	°	°	°	°
A 1	20 36 8	8♌10 51	13♓32	28♌	11♋	24♎	6♓R	17♍	7♋	15♎	18♌
U 2	20 40 4	9 8 14	26 19	0♍	12	25	5	17	7	15	18
G 3	20 44 1	10 5 38	8♈46	1	14	25	5	17	7	15	18
U 4	20 47 58	11 3 4	20 57	3	15	26	5	18	7	15	18
S 5	20 51 54	12 0 31	2♉56	4	16	27	5	18	7	15	18
T 6	20 55 51	12 57 59	14 49	6	17	27	5	18	7	15	18
7	20 59 47	13 55 28	26 40	7	18	28	5	18	8	15	18
8	21 3 44	14 52 59	8♊34	9	20	28	5	18	8	15	18
9	21 7 40	15 50 31	20 37	10	21	29	5	18	8	15	18
10	21 11 37	16 48 4	2♋51	12	22	0♏	5	18	8	15	18
11	21 15 33	17 45 39	15 19	13	23	0	4	18	8	15	18
12	21 19 30	18 43 14	28 4	14	24	1	4	18	8	15	18
13	21 23 27	19 40 52	11♌ 5	16	26	1	4	19	8	15	18
14	21 27 23	20 38 30	24 22	17	27	2	4	19	8	15	18
15	21 31 20	21 36 9	7♍53	18	28	3	4	19	8	15	18
16	21 35 16	22 33 50	21 37	19	29	3	4	19	8	15	18
17	21 39 13	23 31 31	5♎30	20	0♌	4	4	19	8	15	18
18	21 43 9	24 29 14	19 32	22	2	4	4	19	8	15	18
19	21 47 6	25 26 58	3♏38	23	3	5	3	19	8	15	18
20	21 51 2	26 24 43	17 49	24	4	6	3	19	8	15	18
21	21 54 59	27 22 29	2♐ 1	25	5	6	3	19	8	15	18
22	21 58 56	28 20 17	16 12	26	7	7	3	20	8	15	18
23	22 2 52	29 18 5	0♑22	27	8	8	3	20	8	15	18
24	22 6 49	0♍15 55	14 25	27	9	8	3	20	8	15	18
25	22 10 45	1 13 46	28 20	28	10	9	3	20	8	15	18
26	22 14 42	2 11 38	12♒ 4	29	11	9	3	20	8	16	18
27	22 18 38	3 9 31	25 33	0♎	13	10	2	20	8	16	18
28	22 22 35	4 7 26	8♓45	0	14	11	2	20	8	16	18
29	22 26 31	5 5 23	21 41	1	15	11	2	20	9	16	18
30	22 30 28	6 3 21	4♈19	1	16	12	2	21	9	16	18
31	22 34 25	7 1 20	16 41	2	18	13	2	21	9	16	18

THE SUN ENTERS THE SIGN OF VIRGO ON AUG 23 AT 17:24.

DAY	TIME	☉	☽	☿	♀	♂	♃	♄	♅	♆	♇
	h m s	° ' "	° '	°	°	°	°	°	°	°	°
S 1	22 38 21	7♍59 22	28♈50	2♎	19♌	13♏	2♓R	21♍	9♋	16♎	18♌
E 2	22 42 18	8 57 26	10♉49	2	20	14	2	21	9	16	18
P 3	22 46 14	9 55 31	22 42	2	21	15	1	21	9	16	19
T 4	22 50 11	10 53 38	4♊34	2 R	23	15	1	21	9	16	19
E 5	22 54 7	11 51 48	16 29	2	24	16	1	21	9	16	19
M 6	22 58 4	12 49 59	28 32	2	25	17	1	21	9	16	19
B 7	23 2 0	13 48 13	10♋47	2	26	17	1	22	9	16	19
E 8	23 5 57	14 46 28	23 19	2	27	18	1	22	9	16	19
R 9	23 9 54	15 44 46	6♌ 9	1	29	19	1	22	9	16	19
10	23 13 50	16 43 5	19 21	1	0♍	19	1	22	9	16	19
11	23 17 47	17 41 26	2♍54	0	1	20	0	22	9	16	19
12	23 21 43	18 39 49	16 46	29♍	2	21	0	22	9	16	19
13	23 25 40	19 38 14	0♎55	28	4	21	0	22	9	16	19
14	23 29 36	20 36 41	15 16	27	5	22	0	22	9	16	19
15	23 33 33	21 35 9	29 44	26	6	23	0	23	9	16	19
16	23 37 29	22 33 39	14♏13	25	7	23	0	23	9	16	19
17	23 41 26	23 32 11	28 40	24	9	24	0	23	9	16	19
18	23 45 23	24 30 44	13♐ 1	23	10	25	0	23	9	16	19
19	23 49 19	25 29 20	27 11	22	11	25	0	23	9	16	19
20	23 53 16	26 27 57	11♑ 9	21	12	26	29♒	23	9	16	19
21	23 57 12	27 26 35	24 54	20	14	27	29	23	9	16	19
22	0 1 9	28 25 15	8♒26	20	15	27	29	23	9	16	19
23	0 5 5	29 23 57	21 43	19	16	28	29	24	9	16	19
24	0 9 2	0♎22 40	4♓47	18	17	29	29	24	9	16	19
25	0 12 58	1 21 25	17 37	18	18	29	29	24	9	17	19
26	0 16 55	2 20 12	0♈15	18 D	20	0♐	29	24	9	17	19
27	0 20 52	3 19 2	12 39	18	21	1	29	24	9	17	19
28	0 24 48	4 17 53	24 53	18	22	2	29	24	9	17	19
29	0 28 45	5 16 46	6♉57	18	23	2	29	24	9	17	19
30	0 32 41	6 15 42	18 54	19	25	3	29	24	9	17	19

THE SUN ENTERS THE SIGN OF LIBRA ON SEP 23 AT 14:44.

SIDEREAL SUN MOON MERCURY VENUS MARS JUPITER SATURN URANUS NEPTUNE PLUTO

DAY	TIME	☉	☽	☿	♀	♂	♃	♄	♅	♆	♇
	h m s	° ' "	° '	°	°	°	°	°	°	°	°
O 1	0 36 38	7♎14 39	0♊46	20♍	26♍	4♐	28♒R	25♍	9♋	17♎	19♌
C 2	0 40 34	8 13 39	12 37	20	27	4	28	25	9	17	19
T 3	0 44 31	9 12 42	24 31	21	28	5	28	25	9	17	19
O 4	0 48 27	10 11 46	6♋32	22	0♎	6	28	25	9	17	19
B 5	0 52 24	11 10 53	18 45	24	1	6	28	25	9	17	19
E 6	0 56 21	12 10 2	1♌13	25	2	7	28	25	9	17	19
R 7	1 0 17	13 9 14	14 2	26	3	8	28	25	9	17	19
8	1 4 14	14 8 28	27 15	28	5	9	28	25	9	17	19
9	1 8 10	15 7 43	10♍53	29	6	9	28	26	9	17	19
10	1 12 7	16 7 2	24 56	1♎	7	10	28	26	9	17	19
11	1 16 3	17 6 22	9♎22	2	8	11	28	26	9	17	19
12	1 20 0	18 5 44	24 6	4	10	11	28	26	9	17	19
13	1 23 56	19 5 9	9♏ 0	5	11	12	28	26	9	17	19
14	1 27 53	20 4 35	23 57	7	12	13	28	26	9	17	20
15	1 31 50	21 4 3	8♐48	9	13	14	28	26	9	17	20
16	1 35 46	22 3 33	23 26	11	15	14	28	26	9 R	17	20
17	1 39 43	23 3 5	7♑46	12	16	15	28	26	9	17	20
18	1 43 39	24 2 39	21 45	14	17	16	28	27	9	17	20
19	1 47 36	25 2 14	5♒23	16	18	16	28	27	9	17	20
20	1 51 32	26 1 51	18 41	17	20	17	28	27	9	17	20
21	1 55 29	27 1 30	1♓40	19	21	18	28	27	9	17	20
22	1 59 25	28 1 10	14 24	21	22	19	28	27	9	18	20
23	2 3 22	29 0 52	26 55	22	23	19	28	27	9	18	20
24	2 7 19	0♏ 0 36	9♈14	24	25	20	28 D	27	9	18	20
25	2 11 15	1 0 22	21 25	26	26	21	28	27	9	18	20
26	2 15 12	2 0 10	3♉29	28	27	22	28	27	9	18	20
27	2 19 8	3 0 0	15 27	29	28	22	28	28	9	18	20
28	2 23 5	3 59 51	27 20	1♏	0♏	23	28	28	9	18	20
29	2 27 1	4 59 45	9♊12	3	1	24	28	28	9	18	20
30	2 30 58	5 59 41	21 3	4	2	25	28	28	9	18	20
31	2 34 54	6 59 39	2♋57	6	3	25	28	28	9	18	20

THE SUN ENTERS THE SIGN OF SCORPIO ON OCT 23 AT 23:45.

DAY	TIME	☉	☽	☿	♀	♂	♃	♄	♅	♆	♇
	h m s	° ' "	° '	°	°	°	°	°	°	°	°
N 1	2 38 51	7♏59 40	14♋57	8♏	5♏	26♐	28♒	28♍	9♋R	18♎	20♌
O 2	2 42 48	8 59 42	27 7	9	6	27	28	28	9	18	20
V 3	2 46 44	9 59 46	9♌31	11	7	28	28	28	9	18	20
E 4	2 50 41	10 59 53	22 13	12	8	28	28	28	9	18	20
M 5	2 54 37	12 0 1	5♍19	14	10	29	28	29	9	18	20
B 6	2 58 34	13 0 12	18 51	16	11	0♑	28	29	9	18	20
E 7	3 2 30	14 0 24	2♎51	17	12	1	28	29	9	18	20
R 8	3 6 27	15 0 39	17 20	19	14	1	28	29	9	18	20
9	3 10 23	16 0 56	2♏12	20	15	2	28	29	9	18	20
10	3 14 20	17 1 14	17 21	22	16	3	28	29	9	18	20
11	3 18 16	18 1 34	2♐38	24	17	4	28	29	9	18	20
12	3 22 13	19 1 56	17 51	25	19	4	28	29	9	18	20
13	3 26 10	20 2 20	2♑50	27	20	5	28	29	9	18	20
14	3 30 6	21 2 45	17 26	28	21	6	28	29	9	18	20
15	3 34 3	22 3 11	1♒36	0♐	22	7	28	0♎	9	18	20
16	3 37 59	23 3 38	15 18	1	24	7	28	0	9	18	20
17	3 41 56	24 4 7	28 34	3	25	8	29	0	9	18	20
18	3 45 52	25 4 37	11♓26	4	26	9	29	0	9	18	20
19	3 49 49	26 5 9	23 59	6	27	10	29	0	9	18	20
20	3 53 46	27 5 41	6♈18	7	29	10	29	0	9	18	20
21	3 57 42	28 6 15	18 26	9	0♐	11	29	0	9	19	20 R
22	4 1 39	29 6 50	0♉26	11	1	12	29	0	9	19	20
23	4 5 35	0♐ 7 26	12 21	12	2	13	29	0	9	19	20
24	4 9 32	1 8 4	24 14	14	4	13	29	0	9	19	20
25	4 13 28	2 8 44	6♊ 6	15	5	14	29	0	9	19	20
26	4 17 25	3 9 24	17 59	17	6	15	29	0	9	19	20
27	4 21 21	4 10 6	29 53	18	7	16	29	1	9	19	20
28	4 25 18	5 10 50	11♋51	20	9	17	0♓	1	9	19	20
29	4 29 15	6 11 35	23 54	21	10	17	0	1	9	19	20
30	4 33 11	7 12 21	6♌ 6	23	11	18	0	1	9	19	20

THE SUN ENTERS THE SIGN OF SAGITTARIUS ON NOV 22 AT 21:03.

DAY	TIME	☉	☽	☿	♀	♂	♃	♄	♅	♆	♇
	h m s	° ' "	° '	°	°	°	°	°	°	°	°
D 1	4 37 8	8♐13 9	18♌29	24♐	12♐	19♑	0♓	1♎	9♋R	19♎	20♌R
E 2	4 41 4	9 13 58	1♍ 7	26	14	20	0	1	9	19	20
C 3	4 45 1	10 14 49	14 5	27	15	20	0	1	9	19	20
E 4	4 48 57	11 15 41	27 27	28	16	21	0	1	9	19	20
M 5	4 52 54	12 16 34	11♎16	0♑	17	22	0	1	8	19	20
B 6	4 56 50	13 17 29	25 33	1	19	23	1	1	8	19	20
E 7	5 0 47	14 18 25	10♏17	3	20	23	1	1	8	19	20
R 8	5 4 44	15 19 22	25 22	4	21	24	1	1	8	19	20
9	5 8 40	16 20 21	10♐40	5	22	25	1	1	8	19	20
10	5 12 37	17 21 20	26 1	7	24	26	1	1	8	19	20
11	5 16 33	18 22 21	11♑11	8	25	27	1	1	8	19	20
12	5 20 30	19 23 22	26 1	9	26	27	1	1	8	19	20
13	5 24 26	20 24 23	10♒24	11	27	28	2	2	8	19	20
14	5 28 23	21 25 25	24 16	12	29	29	2	2	8	19	20
15	5 32 20	22 26 28	7♓39	13	0♑	0♒	2	2	8	19	20
16	5 36 16	23 27 31	20 34	14	1	0	2	2	8	19	20
17	5 40 13	24 28 34	3♈ 7	15	3	1	2	2	8	19	20
18	5 44 9	25 29 38	15 23	16	4	2	2	2	8	19	20
19	5 48 6	26 30 42	27 26	16	5	3	2	2	8	19	20
20	5 52 2	27 31 47	9♉21	17	6	4	3	2	8	19	20
21	5 55 59	28 32 52	21 12	18	8	4	3	2	8	19	20
22	5 59 55	29 33 57	3♊ 3	18	9	5	3	2	8	19	20
23	6 3 52	0♑35 3	14 55	18 R	10	6	3	2	8	19	20
24	6 7 49	1 36 9	26 51	18	11	7	3	2	8	19	20
25	6 11 45	2 37 15	8♋52	18	13	8	3	2	8	19	20
26	6 15 42	3 38 22	20 58	18	14	8	4	2	8	19	20
27	6 19 38	4 39 29	3♌11	17	15	9	4	2	8	19	20
28	6 23 35	5 40 37	15 32	16	16	10	4	2	8	19	20
29	6 27 31	6 41 44	28 3	15	18	11	4	2	7	19	20
30	6 31 28	7 42 53	10♍47	14	19	11	4	2	7	19	20
31	6 35 24	8 44 2	23 46	13	20	12	5	2	7	19	20

THE SUN ENTERS THE SIGN OF CAPRICORN ON DEC 22 AT 10:14.

♈ ARIES ♉ TAURUS ♊ GEMINI ♋ CANCER ♌ LEO ♍ VIRGO ♎ LIBRA ♏ SCORPIO ♐ SAGITTARIUS ♑ CAPRICORN ♒ AQUARIUS ♓ PISCES

SIDEREAL SUN MOON MERCURY VENUS MARS JUPITER SATURN URANUS NEPTUNE PLUTO

DAY	TIME	☉	☽	☿	♀	♂	♃	♄	♅	♆	♇
	h m s	° ' "	° '	°	°	°	°	°	°	°	°
J 1	6 39 21	9♑45 11	7♎ 3	12♑R	21♑	13♒	5♓	2♎	7♋R	19♎	19♌R
A 2	6 43 18	10 46 20	20 42	10	23	14	5	2	7	19	19
N 3	6 47 14	11 47 30	4♏44	9	24	15	5	2	7	19	19
U 4	6 51 11	12 48 40	19 10	8	25	15	5	2	7	19	19
A 5	6 55 7	13 49 51	3♐56	7	26	16	5	2	7	19	19
R 6	6 59 4	14 51 2	18 57	5	28	17	6	2	7	19	19
Y 7	7 3 0	15 52 13	4♑ 4	4	29	18	6	2	7	19	19
8	7 6 57	16 53 24	19 7	4	0♒	19	6	2	7	19	19
9	7 10 53	17 54 34	3♒55	3	1	19	6	2	7	19	19
10	7 14 50	18 55 44	18 21	2	3	20	6	2	7	19	19
11	7 18 47	19 56 54	2♓20	2	4	21	7	2	7	20	19
12	7 22 43	20 58 3	15 50	2 D	5	22	7	2 R	7	20	19
13	7 26 40	21 59 12	28 53	2	6	22	7	2	7	20	19
14	7 30 36	23 0 20	11♈32	2	8	23	7	2	7	20	19
15	7 34 33	24 1 27	23 51	2	9	24	7	2	7	20	19
16	7 38 29	25 2 34	5♉55	3	10	25	8	2	7	20	19
17	7 42 26	26 3 40	17 51	3	11	26	8	2	7	20	19
18	7 46 22	27 4 45	29 42	4	13	26	8	2	7	20	19
19	7 50 19	28 5 50	11♊33	4	14	27	8	2	7	20	19
20	7 54 16	29 6 53	23 27	5	15	28	9	2	7	20	19
21	7 58 12	0♒ 7 56	5♋28	6	16	29	9	2	7	20 R	19
22	8 2 9	1 8 58	17 36	7	18	0♓	9	2	6	20	19
23	8 6 5	2 10 0	29 54	8	19	0	9	2	6	20	19
24	8 10 2	3 11 0	12♌21	9	20	1	9	2	6	20	19
25	8 13 58	4 12 0	24 59	10	21	2	10	2	6	20	19
26	8 17 55	5 12 59	7♍48	11	23	3	10	2	6	20	19
27	8 21 52	6 13 58	20 48	12	24	4	10	2	6	20	19
28	8 25 48	7 14 56	4♎ 0	13	25	4	10	2	6	20	19
29	8 29 45	8 15 53	17 26	14	26	5	10	2	6	20	19
30	8 33 41	9 16 49	1♏ 7	15	28	6	11	2	6	20	19
31	8 37 38	10 17 45	15 3	17	29	7	11	2	6	20	19

THE SUN ENTERS THE SIGN OF AQUARIUS ON JAN 20 AT 20:53.

DAY	TIME	☉	☽	☿	♀	♂	♃	♄	♅	♆	♇
	h m s	° ' "	° '	°	°	°	°	°	°	°	°
F 1	8 41 34	11♒18 40	29♏14	18♑	0♓	7♓	11♓	2♎R	6♋R	20♎R	19♌R
E 2	8 45 31	12 19 35	13♐39	19	1	8	11	2	6	19	19
B 3	8 49 27	13 20 29	28 14	21	3	9	12	2	6	19	19
R 4	8 53 24	14 21 22	12♑54	22	4	10	12	2	6	19	19
U 5	8 57 21	15 22 14	27 32	23	5	11	12	2	6	19	19
A 6	9 1 17	16 23 4	12♒ 0	25	6	11	12	2	6	19	19
R 7	9 5 14	17 23 54	26 13	26	8	12	13	2	6	19	19
Y 8	9 9 10	18 24 42	10♓ 5	27	9	13	13	2	6	19	19
9	9 13 7	19 25 29	23 34	29	10	14	13	2	6	19	19
10	9 17 3	20 26 14	6♈39	0♒	11	14	13	2	6	19	19
11	9 21 0	21 26 58	19 22	2	13	15	13	2	6	19	19
12	9 24 56	22 27 41	1♉46	3	14	16	14	2	6	19	19
13	9 28 53	23 28 21	13 54	5	15	17	14	1	6	19	19
14	9 32 50	24 29 0	25 53	6	16	18	14	1	6	19	19
15	9 36 46	25 29 38	7♊46	8	18	18	14	1	6	19	18
16	9 40 43	26 30 14	19 38	9	19	19	15	1	6	19	18
17	9 44 39	27 30 48	1♋34	11	20	20	15	1	6	19	18
18	9 48 36	28 31 20	13 38	13	21	21	15	1	6	19	18
19	9 52 32	29 31 51	25 52	14	23	22	15	1	6	19	18
20	9 56 29	0♓32 19	8♌19	16	24	22	16	1	6	19	18
21	10 0 25	1 32 47	21 1	17	25	23	16	1	6	19	18
22	10 4 22	2 33 12	3♍57	19	26	24	16	1	6	19	18
23	10 8 19	3 33 36	17 8	21	28	25	16	1	6	19	18
24	10 12 15	4 33 58	0♎33	22	29	25	17	1	6	19	18
25	10 16 12	5 34 19	14 10	24	0♈	26	17	1	6	19	18
26	10 20 8	6 34 38	27 58	26	1	27	17	1	6	19	18
27	10 24 5	7 34 56	11♏54	27	2	28	17	1	6	19	18
28	10 28 1	8 35 12	25 59	29	4	29	17	1	5	19	18

THE SUN ENTERS THE SIGN OF PISCES ON FEB 19 AT 11:10.

DAY	TIME	☉	☽	☿	♀	♂	♃	♄	♅	♆	♇
	h m s	° ' "	° '	°	°	°	°	°	°	°	°
M 1	10 31 58	9♓35 27	10♐ 8	1♓	5♈	29♓	18♓	0♎R	5♋R	19♎R	18♌R
A 2	10 35 54	10 35 41	24 22	3	6	0♈	18	0	5	19	18
R 3	10 39 51	11 35 53	8♑36	4	7	1	18	0	5	19	18
C 4	10 43 48	12 36 3	22 49	6	9	2	18	0	5	19	18
H 5	10 47 44	13 36 12	6♒56	8	10	2	19	0	5	19	18
6	10 51 41	14 36 19	20 55	10	11	3	19	0	5	19	18
7	10 55 37	15 36 25	4♓42	12	12	4	19	0	5	19	18
8	10 59 34	16 36 28	18 14	14	14	5	19	0	5	19	18
9	11 3 30	17 36 30	1♈29	15	15	5	20	0	5	19	18
10	11 7 27	18 36 30	14 27	17	16	6	20	0	5	19	18
11	11 11 23	19 36 28	27 7	19	17	7	20	0	5	19	18
12	11 15 20	20 36 23	9♉30	21	18	8	20	0	5	19	18
13	11 19 16	21 36 17	21 41	23	20	9	21	0	5	19	18
14	11 23 13	22 36 8	3♊41	25	21	9	21	0	5 D	19	18
15	11 27 10	23 35 57	15 35	27	22	10	21	29♍	5	19	18
16	11 31 6	24 35 44	27 28	29	23	11	21	29	5	19	18
17	11 35 3	25 35 29	9♋24	1♈	25	12	22	29	5	19	18
18	11 38 59	26 35 12	21 28	3	26	12	22	29	5	19	18
19	11 42 56	27 34 52	3♌44	5	27	13	22	29	5	19	18
20	11 46 52	28 34 30	16 16	7	28	14	22	29	5	19	18
21	11 50 49	29 34 6	29 6	9	29	15	23	29	5	19	18
22	11 54 45	0♈33 39	12♍17	11	1♉	15	23	29	5	19	18
23	11 58 42	1 33 11	25 48	13	2	16	23	29	5	19	18
24	12 2 39	2 32 40	9♎37	15	3	17	23	29	5	19	18
25	12 6 35	3 32 7	23 43	17	4	18	24	29	5	19	18
26	12 10 32	4 31 33	8♏ 0	19	6	18	24	29	5	19	18
27	12 14 28	5 30 56	22 23	20	7	19	24	28	5	19	18
28	12 18 25	6 30 18	6♐48	22	8	20	24	28	5	18	18
29	12 22 21	7 29 39	21 10	24	9	21	24	28	5	18	18
30	12 26 18	8 28 57	5♑25	25	10	21	25	28	6	18	18
31	12 30 14	9 28 14	19 31	27	12	22	25	28	6	18	18

THE SUN ENTERS THE SIGN OF ARIES ON MAR 21 AT 10:26.

SIDEREAL SUN MOON MERCURY VENUS MARS JUPITER SATURN URANUS NEPTUNE PLUTO

DAY	TIME	☉	☽	☿	♀	♂	♃	♄	♅	♆	♇
	h m s	° ' "	° '	°	°	°	°	°	°	°	°
A 1	12 34 11	10♈27 29	3♒26	28♈	13♉	23♈	25♓	28♍R	6♋	18♎R	18♌R
P 2	12 38 8	11 26 42	17 10	0♉	14	24	25	28	6	18	18
R 3	12 42 4	12 25 53	0♓42	1	15	24	26	28	6	18	18
I 4	12 46 1	13 25 2	14 2	2	16	25	26	28	6	18	18
L 5	12 49 57	14 24 10	27 9	3	18	26	26	28	6	18	18
6	12 53 54	15 23 15	10♈ 3	4	19	27	26	28	6	18	18
7	12 57 50	16 22 19	22 45	5	20	27	27	28	6	18	18
8	13 1 47	17 21 20	5♉15	6	21	28	27	28	6	18	18
9	13 5 43	18 20 20	17 32	7	22	29	27	28	6	18	18
10	13 9 40	19 19 17	29 39	7	24	0♉	27	27	6	18	18
11	13 13 37	20 18 12	11♊38	8	25	0	28	27	6	18	18
12	13 17 33	21 17 5	23 32	8	26	1	28	27	6	18	17
13	13 21 30	22 15 56	5♋24	8	27	2	28	27	6	18	17
14	13 25 26	23 14 44	17 19	9 R	28	3	28	27	6	18	17
15	13 29 23	24 13 30	29 20	9	0♊	3	28	27	6	18	17
16	13 33 19	25 12 14	11♌34	8	1	4	29	27	6	18	17
17	13 37 16	26 10 56	24 5	8	2	5	29	27	6	18	17
18	13 41 12	27 9 35	6♍57	8	3	6	29	27	6	18	17
19	13 45 9	28 8 13	20 13	8	4	6	29	27	6	18	17
20	13 49 6	29 6 48	3♎54	7	5	7	0☉	27	6	18	17
21	13 53 2	0♉ 5 21	18 1	7	7	8	0	27	6	18	17
22	13 56 59	1 3 52	2♏29	6	8	9	0♈	27	6	18	17
23	14 0 55	2 2 21	17 12	6	9	9	0	27	6	18	17
24	14 4 52	3 0 48	2♐ 4	5	10	10	1	27	6	18	17
25	14 8 48	3 59 14	16 55	4	11	11	1	26	6	18	17
26	14 12 45	4 57 38	1♑37	4	13	12	1	26	6	18	17
27	14 16 41	5 56 1	16 6	3	14	12	1	26	6	18	17
28	14 20 38	6 54 22	0♒16	2	15	13	1	26	6	18	17
29	14 24 35	7 52 42	14 7	2	16	14	2	26	6	18	17
30	14 28 31	8 50 59	27 39	1	17	14	2	26	6	18	17 D

THE SUN ENTERS THE SIGN OF TAURUS ON APR 20 AT 21:48.

DAY	TIME	☉	☽	☿	♀	♂	♃	♄	♅	♆	♇
	h m s	° ' "	° '	°	°	°	°	°	°	°	°
M 1	14 32 28	9♉49 16	10♓54	0♉R	18♊	15♉	2♈	26♍R	6♋	18♎R	17♌
A 2	14 36 24	10 47 31	23 53	0	20	16	2	26	6	18	17
Y 3	14 40 21	11 45 44	6♈39	0	21	17	2	26	6	18	17
4	14 44 17	12 43 55	19 14	29♈	22	17	3	26	6	18	17
5	14 48 14	13 42 6	1♉39	29	23	18	3	26	7	17	17
6	14 52 10	14 40 14	13 55	29	24	19	3	26	7	17	17
7	14 56 7	15 38 21	26 3	28	25	20	3	26	7	17	17
8	15 0 4	16 36 26	8♊ 4	28 D	26	20	4	26	7	17	17
9	15 4 0	17 34 30	20 0	28	28	21	4	26	7	17	17
10	15 7 57	18 32 31	1♋52	28	29	22	4	26	7	17	17
11	15 11 53	19 30 31	13 43	29	0♋	22	4	26	7	17	17
12	15 15 50	20 28 29	25 36	29	1	23	4	26	7	17	17
13	15 19 46	21 26 26	7♌36	29	2	24	5	26	7	17	17
14	15 23 43	22 24 20	19 47	0♉	3	25	5	26	7	17	17
15	15 27 39	23 22 13	2♍14	0	4	25	5	26	7	17	17
16	15 31 36	24 20 4	15 2	0	6	26	5	26	7	17	17
17	15 35 33	25 17 53	28 16	1	7	27	5	26	7	17	17
18	15 39 29	26 15 40	11♎58	2	8	27	6	26	7	17	17
19	15 43 26	27 13 26	26 9	2	9	28	6	26	7	17	17
20	15 47 22	28 11 10	10♏46	3	10	29	6	26	7	17	18
21	15 51 19	29 8 53	25 45	4	11	0♊	6	26	7	17	18
22	15 55 15	0♊ 6 35	10♐56	5	12	0	6	26	7	17	18
23	15 59 12	1 4 15	26 8	6	13	1	7	26	7	17	18
24	16 3 8	2 1 54	11♑11	7	15	2	7	26	7	17	18
25	16 7 5	2 59 32	25 57	8	16	2	7	26	7	17	18
26	16 11 2	3 57 9	10♒19	9	17	3	7	26	8	17	18
27	16 14 58	4 54 46	24 16	10	18	4	7	26	8	17	18
28	16 18 55	5 52 21	7♓47	11	19	4	7	26	8	17	18
29	16 22 51	6 49 55	20 56	13	20	5	8	26 D	8	17	18
30	16 26 48	7 47 28	3♈46	14	21	6	8	26	8	17	18
31	16 30 44	8 45 1	16 20	15	22	7	8	26	8	17	18

THE SUN ENTERS THE SIGN OF GEMINI ON MAY 21 AT 21:16.

DAY	TIME	☉	☽	☿	♀	♂	♃	♄	♅	♆	♇
	h m s	° ' "	° '	°	°	°	°	°	°	°	°
J 1	16 34 41	9♊42 32	28♈42	17♉	23♋	7♊	8♈	26♍	8♋	17♎R	18♌
U 2	16 38 37	10 40 3	10♉54	18	24	8	8	26	8	17	18
N 3	16 42 34	11 37 33	22 58	20	25	9	8	26	8	17	18
E 4	16 46 31	12 35 2	4♊58	21	27	9	9	26	8	17	18
5	16 50 27	13 32 31	16 53	23	28	10	9	26	8	17	18
6	16 54 24	14 29 58	28 45	24	29	11	9	26	8	17	18
7	16 58 20	15 27 24	10♋36	26	0♌	11	9	26	8	17	18
8	17 2 17	16 24 49	22 28	28	1	12	9	26	8	17	18
9	17 6 13	17 22 14	4♌23	29	2	13	9	26	8	17	18
10	17 10 10	18 19 37	16 23	1♊	3	14	10	26	8	17	18
11	17 14 7	19 16 59	28 34	3	4	14	10	26	8	17	18
12	17 18 3	20 14 20	11♍ 0	5	5	15	10	26	8	17	18
13	17 22 0	21 11 40	23 45	7	6	16	10	26	9	17	18
14	17 25 56	22 8 59	6♎53	9	7	16	10	26	9	17	18
15	17 29 53	23 6 17	20 29	11	8	17	10	26	9	17	18
16	17 33 49	24 3 34	4♏35	13	9	18	10	26	9	17	18
17	17 37 46	25 0 51	19 9	15	10	18	11	26	9	17	18
18	17 41 42	25 58 7	4♐ 7	17	11	19	11	26	9	17	18
19	17 45 39	26 55 22	19 22	19	12	20	11	26	9	17	18
20	17 49 36	27 52 37	4♑42	21	13	20	11	26	9	17	18
21	17 53 32	28 49 51	19 57	23	14	21	11	26	9	17	18
22	17 57 29	29 47 4	4♒54	25	15	22	11	26	9	17	18
23	18 1 25	0♋44 18	19 29	28	16	23	11	26	9	17	18
24	18 5 22	1 41 31	3♓35	0♋	17	23	12	26	9	17	18
25	18 9 18	2 38 44	17 13	2	18	24	12	26	9	17	18
26	18 13 15	3 35 57	0♈25	4	19	25	12	26	9	17	18
27	18 17 11	4 33 10	13 14	6	20	25	12	26	9	17	18
28	18 21 8	5 30 24	25 44	8	21	26	12	26	9	17 D	18
29	18 25 5	6 27 37	8♉ 0	11	22	27	12	26	9	17	18
30	18 29 1	7 24 50	20 5	13	23	27	12	26	10	17	18

THE SUN ENTERS THE SIGN OF CANCER ON JUN 22 AT 05:25.

♈ ARIES ♉ TAURUS ♊ GEMINI ♋ CANCER ♌ LEO ♍ VIRGO ♎ LIBRA ♏ SCORPIO ♐ SAGITTARIUS ♑ CAPRICORN ♒ AQUARIUS ♓ PISCES

SIDEREAL SUN MOON MERCURY VENUS MARS JUPITER SATURN URANUS NEPTUNE PLUTO

DAY	TIME	☉	☽	☿	♀	♂	♃	♄	♅	♆	♇
	h m s	° ' "	° '	°	°	°	°	°	°	°	°
J 1	18 32 58	8♋22 3	2♊ 3	15♋	24♌	28♊	12♈	26♍	10♋	17♎	18♌
U 2	18 36 54	9 19 17	13 57	17	25	29	12	26	10	17	18
L 3	18 40 51	10 16 30	25 49	19	25	29	13	27	10	17	18
Y 4	18 44 47	11 13 43	7♋41	21	26	0♋	13	27	10	17	18
5	18 48 44	12 10 57	19 34	23	27	1	13	27	10	17	18
6	18 52 40	13 8 10	1♌29	25	28	1	13	27	10	17	18
7	18 56 37	14 5 23	13 30	27	29	2	13	27	10	17	18
8	19 0 34	15 2 36	25 37	29	0♍	3	13	27	10	17	18
9	19 4 30	15 59 50	7♍54	1♌	1	3	13	27	10	17	18
10	19 8 27	16 57 2	20 24	3	1	4	13	27	10	17	18
11	19 12 23	17 54 15	3♎11	4	2	5	13	27	10	17	19
12	19 16 20	18 51 28	16 18	6	3	5	13	27	10	17	19
13	19 20 16	19 48 41	29 49	8	4	6	13	27	10	17	19
14	19 24 13	20 45 53	13♏46	10	5	7	13	27	10	17	19
15	19 28 9	21 43 6	28 8	11	5	7	14	27	10	17	19
16	19 32 6	22 40 19	12♐54	13	6	8	14	27	11	17	19
17	19 36 3	23 37 32	27 57	15	7	9	14	27	11	17	19
18	19 39 59	24 34 45	13♑ 9	16	8	9	14	28	11	17	19
19	19 43 56	25 31 59	28 18	18	8	10	14	28	11	17	19
20	19 47 52	26 29 13	13♒16	19	9	11	14	28	11	17	19
21	19 51 49	27 26 27	27 55	21	10	11	14	28	11	17	19
22	19 55 45	28 23 43	12♓ 7	22	10	12	14	28	11	17	19
23	19 59 42	29 20 59	25 52	24	11	13	14	28	11	17	19
24	20 3 39	0♌18 15	9♈10	25	12	13	14	28	11	17	19
25	20 7 35	1 15 33	22 4	27	12	14	14	28	11	17	19
26	20 11 32	2 12 51	4♉36	28	13	15	14	28	11	17	19
27	20 15 28	3 10 11	16 52	29	13	15	14	28	11	17	19
28	20 19 25	4 7 31	28 56	0♍	14	16	14	28	11	17	19
29	20 23 21	5 4 53	10♊52	2	14	17	14	28	11	17	19
30	20 27 18	6 2 15	22 44	3	15	17	14	29	11	17	19
31	20 31 14	6 59 39	4♋35	4	15	18	14	29	11	17	19

THE SUN ENTERS THE SIGN OF LEO ON JUL 23 AT 16:21.

DAY	TIME	☉	☽	☿	♀	♂	♃	♄	♅	♆	♇
	h m s	° ' "	° '	°	°	°	°	°	°	°	°
A 1	20 35 11	7♌57 3	16♋29	5♍	16♍	19♋	14♈	29♍	11♋	17♎	19♌
U 2	20 39 8	8 54 29	28 26	6	16	19	14	29	11	17	19
G 3	20 43 4	9 51 55	10♌29	7	16	20	14	29	12	17	19
U 4	20 47 1	10 49 22	22 40	8	17	21	14 R	29	12	17	19
S 5	20 50 57	11 46 50	5♍ 0	9	17	21	14	29	12	17	19
T 6	20 54 54	12 44 19	17 31	10	17	22	14	29	12	17	19
7	20 58 50	13 41 48	0♎14	11	18	23	14	29	12	17	19
8	21 2 47	14 39 19	13 11	11	18	23	14	29	12	17	19
9	21 6 43	15 36 50	26 25	12	18	24	14	0♎	12	17	19
10	21 10 40	16 34 22	9♏57	13	18	25	14	0	12	17	19
11	21 14 37	17 31 55	23 49	13	18	25	14	0	12	17	19
12	21 18 33	18 29 29	8♐ 0	14	18	26	14	0	12	17	19
13	21 22 30	19 27 3	22 29	14	18 R	26	14	0	12	17	19
14	21 26 26	20 24 39	7♑11	15	18	27	14	0	12	17	20
15	21 30 23	21 22 16	22 1	15	18	28	14	0	12	17	20
16	21 34 19	22 19 54	6♒52	15	18	28	14	0	12	17	20
17	21 38 16	23 17 32	21 35	15 R	18	29	14	0	12	17	20
18	21 42 12	24 15 12	6♓ 4	15	18	0♌	14	0	12	17	20
19	21 46 9	25 12 54	20 13	15	18	0	14	1	12	17	20
20	21 50 6	26 10 37	3♈59	15	17	1	14	1	12	17	20
21	21 54 2	27 8 21	17 20	15	17	2	14	1	12	17	20
22	21 57 59	28 6 7	0♉18	14	17	2	14	1	13	18	20
23	22 1 55	29 3 55	12 54	14	16	3	14	1	13	18	20
24	22 5 52	0♍ 1 44	25 13	13	16	4	14	1	13	18	20
25	22 9 48	0 59 36	7♊18	13	16	4	13	1	13	18	20
26	22 13 45	1 57 29	19 15	12	15	5	13	1	13	18	20
27	22 17 41	2 55 24	1♋ 7	11	15	5	13	1	13	18	20
28	22 21 38	3 53 20	12 59	10	14	6	13	2	13	18	20
29	22 25 35	4 51 18	24 55	9	14	7	13	2	13	18	20
30	22 29 31	5 49 18	6♌57	8	13	7	13	2	13	18	20
31	22 33 28	6 47 20	19 10	7	13	8	13	2	13	18	20

THE SUN ENTERS THE SIGN OF VIRGO ON AUG 23 AT 23:17.

DAY	TIME	☉	☽	☿	♀	♂	♃	♄	♅	♆	♇
	h m s	° ' "	° '	°	°	°	°	°	°	°	°
S 1	22 37 24	7♍45 24	1♍34	7♍R	12♍R	9♌	13♈R	2♎	13♋	18♎	20♌
E 2	22 41 21	8 43 29	14 10	6	11	9	13	2	13	18	20
P 3	22 45 17	9 41 35	27 0	5	11	10	13	2	13	18	20
T 4	22 49 14	10 39 44	10♎ 4	4	10	11	13	2	13	18	20
E 5	22 53 10	11 37 53	23 22	3	9	11	13	2	13	18	20
M 6	22 57 7	12 36 5	6♏53	3	9	12	12	3	13	18	20
B 7	23 1 3	13 34 18	20 37	2	8	12	12	3	13	18	20
E 8	23 5 0	14 32 32	4♐33	2	8	13	12	3	13	18	20
R 9	23 8 57	15 30 48	18 40	2 D	7	14	12	3	13	18	20
10	23 12 53	16 29 6	2♑55	2	7	14	12	3	13	18	20
11	23 16 50	17 27 25	17 16	2	6	15	12	3	13	18	20
12	23 20 46	18 25 45	1♒41	2	5	16	12	3	13	18	20
13	23 24 43	19 24 7	16 5	2	5	16	12	3	13	18	20
14	23 28 39	20 22 31	0♓23	3	5	17	12	4	13	18	20
15	23 32 36	21 20 56	14 30	4	4	18	11	4	13	18	20
16	23 36 33	22 19 23	28 24	4	4	18	11	4	13	18	21
17	23 40 29	23 17 52	12♈ 0	5	3	19	11	4	13	18	21
18	23 44 26	24 16 23	25 16	7	3	19	11	4	14	18	21
19	23 48 22	25 14 57	8♉13	8	3	20	11	4	14	18	21
20	23 52 19	26 13 32	20 50	9	3	21	11	4	14	18	21
21	23 56 15	27 12 10	3♊10	10	2	21	11	4	14	18	21
22	0 0 12	28 10 49	15 17	12	2	22	11	5	14	18	21
23	0 4 8	29 9 31	27 14	13	2	23	10	5	14	19	21
24	0 8 5	0♎ 8 16	9♋ 7	15	2	23	10	5	14	19	21
25	0 12 1	1 7 2	20 59	17	2 D	24	10	5	14	19	21
26	0 15 58	2 5 51	2♌56	18	2	24	10	5	14	19	21
27	0 19 55	3 4 42	15 2	20	2	25	10	5	14	19	21
28	0 23 51	4 3 35	27 21	22	2	26	10	5	14	19	21
29	0 27 48	5 2 30	9♍56	24	2	26	10	5	14	19	21
30	0 31 44	6 1 28	22 49	25	3	27	10	6	14	19	21

THE SUN ENTERS THE SIGN OF LIBRA ON SEP 23 AT 20:38.

SIDEREAL SUN MOON MERCURY VENUS MARS JUPITER SATURN URANUS NEPTUNE PLUTO

DAY	TIME	☉	☽	☿	♀	♂	♃	♄	♅	♆	♇
	h m s	° ' "	° '	°	°	°	°	°	°	°	°
O 1	0 35 41	7♎ 0 27	6♎ 0	27♍	3♍	28♌	9♈R	6♎	14♋	19♎	21♌
C 2	0 39 37	7 59 28	19 29	29	3	28	9	6	14	19	21
T 3	0 43 34	8 58 32	3♏14	1♎	3	29	9	6	14	19	21
O 4	0 47 30	9 57 37	17 11	3	4	29	9	6	14	19	21
B 5	0 51 27	10 56 45	1♐17	4	4	0♍	9	6	14	19	21
E 6	0 55 24	11 55 54	15 29	6	4	1	9	6	14	19	21
R 7	0 59 20	12 55 5	29 42	8	5	1	9	6	14	19	21
8	1 3 17	13 54 18	13♑54	10	5	2	8	7	14	19	21
9	1 7 13	14 53 32	28 3	11	6	2	8	7	14	19	21
10	1 11 10	15 52 48	12♒ 7	13	6	3	8	7	14	19	21
11	1 15 6	16 52 6	26 5	15	7	4	8	7	14	19	21
12	1 19 3	17 51 26	9♓55	17	7	4	8	7	14	19	21
13	1 22 59	18 50 47	23 36	18	8	5	8	7	14	19	21
14	1 26 56	19 50 10	7♈ 6	20	8	6	8	7	14	19	21
15	1 30 53	20 49 36	20 24	22	9	6	8	7	14	19	21
16	1 34 49	21 49 3	3♉27	23	9	7	7	8	14	19	21
17	1 38 46	22 48 33	16 14	25	10	7	7	8	14	19	21
18	1 42 42	23 48 4	28 46	27	11	8	7	8	14	19	21
19	1 46 39	24 47 38	11♊ 4	28	11	9	7	8	14	19	21
20	1 50 35	25 47 14	23 10	0♏	12	9	7	8	14 R	20	21
21	1 54 32	26 46 53	5♋ 6	2	13	10	7	8	14	20	21
22	1 58 28	27 46 33	16 57	3	14	10	7	8	14	20	21
23	2 2 25	28 46 16	28 48	5	14	11	7	8	14	20	21
24	2 6 22	29 46 1	10♌44	7	15	12	7	8	14	20	21
25	2 10 18	0♏45 49	22 49	8	16	12	6	9	14	20	21
26	2 14 15	1 45 38	5♍10	10	17	13	6	9	14	20	21
27	2 18 11	2 45 30	17 50	11	18	13	6	9	14	20	21
28	2 22 8	3 45 24	0♎52	13	18	14	6	9	14	20	21
29	2 26 4	4 45 19	14 19	15	19	15	6	9	14	20	21
30	2 30 1	5 45 17	28 9	16	20	15	6	9	14	20	21
31	2 33 57	6 45 17	12♏20	18	21	16	6	9	14	20	21

THE SUN ENTERS THE SIGN OF SCORPIO ON OCT 24 AT 05:37.

DAY	TIME	☉	☽	☿	♀	♂	♃	♄	♅	♆	♇
	h m s	° ' "	° '	°	°	°	°	°	°	°	°
N 1	2 37 54	7♏45 19	26♏46	19♏	22♍	16♍	6♈R	9♎	14♋R	20♎	21♌
O 2	2 41 51	8 45 23	11♐21	21	23	17	6	10	14	20	21
V 3	2 45 47	9 45 28	25 57	22	24	18	5	10	14	20	21
E 4	2 49 44	10 45 35	10♑28	24	25	18	5	10	14	20	21
M 5	2 53 40	11 45 44	24 50	25	25	19	5	10	14	20	21
B 6	2 57 37	12 45 54	8♒59	27	26	19	5	10	14	20	21
E 7	3 1 33	13 46 5	22 54	28	27	20	5	10	14	20	21
R 8	3 5 30	14 46 18	6♓36	0♐	28	21	5	10	14	20	21
9	3 9 26	15 46 33	20 5	1	29	21	5	10	14	20	21
10	3 13 23	16 46 49	3♈22	3	0♎	22	5	10	14	20	22
11	3 17 20	17 47 6	16 28	4	1	22	5	10	14	20	22
12	3 21 16	18 47 25	29 24	6	2	23	5	11	14	20	22
13	3 25 13	19 47 46	12♉ 8	7	3	23	5	11	14	20	22
14	3 29 9	20 48 8	24 41	8	4	24	5	11	14	20	22
15	3 33 6	21 48 32	7♊ 3	10	5	25	5	11	14	20	22
16	3 37 2	22 48 58	19 14	11	6	25	5	11	14	20	22
17	3 40 59	23 49 25	1♋16	13	7	26	5	11	14	21	22
18	3 44 55	24 49 54	13 10	14	8	26	5	11	14	21	22
19	3 48 52	25 50 25	24 59	15	9	27	4	11	14	21	22
20	3 52 49	26 50 58	6♌47	17	10	28	4	11	14	21	22
21	3 56 45	27 51 32	18 40	18	11	28	4	12	14	21	22
22	4 0 42	28 52 8	0♍43	19	12	29	4	12	14	21	22
23	4 4 38	29 52 46	13 0	21	13	29	4	12	14	21	22 R
24	4 8 35	0♐53 25	25 37	22	15	0♎	4	12	13	21	22
25	4 12 31	1 54 6	8♎40	23	16	0	4	12	13	21	22
26	4 16 28	2 54 49	22 10	24	17	1	4	12	13	21	22
27	4 20 24	3 55 33	6♏ 9	25	18	2	4	12	13	21	22
28	4 24 21	4 56 19	20 35	26	19	2	4	12	13	21	22
29	4 28 18	5 57 7	5♐22	27	20	3	4	12	13	21	22
30	4 32 14	6 57 55	20 21	28	21	3	4 D	12	13	21	22

THE SUN ENTERS THE SIGN OF SAGITTARIUS ON NOV 23 AT 02:52.

DAY	TIME	☉	☽	☿	♀	♂	♃	♄	♅	♆	♇
	h m s	° ' "	° '	°	°	°	°	°	°	°	°
D 1	4 36 11	7♐58 45	5♑24	29♐	22♎	4♎	4♈	12♎	13♋R	21♎	22♌R
E 2	4 40 7	8 59 35	20 20	0♑	23	4	4	13	13	21	22
C 3	4 44 4	10 0 27	5♒ 1	1	24	5	4	13	13	21	22
E 4	4 48 0	11 1 20	19 23	1	25	6	4	13	13	21	22
M 5	4 51 57	12 2 13	3♓23	2	27	6	4	13	13	21	22
B 6	4 55 54	13 3 7	17 3	2	28	7	4	13	13	21	22
E 7	4 59 50	14 4 1	0♈23	2 R	29	7	4	13	13	21	22
R 8	5 3 47	15 4 57	13 26	2	0♏	8	4	13	13	21	22
9	5 7 43	16 5 53	26 15	2	1	8	4	13	13	21	21
10	5 11 40	17 6 50	8♉53	2	2	9	4	13	13	21	21
11	5 15 36	18 7 47	21 19	1	3	9	4	13	13	21	21
12	5 19 33	19 8 46	3♊37	0	5	10	4	13	13	21	21
13	5 23 29	20 9 45	15 47	0	6	11	5	13	13	21	21
14	5 27 26	21 10 45	27 49	28♐	7	11	5	13	13	21	21
15	5 31 23	22 11 46	9♋45	27	8	12	5	14	13	21	21
16	5 35 19	23 12 47	21 36	26	9	12	5	14	13	21	21
17	5 39 16	24 13 50	3♌24	25	10	13	5	14	13	21	21
18	5 43 12	25 14 53	15 12	23	11	13	5	14	13	21	21
19	5 47 9	26 15 57	27 5	22	13	14	5	14	13	21	21
20	5 51 5	27 17 2	9♍ 5	21	14	14	5	14	13	21	21
21	5 55 2	28 18 7	21 19	19	15	15	5	14	13	21	21
22	5 58 58	29 19 14	3♎52	18	16	15	5	14	12	21	21
23	6 2 55	0♑20 21	16 48	18	17	16	5	14	12	21	21
24	6 6 52	1 21 28	0♏12	17	18	16	5	14	12	21	21
25	6 10 48	2 22 37	14 6	16	20	17	5	14	12	21	21
26	6 14 45	3 23 46	28 30	16	21	18	5	14	12	21	21
27	6 18 41	4 24 56	13♐20	16 D	22	18	5	14	12	21	21
28	6 22 38	5 26 6	28 28	16	23	19	6	14	12	22	21
29	6 26 34	6 27 17	13♑45	16	24	19	6	14	12	22	21
30	6 30 31	7 28 27	28 59	17	26	20	6	14	12	22	21
31	6 34 27	8 29 38	14♒ 1	17	27	20	6	14	12	22	21

THE SUN ENTERS THE SIGN OF CAPRICORN ON DEC 22 AT 16:01.

♈ ARIES ♉ TAURUS ♊ GEMINI ♋ CANCER ♌ LEO ♍ VIRGO ♎ LIBRA ♏ SCORPIO ♐ SAGITTARIUS ♑ CAPRICORN ♒ AQUARIUS ♓ PISCES

1952

SIDEREAL SUN MOON MERCURY VENUS MARS JUPITER SATURN URANUS NEPTUNE PLUTO

DAY	TIME	☉	☽	☿	♀	♂	♃	♄	♅	♆	♇
	h m s	° ' "	° '	°	°	°	°	°	°	°	°
J 1	6 38 24	9♑30 49	28♒41	18♐	28♏	21♎	6♈	14♎	12♋R	22♎	21♌R
A 2	6 42 21	10 31 59	12♓57	18	29	21	6	15	12	22	21
N 3	6 46 17	11 33 9	26 47	19	0♐	22	6	15	12	22	21
U 4	6 50 14	12 34 19	10♈11	20	1	22	6	15	12	22	21
A 5	6 54 10	13 35 28	23 13	21	3	23	6	15	12	22	21
R 6	6 58 7	14 36 37	5♉56	22	4	23	6	15	12	22	21
Y 7	7 2 3	15 37 46	18 24	23	5	24	7	15	12	22	21
8	7 6 0	16 38 55	0♊39	24	6	24	7	15	12	22	21
9	7 9 56	17 40 3	12 45	25	7	25	7	15	12	22	21
10	7 13 53	18 41 11	24 45	26	9	25	7	15	12	22	21
11	7 17 50	19 42 19	6♋39	27	10	26	7	15	12	22	21
12	7 21 46	20 43 26	18 30	28	11	26	7	15	12	22	21
13	7 25 43	21 44 33	0♌20	0♑	12	27	7	15	12	22	21
14	7 29 39	22 45 39	12 10	1	13	27	8	15	11	22	21
15	7 33 36	23 46 45	24 2	2	15	28	8	15	11	22	21
16	7 37 32	24 47 51	5♍59	4	16	28	8	15	11	22	21
17	7 41 29	25 48 56	18 4	5	17	29	8	15	11	22	21
18	7 45 26	26 50 2	0♎21	6	18	29	8	15	11	22	21
19	7 49 22	27 51 6	12 53	8	19	0♏	8	15	11	22	21
20	7 53 19	28 52 11	25 46	9	21	0	8	15	11	22	21
21	7 57 15	29 53 15	9♏ 2	10	22	0	9	15	11	22	21
22	8 1 12	0♒54 19	22 45	12	23	1	9	15	11	22	21
23	8 5 8	1 55 23	6♐55	13	24	1	9	15	11	22 R	21
24	8 9 5	2 56 26	21 32	15	26	2	9	15 R	11	22	21
25	8 13 1	3 57 29	6♑29	16	27	2	9	15	11	22	21
26	8 16 58	4 58 31	21 40	18	28	3	9	15	11	22	21
27	8 20 55	5 59 32	6♒55	19	29	3	10	15	11	22	21
28	8 24 51	7 0 33	22 3	21	0♑	4	10	15	11	22	21
29	8 28 48	8 1 32	6♓55	22	2	4	10	15	11	22	21
30	8 32 44	9 2 30	21 25	24	3	4	10	15	11	22	21
31	8 36 41	10 3 27	5♈29	25	4	5	10	15	11	22	21

THE SUN ENTERS THE SIGN OF AQUARIUS ON JAN 21 AT 02:39.

DAY	TIME	☉	☽	☿	♀	♂	♃	♄	♅	♆	♇
	h m s	° ' "	° '	°	°	°	°	°	°	°	°
F 1	8 40 37	11♒ 4 23	19♈ 5	27♑	5♑	5♏	10♈	15♎R	11♋R	22♎R	21♌R
E 2	8 44 34	12 5 17	2♉15	28	7	6	11	15	11	22	21
B 3	8 48 30	13 6 10	15 1	0♒	8	6	11	15	11	22	21
R 4	8 52 27	14 7 2	27 29	1	9	7	11	15	11	22	20
U 5	8 56 24	15 7 53	9♊41	3	10	7	11	15	11	22	20
A 6	9 0 20	16 8 42	21 42	5	11	7	11	15	11	22	20
R 7	9 4 17	17 9 29	3♋35	6	13	8	11	15	11	22	20
Y 8	9 8 13	18 10 15	15 25	8	14	8	12	15	11	22	20
9	9 12 10	19 11 0	27 14	10	15	8	12	15	11	22	20
10	9 16 6	20 11 44	9♌ 5	11	16	9	12	15	10	22	20
11	9 20 3	21 12 26	20 59	13	17	9	12	15	10	22	20
12	9 23 59	22 13 6	3♍ 0	15	19	10	12	15	10	22	20
13	9 27 56	23 13 46	15 7	16	20	10	13	15	10	22	20
14	9 31 53	24 14 24	27 25	18	21	10	13	15	10	22	20
15	9 35 49	25 15 0	9♎54	20	22	11	13	15	10	22	20
16	9 39 46	26 15 36	22 36	21	24	11	13	15	10	22	20
17	9 43 42	27 16 10	5♏34	23	25	11	13	15	10	22	20
18	9 47 39	28 16 43	18 51	25	26	12	14	14	10	22	20
19	9 51 35	29 17 15	2♐27	27	27	12	14	14	10	22	20
20	9 55 32	0♓17 46	16 25	29	29	12	14	14	10	22	20
21	9 59 28	1 18 15	0♑42	0♓	0♒	13	14	14	10	21	20
22	10 3 25	2 18 43	15 18	2	1	13	14	14	10	21	20
23	10 7 22	3 19 10	0♒ 7	4	2	13	15	14	10	21	20
24	10 11 18	4 19 35	15 3	6	3	14	15	14	10	21	20
25	10 15 15	5 19 59	29 59	8	5	14	15	14	10	21	20
26	10 19 11	6 20 21	14♓46	10	6	14	15	14	10	21	20
27	10 23 8	7 20 41	29 17	12	7	14	16	14	10	21	20
28	10 27 4	8 20 59	13♈26	13	8	15	16	14	10	21	20
29	10 31 1	9 21 16	27 10	15	10	15	16	14	10	21	20

THE SUN ENTERS THE SIGN OF PISCES ON FEB 19 AT 16:57.

DAY	TIME	☉	☽	☿	♀	♂	♃	♄	♅	♆	♇
	h m s	° ' "	° '	°	°	°	°	°	°	°	°
M 1	10 34 57	10♓21 30	10♉29	17♓	11♒	15♏	16♈	14♎R	10♋R	21♎R	20♌R
A 2	10 38 54	11 21 42	23 22	19	12	15	16	14	10	21	20
R 3	10 42 51	12 21 53	5♊54	21	13	16	17	14	10	21	20
C 4	10 46 47	13 22 1	18 9	23	15	16	17	14	10	21	20
H 5	10 50 44	14 22 7	0♋10	25	16	16	17	14	10	21	20
6	10 54 40	15 22 12	12 2	27	17	16	17	14	10	21	20
7	10 58 37	16 22 14	23 51	29	18	17	17	13	10	21	20
8	11 2 33	17 22 13	5♌40	1♈	19	17	18	13	10	21	20
9	11 6 30	18 22 11	17 33	2	21	17	18	13	10	21	20
10	11 10 26	19 22 7	29 34	4	22	17	18	13	10	21	20
11	11 14 23	20 22 1	11♍44	6	23	17	18	13	10	21	20
12	11 18 20	21 21 52	24 7	7	24	17	19	13	10	21	20
13	11 22 16	22 21 42	6♎42	9	26	18	19	13	10	21	20
14	11 26 13	23 21 30	19 30	11	27	18	19	13	10	21	20
15	11 30 9	24 21 16	2♏33	12	28	18	19	13	10	21	20
16	11 34 6	25 21 0	15 48	13	29	18	20	13	10	21	20
17	11 38 2	26 20 43	29 17	15	0♓	18	20	13	10	21	20
18	11 41 59	27 20 24	12♐59	16	2	18	20	13	10 D	21	20
19	11 45 55	28 20 3	26 53	17	3	18	20	13	10	21	20
20	11 49 52	29 19 41	10♑59	18	4	18	20	13	10	21	19
21	11 53 49	0♈19 16	25 15	18	5	18	21	13	10	21	19
22	11 57 45	1 18 50	9♒40	19	7	18	21	12	10	21	19
23	12 1 42	2 18 23	24 10	20	8	18	21	12	10	21	19
24	12 5 38	3 17 53	8♓40	20	9	18	21	12	10	21	19
25	12 9 35	4 17 21	23 6	20	10	18 R	22	12	10	21	19
26	12 13 31	5 16 48	7♈21	20 R	12	18	22	12	10	21	19
27	12 17 28	6 16 12	21 21	20	13	18	22	12	10	21	19
28	12 21 24	7 15 34	5♉ 2	20	14	18	22	12	10	21	19
29	12 25 21	8 14 55	18 21	20	15	18	23	12	10	21	19
30	12 29 17	9 14 13	1♊17	20	17	18	23	12	10	21	19
31	12 33 14	10 13 28	13 52	19	18	18	23	12	10	21	19

THE SUN ENTERS THE SIGN OF ARIES ON MAR 20 AT 16:14.

SIDEREAL SUN MOON MERCURY VENUS MARS JUPITER SATURN URANUS NEPTUNE PLUTO

DAY	TIME	☉	☽	☿	♀	♂	♃	♄	♅	♆	♇
	h m s	° ' "	° '	°	°	°	°	°	°	°	°
A 1	12 37 11	11♈12 42	26♊ 8	19♈R	19♓	18♏R	23♈	12♎R	10♋	21♎R	19♌R
P 2	12 41 7	12 11 53	8♋11	18	20	18	24	12	10	21	19
R 3	12 45 4	13 11 2	20 4	17	21	18	24	12	10	21	19
I 4	12 49 0	14 10 8	1♌53	17	23	18	24	11	10	21	19
L 5	12 52 57	15 9 12	13 43	16	24	18	24	11	10	20	19
6	12 56 53	16 8 14	25 39	15	25	18	25	11	10	20	19
7	13 0 50	17 7 14	7♍45	14	26	17	25	11	10	20	19
8	13 4 46	18 6 11	20 5	14	28	17	25	11	10	20	19
9	13 8 43	19 5 6	2♎41	13	29	17	25	11	10	20	19
10	13 12 40	20 3 59	15 35	12	0♈	17	25	11	10	20	19
11	13 16 36	21 2 50	28 46	11	1	17	26	11	10	20	19
12	13 20 33	22 1 40	12♏13	11	2	17	26	11	10	20	19
13	13 24 29	23 0 27	25 54	10	4	16	26	11	10	20	19
14	13 28 26	23 59 12	9♐45	10	5	16	26	11	10	20	19
15	13 32 22	24 57 56	23 44	9	6	16	27	11	10	20	19
16	13 36 19	25 56 39	7♑48	9	7	16	27	11	10	20	19
17	13 40 15	26 55 19	21 55	9	9	15	27	10	10	20	19
18	13 44 12	27 53 58	6♒ 3	9	10	15	27	10	10	20	19
19	13 48 9	28 52 35	20 11	9 D	11	15	28	10	10	20	19
20	13 52 5	29 51 10	4♓18	9	12	14	28	10	10	20	19
21	13 56 2	0♉49 44	18 22	9	14	14	28	10	10	20	19
22	13 59 58	1 48 16	2♈21	9	15	14	28	10	10	20	19
23	14 3 55	2 46 46	16 12	9	16	13	29	10	10	20	19
24	14 7 51	3 45 15	29 51	10	17	13	29	10	10	20	19
25	14 11 48	4 43 41	13♉16	10	18	13	29	10	11	20	19
26	14 15 44	5 42 6	26 24	11	20	12	29	10	11	20	19
27	14 19 41	6 40 29	9♊14	11	21	12	0♉	10	11	20	19
28	14 23 38	7 38 50	21 45	12	22	12	0	10	11	20	19
29	14 27 34	8 37 9	4♋ 0	13	23	11	0	10	11	20	19
30	14 31 31	9 35 26	16 2	13	25	11	0	10	11	20	19 D

THE SUN ENTERS THE SIGN OF TAURUS ON APR 20 AT 03:36.

DAY	TIME	☉	☽	☿	♀	♂	♃	♄	♅	♆	♇
	h m s	° ' "	° '	°	°	°	°	°	°	°	°
M 1	14 35 27	10♉33 41	27♋55	14♈	26♈	11♏R	1♉	10♎R	11♋	20♎R	19♌
A 2	14 39 24	11 31 54	9♌44	15	27	10	1	9	11	20	19
Y 3	14 43 20	12 30 5	21 34	16	28	10	1	9	11	20	19
4	14 47 17	13 28 13	3♍31	17	0♉	10	1	9	11	20	19
5	14 51 13	14 26 20	15 40	18	1	9	1	9	11	20	19
6	14 55 10	15 24 25	28 5	19	2	9	2	9	11	20	19
7	14 59 7	16 22 28	10♎50	20	3	8	2	9	11	20	19
8	15 3 3	17 20 29	23 58	21	4	8	2	9	11	20	19
9	15 7 0	18 18 29	7♏27	22	6	8	2	9	11	20	19
10	15 10 56	19 16 27	21 18	24	7	7	3	9	11	20	19
11	15 14 53	20 14 23	5♐25	25	8	7	3	9	11	20	19
12	15 18 49	21 12 18	19 43	26	9	7	3	9	11	20	19
13	15 22 46	22 10 12	4♑ 7	28	11	6	3	9	11	20	19
14	15 26 42	23 8 4	18 30	29	12	6	4	9	11	19	19
15	15 30 39	24 5 55	2♒50	1♉	13	6	4	9	11	19	19
16	15 34 36	25 3 45	17 2	2	14	5	4	9	11	19	19
17	15 38 32	26 1 34	1♓ 7	4	16	5	4	9	11	19	19
18	15 42 29	26 59 21	15 2	5	17	5	5	9	11	19	19
19	15 46 25	27 57 8	28 47	7	18	4	5	9	11	19	19
20	15 50 22	28 54 53	12♈24	8	19	4	5	9	12	19	19
21	15 54 18	29 52 37	25 50	10	20	4	5	9	12	19	19
22	15 58 15	0♊50 20	9♉ 6	12	22	4	5	9	12	19	19
23	16 2 11	1 48 2	22 9	13	23	3	6	8	12	19	19
24	16 6 8	2 45 42	4♊59	15	24	3	6	8	12	19	19
25	16 10 5	3 43 22	17 35	17	25	3	6	8	12	19	19
26	16 14 1	4 41 0	29 57	19	27	3	6	8	12	19	19
27	16 17 58	5 38 36	12♋ 6	21	28	3	7	8	12	19	19
28	16 21 54	6 36 12	24 4	23	29	2	7	8	12	19	19
29	16 25 51	7 33 46	5♌55	25	0♊	2	7	8	12	19	19
30	16 29 47	8 31 19	17 42	27	1	2	7	8	12	19	19
31	16 33 44	9 28 50	29 32	29	3	2	7	8	12	19	19

THE SUN ENTERS THE SIGN OF GEMINI ON MAY 21 AT 03:04.

DAY	TIME	☉	☽	☿	♀	♂	♃	♄	♅	♆	♇
	h m s	° ' "	° '	°	°	°	°	°	°	°	°
J 1	16 37 41	10♊26 20	11♍28	1♊	4♊	2♏R	8♉	8♎R	12♋	19♎R	19♌
U 2	16 41 37	11 23 49	23 36	3	5	2	8	8	12	19	19
N 3	16 45 34	12 21 16	6♎ 2	5	6	2	8	8	12	19	19
E 4	16 49 30	13 18 42	18 50	7	8	1	8	8	12	19	19
5	16 53 27	14 16 7	2♏ 3	9	9	1	9	8	12	19	19
6	16 57 23	15 13 31	15 43	11	10	1	9	8	12	19	19
7	17 1 20	16 10 54	29 47	14	11	1	9	8	12	19	19
8	17 5 16	17 8 16	14♐13	16	13	1	9	8	13	19	19
9	17 9 13	18 5 38	28 54	18	14	1	9	8	13	19	19
10	17 13 10	19 2 58	13♑42	20	15	1 D	10	8 D	13	19	19
11	17 17 6	20 0 18	28 30	22	16	1	10	8	13	19	19
12	17 21 3	20 57 37	13♒ 9	25	17	1	10	8	13	19	19
13	17 24 59	21 54 56	27 36	27	19	1	10	8	13	19	20
14	17 28 56	22 52 15	11♓48	29	20	1	10	8	13	19	20
15	17 32 52	23 49 32	25 43	1♋	21	1	11	8	13	19	20
16	17 36 49	24 46 50	9♈22	3	22	1	11	8	13	19	20
17	17 40 45	25 44 7	22 45	5	24	1	11	8	13	19	20
18	17 44 42	26 41 25	5♉54	7	25	2	11	8	13	19	20
19	17 48 39	27 38 41	18 50	9	26	2	11	8	13	19	20
20	17 52 35	28 35 58	1♊33	11	27	2	12	8	13	19	20
21	17 56 32	29 33 14	14 4	13	28	2	12	8	13	19	20
22	18 0 28	0♋30 30	26 24	15	0♋	2	12	8	13	19	20
23	18 4 25	1 27 46	8♋34	17	1	2	12	8	13	19	20
24	18 8 21	2 25 1	20 34	19	2	2	12	8	13	19	20
25	18 12 18	3 22 15	2♌27	21	3	3	13	8	14	19	20
26	18 16 14	4 19 30	14 15	23	5	3	13	8	14	19	20
27	18 20 11	5 16 43	26 1	24	6	3	13	8	14	19	20
28	18 24 8	6 13 57	7♍50	26	7	3	13	8	14	19	20
29	18 28 4	7 11 10	19 45	28	8	3	13	8	14	19	20
30	18 32 1	8 8 22	1♎53	29	10	4	14	9	14	19 D	20

THE SUN ENTERS THE SIGN OF CANCER ON JUN 21 AT 11:13.

♈ ARIES ♉ TAURUS ♊ GEMINI ♋ CANCER ♌ LEO ♍ VIRGO ♎ LIBRA ♏ SCORPIO ♐ SAGITTARIUS ♑ CAPRICORN ♒ AQUARIUS ♓ PISCES

1952

SIDEREAL SUN MOON MERCURY VENUS MARS JUPITER SATURN URANUS NEPTUNE PLUTO

DAY	TIME	☉	☽	☿	♀	♂	♃	♄	♅	♆	♇
	h m s	° ' "	° '	°	°	°	°	°	°	°	°
J 1	18 35 57	9♋ 5 34	14♎17	1♌	11♋	4♏	14♉	9♎	14♋	19♎	20♌
U 2	18 39 54	10 2 46	27 3	2	12	4	14	9	14	19	20
L 3	18 43 50	10 59 57	10♏15	4	13	4	14	9	14	19	20
Y 4	18 47 47	11 57 8	23 54	5	14	5	14	9	14	19	20
5	18 51 43	12 54 19	8♐ 2	7	16	5	14	9	14	19	20
6	18 55 40	13 51 30	22 34	8	17	5	15	9	14	19	20
7	18 59 37	14 48 41	7♑26	10	18	6	15	9	14	19	20
8	19 3 33	15 45 51	22 30	11	19	6	15	9	14	19	20
9	19 7 30	16 43 2	7♒36	12	21	6	15	9	14	19	20
10	19 11 26	17 40 13	22 36	14	22	6	15	9	14	19	20
11	19 15 23	18 37 25	7♓21	15	23	7	15	9	14	19	20
12	19 19 19	19 34 37	21 47	16	24	7	16	9	15	19	20
13	19 23 16	20 31 49	5♈51	17	26	7	16	9	15	19	20
14	19 27 13	21 29 2	19 33	18	27	8	16	9	15	19	20
15	19 31 9	22 26 16	2♉53	19	28	8	16	9	15	19	20
16	19 35 6	23 23 30	15 54	20	29	9	16	9	15	19	20
17	19 39 2	24 20 45	28 37	21	0♌	9	16	9	15	19	20
18	19 42 59	25 18 0	11♊ 6	22	2	9	17	9	15	19	20
19	19 46 55	26 15 17	23 23	23	3	10	17	9	15	19	20
20	19 50 52	27 12 33	5♋29	23	4	10	17	9	15	19	20
21	19 54 48	28 9 51	17 28	24	5	11	17	10	15	19	20
22	19 58 45	29 7 9	29 20	25	7	11	17	10	15	19	20
23	20 2 42	0♌ 4 27	11♌ 9	25	8	11	17	10	15	19	21
24	20 6 38	1 1 47	22 55	26	9	12	17	10	15	19	21
25	20 10 35	1 59 6	4♍43	26	10	12	18	10	15	19	21
26	20 14 31	2 56 26	16 34	27	12	13	18	10	15	19	21
27	20 18 28	3 53 47	28 32	27	13	13	18	10	15	19	21
28	20 22 24	4 51 8	10♎42	27	14	14	18	10	16	19	21
29	20 26 21	5 48 29	23 6	27 R	15	14	18	10	16	19	21
30	20 30 17	6 45 51	5♏50	27	16	15	18	10	16	19	21
31	20 34 14	7 43 14	18 57	27	18	15	18	10	16	19	21

THE SUN ENTERS THE SIGN OF LEO ON JUL 22 AT 22:08.

DAY	TIME	☉	☽	☿	♀	♂	♃	♄	♅	♆	♇
	h m s	° ' "	° '	°	°	°	°	°	°	°	°
A 1	20 38 11	8♌40 37	2♐30	27♌R	19♌	15♏	19♉	10♎	16♋	19♎	21♌
U 2	20 42 7	9 38 1	16 30	27	20	16	19	10	16	19	21
G 3	20 46 4	10 35 26	0♑56	26	21	16	19	10	16	19	21
U 4	20 50 0	11 32 51	15 45	26	23	17	19	11	16	19	21
S 5	20 53 57	12 30 18	0♒50	26	24	17	19	11	16	19	21
T 6	20 57 53	13 27 45	16 2	25	25	18	19	11	16	19	21
7	21 1 50	14 25 13	1♓12	24	26	18	19	11	16	19	21
8	21 5 46	15 22 42	16 12	24	28	19	19	11	16	19	21
9	21 9 43	16 20 12	0♈52	23	29	19	19	11	16	19	21
10	21 13 40	17 17 44	15 9	22	0♍	20	19	11	16	19	21
11	21 17 36	18 15 17	29 0	21	1	21	20	11	16	19	21
12	21 21 33	19 12 51	12♉25	21	2	21	20	11	16	19	21
13	21 25 29	20 10 27	25 25	20	4	22	20	11	16	19	21
14	21 29 26	21 8 5	8♊ 5	19	5	22	20	11	16	19	21
15	21 33 22	22 5 44	20 26	18	6	23	20	12	16	19	21
16	21 37 19	23 3 24	2♋34	17	7	23	20	12	17	19	21
17	21 41 15	24 1 6	14 32	17	9	24	20	12	17	20	21
18	21 45 12	24 58 50	26 24	16	10	24	20	12	17	20	21
19	21 49 9	25 56 35	8♌12	16	11	25	20	12	17	20	21
20	21 53 5	26 54 21	19 59	15	12	25	20	12	17	20	21
21	21 57 2	27 52 9	1♍47	15	14	26	20	12	17	20	21
22	22 0 58	28 49 58	13 39	15 D	15	27	20	12	17	20	21
23	22 4 55	29 47 49	25 38	15	16	27	20	12	17	20	21
24	22 8 51	0♍45 40	7♎44	15	17	28	21	12	17	20	22
25	22 12 48	1 43 34	20 2	15	18	28	21	12	17	20	22
26	22 16 44	2 41 28	2♏32	16	20	29	21	13	17	20	22
27	22 20 41	3 39 24	15 19	16	21	0♐	21	13	17	20	22
28	22 24 38	4 37 21	28 24	17	22	0	21	13	17	20	22
29	22 28 34	5 35 19	11♐50	17	23	1	21	13	17	20	22
30	22 32 31	6 33 19	25 40	18	25	1	21	13	17	20	22
31	22 36 27	7 31 20	9♑52	19	26	2	21	13	17	20	22

THE SUN ENTERS THE SIGN OF VIRGO ON AUG 23 AT 05:04.

DAY	TIME	☉	☽	☿	♀	♂	♃	♄	♅	♆	♇
	h m s	° ' "	° '	°	°	°	°	°	°	°	°
S 1	22 40 24	8♍29 23	24♑2[illegible]	[illegible]	[illegible]	[illegible]	[illegible]	13♎	17♋	20♎	22♌
E 2	22 44 20	9 27 27	9♒1[illegible]	[illegible]	[illegible]	[illegible]	[illegible]	[illegible]	[illegible]	20	22
P 3	22 48 17	10 25 32	24 2[illegible]	[illegible]	[illegible]	[illegible]	[illegible]	[illegible]	[illegible]	[illegible]	[illegible]
T 4	22 52 13	11 23 39	9♓[illegible]	[illegible]	[illegible]	[illegible]	[illegible]	[illegible]	[illegible]	[illegible]	[illegible]
E 5	22 56 10	12 21 48	24 [illegible]	[illegible]	[illegible]	[illegible]	[illegible]	[illegible]	[illegible]	[illegible]	[illegible]
M 6	23 0 7	13 19 58	9♈[illegible]	[illegible]	[illegible]	[illegible]	[illegible]	[illegible]	[illegible]	[illegible]	[illegible]
B 7	23 4 3	14 18 10	23 [illegible]	[illegible]	[illegible]	[illegible]	[illegible]	[illegible]	[illegible]	[illegible]	[illegible]
E 8	23 8 0	15 16 25	7[illegible]	[illegible]	[illegible]	[illegible]	[illegible]	[illegible]	[illegible]	[illegible]	[illegible]
R 9	23 11 56	16 14 41	21 [illegible]	[illegible]	[illegible]	[illegible]	[illegible]	[illegible]	[illegible]	[illegible]	[illegible]
10	23 15 53	17 12 59	4[illegible]	[illegible]	[illegible]	[illegible]	[illegible]	[illegible]	[illegible]	[illegible]	[illegible]
11	23 19 49	18 11 20	1[illegible]	[illegible]	[illegible]	[illegible]	[illegible]	[illegible]	[illegible]	[illegible]	[illegible]
12	23 23 46	19 9 43	2[illegible]	[illegible]	[illegible]	[illegible]	[illegible]	[illegible]	[illegible]	[illegible]	[illegible]
13	23 27 42	20 8 7	1[illegible]	[illegible]	[illegible]	[illegible]	[illegible]	[illegible]	[illegible]	[illegible]	[illegible]
14	23 31 39	21 6 34	2[illegible]	[illegible]	[illegible]	[illegible]	[illegible]	[illegible]	[illegible]	[illegible]	[illegible]
15	23 35 36	22 5 3	[illegible]	[illegible]	[illegible]	[illegible]	[illegible]	[illegible]	[illegible]	[illegible]	[illegible]
16	23 39 32	23 3 34	[illegible]	[illegible]	[illegible]	[illegible]	[illegible]	[illegible]	[illegible]	[illegible]	[illegible]
17	23 43 29	24 2 7	[illegible]	[illegible]	[illegible]	[illegible]	[illegible]	[illegible]	[illegible]	[illegible]	[illegible]
18	23 47 25	25 0 42	[illegible]	[illegible]	[illegible]	[illegible]	[illegible]	[illegible]	[illegible]	[illegible]	[illegible]
19	23 51 22	25 59 19	[illegible]	[illegible]	[illegible]	[illegible]	[illegible]	[illegible]	[illegible]	[illegible]	[illegible]
20	23 55 18	26 57 58	[illegible]	[illegible]	[illegible]	[illegible]	[illegible]	[illegible]	[illegible]	[illegible]	[illegible]
21	23 59 15	27 56 39	[illegible]	[illegible]	[illegible]	[illegible]	[illegible]	[illegible]	[illegible]	[illegible]	[illegible]
22	0 3 11	28 55 2[illegible]	[illegible]	[illegible]	[illegible]	[illegible]	[illegible]	[illegible]	[illegible]	[illegible]	[illegible]
23	0 7 8	29 54 [illegible]	[illegible]	[illegible]	[illegible]	[illegible]	[illegible]	[illegible]	[illegible]	[illegible]	[illegible]
24	0 11 4	0♎52 5[illegible]	[illegible]	[illegible]	[illegible]	[illegible]	[illegible]	[illegible]	[illegible]	[illegible]	[illegible]
25	0 15 1	1 51 [illegible]	[illegible]	[illegible]	[illegible]	[illegible]	[illegible]	[illegible]	[illegible]	[illegible]	[illegible]
26	0 18 58	2 50 [illegible]	[illegible]	[illegible]	[illegible]	[illegible]	[illegible]	[illegible]	[illegible]	[illegible]	[illegible]
27	0 22 54	3 49 [illegible]	[illegible]	[illegible]	[illegible]	[illegible]	[illegible]	[illegible]	[illegible]	[illegible]	[illegible]
28	0 26 51	4 48 [illegible]	[illegible]	[illegible]	[illegible]	[illegible]	[illegible]	[illegible]	[illegible]	[illegible]	[illegible]
29	0 30 47	5 47 [illegible]	[illegible]	[illegible]	[illegible]	[illegible]	[illegible]	[illegible]	[illegible]	[illegible]	[illegible]
30	0 34 44	6 46 [illegible]	[illegible]	[illegible]	[illegible]	[illegible]	[illegible]	[illegible]	[illegible]	[illegible]	[illegible]

THE SUN ENTERS TH[illegible]

SIDEREAL SUN MOON MERCURY VENUS MARS JUPITER SATURN URANUS NEPTUNE PLUTO

DAY	TIME	☉	☽	☿	♀	♂	♃	♄	♅	♆	♇
	h m s	° ' "	° '	°	°	°	°	°	°	°	°
O 1	0 38 40	7♎45 7	3♓ 9	13♎	4♏	22♐	20♉R	17♎	18♋	21♎	23♌
C 2	0 42 37	8 44 8	17 56	14	5	23	20	17	18	21	23
T 3	0 46 33	9 43 10	2♈43	16	6	24	20	17	18	21	23
O 4	0 50 30	10 42 14	17 21	18	8	24	20	17	18	21	23
B 5	0 54 27	11 41 21	1♉43	19	9	25	20	17	18	21	23
E 6	0 58 23	12 40 29	15 43	21	10	26	20	17	18	21	23
R 7	1 2 20	13 39 40	29 18	23	11	26	20	17	18	21	23
8	1 6 16	14 38 53	12♊27	24	13	27	20	18	18	21	23
9	1 10 13	15 38 9	25 11	26	14	28	20	18	18	21	23
10	1 14 9	16 37 27	7♋33	28	15	28	20	18	18	21	23
11	1 18 6	17 36 47	19 39	29	16	29	19	18	18	21	23
12	1 22 2	18 36 9	1♌34	1♏	18	0♑	19	18	18	21	23
13	1 25 59	19 35 34	13 22	2	19	1	19	18	18	21	23
14	1 29 56	20 35 1	25 9	4	20	1	19	18	18	21	23
15	1 33 52	21 34 30	7♍ 0	5	21	2	19	18	18	21	23
16	1 37 49	22 34 1	18 59	7	22	3	19	19	18	21	23
17	1 41 45	23 33 35	1♎ 9	8	24	3	19	19	19	22	23
18	1 45 42	24 33 10	13 33	10	25	4	19	19	19	22	23
19	1 49 38	25 32 48	26 11	11	26	5	19	19	19	22	23
20	1 53 35	26 32 28	9♏ 3	13	27	6	18	19	19	22	23
21	1 57 31	27 32 10	22 9	14	29	6	18	19	19	22	23
22	2 1 28	28 31 53	5♐27	16	0♐	7	18	19	19	22	23
23	2 5 25	29 31 39	18 56	17	1	8	18	19	19	22	23
24	2 9 21	0♏31 26	2♑35	19	2	9	18	19	19 R	22	23
25	2 13 18	1 31 15	16 22	20	3	9	18	20	19	22	23
26	2 17 14	2 31 6	0♒18	22	5	10	18	20	19	22	23
27	2 21 11	3 30 58	14 23	23	6	11	18	20	19	22	23
28	2 25 7	4 30 52	28 35	24	7	11	17	20	19	22	23
29	2 29 4	5 30 47	12♓53	26	8	12	17	20	19	22	23
30	2 33 0	6 30 45	27 15	27	10	13	17	20	19	22	23
31	2 36 57	7 30 43	11♈37	28	11	14	17	20	19	22	23

THE SUN ENTERS THE SIGN OF SCORPIO ON OCT 23 AT 11:23.

DAY	TIME	☉	☽	☿	♀	♂	♃	♄	♅	♆	♇
	h m s	° ' "	° '	°	°	°	°	°	°	°	°
N 1	2 40 54	8♏30 44	25♈53	0♐	12♐	14♑	17♉R	20♎	19♋R	22♎	23♌
O 2	2 44 50	9 30 46	9♉58	1	13	15	17	21	19	22	23
V 3	2 48 47	10 30 51	23 46	2	14	16	17	21	18	22	23
E 4	2 52 43	11 30 57	7♊14	4	16	17	17	21	18	22	23
M 5	2 56 40	12 31 5	20 19	5	17	17	16	21	18	22	23
B 6	3 0 36	13 31 16	3♋ 2	6	18	18	16	21	18	22	23
E 7	3 4 33	14 31 28	15 25	7	19	19	16	21	18	22	23
R 8	3 8 29	15 31 42	27 32	8	20	20	16	21	18	22	23
9	3 12 26	16 31 58	9♌27	9	22	20	16	21	18	22	23
10	3 16 23	17 32 16	21 15	10	23	21	16	22	18	22	23
11	3 20 19	18 32 36	3♍ 3	11	24	22	16	22	18	22	23
12	3 24 16	19 32 58	14 56	12	25	23	15	22	18	22	23
13	3 28 12	20 33 22	26 59	13	27	23	15	22	18	22	23
14	3 32 9	21 33 48	9♎15	14	28	24	15	22	18	23	23
15	3 36 5	22 34 16	21 49	15	29	25	15	22	18	23	23
16	3 40 2	23 34 45	4♏42	15	0♑	26	15	22	18	23	23
17	3 43 58	24 35 16	17 54	16	1	26	15	22	18	23	23
18	3 47 55	25 35 49	1♐23	16	3	27	15	22	18	23	23
19	3 51 52	26 36 24	15 7	16	4	28	14	23	18	23	23
20	3 55 48	27 36 59	29 1	17 R	5	29	14	23	18	23	23
21	3 59 45	28 37 37	13♑ 3	16	6	29	14	23	18	23	23
22	4 3 41	29 38 15	27 8	16	7	0♒	14	23	18	23	23
23	4 7 38	0♐38 54	11♒15	16	9	1	14	23	18	23	23
24	4 11 34	1 39 35	25 21	15	10	2	14	23	18	23	23 R
25	4 15 31	2 40 16	9♓26	15	11	2	14	23	18	23	23
26	4 19 27	3 40 59	23 29	14	12	3	14	23	18	23	23
27	4 23 24	4 41 42	7♈29	13	14	4	13	23	18	23	23
28	4 27 21	5 42 27	21 24	11	15	5	13	23	18	23	23
29	4 31 17	6 43 13	5♉13	10	16	5	13	24	18	23	23
30	4 35 14	7 44 0	18 51	9	17	6	13	24	18	23	23

THE SUN ENTERS THE SIGN OF SAGITTARIUS ON NOV 22 AT 08:37.

DAY	TIME	☉	☽	☿	♀	♂	♃	♄	♅	♆	♇
	h m s	° ' "	° '	°	°	°	°	°	°	°	°
D 1	4 39 10	8♐44 48	2♊17	7♐R	18♑	7♒	13♉R	24♎	18♋R	23♎	23♌R
E 2	4 43 7	9 45 37	15 27	6	20	8	13	24	18	23	23
C 3	4 47 3	10 46 27	28 20	5	21	9	13	24	18	23	23
E 4	4 51 0	11 47 19	10♋55	4	22	9	13	24	18	23	23
[illegible]	[illegible] 54 57	12 48 11	23 14	3	23	10	13	24	18	23	23
[illegible]	[illegible] 53	13 49 5	5♌19	2	24	11	13	24	18	23	23
[illegible]	[illegible] 2 50	14 50 0	17 14	1	26	12	12	24	18	23	23
[illegible]	[illegible] 6 46	15 50 56	29 2	1	27	12	12	24	18	23	23
[illegible]	[illegible] 43	16 51 54	10♍50	0	28	13	12	24	18	23	23
[illegible]	[illegible] 14 39	17 52 52	22 42	0 D	29	14	12	25	18	23	23
[illegible]	[illegible] 18 36	18 53 52	4♎45	0	0♒	15	12	25	18	23	23
[illegible]	[illegible] 22 32	19 54 53	17 2	1	1	15	12	25	18	23	23
[illegible]	[illegible] 26 29	20 55 55	29 39	1	3	16	12	25	18	23	23
[illegible]	[illegible] 30 26	21 56 57	12♏38	1	4	17	12	25	17	23	23
[illegible]	[illegible] 34 22	22 58 1	26 1	2	5	18	12	25	17	23	23
[illegible]	[illegible] 38 19	23 59 6	9♐47	3	6	19	12	25	17	23	23
[illegible]	5 42 15	25 0 12	23 52	4	7	19	12	25	17	23	23
[illegible]	5 46 12	26 1 18	8♑13	5	9	20	12	25	17	23	23
[illegible]	5 50 8	27 2 25	22 42	6	10	21	11	25	17	24	23
[illegible]	5 54 5	28 3 32	7♒15	7	11	22	11	25	17	24	23
[illegible]	5 58 1	29 4 39	21 44	8	12	22	11	25	17	24	23
[illegible]	6 1 58	0♑ 5 47	6♓ 7	9	13	23	11	26	17	24	23
[illegible]	6 5 55	1 6 54	20 20	10	14	24	11	26	17	24	23
[illegible]	6 9 51	2 8 2	4♈22	11	16	25	11	26	17	24	23
[illegible]	6 13 48	3 9 10	18 12	12	17	25	11	26	17	24	23
[illegible]	6 17 44	4 10 18	1♉49	14	18	26	11	26	17	24	23
[illegible]	6 21 41	5 11 25	15 15	15	19	27	11	26	17	24	23
[illegible]	6 25 37	6 12 33	28 28	16	20	28	11	26	17	24	23
[illegible]	6 29 34	7 13 41	11♊29	18	21	29	11	26	17	24	23
[illegible]	6 33 30	8 14 50	24 16	19	23	29	11	26	17	24	23
31	6 37 27	9 15 58	6♋50	21	24	0♓	11	26	17	24	23

THE SUN ENTERS THE SIGN OF CAPRICORN ON DEC 21 AT 21:44.

♈ ARIES ♉ TAURUS ♊ [illegible] ♏ SCORPIO ♐ SAGITTARIUS ♑ CAPRICORN ♒ AQUARIUS ♓ PISCES

please return in a month or two.
Thanks!
2-15-91

1953

SIDEREAL SUN MOON MERCURY VENUS MARS JUPITER SATURN URANUS NEPTUNE PLUTO

DAY	TIME	☉	☽	☿	♀	♂	♃	♄	♅	♆	♇
	h m s	° ' "	° '	°	°	°	°	°	°	°	°
J 1	6 41 24	10♑17 6	19♋12	22♐	25♒	1♓	11♉R	26♎	17♋R	24♎	23♌R
A 2	6 45 20	11 18 14	1♌22	23	26	2	11	26	17	24	23
N 3	6 49 17	12 19 23	13 22	25	27	2	11	26	17	24	23
U 4	6 53 13	13 20 31	25 14	26	28	3	11	26	17	24	23
A 5	6 57 10	14 21 40	7♍ 2	28	29	4	11 D	26	17	24	23
R 6	7 1 6	15 22 49	18 49	29	1♓	5	11	27	17	24	23
Y 7	7 5 3	16 23 58	0♎41	1♑	2	5	11	27	16	24	23
8	7 8 59	17 25 7	12 42	2	3	6	11	27	16	24	23
9	7 12 56	18 26 16	24 57	4	4	7	11	27	16	24	23
10	7 16 53	19 27 25	7♏30	5	5	8	11	27	16	24	23
11	7 20 49	20 28 34	20 27	7	6	9	11	27	16	24	23
12	7 24 46	21 29 43	3♐48	8	7	9	11	27	16	24	23
13	7 28 42	22 30 52	17 37	10	8	10	11	27	16	24	23
14	7 32 39	23 32 1	1♑51	11	10	11	11	27	16	24	23
15	7 36 35	24 33 9	16 26	13	11	12	11	27	16	24	23
16	7 40 32	25 34 17	1♒16	14	12	12	11	27	16	24	23
17	7 44 29	26 35 25	16 13	16	13	13	11	27	16	24	23
18	7 48 25	27 36 31	1♓10	17	14	14	11	27	16	24	23
19	7 52 22	28 37 37	15 58	19	15	15	11	27	16	24	23
20	7 56 18	29 38 42	0♈31	21	16	15	11	27	16	24	23
21	8 0 15	0♒39 46	14 45	22	17	16	11	27	16	24	23
22	8 4 11	1 40 50	28 40	24	18	17	11	27	16	24	23
23	8 8 8	2 41 52	12♉13	25	19	18	12	27	16	24	23
24	8 12 4	3 42 53	25 28	27	20	19	12	27	16	24	22
25	8 16 1	4 43 53	8♊24	29	22	19	12	27	16	24 R	22
26	8 19 58	5 44 52	21 5	0♒	23	20	12	27	16	24	22
27	8 23 54	6 45 51	3♋33	2	24	21	12	27	16	24	22
28	8 27 51	7 46 48	15 50	4	25	22	12	27	16	24	22
29	8 31 47	8 47 44	27 56	5	26	22	12	27	16	24	22
30	8 35 44	9 48 38	9♌56	7	27	23	12	27	16	24	22
31	8 39 40	10 49 32	21 49	9	28	24	12	27	15	24	22

THE SUN ENTERS THE SIGN OF AQUARIUS ON JAN 20 AT 08:22.

DAY	TIME	☉	☽	☿	♀	♂	♃	♄	♅	♆	♇
	h m s	° ' "	° '	°	°	°	°	°	°	°	°
F 1	8 43 37	11♒50 25	3♍39	10♒	29♓	25♓	12♉	27♎	15♋R	24♎R	22♌R
E 2	8 47 33	12 51 17	15 27	12	0⊙	25	12	27	15	24	22
B 3	8 51 30	13 52 8	27 16	14	1♈	26	12	27	15	24	22
R 4	8 55 27	14 52 58	9♎10	16	2	27	12	27	15	24	22
U 5	8 59 23	15 53 47	21 11	17	3	28	13	27 R	15	24	22
A 6	9 3 20	16 54 35	3♏25	19	4	28	13	27	15	24	22
R 7	9 7 16	17 55 22	15 54	21	5	29	13	27	15	24	22
Y 8	9 11 13	18 56 9	28 44	23	6	0⊙	13	27	15	24	22
9	9 15 9	19 56 54	11♐57	25	7	1♈	13	27	15	24	22
10	9 19 6	20 57 38	25 37	26	8	1	13	27	15	24	22
11	9 23 2	21 58 22	9♑44	28	8	2	13	27	15	24	22
12	9 26 59	22 59 4	24 16	0♓	9	3	13	27	15	24	22
13	9 30 56	23 59 45	9♒10	2	10	4	13	27	15	24	22
14	9 34 52	25 0 24	24 19	4	11	5	14	27	15	24	22
15	9 38 49	26 1 2	9♓32	5	12	5	14	27	15	24	22
16	9 42 45	27 1 38	24 41	7	13	6	14	27	15	24	22
17	9 46 42	28 2 13	9♈35	9	14	7	14	27	15	24	22
18	9 50 38	29 2 46	24 9	11	15	8	14	27	15	24	22
19	9 54 35	0♓ 3 17	8♉17	13	16	8	14	27	15	24	22
20	9 58 31	1 3 47	21 58	15	16	9	14	27	15	24	22
21	10 2 28	2 4 14	5♊13	16	17	10	14	27	15	24	22
22	10 6 25	3 4 40	18 5	18	18	11	15	27	15	24	22
23	10 10 21	4 5 4	0♋37	20	19	11	15	27	15	24	22
24	10 14 18	5 5 26	12 53	21	19	12	15	27	15	24	22
25	10 18 14	6 5 46	24 58	23	20	13	15	27	15	24	22
26	10 22 11	7 6 4	6♌54	24	21	14	15	27	15	24	22
27	10 26 7	8 6 20	18 45	26	22	14	15	27	15	24	22
28	10 30 4	9 6 34	0♍34	27	22	15	16	27	15	24	22

THE SUN ENTERS THE SIGN OF PISCES ON FEB 18 AT 22:42.

DAY	TIME	☉	☽	☿	♀	♂	♃	♄	♅	♆	♇
	h m s	° ' "	° '	°	°	°	°	°	°	°	°
M 1	10 34 0	10♓ 6 47	12♍22	28♓	23♈	16♈	16♉	27♎R	15♋R	24♎R	22♌R
A 2	10 37 57	11 6 57	24 13	29	24	17	16	27	15	24	22
R 3	10 41 54	12 7 6	6♎ 7	0♈	24	17	16	27	15	24	22
C 4	10 45 50	13 7 13	18 7	1	25	18	16	27	15	24	22
H 5	10 49 47	14 7 19	0♏15	2	26	19	16	27	15	23	22
6	10 53 43	15 7 23	12 33	2	26	19	16	27	15	23	22
7	10 57 40	16 7 25	25 4	3	27	20	17	27	15	23	21
8	11 1 36	17 7 26	7♐51	3	27	21	17	26	15	23	21
9	11 5 33	18 7 25	20 57	3 R	28	22	17	26	15	23	21
10	11 9 29	19 7 23	4♑26	3	28	22	17	26	15	23	21
11	11 13 26	20 7 19	18 20	3	29	23	17	26	14	23	21
12	11 17 23	21 7 13	2♒38	2	29	24	18	26	14	23	21
13	11 21 19	22 7 6	17 20	2	29	25	18	26	14	23	21
14	11 25 16	23 6 57	2♓20	1	0♉	25	18	26	14	23	21
15	11 29 12	24 6 45	17 32	1	0	26	18	26	14	23	21
16	11 33 9	25 6 32	2♈45	0⊙	0	27	18	26	14	23	21
17	11 37 5	26 6 17	17 49	29♓	1	28	18	26	14	23	21
18	11 41 2	27 6 0	2♉35	28	1	28	19	26	14	23	21
19	11 44 58	28 5 41	16 56	27	1	29	19	26	14	23	21
20	11 48 55	29 5 19	0♊48	26	1	0♉	19	26	14	23	21
21	11 52 51	0♈ 4 55	14 11	25	1	1	19	26	14	23	21
22	11 56 48	1 4 29	27 6	25	1	1	19	26	14 D	23	21
23	12 0 45	2 4 1	9♋38	24	1 R	2	20	26	14	23	21
24	12 4 41	3 3 30	21 52	23	1	3	20	26	14	23	21
25	12 8 38	4 2 57	3♌52	22	1	3	20	25	14	23	21
26	12 12 34	5 2 22	15 43	22	1	4	20	25	14	23	21
27	12 16 31	6 1 44	27 31	21	1	5	20	25	14	23	21
28	12 20 27	7 1 5	9♍18	21	1	6	21	25	14	23	21
29	12 24 24	8 0 23	21 8	20	1	6	21	25	14	23	21
30	12 28 20	8 59 38	3♎ 4	20	0	7	21	25	14	23	21
31	12 32 17	9 58 52	15 6	20	0	8	21	25	14	23	21

THE SUN ENTERS THE SIGN OF ARIES ON MAR 20 AT 22:01.

DAY	TIME	☉	☽	☿	♀	♂	♃	♄	♅	♆	♇
	h m s	° ' "	° '	°	°	°	°	°	°	°	°
A 1	12 36 14	10♈58 4	27♎17	20♓D	0♉R	9♉	21♉	25♎R	14♋	23♎R	21♌R
P 2	12 40 10	11 57 14	9♏36	20	29♈	9	22	25	14	23	21
R 3	12 44 7	12 56 22	22 6	20	29	10	22	25	14	23	21
I 4	12 48 3	13 55 28	4♐47	20	28	11	22	25	14	23	21
L 5	12 52 0	14 54 32	17 41	20	28	11	22	25	15	23	21
6	12 55 56	15 53 35	0♑50	21	27	12	22	25	15	23	21
7	12 59 53	16 52 36	14 15	21	27	13	23	25	15	23	21
8	13 3 49	17 51 35	27 59	22	26	14	23	24	15	23	21
9	13 7 46	18 50 33	12♒ 4	22	26	14	23	24	15	23	21
10	13 11 43	19 49 28	26 27	23	25	15	23	24	15	23	21
11	13 15 39	20 48 22	11♓ 9	24	25	16	24	24	15	23	21
12	13 19 36	21 47 14	26 3	25	24	16	24	24	15	23	21
13	13 23 32	22 46 4	11♈ 3	25	23	17	24	24	15	23	21
14	13 27 29	23 44 52	25 58	26	23	18	24	24	15	22	21
15	13 31 25	24 43 39	10♉41	27	22	19	24	24	15	22	21
16	13 35 22	25 42 23	25 3	28	21	19	25	24	15	22	21
17	13 39 18	26 41 5	8♊58	29	21	20	25	24	15	22	21
18	13 43 15	27 39 45	22 26	0♈	20	21	25	24	15	22	21
19	13 47 12	28 38 23	5♋25	1	20	21	25	24	15	22	21
20	13 51 8	29 36 59	18 1	3	19	22	25	24	15	22	21
21	13 55 5	0♉35 33	0♌17	4	19	23	26	23	15	22	21
22	13 59 1	1 34 4	12 17	5	18	24	26	23	15	22	21
23	14 2 58	2 32 33	24 9	6	18	24	26	23	15	22	21
24	14 6 54	3 31 0	5♍57	8	17	25	26	23	15	22	21
25	14 10 51	4 29 25	17 46	9	17	26	27	23	15	22	21
26	14 14 47	5 27 48	29 40	10	16	26	27	23	15	22	21
27	14 18 44	6 26 8	11♎42	12	16	27	27	23	15	22	21
28	14 22 41	7 24 27	23 54	13	16	28	27	23	15	22	21
29	14 26 37	8 22 44	6♏17	15	16	28	28	23	15	22	21
30	14 30 34	9 21 0	18 53	16	15	29	28	23	15	22	21

THE SUN ENTERS THE SIGN OF TAURUS ON APR 20 AT 09:25.

DAY	TIME	☉	☽	☿	♀	♂	♃	♄	♅	♆	♇
	h m s	° ' "	° '	°	°	°	°	°	°	°	°
M 1	14 34 30	10♉19 13	1♐41	18♈	15♈R	0♊	28♉	23♎R	15♋	22♎R	21♌R
A 2	14 38 27	11 17 25	14 40	19	15	1	28	23	15	22	21 D
Y 3	14 42 23	12 15 36	27 50	21	15	1	28	23	15	22	21
4	14 46 20	13 13 45	11♑11	23	15 D	2	29	22	15	22	21
5	14 50 16	14 11 52	24 45	24	15	3	29	22	15	22	21
6	14 54 13	15 9 59	8♒30	26	15	3	29	22	15	22	21
7	14 58 10	16 8 3	22 28	28	15	4	29	22	15	22	21
8	15 2 6	17 6 6	6♓40	0♉	15	5	0♊	22	15	22	21
9	15 6 3	18 4 8	21 2	1	15	5	0	22	15	22	21
10	15 9 59	19 2 9	5♈34	3	16	6	0	22	15	22	21
11	15 13 56	20 0 8	20 10	5	16	7	0	22	15	22	21
12	15 17 52	20 58 6	4♉43	7	16	7	1	22	16	22	21
13	15 21 49	21 56 2	19 7	9	16	8	1	22	16	22	21
14	15 25 45	22 53 57	3♊14	11	17	9	1	22	16	22	21
15	15 29 42	23 51 51	17 1	13	17	10	1	22	16	22	21
16	15 33 39	24 49 43	0♋24	15	17	10	1	22	16	22	21
17	15 37 35	25 47 33	13 23	17	18	11	2	22	16	22	21
18	15 41 32	26 45 22	25 59	19	18	12	2	22	16	22	21
19	15 45 28	27 43 9	8♌16	21	19	12	2	22	16	22	21
20	15 49 25	28 40 54	20 19	23	19	13	2	22	16	22	21
21	15 53 21	29 38 38	2♍13	25	20	14	3	21	16	22	21
22	15 57 18	0♊36 20	14 3	27	20	14	3	21	16	22	21
23	16 1 14	1 34 0	25 54	0♊	21	15	3	21	16	22	21
24	16 5 11	2 31 39	7♎51	2	21	16	3	21	16	22	21
25	16 9 8	3 29 17	19 58	4	22	16	4	21	16	21	21
26	16 13 4	4 26 53	2♏19	6	23	17	4	21	16	21	21
27	16 17 1	5 24 28	14 54	8	23	18	4	21	16	21	21
28	16 20 57	6 22 1	27 45	11	24	18	4	21	16	21	21
29	16 24 54	7 19 34	10♐52	13	24	19	5	21	16	21	21
30	16 28 50	8 17 5	24 13	15	25	20	5	21	16	21	21
31	16 32 47	9 14 36	7♑46	17	26	20	5	21	16	21	21

THE SUN ENTERS THE SIGN OF GEMINI ON MAY 21 AT 08:53.

DAY	TIME	☉	☽	☿	♀	♂	♃	♄	♅	♆	♇
	h m s	° ' "	° '	°	°	°	°	°	°	°	°
J 1	16 36 43	10♊12 5	21♑29	19♊	27♈	21♊	5♊	21♎R	16♋	21♎R	21♌
U 2	16 40 40	11 9 34	5♒21	21	27	22	5	21	16	21	21
N 3	16 44 37	12 7 1	19 20	23	28	22	6	21	17	21	21
E 4	16 48 33	13 4 28	3♓24	25	29	23	6	21	17	21	21
5	16 52 30	14 1 55	17 33	27	0♉	24	6	21	17	21	21
6	16 56 26	14 59 21	1♈46	29	0	25	6	21	17	21	21
7	17 0 23	15 56 46	15 59	1♋	1	25	7	21	17	21	21
8	17 4 19	16 54 10	0♉11	3	2	26	7	21	17	21	21
9	17 8 16	17 51 34	14 17	5	3	27	7	21	17	21	21
10	17 12 12	18 48 58	28 14	7	4	27	7	21	17	21	21
11	17 16 9	19 46 21	11♊58	9	5	28	8	21	17	21	21
12	17 20 6	20 43 43	25 25	10	5	29	8	21	17	21	21
13	17 24 2	21 41 4	8♋34	12	6	29	8	21	17	21	21
14	17 27 59	22 38 25	21 23	14	7	0♋	8	21	17	21	21
15	17 31 55	23 35 45	3♌54	15	8	1	8	21	17	21	21
16	17 35 52	24 33 4	16 9	17	9	1	9	21	17	21	21
17	17 39 48	25 30 22	28 12	18	10	2	9	21	17	21	21
18	17 43 45	26 27 39	10♍ 6	20	11	3	9	21	17	21	21
19	17 47 42	27 24 55	21 57	21	12	3	9	21	17	21	21
20	17 51 38	28 22 11	3♎50	22	13	4	10	21	17	21	21
21	17 55 35	29 19 26	15 48	24	14	5	10	21	18	21	21
22	17 59 31	0♋16 41	27 58	25	15	5	10	21	18	21	21
23	18 3 28	1 13 54	10♏23	26	16	6	10	21 D	18	21	21
24	18 7 24	2 11 8	23 5	27	17	7	11	21	18	21	21
25	18 11 21	3 8 21	6♐ 7	28	17	7	11	21	18	21	21
26	18 15 17	4 5 33	19 29	0♌	18	8	11	21	18	21	21
27	18 19 14	5 2 45	3♑10	1	19	9	11	21	18	21	21
28	18 23 11	5 59 57	17 7	2	20	9	11	21	18	21	22
29	18 27 7	6 57 8	1♒16	2	21	10	12	21	18	21	22
30	18 31 4	7 54 20	15 33	3	22	11	12	21	18	21	22

THE SUN ENTERS THE SIGN OF CANCER ON JUN 21 AT 17:00.

♈ ARIES ♉ TAURUS ♊ GEMINI ♋ CANCER ♌ LEO ♍ VIRGO ♎ LIBRA ♏ SCORPIO ♐ SAGITTARIUS ♑ CAPRICORN ♒ AQUARIUS ♓ PISCES

SIDEREAL SUN MOON MERCURY VENUS MARS JUPITER SATURN URANUS NEPTUNE PLUTO

DAY	TIME	☉	☽	☿	♀	♂	♃	♄	♅	♆	♇
	h m s	° ' "	° '	°	°	°	°	°	°	°	°
J 1	18 35 0	8♋51 31	29♒55	4♌	23♉	11♋	12♊	21♎	18♋	21♎R	22♌
U 2	18 38 57	9 48 43	14♓16	5	24	12	12	21	18	21 D	22
L 3	18 42 53	10 45 55	28 34	5	25	13	13	21	18	21	22
Y 4	18 46 50	11 43 7	12♈47	6	26	13	13	21	18	21	22
5	18 50 46	12 40 19	26 52	7	27	14	13	21	18	21	22
6	18 54 43	13 37 32	10♉46	7	29	14	13	21	18	21	22
7	18 58 40	14 34 45	24 30	8	0♊	15	13	21	19	21	22
8	19 2 36	15 31 58	8♊ 1	8	1	16	14	21	19	21	22
9	19 6 33	16 29 12	21 19	8	2	16	14	21	19	21	22
10	19 10 29	17 26 26	4♋22	8	3	17	14	21	19	21	22
11	19 14 26	18 23 40	17 11	8 R	4	18	14	21	19	21	22
12	19 18 22	19 20 55	29 45	8	5	18	14	21	19	21	22
13	19 22 19	20 18 9	12♌ 6	8	6	19	15	21	19	21	22
14	19 26 15	21 15 24	24 15	8	7	20	15	21	19	21	22
15	19 30 12	22 12 39	6♍14	8	8	20	15	21	19	21	22
16	19 34 9	23 9 54	18 7	8	9	21	15	21	19	21	22
17	19 38 5	24 7 9	29 58	7	10	22	16	21	19	21	22
18	19 42 2	25 4 24	11♎50	7	11	22	16	21	19	21	22
19	19 45 58	26 1 40	23 48	6	12	23	16	21	19	21	22
20	19 49 55	26 58 56	5♏57	6	13	24	16	21	19	21	22
21	19 53 51	27 56 12	18 22	5	14	24	16	21	19	21	22
22	19 57 48	28 53 28	1♐ 5	5	16	25	17	21	19	21	22
23	20 1 44	29 50 45	14 10	4	17	26	17	21	19	21	22
24	20 5 41	0♌48 2	27 39	3	18	26	17	21	20	21	22
25	20 9 38	1 45 19	11♑31	2	19	27	17	21	20	21	22
26	20 13 34	2 42 37	25 45	2	20	28	17	21	20	21	22
27	20 17 31	3 39 56	10♒17	1	21	28	18	21	20	21	22
28	20 21 27	4 37 15	25 0	0	22	29	18	22	20	21	22
29	20 25 24	5 34 35	9♓47	0	23	29	18	22	20	21	22
30	20 29 20	6 31 56	24 32	29♋	24	0♌	18	22	20	21	22
31	20 33 17	7 29 19	9♈ 9	29	25	1	18	22	20	21	22

THE SUN ENTERS THE SIGN OF LEO ON JUL 23 AT 03:53.

DAY	TIME	☉	☽	☿	♀	♂	♃	♄	♅	♆	♇
	h m s	° ' "	° '	°	°	°	°	°	°	°	°
A 1	20 37 13	8♌26 42	23♈32	28♋R	27♊	1♌	18♊	22♎	20♋	21♎	22♌
U 2	20 41 10	9 24 6	7♉38	28	28	2	19	22	20	21	22
G 3	20 45 7	10 21 32	21 26	28	29	3	19	22	20	21	23
U 4	20 49 3	11 18 59	4♊55	28 D	0♋	3	19	22	20	21	23
S 5	20 53 0	12 16 27	18 8	28	1	4	19	22	20	21	23
T 6	20 56 56	13 13 57	1♋ 4	28	2	5	19	22	20	21	23
7	21 0 53	14 11 27	13 46	28	3	5	20	22	20	21	23
8	21 4 49	15 8 59	26 15	28	4	6	20	22	20	21	23
9	21 8 46	16 6 32	8♌33	28	6	7	20	22	20	21	23
10	21 12 43	17 4 6	20 42	29	7	7	20	22	21	21	23
11	21 16 39	18 1 41	2♍43	0♌	8	8	20	22	21	22	23
12	21 20 36	18 59 17	14 38	0	9	9	20	22	21	22	23
13	21 24 32	19 56 54	26 29	1	10	9	21	23	21	22	23
14	21 28 29	20 54 32	8♎19	2	11	10	21	23	21	22	23
15	21 32 25	21 52 11	20 11	3	12	10	21	23	21	22	23
16	21 36 22	22 49 52	2♏ 8	4	14	11	21	23	21	22	23
17	21 40 18	23 47 33	14 15	6	15	12	21	23	21	22	23
18	21 44 15	24 45 15	26 36	7	16	12	21	23	21	22	23
19	21 48 11	25 42 59	9♐15	8	17	13	22	23	21	22	23
20	21 52 8	26 40 43	22 16	10	18	14	22	23	21	22	23
21	21 56 5	27 38 29	5♑43	12	19	14	22	23	21	22	23
22	22 0 1	28 36 16	19 36	13	21	15	22	23	21	22	23
23	22 3 58	29 34 4	3♒56	15	22	16	22	23	21	22	23
24	22 7 54	0♍31 54	18 39	17	23	16	22	23	21	22	23
25	22 11 51	1 29 44	3♓38	19	24	17	22	24	21	22	23
26	22 15 47	2 27 36	18 47	20	25	17	23	24	21	22	23
27	22 19 44	3 25 30	3♈55	22	26	18	23	24	21	22	23
28	22 23 40	4 23 26	18 52	24	28	19	23	24	21	22	23
29	22 27 37	5 21 23	3♉31	26	29	19	23	24	22	22	23
30	22 31 34	6 19 22	17 48	28	0♌	20	23	24	22	22	23
31	22 35 30	7 17 23	1♊38	0♍	1	21	23	24	22	22	23

THE SUN ENTERS THE SIGN OF VIRGO ON AUG 23 AT 10:46.

DAY	TIME	☉	☽	☿	♀	♂	♃	♄	♅	♆	♇
	h m s	° ' "	° '	°	°	°	°	°	°	°	°
S 1	22 39 27	8♍15 27	15♊ 4	2♍	2♌	21♌	23♊	24♎	22♋	22♎	23♌
E 2	22 43 23	9 13 32	28 7	4	3	22	24	24	22	22	23
P 3	22 47 20	10 11 39	10♋51	6	5	23	24	24	22	22	23
T 4	22 51 16	11 9 48	23 18	8	6	23	24	24	22	22	24
E 5	22 55 13	12 7 58	5♌33	10	7	24	24	25	22	22	24
M 6	22 59 9	13 6 11	17 38	12	8	24	24	25	22	22	24
B 7	23 3 6	14 4 26	29 36	14	9	25	24	25	22	22	24
E 8	23 7 3	15 2 42	11♍30	16	11	26	24	25	22	22	24
R 9	23 10 59	16 1 0	23 22	17	12	26	24	25	22	22	24
10	23 14 56	16 59 20	5♎12	19	13	27	25	25	22	22	24
11	23 18 52	17 57 41	17 3	21	14	28	25	25	22	22	24
12	23 22 49	18 56 4	28 57	23	15	28	25	25	22	22	24
13	23 26 45	19 54 29	10♏57	25	17	29	25	25	22	22	24
14	23 30 42	20 52 56	23 5	27	18	0♍	25	26	22	22	24
15	23 34 38	21 51 24	5♐24	28	19	0	25	26	22	22	24
16	23 38 35	22 49 54	17 59	0♎	20	1	25	26	22	22	24
17	23 42 32	23 48 26	0♑54	2	21	1	25	26	22	23	24
18	23 46 28	24 46 59	14 12	4	23	2	25	26	22	23	24
19	23 50 25	25 45 34	27 57	5	24	3	25	26	22	23	24
20	23 54 21	26 44 10	12♒10	7	25	3	25	26	22	23	24
21	23 58 18	27 42 48	26 49	9	26	4	26	26	22	23	24
22	0 2 14	28 41 28	11♓51	10	27	5	26	26	22	23	24
23	0 6 11	29 40 10	27 7	12	29	5	26	26	23	23	24
24	0 10 7	0♎38 53	12♈27	14	0♍	6	26	27	23	23	24
25	0 14 4	1 37 39	27 39	15	1	6	26	27	23	23	24
26	0 18 1	2 36 27	12♉33	17	2	7	26	27	23	23	24
27	0 21 57	3 35 17	27 2	18	3	8	26	27	23	23	24
28	0 25 54	4 34 9	11♊ 2	20	5	8	26	27	23	23	24
29	0 29 50	5 33 4	24 32	21	6	9	26	27	23	23	24
30	0 33 47	6 32 1	7♋35	23	7	10	26	27	23	23	24

THE SUN ENTERS THE SIGN OF LIBRA ON SEP 23 AT 08:07.

SIDEREAL SUN MOON MERCURY VENUS MARS JUPITER SATURN URANUS NEPTUNE PLUTO

DAY	TIME	☉	☽	☿	♀	♂	♃	♄	♅	♆	♇
	h m s	° ' "	° '	°	°	°	°	°	°	°	°
O 1	0 37 43	7♎31 1	20♋15	25♎	8♍	10♍	26♊	27♎	23♋	23♎	24♌
C 2	0 41 40	8 30 2	2♌36	26	10	11	26	28	23	23	24
T 3	0 45 36	9 29 6	14 44	28	11	12	26	28	23	23	24
O 4	0 49 33	10 28 12	26 41	29	12	12	26	28	23	23	24
B 5	0 53 30	11 27 20	8♍34	0♏	13	13	26	28	23	23	24
E 6	0 57 26	12 26 31	20 24	2	14	13	26	28	23	23	24
R 7	1 1 23	13 25 43	2♎14	3	16	14	26	28	23	23	24
8	1 5 19	14 24 58	14 6	5	17	15	26	28	23	23	24
9	1 9 16	15 24 15	26 2	6	18	15	26	28	23	23	24
10	1 13 12	16 23 34	8♏ 3	8	19	16	26	28	23	23	24
11	1 17 9	17 22 54	20 9	9	21	17	26	29	23	23	24
12	1 21 5	18 22 17	2♐24	10	22	17	26	29	23	23	25
13	1 25 2	19 21 42	14 48	12	23	18	26	29	23	23	25
14	1 28 58	20 21 8	27 25	13	24	18	26	29	23	23	25
15	1 32 55	21 20 36	10♑18	14	26	19	26 R	29	23	24	25
16	1 36 52	22 20 6	23 30	15	27	20	26	29	23	24	25
17	1 40 48	23 19 38	7♒ 5	17	28	20	26	29	23	24	25
18	1 44 45	24 19 11	21 5	18	29	21	26	29	23	24	25
19	1 48 41	25 18 46	5♓30	19	0♎	22	26	0♏	23	24	25
20	1 52 38	26 18 23	20 18	20	2	22	26	0	23	24	25
21	1 56 34	27 18 1	5♈24	21	3	23	26	0	23	24	25
22	2 0 31	28 17 42	20 38	22	4	23	26	0	23	24	25
23	2 4 27	29 17 24	5♉49	23	5	24	26	0	23	24	25
24	2 8 24	0♏17 8	20 47	24	7	25	26	0	23	24	25
25	2 12 21	1 16 55	5♊23	25	8	25	26	0	23	24	25
26	2 16 17	2 16 44	19 30	26	9	26	26	0	23	24	25
27	2 20 14	3 16 35	3♋ 8	27	10	27	26	1	23	24	25
28	2 24 10	4 16 28	16 17	28	12	27	26	1	23	24	25
29	2 28 7	5 16 23	29 0	29	13	28	26	1	23 R	24	25
30	2 32 3	6 16 21	11♌22	29	14	28	26	1	23	24	25
31	2 36 0	7 16 20	23 29	0♐	15	29	26	1	23	24	25

THE SUN ENTERS THE SIGN OF SCORPIO ON OCT 23 AT 17:07.

DAY	TIME	☉	☽	☿	♀	♂	♃	♄	♅	♆	♇
	h m s	° ' "	° '	°	°	°	°	°	°	°	°
N 1	2 39 56	8♏16 22	5♍25	0♐	17♎	0♎	26♊R	1♏	23♋R	24♎	25♌
O 2	2 43 53	9 16 26	17 16	0	18	0	26	1	23	24	25
V 3	2 47 50	10 16 32	29 5	1 R	19	1	26	1	23	24	25
E 4	2 51 46	11 16 40	10♎57	1	20	1	26	1	23	24	25
M 5	2 55 43	12 16 50	22 53	1	22	2	26	2	23	24	25
B 6	2 59 39	13 17 1	4♏56	0	23	3	26	2	23	24	25
E 7	3 3 36	14 17 15	17 6	0	24	3	26	2	23	24	25
R 8	3 7 32	15 17 30	29 25	29♏	25	4	26	2	23	24	25
9	3 11 29	16 17 48	11♐53	29	27	5	25	2	23	24	25
10	3 15 25	17 18 7	24 31	28	28	5	25	2	23	24	25
11	3 19 22	18 18 27	7♑20	27	29	6	25	2	23	25	25
12	3 23 19	19 18 49	20 21	26	0♏	6	25	2	23	25	25
13	3 27 15	20 19 12	3♒36	24	2	7	25	3	23	25	25
14	3 31 12	21 19 37	17 9	23	3	8	25	3	23	25	25
15	3 35 8	22 20 3	1♓ 0	22	4	8	25	3	23	25	25
16	3 39 5	23 20 30	15 10	20	5	9	25	3	23	25	25
17	3 43 1	24 20 58	29 38	19	7	10	25	3	23	25	25
18	3 46 58	25 21 28	14♈21	18	8	10	25	3	23	25	25
19	3 50 54	26 21 59	29 13	17	9	11	25	3	23	25	25
20	3 54 51	27 22 32	14♉ 6	16	10	11	24	3	23	25	25
21	3 58 48	28 23 6	28 50	15	12	12	24	3	23	25	25
22	4 2 44	29 23 41	13♊18	15	13	13	24	4	23	25	25
23	4 6 41	0♐24 18	27 23	15 D	14	13	24	4	23	25	25
24	4 10 37	1 24 57	11♋ 3	15	15	14	24	4	23	25	25
25	4 14 34	2 25 37	24 15	15	17	14	24	4	23	25	25
26	4 18 30	3 26 18	7♌ 3	15	18	15	24	4	23	25	25 R
27	4 22 27	4 27 2	19 30	15	19	16	24	4	23	25	25
28	4 26 24	5 27 46	1♍40	16	20	16	23	4	23	25	25
29	4 30 20	6 28 33	13 38	17	22	17	23	4	23	25	25
30	4 34 17	7 29 20	25 31	17	23	18	23	4	23	25	25

THE SUN ENTERS THE SIGN OF SAGITTARIUS ON NOV 22 AT 14:23.

DAY	TIME	☉	☽	☿	♀	♂	♃	♄	♅	♆	♇
	h m s	° ' "	° '	°	°	°	°	°	°	°	°
D 1	4 38 13	8♐30 10	7♎21	18♏	24♏	18♎	23♊R	5♏	23♋R	25♎	25♌R
E 2	4 42 10	9 31 0	19 15	19	25	19	23	5	23	25	25
C 3	4 46 6	10 31 52	1♏15	20	27	19	23	5	23	25	25
E 4	4 50 3	11 32 45	13 25	21	28	20	23	5	23	25	25
M 5	4 53 59	12 33 40	25 46	23	29	21	23	5	23	25	25
B 6	4 57 56	13 34 36	8♐19	24	0♐	21	22	5	23	25	25
E 7	5 1 53	14 35 33	21 5	25	2	22	22	5	22	25	25
R 8	5 5 49	15 36 30	4♑ 3	26	3	22	22	5	22	25	25
9	5 9 46	16 37 29	17 13	28	4	23	22	5	22	25	25
10	5 13 42	17 38 28	0♒34	29	5	24	22	6	22	25	25
11	5 17 39	18 39 28	14 6	1♐	7	24	22	6	22	25	25
12	5 21 35	19 40 29	27 49	2	8	25	22	6	22	25	25
13	5 25 32	20 41 30	11♓44	3	9	25	21	6	22	25	25
14	5 29 28	21 42 31	25 48	5	10	26	21	6	22	26	25
15	5 33 25	22 43 33	10♈ 2	6	12	27	21	6	22	26	25
16	5 37 22	23 44 36	24 22	8	13	27	21	6	22	26	25
17	5 41 18	24 45 39	8♉47	9	14	28	21	6	22	26	25
18	5 45 15	25 46 42	23 10	11	15	29	21	6	22	26	25
19	5 49 11	26 47 46	7♊26	12	17	29	21	6	22	26	25
20	5 53 8	27 48 50	21 31	14	18	0♏	21	6	22	26	25
21	5 57 4	28 49 55	5♋20	15	19	0	20	7	22	26	25
22	6 1 1	29 51 0	18 49	17	21	1	20	7	22	26	25
23	6 4 57	0♑52 6	1♌57	18	22	2	20	7	22	26	25
24	6 8 54	1 53 12	14 45	20	23	2	20	7	22	26	25
25	6 12 51	2 54 19	27 14	21	24	3	20	7	22	26	25
26	6 16 47	3 55 26	9♍27	23	26	3	20	7	22	26	25
27	6 20 44	4 56 34	21 28	24	27	4	20	7	22	26	25
28	6 24 40	5 57 42	3♎22	26	28	5	20	7	22	26	25
29	6 28 37	6 58 51	15 14	27	29	5	19	7	22	26	25
30	6 32 33	8 0 1	27 9	29	1♑	6	19	7	22	26	25
31	6 36 30	9 1 10	9♏10	0♑	2	6	19	7	22	26	25

THE SUN ENTERS THE SIGN OF CAPRICORN ON DEC 22 AT 03:32.

♈ ARIES ♉ TAURUS ♊ GEMINI ♋ CANCER ♌ LEO ♍ VIRGO ♎ LIBRA ♏ SCORPIO ♐ SAGITTARIUS ♑ CAPRICORN ♒ AQUARIUS ♓ PISCES

1954

SIDEREAL SUN MOON MERCURY VENUS MARS JUPITER SATURN URANUS NEPTUNE PLUTO

DAY	TIME	☉	☽	☿	♀	♂	♃	♄	♅	♆	♇
	h m s	° ' "	° '	°	°	°	°	°	°	°	°
J 1	6 40 26	10♑ 2 21	21♍23	2♑	3♑	7♏	19♊R	7♏	22♋R	26♎	25♌R
A 2	6 44 23	11 3 31	3♐50	4	4	8	19	8	21	26	25
N 3	6 48 20	12 4 42	16 34	5	6	8	19	8	21	26	25
U 4	6 52 16	13 5 53	29 35	7	7	9	19	8	21	26	25
A 5	6 56 13	14 7 4	12♑54	8	8	9	19	8	21	26	25
R 6	7 0 9	15 8 14	26 29	10	9	10	18	8	21	26	25
Y 7	7 4 6	16 9 25	10♒17	11	11	10	18	8	21	26	25
8	7 8 2	17 10 35	24 17	13	12	11	18	8	21	26	25
9	7 11 59	18 11 45	8♓25	15	13	12	18	8	21	26	25
10	7 15 56	19 12 55	22 37	16	14	12	18	8	21	26	25
11	7 19 52	20 14 3	6♈51	18	16	13	18	8	21	26	25
12	7 23 49	21 15 11	21 3	20	17	13	18	8	21	26	25
13	7 27 45	22 16 19	5♉12	21	18	14	18	8	21	26	25
14	7 31 42	23 17 26	19 15	23	19	15	18	8	21	26	24
15	7 35 38	24 18 32	3♊11	24	21	15	18	8	21	26	24
16	7 39 35	25 19 38	16 58	26	22	16	17	8	21	26	24
17	7 43 31	26 20 43	0♋33	28	23	16	17	9	21	26	24
18	7 47 28	27 21 47	13 56	29	24	17	17	9	21	26	24
19	7 51 25	28 22 51	27 4	1♒	26	18	17	9	21	26	24
20	7 55 21	29 23 54	9♌58	3	27	18	17	9	21	26	24
21	7 59 18	0♒24 56	22 37	5	28	19	17	9	21	26	24
22	8 3 14	1 25 58	5♍ 1	6	0♒	19	17	9	21	26	24
23	8 7 11	2 26 59	17 13	8	1	20	17	9	21	26	24
24	8 11 7	3 27 59	29 15	10	2	20	17	9	21	26	24
25	8 15 4	4 28 59	11♎10	11	3	21	17	9	20	26	24
26	8 19 0	5 29 59	23 2	13	5	22	17	9	20	26	24
27	8 22 57	6 30 58	4♏56	15	6	22	17	9	20	26 R	24
28	8 26 54	7 31 56	16 56	17	7	23	17	9	20	26	24
29	8 30 50	8 32 54	29 7	18	8	23	17	9	20	26	24
30	8 34 47	9 33 51	11♐34	20	10	24	17	9	20	26	24
31	8 38 43	10 34 47	24 20	22	11	24	17	9	20	26	24

THE SUN ENTERS THE SIGN OF AQUARIUS ON JAN 20 AT 14:12.

DAY	TIME	☉	☽	☿	♀	♂	♃	♄	♅	♆	♇
	h m s	° ' "	° '	°	°	°	°	°	°	°	°
F 1	8 42 40	11♒35 43	7♑28	24♒	12♒	25♏	17♊R	9♏	20♋R	26♎R	24♌R
E 2	8 46 36	12 36 37	20 59	25	13	26	17	9	20	26	24
B 3	8 50 33	13 37 31	4♒53	27	15	26	17	9	20	26	24
R 4	8 54 29	14 38 23	19 7	29	16	27	16	9	20	26	24
U 5	8 58 26	15 39 14	3♓36	0♓	17	27	16	9	20	26	24
A 6	9 2 23	16 40 4	18 14	2	18	28	16	9	20	26	24
R 7	9 6 19	17 40 53	2♈54	4	20	28	16	9	20	26	24
Y 8	9 10 16	18 41 40	17 30	5	21	29	16	9	20	26	24
9	9 14 12	19 42 25	1♉55	7	22	0♐	16	9	20	26	24
10	9 18 9	20 43 10	16 7	8	23	0	16 D	9	20	26	24
11	9 22 5	21 43 52	0♊ 3	9	25	1	16	9	20	26	24
12	9 26 2	22 44 33	13 43	11	26	1	16	9	20	26	24
13	9 29 58	23 45 12	27 8	12	27	2	16	9	20	26	24
14	9 33 55	24 45 49	10♋19	13	28	2	16	9	20	26	24
15	9 37 52	25 46 25	23 17	14	0♓	3	16	9	20	26	24
16	9 41 48	26 46 59	6♌ 2	15	1	3	16	9	20	26	24
17	9 45 45	27 47 32	18 37	15	2	4	16	9 R	20	26	24
18	9 49 41	28 48 3	1♍ 1	16	3	5	17	9	20	26	24
19	9 53 38	29 48 32	13 16	16	5	5	17	9	20	26	24
20	9 57 34	0♓49 0	25 22	16 R	6	6	17	9	20	26	24
21	10 1 31	1 49 27	7♎21	16	7	6	17	9	20	26	24
22	10 5 27	2 49 51	19 16	16	8	7	17	9	19	26	24
23	10 9 24	3 50 15	1♏ 7	16	10	7	17	9	19	26	24
24	10 13 21	4 50 37	13 0	15	11	8	17	9	19	26	24
25	10 17 17	5 50 58	24 58	14	12	8	17	9	19	26	24
26	10 21 14	6 51 17	7♐ 6	14	13	9	17	9	19	26	23
27	10 25 10	7 51 35	19 28	13	15	9	17	9	19	26	23
28	10 29 7	8 51 52	2♑ 9	12	16	10	17	9	19	26	23

THE SUN ENTERS THE SIGN OF PISCES ON FEB 19 AT 04:32.

DAY	TIME	☉	☽	☿	♀	♂	♃	♄	♅	♆	♇
	h m s	° ' "	° '	°	°	°	°	°	°	°	°
M 1	10 33 3	9♓52 7	15♑15	11♓R	17♓	10♐	17♊	9♏R	19♋R	26♎R	23♌R
A 2	10 37 0	10 52 20	28 47	10	18	11	17	9	19	26	23
R 3	10 40 56	11 52 32	12♒47	9	20	11	17	9	19	26	23
C 4	10 44 53	12 52 42	27 13	8	21	12	17	9	19	26	23
H 5	10 48 50	13 52 50	12♓ 1	7	22	12	17	9	19	26	23
6	10 52 46	14 52 57	27 3	6	23	13	17	9	19	26	23
7	10 56 43	15 53 1	12♈10	5	25	14	17	9	19	26	23
8	11 0 39	16 53 4	27 11	4	26	14	17	9	19	26	23
9	11 4 36	17 53 4	11♉57	3	27	15	18	9	19	26	23
10	11 8 32	18 53 2	26 23	3	28	15	18	9	19	26	23
11	11 12 29	19 52 59	10♊26	2	0☉	16	18	9	19	26	23
12	11 16 25	20 52 53	24 5	2	1♈	16	18	9	19	26	23
13	11 20 22	21 52 44	7♋21	2	2	17	18	9	19	26	23
14	11 24 19	22 52 34	20 19	2 D	3	17	18	9	19	26	23
15	11 28 15	23 52 21	3♌ 0	2	5	17	18	9	19	26	23
16	11 32 12	24 52 6	15 28	2	6	18	18	9	19	25	23
17	11 36 8	25 51 49	27 47	2	7	18	18	9	19	25	23
18	11 40 5	26 51 30	9♍57	2	8	19	18	9	19	25	23
19	11 44 1	27 51 8	22 1	3	10	19	19	9	19	25	23
20	11 47 58	28 50 45	4♎ 0	3	11	20	19	9	19	25	23
21	11 51 54	29 50 20	15 56	4	12	20	19	9	19	25	23
22	11 55 51	0♈49 52	27 48	4	13	21	19	8	19	25	23
23	11 59 47	1 49 23	9♏40	5	15	21	19	8	19	25	23
24	12 3 44	2 48 52	21 34	6	16	22	19	8	19	25	23
25	12 7 41	3 48 19	3♐32	6	17	22	19	8	19	25	23
26	12 11 37	4 47 45	15 38	7	18	23	19	8	19	25	23
27	12 15 34	5 47 8	27 58	8	19	23	20	8	19 D	25	23
28	12 19 30	6 46 30	10♑34	9	21	24	20	8	19	25	23
29	12 23 27	7 45 50	23 33	10	22	24	20	8	19	25	23
30	12 27 23	8 45 9	6♒59	11	23	24	20	8	19	25	23
31	12 31 20	9 44 25	20 53	12	24	25	20	8	19	25	23

THE SUN ENTERS THE SIGN OF ARIES ON MAR 21 AT 03:53.

SIDEREAL SUN MOON MERCURY VENUS MARS JUPITER SATURN URANUS NEPTUNE PLUTO

DAY	TIME	☉	☽	☿	♀	♂	♃	♄	♅	♆	♇
	h m s	° ' "	° '	°	°	°	°	°	°	°	°
A 1	12 35 16	10♈43 40	5♓17	13♓	26♈	25♐	20♊	8♏R	19♋	25♎R	23♌R
P 2	12 39 13	11 42 53	20 7	14	27	26	20	8	19	25	23
R 3	12 43 10	12 42 3	5♈17	16	28	26	20	8	19	25	23
I 4	12 47 6	13 41 12	20 37	17	29	27	21	8	19	25	23
L 5	12 51 3	14 40 19	5♉54	18	1♉	27	21	8	19	25	23
6	12 54 59	15 39 24	20 58	19	2	27	21	8	19	25	23
7	12 58 56	16 38 26	5♊40	21	3	28	21	7	19	25	23
8	13 2 52	17 37 27	19 55	22	4	28	21	7	19	25	23
9	13 6 49	18 36 25	3♋42	23	6	29	21	7	19	25	23
10	13 10 45	19 35 20	17 1	25	7	29	22	7	19	25	23
11	13 14 42	20 34 14	29 57	26	8	29	22	7	19	25	23
12	13 18 39	21 33 5	12♌33	28	9	0♑	22	7	19	25	23
13	13 22 35	22 31 54	24 53	29	10	0	22	7	19	25	23
14	13 26 32	23 30 40	7♍ 3	1♈	12	0	22	7	19	25	23
15	13 30 28	24 29 25	19 4	2	13	1	22	7	19	25	23
16	13 34 25	25 28 7	1♎ 1	4	14	1	23	7	19	25	23
17	13 38 21	26 26 47	12 54	6	15	2	23	7	19	25	23
18	13 42 18	27 25 25	24 47	7	17	2	23	7	19	25	23
19	13 46 14	28 24 1	6♏40	9	18	2	23	7	19	25	23
20	13 50 11	29 22 36	18 34	11	19	3	23	7	19	25	23
21	13 54 8	0♉21 8	0♐32	12	20	3	23	6	19	25	23
22	13 58 4	1 19 39	12 35	14	22	3	24	6	19	25	23
23	14 2 1	2 18 8	24 46	16	23	3	24	6	19	24	23
24	14 5 57	3 16 36	7♑ 9	18	24	4	24	6	19	24	23
25	14 9 54	4 15 2	19 46	19	25	4	24	6	19	24	23
26	14 13 50	5 13 26	2♒42	21	26	4	24	6	19	24	23
27	14 17 47	6 11 49	16 2	23	28	5	25	6	19	24	23
28	14 21 43	7 10 10	29 47	25	29	5	25	6	19	24	23
29	14 25 40	8 8 29	14♓ 1	27	0♊	5	25	6	19	24	23
30	14 29 37	9 6 47	28 40	29	1	5	25	6	19	24	23

THE SUN ENTERS THE SIGN OF TAURUS ON APR 20 AT 15:20.

DAY	TIME	☉	☽	☿	♀	♂	♃	♄	♅	♆	♇
	h m s	° ' "	° '	°	°	°	°	°	°	°	°
M 1	14 33 33	10♉ 5 4	13♈41	1♉	3♊	6♑	25♊	6♏R	20♋	24♎R	23♌R
A 2	14 37 30	11 3 19	28 54	3	4	6	25	6	20	24	23
Y 3	14 41 26	12 1 32	14♉11	5	5	6	26	6	20	24	23
4	14 45 23	12 59 43	29 18	7	6	6	26	5	20	24	23 D
5	14 49 19	13 57 53	14♊ 7	9	7	7	26	5	20	24	23
6	14 53 16	14 56 1	28 31	11	9	7	26	5	20	24	23
7	14 57 12	15 54 7	12♋27	14	10	7	26	5	20	24	23
8	15 1 9	16 52 11	25 54	16	11	7	27	5	20	24	23
9	15 5 6	17 50 14	8♌55	18	12	7	27	5	20	24	23
10	15 9 2	18 48 14	21 33	20	14	7	27	5	20	24	23
11	15 12 59	19 46 12	3♍53	22	15	8	27	5	20	24	23
12	15 16 55	20 44 9	16 1	24	16	8	27	5	20	24	23
13	15 20 52	21 42 4	27 59	27	17	8	28	5	20	24	23
14	15 24 48	22 39 57	9♎52	29	18	8	28	5	20	24	23
15	15 28 45	23 37 48	21 44	1♊	20	8	28	5	20	24	23
16	15 32 41	24 35 38	3♏37	3	21	8	28	5	20	24	23
17	15 36 38	25 33 26	15 32	5	22	8	28	5	20	24	23
18	15 40 35	26 31 13	27 32	7	23	8	29	4	20	24	23
19	15 44 31	27 28 58	9♐38	9	24	8	29	4	20	24	23
20	15 48 28	28 26 43	21 52	11	26	8	29	4	20	24	23
21	15 52 24	29 24 26	4♑14	13	27	8	29	4	20	24	23
22	15 56 21	0♊22 7	16 47	15	28	9	0♋	4	20	24	23
23	16 0 17	1 19 48	29 34	17	29	9 R	0	4	20	24	23
24	16 4 14	2 17 28	12♒36	19	0♋	9	0	4	20	24	23
25	16 8 10	3 15 6	25 57	21	2	9	0	4	20	24	23
26	16 12 7	4 12 44	9♓39	22	3	8	0	4	20	24	23
27	16 16 4	5 10 20	23 43	24	4	8	1	4	21	24	23
28	16 20 0	6 7 56	8♈ 8	26	5	8	1	4	21	24	23
29	16 23 57	7 5 31	22 50	27	6	8	1	4	21	24	23
30	16 27 53	8 3 5	7♉45	29	8	8	1	4	21	24	23
31	16 31 50	9 0 38	22 44	0♋	9	8	1	4	21	24	23

THE SUN ENTERS THE SIGN OF GEMINI ON MAY 21 AT 14:48.

DAY	TIME	☉	☽	☿	♀	♂	♃	♄	♅	♆	♇
	h m s	° ' "	° '	°	°	°	°	°	°	°	°
J 1	16 35 46	9♊58 10	7♊38	2♋	10♋	8♑R	2♋	4♏R	21♋	24♎R	23♌
U 2	16 39 43	10 55 42	22 19	3	11	8	2	4	21	24	23
N 3	16 43 39	11 53 12	6♋40	5	12	8	2	4	21	24	23
E 4	16 47 36	12 50 41	20 37	6	14	8	2	3	21	24	23
5	16 51 33	13 48 9	4♌ 8	7	15	8	3	3	21	24	23
6	16 55 29	14 45 35	17 14	8	16	7	3	3	21	24	23
7	16 59 26	15 43 1	29 57	10	17	7	3	3	21	23	23
8	17 3 22	16 40 25	12♍20	11	18	7	3	3	21	23	23
9	17 7 19	17 37 48	24 30	12	20	7	3	3	21	23	23
10	17 11 15	18 35 10	6♎29	13	21	7	4	3	21	23	23
11	17 15 12	19 32 32	18 23	13	22	6	4	3	21	23	23
12	17 19 8	20 29 52	0♏15	14	23	6	4	3	21	23	23
13	17 23 5	21 27 11	12 9	15	24	6	4	3	21	23	23
14	17 27 2	22 24 30	24 9	16	26	6	5	3	21	23	23
15	17 30 58	23 21 47	6♐16	16	27	5	5	3	21	23	23
16	17 34 55	24 19 4	18 32	17	28	5	5	3	22	23	23
17	17 38 51	25 16 21	1♑ 0	17	29	5	5	3	22	23	23
18	17 42 48	26 13 37	13 39	18	0♌	5	5	3	22	23	23
19	17 46 44	27 10 52	26 31	18	2	4	6	3	22	23	23
20	17 50 41	28 8 7	9♒36	18	3	4	6	3	22	23	23
21	17 54 37	29 5 22	22 54	19	4	4	6	3	22	23	23
22	17 58 34	0♋ 2 36	6♓27	19	5	3	6	3	22	23	23
23	18 2 31	0 59 51	20 15	19 R	6	3	7	3	22	23	23
24	18 6 27	1 57 5	4♈16	19	7	3	7	3	22	23	23
25	18 10 24	2 54 19	18 31	19	9	3	7	3	22	23	23
26	18 14 20	3 51 33	2♉55	19	10	2	7	3	22	23	23
27	18 18 17	4 48 47	17 27	18	11	2	8	3	22	23	23
28	18 22 13	5 46 2	2♊ 0	18	12	2	8	3	22	23	23
29	18 26 10	6 43 16	16 30	18	13	1	8	3	22	23	23
30	18 30 7	7 40 30	0♋50	17	14	1	8	3	22	23	23

THE SUN ENTERS THE SIGN OF CANCER ON JUN 21 AT 22:54.

♈ ARIES ♉ TAURUS ♊ GEMINI ♋ CANCER ♌ LEO ♍ VIRGO ♎ LIBRA ♏ SCORPIO ♐ SAGITTARIUS ♑ CAPRICORN ♒ AQUARIUS ♓ PISCES

SIDEREAL SUN MOON MERCURY VENUS MARS JUPITER SATURN URANUS NEPTUNE PLUTO

SIDEREAL SUN MOON MERCURY VENUS MARS JUPITER SATURN URANUS NEPTUNE PLUTO

DAY	TIME	☉	☽	☿	♀	♂	♃	♄	♅	♆	♇
	h m s	° ' "	° '	°	°	°	°	°	°	°	°
J 1	18 34 3	8♋37 45	14♋55	17♋R	16♌	1♑R	8♋	3♏R	22♋	23♎R	23♌
U 2	18 38 0	9 34 59	28 42	16	17	0	9	3	22	23	23
L 3	18 41 56	10 32 12	12♌ 9	16	18	0	9	3	23	23	23
Y 4	18 45 53	11 29 26	25 13	15	19	0	9	3	23	23	23
5	18 49 49	12 26 39	7♍57	14	20	0	9	3	23	23 D	23
6	18 53 46	13 23 52	20 23	14	21	29♐	10	3 D	23	23	23
7	18 57 42	14 21 5	2♎35	13	23	29	10	3	23	23	23
8	19 1 39	15 18 17	14 35	12	24	29	10	3	23	23	23
9	19 5 36	16 15 30	26 30	12	25	28	10	3	23	23	23
10	19 9 32	17 12 42	8♏23	11	26	28	10	3	23	23	23
11	19 13 29	18 9 54	20 19	11	27	28	11	3	23	23	24
12	19 17 25	19 7 7	2♐22	10	28	28	11	3	23	23	24
13	19 21 22	20 4 19	14 35	10	0♍	27	11	3	23	23	24
14	19 25 18	21 1 32	27 1	10	1	27	11	3	23	23	24
15	19 29 15	21 58 44	9♑43	10	2	27	12	3	23	23	24
16	19 33 11	22 55 57	22 41	9	3	27	12	3	23	23	24
17	19 37 8	23 53 11	5♒55	9 D	4	27	12	3	23	23	24
18	19 41 5	24 50 24	19 25	9	5	27	12	3	23	23	24
19	19 45 1	25 47 38	3♓ 8	9	6	26	13	3	24	23	24
20	19 48 58	26 44 53	17 3	10	8	26	13	3	24	23	24
21	19 52 54	27 42 9	1♈ 6	10	9	26	13	3	24	23	24
22	19 56 51	28 39 25	15 16	10	10	26	13	3	24	23	24
23	20 0 47	29 36 42	29 29	11	11	26	13	3	24	23	24
24	20 4 44	0♌34 1	13♉43	11	12	26	14	3	24	23	24
25	20 8 40	1 31 20	27 56	12	13	26	14	3	24	23	24
26	20 12 37	2 28 40	12♊ 4	13	14	26	14	3	24	23	24
27	20 16 34	3 26 1	26 7	14	16	26	14	3	24	23	24
28	20 20 30	4 23 23	10♋ 0	15	17	26	14	3	24	23	24
29	20 24 27	5 20 45	23 42	16	18	26 D	15	3	24	23	24
30	20 28 23	6 18 9	7♌10	17	19	26	15	3	24	23	24
31	20 32 20	7 15 33	20 22	18	20	26	15	3	24	23	24

THE SUN ENTERS THE SIGN OF LEO ON JUL 23 AT 09:46.

DAY	TIME	☉	☽	☿	♀	♂	♃	♄	♅	♆	♇
	h m s	° ' "	° '	°	°	°	°	°	°	°	°
A 1	20 36 16	8♌12 58	3♍18	19♋	21♍	26♐	15♋	3♏	24♋	23♎	24♌
U 2	20 40 13	9 10 24	15 57	21	22	26	16	3	24	23	24
G 3	20 44 9	10 7 50	28 21	22	23	26	16	3	24	24	24
U 4	20 48 6	11 5 17	10♎31	24	24	26	16	3	24	24	24
S 5	20 52 3	12 2 45	22 32	25	26	26	16	3	25	24	24
T 6	20 55 59	13 0 14	4♏26	27	27	26	16	3	25	24	24
7	20 59 56	13 57 43	16 18	29	28	26	17	3	25	24	24
8	21 3 52	14 55 13	28 14	1♌	29	26	17	3	25	24	24
9	21 7 49	15 52 44	10♐17	3	0♎	26	17	4	25	24	24
10	21 11 45	16 50 16	22 33	4	1	26	17	4	25	24	24
11	21 15 42	17 47 49	5♑ 5	6	2	27	18	4	25	24	24
12	21 19 38	18 45 22	17 57	8	3	27	18	4	25	24	24
13	21 23 35	19 42 57	1♒10	10	4	27	18	4	25	24	25
14	21 27 32	20 40 33	14 45	12	5	27	18	4	25	24	25
15	21 31 28	21 38 10	28 39	14	6	27	18	4	25	24	25
16	21 35 25	22 35 48	12♓50	16	8	28	19	4	25	24	25
17	21 39 21	23 33 27	27 13	18	9	28	19	4	25	24	25
18	21 43 18	24 31 8	11♈40	20	10	28	19	4	25	24	25
19	21 47 14	25 28 51	26 8	23	11	28	19	4	25	24	25
20	21 51 11	26 26 35	10♉30	25	12	29	19	4	25	24	25
21	21 55 7	27 24 21	24 44	27	13	29	20	4	25	24	25
22	21 59 4	28 22 9	8♊48	29	14	29	20	4	25	24	25
23	22 3 1	29 19 58	22 40	1♍	15	0♑	20	4	26	24	25
24	22 6 57	0♍17 49	6♋20	2	16	0	20	4	26	24	25
25	22 10 54	1 15 42	19 49	4	17	0	20	5	26	24	25
26	22 14 50	2 13 37	3♌ 6	6	18	0	21	5	26	24	25
27	22 18 47	3 11 33	16 11	8	19	1	21	5	26	24	25
28	22 22 43	4 9 30	29 5	10	20	1	21	5	26	24	25
29	22 26 40	5 7 30	11♍46	12	21	2	21	5	26	24	25
30	22 30 36	6 5 30	24 14	14	22	2	21	5	26	24	25
31	22 34 33	7 3 32	6♎31	16	23	2	21	5	26	24	25

THE SUN ENTERS THE SIGN OF VIRGO ON AUG 23 AT 16:37.

DAY	TIME	☉	☽	☿	♀	♂	♃	♄	♅	♆	♇
	h m s	° ' "	° '	°	°	°	°	°	°	°	°
S 1	22 38 30	8♍ 1 36	18♎38	17♍	24♎	3♑	22♋	5♏	26♋	24♎	25♌
E 2	22 42 26	8 59 41	0♏35	19	25	3	22	5	26	24	25
P 3	22 46 23	9 57 48	12 27	21	26	3	22	5	26	24	25
T 4	22 50 19	10 55 56	24 18	23	27	4	22	5	26	24	25
E 5	22 54 16	11 54 6	6♐11	24	28	4	22	5	26	24	25
M 6	22 58 12	12 52 17	18 12	26	29	5	23	6	26	24	25
B 7	23 2 9	13 50 30	0♑26	28	0♏	5	23	6	26	24	25
E 8	23 6 5	14 48 44	12 58	29	1	6	23	6	26	24	25
R 9	23 10 2	15 46 59	25 52	1♎	2	6	23	6	26	24	25
10	23 13 59	16 45 17	9♒12	3	3	6	23	6	26	24	25
11	23 17 55	17 43 35	22 59	4	4	7	23	6	26	24	25
12	23 21 52	18 41 56	7♓12	6	5	7	24	6	27	24	25
13	23 25 48	19 40 18	21 46	7	6	8	24	6	27	24	25
14	23 29 45	20 38 42	6♈35	9	7	8	24	6	27	25	26
15	23 33 41	21 37 8	21 29	10	7	9	24	6	27	25	26
16	23 37 38	22 35 36	6♉20	12	8	9	24	6	27	25	26
17	23 41 34	23 34 6	21 1	13	9	10	24	7	27	25	26
18	23 45 31	24 32 38	5♊25	15	10	10	25	7	27	25	26
19	23 49 28	25 31 13	19 31	16	11	11	25	7	27	25	26
20	23 53 24	26 29 50	3♋17	18	12	11	25	7	27	25	26
21	23 57 21	27 28 29	16 46	19	13	12	25	7	27	25	26
22	0 1 17	28 27 10	29 58	21	13	12	25	7	27	25	26
23	0 5 14	29 25 54	12♌56	22	14	13	25	7	27	25	26
24	0 9 10	0♎24 39	25 41	23	15	14	26	7	27	25	26
25	0 13 7	1 23 27	8♍16	25	16	14	26	7	27	25	26
26	0 17 3	2 22 17	20 41	26	17	15	26	7	27	25	26
27	0 21 0	3 21 8	2♎57	27	17	15	26	8	27	25	26
28	0 24 56	4 20 2	15 5	29	18	16	26	8	27	25	26
29	0 28 53	5 18 58	27 5	0♏	19	16	26	8	27	25	26
30	0 32 50	6 17 56	8♏59	1	20	17	26	8	27	25	26

THE SUN ENTERS THE SIGN OF LIBRA ON SEP 23 AT 13:56.

DAY	TIME	☉	☽	☿	♀	♂	♃	♄	♅	♆	♇
	h m s	° ' "	° '	°	°	°	°	°	°	°	°
O 1	0 36 46	7♎16 55	20♏48	2♏	20♏	17♑	27♋	8♏	27♋	25♎	26♌
C 2	0 40 43	8 15 57	2♐37	3	21	18	27	8	27	25	26
T 3	0 44 39	9 15 0	14 28	4	22	19	27	8	27	25	26
O 4	0 48 36	10 14 5	26 26	6	22	19	27	8	27	25	26
B 5	0 52 32	11 13 12	8♑36	7	23	20	27	8	27	25	26
E 6	0 56 29	12 12 21	21 4	8	24	20	27	9	27	25	26
R 7	1 0 25	13 11 31	3♒55	9	24	21	27	9	27	25	26
8	1 4 22	14 10 43	17 13	9	25	22	27	9	27	25	26
9	1 8 19	15 9 57	1♓ 0	10	25	22	28	9	27	25	26
10	1 12 15	16 9 13	15 17	11	26	23	28	9	27	25	26
11	1 16 12	17 8 30	0♈ 1	12	26	23	28	9	27	25	26
12	1 20 8	18 7 50	15 4	13	27	24	28	9	27	26	26
13	1 24 5	19 7 12	0♉18	13	27	25	28	9	27	26	26
14	1 28 1	20 6 35	15 30	14	28	25	28	9	28	26	26
15	1 31 58	21 6 1	0♊31	14	28	26	28	10	28	26	26
16	1 35 54	22 5 29	15 13	14	28	26	28	10	28	26	26
17	1 39 51	23 5 0	29 31	15	29	27	28	10	28	26	26
18	1 43 48	24 4 33	13♋23	15 R	29	28	29	10	28	26	26
19	1 47 44	25 4 8	26 52	15	29	28	29	10	28	26	26
20	1 51 41	26 3 45	9♌58	15	29	29	29	10	28	26	26
21	1 55 37	27 3 25	22 47	14	0♐	0♒	29	10	28	26	26
22	1 59 34	28 3 7	5♍20	14	0	0	29	10	28	26	26
23	2 3 30	29 2 51	17 42	13	0	1	29	11	28	26	26
24	2 7 27	0♏ 2 37	29 54	13	0	2	29	11	28	26	26
25	2 11 23	1 2 25	11♎58	12	0 R	2	29	11	28	26	27
26	2 15 20	2 2 15	23 57	11	0	3	29	11	28	26	27
27	2 19 17	3 2 8	5♏51	10	0	4	29	11	28	26	27
28	2 23 13	4 2 2	17 42	8	0	4	29	11	28	26	27
29	2 27 10	5 1 58	29 31	7	0	5	29	11	28	26	27
30	2 31 6	6 1 56	11♐20	6	0	6	29	11	28	26	27
31	2 35 3	7 1 56	23 13	5	29♏	6	29	11	28	26	27

THE SUN ENTERS THE SIGN OF SCORPIO ON OCT 23 AT 22:57.

DAY	TIME	☉	☽	☿	♀	♂	♃	♄	♅	♆	♇
	h m s	° ' "	° '	°	°	°	°	°	°	°	°
N 1	2 38 59	8♏ 1 58	5♑13	3♏R	29♏R	7♒	0♌	12♏	28♋	26♎	27♌
O 2	2 42 56	9 2 1	17 23	2	29	8	0	12	28	26	27
V 3	2 46 52	10 2 6	29 48	1	29	8	0	12	28 R	26	27
E 4	2 50 49	11 2 12	12♒34	0	28	9	0	12	28	26	27
M 5	2 54 46	12 2 20	25 45	0	28	10	0	12	28	26	27
B 6	2 58 42	13 2 29	9♓23	29♎	28	10	0	12	28	26	27
E 7	3 2 39	14 2 40	23 32	29 D	27	11	0	12	28	26	27
R 8	3 6 35	15 2 52	8♈ 9	29	27	12	0	12	28	27	27
9	3 10 32	16 3 6	23 9	29	26	12	0	13	28	27	27
10	3 14 28	17 3 22	8♉24	29	26	13	0	13	28	27	27
11	3 18 25	18 3 39	23 44	0♏	25	14	0	13	28	27	27
12	3 22 21	19 3 58	8♊57	0	24	14	0	13	28	27	27
13	3 26 18	20 4 19	23 53	1	24	15	0	13	28	27	27
14	3 30 15	21 4 42	8♋26	2	23	16	0	13	28	27	27
15	3 34 11	22 5 7	22 32	3	23	16	0	13	28	27	27
16	3 38 8	23 5 33	6♌10	4	22	17	0	13	28	27	27
17	3 42 4	24 6 2	19 21	5	21	18	0 R	14	28	27	27
18	3 46 1	25 6 32	2♍11	6	21	19	0	14	28	27	27
19	3 49 57	26 7 4	14 41	8	20	19	0	14	28	27	27
20	3 53 54	27 7 37	26 57	9	20	20	0	14	28	27	27
21	3 57 50	28 8 13	9♎ 1	10	19	21	0	14	28	27	27
22	4 1 47	29 8 50	20 59	12	19	21	0	14	28	27	27
23	4 5 44	0♐ 9 29	2♏51	13	18	22	0	14	28	27	27
24	4 9 40	1 10 9	14 42	14	18	23	0	14	28	27	27
25	4 13 37	2 10 51	26 32	16	17	23	0	14	27	27	27
26	4 17 33	3 11 34	8♐23	17	17	24	0	15	27	27	27
27	4 21 30	4 12 19	20 18	19	16	25	0	15	27	27	27
28	4 25 26	5 13 5	2♑18	20	16	26	0	15	27	27	27 R
29	4 29 23	6 13 52	14 26	22	16	26	0	15	27	27	27
30	4 33 19	7 14 40	26 44	23	15	27	0	15	27	27	27

THE SUN ENTERS THE SIGN OF SAGITTARIUS ON NOV 22 AT 20:15.

DAY	TIME	☉	☽	☿	♀	♂	♃	♄	♅	♆	♇
	h m s	° ' "	° '	°	°	°	°	°	°	°	°
D 1	4 37 16	8♐15 29	9♒14	25♏	15♏R	28♒	0♌R	15♏	27♋R	27♎	27♌R
E 2	4 41 13	9 16 19	22 2	26	15	28	0	15	27	27	27
C 3	4 45 9	10 17 10	5♓10	28	15	29	0	15	27	27	27
E 4	4 49 6	11 18 2	18 40	0♐	15	0♓	29♋	15	27	27	27
M 5	4 53 2	12 18 54	2♈35	1	15 D	0	29	16	27	27	27
B 6	4 56 59	13 19 47	16 55	3	15	1	29	16	27	27	27
E 7	5 0 55	14 20 41	1♉37	4	15	2	29	16	27	27	27
R 8	5 4 52	15 21 36	16 36	6	15	3	29	16	27	27	27
9	5 8 48	16 22 32	1♊43	7	15	3	29	16	27	28	27
10	5 12 45	17 23 29	16 50	9	15	4	29	16	27	28	27
11	5 16 42	18 24 26	1♋47	10	15	5	29	16	27	28	27
12	5 20 38	19 25 25	16 26	12	15	5	29	16	27	28	27
13	5 24 35	20 26 24	0♌42	14	16	6	29	16	27	28	27
14	5 28 31	21 27 25	14 30	15	16	7	29	17	27	28	27
15	5 32 28	22 28 26	27 52	17	16	8	29	17	27	28	27
16	5 36 24	23 29 28	10♍49	18	17	8	29	17	27	28	27
17	5 40 21	24 30 31	23 23	20	17	9	28	17	27	28	27
18	5 44 17	25 31 36	5♎40	21	17	10	28	17	27	28	27
19	5 48 14	26 32 41	17 44	23	18	10	28	17	27	28	27
20	5 52 11	27 33 47	29 38	24	18	11	28	17	27	28	27
21	5 56 7	28 34 53	11♏28	26	19	12	28	17	27	28	27
22	6 0 4	29 36 1	23 18	28	19	13	28	17	27	28	27
23	6 4 0	0♑37 9	5♐ 9	29	20	13	28	17	27	28	27
24	6 7 57	1 38 17	17 6	1♑	20	14	28	18	27	28	27
25	6 11 53	2 39 27	29 9	2	21	15	28	18	27	28	27
26	6 15 50	3 40 36	11♑21	4	22	15	28	18	27	28	27
27	6 19 47	4 41 46	23 44	6	22	16	27	18	27	28	27
28	6 23 43	5 42 56	6♒18	7	23	17	27	18	26	28	27
29	6 27 40	6 44 6	19 5	9	24	18	27	18	26	28	27
30	6 31 36	7 45 16	2♓ 6	10	24	18	27	18	26	28	27
31	6 35 33	8 46 26	15 22	12	25	19	27	18	26	28	27

THE SUN ENTERS THE SIGN OF CAPRICORN ON DEC 22 AT 09:25.

♈ ARIES ♉ TAURUS ♊ GEMINI ♋ CANCER ♌ LEO ♍ VIRGO ♎ LIBRA ♏ SCORPIO ♐ SAGITTARIUS ♑ CAPRICORN ♒ AQUARIUS ♓ PISCES

230 Appendix X

1955

SIDEREAL SUN MOON MERCURY VENUS MARS JUPITER SATURN URANUS NEPTUNE PLUTO

DAY	TIME	☉	☽	☿	♀	♂	♃	♄	♅	♆	♇
	h m s	° ' "	° '	°	°	°	°	°	°	°	°
J 1	6 39 29	9♑47 36	28♓54	14♑	26♏	20♓	27♋R	18♏	26♋R	28♎	27♌R
A 2	6 43 26	10 48 45	12♈42	15	27	21	27	18	26	28	27
N 3	6 47 22	11 49 54	26 47	17	27	21	27	19	26	28	27
U 4	6 51 19	12 51 4	11♉ 8	18	28	22	26	19	26	28	26
A 5	6 55 16	13 52 12	25 41	20	29	23	26	19	26	28	26
R 6	6 59 12	14 53 21	10♊22	22	0♐	23	26	19	26	28	26
Y 7	7 3 9	15 54 29	25 6	23	1	24	26	19	26	28	26
8	7 7 5	16 55 37	9♋45	25	1	25	26	19	26	28	26
9	7 11 2	17 56 45	24 14	27	2	26	26	19	26	28	26
10	7 14 58	18 57 53	8♌25	28	3	26	26	19	26	28	26
11	7 18 55	19 59 0	22 16	0♒	4	27	26	19	26	28	26
12	7 22 51	21 0 7	5♍43	2	5	28	25	19	26	28	26
13	7 26 48	22 1 14	18 45	3	6	28	25	19	26	28	26
14	7 30 45	23 2 21	1♎26	5	7	29	25	19	26	28	26
15	7 34 41	24 3 28	13 47	7	8	0♈	25	19	26	28	26
16	7 38 38	25 4 35	25 53	8	9	1♈	25	20	26	28	26
17	7 42 34	26 5 41	7♏49	10	10	1	25	20	26	28	26
18	7 46 31	27 6 48	19 39	12	11	2	25	20	26	28	26
19	7 50 27	28 7 54	1♐28	13	11	3	24	20	26	28	26
20	7 54 24	29 8 59	13 21	15	12	3	24	20	26	28	26
21	7 58 20	0♒10 4	25 22	16	13	4	24	20	25	28	26
22	8 2 17	1 11 9	7♑34	18	14	5	24	20	25	28	26
23	8 6 14	2 12 13	20 0	19	15	6	24	20	25	28	26
24	8 10 10	3 13 17	2♒40	21	16	6	24	20	25	28	26
25	8 14 7	4 14 19	15 36	22	17	7	24	20	25	28	26
26	8 18 3	5 15 21	28 47	23	18	8	24	20	25	28	26
27	8 22 0	6 16 22	12♓12	25	19	8	23	20	25	28	26
28	8 25 56	7 17 21	25 48	26	20	9	23	20	25	28	26
29	8 29 53	8 18 20	9♈35	27	21	10	23	20	25	28 R	26
30	8 33 49	9 19 17	23 31	28	23	11	23	20	25	28	26
31	8 37 46	10 20 13	7♉33	28	24	11	23	20	25	28	26

THE SUN ENTERS THE SIGN OF AQUARIUS ON JAN 20 AT 20:03.

DAY	TIME	☉	☽	☿	♀	♂	♃	♄	♅	♆	♇
	h m s	° ' "	° '	°	°	°	°	°	°	°	°
F 1	8 41 43	11♒21 8	21♉42	29♒	25♐	12♈	23♋R	20♏	25♋R	28♎R	26♌R
E 2	8 45 39	12 22 2	5♊54	29	26	13	23	21	25	28	26
B 3	8 49 36	13 22 54	20 8	0♓R	27	13	23	21	25	28	26
R 4	8 53 32	14 23 44	4♋23	0	28	14	22	21	25	28	26
U 5	8 57 29	15 24 34	18 34	0	29	15	22	21	25	28	26
A 6	9 1 25	16 25 22	2♌38	29♒	0♑	16	22	21	25	28	26
R 7	9 5 22	17 26 9	16 31	29	1	16	22	21	25	28	26
Y 8	9 9 18	18 26 54	0♍ 9	28	2	17	22	21	25	28	26
9	9 13 15	19 27 39	13 29	27	3	18	22	21	25	28	26
10	9 17 12	20 28 22	26 30	26	4	18	22	21	25	28	26
11	9 21 8	21 29 4	9♎11	25	5	19	22	21	25	28	26
12	9 25 5	22 29 45	21 34	24	6	20	22	21	25	28	26
13	9 29 1	23 30 24	3♏42	23	8	21	21	21	25	28	26
14	9 32 58	24 31 3	15 38	22	9	21	21	21	24	28	26
15	9 36 54	25 31 40	27 29	21	10	22	21	21	24	28	26
16	9 40 51	26 32 17	9♐18	20	11	23	21	21	24	28	26
17	9 44 47	27 32 52	21 12	19	12	23	21	21	24	28	26
18	9 48 44	28 33 25	3♑15	18	13	24	21	21	24	28	25
19	9 52 41	29 33 58	15 32	17	14	25	21	21	24	28	25
20	9 56 37	0♓34 29	28 6	16	15	25	21	21	24	28	25
21	10 0 34	1 34 59	11♒ 1	16	16	26	21	21	24	28	25
22	10 4 30	2 35 27	24 17	15	18	27	21	21	24	28	25
23	10 8 27	3 35 53	7♓52	15	19	28	21	21	24	28	25
24	10 12 23	4 36 18	21 45	14	20	28	21	21	24	28	25
25	10 16 20	5 36 41	5♈49	14 D	21	29	21	21	24	28	25
26	10 20 16	6 37 2	20 2	14	22	0♉	20	21	24	28	25
27	10 24 13	7 37 22	4♉17	14	23	0	20	21	24	28	25
28	10 28 10	8 37 39	18 32	15	24	1	20	21	24	28	25

THE SUN ENTERS THE SIGN OF PISCES ON FEB 19 AT 10:19.

DAY	TIME	☉	☽	☿	♀	♂	♃	♄	♅	♆	♇
	h m s	° ' "	° '	°	°	°	°	°	°	°	°
M 1	10 32 6	9♓37 54	2♊42	15♒	26♑	2♉	20♋R	21♏R	24♋R	28♎R	25♌R
A 2	10 36 3	10 38 8	16 48	15	27	2	20	21	24	28	25
R 3	10 39 59	11 38 19	0♋46	16	28	3	20	21	24	28	25
C 4	10 43 56	12 38 28	14 39	16	29	4	20	21	24	28	25
H 5	10 47 52	13 38 35	28 24	17	0♒	5	20	21	24	28	25
6	10 51 49	14 38 40	12♌ 1	18	1	5	20	21	24	28	25
7	10 55 45	15 38 43	25 28	19	2	6	20	21	24	28	25
8	10 59 42	16 38 43	8♍44	19	4	7	20	21	24	28	25
9	11 3 39	17 38 42	21 47	20	5	7	20	21	24	28	25
10	11 7 35	18 38 39	4♎36	21	6	8	20	21	24	28	25
11	11 11 32	19 38 34	17 9	22	7	9	20	21	24	28	25
12	11 15 28	20 38 28	29 27	23	8	9	20	21	24	28	25
13	11 19 25	21 38 19	11♏33	24	9	10	20	21	24	28	25
14	11 23 21	22 38 9	23 28	25	11	11	20	21	24	28	25
15	11 27 18	23 37 58	5♐18	27	12	12	20	21	24	28	25
16	11 31 14	24 37 44	17 7	28	13	12	20 D	21	24	28	25
17	11 35 11	25 37 29	28 59	29	14	13	20	21	24	28	25
18	11 39 8	26 37 12	11♑ 2	0♓	15	14	20	21	24	28	25
19	11 43 4	27 36 53	23 19	1	16	14	20	21	24	28	25
20	11 47 1	28 36 33	5♒57	3	18	15	20	21	24	28	25
21	11 50 57	29 36 11	18 58	4	19	16	20	21	24	28	25
22	11 54 54	0♈35 46	2♓24	5	20	16	20	21	24	28	25
23	11 58 50	1 35 20	16 16	7	21	17	20	21	24	28	25
24	12 2 47	2 34 52	0♈30	8	22	18	20	21	24	28	25
25	12 6 43	3 34 22	15 1	10	24	18	20	21	24	28	25
26	12 10 40	4 33 50	29 41	11	25	19	20	21	24	27	25
27	12 14 36	5 33 16	14♉22	13	26	20	20	21	24	27	25
28	12 18 33	6 32 39	28 58	14	27	20	20	21	24	27	25
29	12 22 30	7 32 1	13♊24	16	28	21	20	21	24	27	25
30	12 26 26	8 31 20	27 36	17	29	22	20	20	24	27	25
31	12 30 23	9 30 36	11♋34	19	1♓	23	20	20	24	27	25

THE SUN ENTERS THE SIGN OF ARIES ON MAR 21 AT 09:35.

DAY	TIME	☉	☽	☿	♀	♂	♃	♄	♅	♆	♇
	h m s	° ' "	° '	°	°	°	°	°	°	°	°
A 1	12 34 19	10♈29 51	25♋17	20♓	2♓	23♉	20♋	20♏R	24♋D	27♎R	25♌R
P 2	12 38 16	11 29 3	8♌46	22	3	24	20	20	24	27	25
R 3	12 42 12	12 28 12	22 3	24	4	25	20	20	24	27	25
I 4	12 46 9	13 27 19	5♍ 9	25	5	25	20	20	24	27	25
L 5	12 50 5	14 26 24	18 3	27	7	26	20	20	24	27	25
6	12 54 2	15 25 27	0♎45	29	8	27	21	20	24	27	25
7	12 57 59	16 24 28	13 16	1♈	9	27	21	20	24	27	25
8	13 1 55	17 23 26	25 36	2	10	28	21	20	24	27	24
9	13 5 52	18 22 23	7♏46	4	11	29	21	20	24	27	24
10	13 9 48	19 21 18	19 45	6	12	29	21	20	24	27	24
11	13 13 45	20 20 11	1♐38	8	14	0♊	21	20	24	27	24
12	13 17 41	21 19 2	13 26	10	15	1	21	20	24	27	24
13	13 21 38	22 17 51	25 14	12	16	1	21	20	24	27	24
14	13 25 34	23 16 39	7♑ 6	14	17	2	21	20	24	27	24
15	13 29 31	24 15 25	19 7	15	18	3	21	20	24	27	24
16	13 33 28	25 14 9	1♒22	17	20	3	21	20	24	27	24
17	13 37 24	26 12 51	13 58	19	21	4	21	19	24	27	24
18	13 41 21	27 11 32	26 58	21	22	5	21	19	24	27	24
19	13 45 17	28 10 11	10♓26	23	23	5	22	19	24	27	24
20	13 49 14	29 8 48	24 22	26	24	6	22	19	24	27	24
21	13 53 10	0♉ 7 24	8♈44	28	26	7	22	19	24	27	24
22	13 57 7	1 5 57	23 28	0♉	27	7	22	19	24	27	24
23	14 1 3	2 4 29	8♉27	2	28	8	22	19	24	27	24
24	14 5 0	3 2 59	23 30	4	29	9	22	19	24	27	24
25	14 8 57	4 1 27	8♊28	6	0♈	9	22	19	24	27	24
26	14 12 53	4 59 53	23 14	8	2	10	22	19	24	27	24
27	14 16 50	5 58 17	7♋42	10	3	11	22	19	24	27	24
28	14 20 46	6 56 39	21 50	13	4	11	23	19	24	27	24
29	14 24 43	7 54 59	5♌37	15	5	12	23	19	24	27	24
30	14 28 39	8 53 16	19 3	17	6	13	23	19	24	27	24

THE SUN ENTERS THE SIGN OF TAURUS ON APR 20 AT 20:58.

DAY	TIME	☉	☽	☿	♀	♂	♃	♄	♅	♆	♇
	h m s	° ' "	° '	°	°	°	°	°	°	°	°
M 1	14 32 36	9♉51 32	2♍11	19♉	8♈	13♊	23♋	18♏R	24♋	27♎R	24♌R
A 2	14 36 32	10 49 45	15 3	21	9	14	23	18	24	26	24
Y 3	14 40 29	11 47 56	27 41	23	10	15	23	18	24	26	24
4	14 44 26	12 46 6	10♎ 7	25	11	15	23	18	24	26	24
5	14 48 22	13 44 13	22 23	27	12	16	23	18	24	26	24
6	14 52 19	14 42 19	4♏29	29	14	17	24	18	24	26	24 D
7	14 56 15	15 40 23	16 29	1♊	15	17	24	18	24	26	24
8	15 0 12	16 38 26	28 22	3	16	18	24	18	24	26	24
9	15 4 8	17 36 27	10♐11	4	17	19	24	18	24	26	24
10	15 8 5	18 34 26	21 58	6	18	19	24	18	24	26	24
11	15 12 1	19 32 24	3♑47	8	20	20	24	18	24	26	24
12	15 15 58	20 30 21	15 41	10	21	21	24	18	24	26	24
13	15 19 55	21 28 16	27 43	11	22	21	25	18	24	26	24
14	15 23 51	22 26 10	9♒59	13	23	22	25	18	24	26	24
15	15 27 48	23 24 3	22 34	14	24	23	25	17	24	26	24
16	15 31 44	24 21 54	5♓30	15	26	23	25	17	24	26	24
17	15 35 41	25 19 44	18 53	17	27	24	25	17	24	26	24
18	15 39 37	26 17 33	2♈43	18	28	25	25	17	25	26	24
19	15 43 34	27 15 21	17 1	19	29	25	26	17	25	26	24
20	15 47 30	28 13 8	1♉44	20	1♉	26	26	17	25	26	24
21	15 51 27	29 10 53	16 45	21	2	27	26	17	25	26	24
22	15 55 24	0♊ 8 38	1♊56	22	3	27	26	17	25	26	24
23	15 59 20	1 6 21	17 7	23	4	28	26	17	25	26	24
24	16 3 17	2 4 3	2♋ 9	24	5	29	26	17	25	26	24
25	16 7 13	3 1 43	16 53	25	7	29	27	17	25	26	24
26	16 11 10	3 59 22	1♌15	26	8	0♋	27	17	25	26	24
27	16 15 6	4 56 59	15 12	26	9	1	27	17	25	26	24
28	16 19 3	5 54 35	28 44	27	10	1	27	17	25	26	24
29	16 22 59	6 52 9	11♍53	27	11	2	27	16	25	26	24
30	16 26 56	7 49 42	24 41	28	13	3	27	16	25	26	24
31	16 30 53	8 47 13	7♎12	28	14	3	28	16	25	26	24

THE SUN ENTERS THE SIGN OF GEMINI ON MAY 21 AT 20:25.

DAY	TIME	☉	☽	☿	♀	♂	♃	♄	♅	♆	♇
	h m s	° ' "	° '	°	°	°	°	°	°	°	°
J 1	16 34 49	9♊44 43	19♎28	29♊	15♉	4♋	28♋	16♏R	25♋	26♎R	24♌
U 2	16 38 46	10 42 12	1♏33	29	16	5	28	16	25	26	24
N 3	16 42 42	11 39 40	13 30	29 R	17	5	28	16	25	26	24
E 4	16 46 39	12 37 6	25 22	29	19	6	28	16	25	26	24
5	16 50 35	13 34 32	7♐11	29	20	7	28	16	25	26	25
6	16 54 32	14 31 57	18 59	29	21	7	29	16	25	26	25
7	16 58 28	15 29 20	0♑49	29	22	8	29	16	25	26	25
8	17 2 25	16 26 43	12 42	28	24	8	29	16	25	26	25
9	17 6 22	17 24 6	24 42	28	25	9	29	16	26	26	25
10	17 10 18	18 21 27	6♒51	28	26	10	29	16	26	26	25
11	17 14 15	19 18 48	19 13	27	27	10	0♌	16	26	26	25
12	17 18 11	20 16 9	1♓50	27	28	11	0	16	26	26	25
13	17 22 8	21 13 28	14 47	26	0♊	12	0	16	26	26	25
14	17 26 4	22 10 48	28 5	26	1	12	0	15	26	26	25
15	17 30 1	23 8 7	11♈47	25	2	13	0	15	26	26	25
16	17 33 57	24 5 26	25 54	24	3	14	1	15	26	26	25
17	17 37 54	25 2 44	10♉25	24	4	14	1	15	26	26	25
18	17 41 51	26 0 2	25 14	23	6	15	1	15	26	26	25
19	17 45 47	26 57 20	10♊18	23	7	16	1	15	26	26	25
20	17 49 44	27 54 38	25 26	22	8	16	1	15	26	26	25
21	17 53 40	28 51 55	10♋30	22	9	17	2	15	26	26	25
22	17 57 37	29 49 11	25 21	21	10	18	2	15	26	26	25
23	18 1 33	0♋46 27	9♌53	21	12	18	2	15	26	26	25
24	18 5 30	1 43 42	24 0	21	13	19	2	15	26	26	25
25	18 9 26	2 40 57	7♍40	20	14	19	2	15	26	26	25
26	18 13 23	3 38 11	20 54	20	15	20	3	15	26	26	25
27	18 17 20	4 35 25	3♎45	20 D	17	21	3	15	27	25	25
28	18 21 16	5 32 37	16 14	20	18	21	3	15	27	25	25
29	18 25 13	6 29 50	28 27	20	19	22	3	15	27	25	25
30	18 29 9	7 27 2	10♏27	20	20	23	3	15	27	25	25

THE SUN ENTERS THE SIGN OF CANCER ON JUN 22 AT 04:32.

♈ ARIES ♉ TAURUS ♊ GEMINI ♋ CANCER ♌ LEO ♍ VIRGO ♎ LIBRA ♏ SCORPIO ♐ SAGITTARIUS ♑ CAPRICORN ♒ AQUARIUS ♓ PISCES

1955

SIDEREAL SUN MOON MERCURY VENUS MARS JUPITER SATURN URANUS NEPTUNE PLUTO

DAY	TIME	☉	☽	☿	♀	♂	♃	♄	♅	♆	♇
	h m s	° ' "	° '	°	°	°	°	°	°	°	°
J 1	18 33 6	8♋24 13	22♏20	21♊	21♊	23♋	4♌	15♏R	27♋	25♎R	25♌
U 2	18 37 2	9 21 25	4♐ 8	21	23	24	4	15	27	25	25
L 3	18 40 59	10 18 36	15 56	21	24	25	4	15	27	25	25
Y 4	18 44 55	11 15 47	27 46	22	25	25	4	15	27	25	25
5	18 48 52	12 12 58	9♑42	22	26	26	4	15	27	25	25
6	18 52 49	13 10 9	21 44	23	28	27	5	15	27	25	25
7	18 56 45	14 7 20	3♒55	23	29	27	5	15	27	25 D	25
8	19 0 42	15 4 31	16 17	24	0♋	28	5	15	27	25	25
9	19 4 38	16 1 42	28 52	25	1	28	5	15	27	25	25
10	19 8 35	16 58 54	11♓40	26	2	29	6	15	27	25	25
11	19 12 31	17 56 5	24 43	27	4	0♌	6	15	27	25	25
12	19 16 28	18 53 18	8♈ 4	28	5	0	6	15	27	25	25
13	19 20 24	19 50 31	21 42	29	6	1	6	15	27	25	25
14	19 24 21	20 47 44	5♉39	0♋	7	2	6	15	28	25	25
15	19 28 18	21 44 58	19 54	2	9	2	7	15	28	25	25
16	19 32 14	22 42 13	4♊26	3	10	3	7	15	28	25	25
17	19 36 11	23 39 29	19 10	5	11	4	7	15	28	25	25
18	19 40 7	24 36 45	4♋ 2	6	12	4	7	15	28	25	25
19	19 44 4	25 34 1	18 53	8	13	5	8	15 D	28	25	25
20	19 48 0	26 31 18	3♌38	9	15	6	8	15	28	26	25
21	19 51 57	27 28 35	18 7	11	16	6	8	15	28	26	26
22	19 55 54	28 25 53	2♍16	13	17	7	8	15	28	26	26
23	19 59 50	29 23 11	16 0	15	18	7	8	15	28	26	26
24	20 3 47	0♌20 30	29 18	16	20	8	9	15	28	26	26
25	20 7 43	1 17 48	12♎12	18	21	9	9	15	28	26	26
26	20 11 40	2 15 7	24 43	20	22	9	9	15	28	26	26
27	20 15 36	3 12 27	6♏56	22	23	10	9	15	28	26	26
28	20 19 33	4 9 47	18 56	24	24	11	9	15	28	26	26
29	20 23 29	5 7 8	0♐47	26	26	11	10	15	28	26	26
30	20 27 26	6 4 29	12 35	28	27	12	10	15	28	26	26
31	20 31 23	7 1 50	24 24	1♌	28	13	10	15	29	26	26

THE SUN ENTERS THE SIGN OF LEO ON JUL 23 AT 15:25.

DAY	TIME	☉	☽	☿	♀	♂	♃	♄	♅	♆	♇
	h m s	° ' "	° '	°	°	°	°	°	°	°	°
A 1	20 35 19	7♌59 13	6♑18	3♌	29♋	13♌	10♌	15♏	29♋	26♎	26♌
U 2	20 39 16	8 56 36	18 21	5	1♌	14	11	15	29	26	26
G 3	20 43 12	9 54 0	0♒35	7	2	14	11	15	29	26	26
U 4	20 47 9	10 51 24	13 1	9	3	15	11	15	29	26	26
S 5	20 51 5	11 48 50	25 41	11	4	16	11	15	29	26	26
T 6	20 55 2	12 46 16	8♓35	13	6	16	11	15	29	26	26
7	20 58 58	13 43 44	21 42	15	7	17	12	15	29	26	26
8	21 2 55	14 41 13	5♈ 1	17	8	18	12	15	29	26	26
9	21 6 52	15 38 43	18 33	19	9	18	12	15	29	26	26
10	21 10 48	16 36 14	2♉16	21	10	19	12	15	29	26	26
11	21 14 45	17 33 47	16 10	23	12	20	13	15	29	26	26
12	21 18 41	18 31 22	0♊15	25	13	20	13	15	29	26	26
13	21 22 38	19 28 57	14 30	27	14	21	13	15	29	26	26
14	21 26 34	20 26 35	28 53	29	15	21	13	15	29	26	26
15	21 30 31	21 24 14	13♋22	1♍	17	22	13	15	29	26	26
16	21 34 27	22 21 54	27 51	3	18	23	14	15	0♌	26	26
17	21 38 24	23 19 36	12♌16	5	19	23	14	15	0	26	26
18	21 42 21	24 17 19	26 30	6	20	24	14	15	0	26	26
19	21 46 17	25 15 3	10♍28	8	22	25	14	15	0	26	26
20	21 50 14	26 12 48	24 7	10	23	25	15	15	0	26	26
21	21 54 10	27 10 35	7♎22	12	24	26	15	15	0	26	26
22	21 58 7	28 8 23	20 15	13	25	27	15	15	0	26	27
23	22 2 3	29 6 12	2♏47	15	27	27	15	15	0	26	27
24	22 6 0	0♍ 4 2	15 0	17	28	28	15	16	0	26	27
25	22 9 56	1 1 54	27 0	18	29	28	16	16	0	26	27
26	22 13 53	1 59 47	8♐51	20	0♍	29	16	16	0	26	27
27	22 17 50	2 57 41	20 39	22	2	0♍	16	16	0	26	27
28	22 21 46	3 55 36	2♑30	23	3	0	16	16	0	26	27
29	22 25 43	4 53 33	14 28	25	4	1	16	16	0	26	27
30	22 29 39	5 51 31	26 37	26	5	2	17	16	0	26	27
31	22 33 36	6 49 30	9♒ 1	28	6	2	17	16	0	26	27

THE SUN ENTERS THE SIGN OF VIRGO ON AUG 23 AT 22:20.

DAY	TIME	☉	☽	☿	♀	♂	♃	♄	♅	♆	♇
	h m s	° ' "	° '	°	°	°	°	°	°	°	°
S 1	22 37 32	7♍47 31	21♒43	29♍	8♍	3♍	17♌	16♏	0♌	26♎	27♌
E 2	22 41 29	8 45 33	4♓42	1♎	9	4	17	16	0	26	27
P 3	22 45 25	9 43 38	17 57	2	10	4	18	16	0	26	27
T 4	22 49 22	10 41 43	1♈28	4	11	5	18	16	1	26	27
E 5	22 53 18	11 39 51	15 11	5	13	5	18	16	1	26	27
M 6	22 57 15	12 38 0	29 4	6	14	6	18	16	1	26	27
B 7	23 1 12	13 36 12	13♉ 2	8	15	7	18	16	1	26	27
E 8	23 5 8	14 34 25	27 5	9	16	7	19	17	1	26	27
R 9	23 9 5	15 32 41	11♊10	10	18	8	19	17	1	26	27
10	23 13 1	16 30 58	25 17	12	19	9	19	17	1	27	27
11	23 16 58	17 29 18	9♋24	13	20	9	19	17	1	27	27
12	23 20 54	18 27 40	23 31	14	21	10	19	17	1	27	27
13	23 24 51	19 26 4	7♌36	15	23	11	20	17	1	27	27
14	23 28 47	20 24 30	21 35	16	24	11	20	17	1	27	27
15	23 32 44	21 22 58	5♍25	18	25	12	20	17	1	27	27
16	23 36 41	22 21 28	19 4	19	26	12	20	17	1	27	27
17	23 40 37	23 20 0	2♎26	20	28	13	20	17	1	27	27
18	23 44 34	24 18 33	15 30	21	29	14	21	17	1	27	27
19	23 48 30	25 17 9	28 16	22	0♎	14	21	17	1	27	27
20	23 52 27	26 15 46	10♏43	23	1	15	21	17	1	27	27
21	23 56 23	27 14 25	22 54	24	3	16	21	18	1	27	27
22	0 0 20	28 13 6	4♐52	24	4	16	21	18	1	27	27
23	0 4 16	29 11 48	16 43	25	5	17	22	18	1	27	28
24	0 8 13	0♎10 33	28 31	26	6	18	22	18	1	27	28
25	0 12 10	1 9 19	10♑21	26	8	18	22	18	1	27	28
26	0 16 6	2 8 6	22 20	27	9	19	22	18	2	27	28
27	0 20 3	3 6 56	4♒32	28	10	19	22	18	2	27	28
28	0 23 59	4 5 47	17 2	28	11	20	23	18	2	27	28
29	0 27 56	5 4 40	29 53	28	13	21	23	18	2	27	28
30	0 31 52	6 3 34	13♓ 6	28	14	21	23	18	2	27	28

THE SUN ENTERS THE SIGN OF LIBRA ON SEP 23 AT 19:42.

DAY	TIME	☉	☽	☿	♀	♂	♃	♄	♅	♆	♇
	h m s	° ' "	° '	°	°	°	°	°	°	°	°
O 1	0 35 49	7♎ 2 31	26♓41	29♎R	15♎	22♍	23♌	19♏	2♌	27♎	28♌
C 2	0 39 45	8 1 30	10♈35	29	16	23	23	19	2	27	28
T 3	0 43 42	9 0 30	24 44	29	18	23	24	19	2	27	28
O 4	0 47 38	9 59 33	9♉ 2	28	19	24	24	19	2	27	28
B 5	0 51 35	10 58 38	23 25	28	20	25	24	19	2	27	28
E 6	0 55 32	11 57 45	7♊47	27	21	25	24	19	2	27	28
R 7	0 59 28	12 56 55	22 5	27	22	26	24	19	2	27	28
8	1 3 25	13 56 7	6♋15	26	24	26	24	19	2	27	28
9	1 7 21	14 55 21	20 19	25	25	27	25	19	2	27	28
10	1 11 18	15 54 38	4♌13	24	26	28	25	19	2	28	28
11	1 15 14	16 53 57	17 59	23	27	28	25	20	2	28	28
12	1 19 11	17 53 18	1♍35	22	29	29	25	20	2	28	28
13	1 23 7	18 52 42	15 0	21	0♏	0♎	25	20	2	28	28
14	1 27 4	19 52 7	28 14	20	1	0	25	20	2	28	28
15	1 31 1	20 51 35	11♎15	18	2	1	26	20	2	28	28
16	1 34 57	21 51 5	24 1	17	4	2	26	20	2	28	28
17	1 38 54	22 50 37	6♏33	16	5	2	26	20	2	28	28
18	1 42 50	23 50 11	18 51	15	6	3	26	20	2	28	28
19	1 46 47	24 49 47	0♐56	15	7	4	26	20	2	28	28
20	1 50 43	25 49 25	12 51	14	9	4	26	21	2	28	28
21	1 54 40	26 49 4	24 40	13	10	5	27	21	2	28	28
22	1 58 36	27 48 45	6♑27	13 D	11	5	27	21	2	28	28
23	2 2 33	28 48 29	18 16	13	12	6	27	21	2	28	28
24	2 6 30	29 48 13	0♒13	13	14	7	27	21	2	28	28
25	2 10 26	0♏48 0	12 24	14	15	7	27	21	2	28	28
26	2 14 23	1 47 48	24 53	14	16	8	27	21	2	28	28
27	2 18 19	2 47 38	7♓45	15	17	9	27	21	2	28	28
28	2 22 16	3 47 29	21 2	15	19	9	28	21	2	28	28
29	2 26 12	4 47 23	4♈45	16	20	10	28	22	2	28	28
30	2 30 9	5 47 18	18 52	17	21	11	28	22	2	28	28
31	2 34 5	6 47 15	3♉20	18	22	11	28	22	2	28	28

THE SUN ENTERS THE SIGN OF SCORPIO ON OCT 24 AT 04:44.

DAY	TIME	☉	☽	☿	♀	♂	♃	♄	♅	♆	♇
	h m s	° ' "	° '	°	°	°	°	°	°	°	°
N 1	2 38 2	7♏47 13	18♉ 2	20♎	24♏	12♎	28♌	22♏	2♌	28♎	28♌
O 2	2 41 59	8 47 14	2♊51	21	25	13	28	22	2	28	28
V 3	2 45 55	9 47 17	17 39	22	26	13	28	22	2	28	28
E 4	2 49 52	10 47 22	2♋19	24	27	14	29	22	2	28	28
M 5	2 53 48	11 47 29	16 46	25	29	14	29	22	2	28	28
B 6	2 57 45	12 47 38	0♌59	27	0♐	15	29	22	2	29	28
E 7	3 1 41	13 47 49	14 54	28	1	16	29	23	2	29	28
R 8	3 5 38	14 48 2	28 32	0♏	2	16	29	23	2 R	29	28
9	3 9 34	15 48 18	11♍54	1	4	17	29	23	2	29	28
10	3 13 31	16 48 35	25 0	3	5	18	29	23	2	29	29
11	3 17 28	17 48 54	7♎53	4	6	18	29	23	2	29	29
12	3 21 24	18 49 15	20 32	6	7	19	29	23	2	29	29
13	3 25 21	19 49 38	2♏59	7	9	20	0♍	23	2	29	29
14	3 29 17	20 50 3	15 15	9	10	20	0	23	2	29	29
15	3 33 14	21 50 29	27 21	11	11	21	0	24	2	29	29
16	3 37 10	22 50 57	9♐19	12	12	22	0	24	2	29	29
17	3 41 7	23 51 27	21 10	14	14	22	0	24	2	29	29
18	3 45 3	24 51 58	2♑57	15	15	23	0	24	2	29	29
19	3 49 0	25 52 30	14 43	17	16	23	0	24	2	29	29
20	3 52 57	26 53 4	26 32	19	17	24	0	24	2	29	29
21	3 56 53	27 53 39	8♒29	20	19	25	0	24	2	29	29
22	4 0 50	28 54 15	20 37	22	20	25	0	24	2	29	29
23	4 4 46	29 54 53	3♓ 2	23	21	26	1	25	2	29	29
24	4 8 43	0♐55 31	15 49	25	22	27	1	25	2	29	29
25	4 12 39	1 56 11	29 0	27	24	27	1	25	2	29	29
26	4 16 36	2 56 52	12♈38	28	25	28	1	25	2	29	29
27	4 20 32	3 57 33	26 44	0♐	26	29	1	25	2	29	29
28	4 24 29	4 58 16	11♉16	1	27	29	1	25	2	29	29
29	4 28 26	5 59 1	26 8	3	29	0♏	1	25	2	29	29
30	4 32 22	6 59 46	11♊13	4	0♑	1	1	25	2	29	29

THE SUN ENTERS THE SIGN OF SAGITTARIUS ON NOV 23 AT 02:02.

DAY	TIME	☉	☽	☿	♀	♂	♃	♄	♅	♆	♇
	h m s	° ' "	° '	°	°	°	°	°	°	°	°
D 1	4 36 19	8♐ 0 33	26♊22	6♐	1♑	1♏	1♍	25♏	2♌R	29♎	29♌R
E 2	4 40 15	9 1 21	11♋25	8	2	2	1	26	2	29	29
C 3	4 44 12	10 2 10	26 16	9	4	3	1	26	2	29	29
E 4	4 48 8	11 3 1	10♌46	11	5	3	1	26	2	29	29
M 5	4 52 5	12 3 53	24 54	12	6	4	1	26	2	29	29
B 6	4 56 1	13 4 47	8♍37	14	7	4	1	26	2	0♏	29
E 7	4 59 58	14 5 41	21 57	15	9	5	1	26	2	0	29
R 8	5 3 55	15 6 37	4♎56	17	10	6	1	26	2	0	29
9	5 7 51	16 7 35	17 36	19	11	6	1	26	2	0	29
10	5 11 48	17 8 33	0♏ 0	20	12	7	1	27	2	0	29
11	5 15 44	18 9 33	12 12	22	13	8	1	27	2	0	29
12	5 19 41	19 10 33	24 14	23	15	8	1	27	2	0	29
13	5 23 37	20 11 35	6♐10	25	16	9	1	27	2	0	29
14	5 27 34	21 12 38	18 0	26	17	10	1	27	2	0	29
15	5 31 30	22 13 41	29 48	28	18	10	1	27	2	0	29
16	5 35 27	23 14 45	11♑36	0♑	20	11	1	27	2	0	29
17	5 39 24	24 15 49	23 25	1	21	12	2	27	2	0	29
18	5 43 20	25 16 55	5♒18	3	22	12	2 R	27	2	0	29
19	5 47 17	26 18 0	17 18	4	23	13	2	28	2	0	29
20	5 51 13	27 19 6	29 28	6	25	14	2	28	2	0	29
21	5 55 10	28 20 12	11♓52	8	26	14	1	28	2	0	29
22	5 59 6	29 21 19	24 34	9	27	15	1	28	2	0	29
23	6 3 3	0♑22 25	7♈36	11	28	16	1	28	1	0	28
24	6 7 0	1 23 32	21 3	12	0♒	16	1	28	1	0	28
25	6 10 56	2 24 39	4♉56	14	1	17	1	28	1	0	28
26	6 14 53	3 25 46	19 16	15	2	18	1	28	1	0	28
27	6 18 49	4 26 53	3♊59	17	3	18	1	28	1	0	28
28	6 22 46	5 28 1	19 2	19	5	19	1	28	1	0	28
29	6 26 42	6 29 8	4♋16	20	6	19	1	29	1	0	28
30	6 30 39	7 30 16	19 31	22	7	20	1	29	1	0	28
31	6 34 35	8 31 24	4♌38	23	8	21	1	29	1	0	28

THE SUN ENTERS THE SIGN OF CAPRICORN ON DEC 22 AT 15:12.

♈ ARIES ♉ TAURUS ♊ GEMINI ♋ CANCER ♌ LEO ♍ VIRGO ♎ LIBRA ♏ SCORPIO ♐ SAGITTARIUS ♑ CAPRICORN ♒ AQUARIUS ♓ PISCES

1956

232 Appendix X

SIDEREAL SUN MOON MERCURY VENUS MARS JUPITER SATURN URANUS NEPTUNE PLUTO

DAY	TIME	☉	☽	☿	♀	♂	♃	♄	♅	♆	♇
	h m s	° ' "	° '	°	°	°	°	°	°	°	°
J 1	6 38 32	9♑32 33	19♌26	25♑	10♒	21♏	1♍R	29♏	1♌R	0♏	28♌R
A 2	6 42 29	10 33 41	3♍51	26	11	22	1	29	1	0	28
N 3	6 46 25	11 34 50	17 47	28	12	23	1	29	1	0	28
U 4	6 50 22	12 35 59	1♎15	29	13	23	1	29	1	0	28
A 5	6 54 18	13 37 8	14 16	1♒	14	24	1	29	1	0	28
R 6	6 58 15	14 38 18	26 54	2	16	25	1	29	1	0	28
Y 7	7 2 11	15 39 28	9♏12	4	17	25	1	29	1	0	28
8	7 6 8	16 40 37	21 17	5	18	26	1	0♐	1	0	28
9	7 10 4	17 41 48	3♐11	6	19	27	1	0	1	0	28
10	7 14 1	18 42 58	15 0	8	21	27	1	0	1	0	28
11	7 17 58	19 44 8	26 47	9	22	28	1	0	1	0	28
12	7 21 54	20 45 17	8♑34	10	23	29	1	0	1	0	28
13	7 25 51	21 46 27	20 24	11	24	29	0	0	1	0	28
14	7 29 47	22 47 36	2♒20	12	26	0♐	0	0	1	0	28
15	7 33 44	23 48 45	14 22	12	27	1	0	0	1	0	28
16	7 37 40	24 49 53	26 32	13	28	1	0	0	1	0	28
17	7 41 37	25 51 0	8♓51	13	29	2	0	0	0	0	28
18	7 45 33	26 52 7	21 22	13 R	0♓	3	0	0	0	0	28
19	7 49 30	27 53 13	4♈ 7	13	2	3	0	1	0	0	28
20	7 53 27	28 54 18	17 8	13	3	4	0	1	0	0	28
21	7 57 23	29 55 23	0♉27	13	4	5	0	1	0	0	28
22	8 1 20	0♒56 26	14 7	12	5	5	0	1	0	0	28
23	8 5 16	1 57 28	28 10	12	7	6	0	1	0	0	28
24	8 9 13	2 58 30	12♊34	11	8	6	29♌	1	0	0	28
25	8 13 9	3 59 30	27 18	10	9	7	29	1	0	0	28
26	8 17 6	5 0 30	12♋18	9	10	8	29	1	0	0	28
27	8 21 2	6 1 28	27 25	7	11	8	29	1	0	0	28
28	8 24 59	7 2 26	12♌29	6	13	9	29	1	0	0	28
29	8 28 56	8 3 23	27 22	5	14	10	29	1	0	0	28
30	8 32 52	9 4 18	11♍55	4	15	10	29	1	0	0	28
31	8 36 49	10 5 13	26 1	2	16	11	29	1	0	0	28

THE SUN ENTERS THE SIGN OF AQUARIUS ON JAN 21 AT 01:49.

DAY	TIME	☉	☽	☿	♀	♂	♃	♄	♅	♆	♇
	h m s	° ' "	° '	°	°	°	°	°	°	°	°
F 1	8 40 45	11♒ 6 8	9♎38	1♒R	18♓	12♐	28♌R	1♐	0♌R	0♏R	28♌R
E 2	8 44 42	12 7 1	22 46	0	19	12	28	2	0	0	28
B 3	8 48 38	13 7 54	5♏29	0	20	13	28	2	0	0	28
R 4	8 52 35	14 8 46	17 49	29♑	21	14	28	2	0	0	28
U 5	8 56 31	15 9 37	29 53	28	22	14	28	2	0	0	28
A 6	9 0 28	16 10 27	11♐46	28	24	15	28	2	0	0	28
R 7	9 4 25	17 11 16	23 33	28	25	16	28	2	0	0	28
Y 8	9 8 21	18 12 4	5♑19	28 D	26	16	28	2	0	0	28
9	9 12 18	19 12 51	17 9	28	27	17	27	2	29♋	0	28
10	9 16 14	20 13 37	29 4	28	28	18	27	2	29	0	28
11	9 20 11	21 14 22	11♒ 8	28	0☉	18	27	2	29	0	28
12	9 24 7	22 15 5	23 22	28	1♈	19	27	2	29	0	28
13	9 28 4	23 15 47	5♓47	29	2	20	27	2	29	0	27
14	9 32 0	24 16 28	18 23	29	3	20	27	2	29	0	27
15	9 35 57	25 17 7	1♈10	0♒	4	21	27	2	29	0	27
16	9 39 54	26 17 44	14 9	0	6	22	27	2	29	0	27
17	9 43 50	27 18 20	27 20	1	7	22	26	2	29	0	27
18	9 47 47	28 18 54	10♉43	2	8	23	26	2	29	0	27
19	9 51 43	29 19 26	24 20	3	9	24	26	2	29	0	27
20	9 55 40	0♓19 56	8♊13	4	10	24	26	2	29	0	27
21	9 59 36	1 20 25	22 20	5	12	25	26	2	29	0	27
22	10 3 33	2 20 52	6♋43	6	13	26	26	3	29	0	27
23	10 7 29	3 21 16	21 19	7	14	26	26	3	29	0	27
24	10 11 26	4 21 39	6♌ 2	8	15	27	26	3	29	0	27
25	10 15 23	5 22 0	20 47	9	16	27	25	3	29	0	27
26	10 19 19	6 22 19	5♍25	10	17	28	25	3	29	0	27
27	10 23 16	7 22 37	19 48	11	19	29	25	3	29	0	27
28	10 27 12	8 22 53	3♎51	13	20	29	25	3	29	0	27
29	10 31 9	9 23 7	17 29	14	21	0♑	25	3	29	0	27

THE SUN ENTERS THE SIGN OF PISCES ON FEB 19 AT 16:05.

DAY	TIME	☉	☽	☿	♀	♂	♃	♄	♅	♆	♇
	h m s	° ' "	° '	°	°	°	°	°	°	°	°
M 1	10 35 5	10♓23 19	0♏40	15♒	22♈	1♑	25♌R	3♐	29♋R	0♏R	27♌R
A 2	10 39 2	11 23 30	13 27	16	23	1	25	3	29	0	27
R 3	10 42 58	12 23 40	25 51	18	24	2	25	3	29	0	27
C 4	10 46 55	13 23 48	7♐58	19	26	3	24	3	29	0	27
H 5	10 50 52	14 23 54	19 53	21	27	3	24	3	29	0	27
6	10 54 48	15 23 59	1♑42	22	28	4	24	3	29	0	27
7	10 58 45	16 24 2	13 29	23	29	5	24	3	29	0	27
8	11 2 41	17 24 4	25 21	25	0♉	5	24	3	29	0	27
9	11 6 38	18 24 4	7♒21	26	1	6	24	3	29	0	27
10	11 10 34	19 24 2	19 33	28	2	7	24	3	29	0	27
11	11 14 31	20 23 58	1♓59	29	4	7	24	3	29	0	27
12	11 18 27	21 23 53	14 40	1♓	5	8	23	3 R	28	0	27
13	11 22 24	22 23 45	27 35	2	6	9	23	3	28	0	27
14	11 26 21	23 23 35	10♈44	4	7	9	23	3	28	0	27
15	11 30 17	24 23 24	24 5	6	8	10	23	3	28	0	27
16	11 34 14	25 23 10	7♉36	7	9	11	23	3	28	0	27
17	11 38 10	26 22 54	21 16	9	10	11	23	3	28	0	27
18	11 42 7	27 22 36	5♊ 5	10	11	12	23	3	28	0	27
19	11 46 3	28 22 16	19 0	12	13	13	23	3	28	0	27
20	11 50 0	29 21 54	3♋ 3	14	14	13	23	3	28	0	27
21	11 53 56	0♈21 29	17 13	16	15	14	23	3	28	0	27
22	11 57 53	1 21 1	1♌29	17	16	14	23	3	28	0	27
23	12 1 49	2 20 32	15 47	19	17	15	22	3	28	0	27
24	12 5 46	3 20 0	0♍ 4	21	18	16	22	3	28	0	27
25	12 9 43	4 19 26	14 15	23	19	16	22	3	28	0	27
26	12 13 39	5 18 49	28 16	24	20	17	22	3	28	0	27
27	12 17 36	6 18 11	12♎ 1	26	21	18	22	3	28	0	26
28	12 21 32	7 17 30	25 26	28	22	18	22	3	28	0	26
29	12 25 29	8 16 48	8♏30	0♈	23	19	22	3	28	0	26
30	12 29 25	9 16 4	21 13	2	24	20	22	3	28	0	26
31	12 33 22	10 15 18	3♐37	4	26	20	22	3	28	0	26

THE SUN ENTERS THE SIGN OF ARIES ON MAR 20 AT 15:21.

DAY	TIME	☉	☽	☿	♀	♂	♃	♄	♅	♆	♇
	h m s	° ' "	° '	°	°	°	°	°	°	°	°
A 1	12 37 18	11♈14 30	15♐46	6♈	27♉	21♑	22♌R	2♐R	28♋R	0♏R	26♌R
P 2	12 41 15	12 13 40	27 43	8	28	22	22	2	28	0	26
R 3	12 45 12	13 12 49	9♑33	10	29	22	22	2	28	29♎	26
I 4	12 49 8	14 11 56	21 23	12	0♊	23	22	2	28	29	26
L 5	12 53 5	15 11 1	3♒17	14	1	24	22	2	28 D	29	26
6	12 57 1	16 10 4	15 20	16	2	24	22	2	28	29	26
7	13 0 58	17 9 5	27 36	18	3	25	22	2	28	29	26
8	13 4 54	18 8 4	10♓ 9	20	4	26	22	2	28	29	26
9	13 8 51	19 7 2	23 1	22	5	26	22	2	28	29	26
10	13 12 47	20 5 58	6♈12	24	6	27	22	2	28	29	26
11	13 16 44	21 4 51	19 41	26	7	27	22	2	28	29	26
12	13 20 41	22 3 43	3♉25	29	8	28	22	2	28	29	26
13	13 24 37	23 2 33	17 22	1♉	9	29	22	2	28	29	26
14	13 28 34	24 1 21	1♊28	3	10	29	22	2	28	29	26
15	13 32 30	25 0 6	15 38	5	11	0♒	21	2	28	29	26
16	13 36 27	25 58 49	29 51	7	12	1	21	2	28	29	26
17	13 40 23	26 57 31	14♋ 3	9	13	1	21 D	2	28	29	26
18	13 44 20	27 56 9	28 13	11	14	2	21	2	28	29	26
19	13 48 16	28 54 46	12♌20	13	14	3	21	2	28	29	26
20	13 52 13	29 53 20	26 21	15	15	3	21	2	28	29	26
21	13 56 10	0♉51 52	10♍15	16	16	4	22	2	28	29	26
22	14 0 6	1 50 22	23 59	18	17	4	22	2	28	29	26
23	14 4 3	2 48 50	7♎32	20	18	5	22	1	28	29	26
24	14 7 59	3 47 15	20 51	22	19	6	22	1	28	29	26
25	14 11 56	4 45 39	3♏55	23	20	6	22	1	28	29	26
26	14 15 52	5 44 1	16 43	25	21	7	22	1	28	29	26
27	14 19 49	6 42 22	29 16	26	22	8	22	1	28	29	26
28	14 23 45	7 40 40	11♐33	28	22	8	22	1	28	29	26
29	14 27 42	8 38 57	23 39	29	23	9	22	1	28	29	26
30	14 31 39	9 37 13	5♑35	0♊	24	10	22	1	28	29	26

THE SUN ENTERS THE SIGN OF TAURUS ON APR 20 AT 02:43.

DAY	TIME	☉	☽	☿	♀	♂	♃	♄	♅	♆	♇
	h m s	° ' "	° '	°	°	°	°	°	°	°	°
M 1	14 35 35	10♉35 26	17♑26	1♊	25♊	10♒	22♌	1♐R	29♋	29♎R	26♌R
A 2	14 39 32	11 33 39	29 17	2	26	11	22	1	29	29	26
Y 3	14 43 28	12 31 49	11♒11	3	26	11	22	1	29	29	26
4	14 47 25	13 29 59	23 15	4	27	12	22	1	29	29	26
5	14 51 21	14 28 6	5♓32	5	28	13	22	1	29	29	26
6	14 55 18	15 26 13	18 7	6	29	13	22	1	29	29	26
7	14 59 14	16 24 17	1♈ 2	7	29	14	22	1	29	29	26 D
8	15 3 11	17 22 21	14 21	7	0♋	14	22	0	29	29	26
9	15 7 7	18 20 23	28 2	8	1	15	22	0	29	29	26
10	15 11 4	19 18 24	12♉ 4	8	1	16	22	0	29	29	26
11	15 15 1	20 16 23	26 23	8	2	16	22	0	29	28	26
12	15 18 57	21 14 20	10♊54	9	2	17	22	0	29	28	26
13	15 22 54	22 12 16	25 31	9	3	18	22	0	29	28	26
14	15 26 50	23 10 10	10♋ 8	9 R	4	18	23	0	29	28	26
15	15 30 47	24 8 3	24 40	9	4	19	23	0	29	28	26
16	15 34 43	25 5 53	9♌ 2	9	5	19	23	0	29	28	26
17	15 38 40	26 3 42	23 12	9	5	20	23	0	29	28	26
18	15 42 37	27 1 29	7♍ 7	8	6	21	23	0	29	28	26
19	15 46 33	27 59 15	20 47	8	6	21	23	0	29	28	26
20	15 50 30	28 56 58	4♎12	8	7	22	23	0	29	28	26
21	15 54 26	29 54 40	17 22	7	7	22	23	29♏	29	28	26
22	15 58 23	0♊52 21	0♏18	7	7	23	23	29	29	28	26
23	16 2 19	1 50 0	13 0	6	8	24	23	29	29	28	26
24	16 6 16	2 47 38	25 29	6	8	24	23	29	29	28	26
25	16 10 12	3 45 15	7♐47	5	8	25	24	29	29	28	26
26	16 14 9	4 42 50	19 54	5	8	25	24	29	29	28	26
27	16 18 6	5 40 25	1♑54	4	9	26	24	29	29	28	26
28	16 22 2	6 37 58	13 47	4	9	26	24	29	29	28	26
29	16 25 59	7 35 30	25 38	3	9	27	24	29	29	28	26
30	16 29 55	8 33 1	7♒28	3	9	28	24	29	29	28	26
31	16 33 52	9 30 32	19 23	2	9 R	28	24	29	0♌	28	26

THE SUN ENTERS THE SIGN OF GEMINI ON MAY 21 AT 02:12.

DAY	TIME	☉	☽	☿	♀	♂	♃	♄	♅	♆	♇
	h m s	° ' "	° '	°	°	°	°	°	°	°	°
J 1	16 37 48	10♊28 1	1♓26	2♊R	9♋R	29♒	24♌	29♏R	0♌	28♎R	26♌
U 2	16 41 45	11 25 30	13 42	1	9	29	24	29	0	28	26
N 3	16 45 41	12 22 58	26 14	1	9	0♓	25	29	0	28	26
E 4	16 49 38	13 20 26	9♈ 7	1	9	0	25	28	0	28	26
5	16 53 35	14 17 52	22 25	0	9	1	25	28	0	28	26
6	16 57 31	15 15 18	6♉ 8	0	8	1	25	28	0	28	26
7	17 1 28	16 12 44	20 16	0 D	8	2	25	28	0	28	26
8	17 5 24	17 10 8	4♊47	0	8	3	25	28	0	28	26
9	17 9 21	18 7 33	19 35	0	8	3	25	28	0	28	26
10	17 13 17	19 4 56	4♋34	0	7	4	25	28	0	28	26
11	17 17 14	20 2 18	19 35	1	7	4	26	28	0	28	26
12	17 21 10	20 59 40	4♌29	1	7	5	26	28	0	28	26
13	17 25 7	21 57 0	19 10	1	6	5	26	28	0	28	26
14	17 29 4	22 54 19	3♍31	2	6	6	26	28	0	28	26
15	17 33 0	23 51 38	17 31	2	5	6	26	28	0	28	26
16	17 36 57	24 48 56	1♎ 8	3	5	7	26	28	0	28	26
17	17 40 53	25 46 12	14 23	4	4	7	27	28	0	28	26
18	17 44 50	26 43 28	27 19	4	3	8	27	28	0	28	26
19	17 48 46	27 40 43	9♏58	5	3	8	27	27	0	28	27
20	17 52 43	28 37 58	22 23	6	2	9	27	27	1	28	27
21	17 56 39	29 35 12	4♐36	7	2	9	27	27	1	28	27
22	18 0 36	0♋32 25	16 41	8	1	10	27	27	1	28	27
23	18 4 33	1 29 38	28 39	9	0	10	27	27	1	28	27
24	18 8 29	2 26 51	10♑32	10	0	11	28	27	1	28	27
25	18 12 26	3 24 3	22 23	11	29♊	11	28	27	1	28	27
26	18 16 22	4 21 15	4♒14	13	28	12	28	27	1	28	27
27	18 20 19	5 18 27	16 6	14	28	12	28	27	1	28	27
28	18 24 15	6 15 39	28 3	15	27	13	28	27	1	28	27
29	18 28 12	7 12 50	10♓ 7	17	27	13	28	27	1	28	27
30	18 32 8	8 10 2	22 22	18	26	13	29	27	1	28	27

THE SUN ENTERS THE SIGN OF CANCER ON JUN 21 AT 10:24.

♈ ARIES ♉ TAURUS ♊ GEMINI ♋ CANCER ♌ LEO ♍ VIRGO ♎ LIBRA ♏ SCORPIO ♐ SAGITTARIUS ♑ CAPRICORN ♒ AQUARIUS ♓ PISCES

SIDEREAL SUN MOON MERCURY VENUS MARS JUPITER SATURN URANUS NEPTUNE PLUTO

DAY	TIME	☉	☽	☿	♀	♂	♃	♄	♅	♆	♇
	h m s	° ' "	° '	°	°	°	°	°	°	°	°
J 1	18 36 5	9♋ 7 14	4♈52	20♊	26♊R	14♓	29♌	27♏R	1♌	28♎R	27♌
U 2	18 40 2	10 4 26	17 41	22	25	14	29	27	1	28	27
L 3	18 43 58	11 1 39	0♉52	23	25	15	29	27	1	28	27
Y 4	18 47 55	11 58 52	14 29	25	24	15	29	27	1	28	27
5	18 51 51	12 56 4	28 33	27	24	16	29	27	1	28	27
6	18 55 48	13 53 18	13♊ 2	29	24	16	0♍	27	1	28	27
7	18 59 44	14 50 31	27 55	0♋	23	16	0	27	1	28	27
8	19 3 41	15 47 45	13♋ 2	2	23	17	0	27	2	28	27
9	19 7 37	16 44 59	28 17	4	23	17	0	27	2	28 D	27
10	19 11 34	17 42 13	13♌28	6	23	17	0	27	2	28	27
11	19 15 31	18 39 26	28 25	8	23	18	1	26	2	28	27
12	19 19 27	19 36 40	13♍ 0	10	23	18	1	26	2	28	27
13	19 23 24	20 33 54	27 10	12	23 D	18	1	26	2	28	27
14	19 27 20	21 31 8	10♎51	15	23	19	1	26	2	28	27
15	19 31 17	22 28 22	24 6	17	23	19	1	26	2	28	27
16	19 35 13	23 25 36	6♏56	19	23	19	2	26	2	28	27
17	19 39 10	24 22 50	19 27	21	23	20	2	26	2	28	27
18	19 43 6	25 20 4	1♐42	23	23	20	2	26	2	28	27
19	19 47 3	26 17 19	13 46	25	23	20	2	26	2	28	27
20	19 51 0	27 14 34	25 42	27	23	21	2	26	2	28	27
21	19 54 56	28 11 49	7♑34	0♌	23	21	3	26	2	28	27
22	19 58 53	29 9 5	19 24	2	24	21	3	26	2	28	27
23	20 2 49	0♌ 6 21	1♒15	4	24	21	3	26	2	28	27
24	20 6 46	1 3 37	13 8	6	24	22	3	26	3	28	27
25	20 10 42	2 0 55	25 4	8	25	22	3	26	3	28	27
26	20 14 39	2 58 13	7♓ 7	10	25	22	3	26	3	28	27
27	20 18 35	3 55 32	19 17	12	26	22	4	26	3	28	27
28	20 22 32	4 52 52	1♈36	14	26	22	4	26	3	28	28
29	20 26 29	5 50 13	14 8	16	26	23	4	26	3	28	28
30	20 30 25	6 47 35	26 56	18	27	23	4	26 D	3	28	28
31	20 34 22	7 44 58	10♉ 2	20	27	23	5	26	3	28	28

THE SUN ENTERS THE SIGN OF LEO ON JUL 22 AT 21:20.

DAY	TIME	☉	☽	☿	♀	♂	♃	♄	♅	♆	♇
	h m s	° ' "	° '	°	°	°	°	°	°	°	°
A 1	20 38 18	8♌42 22	23♉32	21♌	28♊	23♓	5♍	26♏	3♌	28♎	28♌
U 2	20 42 15	9 39 48	7♊25	23	29	23	5	26	3	28	28
G 3	20 46 11	10 37 14	21 44	25	29	23	5	26	3	28	28
U 4	20 50 8	11 34 42	6♋27	27	0♋	23	5	26	3	28	28
S 5	20 54 4	12 32 11	21 29	29	0	23	6	26	3	28	28
T 6	20 58 1	13 29 41	6♌42	0♍	1	24	6	26	3	28	28
7	21 1 58	14 27 12	21 55	2	2	24	6	26	3	28	28
8	21 5 54	15 24 44	6♍58	4	2	24	6	26	3	28	28
9	21 9 51	16 22 17	21 42	5	3	24	6	26	3	28	28
10	21 13 47	17 19 51	5♎59	7	4	24 R	7	26	4	28	28
11	21 17 44	18 17 26	19 47	9	5	24	7	26	4	28	28
12	21 21 40	19 15 2	3♏ 6	10	5	24	7	26	4	28	28
13	21 25 37	20 12 38	15 58	12	6	24	7	26	4	28	28
14	21 29 33	21 10 16	28 27	13	7	24	7	26	4	28	28
15	21 33 30	22 7 55	10♐40	15	8	24	8	26	4	28	28
16	21 37 27	23 5 34	22 40	16	8	23	8	26	4	28	28
17	21 41 23	24 3 15	4♑33	18	9	23	8	26	4	28	28
18	21 45 20	25 0 57	16 22	19	10	23	8	26	4	28	28
19	21 49 16	25 58 40	28 12	20	11	23	8	26	4	28	28
20	21 53 13	26 56 24	10♒ 5	22	12	23	9	26	4	28	28
21	21 57 9	27 54 10	22 4	23	13	23	9	27	4	28	28
22	22 1 6	28 51 56	4♓ 9	24	13	23	9	27	4	28	28
23	22 5 2	29 49 45	16 21	26	14	23	9	27	4	28	28
24	22 8 59	0♍47 35	28 42	27	15	22	10	27	4	28	28
25	22 12 56	1 45 26	11♈13	28	16	22	10	27	4	28	28
26	22 16 52	2 43 19	23 54	29	17	22	10	27	4	28	28
27	22 20 49	3 41 14	6♉48	0♎	18	22	10	27	5	28	28
28	22 24 45	4 39 11	19 57	2	19	22	10	27	5	28	29
29	22 28 42	5 37 9	3♊24	3	20	22	11	27	5	28	29
30	22 32 38	6 35 10	17 9	4	21	21	11	27	5	28	29
31	22 36 35	7 33 12	1♋16	5	22	21	11	27	5	28	29

THE SUN ENTERS THE SIGN OF VIRGO ON AUG 23 AT 04:16.

DAY	TIME	☉	☽	☿	♀	♂	♃	♄	♅	♆	♇
	h m s	° ' "	° '	°	°	°	°	°	°	°	°
S 1	22 40 31	8♍31 17	15♋44	6♎	23♋	21♓R	11♍	27♏	5♌	28♎	29♌
E 2	22 44 28	9 29 23	0♌28	7	24	21	12	27	5	28	29
P 3	22 48 25	10 27 31	15 25	7	25	20	12	27	5	28	29
T 4	22 52 21	11 25 41	0♍24	8	26	20	12	27	5	28	29
E 5	22 56 18	12 23 53	15 18	9	27	20	12	27	5	28	29
M 6	23 0 14	13 22 6	29 57	10	28	19	12	27	5	29	29
B 7	23 4 11	14 20 21	14♎13	10	29	19	13	27	5	29	29
E 8	23 8 7	15 18 38	28 3	11	0♌	19	13	27	5	29	29
R 9	23 12 4	16 16 56	11♏25	11	1	19	13	27	5	29	29
10	23 16 0	17 15 16	24 20	12	2	18	13	28	5	29	29
11	23 19 57	18 13 38	6♐52	12	3	18	13	28	5	29	29
12	23 23 54	19 12 1	19 6	12	4	18	14	28	5	29	29
13	23 27 50	20 10 25	1♑ 7	12 R	5	18	14	28	5	29	29
14	23 31 47	21 8 52	13 0	12	6	17	14	28	5	29	29
15	23 35 43	22 7 19	24 50	12	7	17	14	28	6	29	29
16	23 39 40	23 5 49	6♒42	12	8	17	15	28	6	29	29
17	23 43 36	24 4 20	18 39	12	9	17	15	28	6	29	29
18	23 47 33	25 2 53	0♓44	11	10	16	15	28	6	29	29
19	23 51 29	26 1 28	12 58	11	11	16	15	28	6	29	29
20	23 55 26	27 0 4	25 24	10	12	16	15	28	6	29	29
21	23 59 22	27 58 43	8♈ 1	9	13	16	16	28	6	29	29
22	0 3 19	28 57 23	20 49	8	14	15	16	28	6	29	29
23	0 7 16	29 56 6	3♉48	7	15	15	16	28	6	29	29
24	0 11 12	0♎54 51	16 58	6	16	15	16	29	6	29	29
25	0 15 9	1 53 38	0♊20	5	18	15	16	29	6	29	29
26	0 19 5	2 52 27	13 54	4	19	15	17	29	6	29	29
27	0 23 2	3 51 19	27 41	3	20	14	17	29	6	29	29
28	0 26 58	4 50 12	11♋41	2	21	14	17	29	6	29	29
29	0 30 55	5 49 9	25 55	1	22	14	17	29	6	29	29
30	0 34 51	6 48 7	10♌20	0	23	14	18	29	6	29	0♍

THE SUN ENTERS THE SIGN OF LIBRA ON SEP 23 AT 01:37.

DAY	TIME	☉	☽	☿	♀	♂	♃	♄	♅	♆	♇
	h m s	° ' "	° '	°	°	°	°	°	°	°	°
O 1	0 38 48	7♎47 8	24♌53	29♍R	24♌	14♓R	18♍	29♏	6♌	29♎	0♍
C 2	0 42 45	8 46 11	9♍28	28	25	14	18	29	6	29	0
T 3	0 46 41	9 45 16	23 59	28	26	14	18	29	6	29	0
O 4	0 50 38	10 44 23	8♎19	28	28	13	18	29	6	29	0
B 5	0 54 34	11 43 32	22 21	27 D	29	13	19	29	6	29	0
E 6	0 58 31	12 42 44	6♏ 3	27	0♍	13	19	0♐	6	0♏	0
R 7	1 2 27	13 41 57	19 20	27	1	13	19	0	6	0	0
8	1 6 24	14 41 12	2♐15	28	2	13	19	0	6	0	0
9	1 10 20	15 40 29	14 48	28	3	13	19	0	6	0	0
10	1 14 17	16 39 48	27 4	29	4	13 D	20	0	6	0	0
11	1 18 14	17 39 9	9♑ 7	0♎	6	13	20	0	7	0	0
12	1 22 10	18 38 31	21 2	1	7	13	20	0	7	0	0
13	1 26 7	19 37 55	2♒53	2	8	13	20	0	7	0	0
14	1 30 3	20 37 21	14 46	3	9	13	20	0	7	0	0
15	1 34 0	21 36 49	26 46	4	10	13	21	0	7	0	0
16	1 37 56	22 36 18	8♓56	5	11	13	21	1	7	0	0
17	1 41 53	23 35 50	21 18	7	12	13	21	1	7	0	0
18	1 45 49	24 35 23	3♈55	8	14	14	21	1	7	0	0
19	1 49 46	25 34 58	16 48	10	15	14	21	1	7	0	0
20	1 53 42	26 34 35	29 56	11	16	14	22	1	7	0	0
21	1 57 39	27 34 14	13♉18	13	17	14	22	1	7	0	0
22	2 1 36	28 33 56	26 52	14	18	14	22	1	7	0	0
23	2 5 32	29 33 39	10♊38	16	20	14	22	1	7	0	0
24	2 9 29	0♏33 25	24 31	18	21	14	22	1	7	0	0
25	2 13 25	1 33 13	8♋33	19	22	15	23	1	7	0	0
26	2 17 22	2 33 3	22 39	21	23	15	23	2	7	0	0
27	2 21 18	3 32 55	6♌49	23	24	15	23	2	7	0	0
28	2 25 15	4 32 49	21 2	24	25	15	23	2	7	0	0
29	2 29 12	5 32 46	5♍13	26	27	15	23	2	7	0	0
30	2 33 8	6 32 45	19 22	28	28	16	23	2	7	0	0
31	2 37 5	7 32 46	3♎24	29	29	16	24	2	7	0	0

THE SUN ENTERS THE SIGN OF SCORPIO ON OCT 23 AT 10:35.

DAY	TIME	☉	☽	☿	♀	♂	♃	♄	♅	♆	♇
	h m s	° ' "	° '	°	°	°	°	°	°	°	°
N 1	2 41 1	8♏32 49	17♎15	1♏	0♎	16♓	24♍	2♐	7♌	0♏	0♍
O 2	2 44 58	9 32 54	0♏54	3	1	16	24	2	7	1	0
V 3	2 48 54	10 33 1	14 16	4	3	17	24	2	7	1	0
E 4	2 52 51	11 33 10	27 21	6	4	17	24	3	7	1	0
M 5	2 56 47	12 33 20	10♐ 7	8	5	17	25	3	7	1	0
B 6	3 0 44	13 33 33	22 37	9	6	17	25	3	7	1	0
E 7	3 4 40	14 33 47	4♑52	11	7	18	25	3	7	1	0
R 8	3 8 37	15 34 2	16 55	13	9	18	25	3	7	1	0
9	3 12 34	16 34 19	28 51	14	10	18	25	3	7	1	0
10	3 16 30	17 34 38	10♒43	16	11	19	25	3	7	1	0
11	3 20 27	18 34 57	22 36	17	12	19	26	3	7	1	0
12	3 24 23	19 35 19	4♓35	19	13	19	26	4	7 R	1	0
13	3 28 20	20 35 41	16 45	21	15	20	26	4	7	1	0
14	3 32 16	21 36 5	29 9	22	16	20	26	4	7	1	0
15	3 36 13	22 36 31	11♈52	24	17	21	26	4	7	1	0
16	3 40 9	23 36 58	24 54	25	18	21	26	4	7	1	0
17	3 44 6	24 37 26	8♉17	27	20	21	27	4	7	1	0
18	3 48 3	25 37 56	22 0	29	21	22	27	4	7	1	0
19	3 51 59	26 38 27	6♊ 1	0♐	22	22	27	4	7	1	0
20	3 55 56	27 39 0	20 15	2	23	23	27	4	7	1	0
21	3 59 52	28 39 35	4♋37	3	24	23	27	5	7	1	0
22	4 3 49	29 40 11	19 4	5	26	23	27	5	7	1	0
23	4 7 45	0♐40 49	3♌30	6	27	24	27	5	7	1	0
24	4 11 42	1 41 29	17 50	8	28	24	28	5	7	1	0
25	4 15 38	2 42 10	2♍ 2	10	29	25	28	5	7	1	0
26	4 19 35	3 42 53	16 4	11	1♏	25	28	5	7	1	0
27	4 23 32	4 43 37	29 53	13	2	26	28	5	7	1	0
28	4 27 28	5 44 23	13♎31	14	3	26	28	5	7	1	0
29	4 31 25	6 45 11	26 55	16	4	26	28	6	7	1	0
30	4 35 21	7 46 0	10♏ 6	17	5	27	28	6	7	1	0

THE SUN ENTERS THE SIGN OF SAGITTARIUS ON NOV 22 AT 07:51.

DAY	TIME	☉	☽	☿	♀	♂	♃	♄	♅	♆	♇
	h m s	° ' "	° '	°	°	°	°	°	°	°	°
D 1	4 39 18	8♐46 50	23♏ 4	19♐	7♏	27♓	29♍	6♐	7♌R	2♏	0♍
E 2	4 43 14	9 47 42	5♐49	20	8	28	29	6	7	2	0 R
C 3	4 47 11	10 48 34	18 22	22	9	28	29	6	7	2	0
E 4	4 51 8	11 49 28	0♑43	23	10	29	29	6	7	2	0
M 5	4 55 4	12 50 23	12 53	25	12	29	29	6	7	2	0
B 6	4 59 1	13 51 19	24 53	26	13	0O	29	6	7	2	0
E 7	5 2 57	14 52 15	6♒48	28	14	0♈	29	6	7	2	0
R 8	5 6 54	15 53 13	18 39	0♑	15	1	29	7	7	2	0
9	5 10 50	16 54 11	0♓31	1	17	1	0♎	7	7	2	0
10	5 14 47	17 55 9	12 28	3	18	2	0	7	7	2	0
11	5 18 43	18 56 9	24 34	4	19	2	0	7	7	2	0
12	5 22 40	19 57 8	6♈55	6	20	3	0	7	7	2	0
13	5 26 37	20 58 9	19 34	7	22	3	0	7	7	2	0
14	5 30 33	21 59 10	2♉36	9	23	4	0	7	7	2	0
15	5 34 30	23 0 11	16 3	10	24	4	0	7	7	2	0
16	5 38 26	24 1 13	29 56	11	25	5	0	8	6	2	0
17	5 42 23	25 2 16	14♊13	13	27	5	0	8	6	2	0
18	5 46 19	26 3 19	28 51	14	28	6	0	8	6	2	0
19	5 50 16	27 4 23	13♋42	16	29	6	1	8	6	2	0
20	5 54 12	28 5 27	28 38	17	0♐	7	1	8	6	2	0
21	5 58 9	29 6 32	13♌31	18	1	8	1	8	6	2	0
22	6 2 6	0♑ 7 38	28 13	20	3	8	1	8	6	2	0
23	6 6 2	1 8 44	12♍39	21	4	9	1	8	6	2	0
24	6 9 59	2 9 51	26 44	22	5	9	1	8	6	2	0
25	6 13 55	3 10 59	10♎28	23	6	10	1	9	6	2	0
26	6 17 52	4 12 7	23 53	24	8	10	1	9	6	2	0
27	6 21 48	5 13 16	6♏59	25	9	11	1	9	6	2	0
28	6 25 45	6 14 26	19 49	26	10	11	1	9	6	2	0
29	6 29 41	7 15 36	2♐26	26	11	12	1	9	6	2	0
30	6 33 38	8 16 46	14 52	27	13	13	1	9	6	2	0
31	6 37 35	9 17 57	27 9	27	14	13	1	9	6	2	0

THE SUN ENTERS THE SIGN OF CAPRICORN ON DEC 21 AT 21:00.

♈ ARIES ♉ TAURUS ♊ GEMINI ♋ CANCER ♌ LEO ♍ VIRGO ♎ LIBRA ♏ SCORPIO ♐ SAGITTARIUS ♑ CAPRICORN ♒ AQUARIUS ♓ PISCES

SIDEREAL · SUN · MOON · MERCURY · VENUS · MARS · JUPITER · SATURN · URANUS · NEPTUNE · PLUTO

January

DAY	TIME h m s	☉ ° ' "	☽ ° '	☿ ° '	♀ ° '	♂ ° '	♃ ° '	♄ ° '	♅ °	♆ °	♇ °
J 1	6 41 31	10♑19 8	9♒17	27♐R	15♐	14♈	1♎	9♐	6♌R	2♏	0♍R
A 2	6 45 28	11 20 19	21 19	27	16	14	1	9	6	2	0
N 3	6 49 24	12 21 29	3♓16	27	18	15	2	10	6	2	0
U 4	6 53 21	13 22 40	15 9	27	19	15	2	10	6	2	0
A 5	6 57 17	14 23 50	27 0	26	20	16	2	10	6	2	0
R 6	7 1 14	15 25 1	8♈51	26	21	17	2	10	6	2	0
Y 7	7 5 10	16 26 10	20 47	25	23	17	2	10	6	2	0
8	7 9 7	17 27 20	2♉50	24	24	18	2	10	6	2	0
9	7 13 4	18 28 29	15 6	22	25	18	2	10	6	2	0
10	7 17 0	19 29 37	27 38	21	26	19	2	10	6	2	0
11	7 20 57	20 30 45	10♊33	20	28	19	2	10	6	2	0
12	7 24 53	21 31 53	23 53	18	29	20	2	10	6	2	0
13	7 28 50	22 32 59	7♋42	17	0♉	21	2	11	5	2	0
14	7 32 46	23 34 6	22 0	16	1	21	2	11	5	2	0
15	7 36 43	24 35 11	6♌45	15	3	22	2	11	5	2	0
16	7 40 39	25 36 16	21 50	14	4	22	2 R	11	5	2	0
17	7 44 36	26 37 21	7♍ 7	13	5	23	2	11	5	2	0
18	7 48 33	27 38 25	22 23	12	6	24	2	11	5	2	0
19	7 52 29	28 39 29	7♍28	12	8	24	2	11	5	2	0
20	7 56 26	29 40 32	22 14	11	9	25	2	11	5	2	0
21	8 0 22	0♒41 34	6♎33	11 D	10	25	2	11	5	2	0
22	8 4 19	1 42 37	20 25	11	11	26	2	11	5	3	0
23	8 8 15	2 43 39	3♏51	11	13	27	2	11	5	3	0
24	8 12 12	3 44 40	16 52	12	14	27	2	12	5	3	0
25	8 16 8	4 45 41	29 33	12	15	28	2	12	5	3	0
26	8 20 5	5 46 42	11♐58	12	16	28	2	12	5	3	0
27	8 24 2	6 47 41	24 11	13	18	29	2	12	5	3	0
28	8 27 58	7 48 41	6♑15	13	19	0♉	2	12	5	3	0
29	8 31 55	8 49 39	18 14	14	20	0	2	12	5	3	0
30	8 35 51	9 50 36	0♒ 9	15	21	1	2	12	5	3	0
31	8 39 48	10 51 33	12 6	16	23	1	2	12	5	3	0

THE SUN ENTERS THE SIGN OF AQUARIUS ON JAN 20 AT 07:39.

February

DAY	TIME h m s	☉ ° ' "	☽ ° '	☿ ° '	♀ ° '	♂ ° '	♃ ° '	♄ ° '	♅ °	♆ °	♇ °
F 1	8 43 44	11♒52 28	23♒54	17♑	24♒	2♉	1♎R	12♐	5♌R	3♏ R	0♍R
E 2	8 47 41	12 53 23	5♓46	18	25	3	1	12	5	3	0
B 3	8 51 37	13 54 16	17 40	19	26	3	1	12	5	3	0
R 4	8 55 34	14 55 8	29 39	20	28	4	1	12	5	3	0
U 5	8 59 31	15 55 58	11♈44	21	29	5	1	13	4	3	0
A 6	9 3 27	16 56 47	23 59	22	0♓	5	1	13	4	3	0
R 7	9 7 24	17 57 35	6♉28	23	1	6	1	13	4	3	29♌
Y 8	9 11 20	18 58 21	19 16	24	3	6	1	13	4	3	29
9	9 15 17	19 59 5	2♊25	25	4	7	1	13	4	3	29
10	9 19 13	20 59 48	16 6	26	6	8	1	13	4	3	29
11	9 23 10	22 0 30	0♋12	28	6	8	1	13	4	3	29
12	9 27 6	23 1 10	14 48	29	8	9	1	13	4	3	29
13	9 31 3	24 1 48	29 48	1♓W	9	9	1	13	4	3	29
14	9 35 0	25 2 25	15♌ 5	2	10	10	1	13	4	3	29
15	9 38 56	26 3 0	0♍27	3	11	11	0	13	4	3	29
16	9 42 53	27 3 33	15 44	5	13	11	0	13	4	3	29
17	9 46 49	28 4 6	0♎43	6	14	12	0	13	4	3	29
18	9 50 46	29 4 36	15 17	7	15	13	0	14	4	3	29
19	9 54 42	0♓ 5 6	29 22	9	16	13	0	14	4	3	29
20	9 58 39	1 5 34	12♏56	10	18	14	0	14	4	3	29
21	10 2 35	2 6 1	26 3	12	19	14	0	14	4	2	29
22	10 6 32	3 6 27	8♐45	13	20	15	0	14	4	2	29
23	10 10 29	4 6 51	21 9	15	21	16	0	14	4	2	29
24	10 14 25	5 7 14	3♑18	16	23	16	0	14	4	2	29
25	10 18 22	6 7 36	15 17	18	24	17	29♍	14	4	2	29
26	10 22 18	7 7 56	27 11	19	25	18	29	14	4	2	29
27	10 26 15	8 8 14	9♒ 2	21	26	18	29	14	4	2	29
28	10 30 11	9 8 31	20 53	23	28	19	29	14	4	2	29

THE SUN ENTERS THE SIGN OF PISCES ON FEB 18 AT 21:59.

March

DAY	TIME h m s	☉ ° ' "	☽ ° '	☿ ° '	♀ ° '	♂ ° '	♃ ° '	♄ ° '	♅ °	♆ °	♇ °
M 1	10 34 8	10♓ 8 46	2♓46	24♒	29♓	19♓	29♍R	14♐	4♌R	2♏R	29♌R
A 2	10 38 4	11 8 59	14 42	26	0♈	20	29	14	4	2	29
R 3	10 42 1	12 9 11	26 43	28	1	21	29	14	3	2	29
C 4	10 45 58	13 9 21	8♈50	29	3	21	29	14	3	2	29
H 5	10 49 54	14 9 28	21 4	1♓	4	22	29	14	3	2	29
6	10 53 51	15 9 34	3♉27	3	5	23	28	14	3	2	29
7	10 57 47	16 9 38	16 2	4	6	23	28	14	3	2	29
8	11 1 44	17 9 39	28 53	6	8	24	28	14	3	2	29
9	11 5 40	18 9 38	12♊11	8	9	25	28	14	3	2	28
10	11 9 37	19 9 36	25 33	10	10	25	28	14	3	2	29
11	11 13 33	20 9 31	9♋55	11	11	26	28	14	3	2	29
12	11 17 30	21 9 24	23 48	13	13	27	27	14	3	2	29
13	11 21 27	22 9 14	8♌30	15	14	27	27	14	3	2	29
14	11 25 23	23 9 2	23 29	17	15	28	27	14	3	2	28
15	11 29 20	24 8 49	8♍38	19	16	28	27	14	3	2	28
16	11 33 16	25 8 33	23 45	21	18	29	27	14	3	2	28
17	11 37 13	26 8 15	8♎41	23	19	29	27	14	3	2	28
18	11 41 9	27 7 55	23 18	24	20	0♊	27	14	3	2	28
19	11 45 6	28 7 33	7♏28	26	1	1	27	14	3	2	28
20	11 49 2	29 7 10	21 11	28	23	1	27	14	3	2	28
21	11 52 59	0♈ 6 45	4♐27	0♈	24	2	26	14	2	2	28
22	11 56 55	1 6 18	17 14	2	25	3	26	14	2	2	28
23	12 0 52	2 5 49	29 42	4	26	4	26	14	2	2	28
24	12 4 49	3 5 19	11♑54	6	28	4	26	14 R	2	2	28
25	12 8 45	4 4 46	23 54	8	29	5	26	14	2	2	28
26	12 12 42	5 4 12	5♒47	10	0♈	5	26	14	2	2	28
27	12 16 38	6 3 36	17 38	12	1	6	26	14	2	2	28
28	12 20 35	7 2 59	29 30	14	3	6	26	14	2	2	28
29	12 24 31	8 2 19	11♓26	17	4	7	26	14	2	2	28
30	12 28 28	9 1 37	23 28	19	5	8	26	14	2	2	28
31	12 32 24	10 0 54	5♈38	21	6	8	25	14	2	2	28

THE SUN ENTERS THE SIGN OF ARIES ON MAR 20 AT 21:17.

April

DAY	TIME h m s	☉ ° ' "	☽ ° '	☿ ° '	♀ ° '	♂ ° '	♃ ° '	♄ ° '	♅ °	♆ °	♇ °
A 1	12 36 21	11♈ 0 8	17♈57	22♈	8♉	9♈	25♍R	14♐R	3♌R	2♏R	28♌R
P 2	12 40 18	11 59 20	0♉25	24	9	9	25	14	3	2	28
R 3	12 44 14	12 58 31	13 5	26	10	10	25	14	3	2	28
I 4	12 48 11	13 57 39	25 56	28	11	11	25	14	3	2	28
L 5	12 52 7	14 56 45	9♊ 0	0♉	12	11	25	14	3	2	28
6	12 56 4	15 55 48	22 19	2	14	12	24	14	3	2	28
7	13 0 0	16 54 50	5♋54	3	15	13	24	14	3	2	28
8	13 3 57	17 53 49	19 46	5	16	13	24	14	3	2	28
9	13 7 53	18 52 45	3♋55	7	17	15	24	14	3 D	2	28
10	13 11 50	19 51 40	18 19	8	19	15	24	14	3	2	28
11	13 15 47	20 50 32	2♍55	10	20	15	24	14	3	1	28
12	13 19 43	21 49 21	17 38	11	21	16	24	14	3	1	28
13	13 23 40	22 48 9	2♎22	12	22	16	24	14	3	1	28
14	13 27 36	23 46 54	16 58	13	24	17	24	14	3	1	28
15	13 31 33	24 45 37	1♏20	14	25	18	24	14	3	1	28
16	13 35 29	25 44 18	15 22	15	26	18	24	14	3	1	28
17	13 39 26	26 42 59	29 2	16	27	19	24	14	3	1	28
18	13 43 22	27 41 37	12♐17	18	29	19	24	14	3	1	28
19	13 47 19	28 40 13	25 11	18	0♊	20	24	14	3	1	28
20	13 51 16	29 38 47	7♑44	1	1	21	24	14	3	1	28
21	13 55 12	0♉37 20	20 0	19	2	21	24	14	3	1	28
22	13 59 9	1 35 51	2♒ 3	19	4	22	24	13	3	1	28
23	14 3 5	2 34 21	13 58	19	5	23	24	13	3	1	28
24	14 7 2	3 32 48	25 47	19 R	6	23	24	13	3	1	28
25	14 10 58	4 31 15	7♓45	7	24	24	13	3	1	28	28
26	14 14 55	5 29 39	19 43	19	9	25	24	13	3	1	28
27	14 18 51	6 28 2	1♈51	19	10	25	24	13	3	1	28
28	14 22 48	7 26 23	14 9	19	11	26	24	13	3	1	28
29	14 26 44	8 24 43	26 40	19	12	26	24	13	3	1	28
30	14 30 41	9 23 0	9♉26	18	13	27	24	13	3	1	28

THE SUN ENTERS THE SIGN OF TAURUS ON APR 20 AT 08:41.

May

DAY	TIME h m s	☉ ° ' "	☽ ° '	☿ ° '	♀ ° '	♂ ° '	♃ ° '	♄ ° '	♅ °	♆ °	♇ °
M 1	14 34 38	10♉21 16	22♉26	18♉R	15♉	28♊	22♍R	13♐R	3♌	1♏R	28♌R
A 2	14 38 34	11 19 31	5♊40	18	16	28	22	13	3	1	28
Y 3	14 42 31	12 17 43	19 7	17	17	29	22	13	3	1	28
4	14 46 27	13 15 54	2♋47	16	18	0♋	22	13	3	1	28
5	14 50 24	14 14 2	16 38	16	20	0	22	13	3	1	28
6	14 54 20	15 12 9	0♌39	15	21	1	22	13	3	1	28
7	14 58 17	16 10 14	14 47	15	22	1	22	13	3	1	28
8	15 2 13	17 8 16	29 2	14	23	2	22	13	3	1	28
9	15 6 10	18 6 17	13♍20	13	25	3	22	13	3	1	28 D
10	15 10 7	19 4 16	27 39	13	26	3	22	13	3	1	28
11	15 14 3	20 2 12	11♎54	12	27	4	22	13	3	1	28
12	15 18 0	21 0 7	26 1	12	29	5	22	13	3	1	28
13	15 21 56	21 58 1	9♏58	11	0♋	5	22	13	3	1	28
14	15 25 53	22 55 53	23 41	11	1♊	6	22	13	3	1	28
15	15 29 49	23 53 44	7♐ 6	11	2	6	22	13	3	1	28
16	15 33 46	24 51 33	20 13	11	3	7	22	13	3	1	28
17	15 37 42	25 49 21	3♑ 3	11	4	8	22	13	3	1	28
18	15 41 39	26 47 7	15 35	12	5	8	22	13	3	1	28
19	15 45 36	27 44 53	27 52	9	7	9	22 D	12	3	1	28
20	15 49 32	28 42 37	9♒57	12	9	10	22	12	4	1	28
21	15 53 29	29 40 20	21 54	13	9	10	22	12	4	0	28
22	15 57 25	0♊38 2	3♓47	14	10	11	22	12	4	0	28
23	16 1 22	1 35 43	15 42	15	12	12	22	12	4	0	28
24	16 5 18	2 33 22	27 42	17	13	13	22	12	4	0	28
25	16 9 15	3 31 1	9♈52	18	14	13	21	12	4	0	28
26	16 13 11	4 28 39	22 14	20	16	14	21	12	4	0	28
27	16 17 8	5 26 16	4♉56	22	17	14	21	11	4	0	28
28	16 21 5	6 23 52	17 55	23	19	15	21	11	4	0	28
29	16 25 1	7 21 27	1♊14	24	19	15	21	11	4	0	28
30	16 28 58	8 19 0	14 52	26	20	16	21	11	4	0	28
31	16 32 54	9 16 33	28 46	27	22	17	22	11	4	0	28

THE SUN ENTERS THE SIGN OF GEMINI ON MAY 21 AT 08:11.

June

DAY	TIME h m s	☉ ° ' "	☽ ° '	☿ ° '	♀ ° '	♂ ° '	♃ ° '	♄ ° '	♅ °	♆ °	♇ °
J 1	16 36 51	10♊14 5	12♋54	16♉R	23♊	17♋	22♍R	11♐R	4♌	0♏R	28♌
U 2	16 40 47	11 11 35	27 10	17	24	18	22	11	4	0	28
N 3	16 44 44	12 9 4	11♌30	18	25	18	22	11	4	0	28
E 4	16 48 40	13 6 31	25 50	20	26	19	22	11	4	0	28
5	16 52 37	14 3 58	10♍ 6	20	28	20	22	11	4	0	28
6	16 56 34	15 1 23	24 16	22	29	20	22	11	4	0	28
7	17 0 30	15 58 47	8♎18	22	0♋	21	22	10	4	0	28
8	17 4 27	16 56 10	22 10	24	1	22	22	10	4	0	28
9	17 8 23	17 53 32	5♏52	25	2	22	22	10	4	0	28
10	17 12 20	18 50 53	19 22	26	4	23	23	10	4	0	28
11	17 16 16	19 48 13	2♐40	28	5	23	23	10	4	0	28
12	17 20 13	20 45 32	15 45	0♋	6	24	23	10	4	0	28
13	17 24 9	21 42 50	28 37	1♊	7	25	23	10	5	0	28
14	17 28 6	22 40 6	11♑15	4	8	26	23	10	5	0	28
15	17 32 3	23 37 22	23 40	4	10	26	23	10	5	0	28
16	17 35 59	24 34 37	5♒53	5	11	27	23	10	5	0	28
17	17 39 56	25 31 51	17 56	7	12	27	23	9	5	0	28
18	17 43 52	26 29 14	29 52	9	14	28	23	9	5	0	28
19	17 47 49	27 26 23	11♓45	11	15	29	23	9	5	0	28
20	17 51 45	28 23 45	23 39	12	16	29	23	9	5	0	28
21	17 55 42	29 21 0	5♈37	14	18	0♌	23	9	5	0	28
22	17 59 38	0♋18 15	17 47	15	19	0	23	9	5	0	28
23	18 3 35	1 15 30	0♉11	18	20	1	23	9	5	0	28
24	18 7 32	2 12 45	12 55	20	21	2	24	9	5	0	28
25	18 11 28	3 9 58	26 0	21	22	2	24	9	5	0	28
26	18 15 25	4 7 14	9♊33	23	24	3	24	9	5	0	28
27	18 19 21	5 4 25	23 28	25	25	3	24	9	5	0	28
28	18 23 18	6 1 42	7♋46	26	26	4	24	9	5	0	28
29	18 27 14	6 58 56	22 20	1♋	27	5	25	9	5	0	29
30	18 31 11	7 56 10	7♍ 3	3	29	5	25	9	5	0	29

THE SUN ENTERS THE SIGN OF CANCER ON JUN 21 AT 16:21.

♈ ARIES ♉ TAURUS ♊ GEMINI ♋ CANCER ♌ LEO ♍ VIRGO ♎ LIBRA ♏ SCORPIO ♐ SAGITTARIUS ♑ CAPRICORN ♒ AQUARIUS ♓ PISCES

SIDEREAL SUN MOON MERCURY VENUS MARS JUPITER SATURN URANUS NEPTUNE PLUTO

DAY	TIME	☉	☽	☿	♀	♂	♃	♄	♅	♆	♇
	h m s	° ' "	° '	°	°	°	°	°	°	°	°
J 1	18 35 8	8♋53 24	21♌48	5♋	29♋	6♌	24♍	9♐R	6♌	0♏R	29♌
U 2	18 39 4	9 50 37	6♍27	7	1♌	7	25	9	6	0	29
L 3	18 43 1	10 47 49	20 55	9	2	7	25	9	6	0	29
Y 4	18 46 57	11 45 2	5♎ 8	11	3	8	25	9	6	0	29
5	18 50 54	12 42 14	19 4	14	4	8	25	9	6	0	29
6	18 54 50	13 39 25	2♏43	16	6	9	25	9	6	0	29
7	18 58 47	14 36 37	16 7	18	7	10	25	9	6	0	29
8	19 2 43	15 33 48	29 16	20	8	10	25	9	6	0	29
9	19 6 40	16 31 0	12♐13	22	9	11	25	9	6	0	29
10	19 10 37	17 28 11	24 57	24	10	12	26	9	6	0	29
11	19 14 33	18 25 23	7♑32	26	12	12	26	8	6	0 D	29
12	19 18 30	19 22 34	19 56	28	13	13	26	8	6	0	29
13	19 22 26	20 19 46	2♒10	0♌	14	13	26	8	6	0	29
14	19 26 23	21 16 58	14 16	2	15	14	26	8	6	0	29
15	19 30 19	22 14 11	26 15	4	16	15	26	8	6	0	29
16	19 34 16	23 11 24	8♓ 9	6	18	15	26	8	6	0	29
17	19 38 12	24 8 37	20 0	8	19	16	27	8	6	0	29
18	19 42 9	25 5 52	1♈52	10	20	17	27	8	7	0	29
19	19 46 6	26 3 6	13 49	12	21	17	27	8	7	0	29
20	19 50 2	27 0 22	25 56	14	23	18	27	8	7	0	29
21	19 53 59	27 57 38	8♉18	15	24	19	27	8	7	0	29
22	19 57 55	28 54 55	21 0	17	25	19	27	8	7	0	29
23	20 1 52	29 52 14	4♊ 6	19	26	20	27	8	7	0	29
24	20 5 48	0♌49 32	17 41	20	27	20	28	8	7	0	29
25	20 9 45	1 46 52	1♋44	22	29	21	28	8	7	0	29
26	20 13 41	2 44 13	16 13	24	0♍	22	28	8	7	0	29
27	20 17 38	3 41 34	1♌ 4	25	1	22	28	8	7	0	29
28	20 21 35	4 38 56	16 9	27	2	23	28	8	7	0	29
29	20 25 31	5 36 19	1♍16	28	3	24	28	8	7	0	29
30	20 29 28	6 33 42	16 16	0♍	5	24	29	8	7	0	29
31	20 33 24	7 31 6	1♎ 1	1	6	25	29	8	7	0	29

THE SUN ENTERS THE SIGN OF LEO ON JUL 23 AT 03:16.

DAY	TIME	☉	☽	☿	♀	♂	♃	♄	♅	♆	♇
	h m s	° ' "	° '	°	°	°	°	°	°	°	°
A 1	20 37 21	8♌28 30	15♎24	3♍	7♍	25♌	29♍	8♐R	7♌	0♏	29♌
U 2	20 41 17	9 25 55	29 25	4	8	26	29	8	7	0	29
G 3	20 45 14	10 23 21	13♏ 2	6	10	27	29	8	7	0	29
U 4	20 49 10	11 20 47	26 18	7	11	27	29	8	8	0	0♍
S 5	20 53 7	12 18 14	9♐16	8	12	28	0♎	8	8	0	0
T 6	20 57 4	13 15 42	21 58	9	13	29	0	8	8	0	0
7	21 1 0	14 13 11	4♑27	11	14	29	0	8	8	0	0
8	21 4 57	15 10 40	16 47	12	16	0♍	0	8	8	0	0
9	21 8 53	16 8 11	28 58	13	17	0	0	8	8	0	0
10	21 12 50	17 5 42	11♒ 3	14	18	1	1	8	8	0	0
11	21 16 46	18 3 15	23 2	15	19	2	1	8 D	8	0	0
12	21 20 43	19 0 48	4♓56	16	20	2	1	8	8	0	0
13	21 24 39	19 58 23	16 47	17	22	3	1	8	8	0	0
14	21 28 36	20 55 59	28 38	18	23	4	1	8	8	0	0
15	21 32 33	21 53 37	10♈30	19	24	4	1	8	8	0	0
16	21 36 29	22 51 16	22 27	20	25	5	2	8	8	0	0
17	21 40 26	23 48 56	4♉33	21	26	6	2	8	8	0	0
18	21 44 22	24 46 38	16 53	22	28	6	2	8	8	0	0
19	21 48 19	25 44 22	29 32	22	29	7	2	8	8	0	0
20	21 52 15	26 42 7	12♊35	23	0♎	7	2	8	9	0	0
21	21 56 12	27 39 54	26 5	23	1	8	3	8	9	0	0
22	22 0 8	28 37 43	10♋ 4	24	2	9	3	8	9	0	0
23	22 4 5	29 35 34	24 33	24	4	9	3	8	9	0	0
24	22 8 2	0♍33 26	9♌26	25	5	10	3	8	9	0	0
25	22 11 58	1 31 19	24 37	25	6	11	3	8	9	0	0
26	22 15 55	2 29 14	9♍56	25	7	11	4	8	9	0	0
27	22 19 51	3 27 11	25 10	25 R	8	12	4	8	9	0	0
28	22 23 48	4 25 9	10♎ 9	25	10	13	4	8	9	0	0
29	22 27 44	5 23 8	24 46	25	11	13	4	8	9	0	0
30	22 31 41	6 21 9	8♏57	25	12	14	4	8	9	0	0
31	22 35 37	7 19 11	22 41	25	13	14	5	8	9	0	0

THE SUN ENTERS THE SIGN OF VIRGO ON AUG 23 AT 10:08.

DAY	TIME	☉	☽	☿	♀	♂	♃	♄	♅	♆	♇
	h m s	° ' "	° '	°	°	°	°	°	°	°	°
S 1	22 39 34	8♍17 15	5♐59	24♍R	14♎	15♍	5♎	8♐	9♌	1♏	0♍
E 2	22 43 30	9 15 20	18 54	24	15	16	5	8	9	1	0
P 3	22 47 27	10 13 26	1♑31	23	17	16	5	8	9	1	0
T 4	22 51 24	11 11 34	13 53	22	18	17	5	8	9	1	1
E 5	22 55 20	12 9 43	26 3	22	19	18	6	8	9	1	1
M 6	22 59 17	13 7 54	8♒ 6	21	20	18	6	8	9	1	1
B 7	23 3 13	14 6 6	20 3	20	21	19	6	8	10	1	1
E 8	23 7 10	15 4 20	1♓57	19	23	20	6	8	10	1	1
R 9	23 11 6	16 2 35	13 49	18	24	20	6	8	10	1	1
10	23 15 3	17 0 53	25 40	17	25	21	7	8	10	1	1
11	23 18 59	17 59 12	7♈33	16	26	22	7	8	10	1	1
12	23 22 56	18 57 33	19 30	15	27	22	7	8	10	1	1
13	23 26 53	19 55 56	1♉32	14	29	23	7	8	10	1	1
14	23 30 49	20 54 21	13 43	13	0♏	23	7	9	10	1	1
15	23 34 46	21 52 49	26 6	12	1	24	8	9	10	1	1
16	23 38 42	22 51 18	8♊46	12	2	25	8	9	10	1	1
17	23 42 39	23 49 50	21 46	12	3	25	8	9	10	1	1
18	23 46 35	24 48 24	5♋10	11	4	26	8	9	10	1	1
19	23 50 32	25 47 0	19 1	11 D	6	27	9	9	10	1	1
20	23 54 28	26 45 38	3♌18	11	7	27	9	9	10	1	1
21	23 58 25	27 44 19	18 0	11	8	28	9	9	10	1	1
22	0 2 22	28 43 1	3♍ 2	12	9	29	9	9	10	1	1
23	0 6 18	29 41 46	18 14	12	10	29	9	9	10	1	1
24	0 10 15	0♎40 33	3♎27	13	11	0♎	10	9	10	1	1
25	0 14 11	1 39 21	18 30	14	13	1	10	9	10	1	1
26	0 18 8	2 38 12	3♏14	15	14	1	10	9	10	1	1
27	0 22 4	3 37 4	17 34	16	15	2	10	9	11	1	1
28	0 26 1	4 35 59	1♐27	17	16	2	10	9	11	1	1
29	0 29 57	5 34 55	14 52	18	17	3	11	9	11	1	1
30	0 33 54	6 33 53	27 52	20	18	4	11	10	11	1	1

THE SUN ENTERS THE SIGN OF LIBRA ON SEP 23 AT 07:27.

SIDEREAL SUN MOON MERCURY VENUS MARS JUPITER SATURN URANUS NEPTUNE PLUTO

DAY	TIME	☉	☽	☿	♀	♂	♃	♄	♅	♆	♇
	h m s	° ' "	° '	°	°	°	°	°	°	°	°
O 1	0 37 51	7♎32 52	10♑31	21♍	20♏	4♎	11♎	10♐	11♌	1♏	1♍
C 2	0 41 47	8 31 54	22 52	23	21	5	11	10	11	1	1
T 3	0 45 44	9 30 57	5♒ 0	24	22	6	12	10	11	1	1
O 4	0 49 40	10 30 1	16 58	26	23	6	12	10	11	2	1
B 5	0 53 37	11 29 8	28 52	28	24	7	12	10	11	2	1
E 6	0 57 33	12 28 16	10♓43	29	25	8	12	10	11	2	1
R 7	1 1 30	13 27 27	22 35	1♎	26	8	12	10	11	2	2
8	1 5 26	14 26 39	4♈30	3	28	9	13	10	11	2	2
9	1 9 23	15 25 53	16 29	4	29	10	13	10	11	2	2
10	1 13 19	16 25 10	28 35	6	0♐	10	13	10	11	2	2
11	1 17 16	17 24 28	10♉48	8	1	11	13	10	11	2	2
12	1 21 13	18 23 49	23 12	10	2	12	14	11	11	2	2
13	1 25 9	19 23 12	5♊47	11	3	12	14	11	11	2	2
14	1 29 6	20 22 37	18 36	13	5	13	14	11	11	2	2
15	1 33 2	21 22 5	1♋42	15	6	14	14	11	11	2	2
16	1 36 59	22 21 34	15 6	17	7	14	14	11	11	2	2
17	1 40 55	23 21 6	28 50	18	8	15	15	11	11	2	2
18	1 44 52	24 20 41	12♌55	20	9	16	15	11	11	2	2
19	1 48 48	25 20 18	27 20	22	10	16	15	11	11	2	2
20	1 52 45	26 19 57	12♍ 0	23	11	17	15	11	11	2	2
21	1 56 42	27 19 38	26 51	25	12	17	15	11	11	2	2
22	2 0 38	28 19 21	11♎46	27	14	18	16	11	11	2	2
23	2 4 35	29 19 6	26 37	29	15	19	16	12	11	2	2
24	2 8 31	0♏18 54	11♏15	0♏	16	19	16	12	11	2	2
25	2 12 28	1 18 43	25 34	2	17	20	16	12	11	2	2
26	2 16 24	2 18 34	9♐30	4	18	21	17	12	11	2	2
27	2 20 21	3 18 28	23 1	5	19	21	17	12	11	2	2
28	2 24 17	4 18 22	6♑ 8	7	20	22	17	12	11	2	2
29	2 28 14	5 18 19	18 51	8	21	23	17	12	11	2	2
30	2 32 11	6 18 17	1♒15	10	22	23	17	12	12	2	2
31	2 36 7	7 18 16	13 25	12	24	24	18	12	12	3	2

THE SUN ENTERS THE SIGN OF SCORPIO ON OCT 23 AT 16:25.

DAY	TIME	☉	☽	☿	♀	♂	♃	♄	♅	♆	♇
	h m s	° ' "	° '	°	°	°	°	°	°	°	°
N 1	2 40 4	8♏18 18	25♒23	13♏	25♐	25♎	18♎	12♐	12♌	3♏	2♍
O 2	2 44 0	9 18 21	7♓16	15	26	25	18	13	12	3	2
V 3	2 47 57	10 18 25	19 6	16	27	26	18	13	12	3	2
E 4	2 51 53	11 18 31	0♈59	18	28	27	18	13	12	3	2
M 5	2 55 50	12 18 39	12 58	20	29	27	19	13	12	3	2
B 6	2 59 46	13 18 48	25 5	21	0♑	28	19	13	12	3	2
E 7	3 3 43	14 18 59	7♉23	23	1	29	19	13	12	3	2
R 8	3 7 40	15 19 12	19 52	24	2	29	19	13	12	3	2
9	3 11 36	16 19 27	2♊35	26	3	0♏	19	13	12	3	2
10	3 15 33	17 19 44	15 31	27	4	1	20	13	12	3	2
11	3 19 29	18 20 2	28 40	29	5	1	20	14	12	3	2
12	3 23 26	19 20 22	12♋ 3	0♐	6	2	20	14	12	3	2
13	3 27 22	20 20 45	25 39	2	7	3	20	14	12	3	2
14	3 31 19	21 21 9	9♌27	3	8	3	20	14	12	3	2
15	3 35 15	22 21 35	23 27	5	9	4	21	14	12	3	2
16	3 39 12	23 22 3	7♍37	6	10	5	21	14	12	3	2
17	3 43 9	24 22 33	21 57	8	12	5	21	14	12 R	3	2
18	3 47 5	25 23 4	6♎21	9	13	6	21	14	12	3	2
19	3 51 2	26 23 38	20 48	11	14	7	21	14	12	3	2
20	3 54 58	27 24 13	5♏13	12	15	7	22	15	12	3	2
21	3 58 55	28 24 50	19 30	14	16	8	22	15	12	3	2
22	4 2 51	29 25 28	3♐34	15	17	9	22	15	12	3	2
23	4 6 48	0♐26 8	17 22	17	18	9	22	15	12	3	2
24	4 10 44	1 26 49	0♑50	18	18	10	22	15	12	3	2
25	4 14 41	2 27 31	13 57	20	19	11	23	15	12	3	2
26	4 18 38	3 28 15	26 43	21	20	12	23	15	12	3	2
27	4 22 34	4 28 59	9♒10	23	21	12	23	15	12	3	2
28	4 26 31	5 29 45	21 21	24	22	13	23	15	12	4	2
29	4 30 27	6 30 31	3♓21	25	23	14	23	16	12	4	2
30	4 34 24	7 31 19	15 13	27	24	14	24	16	12	4	2

THE SUN ENTERS THE SIGN OF SAGITTARIUS ON NOV 22 AT 13:40.

DAY	TIME	☉	☽	☿	♀	♂	♃	♄	♅	♆	♇
	h m s	° ' "	° '	°	°	°	°	°	°	°	°
D 1	4 38 20	8♐32 7	27♓ 4	28♐	25♑	15♏	24♎	16♐	12♌R	4♏	2♍
E 2	4 42 17	9 32 57	8♈57	29	26	16	24	16	12	4	2
C 3	4 46 13	10 33 47	20 58	1♑	27	16	24	16	12	4	2
E 4	4 50 10	11 34 38	3♉10	2	28	17	24	16	12	4	2 R
M 5	4 54 7	12 35 30	15 38	3	29	18	24	16	12	4	2
B 6	4 58 3	13 36 24	28 23	4	29	18	25	16	12	4	2
E 7	5 2 0	14 37 18	11♊26	5	0♒	19	25	17	11	4	2
R 8	5 5 56	15 38 13	24 46	7	1	20	25	17	11	4	2
9	5 9 53	16 39 9	8♋23	7	2	20	25	17	11	4	2
10	5 13 49	17 40 6	22 12	8	3	21	25	17	11	4	2
11	5 17 46	18 41 4	6♌12	9	4	22	25	17	11	4	2
12	5 21 42	[illegible] 42 3	20 17	10	4	22	26	17	11	4	2
13	5 25 39	2[illegible] 43 4	4♍26	11	5	23	26	17	11	4	2
14	5 29 36	21 44 5	18 35	11	6	24	26	17	11	4	2
15	5 33 32	22 45 7	2♎43	11	7	24	26	17	11	4	2
16	5 37 29	23 46 10	16 48	12 R	7	25	26	18	11	4	2
17	5 41 25	24 47 15	0♏49	12	8	26	26	18	11	4	2
18	5 45 22	25 48 20	14 45	11	9	27	27	18	11	4	2
19	5 49 18	26 49 26	28 34	11	9	27	27	18	11	4	2
20	5 53 15	27 50 33	12♐13	10	10	28	27	18	11	4	2
21	5 57 11	28 51 40	25 41	10	10	29	27	18	11	4	2
22	6 1 8	29 52 48	8♑54	9	11	29	27	18	11	4	2
23	6 5 5	0♑53 57	21 52	8	12	0♐	27	18	11	4	2
24	6 9 1	1 55 6	4♒33	6	12	1	27	19	11	4	2
25	6 12 58	2 56 14	16 58	5	13	1	28	19	11	4	2
26	6 16 54	3 57 23	29 9	4	13	2	28	19	11	4	2
27	6 20 51	4 58 32	11♓ 8	2	14	3	28	19	11	4	2
28	6 24 47	5 59 41	23 0	1	14	3	28	19	11	4	2
29	6 28 44	7 0 50	4♈49	0	14	4	28	19	11	4	2
30	6 32 40	8 1 59	16 41	29♐	15	5	28	19	11	4	2
31	6 36 37	9 3 8	28 41	28	15	5	28	19	11	4	2

THE SUN ENTERS THE SIGN OF CAPRICORN ON DEC 22 AT 02:50.

♈ ARIES ♉ TAURUS ♊ GEMINI ♋ CANCER ♌ LEO ♍ VIRGO ♎ LIBRA ♏ SCORPIO ♐ SAGITTARIUS ♑ CAPRICORN ♒ AQUARIUS ♓ PISCES

SIDEREAL SUN MOON MERCURY VENUS MARS JUPITER SATURN URANUS NEPTUNE PLUTO

DAY	TIME	☉	☽	☿	♀	♂	♃	♄	♅	♆	♇
	h m s	° ' "	° '	°	°	°	°	°	°	°	°
J 1	6 40 34	10♑ 4 17	10♉54	27♐R	15♒	6♐	29♎	19♐	11♌R	4♏	2♍R
A 2	6 44 30	11 5 25	23 25	26	16	7	29	20	11	4	2
N 3	6 48 27	12 6 34	6♊18	26	16	8	29	20	11	4	2
U 4	6 52 23	13 7 42	19 34	25	16	8	29	20	11	4	2
A 5	6 56 20	14 8 50	3♋15	25 D	16	9	29	20	11	5	2
R 6	7 0 16	15 9 58	17 16	25	16	10	29	20	11	5	2
Y 7	7 4 13	16 11 6	1♌35	25	16	10	29	20	11	5	2
8	7 8 9	17 12 14	16 4	26	16 R	11	29	20	11	5	2
9	7 12 6	18 13 22	0♍37	26	16	12	0♏	20	11	5	2
10	7 16 3	19 14 29	15 7	27	16	12	0	20	10	5	2
11	7 19 59	20 15 37	29 29	27	16	13	0	21	10	5	2
12	7 23 56	21 16 45	13♎41	28	16	14	0	21	10	5	2
13	7 27 52	22 17 52	27 40	29	16	15	0	21	10	5	2
14	7 31 49	23 19 0	11♏27	0♑	16	15	0	21	10	5	2
15	7 35 45	24 20 7	25 3	1	15	16	0	21	10	5	2
16	7 39 42	25 21 15	8♐27	2	15	17	0	21	10	5	2
17	7 43 38	26 22 22	21 42	3	15	17	0	21	10	5	2
18	7 47 35	27 23 28	4♑46	4	14	18	0	21	10	5	2
19	7 51 32	28 24 35	17 38	5	14	19	0	21	10	5	2
20	7 55 28	29 25 40	0♒20	6	13	20	1	21	10	5	2
21	7 59 25	0♒26 45	12 49	7	13	20	1	22	10	5	2
22	8 3 21	1 27 50	25 5	8	12	21	1	22	10	5	2
23	8 7 18	2 28 53	7♓11	10	12	22	1	22	10	5	2
24	8 11 14	3 29 55	19 7	11	11	22	1	22	10	5	2
25	8 15 11	4 30 57	0♈57	12	11	23	1	22	10	5	2
26	8 19 7	5 31 57	12 45	13	10	24	1	22	10	5	2
27	8 23 4	6 32 57	24 34	15	10	24	1	22	10	5	2
28	8 27 1	7 33 55	6♉31	16	9	25	1	22	10	5	2
29	8 30 57	8 34 52	18 41	17	8	26	1	22	10	5	2
30	8 34 54	9 35 48	1♊10	19	8	27	1	22	10	5	2
31	8 38 50	10 36 43	14 2	20	7	27	1	23	10	5	2

THE SUN ENTERS THE SIGN OF AQUARIUS ON JAN 20 AT 13:29.

DAY	TIME	☉	☽	☿	♀	♂	♃	♄	♅	♆	♇
	h m s	° ' "	° '	°	°	°	°	°	°	°	°
F 1	8 42 47	11♒37 36	27♊21	22♑	6♒R	28♐	1♏	23♐	10♌R	5♏	2♍R
E 2	8 46 43	12 38 29	11♋ 8	23	6	29	1	23	9	5	2
B 3	8 50 40	13 39 20	25 23	25	5	29	1	23	9	5	2
R 4	8 54 37	14 40 9	10♌ 1	26	5	0♑	1	23	9	5	1
U 5	8 58 33	15 40 58	24 54	28	4	1	1	23	9	5 R	1
A 6	9 2 30	16 41 45	9♍53	29	4	2	2	23	9	5	1
R 7	9 6 26	17 42 31	24 49	1♒	3	2	2	23	9	5	1
Y 8	9 10 23	18 43 17	9♎34	2	3	3	2	23	9	5	1
9	9 14 19	19 44 1	24 2	4	2	4	2	23	9	5	1
10	9 18 16	20 44 44	8♏11	5	2	4	2	23	9	5	1
11	9 22 12	21 45 26	21 59	7	2	5	2	23	9	5	1
12	9 26 9	22 46 8	5♐29	8	1	6	2	24	9	5	1
13	9 30 5	23 46 48	18 41	10	1	7	2	24	9	5	1
14	9 34 2	24 47 27	1♑39	12	1	7	2	24	9	5	1
15	9 37 59	25 48 5	14 24	13	1	8	2 R	24	9	5	1
16	9 41 55	26 48 41	26 57	15	1	9	2	24	9	5	1
17	9 45 52	27 49 16	9♒21	16	1	9	2	24	9	5	1
18	9 49 48	28 49 50	21 35	18	1 D	10	2	24	9	5	1
19	9 53 45	29 50 22	3♓41	20	1	11	2	24	9	5	1
20	9 57 41	0♓50 53	15 39	21	1	12	2	24	9	5	1
21	10 1 38	1 51 22	27 31	23	1	12	2	24	9	5	1
22	10 5 34	2 51 49	9♈19	25	1	13	2	24	9	5	1
23	10 9 31	3 52 14	21 6	27	1	14	2	24	9	5	1
24	10 13 28	4 52 38	2♉55	28	1	15	2	24	9	5	1
25	10 17 24	5 53 0	14 51	0♓	2	15	2	24	9	5	1
26	10 21 21	6 53 20	26 59	2	2	16	1	25	9	5	1
27	10 25 17	7 53 37	9♊24	4	2	17	1	25	8	5	1
28	10 29 14	8 53 53	22 11	6	2	17	1	25	8	5	1

THE SUN ENTERS THE SIGN OF PISCES ON FEB 19 AT 03:49.

DAY	TIME	☉	☽	☿	♀	♂	♃	♄	♅	♆	♇
	h m s	° ' "	° '	°	°	°	°	°	°	°	°
M 1	10 33 10	9♓54 7	5♋24	7♓	3♒	18♑	1♏R	25♐	8♌R	5♏R	1♍R
A 2	10 37 7	10 54 19	19 7	9	3	19	1	25	8	5	1
R 3	10 41 3	11 54 29	3♌19	11	4	20	1	25	8	5	1
C 4	10 45 0	12 54 36	17 59	13	4	20	1	25	8	5	1
H 5	10 48 57	13 54 42	2♍59	15	5	21	1	25	8	5	1
6	10 52 53	14 54 46	18 12	17	5	22	1	25	8	5	1
7	10 56 50	15 54 48	3♎25	19	6	22	1	25	8	5	1
8	11 0 46	16 54 48	18 31	21	6	23	1	25	8	5	1
9	11 4 43	17 54 47	3♏19	23	7	24	1	25	8	5	1
10	11 8 39	18 54 43	17 45	25	7	25	1	25	8	4	1
11	11 12 36	19 54 39	1♐46	27	8	25	1	25	8	4	1
12	11 16 32	20 54 33	15 22	29	9	26	1	25	8	4	1
13	11 20 29	21 54 25	28 35	1♈	9	27	1	25	8	4	1
14	11 24 26	22 54 15	11♑28	2	10	28	1	25	8	4	1
15	11 28 22	23 54 4	24 4	4	11	28	1	25	8	4	1
16	11 32 19	24 53 51	6♒26	6	11	29	0	25	8	4	0
17	11 36 15	25 53 36	18 37	8	12	0♒	0	25	8	4	0
18	11 40 12	26 53 19	0♓39	10	13	1	0	25	8	4	0
19	11 44 8	27 53 0	12 35	12	14	1	0	25	8	4	0
20	11 48 5	28 52 40	24 26	14	14	2	0	26	8	4	0
21	11 52 1	29 52 17	6♈15	15	15	3	0	26	8	4	0
22	11 55 58	0♈51 53	18 3	17	16	3	0	26	8	4	0
23	11 59 54	1 51 26	29 52	19	17	4	0	26	8	4	0
24	12 3 51	2 50 57	11♉45	20	18	5	0	26	8	4	0
25	12 7 48	3 50 26	23 46	22	18	6	0	26	8	4	0
26	12 11 44	4 49 53	5♊57	23	19	6	29♎	26	8	4	0
27	12 15 41	5 49 17	18 23	24	20	7	29	26	8	4	0
28	12 19 37	6 48 40	1♋ 8	25	21	8	29	26	8	4	0
29	12 23 34	7 48 0	14 16	27	22	9	29	26	8	4	0
30	12 27 30	8 47 17	27 50	27	23	9	29	26	8	4	0
31	12 31 27	9 46 33	11♌51	28	24	10	29	26	8	4	0

THE SUN ENTERS THE SIGN OF ARIES ON MAR 21 AT 03:06.

DAY	TIME	☉	☽	☿	♀	♂	♃	♄	♅	♆	♇
	h m s	° ' "	° '	°	°	°	°	°	°	°	°
A 1	12 35 23	10♈45 45	26♌18	29♈	25♒	11♒	29♎R	26♐	8♌R	4♏R	0♍R
P 2	12 39 20	11 44 56	11♍ 9	0♉	26	12	29	26	8	4	0
R 3	12 43 17	12 44 4	26 15	0	27	12	29	26	8	4	0
I 4	12 47 13	13 43 11	11♎29	0	27	13	28	26 R	8	4	0
L 5	12 51 10	14 42 15	26 41	1	28	14	28	26	8	4	0
6	12 55 6	15 41 17	11♏40	1 R	29	14	28	26	8	4	0
7	12 59 3	16 40 18	26 20	1	0♓	15	28	26	8	4	0
8	13 2 59	17 39 16	10♐34	1	1	16	28	26	8	4	0
9	13 6 56	18 38 13	24 22	1	2	17	28	26	8	4	0
10	13 10 52	19 37 8	7♑44	0	3	17	28	26	8	4	0
11	13 14 49	20 36 2	20 41	0	4	18	28	26	8	4	0
12	13 18 46	21 34 54	3♒17	29♈	5	19	27	26	8	4	0
13	13 22 42	22 33 43	15 35	29	6	20	27	26	8	4	0
14	13 26 39	23 32 32	27 41	28	7	20	27	26	8	4	0
15	13 30 35	24 31 18	9♓37	28	8	21	27	26	8 D	4	0
16	13 34 32	25 30 2	21 27	27	9	22	27	26	8	4	0
17	13 38 28	26 28 45	3♈15	26	10	23	27	26	8	4	0
18	13 42 25	27 27 26	15 3	25	11	23	27	26	8	4	0
19	13 46 21	28 26 5	26 53	25	12	24	27	26	8	4	0
20	13 50 18	29 24 42	8♉49	24	13	25	26	26	8	4	0
21	13 54 14	0♉23 17	20 51	23	14	26	26	25	8	4	0
22	13 58 11	1 21 51	3♊ 2	23	16	26	26	25	8	3	0
23	14 2 8	2 20 22	15 24	22	17	27	26	25	8	3	0
24	14 6 4	3 18 51	28 0	22	18	28	26	25	8	3	0
25	14 10 1	4 17 18	10♋51	21	19	28	26	25	8	3	0
26	14 13 57	5 15 43	24 0	21	20	29	26	25	8	3	0
27	14 17 54	6 14 6	7♌30	20	21	0♓	26	25	8	3	0
28	14 21 50	7 12 26	21 21	20	22	1	25	25	8	3	0
29	14 25 47	8 10 45	5♍33	20	23	1	25	25	8	3	0
30	14 29 43	9 9 1	20 5	20 D	24	2	25	25	8	3	0

THE SUN ENTERS THE SIGN OF TAURUS ON APR 20 AT 14:27.

DAY	TIME	☉	☽	☿	♀	♂	♃	♄	♅	♆	♇
	h m s	° ' "	° '	°	°	°	°	°	°	°	°
M 1	14 33 40	10♉ 7 15	4♎53	20♈	25♓	3♓	25♎R	25♐R	8♌	3♏R	0♍R
A 2	14 37 37	11 5 28	19 51	20	26	4	25	25	8	3	0
Y 3	14 41 33	12 3 38	4♏51	20	27	4	25	25	8	3	0
4	14 45 30	13 1 47	19 45	21	28	5	25	25	8	3	0
5	14 49 26	13 59 54	4♐25	21	29	6	25	25	8	3	0
6	14 53 23	14 58 0	18 45	21	1♈	7	24	25	8	3	0
7	14 57 19	15 56 4	2♑40	22	2	7	24	25	8	3	0
8	15 1 16	16 54 7	16 9	22	3	8	24	25	8	3	0
9	15 5 12	17 52 8	29 12	23	4	9	24	25	8	3	0
10	15 9 9	18 50 8	11♒52	24	5	9	24	25	8	3	0
11	15 13 6	19 48 6	24 12	24	6	10	24	25	8	3	0 D
12	15 17 2	20 46 4	6♓17	25	7	11	24	25	8	3	0
13	15 20 59	21 44 0	18 12	26	8	12	24	25	8	3	0
14	15 24 55	22 41 54	0♈ 1	27	9	12	24	25	8	3	0
15	15 28 52	23 39 48	11 48	28	11	13	24	24	8	3	0
16	15 32 48	24 37 40	23 38	29	12	14	23	24	8	3	0
17	15 36 45	25 35 30	5♉34	0♉	13	15	23	24	8	3	0
18	15 40 41	26 33 20	17 38	1	14	15	23	24	8	3	0
19	15 44 38	27 31 8	29 53	2	15	16	23	24	8	3	0
20	15 48 35	28 28 54	12♊19	3	16	17	23	24	8	3	0
21	15 52 31	29 26 40	24 59	5	17	18	23	24	8	3	0
22	15 56 28	0♊24 23	7♋52	6	18	18	23	24	8	3	0
23	16 0 24	1 22 6	20 59	7	20	19	23	24	8	3	0
24	16 4 21	2 19 47	4♌20	9	21	20	23	24	8	3	0
25	16 8 17	3 17 26	17 55	10	22	20	23	24	8	3	0
26	16 12 14	4 15 4	1♍44	12	23	21	23	24	8	3	0
27	16 16 10	5 12 40	15 47	13	24	22	23	24	8	3	0
28	16 20 7	6 10 14	0♎ 3	15	25	23	22	24	8	3	0
29	16 24 4	7 7 48	14 29	16	26	23	22	24	8	3	0
30	16 28 0	8 5 19	29 3	18	28	24	22	24	8	3	0
31	16 31 57	9 2 50	13♏40	19	29	25	22	23	8	2	0

THE SUN ENTERS THE SIGN OF GEMINI ON MAY 21 AT 13:51.

DAY	TIME	☉	☽	☿	♀	♂	♃	♄	♅	♆	♇
	h m s	° ' "	° '	°	°	°	°	°	°	°	°
J 1	16 35 53	10♊ 0 19	28♏15	21♉	0♉	26♓	22♎R	23♐R	8♌	2♏R	0♍
U 2	16 39 50	10 57 48	12♐41	23	1	26	22	23	9	2	0
N 3	16 43 46	11 55 15	26 52	25	2	27	22	23	9	2	0
E 4	16 47 43	12 52 42	10♑43	26	3	28	22	23	9	2	0
5	16 51 39	13 50 7	24 12	28	4	28	22	23	9	2	0
6	16 55 36	14 47 32	7♒16	0♊	6	29	22	23	9	2	0
7	16 59 33	15 44 56	19 59	2	7	0⊙	22	23	9	2	0
8	17 3 29	16 42 20	2♓21	4	8	1♈	22	23	9	2	0
9	17 7 26	17 39 43	14 27	6	9	1	22	23	9	2	0
10	17 11 22	18 37 5	26 22	8	10	2	22	23	9	2	0
11	17 15 19	19 34 27	8♈12	10	11	3	22	23	9	2	0
12	17 19 15	20 31 48	20 0	12	13	3	22	23	9	2	0
13	17 23 12	21 29 9	1♉53	15	14	4	22	22	9	2	0
14	17 27 8	22 26 29	13 54	17	15	5	22	22	9	2	0
15	17 31 5	23 23 49	26 7	19	16	6	22	22	9	2	0
16	17 35 2	24 21 8	8♊35	21	17	6	22	22	9	2	0
17	17 38 58	25 18 27	21 19	23	18	7	22	22	9	2	0
18	17 42 55	26 15 45	4♋20	25	19	8	22	22	9	2	0
19	17 46 51	27 13 3	17 36	28	21	8	22 D	22	9	2	0
20	17 50 48	28 10 20	1♌ 5	0♋	22	9	22	22	9	2	0
21	17 54 44	29 7 37	14 47	2	23	10	22	22	9	2	0
22	17 58 41	0♋ 4 52	28 37	4	24	10	22	22	9	2	0
23	18 2 37	1 2 7	12♍35	6	25	11	22	22	9	2	0
24	18 6 34	1 59 22	26 39	8	27	12	22	22	10	2	0
25	18 10 31	2 56 36	10♎46	11	28	12	22	22	10	2	0
26	18 14 27	3 53 49	24 57	13	29	13	22	22	10	2	0
27	18 18 24	4 51 1	9♏10	15	0♊	14	22	21	10	2	0
28	18 22 20	5 48 13	23 23	17	1	15	22	21	10	2	0
29	18 26 17	6 45 25	7♐32	19	2	15	22	21	10	2	0
30	18 30 13	7 42 36	21 35	21	4	16	22	21	10	2	0

THE SUN ENTERS THE SIGN OF CANCER ON JUN 21 AT 21:57.

♈ ARIES ♉ TAURUS ♊ GEMINI ♋ CANCER ♌ LEO ♍ VIRGO ♎ LIBRA ♏ SCORPIO ♐ SAGITTARIUS ♑ CAPRICORN ♒ AQUARIUS ♓ PISCES

SIDEREAL SUN MOON MERCURY VENUS MARS JUPITER SATURN URANUS NEPTUNE PLUTO

DAY	TIME	☉	☽	☿	♀	♂	♃	♄	♅	♆	♇
	h m s	° ' "	° '	°	°	°	°	°	°	°	°
J 1	18 34 10	8♋39 48	5♑26	23♋	5♊	17♈	22♎	21♐R	10♌	2♏R	0♍
U 2	18 38 7	9 36 59	19 2	25	6	17	22	21	10	2	0
L 3	18 42 3	10 34 10	2♒20	26	7	18	22	21	10	2	0
Y 4	18 46 0	11 31 21	15 18	28	8	19	22	21	10	2	0
5	18 49 56	12 28 32	27 57	0♌	9	19	22	21	10	2	0
6	18 53 53	13 25 43	10♓17	2	11	20	22	21	10	2	0
7	18 57 49	14 22 54	22 23	4	12	21	22	21	10	2	1
8	19 1 46	15 20 6	4♈18	5	13	21	22	21	10	2	1
9	19 5 42	16 17 18	16 8	7	14	22	22	21	10	2	1
10	19 9 39	17 14 31	27 57	8	15	23	22	21	10	2	1
11	19 13 36	18 11 44	9♉51	10	17	23	22	21	10	2	1
12	19 17 32	19 8 57	21 56	12	18	24	23	20	11	2	1
13	19 21 29	20 6 11	4♊15	13	19	25	23	20	11	2	1
14	19 25 25	21 3 26	16 53	15	20	25	23	20	11	2 D	1
15	19 29 22	22 0 41	29 51	16	21	26	23	20	11	2	1
16	19 33 18	22 57 56	13♋11	18	23	27	23	20	11	2	1
17	19 37 15	23 55 12	26 49	19	24	27	23	20	11	2	1
18	19 41 11	24 52 28	10♌44	20	25	28	23	20	11	2	1
19	19 45 8	25 49 44	24 51	22	26	29	23	20	11	2	1
20	19 49 5	26 47 1	9♍ 5	23	27	29	23	20	11	2	1
21	19 53 1	27 44 18	23 21	24	29	0♉	23	20	11	2	1
22	19 56 58	28 41 35	7♎36	25	0♋	0	23	20	11	2	1
23	20 0 54	29 38 52	21 47	26	1	1	23	20	11	2	1
24	20 4 51	0♌36 10	5♏53	28	2	2	24	20	11	2	1
25	20 8 47	1 33 28	19 54	29	3	2	24	20	11	2	1
26	20 12 44	2 30 46	3♐47	0♍	5	3	24	20	11	2	1
27	20 16 40	3 28 5	17 34	1	6	4	24	20	11	2	1
28	20 20 37	4 25 25	1♑12	1	7	4	24	20	11	2	1
29	20 24 34	5 22 45	14 39	2	8	5	24	20	12	2	1
30	20 28 30	6 20 5	27 53	3	9	5	24	20	12	2	1
31	20 32 27	7 17 27	10♒53	4	11	6	24	20	12	2	1

THE SUN ENTERS THE SIGN OF LEO ON JUL 23 AT 08:51.

DAY	TIME	☉	☽	☿	♀	♂	♃	♄	♅	♆	♇
	h m s	° ' "	° '	°	°	°	°	°	°	°	°
A 1	20 36 23	8♌14 49	23♒37	5♍	12♋	7♉	24♎	20♐R	12♌	2♏	1♍
U 2	20 40 20	9 12 12	6♓ 6	5	13	7	24	19	12	2	1
G 3	20 44 16	10 9 36	18 21	6	14	8	25	19	12	2	1
U 4	20 48 13	11 7 1	0♈23	6	15	8	25	19	12	2	1
S 5	20 52 9	12 4 27	12 16	7	17	9	25	19	12	2	1
T 6	20 56 6	13 1 55	24 4	7	18	10	25	19	12	2	1
7	21 0 3	13 59 24	5♉52	7	19	10	25	19	12	2	1
8	21 3 59	14 56 54	17 46	8	20	11	25	19	12	2	1
9	21 7 56	15 54 25	29 51	8 R	21	11	25	19	12	2	1
10	21 11 52	16 51 58	12♊13	8	23	12	25	19	12	2	2
11	21 15 49	17 49 32	24 54	8	24	12	26	19	12	2	2
12	21 19 45	18 47 7	8♋ 0	7	25	13	26	19	12	2	2
13	21 23 42	19 44 44	21 30	7	26	13	26	19	12	2	2
14	21 27 38	20 42 22	5♌25	7	27	14	26	19	13	2	2
15	21 31 35	21 40 2	19 40	6	29	15	26	19	13	2	2
16	21 35 32	22 37 43	4♍11	6	0♌	15	26	19	13	2	2
17	21 39 28	23 35 24	18 49	5	1	16	26	19	13	2	2
18	21 43 25	24 33 7	3♎29	5	2	16	27	19	13	2	2
19	21 47 21	25 30 51	18 4	4	4	17	27	19	13	2	2
20	21 51 18	26 28 37	2♏29	3	5	17	27	19	13	2	2
21	21 55 14	27 26 23	16 42	2	6	18	27	19	13	2	2
22	21 59 11	28 24 11	0♐41	1	7	18	27	19	13	2	2
23	22 3 7	29 21 59	14 27	1	8	19	27	19	13	2	2
24	22 7 4	0♍19 49	27 58	0	10	19	28	19 D	13	2	2
25	22 11 0	1 17 40	11♑16	29♌	11	20	28	19	13	2	2
26	22 14 57	2 15 32	24 21	28	12	20	28	19	13	2	2
27	22 18 54	3 13 26	7♒14	27	13	21	28	19	13	3	2
28	22 22 50	4 11 21	19 54	27	15	21	28	19	13	3	2
29	22 26 47	5 9 17	2♓22	26	16	22	28	19	13	3	2
30	22 30 43	6 7 15	14 37	25	17	22	29	19	14	3	2
31	22 34 40	7 5 15	26 42	25	18	22	29	19	14	3	2

THE SUN ENTERS THE SIGN OF VIRGO ON AUG 23 AT 15:47.

DAY	TIME	☉	☽	☿	♀	♂	♃	♄	♅	♆	♇
	h m s	° ' "	° '	°	°	°	°	°	°	°	°
S 1	22 38 36	8♍ 3 16	8♈39	25♌R	19♌	23♉	29♎	19♐	14♌	3♏	2♍
E 2	22 42 33	9 1 19	20 28	25 D	21	23	29	19	14	3	2
P 3	22 46 29	9 59 24	2♉15	25	22	24	29	19	14	3	2
T 4	22 50 26	10 57 31	14 3	25	23	24	29	19	14	3	2
E 5	22 54 23	11 55 40	25 57	25	24	25	0♏	19	14	3	2
M 6	22 58 19	12 53 51	8♊ 1	26	26	25	0	19	14	3	2
B 7	23 2 16	13 52 4	20 20	26	27	25	0	19	14	3	2
E 8	23 6 12	14 50 18	3♋ 0	27	28	26	0	19	14	3	2
R 9	23 10 9	15 48 35	16 5	28	29	26	0	19	14	3	2
10	23 14 5	16 46 54	29 36	29	1♍	27	0	19	14	3	3
11	23 18 2	17 45 15	13♌35	0♍	2	27	1	19	14	3	3
12	23 21 58	18 43 38	27 58	1	3	27	1	19	14	3	3
13	23 25 55	19 42 3	12♍42	2	4	28	1	19	14	3	3
14	23 29 52	20 40 30	27 39	4	6	28	1	19	14	3	3
15	23 33 48	21 38 58	12♎41	5	7	28	1	19	14	3	3
16	23 37 45	22 37 28	27 38	7	8	29	2	20	14	3	3
17	23 41 41	23 36 1	12♏23	9	9	29	2	20	14	3	3
18	23 45 38	24 34 34	26 52	10	10	29	2	20	15	3	3
19	23 49 34	25 33 10	11♐ 0	12	12	29	2	20	15	3	3
20	23 53 31	26 31 47	24 48	14	13	0♊	2	20	15	3	3
21	23 57 27	27 30 26	8♑15	15	14	0	3	20	15	3	3
22	0 1 24	28 29 6	21 22	17	15	0	3	20	15	3	3
23	0 5 21	29 27 48	4♒13	19	17	0	3	20	15	3	3
24	0 9 17	0♎26 32	16 49	21	18	1	3	20	15	3	3
25	0 13 14	1 25 17	29 12	23	19	1	3	20	15	3	3
26	0 17 10	2 24 5	11♓24	25	20	1	4	20	15	3	3
27	0 21 7	3 22 54	23 27	26	22	1	4	20	15	3	3
28	0 25 3	4 21 45	5♈23	28	23	1	4	20	15	3	3
29	0 29 0	5 20 38	17 14	0♎	24	2	4	20	15	3	3
30	0 32 56	6 19 33	29 2	2	25	2	4	20	15	3	3

THE SUN ENTERS THE SIGN OF LIBRA ON SEP 23 AT 13:10.

SIDEREAL SUN MOON MERCURY VENUS MARS JUPITER SATURN URANUS NEPTUNE PLUTO

DAY	TIME	☉	☽	☿	♀	♂	♃	♄	♅	♆	♇
	h m s	° ' "	° '	°	°	°	°	°	°	°	°
O 1	0 36 53	7♎18 31	10♉49	4♎	27♍	2♊	5♏	20♐	15♌	4♏	3♍
C 2	0 40 49	8 17 30	22 38	6	28	2	5	20	15	4	3
T 3	0 44 46	9 16 32	4♊34	7	29	2	5	20	15	4	3
O 4	0 48 43	10 15 36	16 39	9	0♎	2	5	20	15	4	3
B 5	0 52 39	11 14 43	28 57	11	2	2	5	20	15	4	3
E 6	0 56 36	12 13 52	11♋34	13	3	2	6	21	15	4	3
R 7	1 0 32	13 13 3	24 33	14	4	2	6	21	15	4	3
8	1 4 29	14 12 16	7♌57	16	5	2	6	21	15	4	3
9	1 8 25	15 11 32	21 49	18	7	3	6	21	15	4	3
10	1 12 22	16 10 50	6♍ 7	19	8	3 R	6	21	16	4	3
11	1 16 18	17 10 10	20 49	21	9	3	7	21	16	4	3
12	1 20 15	18 9 32	5♎49	23	10	3	7	21	16	4	3
13	1 24 12	19 8 57	21 0	24	12	2	7	21	16	4	4
14	1 28 8	20 8 23	6♏12	26	13	2	7	21	16	4	4
15	1 32 5	21 7 52	21 15	28	14	2	8	21	16	4	4
16	1 36 1	22 7 22	6♐ 1	29	15	2	8	21	16	4	4
17	1 39 58	23 6 54	20 25	1♏	17	2	8	21	16	4	4
18	1 43 54	24 6 28	4♑23	3	18	2	8	21	16	4	4
19	1 47 51	25 6 4	17 55	4	19	2	8	22	16	4	4
20	1 51 47	26 5 42	1♒ 2	6	20	2	9	22	16	4	4
21	1 55 44	27 5 21	13 48	7	22	2	9	22	16	4	4
22	1 59 41	28 5 2	26 15	9	23	2	9	22	16	4	4
23	2 3 37	29 4 44	8♓27	10	24	1	9	22	16	4	4
24	2 7 34	0♏ 4 29	20 29	12	25	1	9	22	16	4	4
25	2 11 30	1 4 15	2♈23	14	27	1	10	22	16	4	4
26	2 15 27	2 4 3	14 12	15	28	1	10	22	16	4	4
27	2 19 23	3 3 52	26 0	17	29	1	10	22	16	4	4
28	2 23 20	4 3 44	7♉48	18	0♏	0	10	22	16	5	4
29	2 27 16	5 3 38	19 39	20	2	0	11	22	16	5	4
30	2 31 13	6 3 34	1♊35	21	3	0	11	22	16	5	4
31	2 35 9	7 3 32	13 37	23	4	29♉	11	23	16	5	4

THE SUN ENTERS THE SIGN OF SCORPIO ON OCT 23 AT 22:12.

DAY	TIME	☉	☽	☿	♀	♂	♃	♄	♅	♆	♇
	h m s	° ' "	° '	°	°	°	°	°	°	°	°
N 1	2 39 6	8♏ 3 32	25♊49	24♏	5♏	29♉R	11♏	23♐	16♌	5♏	4♍
O 2	2 43 3	9 3 34	8♋12	26	7	29	11	23	16	5	4
V 3	2 46 59	10 3 38	20 51	27	8	29	12	23	16	5	4
E 4	2 50 56	11 3 44	3♌47	28	9	28	12	23	16	5	4
M 5	2 54 52	12 3 52	17 3	0♐	10	28	12	23	16	5	4
B 6	2 58 49	13 4 2	0♍43	1	12	28	12	23	16	5	4
E 7	3 2 45	14 4 15	14 46	3	13	27	13	23	16	5	4
R 8	3 6 42	15 4 29	29 13	4	14	27	13	23	16	5	4
9	3 10 38	16 4 46	14♎ 1	5	15	27	13	23	16	5	4
10	3 14 35	17 5 4	29 3	7	17	26	13	24	16	5	4
11	3 18 32	18 5 25	14♏13	8	18	26	13	24	16	5	4
12	3 22 28	19 5 47	29 20	10	19	25	14	24	16	5	4
13	3 26 25	20 6 10	14♐16	11	20	25	14	24	16	5	4
14	3 30 21	21 6 36	28 51	12	22	25	14	24	16	5	4
15	3 34 18	22 7 2	13♑ 1	13	23	24	14	24	16	5	4
16	3 38 14	23 7 30	26 43	15	24	24	15	24	16	5	4
17	3 42 11	24 8 0	9♒56	16	25	24	15	24	16	5	4
18	3 46 7	25 8 30	22 44	17	27	23	15	24	16	5	4
19	3 50 4	26 9 2	5♓10	18	28	23	15	24	16	5	4
20	3 54 1	27 9 35	17 19	19	29	23	15	25	16	5	4
21	3 57 57	28 10 10	29 16	20	1♐	22	16	25	16	5	4
22	4 1 54	29 10 45	11♈ 6	21	2	22	16	25	16 R	5	4
23	4 5 50	0♐11 22	22 52	22	3	21	16	25	16	5	4
24	4 9 47	1 12 0	4♉40	23	4	21	16	25	16	5	4
25	4 13 43	2 12 40	16 31	24	6	21	16	25	16	6	4
26	4 17 40	3 13 20	28 29	24	7	21	17	25	16	6	4
27	4 21 36	4 14 2	10♊35	25	8	20	17	25	16	6	4
28	4 25 33	5 14 46	22 51	25	9	20	17	25	16	6	4
29	4 29 30	6 15 31	5♋16	26	11	20	17	26	16	6	4
30	4 33 26	7 16 17	17 53	26 R	12	19	18	26	16	6	4

THE SUN ENTERS THE SIGN OF SAGITTARIUS ON NOV 22 AT 19:30.

DAY	TIME	☉	☽	☿	♀	♂	♃	♄	♅	♆	♇
	h m s	° ' "	° '	°	°	°	°	°	°	°	°
D 1	4 37 23	8♐17 4	0♌42	26♐R	13♐	19♉R	18♏	26♐	16♌R	6♏	4♍
E 2	4 41 19	9 17 53	13 45	25	14	19	18	26	16	6	4
C 3	4 45 16	10 18 44	27 2	25	16	19	18	26	16	6	4
E 4	4 49 12	11 19 35	10♍35	24	17	18	18	26	16	6	4
M 5	4 53 9	12 20 29	24 26	24	18	18	19	26	16	6	4
B 6	4 57 5	13 21 23	8♎34	23	19	18	19	26	16	6	4 R
E 7	5 1 2	14 22 19	23 0	22	21	18	19	27	16	6	4
R 8	5 4 59	15 23 16	7♏41	20	22	18	19	27	16	6	4
9	5 8 55	16 24 14	22 32	19	23	17	19	27	16	6	4
10	5 12 52	17 25 14	7♐25	18	24	17	20	27	16	6	4
11	5 16 48	18 26 14	22 13	16	26	17	20	27	16	6	4
12	5 20 45	19 27 15	6♑46	15	27	17	20	27	16	6	4
13	5 24 41	20 28 17	20 58	14	28	17	20	27	16	6	4
14	5 28 38	21 29 20	4♒45	13	29	17	20	27	16	6	4
15	5 32 35	22 30 23	18 4	12	1♑	17	21	27	16	6	4
16	5 36 31	23 31 26	0♓57	11	2	17	21	28	16	6	4
17	5 40 28	24 32 30	13 26	10	3	17	21	28	16	6	4
18	5 44 24	25 33 35	25 37	10	4	17	21	28	16	6	4
19	5 48 21	26 34 39	7♈34	10	6	17	21	28	16	6	4
20	5 52 17	27 35 44	19 23	9 D	7	17 D	22	28	16	6	4
21	5 56 14	28 36 49	1♉10	9	8	17	22	28	16	6	4
22	6 0 10	29 37 55	12 59	10	9	17	22	28	16	6	4
23	6 4 7	0♑39 1	24 54	10	11	17	22	28	16	6	4
24	6 8 4	1 40 7	7♊ 0	11	12	17	22	29	16	6	4
25	6 12 0	2 41 13	19 18	11	13	17	23	29	16	6	4
26	6 15 57	3 42 20	1♋49	12	15	17	23	29	16	6	4
27	6 19 53	4 43 27	14 33	13	16	17	23	29	16	6	4
28	6 23 50	5 44 35	27 31	14	17	17	23	29	16	6	4
29	6 27 46	6 45 42	10♌40	14	18	17	23	29	16	6	4
30	6 31 43	7 46 50	24 1	15	20	17	24	29	16	7	4
31	6 35 39	8 47 59	7♍31	17	21	17	24	29	16	7	4

THE SUN ENTERS THE SIGN OF CAPRICORN ON DEC 22 AT 08:41.

♈ ARIES ♉ TAURUS ♊ GEMINI ♋ CANCER ♌ LEO ♍ VIRGO ♎ LIBRA ♏ SCORPIO ♐ SAGITTARIUS ♑ CAPRICORN ♒ AQUARIUS ♓ PISCES

SIDEREAL SUN MOON MERCURY VENUS MARS JUPITER SATURN URANUS NEPTUNE PLUTO

DAY	TIME	☉	☽	☿	♀	♂	♃	♄	♅	♆	♇
	h m s	° ' "	° '	°	°	°	°	°	°	°	°
J 1	6 39 36	9♑49 8	21♍10	18♐	22♑	17♉	24♏	29♐	16♌R	7♏	4♍R
A 2	6 43 33	10 50 17	5♎ 0	19	23	18	24	0♑	16	7	4
N 3	6 47 29	11 51 26	18 59	20	25	18	24	0	16	7	4
U 4	6 51 26	12 52 36	3♏ 8	21	26	18	25	0	16	7	4
A 5	6 55 22	13 53 46	17 26	22	27	18	25	0	16	7	4
R 6	6 59 19	14 54 57	1♐51	24	28	18	25	0	16	7	4
Y 7	7 3 15	15 56 7	16 18	25	0♒	18	25	0	15	7	4
8	7 7 12	16 57 18	0♑42	26	1	19	25	0	15	7	4
9	7 11 8	17 58 28	14 56	28	2	19	25	0	15	7	4
10	7 15 5	18 59 38	28 56	29	3	19	26	1	15	7	4
11	7 19 2	20 0 48	12♒35	0♑	5	19	26	1	15	7	4
12	7 22 58	21 1 58	25 51	2	6	20	26	1	15	7	4
13	7 26 55	22 3 7	8♓43	3	7	20	26	1	15	7	4
14	7 30 51	23 4 15	21 14	5	8	20	26	1	15	7	4
15	7 34 48	24 5 23	3♈27	6	10	20	26	1	15	7	4
16	7 38 44	25 6 30	15 26	8	11	21	27	1	15	7	4
17	7 42 41	26 7 36	27 16	9	12	21	27	1	15	7	4
18	7 46 37	27 8 41	9♉ 4	10	13	21	27	1	15	7	4
19	7 50 34	28 9 46	20 54	12	15	22	27	2	15	7	4
20	7 54 31	29 10 50	2♊52	13	16	22	27	2	15	7	4
21	7 58 27	0♒11 53	15 3	15	17	22	27	2	15	7	4
22	8 2 24	1 12 55	27 29	16	18	23	27	2	15	7	4
23	8 6 20	2 13 57	10♋13	18	20	23	28	2	15	7	4
24	8 10 17	3 14 57	23 15	20	21	23	28	2	15	7	4
25	8 14 13	4 15 57	6♌34	21	22	24	28	2	15	7	4
26	8 18 10	5 16 56	20 8	23	23	24	28	2	15	7	4
27	8 22 6	6 17 54	3♍54	24	25	24	28	2	15	7	4
28	8 26 3	7 18 51	17 48	26	26	25	28	2	15	7	4
29	8 30 0	8 19 48	1♎48	27	27	25	28	3	15	7	4
30	8 33 56	9 20 44	15 52	29	28	25	29	3	15	7	4
31	8 37 53	10 21 39	29 57	1♒	0♓	26	29	3	14	7	4

THE SUN ENTERS THE SIGN OF AQUARIUS ON JAN 20 AT 19:20.

DAY	TIME	☉	☽	☿	♀	♂	♃	♄	♅	♆	♇
	h m s	° ' "	° '	°	°	°	°	°	°	°	°
F 1	8 41 49	11♒22 34	14♏ 2	2♒	1♓	26♉	29♏	3♑	14♌R	7♏	4♍R
E 2	8 45 46	12 23 28	28 8	4	2	26	29	3	14	7	3
B 3	8 49 42	13 24 21	12♐12	5	3	27	29	3	14	7	3
R 4	8 53 39	14 25 13	26 13	7	5	27	29	3	14	7	3
U 5	8 57 35	15 26 5	10♑ 9	9	6	28	29	3	14	7	3
A 6	9 1 32	16 26 55	23 56	10	7	28	29	3	14	7	3
R 7	9 5 29	17 27 44	7♒30	12	8	28	0♐	3	14	7 R	3
Y 8	9 9 25	18 28 33	20 49	14	10	29	0	4	14	7	3
9	9 13 22	19 29 19	3♓51	16	11	29	0	4	14	7	3
10	9 17 18	20 30 5	16 35	17	12	0♊	0	4	14	7	3
11	9 21 15	21 30 49	29 1	19	13	0	0	4	14	7	3
12	9 25 11	22 31 31	11♈12	21	15	1	0	4	14	7	3
13	9 29 8	23 32 12	23 11	23	16	1	0	4	14	7	3
14	9 33 4	24 32 51	5♉ 2	24	17	1	0	4	14	7	3
15	9 37 1	25 33 29	16 50	26	18	2	0	4	14	7	3
16	9 40 58	26 34 5	28 41	28	20	2	1	4	14	7	3
17	9 44 54	27 34 39	10♊39	0♓	21	3	1	4	14	7	3
18	9 48 51	28 35 12	22 50	2	22	3	1	4	14	7	3
19	9 52 47	29 35 42	5♋19	4	23	4	1	5	14	7	3
20	9 56 44	0♓36 11	18 8	5	24	4	1	5	14	7	3
21	10 0 40	1 36 39	1♌19	7	26	5	1	5	14	7	3
22	10 4 37	2 37 4	14 52	9	27	5	1	5	14	7	3
23	10 8 33	3 37 28	28 46	11	28	6	1	5	13	7	3
24	10 12 30	4 37 49	12♍56	13	29	6	1	5	13	7	3
25	10 16 27	5 38 10	27 18	15	1♈	7	1	5	13	7	3
26	10 20 23	6 38 28	11♎46	17	2	7	1	5	13	7	3
27	10 24 20	7 38 46	26 14	18	3	8	1	5	13	7	3
28	10 28 16	8 39 1	10♏39	20	4	8	1	5	13	7	3

THE SUN ENTERS THE SIGN OF PISCES ON FEB 19 AT 09:38.

DAY	TIME	☉	☽	☿	♀	♂	♃	♄	♅	♆	♇
	h m s	° ' "	° '	°	°	°	°	°	°	°	°
M 1	10 32 13	9♓39 16	24♏56	22♓	6♈	9♊	1♐	5♑	13♌R	7♏R	3♍R
A 2	10 36 9	10 39 29	9♐ 5	24	7	9	2	5	13	7	3
R 3	10 40 6	11 39 40	23 2	26	8	10	2	5	13	7	3
C 4	10 44 2	12 39 50	6♑48	27	9	10	2	6	13	7	3
H 5	10 47 59	13 39 58	20 22	29	11	11	2	6	13	7	3
6	10 51 55	14 40 5	3♒43	1♈	12	11	2	6	13	7	3
7	10 55 52	15 40 10	16 51	2	13	12	2	6	13	7	3
8	10 59 49	16 40 13	29 46	4	14	12	2	6	13	7	3
9	11 3 45	17 40 15	12♓27	5	15	13	2	6	13	7	3
10	11 7 42	18 40 14	24 55	7	17	13	2	6	13	7	3
11	11 11 38	19 40 12	7♈11	8	18	14	2	6	13	7	3
12	11 15 35	20 40 8	19 15	9	19	14	2	6	13	7	3
13	11 19 31	21 40 1	1♉11	10	20	15	2	6	13	7	3
14	11 23 28	22 39 53	13 1	11	22	15	2	6	13	7	2
15	11 27 24	23 39 42	24 49	11	23	16	2	6	13	7	2
16	11 31 21	24 39 29	6♊40	12	24	16	2	6	13	7	2
17	11 35 18	25 39 14	18 37	12	25	17	2	6	13	7	2
18	11 39 14	26 38 57	0♋47	13	26	17	2 R	6	13	7	2
19	11 43 11	27 38 38	13 13	13 R	28	18	2	6	13	7	2
20	11 47 7	28 38 16	25 59	13	29	18	2	6	13	7	2
21	11 51 4	29 37 52	9♌10	13	0♉	19	2	6	13	7	2
22	11 55 0	0♈37 25	22 46	13	1	19	2	7	13	6	2
23	11 58 57	1 36 57	6♍47	12	3	20	2	7	13	6	2
24	12 2 53	2 36 26	21 11	12	4	20	2	7	13	6	2
25	12 6 50	3 35 53	5♎52	11	5	21	2	7	13	6	2
26	12 10 47	4 35 18	20 44	11	6	22	2	7	13	6	2
27	12 14 43	5 34 42	5♏39	10	7	22	2	7	12	6	2
28	12 18 40	6 34 3	20 30	9	9	23	2	7	12	6	2
29	12 22 36	7 33 23	5♐ 9	8	10	23	2	7	12	6	2
30	12 26 33	8 32 40	19 32	7	11	24	2	7	12	6	2
31	12 30 29	9 31 57	3♑35	7	12	24	2	7	12	6	2

THE SUN ENTERS THE SIGN OF ARIES ON MAR 21 AT 08:55.

SIDEREAL SUN MOON MERCURY VENUS MARS JUPITER SATURN URANUS NEPTUNE PLUTO

DAY	TIME	☉	☽	☿	♀	♂	♃	♄	♅	♆	♇
	h m s	° ' "	° '	°	°	°	°	°	°	°	°
A 1	12 34 26	10♈31 11	17♑19	6♈R	13♉	25♊	2♐R	7♑	12♌R	6♏R	2♍R
P 2	12 38 22	11 30 24	0♒43	5	15	25	2	7	12	6	2
R 3	12 42 19	12 29 34	13 49	4	16	26	2	7	12	6	2
I 4	12 46 15	13 28 43	26 38	4	17	26	2	7	12	6	2
L 5	12 50 12	14 27 51	9♓12	3	18	27	2	7	12	6	2
6	12 54 9	15 26 56	21 34	2	19	28	1	7	12	6	2
7	12 58 5	16 25 59	3♈46	2	21	28	1	7	12	6	2
8	13 2 2	17 25 0	15 49	1	22	29	1	7	12	6	2
9	13 5 58	18 24 0	27 45	1	23	29	1	7	12	6	2
10	13 9 55	19 22 57	9♉37	1	24	0♋	1	7	12	6	2
11	13 13 51	20 21 52	21 26	1	25	0	1	7	12	6	2
12	13 17 48	21 20 45	3♊14	1 D	27	1	1	7	12	6	2
13	13 21 44	22 19 36	15 6	1	28	1	1	7	12	6	2
14	13 25 41	23 18 25	27 5	1	29	2	1	7	12	6	2
15	13 29 38	24 17 12	9♋14	1	0♊	3	1	7	12	6	2
16	13 33 34	25 15 56	21 37	1	1	3	1	7 R	12	6	2
17	13 37 31	26 14 38	4♌19	2	3	4	1	7	12	6	2
18	13 41 27	27 13 18	17 23	2	4	4	1	7	12	6	2
19	13 45 24	28 11 55	0♍53	3	5	5	1	7	12	6	2
20	13 49 20	29 10 31	14 49	3	6	5	0	7	12 D	6	2
21	13 53 17	0♉ 9 4	29 12	4	7	6	0	7	12	6	2
22	13 57 13	1 7 35	13♎58	5	8	7	0	7	12	6	2
23	14 1 10	2 6 4	29 1	5	10	7	0	7	12	6	2
24	14 5 7	3 4 31	14♏12	6	11	8	0	7	12	6	2
25	14 9 3	4 2 57	29 23	7	12	8	0	7	12	6	2
26	14 13 0	5 1 21	14♐23	8	13	9	0	7	12	6	2
27	14 16 56	5 59 43	29 4	9	14	9	0	7	12	6	2
28	14 20 53	6 58 4	13♑21	10	15	10	0	7	12	6	2
29	14 24 49	7 56 23	27 13	11	17	11	0	7	12	6	2
30	14 28 46	8 54 40	10♒37	12	18	11	29♏	7	12	6	2

THE SUN ENTERS THE SIGN OF TAURUS ON APR 20 AT 20:17.

DAY	TIME	☉	☽	☿	♀	♂	♃	♄	♅	♆	♇
	h m s	° ' "	° '	°	°	°	°	°	°	°	°
M 1	14 32 42	9♉52 56	23♒38	13♈	19♊	12♋	29♏R	7♑R	12♌	5♏R	2♍R
A 2	14 36 39	10 51 11	6♓18	15	20	12	29	7	12	5	2
Y 3	14 40 36	11 49 24	18 41	16	21	13	29	7	12	5	2
4	14 44 32	12 47 35	0♈51	17	22	13	29	7	12	5	2
5	14 48 29	13 45 45	12 51	18	24	14	29	7	12	5	2
6	14 52 25	14 43 53	24 44	20	25	15	29	7	12	5	2
7	14 56 22	15 42 0	6♉34	21	26	15	29	7	12	5	2
8	15 0 18	16 40 5	18 23	23	27	16	28	7	12	5	2
9	15 4 15	17 38 9	0♊12	24	28	16	28	7	12	5	2
10	15 8 11	18 36 11	12 4	26	29	17	28	7	12	5	2
11	15 12 8	19 34 11	24 1	27	0♋	18	28	7	12	5	2
12	15 16 4	20 32 9	6♋ 4	29	2	18	28	7	12	5	2
13	15 20 1	21 30 6	18 17	0♉	3	19	28	7	12	5	2 D
14	15 23 58	22 28 1	0♌41	2	4	19	28	6	12	5	2
15	15 27 54	23 25 54	13 22	4	5	20	28	6	12	5	2
16	15 31 51	24 23 46	26 21	5	6	20	27	6	13	5	2
17	15 35 47	25 21 35	9♍42	7	7	21	27	6	13	5	2
18	15 39 44	26 19 23	23 28	9	8	22	27	6	13	5	2
19	15 43 40	27 17 9	7♎41	11	9	22	27	6	13	5	2
20	15 47 37	28 14 54	22 18	12	11	23	27	6	13	5	2
21	15 51 33	29 12 37	7♏16	14	12	23	27	6	13	5	2
22	15 55 30	0♊10 19	22 27	16	13	24	27	6	13	5	2
23	15 59 27	1 7 59	7♐43	18	14	25	27	6	13	5	2
24	16 3 23	2 5 38	22 53	20	15	25	26	6	13	5	2
25	16 7 20	3 3 16	7♑46	22	16	26	26	6	13	5	2
26	16 11 16	4 0 53	22 15	24	17	26	26	6	13	5	2
27	16 15 13	4 58 29	6♒16	26	18	27	26	6	13	5	2
28	16 19 9	5 56 4	19 47	28	19	28	26	6	13	5	2
29	16 23 6	6 53 38	2♓50	1♊	20	28	26	6	13	5	2
30	16 27 3	7 51 11	15 29	3	22	29	26	6	13	5	2
31	16 30 59	8 48 43	27 49	5	23	29	26	6	13	5	2

THE SUN ENTERS THE SIGN OF GEMINI ON MAY 21 AT 19:43.

DAY	TIME	☉	☽	☿	♀	♂	♃	♄	♅	♆	♇
	h m s	° ' "	° '	°	°	°	°	°	°	°	°
J 1	16 34 56	9♊46 14	9♈54	7♊	24♋	0♌	25♏R	6♑R	13♌	5♏R	2♍
U 2	16 38 52	10 43 45	21 48	9	25	1	25	5	13	5	2
N 3	16 42 49	11 41 15	3♉38	11	26	1	25	5	13	5	2
E 4	16 46 45	12 38 44	15 25	14	27	2	25	5	13	5	2
5	16 50 42	13 36 12	27 14	16	28	2	25	5	13	5	2
6	16 54 38	14 33 39	9♊ 7	18	29	3	25	5	13	5	2
7	16 58 35	15 31 5	21 5	20	0♌	4	25	5	13	5	2
8	17 2 32	16 28 31	3♋10	22	1	4	25	5	13	5	2
9	17 6 28	17 25 55	15 23	25	2	5	25	5	13	5	2
10	17 10 25	18 23 19	27 45	27	3	5	24	5	13	5	2
11	17 14 21	19 20 42	10♌18	29	4	6	24	5	13	5	2
12	17 18 18	20 18 3	23 4	1♋	5	7	24	5	13	4	2
13	17 22 14	21 15 24	6♍ 5	3	6	7	24	5	13	4	2
14	17 26 11	22 12 44	19 24	5	7	8	24	5	13	4	2
15	17 30 7	23 10 2	3♎ 2	7	8	8	24	5	14	4	2
16	17 34 4	24 7 20	17 3	9	9	9	24	5	14	4	2
17	17 38 1	25 4 37	1♏26	11	10	10	24	4	14	4	2
18	17 41 57	26 1 53	16 8	13	11	10	24	4	14	4	2
19	17 45 54	26 59 8	1♐ 6	14	12	11	24	4	14	4	2
20	17 49 50	27 56 23	16 11	16	13	11	23	4	14	4	2
21	17 53 47	28 53 37	1♑14	18	14	12	23	4	14	4	2
22	17 57 43	29 50 51	16 5	20	15	13	23	4	14	4	2
23	18 1 40	0♋48 4	0♒35	21	16	13	23	4	14	4	2
24	18 5 36	1 45 17	14 39	23	17	14	23	4	14	4	2
25	18 9 33	2 42 30	28 15	24	18	14	23	4	14	4	2
26	18 13 30	3 39 43	11♓22	26	19	15	23	4	14	4	2
27	18 17 26	4 36 56	24 4	28	20	16	23	4	14	4	2
28	18 21 23	5 34 9	6♈25	29	21	16	23	4	14	4	2
29	18 25 19	6 31 21	18 29	0♌	22	17	23	4	14	4	2
30	18 29 16	7 28 34	0♉24	2	23	17	23	3	14	4	2

THE SUN ENTERS THE SIGN OF CANCER ON JUN 22 AT 03:50.

♈ ARIES ♉ TAURUS ♊ GEMINI ♋ CANCER ♌ LEO ♍ VIRGO ♎ LIBRA ♏ SCORPIO ♐ SAGITTARIUS ♑ CAPRICORN ♒ AQUARIUS ♓ PISCES

SIDEREAL SUN MOON MERCURY VENUS MARS JUPITER SATURN URANUS NEPTUNE PLUTO

DAY	TIME	☉	☽	☿	♀	♂	♃	♄	♅	♆	♇
	h m s	° ' "	° '	°	°	°	°	°	°	°	°
J 1	18 33 12	8♋25 47	12♉13	3♌	24♌	18♌	23♏R	3♑R	14♌	4♏R	2♍
U 2	18 37 9	9 23 0	24 2	4	24	19	23	3	14	4	2
L 3	18 41 5	10 20 14	5♊54	6	25	19	23	3	14	4	2
Y 4	18 45 2	11 17 27	17 52	7	26	20	23	3	14	4	2
5	18 48 59	12 14 40	29 58	8	27	20	22	3	15	4	2
6	18 52 55	13 11 54	12♋14	9	28	21	22	3	15	4	2
7	18 56 52	14 9 7	24 41	10	29	22	22	3	15	4	2
8	19 0 48	15 6 20	7♌19	11	0♍	22	22	3	15	4	2
9	19 4 45	16 3 34	20 8	12	0	23	22	3	15	4	2
10	19 8 41	17 0 47	3♍ 8	13	1	24	22	3	15	4	2
11	19 12 38	17 58 0	16 20	14	2	24	22	3	15	4	2
12	19 16 34	18 55 13	29 45	15	3	25	22	3	15	4	2
13	19 20 31	19 52 27	13♎24	16	4	25	22	3	15	4	3
14	19 24 28	20 49 40	27 20	16	4	26	22	2	15	4	3
15	19 28 24	21 46 53	11♏30	17	5	27	22	2	15	4	3
16	19 32 21	22 44 6	25 56	18	6	27	22	2	15	4 D	3
17	19 36 17	23 41 19	10♐33	18	6	28	22	2	15	4	3
18	19 40 14	24 38 33	25 16	18	7	28	22	2	15	4	3
19	19 44 10	25 35 46	9♑59	19	8	29	22	2	15	4	3
20	19 48 7	26 33 1	24 33	19	8	0♍	22 D	2	15	4	3
21	19 52 3	27 30 15	8♒51	19	9	0	22	2	15	4	3
22	19 56 0	28 27 30	22 48	19 R	10	1	22	2	16	4	3
23	19 59 57	29 24 46	6♓19	19	10	2	22	2	16	4	3
24	20 3 53	0♌22 2	19 26	19	11	2	22	2	16	4	3
25	20 7 50	1 19 19	2♈ 9	19	11	3	22	2	16	4	3
26	20 11 46	2 16 37	14 31	19	12	3	22	2	16	4	3
27	20 15 43	3 13 56	26 38	19	12	4	22	2	16	4	3
28	20 19 39	4 11 16	8♉35	18	13	5	22	2	16	4	3
29	20 23 36	5 8 37	20 26	18	13	5	22	2	16	4	3
30	20 27 32	6 5 59	2♊16	17	14	6	22	2	16	4	3
31	20 31 29	7 3 22	14 12	17	14	7	22	1	16	4	3

THE SUN ENTERS THE SIGN OF LEO ON JUL 23 AT 14:46.

DAY	TIME	☉	☽	☿	♀	♂	♃	♄	♅	♆	♇
	h m s	° ' "	° '	°	°	°	°	°	°	°	°
A 1	20 35 26	8♌ 0 46	26♊15	16♌R	14♍	7♍	22♏	1♑R	16♌	4♏	3♍
U 2	20 39 22	8 58 11	8♋29	15	15	8	22	1	16	4	3
G 3	20 43 19	9 55 38	20 57	15	15	8	22	1	16	4	3
U 4	20 47 15	10 53 5	3♌39	14	15	9	22	1	16	4	3
S 5	20 51 12	11 50 33	16 34	13	15	10	22	1	16	4	3
T 6	20 55 8	12 48 2	29 43	12	16	10	23	1	16	4	3
7	20 59 5	13 45 31	13♍ 5	12	16	11	23	1	16	4	3
8	21 3 1	14 43 2	26 37	11	16	12	23	1	17	4	3
9	21 6 58	15 40 34	10♎19	10	16	12	23	1	17	4	3
10	21 10 55	16 38 6	24 11	10	16 R	13	23	1	17	4	3
11	21 14 51	17 35 39	8♏11	9	16	13	23	1	17	4	3
12	21 18 48	18 33 13	22 19	9	16	14	23	1	17	4	3
13	21 22 44	19 30 48	6♐33	8	16	15	23	1	17	4	3
14	21 26 41	20 28 24	20 51	8	16	15	23	1	17	4	3
15	21 30 37	21 26 1	5♑11	8 D	16	16	23	1	17	4	4
16	21 34 34	22 23 39	19 27	8	16	17	23	1	17	4	4
17	21 38 30	23 21 18	3♒35	8	15	17	23	1	17	4	4
18	21 42 27	24 18 58	17 29	8	15	18	23	1	17	4	4
19	21 46 24	25 16 39	1♓ 8	8	15	19	23	1	17	4	4
20	21 50 20	26 14 22	14 26	9	15	19	24	1	17	4	4
21	21 54 17	27 12 6	27 25	9	14	20	24	1	17	5	4
22	21 58 13	28 9 51	10♈ 3	10	14	20	24	1	17	5	4
23	22 2 10	29 7 38	22 25	11	13	21	24	1	17	5	4
24	22 6 6	0♍ 5 27	4♉32	12	13	22	24	1	18	5	4
25	22 10 3	1 3 18	16 29	13	12	22	24	1	18	5	4
26	22 13 59	2 1 10	28 22	14	12	23	24	1	18	5	4
27	22 17 56	2 59 4	10♊14	15	11	24	24	1	18	5	4
28	22 21 52	3 57 0	22 11	16	11	24	24	1	18	5	4
29	22 25 49	4 54 58	4♋16	18	10	25	24	0	18	5	4
30	22 29 46	5 52 58	16 35	19	9	26	25	0	18	5	4
31	22 33 42	6 50 59	29 10	21	9	26	25	0	18	5	4

THE SUN ENTERS THE SIGN OF VIRGO ON AUG 23 AT 21:44.

DAY	TIME	☉	☽	☿	♀	♂	♃	♄	♅	♆	♇
	h m s	° ' "	° '	°	°	°	°	°	°	°	°
S 1	22 37 39	7♍49 2	12♌ 3	23♌	8♍R	27♍	25♏	0♑R	18♌	5♏	4♍
E 2	22 41 35	8 47 7	25 15	24	8	27	25	0	18	5	4
P 3	22 45 32	9 45 14	8♍44	26	7	28	25	0	18	5	4
T 4	22 49 28	10 43 22	22 29	28	6	29	25	0	18	5	4
E 5	22 53 25	11 41 32	6♎27	0♍	6	29	25	0 D	18	5	4
M 6	22 57 21	12 39 43	20 35	2	5	0♎	25	0	18	5	4
B 7	23 1 18	13 37 56	4♏49	4	5	1	25	0	18	5	4
E 8	23 5 15	14 36 11	19 5	5	4	1	26	0	18	5	4
R 9	23 9 11	15 34 27	3♐22	7	4	2	26	0	18	5	4
10	23 13 8	16 32 45	17 35	9	3	3	26	0	19	5	4
11	23 17 4	17 31 4	1♑43	11	3	3	26	0	19	5	4
12	23 21 1	18 29 25	15 43	13	2	4	26	0	19	5	4
13	23 24 57	19 27 47	29 35	15	2	5	26	1	19	5	4
14	23 28 54	20 26 11	13♒15	17	1	5	26	1	19	5	5
15	23 32 50	21 24 36	26 43	19	1	6	27	1	19	5	5
16	23 36 47	22 23 3	9♓57	21	1	7	27	1	19	5	5
17	23 40 44	23 21 32	22 56	23	1	7	27	1	19	5	5
18	23 44 40	24 20 3	5♈39	24	0	8	27	1	19	5	5
19	23 48 37	25 18 36	18 8	26	0	8	27	1	19	5	5
20	23 52 33	26 17 11	0♉24	28	0	9	27	1	19	5	5
21	23 56 30	27 15 48	12 29	0♎	0	10	28	1	19	5	5
22	0 0 26	28 14 27	24 25	2	0 D	10	28	1	19	5	5
23	0 4 23	29 13 8	6♊17	3	0	11	28	1	19	5	5
24	0 8 19	0♎11 52	18 9	5	0	12	28	1	19	5	5
25	0 12 16	1 10 38	0♋ 5	7	0	12	28	1	19	5	5
26	0 16 13	2 9 26	12 10	9	0	13	28	1	19	5	5
27	0 20 9	3 8 16	24 28	10	0	14	28	1	19	5	5
28	0 24 6	4 7 9	7♌ 4	12	0	14	29	1	20	6	5
29	0 28 2	5 6 4	20 0	14	1	15	29	1	20	6	5
30	0 31 59	6 5 1	3♍19	15	1	16	29	1	20	6	5

THE SUN ENTERS THE SIGN OF LIBRA ON SEP 23 AT 19:09.

SIDEREAL SUN MOON MERCURY VENUS MARS JUPITER SATURN URANUS NEPTUNE PLUTO

DAY	TIME	☉	☽	☿	♀	♂	♃	♄	♅	♆	♇
	h m s	° ' "	° '	°	°	°	°	°	°	°	°
O 1	0 35 55	7♎ 4 0	17♍ 2	17♎	1♍	16♎	29♏	1♑	20♌	6♏	5♍
C 2	0 39 52	8 3 1	1♎ 6	19	1	17	29	1	20	6	5
T 3	0 43 48	9 2 5	15 28	20	2	18	0♐	1	20	6	5
O 4	0 47 45	10 1 10	0♏ 3	22	2	18	0	1	20	6	5
B 5	0 51 41	11 0 17	14 45	24	3	19	0	1	20	6	5
E 6	0 55 38	11 59 27	29 27	25	3	20	0	1	20	6	5
R 7	0 59 35	12 58 38	14♐ 2	27	4	20	0	1	20	6	5
8	1 3 31	13 57 51	28 26	28	4	21	0	1	20	6	5
9	1 7 28	14 57 6	12♑35	0♏	5	22	1	1	20	6	5
10	1 11 24	15 56 22	26 27	1	5	22	1	1	20	6	5
11	1 15 21	16 55 40	10♒ 3	3	6	23	1	1	20	6	5
12	1 19 17	17 55 0	23 23	4	6	24	1	2	20	6	5
13	1 23 14	18 54 22	6♓27	6	7	24	1	2	20	6	5
14	1 27 10	19 53 45	19 17	7	7	25	2	2	20	6	5
15	1 31 7	20 53 11	1♈55	9	8	26	2	2	20	6	5
16	1 35 4	21 52 38	14 21	10	9	26	2	2	20	6	5
17	1 39 0	22 52 7	26 37	12	9	27	2	2	20	6	5
18	1 42 57	23 51 39	8♉44	13	10	28	2	2	20	6	5
19	1 46 53	24 51 12	20 44	14	11	28	3	2	20	6	6
20	1 50 50	25 50 48	2♊38	16	12	29	3	2	20	6	6
21	1 54 46	26 50 26	14 29	17	12	0♏	3	2	20	6	6
22	1 58 43	27 50 6	26 21	19	13	0	3	2	20	6	6
23	2 2 39	28 49 48	8♋16	20	14	1	3	2	21	6	6
24	2 6 36	29 49 33	20 18	21	15	2	4	2	21	6	6
25	2 10 33	0♏49 20	2♌32	23	16	2	4	2	21	6	6
26	2 14 29	1 49 9	15 3	24	16	3	4	2	21	7	6
27	2 18 26	2 49 0	27 55	25	17	4	4	3	21	7	6
28	2 22 22	3 48 54	11♍11	26	18	4	4	3	21	7	6
29	2 26 19	4 48 49	24 55	28	19	5	5	3	21	7	6
30	2 30 15	5 48 47	9♎ 5	29	20	6	5	3	21	7	6
31	2 34 12	6 48 47	23 40	0♐	21	7	5	3	21	7	6

THE SUN ENTERS THE SIGN OF SCORPIO ON OCT 24 AT 04:12.

DAY	TIME	☉	☽	☿	♀	♂	♃	♄	♅	♆	♇
	h m s	° ' "	° '	°	°	°	°	°	°	°	°
N 1	2 38 8	7♏48 49	8♏35	1♐	22♍	7♏	5♐	3♑	21♌	7♏	6♍
O 2	2 42 5	8 48 52	23 40	2	23	8	5	3	21	7	6
V 3	2 46 1	9 48 58	8♐47	3	24	9	6	3	21	7	6
E 4	2 49 58	10 49 5	23 47	4	24	9	6	3	21	7	6
M 5	2 53 55	11 49 14	8♑29	5	25	10	6	3	21	7	6
B 6	2 57 51	12 49 25	22 50	6	26	11	6	3	21	7	6
E 7	3 1 48	13 49 37	6♒47	7	27	11	6	3	21	7	6
R 8	3 5 44	14 49 50	20 19	8	28	12	7	4	21	7	6
9	3 9 41	15 50 5	3♓29	8	29	13	7	4	21	7	6
10	3 13 37	16 50 21	16 19	9	0♎	13	7	4	21	7	6
11	3 17 34	17 50 39	28 52	9	1	14	7	4	21	7	6
12	3 21 30	18 50 59	11♈14	10	2	15	8	4	21	7	6
13	3 25 27	19 51 19	23 25	10	3	15	8	4	21	7	6
14	3 29 24	20 51 42	5♉29	10 R	4	16	8	4	21	7	6
15	3 33 20	21 52 6	17 27	10	5	17	8	4	21	7	6
16	3 37 17	22 52 31	29 22	10	6	18	8	4	21	7	6
17	3 41 13	23 52 59	11♊14	9	7	18	9	4	21	7	6
18	3 45 10	24 53 28	23 6	9	8	19	9	5	21	7	6
19	3 49 6	25 53 59	4♋59	8	9	20	9	5	21	7	6
20	3 53 3	26 54 31	16 55	7	11	20	9	5	21	7	6
21	3 56 59	27 55 5	28 57	6	12	21	10	5	21	7	6
22	4 0 56	28 55 41	11♌ 9	5	13	22	10	5	21	8	6
23	4 4 53	29 56 18	23 36	3	14	22	10	5	21	8	6
24	4 8 49	0♐56 57	6♍21	2	15	23	10	5	21	8	6
25	4 12 46	1 57 38	19 28	1	16	24	10	5	21	8	6
26	4 16 42	2 58 21	3♎ 2	29♏	17	25	11	5	21	8	6
27	4 20 39	3 59 5	17 5	28	18	25	11	5	21 R	8	6
28	4 24 35	4 59 51	1♏37	27	19	26	11	6	21	8	6
29	4 28 32	6 0 38	16 33	26	20	27	11	6	21	8	6
30	4 32 28	7 1 26	1♐47	25	21	27	12	6	21	8	6

THE SUN ENTERS THE SIGN OF SAGITTARIUS ON NOV 23 AT 01:28.

DAY	TIME	☉	☽	☿	♀	♂	♃	♄	♅	♆	♇
	h m s	° ' "	° '	°	°	°	°	°	°	°	°
D 1	4 36 25	8♐ 2 16	17♐ 8	24♏R	22♎	28♏	12♐	6♑	21♌R	8♏	6♍
E 2	4 40 22	9 3 7	2♑25	24	24	29	12	6	21	8	6
C 3	4 44 18	10 4 0	17 26	24 D	25	29	12	6	21	8	6
E 4	4 48 15	11 4 53	2♒ 3	24	26	0♐	12	6	21	8	6
M 5	4 52 11	12 5 46	16 12	24	27	1	13	6	21	8	6
B 6	4 56 8	13 6 41	29 51	24	28	2	13	6	21	8	6
E 7	5 0 4	14 7 36	13♓ 2	24	29	2	13	7	21	8	6
R 8	5 4 1	15 8 32	25 49	25	0♏	3	13	7	21	8	6 R
9	5 7 58	16 9 29	8♈16	26	1	4	14	7	21	8	6
10	5 11 54	17 10 27	20 29	26	3	4	14	7	21	8	6
11	5 15 51	18 11 25	2♉32	27	4	5	14	7	21	8	6
12	5 19 47	19 12 23	14 28	28	5	6	14	7	21	8	6
13	5 23 44	20 13 23	26 20	29	6	7	15	7	21	8	6
14	5 27 40	21 14 23	8♊12	0♐	7	7	15	7	21	8	6
15	5 31 37	22 15 24	20 4	2	8	8	15	7	21	8	6
16	5 35 33	23 16 26	1♋59	3	10	9	15	8	21	8	6
17	5 39 30	24 17 28	13 57	4	11	9	15	8	21	8	6
18	5 43 27	25 18 32	25 59	5	12	10	16	8	21	8	6
19	5 47 23	26 19 35	8♌ 7	6	13	11	16	8	21	8	6
20	5 51 20	27 20 40	20 24	8	14	12	16	8	21	8	6
21	5 55 16	28 21 46	2♍53	9	15	12	16	8	21	8	6
22	5 59 13	29 22 52	15 36	11	17	13	17	8	21	8	6
23	6 3 9	0♑23 59	28 38	12	18	14	17	8	21	8	6
24	6 7 6	1 25 6	12♎ 2	13	19	14	17	9	21	9	6
25	6 11 2	2 26 15	25 52	15	20	15	17	9	21	9	6
26	6 14 59	3 27 24	10♏ 9	16	21	16	17	9	21	9	6
27	6 18 56	4 28 33	24 51	18	22	17	18	9	21	9	6
28	6 22 52	5 29 43	9♐54	19	24	17	18	9	21	9	6
29	6 26 49	6 30 54	25 8	21	25	18	18	9	21	9	6
30	6 30 45	7 32 5	10♑24	22	26	19	18	9	21	9	6
31	6 34 42	8 33 16	25 30	23	27	20	19	9	21	9	6

THE SUN ENTERS THE SIGN OF CAPRICORN ON DEC 22 AT 14:35.

♈ ARIES ♉ TAURUS ♊ GEMINI ♋ CANCER ♌ LEO ♍ VIRGO ♎ LIBRA ♏ SCORPIO ♐ SAGITTARIUS ♑ CAPRICORN ♒ AQUARIUS ♓ PISCES

SIDEREAL SUN MOON MERCURY VENUS MARS JUPITER SATURN URANUS NEPTUNE PLUTO

SIDEREAL SUN MOON MERCURY VENUS MARS JUPITER SATURN URANUS NEPTUNE PLUTO

DAY	TIME	☉	☽	☿	♀	♂	♃	♄	♅	♆	♇
	h m s	° ' "	° '	°	°	°	°	°	°	°	°
J 1	6 38 38	9♑34 27	10♒16	25♐	28♏	20♐	19♐	9♑	21♌R	9♏	6♍R
A 2	6 42 35	10 35 38	24 34	26	0♐	21	19	10	21	9	6
N 3	6 46 31	11 36 49	8♓23	28	1	22	19	10	20	9	6
U 4	6 50 28	12 37 59	21 43	29	2	22	19	10	20	9	6
A 5	6 54 25	13 39 9	4♈35	1♑	3	23	20	10	20	9	6
R 6	6 58 21	14 40 19	17 5	3	4	24	20	10	20	9	6
Y 7	7 2 18	15 41 29	29 18	4	6	25	20	10	20	9	6
8	7 6 14	16 42 38	11♉19	6	7	25	20	10	20	9	6
9	7 10 11	17 43 47	23 12	7	8	26	20	10	20	9	6
10	7 14 7	18 44 55	5♊ 3	9	9	27	21	11	20	9	6
11	7 18 4	19 46 3	16 54	10	10	28	21	11	20	9	6
12	7 22 0	20 47 10	28 48	12	12	28	21	11	20	9	6
13	7 25 57	21 48 18	10♋48	13	13	29	21	11	20	9	6
14	7 29 54	22 49 24	22 54	15	14	0♑	22	11	20	9	6
15	7 33 50	23 50 31	5♌ 7	17	15	1	22	11	20	9	6
16	7 37 47	24 51 36	17 28	18	16	1	22	11	20	9	6
17	7 41 43	25 52 42	29 58	20	18	2	22	11	20	9	6
18	7 45 40	26 53 47	12♍39	21	19	3	22	11	20	9	6
19	7 49 36	27 54 52	25 31	23	20	4	23	12	20	9	6
20	7 53 33	28 55 56	8♎39	25	21	4	23	12	20	9	6
21	7 57 29	29 57 0	22 3	26	22	5	23	12	20	9	6
22	8 1 26	0♒58 4	5♏46	28	24	6	23	12	20	9	6
23	8 5 23	1 59 7	19 49	0♒	25	7	23	12	20	9	6
24	8 9 19	3 0 10	4♐12	1	26	7	24	12	20	9	6
25	8 13 16	4 1 13	18 52	3	27	8	24	12	20	9	6
26	8 17 12	5 2 15	3♑44	5	29	9	24	12	20	9	6
27	8 21 9	6 3 16	18 39	6	0♑	10	24	12	20	9	6
28	8 25 5	7 4 16	3♒30	8	1	10	24	13	20	9	6
29	8 29 2	8 5 16	18 7	10	2	11	25	13	19	9	6
30	8 32 58	9 6 14	2♓23	11	3	12	25	13	19	9	6
31	8 36 55	10 7 12	16 14	13	5	12	25	13	19	9	6

THE SUN ENTERS THE SIGN OF AQUARIUS ON JAN 21 AT 01:11.

DAY	TIME	☉	☽	☿	♀	♂	♃	♄	♅	♆	♇
	h m s	° ' "	° '	°	°	°	°	°	°	°	°
F 1	8 40 52	11♒ 8 8	29♓38	15♒	6♑	13♑	25♐	13♑	19♌R	9♏	5♍R
E 2	8 44 48	12 9 3	12♈37	17	7	14	25	13	19	9	5
B 3	8 48 45	13 9 57	25 13	18	8	15	25	13	19	9	5
R 4	8 52 41	14 10 49	7♉31	20	10	15	26	13	19	9	5
U 5	8 56 38	15 11 40	19 34	22	11	16	26	13	19	9	5
A 6	9 0 34	16 12 29	1♊30	24	12	17	26	14	19	9	5
R 7	9 4 31	17 13 17	13 21	26	13	18	26	14	19	9	5
Y 8	9 8 27	18 14 4	25 13	27	14	19	26	14	19	9	5
9	9 12 24	19 14 49	7♋10	29	16	19	27	14	19	9	5
10	9 16 21	20 15 33	19 14	1♓	17	20	27	14	19	9 R	5
11	9 20 17	21 16 15	1♌28	3	18	21	27	14	19	9	5
12	9 24 14	22 16 56	13 53	5	19	22	27	14	19	9	5
13	9 28 10	23 17 35	26 30	6	21	22	27	14	19	9	5
14	9 32 7	24 18 13	9♍19	8	22	23	27	14	19	9	5
15	9 36 3	25 18 50	22 21	10	23	24	28	14	19	9	5
16	9 40 0	26 19 25	5♎34	11	24	25	28	15	19	9	5
17	9 43 56	27 19 59	19 0	13	25	25	28	15	19	9	5
18	9 47 53	28 20 32	2♏38	15	27	26	28	15	19	9	5
19	9 51 50	29 21 3	16 27	16	28	27	28	15	19	9	5
20	9 55 46	0♓21 33	0♐28	18	29	28	28	15	19	9	5
21	9 59 43	1 22 2	14 40	19	0♒	28	29	15	18	9	5
22	10 3 39	2 22 30	29 0	20	2	29	29	15	18	9	5
23	10 7 36	3 22 57	13♑26	21	3	0♒	29	15	18	9	5
24	10 11 32	4 23 21	27 52	22	4	1	29	15	18	9	5
25	10 15 29	5 23 45	12♒14	23	5	1	29	15	18	9	5
26	10 19 25	6 24 7	26 27	24	7	2	29	16	18	9	5
27	10 23 22	7 24 27	10♓24	25	8	3	29	16	18	9	5
28	10 27 19	8 24 45	24 4	25	9	4	0♑	16	18	9	5
29	10 31 15	9 25 2	7♈22	26	10	4	0	16	18	9	5

THE SUN ENTERS THE SIGN OF PISCES ON FEB 19 AT 15:27.

DAY	TIME	☉	☽	☿	♀	♂	♃	♄	♅	♆	♇
	h m s	° ' "	° '	°	°	°	°	°	°	°	°
M 1	10 35 12	10♓25 17	20♈20	26♓R	11♒	5♒	0♑	16♑	18♌R	9♏R	5♍R
A 2	10 39 8	11 25 29	2♉58	26	13	6	0	16	18	9	5
R 3	10 43 5	12 25 40	15 19	26	14	7	0	16	18	9	5
C 4	10 47 1	13 25 49	27 26	25	15	7	0	16	18	9	5
H 5	10 50 58	14 25 55	9♊24	25	16	8	0	16	18	9	5
6	10 54 54	15 26 0	21 17	24	18	9	1	16	18	9	5
7	10 58 51	16 26 2	3♋10	24	19	10	1	16	18	9	5
8	11 2 47	17 26 2	15 8	23	20	11	1	16	18	9	5
9	11 6 44	18 26 0	27 14	22	21	11	1	16	18	9	5
10	11 10 41	19 25 56	9♌33	21	23	12	1	17	18	9	5
11	11 14 37	20 25 50	22 7	20	24	13	1	17	18	9	5
12	11 18 34	21 25 42	4♍57	19	25	14	1	17	18	9	4
13	11 22 30	22 25 31	18 5	18	26	14	1	17	18	9	4
14	11 26 27	23 25 19	1♎30	17	27	15	2	17	18	9	4
15	11 30 23	24 25 5	15 10	16	29	16	2	17	18	9	4
16	11 34 20	25 24 49	29 3	16	0♓	17	2	17	18	9	4
17	11 38 16	26 24 31	13♏ 6	15	1	17	2	17	18	9	4
18	11 42 13	27 24 11	27 16	14	2	18	2	17	18	9	4
19	11 46 10	28 23 50	11♐29	14	4	19	2	17	17	9	4
20	11 50 6	29 23 27	25 43	13	5	20	2	17	17	9	4
21	11 54 3	0♈23 2	9♑55	13	6	21	2	17	17	9	4
22	11 57 59	1 22 36	24 2	12	7	21	2	17	17	9	4
23	12 1 56	2 22 8	8♒ 4	12	9	22	2	17	17	9	4
24	12 5 52	3 21 38	21 57	12 D	10	23	2	17	17	9	4
25	12 9 49	4 21 6	5♓40	12	11	24	3	18	17	9	4
26	12 13 45	5 20 32	19 11	12	12	24	3	18	17	9	4
27	12 17 42	6 19 56	2♈28	12	13	25	3	18	17	9	4
28	12 21 39	7 19 18	15 31	13	15	26	3	18	17	9	4
29	12 25 35	8 18 38	28 18	13	16	27	3	18	17	9	4
30	12 29 32	9 17 56	10♉50	14	17	27	3	18	17	9	4
31	12 33 28	10 17 12	23 9	14	18	28	3	18	17	9	4

THE SUN ENTERS THE SIGN OF ARIES ON MAR 20 AT 14:43.

DAY	TIME	☉	☽	☿	♀	♂	♃	♄	♅	♆	♇
	h m s	° ' "	° '	°	°	°	°	°	°	°	°
A 1	12 37 25	11♈16 26	5♊16	15♓	20♓	29♒	3♑	18♑	17♌R	8♏R	4♍R
P 2	12 41 21	12 15 37	17 14	15	21	0♓	3	18	17	8	4
R 3	12 45 18	13 14 46	29 7	16	22	1	3	18	17	8	4
I 4	12 49 14	14 13 53	11♋ 0	17	23	1	3	18	17	8	4
L 5	12 53 11	15 12 57	22 57	18	25	2	3	18	17	8	4
6	12 57 7	16 11 59	5♌ 3	19	26	3	3	18	17	8	4
7	13 1 4	17 10 59	17 22	19	27	4	3	18	17	8	4
8	13 5 1	18 9 57	29 59	20	28	4	3	18	17	8	4
9	13 8 57	19 8 52	12♍56	22	29	5	3	18	17	8	4
10	13 12 54	20 7 45	26 16	23	1♈	6	3	18	17	8	4
11	13 16 50	21 6 36	9♎59	24	2	7	3	18	17	8	4
12	13 20 47	22 5 25	24 2	25	3	8	4	18	17	8	4
13	13 24 43	23 4 12	8♏23	26	4	8	4	18	17	8	4
14	13 28 40	24 2 57	22 55	27	6	9	4	18	17	8	4
15	13 32 36	25 1 40	7♐32	29	7	10	4	18	17	8	4
16	13 36 33	26 0 22	22 8	0⊙	8	11	4	18	17	8	4
17	13 40 30	26 59 2	6♑36	1♈	9	11	4	18	17	8	4
18	13 44 26	27 57 40	20 53	3	11	12	4	18	17	8	4
19	13 48 23	28 56 17	4♒55	4	12	13	4	18	17	8	4
20	13 52 19	29 54 52	18 44	5	13	14	4 R	18	17	8	4
21	13 56 16	0♉53 25	2♓17	7	14	14	4	18	17	8	4
22	14 0 12	1 51 56	15 36	8	15	15	4	18	17	8	4
23	14 4 9	2 50 26	28 42	10	17	16	4	18	17	8	4
24	14 8 5	3 48 54	11♈36	11	18	17	4	18	17 D	8	4
25	14 12 2	4 47 21	24 19	13	19	18	4	18	17	8	4
26	14 15 59	5 45 45	6♉50	15	20	18	4	18	17	8	4
27	14 19 55	6 44 8	19 11	16	22	19	4	18 R	17	8	4
28	14 23 52	7 42 29	1♊22	18	23	20	4	18	17	8	4
29	14 27 48	8 40 48	13 25	20	24	21	3	18	17	8	4
30	14 31 45	9 39 5	25 21	21	25	21	3	18	17	8	4

THE SUN ENTERS THE SIGN OF TAURUS ON APR 20 AT 02:06.

DAY	TIME	☉	☽	☿	♀	♂	♃	♄	♅	♆	♇
	h m s	° ' "	° '	°	°	°	°	°	°	°	°
M 1	14 35 41	10♉37 20	7♋13	23♈	27♈	22♓	3♑R	18♑R	17♌	8♏R	4♍R
A 2	14 39 38	11 35 34	19 5	25	28	23	3	18	17	8	4
Y 3	14 43 34	12 33 45	1♌ 0	27	29	24	3	18	17	8	4
4	14 47 31	13 31 54	13 4	29	0♉	24	3	18	17	8	4
5	14 51 28	14 30 1	25 20	1♉	1	25	3	18	17	8	4
6	14 55 24	15 28 6	7♍54	2	3	26	3	18	17	8	4
7	14 59 21	16 26 10	20 51	4	4	27	3	18	17	8	4
8	15 3 17	17 24 11	4♎13	6	5	27	3	18	17	8	4
9	15 7 14	18 22 11	18 3	8	6	28	3	18	17	7	4
10	15 11 10	19 20 9	2♏20	10	8	29	3	18	17	7	4
11	15 15 7	20 18 5	17 0	12	9	0⊙	3	18	17	7	4
12	15 19 3	21 15 59	1♐55	15	10	1♈	3	18	17	7	4
13	15 23 0	22 13 53	16 58	17	11	1	3	18	17	7	4
14	15 26 57	23 11 45	1♑58	19	12	2	3	18	17	7	4
15	15 30 53	24 9 35	16 46	21	14	3	3	18	17	7	4 D
16	15 34 50	25 7 25	1♒17	23	15	4	3	18	17	7	4
17	15 38 46	26 5 13	15 26	25	16	4	3	18	17	7	4
18	15 42 43	27 3 0	29 12	27	17	5	2	18	17	7	4
19	15 46 39	28 0 46	12♓38	0♊	19	6	2	18	17	7	4
20	15 50 36	28 58 30	25 44	2	20	7	2	18	17	7	4
21	15 54 32	29 56 14	8♈34	4	21	7	2	18	17	7	4
22	15 58 29	0♊53 56	21 11	6	22	8	2	18	17	7	4
23	16 2 26	1 51 38	3♉36	8	24	9	2	18	17	7	4
24	16 6 22	2 49 18	15 53	11	25	10	2	18	17	7	4
25	16 10 19	3 46 57	28 2	13	26	10	2	18	17	7	4
26	16 14 15	4 44 36	10♊ 4	15	27	11	2	18	17	7	4
27	16 18 12	5 42 12	22 1	17	28	12	2	18	17	7	4
28	16 22 8	6 39 48	3♋54	19	0♊	13	2	18	17	7	4
29	16 26 5	7 37 22	15 45	21	1	13	1	18	17	7	4
30	16 30 1	8 34 55	27 36	23	2	14	1	18	17	7	4
31	16 33 58	9 32 27	9♌31	25	3	15	1	18	18	7	4

THE SUN ENTERS THE SIGN OF GEMINI ON MAY 21 AT 01:34.

DAY	TIME	☉	☽	☿	♀	♂	♃	♄	♅	♆	♇
	h m s	° ' "	° '	°	°	°	°	°	°	°	°
J 1	16 37 55	10♊29 57	21♌33	27♊	5♊	16♈	1♑R	18♑R	18♌	7♏R	4♍
U 2	16 41 51	11 27 27	3♍47	28	6	16	1	17	18	7	4
N 3	16 45 48	12 24 54	16 17	0♋	7	17	1	17	18	7	4
E 4	16 49 44	13 22 21	29 10	2	8	18	1	17	18	7	4
5	16 53 41	14 19 46	12♎29	4	10	19	1	17	18	7	4
6	16 57 37	15 17 10	26 16	5	11	19	0	17	18	7	4
7	17 1 34	16 14 34	10♏34	7	12	20	0	17	18	7	4
8	17 5 30	17 11 56	25 18	9	13	21	0	17	18	7	4
9	17 9 27	18 9 17	10♐23	10	14	22	0	17	18	7	4
10	17 13 24	19 6 37	25 40	12	16	22	0	17	18	7	4
11	17 17 20	20 3 57	10♑56	13	17	23	0	17	18	7	4
12	17 21 17	21 1 16	26 2	14	18	24	0	17	18	7	4
13	17 25 13	21 58 35	10♒48	16	19	25	0	17	18	7	4
14	17 29 10	22 55 53	25 9	17	21	25	0	17	18	7	4
15	17 33 6	23 53 10	9♓ 2	18	22	26	29♐	17	18	7	4
16	17 37 3	24 50 27	22 30	19	23	27	29	17	18	7	4
17	17 40 59	25 47 44	5♈33	20	24	28	29	17	18	7	4
18	17 44 56	26 45 1	18 17	22	25	28	29	17	18	7	4
19	17 48 53	27 42 17	0♉44	23	27	29	29	16	18	7	4
20	17 52 49	28 39 34	13 0	24	28	0♉	29	16	18	7	4
21	17 56 46	29 36 49	25 6	24	29	0	29	16	18	7	4
22	18 0 42	0♋34 5	7♊ 6	25	0♋	1	28	16	18	7	4
23	18 4 39	1 31 21	19 2	26	2	2	28	16	18	7	4
24	18 8 35	2 28 36	0♋54	27	3	3	28	16	18	7	4
25	18 12 32	3 25 50	12 46	27	4	3	28	16	19	7	4
26	18 16 28	4 23 5	24 37	28	5	4	28	16	19	6	4
27	18 20 25	5 20 19	6♌31	29	7	5	28	16	19	6	4
28	18 24 22	6 17 33	18 29	29	8	6	28	16	19	6	4
29	18 28 18	7 14 46	0♍34	29	9	6	28	16	19	6	4
30	18 32 15	8 11 59	12 50	0♌	10	7	27	16	19	6	4

THE SUN ENTERS THE SIGN OF CANCER ON JUN 21 AT 09:43.

♈ ARIES ♉ TAURUS ♊ GEMINI ♋ CANCER ♌ LEO ♍ VIRGO ♎ LIBRA ♏ SCORPIO ♐ SAGITTARIUS ♑ CAPRICORN ♒ AQUARIUS ♓ PISCES

1960

SIDEREAL SUN MOON MERCURY VENUS MARS JUPITER SATURN URANUS NEPTUNE PLUTO

DAY	TIME	☉	☽	☿	♀	♂	♃	♄	♅	♆	♇
	h m s	° ' "	° '	°	°	°	°	°	°	°	°
J 1	18 36 11	9♋ 9 11	25♍21	0♌	11♋	8♉	27♐R	16♑R	19♌	6♏R	4♍
U 2	18 40 8	10 6 23	8♎11	0	13	8	27	16	19	6	4
L 3	18 44 4	11 3 35	21 25	0 R	14	9	27	15	19	6	4
Y 4	18 48 1	12 0 46	5♏ 6	0	15	10	27	15	19	6	4
5	18 51 57	12 57 58	19 15	0	16	11	27	15	19	6	4
6	18 55 54	13 55 9	3♐52	0	18	11	27	15	19	6	4
7	18 59 51	14 52 20	18 51	0	19	12	27	15	19	6	4
8	19 3 47	15 49 30	4♑ 5	29♋	20	13	27	15	19	6	4
9	19 7 44	16 46 41	19 24	29	21	13	26	15	19	6	4
10	19 11 40	17 43 52	4♒35	29	23	14	26	15	19	6	4
11	19 15 37	18 41 4	19 29	28	24	15	26	15	19	6	4
12	19 19 33	19 38 15	3♓59	28	25	15	26	15	19	6	4
13	19 23 30	20 35 27	18 2	27	26	16	26	15	19	6	4
14	19 27 26	21 32 40	1♈36	26	27	17	26	15	20	6	4
15	19 31 23	22 29 53	14 44	26	29	18	26	15	20	6	4
16	19 35 20	23 27 7	27 29	25	0♌	18	26	14	20	6	4
17	19 39 16	24 24 21	9♉55	24	1	19	26	14	20	6	5
18	19 43 13	25 21 36	22 7	24	2	20	25	14	20	6 D	5
19	19 47 9	26 18 52	4♊ 9	23	4	20	25	14	20	6	5
20	19 51 6	27 16 9	16 5	23	5	21	25	14	20	6	5
21	19 55 2	28 13 26	27 57	22	6	22	25	14	20	6	5
22	19 58 59	29 10 44	9♋48	21	7	22	25	14	20	6	5
23	20 2 55	0♌ 8 2	21 41	21	9	23	25	14	20	6	5
24	20 6 52	1 5 21	3♌36	21	10	24	25	14	20	6	5
25	20 10 49	2 2 41	15 36	20	11	24	25	14	20	6	5
26	20 14 45	3 0 1	27 42	20	12	25	25	14	20	6	5
27	20 18 42	3 57 22	9♍57	20 D	13	26	25	14	20	6	5
28	20 22 38	4 54 44	22 22	20	15	27	25	14	20	6	5
29	20 26 35	5 52 6	5♎ 0	20	16	27	25	14	20	6	5
30	20 30 31	6 49 28	17 55	20	17	28	24	14	20	6	5
31	20 34 28	7 46 51	1♏10	20	18	29	24	13	21	6	5

THE SUN ENTERS THE SIGN OF LEO ON JUL 22 AT 20:38.

DAY	TIME	☉	☽	☿	♀	♂	♃	♄	♅	♆	♇
	h m s	° ' "	° '	°	°	°	°	°	°	°	°
A 1	20 38 24	8♌44 15	14♏46	21♋	20♌	29♉	24♐R	13♑R	21♌	6♏	5♍
U 2	20 42 21	9 41 39	28 46	21	21	0♊	24	13	21	6	5
G 3	20 46 18	10 39 4	13♐ 9	22	22	1	24	13	21	6	5
U 4	20 50 14	11 36 29	27 52	23	23	1	24	13	21	6	5
S 5	20 54 11	12 33 56	12♑50	23	25	2	24	13	21	6	5
T 6	20 58 7	13 31 23	27 54	24	26	3	24	13	21	6	5
7	21 2 4	14 28 51	12♒55	25	27	3	24	13	21	6	5
8	21 6 0	15 26 20	27 44	26	28	4	24	13	21	6	5
9	21 9 57	16 23 50	12♓14	28	29	4	24	13	21	6	5
10	21 13 53	17 21 21	26 20	29	1♍	5	24	13	21	7	5
11	21 17 50	18 18 54	10♈ 0	0♌	2	6	24	13	21	7	5
12	21 21 47	19 16 28	23 13	2	3	6	24	13	21	7	5
13	21 25 43	20 14 3	6♉ 3	3	4	7	24	13	21	7	5
14	21 29 40	21 11 40	18 32	5	6	8	24	13	21	7	5
15	21 33 36	22 9 19	0♊46	7	7	8	24	13	21	7	5
16	21 37 33	23 6 59	12 47	8	8	9	24	13	22	7	5
17	21 41 29	24 4 40	24 42	10	9	10	24	13	22	7	5
18	21 45 26	25 2 23	6♋33	12	11	10	24	12	22	7	6
19	21 49 22	26 0 8	18 25	14	12	11	24	12	22	7	6
20	21 53 19	26 57 54	0♌21	16	13	11	24 D	12	22	7	6
21	21 57 16	27 55 42	12 22	18	14	12	24	12	22	7	6
22	22 1 12	28 53 31	24 32	20	15	13	24	12	22	7	6
23	22 5 9	29 51 21	6♍51	22	17	13	24	12	22	7	6
24	22 9 5	0♍49 13	19 21	24	18	14	24	12	22	7	6
25	22 13 2	1 47 7	2♎ 3	26	19	15	24	12	22	7	6
26	22 16 58	2 45 1	14 58	28	20	15	24	12	22	7	6
27	22 20 55	3 42 57	28 7	0♍	22	16	24	12	22	7	6
28	22 24 51	4 40 55	11♏31	2	23	16	24	12	22	7	6
29	22 28 48	5 38 53	25 12	4	24	17	24	12	22	7	6
30	22 32 44	6 36 53	9♐ 8	6	25	18	24	12	22	7	6
31	22 36 41	7 34 55	23 20	8	27	18	24	12	22	7	6

THE SUN ENTERS THE SIGN OF VIRGO ON AUG 23 AT 03:36.

DAY	TIME	☉	☽	☿	♀	♂	♃	♄	♅	♆	♇
	h m s	° ' "	° '	°	°	°	°	°	°	°	°
S 1	22 40 38	8♍32 57	7♑44	10♍	28♍	19♊	24♐	12♑R	23♌	7♏	6♍
E 2	22 44 34	9 31 2	22 19	11	29	19	24	12	23	7	6
P 3	22 48 31	10 29 7	6♒58	13	0♎	20	24	12	23	7	6
T 4	22 52 27	11 27 14	21 36	15	1	21	24	12	23	7	6
E 5	22 56 24	12 25 23	6♓ 7	17	3	21	24	12	23	7	6
M 6	23 0 20	13 23 33	20 23	19	4	22	24	12	23	7	6
B 7	23 4 17	14 21 45	4♈22	21	5	22	24	12	23	7	6
E 8	23 8 13	15 19 59	17 59	23	6	23	24	12	23	7	6
R 9	23 12 10	16 18 14	1♉14	24	8	23	24	12	23	7	6
10	23 16 7	17 16 32	14 6	26	9	24	24	12	23	7	6
11	23 20 3	18 14 52	26 38	28	10	25	24	12	23	7	6
12	23 24 0	19 13 14	8♊54	0♎	11	25	25	12	23	7	6
13	23 27 56	20 11 38	20 58	1	13	26	25	12	23	7	6
14	23 31 53	21 10 4	2♋53	3	14	26	25	12	23	7	6
15	23 35 49	22 8 33	14 45	5	15	27	25	12 D	23	7	6
16	23 39 46	23 7 3	26 38	6	16	27	25	12	23	7	6
17	23 43 42	24 5 36	8♌36	8	17	28	25	12	23	7	7
18	23 47 39	25 4 11	20 43	9	19	28	25	12	23	7	7
19	23 51 36	26 2 47	3♍ 2	11	20	29	25	12	24	7	7
20	23 55 32	27 1 26	15 35	13	21	29	25	12	24	7	7
21	23 59 29	28 0 7	28 24	14	22	0♋	25	12	24	7	7
22	0 3 25	28 58 49	11♎27	16	24	0	25	12	24	7	7
23	0 7 22	29 57 34	24 46	17	25	1	25	12	24	7	7
24	0 11 18	0♎56 21	8♏19	19	26	1	26	12	24	8	7
25	0 15 15	1 55 9	22 4	20	27	2	26	12	24	8	7
26	0 19 11	2 53 59	5♐59	22	29	2	26	12	24	8	7
27	0 23 8	3 52 51	20 2	23	0♏	3	26	12	24	8	7
28	0 27 5	4 51 45	4♑11	25	1	3	26	12	24	8	7
29	0 31 1	5 50 40	18 24	26	2	4	26	12	24	8	7
30	0 34 58	6 49 37	2♒39	28	3	4	26	12	24	8	7

THE SUN ENTERS THE SIGN OF LIBRA ON SEP 23 AT 01:00.

SIDEREAL SUN MOON MERCURY VENUS MARS JUPITER SATURN URANUS NEPTUNE PLUTO

DAY	TIME	☉	☽	☿	♀	♂	♃	♄	♅	♆	♇
	h m s	° ' "	° '	°	°	°	°	°	°	°	°
O 1	0 38 54	7♎48 36	16♒52	29♎	5♏	5♋	26♐	12♑	24♌	8♏	7♍
C 2	0 42 51	8 47 36	1♓ 2	0♏	6	5	26	12	24	8	7
T 3	0 46 47	9 46 38	15 5	2	7	6	27	12	24	8	7
O 4	0 50 44	10 45 43	28 59	3	8	6	27	12	24	8	7
B 5	0 54 40	11 44 49	12♈39	4	10	7	27	12	24	8	7
E 6	0 58 37	12 43 57	26 4	6	11	7	27	12	24	8	7
R 7	1 2 33	13 43 7	9♉11	7	12	8	27	12	24	8	7
8	1 6 30	14 42 20	22 0	8	13	8	27	12	25	8	7
9	1 10 27	15 41 35	4♊31	10	14	8	27	12	25	8	7
10	1 14 23	16 40 52	16 47	11	16	9	27	12	25	8	7
11	1 18 20	17 40 11	28 51	12	17	9	28	12	25	8	7
12	1 22 16	18 39 33	10♋46	13	18	10	28	12	25	8	7
13	1 26 13	19 38 57	22 37	14	19	10	28	12	25	8	7
14	1 30 9	20 38 23	4♌30	15	21	10	28	12	25	8	7
15	1 34 6	21 37 52	16 28	16	22	11	28	13	25	8	7
16	1 38 2	22 37 23	28 38	17	23	11	28	13	25	8	7
17	1 41 59	23 36 56	11♍ 2	18	24	12	29	13	25	8	7
18	1 45 56	24 36 31	23 46	19	25	12	29	13	25	8	7
19	1 49 52	25 36 9	6♎49	20	27	12	29	13	25	8	7
20	1 53 49	26 35 48	20 14	21	28	13	29	13	25	8	7
21	1 57 45	27 35 30	3♏59	22	29	13	29	13	25	8	7
22	2 1 42	28 35 13	18 0	22	0♐	13	29	13	25	8	8
23	2 5 38	29 34 59	2♐13	23	2	14	29	13	25	9	8
24	2 9 35	0♏34 46	16 33	23	3	14	0♑	13	25	9	8
25	2 13 31	1 34 35	0♑55	24	4	14	0	13	25	9	8
26	2 17 28	2 34 26	15 13	24	5	15	0	13	25	9	8
27	2 21 25	3 34 19	29 26	24 R	6	15	0	13	25	9	8
28	2 25 21	4 34 13	13♒31	24	8	15	0	13	25	9	8
29	2 29 18	5 34 9	27 26	24	9	15	0	13	25	9	8
30	2 33 14	6 34 6	11♓13	24	10	16	1	13	25	9	8
31	2 37 11	7 34 5	24 50	23	11	16	1	13	25	9	8

THE SUN ENTERS THE SIGN OF SCORPIO ON OCT 23 AT 10:03.

DAY	TIME	☉	☽	☿	♀	♂	♃	♄	♅	♆	♇
	h m s	° ' "	° '	°	°	°	°	°	°	°	°
N 1	2 41 7	8♏34 5	8♈17	23♏R	13♐	16♋	1♑	14♑	25♌	9♏	8♍
O 2	2 45 4	9 34 8	21 33	22	14	16	1	14	25	9	8
V 3	2 49 0	10 34 12	4♉38	21	15	17	1	14	25	9	8
E 4	2 52 57	11 34 18	17 29	20	16	17	2	14	25	9	8
M 5	2 56 54	12 34 26	0♊ 8	19	17	17	2	14	25	9	8
B 6	3 0 50	13 34 36	12 33	18	19	17	2	14	26	9	8
E 7	3 4 47	14 34 47	24 45	16	20	17	2	14	26	9	8
R 8	3 8 43	15 35 1	6♋46	15	21	18	2	14	26	9	8
9	3 12 40	16 35 17	18 40	14	22	18	3	14	26	9	8
10	3 16 36	17 35 34	0♌30	12	23	18	3	14	26	9	8
11	3 20 33	18 35 54	12 20	11	25	18	3	14	26	9	8
12	3 24 29	19 36 15	24 16	10	26	18	3	14	26	9	8
13	3 28 26	20 36 39	6♍23	9	27	18	3	14	26	9	8
14	3 32 23	21 37 4	18 47	9	28	18	4	15	26	9	8
15	3 36 19	22 37 31	1♎33	8	0♑	18	4	15	26	9	8
16	3 40 16	23 38 1	14 43	8 D	1	19	4	15	26	9	8
17	3 44 12	24 38 31	28 20	8	2	19	4	15	26	9	8
18	3 48 9	25 39 4	12♏22	8	3	19	4	15	26	9	8
19	3 52 5	26 39 38	26 47	8	4	19	5	15	26	10	8
20	3 56 2	27 40 14	11♐28	9	6	19 R	5	15	26	10	8
21	3 59 58	28 40 51	26 16	9	7	19	5	15	26	10	8
22	4 3 55	29 41 30	11♑ 4	10	8	19	5	15	26	10	8
23	4 7 52	0♐42 10	25 43	11	9	19	5	15	26	10	8
24	4 11 48	1 42 50	10♒ 9	12	10	19	6	15	26	10	8
25	4 15 45	2 43 32	24 17	13	12	19	6	16	26	10	8
26	4 19 41	3 44 16	8♓ 9	14	13	18	6	16	26	10	8
27	4 23 38	4 44 59	21 43	15	14	18	6	16	26	10	8
28	4 27 34	5 45 44	5♈ 3	16	15	18	6	16	26	10	8
29	4 31 31	6 46 30	18 9	18	16	18	7	16	26	10	8
30	4 35 27	7 47 17	1♉ 4	19	18	18	7	16	26	10	8

THE SUN ENTERS THE SIGN OF SAGITTARIUS ON NOV 22 AT 07:20.

DAY	TIME	☉	☽	☿	♀	♂	♃	♄	♅	♆	♇
	h m s	° ' "	° '	°	°	°	°	°	°	°	°
D 1	4 39 24	8♐48 5	13♉48	20♏	19♑	18♋R	7♑	16♑	26♌R	10♏	8♍
E 2	4 43 21	9 48 55	26 22	22	20	18	7	16	26	10	8
C 3	4 47 17	10 49 45	8♊45	23	21	18	7	16	26	10	8
E 4	4 51 14	11 50 36	20 59	25	22	17	8	16	26	10	8
M 5	4 55 10	12 51 29	3♋ 4	26	24	17	8	17	26	10	8
B 6	4 59 7	13 52 23	15 1	27	25	17	8	17	26	10	8
E 7	5 3 3	14 53 17	26 52	29	26	17	8	17	26	10	8
R 8	5 7 0	15 54 13	8♌40	0♐	27	17	9	17	26	10	8
9	5 10 56	16 55 10	20 29	2	28	16	9	17	26	10	8
10	5 14 53	17 56 9	2♍23	3	0♒	16	9	17	26	10	8 R
11	5 18 50	18 57 8	14 27	5	1	16	9	17	26	10	8
12	5 22 46	19 58 8	26 46	6	2	15	9	17	26	10	8
13	5 26 43	20 59 10	9♎27	8	3	15	10	17	26	10	8
14	5 30 39	22 0 13	22 34	9	4	15	10	18	26	10	8
15	5 34 36	23 1 16	6♏10	11	5	15	10	18	26	10	8
16	5 38 32	24 2 21	20 16	12	7	14	10	18	26	10	8
17	5 42 29	25 3 26	4♐49	14	8	14	11	18	26	10	8
18	5 46 25	26 4 33	19 45	16	9	14	11	18	26	10	8
19	5 50 22	27 5 40	4♑53	17	10	13	11	18	26	11	8
20	5 54 19	28 6 47	20 4	19	11	13	11	18	26	11	8
21	5 58 15	29 7 55	5♒ 6	20	13	12	12	18	26	11	8
22	6 2 12	0♑ 9 3	19 52	22	14	12	12	18	26	11	8
23	6 6 8	1 10 11	4♓17	23	15	12	12	19	26	11	8
24	6 10 5	2 11 20	18 18	25	16	11	12	19	26	11	8
25	6 14 1	3 12 28	1♈55	26	17	11	12	19	26	11	8
26	6 17 58	4 13 36	15 11	28	18	11	13	19	26	11	8
27	6 21 54	5 14 45	28 8	0♑	20	10	13	19	26	11	8
28	6 25 51	6 15 53	10♉49	1	21	10	13	19	25	11	8
29	6 29 48	7 17 2	23 18	3	22	9	13	19	25	11	8
30	6 33 44	8 18 10	5♊36	4	23	9	14	19	25	11	8
31	6 37 41	9 19 19	17 46	6	24	9	14	19	25	11	8

THE SUN ENTERS THE SIGN OF CAPRICORN ON DEC 21 AT 20:27.

♈ ARIES ♉ TAURUS ♊ GEMINI ♋ CANCER ♌ LEO ♍ VIRGO ♎ LIBRA ♏ SCORPIO ♐ SAGITTARIUS ♑ CAPRICORN ♒ AQUARIUS ♓ PISCES

242 *Appendix X*

1961

SIDEREAL SUN MOON MERCURY VENUS MARS JUPITER SATURN URANUS NEPTUNE PLUTO

DAY	TIME	☉	☽	☿	♀	♂	♃	♄	♅	♆	♇
	h m s	° ' "	° '	°	°	°	°	°	°	°	°
J 1	6 41 37	10♑20 28	29♊49	7♑	25♒	8♋R	14♑	20♑	25♌R	11♏	8♍R
A 2	6 45 34	11 21 36	11♋46	9	26	8	14	20	25	11	8
N 3	6 49 30	12 22 45	23 38	11	28	7	15	20	25	11	8
U 4	6 53 27	13 23 53	5♌28	12	29	7	15	20	25	11	8
A 5	6 57 23	14 25 2	17 16	14	0♓	7	15	20	25	11	8
R 6	7 1 20	15 26 11	29 6	15	1	6	15	20	25	11	8
Y 7	7 5 17	16 27 20	11♍ 2	17	2	6	15	20	25	11	8
8	7 9 13	17 28 28	23 6	19	3	5	16	20	25	11	8
9	7 13 10	18 29 37	5♎24	20	4	5	16	21	25	11	8
10	7 17 6	19 30 46	18 1	22	5	5	16	21	25	11	8
11	7 21 3	20 31 55	1♏ 1	24	7	4	16	21	25	11	8
12	7 24 59	21 33 4	14 28	25	8	4	17	21	25	11	8
13	7 28 56	22 34 13	28 25	27	9	4	17	21	25	11	8
14	7 32 52	23 35 22	12♐50	29	10	4	17	21	25	11	8
15	7 36 49	24 36 30	27 41	0♒	11	3	17	21	25	11	8
16	7 40 46	25 37 39	12♑50	2	12	3	18	21	25	11	8
17	7 44 42	26 38 46	28 8	4	13	3	18	21	25	11	8
18	7 48 39	27 39 54	13♒23	5	14	2	18	22	25	11	8
19	7 52 35	28 41 0	28 26	7	15	2	18	22	25	11	8
20	7 56 32	29 42 6	13♓ 8	9	16	2	19	22	25	11	8
21	8 0 28	0♒43 11	27 24	11	17	2	19	22	25	11	8
22	8 4 25	1 44 15	11♈14	12	19	1	19	22	25	11	8
23	8 8 21	2 45 18	24 37	14	20	1	19	22	25	11	8
24	8 12 18	3 46 20	7♉36	16	21	1	19	22	25	11	8
25	8 16 15	4 47 20	20 16	17	22	1	20	22	25	11	8
26	8 20 11	5 48 20	2♊39	19	23	1	20	23	25	11	8
27	8 24 8	6 49 19	14 49	21	24	1	20	23	24	11	8
28	8 28 4	7 50 16	26 50	22	25	1	20	23	24	11	8
29	8 32 1	8 51 13	8♋44	24	26	0	21	23	24	11	8
30	8 35 57	9 52 8	20 36	26	27	0	21	23	24	11	8
31	8 39 54	10 53 3	2♌25	27	28	0	21	23	24	11	7

THE SUN ENTERS THE SIGN OF AQUARIUS ON JAN 20 AT 07:02.

DAY	TIME	☉	☽	☿	♀	♂	♃	♄	♅	♆	♇
	h m s	° ' "	° '	°	°	°	°	°	°	°	°
F 1	8 43 50	11♒53 56	14♌15	29♒	29♓	0♋R	21♑	23♑	24♌R	11♏	7♍R
E 2	8 47 47	12 54 48	26 7	0♓	0⊙	0	21	23	24	11	7
B 3	8 51 44	13 55 39	8♍ 4	2	1♈	0	22	23	24	11	7
R 4	8 55 40	14 56 29	20 7	3	2	0	22	24	24	11	7
U 5	8 59 37	15 57 18	2♎19	4	3	0	22	24	24	11	7
A 6	9 3 33	16 58 6	14 44	5	4	0 D	22	24	24	11	7
R 7	9 7 30	17 58 53	27 24	6	5	0	23	24	24	11	7
Y 8	9 11 26	18 59 39	10♏23	7	6	0	23	24	24	11	7
9	9 15 23	20 0 25	23 44	8	6	0	23	24	24	11	7
10	9 19 19	21 1 9	7♐29	8	7	0	23	24	24	11	7
11	9 23 16	22 1 52	21 39	9	8	0	23	24	24	11 R	7
12	9 27 13	23 2 34	6♑12	9 R	9	0	24	24	24	11	7
13	9 31 9	24 3 15	21 4	9	10	0	24	25	24	11	7
14	9 35 6	25 3 55	6♒ 8	9	11	0	24	25	24	11	7
15	9 39 2	26 4 33	21 16	9	12	0	24	25	24	11	7
16	9 42 59	27 5 10	6♓19	8	13	1	25	25	24	11	7
17	9 46 55	28 5 45	21 7	8	14	1	25	25	24	11	7
18	9 50 52	29 6 19	5♈33	7	14	1	25	25	24	11	7
19	9 54 48	0♓ 6 50	19 35	6	15	1	25	25	23	11	7
20	9 58 45	1 7 20	3♉ 9	5	16	1	25	25	23	11	7
21	10 2 42	2 7 49	16 17	4	17	1	26	25	23	11	7
22	10 6 38	3 8 15	29 1	3	17	1	26	26	23	11	7
23	10 10 35	4 8 40	11♊26	2	18	2	26	26	23	11	7
24	10 14 31	5 9 2	23 35	1	19	2	26	26	23	11	7
25	10 18 28	6 9 23	5♋33	0	20	2	26	26	23	11	7
26	10 22 24	7 9 41	17 25	29♒	20	2	27	26	23	11	7
27	10 26 21	8 9 58	29 13	28	21	2	27	26	23	11	7
28	10 30 17	9 10 13	11♌ 2	27	22	3	27	26	23	11	7

THE SUN ENTERS THE SIGN OF PISCES ON FEB 18 AT 21:17.

DAY	TIME	☉	☽	☿	♀	♂	♃	♄	♅	♆	♇
	h m s	° ' "	° '	°	°	°	°	°	°	°	°
M 1	10 34 14	10♓10 26	22♌55	26♒R	22♈	3♋	27♑	26♑	23♌R	11♏R	7♍R
A 2	10 38 11	11 10 37	4♍54	26	23	3	27	26	23	11	7
R 3	10 42 7	12 10 46	17 1	25	24	3	28	26	23	11	7
C 4	10 46 4	13 10 53	29 18	25	24	4	28	26	23	11	7
H 5	10 50 0	14 10 58	11♎46	25	25	4	28	27	23	11	7
6	10 53 57	15 11 2	24 26	24 D	25	4	28	27	23	11	7
7	10 57 53	16 11 4	7♏20	24	26	4	28	27	23	11	7
8	11 1 50	17 11 5	20 29	24	26	5	29	27	23	11	7
9	11 5 46	18 11 4	3♐54	25	26	5	29	27	23	11	7
10	11 9 43	19 11 1	17 36	25	27	5	29	27	23	11	7
11	11 13 39	20 10 57	1♑34	25	27	6	29	27	23	11	7
12	11 17 36	21 10 51	15 49	26	28	6	29	27	23	11	6
13	11 21 33	22 10 44	0♒19	26	28	6	0♒	27	23	11	6
14	11 25 29	23 10 34	14 58	27	28	7	0	27	23	11	6
15	11 29 26	24 10 23	29 44	27	28	7	0	27	23	11	6
16	11 33 22	25 10 10	14♓28	28	29	7	0	28	22	11	6
17	11 37 19	26 9 55	29 4	29	29	8	0	28	22	11	6
18	11 41 15	27 9 38	13♈26	0♓	29	8	0	28	22	11	6
19	11 45 12	28 9 19	27 27	1	29	8	1	28	22	11	6
20	11 49 8	29 8 58	11♉ 5	1	29 R	9	1	28	22	11	6
21	11 53 5	0♈ 8 35	24 19	2	29	9	1	28	22	11	6
22	11 57 2	1 8 9	7♊ 9	3	29	9	1	28	22	11	6
23	12 0 58	2 7 41	19 38	5	29	10	1	28	22	11	6
24	12 4 55	3 7 11	1♋49	6	29	10	1	28	22	11	6
25	12 8 51	4 6 39	13 48	7	29	11	2	28	22	11	6
26	12 12 48	5 6 4	25 40	8	29	11	2	28	22	11	6
27	12 16 44	6 5 27	7♌28	9	28	11	2	28	22	11	6
28	12 20 41	7 4 47	19 18	10	28	12	2	28	22	11	6
29	12 24 37	8 4 6	1♍15	12	28	12	2	28	22	11	6
30	12 28 34	9 3 22	13 21	13	27	13	2	29	22	11	6
31	12 32 31	10 2 36	25 40	14	27	13	3	29	22	11	6

THE SUN ENTERS THE SIGN OF ARIES ON MAR 20 AT 20:33.

DAY	TIME	☉	☽	☿	♀	♂	♃	♄	♅	♆	♇
	h m s	° ' "	° '	°	°	°	°	°	°	°	°
A 1	12 36 27	11♈ 1 48	8♎12	16♓	27♈R	13♋	3♒	29♑	22♌R	11♏R	6♍R
P 2	12 40 24	12 0 57	21 0	17	26	14	3	29	22	11	6
R 3	12 44 20	13 0 5	4♏ 2	19	26	14	3	29	22	11	6
I 4	12 48 17	13 59 11	17 19	20	25	15	3	29	22	11	6
L 5	12 52 13	14 58 15	0♐48	22	25	15	3	29	22	11	6
6	12 56 10	15 57 17	14 29	23	24	16	3	29	22	11	6
7	13 0 6	16 56 18	28 20	25	23	16	4	29	22	11	6
8	13 4 3	17 55 16	12♑19	26	23	16	4	29	22	11	6
9	13 8 0	18 54 14	26 26	28	22	17	4	29	22	11	6
10	13 11 56	19 53 9	10♒38	29	21	17	4	29	22	10	6
11	13 15 53	20 52 2	24 55	1♈	21	18	4	29	22	10	6
12	13 19 49	21 50 54	9♓14	3	20	18	4	29	22	10	6
13	13 23 46	22 49 44	23 31	4	20	19	4	29	22	10	6
14	13 27 42	23 48 32	7♈43	6	19	19	5	29	22	10	6
15	13 31 39	24 47 18	21 45	8	18	20	5	29	22	10	6
16	13 35 35	25 46 2	5♉33	10	18	20	5	29	22	10	6
17	13 39 32	26 44 45	19 3	11	17	21	5	29	22	10	6
18	13 43 28	27 43 25	2♊13	13	17	21	5	29	22	10	6
19	13 47 25	28 42 3	15 2	15	16	22	5	0♒	22	10	6
20	13 51 22	29 40 39	27 31	17	16	22	5	0	22	10	6
21	13 55 18	0♉39 13	9♋44	19	15	22	5	0	22	10	6
22	13 59 15	1 37 45	21 44	21	15	23	5	0	22	10	6
23	14 3 11	2 36 14	3♌35	23	14	23	6	0	22	10	6
24	14 7 8	3 34 42	15 24	25	14	24	6	0	22	10	6
25	14 11 4	4 33 7	27 15	27	14	24	6	0	22	10	6
26	14 15 1	5 31 30	9♍14	29	14	25	6	0	22	10	6
27	14 18 57	6 29 51	21 26	1♉	13	25	6	0	22	10	6
28	14 22 54	7 28 10	3♎53	3	13	26	6	0	22	10	6
29	14 26 51	8 26 27	16 39	5	13	26	6	0	22 D	10	6
30	14 30 47	9 24 42	29 45	7	13	27	6	0	22	10	6

THE SUN ENTERS THE SIGN OF TAURUS ON APR 20 AT 07:55.

DAY	TIME	☉	☽	☿	♀	♂	♃	♄	♅	♆	♇
	h m s	° ' "	° '	°	°	°	°	°	°	°	°
M 1	14 34 44	10♉22 56	13♏10	9♉	13♈R	27♋	6♒	0♒	22♌	10♏R	6♍R
A 2	14 38 40	11 21 7	26 52	11	13 D	28	6	0	22	10	6
Y 3	14 42 37	12 19 17	10♐48	14	13	28	6	0	22	10	6
4	14 46 33	13 17 26	24 53	16	13	29	6	0	22	10	6
5	14 50 30	14 15 33	9♑ 4	18	13	29	6	0	22	10	6
6	14 54 26	15 13 39	23 15	20	13	0♌	7	0	22	10	6
7	14 58 23	16 11 43	7♒26	22	13	0	7	0	22	10	6
8	15 2 20	17 9 46	21 34	24	13	1	7	0	22	10	6
9	15 6 16	18 7 47	5♓38	26	14	2	7	0 R	22	10	6
10	15 10 13	19 5 47	19 37	29	14	2	7	0	22	10	6
11	15 14 9	20 3 46	3♈30	1♊	14	3	7	0	22	10	6
12	15 18 6	21 1 43	17 16	3	15	3	7	0	22	10	6
13	15 22 2	21 59 39	0♉53	5	15	4	7	0	22	10	6
14	15 25 59	22 57 34	14 19	7	15	4	7	0	22	10	6
15	15 29 55	23 55 27	27 31	9	16	5	7	0	22	10	6
16	15 33 52	24 53 19	10♊27	10	16	5	7	0	22	10	6
17	15 37 49	25 51 10	23 6	12	17	6	7	0	22	10	6 D
18	15 41 45	26 48 58	5♋30	14	17	6	7	0	22	9	6
19	15 45 42	27 46 45	17 39	16	18	7	7	0	22	9	6
20	15 49 38	28 44 31	29 38	18	18	7	7	0	22	9	6
21	15 53 35	29 42 15	11♌28	19	19	8	7	0	22	9	6
22	15 57 31	0♊39 57	23 16	21	19	8	7	0	22	9	6
23	16 1 28	1 37 38	5♍ 7	22	20	9	7	0	22	9	6
24	16 5 24	2 35 18	17 7	24	21	10	7	0	22	9	6
25	16 9 21	3 32 55	29 20	25	21	10	7 R	0	22	9	6
26	16 13 18	4 30 32	11♎51	27	22	11	7	0	22	9	6
27	16 17 14	5 28 6	24 44	28	23	11	7	0	22	9	6
28	16 21 11	6 25 40	8♏ 2	29	23	12	7	0	22	9	6
29	16 25 7	7 23 12	21 44	0♋	24	12	7	0	22	9	6
30	16 29 4	8 20 43	5♐47	1	25	13	7	0	22	9	6
31	16 33 0	9 18 13	20 8	3	25	13	7	29♑	22	9	6

THE SUN ENTERS THE SIGN OF GEMINI ON MAY 21 AT 07:22.

DAY	TIME	☉	☽	☿	♀	♂	♃	♄	♅	♆	♇
	h m s	° ' "	° '	°	°	°	°	°	°	°	°
J 1	16 36 57	10♊15 43	4♑39	4♋	26♈	14♌	7♒R	29♑R	22♌	9♏R	6♍
U 2	16 40 53	11 13 11	19 14	4	27	15	7	29	22	9	6
N 3	16 44 50	12 10 38	3♒47	5	28	15	7	29	22	9	6
E 4	16 48 47	13 8 5	18 12	6	29	16	7	29	22	9	6
5	16 52 43	14 5 31	2♓27	7	29	16	7	29	22	9	6
6	16 56 40	15 2 56	16 30	8	0♉	17	7	29	22	9	6
7	17 0 36	16 0 20	0♈21	8	1	17	7	29	22	9	6
8	17 4 33	16 57 44	13 59	9	2	18	7	29	22	9	6
9	17 8 29	17 55 8	27 26	9	3	18	7	29	22	9	6
10	17 12 26	18 52 31	10♉40	10	4	19	7	29	22	9	6
11	17 16 22	19 49 53	23 43	10	4	20	7	29	22	9	6
12	17 20 19	20 47 15	6♊34	10	5	20	7	29	22	9	6
13	17 24 16	21 44 36	19 12	10	6	21	7	29	23	9	6
14	17 28 12	22 41 57	1♋38	10 R	7	21	7	29	23	9	6
15	17 32 9	23 39 17	13 51	10	8	22	7	29	23	9	6
16	17 36 5	24 36 36	25 53	10	9	22	6	29	23	9	6
17	17 40 2	25 33 54	7♌47	10	10	23	6	29	23	9	6
18	17 43 58	26 31 12	19 35	10	11	24	6	29	23	9	6
19	17 47 55	27 28 29	1♍22	10	12	24	6	29	23	9	6
20	17 51 51	28 25 45	13 12	9	13	25	6	29	23	9	6
21	17 55 48	29 23 0	25 11	9	14	25	6	29	23	9	6
22	17 59 45	0♋20 15	7♎23	9	15	26	6	28	23	9	6
23	18 3 41	1 17 29	19 54	8	16	26	6	28	23	9	6
24	18 7 38	2 14 42	2♏48	8	17	27	6	28	23	9	6
25	18 11 34	3 11 55	16 9	7	18	28	6	28	23	9	6
26	18 15 31	4 9 7	29 57	6	19	28	6	28	23	9	6
27	18 19 27	5 6 19	14♐10	6	20	29	6	28	23	9	6
28	18 23 24	6 3 31	28 46	5	21	29	5	28	23	9	6
29	18 27 20	7 0 42	13♑37	5	22	0♍	5	28	23	9	6
30	18 31 17	7 57 54	28 34	4	23	1	5	28	23	9	6

THE SUN ENTERS THE SIGN OF CANCER ON JUN 21 AT 15:31.

♈ ARIES ♉ TAURUS ♊ GEMINI ♋ CANCER ♌ LEO ♍ VIRGO ♎ LIBRA ♏ SCORPIO ♐ SAGITTARIUS ♑ CAPRICORN ♒ AQUARIUS ♓ PISCES

1961

SIDEREAL SUN MOON MERCURY VENUS MARS JUPITER SATURN URANUS NEPTUNE PLUTO

DAY	TIME	☉	☽	☿	♀	♂	♃	♄	♅	♆	♇
	h m s	° ' "	° '	°	°	°	°	°	°	°	°
J 1	18 35 14	8♋55 5	13♒29	4♋R	24♉	1♍	5♒R	28♑R	23♌	9♏R	6♍
U 2	18 39 10	9 52 16	28 15	3	25	2	5	28	23	9	6
L 3	18 43 7	10 49 28	12♓45	3	26	2	5	28	23	9	6
Y 4	18 47 3	11 46 39	26 58	2	27	3	5	28	23	9	6
5	18 51 0	12 43 51	10♈51	2	28	4	5	28	23	9	6
6	18 54 56	13 41 3	24 25	2	29	4	5	28	24	9	6
7	18 58 53	14 38 16	7♉41	1	0♊	5	5	27	24	9	6
8	19 2 49	15 35 28	20 42	1 D	1	5	4	27	24	9	6
9	19 6 46	16 32 42	3♊27	1	2	6	4	27	24	9	6
10	19 10 43	17 29 55	16 0	1	3	7	4	27	24	9	6
11	19 14 39	18 27 9	28 21	2	4	7	4	27	24	9	6
12	19 18 36	19 24 24	10♋32	2	5	8	4	27	24	9	6
13	19 22 32	20 21 38	22 34	2	6	8	4	27	24	9	6
14	19 26 29	21 18 53	4♌29	3	7	9	4	27	24	9	6
15	19 30 25	22 16 8	16 18	3	8	10	4	27	24	9	6
16	19 34 22	23 13 23	28 5	4	9	10	3	27	24	9	6
17	19 38 18	24 10 39	9♍52	4	10	11	3	27	24	9	6
18	19 42 15	25 7 54	21 42	5	12	11	3	27	24	9	6
19	19 46 12	26 5 10	3♎41	6	13	12	3	27	24	9	6
20	19 50 8	27 2 26	15 53	7	14	13	3	27	24	9 D	6
21	19 54 5	27 59 42	28 22	8	15	13	3	26	24	9	7
22	19 58 1	28 56 59	11♏13	9	16	14	3	26	24	9	7
23	20 1 58	29 54 16	24 30	10	17	14	3	26	24	9	7
24	20 5 54	0♌51 33	8♐14	11	18	15	2	26	25	9	7
25	20 9 51	1 48 51	22 26	13	19	16	2	26	25	9	7
26	20 13 47	2 46 9	7♑ 4	14	20	16	2	26	25	9	7
27	20 17 44	3 43 27	22 0	16	21	17	2	26	25	9	7
28	20 21 41	4 40 47	7♒ 9	17	23	17	2	26	25	9	7
29	20 25 37	5 38 7	22 19	19	24	18	2	26	25	9	7
30	20 29 34	6 35 28	7♓22	21	25	19	2	26	25	9	7
31	20 33 30	7 32 49	22 10	22	26	19	2	26	25	9	7

THE SUN ENTERS THE SIGN OF LEO ON JUL 23 AT 02:24.

DAY	TIME	☉	☽	☿	♀	♂	♃	♄	♅	♆	♇
	h m s	° ' "	° '	°	°	°	°	°	°	°	°
A 1	20 37 27	8♌30 12	6♈37	24♋	27♊	20♍	1♒R	26♑R	25♌	9♏	7♍
U 2	20 41 23	9 27 36	20 40	26	28	21	1	26	25	9	7
G 3	20 45 20	10 25 1	4♉19	28	29	21	1	25	25	9	7
U 4	20 49 16	11 22 27	17 35	0♌	0♋	22	1	25	25	9	7
S 5	20 53 13	12 19 55	0♊30	2	2	22	1	25	25	9	7
T 6	20 57 10	13 17 24	13 6	4	3	23	1	25	25	9	7
7	21 1 6	14 14 54	25 27	6	4	24	1	25	25	9	7
8	21 5 3	15 12 25	7♋36	8	5	24	1	25	25	9	7
9	21 8 59	16 9 58	19 36	10	6	25	0	25	26	9	7
10	21 12 56	17 7 32	1♌29	12	7	26	0	25	26	9	7
11	21 16 52	18 5 7	13 18	14	8	26	0	25	26	9	7
12	21 20 49	19 2 43	25 5	16	10	27	0	25	26	9	7
13	21 24 45	20 0 20	6♍52	18	11	27	0	25	26	9	7
14	21 28 42	20 57 58	18 42	20	12	28	0	25	26	9	7
15	21 32 39	21 55 38	0♎38	22	13	29	0	25	26	9	7
16	21 36 35	22 53 18	12 42	24	14	29	0	25	26	9	7
17	21 40 32	23 51 0	24 57	26	15	0♎	29♑	25	26	9	7
18	21 44 28	24 48 43	7♏28	28	16	1	29	25	26	9	7
19	21 48 25	25 46 26	20 17	0♍	18	1	29	24	26	9	7
20	21 52 21	26 44 11	3♐29	2	19	2	29	24	26	9	7
21	21 56 18	27 41 57	17 5	4	20	3	29	24	26	9	7
22	22 0 14	28 39 44	1♑ 7	6	21	3	29	24	26	9	8
23	22 4 11	29 37 33	15 33	8	22	4	29	24	26	9	8
24	22 8 8	0♍35 22	0♒21	10	23	4	29	24	26	9	8
25	22 12 4	1 33 13	15 25	12	25	5	29	24	26	9	8
26	22 16 1	2 31 5	0♓36	13	26	6	29	24	27	9	8
27	22 19 57	3 28 59	15 46	15	27	6	29	24	27	9	8
28	22 23 54	4 26 54	0♈44	17	28	7	28	24	27	9	8
29	22 27 50	5 24 51	15 23	19	29	8	28	24	27	9	8
30	22 31 47	6 22 49	29 38	20	0♌	8	28	24	27	9	8
31	22 35 43	7 20 50	13♉26	22	2	9	28	24	27	9	8

THE SUN ENTERS THE SIGN OF VIRGO ON AUG 23 AT 09:20.

DAY	TIME	☉	☽	☿	♀	♂	♃	♄	♅	♆	♇
	h m s	° ' "	° '	°	°	°	°	°	°	°	°
S 1	22 39 40	8♍18 52	26♉48	24♍	3♌	10♎	28♑R	24♑R	27♌	9♏	8♍
E 2	22 43 37	9 16 57	9♊44	25	4	10	28	24	27	9	8
P 3	22 47 33	10 15 3	22 18	27	5	11	28	24	27	9	8
T 4	22 51 30	11 13 12	4♋34	29	6	12	28	24	27	9	8
E 5	22 55 26	12 11 22	16 37	0♎	8	12	28	24	27	9	8
M 6	22 59 23	13 9 34	28 31	2	9	13	28	24	27	9	8
B 7	23 3 19	14 7 48	10♌19	3	10	13	28	24	27	9	8
E 8	23 7 16	15 6 4	22 6	5	11	14	28	24	27	9	8
R 9	23 11 12	16 4 22	3♍54	6	12	15	28	24	27	9	8
10	23 15 9	17 2 42	15 45	8	14	15	28	24	27	9	8
11	23 19 6	18 1 3	27 43	9	15	16	28	23	27	9	8
12	23 23 2	18 59 27	9♎48	11	16	17	28	23	28	9	8
13	23 26 59	19 57 52	22 3	12	17	17	28	23	28	9	8
14	23 30 55	20 56 18	4♏29	13	18	18	27	23	28	9	8
15	23 34 52	21 54 47	17 8	15	20	19	27	23	28	9	8
16	23 38 48	22 53 17	0♐ 3	16	21	19	27	23	28	9	8
17	23 42 45	23 51 48	13 14	18	22	20	27	23	28	9	8
18	23 46 41	24 50 22	26 44	19	23	21	27	23	28	9	8
19	23 50 38	25 48 57	10♑35	20	24	21	27	23	28	9	8
20	23 54 34	26 47 33	24 46	21	26	22	27	23	28	9	9
21	23 58 31	27 46 12	9♒16	23	27	23	27	23	28	10	9
22	0 2 28	28 44 52	24 2	24	28	23	27	23	28	10	9
23	0 6 24	29 43 34	8♓59	25	29	24	27 D	23	28	10	9
24	0 10 21	0♎42 17	23 58	26	0♍	25	27	23	28	10	9
25	0 14 17	1 41 2	8♈53	27	2	25	27	23	28	10	9
26	0 18 14	2 39 50	23 34	28	3	26	27	23	28	10	9
27	0 22 10	3 38 40	7♉53	29	4	27	27	23 D	28	10	9
28	0 26 7	4 37 31	21 48	0♏	5	27	27	23	29	10	9
29	0 30 3	5 36 25	5♊15	1	7	28	27	23	29	10	9
30	0 34 0	6 35 22	18 16	2	8	29	27	23	29	10	9

THE SUN ENTERS THE SIGN OF LIBRA ON SEP 23 AT 06:44.

DAY	TIME	☉	☽	☿	♀	♂	♃	♄	♅	♆	♇
	h m s	° ' "	° '	°	°	°	°	°	°	°	°
O 1	0 37 57	7♎34 20	0♋52	3♏	9♍	29♎	27♑	23♑	29♌	10♏	9♍
C 2	0 41 53	8 33 21	13 9	4	10	0♏	27	23	29	10	9
T 3	0 45 50	9 32 25	25 10	5	11	1	27	23	29	10	9
O 4	0 49 46	10 31 30	7♌ 2	6	13	1	27	23	29	10	9
B 5	0 53 43	11 30 38	18 49	6	14	2	28	23	29	10	9
E 6	0 57 39	12 29 48	0♍36	7	15	3	28	23	29	10	9
R 7	1 1 36	13 29 0	12 27	7	16	4	28	23	29	10	9
8	1 5 32	14 28 14	24 26	8	18	4	28	23	29	10	9
9	1 9 29	15 27 31	6♎33	8	19	5	28	23	29	10	9
10	1 13 26	16 26 49	18 53	8 R	20	6	28	23	29	10	9
11	1 17 22	17 26 10	1♏24	8	21	6	28	23	29	10	9
12	1 21 19	18 25 32	14 8	8	22	7	28	23	29	10	9
13	1 25 15	19 24 57	27 5	8	24	8	28	23	29	10	9
14	1 29 12	20 24 23	10♐14	7	25	8	28	23	29	10	9
15	1 33 8	21 23 52	23 35	7	26	9	28	23	29	10	9
16	1 37 5	22 23 22	7♑ 9	6	27	10	28	24	29	10	9
17	1 41 1	23 22 54	20 55	6	29	10	28	24	29	10	9
18	1 44 58	24 22 27	4♒54	5	0♎	11	28	24	29	10	9
19	1 48 54	25 22 2	19 7	4	1	12	28	24	0♍	10	9
20	1 52 51	26 21 39	3♓31	3	2	12	28	24	0	11	9
21	1 56 48	27 21 18	18 4	1	4	13	29	24	0	11	9
22	2 0 44	28 20 58	2♈41	0	5	14	29	24	0	11	9
23	2 4 41	29 20 40	17 16	29♎	6	15	29	24	0	11	9
24	2 8 37	0♏20 24	1♉43	28	7	15	29	24	0	11	10
25	2 12 34	1 20 10	15 55	26	9	16	29	24	0	11	10
26	2 16 30	2 19 59	29 46	25	10	17	29	24	0	11	10
27	2 20 27	3 19 49	13♊13	24	11	17	29	24	0	11	10
28	2 24 23	4 19 41	26 15	24	12	18	29	24	0	11	10
29	2 28 20	5 19 36	8♋53	23	13	19	29	24	0	11	10
30	2 32 17	6 19 33	21 12	23	15	19	29	24	0	11	10
31	2 36 13	7 19 32	3♌14	22 D	16	20	0♒	24	0	11	10

THE SUN ENTERS THE SIGN OF SCORPIO ON OCT 23 AT 15:48.

DAY	TIME	☉	☽	☿	♀	♂	♃	♄	♅	♆	♇
	h m s	° ' "	° '	°	°	°	°	°	°	°	°
N 1	2 40 10	8♏19 33	15♌ 7	22♎	17♎	21♏	0♒	24♑	0♍	11♏	10♍
O 2	2 44 6	9 19 36	26 54	22	18	22	0	24	0	11	10
V 3	2 48 3	10 19 41	8♍43	23	20	22	0	24	0	11	10
E 4	2 51 59	11 19 49	20 37	23	21	23	0	24	0	11	10
M 5	2 55 56	12 19 58	2♎41	24	22	24	0	24	0	11	10
B 6	2 59 52	13 20 9	14 58	25	23	24	0	24	0	11	10
E 7	3 3 49	14 20 23	27 31	26	25	25	0	25	0	11	10
R 8	3 7 46	15 20 38	10♏21	27	26	26	0	25	0	11	10
9	3 11 42	16 20 55	23 26	28	27	26	1	25	0	11	10
10	3 15 39	17 21 14	6♐47	29	28	27	1	25	0	11	10
11	3 19 35	18 21 34	20 19	0♏	0♏	28	1	25	0	11	10
12	3 23 32	19 21 56	4♑ 1	1	1	29	1	25	0	11	10
13	3 27 28	20 22 19	17 50	3	2	29	1	25	0	11	10
14	3 31 25	21 22 44	1♒45	4	3	0♐	1	25	0	11	10
15	3 35 21	22 23 10	15 45	5	5	1	1	25	0	11	10
16	3 39 18	23 23 38	29 49	7	6	1	2	25	0	12	10
17	3 43 15	24 24 6	13♓57	8	7	2	2	25	0	12	10
18	3 47 11	25 24 36	28 7	10	8	3	2	25	0	12	10
19	3 51 8	26 25 7	12♈18	11	10	4	2	25	0	12	10
20	3 55 4	27 25 40	26 27	13	11	4	2	25	0	12	10
21	3 59 1	28 26 14	10♉28	14	12	5	2	26	0	12	10
22	4 2 57	29 26 49	24 19	16	13	6	3	26	0	12	10
23	4 6 54	0♐27 25	7♊53	18	15	7	3	26	0	12	10
24	4 10 50	1 28 4	21 9	19	16	7	3	26	0	12	10
25	4 14 47	2 28 43	4♋ 5	21	17	8	3	26	0	12	10
26	4 18 44	3 29 24	16 41	22	19	9	3	26	0	12	10
27	4 22 40	4 30 7	28 58	24	20	9	3	26	1	12	10
28	4 26 37	5 30 51	11♌ 1	25	21	10	4	26	1	12	10
29	4 30 33	6 31 37	22 54	27	22	11	4	26	1	12	10
30	4 34 30	7 32 24	4♍42	29	24	12	4	26	1	12	10

THE SUN ENTERS THE SIGN OF SAGITTARIUS ON NOV 22 AT 13:09.

DAY	TIME	☉	☽	☿	♀	♂	♃	♄	♅	♆	♇
	h m s	° ' "	° '	°	°	°	°	°	°	°	°
D 1	4 38 26	8♐33 13	16♍31	0♐	25♏	12♐	4♒	26♑	1♍	12♏	10♍
E 2	4 42 23	9 34 3	28 26	2	26	13	4	27	1	12	10
C 3	4 46 19	10 34 54	10♎32	3	27	14	5	27	1	12	10
E 4	4 50 16	11 35 47	22 54	5	29	15	5	27	1	12	10
M 5	4 54 13	12 36 41	5♏35	6	0♐	15	5	27	1	12	10
B 6	4 58 9	13 37 36	18 38	8	1	16	5	27	1 R	12	10
E 7	5 2 6	14 38 33	2♐ 1	9	2	17	5	27	1	12	10
R 8	5 6 2	15 39 31	15 44	11	4	18	5	27	1	12	10
9	5 9 59	16 40 29	29 42	13	5	18	6	27	1	12	10
10	5 13 55	17 41 29	13♑51	14	6	19	6	27	1	12	10
11	5 17 52	18 42 29	28 6	16	7	20	6	27	1	12	10
12	5 21 48	19 43 30	12♒23	17	9	21	6	28	1	12	10 R
13	5 25 45	20 44 31	26 38	19	10	21	6	28	1	12	10
14	5 29 42	21 45 33	10♓48	20	11	22	7	28	1	12	10
15	5 33 38	22 46 36	24 54	22	12	23	7	28	1	12	10
16	5 37 35	23 47 38	8♈53	24	14	23	7	28	1	13	10
17	5 41 31	24 48 41	22 45	25	15	24	7	28	1	13	10
18	5 45 28	25 49 45	6♉28	27	16	25	7	28	0	13	10
19	5 49 24	26 50 49	20 3	28	17	26	8	28	0	13	10
20	5 53 21	27 51 53	3♊26	0♑	19	26	8	28	0	13	10
21	5 57 17	28 52 58	16 37	2	20	27	8	28	0	13	10
22	6 1 14	29 54 3	29 33	3	21	28	8	29	0	13	10
23	6 5 11	0♑55 9	12♋14	5	22	29	9	29	0	13	10
24	6 9 7	1 56 15	24 40	6	24	29	9	29	0	13	10
25	6 13 4	2 57 21	6♌52	8	25	0♑	9	29	0	13	10
26	6 17 0	3 58 28	18 52	10	26	1	9	29	0	13	10
27	6 20 57	4 59 36	0♍44	11	27	2	9	29	0	13	10
28	6 24 53	6 0 44	12 32	13	29	2	10	29	0	13	10
29	6 28 50	7 1 52	24 21	14	0♑	3	10	29	0	13	10
30	6 32 47	8 3 1	6♎15	16	1	4	10	29	0	13	10
31	6 36 43	9 4 11	18 19	18	3	5	10	0♒	0	13	10

THE SUN ENTERS THE SIGN OF CAPRICORN ON DEC 22 AT 02:20.

♈ ARIES ♉ TAURUS ♊ GEMINI ♋ CANCER ♌ LEO ♍ VIRGO ♎ LIBRA ♏ SCORPIO ♐ SAGITTARIUS ♑ CAPRICORN ♒ AQUARIUS ♓ PISCES

SIDEREAL SUN MOON MERCURY VENUS MARS JUPITER SATURN URANUS NEPTUNE PLUTO

DAY	TIME	☉	☽	☿	♀	♂	♃	♄	♅	♆	♇
	h m s	° ' "	° '	°	°	°	°	°	°	°	°
J 1	6 40 40	10♑ 5 20	0♏40	19♑	4♑	5♑	10♒	0♒	0♍R	13♏	10♍R
A 2	6 44 36	11 6 31	13 22	21	5	6	11	0	0	13	10
N 3	6 48 33	12 7 41	26 27	22	6	7	11	0	0	13	10
U 4	6 52 29	13 8 52	9♐57	24	8	8	11	0	0	13	10
A 5	6 56 26	14 10 3	23 51	26	9	9	11	0	0	13	10
R 6	7 0 22	15 11 14	8♑ 7	27	10	9	12	0	0	13	10
Y 7	7 4 19	16 12 24	22 39	29	11	10	12	0	0	13	10
8	7 8 16	17 13 35	7♒21	1♒	13	11	12	0	0	13	10
9	7 12 12	18 14 45	22 6	2	14	12	12	1	0	13	10
10	7 16 9	19 15 55	6♓47	4	15	12	12	1	0	13	10
11	7 20 5	20 17 5	21 17	5	16	13	13	1	0	13	10
12	7 24 2	21 18 14	5♈35	7	18	14	13	1	0	13	10
13	7 27 58	22 19 22	19 38	8	19	15	13	1	0	13	10
14	7 31 55	23 20 29	3♉24	10	20	15	13	1	0	13	10
15	7 35 51	24 21 36	16 54	11	21	16	14	1	0	13	10
16	7 39 48	25 22 42	0♊10	13	23	17	14	1	0	13	10
17	7 43 45	26 23 47	13 10	14	24	18	14	2	0	13	10
18	7 47 41	27 24 52	25 58	16	25	18	14	2	0	13	10
19	7 51 38	28 25 56	8♋32	17	26	19	15	2	0	13	10
20	7 55 34	29 26 59	20 55	18	28	20	15	2	0	13	10
21	7 59 31	0♒28 2	3♌ 7	19	29	21	15	2	0	13	10
22	8 3 27	1 29 4	15 10	20	0♒	22	15	2	0	13	10
23	8 7 24	2 30 5	27 5	21	1	22	16	2	0	13	10
24	8 11 20	3 31 6	8♍55	22	3	23	16	2	0	13	10
25	8 15 17	4 32 6	20 43	22	4	24	16	3	29♌	13	10
26	8 19 14	5 33 5	2♎32	23	5	25	16	3	29	13	10
27	8 23 10	6 34 4	14 26	23 R	6	25	16	3	29	13	10
28	8 27 7	7 35 2	26 29	23	8	26	17	3	29	13	10
29	8 31 3	8 35 59	8♏47	23	9	27	17	3	29	13	10
30	8 35 0	9 36 56	21 23	22	10	28	17	3	29	13	10
31	8 38 56	10 37 52	4♐23	22	11	28	17	3	29	13	10

THE SUN ENTERS THE SIGN OF AQUARIUS ON JAN 20 AT 12:59.

DAY	TIME	☉	☽	☿	♀	♂	♃	♄	♅	♆	♇
	h m s	° ' "	° '	°	°	°	°	°	°	°	°
F 1	8 42 53	11♒38 47	17♐48	21♒R	13♒	29♑	18♒	3♒	29♌R	13♏	10♍R
E 2	8 46 49	12 39 42	1♑40	20	14	0♒	18	3	29	13	9
B 3	8 50 46	13 40 36	15 58	19	15	1	18	4	29	13	9
R 4	8 54 43	14 41 29	0♒39	18	17	2	18	4	29	13	9
U 5	8 58 39	15 42 21	15 36	17	18	2	19	4	29	13	9
A 6	9 2 36	16 43 11	0♓42	16	19	3	19	4	29	13	9
R 7	9 6 32	17 44 0	15 47	15	20	4	19	4	29	13	9
Y 8	9 10 29	18 44 48	0♈43	13	22	5	19	4	29	13	9
9	9 14 25	19 45 34	15 22	12	23	5	20	4	29	13	9
10	9 18 22	20 46 19	29 39	11	24	6	20	4	29	13	9
11	9 22 18	21 47 2	13♉33	10	25	7	20	5	29	13	9
12	9 26 15	22 47 44	27 4	9	27	8	20	5	29	13	9
13	9 30 12	23 48 24	10♊12	9	28	9	21	5	29	13 R	9
14	9 34 8	24 49 2	23 0	8	29	9	21	5	29	13	9
15	9 38 5	25 49 38	5♋32	8	0♓	10	21	5	29	13	9
16	9 42 1	26 50 13	17 50	7	2	11	21	5	29	13	9
17	9 45 58	27 50 46	29 58	7 D	3	12	21	5	29	13	9
18	9 49 54	28 51 18	11♌57	7	4	12	22	5	28	13	9
19	9 53 51	29 51 48	23 51	7	5	13	22	5	28	13	9
20	9 57 47	0♓52 16	5♍41	7	7	14	22	6	28	13	9
21	10 1 44	1 52 43	17 30	8	8	15	22	6	28	13	9
22	10 5 41	2 53 8	29 20	8	9	16	23	6	28	13	9
23	10 9 37	3 53 31	11♎12	9	10	16	23	6	28	13	9
24	10 13 34	4 53 54	23 9	9	12	17	23	6	28	13	9
25	10 17 30	5 54 14	5♏15	10	13	18	23	6	28	13	9
26	10 21 27	6 54 34	17 33	10	14	19	24	6	28	13	9
27	10 25 23	7 54 51	0♐ 7	11	15	20	24	6	28	13	9
28	10 29 20	8 55 8	13 0	12	17	20	24	6	28	13	9

THE SUN ENTERS THE SIGN OF PISCES ON FEB 19 AT 03:15.

DAY	TIME	☉	☽	☿	♀	♂	♃	♄	♅	♆	♇
	h m s	° ' "	° '	°	°	°	°	°	°	°	°
M 1	10 33 16	9♓55 23	26♐15	13♒	18♓	21♒	24♒	7♒	28♌R	13♏R	9♍R
A 2	10 37 13	10 55 36	9♑56	14	19	22	25	7	28	13	9
R 3	10 41 9	11 55 48	24 4	15	20	23	25	7	28	13	9
C 4	10 45 6	12 55 59	8♒37	16	22	23	25	7	28	13	9
H 5	10 49 3	13 56 7	23 32	17	23	24	25	7	28	13	9
6	10 52 59	14 56 14	8♓41	18	24	25	26	7	28	13	9
7	10 56 56	15 56 19	23 57	19	25	26	26	7	28	13	9
8	11 0 52	16 56 22	9♈ 8	20	27	27	26	7	28	13	9
9	11 4 49	17 56 23	24 5	21	28	27	26	7	28	13	9
10	11 8 45	18 56 22	8♉39	23	29	28	26	7	28	13	9
11	11 12 42	19 56 19	22 47	24	0♈	29	27	8	28	13	9
12	11 16 38	20 56 14	6♊26	25	2	0♓	27	8	28	13	9
13	11 20 35	21 56 7	19 37	27	3	1	27	8	28	13	9
14	11 24 32	22 55 57	2♋24	28	4	1	27	8	27	13	8
15	11 28 28	23 55 45	14 51	29	5	2	28	8	27	13	8
16	11 32 25	24 55 31	27 1	1♓	7	3	28	8	27	13	8
17	11 36 21	25 55 15	9♌ 0	2	8	4	28	8	27	13	8
18	11 40 18	26 54 56	20 52	4	9	4	28	8	27	13	8
19	11 44 14	27 54 35	2♍41	5	10	5	28	8	27	13	8
20	11 48 11	28 54 12	14 28	7	11	6	29	8	27	13	8
21	11 52 7	29 53 47	26 18	8	13	7	29	8	27	13	8
22	11 56 4	0♈53 20	8♎12	10	14	8	29	9	27	13	8
23	12 0 1	1 52 51	20 11	11	15	8	29	9	27	13	8
24	12 3 57	2 52 20	2♏17	13	16	9	0♓	9	27	13	8
25	12 7 54	3 51 47	14 32	14	18	10	0	9	27	13	8
26	12 11 50	4 51 13	26 58	16	19	11	0	9	27	13	8
27	12 15 47	5 50 36	9♐35	18	20	12	0	9	27	13	8
28	12 19 43	6 49 58	22 29	19	21	12	0	9	27	13	8
29	12 23 40	7 49 18	5♑40	21	23	13	1	9	27	13	8
30	12 27 36	8 48 36	19 11	23	24	14	1	9	27	13	8
31	12 31 33	9 47 53	3♒ 5	24	25	15	1	9	27	13	8

THE SUN ENTERS THE SIGN OF ARIES ON MAR 21 AT 02:29.

SIDEREAL SUN MOON MERCURY VENUS MARS JUPITER SATURN URANUS NEPTUNE PLUTO

DAY	TIME	☉	☽	☿	♀	♂	♃	♄	♅	♆	♇
	h m s	° ' "	° '	°	°	°	°	°	°	°	°
A 1	12 35 30	10♈47 8	17♒23	26♓	26♈	15♓	1♓	9♒	27♌R	13♏R	8♍R
P 2	12 39 26	11 46 21	2♓ 2	28	28	16	2	9	27	13	8
R 3	12 43 23	12 45 32	16 58	0♈	29	17	2	10	27	13	8
I 4	12 47 19	13 44 41	2♈ 5	2♈	0♉	18	2	10	27	13	8
L 5	12 51 16	14 43 48	17 14	3	1	19	2	10	27	13	8
6	12 55 12	15 42 53	2♉13	5	3	19	2	10	27	13	8
7	12 59 9	16 41 56	16 54	7	4	20	3	10	27	13	8
8	13 3 5	17 40 57	1♊10	9	5	21	3	10	27	13	8
9	13 7 2	18 39 55	14 57	11	6	22	3	10	27	13	8
10	13 10 58	19 38 52	28 15	13	7	22	3	10	27	13	8
11	13 14 55	20 37 46	11♋ 7	15	9	23	3	10	27	13	8
12	13 18 52	21 36 38	23 35	17	10	24	4	10	27	13	8
13	13 22 48	22 35 27	5♌45	19	11	25	4	10	27	13	8
14	13 26 45	23 34 14	17 42	21	12	26	4	10	27	13	8
15	13 30 41	24 32 59	29 32	23	14	26	4	10	27	13	8
16	13 34 38	25 31 42	11♍19	25	15	27	4	10	27	13	8
17	13 38 34	26 30 23	23 8	28	16	28	5	10	27	13	8
18	13 42 31	27 29 1	5♎ 1	0♉	17	29	5	10	27	13	8
19	13 46 27	28 27 38	17 1	2	19	29	5	11	26	13	8
20	13 50 24	29 26 12	29 10	4	20	0♈	5	11	26	12	8
21	13 54 21	0♉24 45	11♏29	6	21	1	5	11	26	12	8
22	13 58 17	1 23 15	23 59	8	22	2	5	11	26	12	8
23	14 2 14	2 21 44	6♐39	10	23	3	6	11	26	12	8
24	14 6 10	3 20 12	19 30	12	25	3	6	11	26	12	8
25	14 10 7	4 18 37	2♑33	14	26	4	6	11	26	12	8
26	14 14 3	5 17 1	15 50	16	27	5	6	11	26	12	8
27	14 18 0	6 15 24	29 21	18	28	6	6	11	26	12	8
28	14 21 56	7 13 45	13♒ 9	20	0♊	6	7	11	26	12	8
29	14 25 53	8 12 4	27 13	22	1	7	7	11	26	12	8
30	14 29 50	9 10 22	11♓35	24	2	8	7	11	26	12	8

THE SUN ENTERS THE SIGN OF TAURUS ON APR 20 AT 13:51.

DAY	TIME	☉	☽	☿	♀	♂	♃	♄	♅	♆	♇
	h m s	° ' "	° '	°	°	°	°	°	°	°	°
M 1	14 33 46	10♉ 8 38	26♓11	26♉	3♊	9♈	7♓	11♒	26♌R	12♏R	8♍R
A 2	14 37 43	11 6 53	10♈58	28	4	9	7	11	26	12	8
Y 3	14 41 39	12 5 6	25 48	0♊	6	10	7	11	26	12	8
4	14 45 36	13 3 18	10♉32	1	7	11	8	11	26 D	12	8
5	14 49 32	14 1 27	25 4	3	8	12	8	11	26	12	8
6	14 53 29	14 59 36	9♊15	4	9	13	8	11	26	12	8
7	14 57 25	15 57 42	23 1	6	10	13	8	11	26	12	8
8	15 1 22	16 55 47	6♋21	7	12	14	8	11	26	12	8
9	15 5 19	17 53 49	19 14	9	13	15	8	11	26	12	8
10	15 9 15	18 51 50	1♌45	10	14	16	8	11	26	12	8
11	15 13 12	19 49 49	13 57	11	15	16	9	11	26	12	8
12	15 17 8	20 47 46	25 57	12	17	17	9	11	26	12	8
13	15 21 5	21 45 42	7♍48	13	18	18	9	11	26	12	8
14	15 25 1	22 43 35	19 37	14	19	19	9	11	26	12	8
15	15 28 58	23 41 27	1♎28	15	20	19	9	11	26	12	8
16	15 32 54	24 39 17	13 25	16	21	20	9	11	26	12	8
17	15 36 51	25 37 5	25 33	17	23	21	9	11	26	12	8
18	15 40 48	26 34 52	7♏52	18	24	22	10	11	26	12	8
19	15 44 44	27 32 37	20 25	18	25	22	10	11	26	12	8 D
20	15 48 41	28 30 21	3♐11	19	26	23	10	11	27	12	8
21	15 52 37	29 28 4	16 11	19	27	24	10	11 R	27	12	8
22	15 56 34	0♊25 45	29 22	20	29	25	10	11	27	12	8
23	16 0 30	1 23 26	12♑45	20	0♋	25	10	11	27	12	8
24	16 4 27	2 21 5	26 17	20	1	26	10	11	27	12	8
25	16 8 23	3 18 43	10♒ 0	20	2	27	10	11	27	12	8
26	16 12 20	4 16 20	23 53	20 R	3	28	11	11	27	12	8
27	16 16 17	5 13 56	7♓55	20	5	29	11	11	27	11	8
28	16 20 13	6 11 32	22 6	20	6	29	11	11	27	11	8
29	16 24 10	7 9 6	6♈25	20	7	0♉	11	11	27	11	8
30	16 28 6	8 6 40	20 49	20	8	1	11	11	27	11	8
31	16 32 3	9 4 13	5♉14	20	9	2	11	11	27	11	8

THE SUN ENTERS THE SIGN OF GEMINI ON MAY 21 AT 13:17.

DAY	TIME	☉	☽	☿	♀	♂	♃	♄	♅	♆	♇
	h m s	° ' "	° '	°	°	°	°	°	°	°	°
J 1	16 35 59	10♊ 1 44	19♉33	19♊R	11♋	2♉	11♓	11♒R	27♌	11♏R	8♍
U 2	16 39 56	10 59 15	3♊42	19	12	3	11	11	27	11	8
N 3	16 43 52	11 56 45	17 35	18	13	4	11	11	27	11	8
E 4	16 47 49	12 54 14	1♋ 9	18	14	4	11	11	27	11	8
5	16 51 46	13 51 43	14 20	17	15	5	12	11	27	11	8
6	16 55 42	14 49 9	27 10	17	17	6	12	11	27	11	8
7	16 59 39	15 46 35	9♌40	16	18	7	12	11	27	11	8
8	17 3 35	16 44 0	21 52	16	19	7	12	11	27	11	8
9	17 7 32	17 41 23	3♍53	15	20	8	12	11	27	11	8
10	17 11 28	18 38 46	15 46	15	21	9	12	11	27	11	8
11	17 15 25	19 36 7	27 36	14	23	10	12	11	27	11	8
12	17 19 21	20 33 28	9♎29	14	24	10	12	11	27	11	8
13	17 23 18	21 30 47	21 30	13	25	11	12	11	27	11	8
14	17 27 15	22 28 6	3♏42	13	26	12	12	11	27	11	8
15	17 31 11	23 25 23	16 10	13	27	13	12	11	27	11	8
16	17 35 8	24 22 40	28 53	12	29	13	12	11	27	11	8
17	17 39 4	25 19 57	11♐55	12	0♌	14	12	11	27	11	8
18	17 43 1	26 17 12	25 13	12	1	15	12	11	27	11	8
19	17 46 57	27 14 27	8♑47	12 D	2	16	12	11	27	11	8
20	17 50 54	28 11 42	22 34	12	3	16	12	11	27	11	8
21	17 54 50	29 8 56	6♒31	12	4	17	12	11	27	11	8
22	17 58 47	0♋ 6 10	20 35	12	6	18	13	11	27	11	8
23	18 2 44	1 3 24	4♓44	12	7	18	13	11	27	11	8
24	18 6 40	2 0 38	18 55	13	8	19	13	11	27	11	8
25	18 10 37	2 57 51	3♈ 7	13	9	20	13	10	28	11	8
26	18 14 33	3 55 5	17 18	14	10	21	13	10	28	11	8
27	18 18 30	4 52 19	1♉25	14	11	21	13	10	28	11	8
28	18 22 26	5 49 33	15 27	15	13	22	13	10	28	11	8
29	18 26 23	6 46 46	29 20	15	14	23	13	10	28	11	8
30	18 30 19	7 44 0	13♊ 2	16	15	23	13	10	28	11	8

THE SUN ENTERS THE SIGN OF CANCER ON JUN 21 AT 21:25.

♈ ARIES ♉ TAURUS ♊ GEMINI ♋ CANCER ♌ LEO ♍ VIRGO ♎ LIBRA ♏ SCORPIO ♐ SAGITTARIUS ♑ CAPRICORN ♒ AQUARIUS ♓ PISCES

SIDEREAL · SUN · MOON · MERCURY · VENUS · MARS · JUPITER · SATURN · URANUS · NEPTUNE · PLUTO

THE SUN ENTERS THE SIGN OF LEO ON JUL 23 AT 08:19.

THE SUN ENTERS THE SIGN OF VIRGO ON AUG 23 AT 15:13.

THE SUN ENTERS THE SIGN OF LIBRA ON SEP 23 AT 12:36.

THE SUN ENTERS THE SIGN OF SCORPIO ON OCT 23 AT 21:41.

THE SUN ENTERS THE SIGN OF SAGITTARIUS ON NOV 22 AT 19:03.

THE SUN ENTERS THE SIGN OF CAPRICORN ON DEC 22 AT 08:16.

♈ ARIES ♉ TAURUS ♊ GEMINI ♋ CANCER ♌ LEO ♍ VIRGO ♎ LIBRA ♏ SCORPIO ♐ SAGITTARIUS ♑ CAPRICORN ♒ AQUARIUS ♓ PISCES

SIDEREAL SUN MOON MERCURY VENUS MARS JUPITER SATURN URANUS NEPTUNE PLUTO

DAY	TIME	☉	☽	☿	♀	♂	♃	♄	♅	♆	♇
	h m s	° ' "	° '	°	°	°	°	°	°	°	°
J 1	6 39 42	9♑50 31	13♓ 8	29♑	25♏	25♌R	9♓	10♒	5♍R	15♏	12♍R
A 2	6 43 39	10 51 41	27 11	0♒	26	24	9	10	5	15	12
N 3	6 47 35	11 52 51	11♈19	1	27	24	9	10	5	15	12
U 4	6 51 32	12 54 0	25 31	2	28	24	10	10	5	15	12
A 5	6 55 28	13 55 9	9♉45	3	29	24	10	10	5	15	12
R 6	6 59 25	14 56 18	23 57	4	29	24	10	10	5	15	12
Y 7	7 3 21	15 57 26	8♊ 6	5	0♐	24	10	11	5	15	12
8	7 7 18	16 58 34	22 6	6	1	24	10	11	5	15	12
9	7 11 15	17 59 42	5♋54	6	2	24	10	11	5	15	12
10	7 15 11	19 0 50	19 27	6	3	23	11	11	5	15	12
11	7 19 8	20 1 57	2♌44	7 R	4	23	11	11	5	15	12
12	7 23 4	21 3 4	15 42	7	5	23	11	11	5	15	12
13	7 27 1	22 4 11	28 22	6	6	23	11	11	5	15	12
14	7 30 57	23 5 17	10♍46	6	7	22	11	11	5	15	12
15	7 34 54	24 6 24	22 56	6	8	22	12	12	5	15	12
16	7 38 50	25 7 30	4♎56	5	8	22	12	12	5	15	12
17	7 42 47	26 8 36	16 50	4	9	22	12	12	5	15	12
18	7 46 44	27 9 42	28 43	3	10	21	12	12	5	15	12
19	7 50 40	28 10 47	10♏38	2	11	21	12	12	5	15	12
20	7 54 37	29 11 52	22 42	0	12	21	13	12	5	15	12
21	7 58 33	0♒12 57	4♐58	29♑	13	20	13	12	5	15	12
22	8 2 30	1 14 2	17 29	28	14	20	13	12	5	15	12
23	8 6 26	2 15 5	0♑19	26	15	20	13	12	5	15	12
24	8 10 23	3 16 9	13 30	25	16	19	14	13	4	16	12
25	8 14 19	4 17 12	27 1	24	17	19	14	13	4	16	12
26	8 18 16	5 18 14	10♒50	23	18	19	14	13	4	16	12
27	8 22 13	6 19 15	24 55	22	20	18	14	13	4	16	12
28	8 26 9	7 20 15	9♓11	22	21	18	14	13	4	16	12
29	8 30 6	8 21 14	23 33	21	22	18	15	13	4	16	12
30	8 34 2	9 22 11	7♈58	21	23	17	15	13	4	16	12
31	8 37 59	10 23 8	22 19	21	24	17	15	13	4	16	12

THE SUN ENTERS THE SIGN OF AQUARIUS ON JAN 20 AT 18:55.

DAY	TIME	☉	☽	☿	♀	♂	♃	♄	♅	♆	♇
	h m s	° ' "	° '	°	°	°	°	°	°	°	°
F 1	8 41 55	11♒24 3	6♉34	21♑D	25♐	16♌R	15♓	14♒	4♍R	16♏	12♍R
E 2	8 45 52	12 24 57	20 40	21	26	16	15	14	4	16	12
B 3	8 49 48	13 25 50	4♊35	21	27	16	16	14	4	16	12
R 4	8 53 45	14 26 41	18 19	21	28	16	16	14	4	16	12
U 5	8 57 42	15 27 31	1♋52	22	29	15	16	14	4	16	12
A 6	9 1 38	16 28 20	15 12	22	0♑	14	16	14	4	16	11
R 7	9 5 35	17 29 7	28 19	23	1	14	17	14	4	16	11
Y 8	9 9 31	18 29 53	11♌14	23	2	14	17	14	4	16	11
9	9 13 28	19 30 37	23 56	24	3	13	17	14	4	16	11
10	9 17 24	20 31 20	6♍26	25	5	13	17	15	4	16	11
11	9 21 21	21 32 2	18 43	26	6	12	18	15	4	16	11
12	9 25 17	22 32 43	0♎51	27	7	12	18	15	4	16	11
13	9 29 14	23 33 23	12 50	27	8	12	18	15	4	16	11
14	9 33 11	24 34 1	24 44	28	9	11	18	15	4	16	11
15	9 37 7	25 34 38	6♏36	0♒	10	11	18	15	4	16	11
16	9 41 4	26 35 14	18 30	1	11	11	19	15	4	16 R	11
17	9 45 0	27 35 49	0♐32	2	12	10	19	15	4	16	11
18	9 48 57	28 36 22	12 44	3	13	10	19	16	3	16	11
19	9 52 53	29 36 55	25 14	4	15	10	19	16	3	16	11
20	9 56 50	0♓37 26	8♑ 3	5	16	9	20	16	3	16	11
21	10 0 46	1 37 56	21 17	7	17	9	20	16	3	16	11
22	10 4 43	2 38 24	4♒57	8	18	9	20	16	3	16	11
23	10 8 40	3 38 51	19 1	9	19	8	20	16	3	16	11
24	10 12 36	4 39 16	3♓28	10	20	8	21	16	3	16	11
25	10 16 33	5 39 39	18 11	12	21	8	21	16	3	16	11
26	10 20 29	6 40 1	3♈ 3	13	23	8	21	16	3	16	11
27	10 24 26	7 40 21	17 55	15	24	7	21	17	3	16	11
28	10 28 22	8 40 39	2♉40	16	25	7	22	17	3	16	11

THE SUN ENTERS THE SIGN OF PISCES ON FEB 19 AT 09:09.

DAY	TIME	☉	☽	☿	♀	♂	♃	♄	♅	♆	♇
	h m s	° ' "	° '	°	°	°	°	°	°	°	°
M 1	10 32 19	9♓40 55	17♉10	17♒	26♑	7♌R	22♓	17♒	3♍R	16♏R	11♍R
A 2	10 36 15	10 41 9	1♊23	19	27	7	22	17	3	16	11
R 3	10 40 12	11 41 21	15 15	20	28	7	22	17	3	16	11
C 4	10 44 9	12 41 31	28 48	22	29	6	22	17	3	16	11
H 5	10 48 5	13 41 38	12♋ 4	23	1♒	6	23	17	3	16	11
6	10 52 2	14 41 44	25 3	25	2	6	23	17	3	16	11
7	10 55 58	15 41 48	7♌49	26	3	6	23	18	3	16	11
8	10 59 55	16 41 49	20 23	28	4	6	23	18	3	16	11
9	11 3 51	17 41 48	2♍48	0♓	5	6	24	18	3	16	11
10	11 7 48	18 41 46	15 3	1	6	6	24	18	3	16	11
11	11 11 44	19 41 41	27 11	3	8	6	24	18	3	16	11
12	11 15 41	20 41 35	9♎13	5	9	5	24	18	2	16	11
13	11 19 37	21 41 27	21 9	6	10	5	25	18	2	15	11
14	11 23 34	22 41 16	3♏ 2	8	11	5	25	18	2	15	11
15	11 27 31	23 41 5	14 54	10	12	5	25	18	2	15	11
16	11 31 27	24 40 51	26 47	11	13	5 D	25	18	2	15	10
17	11 35 24	25 40 36	8♐47	13	15	5	26	19	2	15	10
18	11 39 20	26 40 19	20 56	15	16	5	26	19	2	15	10
19	11 43 17	27 40 0	3♑21	17	17	5	26	19	2	15	10
20	11 47 13	28 39 40	16 5	18	18	5	26	19	2	15	10
21	11 51 10	29 39 17	29 14	20	19	5	27	19	2	15	10
22	11 55 6	0♈38 54	12♒51	22	20	6	27	19	2	15	10
23	11 59 3	1 38 28	26 57	24	22	6	27	19	2	15	10
24	12 3 0	2 38 0	11♓31	26	23	6	27	19	2	15	10
25	12 6 56	3 37 30	26 27	28	24	6	28	19	2	15	10
26	12 10 53	4 36 59	11♈38	0♈	25	6	28	19	2	15	10
27	12 14 49	5 36 25	26 52	2♈	26	6	28	20	2	15	10
28	12 18 46	6 35 49	11♉59	4	28	6	28	20	2	15	10
29	12 22 42	7 35 11	26 49	6	29	6	29	20	2	15	10
30	12 26 39	8 34 31	11♊16	8	0♓	6	29	20	2	15	10
31	12 30 35	9 33 48	25 18	10	1	7	29	20	2	15	10

THE SUN ENTERS THE SIGN OF ARIES ON MAR 21 AT 08:20.

DAY	TIME	☉	☽	☿	♀	♂	♃	♄	♅	♆	♇
	h m s	° ' "	° '	°	°	°	°	°	°	°	°
A 1	12 34 32	10♈33 4	8♋53	12♈	2♓	7♌	29♓	20♒	2♍R	15♏R	10♍R
P 2	12 38 29	11 32 16	22 4	14	4	7	29	20	2	15	10
R 3	12 42 25	12 31 27	4♌54	16	5	7	0♈	20	2	15	10
I 4	12 46 22	13 30 35	17 28	18	6	7	0	20	2	15	10
L 5	12 50 18	14 29 41	29 49	20	7	7	0♈	20	2	15	10
6	12 54 15	15 28 44	12♍ 1	22	8	8	0	20	2	15	10
7	12 58 11	16 27 45	24 5	24	9	8	1	21	2	15	10
8	13 2 8	17 26 44	6♎ 4	26	11	8	1	21	2	15	10
9	13 6 4	18 25 42	18 0	28	12	8	1	21	2	15	10
10	13 10 1	19 24 37	29 53	0♉	13	9	1	21	2	15	10
11	13 13 58	20 23 30	11♏45	2	14	9	2	21	1	15	10
12	13 17 54	21 22 21	23 39	4	15	9	2	21	1	15	10
13	13 21 51	22 21 10	5♐34	6	17	9	2	21	1	15	10
14	13 25 47	23 19 58	17 36	8	18	10	2	21	1	15	10
15	13 29 44	24 18 44	29 46	10	19	10	3	21	1	15	10
16	13 33 40	25 17 28	12♑ 9	11	20	10	3	21	1	15	10
17	13 37 37	26 16 10	24 50	13	21	10	3	21	1	15	10
18	13 41 33	27 14 51	7♒54	15	23	11	3	21	1	15	10
19	13 45 30	28 13 30	21 23	16	24	11	3	21	1	15	10
20	13 49 27	29 12 7	5♓21	18	25	11	4	22	1	15	10
21	13 53 23	0♉10 43	19 48	19	26	12	4	22	1	15	10
22	13 57 20	1 9 17	4♈41	21	27	12	4	22	1	15	10
23	14 1 16	2 7 49	19 53	22	29	12	4	22	1	15	10
24	14 5 13	3 6 19	5♉12	23	0♈	13	5	22	1	15	10
25	14 9 9	4 4 48	20 29	24	1♈	13	5	22	1	15	10
26	14 13 6	5 3 14	5♊32	25	2	13	5	22	1	15	10
27	14 17 2	6 1 39	20 12	26	3	14	5	22	1	15	10
28	14 20 59	7 0 1	4♋25	27	5	14	6	22	1	15	10
29	14 24 56	7 58 22	18 8	28	6	14	6	22	1	14	10
30	14 28 52	8 56 40	1♌24	28	7	15	6	22	1	14	10

THE SUN ENTERS THE SIGN OF TAURUS ON APR 20 AT 19:37.

DAY	TIME	☉	☽	☿	♀	♂	♃	♄	♅	♆	♇
	h m s	° ' "	° '	°	°	°	°	°	°	°	°
M 1	14 32 49	9♉54 56	14♌16	29♉	8♈	15♌	6♈	22♒	1♍R	14♏R	10♍R
A 2	14 36 45	10 53 10	26 48	0♊	9	16	6	22	1	14	10
Y 3	14 40 42	11 51 22	9♍ 4	0	11	16	7	22	1	14	10
4	14 44 38	12 49 33	21 10	0	12	16	7	22	1	14	10
5	14 48 35	13 47 41	3♎ 8	0	13	17	7	22	1	14	10
6	14 52 31	14 45 47	15 2	1 R	14	17	7	22	1	14	10
7	14 56 28	15 43 51	26 54	1	15	18	8	23	1	14	10
8	15 0 24	16 41 54	8♏46	1	17	18	8	23	1	14	10
9	15 4 21	17 39 55	20 41	0	18	18	8	23	1 D	14	10
10	15 8 18	18 37 55	2♐38	0	19	19	8	23	1	14	10
11	15 12 14	19 35 53	14 41	0	20	19	8	23	1	14	10
12	15 16 11	20 33 49	26 49	0	21	20	9	23	1	14	10
13	15 20 7	21 31 44	9♑ 7	29♉	23	20	9	23	1	14	10
14	15 24 4	22 29 38	21 37	29	24	20	9	23	1	14	10
15	15 28 0	23 27 31	4♒21	28	25	21	9	23	1	14	10
16	15 31 57	24 25 22	17 24	28	26	21	9	23	1	14	10
17	15 35 53	25 23 12	0♓50	27	28	22	10	23	1	14	10
18	15 39 50	26 21 1	14 40	27	29	22	10	23	1	14	10
19	15 43 47	27 18 49	28 55	26	0♉	23	10	23	1	14	10
20	15 47 43	28 16 35	13♈33	25	1	23	10	23	1	14	10
21	15 51 40	29 14 21	28 31	25	2	24	10	23	1	14	10 D
22	15 55 36	0♊12 5	13♉39	24	4	24	11	23	1	14	10
23	15 59 33	1 9 48	28 48	24	5	25	11	23	1	14	10
24	16 3 29	2 7 30	13♊48	23	6	25	11	23	1	14	10
25	16 7 26	3 5 11	28 30	23	7	25	11	23	1	14	10
26	16 11 22	4 2 50	12♋47	23	8	26	11	23	1	14	10
27	16 15 19	5 0 28	26 37	22	10	26	12	23	1	14	10
28	16 19 16	5 58 4	10♌ 0	22	11	27	12	23	1	14	10
29	16 23 12	6 55 39	22 57	22	12	27	12	23	1	14	10
30	16 27 9	7 53 12	5♍32	22 D	13	28	12	23	1	14	10
31	16 31 5	8 50 44	17 50	22	14	28	12	23	1	14	10

THE SUN ENTERS THE SIGN OF GEMINI ON MAY 21 AT 18:59.

DAY	TIME	☉	☽	☿	♀	♂	♃	♄	♅	♆	♇
	h m s	° ' "	° '	°	°	°	°	°	°	°	°
J 1	16 35 2	9♊48 15	29♍55	22♉	16♉	29♌	12♈	23♒	1♍	14♏R	10♍
U 2	16 38 58	10 45 44	11♎52	22	17	29	13	23	1	14	10
N 3	16 42 55	11 43 12	23 45	22	18	0♍	13	23 R	1	14	10
E 4	16 46 51	12 40 39	5♏37	22	19	0	13	23	1	14	10
5	16 50 48	13 38 5	17 31	23	21	1	13	23	1	14	10
6	16 54 45	14 35 29	29 29	23	22	1	13	23	1	14	10
7	16 58 41	15 32 53	11♐34	24	23	2	14	23	2	13	10
8	17 2 38	16 30 16	23 47	24	24	2	14	23	2	13	10
9	17 6 34	17 27 38	6♑ 8	25	25	3	14	23	2	13	10
10	17 10 31	18 24 59	18 40	26	27	3	14	23	2	13	10
11	17 14 27	19 22 20	1♒24	26	28	4	14	23	2	13	10
12	17 18 24	20 19 40	14 22	27	29	4	14	23	2	13	10
13	17 22 21	21 17 0	27 34	28	0♊	5	15	23	2	13	10
14	17 26 17	22 14 19	11♓ 4	29	1	6	15	23	2	13	10
15	17 30 14	23 11 38	24 52	0♊	3	6	15	23	2	13	10
16	17 34 10	24 8 56	8♈59	1	4	7	15	23	2	13	10
17	17 38 7	25 6 14	23 22	2	5	7	15	23	2	13	10
18	17 42 3	26 3 32	8♉ 0	3	6	8	15	23	2	13	10
19	17 46 0	27 0 49	22 46	5	7	8	15	23	2	13	10
20	17 49 56	27 58 6	7♊33	6	9	9	16	23	2	13	10
21	17 53 53	28 55 23	22 15	7	10	9	16	23	2	13	10
22	17 57 50	29 52 40	6♋44	9	11	10	16	23	2	13	10
23	18 1 46	0♋49 56	20 54	10	12	10	16	23	2	13	10
24	18 5 43	1 47 11	4♌42	12	14	11	16	23	2	13	10
25	18 9 39	2 44 26	18 6	13	15	11	16	23	2	13	10
26	18 13 36	3 41 40	1♍ 6	15	16	12	16	23	2	13	10
27	18 17 32	4 38 54	13 45	17	17	13	17	23	2	13	10
28	18 21 29	5 36 7	26 6	18	18	13	17	23	2	13	10
29	18 25 25	6 33 20	8♎13	20	20	14	17	23	2	13	10
30	18 29 22	7 30 32	20 11	22	21	14	17	23	2	13	10

THE SUN ENTERS THE SIGN OF CANCER ON JUN 22 AT 03:04.

♈ ARIES ♉ TAURUS ♊ GEMINI ♋ CANCER ♌ LEO ♍ VIRGO ♎ LIBRA ♏ SCORPIO ♐ SAGITTARIUS ♑ CAPRICORN ♒ AQUARIUS ♓ PISCES

1963

SIDEREAL SUN MOON MERCURY VENUS MARS JUPITER SATURN URANUS NEPTUNE PLUTO

DAY	TIME	☉	☽	☿	♀	♂	♃	♄	♅	♆	♇
	h m s	° ' "	° '	°	°	°	°	°	°	°	°
J 1	18 33 19	8♋27 44	2♏ 5	24♊	22♊	15♍	17♈	23♒R	2♍	13♏R	10♍
U 2	18 37 15	9 24 56	13 58	26	23	15	17	22	2	13	10
L 3	18 41 12	10 22 7	25 54	28	25	16	17	22	2	13	10
Y 4	18 45 8	11 19 18	7♐57	0♋	26	16	17	22	2	13	10
5	18 49 5	12 16 29	20 10	2	27	17	17	22	3	13	10
6	18 53 1	13 13 39	2♑34	4	28	18	18	22	3	13	10
7	18 56 58	14 10 50	15 12	6	29	18	18	22	3	13	10
8	19 0 54	15 8 1	28 3	8	1♋	19	18	22	3	13	10
9	19 4 51	16 5 12	11♒ 8	10	2	19	18	22	3	13	10
10	19 8 48	17 2 23	24 27	12	3	20	18	22	3	13	10
11	19 12 44	17 59 34	7♓59	15	4	20	18	22	3	13	10
12	19 16 41	18 56 46	21 44	17	6	21	18	22	3	13	10
13	19 20 37	19 53 58	5♈40	19	7	22	18	22	3	13	10
14	19 24 34	20 51 11	19 46	21	8	22	18	22	3	13	10
15	19 28 30	21 48 25	4♉ 1	23	9	23	18	22	3	13	10
16	19 32 27	22 45 39	18 21	25	10	23	19	22	3	13	10
17	19 36 23	23 42 54	2♊43	27	12	24	19	22	3	13	10
18	19 40 20	24 40 9	17 4	29	13	25	19	22	3	13	10
19	19 44 17	25 37 25	1♋20	2♌	14	25	19	22	3	13	10
20	19 48 13	26 34 42	15 25	4	15	26	19	21	3	13	10
21	19 52 10	27 31 59	29 17	6	17	26	19	21	3	13	10
22	19 56 6	28 29 17	12♌52	8	18	27	19	21	3	13	10
23	20 0 3	29 26 35	26 8	10	19	27	19	21	3	13	10
24	20 3 59	0♌23 53	9♍ 4	12	20	28	19	21	3	13	10
25	20 7 56	1 21 12	21 42	13	21	29	19	21	4	13 D	11
26	20 11 52	2 18 31	4♎ 4	15	23	29	19	21	4	13	11
27	20 15 49	3 15 51	16 12	17	24	0♎	19	21	4	13	11
28	20 19 46	4 13 11	28 11	19	25	0	19	21	4	13	11
29	20 23 42	5 10 32	10♏ 5	21	26	1	19	21	4	13	11
30	20 27 39	6 7 53	21 58	23	28	2	19	21	4	13	11
31	20 31 35	7 5 15	3♐56	24	29	2	19	21	4	13	11

THE SUN ENTERS THE SIGN OF LEO ON JUL 23 AT 13:60.

DAY	TIME	☉	☽	☿	♀	♂	♃	♄	♅	♆	♇
	h m s	° ' "	° '	°	°	°	°	°	°	°	°
A 1	20 35 32	8♌ 2 37	16♐ 2	26♌	0♌	3♎	19♈	21♒R	4♍	13♏	11♍
U 2	20 39 28	9 0 0	28 20	28	1	4	19	21	4	13	11
G 3	20 43 25	9 57 24	10♑54	29	3	4	19	21	4	13	11
U 4	20 47 21	10 54 48	23 46	1♍	4	5	19	20	4	13	11
S 5	20 51 18	11 52 14	6♒56	3	5	5	19	20	4	13	11
T 6	20 55 15	12 49 40	20 25	4	6	6	19	20	4	13	11
7	20 59 11	13 47 7	4♓10	6	7	7	19	20	4	13	11
8	21 3 8	14 44 35	18 9	7	9	7	19	20	4	13	11
9	21 7 4	15 42 5	2♈18	9	10	8	19 R	20	4	13	11
10	21 11 1	16 39 36	16 32	10	11	8	19	20	4	13	11
11	21 14 57	17 37 8	0♉49	12	12	9	19	20	5	13	11
12	21 18 54	18 34 41	15 4	13	14	10	19	20	5	13	11
13	21 22 50	19 32 17	29 15	14	15	10	19	20	5	13	11
14	21 26 47	20 29 53	13♊20	16	16	11	19	20	5	13	11
15	21 30 44	21 27 31	27 18	17	17	12	19	20	5	13	11
16	21 34 40	22 25 11	11♋ 7	18	19	12	19	20	5	13	11
17	21 38 37	23 22 52	24 46	20	20	13	19	19	5	13	11
18	21 42 33	24 20 35	8♌14	21	21	13	19	19	5	13	11
19	21 46 30	25 18 19	21 28	22	22	14	19	19	5	13	11
20	21 50 26	26 16 4	4♍29	23	24	15	19	19	5	13	11
21	21 54 23	27 13 51	17 15	24	25	15	19	19	5	13	11
22	21 58 19	28 11 39	29 47	25	26	16	19	19	5	13	11
23	22 2 16	29 9 28	12♎ 4	26	27	17	19	19	5	13	11
24	22 6 13	0♍ 7 18	24 11	27	28	17	19	19	5	13	11
25	22 10 9	1 5 10	6♏ 8	28	0♍	18	19	19	5	13	12
26	22 14 6	2 3 3	18 1	29	1	19	19	19	5	13	12
27	22 18 2	3 0 57	29 52	0♎	2	19	19	19	5	13	12
28	22 21 59	3 58 52	11♐48	1	3	20	19	19	6	13	12
29	22 25 55	4 56 49	23 53	2	5	21	19	19	6	13	12
30	22 29 52	5 54 47	6♑13	2	6	21	19	19	6	13	12
31	22 33 48	6 52 47	18 51	3	7	22	19	18	6	13	12

THE SUN ENTERS THE SIGN OF VIRGO ON AUG 23 AT 20:58.

DAY	TIME	☉	☽	☿	♀	♂	♃	♄	♅	♆	♇
	h m s	° ' "	° '	°	°	°	°	°	°	°	°
S 1	22 37 45	7♍50 48	1♒51	4♎	8♍	23♎	19♈R	18♒R	6♍	13♏	12♍
E 2	22 41 42	8 48 50	15 15	4	10	23	19	18	6	13	12
P 3	22 45 38	9 46 54	29 3	4	11	24	19	18	6	13	12
T 4	22 49 35	10 44 59	13♓13	5	12	24	18	18	6	13	12
E 5	22 53 31	11 43 7	27 39	5	13	25	18	18	6	13	12
M 6	22 57 28	12 41 16	12♈16	5 R	15	26	18	18	6	13	12
B 7	23 1 24	13 39 26	26 55	5	16	26	18	18	6	13	12
E 8	23 5 21	14 37 39	11♉31	5	17	27	18	18	6	13	12
R 9	23 9 17	15 35 54	25 58	5	18	28	18	18	6	13	12
10	23 13 14	16 34 11	10♊11	5	20	28	18	18	6	13	12
11	23 17 11	17 32 30	24 10	4	21	29	18	18	6	13	12
12	23 21 7	18 30 52	7♋54	4	22	0♏	18	18	6	13	12
13	23 25 4	19 29 15	21 24	3	23	0	18	18	7	14	12
14	23 29 0	20 27 41	4♌41	2	25	1	17	18	7	14	12
15	23 32 57	21 26 8	17 45	2	26	2	17	18	7	14	12
16	23 36 53	22 24 38	0♍38	1	27	2	17	17	7	14	12
17	23 40 50	23 23 9	13 21	0	28	3	17	17	7	14	12
18	23 44 46	24 21 42	25 52	29♍	29	4	17	17	7	14	12
19	23 48 43	25 20 18	8♎12	28	1♎	4	17	17	7	14	12
20	23 52 39	26 18 55	20 23	27	2	5	17	17	7	14	12
21	23 56 36	27 17 34	2♏24	26	3	6	17	17	7	14	12
22	0 0 33	28 16 15	14 18	25	4	6	17	17	7	14	12
23	0 4 29	29 14 57	26 8	24	6	7	16	17	7	14	13
24	0 8 26	0♎13 42	7♐58	23	7	8	16	17	7	14	13
25	0 12 22	1 12 28	19 51	22	8	9	16	17	7	14	13
26	0 16 19	2 11 16	1♑53	21	9	9	16	17	7	14	13
27	0 20 15	3 10 6	14 10	21	11	10	16	17	7	14	13
28	0 24 12	4 8 57	26 45	21	12	11	16	17	7	14	13
29	0 28 8	5 7 50	9♒45	21 D	13	11	16	17	8	14	13
30	0 32 5	6 6 45	23 13	21	14	12	16	17	8	14	13

THE SUN ENTERS THE SIGN OF LIBRA ON SEP 23 AT 18:24.

DAY	TIME	☉	☽	☿	♀	♂	♃	♄	♅	♆	♇
	h m s	° ' "	° '	°	°	°	°	°	°	°	°
O 1	0 36 2	7♎ 5 42	7♓ 9	21♍	16♎	13♏	15♈R	17♒R	8♍	14♏	13♍
C 2	0 39 58	8 4 40	21 33	21	17	13	15	17	8	14	13
T 3	0 43 55	9 3 41	6♈18	22	18	14	15	17	8	14	13
O 4	0 47 51	10 2 43	21 18	22	19	15	15	17	8	14	13
B 5	0 51 48	11 1 48	6♉23	23	21	15	15	17	8	14	13
E 6	0 55 44	12 0 54	21 22	24	22	16	15	17	8	14	13
R 7	0 59 41	13 0 3	6♊ 8	25	23	17	15	17	8	14	13
8	1 3 37	13 59 15	20 34	26	24	17	15	17	8	14	13
9	1 7 34	14 58 29	4♋38	28	26	18	14	17	8	14	13
10	1 11 31	15 57 45	18 20	29	27	19	14	17	8	14	13
11	1 15 27	16 57 3	1♌42	0♎	28	20	14	17	8	14	13
12	1 19 24	17 56 24	14 46	2	29	20	14	17	8	14	13
13	1 23 20	18 55 47	27 35	3	1♏	21	14	17	8	14	13
14	1 27 17	19 55 12	10♍11	5	2	22	14	16	8	14	13
15	1 31 13	20 54 40	22 37	7	3	22	14	16	8	14	13
16	1 35 10	21 54 9	4♎53	8	4	23	13	16	8	15	13
17	1 39 6	22 53 41	17 2	10	6	24	13	16	8	15	13
18	1 43 3	23 53 15	29 4	12	7	24	13	16	9	15	13
19	1 47 0	24 52 50	10♏59	13	8	25	13	16	9	15	13
20	1 50 56	25 52 28	22 50	15	9	26	13	16	9	15	13
21	1 54 53	26 52 8	4♐39	17	11	27	13	16 D	9	15	13
22	1 58 49	27 51 49	16 28	18	12	27	13	16	9	15	13
23	2 2 46	28 51 33	28 20	20	13	28	13	16	9	15	13
24	2 6 42	29 51 18	10♑20	22	14	29	12	16	9	15	13
25	2 10 39	0♏51 5	22 34	24	16	29	12	16	9	15	13
26	2 14 35	1 50 53	5♒ 5	25	17	0♐	12	16	9	15	14
27	2 18 32	2 50 43	17 59	27	18	1	12	16	9	15	14
28	2 22 29	3 50 35	1♓21	29	19	2	12	16	9	15	14
29	2 26 25	4 50 29	15 13	0♏	21	2	12	16	9	15	14
30	2 30 22	5 50 24	29 35	2	22	3	12	17	9	15	14
31	2 34 18	6 50 21	14♈24	4	23	4	12	17	9	15	14

THE SUN ENTERS THE SIGN OF SCORPIO ON OCT 24 AT 03:30.

DAY	TIME	☉	☽	☿	♀	♂	♃	♄	♅	♆	♇
	h m s	° ' "	° '	°	°	°	°	°	°	°	°
N 1	2 38 15	7♏50 19	29♈33	5♏	24♏	5♐	11♈R	17♒	9♍	15♏	14♍
O 2	2 42 11	8 50 20	14♉51	7	26	5	11	17	9	15	14
V 3	2 46 8	9 50 22	0♊ 7	9	27	6	11	17	9	15	14
E 4	2 50 4	10 50 27	15 11	10	28	7	11	17	9	15	14
M 5	2 54 1	11 50 33	29 55	12	29	7	11	17	9	15	14
B 6	2 57 57	12 50 42	14♋13	13	1♐	8	11	17	9	15	14
E 7	3 1 54	13 50 52	28 4	15	2	9	11	17	9	15	14
R 8	3 5 51	14 51 5	11♌30	17	3	10	11	17	9	15	14
9	3 9 47	15 51 20	24 32	18	4	10	11	17	9	15	14
10	3 13 44	16 51 37	7♍15	20	6	11	11	17	9	15	14
11	3 17 40	17 51 55	19 43	21	7	12	11	17	9	15	14
12	3 21 37	18 52 16	1♎58	23	8	13	10	17	10	16	14
13	3 25 33	19 52 38	14 4	25	9	13	10	17	10	16	14
14	3 29 30	20 53 3	26 3	26	11	14	10	17	10	16	14
15	3 33 26	21 53 29	7♏57	28	12	15	10	17	10	16	14
16	3 37 23	22 53 56	19 49	29	13	15	10	17	10	16	14
17	3 41 20	23 54 26	1♐38	1♐	14	16	10	17	10	16	14
18	3 45 16	24 54 57	13 28	2	16	17	10	17	10	16	14
19	3 49 13	25 55 30	25 20	4	17	18	10	17	10	16	14
20	3 53 9	26 56 3	7♑17	5	18	18	10	17	10	16	14
21	3 57 6	27 56 39	19 21	7	19	19	10	17	10	16	14
22	4 1 2	28 57 15	1♒37	9	20	20	10	17	10	16	14
23	4 4 59	29 57 53	14 8	10	22	21	10	17	10	16	14
24	4 8 56	0♐58 32	26 59	12	23	21	10	17	10	16	14
25	4 12 52	1 59 12	10♓13	13	24	22	10	17	10	16	14
26	4 16 49	2 59 53	23 54	15	25	23	10	17	10	16	14
27	4 20 45	4 0 35	8♈ 4	16	27	24	10	18	10	16	14
28	4 24 42	5 1 18	22 40	18	28	24	10	18	10	16	14
29	4 28 38	6 2 2	7♉38	19	29	25	10	18	10	16	14
30	4 32 35	7 2 47	22 50	21	0♑	26	10	18	10	16	14

THE SUN ENTERS THE SIGN OF SAGITTARIUS ON NOV 23 AT 00:51.

DAY	TIME	☉	☽	☿	♀	♂	♃	♄	♅	♆	♇
	h m s	° ' "	° '	°	°	°	°	°	°	°	°
D 1	4 36 31	8♐ 3 34	8♊ 7	22♐	2♑	27♐	10♈R	18♒	10♍	16♏	14♍
E 2	4 40 28	9 4 22	23 17	24	3	27	10	18	10	16	14
C 3	4 44 25	10 5 11	8♋11	25	4	28	10	18	10	16	14
E 4	4 48 21	11 6 1	22 42	27	5	29	10	18	10	16	14
M 5	4 52 18	12 6 53	6♌47	28	7	0♑	10 D	18	10	16	14
B 6	4 56 14	13 7 46	20 23	0♑	8	0	10	18	10	16	14
E 7	5 0 11	14 8 40	3♍33	1	9	1	10	18	10	16	14
R 8	5 4 7	15 9 35	16 20	3	10	2	10	18	10	16	14
9	5 8 4	16 10 32	28 47	4	12	3	10	18	10	16	14
10	5 12 0	17 11 30	10♎59	5	13	4	10	18	10	17	14
11	5 15 57	18 12 29	23 0	7	14	4	10	19	10	17	14
12	5 19 54	19 13 29	4♏55	8	15	5	10	19	10	17	14
13	5 23 50	20 14 30	16 45	10	17	6	10	19	10	17	14
14	5 27 47	21 15 32	28 34	11	18	7	10	19	10	17	14
15	5 31 43	22 16 35	10♐25	12	19	7	10	19	10	17	14
16	5 35 40	23 17 39	22 20	13	20	8	10	19	10 R	17	14
17	5 39 36	24 18 44	4♑20	14	22	9	10	19	10	17	14 R
18	5 43 33	25 19 49	16 27	16	23	10	10	19	10	17	14
19	5 47 29	26 20 55	28 43	17	24	10	10	19	10	17	14
20	5 51 26	27 22 1	11♒10	18	25	11	10	19	10	17	14
21	5 55 23	28 23 7	23 51	18	27	12	10	19	10	17	14
22	5 59 19	29 24 14	6♓47	19	28	13	10	19	10	17	14
23	6 3 16	0♑25 21	20 1	20	29	13	10	20	10	17	14
24	6 7 12	1 26 28	3♈36	20	0♒	14	10	20	10	17	14
25	6 11 9	2 27 35	17 32	21	2	15	10	20	10	17	14
26	6 15 5	3 28 42	1♉49	21 R	3	16	10	20	10	17	14
27	6 19 2	4 29 50	16 25	21	4	17	10	20	10	17	14
28	6 22 58	5 30 57	1♊15	20	5	17	10	20	10	17	14
29	6 26 55	6 32 5	16 13	20	6	18	10	20	10	17	14
30	6 30 52	7 33 12	1♋10	19	8	19	11	20	10	17	14
31	6 34 48	8 34 20	15 58	19	9	20	11	20	10	17	14

THE SUN ENTERS THE SIGN OF CAPRICORN ON DEC 22 AT 14:03.

♈ ARIES ♉ TAURUS ♊ GEMINI ♋ CANCER ♌ LEO ♍ VIRGO ♎ LIBRA ♏ SCORPIO ♐ SAGITTARIUS ♑ CAPRICORN ♒ AQUARIUS ♓ PISCES

SIDEREAL SUN MOON MERCURY VENUS MARS JUPITER SATURN URANUS NEPTUNE PLUTO

DAY	TIME	☉	☽	☿	♀	♂	♃	♄	♅	♆	♇
	h m s	° ' "	° '	°	°	°	°	°	°	°	°
J 1	6 38 45	9♑35 28	0♌30	18♑R	10♒	20♑	11♈	20♒	10♍R	17♏	14♍R
A 2	6 42 41	10 36 36	14 40	17	11	21	11	21	10	17	14
N 3	6 46 38	11 37 45	28 25	15	13	22	11	21	10	17	14
U 4	6 50 34	12 38 53	11♍44	14	14	23	11	21	10	17	14
A 5	6 54 31	13 40 2	24 39	13	15	24	11	21	10	17	14
R 6	6 58 27	14 41 11	7♎11	11	16	24	11	21	10	17	14
Y 7	7 2 24	15 42 20	19 26	10	18	25	11	21	10	17	14
8	7 6 21	16 43 29	1♏28	9	19	26	11	21	10	17	14
9	7 10 17	17 44 39	13 21	8	20	27	12	21	10	17	14
10	7 14 14	18 45 48	25 10	7	21	27	12	21	10	17	14
11	7 18 10	19 46 58	6♐59	6	22	28	12	21	10	17	14
12	7 22 7	20 48 7	18 53	5	24	29	12	22	10	17	14
13	7 26 3	21 49 16	0♑53	5	25	0♒	12	22	10	17	14
14	7 30 0	22 50 26	13 3	5	26	1	12	22	10	17	14
15	7 33 57	23 51 34	25 25	5 D	27	1	12	22	10	17	14
16	7 37 53	24 52 42	7♒59	5	29	2	12	22	10	18	14
17	7 41 50	25 53 50	20 46	5	0♓	3	13	22	10	18	14
18	7 45 46	26 54 57	3♓47	5	1	4	13	22	10	18	14
19	7 49 43	27 56 3	17 1	5	2	5	13	22	10	18	14
20	7 53 39	28 57 9	0♈28	6	4	5	13	22	10	18	14
21	7 57 36	29 58 13	14 8	6	5	6	13	23	9	18	14
22	8 1 32	0♒59 17	28 1	7	6	7	13	23	9	18	14
23	8 5 29	2 0 20	12♉ 6	8	7	8	13	23	9	18	14
24	8 9 25	3 1 21	26 22	9	8	8	13	23	9	18	14
25	8 13 22	4 2 22	10♊46	9	10	9	14	23	9	18	14
26	8 17 19	5 3 22	25 15	10	11	10	14	23	9	18	14
27	8 21 15	6 4 20	9♋45	11	12	11	14	23	9	18	14
28	8 25 12	7 5 18	24 11	12	13	12	14	23	9	18	14
29	8 29 8	8 6 15	8♌26	13	14	12	14	24	9	18	14
30	8 33 5	9 7 10	22 27	15	16	13	14	24	9	18	14
31	8 37 1	10 8 5	6♍ 9	16	17	14	15	24	9	18	14

THE SUN ENTERS THE SIGN OF AQUARIUS ON JAN 21 AT 00:41.

DAY	TIME	☉	☽	☿	♀	♂	♃	♄	♅	♆	♇
	h m s	° ' "	° '	°	°	°	°	°	°	°	°
F 1	8 40 58	11♒ 8 59	19♍29	17♑	18♓	15♒	15♈	24♒	9♍R	18♏	14♍R
E 2	8 44 55	12 9 52	2♎26	18	19	16	15	24	9	18	14
B 3	8 48 51	13 10 44	15 3	19	21	16	15	24	9	18	14
R 4	8 52 48	14 11 36	27 22	21	22	17	15	24	9	18	14
U 5	8 56 44	15 12 26	9♏25	22	23	18	15	24	9	18	14
A 6	9 0 41	16 13 16	21 20	23	24	19	16	24	9	18	14
R 7	9 4 37	17 14 4	3♐ 9	25	25	19	16	25	9	18	14
Y 8	9 8 34	18 14 52	14 59	26	27	20	16	25	9	18	14
9	9 12 30	19 15 39	26 54	27	28	21	16	25	9	18	14
10	9 16 27	20 16 25	8♑59	29	29	22	16	25	9	18	14
11	9 20 24	21 17 9	21 18	0♒	0♈	23	17	25	9	18	13
12	9 24 20	22 17 53	3♒53	2	1	23	17	25	9	18	13
13	9 28 17	23 18 35	16 45	3	3	24	17	25	9	18	13
14	9 32 13	24 19 16	29 55	4	4	25	17	25	9	18	13
15	9 36 10	25 19 55	13♓21	6	5	26	17	26	9	18	13
16	9 40 6	26 20 32	27 2	7	6	27	17	26	9	18	13
17	9 44 3	27 21 8	10♈53	9	7	27	18	26	8	18	13
18	9 47 59	28 21 43	24 52	11	8	28	18	26	8	18 R	13
19	9 51 56	29 22 15	8♉57	12	10	29	18	26	8	18	13
20	9 55 52	0♓22 46	23 3	14	11	0♓	18	26	8	18	13
21	9 59 49	1 23 15	7♊10	15	12	1	18	26	8	18	13
22	10 3 46	2 23 42	21 17	17	13	1	19	26	8	18	13
23	10 7 42	3 24 8	5♋23	18	14	2	19	27	8	18	13
24	10 11 39	4 24 31	19 25	20	16	3	19	27	8	18	13
25	10 15 35	5 24 52	3♌22	22	17	4	19	27	8	18	13
26	10 19 32	6 25 12	17 12	23	18	4	19	27	8	18	13
27	10 23 28	7 25 29	0♍51	25	19	5	20	27	8	18	13
28	10 27 25	8 25 45	14 16	27	20	6	20	27	8	18	13
29	10 31 21	9 25 59	27 25	28	21	7	20	27	8	18	13

THE SUN ENTERS THE SIGN OF PISCES ON FEB 19 AT 14:58.

DAY	TIME	☉	☽	☿	♀	♂	♃	♄	♅	♆	♇
	h m s	° ' "	° '	°	°	°	°	°	°	°	°
M 1	10 35 18	10♓26 12	10♎17	0♓	23♈	8♓	20♈	27♒	8♍R	18♏R	13♍R
A 2	10 39 15	11 26 23	22 51	2	24	8	21	27	8	18	13
R 3	10 43 11	12 26 32	5♏ 8	4	25	9	21	28	8	18	13
C 4	10 47 8	13 26 40	17 13	5	26	10	21	28	8	18	13
H 5	10 51 4	14 26 46	29 7	7	27	11	21	28	8	18	13
6	10 55 1	15 26 50	10♐56	9	28	12	21	28	8	18	13
7	10 58 57	16 26 53	22 46	11	29	12	22	28	8	18	13
8	11 2 54	17 26 55	4♑41	13	1♉	13	22	28	8	18	13
9	11 6 50	18 26 54	16 48	14	2	14	22	28	8	18	13
10	11 10 47	19 26 52	29 10	16	3	15	22	28	8	18	13
11	11 14 44	20 26 49	11♒52	18	4	16	22	29	7	18	13
12	11 18 40	21 26 43	24 57	20	5	16	23	29	7	18	13
13	11 22 37	22 26 36	8♓24	22	6	17	23	29	7	18	13
14	11 26 33	23 26 27	22 14	24	7	18	23	29	7	18	13
15	11 30 30	24 26 15	6♈21	26	8	19	23	29	7	18	13
16	11 34 26	25 26 2	20 41	28	10	19	24	29	7	18	13
17	11 38 23	26 25 47	5♉ 7	0♈	11	20	24	29	7	18	13
18	11 42 19	27 25 29	19 33	2	12	21	24	29	7	18	13
19	11 46 16	28 25 10	3♊55	4	13	22	24	29	7	18	13
20	11 50 13	29 24 48	18 9	6	14	23	25	0♓	7	18	13
21	11 54 9	0♈24 23	2♋13	8	15	23	25	0	7	18	12
22	11 58 6	1 23 57	16 7	10	16	24	25	0	7	18	12
23	12 2 2	2 23 28	29 51	12	17	25	25	0	7	18	12
24	12 5 59	3 22 57	13♌26	14	18	26	25	0	7	18	12
25	12 9 55	4 22 23	26 50	16	19	27	26	0	7	18	12
26	12 13 52	5 21 48	10♍ 4	18	20	27	26	0	7	17	12
27	12 17 48	6 21 10	23 7	20	22	28	26	0	7	17	12
28	12 21 45	7 20 29	5♎58	22	23	29	26	0	7	17	12
29	12 25 42	8 19 47	18 35	23	24	0⊙	27	1	7	17	12
30	12 29 38	9 19 3	0♏59	25	25	0♈	27	1	7	17	12
31	12 33 35	10 18 17	13 11	27	26	1	27	1	7	17	12

THE SUN ENTERS THE SIGN OF ARIES ON MAR 20 AT 14:10.

SIDEREAL SUN MOON MERCURY VENUS MARS JUPITER SATURN URANUS NEPTUNE PLUTO

DAY	TIME	☉	☽	☿	♀	♂	♃	♄	♅	♆	♇
	h m s	° ' "	° '	°	°	°	°	°	°	°	°
A 1	12 37 31	11♈17 29	25♏12	28♈	27♉	2♈	27♈	1♓	7♍R	17♏R	12♍R
P 2	12 41 28	12 16 40	7♐ 4	0♉	28	3	28	1	7	17	12
R 3	12 45 24	13 15 48	18 53	1	29	4	28	1	7	17	12
I 4	12 49 21	14 14 55	0♑41	3	0♊	4	28	1	7	17	12
L 5	12 53 17	15 14 0	12 35	4	1	5	28	1	7	17	12
6	12 57 14	16 13 3	24 41	5	2	6	28	1	7	17	12
7	13 1 10	17 12 4	7♒ 2	6	3	7	29	1	6	17	12
8	13 5 7	18 11 4	19 45	7	4	7	29	2	6	17	12
9	13 9 4	19 10 1	2♓53	8	5	8	29	2	6	17	12
10	13 13 0	20 8 57	16 29	9	6	9	29	2	6	17	12
11	13 16 57	21 7 51	0♈30	10	7	10	0♉	2	6	17	12
12	13 20 53	22 6 43	14 55	10	8	10	0	2	6	17	12
13	13 24 50	23 5 33	29 37	11	9	11	0	2	6	17	12
14	13 28 46	24 4 22	14♉28	11	10	12	0	2	6	17	12
15	13 32 43	25 3 8	29 19	11	11	13	1	2	6	17	12
16	13 36 39	26 1 52	14♊ 3	11 R	12	14	1	2	6	17	12
17	13 40 36	27 0 34	28 34	12	13	14	1	2	6	17	12
18	13 44 33	27 59 13	12♋48	11	13	15	1	2	6	17	12
19	13 48 29	28 57 51	26 45	11	14	16	2	2	6	17	12
20	13 52 26	29 56 26	10♌24	11	15	17	2	3	6	17	12
21	13 56 22	0♉54 59	23 47	11	16	17	2	3	6	17	12
22	14 0 19	1 53 29	6♍55	10	17	18	2	3	6	17	12
23	14 4 15	2 51 58	19 51	10	18	19	3	3	6	17	12
24	14 8 12	3 50 24	2♎34	9	19	20	3	3	6	17	12
25	14 12 8	4 48 49	15 5	9	20	20	3	3	6	17	12
26	14 16 5	5 47 11	27 26	8	20	21	3	3	6	17	12
27	14 20 2	6 45 32	9♏37	7	21	22	4	3	6	17	12
28	14 23 58	7 43 51	21 40	7	22	23	4	3	6	17	12
29	14 27 55	8 42 8	3♐35	6	23	23	4	3	6	17	12
30	14 31 51	9 40 23	15 24	5	24	24	4	3	6	17	12

THE SUN ENTERS THE SIGN OF TAURUS ON APR 20 AT 01:27.

DAY	TIME	☉	☽	☿	♀	♂	♃	♄	♅	♆	♇
	h m s	° ' "	° '	°	°	°	°	°	°	°	°
M 1	14 35 48	10♉38 37	27♐12	5♉R	24♊	25♈	4♉	3♓	6♍R	17♏R	12♍R
A 2	14 39 44	11 36 49	9♑ 0	4	25	26	5	3	6	17	12
Y 3	14 43 41	12 35 0	20 54	4	26	27	5	4	6	17	12
4	14 47 37	13 33 9	2♒59	3	27	27	5	4	6	17	12
5	14 51 34	14 31 17	15 19	3	27	28	5	4	6	17	12
6	14 55 31	15 29 23	28 0	2	28	29	6	4	6	16	12
7	14 59 27	16 27 28	11♓ 5	2	29	0♉	6	4	6	16	12
8	15 3 24	17 25 32	24 38	2	29	0	6	4	6	16	12
9	15 7 20	18 23 34	8♈40	2	0♋	1	6	4	6	16	12
10	15 11 17	19 21 35	23 8	2 D	1	2	7	4	6	16	12
11	15 15 13	20 19 34	7♉59	2	1	3	7	4	6	16	12
12	15 19 10	21 17 32	23 2	2	2	3	7	4	6	16	12
13	15 23 6	22 15 28	8♊11	2	2	4	7	4	6 D	16	12
14	15 27 3	23 13 23	23 14	2	3	5	8	4	6	16	12
15	15 31 0	24 11 16	8♋ 4	2	3	6	8	4	6	16	12
16	15 34 56	25 9 8	22 34	3	4	6	8	4	6	16	12
17	15 38 53	26 6 58	6♌43	3	4	7	8	4	6	16	12
18	15 42 49	27 4 46	20 28	4	5	8	9	4	6	16	12
19	15 46 46	28 2 32	3♍50	4	5	9	9	4	6	16	12
20	15 50 42	29 0 16	16 53	5	5	9	9	4	6	16	12
21	15 54 39	29 57 59	29 38	5	6	10	9	5	6	16	12
22	15 58 35	0♊55 40	12♎ 8	6	6	11	9	5	6	16	12 D
23	16 2 32	1 53 20	24 26	7	6	11	10	5	6	16	12
24	16 6 29	2 50 58	6♏34	8	6	12	10	5	6	16	12
25	16 10 25	3 48 35	18 34	9	6	13	10	5	6	16	12
26	16 14 22	4 46 11	0♐28	10	7	14	10	5	6	16	12
27	16 18 18	5 43 46	12 18	11	7	14	11	5	6	16	12
28	16 22 15	6 41 19	24 6	12	7	15	11	5	6	16	12
29	16 26 11	7 38 52	5♑54	13	7 R	16	11	5	6	16	12
30	16 30 8	8 36 23	17 46	14	7	17	11	5	6	16	12
31	16 34 4	9 33 53	29 43	16	7	17	11	5	6	16	12

THE SUN ENTERS THE SIGN OF GEMINI ON MAY 21 AT 00:50.

DAY	TIME	☉	☽	☿	♀	♂	♃	♄	♅	♆	♇
	h m s	° ' "	° '	°	°	°	°	°	°	°	°
J 1	16 38 1	10♊31 23	11♒51	17♉	7♋R	18♉	12♉	5♓	6♍	16♏R	12♍
U 2	16 41 58	11 28 52	24 13	18	7	19	12	5	6	16	12
N 3	16 45 54	12 26 20	6♓53	20	6	20	12	5	6	16	12
E 4	16 49 51	13 23 47	19 55	21	6	20	12	5	6	16	12
5	16 53 47	14 21 13	3♈22	23	6	21	13	5	6	16	12
6	16 57 44	15 18 39	17 16	24	6	22	13	5	6	16	12
7	17 1 40	16 16 5	1♉37	26	5	22	13	5	6	16	12
8	17 5 37	17 13 29	16 20	27	5	23	13	5	6	16	12
9	17 9 33	18 10 53	1♊22	29	5	24	13	5	6	16	12
10	17 13 30	19 8 17	16 32	1♊	4	25	14	5	6	16	12
11	17 17 27	20 5 39	1♋43	2	4	25	14	5	6	16	12
12	17 21 23	21 3 1	16 44	4	3	26	14	5	6	16	12
13	17 25 20	22 0 22	1♌28	6	3	27	14	5	6	16	12
14	17 29 16	22 57 43	15 49	8	2	28	15	5	6	16	12
15	17 33 13	23 55 2	29 44	10	2	28	15	5 R	6	16	12
16	17 37 9	24 52 20	13♍14	12	1	29	15	5	6	15	12
17	17 41 6	25 49 37	26 18	14	0	0♊	15	5	6	15	12
18	17 45 3	26 46 54	9♎ 1	16	0	0	15	5	6	15	12
19	17 48 59	27 44 9	21 26	18	29♊	1	16	5	6	15	12
20	17 52 56	28 41 24	3♏37	20	29	2	16	5	7	15	12
21	17 56 52	29 38 39	15 37	22	28	3	16	5	7	15	12
22	18 0 49	0♋35 52	27 30	24	27	3	16	5	7	15	12
23	18 4 45	1 33 5	9♐19	26	27	4	16	5	7	15	12
24	18 8 42	2 30 18	21 7	28	26	5	17	5	7	15	12
25	18 12 38	3 27 31	2♑56	1♋	26	5	17	5	7	15	12
26	18 16 35	4 24 43	14 49	3	25	6	17	5	7	15	12
27	18 20 32	5 21 55	26 48	5	24	7	17	5	7	15	12
28	18 24 28	6 19 6	8♒55	7	24	7	17	5	7	15	12
29	18 28 25	7 16 18	21 12	9	23	8	18	5	7	15	12
30	18 32 21	8 13 30	3♓42	12	23	9	18	5	7	15	12

THE SUN ENTERS THE SIGN OF CANCER ON JUN 21 AT 08:57.

♈ ARIES ♉ TAURUS ♊ GEMINI ♋ CANCER ♌ LEO ♍ VIRGO ♎ LIBRA ♏ SCORPIO ♐ SAGITTARIUS ♑ CAPRICORN ♒ AQUARIUS ♓ PISCES

SIDEREAL SUN MOON MERCURY VENUS MARS JUPITER SATURN URANUS NEPTUNE PLUTO

DAY	TIME	☉	☽	☿	♀	♂	♃	♄	♅	♆	♇
	h m s	° ' "	° '	°	°	°	°	°	°	°	°
J 1	18 36 18	9♋10 41	16♓27	14♋	23♊R	10♊	18♉	5♓R	7♍	15♏R	12♍
U 2	18 40 14	10 7 53	29 31	16	22	10	18	5	7	15	12
L 3	18 44 11	11 5 5	12♈55	18	22	11	18	5	7	15	12
Y 4	18 48 7	12 2 17	26 40	20	21	12	19	5	7	15	12
5	18 52 4	12 59 30	10♉48	22	21	12	19	5	7	15	12
6	18 56 1	13 56 43	25 16	24	21	13	19	5	7	15	12
7	18 59 57	14 53 56	10♊ 3	26	21	14	19	5	7	15	12
8	19 3 54	15 51 9	25 1	28	21	14	19	5	7	15	12
9	19 7 50	16 48 23	10♋ 3	0♌	20	15	19	5	7	15	12
10	19 11 47	17 45 37	25 2	2	20	16	20	5	7	15	12
11	19 15 43	18 42 51	9♌48	4	20 D	17	20	5	7	15	12
12	19 19 40	19 40 6	24 15	6	20	17	20	4	7	15	12
13	19 23 36	20 37 20	8♍17	7	20	18	20	4	7	15	12
14	19 27 33	21 34 34	21 53	9	20	19	20	4	8	15	12
15	19 31 30	22 31 48	5♎ 3	11	21	19	20	4	8	15	12
16	19 35 26	23 29 2	17 49	13	21	20	21	4	8	15	12
17	19 39 23	24 26 17	0♏14	14	21	21	21	4	8	15	12
18	19 43 19	25 23 31	12 23	16	21	21	21	4	8	15	12
19	19 47 16	26 20 46	24 20	18	21	22	21	4	8	15	12
20	19 51 12	27 18 1	6♐10	19	22	23	21	4	8	15	12
21	19 55 9	28 15 17	17 58	21	22	23	21	4	8	15	12
22	19 59 5	29 12 32	29 47	22	22	24	22	4	8	15	12
23	20 3 2	0♌ 9 48	11♑40	24	23	25	22	4	8	15	12
24	20 6 59	1 7 5	23 41	25	23	25	22	4	8	15	13
25	20 10 55	2 4 23	5♒51	27	24	26	22	4	8	15	13
26	20 14 52	3 1 40	18 11	28	24	27	22	4	8	15	13
27	20 18 48	3 58 59	0♓44	29	24	27	22	4	8	15 D	13
28	20 22 45	4 56 19	13 30	1♍	25	28	22	4	8	15	13
29	20 26 41	5 53 39	26 29	2	25	29	23	4	8	15	13
30	20 30 38	6 51 0	9♈42	3	26	29	23	4	8	15	13
31	20 34 34	7 48 23	23 10	4	27	0♋	23	3	8	15	13

THE SUN ENTERS THE SIGN OF LEO ON JUL 22 AT 19:53.

DAY	TIME	☉	☽	☿	♀	♂	♃	♄	♅	♆	♇
	h m s	° ' "	° '	°	°	°	°	°	°	°	°
A 1	20 38 31	8♌45 46	6♉53	6♍	27♊	1♋	23♉	3♓R	8♍	15♏	13♍
U 2	20 42 28	9 43 11	20 51	7	28	1	23	3	9	15	13
G 3	20 46 24	10 40 37	5♊ 5	8	28	2	23	3	9	15	13
U 4	20 50 21	11 38 5	19 31	9	29	3	23	3	9	15	13
S 5	20 54 17	12 35 33	4♋ 8	10	0♋	3	24	3	9	15	13
T 6	20 58 14	13 33 3	18 51	11	0	4	24	3	9	15	13
7	21 2 10	14 30 34	3♌33	12	1	5	24	3	9	15	13
8	21 6 7	15 28 6	18 8	13	2	5	24	3	9	15	13
9	21 10 3	16 25 39	2♍28	13	3	6	24	3	9	15	13
10	21 14 0	17 23 12	16 28	14	3	7	24	3	9	15	13
11	21 17 57	18 20 47	0♎ 4	15	4	7	24	3	9	15	13
12	21 21 53	19 18 23	13 16	16	5	8	24	3	9	15	13
13	21 25 50	20 16 0	26 4	16	6	9	24	3	9	15	13
14	21 29 46	21 13 38	8♏30	17	6	9	25	2	9	15	13
15	21 33 43	22 11 16	20 39	17	7	10	25	2	9	15	13
16	21 37 39	23 8 56	2♐36	17	8	11	25	2	9	15	13
17	21 41 36	24 6 37	14 26	18	9	11	25	2	9	15	13
18	21 45 32	25 4 19	26 14	18	10	12	25	2	9	15	13
19	21 49 29	26 2 2	8♑ 5	18 R	11	13	25	2	10	15	13
20	21 53 26	26 59 46	20 4	18	12	13	25	2	10	15	13
21	21 57 22	27 57 31	2♒13	18	12	14	25	2	10	15	13
22	22 1 19	28 55 18	14 35	18	13	15	25	2	10	15	13
23	22 5 15	29 53 6	27 13	17	14	15	25	2	10	15	13
24	22 9 12	0♍50 56	10♓ 5	17	15	16	25	2	10	15	14
25	22 13 8	1 48 46	23 13	17	16	17	25	2	10	15	14
26	22 17 5	2 46 39	6♈33	16	17	17	25	2	10	15	14
27	22 21 1	3 44 33	20 5	15	18	18	26	2	10	15	14
28	22 24 58	4 42 29	3♉47	15	19	19	26	1	10	15	14
29	22 28 55	5 40 27	17 37	14	20	19	26	1	10	15	14
30	22 32 51	6 38 27	1♊36	13	21	20	26	1	10	15	14
31	22 36 48	7 36 29	15 41	12	22	20	26	1	10	15	14

THE SUN ENTERS THE SIGN OF VIRGO ON AUG 23 AT 02:52.

DAY	TIME	☉	☽	☿	♀	♂	♃	♄	♅	♆	♇
	h m s	° ' "	° '	°	°	°	°	°	°	°	°
S 1	22 40 44	8♍34 32	29♊52	11♍R	23♋	21♋	26♉	1♓R	10♍	15♏	14♍
E 2	22 44 41	9 32 38	14♋ 8	10	24	22	26	1	10	15	14
P 3	22 48 37	10 30 46	28 26	9	25	22	26	1	10	15	14
T 4	22 52 34	11 28 55	12♌44	8	26	23	26	1	11	15	14
E 5	22 56 30	12 27 7	26 56	7	27	24	26	1	11	15	14
M 6	23 0 27	13 25 20	10♍58	7	28	24	26	1	11	16	14
B 7	23 4 24	14 23 34	24 44	6	29	25	26	1	11	16	14
E 8	23 8 20	15 21 51	8♎11	5	0♌	26	26	1	11	16	14
R 9	23 12 17	16 20 9	21 17	5	1	26	26	1	11	16	14
10	23 16 13	17 18 29	4♏ 2	5	2	27	26	0	11	16	14
11	23 20 10	18 16 50	16 27	4 D	3	27	26	0	11	16	14
12	23 24 6	19 15 13	28 36	4	4	28	26	0	11	16	14
13	23 28 3	20 13 38	10♐33	4	5	29	26	0	11	16	14
14	23 31 59	21 12 4	22 22	5	6	29	26 R	0	11	16	14
15	23 35 56	22 10 32	4♑11	5	7	0♌	26	0	11	16	14
16	23 39 53	23 9 2	16 3	6	8	0	26	0	11	16	14
17	23 43 49	24 7 33	28 5	6	9	1	26	0	11	16	14
18	23 47 46	25 6 6	10♒20	7	10	2	26	0	11	16	14
19	23 51 42	26 4 41	22 52	8	11	2	26	0	11	16	14
20	23 55 39	27 3 17	5♓44	9	12	3	26	0	12	16	14
21	23 59 35	28 1 55	18 55	11	14	4	26	0	12	16	14
22	0 3 32	29 0 35	2♈25	12	15	4	26	0	12	16	15
23	0 7 28	29 59 17	16 10	13	16	5	26	0	12	16	15
24	0 11 25	0♎58 1	0♉ 8	15	17	5	26	0	12	16	15
25	0 15 21	1 56 48	14 13	16	18	6	26	29♒	12	16	15
26	0 19 18	2 55 36	28 22	18	19	7	26	29	12	16	15
27	0 23 15	3 54 27	12♊31	20	20	7	26	29	12	16	15
28	0 27 11	4 53 20	26 40	21	21	8	26	29	12	16	15
29	0 31 8	5 52 16	10♋46	23	22	8	26	29	12	16	15
30	0 35 4	6 51 14	24 49	25	23	9	26	29	12	16	15

THE SUN ENTERS THE SIGN OF LIBRA ON SEP 23 AT 00:18.

DAY	TIME	☉	☽	☿	♀	♂	♃	♄	♅	♆	♇
	h m s	° ' "	° '	°	°	°	°	°	°	°	°
O 1	0 39 1	7♎50 14	8♌48	26♍	25♌	10♌	26♉R	29♒R	12♍	16♏	15♍
C 2	0 42 57	8 49 16	22 41	28	26	10	26	29	12	16	15
T 3	0 46 54	9 48 21	6♍28	0♎	27	11	26	29	12	16	15
O 4	0 50 50	10 47 28	20 4	2	28	11	26	29	12	16	15
B 5	0 54 47	11 46 37	3♎28	4	29	12	25	29	12	16	15
E 6	0 58 44	12 45 48	16 37	5	0♍	13	25	29	12	16	15
R 7	1 2 40	13 45 1	29 30	7	1	13	25	29	13	16	15
8	1 6 37	14 44 16	12♏ 5	9	3	14	25	29	13	16	15
9	1 10 33	15 43 33	24 25	11	4	14	25	29	13	16	15
10	1 14 30	16 42 52	6♐30	12	5	15	25	29	13	16	15
11	1 18 26	17 42 12	18 25	14	6	15	25	29	13	16	15
12	1 22 23	18 41 35	0♑14	16	7	16	25	29	13	17	15
13	1 26 19	19 40 59	12 1	18	8	17	25	29	13	17	15
14	1 30 16	20 40 26	23 53	19	9	17	25	29	13	17	15
15	1 34 13	21 39 54	5♒54	21	11	18	25	29	13	17	15
16	1 38 9	22 39 23	18 11	23	12	18	25	29	13	17	15
17	1 42 6	23 38 55	0♓46	25	13	19	24	29	13	17	15
18	1 46 2	24 38 28	13 44	26	14	19	24	29	13	17	15
19	1 49 59	25 38 3	27 7	28	15	20	24	29	13	17	15
20	1 53 55	26 37 40	10♈53	0♏	16	21	24	28	13	17	15
21	1 57 52	27 37 19	24 59	1	18	21	24	28	13	17	15
22	2 1 48	28 36 59	9♉21	3	19	22	24	28	13	17	15
23	2 5 45	29 36 42	23 53	4	20	22	24	28	13	17	16
24	2 9 42	0♏36 27	8♊28	6	21	23	24	28	13	17	16
25	2 13 38	1 36 15	23 0	8	22	23	24	28	13	17	16
26	2 17 35	2 36 4	7♋24	9	24	24	23	28	13	17	16
27	2 21 31	3 35 56	21 39	11	25	25	23	28	14	17	16
28	2 25 28	4 35 50	5♌41	12	26	25	23	28	14	17	16
29	2 29 24	5 35 46	19 31	14	27	26	23	28	14	17	16
30	2 33 21	6 35 45	3♍ 9	16	28	26	23	28	14	17	16
31	2 37 17	7 35 45	16 34	17	0♎	27	23	28	14	17	16

THE SUN ENTERS THE SIGN OF SCORPIO ON OCT 23 AT 09:22.

DAY	TIME	☉	☽	☿	♀	♂	♃	♄	♅	♆	♇
	h m s	° ' "	° '	°	°	°	°	°	°	°	°
N 1	2 41 14	8♏35 48	29♍46	19♏	1♎	27♌	23♉R	28♒D	14♍	17♏	16♍
O 2	2 45 11	9 35 52	12♎47	20	2	28	23	28	14	17	16
V 3	2 49 7	10 35 59	25 34	22	3	28	22	28	14	17	16
E 4	2 53 4	11 36 7	8♏ 8	23	4	29	22	28	14	17	16
M 5	2 57 0	12 36 18	20 30	25	6	29	22	28	14	17	16
B 6	3 0 57	13 36 30	2♐39	26	7	0♍	22	28	14	17	16
E 7	3 4 53	14 36 44	14 39	28	8	0	22	28	14	17	16
R 8	3 8 50	15 37 0	26 30	29	9	1	22	28	14	17	16
9	3 12 46	16 37 17	8♑18	1♐	10	1	22	28	14	18	16
10	3 16 43	17 37 36	20 4	2	12	2	22	28	14	18	16
11	3 20 40	18 37 56	1♒55	4	13	3	21	28	14	18	16
12	3 24 36	19 38 18	13 54	5	14	3	21	28	14	18	16
13	3 28 33	20 38 41	26 8	7	15	4	21	28	14	18	16
14	3 32 29	21 39 5	8♓40	8	16	4	21	28	14	18	16
15	3 36 26	22 39 31	21 36	10	18	5	21	28	14	18	16
16	3 40 22	23 39 58	4♈58	11	19	5	21	29	14	18	16
17	3 44 19	24 40 26	18 47	12	20	6	21	29	14	18	16
18	3 48 15	25 40 56	3♉ 2	14	21	6	20	29	14	18	16
19	3 52 12	26 41 27	17 38	15	23	7	20	29	14	18	16
20	3 56 9	27 42 0	2♊30	17	24	7	20	29	14	18	16
21	4 0 5	28 42 34	17 29	18	25	8	20	29	14	18	16
22	4 4 2	29 43 10	2♋26	19	26	8	20	29	14	18	16
23	4 7 58	0♐43 48	17 15	21	27	9	20	29	15	18	16
24	4 11 55	1 44 27	1♌49	22	29	9	20	29	15	18	16
25	4 15 51	2 45 8	16 4	23	0♏	9	19	29	15	18	16
26	4 19 48	3 45 50	29 58	25	1	10	19	29	15	18	16
27	4 23 44	4 46 34	13♍32	26	2	10	19	29	15	18	16
28	4 27 41	5 47 20	26 47	27	4	11	19	29	15	18	16
29	4 31 38	6 48 7	9♎44	28	5	11	19	29	15	18	16
30	4 35 34	7 48 55	22 26	29	6	12	19	29	15	18	16

THE SUN ENTERS THE SIGN OF SAGITTARIUS ON NOV 22 AT 06:40.

DAY	TIME	☉	☽	☿	♀	♂	♃	♄	♅	♆	♇
	h m s	° ' "	° '	°	°	°	°	°	°	°	°
D 1	4 39 31	8♐49 45	4♏54	0♑	7♏	12♍	19♉R	29♒	15♍	18♏	16♍
E 2	4 43 27	9 50 37	17 11	1	9	13	19	29	15	18	16
C 3	4 47 24	10 51 29	29 18	2	10	13	19	29	15	18	16
E 4	4 51 20	11 52 23	11♐17	3	11	14	18	29	15	18	16
M 5	4 55 17	12 53 18	23 9	3	12	14	18	29	15	18	16
B 6	4 59 13	13 54 14	4♑58	4	13	14	18	29	15	19	16
E 7	5 3 10	14 55 11	16 45	4	15	15	18	29	15	19	16
R 8	5 7 7	15 56 8	28 32	5	16	15	18	29	15	19	16
9	5 11 3	16 57 7	10♒24	5 R	17	16	18	0♓	15	19	16
10	5 15 0	17 58 6	22 24	5	18	16	18	0	15	19	16
11	5 18 56	18 59 5	4♓36	5	20	17	18	0	15	19	16
12	5 22 53	20 0 6	17 4	4	21	17	18	0	15	19	16
13	5 26 49	21 1 6	29 53	4	22	17	17	0	15	19	16
14	5 30 46	22 2 7	13♈ 6	3	23	18	17	0	15	19	16
15	5 34 42	23 3 9	26 46	2	25	18	17	0	15	19	16
16	5 38 39	24 4 11	10♉54	1	26	18	17	0	15	19	16
17	5 42 36	25 5 14	25 27	29♐	27	19	17	0	15	19	16
18	5 46 32	26 6 17	10♊22	28	28	19	17	0	15	19	16 R
19	5 50 29	27 7 21	25 32	27	0♐	20	17	0	15	19	16
20	5 54 25	28 8 25	10♋46	25	1	20	17	0	15 R	19	16
21	5 58 22	29 9 30	25 55	24	2	20	17	0	15	19	16
22	6 2 18	0♑10 35	10♌50	23	3	21	17	0	15	19	16
23	6 6 15	1 11 41	25 25	22	5	21	17	1	15	19	16
24	6 10 12	2 12 48	9♍34	21	6	21	17	1	15	19	16
25	6 14 8	3 13 55	23 16	20	7	22	17	1	15	19	16
26	6 18 5	4 15 3	6♎32	19	8	22	17	1	15	19	16
27	6 22 1	5 16 12	19 25	19	10	22	16	1	15	19	16
28	6 25 58	6 17 21	1♏58	19	11	23	16	1	15	19	16
29	6 29 54	7 18 30	14 15	19 D	12	23	16	1	15	19	16
30	6 33 51	8 19 40	26 20	19	13	23	16	1	15	19	16
31	6 37 47	9 20 51	8♐16	19	15	24	16	1	15	19	16

THE SUN ENTERS THE SIGN OF CAPRICORN ON DEC 21 AT 19:50.

♈ ARIES ♉ TAURUS ♊ GEMINI ♋ CANCER ♌ LEO ♍ VIRGO ♎ LIBRA ♏ SCORPIO ♐ SAGITTARIUS ♑ CAPRICORN ♒ AQUARIUS ♓ PISCES

SIDEREAL SUN MOON MERCURY VENUS MARS JUPITER SATURN URANUS NEPTUNE PLUTO

SIDEREAL SUN MOON MERCURY VENUS MARS JUPITER SATURN URANUS NEPTUNE PLUTO

DAY	TIME	☉	☽	☿	♀	♂	♃	♄	♅	♆	♇
	h m s	° ' "	° '	°	°	°	°	°	°	°	°
J 1	6 41 44	10♑22 1	20♐ 7	19♐	16♐	24♍	16♉R	1♓	15♍R	19♏	16♍R
A 2	6 45 41	11 23 12	1♑54	20	17	24	16	1	15	19	16
N 3	6 49 37	12 24 23	13 42	20	18	24	16	1	15	19	16
U 4	6 53 34	13 25 34	25 31	21	20	25	16	2	15	19	16
A 5	6 57 30	14 26 45	7♒24	22	21	25	16	2	15	19	16
R 6	7 1 27	15 27 55	19 22	22	22	25	16	2	15	19	16
Y 7	7 5 23	16 29 5	1♓28	23	23	25	16	2	15	19	16
8	7 9 20	17 30 15	13 44	24	25	26	16	2	15	19	16
9	7 13 16	18 31 24	26 14	25	26	26	16	2	15	20	16
10	7 17 13	19 32 33	9♈ 0	26	27	26	16 D	2	15	20	16
11	7 21 10	20 33 41	22 5	28	28	26	16	2	15	20	16
12	7 25 6	21 34 49	5♉33	29	0♑	26	16	2	15	20	16
13	7 29 3	22 35 56	19 26	0♑	1	27	16	2	15	20	16
14	7 32 59	23 37 3	3♊43	1	2	27	16	3	15	20	16
15	7 36 56	24 38 9	18 24	2	3	27	16	3	15	20	16
16	7 40 52	25 39 14	3♋24	4	5	27	16	3	15	20	16
17	7 44 49	26 40 19	18 36	5	6	27	16	3	14	20	16
18	7 48 45	27 41 23	3♌49	6	7	27	16	3	14	20	16
19	7 52 42	28 42 26	18 55	8	8	27	16	3	14	20	16
20	7 56 39	29 43 29	3♍43	9	10	28	16	3	14	20	16
21	8 0 35	0♒44 31	18 6	10	11	28	16	3	14	20	16
22	8 4 32	1 45 33	2♎ 1	12	12	28	16	3	14	20	16
23	8 8 28	2 46 34	15 26	13	13	28	16	4	14	20	16
24	8 12 25	3 47 35	28 24	14	15	28	16	4	14	20	16
25	8 16 21	4 48 36	10♏58	16	16	28	16	4	14	20	16
26	8 20 18	5 49 36	23 12	17	17	28	17	4	14	20	16
27	8 24 14	6 50 35	5♐12	19	18	28	17	4	14	20	16
28	8 28 11	7 51 34	17 4	20	20	28 R	17	4	14	20	16
29	8 32 8	8 52 32	28 51	22	21	28	17	4	14	20	16
30	8 36 4	9 53 29	10♑37	23	22	28	17	4	14	20	16
31	8 40 1	10 54 26	22 25	25	23	28	17	4	14	20	16

THE SUN ENTERS THE SIGN OF AQUARIUS ON JAN 20 AT 06:30.

DAY	TIME	☉	☽	☿	♀	♂	♃	♄	♅	♆	♇
	h m s	° ' "	° '	°	°	°	°	°	°	°	°
F 1	8 43 57	11♒55 21	4♒20	26♑	25♑	28♍R	17♉	5♓	14♍R	20♏	16♍R
E 2	8 47 54	12 56 16	16 21	28	26	28	17	5	14	20	16
B 3	8 51 50	13 57 9	28 30	29	27	28	17	5	14	20	16
R 4	8 55 47	14 58 1	10♓49	1♒	28	28	17	5	14	20	16
U 5	8 59 43	15 58 52	23 18	3	0♒	28	17	5	14	20	16
A 6	9 3 40	16 59 41	5♈59	4	1	28	17	5	14	20	16
R 7	9 7 37	18 0 29	18 52	6	2	28	17	5	14	20	16
Y 8	9 11 33	19 1 16	1♉59	7	3	27	17	5	14	20	16
9	9 15 30	20 2 1	15 22	9	5	27	18	5	14	20	16
10	9 19 26	21 2 44	29 4	11	6	27	18	6	14	20	16
11	9 23 23	22 3 26	13♊ 5	12	7	27	18	6	14	20	16
12	9 27 19	23 4 6	27 26	14	8	27	18	6	14	20	16
13	9 31 16	24 4 45	12♋ 5	16	10	27	18	6	14	20	16
14	9 35 12	25 5 21	26 56	17	11	26	18	6	14	20	16
15	9 39 9	26 5 57	11♌55	19	12	26	18	6	14	20	16
16	9 43 6	27 6 30	26 51	21	13	26	18	6	13	20	15
17	9 47 2	28 7 2	11♍36	22	15	26	18	6	13	20	15
18	9 50 59	29 7 33	26 1	24	16	25	19	7	13	20	15
19	9 54 55	0♓ 8 2	10♎ 1	26	17	25	19	7	13	20	15
20	9 58 52	1 8 30	23 32	28	18	25	19	7	13	20 R	15
21	10 2 48	2 8 57	6♏36	0♓	20	25	19	7	13	20	15
22	10 6 45	3 9 22	19 15	1	21	24	19	7	13	20	15
23	10 10 41	4 9 46	1♐33	3	22	24	19	7	13	20	15
24	10 14 38	5 10 8	13 34	5	23	24	19	7	13	20	15
25	10 18 35	6 10 30	25 26	7	25	23	19	7	13	20	15
26	10 22 31	7 10 49	7♑13	9	26	23	20	8	13	20	15
27	10 26 28	8 11 7	19 0	11	27	23	20	8	13	20	15
28	10 30 24	9 11 24	0♒52	13	28	22	20	8	13	20	15

THE SUN ENTERS THE SIGN OF PISCES ON FEB 18 AT 20:49.

DAY	TIME	☉	☽	☿	♀	♂	♃	♄	♅	♆	♇
	h m s	° ' "	° '	°	°	°	°	°	°	°	°
M 1	10 34 21	10♓11 39	12♒52	14♓	0♓	22♍R	20♉	8♓	13♍R	20♏R	15♍R
A 2	10 38 17	11 11 52	25 3	16	1	22	20	8	13	20	15
R 3	10 42 14	12 12 4	7♓26	18	2	21	20	8	13	20	15
C 4	10 46 10	13 12 14	20 1	20	3	21	20	8	13	20	15
H 5	10 50 7	14 12 22	2♈49	22	5	20	21	8	13	20	15
6	10 54 4	15 12 28	15 48	24	6	20	21	9	13	20	15
7	10 58 0	16 12 32	28 59	26	7	20	21	9	13	20	15
8	11 1 57	17 12 34	12♉21	28	8	19	21	9	13	20	15
9	11 5 53	18 12 33	25 53	0♈	10	19	21	9	13	20	15
10	11 9 50	19 12 31	9♊36	2♈	11	19	21	9	13	20	15
11	11 13 46	20 12 27	23 31	4	12	18	22	9	12	20	15
12	11 17 43	21 12 20	7♋38	5	13	18	22	9	12	20	15
13	11 21 39	22 12 11	21 57	7	15	17	22	9	12	20	15
14	11 25 36	23 12 0	6♌24	9	16	17	22	9	12	20	15
15	11 29 33	24 11 46	20 57	10	17	17	22	10	12	20	15
16	11 33 29	25 11 31	5♍29	12	18	16	22	10	12	20	15
17	11 37 26	26 11 13	19 53	14	20	16	23	10	12	20	15
18	11 41 22	27 10 53	4♎ 4	15	21	15	23	10	12	20	15
19	11 45 19	28 10 31	17 54	16	22	15	23	10	12	20	15
20	11 49 15	29 10 8	1♏22	17	23	15	23	10	12	20	15
21	11 53 12	0♈ 9 42	14 25	19	25	14	23	10	12	20	15
22	11 57 8	1 9 15	27 5	20	26	14	24	10	12	20	15
23	12 1 5	2 8 46	9♐25	20	27	14	24	11	12	20	15
24	12 5 1	3 8 15	21 30	21	28	13	24	11	12	20	15
25	12 8 58	4 7 43	3♑24	22	29	13	24	11	12	20	15
26	12 12 55	5 7 8	15 13	22	1♈	13	24	11	12	20	15
27	12 16 51	6 6 32	27 2	23	2	12	24	11	12	20	14
28	12 20 48	7 5 55	8♒57	23	3	12	25	11	12	20	14
29	12 24 44	8 5 15	21 2	23 R	4	12	25	11	12	20	14
30	12 28 41	9 4 33	3♓20	23	6	12	25	11	12	20	14
31	12 32 37	10 3 50	15 54	23	7	11	25	11	12	20	14

THE SUN ENTERS THE SIGN OF ARIES ON MAR 20 AT 20:05.

DAY	TIME	☉	☽	☿	♀	♂	♃	♄	♅	♆	♇
	h m s	° ' "	° '	°	°	°	°	°	°	°	°
A 1	12 36 34	11♈ 3 4	28♓45	23♈R	8♈	11♍R	25♉	12♓	12♍R	20♏R	14♍R
P 2	12 40 30	12 2 17	11♈51	23	9	11	26	12	12	20	14
R 3	12 44 27	13 1 27	25 13	22	11	11	26	12	12	20	14
I 4	12 48 24	14 0 36	8♉48	22	12	10	26	12	12	20	14
L 5	12 52 20	14 59 42	22 33	21	13	10	26	12	11	20	14
6	12 56 17	15 58 46	6♊25	20	14	10	26	12	11	19	14
7	13 0 13	16 57 48	20 24	20	16	10	27	12	11	19	14
8	13 4 10	17 56 48	4♋27	19	17	10	27	12	11	19	14
9	13 8 6	18 55 45	18 34	18	18	9	27	12	11	19	14
10	13 12 3	19 54 40	2♌43	17	19	9	27	13	11	19	14
11	13 15 59	20 53 33	16 53	17	21	9	27	13	11	19	14
12	13 19 56	21 52 23	1♍ 2	16	22	9	28	13	11	19	14
13	13 23 53	22 51 11	15 6	15	23	9	28	13	11	19	14
14	13 27 49	23 49 57	29 3	14	24	9	28	13	11	19	14
15	13 31 46	24 48 41	12♎48	14	26	9	28	13	11	19	14
16	13 35 42	25 47 22	26 17	13	27	9	29	13	11	19	14
17	13 39 39	26 46 2	9♏28	13	28	9	29	13	11	19	14
18	13 43 35	27 44 40	22 21	12	29	9	29	13	11	19	14
19	13 47 32	28 43 16	4♐56	12	0♉	9 D	29	13	11	19	14
20	13 51 28	29 41 50	17 13	12	2	9	29	14	11	19	14
21	13 55 25	0♉40 23	29 18	12	3	9	0♊	14	11	19	14
22	13 59 22	1 38 54	11♑13	12 D	4	9	0	14	11	19	14
23	14 3 18	2 37 23	23 3	12	5	9	0	14	11	19	14
24	14 7 15	3 35 51	4♒54	12	7	9	0	14	11	19	14
25	14 11 11	4 34 17	16 51	12	8	9	1	14	11	19	14
26	14 15 8	5 32 42	28 57	12	9	9	1	14	11	19	14
27	14 19 4	6 31 5	11♓19	13	10	9	1	14	11	19	14
28	14 23 1	7 29 26	23 58	13	12	9	1	14	11	19	14
29	14 26 57	8 27 45	6♈58	14	13	9	1	14	11	19	14
30	14 30 54	9 26 3	20 19	14	14	9	2	14	11	19	14

THE SUN ENTERS THE SIGN OF TAURUS ON APR 20 AT 07:26.

DAY	TIME	☉	☽	☿	♀	♂	♃	♄	♅	♆	♇
	h m s	° ' "	° '	°	°	°	°	°	°	°	°
M 1	14 34 51	10♉24 20	3♉59	15♈	15♉	9♍	2♊	15♓	11♍R	19♏R	14♍R
A 2	14 38 47	11 22 34	17 56	15	17	10	2	15	11	19	14
Y 3	14 42 44	12 20 47	2♊ 6	16	18	10	2	15	11	19	14
4	14 46 40	13 18 58	16 25	17	19	10	3	15	11	19	14
5	14 50 37	14 17 8	0♋48	18	20	10	3	15	11	19	14
6	14 54 33	15 15 15	15 11	19	21	10	3	15	11	19	14
7	14 58 30	16 13 20	29 30	20	23	10	3	15	11	19	14
8	15 2 26	17 11 24	13♌43	21	24	11	3	15	11	19	14
9	15 6 23	18 9 25	27 47	22	25	11	4	15	11	19	14
10	15 10 20	19 7 25	11♍42	23	26	11	4	15	11	19	14
11	15 14 16	20 5 22	25 26	24	28	11	4	15	11	19	14
12	15 18 13	21 3 18	8♎57	25	29	11	4	15	11	19	14
13	15 22 9	22 1 12	22 15	27	0♊	12	5	16	11	19	14
14	15 26 6	22 59 5	5♏20	28	1	12	5	16	11	19	14
15	15 30 2	23 56 56	18 10	29	3	12	5	16	11	18	14
16	15 33 59	24 54 45	0♐46	1♉	4	12	5	16	11	18	14
17	15 37 55	25 52 33	13 8	2	5	13	6	16	11	18	14
18	15 41 52	26 50 20	25 19	3	6	13	6	16	11 D	18	14
19	15 45 49	27 48 5	7♑19	5	7	13	6	16	11	18	14
20	15 49 45	28 45 49	19 13	6	9	14	6	16	11	18	14
21	15 53 42	29 43 32	1♒ 4	8	10	14	6	16	11	18	14
22	15 57 38	0♊41 14	12 55	10	11	14	7	16	11	18	14
23	16 1 35	1 38 55	24 51	11	12	14	7	16	11	18	14
24	16 5 31	2 36 35	6♓58	13	14	15	7	16	11	18	14
25	16 9 28	3 34 14	19 19	15	15	15	7	16	11	18	14 D
26	16 13 24	4 31 51	1♈58	16	16	15	8	16	11	18	14
27	16 17 21	5 29 28	14 59	18	17	16	8	16	11	18	14
28	16 21 18	6 27 4	28 24	20	19	16	8	16	11	18	14
29	16 25 14	7 24 39	12♉13	22	20	17	8	16	11	18	14
30	16 29 11	8 22 13	26 25	24	21	17	9	17	11	18	14
31	16 33 7	9 19 46	10♊55	26	22	17	9	17	11	18	14

THE SUN ENTERS THE SIGN OF GEMINI ON MAY 21 AT 06:50.

DAY	TIME	☉	☽	☿	♀	♂	♃	♄	♅	♆	♇
	h m s	° ' "	° '	°	°	°	°	°	°	°	°
J 1	16 37 4	10♊17 18	25♊38	28♉	23♊	18♍	9♊	17♓	11♍	18♏R	14♍
U 2	16 41 0	11 14 49	10♋26	0♊	25	18	9	17	11	18	14
N 3	16 44 57	12 12 19	25 14	2	26	18	10	17	11	18	14
E 4	16 48 53	13 9 47	9♌53	4	27	19	10	17	11	18	14
5	16 52 50	14 7 15	24 19	6	28	19	10	17	11	18	14
6	16 56 47	15 4 41	8♍29	8	0♋	20	10	17	11	18	14
7	17 0 43	16 2 5	22 21	10	1	20	10	17	11	18	14
8	17 4 40	16 59 29	5♎53	12	2	20	11	17	11	18	14
9	17 8 36	17 56 51	19 8	14	3	21	11	17	11	18	14
10	17 12 33	18 54 13	2♏ 6	17	4	21	11	17	11	18	14
11	17 16 29	19 51 33	14 50	19	6	22	11	17	11	18	14
12	17 20 26	20 48 53	27 20	21	7	22	12	17	11	18	14
13	17 24 22	21 46 12	9♐39	23	8	22	12	17	11	18	14
14	17 28 19	22 43 30	21 48	25	9	23	12	17	11	18	14
15	17 32 16	23 40 47	3♑49	28	11	23	12	17	11	18	14
16	17 36 12	24 38 4	15 45	0♋	12	24	13	17	11	18	14
17	17 40 9	25 35 21	27 36	2	13	24	13	17	11	18	14
18	17 44 5	26 32 36	9♒26	4	14	25	13	17	11	18	14
19	17 48 2	27 29 52	21 18	6	15	25	13	17	11	18	14
20	17 51 58	28 27 7	3♓15	8	17	26	13	17	11	18	14
21	17 55 55	29 24 22	15 21	10	18	26	14	17	11	18	14
22	17 59 51	0♋21 37	27 40	12	19	27	14	17	11	18	14
23	18 3 48	1 18 52	10♈16	14	20	27	14	17	11	18	14
24	18 7 45	2 16 6	23 13	16	22	28	14	17	11	18	14
25	18 11 41	3 13 21	6♉35	18	23	28	15	17	11	18	14
26	18 15 38	4 10 35	20 22	20	24	28	15	17	11	18	14
27	18 19 34	5 7 50	4♊36	22	25	29	15	17	11	18	14
28	18 23 31	6 5 4	19 14	24	26	29	15	17 R	11	17	14
29	18 27 27	7 2 18	4♋10	25	28	0♎	16	17	11	17	14
30	18 31 24	7 59 33	19 17	27	29	0	16	17	11	17	14

THE SUN ENTERS THE SIGN OF CANCER ON JUN 21 AT 14:56.

♈ ARIES ♉ TAURUS ♊ GEMINI ♋ CANCER ♌ LEO ♍ VIRGO ♎ LIBRA ♏ SCORPIO ♐ SAGITTARIUS ♑ CAPRICORN ♒ AQUARIUS ♓ PISCES

SIDEREAL SUN MOON MERCURY VENUS MARS JUPITER SATURN URANUS NEPTUNE PLUTO

DAY	TIME	☉	☽	☿	♀	♂	♃	♄	♅	♆	♇
	h m s	° ' "	° '	°	°	°	°	°	°	°	°
J 1	18 35 21	8♋56 47	4♌25	29♋	0♌	1♎	16♊	17♓R	12♍	17♏R	14♍
U 2	18 39 17	9 54 0	19 25	1♌	1	1	16	17	12	17	14
L 3	18 43 14	10 51 14	4♍ 9	2	3	2	16	17	12	17	14
Y 4	18 47 10	11 48 26	18 30	4	4	3	17	17	12	17	14
5	18 51 7	12 45 39	2♎27	5	5	3	17	17	12	17	14
6	18 55 3	13 42 51	15 59	7	6	4	17	17	12	17	14
7	18 59 0	14 40 4	29 7	8	7	4	17	17	12	17	14
8	19 2 56	15 37 15	11♏54	10	9	5	17	17	12	17	14
9	19 6 53	16 34 27	24 24	11	10	5	18	17	12	17	14
10	19 10 50	17 31 39	6♐40	13	11	6	18	17	12	17	14
11	19 14 46	18 28 51	18 46	14	12	6	18	17	12	17	14
12	19 18 43	19 26 3	0♑45	15	13	7	18	17	12	17	14
13	19 22 39	20 23 15	12 39	16	15	7	19	17	12	17	14
14	19 26 36	21 20 27	24 30	18	16	8	19	17	12	17	14
15	19 30 32	22 17 40	6♒21	19	17	8	19	17	12	17	14
16	19 34 29	23 14 53	18 12	20	18	9	19	17	12	17	14
17	19 38 25	24 12 6	0♓ 7	21	20	9	19	17	12	17	14
18	19 42 22	25 9 20	12 8	22	21	10	20	17	12	17	14
19	19 46 19	26 6 35	24 16	23	22	11	20	17	12	17	14
20	19 50 15	27 3 50	6♈35	24	23	11	20	17	12	17	14
21	19 54 12	28 1 6	19 10	25	24	12	20	17	12	17	14
22	19 58 8	28 58 23	2♉ 2	26	26	12	20	17	12	17	15
23	20 2 5	29 55 40	15 17	26	27	13	21	17	12	17	15
24	20 6 1	0♌52 59	28 57	27	28	13	21	17	13	17	15
25	20 9 58	1 50 18	13♊ 4	28	29	14	21	17	13	17	15
26	20 13 54	2 47 39	27 36	28	0♍	15	21	17	13	17	15
27	20 17 51	3 45 0	12♋31	29	2	15	21	17	13	17	15
28	20 21 48	4 42 22	27 42	29	3	16	22	17	13	17	15
29	20 25 44	5 39 45	12♌58	29	4	16	22	16	13	17 D	15
30	20 29 41	6 37 9	28 10	0♍	5	17	22	16	13	17	15
31	20 33 37	7 34 33	13♍ 7	0	7	17	22	16	13	17	15

THE SUN ENTERS THE SIGN OF LEO ON JUL 23 AT 01:49.

DAY	TIME	☉	☽	☿	♀	♂	♃	♄	♅	♆	♇
	h m s	° ' "	° '	°	°	°	°	°	°	°	°
A 1	20 37 34	8♌31 57	27♍40	0♍R	8♍	18♎	22♊	16♓R	13♍	17♏	15♍
U 2	20 41 30	9 29 23	11♎46	0	9	19	23	16	13	17	15
G 3	20 45 27	10 26 49	25 23	0	10	19	23	16	13	17	15
U 4	20 49 23	11 24 16	8♏32	0	11	20	23	16	13	17	15
S 5	20 53 20	12 21 43	21 16	0	13	20	23	16	13	17	15
T 6	20 57 17	13 19 11	3♐41	29♌	14	21	23	16	13	17	15
7	21 1 13	14 16 40	15 50	29	15	22	24	16	13	17	15
8	21 5 10	15 14 10	27 50	28	16	22	24	16	13	17	15
9	21 9 6	16 11 40	9♑42	28	17	23	24	16	13	17	15
10	21 13 3	17 9 12	21 32	27	19	23	24	16	13	17	15
11	21 16 59	18 6 44	3♒23	27	20	24	24	16	14	17	15
12	21 20 56	19 4 18	15 15	26	21	25	24	16	14	17	15
13	21 24 52	20 1 53	27 11	25	22	25	25	16	14	17	15
14	21 28 49	20 59 28	9♓13	24	23	26	25	16	14	17	15
15	21 32 46	21 57 6	21 21	23	25	27	25	15	14	17	15
16	21 36 42	22 54 44	3♈37	23	26	27	25	15	14	17	15
17	21 40 39	23 52 24	16 3	22	27	28	25	15	14	17	15
18	21 44 35	24 50 6	28 41	21	28	28	26	15	14	17	15
19	21 48 32	25 47 49	11♉35	20	29	29	26	15	14	17	15
20	21 52 28	26 45 33	24 46	20	1♎	0♏	26	15	14	17	15
21	21 56 25	27 43 20	8♊19	19	2	0	26	15	14	17	15
22	22 0 21	28 41 8	22 14	18	3	1	26	15	14	17	15
23	22 4 18	29 38 58	6♋34	18	4	2	26	15	14	17	16
24	22 8 15	0♍36 50	21 16	18	5	2	26	15	14	17	16
25	22 12 11	1 34 43	6♌15	18 D	7	3	27	15	14	17	16
26	22 16 8	2 32 38	21 24	18	8	3	27	15	14	17	16
27	22 20 4	3 30 35	6♍32	18	9	4	27	15	14	17	16
28	22 24 1	4 28 33	21 30	18	10	5	27	15	15	17	16
29	22 27 57	5 26 32	6♎ 7	18	11	5	27	14	15	17	16
30	22 31 54	6 24 33	20 18	19	12	6	27	14	15	17	16
31	22 35 50	7 22 35	4♏ 0	20	14	7	28	14	15	18	16

THE SUN ENTERS THE SIGN OF VIRGO ON AUG 23 AT 08:44.

DAY	TIME	☉	☽	☿	♀	♂	♃	♄	♅	♆	♇
	h m s	° ' "	° '	°	°	°	°	°	°	°	°
S 1	22 39 47	8♍20 39	17♏13	20♌	15♎	7♏	28♊	14♓R	15♍	18♏	16♍
E 2	22 43 44	9 18 44	0♐ 0	21	16	8	28	14	15	18	16
P 3	22 47 40	10 16 50	12 25	22	17	9	28	14	15	18	16
T 4	22 51 37	11 14 58	24 34	23	18	9	28	14	15	18	16
E 5	22 55 33	12 13 7	6♑32	25	20	10	28	14	15	18	16
M 6	22 59 30	13 11 18	18 23	26	21	11	28	14	15	18	16
B 7	23 3 26	14 9 30	0♒13	27	22	11	28	14	15	18	16
E 8	23 7 23	15 7 44	12 4	29	23	12	29	14	15	18	16
R 9	23 11 19	16 6 0	24 1	0♍	24	13	29	14	15	18	16
10	23 15 16	17 4 17	6♓ 4	2	25	13	29	14	15	18	16
11	23 19 13	18 2 36	18 16	4	27	14	29	13	15	18	16
12	23 23 9	19 0 56	0♈36	6	28	15	29	13	15	18	16
13	23 27 6	19 59 19	13 6	7	29	15	29	13	16	18	16
14	23 31 2	20 57 44	25 46	9	0♏	16	29	13	16	18	16
15	23 34 59	21 56 10	8♉37	11	1	17	29	13	16	18	16
16	23 38 55	22 54 39	21 40	13	3	17	29	13	16	18	16
17	23 42 52	23 53 10	4♊57	15	4	18	0♋	13	16	18	16
18	23 46 48	24 51 43	18 29	17	5	19	0	13	16	18	16
19	23 50 45	25 50 18	2♋19	18	6	19	0	13	16	18	16
20	23 54 42	26 48 56	16 26	20	7	20	0	13	16	18	16
21	23 58 38	27 47 36	0♌51	22	8	21	0	13	16	18	17
22	0 2 35	28 46 18	15 30	24	10	21	0	13	16	18	17
23	0 6 31	29 45 2	0♍18	26	11	22	0	13	16	18	17
24	0 10 28	0♎43 48	15 8	28	12	23	0	13	16	18	17
25	0 14 24	1 42 36	29 50	0♎	13	24	0	12	16	18	17
26	0 18 21	2 41 27	14♎18	1	14	24	0	12	16	18	17
27	0 22 17	3 40 19	28 23	3	15	25	0	12	16	18	17
28	0 26 14	4 39 13	12♏ 4	5	17	26	1	12	16	18	17
29	0 30 10	5 38 9	25 18	7	18	26	1	12	17	18	17
30	0 34 7	6 37 7	8♐ 8	9	19	27	1	12	17	18	17

THE SUN ENTERS THE SIGN OF LIBRA ON SEP 23 AT 06:07.

SIDEREAL SUN MOON MERCURY VENUS MARS JUPITER SATURN URANUS NEPTUNE PLUTO

DAY	TIME	☉	☽	☿	♀	♂	♃	♄	♅	♆	♇
	h m s	° ' "	° '	°	°	°	°	°	°	°	°
O 1	0 38 4	7♎36 6	20♐36	10♎	20♏	28♏	1♋	12♓R	17♍	18♏	17♍
C 2	0 42 0	8 35 8	2♑47	12	21	28	1	12	17	18	17
T 3	0 45 57	9 34 11	14 46	14	22	29	1	12	17	18	17
O 4	0 49 53	10 33 16	26 38	15	23	0♐	1	12	17	18	17
B 5	0 53 50	11 32 23	8♒29	17	25	1	1	12	17	18	17
E 6	0 57 46	12 31 31	20 23	19	26	1	1	12	17	18	17
R 7	1 1 43	13 30 41	2♓24	20	27	2	1	12	17	18	17
8	1 5 39	14 29 54	14 34	22	28	3	1	12	17	18	17
9	1 9 36	15 29 8	26 55	24	29	3	1	12	17	19	17
10	1 13 33	16 28 24	9♈30	25	0♐	4	1	12	17	19	17
11	1 17 29	17 27 42	22 17	27	1	5	1	11	17	19	17
12	1 21 26	18 27 2	5♉17	29	3	5	1	11	17	19	17
13	1 25 22	19 26 24	18 29	0♏	4	6	1	11	17	19	17
14	1 29 19	20 25 48	1♊52	2	5	7	1	11	17	19	17
15	1 33 15	21 25 15	15 26	3	6	8	1	11	17	19	17
16	1 37 12	22 24 44	29 10	5	7	8	1	11	18	19	17
17	1 41 8	23 24 16	13♋ 4	6	8	9	1	11	18	19	17
18	1 45 5	24 23 49	27 8	8	9	10	1	11	18	19	17
19	1 49 2	25 23 25	11♌21	9	11	11	1 R	11	18	19	17
20	1 52 58	26 23 3	25 40	11	12	11	1	11	18	19	17
21	1 56 55	27 22 44	10♍ 3	12	13	12	1	11	18	19	18
22	2 0 51	28 22 27	24 25	14	14	13	1	11	18	19	18
23	2 4 48	29 22 11	8♎41	15	15	13	1	11	18	19	18
24	2 8 44	0♏21 58	22 45	17	16	14	1	11	18	19	18
25	2 12 41	1 21 47	6♏33	18	17	15	1	11	18	19	18
26	2 16 37	2 21 38	20 2	20	18	16	1	11	18	19	18
27	2 20 34	3 21 31	3♐10	21	19	16	1	11	18	19	18
28	2 24 31	4 21 26	15 57	23	20	17	1	11	18	19	18
29	2 28 27	5 21 22	28 25	24	22	18	1	11	18	19	18
30	2 32 24	6 21 21	10♑37	26	23	19	1	11	18	19	18
31	2 36 20	7 21 20	22 38	27	24	19	1	11	18	19	18

THE SUN ENTERS THE SIGN OF SCORPIO ON OCT 23 AT 15:11.

DAY	TIME	☉	☽	☿	♀	♂	♃	♄	♅	♆	♇
	h m s	° ' "	° '	°	°	°	°	°	°	°	°
N 1	2 40 17	8♏21 22	4♒32	28♏	25♐	20♐	1♋R	11♓R	18♍	19♏	18♍
O 2	2 44 13	9 21 25	16 24	0♐	26	21	1	11	18	19	18
V 3	2 48 10	10 21 29	28 19	1	27	22	1	11	18	19	18
E 4	2 52 6	11 21 36	10♓21	2	28	22	1	11	18	19	18
M 5	2 56 3	12 21 43	22 34	4	29	23	1	11	18	19	18
B 6	3 0 0	13 21 53	5♈ 2	5	0♑	24	1	11	19	19	18
E 7	3 3 56	14 22 4	17 47	6	1	25	1	11	19	20	18
R 8	3 7 53	15 22 16	0♉49	7	2	25	1	11	19	20	18
9	3 11 49	16 22 31	14 9	9	3	26	1	11	19	20	18
10	3 15 46	17 22 47	27 45	10	4	27	1	11	19	20	18
11	3 19 42	18 23 5	11♊35	11	5	28	0	10	19	20	18
12	3 23 39	19 23 24	25 36	12	6	28	0	10	19	20	18
13	3 27 35	20 23 46	9♋44	13	7	29	0	10	19	20	18
14	3 31 32	21 24 10	23 56	14	9	0♑	0	10 D	19	20	18
15	3 35 29	22 24 35	8♌10	15	10	1	0	10	19	20	18
16	3 39 25	23 25 3	22 22	16	11	1	0	10	19	20	18
17	3 43 22	24 25 32	6♍32	17	12	2	0	10	19	20	18
18	3 47 18	25 26 3	20 35	17	13	3	0	10	19	20	18
19	3 51 15	26 26 36	4♎32	18	14	4	0	11	19	20	18
20	3 55 11	27 27 10	18 19	18	15	4	0	11	19	20	18
21	3 59 8	28 27 47	1♏54	19	15	5	0	11	19	20	18
22	4 3 4	29 28 24	15 16	19	16	6	0	11	19	20	18
23	4 7 1	0♐29 4	28 24	19 R	17	7	29♊	11	19	20	18
24	4 10 58	1 29 45	11♐17	19	18	7	29	11	19	20	18
25	4 14 54	2 30 27	23 54	19	19	8	29	11	19	20	18
26	4 18 51	3 31 11	6♑17	18	20	9	29	11	19	20	18
27	4 22 47	4 31 56	18 27	18	21	10	29	11	19	20	18
28	4 26 44	5 32 42	0♒28	17	22	10	29	11	19	20	18
29	4 30 40	6 33 28	12 22	16	23	11	29	11	19	20	18
30	4 34 37	7 34 16	24 14	15	24	12	29	11	19	20	18

THE SUN ENTERS THE SIGN OF SAGITTARIUS ON NOV 22 AT 12:30.

DAY	TIME	☉	☽	☿	♀	♂	♃	♄	♅	♆	♇
	h m s	° ' "	° '	°	°	°	°	°	°	°	°
D 1	4 38 33	8♐35 5	6♓ 7	14♐R	25♑	13♑	29♊R	11♓	19♍	20♏	18♍
E 2	4 42 30	9 35 55	18 7	12	26	13	28	11	19	20	18
C 3	4 46 27	10 36 45	0♈19	11	27	14	28	11	19	20	18
E 4	4 50 23	11 37 37	12 46	10	27	15	28	11	19	21	18
M 5	4 54 20	12 38 29	25 33	8	28	16	28	11	19	21	18
B 6	4 58 16	13 39 22	8♉42	7	29	17	28	11	19	21	18
E 7	5 2 13	14 40 16	22 14	6	0♒	17	28	11	19	21	18
R 8	5 6 9	15 41 11	6♊ 9	5	1	18	28	11	19	21	18
9	5 10 6	16 42 7	20 23	4	1	19	28	11	20	21	18
10	5 14 2	17 43 4	4♋53	4	2	20	27	11	20	21	18
11	5 17 59	18 44 2	19 31	3	3	20	27	11	20	21	18
12	5 21 56	19 45 1	4♌11	3 D	4	21	27	11	20	21	18
13	5 25 52	20 46 1	18 47	3	4	22	27	11	20	21	18
14	5 29 49	21 47 1	3♍14	3	5	23	27	11	20	21	18
15	5 33 45	22 48 3	17 27	3	6	24	27	11	20	21	18
16	5 37 42	23 49 6	1♎24	4	6	24	27	11	20	21	18
17	5 41 38	24 50 10	15 5	4	7	25	26	11	20	21	18
18	5 45 35	25 51 15	28 31	5	8	26	26	11	20	21	18
19	5 49 32	26 52 20	11♏42	5	8	27	26	12	20	21	18
20	5 53 28	27 53 27	24 39	6	9	27	26	12	20	21	18
21	5 57 25	28 54 34	7♐24	7	9	28	26	12	20	21	18 R
22	6 1 21	29 55 42	19 57	8	10	29	26	12	20	21	18
23	6 5 18	0♑56 50	2♑20	9	10	0♒	26	12	20	21	18
24	6 9 14	1 57 59	14 33	10	11	1	25	12	20	21	18
25	6 13 11	2 59 8	26 38	11	11	1	25	12	20 R	21	18
26	6 17 7	4 0 17	8♒35	13	12	2	25	12	20	21	18
27	6 21 4	5 1 27	20 28	14	12	3	25	12	20	21	18
28	6 25 1	6 2 36	2♓19	15	12	4	25	12	20	21	18
29	6 28 57	7 3 46	14 11	16	13	5	25	12	20	21	18
30	6 32 54	8 4 55	26 9	18	13	5	25	12	20	21	18
31	6 36 50	9 6 4	8♈16	19	13	6	25	12	20	21	18

THE SUN ENTERS THE SIGN OF CAPRICORN ON DEC 22 AT 01:41.

♈ ARIES ♉ TAURUS ♊ GEMINI ♋ CANCER ♌ LEO ♍ VIRGO ♎ LIBRA ♏ SCORPIO ♐ SAGITTARIUS ♑ CAPRICORN ♒ AQUARIUS ♓ PISCES

1966

SIDEREAL SUN MOON MERCURY VENUS MARS JUPITER SATURN URANUS NEPTUNE PLUTO

DAY	TIME	☉	☽	☿	♀	♂	♃	♄	♅	♆	♇
	h m s	° ' "	° '	°	°	°	°	°	°	°	°
J 1	6 40 47	10♑ 7 13	20♈38	20♐	13♒	7♒	24♊R	12♓	20♍R	21♏	18♍R
A 2	6 44 43	11 8 22	3♉20	22	14	8	24	13	20	21	18
N 3	6 48 40	12 9 31	16 25	23	14	8	24	13	20	21	18
U 4	6 52 36	13 10 40	29 56	25	14	9	24	13	20	22	18
A 5	6 56 33	14 11 48	13♊56	26	14 R	10	24	13	20	22	18
R 6	7 0 30	15 12 56	28 22	27	14	11	24	13	20	22	18
Y 7	7 4 26	16 14 4	13♋10	29	14	12	24	13	20	22	18
8	7 8 23	17 15 12	28 13	0♑	14	12	24	13	20	22	18
9	7 12 19	18 16 20	13♌21	2	14	13	23	13	20	22	18
10	7 16 16	19 17 27	28 24	3	13	14	23	13	20	22	18
11	7 20 12	20 18 34	13♍13	5	13	15	23	13	20	22	18
12	7 24 9	21 19 42	27 41	6	13	16	23	13	19	22	18
13	7 28 5	22 20 49	11♎46	8	13	16	23	13	19	22	18
14	7 32 2	23 21 56	25 27	9	12	17	23	14	19	22	18
15	7 35 59	24 23 3	8♏44	11	12	18	23	14	19	22	18
16	7 39 55	25 24 10	21 42	12	12	19	23	14	19	22	18
17	7 43 52	26 25 17	4♐22	14	11	19	23	14	19	22	18
18	7 47 48	27 26 23	16 50	15	11	20	23	14	19	22	18
19	7 51 45	28 27 29	29 6	17	10	21	22	14	19	22	18
20	7 55 41	29 28 35	11♑15	19	10	22	22	14	19	22	18
21	7 59 38	0♒29 40	23 18	20	9	23	22	14	19	22	18
22	8 3 35	1 30 45	5♒15	22	9	23	22	14	19	22	18
23	8 7 31	2 31 48	17 9	23	8	24	22	14	19	22	18
24	8 11 28	3 32 51	29 1	25	7	25	22	15	19	22	18
25	8 15 24	4 33 53	10♓53	26	7	26	22	15	19	22	18
26	8 19 21	5 34 54	22 46	28	6	27	22	15	19	22	18
27	8 23 17	6 35 54	4♈43	0♒	6	27	22	15	19	22	18
28	8 27 14	7 36 52	16 49	1	5	28	22	15	19	22	18
29	8 31 10	8 37 50	29 6	3	4	29	22	15	19	22	18
30	8 35 7	9 38 46	11♉41	5	4	0♓	22	15	19	22	18
31	8 39 3	10 39 42	24 38	6	3	1	22	15	19	22	18

THE SUN ENTERS THE SIGN OF AQUARIUS ON JAN 20 AT 12:20.

DAY	TIME	☉	☽	☿	♀	♂	♃	♄	♅	♆	♇
	h m s	° ' "	° '	°	°	°	°	°	°	°	°
F 1	8 43 0	11♒40 36	8♊ 0	8♒	3♒R	1♓	22♊R	15♓	19♍R	22♏	18♍R
E 2	8 46 57	12 41 28	21 52	10	2	2	22	15	19	22	18
B 3	8 50 53	13 42 20	6♋14	11	2	3	22	16	19	22	18
R 4	8 54 50	14 43 10	21 2	13	1	4	21	16	19	22	18
U 5	8 58 46	15 43 58	6♌12	15	1	5	21	16	19	22	18
A 6	9 2 43	16 44 46	21 33	17	0	5	21	16	19	22	18
R 7	9 6 39	17 45 32	6♍54	18	0	6	21	16	19	22	18
Y 8	9 10 36	18 46 17	22 2	20	29♑	7	21	16	19	22	18
9	9 14 33	19 47 1	6♎49	22	29	8	21	16	19	22	18
10	9 18 29	20 47 44	21 9	24	29	8	21	16	19	22	18
11	9 22 26	21 48 26	4♏59	26	29	9	21	16	19	22	18
12	9 26 22	22 49 7	18 21	27	29	10	21	17	19	22	18
13	9 30 19	23 49 46	1♐18	29	28	11	21	17	19	22	18
14	9 34 15	24 50 25	13 54	1♓	28	12	21	17	19	22	18
15	9 38 12	25 51 3	26 13	3	28 D	12	21 D	17	19	22	18
16	9 42 8	26 51 39	8♑21	5	28	13	21	17	18	22	18
17	9 46 5	27 52 14	20 21	7	28	14	21	17	18	22	18
18	9 50 2	28 52 48	2♒16	8	28	15	21	17	18	22	18
19	9 53 58	29 53 20	14 8	10	28	16	21	17	18	22	18
20	9 57 55	0♓53 51	26 0	12	29	16	21	18	18	22	18
21	10 1 51	1 54 20	7♓52	14	29	17	21	18	18	22	18
22	10 5 48	2 54 47	19 47	16	29	18	21	18	18	22 R	18
23	10 9 44	3 55 13	1♈45	17	29	19	21	18	18	22	18
24	10 13 41	4 55 37	13 47	19	0♒	19	21	18	18	22	17
25	10 17 37	5 55 59	25 58	21	0	20	21	18	18	22	17
26	10 21 34	6 56 19	8♉18	23	0	21	21	18	18	22	17
27	10 25 30	7 56 38	20 53	24	1	22	21	18	18	22	17
28	10 29 27	8 56 54	3♊46	26	1	23	22	19	18	22	17

THE SUN ENTERS THE SIGN OF PISCES ON FEB 19 AT 02:38.

DAY	TIME	☉	☽	☿	♀	♂	♃	♄	♅	♆	♇
	h m s	° ' "	° '	°	°	°	°	°	°	°	°
M 1	10 33 24	9♓57 9	17♊ 1	27♓	1♒	23♓	22♊	19♓	18♍R	22♏R	17♍R
A 2	10 37 20	10 57 21	0♋41	29	2	24	22	19	18	22	17
R 3	10 41 17	11 57 31	14 50	0⊙	2	25	22	19	18	22	17
C 4	10 45 13	12 57 39	29 25	1♈	3	26	22	19	18	22	17
H 5	10 49 10	13 57 45	14♌23	2	3	26	22	19	18	22	17
6	10 53 6	14 57 50	29 36	3	4	27	22	19	18	22	17
7	10 57 3	15 57 52	14♍55	4	5	28	22	19	18	22	17
8	11 0 59	16 57 52	0♎ 7	5	5	29	22	20	18	22	17
9	11 4 56	17 57 50	15 2	5	6	0⊙	22	20	18	22	17
10	11 8 53	18 57 47	29 32	5	6	0♈	22	20	18	22	17
11	11 12 49	19 57 42	13♏33	6	7	1	22	20	17	22	17
12	11 16 46	20 57 35	27 4	6 R	8	2	22	20	17	22	17
13	11 20 42	21 57 27	10♐ 8	6	9	3	22	20	17	22	17
14	11 24 39	22 57 17	22 48	5	9	3	22	20	17	22	17
15	11 28 35	23 57 5	5♑ 9	5	10	4	22	20	17	22	17
16	11 32 32	24 56 52	17 15	5	11	5	23	20	17	22	17
17	11 36 28	25 56 37	29 13	4	12	6	23	21	17	22	17
18	11 40 25	26 56 20	11♒ 5	3	12	7	23	21	17	22	17
19	11 44 22	27 56 1	22 56	3	13	7	23	21	17	22	17
20	11 48 18	28 55 40	4♓47	2	14	8	23	21	17	22	17
21	11 52 15	29 55 18	16 43	1	15	9	23	21	17	22	17
22	11 56 11	0♈54 53	28 43	0	16	10	23	21	17	22	17
23	12 0 8	1 54 27	10♈49	29♓	16	10	23	21	17	22	17
24	12 4 4	2 53 58	23 3	28	17	11	23	21	17	22	17
25	12 8 1	3 53 28	5♉25	27	18	12	23	22	17	22	17
26	12 11 57	4 52 55	17 57	27	19	13	24	22	17	22	17
27	12 15 54	5 52 20	0♊42	26	20	13	24	22	17	22	17
28	12 19 51	6 51 43	13 41	25	21	14	24	22	17	22	17
29	12 23 47	7 51 3	26 58	25	22	15	24	22	17	22	17
30	12 27 44	8 50 21	10♋35	24	23	16	24	22	17	22	17
31	12 31 40	9 49 37	24 33	24	24	17	24	22	17	22	17

THE SUN ENTERS THE SIGN OF ARIES ON MAR 21 AT 01:53.

SIDEREAL SUN MOON MERCURY VENUS MARS JUPITER SATURN URANUS NEPTUNE PLUTO

DAY	TIME	☉	☽	☿	♀	♂	♃	♄	♅	♆	♇
	h m s	° ' "	° '	°	°	°	°	°	°	°	°
A 1	12 35 37	10♈48 51	8♌52	23♓R	25♒	17♈	24♊	22♓	17♍R	22♏R	17♍R
P 2	12 39 33	11 48 2	23 30	23	25	18	24	23	17	22	17
R 3	12 43 30	12 47 10	8♍22	23	26	19	25	23	17	22	17
I 4	12 47 26	13 46 17	23 21	23 D	27	20	25	23	16	22	16
L 5	12 51 23	14 45 21	8♎17	23	28	20	25	23	16	22	16
6	12 55 20	15 44 24	23 2	23	29	21	25	23	16	22	16
7	12 59 16	16 43 24	7♏28	23	0♓	22	25	23	16	22	16
8	13 3 13	17 42 22	21 30	23	1	23	25	23	16	22	16
9	13 7 9	18 41 19	5♐ 6	24	2	23	25	23	16	22	16
10	13 11 6	19 40 14	18 16	24	3	24	26	23	16	22	16
11	13 15 2	20 39 7	1♑ 2	25	4	25	26	24	16	22	16
12	13 18 59	21 37 58	13 28	25	5	26	26	24	16	22	16
13	13 22 55	22 36 48	25 38	26	6	26	26	24	16	22	16
14	13 26 52	23 35 36	7♒37	27	7	27	26	24	16	22	16
15	13 30 49	24 34 22	19 31	27	8	28	26	24	16	22	16
16	13 34 45	25 33 7	1♓22	28	9	29	27	24	16	21	16
17	13 38 42	26 31 49	13 16	29	10	29	27	24	16	21	16
18	13 42 38	27 30 30	25 15	0♈	12	0♉	27	24	16	21	16
19	13 46 35	28 29 9	7♈21	1	13	1	27	25	16	21	16
20	13 50 31	29 27 46	19 38	2	14	2	27	25	16	21	16
21	13 54 28	0♉26 21	2♉ 5	3	15	2	27	25	16	21	16
22	13 58 24	1 24 55	14 44	4	16	3	28	25	16	21	16
23	14 2 21	2 23 26	27 35	5	17	4	28	25	16	21	16
24	14 6 17	3 21 56	10♊39	7	18	5	28	25	16	21	16
25	14 10 14	4 20 24	23 57	8	19	5	28	25	16	21	16
26	14 14 11	5 18 49	7♋27	9	20	6	28	25	16	21	16
27	14 18 7	6 17 12	21 12	11	21	7	28	25	16	21	16
28	14 22 4	7 15 34	5♌10	12	22	8	29	25	16	21	16
29	14 26 0	8 13 53	19 21	13	23	8	29	26	16	21	16
30	14 29 57	9 12 10	3♍42	15	24	9	29	26	16	21	16

THE SUN ENTERS THE SIGN OF TAURUS ON APR 20 AT 13:12.

DAY	TIME	☉	☽	☿	♀	♂	♃	♄	♅	♆	♇
	h m s	° ' "	° '	°	°	°	°	°	°	°	°
M 1	14 33 53	10♉10 24	18♍11	16♈	25♓	10♉	29♊	26♓	16♍R	21♏R	16♍R
A 2	14 37 50	11 8 37	2♎43	18	26	10	29	26	16	21	16
Y 3	14 41 46	12 6 48	17 12	19	28	11	0♋	26	16	21	16
4	14 45 43	13 4 57	1♏33	21	29	12	0	26	16	21	16
5	14 49 40	14 3 5	15 40	22	0⊙	13	0	26	16	21	16
6	14 53 36	15 1 10	29 30	24	1♈	13	0	26	16	21	16
7	14 57 33	15 59 14	12♐59	26	2	14	0	26	16	21	16
8	15 1 29	16 57 17	26 7	27	3	15	0	26	16	21	16
9	15 5 26	17 55 18	8♑54	29	4	16	1	27	16	21	16
10	15 9 22	18 53 18	21 23	1♉	5	16	1	27	16	21	16
11	15 13 19	19 51 16	3♒36	2	6	17	1	27	16	21	16
12	15 17 16	20 49 13	15 39	4	8	18	1	27	16	21	16
13	15 21 12	21 47 9	27 34	6	9	19	1	27	16	21	16
14	15 25 9	22 45 4	9♓27	8	10	19	2	27	16	21	16
15	15 29 5	23 42 57	21 22	10	11	20	2	27	16	21	16
16	15 33 2	24 40 49	3♈23	12	12	21	2	27	16	21	16
17	15 36 58	25 38 39	15 35	14	13	21	2	27	16	21	16
18	15 40 55	26 36 29	28 0	16	14	22	2	27	15	21	16
19	15 44 51	27 34 17	10♉40	18	15	23	3	27	15	21	16
20	15 48 48	28 32 4	23 36	20	17	24	3	27	15	21	16
21	15 52 44	29 29 49	6♊49	22	18	24	3	28	15	21	16
22	15 56 41	0♊27 34	20 18	24	19	25	3	28	15	21	16
23	16 0 38	1 25 16	4♋ 1	26	20	26	3	28	15 D	21	16
24	16 4 34	2 22 58	17 56	28	21	26	4	28	15	20	16
25	16 8 31	3 20 38	1♌59	1♊	22	27	4	28	15	20	16
26	16 12 27	4 18 16	16 9	3	23	28	4	28	15	20	16
27	16 16 24	5 15 53	0♍22	5	25	29	4	28	15	20	16 D
28	16 20 20	6 13 28	14 36	7	26	29	5	28	15	20	16
29	16 24 17	7 11 2	28 49	9	27	0♊	5	28	15	20	16
30	16 28 14	8 8 35	12♎57	12	28	1	5	28	16	20	16
31	16 32 10	9 6 6	26 59	14	29	1	5	28	16	20	16

THE SUN ENTERS THE SIGN OF GEMINI ON MAY 21 AT 12:32.

DAY	TIME	☉	☽	☿	♀	♂	♃	♄	♅	♆	♇
	h m s	° ' "	° '	°	°	°	°	°	°	°	°
J 1	16 36 7	10♊ 3 36	10♏52	16♊	0♉	2♊	5♋	28♓	16♍	20♏R	16♍
U 2	16 40 3	11 1 4	24 33	18	1	3	6	28	16	20	16
N 3	16 44 0	11 58 32	8♐ 1	20	3	4	6	28	16	20	16
E 4	16 47 56	12 55 59	21 14	22	4	4	6	29	16	20	16
5	16 51 53	13 53 24	4♑11	24	5	5	6	29	16	20	16
6	16 55 49	14 50 49	16 52	26	6	6	6	29	16	20	16
7	16 59 46	15 48 14	29 18	28	7	6	7	29	16	20	16
8	17 3 43	16 45 37	11♒31	0♋	8	7	7	29	16	20	16
9	17 7 39	17 43 0	23 33	2	10	8	7	29	16	20	16
10	17 11 36	18 40 22	5♓29	4	11	9	7	29	16	20	16
11	17 15 32	19 37 43	17 22	6	12	9	8	29	16	20	16
12	17 19 29	20 35 5	29 17	8	13	10	8	29	16	20	16
13	17 23 25	21 32 25	11♈19	10	14	11	8	29	16	20	16
14	17 27 22	22 29 45	23 32	11	15	11	8	29	16	20	16
15	17 31 18	23 27 5	6♉ 1	13	17	12	8	29	16	20	16
16	17 35 15	24 24 24	18 49	15	18	13	9	29	16	20	16
17	17 39 12	25 21 44	1♊58	16	19	13	9	29	16	20	16
18	17 43 8	26 19 2	15 30	18	20	14	9	29	16	20	16
19	17 47 5	27 16 20	29 22	20	21	15	9	29	16	20	16
20	17 51 1	28 13 38	13♋31	21	22	16	10	29	16	20	16
21	17 54 58	29 10 55	27 54	22	24	16	10	29	16	20	16
22	17 58 54	0♋ 8 12	12♌23	24	25	17	10	29	16	20	16
23	18 2 51	1 5 27	26 54	25	26	18	10	29	16	20	16
24	18 6 47	2 2 42	11♍20	27	27	18	10	29	16	20	16
25	18 10 44	2 59 57	25 38	28	28	19	11	29	16	20	16
26	18 14 41	3 57 11	9♎45	29	29	20	11	29	16	20	16
27	18 18 37	4 54 24	23 39	0♌	1♊	20	11	0⊙	16	20	16
28	18 22 34	5 51 36	7♏21	1	2	21	11	0	16	20	16
29	18 26 30	6 48 49	20 50	2	3	22	12	0	16	20	16
30	18 30 27	7 46 1	4♐ 7	3	4	22	12	0	16	20	16

THE SUN ENTERS THE SIGN OF CANCER ON JUN 21 AT 20:34.

♈ ARIES ♉ TAURUS ♊ GEMINI ♋ CANCER ♌ LEO ♍ VIRGO ♎ LIBRA ♏ SCORPIO ♐ SAGITTARIUS ♑ CAPRICORN ♒ AQUARIUS ♓ PISCES

1966

SIDEREAL SUN MOON MERCURY VENUS MARS JUPITER SATURN URANUS NEPTUNE PLUTO

DAY	TIME	☉	☽	☿	♀	♂	♃	♄	♅	♆	♇
	h m s	° ' "	° '	°	°	°	°	°	°	°	°
J 1	18 34 23	8♋43 12	17♐12	4♌	5♊	23♊	12♋	0⊙	16♍	20♏R	16♍
U 2	18 38 20	9 40 24	0♑ 4	5	7	24	12	0	16	20	16
L 3	18 42 17	10 37 35	12 45	6	8	24	13	0	16	20	16
Y 4	18 46 13	11 34 46	25 14	7	9	25	13	0	16	20	16
5	18 50 10	12 31 57	7♒32	8	10	26	13	0	16	20	16
6	18 54 6	13 29 9	19 40	8	11	27	13	0	16	20	16
7	18 58 3	14 26 20	1♓40	9	12	27	13	0	16	20	16
8	19 1 59	15 23 32	13 33	10	14	28	14	0	16	20	16
9	19 5 56	16 20 44	25 25	10	15	29	14	0	16	20	16
10	19 9 52	17 17 56	7♈18	11	16	29	14	0	16	20	16
11	19 13 49	18 15 9	19 18	11	17	0♋	14	0 R	16	20	16
12	19 17 46	19 12 22	1♉30	11	18	1	15	0	17	20	16
13	19 21 42	20 9 36	13 59	11	20	1	15	0	17	20	16
14	19 25 39	21 6 50	26 48	11 R	21	2	15	0	17	19	16
15	19 29 35	22 4 5	10♊ 3	11	22	3	15	0	17	19	16
16	19 33 32	23 1 20	23 44	11	23	3	15	0	17	19	16
17	19 37 28	23 58 36	7♋51	11	24	4	16	0	17	19	16
18	19 41 25	24 55 53	22 21	11	26	5	16	0	17	19	16
19	19 45 21	25 53 10	7♌ 8	11	27	5	16	0	17	19	16
20	19 49 18	26 50 27	22 3	10	28	6	16	0	17	19	17
21	19 53 15	27 47 44	6♍57	10	29	7	17	0	17	19	17
22	19 57 11	28 45 2	21 43	9	0♋	7	17	0	17	19	17
23	20 1 8	29 42 20	6♎13	9	2	8	17	0	17	19	17
24	20 5 4	0♌39 38	20 25	8	3	9	17	0	17	19	17
25	20 9 1	1 36 57	4♏16	8	4	9	17	0	17	19	17
26	20 12 57	2 34 16	17 48	7	5	10	18	0	17	19	17
27	20 16 54	3 31 36	1♐ 3	6	6	11	18	29♓	17	19	17
28	20 20 50	4 28 55	14 2	5	8	11	18	29	17	19	17
29	20 24 47	5 26 16	26 48	5	9	12	18	29	17	19	17
30	20 28 44	6 23 37	9♑22	4	10	13	19	29	17	19	17
31	20 32 40	7 20 59	21 47	3	11	13	19	29	17	19	17

THE SUN ENTERS THE SIGN OF LEO ON JUL 23 AT 07:24.

DAY	TIME	☉	☽	☿	♀	♂	♃	♄	♅	♆	♇
	h m s	° ' "	° '	°	°	°	°	°	°	°	°
A 1	20 36 37	8♌18 21	4♒ 3	3♌R	12♋	14♋	19♋	29♓R	17♍	19♏D	17♍
U 2	20 40 33	9 15 44	16 11	2	14	15	19	29	18	19	17
G 3	20 44 30	10 13 8	28 12	2	15	15	19	29	18	19	17
U 4	20 48 26	11 10 33	10♓ 8	1	16	16	20	29	18	19	17
S 5	20 52 23	12 8 0	21 59	1	17	17	20	29	18	19	17
T 6	20 56 19	13 5 27	3♈49	1	18	17	20	29	18	19	17
7	21 0 16	14 2 55	15 42	0 D	20	18	20	29	18	19	17
8	21 4 13	15 0 25	27 40	0	21	19	21	29	18	19	17
9	21 8 9	15 57 56	9♉49	0	22	19	21	29	18	19	17
10	21 12 6	16 55 28	22 15	1	23	20	21	29	18	19	17
11	21 16 2	17 53 2	5♊ 2	1	24	21	21	29	18	19	17
12	21 19 59	18 50 37	18 14	1	26	21	21	29	18	19	17
13	21 23 55	19 48 14	1♋55	2	27	22	22	29	18	19	17
14	21 27 52	20 45 52	16 5	2	28	22	22	29	18	19	17
15	21 31 48	21 43 31	0♌43	3	29	23	22	29	18	19	17
16	21 35 45	22 41 12	15 42	4	1♌	24	22	29	18	19	17
17	21 39 42	23 38 54	0♍54	5	2	24	22	29	18	19	17
18	21 43 38	24 36 38	16 7	6	3	25	23	29	18	19	17
19	21 47 35	25 34 22	1♎11	7	4	26	23	29	18	19	17
20	21 51 31	26 32 8	15 58	9	5	26	23	28	19	20	17
21	21 55 28	27 29 54	0♏21	10	7	27	23	28	19	20	17
22	21 59 24	28 27 42	14 19	11	8	28	23	28	19	20	18
23	22 3 21	29 25 31	27 52	13	9	28	24	28	19	20	18
24	22 7 17	0♍23 21	11♐ 2	14	10	29	24	28	19	20	18
25	22 11 14	1 21 13	23 53	16	12	0♌	24	28	19	20	18
26	22 15 11	2 19 6	6♑28	18	13	0	24	28	19	20	18
27	22 19 7	3 17 0	18 50	20	14	1	24	28	19	20	18
28	22 23 4	4 14 55	1♒ 3	22	15	1	25	28	19	20	18
29	22 27 0	5 12 51	13 8	23	16	2	25	28	19	20	18
30	22 30 57	6 10 49	25 7	25	18	3	25	28	19	20	18
31	22 34 53	7 8 49	7♓ 2	27	19	3	25	28	19	20	18

THE SUN ENTERS THE SIGN OF VIRGO ON AUG 23 AT 14:19.

DAY	TIME	☉	☽	☿	♀	♂	♃	♄	♅	♆	♇
	h m s	° ' "	° '	°	°	°	°	°	°	°	°
S 1	22 38 50	8♍ 6 50	18♓55	29♌	20♌	4♌	25♋	28♓R	19♍	20♏	18♍
E 2	22 42 46	9 4 53	0♈45	1♍	21	5	26	28	19	20	18
P 3	22 46 43	10 2 57	12 37	3	23	5	26	28	19	20	18
T 4	22 50 40	11 1 4	24 31	5	24	6	26	27	19	20	18
E 5	22 54 36	11 59 12	6♉31	7	25	7	26	27	20	20	18
M 6	22 58 33	12 57 22	18 42	9	26	7	26	27	20	20	18
B 7	23 2 29	13 55 35	1♊ 6	11	28	8	27	27	20	20	18
E 8	23 6 26	14 53 49	13 50	13	29	8	27	27	20	20	18
R 9	23 10 22	15 52 5	26 58	15	0♍	9	27	27	20	20	18
10	23 14 19	16 50 24	10♋32	17	1	10	27	27	20	20	18
11	23 18 15	17 48 45	24 35	18	2	10	27	27	20	20	18
12	23 22 12	18 47 7	9♌ 7	20	4	11	27	27	20	20	18
13	23 26 9	19 45 32	24 3	22	5	12	28	27	20	20	18
14	23 30 5	20 43 58	9♍15	24	6	12	28	27	20	20	18
15	23 34 2	21 42 27	24 33	26	7	13	28	27	20	20	18
16	23 37 58	22 40 57	9♎46	28	9	14	28	27	20	20	18
17	23 41 55	23 39 29	24 44	29	10	14	28	26	20	20	18
18	23 45 51	24 38 3	9♏20	1♎	11	15	28	26	20	20	18
19	23 49 48	25 36 38	23 28	3	12	15	29	26	20	20	19
20	23 53 44	26 35 16	7♐ 9	5	14	16	29	26	20	20	19
21	23 57 41	27 33 54	20 23	6	15	17	29	26	21	20	19
22	0 1 38	28 32 35	3♑15	8	16	17	29	26	21	20	19
23	0 5 34	29 31 17	15 47	10	17	18	29	26	21	20	19
24	0 9 31	0♎30 1	28 4	11	19	19	29	26	21	20	19
25	0 13 27	1 28 47	10♒10	13	20	19	0♌	26	21	20	19
26	0 17 24	2 27 34	22 9	15	21	20	0	26	21	20	19
27	0 21 20	3 26 24	4♓ 3	16	22	20	0	26	21	20	19
28	0 25 17	4 25 15	15 55	18	24	21	0	26	21	20	19
29	0 29 13	5 24 7	27 47	19	25	22	0	26	21	20	19
30	0 33 10	6 23 2	9♈40	21	26	22	0	25	21	20	19

THE SUN ENTERS THE SIGN OF LIBRA ON SEP 23 AT 11:44.

SIDEREAL SUN MOON MERCURY VENUS MARS JUPITER SATURN URANUS NEPTUNE PLUTO

DAY	TIME	☉	☽	☿	♀	♂	♃	♄	♅	♆	♇
	h m s	° ' "	° '	°	°	°	°	°	°	°	°
O 1	0 37 6	7♎21 59	21♈36	23♎	27♍	23♌	1♌	25♓R	21♍	20♏	19♍
C 2	0 41 3	8 20 58	3♉37	24	29	23	1	25	21	20	19
T 3	0 45 0	9 20 0	15 46	26	0♎	24	1	25	21	20	19
O 4	0 48 56	10 19 3	28 4	27	1	25	1	25	21	20	19
B 5	0 52 53	11 18 9	10♊35	29	2	25	1	25	21	20	19
E 6	0 56 49	12 17 17	23 22	0♏	4	26	1	25	21	21	19
R 7	1 0 46	13 16 27	6♋29	2	5	26	1	25	21	21	19
8	1 4 42	14 15 40	19 58	3	6	27	1	25	22	21	19
9	1 8 39	15 14 55	3♌51	4	7	28	2	25	22	21	19
10	1 12 35	16 14 12	18 8	6	9	28	2	25	22	21	19
11	1 16 32	17 13 32	2♍48	7	10	29	2	25	22	21	19
12	1 20 29	18 12 54	17 44	9	11	0♍	2	25	22	21	19
13	1 24 25	19 12 18	2♎50	10	12	0	2	25	22	21	19
14	1 28 22	20 11 44	17 56	11	14	1	2	24	22	21	19
15	1 32 18	21 11 12	2♏52	13	15	1	2	24	22	21	19
16	1 36 15	22 10 42	17 31	14	16	2	2	24	22	21	19
17	1 40 11	23 10 14	1♐46	15	17	3	3	24	22	21	19
18	1 44 8	24 9 48	15 34	17	19	3	3	24	22	21	20
19	1 48 4	25 9 24	28 57	18	20	4	3	24	22	21	20
20	1 52 1	26 9 2	11♑54	19	21	4	3	24	22	21	20
21	1 55 58	27 8 41	24 29	20	22	5	3	24	22	21	20
22	1 59 54	28 8 22	6♒48	22	24	6	3	24	22	21	20
23	2 3 51	29 8 4	18 53	23	25	6	3	24	22	21	20
24	2 7 47	0♏ 7 49	0♓49	24	26	7	3	24	22	21	20
25	2 11 44	1 7 35	12 41	25	27	7	3	24	23	21	20
26	2 15 40	2 7 23	24 32	26	29	8	3	24	23	21	20
27	2 19 37	3 7 12	6♈25	27	0♏	8	3	24	23	21	20
28	2 23 33	4 7 4	18 23	28	1	9	4	24	23	21	20
29	2 27 30	5 6 57	0♉27	29	2	10	4	24	23	21	20
30	2 31 27	6 6 52	12 40	0♐	4	10	4	24	23	21	20
31	2 35 23	7 6 49	25 4	1	5	11	4	24	23	21	20

THE SUN ENTERS THE SIGN OF SCORPIO ON OCT 23 AT 20:52.

DAY	TIME	☉	☽	☿	♀	♂	♃	♄	♅	♆	♇
	h m s	° ' "	° '	°	°	°	°	°	°	°	°
N 1	2 39 20	8♏ 6 49	7♊38	1♐	6♏	11♍	4♌	23♓R	23♍	21♏	20♍
O 2	2 43 16	9 6 50	20 25	2	7	12	4	23	23	21	20
V 3	2 47 13	10 6 53	3♋26	2	9	13	4	23	23	21	20
E 4	2 51 9	11 6 59	16 41	3	10	13	4	23	23	22	20
M 5	2 55 6	12 7 6	0♌13	3	11	14	4	23	23	22	20
B 6	2 59 2	13 7 16	14 2	3 R	12	14	4	23	23	22	20
E 7	3 2 59	14 7 28	28 7	3	14	15	4	23	23	22	20
R 8	3 6 56	15 7 41	12♍28	3	15	15	4	23	23	22	20
9	3 10 52	16 7 57	27 0	3	16	16	4	23	23	22	20
10	3 14 49	17 8 15	11♎41	2	17	17	4	23	23	22	20
11	3 18 45	18 8 34	26 24	2	19	17	4	23	23	22	20
12	3 22 42	19 8 56	11♏ 2	1	20	18	4	23	23	22	20
13	3 26 38	20 9 19	25 29	0	21	18	4	23	23	22	20
14	3 30 35	21 9 44	9♐38	29♏	22	19	4	23	23	22	20
15	3 34 31	22 10 11	23 27	28	24	19	4	23	23	22	20
16	3 38 28	23 10 39	6♑53	27	25	20	4	23	24	22	20
17	3 42 25	24 11 8	19 55	25	26	21	4	23	24	22	20
18	3 46 21	25 11 39	2♒35	24	27	21	4	23	24	22	20
19	3 50 18	26 12 11	14 56	23	29	22	4	23	24	22	20
20	3 54 14	27 12 44	27 3	21	0♐	22	4	23	24	22	20
21	3 58 11	28 13 19	9♓ 0	20	1	23	4 R	23	24	22	20
22	4 2 7	29 13 55	20 52	19	2	23	4	23	24	22	20
23	4 6 4	0♐14 31	2♈42	18	4	24	4	23	24	22	20
24	4 10 0	1 15 9	14 37	18	5	25	4	23	24	22	20
25	4 13 57	2 15 49	26 39	17	6	25	4	23	24	22	20
26	4 17 54	3 16 29	8♉52	17 D	7	26	4	23 D	24	22	20
27	4 21 50	4 17 11	21 18	17	9	26	4	23	24	22	20
28	4 25 47	5 17 54	3♊59	17	10	27	4	23	24	22	20
29	4 29 43	6 18 38	16 55	18	11	27	4	23	24	22	20
30	4 33 40	7 19 24	0♋ 5	18	13	28	4	23	24	22	20

THE SUN ENTERS THE SIGN OF SAGITTARIUS ON NOV 22 AT 18:15.

DAY	TIME	☉	☽	☿	♀	♂	♃	♄	♅	♆	♇
	h m s	° ' "	° '	°	°	°	°	°	°	°	°
D 1	4 37 36	8♐20 11	13♋30	19♏	14♐	28♍	4♌R	23♓	24♍	23♏	21♍
E 2	4 41 33	9 20 59	27 7	19	15	29	4	23	24	23	21
C 3	4 45 30	10 21 49	10♌55	20	16	29	4	23	24	23	21
E 4	4 49 26	11 22 40	24 51	21	18	0♎	4	23	24	23	21
M 5	4 53 23	12 23 32	8♍55	22	19	1	4	23	24	23	21
B 6	4 57 19	13 24 26	23 4	23	20	1	4	23	24	23	21
E 7	5 1 16	14 25 21	7♎16	24	21	2	4	23	24	23	21
R 8	5 5 12	15 26 18	21 31	25	23	2	4	23	24	23	21
9	5 9 9	16 27 15	5♏45	27	24	3	4	23	24	23	21
10	5 13 5	17 28 14	19 54	28	25	3	4	23	24	23	21
11	5 17 2	18 29 14	3♐57	29	26	4	4	23	24	23	21
12	5 20 59	19 30 15	17 48	0♐	28	4	4	23	24	23	21
13	5 24 55	20 31 17	1♑24	2	29	5	4	23	24	23	21
14	5 28 52	21 32 20	14 42	3	0♑	5	4	23	24	23	21
15	5 32 48	22 33 23	27 42	5	1	6	4	23	24	23	21
16	5 36 45	23 34 27	10♒22	6	3	6	4	23	24	23	21
17	5 40 41	24 35 31	22 45	7	4	7	3	23	24	23	21
18	5 44 38	25 36 35	4♓53	9	5	7	3	23	24	23	21
19	5 48 34	26 37 40	16 50	10	6	8	3	23	24	23	21
20	5 52 31	27 38 45	28 41	12	8	8	3	23	24	23	21
21	5 56 28	28 39 51	10♈31	13	9	9	3	23	24	23	21
22	6 0 24	29 40 57	22 25	15	10	9	3	23	24	23	21
23	6 4 21	0♑42 3	4♉29	16	11	10	3	24	24	23	21 R
24	6 8 17	1 43 9	16 46	18	13	10	3	24	24	23	21
25	6 12 14	2 44 15	29 21	19	14	11	3	24	24	23	21
26	6 16 10	3 45 22	12♊15	21	15	11	3	24	24	23	21
27	6 20 7	4 46 29	25 31	22	16	12	2	24	24	23	21
28	6 24 3	5 47 36	9♋ 7	24	18	12	2	24	24	23	21
29	6 28 0	6 48 44	23 0	25	19	13	2	24	24	23	21
30	6 31 57	7 49 52	7♌ 6	27	20	13	2	24	24 R	23	21
31	6 35 53	8 51 0	21 20	28	21	14	2	24	24	24	21

THE SUN ENTERS THE SIGN OF CAPRICORN ON DEC 22 AT 07:29.

♈ ARIES ♉ TAURUS ♊ GEMINI ♋ CANCER ♌ LEO ♍ VIRGO ♎ LIBRA ♏ SCORPIO ♐ SAGITTARIUS ♑ CAPRICORN ♒ AQUARIUS ♓ PISCES

1967

SIDEREAL SUN MOON MERCURY VENUS MARS JUPITER SATURN URANUS NEPTUNE PLUTO

DAY	TIME	☉	☽	☿	♀	♂	♃	♄	♅	♆	♇
	h m s	° ' "	° '	°	°	°	°	°	°	°	°
J 1	6 39 50	9♑52 8	5♍37	0♑	23♑	14♎	2♌R	24♓	24♍R	24♏	21♍R
A 2	6 43 46	10 53 17	19 54	1	24	15	2	24	24	24	21
N 3	6 47 43	11 54 26	4♎ 5	3	25	15	2	24	24	24	21
U 4	6 51 39	12 55 35	18 11	5	26	16	2	24	24	24	21
A 5	6 55 36	13 56 45	2♏10	6	28	16	1	24	24	24	21
R 6	6 59 32	14 57 55	16 1	8	29	16	1	24	24	24	21
Y 7	7 3 29	15 59 5	29 44	9	0♒	17	1	24	24	24	21
8	7 7 26	17 0 15	13♐19	11	1	17	1	24	24	24	21
9	7 11 22	18 1 25	26 44	12	3	18	1	25	24	24	21
10	7 15 19	19 2 36	9♑58	14	4	18	1	25	24	24	21
11	7 19 15	20 3 46	22 59	16	5	19	1	25	24	24	21
12	7 23 12	21 4 55	5♒47	17	6	19	1	25	24	24	21
13	7 27 8	22 6 4	18 20	19	8	19	0	25	24	24	21
14	7 31 5	23 7 13	0♓38	21	9	20	0	25	24	24	21
15	7 35 2	24 8 21	12 44	22	10	20	0	25	24	24	21
16	7 38 58	25 9 29	24 40	24	12	21	0	25	24	24	21
17	7 42 55	26 10 35	6♈30	25	13	21	0	25	24	24	20
18	7 46 51	27 11 41	18 18	27	14	22	0	25	24	24	20
19	7 50 48	28 12 46	0♉10	29	15	22	0	25	24	24	20
20	7 54 44	29 13 51	12 11	0♒	17	22	29♋	25	24	24	20
21	7 58 41	0♒14 54	24 27	2	18	23	29	26	24	24	20
22	8 2 37	1 15 57	7♊ 3	4	19	23	29	26	24	24	20
23	8 6 34	2 16 59	20 3	6	20	23	29	26	24	24	20
24	8 10 31	3 18 0	3♋29	7	22	24	29	26	24	24	20
25	8 14 27	4 19 0	17 20	9	23	24	29	26	24	24	20
26	8 18 24	5 19 59	1♌35	11	24	25	29	26	24	24	20
27	8 22 20	6 20 57	16 8	12	25	25	29	26	24	24	20
28	8 26 17	7 21 54	0♍51	14	27	25	28	26	24	24	20
29	8 30 13	8 22 51	15 36	16	28	26	28	26	24	24	20
30	8 34 10	9 23 46	0♎16	18	29	26	28	26	24	24	20
31	8 38 6	10 24 41	14 45	19	0♓	26	28	26	24	24	20

THE SUN ENTERS THE SIGN OF AQUARIUS ON JAN 20 AT 18:08.

DAY	TIME	☉	☽	☿	♀	♂	♃	♄	♅	♆	♇
	h m s	° ' "	° '	°	°	°	°	°	°	°	°
F 1	8 42 3	11♒25 36	28♎59	21♒	2♓	27♎	28♋R	27♓	24♍R	24♏	20♍R
E 2	8 46 0	12 26 29	12♏57	23	3	27	28	27	24	24	20
B 3	8 49 56	13 27 22	26 39	25	4	27	28	27	24	24	20
R 4	8 53 53	14 28 14	10♐ 7	26	5	28	28	27	24	24	20
U 5	8 57 49	15 29 5	23 21	28	6	28	27	27	24	24	20
A 6	9 1 46	16 29 56	6♑24	0♓	8	28	27	27	24	24	20
R 7	9 5 42	17 30 45	19 16	2	9	29	27	27	24	24	20
Y 8	9 9 39	18 31 33	1♒57	3	10	29	27	27	24	24	20
9	9 13 35	19 32 20	14 27	5	11	29	27	27	24	24	20
10	9 17 32	20 33 6	26 47	7	13	29	27	27	24	24	20
11	9 21 29	21 33 50	8♓56	8	14	0♏	27	28	24	24	20
12	9 25 25	22 34 33	20 56	10	15	0	27	28	24	24	20
13	9 29 22	23 35 14	2♈49	11	16	0	26	28	24	24	20
14	9 33 18	24 35 54	14 37	12	18	0	26	28	24	24	20
15	9 37 15	25 36 32	26 24	14	19	1	26	28	23	24	20
16	9 41 11	26 37 9	8♉14	15	20	1	26	28	23	24	20
17	9 45 8	27 37 44	20 13	16	21	1	26	28	23	24	20
18	9 49 4	28 38 17	2♊26	17	23	1	26	28	23	24	20
19	9 53 1	29 38 48	14 58	17	24	1	26	28	23	24	20
20	9 56 58	0♓39 18	27 54	18	25	2	26	29	23	24	20
21	10 0 54	1 39 45	11♋19	18	26	2	26	29	23	24	20
22	10 4 51	2 40 11	25 13	19	28	2	26	29	23	24	20
23	10 8 47	3 40 35	9♌35	19 R	29	2	26	29	23	24	20
24	10 12 44	4 40 58	24 20	19	0♈	2	25	29	23	24 R	20
25	10 16 40	5 41 18	9♍22	19	1	2	25	29	23	24	20
26	10 20 37	6 41 37	24 30	18	3	3	25	29	23	24	20
27	10 24 33	7 41 54	9♎33	18	4	3	25	29	23	24	20
28	10 28 30	8 42 9	24 24	17	5	3	25	0⊙	23	24	20

THE SUN ENTERS THE SIGN OF PISCES ON FEB 19 AT 08:24.

DAY	TIME	☉	☽	☿	♀	♂	♃	♄	♅	♆	♇
	h m s	° ' "	° '	°	°	°	°	°	°	°	°
M 1	10 32 27	9♓42 24	8♏57	16♓R	6♈	3♏	25♋R	0⊙	23♍R	24♏R	20♍R
A 2	10 36 23	10 42 36	23 7	15	7	3	25	0	23	24	20
R 3	10 40 20	11 42 47	6♐55	14	9	3	25	0	23	24	20
C 4	10 44 16	12 42 57	20 21	13	10	3	25	0♈	23	24	20
H 5	10 48 13	13 43 5	3♑28	12	11	3	25	0	23	24	19
6	10 52 9	14 43 12	16 19	11	12	3	25	0	23	24	19
7	10 56 6	15 43 17	28 55	10	14	3	25	0	23	24	19
8	11 0 2	16 43 20	11♒20	9	15	3 R	25	0	23	24	19
9	11 3 59	17 43 22	23 35	8	16	3	25	1	23	24	19
10	11 7 56	18 43 21	5♓41	8	17	3	25	1	23	24	19
11	11 11 52	19 43 19	17 40	7	19	3	25	1	23	24	19
12	11 15 49	20 43 15	29 34	6	20	3	25	1	22	24	19
13	11 19 45	21 43 9	11♈23	6	21	3	25	1	22	24	19
14	11 23 42	22 43 1	23 10	5	22	3	25	1	22	24	19
15	11 27 38	23 42 51	4♉58	5	23	3	24	1	22	24	19
16	11 31 35	24 42 38	16 50	5	25	3	24	1	22	24	19
17	11 35 31	25 42 24	28 50	5 D	26	3	24	2	22	24	19
18	11 39 28	26 42 7	11♊ 2	5	27	3	24	2	22	24	19
19	11 43 24	27 41 49	23 32	5	28	3	24	2	22	24	19
20	11 47 21	28 41 27	6♋23	5	29	2	24	2	22	24	19
21	11 51 18	29 41 4	19 41	5	1♉	2	24 D	2	22	24	19
22	11 55 14	0♈40 38	3♌27	5	2	2	24	2	22	24	19
23	11 59 11	1 40 10	17 42	6	3	2	24	2	22	24	19
24	12 3 7	2 39 40	2♍23	6	4	2	24	2	22	24	19
25	12 7 4	3 39 7	17 25	7	6	2	24	3	22	24	19
26	12 11 0	4 38 33	2♎39	8	7	1	24	3	22	24	19
27	12 14 57	5 37 56	17 54	8	8	1	24	3	22	24	19
28	12 18 53	6 37 17	3♏ 1	9	9	1	24	3	22	24	19
29	12 22 50	7 36 37	17 51	10	10	1	25	3	22	24	19
30	12 26 47	8 35 54	2♐18	11	12	0	25	3	22	24	19
31	12 30 43	9 35 10	16 19	12	13	0	25	3	22	24	19

THE SUN ENTERS THE SIGN OF ARIES ON MAR 21 AT 07:37.

SIDEREAL SUN MOON MERCURY VENUS MARS JUPITER SATURN URANUS NEPTUNE PLUTO

DAY	TIME	☉	☽	☿	♀	♂	♃	♄	♅	♆	♇
	h m s	° ' "	° '	°	°	°	°	°	°	°	°
A 1	12 34 40	10♈34 24	29♐54	13♓	14♉	0♏R	25♋	3♈	22♍R	24♏R	19♍R
P 2	12 38 36	11 33 37	13♑ 4	14	15	29♎	25	4	22	24	19
R 3	12 42 33	12 32 47	25 53	15	16	29	25	4	22	24	19
I 4	12 46 29	13 31 56	8♒24	16	18	29	25	4	21	24	19
L 5	12 50 26	14 31 3	20 41	17	19	29	25	4	21	24	19
6	12 54 22	15 30 8	2♓46	18	20	28	25	4	21	24	19
7	12 58 19	16 29 12	14 43	20	21	28	25	4	21	24	19
8	13 2 16	17 28 13	26 34	21	22	28	25	4	21	24	19
9	13 6 12	18 27 12	8♈23	22	24	27	25	4	21	24	19
10	13 10 9	19 26 10	20 11	23	25	27	25	5	21	24	19
11	13 14 5	20 25 5	2♉ 0	25	26	26	25	5	21	24	19
12	13 18 2	21 23 59	13 53	26	27	26	25	5	21	24	19
13	13 21 58	22 22 50	25 51	28	28	26	25	5	21	24	19
14	13 25 55	23 21 39	7♊58	29	0♊	25	25	5	21	24	18
15	13 29 51	24 20 26	20 17	1♈	1	25	25	5	21	24	18
16	13 33 48	25 19 11	2♋50	2	2	25	25	5	21	24	18
17	13 37 45	26 17 54	15 42	4	3	24	26	5	21	24	18
18	13 41 41	27 16 34	28 56	5	4	24	26	6	21	24	18
19	13 45 38	28 15 13	12♌33	7	5	23	26	6	21	24	18
20	13 49 34	29 13 49	26 36	8	7	23	26	6	21	24	18
21	13 53 31	0♉12 22	11♍ 2	10	8	23	26	6	21	24	18
22	13 57 27	1 10 54	25 49	12	9	22	26	6	21	24	18
23	14 1 24	2 9 23	10♎52	13	10	22	26	6	21	24	18
24	14 5 20	3 7 50	26 1	15	11	22	26	6	21	24	18
25	14 9 17	4 6 16	11♏ 7	17	12	21	26	6	21	24	18
26	14 13 14	5 4 40	26 2	19	14	21	26	6	21	23	18
27	14 17 10	6 3 2	10♐38	21	15	21	26	7	21	23	18
28	14 21 7	7 1 22	24 51	22	16	20	27	7	21	23	18
29	14 25 3	7 59 41	8♑36	24	17	20	27	7	21	23	18
30	14 29 0	8 57 58	21 55	26	18	20	27	7	21	23	18

THE SUN ENTERS THE SIGN OF TAURUS ON APR 20 AT 18:56.

DAY	TIME	☉	☽	☿	♀	♂	♃	♄	♅	♆	♇
	h m s	° ' "	° '	°	°	°	°	°	°	°	°
M 1	14 32 56	9♉56 14	4♒49	28♈	19♊	19♎R	27♋	7♈	21♍R	23♏R	18♍R
A 2	14 36 53	10 54 28	17 21	0♉	21	19	27	7	21	23	18
Y 3	14 40 49	11 52 41	29 36	2	22	19	27	7	21	23	18
4	14 44 46	12 50 52	11♓38	4	23	18	27	7	21	23	18
5	14 48 43	13 49 2	23 31	6	24	18	27	7	21	23	18
6	14 52 39	14 47 10	5♈19	8	25	18	28	8	21	23	18
7	14 56 36	15 45 17	17 7	10	26	17	28	8	20	23	18
8	15 0 32	16 43 22	28 56	12	27	17	28	8	20	23	18
9	15 4 29	17 41 25	10♉50	14	29	17	28	8	20	23	18
10	15 8 25	18 39 27	22 51	17	0♋	17	28	8	20	23	18
11	15 12 22	19 37 28	5♊ 1	19	1	17	28	8	20	23	18
12	15 16 18	20 35 27	17 21	21	2	16	28	8	20	23	18
13	15 20 15	21 33 24	29 54	23	3	16	28	8	20	23	18
14	15 24 12	22 31 20	12♋40	25	4	16	29	8	20	23	18
15	15 28 8	23 29 13	25 42	28	5	16	29	9	20	23	18
16	15 32 5	24 27 5	9♌ 0	0♊	6	16	29	9	20	23	18
17	15 36 1	25 24 56	22 35	2	8	16	29	9	20	23	18
18	15 39 58	26 22 44	6♍29	4	9	15	29	9	20	23	18
19	15 43 54	27 20 31	20 40	6	10	15	29	9	20	23	18
20	15 47 51	28 18 16	5♎ 8	8	11	15	29	9	20	23	18
21	15 51 47	29 15 59	19 49	10	12	15	0♌	9	20	23	18
22	15 55 44	0♊13 41	4♏38	12	13	15	0	9	20	23	18
23	15 59 41	1 11 21	19 28	14	14	15	0	9	20	23	18
24	16 3 37	2 9 1	4♐13	16	15	15	0	9	20	23	18
25	16 7 34	3 6 39	18 44	18	16	15	0	9	20	23	18
26	16 11 30	4 4 15	2♑57	20	18	15 D	0	10	20	23	18
27	16 15 27	5 1 51	16 45	22	19	15	1	10	20	23	18
28	16 19 23	5 59 26	0♒ 9	24	20	15	1	10	20 D	23	18
29	16 23 20	6 57 0	13 7	25	21	15	1	10	20	23	18 D
30	16 27 17	7 54 32	25 43	27	22	15	1	10	20	23	18
31	16 31 13	8 52 4	8♓ 0	29	23	15	1	10	20	23	18

THE SUN ENTERS THE SIGN OF GEMINI ON MAY 21 AT 18:18.

DAY	TIME	☉	☽	☿	♀	♂	♃	♄	♅	♆	♇
	h m s	° ' "	° '	°	°	°	°	°	°	°	°
J 1	16 35 10	9♊49 35	20♓ 2	0♋	24♋	15♎	1♌	10♈	20♍	23♏R	18♍
U 2	16 39 6	10 47 6	1♈55	2	25	15	2	10	20	22	18
N 3	16 43 3	11 44 35	13 43	3	26	15	2	10	20	22	18
E 4	16 46 59	12 42 4	25 31	5	27	15	2	10	20	22	18
5	16 50 56	13 39 32	7♉24	6	28	16	2	10	20	22	18
6	16 54 52	14 36 59	19 24	8	29	16	2	10	20	22	18
7	16 58 49	15 34 26	1♊36	9	0♌	16	3	11	20	22	18
8	17 2 45	16 31 51	14 0	10	1	16	3	11	20	22	18
9	17 6 42	17 29 16	26 38	11	2	16	3	11	20	22	18
10	17 10 39	18 26 40	9♋31	12	3	16	3	11	20	22	18
11	17 14 35	19 24 4	22 38	14	4	16	3	11	20	22	18
12	17 18 32	20 21 26	5♌57	15	5	17	3	11	20	22	18
13	17 22 28	21 18 47	19 29	16	6	17	4	11	20	22	18
14	17 26 25	22 16 7	3♍13	16	7	17	4	11	20	22	18
15	17 30 21	23 13 26	17 7	17	8	17	4	11	20	22	18
16	17 34 18	24 10 45	1♎11	18	9	18	4	11	20	22	18
17	17 38 15	25 8 2	15 24	19	10	18	4	11	20	22	18
18	17 42 11	26 5 19	29 45	19	11	18	5	11	20	22	18
19	17 46 8	27 2 34	14♏10	20	12	18	5	11	20	22	18
20	17 50 4	27 59 49	28 36	20	13	19	5	11	20	22	18
21	17 54 1	28 57 4	12♐58	21	14	19	5	11	21	22	18
22	17 57 57	29 54 18	27 11	21	15	19	5	12	21	22	18
23	18 1 54	0♋51 31	11♑11	22	16	19	6	12	21	22	18
24	18 5 50	1 48 45	24 51	22	17	20	6	12	21	22	18
25	18 9 47	2 45 58	8♒11	22	18	20	6	12	21	22	18
26	18 13 44	3 43 10	21 8	22 R	19	20	6	12	21	22	18
27	18 17 40	4 40 23	3♓44	22	20	21	6	12	21	22	18
28	18 21 37	5 37 35	16 1	22	21	21	7	12	21	22	18
29	18 25 33	6 34 48	28 4	22	22	21	7	12	21	22	18
30	18 29 30	7 32 1	9♈57	21	23	22	7	12	21	22	18

THE SUN ENTERS THE SIGN OF CANCER ON JUN 22 AT 02:23.

♈ ARIES ♉ TAURUS ♊ GEMINI ♋ CANCER ♌ LEO ♍ VIRGO ♎ LIBRA ♏ SCORPIO ♐ SAGITTARIUS ♑ CAPRICORN ♒ AQUARIUS ♓ PISCES

SIDEREAL SUN MOON MERCURY VENUS MARS JUPITER SATURN URANUS NEPTUNE PLUTO

DAY	TIME	☉	☽	☿	♀	♂	♃	♄	♅	♆	♇
	h m s	° ' "	° '	°	°	°	°	°	°	°	°
J 1	18 33 26	8♋29 13	21♈46	21♋R	23♌	22♎	7♌	12♈	21♍	22♏R	18♍
U 2	18 37 23	9 26 26	3♉36	21	24	22	7	12	21	22	18
L 3	18 41 19	10 23 39	15 31	20	25	23	8	12	21	22	18
Y 4	18 45 16	11 20 52	27 38	20	26	23	8	12	21	22	18
5	18 49 13	12 18 6	9♊58	19	27	24	8	12	21	22	18
6	18 53 9	13 15 19	22 36	19	28	24	8	12	21	22	18
7	18 57 6	14 12 33	5♋32	18	28	24	8	12	21	22	18
8	19 1 2	15 9 47	18 46	18	29	25	9	12	21	22	18
9	19 4 59	16 7 1	2♌17	17	0♍	25	9	12	21	22	18
10	19 8 55	17 4 14	16 1	16	1	26	9	12	21	22	18
11	19 12 52	18 1 28	29 55	16	2	26	9	12	21	22	18
12	19 16 48	18 58 42	13♍57	15	2	26	9	12	21	22	18
13	19 20 45	19 55 56	28 2	15	3	27	10	12	21	22	18
14	19 24 42	20 53 9	12♎10	14	4	27	10	12	21	22	18
15	19 28 38	21 50 23	26 17	14	4	28	10	12	21	22	19
16	19 32 35	22 47 37	10♏25	13	5	28	10	12	21	22	19
17	19 36 31	23 44 51	24 30	13	6	29	11	12	21	22	19
18	19 40 28	24 42 4	8♐33	13	6	29	11	12	21	22	19
19	19 44 24	25 39 19	22 30	12	7	0♏	11	12	21	22	19
20	19 48 21	26 36 33	6♑19	12 D	8	0	11	12	21	22	19
21	19 52 18	27 33 48	19 56	12	8	0	11	12	21	22	19
22	19 56 14	28 31 3	3♒19	12	9	1	12	12	22	22	19
23	20 0 11	29 28 19	16 25	13	9	1	12	12	22	22	19
24	20 4 7	0♌25 36	29 13	13	10	2	12	12	22	22	19
25	20 8 4	1 22 53	11♓44	13	10	2	12	12 R	22	22	19
26	20 12 0	2 20 11	23 58	14	11	3	13	12	22	22	19
27	20 15 57	3 17 29	5♈59	14	11	3	13	12	22	22	19
28	20 19 53	4 14 49	17 51	15	12	4	13	12	22	22	19
29	20 23 50	5 12 10	29 40	16	12	4	13	12	22	22	19
30	20 27 47	6 9 32	11♉30	17	12	5	13	12	22	22	19
31	20 31 43	7 6 54	23 26	18	13	6	14	12	22	22	19

THE SUN ENTERS THE SIGN OF LEO ON JUL 23 AT 13:17.

DAY	TIME	☉	☽	☿	♀	♂	♃	♄	♅	♆	♇
	h m s	° ' "	° '	°	°	°	°	°	°	°	°
A 1	20 35 40	8♌ 4 18	5♊35	19♋	13♍	6♏	14♌	12♈R	22♍	22♏R	19♍
U 2	20 39 36	9 1 43	18 1	20	13	7	14	12	22	22	19
G 3	20 43 33	9 59 9	0♋47	21	13	7	14	12	22	22 D	19
U 4	20 47 29	10 56 37	13 56	22	14	8	14	12	22	22	19
S 5	20 51 26	11 54 5	27 27	24	14	8	15	12	22	22	19
T 6	20 55 22	12 51 34	11♌19	25	14	9	15	12	22	22	19
7	20 59 19	13 49 4	25 28	27	14	9	15	12	22	22	19
8	21 3 16	14 46 35	9♍48	28	14 R	10	15	12	22	22	19
9	21 7 12	15 44 8	24 14	0♌	14	10	16	12	22	22	19
10	21 11 9	16 41 40	8♎40	2	14	11	16	12	22	22	19
11	21 15 5	17 39 14	23 1	4	14	12	16	12	23	22	19
12	21 19 2	18 36 49	7♏15	6	14	12	16	12	23	22	19
13	21 22 58	19 34 24	21 21	7	14	13	16	12	23	22	19
14	21 26 55	20 32 1	5♐17	9	13	13	17	12	23	22	19
15	21 30 51	21 29 38	19 3	11	13	14	17	12	23	22	19
16	21 34 48	22 27 16	2♑39	13	13	14	17	12	23	22	19
17	21 38 45	23 24 56	16 4	15	13	15	17	12	23	22	19
18	21 42 41	24 22 36	29 18	17	12	16	18	12	23	22	19
19	21 46 38	25 20 18	12♒19	19	12	16	18	12	23	22	20
20	21 50 34	26 18 1	25 6	21	11	17	18	12	23	22	20
21	21 54 31	27 15 45	7♓40	23	11	17	18	12	23	22	20
22	21 58 27	28 13 31	19 59	25	10	18	18	12	23	22	20
23	22 2 24	29 11 18	2♈ 6	27	10	19	19	12	23	22	20
24	22 6 20	0♍ 9 7	14 3	29	9	19	19	12	23	22	20
25	22 10 17	1 6 57	25 53	1♍	9	20	19	12	23	22	20
26	22 14 14	2 4 49	7♉41	3	8	20	19	12	23	22	20
27	22 18 10	3 2 43	19 30	5	8	21	20	12	23	22	20
28	22 22 7	4 0 38	1♊26	7	7	22	20	12	23	22	20
29	22 26 3	4 58 36	13 34	9	6	22	20	11	24	22	20
30	22 30 0	5 56 35	26 0	11	6	23	20	11	24	22	20
31	22 33 56	6 54 36	8♋48	13	5	24	20	11	24	22	20

THE SUN ENTERS THE SIGN OF VIRGO ON AUG 23 AT 20:13.

DAY	TIME	☉	☽	☿	♀	♂	♃	♄	♅	♆	♇
	h m s	° ' "	° '	°	°	°	°	°	°	°	°
S 1	22 37 53	7♍52 40	22♋ 0	15♍	5♍R	24♏	21♌	11♈R	24♍	22♏	20♍
E 2	22 41 49	8 50 44	5♌39	17	4	25	21	11	24	22	20
P 3	22 45 46	9 48 51	19 44	18	3	25	21	11	24	22	20
T 4	22 49 43	10 46 59	4♍10	20	3	26	21	11	24	22	20
E 5	22 53 39	11 45 10	18 51	22	2	27	21	11	24	22	20
M 6	22 57 36	12 43 21	3♎40	24	2	27	22	11	24	22	20
B 7	23 1 32	13 41 35	18 30	25	1	28	22	11	24	22	20
E 8	23 5 29	14 39 50	3♏12	27	1	29	22	11	24	22	20
R 9	23 9 25	15 38 6	17 43	29	0	29	22	11	24	22	20
10	23 13 22	16 36 24	1♐58	0♎	0	0♐	22	11	24	22	20
11	23 17 18	17 34 44	15 55	2	29♌	1	23	11	24	22	20
12	23 21 15	18 33 5	29 36	4	29	1	23	11	24	22	20
13	23 25 12	19 31 28	13♑ 0	5	29	2	23	11	24	22	20
14	23 29 8	20 29 52	26 8	7	28	3	23	10	25	22	20
15	23 33 5	21 28 18	9♒ 2	9	28	3	24	10	25	22	20
16	23 37 1	22 26 45	21 43	10	28	4	24	10	25	22	21
17	23 40 58	23 25 15	4♓12	12	28	5	24	10	25	22	21
18	23 44 54	24 23 45	16 29	13	28	5	24	10	25	22	21
19	23 48 51	25 22 18	28 36	15	28	6	24	10	25	22	21
20	23 52 47	26 20 53	10♈35	16	28 D	7	25	10	25	22	21
21	23 56 44	27 19 30	22 27	18	28	7	25	10	25	22	21
22	0 0 40	28 18 9	4♉15	19	28	8	25	10	25	22	21
23	0 4 37	29 16 50	16 1	20	28	9	25	10	25	22	21
24	0 8 34	0♎15 33	27 51	22	28	9	25	10	25	22	21
25	0 12 30	1 14 18	9♊46	23	28	10	26	10	25	22	21
26	0 16 27	2 13 6	21 54	25	28	11	26	10	25	22	21
27	0 20 23	3 11 56	4♋17	26	28	11	26	9	25	22	21
28	0 24 20	4 10 48	17 1	27	29	12	26	9	25	22	21
29	0 28 16	5 9 42	0♌10	29	29	13	26	9	25	22	21
30	0 32 13	6 8 39	13 46	0♏	29	13	27	9	26	22	21

THE SUN ENTERS THE SIGN OF LIBRA ON SEP 23 AT 17:39.

SIDEREAL SUN MOON MERCURY VENUS MARS JUPITER SATURN URANUS NEPTUNE PLUTO

DAY	TIME	☉	☽	☿	♀	♂	♃	♄	♅	♆	♇
	h m s	° ' "	° '	°	°	°	°	°	°	°	°
O 1	0 36 9	7♎ 7 38	27♌49	1♏	0♍	14♐	27♌	9♈R	26♍	22♏	21♍
C 2	0 40 6	8 6 39	12♍18	2	0	15	27	9	26	22	21
T 3	0 44 3	9 5 43	27 8	4	1	16	27	9	26	23	21
O 4	0 47 59	10 4 48	12♎12	5	1	16	27	9	26	23	21
B 5	0 51 56	11 3 55	27 20	6	1	17	27	9	26	23	21
E 6	0 55 52	12 3 5	12♏23	7	2	18	28	9	26	23	21
R 7	0 59 49	13 2 16	27 13	8	2	18	28	9	26	23	21
8	1 3 45	14 1 29	11♐45	9	3	19	28	9	26	23	21
9	1 7 42	15 0 44	25 54	10	4	20	28	9	26	23	21
10	1 11 38	16 0 1	9♑40	11	4	21	28	8	26	23	21
11	1 15 35	16 59 20	23 2	12	5	21	29	8	26	23	21
12	1 19 32	17 58 40	6♒ 3	13	5	22	29	8	26	23	21
13	1 23 28	18 58 2	18 46	14	6	23	29	8	26	23	21
14	1 27 25	19 57 25	1♓13	15	7	23	29	8	26	23	22
15	1 31 21	20 56 51	13 27	15	7	24	29	8	26	23	22
16	1 35 18	21 56 18	25 31	16	8	25	29	8	27	23	22
17	1 39 14	22 55 47	7♈28	16	9	26	0♍	8	27	23	22
18	1 43 11	23 55 19	19 20	17	10	26	0	8	27	23	22
19	1 47 7	24 54 52	1♉ 8	17	10	27	0	8	27	23	22
20	1 51 4	25 54 27	12 56	17	11	28	0	8	27	23	22
21	1 55 1	26 54 5	24 44	17 R	12	28	0	8	27	23	22
22	1 58 57	27 53 44	6♊37	17	13	29	0	8	27	23	22
23	2 2 54	28 53 26	18 37	17	14	0♑	1	7	27	23	22
24	2 6 50	29 53 10	0♋47	17	14	1	1	7	27	23	22
25	2 10 47	0♏52 56	13 11	16	15	1	1	7	27	23	22
26	2 14 43	1 52 45	25 52	16	16	2	1	7	27	23	22
27	2 18 40	2 52 35	8♌55	15	17	3	1	7	27	23	22
28	2 22 36	3 52 28	22 21	14	18	4	1	7	27	23	22
29	2 26 33	4 52 23	6♍13	13	19	4	1	7	27	23	22
30	2 30 30	5 52 20	20 32	12	20	5	2	7	27	23	22
31	2 34 26	6 52 20	5♎14	11	21	6	2	7	27	23	22

THE SUN ENTERS THE SIGN OF SCORPIO ON OCT 24 AT 02:45.

DAY	TIME	☉	☽	☿	♀	♂	♃	♄	♅	♆	♇
	h m s	° ' "	° '	°	°	°	°	°	°	°	°
N 1	2 38 23	7♏52 21	20♎14	9♏R	22♍	7♑	2♍	7♈R	27♍	23♏	22♍
O 2	2 42 19	8 52 25	5♏26	8	22	7	2	7	27	24	22
V 3	2 46 16	9 52 30	20 38	7	23	8	2	7	28	24	22
E 4	2 50 12	10 52 37	5♐43	6	24	9	2	7	28	24	22
M 5	2 54 9	11 52 46	20 30	4	25	10	2	7	28	24	22
B 6	2 58 5	12 52 57	4♑54	4	26	10	3	7	28	24	22
E 7	3 2 2	13 53 9	18 51	3	27	11	3	7	28	24	22
R 8	3 5 59	14 53 23	2♒21	2	28	12	3	7	28	24	22
9	3 9 55	15 53 38	15 24	2	29	13	3	6	28	24	22
10	3 13 52	16 53 54	28 4	1 D	0♎	13	3	6	28	24	22
11	3 17 48	17 54 12	10♓25	1	1	14	3	6	28	24	22
12	3 21 45	18 54 31	22 32	2	2	15	3	6	28	24	22
13	3 25 41	19 54 52	4♈28	2	3	16	3	6	28	24	22
14	3 29 38	20 55 14	16 18	2	4	16	4	6	28	24	22
15	3 33 34	21 55 38	28 6	3	5	17	4	6	28	24	22
16	3 37 31	22 56 4	9♉53	4	6	18	4	6	28	24	22
17	3 41 28	23 56 30	21 44	5	8	19	4	6	28	24	22
18	3 45 24	24 56 59	3♊39	6	9	19	4	6	28	24	22
19	3 49 21	25 57 29	15 41	7	10	20	4	6	28	24	22
20	3 53 17	26 58 1	27 51	8	11	21	4	6	28	24	23
21	3 57 14	27 58 34	10♋10	9	12	22	4	6	28	24	23
22	4 1 10	28 59 10	22 42	10	13	22	4	6	28	24	23
23	4 5 7	29 59 46	5♌27	12	14	23	4	6	28	24	23
24	4 9 3	1♐ 0 25	18 29	13	15	24	5	6	28	24	23
25	4 13 0	2 1 5	1♍49	14	16	25	5	6	28	24	23
26	4 16 57	3 1 47	15 29	16	17	26	5	6	29	24	23
27	4 20 53	4 2 30	29 31	17	18	26	5	6	29	24	23
28	4 24 50	5 3 15	13♎55	19	19	27	5	6	29	24	23
29	4 28 46	6 4 1	28 37	20	21	28	5	6	29	25	23
30	4 32 43	7 4 49	13♏34	22	22	29	5	6	29	25	23

THE SUN ENTERS THE SIGN OF SAGITTARIUS ON NOV 23 AT 00:06.

DAY	TIME	☉	☽	☿	♀	♂	♃	♄	♅	♆	♇
	h m s	° ' "	° '	°	°	°	°	°	°	°	°
D 1	4 36 39	8♐ 5 39	28♏38	23♏	23♎	29♑	5♍	6♈R	29♍	25♏	23♍
E 2	4 40 36	9 6 30	13♐40	25	24	0♒	5	6	29	25	23
C 3	4 44 32	10 7 22	28 31	26	25	1	5	6	29	25	23
E 4	4 48 29	11 8 15	13♑ 3	28	26	2	5	6	29	25	23
M 5	4 52 26	12 9 9	27 9	29	27	2	5	6	29	25	23
B 6	4 56 22	13 10 3	10♒47	1♐	28	3	5	6	29	25	23
E 7	5 0 19	14 10 59	23 56	2	0♏	4	5	6	29	25	23
R 8	5 4 15	15 11 55	6♓40	4	1	5	6	6	29	25	23
9	5 8 12	16 12 52	19 3	5	2	6	6	6 D	29	25	23
10	5 12 8	17 13 49	1♈ 8	7	3	6	6	6	29	25	23
11	5 16 5	18 14 47	13 2	8	4	7	6	6	29	25	23
12	5 20 2	19 15 46	24 50	10	5	8	6	6	29	25	23
13	5 23 58	20 16 45	6♉36	11	6	9	6	6	29	25	23
14	5 27 55	21 17 45	18 25	13	8	9	6	6	29	25	23
15	5 31 51	22 18 46	0♊21	15	9	10	6	6	29	25	23
16	5 35 48	23 19 48	12 25	16	10	11	6	6	29	25	23
17	5 39 44	24 20 50	24 39	18	11	12	6	6	29	25	23
18	5 43 41	25 21 53	7♋ 4	19	12	13	6	6	29	25	23
19	5 47 37	26 22 56	19 41	21	13	13	6	6	29	25	23
20	5 51 34	27 24 0	2♌30	22	15	14	6	6	29	25	23
21	5 55 31	28 25 5	15 30	24	16	15	6	6	29	25	23
22	5 59 27	29 26 10	28 41	25	17	16	6 R	6	29	25	23
23	6 3 24	0♑27 17	12♍ 6	27	18	16	6	6	29	25	23
24	6 7 20	1 28 23	25 43	29	19	17	6	6	29	25	23
25	6 11 17	2 29 31	9♎35	0♑	21	18	6	6	29	25	23
26	6 15 13	3 30 39	23 41	2	22	19	6	6	29	25	23 R
27	6 19 10	4 31 48	8♏ 2	3	23	20	6	6	29	25	23
28	6 23 6	5 32 58	22 34	5	24	20	6	6	29	26	23
29	6 27 3	6 34 8	7♐15	7	25	21	6	6	29	26	23
30	6 31 0	7 35 19	21 57	8	26	22	6	6	29	26	23
31	6 34 56	8 36 30	6♑34	10	28	23	6	6	29	26	23

THE SUN ENTERS THE SIGN OF CAPRICORN ON DEC 22 AT 13:17.

♈ ARIES ♉ TAURUS ♊ GEMINI ♋ CANCER ♌ LEO ♍ VIRGO ♎ LIBRA ♏ SCORPIO ♐ SAGITTARIUS ♑ CAPRICORN ♒ AQUARIUS ♓ PISCES

SIDEREAL SUN MOON MERCURY VENUS MARS JUPITER SATURN URANUS NEPTUNE PLUTO

DAY	TIME	☉	☽	☿	♀	♂	♃	♄	♅	♆	♇
	h m s	° ' "	° '	°	°	°	°	°	°	°	°
J 1	6 38 53	9♑37 40	20♑56	11♑	29♏	23♒	6♍R	6♈	29♍	26♏	23♍R
A 2	6 42 49	10 38 51	4♒59	13	0♐	24	6	6	29	26	23
N 3	6 46 46	11 40 2	18 38	15	1	25	6	6	29	26	23
U 4	6 50 42	12 41 13	1♓51	16	2	26	6	6	29 R	26	23
A 5	6 54 39	13 42 23	14 38	18	4	27	6	6	29	26	23
R 6	6 58 35	14 43 33	27 4	20	5	27	5	6	29	26	23
Y 7	7 2 32	15 44 43	9♈11	21	6	28	5	6	29	26	23
8	7 6 29	16 45 52	21 7	23	7	29	5	6	29	26	23
9	7 10 25	17 47 1	2♉55	24	8	0♓	5	6	29	26	23
10	7 14 22	18 48 10	14 43	26	10	0	5	7	29	26	23
11	7 18 18	19 49 18	26 34	28	11	1	5	7	29	26	23
12	7 22 15	20 50 25	8♊33	29	12	2	5	7	29	26	23
13	7 26 11	21 51 33	20 45	1♒	13	3	5	7	29	26	23
14	7 30 8	22 52 39	3♋11	3	15	4	5	7	29	26	23
15	7 34 5	23 53 45	15 52	5	16	4	5	7	29	26	23
16	7 38 1	24 54 51	28 49	6	17	5	5	7	29	26	23
17	7 41 58	25 55 56	12♌ 0	8	18	6	5	7	29	26	23
18	7 45 54	26 57 1	25 23	10	19	7	5	7	29	26	23
19	7 49 51	27 58 5	8♍57	11	21	7	5	7	29	26	23
20	7 53 47	28 59 9	22 39	13	22	8	5	7	29	26	23
21	7 57 44	0♒ 0 13	6♎28	14	23	9	4	7	29	26	23
22	8 1 40	1 1 16	20 23	16	24	10	4	7	29	26	23
23	8 5 37	2 2 19	4♏24	18	25	11	4	7	29	26	23
24	8 9 34	3 3 21	18 32	19	27	11	4	7	29	26	23
25	8 13 30	4 4 23	2♐44	21	28	12	4	8	29	26	23
26	8 17 27	5 5 25	16 58	22	29	13	4	8	29	26	23
27	8 21 23	6 6 26	1♑13	24	0♑	14	4	8	29	26	23
28	8 25 20	7 7 26	15 22	25	2	14	4	8	29	26	23
29	8 29 16	8 8 26	29 22	26	3	15	4	8	29	26	23
30	8 33 13	9 9 24	13♒ 6	27	4	16	4	8	29	26	23
31	8 37 9	10 10 22	26 33	29	5	17	3	8	29	26	23

THE SUN ENTERS THE SIGN OF AQUARIUS ON JAN 20 AT 23:55.

DAY	TIME	☉	☽	☿	♀	♂	♃	♄	♅	♆	♇
	h m s	° ' "	° '	°	°	°	°	°	°	°	°
F 1	8 41 6	11♒11 19	9♓38	0♓	6♑	18♓	3♍R	8♈	29♍R	26♏	23♍R
E 2	8 45 3	12 12 14	22 23	0	8	18	3	8	29	26	22
B 3	8 48 59	13 13 8	4♈48	1	9	19	3	8	29	26	22
R 4	8 52 56	14 14 0	16 56	2	10	20	3	8	29	26	22
U 5	8 56 52	15 14 52	28 53	2	11	21	3	8	29	26	22
A 6	9 0 49	16 15 42	10♉43	2 R	13	21	3	9	29	26	22
R 7	9 4 45	17 16 30	22 31	2	14	22	3	9	29	26	22
Y 8	9 8 42	18 17 17	4♊23	2	15	23	2	9	29	26	22
9	9 12 38	19 18 3	16 25	2	16	24	2	9	29	26	22
10	9 16 35	20 18 47	28 40	1	17	25	2	9	29	26	22
11	9 20 32	21 19 30	11♋13	1	19	25	2	9	29	26	22
12	9 24 28	22 20 11	24 5	0	20	26	2	9	29	26	22
13	9 28 25	23 20 50	7♌17	29♒	21	27	2	9	29	26	22
14	9 32 21	24 21 28	20 48	28	22	28	2	9	28	26	22
15	9 36 18	25 22 5	4♍36	27	24	28	2	9	28	26	22
16	9 40 14	26 22 40	18 36	26	25	29	1	10	28	26	22
17	9 44 11	27 23 14	2♎44	24	26	0☉	1	10	28	27	22
18	9 48 7	28 23 46	16 57	23	27	1♈	1	10	28	27	22
19	9 52 4	29 24 17	1♏11	22	29	1	1	10	28	27	22
20	9 56 1	0♓24 47	15 23	21	0♒	2	1	10	28	27	22
21	9 59 57	1 25 16	29 32	20	1	3	1	10	28	27	22
22	10 3 54	2 25 43	13♐36	19	2	4	1	10	28	27	22
23	10 7 50	3 26 10	27 34	19	3	4	1	10	28	27	22
24	10 11 47	4 26 35	11♑25	18	5	5	0	10	28	27	22
25	10 15 43	5 26 58	25 7	18	6	6	0	11	28	27	22
26	10 19 40	6 27 20	8♒39	17	7	7	0	11	28	27	22
27	10 23 36	7 27 40	21 57	17	8	8	0	11	28	27 R	22
28	10 27 33	8 27 59	5♓ 2	17 D	10	8	0	11	28	27	22
29	10 31 30	9 28 15	17 50	17	11	9	0	11	28	27	22

THE SUN ENTERS THE SIGN OF PISCES ON FEB 19 AT 14:10.

DAY	TIME	☉	☽	☿	♀	♂	♃	♄	♅	♆	♇
	h m s	° ' "	° '	°	°	°	°	°	°	°	°
M 1	10 35 26	10♓28 30	0♈23	17♒	12♒	10♈	0♍R	11♈	28♍R	27♏R	22♍R
A 2	10 39 23	11 28 43	12 41	17	13	11	0	11	28	27	22
R 3	10 43 19	12 28 54	24 47	18	15	11	29♌	11	28	27	22
C 4	10 47 16	13 29 4	6♉43	18	16	12	29	11	28	27	22
H 5	10 51 12	14 29 11	18 32	19	17	13	29	12	28	27	22
6	10 55 9	15 29 16	0♊21	19	18	14	29	12	28	27	22
7	10 59 5	16 29 19	12 13	20	19	14	29	12	28	27	22
8	11 3 2	17 29 20	24 14	21	21	15	29	12	28	27	22
9	11 6 59	18 29 19	6♋29	21	22	16	29	12	28	27	22
10	11 10 55	19 29 15	19 1	22	23	17	29	12	28	26	22
11	11 14 52	20 29 9	1♌56	23	24	17	28	12	27	26	22
12	11 18 48	21 29 2	15 13	24	26	18	28	12	27	26	22
13	11 22 45	22 28 52	28 55	25	27	19	28	12	27	26	22
14	11 26 41	23 28 40	12♍59	26	28	20	28	13	27	26	21
15	11 30 38	24 28 25	27 21	27	29	20	28	13	27	26	21
16	11 34 34	25 28 9	11♎55	28	1♓	21	28	13	27	26	21
17	11 38 31	26 27 51	26 36	29	2	22	28	13	27	26	21
18	11 42 28	27 27 32	11♏16	0♓	3	23	28	13	27	26	21
19	11 46 24	28 27 10	25 50	2	4	23	28	13	27	26	21
20	11 50 21	29 26 47	10♐14	3	5	24	27	13	27	26	21
21	11 54 17	0♈26 22	24 25	4	7	25	27	13	27	26	21
22	11 58 14	1 25 56	8♑20	5	8	26	27	14	27	26	21
23	12 2 10	2 25 27	22 0	7	9	26	27	14	27	26	21
24	12 6 7	3 24 57	5♒24	8	10	27	27	14	27	26	21
25	12 10 3	4 24 25	18 33	10	12	28	27	14	27	26	21
26	12 14 0	5 23 51	1♓28	11	13	29	27	14	27	26	21
27	12 17 57	6 23 16	14 9	12	14	29	27	14	27	26	21
28	12 21 53	7 22 38	26 38	14	15	0♉	27	14	27	26	21
29	12 25 50	8 21 58	8♈55	15	17	1	27	14	27	26	21
30	12 29 46	9 21 16	21 3	17	18	1	27	15	27	26	21
31	12 33 43	10 20 32	3♉ 1	18	19	2	27	15	27	26	21

THE SUN ENTERS THE SIGN OF ARIES ON MAR 20 AT 13:22.

SIDEREAL SUN MOON MERCURY VENUS MARS JUPITER SATURN URANUS NEPTUNE PLUTO

DAY	TIME	☉	☽	☿	♀	♂	♃	♄	♅	♆	♇
	h m s	° ' "	° '	°	°	°	°	°	°	°	°
A 1	12 37 39	11♈19 46	14♉54	20♓	20♓	3♉	27♌R	15♈	27♍R	26♏R	21♍R
P 2	12 41 36	12 18 58	26 43	22	21	4	26	15	27	26	21
R 3	12 45 32	13 18 8	8♊32	23	23	4	26	15	26	26	21
I 4	12 49 29	14 17 15	20 24	25	24	5	26	15	26	26	21
L 5	12 53 25	15 16 21	2♋24	27	25	6	26	15	26	26	21
6	12 57 22	16 15 24	14 37	28	26	7	26	15	26	26	21
7	13 1 19	17 14 24	27 6	0☉	28	7	26	16	26	26	21
8	13 5 15	18 13 22	9♌56	2♈	29	8	26	16	26	26	21
9	13 9 12	19 12 18	23 11	3	0♈	9	26	16	26	26	21
10	13 13 8	20 11 12	6♍51	5	1	10	26	16	26	26	21
11	13 17 5	21 10 3	20 58	7	3	10	26	16	26	26	21
12	13 21 1	22 8 52	5♎28	9	4	11	26	16	26	26	21
13	13 24 58	23 7 39	20 17	11	5	12	26	16	26	26	21
14	13 28 54	24 6 24	5♏18	13	6	12	26	16	26	26	21
15	13 32 51	25 5 8	20 23	15	7	13	26	17	26	26	21
16	13 36 48	26 3 49	5♐21	16	9	14	26	17	26	26	21
17	13 40 44	27 2 29	20 6	18	10	15	26	17	26	26	21
18	13 44 41	28 1 7	4♑32	20	11	15	26	17	26	26	21
19	13 48 37	28 59 43	18 36	22	12	16	26	17	26	26	21
20	13 52 34	29 58 18	2♒17	24	14	17	26	17	26	26	21
21	13 56 30	0♉56 51	15 34	26	15	17	26 D	17	26	26	21
22	14 0 27	1 55 23	28 32	29	16	18	26	17	26	26	21
23	14 4 23	2 53 52	11♓11	1♉	17	19	26	18	26	26	21
24	14 8 20	3 52 20	23 36	3	19	20	26	18	26	26	21
25	14 12 17	4 50 47	5♈48	5	20	20	26	18	26	26	21
26	14 16 13	5 49 11	17 52	7	21	21	26	18	26	26	20
27	14 20 10	6 47 34	29 49	9	22	22	26	18	26	26	20
28	14 24 6	7 45 55	11♉41	11	23	22	26	18	26	26	20
29	14 28 3	8 44 14	23 30	13	25	23	26	18	26	26	20
30	14 31 59	9 42 32	5♊19	16	26	24	26	18	26	26	20

THE SUN ENTEPS THE SIGN OF TAURUS ON APR 20 AT 00:41.

DAY	TIME	☉	☽	☿	♀	♂	♃	♄	♅	♆	♇
	h m s	° ' "	° '	°	°	°	°	°	°	°	°
M 1	14 35 56	10♉40 47	17♊10	18♉	27♈	25♉	26♌	19♈	26♍R	26♏R	20♍R
A 2	14 39 52	11 39 1	29 5	20	28	25	26	19	25	26	20
Y 3	14 43 49	12 37 13	11♋ 7	22	0♉	26	26	19	25	26	20
4	14 47 46	13 35 23	23 20	24	1	27	26	19	25	25	20
5	14 51 42	14 33 31	5♌47	26	2	27	26	19	25	25	20
6	14 55 39	15 31 36	18 33	28	3	28	26	19	25	25	20
7	14 59 35	16 29 40	1♍40	0♊	5	29	26	19	25	25	20
8	15 3 32	17 27 42	15 13	2	6	0♊	26	19	25	25	20
9	15 7 28	18 25 42	29 12	4	7	0	26	20	25	25	20
10	15 11 25	19 23 40	13♎37	6	8	1	26	20	25	25	20
11	15 15 21	20 21 37	28 26	8	9	2	26	20	25	25	20
12	15 19 18	21 19 32	13♏32	9	11	2	26	20	25	25	20
13	15 23 15	22 17 25	28 48	11	12	3	26	20	25	25	20
14	15 27 11	23 15 17	14♐ 1	13	13	4	27	20	25	25	20
15	15 31 8	24 13 7	29 3	14	14	4	27	20	25	25	20
16	15 35 4	25 10 56	13♑46	16	16	5	27	20	25	25	20
17	15 39 1	26 8 44	28 2	17	17	6	27	20	25	25	20
18	15 42 57	27 6 31	11♒50	18	18	7	27	21	25	25	20
19	15 46 54	28 4 17	25 10	20	19	7	27	21	25	25	20
20	15 50 51	29 2 1	8♓ 5	21	21	8	27	21	25	25	20
21	15 54 47	29 59 44	20 39	22	22	9	27	21	25	25	20
22	15 58 44	0♊57 27	2♈55	23	23	9	27	21	25	25	20
23	16 2 40	1 55 8	14 59	24	24	10	27	21	25	25	20
24	16 6 37	2 52 48	26 54	25	25	11	27	21	25	25	20
25	16 10 33	3 50 27	8♉44	26	27	11	27	21	25	25	20
26	16 14 30	4 48 5	20 33	27	28	12	28	21	25	25	20
27	16 18 26	5 45 42	2♊22	28	29	13	28	21	25	25	20
28	16 22 23	6 43 18	14 13	29	0♊	14	28	22	25	25	20
29	16 26 20	7 40 52	26 9	29	2	14	28	22	25	25	20
30	16 30 16	8 38 26	8♋10	0♋	3	15	28	22	25	25	20
31	16 34 13	9 35 58	20 19	1	4	16	28	22	25	25	20 D

THE SUN ENTERS THE SIGN OF GEMINI ON MAY 21 AT 00:06.

DAY	TIME	☉	☽	☿	♀	♂	♃	♄	♅	♆	♇
	h m s	° ' "	° '	°	°	°	°	°	°	°	°
J 1	16 38 9	10♊33 29	2♌38	1♋	5♊	16♊	28♌	22♈	25♍R	25♏R	20♍
U 2	16 42 6	11 30 58	15 9	1	6	17	28	22	25 D	25	20
N 3	16 46 2	12 28 27	27 55	2	8	18	28	22	25	25	20
E 4	16 49 59	13 25 54	10♍59	2	9	18	28	22	25	25	20
5	16 53 55	14 23 20	24 24	2	10	19	29	22	25	25	20
6	16 57 52	15 20 44	8♎12	2 R	11	20	29	22	25	25	20
7	17 1 49	16 18 8	22 25	2	13	20	29	23	25	25	20
8	17 5 45	17 15 30	7♏ 2	2	14	21	29	23	25	25	20
9	17 9 42	18 12 52	21 59	2	15	22	29	23	25	25	20
10	17 13 38	19 10 12	7♐ 9	2	16	22	29	23	25	25	20
11	17 17 35	20 7 32	22 22	1	18	23	29	23	25	24	20
12	17 21 31	21 4 51	7♑28	1	19	24	0♍	23	25	24	20
13	17 25 28	22 2 9	22 16	0	20	24	0	23	25	24	20
14	17 29 24	22 59 27	6♒41	0	21	25	0	23	25	24	20
15	17 33 21	23 56 45	20 36	29♊	22	26	0	23	25	24	20
16	17 37 18	24 54 1	4♓ 2	29	24	26	0	23	25	24	20
17	17 41 14	25 51 18	17 0	28	25	27	0	23	25	24	20
18	17 45 11	26 48 34	29 34	28	26	28	0	23	25	24	20
19	17 49 7	27 45 50	11♈49	27	27	29	0	24	25	24	20
20	17 53 4	28 43 6	23 50	27	29	29	1	24	25	24	20
21	17 57 0	29 40 22	5♉43	26	0♋	0♋	1	24	25	24	20
22	18 0 57	0♋37 37	17 31	26	1	1	1	24	25	24	20
23	18 4 53	1 34 52	29 19	25	2	1	1	24	25	24	20
24	18 8 50	2 32 7	11♊10	25	4	2	1	24	25	24	20
25	18 12 47	3 29 22	23 7	24	5	3	1	24	25	24	20
26	18 16 43	4 26 37	5♋11	24	6	3	2	24	25	24	20
27	18 20 40	5 23 51	17 23	24	7	4	2	24	25	24	20
28	18 24 36	6 21 5	29 44	23	8	5	2	24	25	24	20
29	18 28 33	7 18 19	12♌15	23	10	5	2	24	25	24	20
30	18 32 29	8 15 32	24 57	23 D	11	6	2	24	25	24	20

THE SUN ENTERS THE SIGN OF CANCER ON JUN 21 AT 08:14.

♈ ARIES ♉ TAURUS ♊ GEMINI ♋ CANCER ♌ LEO ♍ VIRGO ♎ LIBRA ♏ SCORPIO ♐ SAGITTARIUS ♑ CAPRICORN ♒ AQUARIUS ♓ PISCES

SIDEREAL SUN MOON MERCURY VENUS MARS JUPITER SATURN URANUS NEPTUNE PLUTO

DAY	TIME h m s	☉ ° ' "	☽ ° '	☿ °	♀ °	♂ °	♃ °	♄ °	♅ °	♆ °	♇ °
J 1	18 36 26	9♋12 45	7♍51	23♊	12♋	7♋	2♍	24♈	25♍	24♏R	20♍
U 2	18 40 22	10 9 58	21 0	23	13	7	3	24	25	24	20
L 3	18 44 19	11 7 10	4♎24	24	15	8	3	25	25	24	20
Y 4	18 48 16	12 4 22	18 7	24	16	9	3	25	26	24	20
5	18 52 12	13 1 33	2♏ 9	24	17	9	3	25	26	24	20
6	18 56 9	13 58 45	16 31	25	18	10	3	25	26	24	21
7	19 0 5	14 55 56	1♐11	25	19	11	3	25	26	24	21
8	19 4 2	15 53 7	16 2	26	21	11	4	25	26	24	21
9	19 7 58	16 50 18	1♑ 0	26	22	12	4	25	26	24	21
10	19 11 55	17 47 30	15 53	27	23	13	4	25	26	24	21
11	19 15 52	18 44 41	0♒34	28	24	13	4	25	26	24	21
12	19 19 48	19 41 53	14 55	29	26	14	4	25	26	24	21
13	19 23 45	20 39 5	28 50	0♋	27	15	4	25	26	24	21
14	19 27 41	21 36 17	12♓17	1	28	15	5	25	26	24	21
15	19 31 38	22 33 30	25 18	2	29	16	5	25	26	24	21
16	19 35 34	23 30 43	7♈54	3	1♌	16	5	25	26	24	21
17	19 39 31	24 27 57	20 12	5	2	17	5	25	26	24	21
18	19 43 27	25 25 12	2♉14	6	3	18	5	25	26	24	21
19	19 47 24	26 22 27	14 7	8	4	18	6	25	26	24	21
20	19 51 21	27 19 44	25 57	9	5	19	6	25	26	24	21
21	19 55 17	28 17 1	7♊47	11	7	20	6	25	26	24	21
22	19 59 14	29 14 19	19 42	12	8	20	6	25	26	24	21
23	20 3 10	0♌11 37	1♋45	14	9	21	6	25	26	24	21
24	20 7 7	1 8 56	13 58	16	10	22	7	25	26	24	21
25	20 11 3	2 6 16	26 23	18	12	22	7	25	26	24	21
26	20 15 0	3 3 37	9♌ 0	20	13	23	7	25	26	24	21
27	20 18 56	4 0 58	21 48	21	14	24	7	25	26	24	21
28	20 22 53	4 58 20	4♍48	23	15	24	7	25	26	24	21
29	20 26 50	5 55 42	18 0	25	17	25	8	25	26	24	21
30	20 30 46	6 53 5	1♎23	27	18	26	8	25	26	24	21
31	20 34 43	7 50 29	14 57	29	19	26	8	26	27	24	21

THE SUN ENTERS THE SIGN OF LEO ON JUL 22 AT 19:08.

DAY	TIME h m s	☉ ° ' "	☽ ° '	☿ °	♀ °	♂ °	♃ °	♄ °	♅ °	♆ °	♇ °
A 1	20 38 39	8♌47 53	28♎44	2♌	20♌	27♋	8♍	26♈	27♍	24♏R	21♍
U 2	20 42 36	9 45 18	12♏43	4	21	28	8	26	27	24	21
G 3	20 46 32	10 42 43	26 54	6	23	28	9	26	27	24	21
U 4	20 50 29	11 40 9	11♐17	8	24	29	9	26	27	24	21
S 5	20 54 25	12 37 36	25 47	10	25	0♌	9	26	27	24 D	21
T 6	20 58 22	13 35 4	10♑20	12	26	0	9	26	27	24	21
7	21 2 19	14 32 32	24 49	14	28	1	9	26 R	27	24	21
8	21 6 15	15 30 1	9♒ 9	16	29	1	10	26	27	24	21
9	21 10 12	16 27 32	23 13	18	0♍	2	10	26	27	24	21
10	21 14 8	17 25 3	6♓57	20	1	3	10	26	27	24	21
11	21 18 5	18 22 36	20 18	22	3	3	10	26	27	24	21
12	21 22 1	19 20 9	3♈16	24	4	4	10	26	27	24	21
13	21 25 58	20 17 45	15 52	26	5	5	11	26	27	24	21
14	21 29 54	21 15 21	28 10	28	6	5	11	26	27	24	22
15	21 33 51	22 13 0	10♉15	0♍	7	6	11	25	27	24	22
16	21 37 48	23 10 39	22 10	2	9	7	11	25	27	24	22
17	21 41 44	24 8 21	4♊ 1	4	10	7	11	25	27	24	22
18	21 45 41	25 6 4	15 53	6	11	8	12	25	27	24	22
19	21 49 37	26 3 48	27 52	7	12	9	12	25	28	24	22
20	21 53 34	27 1 34	9♋59	9	14	9	12	25	28	24	22
21	21 57 30	27 59 22	22 20	11	15	10	12	25	28	24	22
22	22 1 27	28 57 11	4♌56	13	16	10	13	25	28	24	22
23	22 5 23	29 55 2	17 47	14	17	11	13	25	28	24	22
24	22 9 20	0♍52 54	0♍54	16	19	12	13	25	28	24	22
25	22 13 17	1 50 48	14 16	18	20	12	13	25	28	24	22
26	22 17 13	2 48 43	27 51	19	21	13	13	25	28	24	22
27	22 21 10	3 46 39	11♎38	21	22	14	14	25	28	24	22
28	22 25 6	4 44 37	25 32	23	24	14	14	25	28	24	22
29	22 29 3	5 42 36	9♏34	24	25	15	14	25	28	24	22
30	22 32 59	6 40 37	23 42	26	26	16	14	25	28	24	22
31	22 36 56	7 38 39	7♐52	27	27	16	14	25	28	24	22

THE SUN ENTERS THE SIGN OF VIRGO ON AUG 23 AT 02:04.

DAY	TIME h m s	☉ ° ' "	☽ ° '	☿ °	♀ °	♂ °	♃ °	♄ °	♅ °	♆ °	♇ °
S 1	22 40 52	8♍36 42	22♐ 5	29♍	28♍	17♌	15♍	25♈R	28♍	24♏	22♍
E 2	22 44 49	9 34 47	6♑17	0♎	0♎	18	15	25	28	24	22
P 3	22 48 46	10 32 53	20 26	2	1	18	15	25	28	24	22
T 4	22 52 42	11 31 1	4♒28	3	2	19	15	25	28	24	22
E 5	22 56 39	12 29 10	18 21	5	3	19	16	25	29	24	22
M 6	23 0 35	13 27 20	2♓ 0	6	5	20	16	25	29	24	22
B 7	23 4 32	14 25 32	15 23	8	6	21	16	25	29	24	22
E 8	23 8 28	15 23 46	28 29	9	7	21	16	25	29	24	22
R 9	23 12 25	16 22 2	11♈16	10	8	22	16	25	29	24	22
10	23 16 21	17 20 20	23 47	12	9	23	17	25	29	24	22
11	23 20 18	18 18 39	6♉ 3	13	11	23	17	25	29	24	22
12	23 24 15	19 17 1	18 7	14	12	24	17	24	29	24	23
13	23 28 11	20 15 25	0♊ 3	16	13	24	17	24	29	24	23
14	23 32 8	21 13 51	11 54	17	14	25	17	24	29	24	23
15	23 36 4	22 12 19	23 47	18	16	26	18	24	29	24	23
16	23 40 1	23 10 49	5♋46	19	17	26	18	24	29	24	23
17	23 43 57	24 9 22	17 55	20	18	27	18	24	29	24	23
18	23 47 54	25 7 57	0♌18	21	19	28	18	24	29	24	23
19	23 51 50	26 6 33	12 59	22	21	28	19	24	29	24	23
20	23 55 47	27 5 12	25 59	23	22	29	19	24	29	24	23
21	23 59 44	28 3 53	9♍21	24	23	0♍	19	24	0♎	24	23
22	0 3 40	29 2 36	23 2	25	24	0	19	24	0	24	23
23	0 7 37	0♎ 1 21	7♎ 1	26	25	1	19	24	0	24	23
24	0 11 33	1 0 8	21 14	27	27	1	20	24	0	24	23
25	0 15 30	1 58 56	5♏37	28	28	2	20	24	0	24	23
26	0 19 26	2 57 47	20 3	28	29	3	20	24	0	24	23
27	0 23 23	3 56 39	4♐30	29	0♏	3	20	24	0	24	23
28	0 27 19	4 55 33	18 52	0♏	2	4	20	23	0	25	23
29	0 31 16	5 54 29	3♑ 6	0	3	5	21	23	0	25	23
30	0 35 13	6 53 27	17 10	1	4	5	21	23	0	25	23

THE SUN ENTERS THE SIGN OF LIBRA ON SEP 22 AT 23:27.

DAY	TIME h m s	☉ ° ' "	☽ ° '	☿ °	♀ °	♂ °	♃ °	♄ °	♅ °	♆ °	♇ °
O 1	0 39 9	7♎52 26	1♒ 2	1♏	5♏	6♍	21♍	23♈R	0♎	25♏	23♍
C 2	0 43 6	8 51 27	14 42	1	6	6	21	23	0	25	23
T 3	0 47 2	9 50 30	28 8	1 R	8	7	22	23	0	25	23
O 4	0 50 59	10 49 35	11♓21	1	9	8	22	23	0	25	23
B 5	0 54 55	11 48 41	24 20	1	10	8	22	23	0	25	23
E 6	0 58 52	12 47 50	7♈ 6	1	11	9	22	23	0	25	23
R 7	1 2 48	13 47 0	19 39	0	13	10	22	23	1	25	23
8	1 6 45	14 46 13	1♉59	0	14	10	23	23	1	25	23
9	1 10 41	15 45 27	14 9	29♎	15	11	23	23	1	25	24
10	1 14 38	16 44 44	26 9	29	16	11	23	23	1	25	24
11	1 18 35	17 44 3	8♊ 4	28	18	12	23	22	1	25	24
12	1 22 31	18 43 25	19 55	27	19	13	23	22	1	25	24
13	1 26 28	19 42 48	1♋47	26	20	13	24	22	1	25	24
14	1 30 24	20 42 14	13 44	24	21	14	24	22	1	25	24
15	1 34 21	21 41 42	25 50	23	22	14	24	22	1	25	24
16	1 38 17	22 41 13	8♌11	22	24	15	24	22	1	25	24
17	1 42 14	23 40 46	20 50	21	25	16	24	22	1	25	24
18	1 46 10	24 40 21	3♍51	20	26	16	25	22	1	25	24
19	1 50 7	25 39 58	17 16	19	27	17	25	22	1	25	24
20	1 54 4	26 39 37	1♎ 7	18	29	18	25	22	1	25	24
21	1 58 0	27 39 19	15 22	17	0♐	18	25	22	1	25	24
22	2 1 57	28 39 3	29 56	16	1	19	25	22	1	25	24
23	2 5 53	29 38 48	14♏45	16	2	19	26	21	1	25	24
24	2 9 50	0♏38 36	29 40	16 D	3	20	26	21	2	25	24
25	2 13 46	1 38 25	14♐32	16	5	21	26	21	2	25	24
26	2 17 43	2 38 17	29 15	16	6	21	26	21	2	25	24
27	2 21 39	3 38 10	13♑42	16	7	22	26	21	2	25	24
28	2 25 36	4 38 4	27 50	17	8	23	27	21	2	25	24
29	2 29 33	5 38 0	11♒38	17	9	23	27	21	2	26	24
30	2 33 29	6 37 58	25 5	18	11	24	27	21	2	26	24
31	2 37 26	7 37 58	8♓14	19	12	24	27	21	2	26	24

THE SUN ENTERS THE SIGN OF SCORPIO ON OCT 23 AT 08:31.

DAY	TIME h m s	☉ ° ' "	☽ ° '	☿ °	♀ °	♂ °	♃ °	♄ °	♅ °	♆ °	♇ °
N 1	2 41 22	8♏37 58	21♓ 6	20♎	13♐	25♍	27♍	21♈R	2♎	26♏	24♍
O 2	2 45 19	9 38 1	3♈44	21	14	26	28	21	2	26	24
V 3	2 49 15	10 38 5	16 11	22	16	26	28	21	2	26	24
E 4	2 53 12	11 38 11	28 28	24	17	27	28	21	2	26	24
M 5	2 57 8	12 38 19	10♉36	25	18	27	28	21	2	26	24
B 6	3 1 5	13 38 28	22 38	26	19	28	28	20	2	26	24
E 7	3 5 2	14 38 40	4♊34	28	20	29	28	20	2	26	24
R 8	3 8 58	15 38 53	16 27	29	22	29	29	20	2	26	24
9	3 12 55	16 39 9	28 18	1♏	23	0♎	29	20	2	26	24
10	3 16 51	17 39 26	10♋10	2	24	0	29	20	2	26	24
11	3 20 48	18 39 45	22 6	4	25	1	29	20	2	26	25
12	3 24 44	19 40 6	4♌10	5	26	2	29	20	2	26	25
13	3 28 41	20 40 29	16 26	7	28	2	0♎	20	3	26	25
14	3 32 37	21 40 54	28 59	9	29	3	0	20	3	26	25
15	3 36 34	22 41 20	11♍53	10	0♑	3	0	20	3	26	25
16	3 40 31	23 41 49	25 12	12	1	4	0	20	3	26	25
17	3 44 27	24 42 19	8♎59	13	3	5	0	20	3	26	25
18	3 48 24	25 42 51	23 15	15	4	5	0	20	3	26	25
19	3 52 20	26 43 25	7♏57	16	5	6	0	20	3	26	25
20	3 56 17	27 44 1	22 59	18	6	7	1	20	3	26	25
21	4 0 13	28 44 38	8♐13	20	7	7	1	20	3	26	25
22	4 4 10	29 45 17	23 28	21	9	8	1	19	3	26	25
23	4 8 7	0♐45 57	8♑34	23	10	8	1	19	3	26	25
24	4 12 3	1 46 38	23 20	24	11	9	1	19	3	26	25
25	4 16 0	2 47 20	7♒42	26	12	10	1	19	3	27	25
26	4 19 56	3 48 3	21 36	28	13	10	2	19	3	27	25
27	4 23 53	4 48 47	5♓ 4	29	15	11	2	19	3	27	25
28	4 27 49	5 49 33	18 7	1♐	16	11	2	19	3	27	25
29	4 31 46	6 50 19	0♈49	2	17	12	2	19	3	27	25
30	4 35 42	7 51 6	13 15	4	18	13	2	19	3	27	25

THE SUN ENTERS THE SIGN OF SAGITTARIUS ON NOV 22 AT 05:50.

DAY	TIME h m s	☉ ° ' "	☽ ° '	☿ °	♀ °	♂ °	♃ °	♄ °	♅ °	♆ °	♇ °
D 1	4 39 39	8♐51 54	25♈28	5♐	19♑	13♎	2♎	19♈R	3♎	27♏	25♍
E 2	4 43 36	9 52 43	7♉33	7	21	14	2	19	3	27	25
C 3	4 47 32	10 53 33	19 31	9	22	14	3	19	3	27	25
E 4	4 51 29	11 54 24	1♊26	10	23	15	3	19	3	27	25
M 5	4 55 25	12 55 17	13 19	12	24	15	3	19	3	27	25
B 6	4 59 22	13 56 10	25 11	13	25	16	3	19	3	27	25
E 7	5 3 18	14 57 4	7♋ 4	15	27	17	3	19	4	27	25
R 8	5 7 15	15 58 0	18 59	16	28	17	3	19	4	27	25
9	5 11 11	16 58 56	0♌59	18	29	18	3	19	4	27	25
10	5 15 8	17 59 54	13 5	20	0♒	18	3	19	4	27	25
11	5 19 5	19 0 53	25 21	21	1	19	4	19	4	27	25
12	5 23 1	20 1 52	7♍50	23	2	20	4	19	4	27	25
13	5 26 58	21 2 53	20 38	24	4	20	4	19	4	27	25
14	5 30 54	22 3 55	3♎48	26	5	21	4	19	4	27	25
15	5 34 51	23 4 58	17 24	27	6	21	4	19	4	27	25
16	5 38 47	24 6 2	1♏28	29	7	22	4	19	4	27	25
17	5 42 44	25 7 7	16 1	1♑	8	23	4	19	4	27	25
18	5 46 40	26 8 13	0♐58	2	9	23	4	19	4	27	25
19	5 50 37	27 9 19	16 12	4	11	24	4	19	4	27	25
20	5 54 34	28 10 26	1♑34	5	12	24	5	19	4	27	25
21	5 58 30	29 11 34	16 51	7	13	25	5	19 D	4	27	25
22	6 2 27	0♑12 42	1♒51	9	14	25	5	19	4	27	25
23	6 6 23	1 13 51	16 27	10	15	26	5	19	4	27	25
24	6 10 20	2 14 59	0♓34	12	16	27	5	19	4	28	25
25	6 14 16	3 16 8	14 10	13	18	27	5	19	4	28	25
26	6 18 13	4 17 16	27 18	15	19	28	5	19	4	28	25
27	6 22 10	5 18 25	10♈ 1	17	20	28	5	19	4	28	25 R
28	6 26 6	6 19 33	22 24	18	21	29	5	19	4	28	25
29	6 30 3	7 20 42	4♉33	20	22	29	5	19	4	28	25
30	6 33 59	8 21 50	16 32	21	23	0♏	5	19	4	28	25
31	6 37 56	9 22 59	28 25	23	25	1	5	19	4	28	25

THE SUN ENTERS THE SIGN OF CAPRICORN ON DEC 21 AT 19:01.

♈ ARIES ♉ TAURUS ♊ GEMINI ♋ CANCER ♌ LEO ♍ VIRGO ♎ LIBRA ♏ SCORPIO ♐ SAGITTARIUS ♑ CAPRICORN ♒ AQUARIUS ♓ PISCES

SIDEREAL SUN MOON MERCURY VENUS MARS JUPITER SATURN URANUS NEPTUNE PLUTO

DAY	TIME	☉	☽	☿	♀	♂	♃	♄	♅	♆	♇
	h m s	° ' "	° '	°	°	°	°	°	°	°	°
J 1	6 41 52	10♑24 7	10♊16	25♑	26♒	1♏	5♎	19♈	4♎	28♏	25♍R
A 2	6 45 49	11 25 16	22 8	26	27	2	6	19	4	28	25
N 3	6 49 45	12 26 24	4♋ 2	28	28	2	6	19	4	28	25
U 4	6 53 42	13 27 32	15 59	29	29	3	6	19	4	28	25
A 5	6 57 39	14 28 41	28 2	1♒	0♓	3	6	19	4	28	25
R 6	7 1 35	15 29 49	10♌10	2	1	4	6	19	4	28	25
Y 7	7 5 32	16 30 57	22 25	4	2	5	6	19	4	28	25
8	7 9 28	17 32 5	4♍49	5	4	5	6	19	4 R	28	25
9	7 13 25	18 33 13	17 25	7	5	6	6	19	4	28	25
10	7 17 21	19 34 21	0♎15	8	6	6	6	19	4	28	25
11	7 21 18	20 35 30	13 22	9	7	7	6	19	4	28	25
12	7 25 14	21 36 38	26 50	10	8	7	6	19	4	28	25
13	7 29 11	22 37 46	10♏42	12	9	8	6	19	4	28	25
14	7 33 8	23 38 54	24 58	13	10	8	6	19	4	28	25
15	7 37 4	24 40 2	9♐36	13	11	9	6	19	4	28	25
16	7 41 1	25 41 10	24 33	14	12	10	6	19	4	28	25
17	7 44 57	26 42 18	9♑41	15	13	10	6	19	4	28	25
18	7 48 54	27 43 25	24 48	15	14	11	6	19	4	28	25
19	7 52 50	28 44 31	9♒46	16	16	11	6	19	4	28	25
20	7 56 47	29 45 37	24 24	16 R	17	12	6 R	19	4	28	25
21	8 0 43	0♒46 42	8♓37	16	18	12	6	20	4	28	25
22	8 4 40	1 47 46	22 21	16	19	13	6	20	4	28	25
23	8 8 37	2 48 49	5♈37	16	20	13	6	20	4	28	25
24	8 12 33	3 49 51	18 27	15	21	14	6	20	4	28	25
25	8 16 30	4 50 52	0♉55	14	22	14	6	20	4	28	25
26	8 20 26	5 51 52	13 6	13	23	15	6	20	4	28	25
27	8 24 23	6 52 51	25 6	12	24	16	6	20	4	28	25
28	8 28 19	7 53 48	6♊58	11	25	16	6	20	4	28	25
29	8 32 16	8 54 45	18 49	10	26	17	6	20	4	28	25
30	8 36 12	9 55 41	0♋41	8	27	17	6	20	4	28	25
31	8 40 9	10 56 35	12 38	7	28	18	6	20	4	28	25

THE SUN ENTERS THE SIGN OF AQUARIUS ON JAN 20 AT 05:39.

DAY	TIME	☉	☽	☿	♀	♂	♃	♄	♅	♆	♇
	h m s	° ' "	° '	°	°	°	°	°	°	°	°
F 1	8 44 6	11♒57 28	24♋41	6♒R	29♓	18♏	6♎R	20♈	4♎R	28♏	25♍R
E 2	8 48 2	12 58 20	6♌53	5	0☉	19	6	20	4	29	25
B 3	8 51 59	13 59 11	19 14	4	1♈	19	6	20	4	29	25
R 4	8 55 55	15 0 1	1♍44	3	2	20	6	20	4	29	25
U 5	8 59 52	16 0 49	14 25	2	3	20	6	21	4	29	25
A 6	9 3 48	17 1 37	27 17	2	4	21	6	21	4	29	25
R 7	9 7 45	18 2 23	10♎21	1	5	21	6	21	4	29	25
Y 8	9 11 41	19 3 9	23 39	1	5	22	6	21	4	29	25
9	9 15 38	20 3 53	7♏11	0	6	22	5	21	4	29	25
10	9 19 35	21 4 37	21 0	0 D	7	23	5	21	4	29	25
11	9 23 31	22 5 20	5♐ 5	0	8	23	5	21	4	29	25
12	9 27 28	23 6 1	19 25	0	9	24	5	21	3	29	25
13	9 31 24	24 6 42	3♑58	1	10	24	5	21	3	29	25
14	9 35 21	25 7 21	18 39	1	11	25	5	21	3	29	25
15	9 39 17	26 7 59	3♒21	1	12	25	5	21	3	29	24
16	9 43 14	27 8 36	17 57	2	12	26	5	21	3	29	24
17	9 47 11	28 9 11	2♓21	3	13	26	5	22	3	29	24
18	9 51 7	29 9 45	16 25	3	14	27	5	22	3	29	24
19	9 55 4	0♓10 17	0♈ 6	4	15	27	5	22	3	29	24
20	9 59 0	1 10 47	13 23	5	15	28	5	22	3	29	24
21	10 2 57	2 11 16	26 17	6	16	28	5	22	3	29	24
22	10 6 53	3 11 42	8♉50	7	17	29	4	22	3	29	24
23	10 10 50	4 12 7	21 6	7	18	29	4	22	3	29	24
24	10 14 46	5 12 30	3♊ 9	8	18	29	4	22	3	29	24
25	10 18 43	6 12 51	15 4	10	19	0♐	4	22	3	29	24
26	10 22 39	7 13 10	26 56	11	20	0	4	22	3	29	24
27	10 26 36	8 13 27	8♋50	12	20	1	4	23	3	29	24
28	10 30 33	9 13 42	20 49	13	21	1	4	23	3	29 R	24

THE SUN ENTERS THE SIGN OF PISCES ON FEB 18 AT 19:55.

DAY	TIME	☉	☽	☿	♀	♂	♃	♄	♅	♆	♇
	h m s	° ' "	° '	°	°	°	°	°	°	°	°
M 1	10 34 29	10♓13 56	2♌57	14♒	21♈	2♐	4♎R	23♈	3♎R	29♏R	24♍R
A 2	10 38 26	11 14 7	15 16	15	22	2	4	23	3	29	24
R 3	10 42 22	12 14 16	27 49	17	22	3	3	23	3	29	24
C 4	10 46 19	13 14 23	10♍36	18	23	3	3	23	3	29	24
H 5	10 50 15	14 14 29	23 38	19	24	3	3	23	3	29	24
6	10 54 12	15 14 32	6♎54	21	24	4	3	23	3	29	24
7	10 58 8	16 14 34	20 22	22	24	4	3	23	3	29	24
8	11 2 5	17 14 34	4♏ 2	23	25	4	3	23	3	29	24
9	11 6 2	18 14 33	17 53	25	25	5	3	23	3	29	24
10	11 9 58	19 14 30	1♐52	26	25	5	3	24	3	29	24
11	11 13 55	20 14 25	15 59	28	26	6	3	24	2	29	24
12	11 17 51	21 14 19	0♑11	29	26	6	2	24	2	29	24
13	11 21 48	22 14 12	14 27	1♓	26	7	2	24	2	29	24
14	11 25 44	23 14 2	28 43	2	26	7	2	24	2	29	24
15	11 29 41	24 13 51	12♒56	4	27	7	2	24	2	29	24
16	11 33 37	25 13 38	27 2	5	27	8	2	25	2	29	24
17	11 37 34	26 13 23	10♓58	7	27	8	2	25	2	29	24
18	11 41 31	27 13 6	24 40	8	27 R	9	2	25	2	29	24
19	11 45 27	28 12 47	8♈ 6	10	27	9	2	25	2	29	24
20	11 49 24	29 12 26	21 14	12	27	9	1	25	2	29	24
21	11 53 20	0♈12 3	4♉ 3	13	27	10	1	25	2	29	24
22	11 57 17	1 11 38	16 36	15	27	10	1	25	2	29	24
23	12 1 13	2 11 11	28 53	17	26	10	1	25	2	29	24
24	12 5 10	3 10 41	10♊58	18	26	11	1	25	2	29	24
25	12 9 6	4 10 9	22 54	20	26	11	1	25	2	29	24
26	12 13 3	5 9 35	4♋48	22	26	11	1	26	2	29	23
27	12 17 0	6 8 59	16 41	24	25	12	0	26	2	29	23
28	12 20 56	7 8 20	28 41	26	25	12	0	26	2	29	23
29	12 24 53	8 7 39	10♌50	27	25	12	0	26	2	28	23
30	12 28 49	9 6 55	23 13	29	24	12	0	26	2	28	23
31	12 32 46	10 6 10	5♍54	1♈	24	13	0	26	2	28	23

THE SUN ENTERS THE SIGN OF ARIES ON MAR 20 AT 19:09.

SIDEREAL SUN MOON MERCURY VENUS MARS JUPITER SATURN URANUS NEPTUNE PLUTO

DAY	TIME	☉	☽	☿	♀	♂	♃	♄	♅	♆	♇
	h m s	° ' "	° '	°	°	°	°	°	°	°	°
A 1	12 36 42	11♈ 5 22	18♍53	3♈	23♈R	13♐	0♎R	26♈	2♎R	28♏R	23♍R
P 2	12 40 39	12 4 32	2♎13	5	23	13	0	26	2	28	23
R 3	12 44 35	13 3 40	15 51	7	22	13	0	27	1	28	23
I 4	12 48 32	14 2 45	29 47	9	21	14	29♍	27	1	28	23
L 5	12 52 29	15 1 49	13♏56	11	21	14	29	27	1	28	23
6	12 56 25	16 0 52	28 14	13	20	14	29	27	1	28	23
7	13 0 22	16 59 52	12♐36	15	20	14	29	27	1	28	23
8	13 4 18	17 58 50	26 58	17	19	15	29	27	1	28	23
9	13 8 15	18 57 47	11♑16	19	18	15	29	27	1	28	23
10	13 12 11	19 56 43	25 26	21	18	15	29	27	1	28	23
11	13 16 8	20 55 36	9♒28	23	17	15	29	28	1	28	23
12	13 20 4	21 54 28	23 19	25	17	15	29	28	1	28	23
13	13 24 1	22 53 17	6♓59	27	16	16	28	28	1	28	23
14	13 27 58	23 52 5	20 27	29	15	16	28	28	1	28	23
15	13 31 54	24 50 52	3♈43	2♉	15	16	28	28	1	28	23
16	13 35 51	25 49 36	16 47	4	14	16	28	28	1	28	23
17	13 39 47	26 48 18	29 37	6	14	16	28	28	1	28	23
18	13 43 44	27 46 59	12♉14	8	13	16	28	28	1	28	23
19	13 47 40	28 45 37	24 39	10	13	16	28	29	1	28	23
20	13 51 37	29 44 14	6♊51	12	12	16	28	29	1	28	23
21	13 55 33	0♉42 48	18 55	14	12	17	28	29	1	28	23
22	13 59 30	1 41 21	0♋51	16	12	17	28	29	1	28	23
23	14 3 27	2 39 51	12 43	18	11	17	27	29	1	28	23
24	14 7 23	3 38 19	24 36	19	11	17	27	29	1	28	23
25	14 11 20	4 36 45	6♌34	21	11	17	27	29	1	28	23
26	14 15 16	5 35 9	18 42	23	11	17	27	0♉	1	28	23
27	14 19 13	6 33 31	1♍ 4	25	11	17 R	27	0	1	28	23
28	14 23 9	7 31 50	13 45	26	11	17	27	0	1	28	23
29	14 27 6	8 30 8	26 49	28	11 D	17	27	0	1	28	23
30	14 31 2	9 28 23	10♎18	29	10	17	27	0	0	28	23

THE SUN ENTERS THE SIGN OF TAURUS ON APR 20 AT 06:27.

DAY	TIME	☉	☽	☿	♀	♂	♃	♄	♅	♆	♇
	h m s	° ' "	° '	°	°	°	°	°	°	°	°
M 1	14 34 59	10♉26 37	24♎11	0♊	11♈	17♐R	27♍R	0♉	0♎R	28♏R	23♍R
A 2	14 38 55	11 24 48	8♏28	2	11	17	27	0	0	28	23
Y 3	14 42 52	12 22 59	23 3	3	11	17	27	0	0	28	23
4	14 46 49	13 21 7	7♐49	4	11	17	27	1	0	28	23
5	14 50 45	14 19 14	22 38	5	11	16	27	1	0	28	23
6	14 54 42	15 17 20	7♑23	6	11	16	27	1	0	28	23
7	14 58 38	16 15 24	21 56	7	11	16	27	1	0	28	23
8	15 2 35	17 13 26	6♒14	8	12	16	26	1	0	28	23
9	15 6 31	18 11 28	20 14	9	12	16	26	1	0	28	23
10	15 10 28	19 9 28	3♓55	10	12	16	26	1	0	28	23
11	15 14 25	20 7 26	17 19	10	12	16	26	1	0	28	23
12	15 18 21	21 5 23	0♈27	11	13	15	26	2	0	27	23
13	15 22 18	22 3 19	13 22	11	14	15	26	2	0	27	23
14	15 26 14	23 1 14	26 5	11	14	15	26	2	0	27	23
15	15 30 11	23 59 7	8♉36	12	15	15	26	2	0	27	22
16	15 34 7	24 56 59	20 58	12	15	15	26	2	0	27	22
17	15 38 4	25 54 50	3♊12	12 R	16	14	26	2	0	27	22
18	15 42 0	26 52 39	15 17	12	16	14	26	2	0	27	22
19	15 45 57	27 50 27	27 16	12	17	14	26	2	0	27	22
20	15 49 54	28 48 13	9♋ 9	12	17	14	26	2	0	27	22
21	15 53 50	29 45 57	21 0	12	18	13	26	3	0	27	22
22	15 57 47	0♊43 40	2♌52	11	19	13	26	3	0	27	22
23	16 1 43	1 41 22	14 48	11	19	13	26 D	3	0	27	22
24	16 5 40	2 39 2	26 53	11	20	12	26	3	0	27	22
25	16 9 36	3 36 40	9♍12	10	21	12	26	3	0	27	22
26	16 13 33	4 34 17	21 50	10	21	12	26	3	0	27	22
27	16 17 29	5 31 52	4♎52	9	22	12	26	3	0	27	22
28	16 21 26	6 29 26	18 21	9	23	11	26	3	0	27	22
29	16 25 23	7 26 58	2♏18	8	23	11	26	4	0	27	22
30	16 29 19	8 24 30	16 44	8	24	11	26	4	0	27	22
31	16 33 16	9 22 0	1♐33	7	25	10	26	4	0	27	22

THE SUN ENTERS THE SIGN OF GEMINI ON MAY 21 AT 05:50.

DAY	TIME	☉	☽	☿	♀	♂	♃	♄	♅	♆	♇
	h m s	° ' "	° '	°	°	°	°	°	°	°	°
J 1	16 37 12	10♊19 29	16♐38	6♊R	26♈	10♐R	26♍	4♉	0♎R	27♏R	22♍R
U 2	16 41 9	11 16 57	1♑49	6	27	10	26	4	0	27	22 D
N 3	16 45 5	12 14 25	16 56	5	27	9	26	4	0	27	22
E 4	16 49 2	13 11 51	1♒48	5	28	9	26	4	0	27	22
5	16 52 58	14 9 17	16 20	5	29	9	26	4	0	27	22
6	16 56 55	15 6 42	0♓27	4	0♉	8	26	4	0	27	22
7	17 0 52	16 4 6	14 9	4	1	8	26	5	0 D	27	22
8	17 4 48	17 1 30	27 29	4	2	8	26	5	0	27	22
9	17 8 45	17 58 53	10♈28	4	3	7	27	5	0	27	22
10	17 12 41	18 56 15	23 10	3 D	3	7	27	5	0	27	22
11	17 16 38	19 53 37	5♉38	3	4	7	27	5	0	27	22
12	17 20 34	20 50 59	17 56	3	5	6	27	5	0	27	22
13	17 24 31	21 48 20	0♊ 6	4	6	6	27	5	0	27	22
14	17 28 27	22 45 41	12 8	4	7	6	27	5	0	27	22
15	17 32 24	23 43 1	24 6	4	8	5	27	5	0	27	22
16	17 36 21	24 40 20	6♋ 0	5	9	5	27	5	0	27	22
17	17 40 17	25 37 39	17 52	5	10	5	27	6	0	27	22
18	17 44 14	26 34 56	29 42	5	11	4	27	6	0	27	22
19	17 48 10	27 32 14	11♌35	6	12	4	27	6	0	27	22
20	17 52 7	28 29 30	23 32	7	13	4	27	6	0	27	22
21	17 56 3	29 26 46	5♍37	7	14	4	27	6	0	26	22
22	18 0 0	0♋24 1	17 54	8	15	4	27	6	0	26	23
23	18 3 57	1 21 16	0♎30	9	16	3	27	6	0	26	23
24	18 7 53	2 18 30	13 27	10	17	3	28	6	0	26	23
25	18 11 50	3 15 43	26 51	11	18	3	28	6	0	26	23
26	18 15 46	4 12 55	10♏44	12	19	3	28	6	0	26	23
27	18 19 43	5 10 8	25 6	13	20	3	28	6	0	26	23
28	18 23 39	6 7 20	9♐55	14	21	2	28	7	0	26	23
29	18 27 36	7 4 31	25 4	16	22	2	28	7	0	26	23
30	18 31 32	8 1 42	10♑23	17	23	2	28	7	0	26	23

THE SUN ENTERS THE SIGN OF CANCER ON JUN 21 AT 13:56.

♈ ARIES ♉ TAURUS ♊ GEMINI ♋ CANCER ♌ LEO ♍ VIRGO ♎ LIBRA ♏ SCORPIO ♐ SAGITTARIUS ♑ CAPRICORN ♒ AQUARIUS ♓ PISCES

SIDEREAL SUN MOON MERCURY VENUS MARS JUPITER SATURN URANUS NEPTUNE PLUTO

DAY	TIME	☉	☽	☿	♀	♂	♃	♄	♅	♆	♇
	h m s	° ' "	° '	°	°	°	°	°	°	°	°
J 1	18 35 29	8♋58 54	25♑41	18♊	24♉	2♐R	28♍	7♉	0♎	26♏R	23♍
U 2	18 39 26	9 56 5	10♒46	20	25	2	28	7	0	26	23
L 3	18 43 22	10 53 16	25 31	21	26	2	28	7	0	26	23
Y 4	18 47 19	11 50 27	9♓49	23	27	2	29	7	0	26	23
5	18 51 15	12 47 38	23 39	25	28	2	29	7	0	26	23
6	18 55 12	13 44 50	7♈ 2	26	29	2	29	7	0	26	23
7	18 59 8	14 42 2	20 1	28	0♊	2	29	7	0	26	23
8	19 3 5	15 39 15	2♉40	0♋	1	2 D	29	7	0	26	23
9	19 7 1	16 36 27	15 3	2	2	2	29	7	0	26	23
10	19 10 58	17 33 41	27 13	3	3	2	29	7	0	26	23
11	19 14 55	18 30 54	9♊15	5	4	2	29	8	0	26	23
12	19 18 51	19 28 9	21 11	7	5	2	0♎	8	0	26	23
13	19 22 48	20 25 23	3♋ 4	9	6	2	0	8	0	26	23
14	19 26 44	21 22 38	14 56	11	8	2	0	8	0	26	23
15	19 30 41	22 19 53	26 47	13	9	2	0	8	0	26	23
16	19 34 37	23 17 8	8♌41	16	10	2	0	8	1	26	23
17	19 38 34	24 14 24	20 37	18	11	2	0	8	1	26	23
18	19 42 30	25 11 40	2♍40	20	12	2	0	8	1	26	23
19	19 46 27	26 8 56	14 51	22	13	2	0	8	1	26	23
20	19 50 24	27 6 12	27 13	24	14	3	1	8	1	26	23
21	19 54 20	28 3 29	9♎51	26	15	3	1	8	1	26	23
22	19 58 17	29 0 46	22 47	28	16	3	1	8	1	26	23
23	20 2 13	29 58 3	6♏ 7	0♌	17	3	1	8	1	26	23
24	20 6 10	0♌55 21	19 53	3	19	3	1	8	1	26	23
25	20 10 6	1 52 39	4♐ 5	5	20	4	1	8	1	26	23
26	20 14 3	2 49 57	18 42	7	21	4	2	8	1	26	23
27	20 17 59	3 47 16	3♑40	9	22	4	2	8	1	26	23
28	20 21 56	4 44 36	18 50	11	23	4	2	8	1	26	23
29	20 25 53	5 41 56	4♒ 4	13	24	5	2	8	1	26	23
30	20 29 49	6 39 16	19 9	15	25	5	2	9	1	26	23
31	20 33 46	7 36 38	3♓58	17	26	5	2	9	1	26	23

THE SUN ENTERS THE SIGN OF LEO ON JUL 23 AT 00:49.

DAY	TIME	☉	☽	☿	♀	♂	♃	♄	♅	♆	♇
	h m s	° ' "	° '	°	°	°	°	°	°	°	°
A 1	20 37 42	8♌34 1	18♓23	19♌	27♊	5♐	2♎	9♉	1♎	26♏R	23♍
U 2	20 41 39	9 31 24	2♈20	21	29	6	3	9	1	26	23
G 3	20 45 35	10 28 49	15 50	22	0♋	6	3	9	1	26	23
U 4	20 49 32	11 26 15	28 55	24	1	6	3	9	1	26	23
S 5	20 53 28	12 23 42	11♉36	26	2	7	3	9	1	26	23
T 6	20 57 25	13 21 10	23 58	27	3	7	3	9	1	26	23
7	21 1 22	14 18 40	6♊ 8	0♍	4	7	3	9	1	26 D	23
8	21 5 18	15 16 11	18 8	1	5	8	4	9	1	26	24
9	21 9 15	16 13 43	0♋ 1	3	7	8	4	9	2	26	24
10	21 13 11	17 11 17	11 52	5	8	8	4	9	2	26	24
11	21 17 8	18 8 52	23 44	7	9	9	4	9	2	26	24
12	21 21 4	19 6 28	5♌38	8	10	9	4	9	2	26	24
13	21 25 1	20 4 5	17 38	10	11	10	5	9	2	26	24
14	21 28 58	21 1 44	29 43	11	12	10	5	9	2	26	24
15	21 32 54	21 59 23	11♍57	13	13	10	5	9	2	26	24
16	21 36 51	22 57 4	24 20	14	15	11	5	9	2	26	24
17	21 40 47	23 54 46	6♎55	16	16	11	5	9	2	26	24
18	21 44 44	24 52 29	19 43	17	17	12	5	9	2	26	24
19	21 48 40	25 50 13	2♏48	19	18	12	6	9	2	26	24
20	21 52 37	26 47 59	16 10	20	19	13	6	9	2	26	24
21	21 56 33	27 45 45	29 53	22	20	13	6	9 R	2	26	24
22	22 0 30	28 43 33	13♐55	23	22	13	6	9	2	26	24
23	22 4 27	29 41 22	28 17	25	23	14	6	9	2	26	24
24	22 8 23	0♍39 11	12♑56	26	24	14	7	9	2	26	24
25	22 12 20	1 37 3	27 46	27	25	15	7	9	2	26	24
26	22 16 16	2 34 55	12♒40	28	26	15	7	9	2	26	24
27	22 20 13	3 32 49	27 30	0♎	28	16	7	9	2	26	24
28	22 24 9	4 30 44	12♓ 9	1	29	16	7	9	3	26	24
29	22 28 6	5 28 41	26 29	2	0♌	17	8	9	3	26	24
30	22 32 2	6 26 39	10♈28	3	1	17	8	9	3	26	24
31	22 35 59	7 24 40	24 1	4	2	18	8	9	3	26	24

THE SUN ENTERS THE SIGN OF VIRGO ON AUG 23 AT 07:44.

DAY	TIME	☉	☽	☿	♀	♂	♃	♄	♅	♆	♇
	h m s	° ' "	° '	°	°	°	°	°	°	°	°
S 1	22 39 55	8♍22 42	7♉ 9	5♎	3♌	18♐	8♎	9♉R	3♎	26♏	24♍
E 2	22 43 52	9 20 46	19 55	6	5	19	8	9	3	26	24
P 3	22 47 49	10 18 52	2♊22	7	6	19	9	9	3	26	24
T 4	22 51 45	11 17 0	14 33	8	7	20	9	9	3	26	24
E 5	22 55 42	12 15 10	26 33	9	8	21	9	9	3	26	24
M 6	22 59 38	13 13 22	8♋26	10	9	21	9	9	3	26	25
B 7	23 3 35	14 11 36	20 18	11	11	22	9	9	3	26	25
E 8	23 7 31	15 9 52	2♌11	12	12	22	10	9	3	26	25
R 9	23 11 28	16 8 10	14 9	12	13	23	10	9	3	26	25
10	23 15 24	17 6 29	26 16	13	14	23	10	9	3	26	25
11	23 19 21	18 4 51	8♍32	13	15	24	10	9	3	26	25
12	23 23 18	19 3 14	21 1	14	17	24	10	9	3	26	25
13	23 27 14	20 1 40	3♎42	14	18	25	11	8	3	26	25
14	23 31 11	21 0 7	16 37	15	19	26	11	8	4	26	25
15	23 35 7	21 58 36	29 46	15	20	26	11	8	4	26	25
16	23 39 4	22 57 6	13♏ 8	15 R	21	27	11	8	4	26	25
17	23 43 0	23 55 38	26 44	15	23	27	11	8	4	26	25
18	23 46 57	24 54 12	10♐33	15	24	28	12	8	4	26	25
19	23 50 53	25 52 48	24 33	15	25	29	12	8	4	26	25
20	23 54 50	26 51 25	8♑45	14	26	29	12	8	4	26	25
21	23 58 47	27 50 4	23 5	14	27	0♑	12	8	4	26	25
22	0 2 43	28 48 45	7♒30	13	29	0	13	8	4	26	25
23	0 6 40	29 47 27	21 57	12	0♍	1	13	8	4	27	25
24	0 10 36	0♎46 11	6♓22	12	1	2	13	8	4	27	25
25	0 14 33	1 44 56	20 38	11	2	3	13	8	4	27	25
26	0 18 29	2 43 44	4♈42	10	3	3	13	8	4	27	25
27	0 22 26	3 42 34	18 29	9	5	4	14	8	4	27	25
28	0 26 22	4 41 25	1♉57	8	6	4	14	8	4	27	25
29	0 30 19	5 40 19	15 4	7	7	5	14	8	4	27	25
30	0 34 16	6 39 16	27 51	5	8	5	14	8	5	27	25

THE SUN ENTERS THE SIGN OF LIBRA ON SEP 23 AT 05:08.

SIDEREAL SUN MOON MERCURY VENUS MARS JUPITER SATURN URANUS NEPTUNE PLUTO

DAY	TIME	☉	☽	☿	♀	♂	♃	♄	♅	♆	♇
	h m s	° ' "	° '	°	°	°	°	°	°	°	°
O 1	0 38 12	7♎38 14	10♊19	4♎R	10♍	6♑	14♎	8♉R	5♎	27♏	25♍
C 2	0 42 9	8 37 15	22 32	3	11	7	15	8	5	27	25
T 3	0 46 5	9 36 18	4♋33	2	12	7	15	7	5	27	25
O 4	0 50 2	10 35 23	16 27	2	13	8	15	7	5	27	26
B 5	0 53 58	11 34 31	28 18	1	14	9	15	7	5	27	26
E 6	0 57 55	12 33 40	10♌12	0	16	9	16	7	5	27	26
R 7	1 1 51	13 32 53	22 13	0	17	10	16	7	5	27	26
8	1 5 48	14 32 7	4♍25	0 D	18	11	16	7	5	27	26
9	1 9 45	15 31 23	16 51	0	19	11	16	7	5	27	26
10	1 13 41	16 30 42	29 34	0	21	12	16	7	5	27	26
11	1 17 38	17 30 3	12♎35	0	22	13	17	7	5	27	26
12	1 21 34	18 29 26	25 53	1	23	13	17	7	5	27	26
13	1 25 31	19 28 50	9♏28	2	24	14	17	7	5	27	26
14	1 29 27	20 28 17	23 17	2	26	15	17	7	5	27	26
15	1 33 24	21 27 46	7♐16	3	27	15	18	7	5	27	26
16	1 37 20	22 27 17	21 23	4	28	16	18	7	6	27	26
17	1 41 17	23 26 49	5♑33	6	29	17	18	6	6	27	26
18	1 45 14	24 26 24	19 45	7	1♎	17	18	6	6	27	26
19	1 49 10	25 25 59	3♒55	8	2	18	18	6	6	27	26
20	1 53 7	26 25 37	18 2	10	3	19	19	6	6	27	26
21	1 57 3	27 25 16	2♓ 5	11	4	20	19	6	6	27	26
22	2 1 0	28 24 57	16 1	13	5	20	19	6	6	27	26
23	2 4 56	29 24 39	29 50	14	7	21	19	6	6	27	26
24	2 8 53	0♏24 24	13♈29	16	8	22	19	6	6	27	26
25	2 12 49	1 24 10	26 55	17	9	22	20	6	6	27	26
26	2 16 46	2 23 58	10♉ 8	19	10	23	20	6	6	27	26
27	2 20 43	3 23 49	23 5	21	12	24	20	6	6	28	26
28	2 24 39	4 23 41	5♊46	22	13	24	20	6	6	28	26
29	2 28 36	5 23 36	18 12	24	14	25	21	5	6	28	26
30	2 32 32	6 23 32	0♋24	26	15	26	21	5	6	28	26
31	2 36 29	7 23 31	12 24	27	17	27	21	5	6	28	26

THE SUN ENTERS THE SIGN OF SCORPIO ON OCT 23 AT 14:12.

DAY	TIME	☉	☽	☿	♀	♂	♃	♄	♅	♆	♇
	h m s	° ' "	° '	°	°	°	°	°	°	°	°
N 1	2 40 25	8♏23 32	24♋17	29♎	18♎	27♑	21♎	5♉R	6♎	28♏	26♍
O 2	2 44 22	9 23 35	6♌ 7	0♏	19	28	21	5	7	28	26
V 3	2 48 18	10 23 40	18 0	2	20	29	22	5	7	28	27
E 4	2 52 15	11 23 47	0♍ 0	4	22	29	22	5	7	28	27
M 5	2 56 12	12 23 56	12 12	5	23	0♒	22	5	7	28	27
B 6	3 0 8	13 24 7	24 42	7	24	1	22	5	7	28	27
E 7	3 4 5	14 24 21	7♎33	9	25	2	22	5	7	28	27
R 8	3 8 1	15 24 36	20 47	10	27	2	23	5	7	28	27
9	3 11 58	16 24 53	4♏25	12	28	3	23	5	7	28	27
10	3 15 54	17 25 12	18 24	14	29	4	23	5	7	28	27
11	3 19 51	18 25 32	2♐41	15	0♏	4	23	4	7	28	27
12	3 23 47	19 25 55	17 10	17	2	5	23	4	7	28	27
13	3 27 44	20 26 19	1♑44	18	3	6	24	4	7	28	27
14	3 31 41	21 26 44	16 15	20	4	7	24	4	7	28	27
15	3 35 37	22 27 11	0♒40	22	5	7	24	4	7	28	27
16	3 39 34	23 27 39	14 54	23	7	8	24	4	7	28	27
17	3 43 30	24 28 8	28 55	25	8	9	24	4	7	28	27
18	3 47 27	25 28 38	12♓43	26	9	10	25	4	7	28	27
19	3 51 23	26 29 10	26 20	28	10	10	25	4	7	28	27
20	3 55 20	27 29 43	9♈44	0♐	12	11	25	4	7	28	27
21	3 59 16	28 30 17	22 58	1	13	12	25	4	8	28	27
22	4 3 13	29 30 52	6♉ 2	3	14	13	25	4	8	28	27
23	4 7 10	0♐31 29	18 54	4	15	13	26	4	8	29	27
24	4 11 6	1 32 7	1♊35	6	17	14	26	4	8	29	27
25	4 15 3	2 32 47	14 4	7	18	15	26	3	8	29	27
26	4 18 59	3 33 28	26 22	9	19	15	26	3	8	29	27
27	4 22 56	4 34 11	8♋28	11	20	16	26	3	8	29	27
28	4 26 52	5 34 55	20 26	12	22	17	27	3	8	29	27
29	4 30 49	6 35 40	2♌17	14	23	18	27	3	8	29	27
30	4 34 45	7 36 27	14 5	15	24	18	27	3	8	29	27

THE SUN ENTERS THE SIGN OF SAGITTARIUS ON NOV 22 AT 11:32.

DAY	TIME	☉	☽	☿	♀	♂	♃	♄	♅	♆	♇
	h m s	° ' "	° '	°	°	°	°	°	°	°	°
D 1	4 38 42	8♐37 15	25♌55	17♐	25♏	19♒	27♎	3♉R	8♎	29♏	27♍
E 2	4 42 39	9 38 5	7♍52	18	27	20	27	3	8	29	27
C 3	4 46 35	10 38 56	20 1	20	28	21	28	3	8	29	27
E 4	4 50 32	11 39 48	2♎28	21	29	21	28	3	8	29	27
M 5	4 54 28	12 40 42	15 18	23	0♐	22	28	3	8	29	27
B 6	4 58 25	13 41 37	28 35	25	2	23	28	3	8	29	27
E 7	5 2 21	14 42 33	12♏20	26	3	24	28	3	8	29	27
R 8	5 6 18	15 43 31	26 33	28	4	24	29	3	8	29	27
9	5 10 14	16 44 29	11♐ 9	29	6	25	29	3	8	29	27
10	5 14 11	17 45 29	26 2	1♑	7	26	29	3	8	29	27
11	5 18 8	18 46 29	11♑ 2	2	8	27	29	3	8	29	27
12	5 22 4	19 47 31	26 0	4	9	27	29	3	8	29	27
13	5 26 1	20 48 32	10♒47	5	11	28	29	2	8	29	27
14	5 29 57	21 49 35	25 16	7	12	29	0♏	2	8	29	27
15	5 33 54	22 50 37	9♓26	8	13	0♓	0	2	8	29	27
16	5 37 50	23 51 40	23 15	10	14	0	0	2	8	29	27
17	5 41 47	24 52 44	6♈45	11	16	1	0	2	8	29	27
18	5 45 44	25 53 48	19 57	13	17	2	0	2	8	29	27
19	5 49 40	26 54 52	2♉54	14	18	3	0	2	8	29	27
20	5 53 37	27 55 56	15 38	16	19	3	1	2	9	29	27
21	5 57 33	28 57 1	28 12	17	21	4	1	2	9	0♐	27
22	6 1 30	29 58 6	10♊36	18	22	5	1	2	9	0	27
23	6 5 26	0♑59 12	22 51	20	23	6	1	2	9	0	27
24	6 9 23	2 0 18	4♋57	21	24	6	1	2	9	0	27
25	6 13 19	3 1 24	16 57	22	26	7	1	2	9	0	27
26	6 17 16	4 2 31	28 50	24	27	8	1	2	9	0	27
27	6 21 13	5 3 38	10♌39	25	28	9	2	2	9	0	27
28	6 25 9	6 4 46	22 27	26	29	9	2	2	9	0	27
29	6 29 6	7 5 54	4♍16	27	1♑	10	2	2	9	0	27
30	6 33 2	8 7 2	16 12	28	2	11	2	2	9	0	27 R
31	6 36 59	9 8 11	28 19	28	3	11	2	2	9	0	27

THE SUN ENTERS THE SIGN OF CAPRICORN ON DEC 22 AT 00:45.

♈ ARIES ♉ TAURUS ♊ GEMINI ♋ CANCER ♌ LEO ♍ VIRGO ♎ LIBRA ♏ SCORPIO ♐ SAGITTARIUS ♑ CAPRICORN ♒ AQUARIUS ♓ PISCES

1970

SIDEREAL SUN MOON MERCURY VENUS MARS JUPITER SATURN URANUS NEPTUNE PLUTO

DAY	TIME	☉	☽	☿	♀	♂	♃	♄	♅	♆	♇
	h m s	° ' "	° '	°	°	°	°	°	°	°	°
J 1	6 40 55	10♑ 9 20	10♎42	29♑	4♑	12♓	2♏	2♉R	9♎	0♐	27♍R
A 2	6 44 52	11 10 30	23 26	0♒	6	13	2	2	9	0	27
N 3	6 48 48	12 11 40	6♏37	0	7	14	3	2 D	9	0	27
U 4	6 52 45	13 12 50	20 17	0 R	8	14	3	2	9	0	27
A 5	6 56 42	14 14 0	4♐27	0	9	15	3	2	9	0	27
R 6	7 0 38	15 15 11	19 5	0	11	16	3	2	9	0	27
Y 7	7 4 35	16 16 22	4♑ 5	29♑	12	17	3	2	9	0	27
8	7 8 31	17 17 32	19 19	29	13	17	3	2	9	0	27
9	7 12 28	18 18 43	4♒34	28	15	18	3	2	9	0	27
10	7 16 24	19 19 53	19 41	27	16	19	3	2	9	0	27
11	7 20 21	20 21 2	4♓31	26	17	20	4	2	9	0	27
12	7 24 18	21 22 11	18 58	25	18	20	4	2	9	0	27
13	7 28 14	22 23 20	3♈ 0	23	20	21	4	2	9 R	0	27
14	7 32 11	23 24 27	16 36	22	21	22	4	2	9	0	27
15	7 36 7	24 25 34	29 49	21	22	23	4	2	9	0	27
16	7 40 4	25 26 40	12♉41	19	23	23	4	2	9	0	27
17	7 44 0	26 27 46	25 16	18	25	24	4	2	9	0	27
18	7 47 57	27 28 51	7♊38	17	26	25	4	2	9	0	27
19	7 51 53	28 29 55	19 50	16	27	26	4	2	9	0	27
20	7 55 50	29 30 58	1♋53	15	28	26	5	2	9	0	27
21	7 59 47	0♒32 1	13 50	15	0♒	27	5	2	9	0	27
22	8 3 43	1 33 3	25 43	14	1	28	5	2	9	0	27
23	8 7 40	2 34 4	7♌33	14	2	29	5	2	9	0	27
24	8 11 36	3 35 4	19 22	14 D	3	29	5	2	9	0	27
25	8 15 33	4 36 4	1♍12	14	5	0♈	5	2	9	1	27
26	8 19 29	5 37 2	13 6	14	6	1	5	3	9	1	27
27	8 23 26	6 38 0	25 6	14	7	2	5	3	9	1	27
28	8 27 22	7 38 58	7♎16	15	8	2	5	3	9	1	27
29	8 31 19	8 39 55	19 40	15	10	3	5	3	9	1	27
30	8 35 16	9 40 51	2♏22	16	11	4	5	3	9	1	27
31	8 39 12	10 41 46	15 27	16	12	5	5	3	9	1	27

THE SUN ENTERS THE SIGN OF AQUARIUS ON JAN 20 AT 11:25.

DAY	TIME	☉	☽	☿	♀	♂	♃	♄	♅	♆	♇
	h m s	° ' "	° '	°	°	°	°	°	°	°	°
F 1	8 43 9	11♒42 41	28♏57	17♑	13♒	5♈	5♏	3♉	9♎R	1♐	27♍R
E 2	8 47 5	12 43 35	12♐55	18	15	6	5	3	9	1	27
B 3	8 51 2	13 44 28	27 20	18	16	7	6	3	9	1	27
R 4	8 54 58	14 45 21	12♑ 9	19	17	7	6	3	9	1	27
U 5	8 58 55	15 46 12	27 15	20	18	8	6	3	9	1	27
A 6	9 2 51	16 47 3	12♒30	21	20	9	6	3	9	1	27
R 7	9 6 48	17 47 52	27 43	22	21	10	6	3	9	1	27
Y 8	9 10 45	18 48 40	12♓44	23	22	10	6	3	8	1	27
9	9 14 41	19 49 26	27 25	25	23	11	6	3	8	1	27
10	9 18 38	20 50 11	11♈41	26	25	12	6	3	8	1	27
11	9 22 34	21 50 54	25 30	27	26	13	6	3	8	1	27
12	9 26 31	22 51 36	8♉52	28	27	13	6	3	8	1	27
13	9 30 27	23 52 16	21 50	29	28	14	6	4	8	1	27
14	9 34 24	24 52 54	4♊26	1♒	0♓	15	6	4	8	1	27
15	9 38 20	25 53 31	16 45	2	1	16	6	4	8	1	27
16	9 42 17	26 54 6	28 51	3	2	16	6	4	8	1	27
17	9 46 14	27 54 40	10♋48	5	3	17	6	4	8	1	27
18	9 50 10	28 55 11	22 40	6	5	18	6	4	8	1	27
19	9 54 7	29 55 41	4♌29	7	6	18	6 R	4	8	1	27
20	9 58 3	0♓56 10	16 18	9	7	19	6	4	8	1	27
21	10 2 0	1 56 36	28 10	10	8	20	6	4	8	1	27
22	10 5 56	2 57 1	10♍ 6	12	10	21	6	4	8	1	27
23	10 9 53	3 57 24	22 9	13	11	21	6	4	8	1	27
24	10 13 49	4 57 46	4♎20	14	12	22	6	4	8	1	27
25	10 17 46	5 58 6	16 41	16	13	23	6	4	8	1	27
26	10 21 43	6 58 25	29 16	18	15	23	6	5	8	1	27
27	10 25 39	7 58 42	12♏ 5	19	16	24	6	5	8	1	27
28	10 29 36	8 58 58	25 12	21	17	25	6	5	8	1	27

THE SUN ENTERS THE SIGN OF PISCES ON FEB 19 AT 01:42.

DAY	TIME	☉	☽	☿	♀	♂	♃	♄	♅	♆	♇
	h m s	° ' "	° '	°	°	°	°	°	°	°	°
M 1	10 33 32	9♓59 12	8♐38	22♒	18♓	26♈	6♏R	5♉	8♎R	1♐	26♍R
A 2	10 37 29	10 59 25	22 26	24	20	26	6	5	8	1	26
R 3	10 41 25	11 59 37	6♑35	25	21	27	6	5	8	1 R	26
C 4	10 45 22	12 59 47	21 4	27	22	28	6	5	8	1	26
H 5	10 49 18	13 59 55	5♒49	29	23	29	6	5	8	1	26
6	10 53 15	15 0 2	20 45	0♓	25	29	6	5	8	1	26
7	10 57 12	16 0 7	5♓44	2	26	0♉	6	5	8	1	26
8	11 1 8	17 0 10	20 37	4	27	1	6	5	8	1	26
9	11 5 5	18 0 11	5♈18	5	28	1	6	6	8	1	26
10	11 9 1	19 0 10	19 39	7	0☉	2	5	6	8	1	26
11	11 12 58	20 0 7	3♉36	9	1♈	3	5	6	7	1	26
12	11 16 54	21 0 2	17 7	11	2	4	5	6	7	1	26
13	11 20 51	21 59 55	0♊12	12	3	4	5	6	7	1	26
14	11 24 47	22 59 46	12 54	14	5	5	5	6	7	1	26
15	11 28 44	23 59 34	25 16	16	6	6	5	6	7	1	26
16	11 32 41	24 59 21	7♋23	18	7	6	5	6	7	1	26
17	11 36 37	25 59 5	19 19	20	8	7	5	6	7	1	26
18	11 40 34	26 58 46	1♌ 9	22	10	8	5	7	7	1	26
19	11 44 30	27 58 26	12 57	24	11	9	5	7	7	1	26
20	11 48 27	28 58 3	24 47	25	12	9	5	7	7	1	26
21	11 52 23	29 57 38	6♍44	27	13	10	5	7	7	1	26
22	11 56 20	0♈57 11	18 48	29	15	11	5	7	7	1	26
23	12 0 16	1 56 42	1♎ 3	1♈	16	11	5	7	7	1	26
24	12 4 13	2 56 11	13 30	3	17	12	4	7	7	1	26
25	12 8 9	3 55 38	26 10	5	18	13	4	7	7	1	26
26	12 12 6	4 55 3	9♏ 4	7	20	13	4	7	7	1	26
27	12 16 3	5 54 26	22 11	9	21	14	4	8	7	1	26
28	12 19 59	6 53 48	5♐31	11	22	15	4	8	7	1	26
29	12 23 56	7 53 7	19 5	13	23	16	4	8	7	1	26
30	12 27 52	8 52 25	2♑53	16	25	16	4	8	7	1	26
31	12 31 49	9 51 41	16 54	18	26	17	4	8	7	1	26

THE SUN ENTERS THE SIGN OF ARIES ON MAR 21 AT 00:56.

DAY	TIME	☉	☽	☿	♀	♂	♃	♄	♅	♆	♇
	h m s	° ' "	° '	°	°	°	°	°	°	°	°
A 1	12 35 45	10♈50 56	1♒ 6	20♈	27♈	18♉	4♏R	8♉	7♎R	1♐R	26♍R
P 2	12 39 42	11 50 9	15 29	22	28	18	3	8	7	1	26
R 3	12 43 38	12 49 19	29 59	24	29	19	3	8	6	1	26
I 4	12 47 35	13 48 28	14♓33	26	1♉	20	3	8	6	1	26
L 5	12 51 32	14 47 35	29 4	27	2	20	3	9	6	1	26
6	12 55 28	15 46 40	13♈28	29	3	21	3	9	6	1	26
7	12 59 25	16 45 43	27 38	1♉	4	22	3	9	6	1	26
8	13 3 21	17 44 45	11♉30	3	6	23	3	9	6	1	25
9	13 7 18	18 43 43	25 1	5	7	23	3	9	6	1	25
10	13 11 14	19 42 40	8♊ 8	7	8	24	3	9	6	1	25
11	13 15 11	20 41 35	20 53	8	9	25	2	9	6	1	25
12	13 19 7	21 40 27	3♋18	10	11	25	2	9	6	0	25
13	13 23 4	22 39 17	15 27	11	12	26	2	10	6	0	25
14	13 27 1	23 38 5	27 24	13	13	27	2	10	6	0	25
15	13 30 57	24 36 51	9♌14	14	14	27	2	10	6	0	25
16	13 34 54	25 35 34	21 3	15	15	28	2	10	6	0	25
17	13 38 50	26 34 15	2♍55	16	17	29	2	10	6	0	25
18	13 42 47	27 32 54	14 55	17	18	29	2	10	6	0	25
19	13 46 43	28 31 31	27 7	18	19	0♊	1	10	6	0	25
20	13 50 40	29 30 5	9♎34	19	20	1	1	10	6	0	25
21	13 54 36	0♉28 38	22 18	20	22	2	1	11	6	0	25
22	13 58 33	1 27 9	5♏19	21	23	2	1	11	6	0	25
23	14 2 30	2 25 38	18 36	21	24	3	1	11	6	0	25
24	14 6 26	3 24 5	2♐ 8	22	25	4	1	11	6	0	25
25	14 10 23	4 22 30	15 51	22	27	4	1	11	6	0	25
26	14 14 19	5 20 54	29 44	22	28	5	1	11	6	0	25
27	14 18 16	6 19 16	13♑44	22	29	6	0	11	6	0	25
28	14 22 12	7 17 37	27 49	22 R	0♊	6	0	11	6	0	25
29	14 26 9	8 15 56	11♒56	22	1	7	0	12	5	0	25
30	14 30 5	9 14 14	26 5	22	3	8	0	12	5	0	25

THE SUN ENTERS THE SIGN OF TAURUS ON APR 20 AT 12:15.

DAY	TIME	☉	☽	☿	♀	♂	♃	♄	♅	♆	♇
	h m s	° ' "	° '	°	°	°	°	°	°	°	°
M 1	14 34 2	10♉12 30	10♓15	22♉R	4♊	8♊	0♏R	12♉	5♎R	0♐R	25♍R
A 2	14 37 59	11 10 44	24 23	22	5	9	0	12	5	0	25
Y 3	14 41 55	12 8 57	8♈28	22	6	10	0	12	5	0	25
4	14 45 52	13 7 9	22 27	21	7	10	0	12	5	0	25
5	14 49 48	14 5 19	6♉15	21	9	11	29♎	12	5	0	25
6	14 53 45	15 3 27	19 50	20	10	12	29	13	5	0	25
7	14 57 41	16 1 34	3♊ 8	20	11	12	29	13	5	0	25
8	15 1 38	16 59 39	16 8	19	12	13	29	13	5	0	25
9	15 5 34	17 57 42	28 48	19	14	14	29	13	5	0	25
10	15 9 31	18 55 43	11♋11	18	15	14	29	13	5	0	25
11	15 13 28	19 53 43	23 20	17	16	15	29	13	5	0	25
12	15 17 24	20 51 41	5♌16	17	17	16	29	13	5	0	25
13	15 21 21	21 49 37	17 6	16	18	16	28	13	5	0	25
14	15 25 17	22 47 31	28 55	16	20	17	28	14	5	0	25
15	15 29 14	23 45 23	10♍48	15	21	18	28	14	5	0	25
16	15 33 10	24 43 13	22 51	15	22	18	28	14	5	0	25
17	15 37 7	25 41 2	5♎ 7	14	23	19	28	14	5	0	25
18	15 41 3	26 38 50	17 42	14	24	20	28	14	5	0	25
19	15 45 0	27 36 35	0♏38	14	26	20	28	14	5	0	25
20	15 48 57	28 34 19	13 56	13	27	21	28	14	5	0	25
21	15 52 53	29 32 2	27 35	13	28	22	28	14	5	0	25
22	15 56 50	0♊29 44	11♐32	13 D	29	22	28	15	5	29♏	25
23	16 0 46	1 27 24	25 42	13	0♋	23	28	15	5	29	25
24	16 4 43	2 25 3	10♑ 1	13	2	24	27	15	5	29	25
25	16 8 39	3 22 41	24 22	13	3	24	27	15	5	29	25
26	16 12 36	4 20 18	8♒41	14	4	25	27	15	5	29	25
27	16 16 32	5 17 54	22 56	14	5	26	27	15	5	29	25
28	16 20 29	6 15 29	7♓ 3	14	6	26	27	15	5	29	25
29	16 24 26	7 13 3	21 3	15	8	27	27	15	5	29	25
30	16 28 22	8 10 36	4♈55	15	9	28	27	16	5	29	25
31	16 32 19	9 8 9	18 39	16	10	28	27	16	5	29	25

THE SUN ENTERS THE SIGN OF GEMINI ON MAY 21 AT 11:38.

DAY	TIME	☉	☽	☿	♀	♂	♃	♄	♅	♆	♇
	h m s	° ' "	° '	°	°	°	°	°	°	°	°
J 1	16 36 15	10♊ 5 41	2♉13	17♉	11♋	29♊	27♎R	16♉	5♎R	29♏R	25♍R
U 2	16 40 12	11 3 12	15 37	17	12	0♋	27	16	5	29	25
N 3	16 44 8	12 0 42	28 49	18	14	0	27	16	5	29	25
E 4	16 48 5	12 58 11	11♊48	19	15	1	27	16	5	29	25
5	16 52 2	13 55 39	24 32	20	16	2	27	16	5	29	25 D
6	16 55 58	14 53 6	7♋ 2	21	17	2	27	16	5	29	25
7	16 59 55	15 50 32	19 18	22	18	3	26	17	5	29	25
8	17 3 51	16 47 57	1♌21	23	20	4	26	17	5	29	25
9	17 7 48	17 45 21	13 15	24	21	4	26	17	5	29	25
10	17 11 44	18 42 45	25 4	25	22	5	26	17	5	29	25
11	17 15 41	19 40 7	6♍52	27	23	6	26	17	5	29	25
12	17 19 37	20 37 27	18 44	28	24	6	26	17	5 D	29	25
13	17 23 34	21 34 47	0♎46	29	26	7	26	17	5	29	25
14	17 27 31	22 32 6	13 4	1♊	27	8	26	17	5	29	25
15	17 31 27	23 29 24	25 41	2	28	8	26	17	5	29	25
16	17 35 24	24 26 42	8♏42	4	29	9	26	18	5	29	25
17	17 39 20	25 23 58	22 9	5	0♌	10	26	18	5	29	25
18	17 43 17	26 21 14	6♐ 2	7	1	10	26	18	5	29	25
19	17 47 13	27 18 29	20 17	8	3	11	26	18	5	29	25
20	17 51 10	28 15 44	4♑49	10	4	12	26	18	5	29	25
21	17 55 6	29 12 58	19 32	12	5	12	26	18	5	29	25
22	17 59 3	0♋10 12	4♒17	14	6	13	26	18	5	29	25
23	18 3 0	1 7 26	18 58	15	7	14	26 D	18	5	29	25
24	18 6 56	2 4 39	3♓29	17	9	14	26	18	5	29	25
25	18 10 53	3 1 52	17 47	19	10	15	26	19	5	29	25
26	18 14 49	3 59 6	1♈49	21	11	16	26	19	5	29	25
27	18 18 46	4 56 19	15 35	23	12	16	26	19	5	29	25
28	18 22 42	5 53 32	29 7	25	13	17	26	19	5	29	25
29	18 26 39	6 50 45	12♉24	27	14	18	26	19	5	29	25
30	18 30 35	7 47 59	25 28	29	16	18	26	19	5	29	25

THE SUN ENTERS THE SIGN OF CANCER ON JUN 21 AT 19:43.

♈ ARIES ♉ TAURUS ♊ GEMINI ♋ CANCER ♌ LEO ♍ VIRGO ♎ LIBRA ♏ SCORPIO ♐ SAGITTARIUS ♑ CAPRICORN ♒ AQUARIUS ♓ PISCES

SIDEREAL SUN MOON MERCURY VENUS MARS JUPITER SATURN URANUS NEPTUNE PLUTO

DAY	TIME	☉	☽	☿	♀	♂	♃	♄	♅	♆	♇
	h m s	° ' "	° '	°	°	°	°	°	°	°	°
J 1	18 34 32	8♋45 12	8♊20	2♋	17♌	19♋	26♎	19♉	5♎	29♏R	25♍
U 2	18 38 29	9 42 26	20 59	4	18	19	26	19	5	29	25
L 3	18 42 25	10 39 40	3♋26	6	19	20	26	19	5	28	25
Y 4	18 46 22	11 36 53	15 41	8	20	21	26	19	5	28	25
5	18 50 18	12 34 7	27 47	10	21	21	26	19	5	28	25
6	18 54 15	13 31 20	9♌43	12	23	22	26	20	5	28	25
7	18 58 11	14 28 33	21 34	15	24	23	26	20	5	28	25
8	19 2 8	15 25 47	3♍20	17	25	23	26	20	5	28	25
9	19 6 4	16 23 0	15 7	19	26	24	26	20	5	28	25
10	19 10 1	17 20 13	26 59	21	27	25	26	20	5	28	25
11	19 13 58	18 17 25	9♎ 1	23	28	25	27	20	5	28	25
12	19 17 54	19 14 38	21 17	25	29	26	27	20	5	28	25
13	19 21 51	20 11 51	3♏53	27	1♍	27	27	20	5	28	25
14	19 25 47	21 9 4	16 52	29	2	27	27	20	5	28	25
15	19 29 44	22 6 17	0♐19	1♌	3	28	27	20	5	28	25
16	19 33 40	23 3 30	14 14	3	4	29	27	20	5	28	25
17	19 37 37	24 0 43	28 35	5	5	29	27	21	5	28	25
18	19 41 34	24 57 57	13♑18	7	6	0♌	27	21	5	28	25
19	19 45 30	25 55 10	28 17	9	7	0	27	21	5	28	25
20	19 49 27	26 52 25	13♒21	11	9	1	27	21	5	28	25
21	19 53 23	27 49 40	28 22	13	10	2	27	21	5	28	25
22	19 57 20	28 46 55	13♓13	15	11	2	27	21	5	28	25
23	20 1 16	29 44 11	27 46	16	12	3	27	21	5	28	25
24	20 5 13	0♌41 28	12♈ 0	18	13	4	27	21	5	28	25
25	20 9 9	1 38 46	25 51	20	14	4	28	21	5	28	25
26	20 13 6	2 36 5	9♉21	22	15	5	28	21	5	28	25
27	20 17 3	3 33 25	22 31	23	16	6	28	21	6	28	25
28	20 20 59	4 30 46	5♊23	25	17	6	28	21	6	28	25
29	20 24 56	5 28 8	18 0	27	19	7	28	21	6	28	25
30	20 28 52	6 25 30	0♋23	28	20	8	28	21	6	28	25
31	20 32 49	7 22 54	12 36	0♍	21	8	28	22	6	28	25

THE SUN ENTERS THE SIGN OF LEO ON JUL 23 AT 06:38.

DAY	TIME	☉	☽	☿	♀	♂	♃	♄	♅	♆	♇
	h m s	° ' "	° '	°	°	°	°	°	°	°	°
A 1	20 36 45	8♌20 19	24♋39	1♍	22♍	9♌	28♎	22♉	6♎	28♏R	26♍
U 2	20 40 42	9 17 45	6♌35	3	23	9	28	22	6	28	26
G 3	20 44 38	10 15 11	18 25	4	24	10	28	22	6	28	26
U 4	20 48 35	11 12 38	0♍12	6	25	11	29	22	6	28	26
S 5	20 52 32	12 10 7	11 59	7	26	11	29	22	6	28	26
T 6	20 56 28	13 7 36	23 47	8	27	12	29	22	6	28	26
7	21 0 25	14 5 5	5♎41	10	28	13	29	22	6	28	26
8	21 4 21	15 2 36	17 45	11	0♎	13	29	22	6	28	26
9	21 8 18	16 0 7	0♏ 1	12	1	14	29	22	6	28	26
10	21 12 14	16 57 40	12 36	13	2	15	29	22	6	28 D	26
11	21 16 11	17 55 13	25 32	15	3	15	29	22	6	28	26
12	21 20 7	18 52 47	8♐53	16	4	16	29	22	6	28	26
13	21 24 4	19 50 22	22 41	17	5	16	0♏	22	6	28	26
14	21 28 1	20 47 58	6♑56	18	6	17	0	22	6	28	26
15	21 31 57	21 45 35	21 35	19	7	18	0	22	6	28	26
16	21 35 54	22 43 13	6♒34	20	8	18	0	22	6	28	26
17	21 39 50	23 40 52	21 44	21	9	19	0	22	6	28	26
18	21 43 47	24 38 33	6♓57	22	10	20	0	22	6	28	26
19	21 47 43	25 36 14	22 2	23	11	20	0	22	7	28	26
20	21 51 40	26 33 58	6♈51	24	12	21	1	22	7	28	26
21	21 55 36	27 31 42	21 18	24	13	22	1	22	7	28	26
22	21 59 33	28 29 29	5♉21	25	14	22	1	22	7	28	26
23	22 3 30	29 27 17	18 57	26	15	23	1	22	7	28	26
24	22 7 26	0♍25 7	2♊ 8	26	16	24	1	23	7	28	26
25	22 11 23	1 22 59	14 57	27	17	24	1	23	7	28	26
26	22 15 19	2 20 52	27 27	27	18	25	2	23	7	28	26
27	22 19 16	3 18 48	9♋41	28	19	25	2	23	7	28	26
28	22 23 12	4 16 45	21 44	28	20	26	2	23	7	28	26
29	22 27 9	5 14 44	3♌38	28	21	26	2	23	7	28	26
30	22 31 5	6 12 44	15 28	28 R	22	27	2	23	7	28	26
31	22 35 2	7 10 46	27 15	28	23	28	2	23	7	28	26

THE SUN ENTERS THE SIGN OF VIRGO ON AUG 23 AT 13:35.

DAY	TIME	☉	☽	☿	♀	♂	♃	♄	♅	♆	♇
	h m s	° ' "	° '	°	°	°	°	°	°	°	°
S 1	22 38 59	8♍ 8 50	9♍ 2	28♍R	24♎	29♌	2♏	23♉	7♎	28♏	27♍
E 2	22 42 55	9 6 55	20 52	28	25	29	3	23	7	28	27
P 3	22 46 52	10 5 2	2♎46	27	26	0♍	3	23	7	28	27
T 4	22 50 48	11 3 10	14 47	27	27	1	3	23 R	7	28	27
E 5	22 54 45	12 1 21	26 58	26	28	1	3	23	7	28	27
M 6	22 58 41	12 59 32	9♏21	26	29	2	3	23	8	28	27
B 7	23 2 38	13 57 45	21 58	25	0♏	2	4	23	8	28	27
E 8	23 6 34	14 56 0	4♐54	24	1	3	4	23	8	28	27
R 9	23 10 31	15 54 16	18 10	23	2	4	4	23	8	28	27
10	23 14 28	16 52 34	1♑48	22	3	4	4	23	8	28	27
11	23 18 24	17 50 54	15 50	21	4	5	4	23	8	28	27
12	23 22 21	18 49 14	0♒16	20	4	6	4	23	8	28	27
13	23 26 17	19 47 37	15 1	19	5	6	5	23	8	28	27
14	23 30 14	20 46 1	0♓ 2	18	6	7	5	23	8	28	27
15	23 34 10	21 44 26	15 9	17	7	7	5	23	8	28	27
16	23 38 7	22 42 54	0♈15	17	8	8	5	23	8	28	27
17	23 42 3	23 41 23	15 11	16	9	8	5	22	8	29	27
18	23 46 0	24 39 55	29 47	15	9	9	6	22	8	29	27
19	23 49 56	25 38 28	13♉59	15	10	10	6	22	8	29	27
20	23 53 53	26 37 4	27 44	14	11	11	6	22	8	29	27
21	23 57 50	27 35 42	11♊ 1	14	12	11	6	22	8	29	27
22	0 1 46	28 34 23	23 52	14 D	13	12	6	22	9	29	27
23	0 5 43	29 33 5	6♋22	14	13	13	6	22	9	29	27
24	0 9 39	0♎31 50	18 34	14	14	13	7	22	9	29	27
25	0 13 36	1 30 37	0♌32	15	15	14	7	22	9	29	27
26	0 17 32	2 29 26	12 23	15	15	14	7	22	9	29	27
27	0 21 29	3 28 17	24 10	16	16	15	7	22	9	29	27
28	0 25 25	4 27 11	5♍57	17	17	16	7	22	9	29	27
29	0 29 22	5 26 6	17 47	18	17	16	8	22	9	29	28
30	0 33 19	6 25 4	29 43	19	18	17	8	22	9	29	28

THE SUN ENTERS THE SIGN OF LIBRA ON SEP 23 AT 11:00.

SIDEREAL SUN MOON MERCURY VENUS MARS JUPITER SATURN URANUS NEPTUNE PLUTO

DAY	TIME	☉	☽	☿	♀	♂	♃	♄	♅	♆	♇
	h m s	° ' "	° '	°	°	°	°	°	°	°	°
O 1	0 37 15	7♎24 4	11♎48	20♍	19♏	18♍	8♏	22♉R	9♎	29♏	28♍
C 2	0 41 12	8 23 5	24 1	21	19	18	8	22	9	29	28
T 3	0 45 8	9 22 9	6♏26	23	20	19	8	22	9	29	28
O 4	0 49 5	10 21 15	19 3	24	20	20	9	22	9	29	28
B 5	0 53 1	11 20 22	1♐52	26	21	20	9	22	9	29	28
E 6	0 56 58	12 19 32	14 55	27	21	21	9	22	9	29	28
R 7	1 0 54	13 18 43	28 13	29	22	21	9	22	9	29	28
8	1 4 51	14 17 56	11♑47	0♎	22	22	9	22	10	29	28
9	1 8 48	15 17 11	25 39	2	23	23	10	22	10	29	28
10	1 12 44	16 16 27	9♒48	4	23	23	10	22	10	29	28
11	1 16 41	17 15 45	24 13	6	23	24	10	21	10	29	28
12	1 20 37	18 15 5	8♓52	7	24	25	10	21	10	29	28
13	1 24 34	19 14 27	23 41	9	24	25	11	21	10	29	28
14	1 28 30	20 13 50	8♈32	11	24	26	11	21	10	29	28
15	1 32 27	21 13 16	23 18	12	25	27	11	21	10	29	28
16	1 36 23	22 12 44	7♉50	14	25	27	11	21	10	29	28
17	1 40 20	23 12 13	22 3	16	25	28	11	21	10	29	28
18	1 44 17	24 11 46	5♊51	18	25	28	12	21	10	29	28
19	1 48 13	25 11 20	19 13	19	25	29	12	21	10	29	28
20	1 52 10	26 10 56	2♋ 8	21	25 R	0♎	12	21	10	29	28
21	1 56 6	27 10 35	14 40	23	25	0	12	21	10	29	28
22	2 0 3	28 10 16	26 53	25	25	1	12	21	10	29	28
23	2 3 59	29 9 59	8♌52	26	25	2	13	21	10	29	28
24	2 7 56	0♏ 9 45	20 42	28	25	2	13	21	11	0♐	28
25	2 11 52	1 9 33	2♍28	0♏	25	3	13	21	11	0	28
26	2 15 49	2 9 22	14 17	1	25	4	13	20	11	0	28
27	2 19 46	3 9 14	26 11	3	24	4	14	20	11	0	29
28	2 23 42	4 9 8	8♎15	5	24	5	14	20	11	0	29
29	2 27 39	5 9 4	20 31	6	24	5	14	20	11	0	29
30	2 31 35	6 9 3	3♏ 1	8	23	6	14	20	11	0	29
31	2 35 32	7 9 3	15 44	9	23	7	14	20	11	0	29

THE SUN ENTERS THE SIGN OF SCORPIO ON OCT 23 AT 20:05.

DAY	TIME	☉	☽	☿	♀	♂	♃	♄	♅	♆	♇
	h m s	° ' "	° '	°	°	°	°	°	°	°	°
N 1	2 39 28	8♏ 9 5	28♏41	11♏	23♏R	7♎	15♏	20♉R	11♎	0♐	29♍
O 2	2 43 25	9 9 9	11♐51	13	22	8	15	20	11	0	29
V 3	2 47 21	10 9 14	25 12	14	22	9	15	20	11	0	29
E 4	2 51 18	11 9 21	8♑44	16	21	9	15	20	11	0	29
M 5	2 55 15	12 9 30	22 25	17	21	10	16	20	11	0	29
B 6	2 59 11	13 9 41	6♒15	19	20	11	16	20	11	0	29
E 7	3 3 8	14 9 52	20 15	21	20	11	16	20	11	0	29
R 8	3 7 4	15 10 5	4♓24	22	19	12	16	19	11	0	29
9	3 11 1	16 10 20	18 42	24	19	12	16	19	11	0	29
10	3 14 57	17 10 36	3♈ 5	25	18	13	17	19	11	0	29
11	3 18 54	18 10 54	17 30	27	17	14	17	19	12	0	29
12	3 22 50	19 11 13	1♉53	28	17	14	17	19	12	0	29
13	3 26 47	20 11 34	16 7	0♐	16	15	17	19	12	0	29
14	3 30 44	21 11 56	0♊ 6	1	15	16	18	19	12	0	29
15	3 34 40	22 12 20	13 46	3	15	16	18	19	12	0	29
16	3 38 37	23 12 46	27 4	5	14	17	18	19	12	0	29
17	3 42 33	24 13 14	9♋59	6	14	17	18	19	12	0	29
18	3 46 30	25 13 43	22 31	8	13	18	18	19	12	0	29
19	3 50 26	26 14 15	4♌45	9	13	19	19	19	12	0	29
20	3 54 23	27 14 48	16 45	11	12	19	19	18	12	0	29
21	3 58 19	28 15 22	28 36	12	12	20	19	18	12	1	29
22	4 2 16	29 15 59	10♍24	14	11	21	19	18	12	1	29
23	4 6 13	0♐16 37	22 13	15	11	21	19	18	12	1	29
24	4 10 9	1 17 17	4♎10	17	11	22	20	18	12	1	29
25	4 14 6	2 17 58	16 19	18	11	23	20	18	12	1	29
26	4 18 2	3 18 41	28 44	19	10	23	20	18	12	1	29
27	4 21 59	4 19 25	11♏26	21	10	24	20	18	12	1	29
28	4 25 55	5 20 11	24 28	22	10	24	21	18	12	1	29
29	4 29 52	6 20 59	7♐47	24	10	25	21	18	12	1	29
30	4 33 48	7 21 48	21 21	25	10 D	26	21	18	12	1	29

THE SUN ENTERS THE SIGN OF SAGITTARIUS ON NOV 22 AT 17:26.

DAY	TIME	☉	☽	☿	♀	♂	♃	♄	♅	♆	♇
	h m s	° ' "	° '	°	°	°	°	°	°	°	°
D 1	4 37 45	8♐22 37	5♑ 8	27♐	10♏D	26♎	21♏	18♉R	13♎	1♐	29♍
E 2	4 41 42	9 23 28	19 3	28	10	27	21	18	13	1	29
C 3	4 45 38	10 24 20	3♒ 4	29	10	28	22	17	13	1	29
E 4	4 49 35	11 25 13	17 8	1♑	10	28	22	17	13	1	29
M 5	4 53 31	12 26 6	1♓13	2	10	29	22	17	13	1	29
B 6	4 57 28	13 27 0	15 18	3	10	0♏	22	17	13	1	29
E 7	5 1 24	14 27 55	29 23	5	10	0	23	17	13	1	0♎
R 8	5 5 21	15 28 51	13♈26	6	11	1	23	17	13	1	0
9	5 9 18	16 29 47	27 26	7	11	1	23	17	13	1	0
10	5 13 14	17 30 44	11♉21	8	11	2	23	17	13	1	0
11	5 17 11	18 31 41	25 8	9	12	3	23	17	13	1	0
12	5 21 7	19 32 40	8♊43	10	12	3	24	17	13	1	0
13	5 25 4	20 33 39	22 3	11	12	4	24	17	13	1	0
14	5 29 0	21 34 40	5♋ 7	12	13	5	24	17	13	1	0
15	5 32 57	22 35 41	17 52	13	13	5	24	17	13	1	0
16	5 36 53	23 36 42	0♌19	13	14	6	24	17	13	1	0
17	5 40 50	24 37 45	12 31	14	14	7	25	17	13	1	0
18	5 44 47	25 38 48	24 31	14	15	7	25	17	13	2	0
19	5 48 43	26 39 53	6♍22	14 R	16	8	25	16	13	2	0
20	5 52 40	27 40 58	18 10	14	16	8	25	16	13	2	0
21	5 56 36	28 42 3	29 59	14	17	9	25	16	13	2	0
22	6 0 33	29 43 10	11♎56	13	17	10	26	16	13	2	0
23	6 4 29	0♑44 17	24 6	13	18	10	26	16	13	2	0
24	6 8 26	1 45 25	6♏33	12	19	11	26	16	13	2	0
25	6 12 22	2 46 34	19 20	11	19	12	26	16	13	2	0
26	6 16 19	3 47 44	2♐31	10	20	12	26	16	13	2	0
27	6 20 16	4 48 53	16 4	9	21	13	27	16	13	2	0
28	6 24 12	5 50 4	29 59	7	22	14	27	16	13	2	0
29	6 28 9	6 51 14	14♑10	6	22	14	27	16	13	2	0
30	6 32 5	7 52 25	28 33	5	23	15	27	16	13	2	0
31	6 36 2	8 53 36	13♒ 2	3	24	15	27	16	13	2	0

THE SUN ENTERS THE SIGN OF CAPRICORN ON DEC 22 AT 06:37.

♈ ARIES ♉ TAURUS ♊ GEMINI ♋ CANCER ♌ LEO ♍ VIRGO ♎ LIBRA ♏ SCORPIO ♐ SAGITTARIUS ♑ CAPRICORN ♒ AQUARIUS ♓ PISCES

1971

SIDEREAL SUN MOON MERCURY VENUS MARS JUPITER SATURN URANUS NEPTUNE PLUTO

DAY	TIME	☉	☽	☿	♀	♂	♃	♄	♅	♆	♇
	h m s	° ' "	° '	°	°	°	°	°	°	°	°
J 1	6 39 58	9♑54 46	27♒31	2♑R	25♏	16♏	28♏	16♉R	13♎	2♐	0♎R
A 2	6 43 55	10 55 57	11♓55	1	26	17	28	16	13	2	0
N 3	6 47 51	11 57 7	26 11	0	26	17	28	16	13	2	0
U 4	6 51 48	12 58 17	10♈18	29♐	27	18	28	16	13	2	0
A 5	6 55 45	13 59 26	24 14	29	28	19	28	16	13	2	0
R 6	6 59 41	15 0 35	7♉59	28	29	19	29	16	13	2	0
Y 7	7 3 38	16 1 44	21 33	28	0♐	20	29	16	14	2	0
8	7 7 34	17 2 53	4♊54	28 D	1	20	29	16	14	2	0
9	7 11 31	18 4 1	18 3	28	2	21	29	16	14	2	0
10	7 15 27	19 5 9	0♋59	28	3	22	29	16	14	2	0
11	7 19 24	20 6 17	13 42	28	4	22	29	16	14	2	0
12	7 23 21	21 7 24	26 11	29	5	23	0♐	16	14	2	0
13	7 27 17	22 8 31	8♌28	29	6	24	0	16	14	2	0
14	7 31 14	23 9 37	20 33	0♑	6	24	0	16	14	2	0
15	7 35 10	24 10 43	2♍30	1	7	25	0	16	14	2	0
16	7 39 7	25 11 49	14 20	1	8	26	0	16	14	2	0
17	7 43 3	26 12 55	26 7	2	9	26	0	16 D	14	2	0
18	7 47 0	27 14 0	7♎56	3	10	27	1	16	14 R	2	0
19	7 50 56	28 15 5	19 52	4	11	27	1	16	14	2	0
20	7 54 53	29 16 10	2♏ 0	5	12	28	1	16	14	3	0
21	7 58 50	0♒17 14	14 24	6	13	29	1	16	14	3	0
22	8 2 46	1 18 18	27 9	7	14	29	1	16	14	3	0
23	8 6 43	2 19 22	10♐18	9	15	0♐	1	16	14	3	0
24	8 10 39	3 20 25	23 53	10	17	1	2	16	14	3	0
25	8 14 36	4 21 28	7♑54	11	18	1	2	16	14	3	0
26	8 18 32	5 22 30	22 18	12	19	2	2	16	14	3	0
27	8 22 29	6 23 31	7♒ 0	13	20	2	2	16	14	3	0
28	8 26 25	7 24 31	21 53	15	21	3	2	16	14	3	0
29	8 30 22	8 25 31	6♓49	16	22	4	2	16	14	3	0
30	8 34 19	9 26 29	21 40	17	23	4	2	16	14	3	29♍
31	8 38 15	10 27 25	6♈19	19	24	5	3	16	13	3	29

THE SUN ENTERS THE SIGN OF AQUARIUS ON JAN 20 AT 17:14.

DAY	TIME	☉	☽	☿	♀	♂	♃	♄	♅	♆	♇
	h m s	° ' "	° '	°	°	°	°	°	°	°	°
F 1	8 42 12	11♒28 21	20♈42	20♑	25♐	6♐	3♐	16♉	13♎R	3♐	29♍R
E 2	8 46 8	12 29 15	4♉45	22	26	6	3	16	13	3	29
B 3	8 50 5	13 30 8	18 29	23	27	7	3	16	13	3	29
R 4	8 54 1	14 31 0	1♊53	24	28	7	3	16	13	3	29
U 5	8 57 58	15 31 50	14 59	26	29	8	3	16	13	3	29
A 6	9 1 54	16 32 39	27 49	27	0♑	9	3	16	13	3	29
R 7	9 5 51	17 33 27	10♋25	29	2	9	4	16	13	3	29
Y 8	9 9 48	18 34 13	22 48	0♒	3	10	4	16	13	3	29
9	9 13 44	19 34 57	5♌ 1	2	4	11	4	16	13	3	29
10	9 17 41	20 35 40	17 4	3	5	11	4	16	13	3	29
11	9 21 37	21 36 22	29 1	5	6	12	4	16	13	3	29
12	9 25 34	22 37 3	10♍53	6	7	12	4	16	13	3	29
13	9 29 30	23 37 42	22 42	8	8	13	4	16	13	3	29
14	9 33 27	24 38 20	4♎30	9	9	14	4	16	13	3	29
15	9 37 23	25 38 56	16 21	11	10	14	4	16	13	3	29
16	9 41 20	26 39 32	28 19	13	12	15	5	17	13	3	29
17	9 45 17	27 40 6	10♏26	14	13	16	5	17	13	3	29
18	9 49 13	28 40 39	22 47	16	14	16	5	17	13	3	29
19	9 53 10	29 41 11	5♐26	17	15	17	5	17	13	3	29
20	9 57 6	0♓41 42	18 28	19	16	17	5	17	13	3	29
21	10 1 3	1 42 11	1♑55	21	17	18	5	17	13	3	29
22	10 4 59	2 42 39	15 49	22	18	19	5	17	13	3	29
23	10 8 56	3 43 5	0♒10	24	20	19	5	17	13	3	29
24	10 12 52	4 43 30	14 54	26	21	20	5	17	13	3	29
25	10 16 49	5 43 54	29 56	28	22	21	5	17	13	3	29
26	10 20 46	6 44 16	15♓ 8	29	23	21	5	17	13	3	29
27	10 24 42	7 44 35	0♈19	1♓	24	22	6	17	13	3	29
28	10 28 39	8 44 53	15 20	3	25	22	6	17	13	3	29

THE SUN ENTERS THE SIGN OF PISCES ON FEB 19 AT 07:27.

DAY	TIME	☉	☽	☿	♀	♂	♃	♄	♅	♆	♇
	h m s	° ' "	° '	°	°	°	°	°	°	°	°
M 1	10 32 35	9♓45 10	0♉ 3	5♓	26♑	23♐	6♐	17♉	13♎R	3♐	29♍R
A 2	10 36 32	10 45 24	14 23	7	28	24	6	17	13	3	29
R 3	10 40 28	11 45 36	28 17	8	29	24	6	17	13	3	29
C 4	10 44 25	12 45 46	11♊44	10	0♒	25	6	18	13	3	29
H 5	10 48 21	13 45 54	24 47	12	1	25	6	18	13	3 R	29
6	10 52 18	14 46 0	7♋28	14	2	26	6	18	13	3	29
7	10 56 15	15 46 4	19 52	16	3	27	6	18	13	3	29
8	11 0 11	16 46 5	2♌ 3	18	5	27	6	18	13	3	29
9	11 4 8	17 46 5	14 4	20	6	28	6	18	13	3	29
10	11 8 4	18 46 2	25 58	22	7	29	6	18	12	3	29
11	11 12 1	19 45 58	7♍48	24	8	29	6	18	12	3	29
12	11 15 57	20 45 51	19 36	26	9	0♑	6	18	12	3	29
13	11 19 54	21 45 43	1♎26	28	10	0	6	18	12	3	29
14	11 23 50	22 45 32	13 18	0☉	12	1	6	18	12	3	29
15	11 27 47	23 45 20	25 14	2♈	13	2	6	18	12	3	28
16	11 31 44	24 45 6	7♏17	4	14	2	6	19	12	3	28
17	11 35 40	25 44 50	19 29	6	15	3	6	19	12	3	28
18	11 39 37	26 44 32	1♐52	7	16	3	6	19	12	3	28
19	11 43 33	27 44 13	14 31	9	17	4	6	19	12	3	28
20	11 47 30	28 43 52	27 28	11	19	5	6	19	12	3	28
21	11 51 26	29 43 29	10♑46	13	20	5	6	19	12	3	28
22	11 55 23	0♈43 5	24 28	15	21	6	6	19	12	3	28
23	11 59 19	1 42 39	8♒36	17	22	6	6 R	19	12	3	28
24	12 3 16	2 42 11	23 8	18	23	7	6	19	12	3	28
25	12 7 13	3 41 41	8♓ 1	20	25	8	6	19	12	3	28
26	12 11 9	4 41 9	23 10	22	26	8	6	20	12	3	28
27	12 15 6	5 40 35	8♈24	23	27	9	6	20	12	3	28
28	12 19 2	6 39 59	23 34	25	28	9	6	20	12	3	28
29	12 22 59	7 39 21	8♉30	26	29	10	6	20	12	3	28
30	12 26 55	8 38 41	23 3	27	0♓	11	6	20	12	3	28
31	12 30 52	9 37 59	7♊ 8	28	2	11	6	20	12	3	28

THE SUN ENTERS THE SIGN OF ARIES ON MAR 21 AT 06:38.

SIDEREAL SUN MOON MERCURY VENUS MARS JUPITER SATURN URANUS NEPTUNE PLUTO

DAY	TIME	☉	☽	☿	♀	♂	♃	♄	♅	♆	♇
	h m s	° ' "	° '	°	°	°	°	°	°	°	°
A 1	12 34 48	10♈37 14	20♊44	29♈	3♓	12♑	6♐R	20♉	12♎R	3♐R	28♍R
P 2	12 38 45	11 36 28	3♋52	0♉	4	12	6	20	12	3	28
R 3	12 42 42	12 35 38	16 34	1	5	13	6	20	11	3	28
I 4	12 46 38	13 34 47	28 56	2	6	13	6	21	11	3	28
L 5	12 50 35	14 33 53	11♌ 2	3	8	14	6	21	11	3	28
6	12 54 31	15 32 56	22 57	3	9	15	6	21	11	3	28
7	12 58 28	16 31 58	4♍47	3	10	15	6	21	11	3	28
8	13 2 24	17 30 57	16 34	4	11	16	6	21	11	3	28
9	13 6 21	18 29 54	28 23	4 R	12	16	6	21	11	3	28
10	13 10 17	19 28 49	10♎15	4	14	17	6	21	11	3	28
11	13 14 14	20 27 42	22 13	4	15	17	6	21	11	3	28
12	13 18 10	21 26 33	4♏19	3	16	18	6	21	11	3	28
13	13 22 7	22 25 22	16 32	3	17	19	6	22	11	3	28
14	13 26 4	23 24 9	28 56	3	18	19	6	22	11	3	28
15	13 30 0	24 22 55	11♐30	2	20	20	6	22	11	3	28
16	13 33 57	25 21 38	24 16	2	21	20	6	22	11	3	28
17	13 37 53	26 20 20	7♑16	1	22	21	6	22	11	3	28
18	13 41 50	27 19 1	20 32	1	23	21	5	22	11	3	28
19	13 45 46	28 17 39	4♒ 8	0	24	22	5	22	11	3	28
20	13 49 43	29 16 16	18 3	29♈	26	23	5	22	11	3	28
21	13 53 39	0♉14 51	2♓19	29	27	23	5	23	11	3	28
22	13 57 36	1 13 25	16 55	28	28	24	5	23	11	3	28
23	14 1 33	2 11 56	1♈47	27	29	24	5	23	11	2	28
24	14 5 29	3 10 27	16 47	26	0♈	25	5	23	11	2	27
25	14 9 26	4 8 55	1♉48	26	2	25	5	23	11	2	27
26	14 13 22	5 7 22	16 39	25	3	26	5	23	11	2	27
27	14 17 19	6 5 46	1♊13	25	4	26	5	23	10	2	27
28	14 21 15	7 4 9	15 21	24	5	27	5	23	10	2	27
29	14 25 12	8 2 30	29 2	24	6	27	4	24	10	2	27
30	14 29 8	9 0 49	12♋14	24	8	28	4	24	10	2	27

THE SUN ENTERS THE SIGN OF TAURUS ON APR 20 AT 17:55.

DAY	TIME	☉	☽	☿	♀	♂	♃	♄	♅	♆	♇
	h m s	° ' "	° '	°	°	°	°	°	°	°	°
M 1	14 33 5	9♉59 5	25♋ 0	23♈R	9♈	28♑	4♐R	24♉	10♎R	2♐R	27♍R
A 2	14 37 2	10 57 20	7♌25	23	10	29	4	24	10	2	27
Y 3	14 40 58	11 55 32	19 32	23 D	11	0♒	4	24	10	2	27
4	14 44 55	12 53 43	1♍27	23	12	0	4	24	10	2	27
5	14 48 51	13 51 51	13 17	23	14	1	4	24	10	2	27
6	14 52 48	14 49 58	25 4	23	15	1	4	24	10	2	27
7	14 56 44	15 48 2	6♎55	24	16	2	4	25	10	2	27
8	15 0 41	16 46 5	18 53	24	17	2	3	25	10	2	27
9	15 4 37	17 44 6	0♏59	24	18	3	3	25	10	2	27
10	15 8 34	18 42 6	13 16	25	20	3	3	25	10	2	27
11	15 12 31	19 40 4	25 44	25	21	4	3	25	10	2	27
12	15 16 27	20 38 0	8♐23	26	22	4	3	25	10	2	27
13	15 20 24	21 35 55	21 14	27	23	5	3	25	10	2	27
14	15 24 20	22 33 49	4♑17	27	25	5	3	25	10	2	27
15	15 28 17	23 31 41	17 31	28	26	6	3	26	10	2	27
16	15 32 13	24 29 32	0♒56	29	27	6	3	26	10	2	27
17	15 36 10	25 27 21	14 35	0♉	28	7	2	26	10	2	27
18	15 40 6	26 25 10	28 27	1	29	7	2	26	10	2	27
19	15 44 3	27 22 57	12♓33	2	1♉	7	2	26	10	2	27
20	15 48 0	28 20 44	26 52	3	2	8	2	26	10	2	27
21	15 51 56	29 18 29	11♈23	4	3	8	2	26	10	2	27
22	15 55 53	0♊16 13	26 1	5	4	9	2	27	10	2	27
23	15 59 49	1 13 56	10♉39	6	5	9	2	27	10	2	27
24	16 3 46	2 11 37	25 11	8	7	10	2	27	10	2	27
25	16 7 42	3 9 18	9♊29	9	8	10	1	27	10	2	27
26	16 11 39	4 6 57	23 28	10	9	11	1	27	10	2	27
27	16 15 35	5 4 36	7♋ 4	12	10	11	1	27	10	2	27
28	16 19 32	6 2 12	20 14	13	11	11	1	27	10	2	27
29	16 23 29	6 59 48	3♌ 1	14	13	12	1	27	10	2	27
30	16 27 25	7 57 21	15 26	16	14	12	1	28	10	2	27
31	16 31 22	8 54 54	27 35	18	15	13	1	28	10	2	27

THE SUN ENTERS THE SIGN OF GEMINI ON MAY 21 AT 17:16.

DAY	TIME	☉	☽	☿	♀	♂	♃	♄	♅	♆	♇
	h m s	° ' "	° '	°	°	°	°	°	°	°	°
J 1	16 35 18	9♊52 25	9♍33	19♉	16♉	13♒	1♐R	28♉	10♎R	1♐R	27♍R
U 2	16 39 15	10 49 55	21 24	21	18	13	0	28	10	1	27
N 3	16 43 11	11 47 23	3♎14	22	19	14	0	28	10	1	27
E 4	16 47 8	12 44 50	15 8	24	20	14	0	28	10	1	27
5	16 51 4	13 42 16	27 10	26	21	15	0	28	10	1	27
6	16 55 1	14 39 41	9♏23	28	22	15	0	28	9	1	27
7	16 58 58	15 37 5	21 50	29	24	15	0	29	9	1	27 D
8	17 2 54	16 34 28	4♐32	1♊	25	16	0	29	9	1	27
9	17 6 51	17 31 50	17 30	3	26	16	0	29	9	1	27
10	17 10 47	18 29 12	0♑41	5	27	16	29♏	29	9	1	27
11	17 14 44	19 26 32	14 6	7	28	17	29	29	9	1	27
12	17 18 40	20 23 52	27 41	9	0♊	17	29	29	9	1	27
13	17 22 37	21 21 11	11♒26	11	1	17	29	29	9	1	27
14	17 26 34	22 18 30	25 19	13	2	18	29	29	9	1	27
15	17 30 30	23 15 49	9♓20	15	3	18	29	0♊	9	1	27
16	17 34 27	24 13 6	23 26	18	5	18	29	0	9	1	27
17	17 38 23	25 10 24	7♈38	20	6	18	29	0	9 D	1	27
18	17 42 20	26 7 41	21 53	22	7	19	29	0	9	1	27
19	17 46 16	27 4 59	6♉ 9	24	8	19	28	0	9	1	27
20	17 50 13	28 2 16	20 21	26	9	19	28	0	9	1	27
21	17 54 9	28 59 32	4♊26	28	11	19	28	0	9	1	27
22	17 58 6	29 56 49	18 20	1♋	12	20	28	0	9	1	27
23	18 2 3	0♋54 5	1♋58	3	13	20	28	1	9	1	27
24	18 5 59	1 51 20	15 17	5	14	20	28	1	9	1	27
25	18 9 56	2 48 35	28 17	7	15	20	28	1	9	1	27
26	18 13 52	3 45 50	10♌58	9	17	21	28	1	9	1	27
27	18 17 49	4 43 4	23 20	11	18	21	28	1	9	1	27
28	18 21 45	5 40 18	5♍29	14	19	21	28	1	9	1	27
29	18 25 42	6 37 31	17 27	16	20	21	28	1	9	1	27
30	18 29 38	7 34 44	29 19	18	22	21	28	1	10	1	27

THE SUN ENTERS THE SIGN OF CANCER ON JUN 22 AT 01:20.

♈ ARIES ♉ TAURUS ♊ GEMINI ♋ CANCER ♌ LEO ♍ VIRGO ♎ LIBRA ♏ SCORPIO ♐ SAGITTARIUS ♑ CAPRICORN ♒ AQUARIUS ♓ PISCES

SIDEREAL SUN MOON MERCURY VENUS MARS JUPITER SATURN URANUS NEPTUNE PLUTO

DAY	TIME	☉	☽	☿	♀	♂	♃	♄	♅	♆	♇
	h m s	° ' "	° '	°	°	°	°	°	°	°	°
J 1	18 33 35	8♋31 56	11♎10	20♋	23♊	21♒	27♏R	1♊	10♎	1♐R	27♍
U 2	18 37 32	9 29 8	23 6	22	24	21	27	2	10	1	27
L 3	18 41 28	10 26 19	5♏10	24	25	22	27	2	10	1	27
Y 4	18 45 25	11 23 31	17 27	26	26	22	27	2	10	1	27
5	18 49 21	12 20 42	0♐ 0	27	28	22	27	2	10	1	27
6	18 53 18	13 17 53	12 52	29	29	22	27	2	10	1	27
7	18 57 14	14 15 3	26 4	1♌	0♋	22	27	2	10	1	27
8	19 1 11	15 12 14	9♑34	3	1	22	27	2	10	1	27
9	19 5 8	16 9 25	23 20	5	3	22	27	2	10	1	27
10	19 9 4	17 6 36	7♒21	6	4	22	27	2	10	1	27
11	19 13 1	18 3 47	21 32	8	5	22 R	27	3	10	1	27
12	19 16 57	19 0 59	5♓49	10	6	22	27	3	10	1	27
13	19 20 54	19 58 11	20 8	11	7	22	27	3	10	1	27
14	19 24 50	20 55 23	4♈26	13	9	22	27	3	10	1	27
15	19 28 47	21 52 36	18 41	14	10	22	27	3	10	1	27
16	19 32 43	22 49 49	2♉50	16	11	22	27	3	10	1	27
17	19 36 40	23 47 4	16 51	17	12	22	27	3	10	0	27
18	19 40 37	24 44 19	0♊42	19	14	22	27	3	10	0	27
19	19 44 33	25 41 35	14 21	20	15	22	27	3	10	0	27
20	19 48 30	26 38 51	27 48	22	16	21	27	3	10	0	27
21	19 52 26	27 36 8	11♋ 1	23	17	21	27	4	10	0	27
22	19 56 23	28 33 26	23 59	24	18	21	27	4	10	0	27
23	20 0 19	29 30 44	6♌42	26	20	21	27	4	10	0	28
24	20 4 16	0♌28 2	19 11	27	21	21	27 D	4	10	0	28
25	20 8 12	1 25 21	1♍26	28	22	21	27	4	10	0	28
26	20 12 9	2 22 41	13 31	29	23	21	27	4	10	0	28
27	20 16 6	3 20 1	25 27	0♍	25	20	27	4	10	0	28
28	20 20 2	4 17 21	7♎18	1	26	20	27	4	10	0	28
29	20 23 59	5 14 42	19 9	2	27	20	27	4	10	0	28
30	20 27 55	6 12 4	1♏ 4	3	28	20	27	4	10	0	28
31	20 31 52	7 9 26	13 8	4	0♌	20	27	4	10	0	28

THE SUN ENTERS THE SIGN OF LEO ON JUL 23 AT 12:16.

DAY	TIME	☉	☽	☿	♀	♂	♃	♄	♅	♆	♇
	h m s	° ' "	° '	°	°	°	°	°	°	°	°
A 1	20 35 48	8♌ 6 49	25♏25	5♍	1♌	19♒R	27♏	4♊	10♎	0♐R	28♍
U 2	20 39 45	9 4 12	7♐59	6	2	19	27	5	10	0	28
G 3	20 43 41	10 1 36	20 53	7	3	19	27	5	10	0	28
U 4	20 47 38	10 59 0	4♑10	7	4	19	27	5	10	0	28
S 5	20 51 35	11 56 26	17 51	8	6	18	27	5	10	0	28
T 6	20 55 31	12 53 52	1♒54	9	7	18	27	5	10	0	28
7	20 59 28	13 51 19	16 16	9	8	18	27	5	11	0	28
8	21 3 24	14 48 47	0♓52	10	9	18	27	5	11	0	28
9	21 7 21	15 46 16	15 36	10	11	17	27	5	11	0	28
10	21 11 17	16 43 47	0♈20	10	12	17	27	5	11	0	28
11	21 15 14	17 41 38	14 59	10	13	17	27	5	11	0	28
12	21 19 10	18 38 51	29 27	11 R	14	17	27	5	11	0 D	28
13	21 23 7	19 36 26	13♉40	11	16	16	27	5	11	0	28
14	21 27 4	20 34 2	27 36	10	17	16	27	5	11	0	28
15	21 31 0	21 31 40	11♊15	10	18	16	27	5	11	0	28
16	21 34 57	22 29 19	24 36	10	19	16	27	5	11	0	28
17	21 38 53	23 27 0	7♋42	10	20	15	27	6	11	0	28
18	21 42 50	24 24 42	20 32	9	22	15	27	6	11	0	28
19	21 46 46	25 22 26	3♌ 9	9	23	15	28	6	11	0	28
20	21 50 43	26 20 11	15 34	8	24	15	28	6	11	0	28
21	21 54 39	27 17 57	27 49	8	25	14	28	6	11	0	28
22	21 58 36	28 15 45	9♍54	7	27	14	28	6	11	0	28
23	22 2 33	29 13 34	21 53	6	28	14	28	6	11	0	28
24	22 6 29	0♍11 24	3♎46	5	29	14	28	6	11	0	28
25	22 10 26	1 9 16	15 36	4	0♍	13	28	6	11	0	28
26	22 14 22	2 7 9	27 27	3	2	13	28	6	11	0	29
27	22 18 19	3 5 4	9♏21	2	3	13	28	6	11	0	29
28	22 22 15	4 2 59	21 23	2	4	13	28	6	12	0	29
29	22 26 12	5 0 56	3♐37	1	5	13	28	6	12	0	29
30	22 30 8	5 58 55	16 7	0	7	13	29	6	12	0	29
31	22 34 5	6 56 55	28 58	29♌	8	12	29	6	12	0	29

THE SUN ENTERS THE SIGN OF VIRGO ON AUG 23 AT 19:16.

DAY	TIME	☉	☽	☿	♀	♂	♃	♄	♅	♆	♇
	h m s	° ' "	° '	°	°	°	°	°	°	°	°
S 1	22 38 2	7♍54 56	12♑12	29♌R	9♍	12♒R	29♏	6♊	12♎	0♐	29♍
E 2	22 41 58	8 52 58	25 53	28	10	12	29	6	12	0	29
P 3	22 45 55	9 51 2	10♒ 0	28	12	12	29	6	12	0	29
T 4	22 49 51	10 49 7	24 33	27	13	12	29	6	12	0	29
E 5	22 53 48	11 47 14	9♓25	27 D	14	12	29	6	12	0	29
M 6	22 57 44	12 45 23	24 30	27	15	12	29	6	12	0	29
B 7	23 1 41	13 43 33	9♈37	28	17	12	29	6	12	0	29
E 8	23 5 37	14 41 46	24 39	28	18	12	0♐	6	12	0	29
R 9	23 9 34	15 40 0	9♉26	28	19	12 D	0	6	12	1	29
10	23 13 31	16 38 16	23 51	29	20	12	0	6	12	1	29
11	23 17 27	17 36 35	7♊53	0♍	21	12	0	6	12	1	29
12	23 21 24	18 34 56	21 30	1	23	12	0	6	12	1	29
13	23 25 20	19 33 19	4♋43	2	24	12	0	6	12	1	29
14	23 29 17	20 31 43	17 36	3	25	12	0	7	12	1	29
15	23 33 13	21 30 11	0♌11	4	26	12	0	7	13	1	29
16	23 37 10	22 28 40	12 33	5	28	12	1	7	13	1	29
17	23 41 6	23 27 11	24 43	7	29	12	1	7	13	1	29
18	23 45 3	24 25 44	6♍46	8	0♎	12	1	7	13	1	29
19	23 48 59	25 24 19	18 43	10	1	12	1	7 R	13	1	29
20	23 52 56	26 22 56	0♎36	11	3	13	1	7	13	1	29
21	23 56 53	27 21 35	12 27	13	4	13	1	7	13	1	29
22	0 0 49	28 20 16	24 17	15	5	13	1	7	13	1	0♎
23	0 4 46	29 18 58	6♏10	17	6	13	2	7	13	1	0
24	0 8 42	0♎17 43	18 6	18	8	13	2	7	13	1	0
25	0 12 39	1 16 29	0♐ 8	20	9	13	2	6	13	1	0
26	0 16 35	2 15 18	12 21	22	10	14	2	6	13	1	0
27	0 20 32	3 14 8	24 47	24	11	14	2	6	13	1	0
28	0 24 28	4 12 59	7♑32	26	13	14	2	6	13	1	0
29	0 28 25	5 11 53	20 39	27	14	14	3	6	13	1	0
30	0 32 22	6 10 48	4♒12	29	15	15	3	6	13	1	0

THE SUN ENTERS THE SIGN OF LIBRA ON SEP 23 AT 16:46.

SIDEREAL SUN MOON MERCURY VENUS MARS JUPITER SATURN URANUS NEPTUNE PLUTO

DAY	TIME	☉	☽	☿	♀	♂	♃	♄	♅	♆	♇
	h m s	° ' "	° '	°	°	°	°	°	°	°	°
O 1	0 36 18	7♎ 9 45	18♒12	1♎	16♎	15♒	3♐	6♊R	14♎	1♐	0♎
C 2	0 40 15	8 8 43	2♓40	3	18	15	3	6	14	1	0
T 3	0 44 11	9 7 44	17 34	5	19	15	3	6	14	1	0
O 4	0 48 8	10 6 46	2♈45	7	20	16	3	6	14	1	0
B 5	0 52 4	11 5 50	18 5	8	21	16	4	6	14	1	0
E 6	0 56 1	12 4 57	3♉21	10	23	16	4	6	14	1	0
R 7	0 59 57	13 4 5	18 25	12	24	17	4	6	14	1	0
8	1 3 54	14 3 16	3♊ 5	14	25	17	4	6	14	1	0
9	1 7 51	15 2 29	17 18	15	26	17	4	6	14	1	0
10	1 11 47	16 1 45	1♋ 1	17	28	18	4	6	14	1	0
11	1 15 44	17 1 3	14 16	19	29	18	5	6	14	1	0
12	1 19 40	18 0 23	27 6	20	0♏	18	5	6	14	1	0
13	1 23 37	18 59 46	9♌36	22	1	19	5	6	14	1	0
14	1 27 33	19 59 11	21 49	24	3	19	5	6	14	1	0
15	1 31 30	20 58 38	3♍51	25	4	20	5	6	14	1	0
16	1 35 26	21 58 7	15 47	27	5	20	6	6	14	1	0
17	1 39 23	22 57 38	27 38	29	6	20	6	6	15	1	0
18	1 43 20	23 57 12	9♎28	0♏	8	21	6	6	15	1	0
19	1 47 16	24 56 47	21 19	2	9	21	6	6	15	1	0
20	1 51 13	25 56 25	3♏13	4	10	22	6	6	15	1	1
21	1 55 9	26 56 5	15 10	5	11	22	7	6	15	2	1
22	1 59 6	27 55 47	27 13	7	13	22	7	6	15	2	1
23	2 3 2	28 55 30	9♐21	8	14	23	7	6	15	2	1
24	2 6 59	29 55 16	21 39	10	15	23	7	5	15	2	1
25	2 10 55	0♏55 3	4♑ 8	12	16	24	7	5	15	2	1
26	2 14 52	1 54 52	16 52	13	18	24	8	5	15	2	1
27	2 18 49	2 54 43	29 54	15	19	25	8	5	15	2	1
28	2 22 45	3 54 35	13♒17	16	20	25	8	5	15	2	1
29	2 26 42	4 54 29	27 6	18	21	26	8	5	15	2	1
30	2 30 38	5 54 24	11♓20	19	22	26	8	5	15	2	1
31	2 34 35	6 54 21	26 0	21	24	27	9	5	15	2	1

THE SUN ENTERS THE SIGN OF SCORPIO ON OCT 24 AT 01:55.

DAY	TIME	☉	☽	☿	♀	♂	♃	♄	♅	♆	♇
	h m s	° ' "	° '	°	°	°	°	°	°	°	°
N 1	2 38 31	7♏54 20	11♈ 0	22♏	25♏	27♒	9♐	5♊R	15♎	2♐	1♎
O 2	2 42 28	8 54 21	26 14	24	26	28	9	5	16	2	1
V 3	2 46 24	9 54 23	11♉29	25	27	28	9	5	16	2	1
E 4	2 50 21	10 54 28	26 36	27	29	29	9	5	16	2	1
M 5	2 54 18	11 54 34	11♊24	28	0♐	29	10	5	16	2	1
B 6	2 58 14	12 54 42	25 45	0♐	1	0♓	10	5	16	2	1
E 7	3 2 11	13 54 53	9♋37	1	2	0	10	5	16	2	1
R 8	3 6 7	14 55 5	22 59	2	4	1	10	4	16	2	1
9	3 10 4	15 55 19	5♌53	4	5	1	11	4	16	2	1
10	3 14 0	16 55 36	18 25	5	6	2	11	4	16	2	1
11	3 17 57	17 55 54	0♍38	7	7	2	11	4	16	2	1
12	3 21 53	18 56 14	12 39	8	9	3	11	4	16	2	1
13	3 25 50	19 56 37	24 32	9	10	3	11	4	16	2	1
14	3 29 47	20 57 1	6♎21	11	11	4	12	4	16	2	1
15	3 33 43	21 57 27	18 11	12	12	5	12	4	16	2	1
16	3 37 40	22 57 55	0♏ 5	13	14	5	12	4	16	2	1
17	3 41 36	23 58 24	12 4	15	15	6	12	4	16	2	1
18	3 45 33	24 58 55	24 9	16	16	6	12	4	16	3	1
19	3 49 29	25 59 28	6♐23	17	17	7	13	4	16	3	1
20	3 53 26	27 0 3	18 44	19	19	7	13	4	17	3	1
21	3 57 22	28 0 38	1♑15	20	20	8	13	3	17	3	1
22	4 1 19	29 1 15	13 56	21	21	9	13	3	17	3	2
23	4 5 16	0♐ 1 54	26 49	22	22	9	14	3	17	3	2
24	4 9 12	1 2 33	9♒55	23	24	10	14	3	17	3	2
25	4 13 9	2 3 14	23 18	24	25	10	14	3	17	3	2
26	4 17 5	3 3 55	7♓ 0	25	26	11	14	3	17	3	2
27	4 21 2	4 4 38	21 1	26	27	12	14	3	17	3	2
28	4 24 58	5 5 22	5♈23	26	29	12	15	3	17	3	2
29	4 28 55	6 6 7	20 1	27	0♑	13	15	3	17	3	2
30	4 32 51	7 6 52	4♉53	28	1	13	15	3	17	3	2

THE SUN ENTERS THE SIGN OF SAGITTARIUS ON NOV 22 AT 23:15.

DAY	TIME	☉	☽	☿	♀	♂	♃	♄	♅	♆	♇
	h m s	° ' "	° '	°	°	°	°	°	°	°	°
D 1	4 36 48	8♐ 7 39	19♉49	28♐	2♑	14♓	15♐	3♊R	17♎	3♐	2♎
E 2	4 40 45	9 8 27	4♊40	28	4	15	16	3	17	3	2
C 3	4 44 41	10 9 16	19 19	28 R	5	15	16	2	17	3	2
E 4	4 48 38	11 10 7	3♋37	28	6	16	16	2	17	3	2
M 5	4 52 34	12 10 59	17 30	28	7	16	16	2	17	3	2
B 6	4 56 31	13 11 51	0♌57	28	9	17	16	2	17	3	2
E 7	5 0 27	14 12 45	13 56	27	10	18	17	2	17	3	2
R 8	5 4 24	15 13 41	26 33	26	11	18	17	2	17	3	2
9	5 8 20	16 14 37	8♍50	25	12	19	17	2	17	3	2
10	5 12 17	17 15 35	20 54	24	14	19	17	2	17	3	2
11	5 16 14	18 16 34	2♎48	23	15	20	18	2	17	3	2
12	5 20 10	19 17 34	14 39	21	16	21	18	2	18	3	2
13	5 24 7	20 18 35	26 31	20	17	21	18	2	18	3	2
14	5 28 3	21 19 37	8♏27	19	19	22	18	2	18	3	2
15	5 32 0	22 20 40	20 31	17	20	23	19	2	18	4	2
16	5 35 56	23 21 44	2♐45	16	21	23	19	1	18	4	2
17	5 39 53	24 22 49	15 11	15	22	24	19	1	18	4	2
18	5 43 50	25 23 55	27 48	14	23	24	19	1	18	4	2
19	5 47 46	26 25 1	10♑38	13	25	25	19	1	18	4	2
20	5 51 43	27 26 8	23 40	13	26	26	20	1	18	4	2
21	5 55 39	28 27 15	6♒53	12	27	26	20	1	18	4	2
22	5 59 36	29 28 23	20 17	12 D	28	27	20	1	18	4	2
23	6 3 32	0♑29 30	3♓53	12	0♒	28	20	1	18	4	2
24	6 7 29	1 30 38	17 41	12	1	28	21	1	18	4	2
25	6 11 25	2 31 46	1♈40	12	2	29	21	1	18	4	2
26	6 15 22	3 32 54	15 50	13	3	0☉	21	1	18	4	2
27	6 19 19	4 34 2	0♉ 9	13	5	0♈	21	1	18	4	2
28	6 23 15	5 35 10	14 34	14	6	1	21	1	18	4	2
29	6 27 12	6 36 18	29 1	15	7	1	22	1	18	4	2
30	6 31 8	7 37 26	13♊24	15	8	2	22	1	18	4	2
31	6 35 5	8 38 35	27 38	16	10	3	22	0	18	4	2

THE SUN ENTERS THE SIGN OF CAPRICORN ON DEC 22 AT 12:25.

♈ ARIES ♉ TAURUS ♊ GEMINI ♋ CANCER ♌ LEO ♍ VIRGO ♎ LIBRA ♏ SCORPIO ♐ SAGITTARIUS ♑ CAPRICORN ♒ AQUARIUS ♓ PISCES

1972

SIDEREAL SUN MOON MERCURY VENUS MARS JUPITER SATURN URANUS NEPTUNE PLUTO

DAY	TIME	☉	☽	☿	♀	♂	♃	♄	♅	♆	♇
	h m s	° ' "	° '	°	°	°	°	°	°	°	°
J 1	6 39 1	9♑39 43	11♋37	17♐	11♒	3♈	22♐	0♊R	18♎	4♐	2♎
A 2	6 42 58	10 40 52	25 18	18	12	4	23	0	18	4	2
N 3	6 46 54	11 42 0	8♌38	19	13	5	23	0	18	4	2
U 4	6 50 51	12 43 9	21 37	20	14	5	23	0	18	4	2 R
A 5	6 54 48	13 44 18	4♍16	21	16	6	23	0	18	4	2
R 6	6 58 44	14 45 27	16 36	23	17	7	23	0	18	4	2
Y 7	7 2 41	15 46 36	28 43	24	18	7	24	0	18	4	2
8	7 6 37	16 47 45	10♎40	25	19	8	24	0	18	4	2
9	7 10 34	17 48 54	22 33	26	21	9	24	0	18	4	2
10	7 14 30	18 50 4	4♏26	28	22	9	24	0	18	4	2
11	7 18 27	19 51 13	16 23	29	23	10	25	0	18	4	2
12	7 22 23	20 52 22	28 29	0♑	24	11	25	0	18	4	2
13	7 26 20	21 53 32	10♐48	2	26	11	25	0	18	4	2
14	7 30 17	22 54 41	23 22	3	27	12	25	0	18	4	2
15	7 34 13	23 55 50	6♑13	4	28	12	25	0	18	5	2
16	7 38 10	24 56 59	19 22	6	29	13	26	0	18	5	2
17	7 42 6	25 58 7	2♒47	7	0♓	14	26	0	18	5	2
18	7 46 3	26 59 14	16 26	9	2	14	26	0	18	5	2
19	7 49 59	28 0 21	0♓18	10	3	15	26	0	18	5	2
20	7 53 56	29 1 28	14 20	12	4	16	26	0	18	5	2
21	7 57 52	0♒ 2 33	28 28	13	5	16	27	0	18	5	2
22	8 1 49	1 3 37	12♈40	15	7	17	27	0	18	5	2
23	8 5 46	2 4 40	26 52	16	8	18	27	0	18 R	5	2
24	8 9 42	3 5 43	11♉ 3	18	9	18	27	0	18	5	2
25	8 13 39	4 6 44	25 10	19	10	19	27	0	18	5	2
26	8 17 35	5 7 45	9♊12	21	11	20	28	0	18	5	2
27	8 21 32	6 8 44	23 6	22	13	20	28	0	18	5	2
28	8 25 28	7 9 42	6♋49	24	14	21	28	0	18	5	2
29	8 29 25	8 10 39	20 21	25	15	22	28	0	18	5	2
30	8 33 22	9 11 35	3♌39	27	16	22	28	0	18	5	2
31	8 37 18	10 12 30	16 42	28	17	23	29	0 D	18	5	2

THE SUN ENTERS THE SIGN OF AQUARIUS ON JAN 20 AT 22:60.

DAY	TIME	☉	☽	☿	♀	♂	♃	♄	♅	♆	♇
	h m s	° ' "	° '	°	°	°	°	°	°	°	°
F 1	8 41 15	11♒13 24	29♌30	0♒	19♓	24♈	29♐	0♊	18♎R	5♐	2♎R
E 2	8 45 11	12 14 17	12♍ 3	2	20	24	29	0	18	5	2
B 3	8 49 8	13 15 10	24 22	3	21	25	29	0	18	5	2
R 4	8 53 4	14 16 1	6♎29	5	22	26	29	0	18	5	2
U 5	8 57 1	15 16 51	18 27	7	24	26	0♑	0	18	5	2
A 6	9 0 57	16 17 40	0♏21	8	25	27	0	0	18	5	2
R 7	9 4 54	17 18 29	12 13	10	26	28	0	0	18	5	2
Y 8	9 8 51	18 19 16	24 10	11	27	28	0	0	18	5	2
9	9 12 47	19 20 3	6♐15	13	28	29	0	0	18	5	2
10	9 16 44	20 20 49	18 33	15	29	0♉	1	0	18	5	2
11	9 20 40	21 21 33	1♑ 9	17	1♈	0	1	0	18	5	2
12	9 24 37	22 22 17	14 5	18	2	1	1	0	18	5	2
13	9 28 33	23 22 59	27 24	20	3	2	1	0	18	5	2
14	9 32 30	24 23 40	11♒ 5	22	4	2	1	0	18	5	2
15	9 36 26	25 24 19	25 8	24	5	3	1	0	18	5	2
16	9 40 23	26 24 57	9♓28	25	7	4	2	0	18	5	2
17	9 44 20	27 25 34	24 0	27	8	4	2	0	18	5	2
18	9 48 16	28 26 9	8♈37	29	9	5	2	0	18	5	2
19	9 52 13	29 26 42	23 13	1♓	10	6	2	0	18	5	2
20	9 56 9	0♓27 13	7♉42	3	11	6	2	0	18	5	1
21	10 0 6	1 27 43	22 0	5	13	7	3	0	18	5	1
22	10 4 2	2 28 10	6♊ 4	6	14	8	3	0	18	5	1
23	10 7 59	3 28 36	19 52	8	15	8	3	0	18	5	1
24	10 11 55	4 29 0	3♋26	10	16	9	3	0	18	5	1
25	10 15 52	5 29 22	16 46	12	17	10	3	0	18	5	1
26	10 19 49	6 29 42	29 52	14	18	10	3	0	18	5	1
27	10 23 45	7 30 0	12♌45	16	20	11	3	0	18	5	1
28	10 27 42	8 30 16	25 28	18	21	11	4	0	18	5	1
29	10 31 38	9 30 30	7♍59	20	22	12	4	0	18	5	1

THE SUN ENTERS THE SIGN OF PISCES ON FEB 19 AT 13:12.

DAY	TIME	☉	☽	☿	♀	♂	♃	♄	♅	♆	♇
	h m s	° ' "	° '	°	°	°	°	°	°	°	°
M 1	10 35 35	10♓30 43	20♍20	21♓	23♈	13♉	4♑	0♊	18♎R	5♐	1♎R
A 2	10 39 31	11 30 53	2♎31	23	24	13	4	0	18	5	1
R 3	10 43 28	12 31 2	14 35	25	25	14	4	1	18	5	1
C 4	10 47 24	13 31 10	26 31	27	26	15	4	1	18	5	1
H 5	10 51 21	14 31 16	8♏24	29	28	15	5	1	18	5	1
6	10 55 17	15 31 20	20 16	1♈	29	16	5	1	18	5	1
7	10 59 14	16 31 22	2♐11	2	0♉	17	5	1	18	5 R	1
8	11 3 11	17 31 23	14 13	4	1	17	5	1	17	5	1
9	11 7 7	18 31 23	26 28	5	2	18	5	1	17	5	1
10	11 11 4	19 31 20	9♑ 0	7	3	19	5	1	17	5	1
11	11 15 0	20 31 16	21 53	8	4	19	5	1	17	5	1
12	11 18 57	21 31 11	5♒12	10	5	20	5	1	17	5	1
13	11 22 53	22 31 3	18 58	11	7	21	6	1	17	5	1
14	11 26 50	23 30 54	3♓12	12	8	21	6	1	17	5	1
15	11 30 46	24 30 43	17 49	13	9	22	6	1	17	5	1
16	11 34 43	25 30 30	2♈44	14	10	23	6	1	17	5	1
17	11 38 40	26 30 15	17 47	14	11	23	6	1	17	5	1
18	11 42 36	27 29 57	2♉50	15	12	24	6	2	17	5	1
19	11 46 33	28 29 38	17 42	15	13	25	6	2	17	5	1
20	11 50 29	29 29 17	2♊16	16	14	25	6	2	17	5	1
21	11 54 26	0♈28 53	16 29	16 R	15	26	6	2	17	5	1
22	11 58 22	1 28 26	0♋19	16	16	27	7	2	17	5	1
23	12 2 19	2 27 58	13 46	16	18	27	7	2	17	5	1
24	12 6 15	3 27 27	26 53	16	19	28	7	2	17	5	1
25	12 10 12	4 26 54	9♌43	15	20	29	7	2	17	5	1
26	12 14 9	5 26 19	22 19	15	21	29	7	2	17	5	1
27	12 18 5	6 25 41	4♍44	14	22	0♊	7	2	17	5	1
28	12 22 2	7 25 1	17 0	14	23	1	7	2	17	5	1
29	12 25 58	8 24 19	29 8	13	24	1	7	2	17	5	0
30	12 29 55	9 23 34	11♎11	12	25	2	7	3	17	5	0
31	12 33 51	10 22 48	23 9	11	26	2	7	3	17	5	0

THE SUN ENTERS THE SIGN OF ARIES ON MAR 20 AT 12:22.

SIDEREAL SUN MOON MERCURY VENUS MARS JUPITER SATURN URANUS NEPTUNE PLUTO

DAY	TIME	☉	☽	☿	♀	♂	♃	♄	♅	♆	♇
	h m s	° ' "	° '	°	°	°	°	°	°	°	°
A 1	12 37 48	11♈22 0	5♏ 3	10♈R	27♉	3♊	7♑	3♊	17♎R	5♐R	0♎R
P 2	12 41 44	12 21 10	16 55	10	28	4	8	3	16	5	0
R 3	12 45 41	13 20 18	28 47	9	29	4	8	3	16	5	0
I 4	12 49 38	14 19 24	10♐42	8	0♊	5	8	3	16	5	0
L 5	12 53 34	15 18 28	22 44	7	1	6	8	3	16	5	0
6	12 57 31	16 17 31	4♑56	7	2	6	8	3	16	5	0
7	13 1 27	17 16 32	17 24	6	3	7	8	3	16	5	0
8	13 5 24	18 15 31	0♒12	5	4	8	8	3	16	5	0
9	13 9 20	19 14 28	13 25	5	5	8	8	4	16	5	0
10	13 13 17	20 13 24	27 6	4	6	9	8	4	16	5	0
11	13 17 13	21 12 18	11♓17	4	7	10	8	4	16	5	0
12	13 21 10	22 11 9	25 56	4	8	10	8	4	16	5	0
13	13 25 7	23 9 59	10♈58	4	9	11	8	4	16	5	0
14	13 29 3	24 8 48	26 13	4 D	10	12	8	4	16	5	0
15	13 33 0	25 7 34	11♉32	4	11	12	8	4	16	5	0
16	13 36 56	26 6 18	26 42	4	12	13	8	4	16	5	0
17	13 40 53	27 5 0	11♊33	4	13	14	8	4	16	5	0
18	13 44 49	28 3 40	26 0	4	13	14	8	5	16	5	0
19	13 48 46	29 2 18	9♋59	5	14	15	8	5	16	5	0
20	13 52 42	0♉ 0 53	23 31	5	15	15	8	5	16	5	0
21	13 56 39	0 59 26	6♌37	6	16	16	8	5	16	5	0
22	14 0 36	1 57 57	19 23	6	17	17	8	5	16	5	0
23	14 4 32	2 56 26	1♍51	7	18	17	8	5	16	5	0
24	14 8 29	3 54 53	14 6	8	19	18	8	5	16	5	0
25	14 12 25	4 53 17	26 12	8	19	19	8 R	5	15	5	0
26	14 16 22	5 51 40	8♎12	9	20	19	8	5	15	5	0
27	14 20 18	6 50 0	20 7	10	21	20	8	6	15	5	0
28	14 24 15	7 48 19	2♏ 1	11	22	21	8	6	15	5	0
29	14 28 11	8 46 36	13 53	12	23	21	8	6	15	5	0
30	14 32 8	9 44 51	25 46	13	23	22	8	6	15	5	0

THE SUN ENTERS THE SIGN OF TAURUS ON APR 19 AT 23:38.

DAY	TIME	☉	☽	☿	♀	♂	♃	♄	♅	♆	♇
	h m s	° ' "	° '	°	°	°	°	°	°	°	°
M 1	14 36 4	10♉43 5	7♐42	14♈	24♊	23♊	8♑R	6♊	15♎R	5♐R	0♎R
A 2	14 40 1	11 41 17	19 41	15	25	23	8	6	15	4	0
Y 3	14 43 58	12 39 27	1♑47	16	25	24	8	6	15	4	0
4	14 47 54	13 37 36	14 2	17	26	25	8	6	15	4	0
5	14 51 51	14 35 43	26 31	19	27	25	8	7	15	4	0
6	14 55 47	15 33 49	9♒18	20	27	26	8	7	15	4	0
7	14 59 44	16 31 53	22 26	21	28	26	8	7	15	4	0
8	15 3 40	17 29 56	6♓ 0	23	29	27	8	7	15	4	0
9	15 7 37	18 27 58	20 2	24	29	28	8	7	15	4	0
10	15 11 34	19 25 58	4♈31	25	0♋	28	8	7	15	4	0
11	15 15 30	20 23 57	19 24	27	0	29	8	7	15	4	0
12	15 19 27	21 21 55	4♉34	28	1	0♋	8	7	15	4	0
13	15 23 23	22 19 51	19 52	0♉	1	0	8	8	15	4	0
14	15 27 20	23 17 46	5♊ 5	2	2	1	8	8	15	4	29♍
15	15 31 16	24 15 39	20 3	3	2	2	8	8	15	4	29
16	15 35 13	25 13 31	4♋39	5	2	2	8	8	15	4	29
17	15 39 9	26 11 21	18 47	7	3	3	8	8	15	4	29
18	15 43 6	27 9 9	2♌27	8	3	3	8	8	15	4	29
19	15 47 3	28 6 56	15 39	10	4	4	7	8	15	4	29
20	15 50 59	29 4 41	28 27	12	4	5	7	8	15	4	29
21	15 54 56	0♊ 2 24	10♍56	14	4	5	7	9	15	4	29
22	15 58 52	1 0 5	23 9	15	4	6	7	9	15	4	29
23	16 2 49	1 57 45	5♎12	17	4	7	7	9	15	4	29
24	16 6 45	2 55 24	17 7	19	5	7	7	9	15	4	29
25	16 10 42	3 53 1	29 0	21	5	8	7	9	15	4	29
26	16 14 38	4 50 37	10♏52	23	5	9	7	9	14	4	29
27	16 18 35	5 48 11	22 45	25	5 R	9	7	9	14	4	29
28	16 22 32	6 45 45	4♐42	27	5	10	7	10	14	4	29
29	16 26 28	7 43 17	16 44	29	5	11	7	10	14	4	29
30	16 30 25	8 40 48	28 52	2♊	5	11	6	10	14	4	29
31	16 34 21	9 38 18	11♑ 8	4	4	12	6	10	14	4	29

THE SUN ENTERS THE SIGN OF GEMINI ON MAY 20 AT 23:00.

DAY	TIME	☉	☽	☿	♀	♂	♃	♄	♅	♆	♇
	h m s	° ' "	° '	°	°	°	°	°	°	°	°
J 1	16 38 18	10♊35 47	23♑34	6♊	4♋R	12♋	6♑R	10♊	14♎R	4♐R	29♍R
U 2	16 42 14	11 33 16	6♒13	8	4	13	6	10	14	4	29
N 3	16 46 11	12 30 43	19 6	10	4	14	6	10	14	4	29
E 4	16 50 7	13 28 10	2♓17	12	4	14	6	10	14	4	29
5	16 54 4	14 25 36	15 49	15	3	15	6	11	14	4	29
6	16 58 1	15 23 1	29 43	17	3	16	6	11	14	4	29
7	17 1 57	16 20 26	14♈ 0	19	2	16	6	11	14	4	29
8	17 5 54	17 17 50	28 37	21	2	17	6	11	14	4	29
9	17 9 50	18 15 14	13♉29	23	1	18	5	11	14	3	29 D
10	17 13 47	19 12 37	28 29	25	1	18	5	11	14	3	29
11	17 17 43	20 10 0	13♊29	28	0	19	5	11	14	3	29
12	17 21 40	21 7 22	28 19	0♋	0	19	5	11	14	3	29
13	17 25 36	22 4 43	12♋51	2	29♊	20	5	12	14	3	29
14	17 29 33	23 2 3	27 0	4	29	21	5	12	14	3	29
15	17 33 30	23 59 23	10♌44	6	28	21	5	12	14	3	29
16	17 37 26	24 56 42	24 1	8	28	22	5	12	14	3	29
17	17 41 23	25 53 59	6♍54	10	27	23	4	12	14	3	29
18	17 45 19	26 51 16	19 26	12	26	23	4	12	14	3	29
19	17 49 16	27 48 32	1♎42	14	26	24	4	12	14	3	29
20	17 53 12	28 45 47	13 45	16	25	25	4	12	14	3	29
21	17 57 9	29 43 2	25 41	17	24	25	4	13	14 D	3	29
22	18 1 5	0♋40 16	7♏33	19	24	26	4	13	14	3	29
23	18 5 2	1 37 29	19 26	21	23	26	4	13	14	3	29
24	18 8 59	2 34 42	1♐22	23	23	27	4	13	14	3	29
25	18 12 55	3 31 55	13 25	24	22	28	3	13	14	3	29
26	18 16 52	4 29 7	25 35	26	22	28	3	13	14	3	29
27	18 20 48	5 26 19	7♑56	27	21	29	3	13	14	3	29
28	18 24 45	6 23 30	20 27	29	21	0♌	3	13	14	3	29
29	18 28 41	7 20 41	3♒10	0♌	20	0	3	14	14	3	29
30	18 32 38	8 17 53	16 6	2	20	1	3	14	14	3	29

THE SUN ENTERS THE SIGN OF CANCER ON JUN 21 AT 07:07.

♈ ARIES ♉ TAURUS ♊ GEMINI ♋ CANCER ♌ LEO ♍ VIRGO ♎ LIBRA ♏ SCORPIO ♐ SAGITTARIUS ♑ CAPRICORN ♒ AQUARIUS ♓ PISCES

SIDEREAL SUN MOON MERCURY VENUS MARS JUPITER SATURN URANUS NEPTUNE PLUTO

DAY	TIME	☉	☽	☿	♀	♂	♃	♄	♅	♆	♇
	h m s	° ' "	° '	°	°	°	°	°	°	°	°
J 1	18 36 35	9♋15 4	29♒16	3♌	20♊R	1♌	3♑R	14♊	14♎	3♐R	29♍
U 2	18 40 31	10 12 15	12♓40	5	19	2	3	14	14	3	29
L 3	18 44 28	11 9 27	26 20	6	19	3	2	14	14	3	29
Y 4	18 48 24	12 6 39	10♈14	7	19	3	2	14	14	3	29
5	18 52 21	13 3 51	24 23	9	19	4	2	14	14	3	29
6	18 56 17	14 1 3	8♉45	10	18	5	2	14	14	3	0♎
7	19 0 14	14 58 16	23 16	11	18	5	2	15	14	3	0
8	19 4 10	15 55 29	7♊52	12	18	6	2	15	14	3	0
9	19 8 7	16 52 43	22 27	13	18 D	7	2	15	14	3	0
10	19 12 4	17 49 57	6♋55	14	18	7	2	15	14	3	0
11	19 16 0	18 47 11	21 10	15	18	8	1	15	14	3	0
12	19 19 57	19 44 25	5♌ 9	16	18	8	1	15	14	3	0
13	19 23 53	20 41 39	18 46	17	18	9	1	15	14	3	0
14	19 27 50	21 38 54	2♍ 2	18	19	10	1	15	14	3	0
15	19 31 46	22 36 8	14 56	19	19	10	1	16	14	3	0
16	19 35 43	23 33 23	27 31	19	19	11	1	16	14	3	0
17	19 39 39	24 30 38	9♎48	20	19	12	1	16	14	3	0
18	19 43 36	25 27 53	21 54	20	20	12	1	16	14	3	0
19	19 47 33	26 25 8	3♏50	21	20	13	1	16	15	3	0
20	19 51 29	27 22 23	15 44	21	20	14	0	16	15	3	0
21	19 55 26	28 19 39	27 37	22	21	14	0	16	15	3	0
22	19 59 22	29 16 55	9♐36	22	21	15	0	16	15	3	0
23	20 3 19	0♌14 11	21 43	22	22	15	0	16	15	3	0
24	20 7 15	1 11 28	4♑ 2	22 R	22	16	0	16	15	3	0
25	20 11 12	2 8 45	16 35	22	22	17	0	17	15	3	0
26	20 15 8	3 6 3	29 24	22	23	17	0	17	15	3	0
27	20 19 5	4 3 22	12♒28	22	24	18	0	17	15	3	0
28	20 23 2	5 0 41	25 47	22	24	19	0	17	15	3	0
29	20 26 58	5 58 1	9♓21	22	25	19	0	17	15	3	0
30	20 30 55	6 55 22	23 8	21	25	20	0	17	15	3	0
31	20 34 51	7 52 44	7♈ 5	21	26	20	29♐	17	15	3	0

THE SUN ENTERS THE SIGN OF LEO ON JUL 22 AT 18:03.

DAY	TIME	☉	☽	☿	♀	♂	♃	♄	♅	♆	♇
	h m s	° ' "	° '	°	°	°	°	°	°	°	°
A 1	20 38 48	8♌50 7	21♈10	20♌R	26♊	21♌	29♐R	17♊	15♎	3♐R	0♎
U 2	20 42 44	9 47 31	5♉21	20	27	22	29	17	15	3	0
G 3	20 46 41	10 44 57	19 34	19	28	22	29	17	15	3	0
U 4	20 50 37	11 42 24	3♊49	18	29	23	29	18	15	3	0
S 5	20 54 34	12 39 52	18 2	18	29	24	29	18	15	3	0
T 6	20 58 31	13 37 21	2♋10	17	0♋	24	29	18	15	3	0
7	21 2 27	14 34 52	16 11	16	1	25	29	18	15	3	0
8	21 6 24	15 32 23	0♌ 2	15	1	26	29	18	15	2	0
9	21 10 20	16 29 56	13 40	14	2	26	29	18	15	2	0
10	21 14 17	17 27 30	27 2	14	3	27	29	18	15	2	0
11	21 18 13	18 25 5	10♍ 8	13	4	27	29	18	15	2	0
12	21 22 10	19 22 41	22 56	12	5	28	29	18	15	2	0
13	21 26 6	20 20 18	5♎28	12	5	29	29	18	15	2	0
14	21 30 3	21 17 56	17 45	11	6	29	29	18	15	2 D	0
15	21 34 0	22 15 35	29 50	11	7	0♍	29	19	15	2	0
16	21 37 56	23 13 15	11♏47	11	8	1	29	19	15	2	0
17	21 41 53	24 10 56	23 39	11 D	9	1	29	19	16	2	1
18	21 45 49	25 8 38	5♐33	10	10	2	29	19	16	2	1
19	21 49 46	26 6 21	17 31	11	11	3	29	19	16	2	1
20	21 53 42	27 4 6	29 40	11	11	3	29	19	16	2	1
21	21 57 39	28 1 51	12♑ 4	11	12	4	29	19	16	3	1
22	22 1 35	28 59 38	24 46	11	13	4	29	19	16	3	1
23	22 5 32	29 57 26	7♒48	12	14	5	28	19	16	3	1
24	22 9 29	0♍55 15	21 11	13	15	6	28	19	16	3	1
25	22 13 25	1 53 6	4♓54	14	16	6	28 D	19	16	3	1
26	22 17 22	2 50 58	18 56	15	17	7	28	19	16	3	1
27	22 21 18	3 48 52	3♈10	16	18	8	28	19	16	3	1
28	22 25 15	4 46 47	17 33	17	19	8	28	19	16	3	1
29	22 29 11	5 44 45	1♉58	18	20	9	29	20	16	3	1
30	22 33 8	6 42 44	16 21	19	21	10	29	20	16	3	1
31	22 37 4	7 40 45	0♊38	21	22	10	29	20	16	3	1

THE SUN ENTERS THE SIGN OF VIRGO ON AUG 23 AT 01:04.

DAY	TIME	☉	☽	☿	♀	♂	♃	♄	♅	♆	♇
	h m s	° ' "	° '	°	°	°	°	°	°	°	°
S 1	22 41 1	8♍38 48	14♊46	22♌	23♋	11♍	29♐	20♊	16♎	3♐	1♎
E 2	22 44 58	9 36 53	28 44	24	24	11	29	20	16	3	1
P 3	22 48 54	10 35 0	12♋31	26	25	12	29	20	16	3	1
T 4	22 52 51	11 33 9	26 7	27	26	13	29	20	16	3	1
E 5	22 56 47	12 31 20	9♌32	29	27	13	29	20	16	3	1
M 6	23 0 44	13 29 33	22 46	1♍	28	14	29	20	17	3	1
B 7	23 4 40	14 27 48	5♍48	3	29	15	29	20	17	3	1
E 8	23 8 37	15 26 4	18 38	5	0♌	15	29	20	17	3	1
R 9	23 12 33	16 24 22	1♎14	7	1	16	29	20	17	3	1
10	23 16 30	17 22 42	13 38	8	2	17	29	20	17	3	1
11	23 20 27	18 21 3	25 50	10	3	17	29	20	17	3	1
12	23 24 23	19 19 26	7♏52	12	4	18	29	20	17	3	1
13	23 28 20	20 17 51	19 47	14	5	18	29	20	17	3	1
14	23 32 16	21 16 18	1♐37	16	6	19	29	20	17	3	1
15	23 36 13	22 14 46	13 28	18	7	20	29	20	17	3	2
16	23 40 9	23 13 16	25 25	20	8	20	29	20	17	3	2
17	23 44 6	24 11 47	7♑32	22	10	21	29	20	17	3	2
18	23 48 2	25 10 20	19 55	24	11	22	29	20	17	3	2
19	23 51 59	26 8 55	2♒38	25	12	22	29	20	17	3	2
20	23 55 56	27 7 31	15 46	27	13	23	0♑	20	17	3	2
21	23 59 52	28 6 9	29 20	29	14	24	0	20	17	3	2
22	0 3 49	29 4 49	13♓20	1♎	15	24	0	20	17	3	2
23	0 7 45	0♎ 3 31	27 43	3	16	25	0	21	18	3	2
24	0 11 42	1 2 15	12♈24	4	17	26	0	21	18	3	2
25	0 15 38	2 1 1	27 14	6	18	26	0	21	18	3	2
26	0 19 35	2 59 49	12♉ 5	8	19	27	0	21	18	3	2
27	0 23 31	3 58 39	26 48	10	21	27	0	21	18	3	2
28	0 27 28	4 57 31	11♊19	11	22	28	0	21	18	3	2
29	0 31 24	5 56 26	25 32	13	23	29	0	21	18	3	2
30	0 35 21	6 55 24	9♋27	15	24	29	0	21	18	3	2

THE SUN ENTERS THE SIGN OF LIBRA ON SEP 22 AT 22:34.

SIDEREAL SUN MOON MERCURY VENUS MARS JUPITER SATURN URANUS NEPTUNE PLUTO

DAY	TIME	☉	☽	☿	♀	♂	♃	♄	♅	♆	♇
	h m s	° ' "	° '	°	°	°	°	°	°	°	°
O 1	0 39 18	7♎54 23	23♋ 3	16♎	25♌	0♎	1♑	21♊	18♎	3♐	2♎
C 2	0 43 14	8 53 25	6♌24	18	26	1	1	21 R	18	3	2
T 3	0 47 11	9 52 29	19 30	20	27	1	1	21	18	3	2
O 4	0 51 7	10 51 35	2♍23	21	28	2	1	21	18	3	2
B 5	0 55 4	11 50 44	15 6	23	0♍	3	1	21	18	3	2
E 6	0 59 0	12 49 54	27 37	25	1	3	1	21	18	3	2
R 7	1 2 57	13 49 7	10♎ 0	26	2	4	1	21	18	3	2
8	1 6 53	14 48 22	22 12	28	3	5	1	21	18	3	2
9	1 10 50	15 47 39	4♏17	29	4	5	1	21	19	3	2
10	1 14 47	16 46 58	16 14	1♏	5	6	2	21	19	3	2
11	1 18 43	17 46 18	28 5	2	6	6	2	21	19	3	3
12	1 22 40	18 45 41	9♐54	4	8	7	2	21	19	3	3
13	1 26 36	19 45 6	21 43	5	9	8	2	20	19	3	3
14	1 30 33	20 44 32	3♑37	7	10	8	2	20	19	3	3
15	1 34 29	21 44 0	15 40	8	11	9	2	20	19	3	3
16	1 38 26	22 43 30	27 59	10	12	10	2	20	19	4	3
17	1 42 22	23 43 2	10♒39	11	13	10	3	20	19	4	3
18	1 46 19	24 42 35	23 43	13	15	11	3	20	19	4	3
19	1 50 16	25 42 10	7♓17	14	16	12	3	20	19	4	3
20	1 54 12	26 41 47	21 21	16	17	12	3	20	19	4	3
21	1 58 9	27 41 26	5♈52	17	18	13	3	20	19	4	3
22	2 2 5	28 41 7	20 47	18	19	14	3	20	19	4	3
23	2 6 2	29 40 49	5♉56	20	21	14	3	20	19	4	3
24	2 9 58	0♏40 34	21 9	21	22	15	4	20	19	4	3
25	2 13 55	1 40 21	6♊14	23	23	16	4	20	20	4	3
26	2 17 51	2 40 10	21 4	24	24	16	4	20	20	4	3
27	2 21 48	3 40 1	5♋32	25	25	17	4	20	20	4	3
28	2 25 45	4 39 54	19 35	26	27	18	4	20	20	4	3
29	2 29 41	5 39 50	3♌14	28	28	18	4	20	20	4	3
30	2 33 38	6 39 47	16 31	29	29	19	5	20	20	4	3
31	2 37 34	7 39 47	29 28	0♐	0♎	20	5	20	20	4	3

THE SUN ENTERS THE SIGN OF SCORPIO ON OCT 23 AT 07:43.

DAY	TIME	☉	☽	☿	♀	♂	♃	♄	♅	♆	♇
	h m s	° ' "	° '	°	°	°	°	°	°	°	°
N 1	2 41 31	8♏39 50	12♍ 9	1♐	1♎	20♎	5♑	20♊R	20♎	4♐	3♎
O 2	2 45 27	9 39 54	24 37	3	3	21	5	20	20	4	3
V 3	2 49 24	10 40 0	6♎55	4	4	21	5	20	20	4	3
E 4	2 53 20	11 40 8	19 4	5	5	22	5	20	20	4	3
M 5	2 57 17	12 40 18	1♏ 7	6	6	23	6	20	20	4	3
B 6	3 1 14	13 40 30	13 3	7	7	23	6	20	20	4	3
E 7	3 5 10	14 40 44	24 56	8	9	24	6	19	20	4	3
R 8	3 9 7	15 41 0	6♐45	9	10	25	6	19	20	4	3
9	3 13 3	16 41 17	18 34	9	11	25	6	19	20	4	3
10	3 17 0	17 41 36	0♑24	10	12	26	7	19	20	4	4
11	3 20 56	18 41 57	12 19	11	13	27	7	19	21	4	4
12	3 24 53	19 42 19	24 23	11	15	27	7	19	21	4	4
13	3 28 49	20 42 42	6♒40	12	16	28	7	19	21	4	4
14	3 32 46	21 43 7	19 15	12	17	29	7	19	21	4	4
15	3 36 43	22 43 33	2♓13	12 R	18	29	8	19	21	5	4
16	3 40 39	23 44 0	15 39	12	20	0♏	8	19	21	5	4
17	3 44 36	24 44 29	29 34	12	21	1	8	19	21	5	4
18	3 48 32	25 44 59	13♈58	12	22	1	8	19	21	5	4
19	3 52 29	26 45 30	28 49	12	23	2	8	19	21	5	4
20	3 56 25	27 46 3	13♉59	11	24	3	9	19	21	5	4
21	4 0 22	28 46 37	29 18	10	26	3	9	19	21	5	4
22	4 4 18	29 47 13	14♊36	9	27	4	9	18	21	5	4
23	4 8 15	0♐47 50	29 40	8	28	5	9	18	21	5	4
24	4 12 12	1 48 29	14♋24	7	29	5	9	18	21	5	4
25	4 16 8	2 49 10	28 43	6	1♏	6	10	18	21	5	4
26	4 20 5	3 49 52	12♌33	4	2	7	10	18	21	5	4
27	4 24 1	4 50 35	25 57	3	3	7	10	18	21	5	4
28	4 27 58	5 51 20	8♍56	2	4	8	10	18	21	5	4
29	4 31 54	6 52 7	21 35	0	5	9	10	18	22	5	4
30	4 35 51	7 52 55	3♎58	29♏	7	9	11	18	22	5	4

THE SUN ENTERS THE SIGN OF SAGITTARIUS ON NOV 22 AT 05:04.

DAY	TIME	☉	☽	☿	♀	♂	♃	♄	♅	♆	♇
	h m s	° ' "	° '	°	°	°	°	°	°	°	°
D 1	4 39 47	8♐53 45	16♎ 8	28♏R	8♏	10♏	11♑	18♊R	22♎	5♐	4♎
E 2	4 43 44	9 54 36	28 9	27	9	11	11	18	22	5	4
C 3	4 47 41	10 55 28	10♏ 4	27	10	11	11	18	22	5	4
E 4	4 51 37	11 56 22	21 55	26	12	12	11	18	22	5	4
M 5	4 55 34	12 57 17	3♐45	26 D	13	13	12	17	22	5	4
B 6	4 59 30	13 58 13	15 35	26	14	13	12	17	22	5	4
E 7	5 3 27	14 59 10	27 28	26	15	14	12	17	22	5	4
R 8	5 7 23	16 0 8	9♑24	27	17	15	12	17	22	5	4
9	5 11 20	17 1 7	21 26	27	18	15	13	17	22	5	4
10	5 15 16	18 2 6	3♒37	28	19	16	13	17	22	5	4
11	5 19 13	19 3 6	16 0	28	20	17	13	17	22	6	4
12	5 23 10	20 4 7	28 38	29	22	17	13	17	22	6	4
13	5 27 6	21 5 9	11♓35	0♐	23	18	13	17	22	6	4
14	5 31 3	22 6 10	24 54	1	24	19	14	17	22	6	4
15	5 34 59	23 7 12	8♈38	2	25	19	14	17	22	6	4
16	5 38 56	24 8 15	22 47	3	27	20	14	17	22	6	4
17	5 42 52	25 9 18	7♉20	4	28	21	14	16	22	6	4
18	5 46 49	26 10 22	22 12	5	29	21	15	16	22	6	4
19	5 50 45	27 11 26	7♊18	7	0♐	22	15	16	22	6	4
20	5 54 42	28 12 30	22 28	8	2	23	15	16	22	6	4
21	5 58 39	29 13 35	7♋33	9	3	23	15	16	22	6	4
22	6 2 35	0♑14 41	22 22	10	4	24	16	16	22	6	4
23	6 6 32	1 15 47	6♌50	12	5	25	16	16	22	6	4
24	6 10 28	2 16 54	20 52	13	7	25	16	16	23	6	4
25	6 14 25	3 18 1	4♍27	15	8	26	16	16	23	6	4
26	6 18 21	4 19 9	17 35	16	9	27	16	16	23	6	4
27	6 22 18	5 20 17	0♎20	17	10	28	17	16	23	6	4
28	6 26 15	6 21 26	12 45	19	12	28	17	16	23	6	4
29	6 30 11	7 22 35	24 54	20	13	29	17	16	23	6	4
30	6 34 8	8 23 45	6♏53	22	14	0♐	17	15	23	6	4
31	6 38 4	9 24 55	18 44	23	15	0	18	15	23	6	4

THE SUN ENTERS THE SIGN OF CAPRICORN ON DEC 21 AT 18:14.

♈ ARIES ♉ TAURUS ♊ GEMINI ♋ CANCER ♌ LEO ♍ VIRGO ♎ LIBRA ♏ SCORPIO ♐ SAGITTARIUS ♑ CAPRICORN ♒ AQUARIUS ♓ PISCES

1973

266 Appendix X

SIDEREAL SUN MOON MERCURY VENUS MARS JUPITER SATURN URANUS NEPTUNE PLUTO

DAY	TIME	☉	☽	☿	♀	♂	♃	♄	♅	♆	♇
	h m s	° ' "	° '	°	°	°	°	°	°	°	°
J 1	6 42 1	10♑26 6	0♐33	25♐	16♐	1♐	18♑	15♊R	23♎	6♐	4♎
A 2	6 45 57	11 27 17	12 23	26	18	2	18	15	23	6	4
N 3	6 49 54	12 28 28	24 16	28	19	2	18	15	23	6	4
U 4	6 53 50	13 29 39	6♑15	29	20	3	19	15	23	6	4
A 5	6 57 47	14 30 50	18 21	1♑	21	4	19	15	23	6	4
R 6	7 1 44	15 32 1	0♒37	2	23	4	19	15	23	6	4 R
Y 7	7 5 40	16 33 12	13 4	4	24	5	19	15	23	6	4
8	7 9 37	17 34 23	25 42	5	25	6	19	15	23	6	4
9	7 13 33	18 35 33	8♓34	7	26	6	20	15	23	6	4
10	7 17 30	19 36 42	21 41	8	28	7	20	15	23	7	4
11	7 21 26	20 37 51	5♈ 4	10	29	8	20	15	23	7	4
12	7 25 23	21 39 0	18 44	11	0♑	8	20	15	23	7	4
13	7 29 19	22 40 8	2♉41	13	1	9	21	15	23	7	4
14	7 33 16	23 41 15	16 55	14	3	10	21	14	23	7	4
15	7 37 13	24 42 22	1♊24	16	4	10	21	14	23	7	4
16	7 41 9	25 43 27	16 4	18	5	11	21	14	23	7	4
17	7 45 6	26 44 33	0♋50	19	7	12	22	14	23	7	4
18	7 49 2	27 45 37	15 35	21	8	13	22	14	23	7	4
19	7 52 59	28 46 41	0♌12	22	9	13	22	14	23	7	4
20	7 56 55	29 47 44	14 34	24	10	14	22	14	23	7	4
21	8 0 52	0♒48 47	28 37	26	12	15	22	14	23	7	4
22	8 4 48	1 49 49	12♍16	27	13	15	23	14	23	7	4
23	8 8 45	2 50 50	25 31	29	14	16	23	14	23	7	4
24	8 12 42	3 51 51	8♎23	1♒	15	17	23	14	23	7	4
25	8 16 38	4 52 52	20 53	2	17	17	23	14	23	7	4
26	8 20 35	5 53 52	3♏ 6	4	18	18	24	14	23	7	4
27	8 24 31	6 54 51	15 5	6	19	19	24	14	23 R	7	4
28	8 28 28	7 55 50	26 57	7	20	19	24	14	23	7	4
29	8 32 24	8 56 48	8♐46	9	22	20	24	14	23	7	4
30	8 36 21	9 57 45	20 36	11	23	21	25	14	23	7	4
31	8 40 17	10 58 42	2♑33	13	24	21	25	14	23	7	4

THE SUN ENTERS THE SIGN OF AQUARIUS ON JAN 20 AT 04:49.

DAY	TIME	☉	☽	☿	♀	♂	♃	♄	♅	♆	♇
	h m s	° ' "	° '	°	°	°	°	°	°	°	°
F 1	8 44 14	11♒59 38	14♑38	14♒	25♑	22♐	25♑	14♊R	23♎R	7♐	4♎R
E 2	8 48 11	13 0 33	26 56	16	27	23	25	14	23	7	4
B 3	8 52 7	14 1 26	9♒27	18	28	24	25	14	23	7	4
R 4	8 56 4	15 2 19	22 14	20	29	24	26	14	23	7	4
U 5	9 0 0	16 3 10	5♓15	21	0♒	25	26	14	23	7	4
A 6	9 3 57	17 4 1	18 30	23	2	26	26	14	23	7	4
R 7	9 7 53	18 4 49	1♈59	25	3	26	26	14	23	7	4
Y 8	9 11 50	19 5 37	15 39	27	4	27	27	14	23	7	4
9	9 15 46	20 6 22	29 29	29	5	28	27	14	23	7	4
10	9 19 43	21 7 7	13♉27	0♓	7	28	27	14	23	7	4
11	9 23 40	22 7 49	27 32	2	8	29	27	14	23	7	4
12	9 27 36	23 8 30	11♊44	4	9	0♑	28	14	23	7	4
13	9 31 33	24 9 10	25 59	6	10	1	28	14 D	23	7	4
14	9 35 29	25 9 47	10♋16	8	12	1	28	14	23	7	4
15	9 39 26	26 10 23	24 33	9	13	2	28	14	23	7	4
16	9 43 22	27 10 58	8♌44	11	14	3	28	14	23	7	4
17	9 47 19	28 11 30	22 46	13	15	3	29	14	23	7	4
18	9 51 15	29 12 1	6♍34	14	17	4	29	14	23	7	4
19	9 55 12	0♓12 31	20 5	16	18	5	29	14	23	7	4
20	9 59 9	1 12 59	3♎17	18	19	5	29	14	23	7	4
21	10 3 5	2 13 25	16 8	19	20	6	29	14	23	7	4
22	10 7 2	3 13 51	28 40	21	22	7	0♒	14	23	7	4
23	10 10 58	4 14 14	10♏55	22	23	8	0	14	23	7	4
24	10 14 55	5 14 37	22 56	23	24	8	0	14	23	7	4
25	10 18 51	6 14 58	4♐49	24	25	9	0	14	23	7	4
26	10 22 48	7 15 18	16 38	25	27	10	1	14	23	7	4
27	10 26 44	8 15 36	28 29	26	28	10	1	14	23	7	4
28	10 30 41	9 15 53	10♑26	27	29	11	1	14	23	7	4

THE SUN ENTERS THE SIGN OF PISCES ON FEB 18 AT 19:02.

DAY	TIME	☉	☽	☿	♀	♂	♃	♄	♅	♆	♇
	h m s	° ' "	° '	°	°	°	°	°	°	°	°
M 1	10 34 38	10♓16 8	22♑36	28♓	0♓	12♑	1♒	14♊	23♎R	7♐	4♎R
A 2	10 38 34	11 16 21	5♒ 1	28	2	12	1	14	23	7	4
R 3	10 42 31	12 16 33	17 45	28	3	13	2	14	23	7	4
C 4	10 46 27	13 16 43	0♓49	29 R	4	14	2	14	22	7	4
H 5	10 50 24	14 16 52	14 13	29	5	15	2	14	22	7	4
6	10 54 20	15 16 58	27 54	28	7	15	2	14	22	7	4
7	10 58 17	16 17 3	11♈51	28	8	16	2	14	22	7	4
8	11 2 13	17 17 5	25 57	28	9	17	3	14	22	7	4
9	11 6 10	18 17 5	10♉ 9	27	10	17	3	14	22	7 R	3
10	11 10 7	19 17 4	24 22	26	12	18	3	14	22	7	3
11	11 14 3	20 17 0	8♊33	26	13	19	3	14	22	7	3
12	11 18 0	21 16 54	22 41	25	14	19	3	14	22	7	3
13	11 21 56	22 16 46	6♋43	24	15	20	4	14	22	7	3
14	11 25 53	23 16 35	20 41	23	16	21	4	14	22	7	3
15	11 29 49	24 16 23	4♌32	22	18	22	4	14	22	7	3
16	11 33 46	25 16 8	18 16	21	19	22	4	14	22	7	3
17	11 37 42	26 15 50	1♍51	20	20	23	4	15	22	7	3
18	11 41 39	27 15 31	15 16	19	21	24	5	15	22	7	3
19	11 45 36	28 15 9	28 28	18	23	24	5	15	22	7	3
20	11 49 32	29 14 46	11♎26	18	24	25	5	15	22	7	3
21	11 53 29	0♈14 21	24 8	17	25	26	5	15	22	7	3
22	11 57 25	1 13 53	6♏34	16	26	27	5	15	22	7	3
23	12 1 22	2 13 24	18 46	16	28	27	5	15	22	7	3
24	12 5 18	3 12 53	0♐46	16	29	28	6	15	22	7	3
25	12 9 15	4 12 20	12 38	15	0♈	29	6	15	22	7	3
26	12 13 11	5 11 46	24 27	15	1	29	6	15	22	7	3
27	12 17 8	6 11 10	6♑17	15 D	3	0♒	6	15	22	7	3
28	12 21 5	7 10 32	18 14	15	4	1	6	15	22	7	3
29	12 25 1	8 9 52	0♒24	15	5	2	6	15	22	7	3
30	12 28 58	9 9 10	12 51	15	6	2	7	15	22	7	3
31	12 32 54	10 8 26	25 41	16	8	3	7	15	22	7	3

THE SUN ENTERS THE SIGN OF ARIES ON MAR 20 AT 18:13.

SIDEREAL SUN MOON MERCURY VENUS MARS JUPITER SATURN URANUS NEPTUNE PLUTO

DAY	TIME	☉	☽	☿	♀	♂	♃	♄	♅	♆	♇
	h m s	° ' "	° '	°	°	°	°	°	°	°	°
A 1	12 36 51	11♈ 7 41	8♓54	16♓	9♈	4♒	7♒	16♊	21♎R	7♐R	3♎R
P 2	12 40 47	12 6 53	22 33	16	10	4	7	16	21	7	3
R 3	12 44 44	13 6 4	6♈35	17	11	5	7	16	21	7	3
I 4	12 48 40	14 5 13	20 56	18	13	6	7	16	21	7	3
L 5	12 52 37	15 4 19	5♉29	18	14	6	8	16	21	7	3
6	12 56 33	16 3 24	20 8	19	15	7	8	16	21	7	3
7	13 0 30	17 2 26	4♊44	20	16	8	8	16	21	7	3
8	13 4 27	18 1 27	19 13	21	18	9	8	16	21	7	3
9	13 8 23	19 0 24	3♋30	21	19	9	8	16	21	7	3
10	13 12 20	19 59 20	17 34	22	20	10	8	16	21	7	3
11	13 16 16	20 58 13	1♌25	23	21	11	8	16	21	7	3
12	13 20 13	21 57 4	15 2	24	23	11	9	17	21	7	3
13	13 24 9	22 55 52	28 27	25	24	12	9	17	21	7	3
14	13 28 6	23 54 38	11♍41	27	25	13	9	17	21	7	3
15	13 32 2	24 53 22	24 43	28	26	14	9	17	21	7	2
16	13 35 59	25 52 4	7♎33	29	27	14	9	17	21	7	2
17	13 39 56	26 50 44	20 12	0♈	29	15	9	17	21	7	2
18	13 43 52	27 49 22	2♏39	1	0♉	16	9	17	21	7	2
19	13 47 49	28 47 58	14 54	3	1	16	9	17	21	7	2
20	13 51 45	29 46 32	26 59	4	2	17	10	17	21	7	2
21	13 55 42	0♉45 5	8♐55	5	4	18	10	17	21	7	2
22	13 59 38	1 43 35	20 45	7	5	19	10	18	21	7	2
23	14 3 35	2 42 4	2♑32	8	6	19	10	18	21	7	2
24	14 7 31	3 40 32	14 22	10	7	20	10	18	20	7	2
25	14 11 28	4 38 57	26 18	11	9	21	10	18	20	7	2
26	14 15 25	5 37 21	8♒27	13	10	21	10	18	20	7	2
27	14 19 21	6 35 44	20 53	14	11	22	10	18	20	7	2
28	14 23 18	7 34 5	3♓41	16	12	23	10	18	20	7	2
29	14 27 14	8 32 24	16 56	18	14	24	11	18	20	7	2
30	14 31 11	9 30 42	0♈38	19	15	24	11	18	20	7	2

THE SUN ENTERS THE SIGN OF TAURUS ON APR 20 AT 05:31.

DAY	TIME	☉	☽	☿	♀	♂	♃	♄	♅	♆	♇
	h m s	° ' "	° '	°	°	°	°	°	°	°	°
M 1	14 35 7	10♉28 58	14♈48	21♈	16♉	25♒	11♒	18♊	20♎R	7♐R	2♎R
A 2	14 39 4	11 27 12	29 22	23	17	26	11	19	20	7	2
Y 3	14 43 0	12 25 25	14♉13	24	18	26	11	19	20	7	2
4	14 46 57	13 23 36	29 12	26	20	27	11	19	20	7	2
5	14 50 54	14 21 46	14♊11	28	21	28	11	19	20	7	2
6	14 54 50	15 19 54	29 1	0♉	22	28	11	19	20	7	2
7	14 58 47	16 17 59	13♋37	2	23	29	11	19	20	7	2
8	15 2 43	17 16 3	27 53	4	25	0♓	11	19	20	7	2
9	15 6 40	18 14 5	11♌49	5	26	1	11	19	20	7	2
10	15 10 36	19 12 5	25 25	7	27	1	11	20	20	7	2
11	15 14 33	20 10 3	8♍42	9	28	2	12	20	20	7	2
12	15 18 29	21 7 59	21 43	11	0♊	3	12	20	20	6	2
13	15 22 26	22 5 53	4♎29	13	1	3	12	20	20	6	2
14	15 26 23	23 3 46	17 2	16	2	4	12	20	20	6	2
15	15 30 19	24 1 37	29 24	18	3	5	12	20	20	6	2
16	15 34 16	24 59 26	11♏36	20	4	6	12	20	20	6	2
17	15 38 12	25 57 14	23 40	22	6	6	12	20	20	6	2
18	15 42 9	26 55 0	5♐36	24	7	7	12	20	20	6	2
19	15 46 5	27 52 45	17 28	26	8	8	12	21	20	6	2
20	15 50 2	28 50 29	29 15	28	9	8	12	21	20	6	2
21	15 53 58	29 48 12	11♑ 3	1♊	11	9	12	21	20	6	2
22	15 57 55	0♊45 53	22 54	3	12	10	12	21	19	6	2
23	16 1 52	1 43 34	4♒51	5	13	10	12	21	19	6	2
24	16 5 48	2 41 13	17 0	7	14	11	12	21	19	6	2
25	16 9 45	3 38 51	29 25	9	16	12	12	21	19	6	2
26	16 13 41	4 36 28	12♓11	12	17	12	12	21	19	6	2
27	16 17 38	5 34 5	25 22	14	18	13	12	22	19	6	2
28	16 21 34	6 31 40	9♈ 0	16	19	14	12	22	19	6	2
29	16 25 31	7 29 15	23 6	18	20	15	12	22	19	6	2
30	16 29 27	8 26 48	7♉38	20	22	15	12 R	22	19	6	2
31	16 33 24	9 24 21	22 32	22	23	16	12	22	19	6	2

THE SUN ENTERS THE SIGN OF GEMINI ON MAY 21 AT 04:54.

DAY	TIME	☉	☽	☿	♀	♂	♃	♄	♅	♆	♇
	h m s	° ' "	° '	°	°	°	°	°	°	°	°
J 1	16 37 21	10♊21 53	7♊39	24♊	24♊	17♓	12♒R	22♊	19♎R	6♐R	2♎R
U 2	16 41 17	11 19 24	22 50	26	25	17	12	22	19	6	2
N 3	16 45 14	12 16 54	7♋56	28	27	18	12	23	19	6	2
E 4	16 49 10	13 14 22	22 48	0♋	28	19	12	23	19	6	2
5	16 53 7	14 11 50	7♌19	1	29	19	12	23	19	6	2
6	16 57 3	15 9 16	21 27	3	0♋	20	12	23	19	6	2
7	17 1 0	16 6 41	5♍10	5	1	21	12	23	19	6	2
8	17 4 57	17 4 5	18 30	7	3	21	12	23	19	6	2
9	17 8 53	18 1 28	1♎27	8	4	22	12	23	19	6	2
10	17 12 50	18 58 49	14 6	10	5	23	12	23	19	6	2
11	17 16 46	19 56 10	26 30	12	6	23	12	24	19	6	2 D
12	17 20 43	20 53 30	8♏41	13	8	24	12	24	19	6	2
13	17 24 39	21 50 48	20 42	14	9	25	12	24	19	6	2
14	17 28 36	22 48 7	2♐37	16	10	25	12	24	19	6	2
15	17 32 32	23 45 24	14 27	17	11	26	12	24	19	6	2
16	17 36 29	24 42 41	26 15	19	12	27	12	24	19	6	2
17	17 40 26	25 39 57	8♑ 3	20	14	27	12	24	19	6	2
18	17 44 22	26 37 12	19 54	21	15	28	12	24	19	6	2
19	17 48 19	27 34 27	1♒50	22	16	29	12	25	19	5	2
20	17 52 15	28 31 42	13 54	23	17	29	11	25	19	5	2
21	17 56 12	29 28 57	26 8	25	19	0♈	11	25	19	5	2
22	18 0 8	0♋26 11	8♓37	26	20	1	11	25	19	5	2
23	18 4 5	1 23 25	21 23	27	21	1	11	25	19	5	2
24	18 8 1	2 20 39	4♈31	27	22	2	11	25	19	5	2
25	18 11 58	3 17 53	18 3	28	23	3	11	25	19	5	2
26	18 15 55	4 15 7	1♉59	29	25	3	11	25	19 D	5	2
27	18 19 51	5 12 21	16 20	0♌	26	4	11	26	19	5	2
28	18 23 48	6 9 35	1♊ 3	0	27	5	11	26	19	5	2
29	18 27 44	7 6 49	16 2	1	28	5	11	26	19	5	2
30	18 31 41	8 4 3	1♋10	2	0♌	6	11	26	19	5	2

THE SUN ENTERS THE SIGN OF CANCER ON JUN 21 AT 13:01.

♈ ARIES ♉ TAURUS ♊ GEMINI ♋ CANCER ♌ LEO ♍ VIRGO ♎ LIBRA ♏ SCORPIO ♐ SAGITTARIUS ♑ CAPRICORN ♒ AQUARIUS ♓ PISCES

1973

SIDEREAL SUN MOON MERCURY VENUS MARS JUPITER SATURN URANUS NEPTUNE PLUTO

DAY	TIME	☉	☽	☿	♀	♂	♃	♄	♅	♆	♇
	h m s	° ' "	° '	°	°	°	°	°	°	°	°
J 1	18 35 37	9♋ 1 17	16♋18	2♌	1♌	7♈	11♒R	26♊	19♎	5♐R	2♎
U 2	18 39 34	9 58 30	1♌17	2	2	7	11	26	19	5	2
L 3	18 43 30	10 55 44	15 58	3	3	8	10	26	19	5	2
Y 4	18 47 27	11 52 57	0♍17	3	4	8	10	27	19	5	2
5	18 51 24	12 50 10	14 9	3	6	9	10	27	19	5	2
6	18 55 20	13 47 22	27 35	3 R	7	10	10	27	19	5	2
7	18 59 17	14 44 35	10♎36	3	8	10	10	27	19	5	2
8	19 3 13	15 41 47	23 14	3	9	11	10	27	19	5	2
9	19 7 10	16 38 59	5♏34	3	10	12	10	27	19	5	2
10	19 11 6	17 36 11	17 40	3	12	12	10	27	19	5	2
11	19 15 3	18 33 23	29 36	3	13	13	10	27	19	5	2
12	19 18 59	19 30 35	11♐26	2	14	13	10	28	19	5	2
13	19 22 56	20 27 47	23 14	2	15	14	9	28	19	5	2
14	19 26 53	21 24 59	5♑ 2	1	17	15	9	28	19	5	2
15	19 30 49	22 22 12	16 54	1	18	15	9	28	19	5	2
16	19 34 46	23 19 25	28 52	0	19	16	9	28	19	5	2
17	19 38 42	24 16 38	10♒58	0	20	16	9	28	19	5	2
18	19 42 39	25 13 51	23 13	29♋	21	17	9	28	19	5	2
19	19 46 35	26 11 5	5♓40	28	23	17	9	28	19	5	2
20	19 50 32	27 8 20	18 19	28	24	18	9	29	19	5	2
21	19 54 28	28 5 35	1♈14	27	25	19	8	29	19	5	2
22	19 58 25	29 2 52	14 25	26	26	19	8	29	19	5	2
23	20 2 22	0♌ 0 9	27 54	26	27	20	8	29	19	5	2
24	20 6 18	0 57 27	11♉42	25	29	20	8	29	19	5	2
25	20 10 15	1 54 46	25 50	24	0♍	21	8	29	19	5	2
26	20 14 11	2 52 6	10♊16	24	1	21	8	29	19	5	2
27	20 18 8	3 49 27	24 57	24	2	22	8	29	19	5	2
28	20 22 4	4 46 48	9♋49	23	4	22	8	29	19	5	2
29	20 26 1	5 44 11	24 44	23	5	23	7	0♋	19	5	2
30	20 29 57	6 41 34	9♌35	23 D	6	23	7	0	19	5	2
31	20 33 54	7 38 59	24 14	23	7	24	7	0	19	5	2

THE SUN ENTERS THE SIGN OF LEO ON JUL 22 AT 23:56.

DAY	TIME	☉	☽	☿	♀	♂	♃	♄	♅	♆	♇
	h m s	° ' "	° '	°	°	°	°	°	°	°	°
A 1	20 37 51	8♌36 24	8♍34	23♋	8♍	24♈	7♒R	0♋	19♎	5♐R	2♎
U 2	20 41 47	9 33 49	22 31	23	10	25	7	0	20	5	2
G 3	20 45 44	10 31 15	6♎ 1	23	11	26	7	0	20	5	2
U 4	20 49 40	11 28 42	19 6	24	12	26	7	0	20	5	2
S 5	20 53 37	12 26 10	1♏46	24	13	26	6	0	20	5	2
T 6	20 57 33	13 23 38	14 7	25	14	27	6	0	20	5	2
7	21 1 30	14 21 7	26 12	26	16	27	6	1	20	5	2
8	21 5 26	15 18 37	8♐ 7	26	17	28	6	1	20	5	3
9	21 9 23	16 16 8	19 55	27	18	28	6	1	20	5	3
10	21 13 20	17 13 40	1♑43	28	19	29	6	1	20	5	3
11	21 17 16	18 11 12	13 34	29	20	29	6	1	20	5	3
12	21 21 13	19 8 46	25 32	1♌	22	0♉	6	1	20	5	3
13	21 25 9	20 6 20	7♒39	2	23	0	5	1	20	5	3
14	21 29 6	21 3 56	19 58	3	24	1	5	1	20	5	3
15	21 33 2	22 1 33	2♓30	5	25	1	5	1	20	5	3
16	21 36 59	22 59 11	15 15	6	26	1	5	1	20	5 D	3
17	21 40 55	23 56 51	28 13	8	28	2	5	2	20	5	3
18	21 44 52	24 54 32	11♈24	10	29	2	5	2	20	5	3
19	21 48 49	25 52 14	24 47	11	0♎	3	5	2	20	5	3
20	21 52 45	26 49 58	8♉23	13	1	3	5	2	20	5	3
21	21 56 42	27 47 44	22 11	15	2	3	5	2	20	5	3
22	22 0 38	28 45 32	6♊11	17	4	4	4	2	20	5	3
23	22 4 35	29 43 21	20 22	19	5	4	4	2	20	5	3
24	22 8 31	0♍41 13	4♋43	21	6	4	4	2	20	5	3
25	22 12 28	1 39 5	19 12	23	7	5	4	2	20	5	3
26	22 16 24	2 37 0	3♌45	25	8	5	4	2	20	5	3
27	22 20 21	3 34 56	18 16	27	9	5	4	2	20	5	3
28	22 24 18	4 32 54	2♍39	29	11	6	4	3	21	5	3
29	22 28 14	5 30 53	16 48	1♍	12	6	4	3	21	5	3
30	22 32 11	6 28 54	0♎38	3	13	6	4	3	21	5	3
31	22 36 7	7 26 56	14 6	5	14	7	4	3	21	5	3

THE SUN ENTERS THE SIGN OF VIRGO ON AUG 23 AT 06:55.

DAY	TIME	☉	☽	☿	♀	♂	♃	♄	♅	♆	♇
	h m s	° ' "	° '	°	°	°	°	°	°	°	°
S 1	22 40 4	8♍25 0	27♎10	7♍	15♎	7♉	3♒R	3♋	21♎	5♐	3♎
E 2	22 44 0	9 23 5	9♏51	9	17	7	3	3	21	5	3
P 3	22 47 57	10 21 12	22 13	10	18	7	3	3	21	5	3
T 4	22 51 53	11 19 20	4♐18	12	19	7	3	3	21	5	3
E 5	22 55 50	12 17 29	16 12	14	20	8	3	3	21	5	3
M 6	22 59 47	13 15 41	28 1	16	21	8	3	3	21	5	3
B 7	23 3 43	14 13 53	9♑50	18	22	8	3	3	21	5	4
E 8	23 7 40	15 12 7	21 44	20	24	8	3	3	21	5	4
R 9	23 11 36	16 10 23	3♒47	22	25	8	3	3	21	5	4
10	23 15 33	17 8 40	16 3	24	26	9	3	4	21	5	4
11	23 19 29	18 6 59	28 35	25	27	9	3	4	21	5	4
12	23 23 26	19 5 19	11♓24	27	28	9	3	4	21	5	4
13	23 27 22	20 3 41	24 30	29	0♏	9	3	4	21	5	4
14	23 31 19	21 2 5	7♈51	1♎	1	9	3	4	21	5	4
15	23 35 16	22 0 31	21 26	2	2	9	3	4	21	5	4
16	23 39 12	22 59 0	5♉11	4	3	9	3	4	22	5	4
17	23 43 9	23 57 30	19 3	6	4	9	3	4	22	5	4
18	23 47 5	24 56 2	3♊ 2	7	5	9	2	4	22	5	4
19	23 51 2	25 54 37	17 4	9	7	9 R	2	4	22	5	4
20	23 54 58	26 53 14	1♋10	11	8	9	2	4	22	5	4
21	23 58 55	27 51 53	15 17	12	9	9	2	4	22	5	4
22	0 2 51	28 50 35	29 26	14	10	9	2	4	22	5	4
23	0 6 48	29 49 18	13♌35	15	11	9	2	4	22	5	4
24	0 10 45	0♎48 4	27 40	17	12	9	2	4	22	5	4
25	0 14 41	1 46 52	11♍39	18	14	9	2	4	22	5	4
26	0 18 38	2 45 42	25 27	20	15	9	2	4	22	5	4
27	0 22 34	3 44 34	9♎ 0	21	16	9	2	4	22	5	4
28	0 26 31	4 43 28	22 15	23	17	9	2 D	4	22	5	4
29	0 30 27	5 42 24	5♏11	24	18	9	2	4	22	5	4
30	0 34 24	6 41 22	17 47	26	19	9	2	4	22	5	4

THE SUN ENTERS THE SIGN OF LIBRA ON SEP 23 AT 04:23.

SIDEREAL SUN MOON MERCURY VENUS MARS JUPITER SATURN URANUS NEPTUNE PLUTO

DAY	TIME	☉	☽	☿	♀	♂	♃	♄	♅	♆	♇
	h m s	° ' "	° '	°	°	°	°	°	°	°	°
O 1	0 38 20	7♎40 21	0♐ 6	27♎	20♏	8♉R	2♒	5♋	22♎	5♐	4♎
C 2	0 42 17	8 39 23	12 10	29	22	8	2	5	22	5	4
T 3	0 46 13	9 38 26	24 4	0♏	23	8	2	5	23	5	4
O 4	0 50 10	10 37 31	5♑53	2	24	8	2	5	23	5	5
B 5	0 54 7	11 36 38	17 41	3	25	8	2	5	23	5	5
E 6	0 58 3	12 35 47	29 35	4	26	7	2	5	23	5	5
R 7	1 2 0	13 34 57	11♒41	6	27	7	2	5	23	5	5
8	1 5 56	14 34 10	24 2	7	28	7	2	5	23	5	5
9	1 9 53	15 33 24	6♓42	8	0♐	7	2	5	23	5	5
10	1 13 49	16 32 39	19 43	10	1	6	3	5	23	5	5
11	1 17 46	17 31 57	3♈ 6	11	2	6	3	5	23	5	5
12	1 21 42	18 31 17	16 49	12	3	6	3	5	23	5	5
13	1 25 39	19 30 39	0♉49	13	4	6	3	5	23	6	5
14	1 29 36	20 30 3	15 1	15	5	5	3	5	23	6	5
15	1 33 32	21 29 29	29 19	16	6	5	3	5	23	6	5
16	1 37 29	22 28 57	13♊38	17	8	5	3	5	23	6	5
17	1 41 25	23 28 28	27 56	18	9	4	3	5 R	23	6	5
18	1 45 22	24 28 1	12♋ 8	19	10	4	3	5	23	6	5
19	1 49 18	25 27 36	26 15	20	11	4	3	5	24	6	5
20	1 53 15	26 27 14	10♌14	21	12	3	3	5	24	6	5
21	1 57 11	27 26 54	24 5	22	13	3	3	5	24	6	5
22	2 1 8	28 26 36	7♍48	23	14	3	3	5	24	6	5
23	2 5 5	29 26 20	21 21	23	15	2	3	5	24	6	5
24	2 9 1	0♏26 6	4♎43	24	16	2	3	5	24	6	5
25	2 12 58	1 25 55	17 53	25	17	2	3	5	24	6	5
26	2 16 54	2 25 46	0♏49	25	19	1	4	5	24	6	5
27	2 20 51	3 25 38	13 30	26	20	1	4	5	24	6	5
28	2 24 47	4 25 33	25 55	26	21	1	4	5	24	6	5
29	2 28 44	5 25 29	8♐ 7	26	22	0	4	5	24	6	5
30	2 32 40	6 25 27	20 8	27 R	23	0	4	5	24	6	5
31	2 36 37	7 25 27	1♑59	27	24	0	4	5	24	6	6

THE SUN ENTERS THE SIGN OF SCORPIO ON OCT 23 AT 13:31.

DAY	TIME	☉	☽	☿	♀	♂	♃	♄	♅	♆	♇
	h m s	° ' "	° '	°	°	°	°	°	°	°	°
N 1	2 40 34	8♏25 29	13♑47	26♏R	25♐	29♈R	4♒	5♋R	24♎	6♐	6♎
O 2	2 44 30	9 25 32	25 34	26	26	29	4	5	24	6	6
V 3	2 48 27	10 25 37	7♒27	26	27	29	4	4	24	6	6
E 4	2 52 23	11 25 43	19 31	25	28	28	4	4	25	6	6
M 5	2 56 20	12 25 51	1♓51	24	29	28	5	4	25	6	6
B 6	3 0 16	13 26 1	14 31	23	0♑	28	5	4	25	6	6
E 7	3 4 13	14 26 11	27 36	22	1	28	5	4	25	6	6
R 8	3 8 9	15 26 24	11♈ 6	21	2	27	5	4	25	6	6
9	3 12 6	16 26 38	25 1	20	3	27	5	4	25	6	6
10	3 16 3	17 26 54	9♉18	18	5	27	5	4	25	6	6
11	3 19 59	18 27 11	23 52	17	6	27	5	4	25	6	6
12	3 23 56	19 27 31	8♊36	16	7	27	5	4	25	7	6
13	3 27 52	20 27 52	23 23	15	8	26	6	4	25	7	6
14	3 31 49	21 28 15	8♋ 5	14	9	26	6	4	25	7	6
15	3 35 45	22 28 40	22 37	13	10	26	6	4	25	7	6
16	3 39 42	23 29 7	6♌55	12	11	26	6	4	25	7	6
17	3 43 38	24 29 35	20 58	11	12	26	6	4	25	7	6
18	3 47 35	25 30 5	4♍44	11	13	26	6	4	25	7	6
19	3 51 32	26 30 38	18 15	11 D	14	26	6	4	25	7	6
20	3 55 28	27 31 12	1♎30	11	14	26	7	4	25	7	6
21	3 59 25	28 31 47	14 31	11	15	25	7	4	26	7	6
22	4 3 21	29 32 25	27 18	11	16	25	7	4	26	7	6
23	4 7 18	0♐33 4	9♏53	12	17	25	7	4	26	7	6
24	4 11 14	1 33 44	22 16	12	18	25	7	3	26	7	6
25	4 15 11	2 34 27	4♐28	13	19	25	7	3	26	7	6
26	4 19 7	3 35 10	16 30	14	20	25 D	7	3	26	7	6
27	4 23 4	4 35 55	28 25	15	21	25	8	3	26	7	6
28	4 27 1	5 36 41	10♑14	16	22	25	8	3	26	7	6
29	4 30 57	6 37 28	22 0	17	23	25	8	3	26	7	6
30	4 34 54	7 38 16	3♒47	18	24	25	8	3	26	7	6

THE SUN ENTERS THE SIGN OF SAGITTARIUS ON NOV 22 AT 10:55.

DAY	TIME	☉	☽	☿	♀	♂	♃	♄	♅	♆	♇
	h m s	° ' "	° '	°	°	°	°	°	°	°	°
D 1	4 38 50	8♐39 5	15♒40	19♏	24♑	25♈	8♒	3♋R	26♎	7♐	6♎
E 2	4 42 47	9 39 55	27 42	20	25	26	8	3	26	7	6
C 3	4 46 43	10 40 46	9♓58	22	26	26	9	3	26	7	6
E 4	4 50 40	11 41 37	22 34	23	27	26	9	3	26	7	6
M 5	4 54 36	12 42 30	5♈33	24	28	26	9	3	26	7	6
B 6	4 58 33	13 43 23	18 58	26	29	26	9	3	26	7	6
E 7	5 2 30	14 44 17	2♉50	27	29	26	9	3	26	7	7
R 8	5 6 26	15 45 12	17 10	29	0♒	26	10	2	26	7	7
9	5 10 23	16 46 8	1♊52	0♐	1	26	10	2	26	8	7
10	5 14 19	17 47 5	16 51	2	2	27	10	2	27	8	7
11	5 18 16	18 48 2	1♋58	3	2	27	10	2	27	8	7
12	5 22 12	19 49 1	17 4	5	3	27	10	2	27	8	7
13	5 26 9	20 50 0	2♌ 1	6	4	27	10	2	27	8	7
14	5 30 5	21 51 1	16 40	8	4	27	11	2	27	8	7
15	5 34 2	22 52 2	0♍58	9	5	28	11	2	27	8	7
16	5 37 59	23 53 4	14 53	11	5	28	11	2	27	8	7
17	5 41 55	24 54 8	28 24	12	6	28	11	2	27	8	7
18	5 45 52	25 55 12	11♎32	14	7	28	11	2	27	8	7
19	5 49 48	26 56 17	24 21	15	7	28	12	2	27	8	7
20	5 53 45	27 57 23	6♏54	17	8	29	12	2	27	8	7
21	5 57 41	28 58 30	19 12	18	8	29	12	1	27	8	7
22	6 1 38	29 59 38	1♐20	20	9	29	12	1	27	8	7
23	6 5 35	1♑ 0 46	13 20	21	9	0♉	12	1	27	8	7
24	6 9 31	2 1 55	25 13	23	9	0	13	1	27	8	7
25	6 13 28	3 3 4	7♑ 2	24	10	0	13	1	27	8	7
26	6 17 24	4 4 13	18 50	26	10	1	13	1	27	8	7
27	6 21 21	5 5 23	0♒38	27	10	1	13	1	27	8	7
28	6 25 17	6 6 33	12 28	29	11	1	14	1	27	8	7
29	6 29 14	7 7 42	24 24	1♑	11	1	14	1	27	8	7
30	6 33 10	8 8 52	6♓28	2	11	2	14	1	27	8	7
31	6 37 7	9 10 2	18 45	4	11	2	14	1	27	8	7

THE SUN ENTERS THE SIGN OF CAPRICORN ON DEC 22 AT 00:09.

♈ ARIES ♉ TAURUS ♊ GEMINI ♋ CANCER ♌ LEO ♍ VIRGO ♎ LIBRA ♏ SCORPIO ♐ SAGITTARIUS ♑ CAPRICORN ♒ AQUARIUS ♓ PISCES

SIDEREAL SUN MOON MERCURY VENUS MARS JUPITER SATURN URANUS NEPTUNE PLUTO

DAY	TIME	☉	☽	☿	♀	♂	♃	♄	♅	♆	♇
	h m s	° ' "	° '	°	°	°	°	°	°	°	°
J 1	6 41 4	10♑11 12	1♈17	5♑	11♒	3♉	14♒	1♋R	27♎	8♐	7♎
A 2	6 45 0	11 12 21	14 9	7	11	3	15	0	27	8	7
N 3	6 48 57	12 13 30	27 23	8	11 R	3	15	0	27	8	7
U 4	6 52 53	13 14 39	11♉ 4	10	11	4	15	0	27	8	7
A 5	6 56 50	14 15 48	25 11	12	11	4	15	0	27	8	7
R 6	7 0 46	15 16 56	9♊45	13	11	4	16	0	27	8	7
Y 7	7 4 43	16 18 5	24 40	15	11	5	16	0	27	9	7
8	7 8 39	17 19 13	9♋50	16	11	5	16	0	28	9	7
9	7 12 36	18 20 20	25 6	18	11	6	16	0	28	9	7 R
10	7 16 33	19 21 28	10♌18	20	10	6	16	0	28	9	7
11	7 20 29	20 22 35	25 16	21	10	6	17	0	28	9	7
12	7 24 26	21 23 42	9♍52	23	10	7	17	0	28	9	7
13	7 28 22	22 24 49	24 2	25	9	7	17	0	28	9	7
14	7 32 19	23 25 56	7♎43	26	9	8	17	0	28	9	7
15	7 36 15	24 27 3	20 56	28	9	8	18	29♊	28	9	7
16	7 40 12	25 28 10	3♏45	0♒	8	9	18	29	28	9	7
17	7 44 8	26 29 16	16 12	1	8	9	18	29	28	9	7
18	7 48 5	27 30 22	28 23	3	7	9	18	29	28	9	7
19	7 52 2	28 31 28	10♐22	5	6	10	18	29	28	9	7
20	7 55 58	29 32 34	22 14	7	6	10	19	29	28	9	7
21	7 59 55	0♒33 39	4♑ 2	8	5	11	19	29	28	9	7
22	8 3 51	1 34 44	15 48	10	5	11	19	29	28	9	7
23	8 7 48	2 35 48	27 37	12	4	12	19	29	28	9	7
24	8 11 44	3 36 51	9♒29	13	3	12	20	29	28	9	7
25	8 15 41	4 37 53	21 27	15	3	13	20	29	28	9	7
26	8 19 37	5 38 55	3♓32	17	2	13	20	29	28	9	7
27	8 23 34	6 39 55	15 45	19	2	14	20	29	28	9	7
28	8 27 31	7 40 55	28 9	20	1	14	21	29	28	9	7
29	8 31 27	8 41 53	10♈46	22	0	15	21	29	28	9	7
30	8 35 24	9 42 50	23 38	24	0	15	21	29	28	9	7
31	8 39 20	10 43 46	6♉47	25	29♑	16	21	28	28	9	7

THE SUN ENTERS THE SIGN OF AQUARIUS ON JAN 20 AT 10:47.

DAY	TIME	☉	☽	☿	♀	♂	♃	♄	♅	♆	♇
	h m s	° ' "	° '	°	°	°	°	°	°	°	°
F 1	8 43 17	11♒44 41	20♉17	27♒	29♑R	16♉	22♒	28♊R	28♎R	9♐	7♎R
E 2	8 47 13	12 45 34	4♊ 9	29	28	17	22	28	28	9	7
B 3	8 51 10	13 46 26	18 24	0♓	28	17	22	28	28	9	7
R 4	8 55 6	14 47 17	3♋ 0	2	28	18	22	28	28	9	7
U 5	8 59 3	15 48 6	17 55	3	27	18	22	28	28	9	7
A 6	9 3 0	16 48 54	3♌ 2	4	27	19	23	28	28	9	7
R 7	9 6 56	17 49 41	18 10	6	27	19	23	28	28	9	7
Y 8	9 10 53	18 50 26	3♍11	7	26	20	23	28	28	9	7
9	9 14 49	19 51 10	17 55	8	26	20	23	28	28	9	7
10	9 18 46	20 51 53	2♎15	9	26	21	24	28	28	9	7
11	9 22 42	21 52 35	16 6	10	26	21	24	28	28	9	7
12	9 26 39	22 53 16	29 28	11	26	22	24	28	28	9	7
13	9 30 35	23 53 56	12♏22	11	26 D	22	24	28	28	9	6
14	9 34 32	24 54 34	24 53	12	26	23	25	28	28	9	6
15	9 38 29	25 55 12	7♐ 4	12 R	26	23	25	28	28	9	6
16	9 42 25	26 55 48	19 1	12	26	24	25	28	28	9	6
17	9 46 22	27 56 23	0♑51	12	26	24	25	28	28	9	6
18	9 50 18	28 56 57	12 37	11	26	25	26	28	28	9	6
19	9 54 15	29 57 30	24 24	11	26	25	26	28	28	9	6
20	9 58 11	0♓58 1	6♒16	10	27	26	26	28	28	10	6
21	10 2 8	1 58 30	18 15	10	27	26	26	28	28	10	6
22	10 6 4	2 58 58	0♓23	9	27	27	27	28	28	10	6
23	10 10 1	3 59 25	12 41	8	28	28	27	28	28	10	6
24	10 13 58	4 59 49	25 9	7	28	28	27	28	28	10	6
25	10 17 54	6 0 12	7♈49	6	28	29	27	28	28	10	6
26	10 21 51	7 0 33	20 40	5	29	29	28	28	28	10	6
27	10 25 47	8 0 52	3♉43	4	29	0♊	28	28 D	27	10	6
28	10 29 44	9 1 9	16 59	3	0♒	0	28	28	27	10	6

THE SUN ENTERS THE SIGN OF PISCES ON FEB 19 AT 00:59.

DAY	TIME	☉	☽	☿	♀	♂	♃	♄	♅	♆	♇
	h m s	° ' "	° '	°	°	°	°	°	°	°	°
M 1	10 33 40	10♓ 1 25	0♊28	2♓R	0♒	1♊	28♒	28♊	27♎R	10♐	6♎R
A 2	10 37 37	11 1 38	14 13	1	1	1	28	28	27	10	6
R 3	10 41 33	12 1 49	28 14	0	1	2	29	28	27	10	6
C 4	10 45 30	13 1 58	12♋31	29♒	2	3	29	28	27	10	6
H 5	10 49 27	14 2 5	27 3	28	2	3	29	28	27	10	6
6	10 53 23	15 2 10	11♌46	28	3	4	29	28	27	10	6
7	10 57 20	16 2 13	26 34	28	4	4	0♓	28	27	10	6
8	11 1 16	17 2 13	11♍19	27	4	5	0	28	27	10	6
9	11 5 13	18 2 12	25 53	27 D	5	5	0	28	27	10	6
10	11 9 9	19 2 9	10♎ 8	27	6	6	0	28	27	10	6
11	11 13 6	20 2 4	23 59	27	6	6	1	28	27	10	6
12	11 17 2	21 1 58	7♏23	27	7	7	1	28	27	10 R	6
13	11 20 59	22 1 49	20 22	28	8	8	1	28	27	10	6
14	11 24 56	23 1 39	2♐56	28	9	8	1	28	27	10	6
15	11 28 52	24 1 28	15 11	28	10	9	2	28	27	10	6
16	11 32 49	25 1 14	27 11	29	10	9	2	28	27	10	6
17	11 36 45	26 0 59	9♑ 2	29	11	10	2	28	27	10	6
18	11 40 42	27 0 43	20 49	0♓	12	10	2	28	27	10	6
19	11 44 38	28 0 24	2♒39	1	13	11	2	28	27	10	6
20	11 48 35	29 0 4	14 34	2	14	12	3	28	27	10	6
21	11 52 31	29 59 41	26 39	2	14	12	3	28	27	10	6
22	11 56 28	0♈59 17	8♓57	3	15	13	3	28	27	10	6
23	12 0 24	1 58 51	21 29	4	16	13	3	28	27	10	6
24	12 4 21	2 58 23	4♈15	5	17	14	4	28	27	10	6
25	12 8 18	3 57 53	17 15	6	18	15	4	28	27	10	6
26	12 12 14	4 57 21	0♉28	7	19	15	4	28	27	10	5
27	12 16 11	5 56 47	13 51	8	20	16	4	28	27	10	5
28	12 20 7	6 56 10	27 24	10	21	16	4	29	27	10	5
29	12 24 4	7 55 32	11♊ 7	11	22	17	5	29	27	10	5
30	12 28 0	8 54 51	24 58	12	23	17	5	29	26	10	5
31	12 31 57	9 54 7	8♋57	13	24	18	5	29	26	10	5

THE SUN ENTERS THE SIGN OF ARIES ON MAR 21 AT 00:07.

SIDEREAL SUN MOON MERCURY VENUS MARS JUPITER SATURN URANUS NEPTUNE PLUTO

DAY	TIME	☉	☽	☿	♀	♂	♃	♄	♅	♆	♇
	h m s	° ' "	° '	°	°	°	°	°	°	°	°
A 1	12 35 53	10♈53 21	23♋ 5	15♓	25♒	19♊	5♓	29♊	26♎R	10♐R	5♎R
P 2	12 39 50	11 52 33	7♌19	16	25	19	6	29	26	9	5
R 3	12 43 47	12 51 43	21 39	17	26	20	6	29	26	9	5
I 4	12 47 43	13 50 50	6♍ 1	19	27	20	6	29	26	9	5
L 5	12 51 40	14 49 55	20 19	20	28	21	6	29	26	9	5
6	12 55 36	15 48 58	4♎28	21	29	22	6	29	26	9	5
7	12 59 33	16 47 58	18 24	23	0♓	22	7	29	26	9	5
8	13 3 29	17 46 57	2♏ 0	24	1	23	7	29	26	9	5
9	13 7 26	18 45 54	15 16	26	2	23	7	29	26	9	5
10	13 11 22	19 44 49	28 10	27	3	24	7	29	26	9	5
11	13 15 19	20 43 42	10♐43	29	4	24	7	29	26	9	5
12	13 19 16	21 42 33	22 59	1♈	5	25	8	29	26	9	5
13	13 23 12	22 41 23	5♑ 1	2	7	26	8	0♋	26	9	5
14	13 27 9	23 40 11	16 54	4	8	26	8	0	26	9	5
15	13 31 5	24 38 57	28 44	6	9	27	8	0	26	9	5
16	13 35 2	25 37 41	10♒35	7	10	27	8	0	26	9	5
17	13 38 58	26 36 24	22 33	9	11	28	9	0	26	9	5
18	13 42 55	27 35 4	4♓43	11	12	29	9	0	26	9	5
19	13 46 51	28 33 43	17 7	12	13	29	9	0	26	9	5
20	13 50 48	29 32 21	29 49	14	14	0♋	9	0	26	9	5
21	13 54 45	0♉30 56	12♈49	16	15	0	9	0	26	9	5
22	13 58 41	1 29 30	26 7	18	16	1	10	0	26	9	5
23	14 2 38	2 28 2	9♉42	20	17	2	10	0	25	9	5
24	14 6 34	3 26 32	23 30	22	18	2	10	0	25	9	5
25	14 10 31	4 25 0	7♊29	24	19	3	10	1	25	9	5
26	14 14 27	5 23 26	21 34	26	20	3	10	1	25	9	5
27	14 18 24	6 21 50	5♋44	28	21	4	11	1	25	9	5
28	14 22 20	7 20 12	19 55	0♉	22	5	11	1	25	9	5
29	14 26 17	8 18 31	4♌ 6	2	24	5	11	1	25	9	5
30	14 30 14	9 16 49	18 15	4	25	6	11	1	25	9	5

THE SUN ENTERS THE SIGN OF TAURUS ON APR 20 AT 11:19.

DAY	TIME	☉	☽	☿	♀	♂	♃	♄	♅	♆	♇
	h m s	° ' "	° '	°	°	°	°	°	°	°	°
M 1	14 34 10	10♉15 4	2♍20	6♉	26♓	6♋	11♓	1♋	25♎R	9♐R	5♎R
A 2	14 38 7	11 13 18	16 20	8	27	7	11	1	25	9	5
Y 3	14 42 3	12 11 29	0♎12	10	28	8	12	1	25	9	5
4	14 46 0	13 9 38	13 53	12	29	8	12	1	25	9	5
5	14 49 56	14 7 46	27 22	14	0♈	9	12	1	25	9	4
6	14 53 53	15 5 52	10♏36	17	1	9	12	2	25	9	4
7	14 57 49	16 3 56	23 34	19	2	10	12	2	25	9	4
8	15 1 46	17 1 59	6♐15	21	4	11	12	2	25	9	4
9	15 5 43	18 0 0	18 41	23	5	11	13	2	25	9	4
10	15 9 39	18 57 59	0♑53	25	6	12	13	2	25	9	4
11	15 13 36	19 55 57	12 53	27	7	12	13	2	25	9	4
12	15 17 32	20 53 54	24 47	0♊	8	13	13	2	25	9	4
13	15 21 29	21 51 50	6♒37	2	9	14	13	2	25	9	4
14	15 25 25	22 49 44	18 29	4	10	14	13	2	25	9	4
15	15 29 22	23 47 37	0♓28	6	11	15	14	3	25	9	4
16	15 33 18	24 45 28	12 39	8	12	15	14	3	25	9	4
17	15 37 15	25 43 18	25 5	10	14	16	14	3	25	9	4
18	15 41 12	26 41 8	7♈50	12	15	17	14	3	24	9	4
19	15 45 8	27 38 56	20 57	14	16	17	14	3	24	9	4
20	15 49 5	28 36 42	4♉26	15	17	18	14	3	24	9	4
21	15 53 1	29 34 28	18 17	17	18	18	14	3	24	8	4
22	15 56 58	0♊32 12	2♊26	19	19	19	15	3	24	8	4
23	16 0 54	1 29 55	16 49	21	20	20	15	3	24	8	4
24	16 4 51	2 27 37	1♋21	22	22	20	15	4	24	8	4
25	16 8 47	3 25 17	15 56	24	23	21	15	4	24	8	4
26	16 12 44	4 22 56	0♌29	25	24	21	15	4	24	8	4
27	16 16 41	5 20 33	14 54	27	25	22	15	4	24	8	4
28	16 20 37	6 18 9	29 9	28	26	23	15	4	24	8	4
29	16 24 34	7 15 43	13♍12	0♋	27	23	15	4	24	8	4
30	16 28 30	8 13 16	27 0	1	28	24	16	4	24	8	4
31	16 32 27	9 10 47	10♎34	2	0♉	24	16	4	24	8	4

THE SUN ENTERS THE SIGN OF GEMINI ON MAY 21 AT 10:37.

DAY	TIME	☉	☽	☿	♀	♂	♃	♄	♅	♆	♇
	h m s	° ' "	° '	°	°	°	°	°	°	°	°
J 1	16 36 23	10♊ 8 18	23♎53	3♋	1♉	25♋	16♓	5♋	24♎R	8♐R	4♎R
U 2	16 40 20	11 5 46	6♏57	4	2	26	16	5	24	8	4
N 3	16 44 16	12 3 14	19 48	6	3	26	16	5	24	8	4
E 4	16 48 13	13 0 41	2♐25	7	4	27	16	5	24	8	4
5	16 52 10	13 58 6	14 50	7	5	28	16	5	24	8	4
6	16 56 6	14 55 31	27 4	8	7	28	16	5	24	8	4
7	17 0 3	15 52 55	9♑ 8	9	8	29	16	5	24	8	4
8	17 3 59	16 50 18	21 4	10	9	29	16	5	24	8	4
9	17 7 56	17 47 40	2♒56	11	10	0♌	17	6	24	8	4
10	17 11 52	18 45 2	14 47	11	11	1	17	6	24	8	4
11	17 15 49	19 42 23	26 39	12	12	1	17	6	24	8	4
12	17 19 45	20 39 44	8♓38	12	14	2	17	6	24	8	4
13	17 23 42	21 37 4	20 47	13	15	2	17	6	24	8	4
14	17 27 39	22 34 23	3♈11	13	16	3	17	6	24	8	4 D
15	17 31 35	23 31 43	15 55	13	17	4	17	6	24	8	4
16	17 35 32	24 29 2	29 1	14	18	4	17	6	24	8	4
17	17 39 28	25 26 20	12♉31	14 R	19	5	17	7	24	8	4
18	17 43 25	26 23 38	26 27	14	21	5	17	7	24	8	4
19	17 47 21	27 20 56	10♊47	14	22	6	17	7	24	8	4
20	17 51 18	28 18 14	25 27	13	23	7	17	7	24	8	4
21	17 55 14	29 15 31	10♋20	13	24	7	17	7	24	8	4
22	17 59 11	0♋12 47	25 19	13	25	8	17	7	24	8	4
23	18 3 8	1 10 3	10♌15	13	26	9	18	7	24	8	4
24	18 7 4	2 7 19	25 1	12	28	9	18	7	24	8	4
25	18 11 1	3 4 33	9♍30	12	29	10	18	8	24	8	4
26	18 14 57	4 1 47	23 39	11	0♊	10	18	8	24	8	4
27	18 18 54	4 59 1	7♎27	11	1	11	18	8	24	8	4
28	18 22 50	5 56 13	20 52	10	2	12	18	8	24	8	4
29	18 26 47	6 53 26	3♏58	10	4	12	18	8	24	7	4
30	18 30 43	7 50 38	16 45	9	5	13	18	8	24	7	4

THE SUN ENTERS THE SIGN OF CANCER ON JUN 21 AT 18:38.

♈ ARIES ♉ TAURUS ♊ GEMINI ♋ CANCER ♌ LEO ♍ VIRGO ♎ LIBRA ♏ SCORPIO ♐ SAGITTARIUS ♑ CAPRICORN ♒ AQUARIUS ♓ PISCES

SIDEREAL SUN MOON MERCURY VENUS MARS JUPITER SATURN URANUS NEPTUNE PLUTO

DAY	TIME	☉	☽	☿	♀	♂	♃	♄	♅	♆	♇
	h m s	° ' "	° '	°	°	°	°	°	°	°	°
J 1	18 34 40	8♋47 50	29♏18	9♋R	6♊	13♌	18♓	8♋	24♎R	7♐R	4♎
U 2	18 38 37	9 45 1	11♐38	8	7	14	18	9	24 D	7	4
L 3	18 42 33	10 42 12	23 48	7	8	15	18	9	24	7	4
Y 4	18 46 30	11 39 23	5♑50	7	9	15	18	9	24	7	4
5	18 50 26	12 36 34	17 47	6	11	16	18	9	24	7	4
6	18 54 23	13 33 45	29 39	6	12	17	18	9	24	7	4
7	18 58 19	14 30 56	11♒30	5	13	17	18 R	9	24	7	4
8	19 2 16	15 28 7	23 21	5	14	18	18	9	24	7	4
9	19 6 12	16 25 19	5♓15	5	15	18	18	9	24	7	4
10	19 10 9	17 22 30	17 15	5	17	19	18	10	24	7	4
11	19 14 6	18 19 42	29 24	4	18	20	18	10	24	7	4
12	19 18 2	19 16 55	11♈46	4 D	19	20	18	10	24	7	4
13	19 21 59	20 14 8	24 26	4	20	21	18	10	24	7	4
14	19 25 55	21 11 22	7♉26	5	21	22	18	10	24	7	4
15	19 29 52	22 8 36	20 52	5	23	22	18	10	24	7	4
16	19 33 48	23 5 51	4♊43	5	24	23	18	10	24	7	4
17	19 37 45	24 3 6	19 2	5	25	23	18	10	24	7	4
18	19 41 42	25 0 22	3♋45	6	26	24	18	11	24	7	4
19	19 45 38	25 57 39	18 46	7	27	25	18	11	24	7	4
20	19 49 35	26 54 56	3♌59	7	29	25	18	11	24	7	4
21	19 53 31	27 52 14	19 12	8	0♋	26	18	11	24	7	4
22	19 57 28	28 49 31	4♍15	9	1	27	18	11	24	7	4
23	20 1 24	29 46 50	19 1	10	2	27	17	11	24	7	4
24	20 5 21	0♌44 8	3♎21	11	3	28	17	11	24	7	4
25	20 9 17	1 41 27	17 15	12	5	28	17	11	24	7	5
26	20 13 14	2 38 46	0♏41	13	6	29	17	12	24	7	5
27	20 17 11	3 36 5	13 42	14	7	0♍	17	12	24	7	5
28	20 21 7	4 33 26	26 22	16	8	0	17	12	24	7	5
29	20 25 4	5 30 46	8♐44	17	9	1	17	12	24	7	5
30	20 29 0	6 28 7	20 54	19	11	2	17	12	24	7	5
31	20 32 57	7 25 29	2♑54	20	12	2	17	12	24	7	5

THE SUN ENTERS THE SIGN OF LEO ON JUL 23 AT 05:31.

DAY	TIME	☉	☽	☿	♀	♂	♃	♄	♅	♆	♇
	h m s	° ' "	° '	°	°	°	°	°	°	°	°
A 1	20 36 53	8♌22 51	14♑48	22♋	13♋	3♍	17♓R	12♋	24♎	7♐R	5♎
U 2	20 40 50	9 20 14	26 39	24	14	3	17	12	24	7	5
G 3	20 44 46	10 17 38	8♒30	25	15	4	17	13	24	7	5
U 4	20 48 43	11 15 3	20 21	27	17	5	17	13	24	7	5
S 5	20 52 40	12 12 29	2♓16	29	18	5	17	13	24	7	5
T 6	20 56 36	13 9 55	14 14	1♌	19	6	17	13	24	7	5
7	21 0 33	14 7 23	26 19	3	20	7	16	13	24	7	5
8	21 4 29	15 4 52	8♈33	5	21	7	16	13	24	7	5
9	21 8 26	16 2 22	20 57	7	23	8	16	13	24	7	5
10	21 12 22	16 59 54	3♉36	9	24	8	16	13	24	7	5
11	21 16 19	17 57 27	16 33	11	25	9	16	14	24	7	5
12	21 20 15	18 55 2	29 51	13	26	10	16	14	24	7	5
13	21 24 12	19 52 38	13♊34	15	28	10	16	14	24	7	5
14	21 28 9	20 50 15	27 42	17	29	11	16	14	24	7	5
15	21 32 5	21 47 54	12♋16	19	0♌	12	16	14	24	7	5
16	21 36 2	22 45 35	27 12	21	1	12	15	14	25	7	5
17	21 39 58	23 43 17	12♌23	23	2	13	15	14	25	7	5
18	21 43 55	24 41 0	27 38	25	4	13	15	14	25	7	5
19	21 47 51	25 38 44	12♍48	27	5	14	15	14	25	7 D	5
20	21 51 48	26 36 30	27 42	29	6	15	15	15	25	7	5
21	21 55 44	27 34 16	12♎12	1♍	7	15	15	15	25	7	5
22	21 59 41	28 32 4	26 13	3	9	16	15	15	25	7	5
23	22 3 37	29 29 54	9♏44	5	10	17	15	15	25	7	5
24	22 7 34	0♍27 44	22 48	7	11	17	15	15	25	7	5
25	22 11 31	1 25 36	5♐27	9	12	18	14	15	25	7	5
26	22 15 27	2 23 28	17 47	11	13	19	14	15	25	7	5
27	22 19 24	3 21 22	29 52	13	15	19	14	15	25	7	5
28	22 23 20	4 19 18	11♑48	14	16	20	14	15	25	7	5
29	22 27 17	5 17 14	23 39	16	17	20	14	15	25	7	5
30	22 31 13	6 15 13	5♒29	18	18	21	14	16	25	7	6
31	22 35 10	7 13 12	17 20	20	20	22	14	16	25	7	6

THE SUN ENTERS THE SIGN OF VIRGO ON AUG 23 AT 12:30.

DAY	TIME	☉	☽	☿	♀	♂	♃	♄	♅	♆	♇
	h m s	° ' "	° '	°	°	°	°	°	°	°	°
S 1	22 39 6	8♍11 13	29♒15	21♍	21♌	22♍	14♓R	16♋	25♎	7♐	6♎
E 2	22 43 3	9 9 16	11♓16	23	22	23	13	16	25	7	6
P 3	22 47 0	10 7 20	23 24	25	23	24	13	16	25	7	6
T 4	22 50 56	11 5 26	5♈39	26	25	24	13	16	25	7	6
E 5	22 54 53	12 3 33	18 3	28	26	25	13	16	25	7	6
M 6	22 58 49	13 1 43	0♉36	0♎	27	26	13	16	25	7	6
B 7	23 2 46	13 59 55	13 22	1	28	26	13	16	25	7	6
E 8	23 6 42	14 58 8	26 22	3	29	27	13	16	26	7	6
R 9	23 10 39	15 56 24	9♊39	4	1♍	28	12	16	26	7	6
10	23 14 35	16 54 42	23 15	6	2	28	12	17	26	7	6
11	23 18 32	17 53 2	7♋13	7	3	29	12	17	26	7	6
12	23 22 29	18 51 24	21 32	9	4	29	12	17	26	7	6
13	23 26 25	19 49 48	6♌12	10	6	0♎	12	17	26	7	6
14	23 30 22	20 48 14	21 6	12	7	1	12	17	26	7	6
15	23 34 18	21 46 42	6♍ 8	13	8	1	12	17	26	7	6
16	23 38 15	22 45 12	21 9	15	9	2	12	17	26	7	6
17	23 42 11	23 43 44	5♎58	16	11	3	11	17	26	7	6
18	23 46 8	24 42 18	20 26	17	12	3	11	17	26	7	6
19	23 50 4	25 40 53	4♏30	19	13	4	11	17	26	7	6
20	23 54 1	26 39 31	18 4	20	14	5	11	17	26	7	6
21	23 57 58	27 38 10	1♐12	22	16	5	11	17	26	7	6
22	0 1 54	28 36 51	13 54	23	17	6	11	17	26	7	6
23	0 5 51	29 35 33	26 16	24	18	7	11	18	26	7	6
24	0 9 47	0♎34 17	8♑22	25	19	7	11	18	26	7	6
25	0 13 44	1 33 3	20 18	27	21	8	10	18	26	7	6
26	0 17 40	2 31 51	2♒ 9	28	22	9	10	18	27	7	7
27	0 21 37	3 30 40	13 59	29	23	9	10	18	27	7	7
28	0 25 33	4 29 31	25 53	0♏	24	10	10	18	27	7	7
29	0 29 30	5 28 24	7♓53	1	26	11	10	18	27	7	7
30	0 33 27	6 27 19	20 2	2	27	11	10	18	27	7	7

THE SUN ENTERS THE SIGN OF LIBRA ON SEP 23 AT 09:60.

SIDEREAL SUN MOON MERCURY VENUS MARS JUPITER SATURN URANUS NEPTUNE PLUTO

DAY	TIME	☉	☽	☿	♀	♂	♃	♄	♅	♆	♇
	h m s	° ' "	° '	°	°	°	°	°	°	°	°
O 1	0 37 23	7♎26 15	2♈21	3♏	28♍	12♎	10♓R	18♋	27♎	7♐	7♎
C 2	0 41 20	8 25 14	14 51	4	29	13	10	18	27	7	7
T 3	0 45 16	9 24 15	27 31	5	0♎	13	10	18	27	7	7
O 4	0 49 13	10 23 18	10♉22	6	2	14	10	18	27	7	7
B 5	0 53 9	11 22 23	23 24	7	3	14	9	18	27	7	7
E 6	0 57 6	12 21 30	6♊38	7	4	15	9	18	27	7	7
R 7	1 1 2	13 20 40	20 4	8	5	16	9	18	27	7	7
8	1 4 59	14 19 52	3♋43	9	7	16	9	18	27	8	7
9	1 8 55	15 19 6	17 37	9	8	17	9	18	27	8	7
10	1 12 52	16 18 23	1♌45	10	9	18	9	18	27	8	7
11	1 16 49	17 17 42	16 6	10	10	18	9	19	27	8	7
12	1 20 45	18 17 3	0♍39	10	12	19	9	19	28	8	7
13	1 24 42	19 16 27	15 16	11 R	13	20	9	19	28	8	7
14	1 28 38	20 15 53	29 53	11	14	20	9	19	28	8	7
15	1 32 35	21 15 20	14♎22	11	15	21	9	19	28	8	7
16	1 36 31	22 14 50	28 36	10	17	22	9	19	28	8	7
17	1 40 28	23 14 22	12♏29	10	18	22	9	19	28	8	7
18	1 44 24	24 13 56	26 0	9	19	23	8	19	28	8	7
19	1 48 21	25 13 32	9♐ 6	9	20	24	8	19	28	8	7
20	1 52 18	26 13 10	21 50	8	22	24	8	19	28	8	7
21	1 56 14	27 12 49	4♑14	7	23	25	8	19	28	8	7
22	2 0 11	28 12 30	16 23	6	24	26	8	19	28	8	8
23	2 4 7	29 12 13	28 21	5	25	26	8	19	28	8	8
24	2 8 4	0♏11 58	10♒13	4	27	27	8	19	28	8	8
25	2 12 0	1 11 44	22 5	2	28	28	8	19	28	8	8
26	2 15 57	2 11 32	4♓ 1	1	29	28	8	19	28	8	8
27	2 19 53	3 11 22	16 5	0	1♏	29	8	19	28	8	8
28	2 23 50	4 11 13	28 20	29♎	2	0♏	8	19	29	8	8
29	2 27 47	5 11 6	10♈49	28	3	0	8	19	29	8	8
30	2 31 43	6 11 1	23 32	27	4	1	8	19	29	8	8
31	2 35 40	7 10 58	6♉31	26	6	2	8	19 R	29	8	8

THE SUN ENTERS THE SIGN OF SCORPIO ON OCT 23 AT 19:12.

DAY	TIME	☉	☽	☿	♀	♂	♃	♄	♅	♆	♇
	h m s	° ' "	° '	°	°	°	°	°	°	°	°
N 1	2 39 36	8♏10 57	19♉44	25♎R	7♏	2♏	8♓R	19♋R	29♎	8♐	8♎
O 2	2 43 33	9 10 58	3♊ 9	25	8	3	8	19	29	8	8
V 3	2 47 29	10 11 0	16 47	25 D	9	4	8 D	19	29	8	8
E 4	2 51 26	11 11 5	0♋34	25	11	5	8	19	29	8	8
M 5	2 55 22	12 11 12	14 29	25	12	5	8	19	29	8	8
B 6	2 59 19	13 11 21	28 32	25	13	6	8	19	29	8	8
E 7	3 3 16	14 11 32	12♌39	26	14	7	8	19	29	8	8
R 8	3 7 12	15 11 45	26 51	27	16	7	8	19	29	8	8
9	3 11 9	16 12 0	11♍ 5	27	17	8	8	19	29	8	8
10	3 15 5	17 12 17	25 17	28	18	9	8	19	29	9	8
11	3 19 2	18 12 37	9♎25	29	19	9	8	19	29	9	8
12	3 22 58	19 12 58	23 25	0♏	21	10	8	19	29	9	8
13	3 26 55	20 13 20	7♏13	2	22	11	8	19	0♏	9	8
14	3 30 51	21 13 45	20 46	3	23	11	8	19	0	9	8
15	3 34 48	22 14 11	4♐ 1	4	24	12	8	19	0	9	8
16	3 38 45	23 14 39	16 59	5	26	13	8	19	0	9	8
17	3 42 41	24 15 9	29 38	7	27	13	8	19	0	9	8
18	3 46 38	25 15 40	12♑ 1	8	28	14	8	19	0	9	8
19	3 50 34	26 16 12	24 10	10	29	15	8	19	0	9	8
20	3 54 31	27 16 45	6♒ 9	11	1♐	15	8	19	0	9	8
21	3 58 27	28 17 20	18 2	13	2	16	9	19	0	9	9
22	4 2 24	29 17 56	29 54	14	3	17	9	18	0	9	9
23	4 6 20	0♐18 33	11♓50	16	4	18	9	18	0	9	9
24	4 10 17	1 19 11	23 54	17	6	18	9	18	0	9	9
25	4 14 14	2 19 50	6♈10	19	7	19	9	18	0	9	9
26	4 18 10	3 20 30	18 43	20	8	20	9	18	0	9	9
27	4 22 7	4 21 12	1♉35	22	9	20	9	18	0	9	9
28	4 26 3	5 21 55	14 46	23	11	21	9	18	0	9	9
29	4 30 0	6 22 39	28 18	25	12	22	9	18	0	9	9
30	4 33 56	7 23 24	12♊ 8	26	13	22	9	18	0	9	9

THE SUN ENTERS THE SIGN OF SAGITTARIUS ON NOV 22 AT 16:40.

DAY	TIME	☉	☽	☿	♀	♂	♃	♄	♅	♆	♇
	h m s	° ' "	° '	°	°	°	°	°	°	°	°
D 1	4 37 53	8♐24 11	26♊13	28♏	14♐	23♏	9♓	18♋R	1♏	9♐	9♎
E 2	4 41 49	9 24 59	10♋30	0♐	16	24	9	18	1	9	9
C 3	4 45 46	10 25 48	24 53	1	17	24	9	18	1	9	9
E 4	4 49 43	11 26 38	9♌17	3	18	25	10	18	1	9	9
M 5	4 53 39	12 27 30	23 39	4	19	26	10	18	1	9	9
B 6	4 57 36	13 28 23	7♍54	6	21	27	10	18	1	9	9
E 7	5 1 32	14 29 18	22 1	7	22	27	10	18	1	10	9
R 8	5 5 29	15 30 14	5♎57	9	23	28	10	18	1	10	9
9	5 9 25	16 31 11	19 42	11	24	29	10	18	1	10	9
10	5 13 22	17 32 9	3♏14	12	26	29	10	18	1	10	9
11	5 17 18	18 33 8	16 34	14	27	0♐	10	17	1	10	9
12	5 21 15	19 34 9	29 41	15	28	1	10	17	1	10	9
13	5 25 12	20 35 10	12♐35	17	0♑	1	11	17	1	10	9
14	5 29 8	21 36 13	25 16	18	1	2	11	17	1	10	9
15	5 33 5	22 37 16	7♑44	20	2	3	11	17	1	10	9
16	5 37 1	23 38 20	20 0	21	3	4	11	17	1	10	9
17	5 40 58	24 39 24	2♒ 6	23	5	4	11	17	1	10	9
18	5 44 54	25 40 29	14 4	25	6	5	11	17	1	10	9
19	5 48 51	26 41 34	25 57	26	7	6	11	17	1	10	9
20	5 52 47	27 42 39	7♓48	28	8	6	11	17	1	10	9
21	5 56 44	28 43 45	19 42	29	10	7	12	17	1	10	9
22	6 0 41	29 44 51	1♈43	1♑	11	8	12	17	2	10	9
23	6 4 37	0♑45 57	13 56	3	12	9	12	17	2	10	9
24	6 8 34	1 47 4	26 25	4	13	9	12	17	2	10	9
25	6 12 30	2 48 10	9♉16	6	15	10	12	16	2	10	9
26	6 16 27	3 49 17	22 30	7	16	11	12	16	2	10	9
27	6 20 23	4 50 24	6♊10	9	17	11	13	16	2	10	9
28	6 24 20	5 51 31	20 14	11	18	12	13	16	2	10	9
29	6 28 17	6 52 38	4♋41	12	20	13	13	16	2	10	9
30	6 32 13	7 53 46	19 25	14	21	14	13	16	2	10	9
31	6 36 10	8 54 54	4♌17	15	22	14	13	16	2	10	9

THE SUN ENTERS THE SIGN OF CAPRICORN ON DEC 22 AT 05:57.

♈ ARIES ♉ TAURUS ♊ GEMINI ♋ CANCER ♌ LEO ♍ VIRGO ♎ LIBRA ♏ SCORPIO ♐ SAGITTARIUS ♑ CAPRICORN ♒ AQUARIUS ♓ PISCES

1975

SIDEREAL SUN MOON MERCURY VENUS MARS JUPITER SATURN URANUS NEPTUNE PLUTO

DAY	TIME	☉	☽	☿	♀	♂	♃	♄	♅	♆	♇
	h m s	° ' "	° '	°	°	°	°	°	°	°	°
J 1	6 40 6	9♑56 2	19♌11	17♑	23♑	15♐	13♓	16♋R	2♏	10♐	9♎
A 2	6 44 3	10 57 10	3♍57	19	25	16	13	16	2	10	9
N 3	6 47 59	11 58 18	18 29	20	26	16	14	16	2	11	9
U 4	6 51 56	12 59 27	2♎43	22	27	17	14	16	2	11	9
A 5	6 55 52	14 0 36	16 37	24	28	18	14	16	2	11	9
R 6	6 59 49	15 1 46	0♏12	25	0♒	19	14	15	2	11	9
Y 7	7 3 46	16 2 55	13 27	27	1	19	14	15	2	11	9
8	7 7 42	17 4 5	26 26	28	2	20	15	15	2	11	9
9	7 11 39	18 5 15	9♐11	0♒	3	21	15	15	2	11	9
10	7 15 35	19 6 25	21 44	2	5	21	15	15	2	11	9
11	7 19 32	20 7 35	4♑ 7	3	6	22	15	15	2	11	9 R
12	7 23 28	21 8 44	16 21	5	7	23	15	15	2	11	9
13	7 27 25	22 9 53	28 28	7	8	24	15	15	2	11	9
14	7 31 21	23 11 2	10♒28	8	10	24	16	15	2	11	9
15	7 35 18	24 12 11	22 23	10	11	25	16	15	2	11	9
16	7 39 15	25 13 18	4♓15	11	12	26	16	15	2	11	9
17	7 43 11	26 14 26	16 6	13	13	27	16	15	2	11	9
18	7 47 8	27 15 32	27 59	14	15	27	16	14	2	11	9
19	7 51 4	28 16 38	9♈57	16	16	28	17	14	2	11	9
20	7 55 1	29 17 42	22 6	17	17	29	17	14	2	11	9
21	7 58 57	0♒18 46	4♉30	18	18	29	17	14	2	11	9
22	8 2 54	1 19 49	17 13	20	20	0♑	17	14	2	11	9
23	8 6 50	2 20 51	0♊20	21	21	1	17	14	2	11	9
24	8 10 47	3 21 53	13 55	22	22	2	18	14	2	11	9
25	8 14 44	4 22 53	28 0	23	23	2	18	14	2	11	9
26	8 18 40	5 23 52	12♋32	24	25	3	18	14	2	11	9
27	8 22 37	6 24 50	27 28	24	26	4	18	14	2	11	9
28	8 26 33	7 25 48	12♌40	25	27	5	18	14	2	11	9
29	8 30 30	8 26 44	27 57	25	28	5	19	14	2	11	9
30	8 34 26	9 27 40	13♍ 7	25 R	0♓	6	19	14	2	11	9
31	8 38 23	10 28 35	28 1	25	1	7	19	14	2	11	9

THE SUN ENTERS THE SIGN OF AQUARIUS ON JAN 20 AT 16:37.

DAY	TIME	☉	☽	☿	♀	♂	♃	♄	♅	♆	♇
	h m s	° ' "	° '	°	°	°	°	°	°	°	°
F 1	8 42 19	11♒29 28	12♎32	25♒R	2♓	7♑	19♓	13♋R	2♏	11♐	9♎R
E 2	8 46 16	12 30 22	26 37	25	3	8	20	13	2	11	9
B 3	8 50 13	13 31 14	10♏14	24	5	9	20	13	2	11	9
R 4	8 54 9	14 32 6	23 26	24	6	10	20	13	2	11	9
U 5	8 58 6	15 32 57	6♐17	23	7	10	20	13	2	11	9
A 6	9 2 2	16 33 47	18 50	22	8	11	20	13	2 R	11	9
R 7	9 5 59	17 34 36	1♑10	21	10	12	21	13	2	11	9
Y 8	9 9 55	18 35 25	13 20	19	11	13	21	13	2	11	9
9	9 13 52	19 36 12	25 22	18	12	13	21	13	2	11	9
10	9 17 48	20 36 57	7♒19	17	13	14	21	13	2	12	9
11	9 21 45	21 37 42	19 14	16	15	15	22	13	2	12	9
12	9 25 42	22 38 25	1♓ 6	15	16	16	22	13	2	12	9
13	9 29 38	23 39 7	12 58	14	17	16	22	13	2	12	9
14	9 33 35	24 39 47	24 51	13	18	17	22	13	2	12	9
15	9 37 31	25 40 26	6♈46	12	20	18	22	13	2	12	9
16	9 41 28	26 41 3	18 47	11	21	19	23	13	2	12	9
17	9 45 24	27 41 39	0♉56	11	22	19	23	13	2	12	9
18	9 49 21	28 42 12	13 18	10	23	20	23	12	2	12	9
19	9 53 17	29 42 44	25 56	10	25	21	23	12	2	12	9
20	9 57 14	0♓43 15	8♊56	10 D	26	22	24	12	2	12	9
21	10 1 11	1 43 43	22 21	10	27	22	24	12	2	12	9
22	10 5 7	2 44 10	6♋15	10	28	23	24	12	2	12	9
23	10 9 4	3 44 34	20 38	10	29	24	24	12	2	12	9
24	10 13 0	4 44 57	5♌28	11	1♈	25	25	12	2	12	9
25	10 16 57	5 45 18	20 39	11	2	25	25	12	2	12	9
26	10 20 53	6 45 37	6♍ 1	11	3	26	25	12	2	12	9
27	10 24 50	7 45 54	21 21	12	4	27	25	12	2	12	9
28	10 28 46	8 46 10	6♎29	13	6	28	26	12	2	12	9

THE SUN ENTERS THE SIGN OF PISCES ON FEB 19 AT 06:50.

DAY	TIME	☉	☽	☿	♀	♂	♃	♄	♅	♆	♇
	h m s	° ' "	° '	°	°	°	°	°	°	°	°
M 1	10 32 43	9♓46 24	21♎16	13♒	7♈	28♑	26♓	12♋R	2♏R	12♐	9♎R
A 2	10 36 39	10 46 37	5♏34	14	8	29	26	12	2	12	9
R 3	10 40 36	11 46 48	19 22	15	9	0♒	26	12	2	12	9
C 4	10 44 33	12 46 57	2♐41	16	11	1	26	12	2	12	9
H 5	10 48 29	13 47 5	15 34	17	12	1	27	12	2	12	9
6	10 52 26	14 47 12	28 7	18	13	2	27	12	2	12	9
7	10 56 22	15 47 17	10♑22	19	14	3	27	12	2	12	8
8	11 0 19	16 47 21	22 26	20	15	4	27	12	2	12	8
9	11 4 15	17 47 22	4♒23	21	17	4	28	12	2	12	8
10	11 8 12	18 47 22	16 15	22	18	5	28	12	2	12	8
11	11 12 8	19 47 20	28 7	23	19	6	28	12	2	12	8
12	11 16 5	20 47 17	9♓58	24	20	7	28	12	2	12	8
13	11 20 2	21 47 11	21 53	25	22	7	29	12	2	12	8
14	11 23 58	22 47 3	3♈50	27	23	8	29	12 D	2	12 R	8
15	11 27 55	23 46 54	15 53	28	24	9	29	12	2	12	8
16	11 31 51	24 46 42	28 1	29	25	10	29	12	2	12	8
17	11 35 48	25 46 29	10♉18	1♓	26	10	0☉	12	2	12	8
18	11 39 44	26 46 13	22 46	2	28	11	0	12	2	12	8
19	11 43 41	27 45 55	5♊28	3	29	12	0♈	12	2	12	8
20	11 47 37	28 45 35	18 27	5	0♉	13	0	12	2	12	8
21	11 51 34	29 45 12	1♋47	6	1	13	1	12	2	12	8
22	11 55 31	0♈44 47	15 32	8	3	14	1	12	2	12	8
23	11 59 27	1 44 20	29 41	9	4	15	1	12	2	12	8
24	12 3 24	2 43 51	14♌15	11	5	16	1	12	2	12	8
25	12 7 20	3 43 19	29 9	12	6	16	2	12	2	12	8
26	12 11 17	4 42 45	14♍16	14	7	17	2	12	2	12	8
27	12 15 13	5 42 8	29 27	16	9	18	2	12	1	12	8
28	12 19 10	6 41 30	14♎31	17	10	19	2	12	1	12	8
29	12 23 6	7 40 50	29 18	19	11	19	2	12	1	12	8
30	12 27 3	8 40 8	13♏42	20	12	20	3	12	1	12	8
31	12 31 0	9 39 24	27 38	22	13	21	3	12	1	12	8

THE SUN ENTERS THE SIGN OF ARIES ON MAR 21 AT 05:57.

DAY	TIME	☉	☽	☿	♀	♂	♃	♄	♅	♆	♇
	h m s	° ' "	° '	°	°	°	°	°	°	°	°
A 1	12 34 56	10♈38 38	11♐ 5	24♓	15♉	22♒	3♈	12♋	1♏R	12♐R	8♎R
P 2	12 38 53	11 37 50	24 6	26	16	23	3	12	1	12	8
R 3	12 42 49	12 37 1	6♑43	27	17	23	4	12	1	12	8
I 4	12 46 46	13 36 10	19 2	29	18	24	4	12	1	12	8
L 5	12 50 42	14 35 17	1♒ 7	1♈	19	25	4	12	1	12	8
6	12 54 39	15 34 22	13 3	3	21	26	4	12	1	12	8
7	12 58 35	16 33 26	24 55	5	22	26	5	12	1	12	8
8	13 2 32	17 32 27	6♓46	6	23	27	5	13	1	12	8
9	13 6 28	18 31 27	18 40	8	24	28	5	13	1	12	8
10	13 10 25	19 30 25	0♈38	10	25	29	5	13	1	12	8
11	13 14 22	20 29 21	12 42	12	27	29	6	13	1	12	8
12	13 18 18	21 28 15	24 55	14	28	0♓	6	13	1	12	8
13	13 22 15	22 27 7	7♉17	16	29	1	6	13	1	12	7
14	13 26 11	23 25 56	19 49	18	0♊	2	6	13	1	12	7
15	13 30 8	24 24 44	2♊32	20	1	2	7	13	1	12	7
16	13 34 4	25 23 30	15 28	22	2	3	7	13	1	12	7
17	13 38 1	26 22 14	28 38	24	4	4	7	13	1	12	7
18	13 41 57	27 20 55	12♋ 4	26	5	5	7	13	1	11	7
19	13 45 54	28 19 34	25 48	28	6	5	8	13	1	11	7
20	13 49 51	29 18 11	9♌49	1♉	7	6	8	13	0	11	7
21	13 53 47	0♉16 45	24 8	3	8	7	8	13	0	11	7
22	13 57 44	1 15 18	8♍41	5	9	8	8	13	0	11	7
23	14 1 40	2 13 48	23 24	7	11	9	8	13	0	11	7
24	14 5 37	3 12 16	8♎11	9	12	9	9	13	0	11	7
25	14 9 33	4 10 42	22 54	11	13	10	9	13	0	11	7
26	14 13 30	5 9 6	7♏26	13	14	11	9	14	0	11	7
27	14 17 26	6 7 28	21 40	15	15	12	9	14	0	11	7
28	14 21 23	7 5 49	5♐32	17	16	12	10	14	0	11	7
29	14 25 20	8 4 7	19 0	20	18	13	10	14	0	11	7
30	14 29 16	9 2 25	2♑ 4	22	19	14	10	14	0	11	7

THE SUN ENTERS THE SIGN OF TAURUS ON APR 20 AT 17:08.

DAY	TIME	☉	☽	☿	♀	♂	♃	♄	♅	♆	♇
	h m s	° ' "	° '	°	°	°	°	°	°	°	°
M 1	14 33 13	10♉ 0 41	14♑46	23♉	20♊	15♓	10♈	14♋	0♏R	11♐R	7♎R
A 2	14 37 9	10 58 55	27 10	25	21	15	10	14	0	11	7
Y 3	14 41 6	11 57 7	9♒18	27	22	16	11	14	0	11	7
4	14 45 2	12 55 19	21 17	29	23	17	11	14	0	11	7
5	14 48 59	13 53 28	3♓10	1♊	24	18	11	14	0	11	7
6	14 52 55	14 51 36	15 3	3	26	18	11	14	0	11	7
7	14 56 52	15 49 43	26 58	4	27	19	12	14	0	11	7
8	15 0 49	16 47 48	9♈ 1	6	28	20	12	15	0	11	7
9	15 4 45	17 45 52	21 13	7	29	21	12	15	0	11	7
10	15 8 42	18 43 55	3♉36	9	0♋	21	12	15	0	11	7
11	15 12 38	19 41 55	16 13	10	1	22	12	15	0	11	7
12	15 16 35	20 39 55	29 3	12	2	23	13	15	0	11	7
13	15 20 31	21 37 52	12♊ 8	13	4	24	13	15	0	11	7
14	15 24 28	22 35 48	25 26	14	5	24	13	15	0	11	7
15	15 28 24	23 33 43	8♋58	15	6	25	13	15	29♎	11	7
16	15 32 21	24 31 36	22 41	16	7	26	14	15	29	11	7
17	15 36 18	25 29 27	6♌36	17	8	27	14	15	29	11	7
18	15 40 14	26 27 16	20 41	18	9	27	14	15	29	11	7
19	15 44 11	27 25 3	4♍53	19	10	28	14	16	29	11	7
20	15 48 7	28 22 49	19 11	20	11	29	14	16	29	11	7
21	15 52 4	29 20 33	3♎32	21	12	0☉	15	16	29	11	7
22	15 56 0	0♊18 15	17 52	21	14	0♈	15	16	29	11	7
23	15 59 57	1 15 56	2♏ 6	22	15	1	15	16	29	11	7
24	16 3 53	2 13 36	16 12	22	16	2	15	16	29	11	7
25	16 7 50	3 11 14	0♐ 5	23	17	3	15	16	29	11	7
26	16 11 47	4 8 51	13 41	23	18	3	16	16	29	11	7
27	16 15 43	5 6 26	26 59	23	19	4	16	16	29	11	7
28	16 19 40	6 4 1	9♑58	23	20	5	16	17	29	11	7
29	16 23 36	7 1 35	22 39	24 R	21	6	16	17	29	11	7
30	16 27 33	7 59 7	5♒ 3	24	22	6	16	17	29	10	7
31	16 31 29	8 56 39	17 14	24	23	7	17	17	29	10	7

THE SUN ENTERS THE SIGN OF GEMINI ON MAY 21 AT 16:24.

DAY	TIME	☉	☽	☿	♀	♂	♃	♄	♅	♆	♇
	h m s	° ' "	° '	°	°	°	°	°	°	°	°
J 1	16 35 26	9♊54 10	29♒14	23♊R	24♋	8♈	17♈	17♋	29♎R	10♐R	7♎R
U 2	16 39 22	10 51 40	11♓ 8	23	25	9	17	17	29	10	7
N 3	16 43 19	11 49 9	23 2	23	26	9	17	17	29	10	7
E 4	16 47 16	12 46 38	4♈58	23	27	10	17	17	29	10	7
5	16 51 12	13 44 5	17 3	22	28	11	17	17	29	10	7
6	16 55 9	14 41 32	29 19	22	0♌	12	18	18	29	10	7
7	16 59 5	15 38 59	11♉50	21	1	12	18	18	29	10	7
8	17 3 2	16 36 24	24 40	21	2	13	18	18	29	10	7
9	17 6 58	17 33 49	7♊47	20	3	14	18	18	29	10	6
10	17 10 55	18 31 14	21 14	20	4	15	18	18	29	10	6
11	17 14 51	19 28 37	4♋58	19	5	15	19	18	29	10	6
12	17 18 48	20 26 0	18 57	19	6	16	19	18	29	10	6
13	17 22 45	21 23 21	3♌ 6	18	7	17	19	18	29	10	6
14	17 26 41	22 20 42	17 22	17	8	18	19	18	29	10	6
15	17 30 38	23 18 1	1♍41	17	9	18	19	19	29	10	6
16	17 34 34	24 15 20	15 58	17	10	19	19	19	29	10	6
17	17 38 31	25 12 38	0♎11	16	11	20	20	19	29	10	6 D
18	17 42 27	26 9 55	14 18	16	12	21	20	19	29	10	6
19	17 46 24	27 7 11	28 16	16	12	21	20	19	28	10	6
20	17 50 20	28 4 26	12♏ 5	15	13	22	20	19	28	10	6
21	17 54 17	29 1 41	25 44	15	14	23	20	19	28	10	6
22	17 58 14	29 58 55	9♐11	15 D	15	23	20	19	28	10	6
23	18 2 10	0♋56 9	22 25	15	16	24	20	20	28	10	6
24	18 6 7	1 53 22	5♑25	15	17	25	21	20	28	10	6
25	18 10 3	2 50 35	18 12	15	18	26	21	20	28	10	6
26	18 14 0	3 47 47	0♒45	15	19	26	21	20	28	10	7
27	18 17 56	4 44 59	13 4	16	20	27	21	20	28	10	7
28	18 21 53	5 42 11	25 13	16	21	28	21	20	28	10	7
29	18 25 50	6 39 23	7♓12	17	22	28	21	20	28	10	7
30	18 29 46	7 36 36	19 6	17	22	29	21	20	28	10	7

THE SUN ENTERS THE SIGN OF CANCER ON JUN 22 AT 00:27.

♈ ARIES ♉ TAURUS ♊ GEMINI ♋ CANCER ♌ LEO ♍ VIRGO ♎ LIBRA ♏ SCORPIO ♐ SAGITTARIUS ♑ CAPRICORN ♒ AQUARIUS ♓ PISCES

SIDEREAL SUN MOON MERCURY VENUS MARS JUPITER SATURN URANUS NEPTUNE PLUTO

DAY	TIME	☉	☽	☿	♀	♂	♃	♄	♅	♆	♇
	h m s	° ' "	° '	°	°	°	°	°	°	°	°
J 1	18 33 43	8♋33 48	0♈58	18♊	23♌	0♉	22♈	21♋	28♎R	10♐R	7♎
U 2	18 37 39	9 31 0	12 54	18	24	1	22	21	28	10	7
L 3	18 41 36	10 28 12	24 58	19	25	1	22	21	28	10	7
Y 4	18 45 32	11 25 25	7♉14	20	26	2	22	21	28	10	7
5	18 49 29	12 22 38	19 48	21	27	3	22	21	28	10	7
6	18 53 25	13 19 51	2♊44	22	27	3	22	21	28	10	7
7	18 57 22	14 17 4	16 3	23	28	4	22	21	28 D	10	7
8	19 1 19	15 14 18	29 46	24	29	5	22	22	28	10	7
9	19 5 15	16 11 32	13♋52	25	0♍	6	23	22	28	9	7
10	19 9 12	17 8 46	28 16	27	0	6	23	22	28	9	7
11	19 13 8	18 5 59	12♌53	28	1	7	23	22	28	9	7
12	19 17 5	19 3 13	27 35	29	2	8	23	22	28	9	7
13	19 21 1	20 0 27	12♍15	1♋	2	8	23	22	28	9	7
14	19 24 58	20 57 41	26 47	2	3	9	23	22	28	9	7
15	19 28 54	21 54 55	11♎ 5	4	4	10	23	22	28	9	7
16	19 32 51	22 52 9	25 9	6	4	10	23	23	28	9	7
17	19 36 48	23 49 23	8♏56	7	5	11	23	23	28	9	7
18	19 40 44	24 46 37	22 28	9	6	12	23	23	28	9	7
19	19 44 41	25 43 51	5♐46	11	6	12	24	23	28	9	7
20	19 48 37	26 41 6	18 51	13	7	13	24	23	28	9	7
21	19 52 34	27 38 20	1♑43	15	7	14	24	23	28	9	7
22	19 56 30	28 35 36	14 25	17	8	14	24	23	28	9	7
23	20 0 27	29 32 51	26 56	19	8	15	24	23	28	9	7
24	20 4 23	0♌30 7	9♒16	21	9	16	24	24	28	9	7
25	20 8 20	1 27 24	21 28	23	9	17	24	24	28	9	7
26	20 12 17	2 24 42	3♓31	25	9	17	24	24	29	9	7
27	20 16 13	3 22 0	15 27	27	10	18	24	24	29	9	7
28	20 20 10	4 19 19	27 18	29	10	19	24	24	29	9	7
29	20 24 6	5 16 39	9♈ 9	1♌	10	19	24	24	29	9	7
30	20 28 3	6 14 0	21 3	4	11	20	24	24	29	9	7
31	20 31 59	7 11 22	3♉ 4	6	11	21	24	24	29	9	7

THE SUN ENTERS THE SIGN OF LEO ON JUL 23 AT 11:23.

DAY	TIME	☉	☽	☿	♀	♂	♃	♄	♅	♆	♇
	h m s	° ' "	° '	°	°	°	°	°	°	°	°
A 1	20 35 56	8♌ 8 45	15♉19	8♌	11♍	21♉	24♈	25♋	29♎	9♐R	7♎
U 2	20 39 52	9 6 9	27 51	10	11	22	24	25	29	9	7
G 3	20 43 49	10 3 35	10♊46	12	12	22	24	25	29	9	7
U 4	20 47 46	11 1 1	24 8	14	12	23	25	25	29	9	7
S 5	20 51 42	11 58 29	7♋57	16	12	24	25	25	29	9	7
T 6	20 55 39	12 55 58	22 15	18	12 R	24	25	25	29	9	7
7	20 59 35	13 53 28	6♌56	20	12	25	25	25	29	9	7
8	21 3 32	14 50 59	21 54	22	12	26	25	25	29	9	7
9	21 7 28	15 48 31	6♍59	24	12	26	25	26	29	9	7
10	21 11 25	16 46 4	22 1	26	11	27	25	26	29	9	7
11	21 15 21	17 43 37	6♎51	28	11	28	25	26	29	9	7
12	21 19 18	18 41 12	21 23	0♍	11	28	25	26	29	9	7
13	21 23 15	19 38 47	5♏33	1	11	29	25	26	29	9	7
14	21 27 11	20 36 24	19 21	3	11	29	25 R	26	29	9	7
15	21 31 8	21 34 1	2♐46	5	10	0♊	25	26	29	9	7
16	21 35 4	22 31 40	15 53	7	10	1	25	26	29	9	7
17	21 39 1	23 29 19	28 43	8	9	1	25	27	29	9	7
18	21 42 57	24 27 0	11♑20	10	9	2	25	27	29	9	7
19	21 46 54	25 24 41	23 46	12	9	3	25	27	29	9	8
20	21 50 50	26 22 24	6♒ 2	14	8	3	25	27	29	9	8
21	21 54 47	27 20 8	18 11	15	8	4	25	27	29	9 D	8
22	21 58 44	28 17 53	0♓14	17	7	4	25	27	29	9	8
23	22 2 40	29 15 40	12 10	18	6	5	25	27	29	9	8
24	22 6 37	0♍13 28	24 3	20	6	6	25	27	29	9	8
25	22 10 33	1 11 18	5♈53	22	5	6	25	28	29	9	8
26	22 14 30	2 9 9	17 44	23	5	7	24	28	29	9	8
27	22 18 26	3 7 2	29 37	25	4	7	24	28	29	9	8
28	22 22 23	4 4 57	11♉38	26	3	8	24	28	29	9	8
29	22 26 19	5 2 54	23 51	28	3	8	24	28	0♏	9	8
30	22 30 16	6 0 52	6♊20	29	2	9	24	28	0	9	8
31	22 34 12	6 58 53	19 11	0♎	2	10	24	28	0	9	8

THE SUN ENTERS THE SIGN OF VIRGO ON AUG 23 AT 18:25.

DAY	TIME	☉	☽	☿	♀	♂	♃	♄	♅	♆	♇
	h m s	° ' "	° '	°	°	°	°	°	°	°	°
S 1	22 38 9	7♍56 55	2♋28	2♎	1♍R	10♊	24♈R	28♋	0♏	9♐	8♎
E 2	22 42 6	8 54 59	16 15	3	0	11	24	28	0	9	8
P 3	22 46 2	9 53 6	0♌31	4	0	11	24	29	0	9	8
T 4	22 49 59	10 51 14	15 14	6	29♌	12	24	29	0	9	8
E 5	22 53 55	11 49 23	0♍19	7	29	12	24	29	0	9	8
M 6	22 57 52	12 47 35	15 35	8	28	13	24	29	0	9	8
B 7	23 1 48	13 45 48	0♎52	10	28	13	24	29	0	9	8
E 8	23 5 45	14 44 3	15 58	11	27	14	24	29	0	9	8
R 9	23 9 41	15 42 19	0♏45	12	27	14	24	29	0	9	8
10	23 13 38	16 40 37	15 7	13	27	15	24	29	0	9	8
11	23 17 35	17 38 57	29 2	14	26	15	24	29	0	9	8
12	23 21 31	18 37 18	12♐31	15	26	16	23	29	0	9	8
13	23 25 28	19 35 41	25 37	16	26	17	23	0♌	0	9	8
14	23 29 24	20 34 5	8♑22	17	26	17	23	0	0	9	8
15	23 33 21	21 32 31	20 51	18	26	18	23	0	0	9	8
16	23 37 17	22 30 59	3♒ 7	19	26	18	23	0	0	9	8
17	23 41 14	23 29 28	15 14	20	25	18	23	0	0	9	9
18	23 45 10	24 27 59	27 14	21	25 D	19	23	0	1	9	9
19	23 49 7	25 26 32	9♓10	21	25	19	23	0	1	9	9
20	23 53 4	26 25 6	21 3	22	26	20	23	0	1	9	9
21	23 57 0	27 23 42	2♈54	23	26	20	23	0	1	9	9
22	0 0 57	28 22 21	14 46	23	26	21	22	0	1	9	9
23	0 4 53	29 21 1	26 39	24	26	21	22	1	1	9	9
24	0 8 50	0♎19 44	8♉37	24	26	22	22	1	1	9	9
25	0 12 46	1 18 28	20 42	24	26	22	22	1	1	9	9
26	0 16 43	2 17 15	2♊58	24 R	27	23	22	1	1	9	9
27	0 20 39	3 16 5	15 29	24	27	23	22	1	1	9	9
28	0 24 36	4 14 56	28 18	24	27	23	22	1	1	9	9
29	0 28 33	5 13 50	11♋30	24	28	24	22	1	1	9	9
30	0 32 29	6 12 46	25 9	24	28	24	21	1	1	9	9

THE SUN ENTERS THE SIGN OF LIBRA ON SEP 23 AT 15:56.

SIDEREAL SUN MOON MERCURY VENUS MARS JUPITER SATURN URANUS NEPTUNE PLUTO

DAY	TIME	☉	☽	☿	♀	♂	♃	♄	♅	♆	♇
	h m s	° ' "	° '	°	°	°	°	°	°	°	°
O 1	0 36 26	7♎11 44	9♌15	23♎R	28♌	25♊	21♈R	1♌	1♏	9♐	9♎
C 2	0 40 22	8 10 45	23 47	23	29	25	21	1	1	9	9
T 3	0 44 19	9 9 48	8♍42	22	29	25	21	1	1	10	9
O 4	0 48 15	10 8 53	23 52	21	0♍	26	21	1	1	10	9
B 5	0 52 12	11 8 0	9♎ 7	21	0	26	21	1	1	10	9
E 6	0 56 8	12 7 9	24 17	20	1	27	21	2	2	10	9
R 7	1 0 5	13 6 20	9♏11	18	2	27	21	2	2	10	9
8	1 4 1	14 5 34	23 43	17	2	27	20	2	2	10	9
9	1 7 58	15 4 49	7♐49	16	3	28	20	2	2	10	9
10	1 11 55	16 4 6	21 26	15	3	28	20	2	2	10	9
11	1 15 51	17 3 24	4♑38	14	4	28	20	2	2	10	9
12	1 19 48	18 2 45	17 26	13	5	29	20	2	2	10	9
13	1 23 44	19 2 7	29 55	12	5	29	20	2	2	10	10
14	1 27 41	20 1 31	12♒ 8	11	6	29	20	2	2	10	10
15	1 31 37	21 0 56	24 11	10	7	29	19	2	2	10	10
16	1 35 34	22 0 24	6♓ 7	10	8	0♋	19	2	2	10	10
17	1 39 30	22 59 53	17 59	9	8	0	19	2	2	10	10
18	1 43 27	23 59 24	29 50	9 D	9	0	19	2	2	10	10
19	1 47 24	24 58 57	11♈42	9	10	0	19	2	2	10	10
20	1 51 20	25 58 32	23 38	9	11	1	19	2	2	10	10
21	1 55 17	26 58 9	5♉39	10	12	1	19	2	2	10	10
22	1 59 13	27 57 48	17 47	10	12	1	19	2	3	10	10
23	2 3 10	28 57 30	0♊ 4	11	13	1	18	2	3	10	10
24	2 7 6	29 57 13	12 32	12	14	1	18	3	3	10	10
25	2 11 3	0♏56 59	25 12	13	15	2	18	3	3	10	10
26	2 14 59	1 56 46	8♋ 8	14	16	2	18	3	3	10	10
27	2 18 56	2 56 36	21 22	15	17	2	18	3	3	10	10
28	2 22 53	3 56 29	4♌56	16	18	2	18	3	3	10	10
29	2 26 49	4 56 23	18 51	17	19	2	18	3	3	10	10
30	2 30 46	5 56 20	3♍ 8	19	20	2	18	3	3	10	10
31	2 34 42	6 56 19	17 42	20	21	2	17	3	3	10	10

THE SUN ENTERS THE SIGN OF SCORPIO ON OCT 24 AT 01:08.

DAY	TIME	☉	☽	☿	♀	♂	♃	♄	♅	♆	♇
	h m s	° ' "	° '	°	°	°	°	°	°	°	°
N 1	2 38 39	7♏56 20	2♎31	22♎	22♍	2♋	17♈R	3♌	3♏	10♐	10♎
O 2	2 42 35	8 56 23	17 28	23	22	3	17	3	3	10	10
V 3	2 46 32	9 56 28	2♏24	25	23	3	17	3	3	10	10
E 4	2 50 28	10 56 35	17 11	26	24	3	17	3	3	10	10
M 5	2 54 25	11 56 43	1♐41	28	25	3	17	3	3	10	10
B 6	2 58 22	12 56 54	15 50	29	26	3 R	17	3	3	10	10
E 7	3 2 18	13 57 6	29 34	1♏	27	3	17	3	4	11	10
R 8	3 6 15	14 57 20	12♑53	3	28	3	17	3	4	11	10
9	3 10 11	15 57 35	25 47	4	29	3	16	3	4	11	10
10	3 14 8	16 57 52	8♒20	6	0♎	3	16	3	4	11	11
11	3 18 4	17 58 10	20 36	7	1	3	16	3	4	11	11
12	3 22 1	18 58 30	2♓39	9	2	2	16	3	4	11	11
13	3 25 57	19 58 51	14 33	11	4	2	16	3	4	11	11
14	3 29 54	20 59 13	26 24	12	5	2	16	3 R	4	11	11
15	3 33 51	21 59 37	8♈15	14	6	2	16	3	4	11	11
16	3 37 47	23 0 2	20 10	16	7	2	16	3	4	11	11
17	3 41 44	24 0 29	2♉12	17	8	2	16	3	4	11	11
18	3 45 40	25 0 58	14 23	19	9	2	16	3	4	11	11
19	3 49 37	26 1 27	26 45	20	10	2	16	3	4	11	11
20	3 53 33	27 1 59	9♊19	22	11	1	15	3	4	11	11
21	3 57 30	28 2 32	22 6	24	12	1	15	3	4	11	11
22	4 1 26	29 3 7	5♋ 7	25	13	1	15	3	4	11	11
23	4 5 23	0♐ 3 43	18 21	27	14	1	15	3	4	11	11
24	4 9 20	1 4 21	1♌48	28	15	0	15	3	5	11	11
25	4 13 16	2 5 0	15 29	0♐	16	0	15	3	5	11	11
26	4 17 13	3 5 41	29 22	1	18	0	15	3	5	11	11
27	4 21 9	4 6 24	13♍27	3	19	0	15	3	5	11	11
28	4 25 6	5 7 8	27 43	5	20	29♊	15	3	5	11	11
29	4 29 2	6 7 54	12♎ 7	6	21	29	15	3	5	11	11
30	4 32 59	7 8 42	26 36	8	22	29	15	3	5	11	11

THE SUN ENTERS THE SIGN OF SAGITTARIUS ON NOV 22 AT 22:32.

DAY	TIME	☉	☽	☿	♀	♂	♃	♄	♅	♆	♇
	h m s	° ' "	° '	°	°	°	°	°	°	°	°
D 1	4 36 55	8♐ 9 31	11♏ 5	9♐	23♎	28♊R	15♈R	3♌R	5♏	11♐	11♎
E 2	4 40 52	9 10 21	25 30	11	24	28	15	3	5	11	11
C 3	4 44 49	10 11 13	9♐44	12	25	28	15	3	5	11	11
E 4	4 48 45	11 12 6	23 42	14	27	27	15	3	5	12	11
M 5	4 52 42	12 13 0	7♑22	16	28	27	15	3	5	12	11
B 6	4 56 38	13 13 54	20 41	17	29	27	15	3	5	12	11
E 7	5 0 35	14 14 50	3♒38	19	0♏	26	15	3	5	12	11
R 8	5 4 31	15 15 46	16 14	20	1	26	15	2	5	12	11
9	5 8 28	16 16 44	28 33	22	2	26	15	2	5	12	11
10	5 12 24	17 17 41	10♓37	23	3	25	15 D	2	5	12	11
11	5 16 21	18 18 40	22 32	25	5	25	15	2	5	12	11
12	5 20 18	19 19 39	4♈23	27	6	24	15	2	6	12	11
13	5 24 14	20 20 38	16 14	28	7	24	15	2	6	12	11
14	5 28 11	21 21 38	28 10	0♑	8	24	15	2	6	12	11
15	5 32 7	22 22 39	10♉16	1	9	23	15	2	6	12	11
16	5 36 4	23 23 40	22 35	3	10	23	15	2	6	12	11
17	5 40 0	24 24 42	5♊10	4	12	22	15	2	6	12	11
18	5 43 57	25 25 45	18 2	6	13	22	15	2	6	12	11
19	5 47 53	26 26 48	1♋12	8	14	22	15	2	6	12	12
20	5 51 50	27 27 52	14 39	9	15	21	15	2	6	12	12
21	5 55 47	28 28 56	28 20	11	16	21	15	2	6	12	12
22	5 59 43	29 30 1	12♌12	12	17	21	15	2	6	12	12
23	6 3 40	0♑31 7	26 12	14	19	20	15	2	6	12	12
24	6 7 36	1 32 13	10♍18	15	20	20	15	2	6	12	12
25	6 11 33	2 33 20	24 25	17	21	19	15	2	6	12	12
26	6 15 29	3 34 28	8♎34	19	22	19	15	1	6	12	12
27	6 19 26	4 35 36	22 41	20	23	19	15	1	6	12	12
28	6 23 22	5 36 45	6♏45	22	25	19	15	1	6	12	12
29	6 27 19	6 37 55	20 46	23	26	18	15	1	6	12	12
30	6 31 16	7 39 5	4♐41	25	27	18	15	1	6	12	12
31	6 35 12	8 40 15	18 29	26	28	18	15	1	6	12	12

THE SUN ENTERS THE SIGN OF CAPRICORN ON DEC 22 AT 11:47.

♈ ARIES ♉ TAURUS ♊ GEMINI ♋ CANCER ♌ LEO ♍ VIRGO ♎ LIBRA ♏ SCORPIO ♐ SAGITTARIUS ♑ CAPRICORN ♒ AQUARIUS ♓ PISCES

SIDEREAL SUN MOON MERCURY VENUS MARS JUPITER SATURN URANUS NEPTUNE PLUTO

DAY	TIME	☉	☽	☿	♀	♂	♃	♄	♅	♆	♇
	h m s	° ' "	° '	°	°	°	°	°	°	°	°
J 1	6 39 9	9♑41 26	2♑ 6	27♑	29♏	17♊R	16♈	1♌R	6♏	13♐	12♎
A 2	6 43 5	10 42 37	15 29	29	1♐	17	16	1	6	13	12
N 3	6 47 2	11 43 48	28 37	0♒	2	17	16	1	6	13	12
U 4	6 50 58	12 44 58	11♒28	2	3	17	16	1	6	13	12
A 5	6 54 55	13 46 9	24 2	3	4	16	16	1	7	13	12
R 6	6 58 51	14 47 19	6♓20	4	5	16	16	1	7	13	12
Y 7	7 2 48	15 48 29	18 24	5	7	16	16	1	7	13	12
8	7 6 45	16 49 39	0♈19	6	8	16	16	1	7	13	12
9	7 10 41	17 50 48	12 9	7	9	16	16	0	7	13	12
10	7 14 38	18 51 57	23 58	8	10	16	16	0	7	13	12
11	7 18 34	19 53 5	5♉53	8	11	15	16	0	7	13	12
12	7 22 31	20 54 13	17 59	9	13	15	17	0	7	13	12
13	7 26 27	21 55 20	0♊21	9	14	15	17	0	7	13	12
14	7 30 24	22 56 27	13 2	9 R	15	15	17	0	7	13	12 R
15	7 34 20	23 57 33	26 6	9	16	15	17	0	7	13	12
16	7 38 17	24 58 39	9♋34	9	18	15	17	0	7	13	12
17	7 42 14	25 59 44	23 24	9	19	15	17	0	7	13	12
18	7 46 10	27 0 48	7♌32	8	20	15	17	0	7	13	12
19	7 50 7	28 1 52	21 54	7	21	15	17	0	7	13	12
20	7 54 3	29 2 56	6♍23	6	22	15 D	17	0	7	13	12
21	7 58 0	0♒ 3 59	20 52	5	24	15	18	29♋	7	13	12
22	8 1 56	1 5 1	5♎17	4	25	15	18	29	7	13	12
23	8 5 53	2 6 4	19 32	3	26	15	18	29	7	13	12
24	8 9 50	3 7 6	3♏37	1	27	15	18	29	7	13	12
25	8 13 46	4 8 7	17 30	0	28	15	18	29	7	13	12
26	8 17 43	5 9 8	1♐13	29♑	0♑	15	18	29	7	13	12
27	8 21 39	6 10 9	14 45	28	1	15	18	29	7	13	12
28	8 25 36	7 11 9	28 7	27	2	15	19	29	7	13	12
29	8 29 32	8 12 8	11♑19	26	3	15	19	29	7	13	12
30	8 33 29	9 13 6	24 19	25	5	15	19	29	7	13	12
31	8 37 25	10 14 4	7♒ 9	24	6	15	19	29	7	13	12

THE SUN ENTERS THE SIGN OF AQUARIUS ON JAN 20 AT 22:26.

DAY	TIME	☉	☽	☿	♀	♂	♃	♄	♅	♆	♇
	h m s	° ' "	° '	°	°	°	°	°	°	°	°
F 1	8 41 22	11♒15 0	19♒46	24♑R	7♑	15♊	19♈	29♋R	7♏	13♐	12♎R
E 2	8 45 19	12 15 56	2♓10	24	8	16	19	28	7	13	12
B 3	8 49 15	13 16 50	14 22	23 D	9	16	19	28	7	13	12
R 4	8 53 12	14 17 43	26 23	23	11	16	20	28	7	14	12
U 5	8 57 8	15 18 34	8♈15	23	12	16	20	28	7	14	12
A 6	9 1 5	16 19 25	20 3	24	13	16	20	28	7	14	12
R 7	9 5 1	17 20 14	1♉51	24	14	16	20	28	7	14	12
Y 8	9 8 58	18 21 1	13 44	24	16	17	20	28	7	14	12
9	9 12 54	19 21 47	25 47	25	17	17	20	28	7	14	12
10	9 16 51	20 22 31	8♊ 6	25	18	17	21	28	7 R	14	12
11	9 20 47	21 23 14	20 47	26	19	17	21	28	7	14	11
12	9 24 44	22 23 56	3♋52	27	21	18	21	28	7	14	11
13	9 28 41	23 24 36	17 26	27	22	18	21	28	7	14	11
14	9 32 37	24 25 14	1♌27	28	23	18	21	28	7	14	11
15	9 36 34	25 25 50	15 53	29	24	18	22	28	7	14	11
16	9 40 30	26 26 25	0♍37	0♒	25	19	22	27	7	14	11
17	9 44 27	27 26 59	15 32	1	27	19	22	27	7	14	11
18	9 48 23	28 27 31	0♎28	2	28	19	22	27	7	14	11
19	9 52 20	29 28 2	15 17	3	29	19	22	27	7	14	11
20	9 56 16	0♓28 32	29 51	4	0♒	20	22	27	7	14	11
21	10 0 13	1 29 0	14♏ 8	6	2	20	23	27	7	14	11
22	10 4 10	2 29 27	28 6	7	3	20	23	27	7	14	11
23	10 8 6	3 29 53	11♐45	8	4	21	23	27	7	14	11
24	10 12 3	4 30 17	25 6	9	5	21	23	27	7	14	11
25	10 15 59	5 30 40	8♑13	11	7	21	23	27	7	14	11
26	10 19 56	6 31 2	21 5	12	8	22	24	27	7	14	11
27	10 23 52	7 31 22	3♒47	13	9	22	24	27	7	14	11
28	10 27 49	8 31 41	16 17	15	10	22	24	27	7	14	11
29	10 31 45	9 31 58	28 37	16	11	23	24	27	7	14	11

THE SUN ENTERS THE SIGN OF PISCES ON FEB 19 AT 12:41.

DAY	TIME	☉	☽	☿	♀	♂	♃	♄	♅	♆	♇
	h m s	° ' "	° '	°	°	°	°	°	°	°	°
M 1	10 35 42	10♓32 13	10♓48	17♒	13♒	23♊	24♈	27♋R	7♏R	14♐	11♎R
A 2	10 39 39	11 32 26	22 51	19	14	23	25	27	7	14	11
R 3	10 43 35	12 32 37	4♈46	20	15	24	25	27	7	14	11
C 4	10 47 32	13 32 47	16 36	22	16	24	25	27	7	14	11
H 5	10 51 28	14 32 55	28 22	23	18	24	25	26	7	14	11
6	10 55 25	15 33 0	10♉10	25	19	25	25	26	7	14	11
7	10 59 21	16 33 4	22 2	26	20	25	26	26	7	14	11
8	11 3 18	17 33 5	4♊ 4	28	21	26	26	26	7	14	11
9	11 7 14	18 33 5	16 20	29	23	26	26	26	7	14	11
10	11 11 11	19 33 2	28 56	1♓	24	26	26	26	7	14	11
11	11 15 8	20 32 57	11♋57	2	25	27	27	26	7	14	11
12	11 19 4	21 32 49	25 26	4	26	27	27	26	7	14	11
13	11 23 1	22 32 40	9♌25	6	27	28	27	26	7	14	11
14	11 26 57	23 32 28	23 52	7	29	28	27	26	7	14	11
15	11 30 54	24 32 15	8♍43	9	0♓	28	27	26	7	14 R	11
16	11 34 50	25 31 59	23 49	11	1	29	28	26	7	14	11
17	11 38 47	26 31 41	9♎ 2	12	2	29	28	26	7	14	11
18	11 42 43	27 31 21	24 11	14	4	0♋	28	26	7	14	11
19	11 46 40	28 30 59	9♏ 6	16	5	0	28	26	7	14	11
20	11 50 36	29 30 36	23 42	18	6	1	29	26	7	14	11
21	11 54 33	0♈30 11	7♐54	19	7	1	29	26	6	14	11
22	11 58 30	1 29 44	21 41	21	9	2	29	26	6	14	11
23	12 2 26	2 29 16	5♑ 5	23	10	2	29	26	6	14	11
24	12 6 23	3 28 46	18 8	25	11	2	29	26	6	14	11
25	12 10 19	4 28 14	0♒52	27	12	3	0♉	26	6	14	11
26	12 14 16	5 27 40	13 22	29	14	3	0	26	6	14	10
27	12 18 12	6 27 4	25 39	1♈	15	4	0	26 D	6	14	10
28	12 22 9	7 26 26	7♓46	3	16	4	0	26	6	14	10
29	12 26 5	8 25 47	19 46	5	17	5	1	26	6	14	10
30	12 30 2	9 25 5	1♈40	7	18	5	1	26	6	14	10
31	12 33 59	10 24 22	13 30	9	20	6	1	26	6	14	10

THE SUN ENTERS THE SIGN OF ARIES ON MAR 20 AT 11:50.

SIDEREAL SUN MOON MERCURY VENUS MARS JUPITER SATURN URANUS NEPTUNE PLUTO

DAY	TIME	☉	☽	☿	♀	♂	♃	♄	♅	♆	♇
	h m s	° ' "	° '	°	°	°	°	°	°	°	°
A 1	12 37 55	11♈23 36	25♈18	11♈	21♓	6♋	1♉	26♋	6♏R	14♐R	10♎R
P 2	12 41 52	12 22 49	7♉ 6	13	22	7	2	26	6	14	10
R 3	12 45 48	13 21 59	18 56	15	23	7	2	26	6	14	10
I 4	12 49 45	14 21 7	0♊52	17	25	8	2	26	6	14	10
L 5	12 53 41	15 20 13	12 57	19	26	8	2	26	6	14	10
6	12 57 38	16 19 17	25 15	21	27	9	2	26	6	14	10
7	13 1 34	17 18 18	7♋51	23	28	9	3	26	6	14	10
8	13 5 31	18 17 17	20 48	25	0⊙	10	3	26	6	14	10
9	13 9 28	19 16 14	4♌ 9	27	1♈	10	3	26	6	14	10
10	13 13 24	20 15 8	17 58	29	2	11	3	26	6	14	10
11	13 17 21	21 14 0	2♍15	1♉	3	11	4	26	6	14	10
12	13 21 17	22 12 50	16 56	3	4	12	4	26	6	14	10
13	13 25 14	23 11 38	1♎57	5	6	12	4	26	6	14	10
14	13 29 10	24 10 23	17 9	7	7	13	4	26	6	14	10
15	13 33 7	25 9 7	2♏22	9	8	13	5	26	6	14	10
16	13 37 3	26 7 48	17 28	11	9	14	5	26	6	14	10
17	13 41 0	27 6 28	2♐17	13	11	14	5	26	5	14	10
18	13 44 57	28 5 6	16 43	15	12	15	5	26	5	14	10
19	13 48 53	29 3 43	0♑44	16	13	15	6	26	5	14	10
20	13 52 50	0♉ 2 17	14 17	18	14	16	6	27	5	14	10
21	13 56 46	1 0 50	27 25	19	16	16	6	27	5	14	10
22	14 0 43	1 59 22	10♒11	21	17	17	6	27	5	14	10
23	14 4 39	2 57 52	22 37	22	18	17	7	27	5	14	10
24	14 8 36	3 56 20	4♓49	24	19	18	7	27	5	14	10
25	14 12 32	4 54 46	16 49	25	20	18	7	27	5	14	10
26	14 16 29	5 53 11	28 42	26	22	19	7	27	5	14	10
27	14 20 26	6 51 34	10♈31	27	23	19	7	27	5	14	10
28	14 24 22	7 49 55	22 19	28	24	20	8	27	5	13	10
29	14 28 19	8 48 15	4♉ 7	29	25	20	8	27	5	13	10
30	14 32 15	9 46 33	15 59	0♊	27	21	8	27	5	13	10

THE SUN ENTERS THE SIGN OF TAURUS ON APR 19 AT 23:04.

DAY	TIME	☉	☽	☿	♀	♂	♃	♄	♅	♆	♇
	h m s	° ' "	° '	°	°	°	°	°	°	°	°
M 1	14 36 12	10♉44 49	27♉57	1♊	28♈	22♋	8♉	27♋	5♏R	13♐R	10♎R
A 2	14 40 8	11 43 4	10♊ 2	1	29	22	9	27	5	13	10
Y 3	14 44 5	12 41 16	22 17	2	0♉	23	9	27	5	13	9
4	14 48 1	13 39 27	4♋45	3	2	23	9	27	5	13	9
5	14 51 58	14 37 35	17 28	3	3	24	9	27	5	13	9
6	14 55 55	15 35 42	0♌27	3	4	24	10	27	5	13	9
7	14 59 51	16 33 47	13 47	4	5	25	10	27	5	13	9
8	15 3 48	17 31 50	27 28	4	6	25	10	28	5	13	9
9	15 7 44	18 29 50	11♍32	4 R	8	26	10	28	5	13	9
10	15 11 41	19 27 49	25 56	4	9	26	11	28	4	13	9
11	15 15 37	20 25 46	10♎39	4	10	27	11	28	4	13	9
12	15 19 34	21 23 42	25 35	3	11	28	11	28	4	13	9
13	15 23 30	22 21 35	10♏37	3	13	28	11	28	4	13	9
14	15 27 27	23 19 28	25 36	3	14	29	12	28	4	13	9
15	15 31 23	24 17 18	10♐25	2	15	29	12	28	4	13	9
16	15 35 20	25 15 8	24 56	2	16	0♌	12	28	4	13	9
17	15 39 17	26 12 56	9♑ 3	2	18	0	12	28	4	13	9
18	15 43 13	27 10 43	22 44	1	19	1	12	28	4	13	9
19	15 47 10	28 8 28	5♒59	0	20	1	13	28	4	13	9
20	15 51 6	29 6 13	18 50	0	21	2	13	28	4	13	9
21	15 55 3	0♊ 3 56	1♓18	29♉	22	3	13	29	4	13	9
22	15 58 59	1 1 38	13 30	29	24	3	13	29	4	13	9
23	16 2 56	1 59 19	25 29	28	25	4	14	29	4	13	9
24	16 6 52	2 57 0	7♈20	28	26	4	14	29	4	13	9
25	16 10 49	3 54 39	19 7	27	27	5	14	29	4	13	9
26	16 14 46	4 52 17	0♉55	27	29	5	14	29	4	13	9
27	16 18 42	5 49 54	12 47	26	0♊	6	15	29	4	13	9
28	16 22 39	6 47 30	24 46	26	1	7	15	29	4	13	9
29	16 26 35	7 45 5	6♊55	26	2	7	15	29	4	13	9
30	16 30 32	8 42 39	19 14	25	3	8	15	29	4	13	9
31	16 34 28	9 40 11	1♋45	25	5	8	15	29	4	13	9

THE SUN ENTERS THE SIGN OF GEMINI ON MAY 20 AT 22:22.

DAY	TIME	☉	☽	☿	♀	♂	♃	♄	♅	♆	♇
	h m s	° ' "	° '	°	°	°	°	°	°	°	°
J 1	16 38 25	10♊37 43	14♋30	25♉R	6♊	9♌	16♉	0♌	4♏R	13♐R	9♎R
U 2	16 42 22	11 35 13	27 28	25 D	7	9	16	0	4	13	9
N 3	16 46 18	12 32 43	10♌40	25	8	10	16	0	4	13	9
E 4	16 50 15	13 30 10	24 7	25	10	11	16	0	4	13	9
5	16 54 11	14 27 37	7♍49	25	11	11	17	0	4	13	9
6	16 58 8	15 25 2	21 45	26	12	12	17	0	4	13	9
7	17 2 4	16 22 26	5♎56	26	13	12	17	0	4	12	9
8	17 6 1	17 19 49	20 19	26	15	13	17	0	3	12	9
9	17 9 57	18 17 11	4♏53	27	16	13	17	0	3	12	9
10	17 13 54	19 14 32	19 32	27	17	14	18	1	3	12	9
11	17 17 51	20 11 52	4♐12	28	18	15	18	1	3	12	9
12	17 21 47	21 9 12	18 45	29	19	15	18	1	3	12	9
13	17 25 44	22 6 30	3♑ 6	29	21	16	18	1	3	12	9
14	17 29 40	23 3 48	17 9	0♊	22	16	19	1	3	12	9
15	17 33 37	24 1 5	0♒50	1	23	17	19	1	3	12	9
16	17 37 33	24 58 22	14 6	2	24	18	19	1	3	12	9
17	17 41 30	25 55 39	26 59	3	26	18	19	1	3	12	9
18	17 45 26	26 52 55	9♓30	4	27	19	19	1	3	12	9 D
19	17 49 23	27 50 11	21 43	5	28	19	20	2	3	12	9
20	17 53 20	28 47 26	3♈42	6	29	20	20	2	3	12	9
21	17 57 16	29 44 42	15 33	8	1♋	20	20	2	3	12	9
22	18 1 13	0♋41 57	27 22	9	2	21	20	2	3	12	9
23	18 5 9	1 39 12	9♉11	10	3	22	20	2	3	12	9
24	18 9 6	2 36 27	21 8	12	4	22	21	2	3	12	9
25	18 13 2	3 33 42	3♊14	13	5	23	21	2	3	12	9
26	18 16 59	4 30 56	15 34	15	7	23	21	2	3	12	9
27	18 20 55	5 28 11	28 9	16	8	24	21	2	3	12	9
28	18 24 52	6 25 25	10♋59	18	9	25	21	3	3	12	9
29	18 28 49	7 22 39	24 6	20	10	25	22	3	3	12	9
30	18 32 45	8 19 53	7♌26	21	12	26	22	3	3	12	9

THE SUN ENTERS THE SIGN OF CANCER ON JUN 21 AT 06:25.

♈ ARIES ♉ TAURUS ♊ GEMINI ♋ CANCER ♌ LEO ♍ VIRGO ♎ LIBRA ♏ SCORPIO ♐ SAGITTARIUS ♑ CAPRICORN ♒ AQUARIUS ♓ PISCES

SIDEREAL SUN MOON MERCURY VENUS MARS JUPITER SATURN URANUS NEPTUNE PLUTO

DAY	TIME	☉	☽	☿	♀	♂	♃	♄	♅	♆	♇
	h m s	° ' "	° '	°	°	°	°	°	°	°	°
J 1	18 36 42	9♋17 6	20♌59	23♊	13♋	26♌	22♉	3♌	3♏R	12♐R	9♎
U 2	18 40 38	10 14 19	4♍43	25	14	27	22	3	3	12	9
L 3	18 44 35	11 11 32	18 35	27	15	28	22	3	3	12	9
Y 4	18 48 31	12 8 44	2♎35	29	16	28	23	3	3	12	9
5	18 52 28	13 5 56	16 40	1♋	18	29	23	3	3	12	9
6	18 56 24	14 3 8	0♏51	3	19	29	23	4	3	12	9
7	19 0 21	15 0 20	15 5	5	20	0♍	23	4	3	12	9
8	19 4 18	15 57 31	29 21	7	21	1	23	4	3	12	9
9	19 8 14	16 54 43	13♐35	9	23	1	24	4	3	12	9
10	19 12 11	17 51 54	27 45	11	24	2	24	4	3	12	9
11	19 16 7	18 49 5	11♑45	13	25	2	24	4	3 D	12	9
12	19 20 4	19 46 17	25 32	15	26	3	24	4	3	12	9
13	19 24 0	20 43 29	9♒ 1	18	28	4	24	4	3	12	9
14	19 27 57	21 40 41	22 10	20	29	4	25	5	3	12	9
15	19 31 53	22 37 53	4♓58	22	0♌	5	25	5	3	12	9
16	19 35 50	23 35 6	17 27	24	1	5	25	5	3	12	9
17	19 39 47	24 32 20	29 40	26	2	6	25	5	3	12	9
18	19 43 43	25 29 34	11♈39	28	4	7	25	5	3	12	9
19	19 47 40	26 26 49	23 30	0♌	5	7	25	5	3	12	9
20	19 51 36	27 24 5	5♉19	2	6	8	26	5	3	11	9
21	19 55 33	28 21 21	17 10	5	7	9	26	5	3	11	9
22	19 59 29	29 18 39	29 9	7	9	9	26	6	3	11	9
23	20 3 26	0♌15 57	11♊21	9	10	10	26	6	3	11	9
24	20 7 22	1 13 16	23 49	11	11	10	26	6	3	11	9
25	20 11 19	2 10 35	6♋37	12	12	11	26	6	3	11	9
26	20 15 16	3 7 56	19 45	14	14	12	27	6	3	11	9
27	20 19 12	4 5 17	3♌13	16	15	12	27	6	3	11	9
28	20 23 9	5 2 39	16 58	18	16	13	27	6	3	11	9
29	20 27 5	6 0 2	0♍56	20	17	13	27	6	3	11	9
30	20 31 2	6 57 25	15 4	22	18	14	27	7	3	11	9
31	20 34 58	7 54 48	29 16	24	20	15	27	7	3	11	9

THE SUN ENTERS THE SIGN OF LEO ON JUL 22 AT 17:19.

DAY	TIME	☉	☽	☿	♀	♂	♃	♄	♅	♆	♇
	h m s	° ' "	° '	°	°	°	°	°	°	°	°
A 1	20 38 55	8♌52 13	13♎29	25♌	21♌	15♍	27♉	7♌	3♏	11♐R	9♎
U 2	20 42 51	9 49 38	27 41	27	22	16	28	7	3	11	9
G 3	20 46 48	10 47 3	11♏49	29	23	17	28	7	3	11	9
U 4	20 50 45	11 44 29	25 53	1♍	25	17	28	7	3	11	10
S 5	20 54 41	12 41 56	9♐51	2	26	18	28	7	3	11	10
T 6	20 58 38	13 39 24	23 44	4	27	18	28	8	3	11	10
7	21 2 34	14 36 52	7♑29	5	28	19	28	8	3	11	10
8	21 6 31	15 34 22	21 4	7	0♍	20	28	8	3	11	10
9	21 10 27	16 31 52	4♒28	8	1	20	28	8	3	11	10
10	21 14 24	17 29 23	17 37	10	2	21	29	8	3	11	10
11	21 18 20	18 26 55	0♓31	11	3	22	29	8	3	11	10
12	21 22 17	19 24 29	13 9	13	4	22	29	8	3	11	10
13	21 26 14	20 22 3	25 31	14	6	23	29	8	3	11	10
14	21 30 10	21 19 39	7♈39	16	7	23	29	9	4	11	10
15	21 34 7	22 17 17	19 36	17	8	24	29	9	4	11	10
16	21 38 3	23 14 56	1♉26	18	9	25	29	9	4	11	10
17	21 42 0	24 12 37	13 13	20	11	25	29	9	4	11	10
18	21 45 56	25 10 19	25 4	21	12	26	29	9	4	11	10
19	21 49 53	26 8 2	7♊ 4	22	13	27	0♊	9	4	11	10
20	21 53 49	27 5 48	19 17	24	14	27	0	9	4	11	10
21	21 57 46	28 3 35	1♋49	25	16	28	0	9	4	11	10
22	22 1 43	29 1 23	14 43	26	17	29	0	10	4	11	10
23	22 5 39	29 59 14	28 1	27	18	29	0	10	4	11 D	10
24	22 9 36	0♍57 6	11♌43	28	19	0♎	0	10	4	11	10
25	22 13 32	1 54 59	25 48	29	20	0	0	10	4	11	10
26	22 17 29	2 52 54	10♍ 9	0♎	22	1	0	10	4	11	10
27	22 21 25	3 50 50	24 42	1	23	2	0	10	4	11	10
28	22 25 22	4 48 48	9♎19	2	24	2	0	10	4	11	10
29	22 29 18	5 46 47	23 54	3	25	3	0	10	4	11	10
30	22 33 15	6 44 48	8♏22	4	27	4	1	11	4	11	10
31	22 37 11	7 42 50	22 39	4	28	4	1	11	4	11	10

THE SUN ENTERS THE SIGN OF VIRGO ON AUG 23 AT 00:20.

DAY	TIME	☉	☽	☿	♀	♂	♃	♄	♅	♆	♇
	h m s	° ' "	° '	°	°	°	°	°	°	°	°
S 1	22 41 8	8♍40 53	6♐44	5♎	29♍	5♎	1♊	11♌	4♏	11♐	10♎
E 2	22 45 5	9 38 58	20 36	6	0♎	6	1	11	4	11	10
P 3	22 49 1	10 37 4	4♑15	6	2	6	1	11	4	11	10
T 4	22 52 58	11 35 11	17 41	7	3	7	1	11	4	11	10
E 5	22 56 54	12 33 20	0♒54	7	4	8	1	11	4	11	10
M 6	23 0 51	13 31 31	13 55	7	5	8	1	11	4	11	11
B 7	23 4 47	14 29 43	26 44	8	6	9	1	11	4	11	11
E 8	23 8 44	15 27 56	9♓19	8 R	8	10	1	12	4	11	11
R 9	23 12 40	16 26 12	21 42	8	9	10	1	12	5	11	11
10	23 16 37	17 24 29	3♈53	8	10	11	1	12	5	11	11
11	23 20 34	18 22 48	15 54	8	11	11	1	12	5	11	11
12	23 24 30	19 21 9	27 47	7	13	12	1	12	5	11	11
13	23 28 27	20 19 32	9♉35	7	14	13	1	12	5	11	11
14	23 32 23	21 17 57	21 21	6	15	13	1	12	5	11	11
15	23 36 20	22 16 24	8♊11	6	16	14	1	12	5	11	11
16	23 40 16	23 14 54	15 10	5	18	15	1	12	5	11	11
17	23 44 13	24 13 25	27 22	4	19	15	1	13	5	11	11
18	23 48 9	25 11 59	9♋52	3	20	16	1	13	5	11	11
19	23 52 6	26 10 35	22 44	2	21	17	1 R	13	5	11	11
20	23 56 3	27 9 13	6♌ 3	1	22	17	1	13	5	11	11
21	23 59 59	28 7 53	19 49	0	24	18	1	13	5	11	11
22	0 3 56	29 6 36	4♍ 1	29♍	25	19	1	13	5	11	11
23	0 7 52	0♎ 5 20	18 36	28	26	19	1	13	5	11	11
24	0 11 49	1 4 7	3♎26	27	27	20	1	13	5	11	11
25	0 15 45	2 2 55	18 25	26	29	21	1	13	5	11	11
26	0 19 42	3 1 46	3♏23	25	0♏	21	1	13	5	12	11
27	0 23 38	4 0 38	18 12	25	1	22	1	14	5	12	11
28	0 27 35	4 59 32	2♐48	24	2	23	1	14	5	12	11
29	0 31 32	5 58 28	17 4	24	3	23	1	14	6	12	11
30	0 35 28	6 57 25	1♑ 1	23	5	24	1	14	6	12	11

THE SUN ENTERS THE SIGN OF LIBRA ON SEP 22 AT 21:49.

SIDEREAL SUN MOON MERCURY VENUS MARS JUPITER SATURN URANUS NEPTUNE PLUTO

DAY	TIME	☉	☽	☿	♀	♂	♃	♄	♅	♆	♇
	h m s	° ' "	° '	°	°	°	°	°	°	°	°
O 1	0 39 25	7♎56 25	14♑37	23♍D	6♏	25♎	1♊R	14♌	6♏	12♐	11♎
C 2	0 43 21	8 55 26	27 54	23	7	25	1	14	6	12	11
T 3	0 47 18	9 54 29	10♒54	23	8	26	1	14	6	12	12
O 4	0 51 14	10 53 33	23 38	24	10	27	1	14	6	12	12
B 5	0 55 11	11 52 40	6♓ 8	24	11	27	1	14	6	12	12
E 6	0 59 7	12 51 48	18 27	25	12	28	1	14	6	12	12
R 7	1 3 4	13 50 58	0♈35	26	13	29	1	15	6	12	12
8	1 7 0	14 50 10	12 35	27	14	29	1	15	6	12	12
9	1 10 57	15 49 24	24 29	28	16	0♏	1	15	6	12	12
10	1 14 54	16 48 40	6♉18	29	17	1	1	15	6	12	12
11	1 18 50	17 47 59	18 5	1♎	18	1	0	15	6	12	12
12	1 22 47	18 47 20	29 53	2	19	2	0	15	6	12	12
13	1 26 43	19 46 42	11♊44	3	21	3	0	15	6	12	12
14	1 30 40	20 46 8	23 44	5	22	3	0	15	6	12	12
15	1 34 36	21 45 35	5♋55	6	23	4	0	15	6	12	12
16	1 38 33	22 45 5	18 22	8	24	5	0	15	7	12	12
17	1 42 29	23 44 37	1♌10	10	25	6	0	15	7	12	12
18	1 46 26	24 44 11	14 22	11	27	6	0	15	7	12	12
19	1 50 23	25 43 48	28 1	13	28	7	0	15	7	12	12
20	1 54 19	26 43 27	12♍ 7	14	29	8	0	16	7	12	12
21	1 58 16	27 43 8	26 39	16	0♐	8	0	16	7	12	12
22	2 2 12	28 42 51	11♎32	18	2	9	0	16	7	12	12
23	2 6 9	29 42 36	26 39	20	3	10	29♉	16	7	12	12
24	2 10 5	0♏42 24	11♏51	21	4	10	29	16	7	12	12
25	2 14 2	1 42 13	26 59	23	5	11	29	16	7	12	12
26	2 17 58	2 42 4	11♐53	25	6	12	29	16	7	12	12
27	2 21 55	3 41 57	26 28	26	8	12	29	16	7	12	12
28	2 25 52	4 41 52	10♑37	28	9	13	29	16	7	12	12
29	2 29 48	5 41 48	24 21	0♏	10	14	29	16	7	12	13
30	2 33 45	6 41 46	7♒39	1	11	15	29	16	7	12	13
31	2 37 41	7 41 45	20 35	3	13	15	29	16	7	12	13

THE SUN ENTERS THE SIGN OF SCORPIO ON OCT 23 AT 06:60.

DAY	TIME	☉	☽	☿	♀	♂	♃	♄	♅	♆	♇
	h m s	° ' "	° '	°	°	°	°	°	°	°	°
N 1	2 41 38	8♏41 46	3♓10	5♏	14♐	16♏	28♉R	16♌	8♏	12♐	13♎
O 2	2 45 34	9 41 49	15 30	6	15	17	28	16	8	12	13
V 3	2 49 31	10 41 53	27 37	8	16	17	28	16	8	13	13
E 4	2 53 27	11 41 59	9♈34	10	17	18	28	16	8	13	13
M 5	2 57 24	12 42 7	21 26	11	19	19	28	16	8	13	13
B 6	3 1 21	13 42 16	3♉15	13	20	19	28	16	8	13	13
E 7	3 5 17	14 42 27	15 3	14	21	20	28	16	8	13	13
R 8	3 9 14	15 42 40	26 52	16	22	21	28	17	8	13	13
9	3 13 10	16 42 55	8♊44	18	23	21	27	17	8	13	13
10	3 17 7	17 43 12	20 42	19	25	22	27	17	8	13	13
11	3 21 3	18 43 30	2♋48	21	26	23	27	17	8	13	13
12	3 25 0	19 43 50	15 4	22	27	24	27	17	8	13	13
13	3 28 56	20 44 13	27 34	24	28	24	27	17	8	13	13
14	3 32 53	21 44 37	10♌20	26	29	25	27	17	8	13	13
15	3 36 50	22 45 3	23 26	27	1♑	26	27	17	8	13	13
16	3 40 46	23 45 31	6♍54	29	2	26	26	17	8	13	13
17	3 44 43	24 46 1	20 47	0♐	3	27	26	17	9	13	13
18	3 48 39	25 46 32	5♎ 3	2	4	28	26	17	9	13	13
19	3 52 36	26 47 6	19 43	3	5	29	26	17	9	13	13
20	3 56 32	27 47 41	4♏41	5	7	29	26	17	9	13	13
21	4 0 29	28 48 18	19 50	7	8	0♐	26	17	9	13	13
22	4 4 25	29 48 56	5♐ 1	8	9	1	26	17	9	13	13
23	4 8 22	0♐49 36	20 4	10	10	1	25	17	9	13	13
24	4 12 19	1 50 17	4♑51	11	11	2	25	17	9	13	13
25	4 16 15	2 51 0	19 13	13	13	3	25	17	9	13	13
26	4 20 12	3 51 43	3♒ 9	14	14	4	25	17	9	13	13
27	4 24 8	4 52 28	16 35	16	15	4	25	17 R	9	13	13
28	4 28 5	5 53 13	29 34	17	16	5	25	17	9	13	13
29	4 32 1	6 54 0	12♓10	19	17	6	25	17	9	13	14
30	4 35 58	7 54 47	24 27	20	19	6	25	17	9	13	14

THE SUN ENTERS THE SIGN OF SAGITTARIUS ON NOV 22 AT 04:23.

DAY	TIME	☉	☽	☿	♀	♂	♃	♄	♅	♆	♇
	h m s	° ' "	° '	°	°	°	°	°	°	°	°
D 1	4 39 54	8♐55 35	6♈29	22♐	20♑	7♐	24♉R	17♌R	9♏	14♐	14♎
E 2	4 43 51	9 56 25	18 21	23	21	8	24	17	9	14	14
C 3	4 47 48	10 57 15	0♉ 9	25	22	9	24	17	9	14	14
E 4	4 51 44	11 58 6	11 55	26	23	9	24	17	10	14	14
M 5	4 55 41	12 58 58	23 45	28	25	10	24	17	10	14	14
B 6	4 59 37	13 59 51	5♊39	29	26	11	24	17	10	14	14
E 7	5 3 34	15 0 45	17 40	1♑	27	12	24	17	10	14	14
R 8	5 7 30	16 1 41	29 49	2	28	12	24	17	10	14	14
9	5 11 27	17 2 37	12♋ 8	4	29	13	23	17	10	14	14
10	5 15 23	18 3 34	24 38	5	1♒	14	23	17	10	14	14
11	5 19 20	19 4 32	7♌19	7	2	14	23	17	10	14	14
12	5 23 17	20 5 31	20 13	8	3	15	23	17	10	14	14
13	5 27 13	21 6 32	3♍21	10	4	16	23	17	10	14	14
14	5 31 10	22 7 33	16 45	11	5	17	23	17	10	14	14
15	5 35 6	23 8 36	0♎27	12	6	17	23	17	10	14	14
16	5 39 3	24 9 39	14 27	14	8	18	23	17	10	14	14
17	5 42 59	25 10 43	28 46	15	9	19	23	17	10	14	14
18	5 46 56	26 11 49	13♏23	16	10	20	23	17	10	14	14
19	5 50 52	27 12 55	28 12	17	11	20	22	16	10	14	14
20	5 54 49	28 14 2	13♐ 7	18	12	21	22	16	10	14	14
21	5 58 46	29 15 9	28 1	19	13	22	22	16	10	14	14
22	6 2 42	0♑16 18	12♑45	20	15	23	22	16	10	14	14
23	6 6 39	1 17 26	27 9	21	16	23	22	16	11	14	14
24	6 10 35	2 18 35	11♒10	22	17	24	22	16	11	14	14
25	6 14 32	3 19 43	24 42	22	18	25	22	16	11	14	14
26	6 18 28	4 20 52	7♓48	23	19	26	22	16	11	14	14
27	6 22 25	5 22 1	20 28	23	20	26	22	16	11	14	14
28	6 26 21	6 23 10	2♈46	23 R	21	27	22	16	11	15	14
29	6 30 18	7 24 19	14 49	23	23	28	22	16	11	15	14
30	6 34 15	8 25 28	26 41	23	24	28	22	16	11	15	14
31	6 38 11	9 26 37	8♉28	23	25	29	22	16	11	15	14

THE SUN ENTERS THE SIGN OF CAPRICORN ON DEC 21 AT 17:36.

♈ ARIES ♉ TAURUS ♊ GEMINI ♋ CANCER ♌ LEO ♍ VIRGO ♎ LIBRA ♏ SCORPIO ♐ SAGITTARIUS ♑ CAPRICORN ♒ AQUARIUS ♓ PISCES

SIDEREAL SUN MOON MERCURY VENUS MARS JUPITER SATURN URANUS NEPTUNE PLUTO

DAY	TIME	☉	☽	☿	♀	♂	♃	♄	♅	♆	♇
	h m s	° ' "	° '	°	°	°	°	°	°	°	°
J 1	6 42 8	10♑27 45	20♉16	22♑R	26♒	0♑	22♉R	16♌R	11♏	15♐	14♎
A 2	6 46 4	11 28 54	2♊ 7	21	27	1	21	16	11	15	14
N 3	6 50 1	12 30 2	14 7	20	28	1	21	16	11	15	14
U 4	6 53 57	13 31 11	26 18	19	29	2	21	16	11	15	14
A 5	6 57 54	14 32 19	8♋41	18	1♓	3	21	16	11	15	14
R 6	7 1 50	15 33 27	21 17	16	2	4	21	16	11	15	14
Y 7	7 5 47	16 34 35	4♌ 6	15	3	4	21	15	11	15	14
8	7 9 44	17 35 43	17 8	14	4	5	21	15	11	15	14
9	7 13 40	18 36 50	0♍20	12	5	6	21	15	11	15	14
10	7 17 37	19 37 58	13 43	11	6	7	21	15	11	15	14
11	7 21 33	20 39 6	27 16	10	7	7	21	15	11	15	14
12	7 25 30	21 40 13	10♎59	9	8	8	21	15	11	15	14
13	7 29 26	22 41 21	24 53	9	9	9	21	15	11	15	14
14	7 33 23	23 42 29	8♏58	8	10	10	21	15	11	15	14
15	7 37 19	24 43 36	23 14	7	11	11	21 D	15	11	15	14
16	7 41 16	25 44 44	7♐38	7	13	11	21	15	11	15	14 R
17	7 45 13	26 45 51	22 7	7 D	14	12	21	15	11	15	14
18	7 49 9	27 46 57	6♑37	7	15	13	21	15	11	15	14
19	7 53 6	28 48 4	20 59	7	16	14	21	15	11	15	14
20	7 57 2	29 49 10	5♒ 9	8	17	14	21	15	11	15	14
21	8 0 59	0♒50 15	19 1	8	18	15	21	14	12	15	14
22	8 4 55	1 51 19	2♓29	8	19	16	21	14	12	15	14
23	8 8 52	2 52 22	15 34	9	20	17	21	14	12	15	14
24	8 12 48	3 53 25	28 16	10	21	17	21	14	12	15	14
25	8 16 45	4 54 26	10♈37	10	22	18	21	14	12	15	14
26	8 20 42	5 55 26	22 42	11	23	19	21	14	12	15	14
27	8 24 38	6 56 25	4♉36	12	24	20	21	14	12	15	14
28	8 28 35	7 57 23	16 24	13	25	20	21	14	12	15	14
29	8 32 31	8 58 20	28 13	14	26	21	21	14	12	16	14
30	8 36 28	9 59 16	10♊ 6	15	27	22	22	14	12	16	14
31	8 40 24	11 0 11	22 10	16	28	23	22	14	12	16	14

THE SUN ENTERS THE SIGN OF AQUARIUS ON JAN 20 AT 04:15.

DAY	TIME	☉	☽	☿	♀	♂	♃	♄	♅	♆	♇
	h m s	° ' "	° '	°	°	°	°	°	°	°	°
F 1	8 44 21	12♒ 1 4	4♋28	17♑	29♓	23♑	22♉	14♌R	12♏	16♐	14♎R
E 2	8 48 17	13 1 56	17 2	18	0☉	24	22	13	12	16	14
B 3	8 52 14	14 2 47	29 53	20	1♈	25	22	13	12	16	14
R 4	8 56 11	15 3 37	13♌ 2	21	2	26	22	13	12	16	14
U 5	9 0 7	16 4 25	26 27	22	3	27	22	13	12	16	14
A 6	9 4 4	17 5 13	10♍ 4	23	3	27	22	13	12	16	14
R 7	9 8 0	18 5 59	23 52	25	4	28	22	13	12	16	14
Y 8	9 11 57	19 6 44	7♎46	26	5	29	22	13	12	16	14
9	9 15 53	20 7 28	21 46	27	6	0♒	22	13	12	16	14
10	9 19 50	21 8 11	5♏49	29	7	0	22	13	12	16	14
11	9 23 46	22 8 53	19 54	0♒	8	1	22	13	12	16	14
12	9 27 43	23 9 34	4♐ 0	1	9	2	22	13	12	16	14
13	9 31 40	24 10 15	18 7	3	10	3	23	13	12	16	14
14	9 35 36	25 10 53	2♑12	4	10	3	23	13	12 R	16	14
15	9 39 33	26 11 31	16 14	6	11	4	23	12	12	16	14
16	9 43 29	27 12 8	0♒ 8	7	12	5	23	12	12	16	14
17	9 47 26	28 12 43	13 52	9	13	6	23	12	12	16	14
18	9 51 22	29 13 16	27 22	10	13	7	23	12	12	16	14
19	9 55 19	0♓13 49	10♓34	12	14	7	23	12	12	16	14
20	9 59 15	1 14 19	23 28	13	15	8	23	12	12	16	14
21	10 3 12	2 14 48	6♈ 3	15	16	9	23	12	12	16	14
22	10 7 9	3 15 15	18 22	16	16	10	23	12	12	16	14
23	10 11 5	4 15 40	0♉27	18	17	10	24	12	12	16	14
24	10 15 2	5 16 3	12 21	19	18	11	24	12	12	16	14
25	10 18 58	6 16 25	24 10	21	18	12	24	12	12	16	14
26	10 22 55	7 16 44	6♊ 0	23	19	13	24	12	12	16	14
27	10 26 51	8 17 2	17 54	24	19	14	24	12	12	16	14
28	10 30 48	9 17 17	29 59	26	20	14	24	11	12	16	14

THE SUN ENTERS THE SIGN OF PISCES ON FEB 18 AT 18:31.

DAY	TIME	☉	☽	☿	♀	♂	♃	♄	♅	♆	♇
	h m s	° ' "	° '	°	°	°	°	°	°	°	°
M 1	10 34 44	10♓17 31	12♋18	28♒	20♈	15♒	24♉	11♌R	12♏R	16♐	14♎R
A 2	10 38 41	11 17 42	24 56	29	21	16	24	11	12	16	14
R 3	10 42 38	12 17 52	7♌56	1♓	21	17	25	11	12	16	14
C 4	10 46 34	13 17 59	21 17	3	22	17	25	11	12	16	14
H 5	10 50 31	14 18 5	5♍ 0	5	22	18	25	11	12	16	14
6	10 54 27	15 18 8	19 0	6	23	19	25	11	12	16	14
7	10 58 24	16 18 10	3♎14	8	23	20	25	11	12	16	14
8	11 2 20	17 18 10	17 36	10	23	21	25	11	12	16	14
9	11 6 17	18 18 8	2♏ 2	12	24	21	26	11	12	16	13
10	11 10 13	19 18 5	16 26	14	24	22	26	11	12	16	13
11	11 14 10	20 18 0	0♐46	15	24	23	26	11	12	16	13
12	11 18 7	21 17 53	14 58	17	24	24	26	11	12	16	13
13	11 22 3	22 17 45	29 2	19	24	24	26	11	11	16	13
14	11 26 0	23 17 35	12♑54	21	24	25	26	11	11	16	13
15	11 29 56	24 17 24	26 36	23	25	26	26	11	11	16	13
16	11 33 53	25 17 10	10♒ 6	25	25 R	27	27	11	11	16	13
17	11 37 49	26 16 55	23 23	27	25	28	27	11	11	16	13
18	11 41 46	27 16 38	6♓27	29	24	28	27	10	11	16 R	13
19	11 45 42	28 16 20	19 17	1♈	24	29	27	10	11	16	13
20	11 49 39	29 15 59	1♈53	3	24	0♓	27	10	11	16	13
21	11 53 35	0♈15 36	14 15	5	24	1	27	10	11	16	13
22	11 57 32	1 15 11	26 26	7	24	1	28	10	11	16	13
23	12 1 29	2 14 44	8♉26	9	24	2	28	10	11	16	13
24	12 5 25	3 14 15	20 19	11	23	3	28	10	11	16	13
25	12 9 22	4 13 43	2♊ 8	13	23	4	28	10	11	16	13
26	12 13 18	5 13 10	13 57	15	23	5	28	10	11	16	13
27	12 17 15	6 12 34	25 51	17	22	5	29	10	11	16	13
28	12 21 11	7 11 56	7♋55	19	22	6	29	10	11	16	13
29	12 25 8	8 11 15	20 13	21	21	7	29	10	11	16	13
30	12 29 4	9 10 33	2♌49	23	21	8	29	10	11	16	13
31	12 33 1	10 9 47	15 48	25	20	9	29	10	11	16	13

THE SUN ENTERS THE SIGN OF ARIES ON MAR 20 AT 17:43.

SIDEREAL SUN MOON MERCURY VENUS MARS JUPITER SATURN URANUS NEPTUNE PLUTO

DAY	TIME	☉	☽	☿	♀	♂	♃	♄	♅	♆	♇
	h m s	° ' "	° '	°	°	°	°	°	°	°	°
A 1	12 36 58	11♈ 9 0	29♌11	26♈	20♈R	9♓	29♉	10♌R	11♏R	16♐R	13♎R
P 2	12 40 54	12 8 10	13♍ 0	28	19	10	0♊	10	11	16	13
R 3	12 44 51	13 7 18	27 12	0♉	18	11	0	10	11	16	13
I 4	12 48 47	14 6 24	11♎44	1	18	12	0	10	11	16	13
L 5	12 52 44	15 5 28	26 29	3	17	12	0	10	11	16	13
6	12 56 40	16 4 30	11♏22	4	17	13	0	10	11	16	13
7	13 0 37	17 3 30	26 13	6	16	14	1	10	11	16	13
8	13 4 33	18 2 29	10♐56	7	15	15	1	10	11	16	13
9	13 8 30	19 1 26	25 25	8	15	16	1	10	11	16	13
10	13 12 27	20 0 20	9♑37	9	14	16	1	10	11	16	13
11	13 16 23	20 59 14	23 31	10	13	17	1	10 D	11	16	13
12	13 20 20	21 58 5	7♒ 5	11	13	18	2	10	11	16	13
13	13 24 16	22 56 55	20 20	12	12	19	2	10	10	16	13
14	13 28 13	23 55 43	3♓18	13	12	19	2	10	10	16	13
15	13 32 9	24 54 29	16 1	13	11	20	2	10	10	16	12
16	13 36 6	25 53 13	28 31	14	11	21	3	10	10	16	12
17	13 40 2	26 51 56	10♈49	14	10	22	3	10	10	16	12
18	13 43 59	27 50 37	22 57	14	10	23	3	10	10	16	12
19	13 47 55	28 49 15	4♉58	14	10	23	3	10	10	16	12
20	13 51 52	29 47 52	16 52	15 R	9	24	3	10	10	16	12
21	13 55 49	0♉46 27	28 42	14	9	25	4	10	10	16	12
22	13 59 45	1 45 0	10♊31	14	9	26	4	10	10	16	12
23	14 3 42	2 43 31	22 21	14	9	26	4	10	10	16	12
24	14 7 38	3 42 0	4♋16	14	8	27	4	10	10	16	12
25	14 11 35	4 40 26	16 19	13	8	28	4	10	10	16	12
26	14 15 31	5 38 51	28 35	13	8	29	5	10	10	16	12
27	14 19 28	6 37 14	11♌ 8	12	8 D	29	5	10	10	16	12
28	14 23 24	7 35 34	24 2	12	8	0♈	5	10	10	16	12
29	14 27 21	8 33 52	7♍19	11	8	1	5	10	10	16	12
30	14 31 18	9 32 8	21 3	11	8	2	6	10	10	16	12

THE SUN ENTERS THE SIGN OF TAURUS ON APR 20 AT 04:58.

DAY	TIME	☉	☽	☿	♀	♂	♃	♄	♅	♆	♇
	h m s	° ' "	° '	°	°	°	°	°	°	°	°
M 1	14 35 14	10♉30 22	5♎14	10♉R	8♈	3♈	6♊	10♌	10♏R	16♐R	12♎R
A 2	14 39 11	11 28 35	19 50	9	9	3	6	10	10	16	12
Y 3	14 43 7	12 26 45	4♏45	9	9	4	6	10	10	16	12
4	14 47 4	13 24 54	19 53	8	9	5	6	10	10	16	12
5	14 51 0	14 23 1	5♐ 4	8	9	6	7	10	10	16	12
6	14 54 57	15 21 6	20 8	7	10	6	7	10	10	16	12
7	14 58 53	16 19 10	4♑58	6	10	7	7	11	9	16	12
8	15 2 50	17 17 13	19 25	6	10	8	7	11	9	16	12
9	15 6 47	18 15 14	3♒28	6	11	9	8	11	9	15	12
10	15 10 43	19 13 14	17 5	5	11	9	8	11	9	15	12
11	15 14 40	20 11 13	0♓16	5	12	10	8	11	9	15	12
12	15 18 36	21 9 10	13 6	5	12	11	8	11	9	15	12
13	15 22 33	22 7 6	25 38	5 D	12	12	8	11	9	15	12
14	15 26 29	23 5 1	7♈54	5	13	13	9	11	9	15	12
15	15 30 26	24 2 54	19 59	5	14	13	9	11	9	15	12
16	15 34 22	25 0 46	1♉57	5	14	14	9	11	9	15	12
17	15 38 19	25 58 37	13 49	5	15	15	9	11	9	15	12
18	15 42 16	26 56 26	25 39	5	15	16	10	11	9	15	12
19	15 46 12	27 54 14	7♊28	6	16	16	10	11	9	15	12
20	15 50 9	28 52 1	19 18	6	17	17	10	11	9	15	12
21	15 54 5	29 49 46	1♋11	7	17	18	10	11	9	15	12
22	15 58 2	0♊47 30	13 11	7	18	19	11	11	9	15	12
23	16 1 58	1 45 12	25 18	8	19	19	11	11	9	15	12
24	16 5 55	2 42 53	7♌35	9	19	20	11	12	9	15	12
25	16 9 51	3 40 32	20 7	9	20	21	11	12	9	15	12
26	16 13 48	4 38 10	2♍57	10	21	22	11	12	9	15	12
27	16 17 45	5 35 46	16 8	11	22	22	12	12	9	15	12
28	16 21 41	6 33 20	29 43	12	22	23	12	12	9	15	12
29	16 25 38	7 30 54	13♎44	13	23	24	12	12	9	15	12
30	16 29 34	8 28 26	28 12	14	24	25	12	12	9	15	12
31	16 33 31	9 25 56	13♏ 2	15	25	25	13	12	9	15	12

THE SUN ENTERS THE SIGN OF GEMINI ON MAY 21 AT 04:15.

DAY	TIME	☉	☽	☿	♀	♂	♃	♄	♅	♆	♇
	h m s	° ' "	° '	°	°	°	°	°	°	°	°
J 1	16 37 27	10♊23 26	28♏ 9	16♉	25♈	26♈	13♊	12♌	9♏R	15♐R	12♎R
U 2	16 41 24	11 20 54	13♐25	17	26	27	13	12	8	15	12
N 3	16 45 20	12 18 22	28 39	19	27	28	13	12	8	15	11
E 4	16 49 17	13 15 48	13♑41	20	28	28	14	12	8	15	11
5	16 53 14	14 13 14	28 21	21	29	29	14	12	8	15	11
6	16 57 10	15 10 39	12♒34	23	0♉	0♉	14	13	8	15	11
7	17 1 7	16 8 3	26 18	24	1	1	14	13	8	15	11
8	17 5 3	17 5 27	9♓34	25	2	1	14	13	8	15	11
9	17 9 0	18 2 50	22 23	27	2	2	15	13	8	15	11
10	17 12 56	19 0 13	4♈51	29	3	3	15	13	8	15	11
11	17 16 53	19 57 35	17 2	0♊	4	4	15	13	8	15	11
12	17 20 49	20 54 56	29 2	2	5	4	15	13	8	15	11
13	17 24 46	21 52 18	10♉54	4	6	5	16	13	8	15	11
14	17 28 43	22 49 38	22 42	5	7	6	16	13	8	15	11
15	17 32 39	23 46 58	4♊30	7	8	7	16	13	8	15	11
16	17 36 36	24 44 18	16 21	9	9	7	16	14	8	14	11
17	17 40 32	25 41 37	28 16	11	10	8	17	14	8	14	11
18	17 44 29	26 38 55	10♋16	13	11	9	17	14	8	14	11
19	17 48 25	27 36 13	22 24	15	12	10	17	14	8	14	11
20	17 52 22	28 33 30	4♌40	17	13	10	17	14	8	14	11
21	17 56 18	29 30 47	17 6	19	14	11	17	14	8	14	11 D
22	18 0 15	0♋28 3	29 44	21	15	12	18	14	8	14	11
23	18 4 12	1 25 18	12♍37	23	16	12	18	14	8	14	11
24	18 8 8	2 22 33	25 46	25	17	13	18	14	8	14	11
25	18 12 5	3 19 47	9♎15	27	18	14	18	14	8	14	11
26	18 16 1	4 17 0	23 6	29	19	15	19	15	8	14	11
27	18 19 58	5 14 13	7♏20	2♋	20	15	19	15	8	14	11
28	18 23 54	6 11 25	21 56	4	21	16	19	15	8	14	11
29	18 27 51	7 8 37	6♐50	6	22	17	19	15	8	14	11
30	18 31 47	8 5 49	21 55	8	23	17	20	15	8	14	11

THE SUN ENTERS THE SIGN OF CANCER ON JUN 21 AT 12:15.

♈ ARIES ♉ TAURUS ♊ GEMINI ♋ CANCER ♌ LEO ♍ VIRGO ♎ LIBRA ♏ SCORPIO ♐ SAGITTARIUS ♑ CAPRICORN ♒ AQUARIUS ♓ PISCES

SIDEREAL SUN MOON MERCURY VENUS MARS JUPITER SATURN URANUS NEPTUNE PLUTO

DAY	TIME	☉	☽	☿	♀	♂	♃	♄	♅	♆	♇
	h m s	° ' "	° '	°	°	°	°	°	°	°	°
J 1	18 35 44	9♋ 3 0	7♑ 3	10♋	24♉	18♉	20♊	15♌	8♏R	14♐R	11♎
U 2	18 39 41	10 0 12	22 2	12	25	19	20	15	8	14	11
L 3	18 43 37	10 57 23	6♒43	15	26	20	20	15	8	14	11
Y 4	18 47 34	11 54 34	21 1	17	27	20	20	15	8	14	11
5	18 51 30	12 51 45	4♓49	19	28	21	21	16	8	14	11
6	18 55 27	13 48 57	18 9	21	29	22	21	16	8	14	11
7	18 59 23	14 46 9	1♈ 1	23	0♊	23	21	16	8	14	11
8	19 3 20	15 43 21	13 31	25	1	23	21	16	8	14	11
9	19 7 16	16 40 34	25 42	27	3	24	22	16	8	14	11
10	19 11 13	17 37 47	7♉41	29	4	25	22	16	8	14	11
11	19 15 10	18 35 0	19 32	1♌	5	25	22	16	8	14	12
12	19 19 6	19 32 14	1♊21	3	6	26	22	16	8	14	12
13	19 23 3	20 29 28	13 11	5	7	27	22	16	8	14	12
14	19 26 59	21 26 43	25 5	7	8	27	23	17	8	14	12
15	19 30 56	22 23 59	7♋ 7	8	9	28	23	17	8	14	12
16	19 34 52	23 21 14	19 17	10	10	29	23	17	8 D	14	12
17	19 38 49	24 18 30	1♌37	12	11	0♊	23	17	8	14	12
18	19 42 46	25 15 46	14 8	14	12	0	23	17	8	14	12
19	19 46 42	26 13 3	26 49	15	13	1	24	17	8	14	12
20	19 50 39	27 10 20	9♍41	17	15	2	24	17	8	14	12
21	19 54 35	28 7 37	22 44	19	16	2	24	17	8	14	12
22	19 58 32	29 4 55	6♎ 1	20	17	3	24	18	8	14	12
23	20 2 28	0♌ 2 12	19 33	22	18	4	25	18	8	14	12
24	20 6 25	0 59 30	3♏20	24	19	4	25	18	8	14	12
25	20 10 21	1 56 49	17 25	25	20	5	25	18	8	14	12
26	20 14 18	2 54 8	1♐45	27	21	6	25	18	8	14	12
27	20 18 15	3 51 27	16 20	28	22	6	25	18	8	14	12
28	20 22 11	4 48 47	1♑ 4	29	23	7	26	18	8	14	12
29	20 26 8	5 46 7	15 51	1♍	25	8	26	18	8	14	12
30	20 30 4	6 43 28	0♒33	2	26	9	26	19	8	14	12
31	20 34 1	7 40 49	15 2	3	27	9	26	19	8	14	12

THE SUN ENTERS THE SIGN OF LEO ON JUL 22 AT 23:05.

DAY	TIME	☉	☽	☿	♀	♂	♃	♄	♅	♆	♇
	h m s	° ' "	° '	°	°	°	°	°	°	°	°
A 1	20 37 57	8♌38 12	29♒11	5♍	28♊	10♊	26♊	19♌	8♏	14♐R	12♎
U 2	20 41 54	9 35 35	12♓56	6	29	11	27	19	8	14	12
G 3	20 45 50	10 33 0	26 15	7	0♋	11	27	19	8	14	12
U 4	20 49 47	11 30 25	9♈ 8	8	1	12	27	19	8	13	12
S 5	20 53 43	12 27 52	21 40	10	3	13	27	19	8	13	12
T 6	20 57 40	13 25 20	3♉53	11	4	13	27	19	8	13	12
7	21 1 37	14 22 49	15 54	12	5	14	28	20	8	13	12
8	21 5 33	15 20 19	27 47	13	6	15	28	20	8	13	12
9	21 9 30	16 17 51	9♊37	14	7	15	28	20	8	13	12
10	21 13 26	17 15 25	21 29	15	8	16	28	20	8	13	12
11	21 17 23	18 12 59	3♋28	15	9	17	28	20	8	13	12
12	21 21 19	19 10 35	15 36	16	11	17	28	20	8	13	12
13	21 25 16	20 8 12	27 57	17	12	18	29	20	8	13	12
14	21 29 12	21 5 51	10♌30	18	13	19	29	20	8	13	12
15	21 33 9	22 3 30	23 17	18	14	19	29	21	8	13	12
16	21 37 6	23 1 11	6♍17	19	15	20	29	21	8	13	12
17	21 41 2	23 58 53	19 30	19	16	20	29	21	8	13	12
18	21 44 59	24 56 36	2♎54	20	18	21	0♋	21	8	13	12
19	21 48 55	25 54 21	16 29	20	19	22	0	21	8	13	12
20	21 52 52	26 52 6	0♏14	20	20	22	0	21	8	13	12
21	21 56 48	27 49 53	14 8	21	21	23	0	21	8	13	12
22	22 0 45	28 47 41	28 12	21 R	22	24	0	22	8	13	12
23	22 4 41	29 45 30	12♐24	21	23	24	0	22	8	13	12
24	22 8 38	0♍43 20	26 42	21	25	25	1	22	8	13	12
25	22 12 35	1 41 11	11♑ 4	21	26	26	1	22	8	13 D	12
26	22 16 31	2 39 3	25 25	20	27	26	1	22	8	13	13
27	22 20 28	3 36 57	9♒41	20	28	27	1	22	8	13	13
28	22 24 24	4 34 52	23 45	19	29	27	1	22	8	13	13
29	22 28 21	5 32 49	7♓34	19	0♌	28	1	22	8	13	13
30	22 32 17	6 30 47	21 5	18	2	29	2	23	9	13	13
31	22 36 14	7 28 47	4♈14	17	3	29	2	23	9	13	13

THE SUN ENTERS THE SIGN OF VIRGO ON AUG 23 AT 06:02.

DAY	TIME	☉	☽	☿	♀	♂	♃	♄	♅	♆	♇
	h m s	° ' "	° '	°	°	°	°	°	°	°	°
S 1	22 40 10	8♍26 49	17♈ 3	17♍R	4♌	0♋	2♋	23♌	9♏	13♐	13♎
E 2	22 44 7	9 24 52	29 33	16	5	1	2	23	9	13	13
P 3	22 48 4	10 22 57	11♉47	15	6	1	2	23	9	13	13
T 4	22 52 0	11 21 5	23 49	14	8	2	2	23	9	13	13
E 5	22 55 57	12 19 14	5♊43	13	9	2	2	23	9	13	13
M 6	22 59 53	13 17 25	17 34	12	10	3	3	23	9	13	13
B 7	23 3 50	14 15 38	29 28	11	11	4	3	24	9	13	13
E 8	23 7 46	15 13 54	11♋29	10	12	4	3	24	9	13	13
R 9	23 11 43	16 12 11	23 41	9	14	5	3	24	9	13	13
10	23 15 39	17 10 30	6♌ 8	9	15	5	3	24	9	13	13
11	23 19 36	18 8 51	18 51	8	16	6	3	24	9	13	13
12	23 23 33	19 7 14	1♍52	7	17	7	3	24	9	13	13
13	23 27 29	20 5 39	15 11	7	18	7	3	24	9	13	13
14	23 31 26	21 4 6	28 47	7 D	20	8	4	24	9	13	13
15	23 35 22	22 2 35	12♎36	7	21	8	4	24	9	13	13
16	23 39 19	23 1 5	26 37	7	22	9	4	25	9	13	13
17	23 43 15	23 59 37	10♏45	7	23	10	4	25	9	14	13
18	23 47 12	24 58 11	24 58	8	24	10	4	25	9	14	13
19	23 51 8	25 56 47	9♐13	8	26	11	4	25	9	14	13
20	23 55 5	26 55 24	23 27	9	27	11	4	25	9	14	13
21	23 59 1	27 54 3	7♑37	10	28	12	4	25	10	14	13
22	0 2 58	28 52 43	21 43	11	29	12	4	25	10	14	13
23	0 6 55	29 51 25	5♒41	12	0♍	13	5	25	10	14	14
24	0 10 51	0♎50 9	19 29	13	2	14	5	26	10	14	14
25	0 14 48	1 48 55	3♓ 6	15	3	14	5	26	10	14	14
26	0 18 44	2 47 42	16 29	16	4	15	5	26	10	14	14
27	0 22 41	3 46 31	29 38	18	5	15	5	26	10	14	14
28	0 26 37	4 45 23	12♈31	19	7	16	5	26	10	14	14
29	0 30 34	5 44 16	25 8	21	8	16	5	26	10	14	14
30	0 34 30	6 43 11	7♉31	22	9	17	5	26	10	14	14

THE SUN ENTERS THE SIGN OF LIBRA ON SEP 23 AT 03:31.

SIDEREAL SUN MOON MERCURY VENUS MARS JUPITER SATURN URANUS NEPTUNE PLUTO

DAY	TIME	☉	☽	☿	♀	♂	♃	♄	♅	♆	♇
	h m s	° ' "	° '	°	°	°	°	°	°	°	°
O 1	0 38 27	7♎42 9	19♉42	24♍	10♍	17♋	5♋	26♌	10♏	14♐	14♎
C 2	0 42 24	8 41 9	1♊43	26	11	18	5	26	10	14	14
T 3	0 46 20	9 40 11	13 37	28	13	19	5	27	10	14	14
O 4	0 50 17	10 39 15	25 28	29	14	19	5	27	10	14	14
B 5	0 54 13	11 38 22	7♋22	1♎	15	20	6	27	10	14	14
E 6	0 58 10	12 37 31	19 22	3	16	20	6	27	10	14	14
R 7	1 2 6	13 36 42	1♌33	5	18	21	6	27	10	14	14
8	1 6 3	14 35 56	14 0	6	19	21	6	27	10	14	14
9	1 9 59	15 35 11	26 46	8	20	22	6	27	10	14	14
10	1 13 56	16 34 30	9♍53	10	21	22	6	27	11	14	14
11	1 17 53	17 33 50	23 24	12	23	23	6	27	11	14	14
12	1 21 49	18 33 12	7♎16	13	24	23	6	27	11	14	14
13	1 25 46	19 32 37	21 29	15	25	24	6	27	11	14	14
14	1 29 42	20 32 3	5♏56	17	26	24	6	28	11	14	14
15	1 33 39	21 31 32	20 33	19	27	25	6	28	11	14	14
16	1 37 35	22 31 2	5♐13	20	29	25	6	28	11	14	14
17	1 41 32	23 30 34	19 49	22	0♎	26	6	28	11	14	14
18	1 45 28	24 30 8	4♑17	24	1	26	6	28	11	14	14
19	1 49 25	25 29 44	18 32	26	2	27	6	28	11	14	15
20	1 53 22	26 29 22	2♒32	27	4	27	6	28	11	14	15
21	1 57 18	27 29 1	16 17	29	5	27	6	28	11	14	15
22	2 1 15	28 28 42	29 45	1♏	6	28	6	28	11	14	15
23	2 5 11	29 28 24	12♓58	2	7	28	6	28	11	14	15
24	2 9 8	0♏28 8	25 57	4	9	29	6 R	28	11	14	15
25	2 13 4	1 27 54	8♈43	5	10	29	6	29	11	14	15
26	2 17 1	2 27 42	21 16	7	11	0♌	6	29	12	14	15
27	2 20 57	3 27 32	3♉39	9	12	0	6	29	12	14	15
28	2 24 54	4 27 24	15 52	10	14	1	6	29	12	14	15
29	2 28 50	5 27 18	27 56	12	15	1	6	29	12	14	15
30	2 32 47	6 27 14	9♊53	13	16	1	6	29	12	14	15
31	2 36 44	7 27 11	21 46	15	17	2	6	29	12	15	15

THE SUN ENTERS THE SIGN OF SCORPIO ON OCT 23 AT 12:42.

DAY	TIME	☉	☽	☿	♀	♂	♃	♄	♅	♆	♇
	h m s	° ' "	° '	°	°	°	°	°	°	°	°
N 1	2 40 40	8♏27 11	3♋37	17♏	19♎	2♌	6♋R	29♌	12♏	15♐	15♎
O 2	2 44 37	9 27 14	15 29	18	20	3	6	29	12	15	15
V 3	2 48 33	10 27 18	27 27	20	21	3	6	29	12	15	15
E 4	2 52 30	11 27 24	9♌35	21	22	3	6	29	12	15	15
M 5	2 56 26	12 27 32	21 58	23	24	4	6	29	12	15	15
B 6	3 0 23	13 27 43	4♍39	24	25	4	6	29	12	15	15
E 7	3 4 19	14 27 55	17 43	26	26	4	6	29	12	15	15
R 8	3 8 16	15 28 10	1♎13	27	27	5	6	0♍	12	15	15
9	3 12 13	16 28 26	15 11	29	29	5	6	0	12	15	15
10	3 16 9	17 28 44	29 34	0♐	0♏	5	6	0	12	15	15
11	3 20 6	18 29 5	14♏19	2	1	6	6	0	13	15	15
12	3 24 2	19 29 27	29 20	3	2	6	6	0	13	15	15
13	3 27 59	20 29 50	14♐26	5	4	6	6	0	13	15	15
14	3 31 55	21 30 16	29 28	6	5	7	5	0	13	15	15
15	3 35 52	22 30 42	14♑18	8	6	7	5	0	13	15	16
16	3 39 48	23 31 10	28 48	9	7	7	5	0	13	15	16
17	3 43 45	24 31 40	12♒55	11	9	8	5	0	13	15	16
18	3 47 42	25 32 10	26 38	12	10	8	5	0	13	15	16
19	3 51 38	26 32 42	9♓58	14	11	8	5	0	13	15	16
20	3 55 35	27 33 15	22 58	15	12	8	5	0	13	15	16
21	3 59 31	28 33 49	5♈40	17	14	9	5	0	13	15	16
22	4 3 28	29 34 24	18 8	18	15	9	5	0	13	15	16
23	4 7 24	0♐35 1	0♉25	19	16	9	5	0	13	15	16
24	4 11 21	1 35 39	12 34	21	17	9	5	0	13	15	16
25	4 15 17	2 36 18	24 36	22	19	10	5	0	13	15	16
26	4 19 14	3 36 59	6♊33	23	20	10	4	0	13	15	16
27	4 23 11	4 37 41	18 27	25	21	10	4	0	13	15	16
28	4 27 7	5 38 24	0♋19	26	22	10	4	0	14	15	16
29	4 31 4	6 39 9	12 11	27	24	10	4	0	14	16	16
30	4 35 0	7 39 55	24 5	28	25	11	4	0	14	16	16

THE SUN ENTERS THE SIGN OF SAGITTARIUS ON NOV 22 AT 10:08.

DAY	TIME	☉	☽	☿	♀	♂	♃	♄	♅	♆	♇
	h m s	° ' "	° '	°	°	°	°	°	°	°	°
D 1	4 38 57	8♐40 43	6♌ 3	0♑	26♏	11♌	4♋R	0♍	14♏	16♐	16♎
E 2	4 42 53	9 41 32	18 10	1	27	11	4	0	14	16	16
C 3	4 46 50	10 42 22	0♍28	2	29	11	4	0	14	16	16
E 4	4 50 46	11 43 14	13 3	3	0♐	11	4	0	14	16	16
M 5	4 54 43	12 44 7	25 59	4	1	11	3	1	14	16	16
B 6	4 58 40	13 45 1	9♎20	5	2	11	3	1	14	16	16
E 7	5 2 36	14 45 57	23 10	5	4	11	3	1	14	16	16
R 8	5 6 33	15 46 54	7♏29	6	5	11	3	1	14	16	16
9	5 10 29	16 47 52	22 14	7	6	11	3	1	14	16	16
10	5 14 26	17 48 52	7♐22	7	7	12	3	1	14	16	16
11	5 18 22	18 49 52	22 41	7	9	12	3	1 R	14	16	16
12	5 22 19	19 50 53	8♑ 1	7 R	10	12 R	3	1	14	16	16
13	5 26 15	20 51 55	23 10	7	11	12	2	1	14	16	16
14	5 30 12	21 52 57	7♒58	7	12	12	2	1	14	16	16
15	5 34 9	22 54 0	22 20	7	14	12	2	1	15	16	16
16	5 38 5	23 55 4	6♓12	6	15	11	2	1	15	16	16
17	5 42 2	24 56 7	19 36	5	16	11	2	1	15	16	16
18	5 45 58	25 57 11	2♈34	4	18	11	2	1	15	16	16
19	5 49 55	26 58 16	15 10	3	19	11	2	0	15	16	16
20	5 53 51	27 59 21	27 30	2	20	11	1	0	15	16	16
21	5 57 48	29 0 26	9♉38	0	21	11	1	0	15	16	16
22	6 1 44	0♑ 1 31	21 37	29♐	23	11	1	0	15	16	16
23	6 5 41	1 2 37	3♊32	28	24	11	1	0	15	16	16
24	6 9 38	2 3 43	15 24	26	25	11	1	0	15	16	16
25	6 13 34	3 4 49	27 16	25	26	11	1	0	15	16	17
26	6 17 31	4 5 55	9♋10	24	28	10	1	0	15	17	17
27	6 21 27	5 7 2	21 5	23	29	10	1	0	15	17	17
28	6 25 24	6 8 10	3♌ 4	22	0♑	10	0	0	15	17	17
29	6 29 20	7 9 17	15 8	22	1	10	0	0	15	17	17
30	6 33 17	8 10 25	27 19	21	3	10	0	0	15	17	17
31	6 37 14	9 11 34	9♍40	21 D	4	9	0	0	15	17	17

THE SUN ENTERS THE SIGN OF CAPRICORN ON DEC 21 AT 23:24.

♈ ARIES ♉ TAURUS ♊ GEMINI ♋ CANCER ♌ LEO ♍ VIRGO ♎ LIBRA ♏ SCORPIO ♐ SAGITTARIUS ♑ CAPRICORN ♒ AQUARIUS ♓ PISCES

DAY	TIME (SIDEREAL)	☉ (SUN)	☽ (MOON)	☿ (MERCURY)	♀ (VENUS)	♂ (MARS)	♃ (JUPITER)	♄ (SATURN)	♅ (URANUS)	♆ (NEPTUNE)	♇ (PLUTO)
	h m s	° ' "	° '	°	°	°	°	°	°	°	°
J 1	6 41 10	10♑12 42	22♍15	21♐	5♑	9♌R	0♋R	0♍R	15♏	17♐	17♎
A 2	6 45 7	11 13 51	5♎ 7	21	6	9	0	0	15	17	17
N 3	6 49 3	12 15 1	18 20	21	8	9	0	0	15	17	17
U 4	6 53 0	13 16 10	1♏58	22	9	8	29♊	0	15	17	17
A 5	6 56 56	14 17 20	16 2	22	10	8	29	0	15	17	17
R 6	7 0 53	15 18 31	0♐34	23	11	8	29	0	16	17	17
Y 7	7 4 49	16 19 41	15 29	24	13	7	29	0	16	17	17
8	7 8 46	17 20 51	0♑41	24	14	7	29	0	16	17	17
9	7 12 43	18 22 2	15 59	25	15	7	29	0	16	17	17
10	7 16 39	19 23 12	1♒12	26	16	6	29	0	16	17	17
11	7 20 36	20 24 22	16 9	27	18	6	29	0	16	17	17
12	7 24 32	21 25 31	0♓41	28	19	6	28	0	16	17	17
13	7 28 29	22 26 40	14 44	29	20	5	28	0	16	17	17
14	7 32 25	23 27 48	28 17	0♑	21	5	28	0	16	17	17
15	7 36 22	24 28 55	11♈22	1	23	4	28	29♌	16	17	17
16	7 40 18	25 30 2	24 2	3	24	4	28	29	16	17	17
17	7 44 15	26 31 8	6♉23	4	25	4	28	29	16	17	17
18	7 48 12	27 32 13	18 29	5	27	3	28	29	16	17	17
19	7 52 8	28 33 17	0♊26	6	28	3	28	29	16	17	17 R
20	7 56 5	29 34 21	12 18	8	29	2	28	29	16	17	17
21	8 0 1	0♒35 24	24 9	9	0♒	2	28	29	16	17	17
22	8 3 58	1 36 25	6♋ 1	10	2	2	27	29	16	17	17
23	8 7 54	2 37 27	17 57	12	3	1	27	29	16	17	17
24	8 11 51	3 38 27	29 59	13	4	1	27	29	16	17	17
25	8 15 47	4 39 26	12♌ 7	14	5	0	27	29	16	18	17
26	8 19 44	5 40 25	24 22	16	7	0	27	29	16	18	17
27	8 23 41	6 41 23	6♍46	17	8	0	27	29	16	18	17
28	8 27 37	7 42 20	19 19	19	9	29♋	27	29	16	18	17
29	8 31 34	8 43 17	2♎ 4	20	10	29	27	29	16	18	17
30	8 35 30	9 44 12	15 2	21	12	29	27	28	16	18	17
31	8 39 27	10 45 7	28 17	23	13	28	27	28	16	18	17

THE SUN ENTERS THE SIGN OF AQUARIUS ON JAN 20 AT 10:05.

DAY	TIME	☉	☽	☿	♀	♂	♃	♄	♅	♆	♇
	h m s	° ' "	° '	°	°	°	°	°	°	°	°
F 1	8 43 23	11♒46 2	11♏50	24♑	14♒	28♋R	27♊R	28♌R	16♏	18♐	17♎R
E 2	8 47 20	12 46 55	25 44	26	15	27	27	28	16	18	17
B 3	8 51 16	13 47 48	9♐59	27	17	27	27	28	16	18	17
R 4	8 55 13	14 48 40	24 34	29	18	27	27	28	16	18	17
U 5	8 59 10	15 49 32	9♑23	1♒	19	26	26	28	16	18	17
A 6	9 3 6	16 50 22	24 20	2	20	26	26	28	16	18	17
R 7	9 7 3	17 51 11	9♒17	4	22	26	26	28	16	18	17
Y 8	9 10 59	18 51 59	24 3	5	23	26	26	28	16	18	17
9	9 14 56	19 52 46	8♓31	7	24	25	26	28	16	18	17
10	9 18 52	20 53 31	22 35	8	25	25	26	28	16	18	17
11	9 22 49	21 54 14	6♈13	10	27	25	26	28	16	18	17
12	9 26 45	22 54 56	19 24	12	28	24	26	27	16	18	17
13	9 30 42	23 55 37	2♉11	13	29	24	26	27	16	18	17
14	9 34 39	24 56 16	14 37	15	0♓	24	26	27	16	18	17
15	9 38 35	25 56 53	26 47	17	2	24	26	27	16	18	16
16	9 42 32	26 57 28	8♊46	18	3	24	26	27	16	18	16
17	9 46 28	27 58 2	20 39	20	4	23	26	27	16	18	16
18	9 50 25	28 58 34	2♋30	22	5	23	26	27	16	18	16
19	9 54 21	29 59 5	14 24	23	7	23	26	27	16 R	18	16
20	9 58 18	0♓59 33	26 23	25	8	23	26 D	27	16	18	16
21	10 2 14	2 0 0	8♌31	27	9	23	26	27	16	18	16
22	10 6 11	3 0 25	20 49	29	10	23	26	27	16	18	16
23	10 10 7	4 0 48	3♍19	1♓	12	23	26	27	16	18	16
24	10 14 4	5 1 10	16 0	2	13	23	26	27	16	18	16
25	10 18 1	6 1 30	28 53	4	14	22	26	26	16	18	16
26	10 21 57	7 1 48	11♎58	6	15	22	26	26	16	18	16
27	10 25 54	8 2 5	25 15	8	17	22	26	26	16	18	16
28	10 29 50	9 2 21	8♏45	10	18	22	26	26	16	18	16

THE SUN ENTERS THE SIGN OF PISCES ON FEB 19 AT 00:21.

DAY	TIME	☉	☽	☿	♀	♂	♃	♄	♅	♆	♇
	h m s	° ' "	° '	°	°	°	°	°	°	°	°
M 1	10 33 47	10♓ 2 35	22♏28	12♓	19♓	22♋R	26♊	26♌R	16♏R	18♐	16♎R
A 2	10 37 43	11 2 47	6♐23	14	20	22 D	26	26	16	18	16
R 3	10 41 40	12 2 58	20 30	15	22	22	26	26	16	18	16
C 4	10 45 36	13 3 8	4♑48	17	23	22	26	26	16	18	16
H 5	10 49 33	14 3 16	19 13	19	24	22	26	26	16	18	16
6	10 53 30	15 3 22	3♒43	21	25	22	26	26	16	18	16
7	10 57 26	16 3 27	18 10	23	27	22	26	26	16	18	16
8	11 1 23	17 3 30	2♓31	25	28	22	26	26	16	18	16
9	11 5 19	18 3 31	16 39	27	29	23	26	26	16	18	16
10	11 9 16	19 3 31	0♈29	29	0♈	23	27	25	16	18	16
11	11 13 12	20 3 28	13 59	1♈	2	23	27	25	16	18	16
12	11 17 9	21 3 23	27 8	3	3	23	27	25	16	18	16
13	11 21 5	22 3 17	9♉56	5	4	23	27	25	16	18	16
14	11 25 2	23 3 8	22 26	6	5	23	27	25	16	18	16
15	11 28 59	24 2 57	4♊39	7	7	23	27	25	16	18	16
16	11 32 55	25 2 43	16 41	10	8	23	27	25	16	18	16
17	11 36 52	26 2 28	28 36	12	9	24	27	25	16	18	16
18	11 40 48	27 2 10	10♋29	13	10	24	27	25	16	18	16
19	11 44 45	28 1 50	22 24	15	12	24	27	25	16	18	16
20	11 48 41	29 1 28	4♌25	16	13	24	27	25	16	18 R	16
21	11 52 38	0♈ 1 3	16 37	18	14	24	27	25	16	18	16
22	11 56 34	1 0 37	29 2	19	15	24	28	25	16	18	16
23	12 0 31	2 0 8	11♍43	20	17	25	28	25	16	18	16
24	12 4 27	2 59 37	24 41	22	18	25	28	25	16	18	16
25	12 8 24	3 59 3	7♎55	23	19	25	28	25	16	18	16
26	12 12 21	4 58 28	21 25	23	20	25	28	24	16	18	16
27	12 16 17	5 57 51	5♏ 9	24	21	26	28	24	16	18	16
28	12 20 14	6 57 12	19 5	25	23	26	28	24	16	18	16
29	12 24 10	7 56 32	3♐ 9	25	24	26	28	24	16	18	16
30	12 28 7	8 55 49	17 19	26	25	26	28	24	16	18	16
31	12 32 3	9 55 5	1♑32	26	26	27	28	24	16	18	15

THE SUN ENTERS THE SIGN OF ARIES ON MAR 20 AT 23:34.

DAY	TIME (SIDEREAL)	☉ (SUN)	☽ (MOON)	☿ (MERCURY)	♀ (VENUS)	♂ (MARS)	♃ (JUPITER)	♄ (SATURN)	♅ (URANUS)	♆ (NEPTUNE)	♇ (PLUTO)
	h m s	° ' "	° '	°	°	°	°	°	°	°	°
A 1	12 36 0	10♈54 19	15♑46	26♈R	28♈	27♋	29♊	24♌R	16♏R	18♐R	15♎R
P 2	12 39 56	11 53 31	29 57	26	29	27	29	24	16	18	15
R 3	12 43 53	12 52 42	14♒ 3	26	0♉	27	29	24	16	18	15
I 4	12 47 50	13 51 51	28 3	26	1	28	29	24	16	18	15
L 5	12 51 46	14 50 58	11♓54	26	3	28	29	24	16	18	15
6	12 55 43	15 50 3	25 34	25	4	28	29	24	16	18	15
7	12 59 39	16 49 6	9♈ 1	25	5	29	29	24	16	18	15
8	13 3 36	17 48 7	22 13	24	6	29	29	24	15	18	15
9	13 7 32	18 47 6	5♉10	23	8	29	0♋	24	15	18	15
10	13 11 29	19 46 3	17 50	23	9	0♌	0	24	15	18	15
11	13 15 25	20 44 58	0♊16	22	10	0	0	24	15	18	15
12	13 19 22	21 43 51	12 29	21	11	0	0	24	15	18	15
13	13 23 19	22 42 41	24 32	20	12	1	0	24	15	18	15
14	13 27 15	23 41 30	6♋27	20	14	1	0	24	15	18	15
15	13 31 12	24 40 16	18 20	19	15	2	0	24	15	18	15
16	13 35 8	25 39 0	0♌14	18	16	2	1	24	15	18	15
17	13 39 5	26 37 41	12 15	18	17	2	1	24	15	18	15
18	13 43 1	27 36 21	24 27	17	19	3	1	24	15	18	15
19	13 46 58	28 34 58	6♍55	16	20	3	1	24	15	18	15
20	13 50 54	29 33 33	19 42	16	21	3	1	24	15	18	15
21	13 54 51	0♉32 6	2♎50	16	22	4	1	24	15	18	15
22	13 58 47	1 30 37	16 20	15	23	4	2	24	15	18	15
23	14 2 44	2 29 6	0♏12	15	25	5	2	24	15	18	15
24	14 6 41	3 27 33	14 22	15	26	5	2	24	15	18	15
25	14 10 37	4 25 58	28 47	15 D	27	5	2	24 D	15	18	15
26	14 14 34	5 24 22	13♐20	15	28	6	2	24	15	18	15
27	14 18 30	6 22 44	27 54	15	0♊	6	2	24	15	18	15
28	14 22 27	7 21 4	12♑24	15	1	7	3	24	15	18	15
29	14 26 23	8 19 23	26 45	15	2	7	3	24	15	18	15
30	14 30 20	9 17 41	10♒54	16	3	8	3	24	15	18	15

THE SUN ENTERS THE SIGN OF TAURUS ON APR 20 AT 10:50.

DAY	TIME	☉	☽	☿	♀	♂	♃	♄	♅	♆	♇
	h m s	° ' "	° '	°	°	°	°	°	°	°	°
M 1	14 34 17	10♉15 56	24♒50	16♈	4♊	8♌	3♋	24♌	15♏R	18♐R	15♎R
A 2	14 38 13	11 14 11	8♓32	17	6	8	3	24	15	18	15
Y 3	14 42 10	12 12 24	22 0	17	7	9	3	24	14	18	15
4	14 46 6	13 10 35	5♈14	18	8	9	4	24	14	18	15
5	14 50 3	14 8 45	18 17	18	9	10	4	24	14	18	15
6	14 53 59	15 6 53	1♉ 7	19	11	10	4	24	14	18	15
7	14 57 56	16 5 0	13 46	20	12	11	4	24	14	18	14
8	15 1 52	17 3 5	26 14	21	13	11	4	24	14	18	14
9	15 5 49	18 1 9	8♊31	22	14	12	5	24	14	18	14
10	15 9 45	18 59 10	20 39	23	15	12	5	24	14	18	14
11	15 13 42	19 57 10	2♋38	24	17	12	5	24	14	18	14
12	15 17 39	20 55 9	14 32	25	18	13	5	24	14	18	14
13	15 21 35	21 53 5	26 24	26	19	13	5	24	14	18	14
14	15 25 32	22 51 0	8♌17	27	20	14	5	24	14	18	14
15	15 29 28	23 48 53	20 16	28	21	14	6	24	14	18	14
16	15 33 25	24 46 44	2♍25	0♉	23	15	6	24	14	18	14
17	15 37 21	25 44 34	14 51	1	24	15	6	24	14	18	14
18	15 41 18	26 42 21	27 36	2	25	16	6	24	14	18	14
19	15 45 14	27 40 8	10♎47	4	26	16	6	24	14	17	14
20	15 49 11	28 37 52	24 24	5	27	17	7	24	14	17	14
21	15 53 8	29 35 35	8♏27	6	29	17	7	24	14	17	14
22	15 57 4	0♊33 17	22 56	8	0♋	18	7	24	14	17	14
23	16 1 1	1 30 57	7♐43	9	1	18	7	24	14	17	14
24	16 4 57	2 28 36	22 41	11	2	19	7	24	14	17	14
25	16 8 54	3 26 14	7♑41	13	4	19	8	24	14	17	14
26	16 12 50	4 23 51	22 33	14	5	20	8	24	14	17	14
27	16 16 47	5 21 27	7♒10	16	6	20	8	25	13	17	14
28	16 20 43	6 19 2	21 28	18	7	21	8	25	13	17	14
29	16 24 40	7 16 36	5♓24	19	8	21	8	25	13	17	14
30	16 28 37	8 14 9	18 59	21	9	22	9	25	13	17	14
31	16 32 33	9 11 42	2♈15	23	11	22	9	25	13	17	14

THE SUN ENTERS THE SIGN OF GEMINI ON MAY 21 AT 10:09.

DAY	TIME	☉	☽	☿	♀	♂	♃	♄	♅	♆	♇
	h m s	° ' "	° '	°	°	°	°	°	°	°	°
J 1	16 36 30	10♊ 9 13	15♈14	25♉	12♋	23♌	9♋	25♌	13♏R	17♐R	14♎R
U 2	16 40 26	11 6 44	27 59	27	13	24	9	25	13	17	14
N 3	16 44 23	12 4 14	10♉31	29	14	24	10	25	13	17	14
E 4	16 48 19	13 1 43	22 54	1♊	15	25	10	25	13	17	14
5	16 52 16	13 59 12	5♊ 8	3	17	25	10	25	13	17	14
6	16 56 12	14 56 39	17 14	5	18	26	10	25	13	17	14
7	17 0 9	15 54 6	29 15	7	19	26	10	25	13	17	14
8	17 4 6	16 51 31	11♋10	9	20	27	11	25	13	17	14
9	17 8 2	17 48 56	23 2	11	21	27	11	25	13	17	14
10	17 11 59	18 46 20	4♌52	13	23	28	11	25	13	17	14
11	17 15 55	19 43 42	16 44	15	24	28	11	25	13	17	14
12	17 19 52	20 41 4	28 42	18	25	29	11	26	13	17	14
13	17 23 48	21 38 25	10♍50	20	26	29	12	26	13	17	14
14	17 27 45	22 35 44	23 12	22	27	0♍	12	26	13	17	14
15	17 31 41	23 33 3	5♎54	24	29	0	12	26	13	17	14
16	17 35 38	24 30 21	19 1	26	0♌	1	12	26	13	17	14
17	17 39 35	25 27 38	2♏35	29	1	2	13	26	13	17	14
18	17 43 31	26 24 54	16 40	1♋	2	2	13	26	13	17	14
19	17 47 28	27 22 10	1♐13	3	3	3	13	26	13	17	14
20	17 51 24	28 19 25	16 9	5	4	3	13	26	13	17	14
21	17 55 21	29 16 40	1♑21	7	6	4	13	26	13	17	14
22	17 59 17	0♋13 54	16 38	9	7	4	14	26	13	17	14
23	18 3 14	1 11 7	1♒48	11	8	5	14	26	13	17	14
24	18 7 11	2 8 21	16 42	13	9	5	14	27	13	17	14 D
25	18 11 7	3 5 34	1♓13	15	10	6	14	27	13	16	14
26	18 15 4	4 2 47	15 18	17	11	7	15	27	13	16	14
27	18 19 0	5 0 0	28 57	19	13	7	15	27	13	16	14
28	18 22 57	5 57 14	12♈11	21	14	8	15	27	13	16	14
29	18 26 53	6 54 27	25 3	23	15	8	15	27	13	16	14
30	18 30 50	7 51 40	7♉39	25	16	9	15	27	13	16	14

THE SUN ENTERS THE SIGN OF CANCER ON JUN 21 AT 18:10.

♈ ARIES ♉ TAURUS ♊ GEMINI ♋ CANCER ♌ LEO ♍ VIRGO ♎ LIBRA ♏ SCORPIO ♐ SAGITTARIUS ♑ CAPRICORN ♒ AQUARIUS ♓ PISCES

SIDEREAL SUN MOON MERCURY VENUS MARS JUPITER SATURN URANUS NEPTUNE PLUTO

DAY	TIME	☉	☽	☿	♀	♂	♃	♄	♅	♆	♇
	h m s	° ′ ″	° ′	°	°	°	°	°	°	°	°
J 1	18 34 46	8♋48 54	20♉ 1	27♋	17♌	9♍	16♋	27♌	12♏R	16♐R	14♎
U 2	18 38 43	9 46 7	2♊12	28	18	10	16	27	12	16	14
L 3	18 42 40	10 43 21	14 16	0♌	20	11	16	27	12	16	14
Y 4	18 46 36	11 40 35	26 14	2	21	11	16	28	12	16	14
5	18 50 33	12 37 48	8♋ 9	3	22	12	17	28	12	16	14
6	18 54 29	13 35 2	20 1	5	23	12	17	28	12	16	14
7	18 58 26	14 32 16	1♌52	7	24	13	17	28	12	16	14
8	19 2 22	15 29 30	13 43	8	25	14	17	28	12	16	14
9	19 6 19	16 26 43	25 38	10	26	14	17	28	12	16	14
10	19 10 15	17 23 57	7♍38	11	28	15	18	28	12	16	14
11	19 14 12	18 21 11	19 48	13	29	15	18	28	12	16	14
12	19 18 9	19 18 24	2♎11	14	0♍	16	18	28	12	16	14
13	19 22 5	20 15 38	14 51	15	1	16	18	28	12	16	14
14	19 26 2	21 12 51	27 54	17	2	17	19	29	12	16	14
15	19 29 58	22 10 5	11♏23	18	3	18	19	29	12	16	14
16	19 33 55	23 7 18	25 20	19	4	18	19	29	12	16	14
17	19 37 51	24 4 32	9♐46	20	6	19	19	29	12	16	14
18	19 41 48	25 1 46	24 37	22	7	19	20	29	12	16	14
19	19 45 44	25 59 0	9♑47	23	8	20	20	29	12	16	14
20	19 49 41	26 56 15	25 5	24	9	21	20	29	12	16	14
21	19 53 38	27 53 30	10♒21	25	10	21	20	29	12 D	16	14
22	19 57 34	28 50 45	25 24	26	11	22	20	29	12	16	14
23	20 1 31	29 48 1	10♓ 5	27	12	22	21	0♍	12	16	14
24	20 5 27	0♌45 18	24 20	28	13	23	21	0	12	16	14
25	20 9 24	1 42 36	8♈ 6	28	15	24	21	0	12	16	14
26	20 13 20	2 39 55	21 26	29	16	24	21	0	12	16	14
27	20 17 17	3 37 14	4♉21	0♍	17	25	22	0	12	16	14
28	20 21 13	4 34 35	16 55	0	18	25	22	0	12	16	14
29	20 25 10	5 31 57	29 14	1	19	26	22	0	12	16	14
30	20 29 7	6 29 19	11♊20	2	20	27	22	0	12	16	14
31	20 33 3	7 26 43	23 19	2	21	27	22	1	12	16	14

THE SUN ENTERS THE SIGN OF LEO ON JUL 23 AT 05:01.

DAY	TIME	☉	☽	☿	♀	♂	♃	♄	♅	♆	♇
	h m s	° ′ ″	° ′	°	°	°	°	°	°	°	°
A 1	20 37 0	8♌24 8	5♋12	2♍	22♍	28♍	23♋	1♍	12♏	16♐R	14♎
U 2	20 40 56	9 21 33	17 4	3	23	29	23	1	12	16	14
G 3	20 44 53	10 19 0	28 55	3	24	29	23	1	12	16	14
U 4	20 48 49	11 16 28	10♌48	3 R	26	0♎	23	1	12	16	14
S 5	20 52 46	12 13 56	22 45	3	27	0	24	1	12	16	14
T 6	20 56 42	13 11 25	4♍47	3	28	1	24	1	12	16	14
7	21 0 39	14 8 56	16 55	3	29	2	24	1	12	16	14
8	21 4 36	15 6 27	29 13	3	0♎	2	24	2	12	16	14
9	21 8 32	16 3 59	11♎44	2	1	3	24	2	12	16	14
10	21 12 29	17 1 32	24 29	2	2	3	25	2	12	16	14
11	21 16 25	17 59 5	7♏33	1	3	4	25	2	12	16	15
12	21 20 22	18 56 40	20 59	1	4	5	25	2	13	16	15
13	21 24 18	19 54 15	4♐49	0	5	5	25	2	13	16	15
14	21 28 15	20 51 52	19 3	29♌	6	6	25	2	13	16	15
15	21 32 11	21 49 29	3♑39	29	7	7	26	2	13	16	15
16	21 36 8	22 47 8	18 32	28	8	7	26	3	13	16	15
17	21 40 5	23 44 47	3♒37	27	9	8	26	3	13	16	15
18	21 44 1	24 42 27	18 42	26	10	9	26	3	13	16	15
19	21 47 58	25 40 9	3♓40	25	11	9	27	3	13	16	15
20	21 51 54	26 37 52	18 21	25	12	10	27	3	13	16	15
21	21 55 51	27 35 37	2♈39	24	13	10	27	3	13	16	15
22	21 59 47	28 33 23	16 31	23	14	11	27	3	13	16	15
23	22 3 44	29 31 11	29 57	22	15	12	27	3	13	16	15
24	22 7 40	0♍29 0	12♉57	22	16	12	28	4	13	16	15
25	22 11 37	1 26 52	25 35	21	17	13	28	4	13	16	15
26	22 15 33	2 24 45	7♊55	21	18	14	28	4	13	16	15
27	22 19 30	3 22 40	20 2	21	19	14	28	4	13	16	15
28	22 23 27	4 20 36	1♋59	20 D	20	15	28	4	13	16 D	15
29	22 27 23	5 18 35	13 52	20	21	16	29	4	13	16	15
30	22 31 20	6 16 35	25 43	20	22	16	29	4	13	16	15
31	22 35 16	7 14 37	7♌36	21	23	17	29	4	13	16	15

THE SUN ENTERS THE SIGN OF VIRGO ON AUG 23 AT 11:58.

DAY	TIME	☉	☽	☿	♀	♂	♃	♄	♅	♆	♇
	h m s	° ′ ″	° ′	°	°	°	°	°	°	°	°
S 1	22 39 13	8♍12 40	19♌33	21♌	24♎	18♎	29♋	5♍	13♏	16♐	15♎
E 2	22 43 9	9 10 46	1♍38	22	25	18	29	5	13	16	15
P 3	22 47 6	10 8 53	13 50	22	26	19	0♌	5	13	16	15
T 4	22 51 2	11 7 1	26 13	23	27	19	0	5	13	16	15
E 5	22 54 59	12 5 12	8♎47	24	28	20	0	5	13	16	15
M 6	22 58 56	13 3 23	21 33	25	29	21	0	5	13	16	15
B 7	23 2 52	14 1 37	4♏33	26	0♏	21	0	5	13	16	15
E 8	23 6 49	14 59 52	17 48	27	1	22	1	5	13	16	15
R 9	23 10 45	15 58 8	1♐20	29	2	23	1	6	13	16	15
10	23 14 42	16 56 26	15 8	0♍	2	23	1	6	13	16	15
11	23 18 38	17 54 46	29 12	2	3	24	1	6	13	16	15
12	23 22 35	18 53 7	13♑32	3	4	25	1	6	13	16	16
13	23 26 31	19 51 29	28 5	5	5	25	1	6	14	16	16
14	23 30 28	20 49 53	12♒45	7	6	26	2	6	14	16	16
15	23 34 25	21 48 19	27 27	8	7	27	2	6	14	16	16
16	23 38 21	22 46 47	12♓ 5	10	7	27	2	6	14	16	16
17	23 42 18	23 45 16	26 31	12	8	28	2	7	14	16	16
18	23 46 14	24 43 47	10♈41	14	9	29	2	7	14	16	16
19	23 50 11	25 42 20	24 30	16	10	29	2	7	14	16	16
20	23 54 7	26 40 55	7♉57	18	11	0♏	3	7	14	16	16
21	23 58 4	27 39 33	21 0	19	11	1	3	7	14	16	16
22	0 2 0	28 38 12	3♊42	21	12	1	3	7	14	16	16
23	0 5 57	29 36 54	16 5	23	13	2	3	7	14	16	16
24	0 9 53	0♎35 38	28 14	25	13	3	3	7	14	16	16
25	0 13 50	1 34 24	10♋12	27	14	3	3	8	14	16	16
26	0 17 47	2 33 13	22 5	29	15	4	4	8	14	16	16
27	0 21 43	3 32 4	3♌56	1♎	15	5	4	8	14	16	16
28	0 25 40	4 30 56	15 51	2	16	5	4	8	14	16	16
29	0 29 36	5 29 51	27 53	4	17	6	4	8	14	16	16
30	0 33 33	6 28 49	10♍ 5	6	17	7	4	8	14	16	16

THE SUN ENTERS THE SIGN OF LIBRA ON SEP 23 AT 09:27.

SIDEREAL SUN MOON MERCURY VENUS MARS JUPITER SATURN URANUS NEPTUNE PLUTO

DAY	TIME	☉	☽	☿	♀	♂	♃	♄	♅	♆	♇
	h m s	° ′ ″	° ′	°	°	°	°	°	°	°	°
O 1	0 37 29	7♎27 48	22♍30	8♎	18♏	8♏	4♌	8♍	14♏	16♐	16♎
C 2	0 41 26	8 26 50	5♎ 9	10	18	8	5	8	14	16	16
T 3	0 45 22	9 25 53	18 3	11	19	9	5	8	14	16	16
O 4	0 49 19	10 24 58	1♏13	13	19	10	5	9	15	16	16
B 5	0 53 16	11 24 6	14 36	15	20	10	5	9	15	16	16
E 6	0 57 12	12 23 15	28 13	16	20	11	5	9	15	16	16
R 7	1 1 9	13 22 26	12♐ 1	18	21	12	5	9	15	16	16
8	1 5 5	14 21 39	25 58	20	21	12	5	9	15	16	17
9	1 9 2	15 20 54	10♑ 3	21	21	13	6	9	15	16	17
10	1 12 58	16 20 11	24 14	23	22	14	6	9	15	16	17
11	1 16 55	17 19 29	8♒29	25	22	14	6	9	15	16	17
12	1 20 51	18 18 49	22 45	26	22	15	6	9	15	16	17
13	1 24 48	19 18 10	6♓59	28	22	16	6	10	15	16	17
14	1 28 45	20 17 34	21 9	0♏	22	17	6	10	15	16	17
15	1 32 41	21 16 59	5♈11	1	23	17	6	10	15	16	17
16	1 36 38	22 16 26	19 1	3	23	18	6	10	15	16	17
17	1 40 34	23 15 55	2♉36	4	23	19	7	10	15	16	17
18	1 44 31	24 15 27	15 53	6	23 R	19	7	10	15	16	17
19	1 48 27	25 15 0	28 53	7	23	20	7	10	15	16	17
20	1 52 24	26 14 36	11♊33	9	23	21	7	10	15	16	17
21	1 56 20	27 14 14	23 57	11	23	21	7	10	16	16	17
22	2 0 17	28 13 54	6♋ 7	12	23	22	7	10	16	16	17
23	2 4 14	29 13 36	18 5	14	22	23	7	11	16	16	17
24	2 8 10	0♏13 21	29 58	15	22	24	7	11	16	16	17
25	2 12 7	1 13 8	11♌49	17	22	24	7	11	16	16	17
26	2 16 3	2 12 57	23 43	18	22	25	8	11	16	16	17
27	2 20 0	3 12 48	5♍47	20	21	26	8	11	16	16	17
28	2 23 56	4 12 41	18 3	21	21	26	8	11	16	17	17
29	2 27 53	5 12 37	0♎36	22	20	27	8	11	16	17	17
30	2 31 49	6 12 34	13 29	24	20	28	8	11	16	17	17
31	2 35 46	7 12 34	26 42	25	20	29	8	11	16	17	17

THE SUN ENTERS THE SIGN OF SCORPIO ON OCT 23 AT 18:38.

DAY	TIME	☉	☽	☿	♀	♂	♃	♄	♅	♆	♇
	h m s	° ′ ″	° ′	°	°	°	°	°	°	°	°
N 1	2 39 42	8♏12 36	10♏16	27♏	19♏R	29♏	8♌	11♍	16♏	17♐	17♎
O 2	2 43 39	9 12 39	24 7	28	19	0♐	8	12	16	17	17
V 3	2 47 36	10 12 44	8♐12	0♐	18	1	8	12	16	17	18
E 4	2 51 32	11 12 51	22 26	1	17	1	8	12	16	17	18
M 5	2 55 29	12 13 0	6♑45	2	17	2	8	12	16	17	18
B 6	2 59 25	13 13 10	21 3	4	16	3	8	12	17	17	18
E 7	3 3 22	14 13 22	5♒17	5	16	4	8	12	17	17	18
R 8	3 7 18	15 13 35	19 25	6	15	4	9	12	17	17	18
9	3 11 15	16 13 50	3♓25	8	14	5	9	12	17	17	18
10	3 15 11	17 14 5	17 18	9	14	6	9	12	17	17	18
11	3 19 8	18 14 23	1♈ 1	10	13	6	9	12	17	17	18
12	3 23 5	19 14 42	14 36	11	13	7	9	12	17	17	18
13	3 27 1	20 15 2	28 0	12	12	8	9	12	17	17	18
14	3 30 58	21 15 24	11♉14	14	12	9	9	12	17	17	18
15	3 34 54	22 15 48	24 14	15	11	9	9	13	17	17	18
16	3 38 51	23 16 13	7♊ 2	16	11	10	9	13	17	17	18
17	3 42 47	24 16 40	19 35	17	10	11	9	13	17	17	18
18	3 46 44	25 17 9	1♋54	18	10	12	9	13	17	17	18
19	3 50 40	26 17 39	14 1	18	9	12	9	13	17	17	18
20	3 54 37	27 18 11	25 58	19	9	13	9	13	17	17	18
21	3 58 34	28 18 45	7♌49	20	9	14	9	13	17	17	18
22	4 2 30	29 19 21	19 38	21	8	15	9	13	17	17	18
23	4 6 27	0♐19 58	1♍30	21	8	15	9	13	18	17	18
24	4 10 23	1 20 37	13 32	21	8	16	9	13	18	17	18
25	4 14 20	2 21 18	25 47	22 R	8	17	9 R	13	18	17	18
26	4 18 16	3 22 0	8♎21	22	7	17	9	13	18	17	18
27	4 22 13	4 22 43	21 19	22	7	18	9	13	18	18	18
28	4 26 9	5 23 29	4♏42	21	7 D	19	9	13	18	18	18
29	4 30 6	6 24 16	18 32	21	7	20	9	13	18	18	18
30	4 34 3	7 25 4	2♐45	20	7	20	9	13	18	18	18

THE SUN ENTERS THE SIGN OF SAGITTARIUS ON NOV 22 AT 16:06.

DAY	TIME	☉	☽	☿	♀	♂	♃	♄	♅	♆	♇
	h m s	° ′ ″	° ′	°	°	°	°	°	°	°	°
D 1	4 37 59	8♐25 53	17♐17	19♐R	7♏	21♐	9♌R	13♍	18♏	18♐	18♎
E 2	4 41 56	9 26 44	2♑ 0	18	8	22	9	13	18	18	18
C 3	4 45 52	10 27 36	16 46	17	8	23	9	13	18	18	19
E 4	4 49 49	11 28 28	1♒28	16	8	23	9	14	18	18	19
M 5	4 53 45	12 29 22	15 58	15	8	24	9	14	18	18	19
B 6	4 57 42	13 30 16	0♓14	13	8	25	9	14	18	18	19
E 7	5 1 38	14 31 11	14 13	12	9	26	9	14	18	18	19
R 8	5 5 35	15 32 6	27 55	11	9	26	9	14	18	18	19
9	5 9 32	16 33 2	11♈23	9	9	27	9	14	19	18	19
10	5 13 28	17 33 59	24 37	8	10	28	9	14	19	18	19
11	5 17 25	18 34 57	7♉40	7	10	29	9	14	19	18	19
12	5 21 21	19 35 55	20 31	7	11	29	9	14	19	18	19
13	5 25 18	20 36 54	3♊12	6	11	0♑	9	14	19	18	19
14	5 29 14	21 37 54	15 42	6	12	1	9	14	19	18	19
15	5 33 11	22 38 55	28 2	5 D	12	2	8	14	19	18	19
16	5 37 7	23 39 56	10♋13	5	13	2	8	14	19	18	19
17	5 41 4	24 40 58	22 14	6	13	3	8	14	19	18	19
18	5 45 1	25 42 1	4♌ 8	6	14	4	8	14	19	18	19
19	5 48 57	26 43 5	15 57	6	15	5	8	14	19	18	19
20	5 52 54	27 44 9	27 45	7	15	6	8	14	19	18	19
21	5 56 50	28 45 14	9♍35	7	16	6	8	14	19	18	19
22	6 0 47	29 46 20	21 33	8	17	7	8	14	19	18	19
23	6 4 43	0♑47 27	3♎45	9	17	8	8	14	19	19	19
24	6 8 40	1 48 34	16 15	10	18	9	8	14 R	19	19	19
25	6 12 36	2 49 42	29 9	11	19	9	8	14	19	19	19
26	6 16 33	3 50 51	12♏31	12	20	10	8	14	19	19	19
27	6 20 30	4 52 0	26 23	13	20	11	8	14	19	19	19
28	6 24 26	5 53 10	10♐43	14	21	12	7	14	20	19	19
29	6 28 23	6 54 20	25 28	15	22	12	7	14	20	19	19
30	6 32 19	7 55 31	10♑30	17	23	13	7	14	20	19	19
31	6 36 16	8 56 41	25 39	18	24	14	7	14	20	19	19

THE SUN ENTERS THE SIGN OF CAPRICORN ON DEC 22 AT 05:22.

♈ ARIES ♉ TAURUS ♊ GEMINI ♋ CANCER ♌ LEO ♍ VIRGO ♎ LIBRA ♏ SCORPIO ♐ SAGITTARIUS ♑ CAPRICORN ♒ AQUARIUS ♓ PISCES

278 Appendix X

1979

SIDEREAL SUN MOON MERCURY VENUS MARS JUPITER SATURN URANUS NEPTUNE PLUTO

DAY	TIME	☉	☽	☿	♀	♂	♃	♄	♅	♆	♇
	h m s	° ' "	° '	°	°	°	°	°	°	°	°
J 1	6 40 12	9♑57 52	10♒45	19♐	24♏	15♑	7♌R	14♍R	20♏	19♐	19♎
A 2	6 44 9	10 59 3	25 38	20	25	15	7	14	20	19	19
N 3	6 48 6	12 0 13	10♓11	22	26	16	7	14	20	19	19
U 4	6 52 2	13 1 23	24 23	23	27	17	7	14	20	19	19
A 5	6 55 59	14 2 33	8♈11	24	28	18	7	14	20	19	19
R 6	6 59 55	15 3 42	21 36	26	29	19	6	14	20	19	19
Y 7	7 3 52	16 4 52	4♉43	27	0♐	19	6	14	20	19	19
8	7 7 48	17 6 0	17 33	29	1	20	6	14	20	19	19
9	7 11 45	18 7 8	0♊ 9	0♑	2	21	6	14	20	19	19
10	7 15 41	19 8 16	12 33	2	3	22	6	14	20	19	19
11	7 19 38	20 9 24	24 49	3	4	22	6	14	20	19	19
12	7 23 35	21 10 31	6♋56	4	4	23	6	14	20	19	19
13	7 27 31	22 11 38	18 56	6	5	24	6	14	20	19	19
14	7 31 28	23 12 44	0♌51	7	6	25	5	14	20	19	19
15	7 35 24	24 13 50	12 42	9	7	26	5	14	20	19	19
16	7 39 21	25 14 56	24 30	10	8	26	5	13	20	19	19
17	7 43 17	26 16 1	6♍19	12	9	27	5	13	20	19	19
18	7 47 14	27 17 6	18 10	13	10	28	5	13	20	19	19
19	7 51 10	28 18 11	0♎ 9	15	11	29	5	13	20	19	19
20	7 55 7	29 19 15	12 20	16	12	29	5	13	20	19	19
21	7 59 4	0♒20 19	24 47	18	14	0♒	5	13	20	20	19 R
22	8 3 0	1 21 22	7♏36	20	15	1	4	13	20	20	19
23	8 6 57	2 22 25	20 50	21	16	2	4	13	21	20	19
24	8 10 53	3 23 28	4♐33	23	17	3	4	13	21	20	19
25	8 14 50	4 24 30	18 45	24	18	3	4	13	21	20	19
26	8 18 46	5 25 32	3♑25	26	19	4	4	13	21	20	19
27	8 22 43	6 26 33	18 27	28	20	5	4	13	21	20	19
28	8 26 39	7 27 34	3♒41	29	21	6	4	13	21	20	19
29	8 30 36	8 28 33	18 58	1♒	22	6	3	13	21	20	19
30	8 34 33	9 29 31	4♓ 7	2	23	7	3	13	21	20	19
31	8 38 29	10 30 29	18 59	4	24	8	3	13	21	20	19

THE SUN ENTERS THE SIGN OF AQUARIUS ON JAN 20 AT 16:01.

DAY	TIME	☉	☽	☿	♀	♂	♃	♄	♅	♆	♇
	h m s	° ' "	° '	°	°	°	°	°	°	°	°
F 1	8 42 26	11♒31 25	3♈28	6♒	25♐	9♒	3♌R	13♍R	21♏	20♐	19♎R
E 2	8 46 22	12 32 19	17 30	7	26	10	3	13	21	20	19
B 3	8 50 19	13 33 13	1♉ 5	9	27	10	3	13	21	20	19
R 4	8 54 15	14 34 5	14 16	11	28	11	3	12	21	20	19
U 5	8 58 12	15 34 55	27 4	12	0♑	12	3	12	21	20	19
A 6	9 2 8	16 35 45	9♊35	14	1	13	2	12	21	20	19
R 7	9 6 5	17 36 32	21 52	16	2	14	2	12	21	20	19
Y 8	9 10 2	18 37 19	3♋58	18	3	14	2	12	21	20	19
9	9 13 58	19 38 4	15 56	19	4	15	2	12	21	20	19
10	9 17 55	20 38 47	27 49	21	5	16	2	12	21	20	19
11	9 21 51	21 39 29	9♌39	23	6	17	2	12	21	20	19
12	9 25 48	22 40 10	21 28	25	7	17	2	12	21	20	19
13	9 29 44	23 40 49	3♍18	27	8	18	2	12	21	20	19
14	9 33 41	24 41 27	15 12	28	10	19	1	12	21	20	19
15	9 37 37	25 42 3	27 10	0♓	11	20	1	12	21	20	19
16	9 41 34	26 42 38	9♎17	2	12	21	1	12	21	20	19
17	9 45 31	27 43 12	21 34	4	13	21	1	12	21	20	19
18	9 49 27	28 43 45	4♏ 6	6	14	22	1	11	21	20	19
19	9 53 24	29 44 16	16 55	8	15	23	1	11	21	20	19
20	9 57 20	0♓44 47	0♐ 5	10	16	24	1	11	21	20	19
21	10 1 17	1 45 16	13 38	11	18	25	1	11	21	20	19
22	10 5 13	2 45 43	27 37	13	19	25	1	11	21	20	19
23	10 9 10	3 46 10	12♑ 0	15	20	26	1	11	21	20	19
24	10 13 6	4 46 34	26 45	17	21	27	0	11	21 R	20	19
25	10 17 3	5 46 58	11♒46	19	22	28	0	11	21	20	19
26	10 20 59	6 47 20	26 55	20	23	29	0	11	21	20	19
27	10 24 56	7 47 40	12♓ 2	22	25	29	0	11	21	20	19
28	10 28 53	8 47 58	26 59	24	26	0♓	0	11	21	20	19

THE SUN ENTERS THE SIGN OF PISCES ON FEB 19 AT 06:14.

DAY	TIME	☉	☽	☿	♀	♂	♃	♄	♅	♆	♇
	h m s	° ' "	° '	°	°	°	°	°	°	°	°
M 1	10 32 49	9♓48 15	11♈36	26♓	27♑	1♓	0♌R	11♍R	21♏R	20♐	19♎R
A 2	10 36 46	10 48 29	25 50	27	28	2	0	11	21	20	19
R 3	10 40 42	11 48 42	9♉37	29	29	2	0	10	21	20	19
C 4	10 44 39	12 48 53	22 58	0♈	0♒	3	0	10	21	20	19
H 5	10 48 35	13 49 1	5♊53	2	1	4	0	10	21	20	19
6	10 52 32	14 49 7	18 27	3	3	5	0	10	21	20	19
7	10 56 28	15 49 12	0♋43	4	4	6	0	10	21	20	19
8	11 0 25	16 49 14	12 46	5	5	6	0	10	21	20	19
9	11 4 22	17 49 14	24 40	6	6	7	29♋	10	21	20	19
10	11 8 18	18 49 12	6♌30	7	7	8	29	10	21	20	19
11	11 12 15	19 49 8	18 18	7	9	9	29	10	21	20	19
12	11 16 11	20 49 1	0♍ 8	8	10	10	29	10	21	20	19
13	11 20 8	21 48 53	12 3	8	11	10	29	10	21	20	19
14	11 24 4	22 48 43	24 5	8	12	11	29	10	21	20	19
15	11 28 1	23 48 30	6♎15	9 R	13	12	29	9	21	20	19
16	11 31 57	24 48 16	18 36	8	14	13	29	9	21	20	18
17	11 35 54	25 48 0	1♏ 9	8	16	14	29	9	21	20	18
18	11 39 51	26 47 42	13 54	8	17	14	29	9	21	20	18
19	11 43 47	27 47 23	26 54	7	18	15	29	9	21	20	18
20	11 47 44	28 47 1	10♐10	7	19	16	29	9	21	20	18
21	11 51 40	29 46 38	23 43	6	20	17	29	9	21	20	18
22	11 55 37	0♈46 14	7♑34	6	22	17	29	9	21	20	18
23	11 59 33	1 45 47	21 42	5	23	18	29	9	21	20 R	18
24	12 3 30	2 45 19	6♒ 6	4	24	19	29	9	21	20	18
25	12 7 26	3 44 49	20 44	3	25	20	29	9	21	20	18
26	12 11 23	4 44 17	5♓30	2	26	21	29 D	9	21	20	18
27	12 15 19	5 43 43	20 18	1	27	21	29	9	21	20	18
28	12 19 16	6 43 8	5♈ 1	0	29	22	29	9	21	20	18
29	12 23 13	7 42 30	19 32	0⊙	0♓	23	29	9	21	20	18
30	12 27 9	8 41 50	3♉45	29♓	1	24	29	8	21	20	18
31	12 31 6	9 41 8	17 35	28	2	24	29	8	20	20	18

THE SUN ENTERS THE SIGN OF ARIES ON MAR 21 AT 05:22.

SIDEREAL SUN MOON MERCURY VENUS MARS JUPITER SATURN URANUS NEPTUNE PLUTO

DAY	TIME	☉	☽	☿	♀	♂	♃	♄	♅	♆	♇
	h m s	° ' "	° '	°	°	°	°	°	°	°	°
A 1	12 35 2	10♈40 24	1♊ 1	28♓R	3♓	25♓	29♋	8♍R	20♏R	20♐R	18♎R
P 2	12 38 59	11 39 37	14 2	27	5	26	29	8	20	20	18
R 3	12 42 55	12 38 49	26 41	27	6	27	29	8	20	20	18
I 4	12 46 52	13 37 58	9♋ 0	26	7	28	29	8	20	20	18
L 5	12 50 48	14 37 4	21 4	26	8	28	29	8	20	20	18
6	12 54 45	15 36 8	2♌59	26	9	29	29	8	20	20	18
7	12 58 42	16 35 10	14 48	26 D	11	0⊙	29	8	20	20	18
8	13 2 38	17 34 10	26 36	26	12	1♈	29	8	20	20	18
9	13 6 35	18 33 8	8♍29	26	13	2	29	8	20	20	18
10	13 10 31	19 32 3	20 29	26	14	2	29	8	20	20	18
11	13 14 28	20 30 56	2♎41	26	15	3	29	8	20	20	18
12	13 18 24	21 29 47	15 5	27	17	4	29	8	20	20	18
13	13 22 21	22 28 36	27 43	27	18	5	0♌	8	20	20	18
14	13 26 17	23 27 23	10♏37	28	19	5	0	8	20	20	18
15	13 30 14	24 26 8	23 44	28	20	6	0	8	20	20	18
16	13 34 11	25 24 52	7♐ 5	29	21	7	0	8	20	20	18
17	13 38 7	26 23 33	20 38	0⊙	23	8	0	8	20	20	18
18	13 42 4	27 22 13	4♑22	0♈	24	8	0	7	20	20	18
19	13 46 0	28 20 52	18 16	1	25	9	0	7	20	20	18
20	13 49 57	29 19 28	2♒19	2	26	10	0	7	20	20	18
21	13 53 53	0♉18 3	16 30	3	27	11	0	7	20	20	17
22	13 57 50	1 16 36	0♓47	4	29	12	0	7	20	20	17
23	14 1 46	2 15 8	15 7	5	0⊙	12	0	7	20	20	17
24	14 5 43	3 13 38	29 29	6	1♈	13	0	7	20	20	17
25	14 9 40	4 12 6	13♈48	7	2	14	0	7	20	20	17
26	14 13 36	5 10 33	27 58	8	3	15	0	7	20	20	17
27	14 17 33	6 8 58	11♉56	10	5	15	1	7	20	20	17
28	14 21 29	7 7 20	25 37	11	6	16	1	7	19	20	17
29	14 25 26	8 5 42	8♊58	12	7	17	1	7	19	20	17
30	14 29 22	9 4 1	21 57	13	8	18	1	7	19	20	17

THE SUN ENTERS THE SIGN OF TAURUS ON APR 20 AT 16:36.

DAY	TIME	☉	☽	☿	♀	♂	♃	♄	♅	♆	♇
	h m s	° ' "	° '	°	°	°	°	°	°	°	°
M 1	14 33 19	10♉ 2 18	4♋36	15♈	9♈	18♈	1♌	7♍R	19♏R	20♐R	17♎R
A 2	14 37 15	11 0 33	16 56	16	11	19	1	7	19	20	17
Y 3	14 41 12	11 58 46	29 1	18	12	20	1	7	19	20	17
4	14 45 9	12 56 57	10♌56	19	13	21	1	7	19	20	17
5	14 49 5	13 55 6	22 46	21	14	22	1	7	19	20	17
6	14 53 2	14 53 13	4♍35	22	15	22	2	7	19	20	17
7	14 56 58	15 51 18	16 30	24	17	23	2	7	19	20	17
8	15 0 55	16 49 22	28 34	25	18	24	2	7	19	20	17
9	15 4 51	17 47 23	10♎53	27	19	25	2	7 D	19	20	17
10	15 8 48	18 45 23	23 29	28	20	25	2	7	19	20	17
11	15 12 44	19 43 21	6♏24	0♉	22	26	2	7	19	20	17
12	15 16 41	20 41 17	19 38	2	23	27	2	7	19	20	17
13	15 20 37	21 39 12	3♐10	4	24	28	2	7	19	20	17
14	15 24 34	22 37 5	16 57	5	25	28	3	7	19	20	17
15	15 28 31	23 34 57	0♑55	7	26	29	3	7	19	20	17
16	15 32 27	24 32 48	15 0	9	28	0♉	3	7	19	20	17
17	15 36 24	25 30 37	29 9	11	29	1	3	7	19	20	17
18	15 40 20	26 28 26	13♒19	13	0♉	1	3	7	19	20	17
19	15 44 17	27 26 13	27 27	15	1	2	3	7	19	20	17
20	15 48 13	28 23 59	11♓34	17	2	3	3	7	19	20	17
21	15 52 10	29 21 44	25 37	19	4	4	3	7	19	20	17
22	15 56 6	0♊19 27	9♈36	21	5	4	4	7	18	20	17
23	16 0 3	1 17 10	23 29	23	6	5	4	7	18	20	17
24	16 4 0	2 14 52	7♉14	25	7	6	4	7	18	20	17
25	16 7 56	3 12 32	20 48	27	8	7	4	7	18	20	17
26	16 11 53	4 10 12	4♊10	29	10	7	4	7	18	20	17
27	16 15 49	5 7 50	17 15	1♊	11	8	4	7	18	20	17
28	16 19 46	6 5 27	0♋ 5	4	12	9	5	7	18	19	17
29	16 23 42	7 3 3	12 37	6	13	10	5	7	18	19	17
30	16 27 39	8 0 37	24 53	8	15	10	5	7	18	19	17
31	16 31 35	8 58 10	6♌56	10	16	11	5	7	18	19	17

THE SUN ENTERS THE SIGN OF GEMINI ON MAY 21 AT 15:55.

DAY	TIME	☉	☽	☿	♀	♂	♃	♄	♅	♆	♇
	h m s	° ' "	° '	°	°	°	°	°	°	°	°
J 1	16 35 32	9♊55 42	18♌50	12♊	17♉	12♉	5♌	8♍	18♏R	19♐R	17♎R
U 2	16 39 29	10 53 12	0♍39	15	18	13	5	8	18	19	17
N 3	16 43 25	11 50 41	12 28	17	19	13	6	8	18	19	17
E 4	16 47 22	12 48 9	24 23	19	21	14	6	8	18	19	17
5	16 51 18	13 45 35	6♎29	21	22	15	6	8	18	19	17
6	16 55 15	14 43 1	18 51	23	23	15	6	8	18	19	17
7	16 59 11	15 40 25	1♏34	25	24	16	6	8	18	19	17
8	17 3 8	16 37 48	14 39	27	25	17	6	8	18	19	17
9	17 7 4	17 35 11	28 8	29	27	18	7	8	18	19	17
10	17 11 1	18 32 32	12♐ 0	1♋	28	18	7	8	18	19	17
11	17 14 58	19 29 53	26 11	3	29	19	7	8	18	19	16
12	17 18 54	20 27 12	10♑34	5	0♊	20	7	8	18	19	16
13	17 22 51	21 24 32	25 5	7	2	21	7	8	18	19	16
14	17 26 47	22 21 50	9♒36	9	3	21	7	8	18	19	16
15	17 30 44	23 19 9	24 3	11	4	22	8	8	18	19	16
16	17 34 40	24 16 26	8♓22	13	5	23	8	8	18	19	16
17	17 38 37	25 13 44	22 29	14	6	23	8	8	18	19	16
18	17 42 34	26 11 1	6♈26	16	8	24	8	8	18	19	16
19	17 46 30	27 8 18	20 11	18	9	25	8	8	17	19	16
20	17 50 27	28 5 34	3♉46	19	10	26	9	9	17	19	16
21	17 54 23	29 2 51	17 9	21	11	26	9	9	17	19	16
22	17 58 20	0♋ 0 7	0♊20	22	12	27	9	9	17	19	16
23	18 2 16	0 57 23	13 19	24	14	28	9	9	17	19	16
24	18 6 13	1 54 39	26 6	25	15	29	9	9	17	19	16
25	18 10 9	2 51 54	8♋39	27	16	29	10	9	17	19	16
26	18 14 6	3 49 9	20 59	28	17	0♊	10	9	17	19	16
27	18 18 3	4 46 24	3♌ 7	29	19	1	10	9	17	19	16 D
28	18 21 59	5 43 38	15 5	1♌	20	1	10	9	17	19	16
29	18 25 56	6 40 52	26 56	2	21	2	10	9	17	19	16
30	18 29 52	7 38 5	8♍43	3	22	3	11	9	17	19	16

THE SUN ENTERS THE SIGN OF CANCER ON JUN 21 AT 23:57.

♈ ARIES ♉ TAURUS ♊ GEMINI ♋ CANCER ♌ LEO ♍ VIRGO ♎ LIBRA ♏ SCORPIO ♐ SAGITTARIUS ♑ CAPRICORN ♒ AQUARIUS ♓ PISCES

1979

SIDEREAL SUN MOON MERCURY VENUS MARS JUPITER SATURN URANUS NEPTUNE PLUTO

DAY	TIME	☉	☽	☿	♀	♂	♃	♄	♅	♆	♇
	h m s	° ' "	° '	°	°	°	°	°	°	°	°
J 1	18 33 49	8♋35 18	20♍31	4♌	23♊	3♊	11♌	9♍	17♏R	19♐R	16♎
U 2	18 37 45	9 32 31	2♎25	5	25	4	11	9	17	19	16
L 3	18 41 42	10 29 43	14 31	6	26	5	11	9	17	19	16
Y 4	18 45 38	11 26 55	26 52	7	27	6	11	10	17	19	16
5	18 49 35	12 24 6	9♏36	8	28	6	12	10	17	18	16
6	18 53 32	13 21 18	22 44	9	0♋	7	12	10	17	18	16
7	18 57 28	14 18 29	6♐19	10	1	8	12	10	17	18	16
8	19 1 25	15 15 40	20 21	11	2	8	12	10	17	18	16
9	19 5 21	16 12 51	4♑46	11	3	9	12	10	17	18	16
10	19 9 18	17 10 2	19 28	12	4	10	13	10	17	18	16
11	19 13 14	18 7 14	4♒21	13	6	11	13	10	17	18	16
12	19 17 11	19 4 25	19 15	13	7	11	13	10	17	18	16
13	19 21 7	20 1 37	4♓ 4	13	8	12	13	10	17	18	16
14	19 25 4	20 58 49	18 39	14	9	13	13	10	17	18	17
15	19 29 1	21 56 2	2♈59	14	11	13	14	11	17	18	17
16	19 32 57	22 53 16	17 0	14	12	14	14	11	17	18	17
17	19 36 54	23 50 30	0♉43	14 R	13	15	14	11	17	18	17
18	19 40 50	24 47 44	14 8	14	14	15	14	11	17	18	17
19	19 44 47	25 45 0	27 17	14	15	16	15	11	17	18	17
20	19 48 43	26 42 16	10♊11	14	17	17	15	11	17	18	17
21	19 52 40	27 39 33	22 52	14	18	17	15	11	17	18	17
22	19 56 36	28 36 51	5♋20	14	19	18	15	11	17	18	17
23	20 0 33	29 34 9	17 37	13	20	19	15	11	17	18	17
24	20 4 30	0♌31 28	29 45	13	22	20	16	11	17	18	17
25	20 8 26	1 28 47	11♌43	12	23	20	16	12	17	18	17
26	20 12 23	2 26 7	23 35	12	24	21	16	12	17 D	18	17
27	20 16 19	3 23 28	5♍23	11	25	22	16	12	17	18	17
28	20 20 16	4 20 49	17 9	11	27	22	16	12	17	18	17
29	20 24 12	5 18 11	28 57	10	28	23	17	12	17	18	17
30	20 28 9	6 15 33	10♎52	9	29	24	17	12	17	18	17
31	20 32 5	7 12 55	22 57	8	0♌	24	17	12	17	18	17

THE SUN ENTERS THE SIGN OF LEO ON JUL 23 AT 10:50.

DAY	TIME	☉	☽	☿	♀	♂	♃	♄	♅	♆	♇
	h m s	° ' "	° '	°	°	°	°	°	°	°	°
A 1	20 36 2	8♌10 19	5♏17	8♌R	1♌	25♊	17♌	12♍	17♏	18♐R	17♎
U 2	20 39 59	9 7 43	17 58	7	3	26	18	12	17	18	17
G 3	20 43 55	10 5 7	1♐ 3	6	4	26	18	13	17	18	17
U 4	20 47 52	11 2 32	14 35	6	5	27	18	13	17	18	17
S 5	20 51 48	11 59 58	28 35	5	6	28	18	13	17	18	17
T 6	20 55 45	12 57 25	13♑ 1	4	8	28	18	13	17	18	17
7	20 59 41	13 54 52	27 50	4	9	29	19	13	17	18	17
8	21 3 38	14 52 20	12♒53	4	10	0♋	19	13	17	18	17
9	21 7 34	15 49 50	28 2	3	11	0	19	13	17	18	17
10	21 11 31	16 47 20	13♓ 9	3	13	1	19	13	17	18	17
11	21 15 28	17 44 52	28 3	3 D	14	2	20	13	17	18	17
12	21 19 24	18 42 25	12♈39	3	15	2	20	14	17	18	17
13	21 23 21	19 39 59	26 52	3	16	3	20	14	17	18	17
14	21 27 17	20 37 35	10♉42	4	17	4	20	14	17	18	17
15	21 31 14	21 35 12	24 8	4	19	4	20	14	17	18	17
16	21 35 10	22 32 51	7♊12	5	20	5	21	14	17	18	17
17	21 39 7	23 30 32	19 57	5	21	6	21	14	17	18	17
18	21 43 3	24 28 14	2♋26	6	22	6	21	14	17	18	17
19	21 47 0	25 25 58	14 41	7	24	7	21	14	17	18	17
20	21 50 57	26 23 43	26 46	8	25	8	21	15	17	18	17
21	21 54 53	27 21 29	8♌42	9	26	8	22	15	17	18	17
22	21 58 50	28 19 17	20 34	10	27	9	22	15	17	18	17
23	22 2 46	29 17 7	2♍21	11	29	9	22	15	17	18	17
24	22 6 43	0♍14 57	14 8	13	0♍	10	22	15	17	18	17
25	22 10 39	1 12 50	25 56	14	1	11	23	15	17	18	17
26	22 14 36	2 10 43	7♎48	16	2	11	23	15	17	18	17
27	22 18 32	3 8 38	19 47	17	4	12	23	15	17	18	17
28	22 22 29	4 6 34	1♏56	19	5	13	23	16	17	18	17
29	22 26 25	5 4 32	14 18	21	6	13	23	16	17	18	17
30	22 30 22	6 2 31	26 58	23	7	14	24	16	17	18 D	18
31	22 34 19	7 0 31	9♐58	25	9	15	24	16	17	18	18

THE SUN ENTERS THE SIGN OF VIRGO ON AUG 23 AT 17:48.

DAY	TIME	☉	☽	☿	♀	♂	♃	♄	♅	♆	♇
	h m s	° ' "	° '	°	°	°	°	°	°	°	°
S 1	22 38 15	7♍58 33	23♐23	26♌	10♍	15♋	24♌	16♍	17♏	18♐	18♎
E 2	22 42 12	8 56 36	7♑13	28	11	16	24	16	18	18	18
P 3	22 46 8	9 54 40	21 29	0♍	12	17	25	16	18	18	18
T 4	22 50 5	10 52 46	6♒ 9	2	13	17	25	16	18	18	18
E 5	22 54 1	11 50 53	21 8	4	15	18	25	17	18	18	18
M 6	22 57 58	12 49 2	6♓18	6	16	18	25	17	18	18	18
B 7	23 1 54	13 47 12	21 30	8	17	19	25	17	18	18	18
E 8	23 5 51	14 45 25	6♈35	10	18	20	26	17	18	18	18
R 9	23 9 48	15 43 39	21 24	12	20	20	26	17	18	18	18
10	23 13 44	16 41 55	5♉50	14	21	21	26	17	18	18	18
11	23 17 41	17 40 13	19 51	16	22	22	26	17	18	18	18
12	23 21 37	18 38 33	3♊24	18	23	22	26	17	18	18	18
13	23 25 34	19 36 56	16 31	19	25	23	27	18	18	18	18
14	23 29 30	20 35 20	29 14	21	26	23	27	18	18	18	18
15	23 33 27	21 33 47	11♋38	23	27	24	27	18	18	18	18
16	23 37 23	22 32 16	23 47	25	28	25	27	18	18	18	18
17	23 41 20	23 30 47	5♌45	27	0♎	25	27	18	18	18	18
18	23 45 17	24 29 20	17 35	29	1	26	28	18	18	18	18
19	23 49 13	25 27 55	29 23	0♎	2	26	28	18	18	18	18
20	23 53 10	26 26 32	11♍ 9	2	3	27	28	18	18	18	18
21	23 57 6	27 25 11	22 59	4	5	28	28	19	18	18	18
22	0 1 3	28 23 52	4♎52	6	6	28	29	19	18	18	18
23	0 4 59	29 22 35	16 53	7	7	29	29	19	18	18	18
24	0 8 56	0♎21 19	29 2	9	8	29	29	19	18	18	18
25	0 12 52	1 20 6	11♏21	11	10	0♌	29	19	18	18	18
26	0 16 49	2 18 54	23 52	12	11	1	29	19	18	18	18
27	0 20 45	3 17 45	6♐37	14	12	1	0♍	19	19	18	19
28	0 24 42	4 16 37	19 39	16	13	2	0	19	19	18	19
29	0 28 39	5 15 30	2♑59	17	15	2	0	20	19	18	19
30	0 32 35	6 14 26	16 40	19	16	3	0	20	19	18	19

THE SUN ENTERS THE SIGN OF LIBRA ON SEP 23 AT 15:18.

DAY	TIME	☉	☽	☿	♀	♂	♃	♄	♅	♆	♇
	h m s	° ' "	° '	°	°	°	°	°	°	°	°
O 1	0 36 32	7♎13 23	0♒42	20♎	17♎	4♌	0♍	20♍	19♏	18♐	19♎
C 2	0 40 28	8 12 22	15 4	22	18	4	1	20	19	18	19
T 3	0 44 25	9 11 23	29 45	24	20	5	1	20	19	18	19
O 4	0 48 21	10 10 25	14♓40	25	21	5	1	20	19	18	19
B 5	0 52 18	11 9 30	29 42	27	22	6	1	20	19	18	19
E 6	0 56 14	12 8 36	14♈42	28	23	7	1	20	19	18	19
R 7	1 0 11	13 7 44	29 32	0♏	25	7	1	21	19	18	19
8	1 4 8	14 6 55	14♉ 4	1	26	8	2	21	19	18	19
9	1 8 4	15 6 7	28 11	3	27	8	2	21	19	18	19
10	1 12 1	16 5 22	11♊52	4	28	9	2	21	19	18	19
11	1 15 57	17 4 40	25 4	6	29	9	2	21	19	18	19
12	1 19 54	18 3 59	7♋51	7	1♏	10	2	21	19	18	19
13	1 23 50	19 3 21	20 16	9	2	11	3	21	19	18	19
14	1 27 47	20 2 46	2♌24	10	3	11	3	21	19	18	19
15	1 31 43	21 2 12	14 20	11	4	12	3	21	19	18	19
16	1 35 40	22 1 41	26 8	13	6	12	3	22	20	18	19
17	1 39 37	23 1 12	7♍55	14	7	13	3	22	20	18	19
18	1 43 33	24 0 45	19 43	15	8	13	3	22	20	18	19
19	1 47 30	25 0 20	1♎37	17	9	14	4	22	20	18	19
20	1 51 26	25 59 58	13 39	18	11	14	4	22	20	18	19
21	1 55 23	26 59 37	25 52	19	12	15	4	22	20	18	19
22	1 59 19	27 59 19	8♏16	21	13	16	4	22	20	18	19
23	2 3 16	28 59 2	20 52	22	14	16	4	22	20	18	20
24	2 7 12	29 58 48	3♐40	23	16	17	4	22	20	19	20
25	2 11 9	0♏58 35	16 41	24	17	17	5	23	20	19	20
26	2 15 6	1 58 24	29 53	25	18	18	5	23	20	19	20
27	2 19 2	2 58 15	13♑19	27	19	18	5	23	20	19	20
28	2 22 59	3 58 7	26 58	28	21	19	5	23	20	19	20
29	2 26 55	4 58 2	10♒50	29	22	19	5	23	20	19	20
30	2 30 52	5 57 57	24 57	0♐	23	20	5	23	20	19	20
31	2 34 48	6 57 54	9♓17	1	24	20	6	23	20	19	20

THE SUN ENTERS THE SIGN OF SCORPIO ON OCT 24 AT 00:30.

DAY	TIME	☉	☽	☿	♀	♂	♃	♄	♅	♆	♇
	h m s	° ' "	° '	°	°	°	°	°	°	°	°
N 1	2 38 45	7♏57 53	23♓49	2♐	26♏	21♌	6♍	23♍	20♏	19♐	20♎
O 2	2 42 41	8 57 54	8♈27	2	27	21	6	23	21	19	20
V 3	2 46 38	9 57 56	23 8	3	28	22	6	23	21	19	20
E 4	2 50 34	10 58 0	7♉43	4	29	22	6	24	21	19	20
M 5	2 54 31	11 58 6	22 5	4	1♐	23	6	24	21	19	20
B 6	2 58 28	12 58 14	6♊ 8	5	2	23	6	24	21	19	20
E 7	3 2 24	13 58 23	19 48	5	3	24	7	24	21	19	20
R 8	3 6 21	14 58 35	3♋ 3	6	4	24	7	24	21	19	20
9	3 10 17	15 58 49	15 53	6 R	6	25	7	24	21	19	20
10	3 14 14	16 59 4	28 20	6	7	25	7	24	21	19	20
11	3 18 10	17 59 22	10♌30	6	8	26	7	24	21	19	20
12	3 22 7	18 59 41	22 26	5	9	26	7	24	21	19	20
13	3 26 3	20 0 3	4♍15	5	11	27	7	24	21	19	20
14	3 30 0	21 0 26	16 2	4	12	27	7	25	21	19	20
15	3 33 57	22 0 51	27 52	3	13	28	8	25	21	19	20
16	3 37 53	23 1 19	9♎51	2	14	28	8	25	21	19	20
17	3 41 50	24 1 48	22 1	1	16	29	8	25	21	19	20
18	3 45 46	25 2 18	4♏25	0	17	29	8	25	22	19	20
19	3 49 43	26 2 50	17 5	29♏	18	0♍	8	25	22	19	21
20	3 53 39	27 3 24	0♐ 2	28	19	0	8	25	22	19	21
21	3 57 36	28 4 0	13 12	26	21	0	8	25	22	19	21
22	4 1 32	29 4 37	26 36	25	22	1	8	25	22	19	21
23	4 5 29	0♐ 5 15	10♑10	24	23	1	8	25	22	19	21
24	4 9 26	1 5 55	23 53	23	24	2	9	25	22	20	21
25	4 13 22	2 6 35	7♒43	22	26	2	9	25	22	20	21
26	4 17 19	3 7 17	21 39	21	27	3	9	25	22	20	21
27	4 21 15	4 8 0	5♓41	20	28	3	9	26	22	20	21
28	4 25 12	5 8 43	19 47	20	29	4	9	26	22	20	21
29	4 29 8	6 9 28	3♈58	20 D	1♑	4	9	26	22	20	21
30	4 33 5	7 10 14	18 12	20	2	4	9	26	22	20	21

THE SUN ENTERS THE SIGN OF SAGITTARIUS ON NOV 22 AT 21:55.

DAY	TIME	☉	☽	☿	♀	♂	♃	♄	♅	♆	♇
	h m s	° ' "	° '	°	°	°	°	°	°	°	°
D 1	4 37 1	8♐11 0	2♉25	20♏	3♑	5♍	9♍	26♍	22♏	20♐	21♎
E 2	4 40 58	9 11 48	16 34	20	4	5	9	26	22	20	21
C 3	4 44 55	10 12 37	0♊33	21	5	6	9	26	22	20	21
E 4	4 48 51	11 13 27	14 19	21	7	6	9	26	23	20	21
M 5	4 52 48	12 14 18	27 46	22	8	6	10	26	23	20	21
B 6	4 56 44	13 15 10	10♋53	23	9	7	10	26	23	20	21
E 7	5 0 41	14 16 3	23 39	24	10	7	10	26	23	20	21
R 8	5 4 37	15 16 58	6♌ 6	25	12	7	10	26	23	20	21
9	5 8 34	16 17 54	18 16	26	13	8	10	26	23	20	21
10	5 12 31	17 18 50	0♍13	27	14	8	10	26	23	20	21
11	5 16 27	18 19 49	12 3	28	15	8	10	26	23	20	21
12	5 20 24	19 20 48	23 50	29	17	9	10	26	23	20	21
13	5 24 20	20 21 48	5♎42	1♐	18	9	10	26	23	20	21
14	5 28 17	21 22 49	17 42	2	19	9	10	26	23	20	21
15	5 32 13	22 23 52	29 56	3	20	10	10	27	23	20	21
16	5 36 10	23 24 55	12♏27	5	22	10	10	27	23	20	21
17	5 40 6	24 25 59	25 18	6	23	10	10	27	23	20	21
18	5 44 3	25 27 4	8♐30	7	24	11	10	27	23	20	21
19	5 48 0	26 28 10	22 1	9	25	11	10	27	23	20	21
20	5 51 56	27 29 17	5♑50	10	27	11	10	27	23	20	21
21	5 55 53	28 30 24	19 51	12	28	12	10	27	23	21	21
22	5 59 49	29 31 31	4♒ 0	13	29	12	10	27	24	21	21
23	6 3 46	0♑32 39	18 14	14	0♒	12	10	27	24	21	21
24	6 7 42	1 33 47	2♓28	16	2	12	10	27	24	21	21
25	6 11 39	2 34 55	16 39	17	3	13	10	27	24	21	21
26	6 15 35	3 36 3	0♈46	19	4	13	10 R	27	24	21	22
27	6 19 32	4 37 11	14 49	20	5	13	10	27	24	21	22
28	6 23 29	5 38 19	28 46	22	6	13	10	27	24	21	22
29	6 27 25	6 39 27	12♉36	23	8	13	10	27	24	21	22
30	6 31 22	7 40 35	26 18	25	9	14	10	27	24	21	22
31	6 35 18	8 41 43	9♊49	26	10	14	10	27	24	21	22

THE SUN ENTERS THE SIGN OF CAPRICORN ON DEC 22 AT 11:11.

♈ ARIES ♉ TAURUS ♊ GEMINI ♋ CANCER ♌ LEO ♍ VIRGO ♎ LIBRA ♏ SCORPIO ♐ SAGITTARIUS ♑ CAPRICORN ♒ AQUARIUS ♓ PISCES

1980

280 *Appendix X*

SIDEREAL SUN MOON MERCURY VENUS MARS JUPITER SATURN URANUS NEPTUNE PLUTO

DAY	TIME	☉	☽	☿	♀	♂	♃	♄	♅	♆	♇
	h m s	° ' "	° '	°	°	°	°	°	°	°	°
J 1	6 39 15	9♑42 51	23♊ 9	28♐	11♒	14♍	10♍R	27♍	24♏	21♐	22♎
A 2	6 43 11	10 43 59	6♋15	29	13	14	10	27	24	21	22
N 3	6 47 8	11 45 7	19 5	1♑	14	14	10	27	24	21	22
U 4	6 51 4	12 46 15	1♌40	3	15	14	10	27	24	21	22
A 5	6 55 1	13 47 24	13 59	4	16	15	10	27	24	21	22
R 6	6 58 58	14 48 32	26 6	6	18	15	10	27	24	21	22
Y 7	7 2 54	15 49 40	8♍ 2	7	19	15	10	27 R	24	21	22
8	7 6 51	16 50 49	19 51	9	20	15	10	27	24	21	22
9	7 10 47	17 51 58	1♎39	10	21	15	10	27	24	21	22
10	7 14 44	18 53 6	13 30	12	22	15	10	27	24	21	22
11	7 18 40	19 54 15	25 29	14	24	15	10	27	24	21	22
12	7 22 37	20 55 23	7♏42	15	25	15	10	27	25	21	22
13	7 26 33	21 56 32	20 13	17	26	15	10	27	25	21	22
14	7 30 30	22 57 41	3♐ 6	18	27	15	10	27	25	21	22
15	7 34 27	23 58 49	16 23	20	29	15	10	27	25	21	22
16	7 38 23	24 59 57	0♑ 5	22	0♓	15 R	10	27	25	21	22
17	7 42 20	26 1 5	14 9	23	1	15	10	27	25	22	22
18	7 46 16	27 2 13	28 32	25	2	15	9	27	25	22	22
19	7 50 13	28 3 20	13♒ 8	27	3	15	9	27	25	22	22
20	7 54 9	29 4 27	27 49	28	5	15	9	27	25	22	22
21	7 58 6	0♒ 5 31	12♓30	0♒	6	15	9	27	25	22	22
22	8 2 2	1 6 36	27 4	2	7	15	9	27	25	22	22
23	8 5 59	2 7 39	11♈27	3	8	15	9	27	25	22	22
24	8 9 56	3 8 42	25 36	5	10	15	9	27	25	22	22 R
25	8 13 52	4 9 44	9♉31	7	11	15	9	27	25	22	22
26	8 17 49	5 10 44	23 10	8	12	15	9	27	25	22	22
27	8 21 45	6 11 43	6♊34	10	13	15	9	27	25	22	22
28	8 25 42	7 12 42	19 43	12	14	14	9	27	25	22	22
29	8 29 38	8 13 39	2♋39	14	16	14	9	27	25	22	22
30	8 33 35	9 14 35	15 21	15	17	14	8	27	25	22	22
31	8 37 31	10 15 30	27 51	17	18	14	8	27	25	22	22

THE SUN ENTERS THE SIGN OF AQUARIUS ON JAN 20 AT 21:50.

DAY	TIME	☉	☽	☿	♀	♂	♃	♄	♅	♆	♇
	h m s	° ' "	° '	°	°	°	°	°	°	°	°
F 1	8 41 28	11♒16 24	10♌10	19♒	19♓	14♍R	8♍R	26♍R	25♏	22♐	22♎R
E 2	8 45 25	12 17 17	22 18	21	20	14	8	26	25	22	22
B 3	8 49 21	13 18 9	4♍18	22	22	13	8	26	25	22	22
R 4	8 53 18	14 19 0	16 11	24	23	13	8	26	25	22	22
U 5	8 57 14	15 19 50	28 0	26	24	13	8	26	25	22	22
A 6	9 1 11	16 20 39	9♎48	28	25	13	8	26	25	22	22
R 7	9 5 7	17 21 26	21 39	29	26	12	8	26	25	22	22
Y 8	9 9 4	18 22 13	3♏37	1♓	28	12	7	26	25	22	22
9	9 13 0	19 23 0	15 48	3	29	12	7	26	25	22	22
10	9 16 57	20 23 45	28 15	5	0♈	11	7	26	25	22	22
11	9 20 54	21 24 29	11♐ 3	6	1	11	7	26	25	22	22
12	9 24 50	22 25 12	24 15	8	2	11	7	26	25	22	22
13	9 28 47	23 25 54	7♑54	9	4	10	7	26	25	22	22
14	9 32 43	24 26 34	21 59	11	5	10	7	26	25	22	22
15	9 36 40	25 27 14	6♒29	13	6	10	7	26	25	22	22
16	9 40 36	26 27 52	21 18	14	7	9	6	26	25	22	22
17	9 44 33	27 28 29	6♓20	15	8	9	6	26	26	22	22
18	9 48 29	28 29 4	21 25	16	9	9	6	26	26	22	22
19	9 52 26	29 29 37	6♈24	18	11	8	6	25	26	22	22
20	9 56 23	0♓30 9	21 10	19	12	8	6	25	26	22	22
21	10 0 19	1 30 38	5♉37	19	13	7	6	25	26	22	22
22	10 4 16	2 31 7	19 42	20	14	7	6	25	26	22	22
23	10 8 12	3 31 33	3♊24	21	15	7	6	25	26	22	22
24	10 12 9	4 31 57	16 43	21	16	6	5	25	26	22	22
25	10 16 5	5 32 19	29 41	21	18	6	5	25	26	22	21
26	10 20 2	6 32 40	12♋22	22 R	19	5	5	25	26	22	21
27	10 23 58	7 32 58	24 47	21	20	5	5	25	26	22	21
28	10 27 55	8 33 14	7♌ 1	21	21	5	5	25	26	22	21
29	10 31 52	9 33 29	19 5	21	22	4	5	25	26 R	23	21

THE SUN ENTERS THE SIGN OF PISCES ON FEB 19 AT 12:02.

DAY	TIME	☉	☽	☿	♀	♂	♃	♄	♅	♆	♇
	h m s	° ' "	° '	°	°	°	°	°	°	°	°
M 1	10 35 48	10♓33 42	1♍ 3	20♓R	23♈	4♍R	5♍R	25♍R	26♏R	23♐	21♎R
A 2	10 39 45	11 33 53	12 55	20	25	4	4	25	26	23	21
R 3	10 43 41	12 34 2	24 45	19	26	3	4	25	26	23	21
C 4	10 47 38	13 34 9	6♎34	18	27	3	4	24	26	23	21
H 5	10 51 34	14 34 14	18 24	17	28	2	4	24	26	23	21
6	10 55 31	15 34 18	0♏18	16	29	2	4	24	26	23	21
7	10 59 27	16 34 20	12 20	15	0♉	2	4	24	26	23	21
8	11 3 24	17 34 21	24 31	14	1	1	4	24	26	23	21
9	11 7 20	18 34 20	6♐56	13	2	1	4	24	26	23	21
10	11 11 17	19 34 17	19 39	12	4	1	3	24	26	23	21
11	11 15 14	20 34 13	2♑44	11	5	0	3	24	26	23	21
12	11 19 10	21 34 7	16 13	10	6	0	3	24	26	23	21
13	11 23 7	22 34 0	0♒ 8	10	7	0	3	24	25	23	21
14	11 27 3	23 33 50	14 30	9	8	29♌	3	24	25	23	21
15	11 31 0	24 33 39	29 16	8	9	29	3	24	25	23	21
16	11 34 56	25 33 26	14♓19	8	10	29	3	23	25	23	21
17	11 38 53	26 33 11	29 33	8	11	29	3	23	25	23	21
18	11 42 49	27 32 54	14♈48	8	12	28	3	23	25	23	21
19	11 46 46	28 32 35	29 52	7 D	14	28	2	23	25	23	21
20	11 50 43	29 32 14	14♉37	7	15	28	2	23	25	23	21
21	11 54 39	0♈31 51	28 57	8	16	28	2	23	25	23	21
22	11 58 36	1 31 25	12♊49	8	17	27	2	23	25	23	21
23	12 2 32	2 30 57	26 13	8	18	27	2	23	25	23	21
24	12 6 29	3 30 27	9♋11	8	19	27	2	23	25	23 R	21
25	12 10 25	4 29 54	21 47	9	20	27	2	23	25	23	21
26	12 14 22	5 29 19	4♌ 5	9	21	27	2	23	25	23	21
27	12 18 18	6 28 42	16 9	10	22	27	2	23	25	23	21
28	12 22 15	7 28 2	28 5	10	23	26	2	23	25	23	21
29	12 26 12	8 27 21	9♍55	11	24	26	1	22	25	23	21
30	12 30 8	9 26 37	21 43	12	25	26	1	22	25	23	21
31	12 34 5	10 25 51	3♎32	13	26	26	1	22	25	23	21

THE SUN ENTERS THE SIGN OF ARIES ON MAR 20 AT 11:10.

SIDEREAL SUN MOON MERCURY VENUS MARS JUPITER SATURN URANUS NEPTUNE PLUTO

DAY	TIME	☉	☽	☿	♀	♂	♃	♄	♅	♆	♇
	h m s	° ' "	° '	°	°	°	°	°	°	°	°
A 1	12 38 1	11♈25 3	15♎23	14♓	27♉	26♌R	1♍R	22♍R	25♏R	23♐R	21♎R
P 2	12 41 58	12 24 12	27 19	15	28	26	1	22	25	23	21
R 3	12 45 54	13 23 20	9♏21	16	29	26	1	22	25	23	21
I 4	12 49 51	14 22 26	21 30	17	0♊	26	1	22	25	23	21
L 5	12 53 47	15 21 30	3♐49	18	1	26	1	22	25	23	21
6	12 57 44	16 20 33	16 20	19	2	26 D	1	22	25	23	21
7	13 1 40	17 19 33	29 4	20	3	26	1	22	25	23	20
8	13 5 37	18 18 32	12♑ 6	21	4	26	1	22	25	23	20
9	13 9 34	19 17 29	25 28	22	5	26	1	22	25	23	20
10	13 13 30	20 16 25	9♒12	24	6	26	1	22	25	23	20
11	13 17 27	21 15 18	23 19	25	7	26	1	22	25	23	20
12	13 21 23	22 14 10	7♓50	26	8	26	1	22	25	23	20
13	13 25 20	23 13 0	22 41	28	9	26	1	21	25	23	20
14	13 29 16	24 11 48	7♈46	29	10	26	0	21	25	23	20
15	13 33 13	25 10 34	22 56	0♈	11	26	0	21	25	23	20
16	13 37 9	26 9 18	8♉ 2	2	12	26	0	21	25	23	20
17	13 41 6	27 8 1	22 54	3	12	27	0	21	25	23	20
18	13 45 3	28 6 41	7♊22	5	13	27	0	21	25	23	20
19	13 48 59	29 5 19	21 23	6	14	27	0	21	25	23	20
20	13 52 56	0♉ 3 55	4♋54	8	15	27	0	21	25	22	20
21	13 56 52	1 2 29	17 57	10	16	27	0	21	24	22	20
22	14 0 49	2 1 1	0♌35	11	17	27	0	21	24	22	20
23	14 4 45	2 59 30	12 53	13	17	27	0	21	24	22	20
24	14 8 42	3 57 57	24 56	15	18	28	0	21	24	22	20
25	14 12 38	4 56 22	6♍49	16	19	28	0	21	24	22	20
26	14 16 35	5 54 45	18 37	18	20	28	0 D	21	24	22	20
27	14 20 32	6 53 6	0♎25	20	21	28	0	21	24	22	20
28	14 24 28	7 51 25	12 15	22	21	28	0	21	24	22	20
29	14 28 25	8 49 42	24 11	23	22	29	0	21	24	22	20
30	14 32 21	9 47 57	6♏15	25	23	29	0	21	24	22	20

THE SUN ENTERS THE SIGN OF TAURUS ON APR 19 AT 22:24.

DAY	TIME	☉	☽	☿	♀	♂	♃	♄	♅	♆	♇
	h m s	° ' "	° '	°	°	°	°	°	°	°	°
M 1	14 36 18	10♉46 11	18♏28	27♈	23♊	29♌	0♍	21♍R	24♏R	22♐R	20♎R
A 2	14 40 14	11 44 23	0♐51	29	24	29	0	21	24	22	20
Y 3	14 44 11	12 42 33	13 23	1♉	25	0♍	0	21	24	22	20
4	14 48 7	13 40 41	26 7	3	25	0	0	20	24	22	20
5	14 52 4	14 38 48	9♑ 2	5	26	0	0	20	24	22	20
6	14 56 1	15 36 54	22 11	7	27	1	0	20	24	22	20
7	14 59 57	16 34 58	5♒34	9	27	1	0	20	24	22	20
8	15 3 54	17 33 1	19 14	11	28	1	0	20	24	22	20
9	15 7 50	18 31 2	3♓11	13	28	1	0	20	24	22	20
10	15 11 47	19 29 2	17 27	15	29	2	1	20	24	22	20
11	15 15 43	20 27 1	1♈59	18	29	2	1	20	24	22	20
12	15 19 40	21 24 59	16 44	20	0♋	2	1	20	24	22	20
13	15 23 36	22 22 55	1♉36	22	0	3	1	20	24	22	20
14	15 27 33	23 20 49	16 27	24	0	3	1	20	24	22	20
15	15 31 30	24 18 43	1♊ 8	26	1	3	1	20	24	22	19
16	15 35 26	25 16 34	15 31	28	1	4	1	20	23	22	19
17	15 39 23	26 14 25	29 30	1♊	1	4	1	20	23	22	19
18	15 43 19	27 12 13	13♋ 2	3	2	4	1	20	23	22	19
19	15 47 16	28 10 0	26 8	5	2	5	1	20	23	22	19
20	15 51 12	29 7 46	8♌49	7	2	5	1	20	23	22	19
21	15 55 9	0♊ 5 30	21 9	9	2	6	1	20	23	22	19
22	15 59 5	1 3 12	3♍13	11	3	6	1	20 D	23	22	19
23	16 3 2	2 0 52	15 8	13	3	6	1	20	23	22	19
24	16 6 59	2 58 31	26 57	15	3 R	7	1	20	23	22	19
25	16 10 55	3 56 9	8♎47	17	3	7	1	20	23	22	19
26	16 14 52	4 53 45	20 41	19	3	8	2	20	23	22	19
27	16 18 48	5 51 20	2♏43	21	3	8	2	20	23	22	19
28	16 22 45	6 48 53	14 55	23	2	8	2	20	23	22	19
29	16 26 41	7 46 25	27 20	25	2	9	2	20	23	22	19
30	16 30 38	8 43 56	9♐58	27	2	9	2	20	23	22	19
31	16 34 34	9 41 26	22 49	28	2	10	2	20	23	22	19

THE SUN ENTERS THE SIGN OF GEMINI ON MAY 20 AT 21:43.

DAY	TIME	☉	☽	☿	♀	♂	♃	♄	♅	♆	♇
	h m s	° ' "	° '	°	°	°	°	°	°	°	°
J 1	16 38 31	10♊38 55	5♑52	0♋	2♋R	10♍	2♍	20♍	23♏R	22♐R	19♎R
U 2	16 42 28	11 36 23	19 6	2	1	11	2	20	23	22	19
N 3	16 46 24	12 33 51	2♒32	3	1	11	2	20	23	22	19
E 4	16 50 21	13 31 17	16 7	5	1	11	2	20	23	22	19
5	16 54 17	14 28 43	29 54	6	0	12	3	20	23	21	19
6	16 58 14	15 26 8	13♓51	8	0	12	3	20	23	21	19
7	17 2 10	16 23 33	27 59	9	29♊	13	3	20	23	21	19
8	17 6 7	17 20 56	12♈16	11	29	13	3	20	23	21	19
9	17 10 3	18 18 20	26 41	12	28	14	3	20	23	21	19
10	17 14 0	19 15 43	11♉ 9	13	28	14	3	20	23	21	19
11	17 17 57	20 13 5	25 35	14	27	15	3	21	22	21	19
12	17 21 53	21 10 27	9♊53	15	26	15	3	21	22	21	19
13	17 25 50	22 7 48	23 56	17	26	16	3	21	22	21	19
14	17 29 46	23 5 8	7♋42	18	25	16	4	21	22	21	19
15	17 33 43	24 2 28	21 5	19	25	17	4	21	22	21	19
16	17 37 39	24 59 47	4♌ 6	19	24	17	4	21	22	21	19
17	17 41 36	25 57 5	16 45	20	23	17	4	21	22	21	19
18	17 45 32	26 54 23	29 5	21	23	18	4	21	22	21	19
19	17 49 29	27 51 39	11♍11	22	22	18	4	21	22	21	19
20	17 53 26	28 48 55	23 7	22	21	19	4	21	22	21	19
21	17 57 22	29 46 10	4♎58	23	21	19	5	21	22	21	19
22	18 1 19	0♋43 25	16 50	24	20	20	5	21	22	21	19
23	18 5 15	1 40 38	28 46	24	20	20	5	21	22	21	19
24	18 9 12	2 37 52	10♏53	24	19	21	5	21	22	21	19
25	18 13 8	3 35 4	23 12	25	19	21	5	21	22	21	19
26	18 17 5	4 32 17	5♐47	25	18	22	5	21	22	21	19
27	18 21 1	5 29 28	18 38	25	18	23	5	21	22	21	19
28	18 24 58	6 26 40	1♑47	25 R	18	23	6	21	22	21	19 D
29	18 28 55	7 23 51	15 11	25	17	24	6	21	22	21	19
30	18 32 51	8 21 2	28 49	25	17	24	6	21	22	21	19

THE SUN ENTERS THE SIGN OF CANCER ON JUN 21 AT 05:48.

♈ ARIES ♉ TAURUS ♊ GEMINI ♋ CANCER ♌ LEO ♍ VIRGO ♎ LIBRA ♏ SCORPIO ♐ SAGITTARIUS ♑ CAPRICORN ♒ AQUARIUS ♓ PISCES

SIDEREAL SUN MOON MERCURY VENUS MARS JUPITER SATURN URANUS NEPTUNE PLUTO

DAY	TIME	☉	☽	☿	♀	♂	♃	♄	♅	♆	♇
	h m s	° ' "	° '	°	°	°	°	°	°	°	°
J 1	18 36 48	9♋18 14	12♒38	25♋R	17♊R	25♍	6♍	21♍	22♏R	21♐R	19♎
U 2	18 40 44	10 15 25	26 36	25	17	25	6	22	22	21	19
L 3	18 44 41	11 12 36	10♓40	24	16	26	6	22	22	21	19
Y 4	18 48 37	12 9 48	24 49	24	16	26	7	22	22	21	19
5	18 52 34	13 6 59	9♈ 0	24	16	27	7	22	22	21	19
6	18 56 30	14 4 11	23 12	23	16 D	27	7	22	22	21	19
7	19 0 27	15 1 24	7♉22	23	16	28	7	22	22	21	19
8	19 4 24	15 58 37	21 29	22	16	28	7	22	22	21	19
9	19 8 20	16 55 50	5♊29	21	16	29	7	22	22	21	19
10	19 12 17	17 53 4	19 20	21	16	0♎	8	22	22	21	19
11	19 16 13	18 50 18	2♋58	20	16	0	8	22	22	21	19
12	19 20 10	19 47 32	16 20	19	17	1	8	22	22	21	19
13	19 24 6	20 44 47	29 26	19	17	1	8	22	22	21	19
14	19 28 3	21 42 1	12♌14	18	17	2	8	22	22	20	19
15	19 31 59	22 39 16	24 45	18	17	2	8	23	22	20	19
16	19 35 56	23 36 31	7♍ 2	17	18	3	9	23	22	20	19
17	19 39 53	24 33 47	19 6	17	18	4	9	23	22	20	19
18	19 43 49	25 31 2	1♎ 2	16	18	4	9	23	22	20	19
19	19 47 46	26 28 18	12 53	16	19	5	9	23	22	20	19
20	19 51 42	27 25 34	24 45	16	19	5	9	23	22	20	19
21	19 55 39	28 22 50	6♏43	15	20	6	10	23	22	20	19
22	19 59 35	29 20 6	18 50	15 D	20	6	10	23	22	20	19
23	20 3 32	0♌17 23	1♐11	15	20	7	10	23	22	20	19
24	20 7 28	1 14 40	13 51	15	21	8	10	23	22	20	19
25	20 11 25	2 11 58	26 50	15	22	8	10	23	22	20	19
26	20 15 22	3 9 16	10♑10	16	22	9	10	23	22	20	19
27	20 19 18	4 6 35	23 52	16	23	9	11	24	22	20	19
28	20 23 15	5 3 54	7♒51	17	23	10	11	24	22	20	19
29	20 27 11	6 1 14	22 6	17	24	11	11	24	22	20	19
30	20 31 8	6 58 35	6♓30	18	25	11	11	24	21 D	20	19
31	20 35 4	7 55 57	21 0	19	25	12	11	24	21	20	19

THE SUN ENTERS THE SIGN OF LEO ON JUL 22 AT 16:43.

DAY	TIME	☉	☽	☿	♀	♂	♃	♄	♅	♆	♇
	h m s	° ' "	° '	°	°	°	°	°	°	°	°
A 1	20 39 1	8♌53 20	5♈29	19♋	26♊	12♎	12♍	24♍	22♏	20♐R	19♎
U 2	20 42 57	9 50 44	19 55	20	27	13	12	24	22	20	19
G 3	20 46 54	10 48 9	4♉12	22	27	14	12	24	22	20	19
U 4	20 50 51	11 45 36	18 18	23	28	14	12	24	22	20	19
S 5	20 54 47	12 43 3	2♊12	24	29	15	12	24	22	20	19
T 6	20 58 44	13 40 33	15 53	25	0♋	15	13	25	22	20	19
7	21 2 40	14 38 3	29 20	27	0	16	13	25	22	20	19
8	21 6 37	15 35 35	12♋32	28	1	17	13	25	22	20	19
9	21 10 33	16 33 7	25 31	0♌	2	17	13	25	22	20	19
10	21 14 30	17 30 41	8♌15	1	3	18	13	25	22	20	19
11	21 18 26	18 28 17	20 47	3	4	18	14	25	22	20	19
12	21 22 23	19 25 53	3♍ 6	5	4	19	14	25	22	20	20
13	21 26 20	20 23 30	15 15	7	5	20	14	25	22	20	20
14	21 30 16	21 21 9	27 15	9	6	20	14	25	22	20	20
15	21 34 13	22 18 48	9♎ 8	10	7	21	14	26	22	20	20
16	21 38 9	23 16 29	20 59	12	8	22	15	26	22	20	20
17	21 42 6	24 14 11	2♏50	14	9	22	15	26	22	20	20
18	21 46 2	25 11 53	14 47	16	10	23	15	26	22	20	20
19	21 49 59	26 9 37	26 52	18	11	23	15	26	22	20	20
20	21 53 55	27 7 22	9♐12	20	11	24	16	26	22	20	20
21	21 57 52	28 5 8	21 49	22	12	25	16	26	22	20	20
22	22 1 49	29 2 56	4♑48	24	13	25	16	26	22	20	20
23	22 5 45	0♍ 0 44	18 12	26	14	26	16	26	22	20	20
24	22 9 42	0 58 34	2♒ 0	28	15	27	16	27	22	20	20
25	22 13 38	1 56 25	16 13	0♍	16	27	17	27	22	20	20
26	22 17 35	2 54 17	0♓46	2	17	28	17	27	22	20	20
27	22 21 31	3 52 11	15 35	4	18	29	17	27	22	20	20
28	22 25 28	4 50 7	0♈30	6	19	29	17	27	22	20	20
29	22 29 24	5 48 4	15 25	8	20	0♏	17	27	22	20	20
30	22 33 21	6 46 3	0♉11	10	21	0	18	27	22	20	20
31	22 37 18	7 44 4	14 43	12	22	1	18	27	22	20 D	20

THE SUN ENTERS THE SIGN OF VIRGO ON AUG 22 AT 23:42.

DAY	TIME	☉	☽	☿	♀	♂	♃	♄	♅	♆	♇
	h m s	° ' "	° '	°	°	°	°	°	°	°	°
S 1	22 41 14	8♍42 7	28♉55	14♍	23♋	2♏	18♍	27♍	22♏	20♐	20♎
E 2	22 45 11	9 40 11	12♊47	16	24	2	18	28	22	20	20
P 3	22 49 7	10 38 18	26 18	18	25	3	19	28	22	20	20
T 4	22 53 4	11 36 27	9♋30	19	26	4	19	28	22	20	20
E 5	22 57 0	12 34 38	22 24	21	27	4	19	28	22	20	20
M 6	23 0 57	13 32 51	5♌ 2	23	28	5	19	28	22	20	20
B 7	23 4 53	14 31 5	17 28	25	29	6	19	28	22	20	20
E 8	23 8 50	15 29 22	29 44	26	0♌	6	20	28	22	20	20
R 9	23 12 47	16 27 40	11♍51	28	1	7	20	28	22	20	20
10	23 16 43	17 26 0	23 51	0♎	2	8	20	29	22	20	20
11	23 20 40	18 24 22	5♎45	2	3	8	20	29	22	20	20
12	23 24 36	19 22 45	17 37	3	4	9	20	29	22	20	20
13	23 28 33	20 21 11	29 27	5	6	10	21	29	22	20	20
14	23 32 29	21 19 38	11♏19	6	7	10	21	29	22	20	21
15	23 36 26	22 18 6	23 15	8	8	11	21	29	22	20	21
16	23 40 22	23 16 37	5♐19	10	9	12	21	29	22	20	21
17	23 44 19	24 15 9	17 35	11	10	12	22	29	22	20	21
18	23 48 15	25 13 43	0♑ 8	13	11	13	22	0♎	23	20	21
19	23 52 12	26 12 18	13 1	14	12	14	22	0	23	20	21
20	23 56 9	27 10 55	26 19	16	13	14	22	0	23	20	21
21	0 0 5	28 9 34	10♒ 3	17	14	15	22	0	23	20	21
22	0 4 2	29 8 14	24 16	19	15	16	23	0	23	20	21
23	0 7 58	0♎ 6 56	8♓55	20	16	17	23	0	23	20	21
24	0 11 55	1 5 40	23 55	22	18	17	23	0	23	20	21
25	0 15 51	2 4 26	9♈ 7	23	19	18	23	0	23	20	21
26	0 19 48	3 3 14	24 22	24	20	19	23	1	23	20	21
27	0 23 44	4 2 4	9♉29	26	21	19	24	1	23	20	21
28	0 27 41	5 0 57	24 19	27	22	20	24	1	23	20	21
29	0 31 38	5 59 51	8♊45	29	23	21	24	1	23	20	21
30	0 35 34	6 58 48	22 44	0♏	24	21	24	1	23	20	21

THE SUN ENTERS THE SIGN OF LIBRA ON SEP 22 AT 21:10.

SIDEREAL SUN MOON MERCURY VENUS MARS JUPITER SATURN URANUS NEPTUNE PLUTO

DAY	TIME	☉	☽	☿	♀	♂	♃	♄	♅	♆	♇
	h m s	° ' "	° '	°	°	°	°	°	°	°	°
O 1	0 39 31	7♎57 47	6♋16	1♏	25♌	22♏	25♍	1♎	23♏	20♐	21♎
C 2	0 43 27	8 56 49	19 23	3	27	23	25	1	23	20	21
T 3	0 47 24	9 55 53	2♌ 7	4	28	23	25	1	23	20	21
O 4	0 51 20	10 54 59	14 35	5	29	24	25	2	23	20	21
B 5	0 55 17	11 54 7	26 48	6	0♍	25	25	2	23	20	21
E 6	0 59 13	12 53 18	8♍52	7	1	26	26	2	23	20	21
R 7	1 3 10	13 52 30	20 49	9	2	26	26	2	23	20	21
8	1 7 7	14 51 45	2♎43	10	3	27	26	2	23	20	21
9	1 11 3	15 51 2	14 34	11	5	28	26	2	24	20	21
10	1 15 0	16 50 21	26 25	12	6	28	26	2	24	20	21
11	1 18 56	17 49 42	8♏17	13	7	29	27	2	24	20	22
12	1 22 53	18 49 5	20 12	14	8	0♐	27	3	24	20	22
13	1 26 49	19 48 30	2♐11	15	9	1	27	3	24	20	22
14	1 30 46	20 47 57	14 18	16	10	1	27	3	24	20	22
15	1 34 42	21 47 26	26 34	16	12	2	27	3	24	20	22
16	1 38 39	22 46 56	9♑ 5	17	13	3	28	3	24	20	22
17	1 42 36	23 46 28	21 52	18	14	3	28	3	24	20	22
18	1 46 32	24 46 2	5♒ 2	18	15	4	28	3	24	20	22
19	1 50 29	25 45 38	18 37	19	16	5	28	3	24	21	22
20	1 54 25	26 45 15	2♓39	19	18	6	29	3	24	21	22
21	1 58 22	27 44 54	17 9	20	19	6	29	4	24	21	22
22	2 2 18	28 44 35	2♈ 3	20	20	7	29	4	24	21	22
23	2 6 15	29 44 18	17 16	20 R	21	8	29	4	24	21	22
24	2 10 11	0♏44 2	2♉36	20	22	8	29	4	24	21	22
25	2 14 8	1 43 49	17 53	20	23	9	0♎	4	24	21	22
26	2 18 4	2 43 37	2♊55	19	25	10	0	4	24	21	22
27	2 22 1	3 43 28	17 34	19	26	11	0	4	25	21	22
28	2 25 58	4 43 21	1♋44	18	27	11	0	4	25	21	22
29	2 29 54	5 43 16	15 24	17	28	12	0	5	25	21	22
30	2 33 51	6 43 14	28 34	16	29	13	1	5	25	21	22
31	2 37 47	7 43 13	11♌19	15	1♎	14	1	5	25	21	22

THE SUN ENTERS THE SIGN OF SCORPIO ON OCT 23 AT 06:19.

DAY	TIME	☉	☽	☿	♀	♂	♃	♄	♅	♆	♇
	h m s	° ' "	° '	°	°	°	°	°	°	°	°
N 1	2 41 44	8♏43 15	23♌44	14♏R	2♎	14♐	1♎	5♎	25♏	21♐	22♎
O 2	2 45 40	9 43 19	5♍53	13	3	15	1	5	25	21	22
V 3	2 49 37	10 43 24	17 52	12	4	16	1	5	25	21	22
E 4	2 53 33	11 43 32	29 44	10	5	16	1	5	25	21	22
M 5	2 57 30	12 43 42	11♎34	9	7	17	2	5	25	21	23
B 6	3 1 27	13 43 54	23 24	8	8	18	2	5	25	21	23
E 7	3 5 23	14 44 8	5♏17	7	9	19	2	6	25	21	23
R 8	3 9 20	15 44 23	17 14	6	10	19	2	6	25	21	23
9	3 13 16	16 44 40	29 17	5	12	20	2	6	25	21	23
10	3 17 13	17 44 59	11♐25	5	13	21	3	6	25	21	23
11	3 21 9	18 45 20	23 41	4	14	22	3	6	25	21	23
12	3 25 6	19 45 42	6♑ 5	4 D	15	22	3	6	25	21	23
13	3 29 2	20 46 6	18 41	4	16	23	3	6	26	21	23
14	3 32 59	21 46 31	1♒31	4	18	24	3	6	26	21	23
15	3 36 56	22 46 57	14 38	5	19	25	3	6	26	21	23
16	3 40 52	23 47 25	28 5	5	20	25	4	6	26	21	23
17	3 44 49	24 47 54	11♓55	6	21	26	4	7	26	21	23
18	3 48 45	25 48 24	26 9	6	23	27	4	7	26	21	23
19	3 52 42	26 48 56	10♈46	7	24	28	4	7	26	21	23
20	3 56 38	27 49 28	25 42	8	25	28	4	7	26	21	23
21	4 0 35	28 50 2	10♉48	9	26	29	4	7	26	22	23
22	4 4 31	29 50 38	25 57	11	27	0♑	5	7	26	22	23
23	4 8 28	0♐51 15	10♊56	12	29	1	5	7	26	22	23
24	4 12 25	1 51 53	25 36	13	0♏	1	5	7	26	22	23
25	4 16 21	2 52 33	9♋51	14	1	2	5	7	26	22	23
26	4 20 18	3 53 15	23 38	16	2	3	5	7	26	22	23
27	4 24 14	4 53 58	6♌55	17	4	4	5	7	26	22	23
28	4 28 11	5 54 42	19 46	18	5	5	6	7	26	22	23
29	4 32 7	6 55 28	2♍15	20	6	5	6	8	27	22	23
30	4 36 4	7 56 16	14 26	21	7	6	6	8	27	22	23

THE SUN ENTERS THE SIGN OF SAGITTARIUS ON NOV 22 AT 03:43.

DAY	TIME	☉	☽	☿	♀	♂	♃	♄	♅	♆	♇
	h m s	° ' "	° '	°	°	°	°	°	°	°	°
D 1	4 40 0	8♐57 5	26♍25	23♏	9♏	7♑	6♎	8♎	27♏	22♐	23♎
E 2	4 43 57	9 57 55	8♎17	24	10	8	6	8	27	22	23
C 3	4 47 54	10 58 47	20 7	26	11	8	6	8	27	22	23
E 4	4 51 50	11 59 40	1♏58	27	12	9	6	8	27	22	24
M 5	4 55 47	13 0 34	13 55	29	14	10	7	8	27	22	24
B 6	4 59 43	14 1 30	25 58	0♐	15	11	7	8	27	22	24
E 7	5 3 40	15 2 26	8♐10	2	16	11	7	8	27	22	24
R 8	5 7 36	16 3 24	20 31	3	17	12	7	8	27	22	24
9	5 11 33	17 4 23	3♑ 2	5	18	13	7	8	27	22	24
10	5 15 29	18 5 22	15 43	6	20	14	7	8	27	22	24
11	5 19 26	19 6 22	28 35	8	21	14	7	8	27	22	24
12	5 23 23	20 7 23	11♒39	9	22	15	8	9	27	22	24
13	5 27 19	21 8 25	24 55	11	23	16	8	9	27	22	24
14	5 31 16	22 9 27	8♓26	13	25	17	8	9	27	22	24
15	5 35 12	23 10 29	22 13	14	26	18	8	9	27	22	24
16	5 39 9	24 11 32	6♈15	16	27	18	8	9	28	22	24
17	5 43 5	25 12 35	20 34	17	28	19	8	9	28	22	24
18	5 47 2	26 13 38	5♉ 6	19	0♐	20	8	9	28	23	24
19	5 50 58	27 14 42	19 46	20	1	21	8	9	28	23	24
20	5 54 55	28 15 46	4♊30	22	2	21	8	9	28	23	24
21	5 58 52	29 16 51	19 7	23	3	22	9	9	28	23	24
22	6 2 48	0♑17 56	3♋32	25	5	23	9	9	28	23	24
23	6 6 45	1 19 2	17 39	27	6	24	9	9	28	23	24
24	6 10 41	2 20 8	1♌22	28	7	25	9	9	28	23	24
25	6 14 38	3 21 14	14 41	0♑	8	25	9	9	28	23	24
26	6 18 34	4 22 21	27 36	1	10	26	9	9	28	23	24
27	6 22 31	5 23 29	10♍ 9	3	11	27	9	9	28	23	24
28	6 26 28	6 24 37	22 24	4	12	28	9	9	28	23	24
29	6 30 24	7 25 45	4♎27	6	13	28	9	9	28	23	24
30	6 34 21	8 26 54	16 21	8	15	29	9	9	28	23	24
31	6 38 17	9 28 4	28 13	9	16	0♒	9	9	28	23	24

THE SUN ENTERS THE SIGN OF CAPRICORN ON DEC 21 AT 16:57.

♈ ARIES ♉ TAURUS ♊ GEMINI ♋ CANCER ♌ LEO ♍ VIRGO ♎ LIBRA ♏ SCORPIO ♐ SAGITTARIUS ♑ CAPRICORN ♒ AQUARIUS ♓ PISCES

1981

SIDEREAL SUN MOON MERCURY VENUS MARS JUPITER SATURN URANUS NEPTUNE PLUTO

DAY	TIME	☉	☽	☿	♀	♂	♃	♄	♅	♆	♇
	h m s	° ' "	° '	°	°	°	°	°	°	°	°
J 1	6 42 14	10♑29 14	10♏ 6	11♑	17♐	1♒	10♎	10♎	28♏	23♐	24♎
A 2	6 46 10	11 30 24	22 5	12	18	2	10	10	28	23	24
N 3	6 50 7	12 31 34	4♐13	14	20	2	10	10	29	23	24
U 4	6 54 3	13 32 45	16 33	16	21	3	10	10	29	23	24
A 5	6 58 0	14 33 55	29 6	17	22	4	10	10	29	23	24
R 6	7 1 57	15 35 6	11♑54	19	23	5	10	10	29	23	24
Y 7	7 5 53	16 36 17	24 56	21	25	6	10	10	29	23	24
8	7 9 50	17 37 27	8♒11	22	26	6	10	10	29	23	24
9	7 13 46	18 38 37	21 39	24	27	7	10	10	29	23	24
10	7 17 43	19 39 47	5♓18	26	28	8	10	10	29	23	24
11	7 21 39	20 40 56	19 7	27	0♑	9	10	10	29	23	24
12	7 25 36	21 42 4	3♈ 4	29	1	9	10	10	29	23	24
13	7 29 32	22 43 12	17 9	1♒	2	10	10	10	29	23	24
14	7 33 29	23 44 19	1♉19	2	3	11	10	10	29	24	24
15	7 37 26	24 45 26	15 34	4	5	12	10	10	29	24	24
16	7 41 22	25 46 32	29 49	6	6	13	10	10	29	24	24
17	7 45 19	26 47 37	14♊ 3	7	7	13	10	10	29	24	24
18	7 49 15	27 48 41	28 10	9	8	14	10	10 R	29	24	24
19	7 53 12	28 49 45	12♋ 7	11	10	15	10	10	29	24	24
20	7 57 8	29 50 48	25 51	12	11	16	10	10	29	24	24
21	8 1 5	0♒51 50	9♌18	14	12	17	10	10	29	24	24
22	8 5 1	1 52 52	22 27	16	13	17	10	10	29	24	24
23	8 8 58	2 53 52	5♍17	17	15	18	10	10	29	24	24
24	8 12 55	3 54 53	17 50	19	16	19	10 R	10	29	24	24
25	8 16 51	4 55 52	0♎ 7	21	17	20	10	10	29	24	24
26	8 20 48	5 56 52	12 12	22	18	21	10	10	29	24	24 R
27	8 24 44	6 57 50	24 9	24	20	21	10	10	29	24	24
28	8 28 41	7 58 48	6♏ 1	25	21	22	10	10	0♐	24	24
29	8 32 37	8 59 45	17 55	27	22	23	10	10	0	24	24
30	8 36 34	10 0 42	29 54	28	23	24	10	10	0	24	24
31	8 40 30	11 1 38	12♐ 3	29	25	24	10	10	0	24	24

THE SUN ENTERS THE SIGN OF AQUARIUS ON JAN 20 AT 03:37.

DAY	TIME	☉	☽	☿	♀	♂	♃	♄	♅	♆	♇
	h m s	° ' "	° '	°	°	°	°	°	°	°	°
F 1	8 44 27	12♒ 2 33	24♐26	0♓	26♑	25♒	10♎R	10♎R	0♐	24♐	24♎R
E 2	8 48 24	13 3 27	7♑ 6	1	27	26	10	10	0	24	24
B 3	8 52 20	14 4 21	20 5	2	28	27	10	10	0	24	24
R 4	8 56 17	15 5 13	3♒24	3	0♒	28	10	10	0	24	24
U 5	9 0 13	16 6 4	17 2	4	1	28	10	10	0	24	24
A 6	9 4 10	17 6 54	0♓57	4	2	29	10	9	0	24	24
R 7	9 8 6	18 7 43	15 6	5	3	0♓	10	9	0	24	24
Y 8	9 12 3	19 8 31	29 23	5 R	5	1	10	9	0	24	24
9	9 15 59	20 9 16	13♈44	5	6	2	10	9	0	24	24
10	9 19 56	21 10 1	28 6	5	7	2	10	9	0	24	24
11	9 23 53	22 10 43	12♉23	4	8	3	10	9	0	24	24
12	9 27 49	23 11 25	26 34	4	10	4	10	9	0	24	24
13	9 31 46	24 12 4	10♊35	3	11	5	10	9	0	24	24
14	9 35 42	25 12 42	24 26	2	12	6	10	9	0	24	24
15	9 39 39	26 13 18	8♋ 6	1	13	6	10	9	0	24	24
16	9 43 35	27 13 52	21 35	0	15	7	10	9	0	24	24
17	9 47 32	28 14 25	4♌51	29♒	16	8	10	9	0	24	24
18	9 51 28	29 14 56	17 55	28	17	9	9	9	0	24	24
19	9 55 25	0♓15 25	0♍45	27	18	10	9	9	0	24	24
20	9 59 22	1 15 53	13 23	26	20	10	9	9	0	25	24
21	10 3 18	2 16 19	25 48	25	21	11	9	9	0	25	24
22	10 7 15	3 16 44	8♎ 1	24	22	12	9	9	0	25	24
23	10 11 11	4 17 8	20 5	23	23	13	9	9	0	25	24
24	10 15 8	5 17 29	2♏ 1	22	25	13	9	9	0	25	24
25	10 19 4	6 17 50	13 54	21	26	14	9	9	0	25	24
26	10 23 1	7 18 9	25 47	21	27	15	9	9	0	25	24
27	10 26 57	8 18 26	7♐44	20	28	16	9	8	0	25	24
28	10 30 54	9 18 42	19 51	20	0♓	17	9	8	0	25	24

THE SUN ENTERS THE SIGN OF PISCES ON FEB 18 AT 17:53.

DAY	TIME	☉	☽	☿	♀	♂	♃	♄	♅	♆	♇
	h m s	° ' "	° '	°	°	°	°	°	°	°	°
M 1	10 34 51	10♓18 57	2♑11	20♒R	1♓	17♓	9♎R	8♎R	0♐	25♐	24♎R
A 2	10 38 47	11 19 10	14 51	20 D	2	18	8	8	0	25	24
R 3	10 42 44	12 19 22	27 52	20	3	19	8	8	0	25	24
C 4	10 46 40	13 19 32	11♒18	20	5	20	8	8	0	25	24
H 5	10 50 37	14 19 40	25 10	20	6	21	8	8	0 R	25	24
6	10 54 33	15 19 46	9♓25	21	7	21	8	8	0	25	24
7	10 58 30	16 19 51	23 59	21	8	22	8	8	0	25	24
8	11 2 26	17 19 54	8♈45	21	10	23	8	8	0	25	24
9	11 6 23	18 19 54	23 35	22	11	24	8	8	0	25	24
10	11 10 19	19 19 53	8♉22	23	12	24	8	8	0	25	24
11	11 14 16	20 19 49	22 58	23	13	25	7	8	0	25	24
12	11 18 13	21 19 44	7♊18	24	15	26	7	8	0	25	24
13	11 22 9	22 19 36	21 20	25	16	27	7	8	0	25	24
14	11 26 6	23 19 26	5♋ 3	26	17	28	7	7	0	25	24
15	11 30 2	24 19 13	18 27	27	18	28	7	7	0	25	24
16	11 33 59	25 18 59	1♌36	28	20	29	7	7	0	25	24
17	11 37 55	26 18 42	14 30	29	21	0♈	7	7	0	25	24
18	11 41 52	27 18 23	27 12	0♓	22	1♈	7	7	0	25	24
19	11 45 48	28 18 2	9♍43	1	23	1	6	7	0	25	24
20	11 49 45	29 17 38	22 5	2	25	2	6	7	0	25	24
21	11 53 42	0♈17 13	4♎18	3	26	3	6	7	0	25	24
22	11 57 38	1 16 45	16 24	4	27	4	6	7	0	25	24
23	12 1 35	2 16 16	28 23	6	28	5	6	7	0	25	24
24	12 5 31	3 15 45	10♏18	7	0♈	5	6	7	0	25	24
25	12 9 28	4 15 12	22 10	8	1♈	6	6	7	0	25	23
26	12 13 24	5 14 37	4♐ 2	10	2	7	6	7	0	25	23
27	12 17 21	6 14 0	15 58	11	3	8	5	6	0	25 R	23
28	12 21 17	7 13 21	28 2	12	5	8	5	6	0	25	23
29	12 25 14	8 12 41	10♑19	14	6	9	5	6	0	25	23
30	12 29 11	9 11 59	22 53	15	7	10	5	6	0	25	23
31	12 33 7	10 11 15	5♒50	17	8	11	5	6	0	25	23

THE SUN ENTERS THE SIGN OF ARIES ON MAR 20 AT 17:04.

SIDEREAL SUN MOON MERCURY VENUS MARS JUPITER SATURN URANUS NEPTUNE PLUTO

DAY	TIME	☉	☽	☿	♀	♂	♃	♄	♅	♆	♇
	h m s	° ' "	° '	°	°	°	°	°	°	°	°
A 1	12 37 4	11♈10 30	19♒14	18♓	10♈	12♈	5♎R	6♎R	0♐R	25♐R	23♎R
P 2	12 41 0	12 9 42	3♓ 6	20	11	12	5	6	0	25	23
R 3	12 44 57	13 8 53	17 27	21	12	13	4	6	0	25	23
I 4	12 48 53	14 8 2	2♈13	23	13	14	4	6	0	25	23
L 5	12 52 50	15 7 9	17 17	24	15	15	4	6	0	25	23
6	12 56 46	16 6 13	2♉29	26	16	15	4	6	0	25	23
7	13 0 43	17 5 16	17 39	28	17	16	4	6	0	25	23
8	13 4 39	18 4 16	2♊36	29	18	17	4	6	0	25	23
9	13 8 36	19 3 15	17 13	1♈	19	18	4	5	0	25	23
10	13 12 33	20 2 11	1♋25	3	21	18	4	5	0	25	23
11	13 16 29	21 1 4	15 12	5	22	19	4	5	0	25	23
12	13 20 26	21 59 56	28 34	6	23	20	3	5	0	25	23
13	13 24 22	22 58 45	11♌34	8	24	21	3	5	29♏	25	23
14	13 28 19	23 57 32	24 17	10	26	21	3	5	29	25	23
15	13 32 15	24 56 16	6♍45	12	27	22	3	5	29	25	23
16	13 36 12	25 54 58	19 2	14	28	23	3	5	29	25	23
17	13 40 8	26 53 39	1♎11	16	29	24	3	5	29	25	23
18	13 44 5	27 52 17	13 14	17	1♉	24	3	5	29	25	23
19	13 48 2	28 50 53	25 12	19	2	25	3	5	29	25	23
20	13 51 58	29 49 27	7♏ 7	21	3	26	3	5	29	25	23
21	13 55 55	0♉47 59	18 59	23	4	27	2	5	29	25	23
22	13 59 51	1 46 30	0♐52	25	6	28	2	5	29	25	23
23	14 3 48	2 44 59	12 45	27	7	28	2	4	29	25	23
24	14 7 44	3 43 26	24 43	0♉	8	29	2	4	29	25	23
25	14 11 41	4 41 51	6♑48	2	9	0♉	2	4	29	25	23
26	14 15 37	5 40 15	19 4	4	10	1	2	4	29	25	23
27	14 19 34	6 38 37	1♒36	6	12	1	2	4	29	25	23
28	14 23 31	7 36 58	14 29	8	13	2	2	4	29	25	23
29	14 27 27	8 35 17	27 46	10	14	3	2	4	29	25	23
30	14 31 24	9 33 34	11♓32	12	15	4	2	4	29	25	22

THE SUN ENTERS THE SIGN OF TAURUS ON APR 20 AT 04:19.

DAY	TIME	☉	☽	☿	♀	♂	♃	♄	♅	♆	♇
	h m s	° ' "	° '	°	°	°	°	°	°	°	°
M 1	14 35 20	10♉31 50	25♓46	14♉	17♉	4♉	2♎R	4♎R	29♏R	25♐R	22♎R
A 2	14 39 17	11 30 5	10♈29	17	18	5	1	4	29	25	22
Y 3	14 43 13	12 28 18	25 33	19	19	6	1	4	29	25	22
4	14 47 10	13 26 29	10♉51	21	20	6	1	4	29	24	22
5	14 51 6	14 24 39	26 10	23	22	7	1	4	29	24	22
6	14 55 3	15 22 47	11♊20	25	23	8	1	4	29	24	22
7	14 59 0	16 20 53	26 10	27	24	9	1	4	29	24	22
8	15 2 56	17 18 57	10♋35	29	25	9	1	4	29	24	22
9	15 6 53	18 17 0	24 31	1♊	27	10	1	4	29	24	22
10	15 10 49	19 15 0	7♌59	3	28	11	1	4	28	24	22
11	15 14 46	20 12 59	21 1	5	29	12	1	4	28	24	22
12	15 18 42	21 10 55	3♍42	7	0♊	12	1	3	28	24	22
13	15 22 39	22 8 50	16 6	9	1	13	1	3	28	24	22
14	15 26 35	23 6 43	28 17	11	3	14	1	3	28	24	22
15	15 30 32	24 4 35	10♎19	12	4	15	1	3	28	24	22
16	15 34 29	25 2 24	22 15	14	5	15	1	3	28	24	22
17	15 38 25	26 0 12	4♏ 8	16	6	16	1	3	28	24	22
18	15 42 22	26 57 59	16 1	17	8	17	1	3	28	24	22
19	15 46 18	27 55 44	27 54	19	9	18	1	3	28	24	22
20	15 50 15	28 53 28	9♐49	20	10	18	1	3	28	24	22
21	15 54 11	29 51 10	21 48	21	11	19	1	3	28	24	22
22	15 58 8	0♊48 52	3♑52	23	13	20	0	3	28	24	22
23	16 2 4	1 46 32	16 3	24	14	20	0	3	28	24	22
24	16 6 1	2 44 11	28 26	25	15	21	0	3	28	24	22
25	16 9 58	3 41 49	11♒ 2	26	16	22	0	3	28	24	22
26	16 13 54	4 39 26	23 55	27	17	23	0	3	28	24	22
27	16 17 51	5 37 2	7♓10	28	19	23	0 D	3	28	24	22
28	16 21 47	6 34 37	20 49	29	20	24	0	3	28	24	22
29	16 25 44	7 32 11	4♈54	0♋	21	25	0	3	28	24	22
30	16 29 40	8 29 45	19 24	1	22	26	0	3	28	24	22
31	16 33 37	9 27 17	4♉15	2	24	26	0	3	28	24	22

THE SUN ENTERS THE SIGN OF GEMINI ON MAY 21 AT 03:40.

DAY	TIME	☉	☽	☿	♀	♂	♃	♄	♅	♆	♇
	h m s	° ' "	° '	°	°	°	°	°	°	°	°
J 1	16 37 33	10♊24 49	19♉21	2♋	25♊	27♉	0♎	3♎R	28♏R	24♐R	22♎R
U 2	16 41 30	11 22 20	4♊33	3	26	28	0	3	28	24	22
N 3	16 45 27	12 19 50	19 39	4	27	28	1	3	27	24	22
E 4	16 49 23	13 17 19	4♋31	4	28	29	1	3	27	24	22
5	16 53 20	14 14 47	19 0	4	0♋	0♊	1	3 D	27	24	22
6	16 57 16	15 12 13	3♌ 3	5	1	1	1	3	27	24	22
7	17 1 13	16 9 39	16 38	5	2	1	1	3	27	24	22
8	17 5 9	17 7 3	29 46	5	3	2	1	3	27	24	22
9	17 9 6	18 4 27	12♍31	5 R	5	3	1	3	27	24	22
10	17 13 2	19 1 49	24 56	5	6	3	1	3	27	24	22
11	17 16 59	19 59 10	7♎ 7	5	7	4	1	3	27	24	22
12	17 20 56	20 56 30	19 7	5	8	5	1	3	27	24	22
13	17 24 52	21 53 49	1♏ 2	5	9	6	1	3	27	24	22
14	17 28 49	22 51 7	12 54	4	11	6	1	3	27	24	22
15	17 32 45	23 48 25	24 46	4	12	7	1	3	27	23	22
16	17 36 42	24 45 42	6♐42	4	13	8	1	3	27	23	22
17	17 40 38	25 42 58	18 43	3	14	8	1	3	27	23	22
18	17 44 35	26 40 13	0♑50	3	16	9	1	3	27	23	22
19	17 48 31	27 37 28	13 5	2	17	10	1	3	27	23	22
20	17 52 28	28 34 43	25 30	2	18	10	1	3	27	23	22
21	17 56 25	29 31 57	8♒ 6	1	19	11	1	3	27	23	22
22	18 0 21	0♋29 11	20 55	1	20	12	1	3	27	23	22
23	18 4 18	1 26 25	3♓58	0	22	13	1	3	27	23	22
24	18 8 14	2 23 39	17 19	29♊	23	13	2	3	27	23	22
25	18 12 11	3 20 52	0♈58	29	24	14	2	3	27	23	22
26	18 16 7	4 18 6	14 56	28	25	15	2	3	27	23	22
27	18 20 4	5 15 19	29 14	28	27	15	2	3	27	23	22
28	18 24 0	6 12 33	13♉47	27	28	16	2	3	27	23	22
29	18 27 57	7 9 47	28 32	27	29	17	2	3	27	23	22
30	18 31 54	8 7 0	13♊23	27	0♌	17	2	4	27	23	22

THE SUN ENTERS THE SIGN OF CANCER ON JUN 21 AT 11:46.

♈ ARIES ♉ TAURUS ♊ GEMINI ♋ CANCER ♌ LEO ♍ VIRGO ♎ LIBRA ♏ SCORPIO ♐ SAGITTARIUS ♑ CAPRICORN ♒ AQUARIUS ♓ PISCES

1981

SIDEREAL · SUN · MOON · MERCURY · VENUS · MARS · JUPITER · SATURN · URANUS · NEPTUNE · PLUTO

DAY	TIME	☉	☽	☿	♀	♂	♃	♄	♅	♆	♇
	h m s	° ' "	° '	°	°	°	°	°	°	°	°
J 1	18 35 50	9♋ 4 14	28♊11	27♊R	1♌	18♊	2♎	4♎	27♏R	23♐R	22♎D
U 2	18 39 47	10 1 28	12♋49	26	3	19	2	4	27	23	22
L 3	18 43 43	10 58 42	27 10	26 D	4	20	2	4	26	23	22
Y 4	18 47 40	11 55 55	11♌10	26	5	20	2	4	26	23	22
5	18 51 36	12 53 8	24 46	26	6	21	3	4	26	23	22
6	18 55 33	13 50 21	7♍57	27	7	22	3	4	26	23	22
7	18 59 30	14 47 34	20 46	27	9	22	3	4	26	23	22
8	19 3 26	15 44 47	3♎14	27	10	23	3	4	26	23	22
9	19 7 23	16 41 59	15 28	28	11	24	3	4	26	23	22
10	19 11 19	17 39 12	27 29	28	12	24	3	4	26	23	22
11	19 15 16	18 36 24	9♏24	29	14	25	3	4	26	23	22
12	19 19 12	19 33 36	21 17	29	15	26	3	4	26	23	22
13	19 23 9	20 30 49	3♐11	0♋	16	26	3	4	26	23	22
14	19 27 5	21 28 1	15 10	1	17	27	4	4	26	23	22
15	19 31 2	22 25 14	27 17	2	18	28	4	4	26	23	22
16	19 34 59	23 22 27	9♑34	3	20	28	4	4	26	23	22
17	19 38 55	24 19 40	22 4	4	21	29	4	4	26	23	22
18	19 42 52	25 16 53	4♒46	5	22	0♋	4	4	26	23	22
19	19 46 48	26 14 7	17 42	6	23	0	4	5	26	23	22
20	19 50 45	27 11 22	0♓52	8	24	1	4	5	26	23	22
21	19 54 41	28 8 37	14 15	9	26	2	4	5	26	23	22
22	19 58 38	29 5 53	27 52	11	27	2	5	5	26	23	22
23	20 2 34	0♌ 3 9	11♈41	12	28	3	5	5	26	23	22
24	20 6 31	1 0 27	25 42	14	29	4	5	5	26	23	22
25	20 10 28	1 57 45	9♉52	15	0♍	4	5	5	26	23	22
26	20 14 24	2 55 5	24 11	17	2	5	5	5	26	22	22
27	20 18 21	3 52 25	8♊35	19	3	6	5	5	26	22	22
28	20 22 17	4 49 47	23 0	21	4	6	5	5	26	22	22
29	20 26 14	5 47 9	7♋21	23	5	7	6	5	26	22	22
30	20 30 10	6 44 33	21 35	24	7	8	6	5	26	22	22
31	20 34 7	7 41 57	5♌37	26	8	8	6	5	26	22	22

THE SUN ENTERS THE SIGN OF LEO ON JUL 22 AT 22:41.

DAY	TIME	☉	☽	☿	♀	♂	♃	♄	♅	♆	♇
	h m s	° ' "	° '	°	°	°	°	°	°	°	°
A 1	20 38 3	8♌39 22	19♌22	28♋	9♍	9♋	6♎	6♎	26♏R	22♐R	22♎
U 2	20 42 0	9 36 48	2♍49	0♌	10	10	6	6	26	22	22
G 3	20 45 57	10 34 14	15 56	3	11	10	6	6	26	22	22
U 4	20 49 53	11 31 42	28 44	5	13	11	7	6	26 D	22	22
S 5	20 53 50	12 29 10	11♎13	7	14	12	7	6	26	22	22
T 6	20 57 46	13 26 38	23 28	9	15	12	7	6	26	22	22
7	21 1 43	14 24 8	5♏31	11	16	13	7	6	26	22	22
8	21 5 39	15 21 38	17 26	13	17	14	7	6	26	22	22
9	21 9 36	16 19 9	29 19	15	19	14	7	6	26	22	22
10	21 13 32	17 16 41	11♐13	17	20	15	8	6	26	22	22
11	21 17 29	18 14 14	23 15	19	21	16	8	6	26	22	22
12	21 21 26	19 11 48	5♑26	21	22	16	8	7	26	22	22
13	21 25 22	20 9 23	17 52	23	23	17	8	7	26	22	22
14	21 29 19	21 6 59	0♒34	25	25	18	8	7	26	22	22
15	21 33 15	22 4 36	13 34	27	26	18	8	7	26	22	22
16	21 37 12	23 2 14	26 52	29	27	19	9	7	26	22	22
17	21 41 8	23 59 54	10♓27	1♍	28	20	9	7	26	22	22
18	21 45 5	24 57 35	24 17	3	29	20	9	7	26	22	22
19	21 49 1	25 55 17	8♈18	5	1♎	21	9	7	26	22	22
20	21 52 58	26 53 1	22 27	7	2	22	9	7	26	22	22
21	21 56 54	27 50 46	6♉41	8	3	22	10	7	26	22	22
22	22 0 51	28 48 34	20 55	10	4	23	10	8	26	22	22
23	22 4 48	29 46 23	5♊ 8	12	5	24	10	8	26	22	22
24	22 8 44	0♍44 13	19 17	14	6	24	10	8	26	22	22
25	22 12 41	1 42 6	3♋20	15	8	25	10	8	26	22	22
26	22 16 37	2 40 0	17 16	17	9	25	11	8	26	22	22
27	22 20 34	3 37 57	1♌ 2	19	10	26	11	8	26	22	22
28	22 24 30	4 35 54	14 39	21	11	27	11	8	26	22	22
29	22 28 27	5 33 54	28 3	22	12	27	11	8	26	22	22
30	22 32 23	6 31 55	11♍13	24	14	28	11	8	26	22	22
31	22 36 20	7 29 57	24 8	25	15	29	11	9	26	22	23

THE SUN ENTERS THE SIGN OF VIRGO ON AUG 23 AT 05:40.

DAY	TIME	☉	☽	☿	♀	♂	♃	♄	♅	♆	♇
	h m s	° ' "	° '	°	°	°	°	°	°	°	°
S 1	22 40 17	8♍28 1	6♎48	27♍	16♎	29♋	12♎	9♎	26♏	22♐R	23♎
E 2	22 44 13	9 26 7	19 13	29	17	0♌	12	9	26	22	23
P 3	22 48 10	10 24 14	1♏25	0♎	18	1	12	9	26	22 D	23
T 4	22 52 6	11 22 22	13 27	2	19	1	12	9	26	22	23
E 5	22 56 3	12 20 32	25 21	3	21	2	12	9	26	22	23
M 6	22 59 59	13 18 44	7♐12	5	22	2	13	9	27	22	23
B 7	23 3 56	14 16 57	19 6	6	23	3	13	9	27	22	23
E 8	23 7 52	15 15 12	1♑ 6	7	24	4	13	9	27	22	23
R 9	23 11 49	16 13 28	13 18	9	25	4	13	10	27	22	23
10	23 15 46	17 11 46	25 46	10	27	5	13	10	27	22	23
11	23 19 42	18 10 5	8♒35	12	28	6	14	10	27	22	23
12	23 23 39	19 8 26	21 47	13	29	6	14	10	27	22	23
13	23 27 35	20 6 48	5♓23	14	0♏	7	14	10	27	22	23
14	23 31 32	21 5 13	19 21	16	1	8	14	10	27	22	23
15	23 35 28	22 3 39	3♈38	17	2	8	15	10	27	22	23
16	23 39 25	23 2 7	18 8	18	4	9	15	10	27	22	23
17	23 43 21	24 0 37	2♉44	19	5	9	15	10	27	22	23
18	23 47 18	24 59 9	17 19	21	6	10	15	11	27	22	23
19	23 51 15	25 57 44	1♊48	22	7	11	15	11	27	22	23
20	23 55 11	26 56 20	16 6	23	8	11	16	11	27	22	23
21	23 59 8	27 54 59	0♋11	24	9	12	16	11	27	22	23
22	0 3 4	28 53 40	14 2	25	11	12	16	11	27	22	23
23	0 7 1	29 52 24	27 40	26	12	13	16	11	27	22	23
24	0 10 57	0♎51 10	11♌ 4	27	13	14	16	11	27	22	23
25	0 14 54	1 49 57	24 17	28	14	14	17	11	27	22	23
26	0 18 50	2 48 47	7♍18	29	15	15	17	12	27	22	23
27	0 22 47	3 47 40	20 8	0♏	16	16	17	12	27	22	23
28	0 26 44	4 46 34	2♎47	0	17	16	17	12	27	22	23
29	0 30 40	5 45 30	15 15	1	19	17	17	12	27	22	24
30	0 34 37	6 44 28	27 31	2	20	17	18	12	27	22	24

THE SUN ENTERS THE SIGN OF LIBRA ON SEP 23 AT 03:07.

SIDEREAL · SUN · MOON · MERCURY · VENUS · MARS · JUPITER · SATURN · URANUS · NEPTUNE · PLUTO

DAY	TIME	☉	☽	☿	♀	♂	♃	♄	♅	♆	♇
	h m s	° ' "	° '	°	°	°	°	°	°	°	°
O 1	0 38 33	7♎43 28	9♏38	2♏	21♏	18♌	18♎	12♎	27♏	22♐	24♎
C 2	0 42 30	8 42 30	21 35	3	22	19	18	12	27	22	24
T 3	0 46 26	9 41 34	3♐27	3	23	19	18	12	28	22	24
O 4	0 50 23	10 40 40	15 16	4	24	20	19	13	28	22	24
B 5	0 54 19	11 39 47	27 7	4	25	20	19	13	28	22	24
E 6	0 58 16	12 38 57	9♑ 4	4 R	27	21	19	13	28	22	24
R 7	1 2 12	13 38 8	21 13	4	28	22	19	13	28	22	24
8	1 6 9	14 37 21	3♒39	4	29	22	19	13	28	22	24
9	1 10 6	15 36 35	16 27	3	0♐	23	20	13	28	22	24
10	1 14 2	16 35 52	29 41	3	1	23	20	13	28	22	24
11	1 17 59	17 35 10	13♓24	2	2	24	20	13	28	22	24
12	1 21 55	18 34 30	27 35	2	3	25	20	14	28	22	24
13	1 25 52	19 33 52	12♈10	1	4	25	20	14	28	23	24
14	1 29 48	20 33 16	27 3	0	6	26	21	14	28	23	24
15	1 33 45	21 32 42	12♉ 4	29♎	7	26	21	14	28	23	24
16	1 37 41	22 32 10	27 5	28	8	27	21	14	28	23	24
17	1 41 38	23 31 41	11♊55	27	9	28	21	14	28	23	24
18	1 45 35	24 31 14	26 29	25	10	28	22	14	28	23	24
19	1 49 31	25 30 49	10♋42	24	11	29	22	14	28	23	24
20	1 53 28	26 30 26	24 34	23	12	29	22	15	28	23	24
21	1 57 24	27 30 6	8♌ 5	22	13	0♍	22	15	28	23	24
22	2 1 21	28 29 48	21 18	21	14	1	22	15	28	23	24
23	2 5 17	29 29 32	4♍14	20	16	1	23	15	29	23	24
24	2 9 14	0♏29 19	16 58	19	17	2	23	15	29	23	25
25	2 13 10	1 29 7	29 30	19	18	2	23	15	29	23	25
26	2 17 7	2 28 58	11♎53	18	19	3	23	15	29	23	25
27	2 21 4	3 28 50	24 7	18 D	20	3	24	15	29	23	25
28	2 25 0	4 28 45	6♏13	18	21	4	24	15	29	23	25
29	2 28 57	5 28 42	18 12	18	22	5	24	16	29	23	25
30	2 32 53	6 28 40	0♐ 5	19	23	5	24	16	29	23	25
31	2 36 50	7 28 41	11 55	19	24	6	24	16	29	23	25

THE SUN ENTERS THE SIGN OF SCORPIO ON OCT 23 AT 12:14.

DAY	TIME	☉	☽	☿	♀	♂	♃	♄	♅	♆	♇
	h m s	° ' "	° '	°	°	°	°	°	°	°	°
N 1	2 40 46	8♏28 43	23♐43	20♎	25♐	6♍	25♎	16♎	29♏	23♐	25♎
O 2	2 44 43	9 28 46	5♑32	21	26	7	25	16	29	23	25
V 3	2 48 39	10 28 52	17 28	22	27	7	25	16	29	23	25
E 4	2 52 36	11 28 59	29 34	23	28	8	25	16	29	23	25
M 5	2 56 33	12 29 8	11♒56	24	29	9	25	16	29	23	25
B 6	3 0 29	13 29 18	24 39	25	0♑	9	26	17	29	23	25
E 7	3 4 26	14 29 29	7♓47	27	2	10	26	17	29	23	25
R 8	3 8 22	15 29 42	21 25	28	3	10	26	17	29	23	25
9	3 12 19	16 29 57	5♈34	29	4	11	26	17	0♐	23	25
10	3 16 15	17 30 13	20 11	1♏	5	11	27	17	0	23	25
11	3 20 12	18 30 31	5♉11	2	6	12	27	17	0	23	25
12	3 24 8	19 30 50	20 26	4	7	12	27	17	0	23	25
13	3 28 5	20 31 11	5♊44	5	8	13	27	17	0	23	25
14	3 32 2	21 31 34	20 54	7	9	14	27	17	0	23	25
15	3 35 58	22 31 59	5♋46	8	10	14	28	18	0	23	25
16	3 39 55	23 32 25	20 16	10	11	15	28	18	0	23	25
17	3 43 51	24 32 53	4♌19	11	12	15	28	18	0	23	25
18	3 47 48	25 33 24	17 56	13	12	16	28	18	0	24	25
19	3 51 44	26 33 55	1♍ 9	14	13	16	28	18	0	24	26
20	3 55 41	27 34 29	14 1	16	14	17	29	18	0	24	26
21	3 59 37	28 35 5	26 36	18	15	17	29	18	0	24	26
22	4 3 34	29 35 42	8♎58	19	16	18	29	18	0	24	26
23	4 7 31	0♐36 21	21 8	21	17	18	29	18	0	24	26
24	4 11 27	1 37 1	3♏11	22	18	19	29	18	0	24	26
25	4 15 24	2 37 43	15 9	24	19	19	0♏	19	1	24	26
26	4 19 20	3 38 26	27 2	25	20	20	0	19	1	24	26
27	4 23 17	4 39 11	8♐52	27	21	21	0	19	1	24	26
28	4 27 13	5 39 57	20 41	29	22	21	0	19	1	24	26
29	4 31 10	6 40 45	2♑31	0♐	22	22	0	19	1	24	26
30	4 35 6	7 41 33	14 24	2	23	22	1	19	1	24	26

THE SUN ENTERS THE SIGN OF SAGITTARIUS ON NOV 22 AT 09:37.

DAY	TIME	☉	☽	☿	♀	♂	♃	♄	♅	♆	♇
	h m s	° ' "	° '	°	°	°	°	°	°	°	°
D 1	4 39 3	8♐42 23	26♑24	3♐	24♑	23♍	1♏	19♎	1♐	24♐	26♎
E 2	4 43 0	9 43 13	8♒32	5	25	23	1	19	1	24	26
C 3	4 46 56	10 44 4	20 55	7	26	24	1	19	1	24	26
E 4	4 50 53	11 44 57	3♓35	8	26	24	1	19	1	24	26
M 5	4 54 49	12 45 50	16 37	10	27	25	2	20	1	24	26
B 6	4 58 46	13 46 43	0♈ 6	11	28	25	2	20	1	24	26
E 7	5 2 42	14 47 38	14 3	13	29	26	2	20	1	24	26
R 8	5 6 39	15 48 33	28 27	14	29	26	2	20	1	24	26
9	5 10 35	16 49 29	13♉16	16	0♒	27	2	20	1	24	26
10	5 14 32	17 50 25	28 24	17	1	27	2	20	1	24	26
11	5 18 29	18 51 23	13♊41	19	1	28	3	20	2	24	26
12	5 22 25	19 52 21	28 56	21	2	28	3	20	2	24	26
13	5 26 22	20 53 21	13♋59	22	3	29	3	20	2	24	26
14	5 30 18	21 54 21	28 42	24	3	29	3	20	2	24	26
15	5 34 15	22 55 22	12♌59	25	4	0♎	3	20	2	25	26
16	5 38 11	23 56 24	26 49	27	4	0	4	20	2	25	26
17	5 42 8	24 57 27	10♍11	29	5	0	4	20	2	25	26
18	5 46 4	25 58 30	23 9	0♑	5	1	4	21	2	25	26
19	5 50 1	26 59 35	5♎45	2	6	1	4	21	2	25	26
20	5 53 58	28 0 41	18 4	3	6	2	4	21	2	25	26
21	5 57 54	29 1 47	0♏10	5	7	2	4	21	2	25	26
22	6 1 51	0♑ 2 54	12 7	6	7	3	5	21	2	25	26
23	6 5 47	1 4 2	23 59	8	7	3	5	21	2	25	27
24	6 9 44	2 5 10	5♐49	10	8	4	5	21	2	25	27
25	6 13 40	3 6 19	17 38	11	8	4	5	21	2	25	27
26	6 17 37	4 7 28	29 30	13	8	5	5	21	2	25	27
27	6 21 33	5 8 38	11♑26	14	8	5	5	21	2	25	27
28	6 25 30	6 9 48	23 29	16	9	5	5	21	2	25	27
29	6 29 27	7 10 58	5♒39	18	9	6	6	21	3	25	27
30	6 33 23	8 12 8	17 59	19	9	6	6	21	3	25	27
31	6 37 20	9 13 18	0♓31	21	9 R	7	6	21	3	25	27

THE SUN ENTERS THE SIGN OF CAPRICORN ON DEC 21 AT 22:52.

♈ ARIES ♉ TAURUS ♊ GEMINI ♋ CANCER ♌ LEO ♍ VIRGO ♎ LIBRA ♏ SCORPIO ♐ SAGITTARIUS ♑ CAPRICORN ♒ AQUARIUS ♓ PISCES

SIDEREAL SUN MOON MERCURY VENUS MARS JUPITER SATURN URANUS NEPTUNE PLUTO

DAY	TIME	☉	☽	☿	♀	♂	♃	♄	♅	♆	♇
	h m s	° ' "	° '	°	°	°	°	°	°	°	°
J 1	6 41 16	10♑14 28	13♓18	23♑	9♒R	7♎	6♏	21♎	3♐	25♐	27♎
A 2	6 45 13	11 15 37	26 22	24	9	7	6	21	3	25	27
N 3	6 49 9	12 16 47	9♈46	26	9	8	6	22	3	25	27
U 4	6 53 6	13 17 56	23 32	27	9	8	7	22	3	25	27
A 5	6 57 2	14 19 5	7♉40	29	9	9	7	22	3	25	27
R 6	7 0 59	15 20 13	22 9	0♒	8	9	7	22	3	25	27
Y 7	7 4 56	16 21 21	6♊54	2	8	9	7	22	3	25	27
8	7 8 52	17 22 29	21 51	4	8	10	7	22	3	25	27
9	7 12 49	18 23 37	6♋51	5	8	10	7	22	3	25	27
10	7 16 45	19 24 44	21 47	7	7	11	7	22	3	25	27
11	7 20 42	20 25 51	6♌29	8	7	11	7	22	3	26	27
12	7 24 38	21 26 58	20 51	9	6	11	8	22	3	26	27
13	7 28 35	22 28 4	4♍49	11	6	12	8	22	3	26	27
14	7 32 32	23 29 11	18 21	12	5	12	8	22	3	26	27
15	7 36 28	24 30 17	1♎27	13	5	12	8	22	3	26	27
16	7 40 25	25 31 23	14 10	14	4	13	8	22	3	26	27
17	7 44 21	26 32 28	26 33	15	4	13	8	22	3	26	27
18	7 48 18	27 33 34	8♏40	16	3	13	8	22	3	26	27
19	7 52 14	28 34 39	20 37	17	3	14	8	22	4	26	27
20	7 56 11	29 35 44	2♐27	18	2	14	8	22	4	26	27
21	8 0 7	0♒36 49	14 16	18	1	14	9	22	4	26	27
22	8 4 4	1 37 53	26 6	18	1	14	9	22	4	26	27
23	8 8 1	2 38 56	8♑ 2	19 R	0	15	9	22	4	26	27
24	8 11 57	3 39 59	20 6	19	29♑	15	9	22	4	26	27
25	8 15 54	4 41 2	2♒21	18	29	15	9	22	4	26	27
26	8 19 50	5 42 3	14 47	18	28	16	9	22	4	26	27
27	8 23 47	6 43 3	27 26	17	28	16	9	22	4	26	27
28	8 27 43	7 44 3	10♓17	17	27	16	9	22	4	26	27
29	8 31 40	8 45 1	23 23	16	27	16	9	22	4	26	27 R
30	8 35 36	9 45 59	6♈42	15	26	17	9	22	4	26	27
31	8 39 33	10 46 55	20 14	13	26	17	9	22 R	4	26	27

THE SUN ENTERS THE SIGN OF AQUARIUS ON JAN 20 AT 09:32.

DAY	TIME	☉	☽	☿	♀	♂	♃	♄	♅	♆	♇
	h m s	° ' "	° '	°	°	°	°	°	°	°	°
F 1	8 43 30	11♒47 49	4♉ 0	12♒R	25♑R	17♎	9♏	22♎R	4♐	26♐	27♎R
E 2	8 47 26	12 48 43	17 59	11	25	17	10	22	4	26	27
B 3	8 51 23	13 49 35	2♊10	10	25	17	10	22	4	26	27
R 4	8 55 19	14 50 26	16 32	9	24	18	10	22	4	26	27
U 5	8 59 16	15 51 15	1♋ 1	7	24	18	10	22	4	26	27
A 6	9 3 12	16 52 3	15 34	6	24	18	10	22	4	26	27
R 7	9 7 9	17 52 49	0♌ 6	6	24	18	10	22	4	26	27
Y 8	9 11 5	18 53 35	14 30	5	24	18	10	22	4	26	27
9	9 15 2	19 54 18	28 41	4	23	18	10	22	4	26	27
10	9 18 59	20 55 1	12♍34	4	23 D	18	10	22	4	26	27
11	9 22 55	21 55 42	26 6	3	23	19	10	22	4	26	27
12	9 26 52	22 56 23	9♎15	3	23	19	10	22	4	26	27
13	9 30 48	23 57 2	22 2	3 D	23	19	10	22	4	26	27
14	9 34 45	24 57 39	4♏29	3	24	19	10	22	4	27	27
15	9 38 41	25 58 16	16 40	3	24	19	10	22	4	27	27
16	9 42 38	26 58 52	28 38	3	24	19	10	22	4	27	27
17	9 46 34	27 59 26	10♐29	4	24	19	10	22	4	27	27
18	9 50 31	28 59 59	22 18	4	24	19	10	22	4	27	27
19	9 54 28	0♓ 0 31	4♑ 9	5	25	19	10	22	4	27	27
20	9 58 24	1 1 2	16 9	5	25	19 R	10	22	4	27	27
21	10 2 21	2 1 31	28 20	6	25	19	10	22	4	27	27
22	10 6 17	3 1 59	10♒45	7	26	19	10	22	5	27	27
23	10 10 14	4 2 25	23 27	7	26	19	10	22	5	27	27
24	10 14 10	5 2 49	6♓27	8	27	19	10 R	22	5	27	27
25	10 18 7	6 3 12	19 43	9	27	19	10	22	5	27	27
26	10 22 3	7 3 33	3♈14	10	27	19	10	22	5	27	27
27	10 26 0	8 3 52	16 58	11	28	19	10	22	5	27	27
28	10 29 56	9 4 10	0♉51	12	29	19	10	22	5	27	27

THE SUN ENTERS THE SIGN OF PISCES ON FEB 18 AT 23:48.

DAY	TIME	☉	☽	☿	♀	♂	♃	♄	♅	♆	♇
	h m s	° ' "	° '	°	°	°	°	°	°	°	°
M 1	10 33 53	10♓ 4 25	14♉51	13♒	29♑	19♎R	10♏R	22♎R	5♐	27♐	27♎R
A 2	10 37 50	11 4 38	28 55	14	0♒	19	10	21	5	27	27
R 3	10 41 46	12 4 50	13♊ 2	16	0	19	10	21	5	27	27
C 4	10 45 43	13 4 59	27 10	17	1	18	10	21	5	27	27
H 5	10 49 39	14 5 6	11♋17	18	2	18	10	21	5	27	27
6	10 53 36	15 5 11	25 24	19	2	18	10	21	5	27	27
7	10 57 32	16 5 14	9♌27	21	3	18	10	21	5	27	27
8	11 1 29	17 5 15	23 24	22	4	18	10	21	5	27	27
9	11 5 25	18 5 13	7♍11	23	4	18	10	21	5 R	27	27
10	11 9 22	19 5 10	20 46	25	5	17	10	21	5	27	26
11	11 13 19	20 5 5	4♎ 5	26	6	17	10	21	5	27	26
12	11 17 15	21 4 58	17 7	27	7	17	10	21	5	27	26
13	11 21 12	22 4 49	29 51	29	7	17	10	21	5	27	26
14	11 25 8	23 4 39	12♏17	0♓	8	16	10	21	5	27	26
15	11 29 5	24 4 26	24 27	2	9	16	10	21	5	27	26
16	11 33 1	25 4 12	6♐26	3	10	16	10	21	5	27	26
17	11 36 58	26 3 57	18 17	5	11	15	10	21	5	27	26
18	11 40 54	27 3 39	0♑ 6	6	12	15	10	21	5	27	26
19	11 44 51	28 3 20	11 58	8	12	15	10	20	5	27	26
20	11 48 48	29 2 59	23 58	9	13	15	9	20	5	27	26
21	11 52 44	0♈ 2 37	6♒12	11	14	14	9	20	5	27	26
22	11 56 41	1 2 12	18 44	13	15	14	9	20	5	27	26
23	12 0 37	2 1 46	1♓37	14	16	14	9	20	5	27	26
24	12 4 34	3 1 18	14 52	16	17	13	9	20	5	27	26
25	12 8 30	4 0 48	28 29	18	18	13	9	20	5	27	26
26	12 12 27	5 0 16	12♈26	19	19	12	9	20	5	27	26
27	12 16 23	5 59 41	26 37	21	20	12	9	20	4	27	26
28	12 20 20	6 59 5	10♉58	23	21	12	9	20	4	27	26
29	12 24 17	7 58 26	25 22	25	22	11	9	20	4	27 R	26
30	12 28 13	8 57 46	9♊43	27	23	11	9	20	4	27	26
31	12 32 10	9 57 3	24 0	28	24	11	9	20	4	27	26

THE SUN ENTERS THE SIGN OF ARIES ON MAR 20 AT 22:57.

SIDEREAL SUN MOON MERCURY VENUS MARS JUPITER SATURN URANUS NEPTUNE PLUTO

DAY	TIME	☉	☽	☿	♀	♂	♃	♄	♅	♆	♇
	h m s	° ' "	° '	°	°	°	°	°	°	°	°
A 1	12 36 6	10♈56 17	8♋ 8	0♈	25♒	10♎R	8♏R	20♎R	4♐R	27♐R	26♎R
P 2	12 40 3	11 55 30	22 8	2	25	10	8	19	4	27	26
R 3	12 43 59	12 54 40	5♌58	4	26	9	8	19	4	27	26
I 4	12 47 56	13 53 47	19 39	6	27	9	8	19	4	27	26
L 5	12 51 52	14 52 53	3♍11	8	28	9	8	19	4	27	26
6	12 55 49	15 51 55	16 34	10	29	8	8	19	4	27	26
7	12 59 45	16 50 56	29 45	12	0♓	8	8	19	4	27	26
8	13 3 42	17 49 55	12♎44	14	2	7	8	19	4	27	26
9	13 7 39	18 48 52	25 30	16	3	7	8	19	4	27	26
10	13 11 35	19 47 46	8♏ 2	18	4	7	7	19	4	27	26
11	13 15 32	20 46 39	20 21	20	5	6	7	19	4	27	26
12	13 19 28	21 45 30	2♐27	22	6	6	7	19	4	27	26
13	13 23 25	22 44 19	14 23	24	7	6	7	19	4	27	26
14	13 27 21	23 43 6	26 13	26	8	5	7	19	4	27	26
15	13 31 18	24 41 52	8♑ 1	28	9	5	7	18	4	27	26
16	13 35 14	25 40 36	19 52	0♉	10	5	7	18	4	27	26
17	13 39 11	26 39 18	1♒51	3	11	4	7	18	4	27	26
18	13 43 8	27 37 59	14 5	5	12	4	6	18	4	27	25
19	13 47 4	28 36 38	26 37	7	13	4	6	18	4	27	25
20	13 51 1	29 35 15	9♓33	9	14	3	6	18	4	27	25
21	13 54 57	0♉33 50	22 55	11	15	3	6	18	4	27	25
22	13 58 54	1 32 24	6♈44	13	16	3	6	18	4	27	25
23	14 2 50	2 30 55	20 57	15	17	3	6	18	4	27	25
24	14 6 47	3 29 25	5♉29	17	18	2	6	18	4	27	25
25	14 10 43	4 27 54	20 14	19	20	2	6	18	4	27	25
26	14 14 40	5 26 20	5♊ 3	21	21	2	5	18	4	27	25
27	14 18 37	6 24 44	19 48	22	22	2	5	18	4	27	25
28	14 22 33	7 23 7	4♋24	24	23	2	5	18	4	27	25
29	14 26 30	8 21 27	18 44	26	24	1	5	17	4	27	25
30	14 30 26	9 19 45	2♌49	28	25	1	5	17	4	27	25

THE SUN ENTERS THE SIGN OF TAURUS ON APR 20 AT 10:08.

DAY	TIME	☉	☽	☿	♀	♂	♃	♄	♅	♆	♇
	h m s	° ' "	° '	°	°	°	°	°	°	°	°
M 1	14 34 23	10♉18 1	16♌36	29♉	26♓	1♎R	5♏R	17♎R	4♐R	27♐R	25♎R
A 2	14 38 19	11 16 15	0♍ 8	1♊	27	1	5	17	4	27	25
Y 3	14 42 16	12 14 27	13 25	2	28	1	5	17	3	27	25
4	14 46 12	13 12 36	26 28	3	29	1	4	17	3	27	25
5	14 50 9	14 10 44	9♎19	5	1♈	1	4	17	3	27	25
6	14 54 6	15 8 50	21 58	6	2	1	4	17	3	27	25
7	14 58 2	16 6 55	4♏26	7	3	1	4	17	3	27	25
8	15 1 59	17 4 57	16 44	8	4	0	4	17	3	27	25
9	15 5 55	18 2 58	28 51	9	5	0	4	17	3	27	25
10	15 9 52	19 0 58	10♐50	10	6	0	4	17	3	27	25
11	15 13 48	19 58 55	22 42	11	7	0 D	4	17	3	27	25
12	15 17 45	20 56 52	4♑30	12	8	0	3	17	3	27	25
13	15 21 41	21 54 47	16 17	13	10	0	3	17	3	27	25
14	15 25 38	22 52 41	28 8	13	11	0	3	17	3	27	25
15	15 29 35	23 50 34	10♒ 7	14	12	0	3	16	3	27	25
16	15 33 31	24 48 25	22 20	14	13	0	3	16	3	26	25
17	15 37 28	25 46 15	4♓51	15	14	1	3	16	3	26	25
18	15 41 24	26 44 4	17 45	15	15	1	3	16	3	26	25
19	15 45 21	27 41 52	1♈ 5	15	16	1	3	16	3	26	25
20	15 49 17	28 39 38	14 54	15	17	1	3	16	3	26	25
21	15 53 14	29 37 24	29 10	15 R	19	1	2	16	3	26	25
22	15 57 10	0♊35 8	13♉50	15	20	1	2	16	3	26	25
23	16 1 7	1 32 51	28 48	15	21	1	2	16	3	26	25
24	16 5 4	2 30 33	13♊53	15	22	1	2	16	3	26	25
25	16 9 0	3 28 13	28 58	15	23	1	2	16	3	26	25
26	16 12 57	4 25 53	13♋53	14	24	2	2	16	3	26	25
27	16 16 53	5 23 31	28 31	14	26	2	2	16	3	26	25
28	16 20 50	6 21 7	12♌49	13	27	2	2	16	2	26	24
29	16 24 46	7 18 42	26 44	13	28	2	2	16	2	26	24
30	16 28 43	8 16 15	10♍17	13	29	2	2	16	2	26	24
31	16 32 39	9 13 47	23 29	12	0♉	3	2	16	2	26	24

THE SUN ENTERS THE SIGN OF GEMINI ON MAY 21 AT 09:24.

DAY	TIME	☉	☽	☿	♀	♂	♃	♄	♅	♆	♇
	h m s	° ' "	° '	°	°	°	°	°	°	°	°
J 1	16 36 36	10♊11 17	6♎23	11♊R	1♉	3♎	1♏R	16♎R	2♐R	26♐R	24♎R
U 2	16 40 33	11 8 47	19 1	11	2	3	1	16	2	26	24
N 3	16 44 29	12 6 15	1♏26	10	4	3	1	16	2	26	24
E 4	16 48 26	13 3 41	13 40	10	5	3	1	16	2	26	24
5	16 52 22	14 1 7	25 44	9	6	4	1	16	2	26	24
6	16 56 19	14 58 32	7♐42	9	7	4	1	16	2	26	24
7	17 0 15	15 55 56	19 34	8	8	4	1	16	2	26	24
8	17 4 12	16 53 19	1♑22	8	9	5	1	16	2	26	24
9	17 8 8	17 50 41	13 10	7	11	5	1	16	2	26	24
10	17 12 5	18 48 3	24 59	7	12	5	1	16	2	26	24
11	17 16 2	19 45 24	6♒53	7	13	5	1	16	2	26	24
12	17 19 58	20 42 44	18 55	7	14	6	1	16	2	26	24
13	17 23 55	21 40 4	1♓10	7 D	15	6	1	16	2	26	24
14	17 27 51	22 37 23	13 41	7	16	6	1	16	2	26	24
15	17 31 48	23 34 42	26 32	7	18	7	1	16	2	26	24
16	17 35 44	24 32 0	9♈48	7	19	7	1	16	2	26	24
17	17 39 41	25 29 19	23 30	7	20	7	1	15	2	26	24
18	17 43 37	26 26 36	7♉39	7	21	8	1	15 D	2	26	24
19	17 47 34	27 23 54	22 13	8	22	8	1	15	2	26	24
20	17 51 31	28 21 11	7♊ 8	8	23	9	1	15	2	26	24
21	17 55 27	29 18 29	22 16	8	25	9	1	16	2	26	24
22	17 59 24	0♋15 45	7♋27	9	26	9	0	16	1	26	24
23	18 3 20	1 13 1	22 33	10	27	10	0	16	1	26	24
24	18 7 17	2 10 17	7♌25	10	28	10	0	16	1	25	24
25	18 11 13	3 7 32	21 57	11	29	10	0	16	1	25	24
26	18 15 10	4 4 47	6♍ 3	12	1♊	11	0	16	1	25	24
27	18 19 7	5 2 1	19 44	13	2	11	0 D	16	1	25	24
28	18 23 3	5 59 14	3♎ 0	14	3	12	0	16	1	25	24
29	18 27 0	6 56 27	15 53	15	4	12	0	16	1	25	24
30	18 30 56	7 53 39	28 26	16	5	13	0	16	1	25	24

THE SUN ENTERS THE SIGN OF CANCER ON JUN 21 AT 17:24.

♈ ARIES ♉ TAURUS ♊ GEMINI ♋ CANCER ♌ LEO ♍ VIRGO ♎ LIBRA ♏ SCORPIO ♐ SAGITTARIUS ♑ CAPRICORN ♒ AQUARIUS ♓ PISCES

SIDEREAL SUN MOON MERCURY VENUS MARS JUPITER SATURN URANUS NEPTUNE PLUTO

DAY	TIME	☉	☽	☿	♀	♂	♃	♄	♅	♆	♇
	h m s	° ' "	° '	°	°	°	°	°	°	°	°
J 1	18 34 53	8♋50 51	10♏43	17♊	7♊	13♎	0♏	16♎	1♐R	25♐R	24♎R
U 2	18 38 49	9 48 3	22 48	19	8	13	0	16	1	25	24
L 3	18 42 46	10 45 14	4♐45	20	9	14	0	16	1	25	24
Y 4	18 46 42	11 42 25	16 36	21	10	14	0	16	1	25	24 D
5	18 50 39	12 39 36	28 24	23	11	15	1	16	1	25	24
6	18 54 36	13 36 47	10♑12	24	12	15	1	16	1	25	24
7	18 58 32	14 33 58	22 2	26	14	16	1	16	1	25	24
8	19 2 29	15 31 9	3♒57	27	15	16	1	16	1	25	24
9	19 6 25	16 28 20	15 59	29	16	17	1	16	1	25	24
10	19 10 22	17 25 32	28 9	1♋	17	17	1	16	1	25	24
11	19 14 18	18 22 44	10♓32	3	18	18	1	16	1	25	24
12	19 18 15	19 19 56	23 9	5	20	18	1	16	1	25	24
13	19 22 11	20 17 8	6♈ 2	6	21	19	1	16	1	25	24
14	19 26 8	21 14 21	19 16	8	22	19	1	16	1	25	24
15	19 30 5	22 11 35	2♉51	10	23	20	1	16	1	25	24
16	19 34 1	23 8 50	16 50	12	24	20	1	16	1	25	24
17	19 37 58	24 6 5	1♊10	14	26	21	1	16	1	25	24
18	19 41 54	25 3 20	15 50	16	27	21	1	16	1	25	24
19	19 45 51	26 0 37	0♋46	19	28	22	1	16	1	25	24
20	19 49 47	26 57 54	15 49	21	29	22	1	16	1	25	24
21	19 53 44	27 55 11	0♌52	23	0♋	23	1	16	1	25	24
22	19 57 40	28 52 29	15 46	25	2	23	1	16	1	25	24
23	20 1 37	29 49 48	0♍24	27	3	24	1	16	1	25	24
24	20 5 34	0♌47 6	14 38	29	4	24	1	17	1	25	24
25	20 9 30	1 44 26	28 26	1♌	5	25	2	17	1	25	24
26	20 13 27	2 41 45	11♎48	3	6	25	2	17	1	25	24
27	20 17 23	3 39 5	24 44	6	8	26	2	17	1	25	24
28	20 21 20	4 36 25	7♏18	8	9	26	2	17	1	25	24
29	20 25 16	5 33 46	19 33	10	10	27	2	17	1	25	24
30	20 29 13	6 31 7	1♐35	12	11	27	2	17	1	25	24
31	20 33 9	7 28 29	13 28	14	12	28	2	17	1	25	24

THE SUN ENTERS THE SIGN OF LEO ON JUL 23 AT 04:17.

DAY	TIME	☉	☽	☿	♀	♂	♃	♄	♅	♆	♇
	h m s	° ' "	° '	°	°	°	°	°	°	°	°
A 1	20 37 6	8♌25 52	25♐17	16♌	14♋	29♎	2♏	17♎	1♐R	25♐R	24♎
U 2	20 41 3	9 23 15	7♑ 4	18	15	29	2	17	1	25	24
G 3	20 44 59	10 20 39	18 55	20	16	0♏	2	17	1	25	24
U 4	20 48 56	11 18 4	0♒51	22	17	0	2	17	1	25	24
S 5	20 52 52	12 15 29	12 55	23	18	1	3	17	1	25	24
T 6	20 56 49	13 12 56	25 9	25	20	1	3	17	1	25	24
7	21 0 45	14 10 24	7♓35	27	21	2	3	17	1	25	24
8	21 4 42	15 7 53	20 12	29	22	3	3	18	1	24	24
9	21 8 38	16 5 22	3♈ 2	1♍	23	3	3	18	1 D	24	24
10	21 12 35	17 2 53	16 7	2	25	4	3	18	1	24	24
11	21 16 32	18 0 26	29 26	4	26	4	3	18	1	24	24
12	21 20 28	18 58 0	13♉ 1	6	27	5	3	18	1	24	25
13	21 24 25	19 55 35	26 52	8	28	6	3	18	1	24	25
14	21 28 21	20 53 12	10♊59	9	29	6	4	18	1	24	25
15	21 32 18	21 50 51	25 21	11	1♌	7	4	18	1	24	25
16	21 36 14	22 48 31	9♋56	13	2	7	4	18	1	24	25
17	21 40 11	23 46 13	24 39	14	3	8	4	18	1	24	25
18	21 44 7	24 43 56	9♌26	16	4	9	4	18	1	24	25
19	21 48 4	25 41 40	24 7	17	6	9	4	19	1	24	25
20	21 52 1	26 39 26	8♍38	19	7	10	4	19	1	24	25
21	21 55 57	27 37 13	22 49	20	8	10	4	19	1	24	25
22	21 59 54	28 35 1	6♎38	22	9	11	5	19	1	24	25
23	22 3 50	29 32 50	20 2	23	10	12	5	19	1	24	25
24	22 7 47	0♍30 41	3♏ 1	24	12	12	5	19	1	24	25
25	22 11 43	1 28 33	15 36	26	13	13	5	19	1	24	25
26	22 15 40	2 26 26	27 53	27	14	14	5	19	1	24	25
27	22 19 36	3 24 20	9♐55	29	15	14	5	19	1	24	25
28	22 23 33	4 22 16	21 47	0♎	17	15	6	19	1	24	25
29	22 27 30	5 20 13	3♑35	1	18	15	6	19	1	24	25
30	22 31 26	6 18 11	15 24	2	19	16	6	19	1	24	25
31	22 35 23	7 16 11	27 18	4	20	17	6	20	1	24	25

THE SUN ENTERS THE SIGN OF VIRGO ON AUG 23 AT 11:17.

DAY	TIME	☉	☽	☿	♀	♂	♃	♄	♅	♆	♇
	h m s	° ' "	° '	°	°	°	°	°	°	°	°
S 1	22 39 19	8♍14 12	9♒21	5♎	21♌	17♏	6♏	20♎	1♐	24♐R	25♎
E 2	22 43 16	9 12 15	21 36	6	23	18	6	20	1	24	25
P 3	22 47 12	10 10 19	4♓ 5	7	24	19	6	20	1	24	25
T 4	22 51 9	11 8 25	16 49	8	25	19	7	20	1	24	25
E 5	22 55 5	12 6 32	29 47	9	26	20	7	20	1	24 D	25
M 6	22 59 2	13 4 42	12♈58	10	28	21	7	20	1	24	25
B 7	23 2 58	14 2 53	26 22	11	29	21	7	20	1	24	25
E 8	23 6 55	15 1 6	9♉56	12	0♍	22	7	20	1	24	25
R 9	23 10 52	15 59 21	23 40	13	1	23	7	21	1	24	25
10	23 14 48	16 57 39	7♊33	14	3	23	8	21	1	24	25
11	23 18 45	17 55 58	21 34	14	4	24	8	21	1	24	25
12	23 22 41	18 54 20	5♋43	15	5	25	8	21	1	24	25
13	23 26 38	19 52 44	19 59	16	6	25	8	21	1	24	25
14	23 30 34	20 51 9	4♌19	16	8	26	8	21	1	24	25
15	23 34 31	21 49 37	18 41	17	9	27	9	21	1	24	26
16	23 38 27	22 48 7	3♍ 0	17	10	27	9	21	1	24	26
17	23 42 24	23 46 39	17 10	17	11	28	9	21	1	24	26
18	23 46 21	24 45 13	1♎ 7	17	13	29	9	21	1	24	26
19	23 50 17	25 43 49	14 46	18 R	14	29	9	22	1	24	26
20	23 54 14	26 42 26	28 4	18	15	0♐	9	22	1	24	26
21	23 58 10	27 41 5	10♏59	17	16	1	10	22	1	24	26
22	0 2 7	28 39 46	23 34	17	17	1	10	22	1	24	26
23	0 6 3	29 38 29	5♐50	17	19	2	10	22	1	24	26
24	0 10 0	0♎37 14	17 52	16	20	3	10	22	1	24	26
25	0 13 56	1 36 0	29 44	16	21	3	10	22	1	24	26
26	0 17 53	2 34 48	11♑32	15	22	4	11	22	2	24	26
27	0 21 50	3 33 38	23 22	14	24	5	11	23	2	24	26
28	0 25 46	4 32 30	5♒18	13	25	5	11	23	2	24	26
29	0 29 43	5 31 23	17 27	12	26	6	11	23	2	24	26
30	0 33 39	6 30 18	29 50	11	27	7	11	23	2	24	26

THE SUN ENTERS THE SIGN OF LIBRA ON SEP 23 AT 08:48.

SIDEREAL SUN MOON MERCURY VENUS MARS JUPITER SATURN URANUS NEPTUNE PLUTO

DAY	TIME	☉	☽	☿	♀	♂	♃	♄	♅	♆	♇
	h m s	° ' "	° '	°	°	°	°	°	°	°	°
O 1	0 37 36	7♎29 15	12♓31	10♎R	29♍	8♐	12♏	23♎	2♐	24♐	26♎
C 2	0 41 32	8 28 14	25 32	9	0♎	8	12	23	2	24	26
T 3	0 45 29	9 27 15	8♈51	8	1	9	12	23	2	24	26
O 4	0 49 25	10 26 18	22 27	7	2	10	12	23	2	24	26
B 5	0 53 22	11 25 23	6♉16	6	4	10	12	23	2	25	26
E 6	0 57 19	12 24 30	20 14	5	5	11	13	24	2	25	26
R 7	1 1 15	13 23 39	4♊19	4	6	12	13	24	2	25	26
8	1 5 12	14 22 51	18 25	3	7	13	13	24	2	25	26
9	1 9 8	15 22 5	2♋33	3	9	13	13	24	2	25	26
10	1 13 5	16 21 21	16 39	3	10	14	13	24	2	25	26
11	1 17 1	17 20 40	0♌44	2 D	11	15	14	24	2	25	26
12	1 20 58	18 20 1	14 46	2	12	15	14	24	2	25	27
13	1 24 54	19 19 25	28 45	2	14	16	14	24	2	25	27
14	1 28 51	20 18 50	12♍38	3	15	17	14	25	2	25	27
15	1 32 48	21 18 18	26 22	4	16	18	14	25	2	25	27
16	1 36 44	22 17 48	9♎56	4	17	18	15	25	2	25	27
17	1 40 41	23 17 20	23 15	5	19	19	15	25	2	25	27
18	1 44 37	24 16 54	6♏18	6	20	20	15	25	3	25	27
19	1 48 34	25 16 30	19 3	7	21	20	15	25	3	25	27
20	1 52 30	26 16 8	1♐31	8	22	21	16	25	3	25	27
21	1 56 27	27 15 48	13 43	10	24	22	16	25	3	25	27
22	2 0 23	28 15 30	25 43	11	25	23	16	26	3	25	27
23	2 4 20	29 15 14	7♑34	12	26	23	16	26	3	25	27
24	2 8 16	0♏14 59	19 22	14	27	24	16	26	3	25	27
25	2 12 13	1 14 46	1♒11	15	29	25	17	26	3	25	27
26	2 16 10	2 14 35	13 7	17	0♏	26	17	26	3	25	27
27	2 20 6	3 14 25	25 16	19	1	26	17	26	3	25	27
28	2 24 3	4 14 17	7♓42	20	2	27	17	26	3	25	27
29	2 27 59	5 14 11	20 28	22	4	28	17	26	3	25	27
30	2 31 56	6 14 6	3♈39	23	5	29	18	27	3	25	27
31	2 35 52	7 14 3	17 12	25	6	29	18	27	3	25	27

THE SUN ENTERS THE SIGN OF SCORPIO ON OCT 23 AT 17:59.

DAY	TIME	☉	☽	☿	♀	♂	♃	♄	♅	♆	♇
	h m s	° ' "	° '	°	°	°	°	°	°	°	°
N 1	2 39 49	8♏14 2	1♉ 8	27♎	7♏	0♑	18♏	27♎	3♐	25♐	27♎
O 2	2 43 45	9 14 3	15 21	28	9	1	18	27	3	25	27
V 3	2 47 42	10 14 6	29 46	0♏	10	2	19	27	3	25	27
E 4	2 51 39	11 14 11	14♊17	2	11	2	19	27	3	25	27
M 5	2 55 35	12 14 17	28 48	3	12	3	19	27	4	25	27
B 6	2 59 32	13 14 26	13♋14	5	14	4	19	27	4	25	28
E 7	3 3 28	14 14 37	27 32	7	15	5	19	27	4	25	28
R 8	3 7 25	15 14 50	11♌39	8	16	5	20	28	4	25	28
9	3 11 21	16 15 5	25 35	10	17	6	20	28	4	25	28
10	3 15 18	17 15 22	9♍19	11	19	7	20	28	4	25	28
11	3 19 14	18 15 41	22 52	13	20	8	20	28	4	25	28
12	3 23 11	19 16 2	6♎13	15	21	8	21	28	4	25	28
13	3 27 8	20 16 25	19 22	16	23	9	21	28	4	25	28
14	3 31 4	21 16 50	2♏17	18	24	10	21	28	4	25	28
15	3 35 1	22 17 16	15 0	19	25	11	21	28	4	26	28
16	3 38 57	23 17 44	27 29	21	26	11	21	29	4	26	28
17	3 42 54	24 18 14	9♐46	23	28	12	22	29	4	26	28
18	3 46 50	25 18 46	21 51	24	29	13	22	29	4	26	28
19	3 50 47	26 19 18	3♑47	26	0♐	14	22	29	4	26	28
20	3 54 43	27 19 52	15 36	27	1	14	22	29	4	26	28
21	3 58 40	28 20 28	27 22	29	3	15	23	29	4	26	28
22	4 2 37	29 21 4	9♒10	1♐	4	16	23	29	5	26	28
23	4 6 33	0♐21 42	21 5	2	5	17	23	29	5	26	28
24	4 10 30	1 22 21	3♓11	4	6	17	23	29	5	26	28
25	4 14 26	2 23 1	15 34	5	8	18	23	0♏	5	26	28
26	4 18 23	3 23 42	28 19	7	9	19	24	0	5	26	28
27	4 22 19	4 24 25	11♈28	8	10	20	24	0	5	26	28
28	4 26 16	5 25 8	25 3	10	11	21	24	0	5	26	28
29	4 30 12	6 25 52	9♉ 5	12	13	21	24	0	5	26	28
30	4 34 9	7 26 38	23 31	13	14	22	24	0	5	26	28

THE SUN ENTERS THE SIGN OF SAGITTARIUS ON NOV 22 AT 15:25.

DAY	TIME	☉	☽	☿	♀	♂	♃	♄	♅	♆	♇
	h m s	° ' "	° '	°	°	°	°	°	°	°	°
D 1	4 38 6	8♐27 25	8♊15	15♐	15♐	23♑	25♏	0♏	5♐	26♐	28♎
E 2	4 42 2	9 28 13	23 10	16	16	24	25	0	5	26	28
C 3	4 45 59	10 29 2	8♋ 7	18	18	24	25	0	5	26	28
E 4	4 49 55	11 29 53	22 59	19	19	25	25	0	5	26	29
M 5	4 53 52	12 30 44	7♌38	21	20	26	26	1	5	26	29
B 6	4 57 48	13 31 37	22 1	22	21	27	26	1	5	26	29
E 7	5 1 45	14 32 32	6♍ 5	24	23	27	26	1	5	26	29
R 8	5 5 42	15 33 28	19 49	26	24	28	26	1	6	26	29
9	5 9 38	16 34 24	3♎13	27	25	29	26	1	6	26	29
10	5 13 35	17 35 23	16 19	29	26	0♒	27	1	6	26	29
11	5 17 31	18 36 22	29 10	0♑	28	1	27	1	6	26	29
12	5 21 28	19 37 22	11♏45	2	29	1	27	1	6	26	29
13	5 25 24	20 38 24	24 9	3	0♑	2	27	1	6	27	29
14	5 29 21	21 39 26	6♐22	5	1	3	28	1	6	27	29
15	5 33 17	22 40 29	18 25	6	3	4	28	2	6	27	29
16	5 37 14	23 41 33	0♑22	8	4	4	28	2	6	27	29
17	5 41 11	24 42 38	12 13	9	5	5	28	2	6	27	29
18	5 45 7	25 43 43	24 0	11	6	6	28	2	6	27	29
19	5 49 4	26 44 49	5♒47	13	8	7	29	2	6	27	29
20	5 53 0	27 45 55	17 36	14	9	8	29	2	6	27	29
21	5 56 57	28 47 2	29 32	15	10	8	29	2	6	27	29
22	6 0 53	29 48 9	11♓37	17	11	9	29	2	6	27	29
23	6 4 50	0♑49 15	23 57	18	13	10	29	2	6	27	29
24	6 8 46	1 50 22	6♈35	20	14	11	0♐	2	6	27	29
25	6 12 43	2 51 30	19 36	21	15	12	0	2	7	27	29
26	6 16 40	3 52 37	3♉ 3	23	17	12	0	2	7	27	29
27	6 20 36	4 53 44	16 58	24	18	13	0	3	7	27	29
28	6 24 33	5 54 52	1♊19	25	19	14	0	3	7	27	29
29	6 28 29	6 55 59	16 5	26	20	15	1	3	7	27	29
30	6 32 26	7 57 7	1♋ 8	27	22	15	1	3	7	27	29
31	6 36 22	8 58 15	16 20	29	23	16	1	3	7	27	29

THE SUN ENTERS THE SIGN OF CAPRICORN ON DEC 22 AT 04:39.

♈ ARIES ♉ TAURUS ♊ GEMINI ♋ CANCER ♌ LEO ♍ VIRGO ♎ LIBRA ♏ SCORPIO ♐ SAGITTARIUS ♑ CAPRICORN ♒ AQUARIUS ♓ PISCES

SIDEREAL SUN MOON MERCURY VENUS MARS JUPITER SATURN URANUS NEPTUNE PLUTO

DAY	TIME	☉	☽	☿	♀	♂	♃	♄	♅	♆	♇
	h m s	° ' "	° '	°	°	°	°	°	°	°	°
J 1	6 40 19	9♑59 23	1♌32	0♒	24♑	17♒	1♐	3♏	7♐	27♐	29♎
A 2	6 44 15	11 0 31	16 35	0	25	18	1	3	7	27	29
N 3	6 48 12	12 1 40	1♍19	1	27	19	2	3	7	27	29
U 4	6 52 9	13 2 48	15 40	2	28	19	2	3	7	27	29
A 5	6 56 5	14 3 57	29 34	2	29	20	2	3	7	27	29
R 6	7 0 2	15 5 6	13♎ 3	2	0♒	21	2	3	7	27	29
Y 7	7 3 58	16 6 15	26 7	3 R	2	22	2	3	7	27	29
8	7 7 55	17 7 25	8♏49	3	3	22	3	3	7	28	29
9	7 11 51	18 8 34	21 14	2	4	23	3	3	7	28	29
10	7 15 48	19 9 44	3♐25	2	5	24	3	3	7	28	29
11	7 19 44	20 10 54	15 25	1	7	25	3	4	7	28	29
12	7 23 41	21 12 3	27 19	0	8	26	3	4	7	28	29
13	7 27 38	22 13 12	9♑ 8	29♑	9	26	3	4	8	28	29
14	7 31 34	23 14 21	20 56	28	10	27	4	4	8	28	29
15	7 35 31	24 15 30	2♒44	27	12	28	4	4	8	28	29
16	7 39 27	25 16 38	14 34	26	13	29	4	4	8	28	29
17	7 43 24	26 17 45	26 29	24	14	0♓	4	4	8	28	29
18	7 47 20	27 18 52	8♓30	23	15	0	4	4	8	28	29
19	7 51 17	28 19 58	20 40	22	17	1	4	4	8	28	29
20	7 55 13	29 21 3	3♈ 2	21	18	2	5	4	8	28	29
21	7 59 10	0♒22 8	15 39	20	19	3	5	4	8	28	29
22	8 3 7	1 23 11	28 34	19	20	3	5	4	8	28	29
23	8 7 3	2 24 14	11♉51	18	22	4	5	4	8	28	0♏
24	8 11 0	3 25 15	25 32	17	23	5	5	4	8	28	0
25	8 14 56	4 26 16	9♊38	17	24	6	5	4	8	28	0
26	8 18 53	5 27 15	24 9	17	25	7	6	4	8	28	0
27	8 22 49	6 28 14	9♋ 2	16 D	27	7	6	4	8	28	0
28	8 26 46	7 29 11	24 10	16	28	8	6	4	8	28	0
29	8 30 43	8 30 8	9♌25	17	29	9	6	4	8	28	0
30	8 34 39	9 31 3	24 37	17	0♓	10	6	4	8	28	0
31	8 38 36	10 31 58	9♍34	17	2	11	6	4	8	28	0

THE SUN ENTERS THE SIGN OF AQUARIUS ON JAN 20 AT 15:18.

DAY	TIME	☉	☽	☿	♀	♂	♃	♄	♅	♆	♇
	h m s	° ' "	° '	°	°	°	°	°	°	°	°
F 1	8 42 32	11♒32 52	24♍10	18♑	3♓	11♓	7♐	4♏	8♐	28♐	0♏R
E 2	8 46 29	12 33 44	8♎19	18	4	12	7	4	8	28	0
B 3	8 50 25	13 34 36	21 58	19	5	13	7	4	8	28	0
R 4	8 54 22	14 35 27	5♏ 8	20	7	14	7	4	8	28	0
U 5	8 58 18	15 36 18	17 52	20	8	14	7	4	8	28	0
A 6	9 2 15	16 37 7	0♐16	21	9	15	7	4	9	28	0
R 7	9 6 12	17 37 56	12 22	22	10	16	7	4	9	28	0
Y 8	9 10 8	18 38 44	24 18	23	12	17	8	4	9	29	0
9	9 14 5	19 39 30	6♑ 6	24	13	18	8	4	9	29	0
10	9 18 1	20 40 16	17 53	25	14	18	8	4	9	29	0
11	9 21 58	21 41 0	29 40	26	15	19	8	4	9	29	0
12	9 25 54	22 41 44	11♒31	27	17	20	8	4 R	9	29	29♎
13	9 29 51	23 42 25	23 27	28	18	21	8	4	9	29	29
14	9 33 47	24 43 6	5♓32	0♒	19	21	8	4	9	29	29
15	9 37 44	25 43 44	17 45	1	20	22	8	4	9	29	29
16	9 41 40	26 44 22	0♈ 7	2	21	23	9	4	9	29	29
17	9 45 37	27 44 57	12 40	3	23	24	9	4	9	29	29
18	9 49 34	28 45 31	25 25	5	24	25	9	4	9	29	29
19	9 53 30	29 46 4	8♉24	6	25	25	9	4	9	29	29
20	9 57 27	0♓46 34	21 39	7	26	26	9	4	9	29	29
21	10 1 23	1 47 3	5♊11	9	28	27	9	4	9	29	29
22	10 5 20	2 47 29	19 3	10	29	28	9	4	9	29	29
23	10 9 16	3 47 54	3♋16	11	0♈	28	9	4	9	29	29
24	10 13 13	4 48 17	17 48	13	1	29	9	4	9	29	29
25	10 17 9	5 48 38	2♌37	14	3	0☉	9	4	9	29	29
26	10 21 6	6 48 57	17 35	16	4	1♈	10	4	9	29	29
27	10 25 3	7 49 15	2♍36	17	5	2	10	4	9	29	29
28	10 28 59	8 49 30	17 29	19	6	2	10	4	9	29	29

THE SUN ENTERS THE SIGN OF PISCES ON FEB 19 AT 05:31.

DAY	TIME	☉	☽	☿	♀	♂	♃	♄	♅	♆	♇
	h m s	° ' "	° '	°	°	°	°	°	°	°	°
M 1	10 32 56	9♓49 44	2♎ 6	20♒	8♈	3♈	10♐	4♏R	9♐	29♐	29♎R
A 2	10 36 52	10 49 56	16 19	22	9	4	10	4	9	29	29
R 3	10 40 49	11 50 6	0♏ 5	23	10	5	10	4	9	29	29
C 4	10 44 45	12 50 15	13 22	25	11	5	10	4	9	29	29
H 5	10 48 42	13 50 23	26 12	26	12	6	10	4	9	29	29
6	10 52 38	14 50 29	8♐39	28	14	7	10	4	9	29	29
7	10 56 35	15 50 33	20 47	0♓	15	8	10	4	9	29	29
8	11 0 32	16 50 36	2♑43	1	16	8	10	4	9	29	29
9	11 4 28	17 50 37	14 32	3	17	9	10	4	9	29	29
10	11 8 25	18 50 36	26 18	5	19	10	10	4	9	29	29
11	11 12 21	19 50 34	8♒ 8	6	20	11	10	4	9	29	29
12	11 16 18	20 50 30	20 3	8	21	11	11	4	9	29	29
13	11 20 14	21 50 24	2♓ 8	10	22	12	11	4	9	29	29
14	11 24 11	22 50 16	14 23	12	23	13	11	4	9 R	29	29
15	11 28 7	23 50 7	26 51	13	25	14	11	4	9	29	29
16	11 32 4	24 49 55	9♈30	15	26	15	11	4	9	29	29
17	11 36 1	25 49 41	22 22	17	27	15	11	4	9	29	29
18	11 39 57	26 49 25	5♉25	19	28	16	11	4	9	29	29
19	11 43 54	27 49 8	18 38	21	0♉	17	11	3	9	29	29
20	11 47 50	28 48 47	2♊ 3	23	1	18	11	3	9	29	29
21	11 51 47	29 48 25	15 40	24	2	18	11	3	9	29	29
22	11 55 43	0♈48 0	29 29	26	3	19	11	3	9	29	29
23	11 59 40	1 47 34	13♋31	28	4	20	11	3	9	29	29
24	12 3 36	2 47 4	27 46	0♈	6	21	11	3	9	29	29
25	12 7 33	3 46 33	12♌12	2	7	21	11	3	9	29	29
26	12 11 30	4 45 59	26 46	4	8	22	11	3	9	29	29
27	12 15 26	5 45 23	11♍22	6	9	23	11 R	3	9	29	29
28	12 19 23	6 44 44	25 54	8	10	24	11	3	9	29	29
29	12 23 19	7 44 4	10♎14	10	12	24	11	3	9	29	29
30	12 27 16	8 43 21	24 17	12	13	25	11	3	9	29	29
31	12 31 12	9 42 36	7♏57	14	14	26	11	3	9	29	29

THE SUN ENTERS THE SIGN OF ARIES ON MAR 21 AT 04:39.

SIDEREAL SUN MOON MERCURY VENUS MARS JUPITER SATURN URANUS NEPTUNE PLUTO

DAY	TIME	☉	☽	☿	♀	♂	♃	♄	♅	♆	♇
	h m s	° ' "	° '	°	°	°	°	°	°	°	°
A 1	12 35 9	10♈41 50	21♏12	16♈	15♉	27♈	11♐R	3♏R	9♐R	29♐R	29♎R
P 2	12 39 5	11 41 2	4♐ 4	19	16	27	11	3	9	29	29
R 3	12 43 2	12 40 12	16 33	21	18	28	11	3	9	29	29
I 4	12 46 58	13 39 20	28 44	23	19	29	11	2	9	29	29
L 5	12 50 55	14 38 27	10♑43	25	20	0♉	11	2	9	29	29
6	12 54 52	15 37 31	22 34	27	21	0	11	2	9	29	29
7	12 58 48	16 36 34	4♒22	29	22	1	11	2	9	29	28
8	13 2 45	17 35 35	16 14	1♉	24	2	11	2	9	29	28
9	13 6 41	18 34 35	28 14	2	25	3	11	2	9	29	28
10	13 10 38	19 33 32	10♓25	4	26	3	11	2	9	29	28
11	13 14 34	20 32 28	22 50	6	27	4	11	2	9	29	28
12	13 18 31	21 31 21	5♈31	8	28	5	11	2	9	29	28
13	13 22 27	22 30 13	18 28	10	29	5	11	2	9	29	28
14	13 26 24	23 29 3	1♉40	11	1♊	6	10	2	9	29	28
15	13 30 21	24 27 51	15 6	13	2	7	10	2	9	29	28
16	13 34 17	25 26 36	28 43	14	3	8	10	2	9	29	28
17	13 38 14	26 25 20	12♊29	16	4	8	10	1	9	29	28
18	13 42 10	27 24 2	26 22	17	5	9	10	1	9	29	28
19	13 46 7	28 22 41	10♋22	18	6	10	10	1	9	29	28
20	13 50 3	29 21 18	24 26	19	8	11	10	1	9	29	28
21	13 54 0	0♉19 53	8♌35	20	9	11	10	1	9	29	28
22	13 57 56	1 18 25	22 46	21	10	12	10	1	8	29	28
23	14 1 53	2 16 56	6♍59	22	11	13	10	1	8	29	28
24	14 5 50	3 15 24	21 9	23	12	14	10	1	8	29	28
25	14 9 46	4 13 50	5♎13	23	13	14	10	1	8	29	28
26	14 13 43	5 12 14	19 7	24	15	15	10	1	8	29	28
27	14 17 39	6 10 36	2♏46	25	16	16	10	1	8	29	28
28	14 21 36	7 8 57	16 9	25	17	16	9	1	8	29	28
29	14 25 32	8 7 15	29 12	25	18	17	9	1	8	29	28
30	14 29 29	9 5 32	11♐56	25	19	18	9	1	8	29	28

THE SUN ENTERS THE SIGN OF TAURUS ON APR 20 AT 15:51.

DAY	TIME	☉	☽	☿	♀	♂	♃	♄	♅	♆	♇
	h m s	° ' "	° '	°	°	°	°	°	°	°	°
M 1	14 33 25	10♉ 3 47	24♐22	26♉R	20♊	19♉	9♐R	0♏R	8♐R	29♐R	28♎R
A 2	14 37 22	11 2 1	6♑33	26	22	19	9	0	8	29	28
Y 3	14 41 19	12 0 13	18 32	25	23	20	9	0	8	29	28
4	14 45 15	12 58 24	0♒25	25	24	21	9	0	8	29	28
5	14 49 12	13 56 33	12 15	25	25	22	9	0	8	29	28
6	14 53 8	14 54 41	24 8	25	26	22	9	0	8	29	28
7	14 57 5	15 52 47	6♓10	24	27	23	9	0	8	29	28
8	15 1 1	16 50 52	18 24	24	28	24	8	0	8	29	28
9	15 4 58	17 48 56	0♈54	23	29	24	8	0	8	29	28
10	15 8 54	18 46 57	13 43	23	1♋	25	8	0	8	29	28
11	15 12 51	19 44 58	26 53	22	2	26	8	0	8	29	28
12	15 16 48	20 42 57	10♉22	22	3	27	8	0	8	29	28
13	15 20 44	21 40 55	24 8	21	4	27	8	0	8	29	27
14	15 24 41	22 38 51	8♊10	21	5	28	8	29♎	8	29	27
15	15 28 37	23 36 46	22 22	20	6	29	8	29	8	29	27
16	15 32 34	24 34 39	6♋41	19	7	29	8	29	8	29	27
17	15 36 30	25 32 30	21 2	19	8	0♊	7	29	8	29	27
18	15 40 27	26 30 20	5♌21	18	10	1	7	29	8	29	27
19	15 44 23	27 28 7	19 36	18	11	1	7	29	8	29	27
20	15 48 20	28 25 53	3♍45	18	12	2	7	29	7	29	27
21	15 52 17	29 23 38	17 45	17	13	3	7	29	7	29	27
22	15 56 13	0♊21 21	1♎36	17	14	4	7	29	7	29	27
23	16 0 10	1 19 2	15 16	17	15	4	7	29	7	29	27
24	16 4 6	2 16 41	28 43	17	16	5	7	29	7	29	27
25	16 8 3	3 14 20	11♏57	16 D	17	6	6	29	7	29	27
26	16 11 59	4 11 56	24 57	16	18	6	6	29	7	29	27
27	16 15 56	5 9 32	7♐41	16	19	7	6	29	7	28	27
28	16 19 52	6 7 7	20 12	17	20	8	6	29	7	28	27
29	16 23 49	7 4 40	2♑29	17	21	9	6	29	7	28	27
30	16 27 46	8 2 12	14 35	17	22	9	6	29	7	28	27
31	16 31 42	8 59 44	26 32	18	24	10	6	29	7	28	27

THE SUN ENTERS THE SIGN OF GEMINI ON MAY 21 AT 15:07.

DAY	TIME	☉	☽	☿	♀	♂	♃	♄	♅	♆	♇
	h m s	° ' "	° '	°	°	°	°	°	°	°	°
J 1	16 35 39	9♊57 14	8♒24	18♉	25♋	11♊	6♐R	28♎R	7♐R	28♐R	27♎R
U 2	16 39 35	10 54 44	20 14	18	26	11	5	28	7	28	27
N 3	16 43 32	11 52 13	2♓ 8	19	27	12	5	28	7	28	27
E 4	16 47 28	12 49 41	14 9	20	28	13	5	28	7	28	27
5	16 51 25	13 47 8	26 23	20	29	13	5	28	7	28	27
6	16 55 21	14 44 35	8♈53	21	0♌	14	5	28	7	28	27
7	16 59 18	15 42 1	21 44	22	1	15	5	28	7	28	27
8	17 3 15	16 39 26	4♉57	23	2	15	5	28	7	28	27
9	17 7 11	17 36 51	18 34	24	3	16	5	28	7	28	27
10	17 11 8	18 34 15	2♊34	25	4	17	4	28	7	28	27
11	17 15 4	19 31 38	16 55	26	5	18	4	28	7	28	27
12	17 19 1	20 29 1	1♋30	27	6	18	4	28	7	28	27
13	17 22 57	21 26 23	16 14	28	7	19	4	28	6	28	27
14	17 26 54	22 23 44	1♌ 0	0♊	8	20	4	28	6	28	27
15	17 30 51	23 21 4	15 42	1	9	20	4	28	6	28	27
16	17 34 47	24 18 23	0♍13	2	10	21	4	28	6	28	27
17	17 38 44	25 15 42	14 30	4	11	22	4	28	6	28	27
18	17 42 40	26 12 59	28 29	5	12	22	4	28	6	28	27
19	17 46 37	27 10 15	12♎11	7	13	23	3	28	6	28	27
20	17 50 33	28 7 31	25 36	8	13	24	3	28	6	28	27
21	17 54 30	29 4 46	8♏43	10	14	24	3	28	6	28	27
22	17 58 26	0♋ 2 0	21 35	11	15	25	3	28	6	28	27
23	18 2 23	0 59 14	4♐13	13	16	26	3	28	6	28	27
24	18 6 20	1 56 27	16 39	15	17	26	3	28	6	28	27
25	18 10 16	2 53 40	28 55	17	18	27	3	28	6	28	27
26	18 14 13	3 50 52	11♑ 1	18	19	28	3	28	6	28	27
27	18 18 9	4 48 5	23 0	20	20	28	3	28	6	28	27
28	18 22 6	5 45 17	4♒53	22	21	29	3	28	6	28	27
29	18 26 2	6 42 28	16 44	24	21	0♋	2	28	6	28	27
30	18 29 59	7 39 40	28 35	26	22	0	2	28	6	28	27

THE SUN ENTERS THE SIGN OF CANCER ON JUN 21 AT 23:10.

♈ ARIES ♉ TAURUS ♊ GEMINI ♋ CANCER ♌ LEO ♍ VIRGO ♎ LIBRA ♏ SCORPIO ♐ SAGITTARIUS ♑ CAPRICORN ♒ AQUARIUS ♓ PISCES

SIDEREAL SUN MOON MERCURY VENUS MARS JUPITER SATURN URANUS NEPTUNE PLUTO

DAY	TIME	☉	☽	☿	♀	♂	♃	♄	♅	♆	♇
	h m s	° ' "	° '	°	°	°	°	°	°	°	°
J 1	18 33 55	8♋36 52	10♓29	28♊	23♌	1♋	2♐R	28♎D	6♐R	28♐R	27♎R
U 2	18 37 52	9 34 4	22 30	0♋	24	2	2	28	6	28	27
L 3	18 41 49	10 31 16	4♈42	3	25	3	2	28	6	28	27
Y 4	18 45 45	11 28 28	17 10	5	25	3	2	28	6	27	27
5	18 49 42	12 25 40	29 57	7	26	4	2	28	6	27	27
6	18 53 38	13 22 53	13♉ 7	9	27	5	2	28	6	27	27
7	18 57 35	14 20 6	26 42	11	28	5	2	28	6	27	27 D
8	19 1 31	15 17 19	10♊45	13	28	6	2	28	6	27	27
9	19 5 28	16 14 33	25 12	15	29	7	2	28	6	27	27
10	19 9 24	17 11 47	9♋59	18	0♍	7	2	28	6	27	27
11	19 13 21	18 9 1	25 1	20	1	8	2	28	6	27	27
12	19 17 18	19 6 15	10♌ 8	22	1	9	2	28	6	27	27
13	19 21 14	20 3 29	25 12	24	2	9	1	28	5	27	27
14	19 25 11	21 0 43	10♍ 2	26	2	10	1	28	5	27	27
15	19 29 7	21 57 58	24 33	28	3	11	1	28	5	27	27
16	19 33 4	22 55 12	8♎40	0♌	4	11	1	28	5	27	27
17	19 37 0	23 52 26	22 23	2	4	12	1	28	5	27	27
18	19 40 57	24 49 41	5♏42	4	5	13	1	28	5	27	27
19	19 44 53	25 46 55	18 39	6	5	13	1	28	5	27	27
20	19 48 50	26 44 10	1♐17	8	6	14	1	28	5	27	27
21	19 52 47	27 41 25	13 41	10	6	15	1	28	5	27	27
22	19 56 43	28 38 40	25 52	12	7	15	1	28	5	27	27
23	20 0 40	29 35 56	7♑55	14	7	16	1	28	5	27	27
24	20 4 36	0♌33 12	19 52	16	7	16	1	28	5	27	27
25	20 8 33	1 30 29	1♒45	18	8	17	1	28	5	27	27
26	20 12 29	2 27 46	13 36	19	8	18	1	28	5	27	27
27	20 16 26	3 25 4	25 27	21	8	18	1	28	5	27	27
28	20 20 22	4 22 23	7♓20	23	9	19	1	28	5	27	27
29	20 24 19	5 19 43	19 17	24	9	20	1 D	28	5	27	27
30	20 28 16	6 17 3	1♈20	26	9	20	1	28	5	27	27
31	20 32 12	7 14 25	13 33	28	9	21	1	28	5	27	27

THE SUN ENTERS THE SIGN OF LEO ON JUL 23 AT 10:05.

DAY	TIME	☉	☽	☿	♀	♂	♃	♄	♅	♆	♇
	h m s	° ' "	° '	°	°	°	°	°	°	°	°
A 1	20 36 9	8♌11 47	25♈59	29♌	9♍	22♋	1♐	28♎	5♐R	27♐R	27♎
U 2	20 40 5	9 9 11	8♉43	1♍	9	22	1	29	5	27	27
G 3	20 44 2	10 6 36	21 47	2	9 R	23	1	29	5	27	27
U 4	20 47 58	11 4 2	5♊15	4	9	24	1	29	5	27	27
S 5	20 51 55	12 1 29	19 10	5	9	24	1	29	5	27	27
T 6	20 55 51	12 58 58	3♋32	7	9	25	1	29	5	27	27
7	20 59 48	13 56 28	18 18	8	9	26	1	29	5	27	27
8	21 3 45	14 53 59	3♌24	10	9	26	1	29	5	27	27
9	21 7 41	15 51 31	18 39	11	9	27	1	29	5	27	27
10	21 11 38	16 49 4	3♍55	12	9	28	1	29	5	27	27
11	21 15 34	17 46 38	18 59	14	8	28	1	29	5	27	27
12	21 19 31	18 44 13	3♎44	15	8	29	1	29	5	27	27
13	21 23 27	19 41 48	18 2	16	8	0♌	1	29	5	27	27
14	21 27 24	20 39 25	1♏51	17	7	0	1	29	5 D	27	27
15	21 31 20	21 37 3	15 12	19	7	1	1	29	5	27	27
16	21 35 17	22 34 41	28 7	20	7	1	2	29	5	27	27
17	21 39 14	23 32 21	10♐40	21	6	2	2	29	5	27	27
18	21 43 10	24 30 2	22 56	22	6	3	2	0♏	5	27	27
19	21 47 7	25 27 44	5♑ 0	23	5	3	2	0	5	27	27
20	21 51 3	26 25 27	16 56	24	5	4	2	0	5	27	27
21	21 55 0	27 23 11	28 48	25	4	5	2	0	5	27	27
22	21 58 56	28 20 56	10♒38	26	3	5	2	0	5	27	27
23	22 2 53	29 18 43	22 29	26	3	6	2	0	5	27	27
24	22 6 49	0♍16 31	4♓23	27	2	7	2	0	5	27	27
25	22 10 46	1 14 20	16 21	28	2	7	2	0	5	27	27
26	22 14 43	2 12 11	28 25	28	1	8	2	0	5	27	27
27	22 18 39	3 10 4	10♈35	29	0	9	2	0	5	27	27
28	22 22 36	4 7 58	22 55	29	0	9	2	0	5	27	27
29	22 26 32	5 5 54	5♉25	0♎	29♌	10	2	0	5	26	27
30	22 30 29	6 3 52	18 10	0	28	10	3	0	5	26	27
31	22 34 25	7 1 52	1♊12	1	28	11	3	1	5	26	28

THE SUN ENTERS THE SIGN OF VIRGO ON AUG 23 AT 17:09.

DAY	TIME	☉	☽	☿	♀	♂	♃	♄	♅	♆	♇
	h m s	° ' "	° '	°	°	°	°	°	°	°	°
S 1	22 38 22	7♍59 54	14♊34	1♎	27♌R	12♌	3♐	1♏	5♐	26♐R	28♎
E 2	22 42 18	8 57 58	28 19	1 R	27	12	3	1	5	26	28
P 3	22 46 15	9 56 4	12♋29	1	26	13	3	1	5	26	28
T 4	22 50 12	10 54 11	27 3	1	26	14	3	1	5	26	28
E 5	22 54 8	11 52 21	11♌57	0	25	14	3	1	5	26	28
M 6	22 58 5	12 50 32	27 5	0	25	15	3	1	5	26	28
B 7	23 2 1	13 48 45	12♍17	0	25	16	3	1	5	26	28
E 8	23 5 58	14 47 0	27 22	29♍	24	16	3	1	5	26 D	28
R 9	23 9 54	15 45 17	12♎10	28	24	17	4	1	5	26	28
10	23 13 51	16 43 35	26 34	28	24	17	4	1	5	26	28
11	23 17 47	17 41 55	10♏30	27	24	18	4	2	5	26	28
12	23 21 44	18 40 16	23 55	26	23	19	4	2	5	26	28
13	23 25 41	19 38 39	6♐54	25	23	19	4	2	5	26	28
14	23 29 37	20 37 4	19 28	24	23	20	4	2	5	26	28
15	23 33 34	21 35 30	1♑44	23	23 D	21	4	2	5	26	28
16	23 37 30	22 33 58	13 46	22	23	21	4	2	6	26	28
17	23 41 27	23 32 28	25 40	21	23	22	5	2	6	26	28
18	23 45 23	24 30 59	7♒30	20	23	22	5	2	6	26	28
19	23 49 20	25 29 32	19 21	19	23	23	5	2	6	26	28
20	23 53 16	26 28 6	1♓14	18	24	24	5	2	6	27	28
21	23 57 13	27 26 43	13 13	18	24	24	5	3	6	27	28
22	0 1 10	28 25 21	25 20	17	24	25	5	3	6	27	28
23	0 5 6	29 24 1	7♈34	17	24	26	5	3	6	27	28
24	0 9 3	0♎22 43	19 58	16 D	24	26	6	3	6	27	28
25	0 12 59	1 21 28	2♉31	16	25	27	6	3	6	27	28
26	0 16 56	2 20 14	15 14	16	25	28	6	3	6	27	28
27	0 20 52	3 19 3	28 9	17	26	28	6	3	6	27	28
28	0 24 49	4 17 54	11♊17	17	26	29	6	3	6	27	28
29	0 28 45	5 16 47	24 40	18	26	29	6	3	6	27	28
30	0 32 42	6 15 43	8♋21	19	27	0♍	7	4	6	27	29

THE SUN ENTERS THE SIGN OF LIBRA ON SEP 23 AT 14:43.

SIDEREAL SUN MOON MERCURY VENUS MARS JUPITER SATURN URANUS NEPTUNE PLUTO

DAY	TIME	☉	☽	☿	♀	♂	♃	♄	♅	♆	♇
	h m s	° ' "	° '	°	°	°	°	°	°	°	°
O 1	0 36 38	7♎14 40	22♋20	19♍	27♌	1♍	7♐	4♏	6♐	27♐	29♎
C 2	0 40 35	8 13 41	6♌38	20	28	1	7	4	6	27	29
T 3	0 44 32	9 12 43	21 14	22	28	2	7	4	6	27	29
O 4	0 48 28	10 11 48	6♍ 1	23	29	2	7	4	6	27	29
B 5	0 52 25	11 10 55	20 54	24	0♍	3	7	4	6	27	29
E 6	0 56 21	12 10 4	5♎44	25	0	4	8	4	6	27	29
R 7	1 0 18	13 9 15	20 21	27	1	4	8	4	6	27	29
8	1 4 14	14 8 28	4♏40	28	1	5	8	4	6	27	29
9	1 8 11	15 7 44	18 34	0♎	2	6	8	5	6	27	29
10	1 12 7	16 7 1	2♐ 1	2	3	6	8	5	6	27	29
11	1 16 4	17 6 20	15 2	3	3	7	8	5	6	27	29
12	1 20 1	18 5 41	27 40	5	4	7	9	5	6	27	29
13	1 23 57	19 5 3	9♑58	7	5	8	9	5	7	27	29
14	1 27 54	20 4 28	22 2	8	6	9	9	5	7	27	29
15	1 31 50	21 3 54	3♒57	10	6	9	9	5	7	27	29
16	1 35 47	22 3 22	15 48	12	7	10	9	5	7	27	29
17	1 39 43	23 2 51	27 40	14	8	10	9	6	7	27	29
18	1 43 40	24 2 23	9♓37	15	9	11	10	6	7	27	29
19	1 47 36	25 1 56	21 41	17	10	12	10	6	7	27	29
20	1 51 33	26 1 31	3♈56	19	11	12	10	6	7	27	29
21	1 55 30	27 1 8	16 23	20	11	13	10	6	7	27	29
22	1 59 26	28 0 47	29 2	22	12	14	10	6	7	27	29
23	2 3 23	29 0 28	11♉54	24	13	14	11	6	7	27	29
24	2 7 19	0♏ 0 11	24 57	26	14	15	11	6	7	27	29
25	2 11 16	0 59 57	8♊12	27	15	15	11	6	7	27	0♏
26	2 15 12	1 59 44	21 38	29	16	16	11	7	7	27	0
27	2 19 9	2 59 34	5♋14	1♏	17	17	11	7	7	27	0
28	2 23 5	3 59 26	19 2	2	18	17	12	7	7	27	0
29	2 27 2	4 59 20	3♌ 1	4	19	18	12	7	7	27	0
30	2 30 59	5 59 16	17 10	6	20	18	12	7	7	27	0
31	2 34 55	6 59 15	1♍27	7	21	19	12	7	7	27	0

THE SUN ENTERS THE SIGN OF SCORPIO ON OCT 23 AT 23:55.

DAY	TIME	☉	☽	☿	♀	♂	♃	♄	♅	♆	♇
	h m s	° ' "	° '	°	°	°	°	°	°	°	°
N 1	2 38 52	7♏59 16	15♍51	9♏	21♍	20♍	12♐	7♏	8♐	27♐	0♏
O 2	2 42 48	8 59 18	0♎17	10	22	20	13	7	8	27	0
V 3	2 46 45	9 59 23	14 40	12	23	21	13	8	8	27	0
E 4	2 50 41	10 59 30	28 53	14	24	21	13	8	8	27	0
M 5	2 54 38	11 59 39	12♏52	15	25	22	13	8	8	27	0
B 6	2 58 34	12 59 50	26 33	17	26	23	13	8	8	27	0
E 7	3 2 31	14 0 2	9♐52	18	27	23	14	8	8	27	0
R 8	3 6 28	15 0 16	22 50	20	29	24	14	8	8	27	0
9	3 10 24	16 0 32	5♑28	22	0♎	24	14	8	8	27	0
10	3 14 21	17 0 50	17 48	23	1	25	14	8	8	27	0
11	3 18 17	18 1 8	29 54	25	2	26	14	9	8	28	0
12	3 22 14	19 1 29	11♒51	26	3	26	15	9	8	28	0
13	3 26 10	20 1 50	23 43	28	4	27	15	9	8	28	0
14	3 30 7	21 2 14	5♓36	29	5	27	15	9	8	28	0
15	3 34 3	22 2 38	17 34	1♐	6	28	15	9	8	28	0
16	3 38 0	23 3 4	29 41	3	7	29	16	9	8	28	0
17	3 41 57	24 3 31	12♈ 1	4	8	29	16	9	8	28	0
18	3 45 53	25 4 0	24 36	6	9	0♎	16	9	8	28	0
19	3 49 50	26 4 30	7♉29	7	10	0	16	9	9	28	1
20	3 53 46	27 5 1	20 39	9	11	1	16	10	9	28	1
21	3 57 43	28 5 34	4♊ 5	10	12	2	17	10	9	28	1
22	4 1 39	29 6 9	17 45	12	13	2	17	10	9	28	1
23	4 5 36	0♐ 6 45	1♋38	13	15	3	17	10	9	28	1
24	4 9 32	1 7 23	15 40	15	16	3	17	10	9	28	1
25	4 13 29	2 8 3	29 48	16	17	4	18	10	9	28	1
26	4 17 26	3 8 44	14♌ 0	18	18	4	18	10	9	28	1
27	4 21 22	4 9 26	28 12	19	19	5	18	10	9	28	1
28	4 25 19	5 10 11	12♍23	21	20	6	18	11	9	28	1
29	4 29 15	6 10 56	26 30	22	21	6	18	11	9	28	1
30	4 33 12	7 11 44	10♎32	24	22	7	19	11	9	28	1

THE SUN ENTERS THE SIGN OF SAGITTARIUS ON NOV 22 AT 21:20.

DAY	TIME	☉	☽	☿	♀	♂	♃	♄	♅	♆	♇
	h m s	° ' "	° '	°	°	°	°	°	°	°	°
D 1	4 37 8	8♐12 33	24♎26	25♐	24♎	7♎	19♐	11♏	9♐	28♐	1♏
E 2	4 41 5	9 13 23	8♏10	26	25	8	19	11	9	28	1
C 3	4 45 1	10 14 15	21 41	28	26	8	19	11	9	28	1
E 4	4 48 58	11 15 8	4♐59	29	27	9	20	11	9	28	1
M 5	4 52 55	12 16 2	18 1	1♑	28	10	20	11	10	28	1
B 6	4 56 51	13 16 57	0♑48	2	29	10	20	11	10	28	1
E 7	5 0 48	14 17 53	13 19	3	0♏	11	20	12	10	28	1
R 8	5 4 44	15 18 50	25 37	5	2	11	20	12	10	28	1
9	5 8 41	16 19 48	7♒42	6	3	12	21	12	10	28	1
10	5 12 37	17 20 47	19 40	7	4	12	21	12	10	29	1
11	5 16 34	18 21 46	1♓32	9	5	13	21	12	10	29	1
12	5 20 30	19 22 46	13 24	10	6	14	21	12	10	29	1
13	5 24 27	20 23 46	25 20	11	7	14	22	12	10	29	1
14	5 28 24	21 24 47	7♈26	12	9	15	22	12	10	29	1
15	5 32 20	22 25 48	19 45	13	10	15	22	12	10	29	1
16	5 36 17	23 26 50	2♉21	14	11	16	22	12	10	29	1
17	5 40 13	24 27 53	15 19	15	12	16	23	13	10	29	1
18	5 44 10	25 28 56	28 39	15	13	17	23	13	10	29	1
19	5 48 6	26 29 59	12♊21	16	14	18	23	13	10	29	1
20	5 52 3	27 31 3	26 24	16	16	18	23	13	10	29	2
21	5 56 0	28 32 8	10♋45	17	17	19	23	13	11	29	2
22	5 59 56	29 33 13	25 17	17 R	18	19	24	13	11	29	2
23	6 3 53	0♑34 19	9♌55	17	19	20	24	13	11	29	2
24	6 7 49	1 35 26	24 31	16	20	20	24	13	11	29	2
25	6 11 46	2 36 33	9♍ 1	16	22	21	24	13	11	29	2
26	6 15 42	3 37 40	23 20	15	23	21	25	13	11	29	2
27	6 19 39	4 38 49	7♎24	14	24	22	25	14	11	29	2
28	6 23 35	5 39 57	21 14	13	25	23	25	14	11	29	2
29	6 27 32	6 41 7	4♏48	12	26	23	25	14	11	29	2
30	6 31 29	7 42 17	18 8	11	27	24	25	14	11	29	2
31	6 35 25	8 43 27	1♐13	9	29	24	26	14	11	29	2

THE SUN ENTERS THE SIGN OF CAPRICORN ON DEC 22 AT 10:31.

♈ ARIES ♉ TAURUS ♊ GEMINI ♋ CANCER ♌ LEO ♍ VIRGO ♎ LIBRA ♏ SCORPIO ♐ SAGITTARIUS ♑ CAPRICORN ♒ AQUARIUS ♓ PISCES

SIDEREAL SUN MOON MERCURY VENUS MARS JUPITER SATURN URANUS NEPTUNE PLUTO

DAY	TIME	☉	☽	☿	♀	♂	♃	♄	♅	♆	♇
	h m s	° ' "	° '	°	°	°	°	°	°	°	°
J 1	6 39 22	9♑44 38	14♐ 6	8♑R	0♐	25♎	26♐	14♏	11♐	29♐	2♏
A 2	6 43 18	10 45 49	26 47	7	1	25	26	14	11	29	2
N 3	6 47 15	11 47 0	9♑17	6	2	26	26	14	11	29	2
U 4	6 51 11	12 48 12	21 37	4	4	26	27	14	11	29	2
A 5	6 55 8	13 49 23	3♒46	3	5	27	27	14	11	29	2
R 6	6 59 4	14 50 34	15 48	2	6	27	27	14	11	0♑	2
Y 7	7 3 1	15 51 44	27 44	2	7	28	27	14	11	0	2
8	7 6 58	16 52 55	9♓36	1	8	28	27	15	12	0	2
9	7 10 54	17 54 5	21 27	1	10	29	28	15	12	0	2
10	7 14 51	18 55 14	3♈21	0	11	29	28	15	12	0	2
11	7 18 47	19 56 23	15 23	0 D	12	0♏	28	15	12	0	2
12	7 22 44	20 57 32	27 37	0	13	0	28	15	12	0	2
13	7 26 40	21 58 40	10♉ 8	1	14	1	29	15	12	0	2
14	7 30 37	22 59 47	23 1	1	16	1	29	15	12	0	2
15	7 34 33	24 0 54	6♊20	1	17	2	29	15	12	0	2
16	7 38 30	25 2 0	20 5	2	18	2	29	15	12	0	2
17	7 42 27	26 3 6	4♋18	3	19	3	29	15	12	0	2
18	7 46 23	27 4 11	18 56	3	20	3	0♑	15	12	0	2
19	7 50 20	28 5 15	3♌51	4	22	4	0	15	12	0	2
20	7 54 16	29 6 19	18 56	5	23	4	0	15	12	0	2
21	7 58 13	0♒ 7 22	4♍ 1	6	24	5	0	15	12	0	2
22	8 2 9	1 8 25	18 55	7	25	5	1	15	12	0	2
23	8 6 6	2 9 27	3♎33	8	27	6	1	15	12	0	2
24	8 10 2	3 10 29	17 48	9	28	6	1	16	12	0	2
25	8 13 59	4 11 30	1♏40	10	29	7	1	16	12	0	2
26	8 17 56	5 12 31	15 8	11	0♑	7	1	16	12	0	2
27	8 21 52	6 13 31	28 16	12	1	8	2	16	12	0	2
28	8 25 49	7 14 31	11♐ 5	14	3	8	2	16	12	0	2
29	8 29 45	8 15 30	23 40	15	4	9	2	16	13	0	2
30	8 33 42	9 16 29	6♑ 3	16	5	9	2	16	13	0	2
31	8 37 38	10 17 26	18 17	17	6	10	2	16	13	0	2

THE SUN ENTERS THE SIGN OF AQUARIUS ON JAN 20 AT 21:06.

DAY	TIME	☉	☽	☿	♀	♂	♃	♄	♅	♆	♇
	h m s	° ' "	° '	°	°	°	°	°	°	°	°
F 1	8 41 35	11♒18 23	0♒24	19♑	8♑	10♏	3♑	16♏	13♐	0♑	2♏
E 2	8 45 32	12 19 19	12 25	20	9	11	3	16	13	0	2
B 3	8 49 28	13 20 13	24 22	21	10	11	3	16	13	0	2
R 4	8 53 25	14 21 7	6♓15	23	11	12	3	16	13	1	2 R
U 5	8 57 21	15 21 59	18 6	24	13	12	3	16	13	1	2
A 6	9 1 18	16 22 50	29 58	26	14	12	4	16	13	1	2
R 7	9 5 14	17 23 39	11♈52	27	15	13	4	16	13	1	2
Y 8	9 9 11	18 24 27	23 53	28	16	13	4	16	13	1	2
9	9 13 7	19 25 14	6♉ 4	0♒	17	14	4	16	13	1	2
10	9 17 4	20 25 59	18 30	1	19	14	4	16	13	1	2
11	9 21 0	21 26 42	1♊15	3	20	15	5	16	13	1	2
12	9 24 57	22 27 24	14 25	4	21	15	5	16	13	1	2
13	9 28 54	23 28 5	28 3	6	22	16	5	16	13	1	2
14	9 32 50	24 28 43	12♋11	7	24	16	5	16	13	1	2
15	9 36 47	25 29 20	26 48	9	25	16	5	16	13	1	2
16	9 40 43	26 29 56	11♌49	11	26	17	5	16	13	1	2
17	9 44 40	27 30 30	27 5	12	27	17	6	16	13	1	2
18	9 48 36	28 31 2	12♍27	14	29	18	6	16	13	1	2
19	9 52 33	29 31 33	27 42	15	0♒	18	6	16	13	1	2
20	9 56 29	0♓32 2	12♎39	17	1	18	6	16	13	1	2
21	10 0 26	1 32 30	27 11	19	2	19	6	16	13	1	2
22	10 4 23	2 32 57	11♏14	20	3	19	7	16	13	1	2
23	10 8 19	3 33 22	24 49	22	5	19	7	16	13	1	2
24	10 12 16	4 33 46	7♐57	24	6	20	7	16 R	13	1	2
25	10 16 12	5 34 9	20 43	25	7	20	7	16	13	1	2
26	10 20 9	6 34 30	3♑10	27	8	21	7	16	13	1	2
27	10 24 5	7 34 50	15 24	29	10	21	7	16	13	1	2
28	10 28 2	8 35 9	27 29	0♓	11	21	8	16	13	1	2
29	10 31 58	9 35 26	9♒26	2	12	22	8	16	13	1	2

THE SUN ENTERS THE SIGN OF PISCES ON FEB 19 AT 11:17.

DAY	TIME	☉	☽	☿	♀	♂	♃	♄	♅	♆	♇
	h m s	° ' "	° '	°	°	°	°	°	°	°	°
M 1	10 35 55	10♓35 41	21♒20	4♓	13♒	22♏	8♑	16♏R	13♐	1♑	2♏R
A 2	10 39 52	11 35 54	3♓13	6	15	22	8	16	13	1	2
R 3	10 43 48	12 36 6	15 5	8	16	23	8	16	13	1	2
C 4	10 47 45	13 36 15	26 58	9	17	23	8	16	13	1	2
H 5	10 51 41	14 36 23	8♈53	11	18	23	8	16	13	1	2
6	10 55 38	15 36 29	20 52	13	19	23	9	16	13	1	2
7	10 59 34	16 36 33	2♉57	15	21	24	9	16	14	1	2
8	11 3 31	17 36 35	15 11	17	22	24	9	16	14	1	2
9	11 7 27	18 36 34	27 38	19	23	24	9	16	14	1	2
10	11 11 24	19 36 32	10♊21	21	24	25	9	16	14	1	2
11	11 15 21	20 36 27	23 25	23	26	25	9	16	14	1	2
12	11 19 17	21 36 21	6♋54	25	27	25	9	16	14	1	2
13	11 23 14	22 36 12	20 50	27	28	25	10	16	14	1	2
14	11 27 10	23 36 0	5♌14	29	29	26	10	16	14	1	2
15	11 31 7	24 35 47	20 4	1♈	1♓	26	10	16	14	1	2
16	11 35 3	25 35 31	5♍12	3	2	26	10	16	14	1	2
17	11 39 0	26 35 13	20 31	5	3	26	10	16	14	1	2
18	11 42 56	27 34 53	5♎48	7	4	26	10	16	14 R	1	2
19	11 46 53	28 34 31	20 52	9	6	27	10	16	14	1	2
20	11 50 50	29 34 8	5♏34	10	7	27	10	16	14	1	2
21	11 54 46	0♈33 42	19 49	12	8	27	11	16	14	1	2
22	11 58 43	1 33 15	3♐34	14	9	27	11	16	14	1	2
23	12 2 39	2 32 46	16 50	16	10	27	11	16	14	1	2
24	12 6 36	3 32 15	29 41	18	12	27	11	16	14	1	1
25	12 10 32	4 31 42	12♑10	20	13	28	11	16	14	1	1
26	12 14 29	5 31 8	24 23	21	14	28	11	16	14	1	1
27	12 18 25	6 30 32	6♒25	23	15	28	11	16	14	1	1
28	12 22 22	7 29 54	18 20	25	17	28	11	16	14	1	1
29	12 26 19	8 29 14	0♓11	26	18	28	11	15	14	1	1
30	12 30 15	9 28 33	12 2	28	19	28	12	15	14	1	1
31	12 34 12	10 27 49	23 55	29	20	28	12	15	13	1	1

THE SUN ENTERS THE SIGN OF ARIES ON MAR 20 AT 10:25.

DAY	TIME	☉	☽	☿	♀	♂	♃	♄	♅	♆	♇
	h m s	° ' "	° '	°	°	°	°	°	°	°	°
A 1	12 38 8	11♈27 3	5♈52	0♉	22♓	28♏	12♑	15♏R	13♐R	1♑	1♏R
P 2	12 42 5	12 26 15	17 54	1	23	28	12	15	13	1 R	1
R 3	12 46 1	13 25 26	0♉ 2	2	24	28	12	15	13	1	1
I 4	12 49 58	14 24 34	12 18	3	25	28	12	15	13	1	1
L 5	12 53 54	15 23 40	24 43	4	26	28 R	12	15	13	1	1
6	12 57 51	16 22 44	7♊20	5	28	28	12	15	13	1	1
7	13 1 47	17 21 45	20 11	5	29	28	12	15	13	1	1
8	13 5 44	18 20 45	3♋18	6	0♈	28	12	15	13	1	1
9	13 9 41	19 19 42	16 45	6	1	28	12	15	13	1	1
10	13 13 37	20 18 37	0♌34	7	3	28	12	15	13	1	1
11	13 17 34	21 17 29	14 44	7 R	4	28	12	15	13	1	1
12	13 21 30	22 16 19	29 16	7	5	28	12	15	13	1	1
13	13 25 27	23 15 7	14♍ 5	7	6	28	13	15	13	1	1
14	13 29 23	24 13 52	29 4	6	8	28	13	14	13	1	1
15	13 33 20	25 12 35	14♎ 4	6	9	28	13	14	13	1	1
16	13 37 16	26 11 17	28 57	6	10	28	13	14	13	1	1
17	13 41 13	27 9 56	13♏34	5	11	28	13	14	13	1	1
18	13 45 10	28 8 34	27 49	5	13	27	13	14	13	1	1
19	13 49 6	29 7 10	11♐38	4	14	27	13	14	13	1	1
20	13 53 3	0♉ 5 44	25 0	4	15	27	13	14	13	1	1
21	13 56 59	1 4 16	7♑57	3	16	27	13	14	13	1	1
22	14 0 56	2 2 47	20 32	2	17	27	13	14	13	1	1
23	14 4 52	3 1 17	2♒49	2	19	26	13	14	13	1	1
24	14 8 49	3 59 44	14 53	1	20	26	13	14	13	1	1
25	14 12 45	4 58 10	26 48	0	21	26	13	14	13	1	1
26	14 16 42	5 56 34	8♓40	0	22	26	13	14	13	1	1
27	14 20 39	6 54 57	20 32	29♈	24	25	13	14	13	1	1
28	14 24 35	7 53 18	2♈28	28	25	25	13	13	13	1	1
29	14 28 32	8 51 37	14 30	28	26	25	13 R	13	13	1	1
30	14 32 28	9 49 55	26 40	28	27	25	13	13	13	1	0

THE SUN ENTERS THE SIGN OF TAURUS ON APR 19 AT 21:39.

DAY	TIME	☉	☽	☿	♀	♂	♃	♄	♅	♆	♇
	h m s	° ' "	° '	°	°	°	°	°	°	°	°
M 1	14 36 25	10♉48 11	9♉ 0	27♈R	29♈	24♏R	13♑R	13♏R	13♐R	1♑R	0♏R
A 2	14 40 21	11 46 25	21 31	27	0♉	24	13	13	13	1	0
Y 3	14 44 18	12 44 37	4♊14	27	1	24	13	13	13	1	0
4	14 48 14	13 42 48	17 10	26	2	23	13	13	13	1	0
5	14 52 11	14 40 57	0♋18	26 D	3	23	13	13	13	1	0
6	14 56 8	15 39 4	13 41	26	5	23	13	13	13	1	0
7	15 0 4	16 37 9	27 17	26	6	22	13	13	13	1	0
8	15 4 1	17 35 12	11♌ 8	27	7	22	13	13	13	1	0
9	15 7 57	18 33 13	25 14	27	8	22	13	13	13	1	0
10	15 11 54	19 31 12	9♍32	27	10	21	13	13	12	1	0
11	15 15 50	20 29 10	23 59	27	11	21	13	13	12	1	0
12	15 19 47	21 27 5	8♎33	28	12	21	13	12	12	1	0
13	15 23 43	22 24 59	23 7	28	13	20	13	12	12	1	0
14	15 27 40	23 22 51	7♏36	29	15	20	13	12	12	1	0
15	15 31 37	24 20 41	21 53	0♉	16	20	13	12	12	1	0
16	15 35 33	25 18 30	5♐54	0	17	19	13	12	12	1	0
17	15 39 30	26 16 18	19 34	1	18	19	13	12	12	1	0
18	15 43 26	27 14 4	2♑53	2	19	18	12	12	12	1	0
19	15 47 23	28 11 50	15 51	3	21	18	12	12	12	1	0
20	15 51 19	29 9 33	28 28	4	22	18	12	12	12	1	0
21	15 55 16	0♊ 7 16	10♒49	5	23	17	12	12	12	1	0
22	15 59 12	1 4 58	22 56	6	24	17	12	12	12	1	0
23	16 3 9	2 2 39	4♓54	7	26	17	12	12	12	1	0
24	16 7 6	3 0 18	16 47	8	27	16	12	12	12	1	0
25	16 11 2	3 57 57	28 40	9	28	16	12	12	12	1	0
26	16 14 59	4 55 34	10♈38	11	29	16	12	11	12	1	0
27	16 18 55	5 53 11	22 44	12	0♊	15	12	11	12	1	0
28	16 22 52	6 50 46	5♉ 1	13	2	15	12	11	12	1	0
29	16 26 48	7 48 21	17 33	15	3	15	12	11	12	1	0
30	16 30 45	8 45 55	0♊19	16	4	15	12	11	12	1	0
31	16 34 41	9 43 28	13 22	17	5	14	11	11	12	1	0

THE SUN ENTERS THE SIGN OF GEMINI ON MAY 20 AT 20:58.

DAY	TIME	☉	☽	☿	♀	♂	♃	♄	♅	♆	♇
	h m s	° ' "	° '	°	°	°	°	°	°	°	°
J 1	16 38 38	10♊40 59	26♊41	19♉	7♊	14♏R	11♑R	11♏R	12♐R	1♑R	0♏R
U 2	16 42 35	11 38 30	10♋15	20	8	14	11	11	12	1	0
N 3	16 46 31	12 35 59	24 1	22	9	14	11	11	12	1	0
E 4	16 50 28	13 33 27	7♌58	24	10	13	11	11	11	1	0
5	16 54 24	14 30 54	22 3	25	12	13	11	11	11	0	0
6	16 58 21	15 28 20	6♍14	27	13	13	11	11	11	0	0
7	17 2 17	16 25 44	20 28	29	14	13	11	11	11	0	0
8	17 6 14	17 23 7	4♎42	1♊	15	13	11	11	11	0	0
9	17 10 11	18 20 29	18 55	2	16	12	11	11	11	0	0
10	17 14 7	19 17 50	3♏ 3	4	18	12	10	11	11	0	0
11	17 18 4	20 15 11	17 3	6	19	12	10	11	11	0	0
12	17 22 0	21 12 30	0♐53	8	20	12	10	10	11	0	0
13	17 25 57	22 9 48	14 31	10	21	12	10	10	11	0	0
14	17 29 53	23 7 6	27 54	12	23	12	10	10	11	0	29♎
15	17 33 50	24 4 23	11♑ 1	14	24	12	10	10	11	0	29
16	17 37 46	25 1 40	23 51	16	25	12	10	10	11	0	29
17	17 41 43	25 58 56	6♒25	19	26	12	10	10	11	0	29
18	17 45 40	26 56 12	18 44	21	28	12	10	10	11	0	29
19	17 49 36	27 53 27	0♓51	23	29	12 D	9	10	11	0	29
20	17 53 33	28 50 42	12 49	25	0♋	12	9	10	11	0	29
21	17 57 29	29 47 57	24 43	27	1	12	9	10	11	0	29
22	18 1 26	0♋45 11	6♈36	29	2	12	9	10	11	0	29
23	18 5 22	1 42 26	18 34	2♋	4	12	9	10	11	0	29
24	18 9 19	2 39 40	0♉41	4	5	12	9	10	11	0	29
25	18 13 15	3 36 55	13 2	6	6	12	9	10	11	0	29
26	18 17 12	4 34 9	25 40	8	7	12	9	10	11	0	29
27	18 21 9	5 31 23	8♊39	10	9	12	8	10	11	0	29
28	18 25 5	6 28 37	21 58	12	10	12	8	10	11	0	29
29	18 29 2	7 25 51	5♋39	15	11	12	8	10	11	0	29
30	18 32 58	8 23 5	19 38	17	12	12	8	10	10	0	29

THE SUN ENTERS THE SIGN OF CANCER ON JUN 21 AT 05:03.

♈ ARIES ♉ TAURUS ♊ GEMINI ♋ CANCER ♌ LEO ♍ VIRGO ♎ LIBRA ♏ SCORPIO ♐ SAGITTARIUS ♑ CAPRICORN ♒ AQUARIUS ♓ PISCES

SIDEREAL SUN MOON MERCURY VENUS MARS JUPITER SATURN URANUS NEPTUNE PLUTO

DAY	TIME	☉	☽	☿	♀	♂	♃	♄	♅	♆	♇
	h m s	° ' "	° '	°	°	°	°	°	°	°	°
J 1	18 36 55	9♋20 19	3♌52	19♋	13♋	13♏	8♑R	10♏R	10♐R	0♑R	29♎R
U 2	18 40 51	10 17 32	18 16	21	15	13	8	10	10	0	29
L 3	18 44 48	11 14 45	2♍44	23	16	13	8	10	10	0	29
Y 4	18 48 44	12 11 58	17 10	25	17	13	8	10	10	0	29
5	18 52 41	13 9 10	1♎31	27	18	13	7	10	10	0	29
6	18 56 38	14 6 22	15 42	29	20	13	7	10	10	0	29
7	19 0 34	15 3 34	29 43	0♌	21	14	7	10	10	0	29
8	19 4 31	16 0 46	13♏32	2	22	14	7	10	10	0	29
9	19 8 27	16 57 57	27 9	4	23	14	7	10	10	0	29 D
10	19 12 24	17 55 9	10♐34	6	25	14	7	10	10	0	29
11	19 16 20	18 52 20	23 48	8	26	15	7	10	10	0	29
12	19 20 17	19 49 32	6♑49	9	27	15	7	10	10	0	29
13	19 24 13	20 46 44	19 38	11	28	15	6	10 D	10	29♐	29
14	19 28 10	21 43 56	2♒15	13	29	15	6	10	10	29	29
15	19 32 7	22 41 8	14 39	14	1♌	16	6	10	10	29	29
16	19 36 3	23 38 21	26 53	16	2	16	6	10	10	29	29
17	19 40 0	24 35 34	8♓56	17	3	16	6	10	10	29	29
18	19 43 56	25 32 48	20 53	19	4	17	6	10	10	29	29
19	19 47 53	26 30 3	2♈45	20	6	17	6	10	10	29	29
20	19 51 49	27 27 18	14 37	22	7	17	6	10	10	29	29
21	19 55 46	28 24 34	26 33	23	8	18	5	10	10	29	29
22	19 59 42	29 21 50	8♉39	25	9	18	5	10	10	29	29
23	20 3 39	0♌19 8	20 59	26	11	18	5	10	10	29	29
24	20 7 36	1 16 26	3♊38	27	12	19	5	10	10	29	29
25	20 11 32	2 13 46	16 40	28	13	19	5	10	10	29	29
26	20 15 29	3 11 6	0♋ 9	0♍	14	19	5	10	10	29	29
27	20 19 25	4 8 27	14 3	1	15	20	5	10	10	29	29
28	20 23 22	5 5 49	28 22	2	17	20	5	10	10	29	29
29	20 27 18	6 3 12	13♌ 0	3	18	21	5	10	10	29	29
30	20 31 15	7 0 35	27 50	4	19	21	5	10	10	29	29
31	20 35 12	7 57 59	12♍43	5	20	21	4	10	10	29	29

THE SUN ENTERS THE SIGN OF LEO ON JUL 22 AT 15:59.

DAY	TIME	☉	☽	☿	♀	♂	♃	♄	♅	♆	♇
	h m s	° ' "	° '	°	°	°	°	°	°	°	°
A 1	20 39 8	8♌55 23	27♍31	6♍	22♌	22♏	4♑R	10♏	10♐R	29♐R	29♎
U 2	20 43 5	9 52 49	12♎ 6	7	23	22	4	10	10	29	29
G 3	20 47 1	10 50 15	26 25	8	24	23	4	10	10	29	29
U 4	20 50 58	11 47 41	10♏25	9	25	23	4	10	10	29	29
S 5	20 54 54	12 45 8	24 6	10	27	24	4	10	10	29	0♏
T 6	20 58 51	13 42 36	7♐29	10	28	24	4	10	10	29	0
7	21 2 47	14 40 5	20 37	11	29	25	4	10	10	29	0
8	21 6 44	15 37 34	3♑31	11	0♍	25	4	10	10	29	0
9	21 10 41	16 35 5	16 13	12	1	26	4	10	10	29	0
10	21 14 37	17 32 36	28 44	12	3	26	4	10	10	29	0
11	21 18 34	18 30 8	11♒ 6	13	4	27	4	10	10	29	0
12	21 22 30	19 27 42	23 19	13	5	27	4	10	10	29	0
13	21 26 27	20 25 16	5♓25	13	6	28	4	10	10	29	0
14	21 30 23	21 22 52	17 23	13 R	8	28	4	11	10	29	0
15	21 34 20	22 20 29	29 16	13	9	29	3	11	10	29	0
16	21 38 16	23 18 7	11♈ 6	13	10	29	3	11	10	29	0
17	21 42 13	24 15 47	22 57	13	11	0♐	3	11	10	29	0
18	21 46 9	25 13 29	4♉52	13	13	0	3	11	10 D	29	0
19	21 50 6	26 11 12	16 55	13	14	1	3	11	10	29	0
20	21 54 3	27 8 57	29 12	12	15	1	3	11	10	29	0
21	21 57 59	28 6 43	11♊48	12	16	2	3	11	10	29	0
22	22 1 56	29 4 32	24 49	11	17	2	3	11	10	29	0
23	22 5 52	0♍ 2 22	8♋16	10	19	3	3	11	10	29	0
24	22 9 49	1 0 13	22 14	10	20	3	3	11	10	29	0
25	22 13 45	1 58 6	6♌40	9	21	4	3	11	10	29	0
26	22 17 42	2 56 1	21 30	8	22	4	3	11	10	29	0
27	22 21 39	3 53 58	6♍36	7	24	5	3	11	10	29	0
28	22 25 35	4 51 55	21 48	6	25	6	3	11	10	29	0
29	22 29 32	5 49 55	6♎56	5	26	6	3 D	11	10	29	0
30	22 33 28	6 47 55	21 50	4	27	7	3	11	10	29	0
31	22 37 25	7 45 58	6♏23	3	29	7	3	12	10	29	0

THE SUN ENTERS THE SIGN OF VIRGO ON AUG 22 AT 23:01.

DAY	TIME	☉	☽	☿	♀	♂	♃	♄	♅	♆	♇
	h m s	° ' "	° '	°	°	°	°	°	°	°	°
S 1	22 41 21	8♍44 1	20♏31	3♍R	0♎	8♐	3♑	12♏	10♐	29♐R	0♏
E 2	22 45 18	9 42 6	4♐14	2	1	9	3	12	10	29	0
P 3	22 49 14	10 40 12	17 35	1	2	9	3	12	10	29	0
T 4	22 53 11	11 38 20	0♑35	1	3	10	3	12	10	29	0
E 5	22 57 7	12 36 29	13 17	0	5	10	3	12	10	29	0
M 6	23 1 4	13 34 40	25 46	0	6	11	3	12	10	29	0
B 7	23 5 1	14 32 52	8♒ 5	0 D	7	12	3	12	10	29	0
E 8	23 8 57	15 31 6	20 15	0	8	12	3	12	10	29	0
R 9	23 12 54	16 29 21	2♓18	0	10	13	3	12	10	29 D	0
10	23 16 50	17 27 38	14 15	1	11	13	3	12	10	29	0
11	23 20 47	18 25 57	26 9	1	12	14	3	12	10	29	0
12	23 24 43	19 24 18	8♈ 0	2	13	15	3	13	10	29	0
13	23 28 40	20 22 41	19 50	3	14	15	3	13	10	29	0
14	23 32 36	21 21 5	1♉42	3	16	16	3	13	10	29	1
15	23 36 33	22 19 32	13 38	4	17	17	3	13	10	29	1
16	23 40 30	23 18 1	25 43	6	18	17	4	13	10	29	1
17	23 44 26	24 16 32	7♊59	7	19	18	4	13	10	29	1
18	23 48 23	25 15 5	20 33	8	21	18	4	13	10	29	1
19	23 52 19	26 13 40	3♋29	10	22	19	4	13	10	29	1
20	23 56 16	27 12 18	16 51	11	23	20	4	13	10	29	1
21	0 0 12	28 10 58	0♌41	13	24	20	4	13	10	29	1
22	0 4 9	29 9 40	15 1	14	26	21	4	13	10	29	1
23	0 8 5	0♎ 8 24	29 48	16	27	22	4	14	10	29	1
24	0 12 2	1 7 10	14♍54	18	28	22	4	14	10	29	1
25	0 15 59	2 5 59	0♎12	20	29	23	4	14	10	29	1
26	0 19 55	3 4 49	15 29	21	0♏	24	4	14	10	29	1
27	0 23 52	4 3 41	0♏34	23	2	24	4	14	10	29	1
28	0 27 48	5 2 35	15 20	25	3	25	4	14	10	29	1
29	0 31 45	6 1 32	29 41	27	4	26	5	14	10	29	1
30	0 35 41	7 0 29	13♐34	29	5	26	5	14	10	29	1

THE SUN ENTERS THE SIGN OF LIBRA ON SEP 22 AT 20:34.

DAY	TIME	☉	☽	☿	♀	♂	♃	♄	♅	♆	♇
	h m s	° ' "	° '	°	°	°	°	°	°	°	°
O 1	0 39 38	7♎59 29	27♐ 0	0♎	7♏	27♐	5♑	14♏	10♐	29♐	1♏
C 2	0 43 34	8 58 30	10♑ 1	2	8	28	5	14	10	29	1
T 3	0 47 31	9 57 34	22 42	4	9	28	5	15	10	29	1
O 4	0 51 28	10 56 38	5♒ 6	6	10	29	5	15	10	29	1
B 5	0 55 24	11 55 45	17 18	8	11	0♑	5	15	10	29	1
E 6	0 59 21	12 54 53	29 20	9	13	1	5	15	11	29	1
R 7	1 3 17	13 54 4	11♓16	11	14	1	5	15	11	29	1
8	1 7 14	14 53 16	23 9	13	15	2	5	15	11	29	1
9	1 11 10	15 52 30	5♈ 1	15	16	3	6	15	11	29	1
10	1 15 7	16 51 46	16 52	16	18	3	6	15	11	29	1
11	1 19 3	17 51 4	28 46	18	19	4	6	15	11	29	1
12	1 23 0	18 50 24	10♉43	20	20	5	6	16	11	29	2
13	1 26 57	19 49 47	22 47	21	21	5	6	16	11	29	2
14	1 30 53	20 49 11	4♊59	23	22	6	6	16	11	29	2
15	1 34 50	21 48 38	17 22	25	24	7	6	16	11	29	2
16	1 38 46	22 48 8	0♋ 0	26	25	8	6	16	11	29	2
17	1 42 43	23 47 39	12 56	28	26	8	7	16	11	29	2
18	1 46 39	24 47 13	26 13	0♏	27	9	7	16	11	29	2
19	1 50 36	25 46 49	9♌55	1	28	10	7	16	11	29	2
20	1 54 32	26 46 28	24 2	3	0♐	10	7	16	11	29	2
21	1 58 29	27 46 8	8♍33	5	1	11	7	17	11	29	2
22	2 2 26	28 45 51	23 24	6	2	12	7	17	11	29	2
23	2 6 22	29 45 36	8♎28	8	3	13	7	17	11	29	2
24	2 10 19	0♏45 23	23 37	9	5	13	8	17	11	29	2
25	2 14 15	1 45 12	8♏40	11	6	14	8	17	11	29	2
26	2 18 12	2 45 4	23 29	13	7	15	8	17	11	29	2
27	2 22 8	3 44 57	7♐57	14	8	15	8	17	11	29	2
28	2 26 5	4 44 52	21 58	16	9	16	8	17	12	29	2
29	2 30 1	5 44 48	5♑33	17	11	17	8	17	12	29	2
30	2 33 58	6 44 47	18 42	19	12	18	9	18	12	29	2
31	2 37 55	7 44 46	1♒27	20	13	18	9	18	12	29	2

THE SUN ENTERS THE SIGN OF SCORPIO ON OCT 23 AT 05:47.

DAY	TIME	☉	☽	☿	♀	♂	♃	♄	♅	♆	♇
	h m s	° ' "	° '	°	°	°	°	°	°	°	°
N 1	2 41 51	8♏44 48	13♒53	22♏	14♐	19♑	9♑	18♏	12♐	29♐	2♏
O 2	2 45 48	9 44 51	26 4	23	16	20	9	18	12	29	2
V 3	2 49 44	10 44 56	8♓ 4	25	17	21	9	18	12	29	2
E 4	2 53 41	11 45 2	19 57	26	18	21	9	18	12	29	2
M 5	2 57 37	12 45 9	1♈48	28	19	22	10	18	12	29	2
B 6	3 1 34	13 45 19	13 39	29	20	23	10	18	12	0♑	3
E 7	3 5 30	14 45 30	25 34	1♐	22	23	10	19	12	0	3
R 8	3 9 27	15 45 43	7♉34	2	23	24	10	19	12	0	3
9	3 13 23	16 45 58	19 41	4	24	25	10	19	12	0	3
10	3 17 20	17 46 14	1♊58	5	25	26	10	19	12	0	3
11	3 21 17	18 46 32	14 25	7	26	26	11	19	12	0	3
12	3 25 13	19 46 52	27 3	8	28	27	11	19	12	0	3
13	3 29 10	20 47 14	9♋55	9	29	28	11	19	12	0	3
14	3 33 6	21 47 38	23 2	11	0♑	29	11	19	12	0	3
15	3 37 3	22 48 4	6♌24	12	1	29	11	20	13	0	3
16	3 40 59	23 48 31	20 4	13	2	0♒	12	20	13	0	3
17	3 44 56	24 49 1	4♍ 1	15	4	1	12	20	13	0	3
18	3 48 53	25 49 32	18 15	16	5	2	12	20	13	0	3
19	3 52 49	26 50 5	2♎44	17	6	2	12	20	13	0	3
20	3 56 46	27 50 40	17 23	19	7	3	12	20	13	0	3
21	4 0 42	28 51 17	2♏ 8	20	8	4	12	20	13	0	3
22	4 4 39	29 51 55	16 52	21	10	5	13	20	13	0	3
23	4 8 35	0♐52 35	1♐28	22	11	5	13	20	13	0	3
24	4 12 32	1 53 16	15 49	23	12	6	13	21	13	0	3
25	4 16 28	2 53 59	29 50	25	13	7	13	21	13	0	3
26	4 20 25	3 54 43	13♑28	26	14	8	14	21	13	0	3
27	4 24 22	4 55 28	26 42	27	16	8	14	21	13	0	3
28	4 28 18	5 56 14	9♒32	27	17	9	14	21	13	0	3
29	4 32 15	6 57 1	22 3	28	18	10	14	21	13	0	3
30	4 36 11	7 57 49	4♓16	29	19	11	14	21	13	0	3

THE SUN ENTERS THE SIGN OF SAGITTARIUS ON NOV 22 AT 03:12.

DAY	TIME	☉	☽	☿	♀	♂	♃	♄	♅	♆	♇
	h m s	° ' "	° '	°	°	°	°	°	°	°	°
D 1	4 40 8	8♐58 38	16♓17	0♑	20♑	11♒	15♑	21♏	14♐	0♑	3♏
E 2	4 44 4	9 59 28	28 10	0	22	12	15	22	14	0	4
C 3	4 48 1	11 0 18	10♈ 0	1	23	13	15	22	14	0	4
E 4	4 51 57	12 1 10	21 52	1 R	24	14	15	22	14	0	4
M 5	4 55 54	13 2 2	3♉49	1	25	15	15	22	14	0	4
B 6	4 59 51	14 2 56	15 56	1	26	15	16	22	14	1	4
E 7	5 3 47	15 3 50	28 14	0	27	16	16	22	14	1	4
R 8	5 7 44	16 4 45	10♊46	0	29	17	16	22	14	1	4
9	5 11 40	17 5 42	23 33	29♐	0♒	18	16	22	14	1	4
10	5 15 37	18 6 39	6♋34	28	1	18	16	22	14	1	4
11	5 19 33	19 7 37	19 50	27	2	19	17	23	14	1	4
12	5 23 30	20 8 36	3♌18	26	3	20	17	23	14	1	4
13	5 27 26	21 9 37	16 58	25	5	21	17	23	14	1	4
14	5 31 23	22 10 38	0♍49	24	6	21	17	23	14	1	4
15	5 35 20	23 11 40	14 48	22	7	22	18	23	14	1	4
16	5 39 16	24 12 43	28 54	21	8	23	18	23	14	1	4
17	5 43 13	25 13 47	13♎ 5	20	9	24	18	23	14	1	4
18	5 47 9	26 14 52	27 20	18	10	24	18	23	15	1	4
19	5 51 6	27 15 59	11♏37	17	12	25	18	23	15	1	4
20	5 55 2	28 17 6	25 52	16	13	26	19	24	15	1	4
21	5 58 59	29 18 13	10♐ 2	16	14	27	19	24	15	1	4
22	6 2 55	0♑19 21	24 1	15	15	27	19	24	15	1	4
23	6 6 52	1 20 30	7♑48	15	16	28	19	24	15	1	4
24	6 10 49	2 21 39	21 17	15 D	17	29	20	24	15	1	4
25	6 14 45	3 22 49	4♒28	15	18	0♓	20	24	15	1	4
26	6 18 42	4 23 59	17 18	15	20	1	20	24	15	1	4
27	6 22 38	5 25 8	29 50	15	21	1	20	24	15	1	4
28	6 26 35	6 26 18	12♓ 5	15	22	2	21	24	15	1	4
29	6 30 31	7 27 27	24 7	16	23	3	21	24	15	1	4
30	6 34 28	8 28 37	6♈ 1	16	24	4	21	25	15	1	4
31	6 38 25	9 29 46	17 50	17	25	4	21	25	15	1	4

THE SUN ENTERS THE SIGN OF CAPRICORN ON DEC 21 AT 16:24.

♈ ARIES ♉ TAURUS ♊ GEMINI ♋ CANCER ♌ LEO ♍ VIRGO ♎ LIBRA ♏ SCORPIO ♐ SAGITTARIUS ♑ CAPRICORN ♒ AQUARIUS ♓ PISCES

1985

290 *Appendix X*

SIDEREAL SUN MOON MERCURY VENUS MARS JUPITER SATURN URANUS NEPTUNE PLUTO

DAY	TIME	☉	☽	☿	♀	♂	♃	♄	♅	♆	♇
	h m s	° ' "	° '	°	°	°	°	°	°	°	°
J 1	6 42 21	10♑30 56	29♈42	18♐	26♒	5♓	21♑	25♏	15♐	1♑	4♏
A 2	6 46 18	11 32 5	11♉40	19	27	6	22	25	15	2	4
N 3	6 50 14	12 33 14	23 49	20	29	7	22	25	15	2	4
U 4	6 54 11	13 34 23	6♊14	21	0♓	7	22	25	16	2	4
A 5	6 58 7	14 35 32	18 58	22	1	8	22	25	16	2	4
R 6	7 2 4	15 36 40	2♋ 2	23	2	9	23	25	16	2	4
Y 7	7 6 0	16 37 49	15 26	24	3	10	23	25	16	2	4
8	7 9 57	17 38 57	29 9	25	4	10	23	25	16	2	4
9	7 13 54	18 40 5	13♌ 6	26	5	11	23	25	16	2	5
10	7 17 50	19 41 13	27 14	28	6	12	24	26	16	2	5
11	7 21 47	20 42 20	11♍28	29	7	13	24	26	16	2	5
12	7 25 43	21 43 28	25 43	0♑	8	14	24	26	16	2	5
13	7 29 40	22 44 36	9♎55	2	10	14	24	26	16	2	5
14	7 33 36	23 45 43	24 3	3	11	15	24	26	16	2	5
15	7 37 33	24 46 51	8♏ 6	4	12	16	25	26	16	2	5
16	7 41 29	25 47 58	22 2	6	13	17	25	26	16	2	5
17	7 45 26	26 49 5	5♐51	7	14	17	25	26	16	2	5
18	7 49 23	27 50 12	19 33	8	15	18	25	26	16	2	5
19	7 53 19	28 51 19	3♑ 6	10	16	19	26	26	16	2	5
20	7 57 16	29 52 25	16 28	11	17	20	26	26	16	2	5
21	8 1 12	0♒53 30	29 39	13	18	20	26	26	16	2	5
22	8 5 9	1 54 35	12♒35	14	19	21	26	26	16	2	5
23	8 9 5	2 55 39	25 17	16	20	22	27	27	17	2	5
24	8 13 2	3 56 42	7♓43	17	21	23	27	27	17	2	5
25	8 16 58	4 57 44	19 56	19	22	23	27	27	17	2	5
26	8 20 55	5 58 45	1♈56	20	23	24	27	27	17	2	5
27	8 24 52	6 59 46	13 49	22	24	25	28	27	17	2	5
28	8 28 48	8 0 44	25 37	23	25	26	28	27	17	2	5
29	8 32 45	9 1 42	7♉27	25	26	26	28	27	17	2	5
30	8 36 41	10 2 39	19 23	26	27	27	28	27	17	3	5
31	8 40 38	11 3 34	1♊31	28	28	28	28	27	17	3	5

THE SUN ENTERS THE SIGN OF AQUARIUS ON JAN 20 AT 02:59.

DAY	TIME	☉	☽	☿	♀	♂	♃	♄	♅	♆	♇
	h m s	° ' "	° '	°	°	°	°	°	°	°	°
F 1	8 44 34	12♒ 4 28	13♊57	29♑	29♓	29♓	29♑	27♏	17♐	3♑	5♏
E 2	8 48 31	13 5 21	26 44	1♒	0⊙	29	29	27	17	3	5
B 3	8 52 27	14 6 13	9♋57	3	1♈	0♈	29	27	17	3	5
R 4	8 56 24	15 7 3	23 35	4	2	1	29	27	17	3	5
U 5	9 0 21	16 7 52	7♌38	6	2	2	0♒	27	17	3	5 R
A 6	9 4 17	17 8 40	22 0	8	3	2	0	27	17	3	5
R 7	9 8 14	18 9 26	6♍37	9	4	3	0	27	17	3	5
Y 8	9 12 10	19 10 12	21 19	11	5	4	0	27	17	3	5
9	9 16 7	20 10 56	5♎59	13	6	5	1	28	17	3	5
10	9 20 3	21 11 39	20 31	14	7	5	1	28	17	3	5
11	9 24 0	22 12 21	4♏51	16	8	6	1	28	17	3	5
12	9 27 56	23 13 2	18 56	18	8	7	1	28	17	3	5
13	9 31 53	24 13 42	2♐46	19	9	8	1	28	17	3	5
14	9 35 50	25 14 21	16 22	21	10	8	2	28	17	3	5
15	9 39 46	26 14 59	29 45	23	11	9	2	28	17	3	5
16	9 43 43	27 15 36	12♑55	25	11	10	2	28	17	3	5
17	9 47 39	28 16 11	25 55	26	12	11	2	28	17	3	5
18	9 51 36	29 16 45	8♒43	28	13	11	3	28	18	3	5
19	9 55 32	0♓17 18	21 21	0♓	14	12	3	28	18	3	5
20	9 59 29	1 17 49	3♓48	2	14	13	3	28	18	3	5
21	10 3 25	2 18 18	16 3	4	15	14	3	28	18	3	5
22	10 7 22	3 18 45	28 8	6	16	14	3	28	18	3	5
23	10 11 19	4 19 11	10♈ 5	7	16	15	4	28	18	3	5
24	10 15 15	5 19 35	21 55	9	17	16	4	28	18	3	5
25	10 19 12	6 19 57	3♉42	11	17	17	4	28	18	3	5
26	10 23 8	7 20 18	15 30	13	18	17	4	28	18	3	5
27	10 27 5	8 20 36	27 24	15	18	18	5	28	18	3	5
28	10 31 1	9 20 52	9♊30	17	19	19	5	28	18	3	5

THE SUN ENTERS THE SIGN OF PISCES ON FEB 18 AT 17:08.

DAY	TIME	☉	☽	☿	♀	♂	♃	♄	♅	♆	♇
	h m s	° ' "	° '	°	°	°	°	°	°	°	°
M 1	10 34 58	10♓21 7	21♊52	19♓	19♈	20♈	5♒	28♏	18♐	3♑	5♏R
A 2	10 38 54	11 21 19	4♋37	21	20	20	5	28	18	3	5
R 3	10 42 51	12 21 29	17 48	23	20	21	5	28	18	3	5
C 4	10 46 48	13 21 37	1♌27	24	20	22	6	28	18	3	5
H 5	10 50 44	14 21 43	15 36	26	21	23	6	28	18	3	5
6	10 54 41	15 21 47	0♍10	28	21	23	6	28	18	3	5
7	10 58 37	16 21 49	15 4	0⊙	21	24	6	28 R	18	3	5
8	11 2 34	17 21 50	0♎ 7	2♈	22	25	6	28	18	3	4
9	11 6 30	18 21 48	15 12	3	22	25	7	28	18	3	4
10	11 10 27	19 21 45	0♏ 7	5	22	26	7	28	18	3	4
11	11 14 23	20 21 39	14 47	7	22	27	7	28	18	3	4
12	11 18 20	21 21 33	29 7	8	22	28	7	28	18	3	4
13	11 22 17	22 21 24	13♐ 5	10	22 R	28	7	28	18	3	4
14	11 26 13	23 21 15	26 42	11	22	29	8	28	18	3	4
15	11 30 10	24 21 3	9♑58	12	22	0♉	8	28	18	3	4
16	11 34 6	25 20 50	22 58	14	22	1	8	28	18	4	4
17	11 38 3	26 20 34	5♒42	15	22	1	8	28	18	4	4
18	11 41 59	27 20 18	18 14	16	22	2	8	28	18	4	4
19	11 45 56	28 19 59	0♓35	16	22	3	9	28	18	4	4
20	11 49 52	29 19 38	12 47	17	21	3	9	28	18	4	4
21	11 53 49	0♈19 15	24 50	18	21	4	9	28	18	4	4
22	11 57 46	1 18 51	6♈47	18	21	5	9	28	18 R	4	4
23	12 1 42	2 18 24	18 38	18	21	6	9	28	18	4	4
24	12 5 39	3 17 55	0♉26	19 R	20	6	10	28	18	4	4
25	12 9 35	4 17 24	12 13	19	20	7	10	28	18	4	4
26	12 13 32	5 16 51	24 2	19	19	8	10	28	18	4	4
27	12 17 28	6 16 16	5♊57	18	19	9	10	28	18	4	4
28	12 21 25	7 15 38	18 3	18	18	9	10	28	18	4	4
29	12 25 21	8 14 59	0♋24	18	18	10	10	28	18	4	4
30	12 29 18	9 14 16	13 5	17	17	11	11	28	18	4	4
31	12 33 15	10 13 32	26 10	16	17	11	11	28	18	4	4

THE SUN ENTERS THE SIGN OF ARIES ON MAR 20 AT 16:15.

SIDEREAL SUN MOON MERCURY VENUS MARS JUPITER SATURN URANUS NEPTUNE PLUTO

DAY	TIME	☉	☽	☿	♀	♂	♃	♄	♅	♆	♇
	h m s	° ' "	° '	°	°	°	°	°	°	°	°
A 1	12 37 11	11♈12 45	9♌43	16♈R	16♈R	12♉	11♒	28♏R	18♐R	4♑	4♏R
P 2	12 41 8	12 11 56	23 45	15	15	13	11	28	18	4	4
R 3	12 45 4	13 11 4	8♍15	14	15	14	11	28	18	4	4
I 4	12 49 1	14 10 11	23 8	13	14	14	11	28	18	4	4
L 5	12 52 57	15 9 15	8♎17	13	13	15	12	27	18	4 R	4
6	12 56 54	16 8 17	23 32	12	13	16	12	27	18	4	4
7	13 0 50	17 7 17	8♏43	11	12	16	12	27	18	4	4
8	13 4 47	18 6 15	23 41	10	12	17	12	27	18	4	4
9	13 8 43	19 5 11	8♐18	10	11	18	12	27	18	4	4
10	13 12 40	20 4 6	22 30	9	10	19	12	27	18	4	4
11	13 16 37	21 2 59	6♑17	8	10	19	13	27	18	4	4
12	13 20 33	22 1 50	19 39	8	9	20	13	27	18	4	4
13	13 24 30	23 0 39	2♒38	8	9	21	13	27	18	4	4
14	13 28 26	23 59 27	15 18	7	8	21	13	27	18	4	4
15	13 32 23	24 58 13	27 41	7	8	22	13	27	18	4	4
16	13 36 19	25 56 57	9♓52	7	8	23	13	27	18	4	4
17	13 40 16	26 55 39	21 54	7 D	7	23	13	27	18	4	4
18	13 44 12	27 54 20	3♈48	7	7	24	14	27	18	4	4
19	13 48 9	28 52 58	15 38	7	7	25	14	27	18	4	3
20	13 52 6	29 51 35	27 26	7	7	26	14	27	18	4	3
21	13 56 2	0♉50 10	9♉14	7	6	26	14	27	18	4	3
22	13 59 59	1 48 43	21 4	8	6	27	14	27	18	4	3
23	14 3 55	2 47 14	2♊58	8	6	28	14	26	18	4	3
24	14 7 52	3 45 43	15 0	9	6	28	14	26	18	4	3
25	14 11 48	4 44 10	27 12	9	6 D	29	14	26	18	4	3
26	14 15 45	5 42 35	9♋37	10	6	0♊	15	26	18	4	3
27	14 19 41	6 40 58	22 20	10	6	0	15	26	17	3	3
28	14 23 38	7 39 19	5♌23	11	6	1	15	26	17	3	3
29	14 27 35	8 37 38	18 49	12	6	2	15	26	17	3	3
30	14 31 31	9 35 54	2♍41	13	6	3	15	26	17	3	3

THE SUN ENTERS THE SIGN OF TAURUS ON APR 20 AT 03:26.

DAY	TIME	☉	☽	☿	♀	♂	♃	♄	♅	♆	♇
	h m s	° ' "	° '	°	°	°	°	°	°	°	°
M 1	14 35 28	10♉34 8	16♍57	14♈	7♈	3♊	15♒	26♏R	17♐R	3♑R	3♏R
A 2	14 39 24	11 32 21	1♎37	15	7	4	15	26	17	3	3
Y 3	14 43 21	12 30 31	16 34	16	7	5	15	26	17	3	3
4	14 47 17	13 28 40	1♏42	17	7	5	15	26	17	3	3
5	14 51 14	14 26 47	16 52	18	8	6	15	26	17	3	3
6	14 55 10	15 24 52	1♐54	19	8	7	16	26	17	3	3
7	14 59 7	16 22 56	16 40	20	9	7	16	25	17	3	3
8	15 3 4	17 20 58	1♑ 4	22	9	8	16	25	17	3	3
9	15 7 0	18 18 59	15 1	23	9	9	16	25	17	3	3
10	15 10 57	19 16 58	28 32	24	10	9	16	25	17	3	3
11	15 14 53	20 14 56	11♒37	26	10	10	16	25	17	3	3
12	15 18 50	21 12 53	24 19	27	11	11	16	25	17	3	3
13	15 22 46	22 10 48	6♓42	28	11	11	16	25	17	3	3
14	15 26 43	23 8 43	18 50	0♉	12	12	16	25	17	3	3
15	15 30 39	24 6 35	0♈46	1	13	13	16	25	17	3	3
16	15 34 36	25 4 27	12 37	3	13	14	16	25	17	3	3
17	15 38 33	26 2 17	24 24	5	14	14	16	25	17	3	3
18	15 42 29	27 0 6	6♉12	6	15	15	16	25	17	3	3
19	15 46 26	27 57 54	18 3	8	15	16	17	25	17	3	3
20	15 50 22	28 55 41	29 59	9	16	16	17	25	17	3	3
21	15 54 19	29 53 26	12♊ 3	11	17	17	17	24	17	3	3
22	15 58 15	0♊51 10	24 17	13	17	18	17	24	17	3	3
23	16 2 12	1 48 52	6♋42	15	18	18	17	24	17	3	3
24	16 6 9	2 46 33	19 20	17	19	19	17	24	17	3	3
25	16 10 5	3 44 12	2♌13	18	20	20	17	24	17	3	3
26	16 14 2	4 41 50	15 21	20	20	20	17	24	16	3	3
27	16 17 58	5 39 27	28 48	22	21	21	17	24	16	3	2
28	16 21 55	6 37 2	12♍33	24	22	22	17	24	16	3	2
29	16 25 51	7 34 35	26 37	26	23	22	17	24	16	3	2
30	16 29 48	8 32 7	10♎59	28	24	23	17	24	16	3	2
31	16 33 44	9 29 38	25 37	0♊	24	24	17	24	16	3	2

THE SUN ENTERS THE SIGN OF GEMINI ON MAY 21 AT 02:43.

DAY	TIME	☉	☽	☿	♀	♂	♃	♄	♅	♆	♇
	h m s	° ' "	° '	°	°	°	°	°	°	°	°
J 1	16 37 41	10♊27 7	10♏25	2♊	25♈	24♊	17♒	24♏R	16♐R	3♑R	2♏R
U 2	16 41 38	11 24 35	25 18	5	26	25	17	24	16	3	2
N 3	16 45 34	12 22 3	10♐ 9	7	27	26	17	24	16	3	2
E 4	16 49 31	13 19 29	24 49	9	28	26	17 R	23	16	3	2
5	16 53 27	14 16 54	9♑12	11	29	27	17	23	16	3	2
6	16 57 24	15 14 19	23 13	13	0♉	28	17	23	16	3	2
7	17 1 20	16 11 43	6♒49	15	1	28	17	23	16	3	2
8	17 5 17	17 9 6	19 59	18	1	29	17	23	16	3	2
9	17 9 13	18 6 28	2♓44	20	2	0♋	17	23	16	3	2
10	17 13 10	19 3 50	15 9	22	3	0	17	23	16	3	2
11	17 17 7	20 1 12	27 18	24	4	1	17	23	16	3	2
12	17 21 3	20 58 33	9♈14	26	5	2	17	23	16	3	2
13	17 25 0	21 55 53	21 3	29	6	2	17	23	16	3	2
14	17 28 56	22 53 13	2♉51	1♋	7	3	17	23	16	3	2
15	17 32 53	23 50 33	14 41	3	8	4	17	23	16	2	2
16	17 36 49	24 47 52	26 37	5	9	4	17	23	16	2	2
17	17 40 46	25 45 11	8♊42	7	10	5	17	23	16	2	2
18	17 44 42	26 42 29	20 58	9	11	6	17	23	16	2	2
19	17 48 39	27 39 47	3♋28	11	12	6	17	23	15	2	2
20	17 52 36	28 37 4	16 12	13	13	7	17	22	15	2	2
21	17 56 32	29 34 20	29 9	15	14	8	17	22	15	2	2
22	18 0 29	0♋31 37	12♌20	17	15	8	17	22	15	2	2
23	18 4 25	1 28 52	25 44	18	16	9	16	22	15	2	2
24	18 8 22	2 26 7	9♍21	20	17	10	16	22	15	2	2
25	18 12 18	3 23 21	23 9	22	18	10	16	22	15	2	2
26	18 16 15	4 20 34	7♎ 8	24	19	11	16	22	15	2	2
27	18 20 11	5 17 47	21 17	25	20	12	16	22	15	2	2
28	18 24 8	6 15 0	5♏36	27	21	12	16	22	15	2	2
29	18 28 5	7 12 12	20 2	29	22	13	16	22	15	2	2
30	18 32 1	8 9 23	4♐31	0♌	23	14	16	22	15	2	2

THE SUN ENTERS THE SIGN OF CANCER ON JUN 21 AT 10:45.

♈ ARIES ♉ TAURUS ♊ GEMINI ♋ CANCER ♌ LEO ♍ VIRGO ♎ LIBRA ♏ SCORPIO ♐ SAGITTARIUS ♑ CAPRICORN ♒ AQUARIUS ♓ PISCES

SIDEREAL SUN MOON MERCURY VENUS MARS JUPITER SATURN URANUS NEPTUNE PLUTO

DAY	TIME	☉	☽	☿	♀	♂	♃	♄	♅	♆	♇
	h m s	° ′ ″	° ′	°	°	°	°	°	°	°	°
J 1	18 35 58	9♋ 6 35	18♐59	2♌	24♉	14♋	16♒R	22♏R	15♐R	2♑R	2♏R
U 2	18 39 54	10 3 46	3♑21	3	25	15	16	22	15	2	2
L 3	18 43 51	11 0 57	17 30	5	26	16	16	22	15	2	2
Y 4	18 47 47	11 58 8	1♒22	6	28	16	16	22	15	2	2
5	18 51 44	12 55 19	14 53	8	29	17	16	22	15	2	2
6	18 55 41	13 52 30	28 1	9	0♊	18	15	22	15	2	2
7	18 59 37	14 49 41	10♓47	10	1	18	15	22	15	2	2
8	19 3 34	15 46 53	23 13	11	2	19	15	22	15	2	2
9	19 7 30	16 44 5	5♈22	13	3	19	15	22	15	2	2
10	19 11 27	17 41 17	17 18	14	4	20	15	22	15	2	2
11	19 15 23	18 38 30	29 8	15	5	21	15	22	15	2	2
12	19 19 20	19 35 43	10♉57	16	6	21	15	22	15	2	2 D
13	19 23 16	20 32 57	22 49	17	7	22	15	22	15	2	2
14	19 27 13	21 30 11	4♊49	18	8	23	15	22	15	2	2
15	19 31 10	22 27 26	17 2	19	9	23	15	22	15	2	2
16	19 35 6	23 24 42	29 31	20	11	24	14	22	15	2	2
17	19 39 3	24 21 57	12♋17	21	12	25	14	22	15	2	2
18	19 42 59	25 19 14	25 21	21	13	25	14	22	14	2	2
19	19 46 56	26 16 30	8♌41	22	14	26	14	22	14	2	2
20	19 50 52	27 13 47	22 16	23	15	27	14	21	14	2	2
21	19 54 49	28 11 5	6♍ 3	23	16	27	14	21	14	2	2
22	19 58 45	29 8 22	19 58	24	17	28	14	21	14	2	2
23	20 2 42	0♌ 5 40	3♎59	24	18	29	14	21	14	1	2
24	20 6 39	1 2 58	18 4	25	19	29	14	21	14	1	2
25	20 10 35	2 0 17	2♏11	25	21	0♌	13	21 D	14	1	2
26	20 14 32	2 57 36	16 19	25	22	1	13	21	14	1	2
27	20 18 28	3 54 55	0♐27	25	23	1	13	21	14	1	2
28	20 22 25	4 52 15	14 34	25 R	24	2	13	21	14	1	2
29	20 26 21	5 49 36	28 37	25	25	2	13	21	14	1	2
30	20 30 18	6 46 57	12♑34	25	26	3	13	21	14	1	2
31	20 34 14	7 44 18	26 20	25	27	4	13	21	14	1	2

THE SUN ENTERS THE SIGN OF LEO ON JUL 22 AT 21:38.

DAY	TIME	☉	☽	☿	♀	♂	♃	♄	♅	♆	♇
	h m s	° ′ ″	° ′	°	°	°	°	°	°	°	°
A 1	20 38 11	8♌41 41	9♒54	25♌R	28♊	4♌	12♒R	21♏	14♐R	1♑R	2♏
U 2	20 42 8	9 39 4	23 10	24	0♋	5	12	22	14	1	2
G 3	20 46 4	10 36 28	6♓ 8	24	1	6	12	22	14	1	2
U 4	20 50 1	11 33 53	18 48	23	2	6	12	22	14	1	2
S 5	20 53 57	12 31 19	1♈10	23	3	7	12	22	14	1	2
T 6	20 57 54	13 28 46	13 17	22	4	8	12	22	14	1	2
7	21 1 50	14 26 15	25 13	21	5	8	12	22	14	1	2
8	21 5 47	15 23 45	7♉ 2	21	6	9	12	22	14	1	2
9	21 9 43	16 21 16	18 51	20	8	10	11	22	14	1	2
10	21 13 40	17 18 49	0♊44	19	9	10	11	22	14	1	2
11	21 17 37	18 16 23	12 46	18	10	11	11	22	14	1	2
12	21 21 33	19 13 58	25 4	17	11	11	11	22	14	1	2
13	21 25 30	20 11 35	7♋40	17	12	12	11	22	14	1	2
14	21 29 26	21 9 13	20 37	16	13	13	11	22	14	1	2
15	21 33 23	22 6 53	3♌57	15	15	13	11	22	14	1	2
16	21 37 19	23 4 33	17 38	15	16	14	11	22	14	1	2
17	21 41 16	24 2 16	1♍36	14	17	15	10	22	14	1	2
18	21 45 12	24 59 59	15 49	14	18	15	10	22	14	1	2
19	21 49 9	25 57 43	0♎ 9	13	19	16	10	22	14	1	2
20	21 53 6	26 55 29	14 32	13 D	20	17	10	22	14	1	2
21	21 57 2	27 53 16	28 53	13	22	17	10	22	14	1	2
22	22 0 59	28 51 4	13♏ 9	13	23	18	10	22	14	1	2
23	22 4 55	29 48 53	27 18	13	24	19	10	22	14 D	1	2
24	22 8 52	0♍46 43	11♐18	14	25	19	10	22	14	1	2
25	22 12 48	1 44 35	25 10	14	26	20	9	22	14	1	2
26	22 16 45	2 42 28	8♑53	15	27	20	9	22	14	1	2
27	22 20 41	3 40 22	22 26	16	29	21	9	22	14	1	3
28	22 24 38	4 38 17	5♒48	16	0♌	22	9	22	14	1	3
29	22 28 35	5 36 14	18 58	17	1	22	9	22	14	1	3
30	22 32 31	6 34 12	1♓55	18	2	23	9	22	14	1	3
31	22 36 28	7 32 11	14 37	20	3	24	9	23	14	1	3

THE SUN ENTERS THE SIGN OF VIRGO ON AUG 23 AT 04:37.

DAY	TIME	☉	☽	☿	♀	♂	♃	♄	♅	♆	♇
	h m s	° ′ ″	° ′	°	°	°	°	°	°	°	°
S 1	22 40 24	8♍30 13	27♓ 4	21♌	5♌	24♌	9♒R	23♏	14♐	1♑R	3♏
E 2	22 44 21	9 28 16	9♈18	22	6	25	9	23	14	1	3
P 3	22 48 17	10 26 21	21 20	24	7	26	9	23	14	1	3
T 4	22 52 14	11 24 27	3♉13	25	8	26	8	23	14	1	3
E 5	22 56 10	12 22 36	15 1	27	9	27	8	23	14	1	3
M 6	23 0 7	13 20 46	26 49	29	11	27	8	23	14	1	3
B 7	23 4 4	14 18 59	8♊41	0♍	12	28	8	23	14	1	3
E 8	23 8 0	15 17 14	20 43	2	13	29	8	23	14	1	3
R 9	23 11 57	16 15 30	3♋ 0	4	14	29	8	23	14	1	3
10	23 15 53	17 13 49	15 37	6	15	0♍	8	23	14	1	3
11	23 19 50	18 12 10	28 38	8	17	1	8	23	14	1	3
12	23 23 46	19 10 33	12♌ 5	9	18	1	8	23	14	1 D	3
13	23 27 43	20 8 58	25 57	11	19	2	8	23	14	1	3
14	23 31 39	21 7 24	10♍12	13	20	2	8	23	14	1	3
15	23 35 36	22 5 53	24 45	15	21	3	8	24	14	1	3
16	23 39 33	23 4 23	9♎29	17	23	4	8	24	14	1	3
17	23 43 29	24 2 55	24 17	19	24	4	8	24	14	1	3
18	23 47 26	25 1 29	9♏ 1	21	25	5	8	24	14	1	3
19	23 51 22	26 0 5	23 35	23	26	6	7	24	14	1	3
20	23 55 19	26 58 43	7♐56	25	27	6	7	24	14	1	3
21	23 59 15	27 57 22	22 0	26	29	7	7	24	14	1	3
22	0 3 12	28 56 3	5♑49	28	0♍	8	7	24	14	1	3
23	0 7 8	29 54 45	19 21	0♎	1	8	7	24	14	1	3
24	0 11 5	0♎53 29	2♒38	2	2	9	7	24	14	1	3
25	0 15 2	1 52 15	15 40	4	4	9	7	24	14	1	3
26	0 18 58	2 51 3	28 29	5	5	10	7	24	14	1	3
27	0 22 55	3 49 52	11♓ 6	7	6	11	7	24	14	1	3
28	0 26 51	4 48 43	23 30	9	7	11	7	25	15	1	3
29	0 30 48	5 47 36	5♈43	11	8	12	7	25	15	1	4
30	0 34 44	6 46 31	17 47	12	10	13	7	25	15	1	4

THE SUN ENTERS THE SIGN OF LIBRA ON SEP 23 AT 02:09.

SIDEREAL SUN MOON MERCURY VENUS MARS JUPITER SATURN URANUS NEPTUNE PLUTO

DAY	TIME	☉	☽	☿	♀	♂	♃	♄	♅	♆	♇
	h m s	° ′ ″	° ′	°	°	°	°	°	°	°	°
O 1	0 38 41	7♎45 29	29♈42	14♎	11♍	13♍	7♒R	25♏	15♐	1♑	4♏
C 2	0 42 37	8 44 28	11♉32	16	12	14	7	25	15	1	4
T 3	0 46 34	9 43 30	23 19	17	13	15	7 D	25	15	1	4
O 4	0 50 30	10 42 33	5♊ 6	19	15	15	7	25	15	1	4
B 5	0 54 27	11 41 39	16 58	21	16	16	7	25	15	1	4
E 6	0 58 24	12 40 48	28 59	22	17	16	7	25	15	1	4
R 7	1 2 20	13 39 59	11♋15	24	18	17	7	25	15	1	4
8	1 6 17	14 39 12	23 48	26	19	18	7	26	15	1	4
9	1 10 13	15 38 27	6♌45	27	21	18	7	26	15	1	4
10	1 14 10	16 37 44	20 8	29	22	19	7	26	15	1	4
11	1 18 6	17 37 4	3♍59	0♏	23	20	7	26	15	1	4
12	1 22 3	18 36 26	18 17	2	24	20	7	26	15	1	4
13	1 25 59	19 35 51	2♎57	3	26	21	7	26	15	1	4
14	1 29 56	20 35 17	17 55	5	27	21	7	26	15	1	4
15	1 33 53	21 34 45	3♏ 0	6	28	22	7	26	15	1	4
16	1 37 49	22 34 16	18 6	8	29	23	7	26	15	1	4
17	1 41 46	23 33 48	3♐ 2	9	1♎	23	7	26	15	1	4
18	1 45 42	24 33 23	17 41	11	2	24	7	27	15	1	4
19	1 49 39	25 32 59	2♑ 0	12	3	25	8	27	15	1	4
20	1 53 35	26 32 36	15 56	14	4	25	8	27	15	1	4
21	1 57 32	27 32 16	29 29	15	6	26	8	27	15	1	4
22	2 1 28	28 31 57	12♒40	17	7	26	8	27	15	1	4
23	2 5 25	29 31 40	25 32	18	8	27	8	27	15	1	4
24	2 9 22	0♏31 24	8♓ 7	20	9	28	8	27	16	1	5
25	2 13 18	1 31 10	20 28	21	10	28	8	27	16	1	5
26	2 17 15	2 30 58	2♈37	22	12	29	8	27	16	1	5
27	2 21 11	3 30 48	14 38	24	13	0♎	8	28	16	1	5
28	2 25 8	4 30 40	26 32	25	14	0	8	28	16	1	5
29	2 29 4	5 30 33	8♉23	26	15	1	8	28	16	1	5
30	2 33 1	6 30 29	20 10	28	17	1	8	28	16	1	5
31	2 36 57	7 30 26	1♊58	29	18	2	8	28	16	1	5

THE SUN ENTERS THE SIGN OF SCORPIO ON OCT 23 AT 11:23.

DAY	TIME	☉	☽	☿	♀	♂	♃	♄	♅	♆	♇
	h m s	° ′ ″	° ′	°	°	°	°	°	°	°	°
N 1	2 40 54	8♏30 26	13♊48	0♐	19♎	3♎	8♒	28♏	16♐	2♑	5♏
O 2	2 44 51	9 30 28	25 44	2	20	3	9	28	16	2	5
V 3	2 48 47	10 30 31	7♋48	3	22	4	9	28	16	2	5
E 4	2 52 44	11 30 37	20 4	4	23	5	9	28	16	2	5
M 5	2 56 40	12 30 45	2♌36	5	24	5	9	29	16	2	5
B 6	3 0 37	13 30 55	15 27	6	25	6	9	29	16	2	5
E 7	3 4 33	14 31 7	28 42	7	27	6	9	29	16	2	5
R 8	3 8 30	15 31 21	12♍22	9	28	7	9	29	16	2	5
9	3 12 26	16 31 37	26 29	10	29	8	9	29	16	2	5
10	3 16 23	17 31 55	11♎ 1	10	0♏	8	9	29	16	2	5
11	3 20 20	18 32 14	25 54	11	2	9	9	29	16	2	5
12	3 24 16	19 32 36	11♏ 2	12	3	10	10	29	17	2	5
13	3 28 13	20 33 0	26 16	13	4	10	10	0♐	17	2	5
14	3 32 9	21 33 25	11♐26	14	5	11	10	0	17	2	5
15	3 36 6	22 33 52	26 23	14	7	11	10	0	17	2	5
16	3 40 2	23 34 20	10♑58	14	8	12	10	0	17	2	5
17	3 43 59	24 34 50	25 8	15	9	13	10	0	17	2	5
18	3 47 55	25 35 21	8♒50	15 R	10	13	10	0	17	2	6
19	3 51 52	26 35 53	22 5	15	12	14	11	0	17	2	6
20	3 55 49	27 36 26	4♓55	15	13	15	11	0	17	2	6
21	3 59 45	28 37 1	17 25	15	14	15	11	0	17	2	6
22	4 3 42	29 37 36	29 38	14	16	16	11	1	17	2	6
23	4 7 38	0♐38 13	11♈39	13	17	16	11	1	17	2	6
24	4 11 35	1 38 51	23 32	13	18	17	11	1	17	2	6
25	4 15 31	2 39 31	5♉21	12	19	18	11	1	17	2	6
26	4 19 28	3 40 11	17 8	10	21	18	12	1	17	2	6
27	4 23 24	4 40 53	28 56	9	22	19	12	1	17	2	6
28	4 27 21	5 41 36	10♊49	8	23	20	12	1	17	2	6
29	4 31 18	6 42 21	22 46	7	24	20	12	1	18	2	6
30	4 35 14	7 43 7	4♋51	5	26	21	12	2	18	2	6

THE SUN ENTERS THE SIGN OF SAGITTARIUS ON NOV 22 AT 08:52.

DAY	TIME	☉	☽	☿	♀	♂	♃	♄	♅	♆	♇
	h m s	° ′ ″	° ′	°	°	°	°	°	°	°	°
D 1	4 39 11	8♐43 54	17♋ 4	4♐R	27♏	21♎	12♒	2♐	18♐	2♑	6♏
E 2	4 43 7	9 44 43	29 29	3	28	22	12	2	18	2	6
C 3	4 47 4	10 45 33	12♌ 6	2	29	23	13	2	18	3	6
E 4	4 51 0	11 46 24	24 58	1	1♐	23	13	2	18	3	6
M 5	4 54 57	12 47 17	8♍ 8	0	2	24	13	2	18	3	6
B 6	4 58 54	13 48 11	21 38	29♏	3	25	13	2	18	3	6
E 7	5 2 50	14 49 6	5♎29	29	4	25	13	2	18	3	6
R 8	5 6 47	15 50 3	19 44	29 D	6	26	14	2	18	3	6
9	5 10 43	16 51 0	4♏19	29	7	26	14	3	18	3	6
10	5 14 40	17 51 59	19 12	29	8	27	14	3	18	3	6
11	5 18 36	18 53 0	4♐15	29	9	28	14	3	18	3	6
12	5 22 33	19 54 1	19 22	0♐	11	28	14	3	18	3	6
13	5 26 29	20 55 3	4♑21	0	12	29	14	3	18	3	6
14	5 30 26	21 56 6	19 4	1	13	0♏	15	3	18	3	6
15	5 34 23	22 57 9	3♒23	2	14	0	15	3	18	3	6
16	5 38 19	23 58 13	17 15	3	16	1	15	3	19	3	6
17	5 42 16	24 59 17	0♓38	4	17	1	15	4	19	3	7
18	5 46 12	26 0 21	13 34	5	18	2	15	4	19	3	7
19	5 50 9	27 1 26	26 5	6	19	3	16	4	19	3	7
20	5 54 5	28 2 31	8♈18	7	21	3	16	4	19	3	7
21	5 58 2	29 3 37	20 17	8	22	4	16	4	19	3	7
22	6 1 58	0♑ 4 43	2♉ 7	9	23	4	16	4	19	3	7
23	6 5 55	1 5 49	13 54	11	24	5	16	4	19	3	7
24	6 9 52	2 6 55	25 41	12	26	6	17	4	19	3	7
25	6 13 48	3 8 1	7♊32	13	27	6	17	4	19	3	7
26	6 17 45	4 9 8	19 31	14	28	7	17	5	19	3	7
27	6 21 41	5 10 15	1♋39	16	0♑	8	17	5	19	3	7
28	6 25 38	6 11 23	13 58	17	1	8	17	5	19	3	7
29	6 29 34	7 12 30	26 27	19	2	9	18	5	19	3	7
30	6 33 31	8 13 38	9♌ 8	20	3	9	18	5	19	4	7
31	6 37 27	9 14 46	22 0	21	5	10	18	5	19	4	7

THE SUN ENTERS THE SIGN OF CAPRICORN ON DEC 21 AT 22:09.

♈ ARIES ♉ TAURUS ♊ GEMINI ♋ CANCER ♌ LEO ♍ VIRGO ♎ LIBRA ♏ SCORPIO ♐ SAGITTARIUS ♑ CAPRICORN ♒ AQUARIUS ♓ PISCES

APPENDIX XI Longitudes and Latitudes of Major Cities in the World

Aberdeen, SD	98w30	45n28	6:34:00
Abilene, TX	99w43	32n28	6:38:52
Akron, OH	81w31	41n05	5:26:04
Alameda, CA	122w15	37n46	8:09:00
Albany, GA	84w10	31n35	5:36:40
Albany, NY	73w45	42n39	4:55:00
Albuquerque, NM	106w39	35n05	7:06:36
Alexandria, LA	92w27	31n18	6:09:48
Alexandria, VA	77w03	38n48	5:08:12
Alhambra, CA	118w06	34n08	7:52:24
Allen Park, MI	83w13	42n16	5:32:52
Allentown, PA	75w29	40n37	5:01:56
Alliance, OH	81w06	40n55	5:24:24
Altadena, CA	118w08	34n11	7:52:32
Alton, IL	90w11	38n53	6:00:44
Altoona, PA	78w24	40n31	5:13:36
Amarillo, TX	101w50	35n13	6:47:20
Ames, IA	93w37	42n02	6:14:28
Amherst, NY	78w48	42n59	5:15:12
Amsterdam, NY	74w11	42n56	4:56:44
Anaheim, CA	117w55	33n50	7:51:40
Anchorage, AK	149w54	61n13	9:59:36
Anderson, IN	85w41	40n10	5:42:44
Anderson, SC	82w39	34n31	5:30:36
Annandale, VA	77w12	38n50	5:08:48
Annapolis, MD	76w30	38n59	5:06:00
Ann Arbor, MI	83w45	42n17	5:35:00
Anniston, AL	85w50	33n39	5:43:20
Antioch, CA	121w48	38n01	8:07:12
Appleton, WI	88w25	44n16	5:53:40
Arcade, CA	121w26	38n37	8:05:44
Arcadia, CA	118w02	34n08	7:52:08
Arden, CA	121w23	38n36	8:05:32
Arlington, MA	71w09	42n25	4:44:36
Arlington, TX	97w07	32n44	6:28:28
Arlington, VA	77w07	38n53	5:08:28
Arlington Heights, IL	87w59	42n05	5:51:56
Arvada, CO	105w05	39n48	7:00:20
Asheville, NC	82w33	35n36	5:30:12
Ashland, KY	82w38	38n28	5:30:32
Astoria, NY	73w55	40n46	4:55:40
Athens, GA	83w23	33n57	5:33:32
Atlanta, GA	84w23	33n45	5:37:32
Atlantic City, NJ	74w27	39n21	4:57:48
Attleboro, MA	71w17	41n57	4:45:08
Auburn, NY	76w34	42n56	5:06:16
Augusta, GA	81w58	33n28	5:27:52
Augusta, ME	69w47	44n19	4:39:08
Aurora, CO	104w52	39n44	6:59:28
Aurora, IL	88w19	41n45	5:53:16
Austin, MN	92w58	43n40	6:11:52
Austin, TX	97w45	30n17	6:31:00
Azusa, CA	117w52	34n08	7:51:28
Bakersfield, CA	119w01	35n23	7:56:04
Baldwin, NY	73w36	40n39	4:54:24
Baldwin, PA	79w58	40n23	5:19:52
Baldwin Park, CA	117w58	34n04	7:51:52
Baltimore, MD	76w37	39n17	5:06:28
Bangor, ME	68w46	44n48	4:35:04
Barberton, OH	81w39	41n00	5:26:36
Bartlesville, OK	95w59	36n45	6:23:56
Baton Rouge, LA	91w11	30n27	6:04:44
Battle Creek, MI	85w11	42n19	5:40:44
Bay City, MI	83w54	43n36	5:35:36
Bayonne, NJ	74w07	40n40	4:36:28
Bay Shore, NY	73w15	40n43	4:53:00
Bayside, NY	73w46	40n46	4:55:04
Baytown, TX	94w59	29n43	6:19:56
Beaumont, TX	94w06	30n05	6:16:24
Bell, CA	118w11	33n59	7:52:44
Belleville, IL	89w59	38n31	5:59:56
Belleville, NJ	74w09	40n47	4:56:36
Bellevue, WA	122w12	47n37	8:08:48
Bellflower, CA	118w09	33n53	7:52:36
Bell Gardens, CA	118w10	33n58	7:52:40
Bellingham, WA	122w29	48n46	8:09:56
Belmont, CA	122w16	37n31	8:09:04
Belmont, MA	71w11	42n24	4:44:44
Beloit, WI	89w02	42n31	5:56:08
Bergenfield, NJ	74w00	40n56	4:56:00
Berkeley, CA	122w16	37n52	8:09:04
Berwyn, IL	87w47	41n51	5:51:08
Bessemer, AL	86w58	33n24	5:47:52
Bethel Park, PA	80w01	40n20	5:20:04
Bethesda, MD	77w06	38n59	5:08:24
Bethlehem, PA	75w23	40n37	5:01:32
Bethpage, NY	73w30	40n44	4:54:00
Beverly, MA	70w53	42n33	4:43:32
Beverly Hills, CA	118w25	34n04	7:53:40
Big Spring, TX	101w28	32n15	6:45:52
Billings, MT	108w30	45n47	7:14:00
Biloxi, MS	88w53	30n24	5:55:32
Binghamton, NY	75w55	42n06	5:03:40
Birmingham, AL	86w48	33n31	5:47:12
Birmingham, MI	83w13	42n33	5:32:52
Bismarck, ND	100w47	46n48	6:43:08
Bloomfield, NJ	74w12	40n48	4:56:48
Bloomington, IL	89w00	40n29	5:56:00
Bloomington, IN	86w32	39n10	5:46:08
Bloomington, MN	93w17	44n50	6:13:08
Boardman, OH	80w40	41n02	5:22:40
Boca Raton, FL	80w05	26n21	5:20:20
Boise, ID	116w13	43n37	7:44:52
Bossier City, LA	93w44	32n31	6:14:56
Boston, MA	71w04	42n22	4:44:16
Boulder, CO	105w17	40n01	7:01:08
Bountiful, UT	111w53	40n53	7:27:32
Bowie, MD	76w47	39n00	5:07:08
Bowling Green, KY	86w27	36n59	5:45:48
Braintree, MA	71w00	42n13	4:44:00
Bremerton, WA	122w38	47n34	8:10:32
Brentwood, NY	73w15	40n47	4:53:00
Bridgeport, CT	73w12	41n11	4:52:48
Brighton, NY	77w34	43n08	5:10:16
Bristol, CT	72w57	41n40	4:51:48
Brockton, MA	71w01	42n05	4:44:04
Bronx, NY	73w54	40n51	4:55:36
Brookfield, WI	88w09	43n04	5:52:36
Brookline, MA	71w07	42n20	4:44:28
Brooklyn, NY	73w56	40n38	4:55:44
Brooklyn Center, MN	93w20	45n05	6:13:20
Brooklyn Park, MN	93w23	45n05	6:13:32
Brook Park, OH	80w51	41n24	5:23:24
Broomall, PA	75w22	39n59	5:01:28
Brownsville, TX	97w30	25n54	6:30:00
Bryan, TX	96w22	30n40	6:25:28
Buena Park, CA	118w00	33n52	7:52:00
Buffalo, NY	78w53	42n53	5:15:32
Burbank, CA	118w19	34n11	7:53:16
Burbank, IL	87w45	41n44	5:51:00
Burlingame, CA	122w21	37n35	8:09:24
Burlington, IA	91w14	40n49	6:04:56
Burlington, NC	79w26	36n06	5:17:44
Burlington, VT	73w12	44n29	4:52:48
Calumet City, IL	87w32	41n37	5:50:08
Cambridge, MA	71w06	42n22	4:44:24
Camden, NJ	75w07	39n56	5:00:28
Campbell, CA	121w57	37n17	8:07:48
Canton, OH	81w23	40n48	5:25:32
Cape Girardeau, MO	89w32	37n19	5:58:08
Carmichael, CA	121w19	38n38	8:05:16
Carol City, FL	80w16	25n56	5:21:04
Carson, CA	118w17	33n48	7:53:08
Carson City, NV	119w46	39n10	7:59:04
Casper, WY	106w19	42n51	7:05:16
Castro Valley, CA	122w04	37n42	8:08:16
Catonsville, MD	76w44	39n17	5:06:56
Cedar Falls, IA	92w27	42n32	6:09:48
Cedar Rapids, IA	91w40	41n59	6:06:40
Central Islip, NY	73w12	40n47	4:52:48
Champaign, IL	88w15	40n07	5:53:00
Chapel Hill, NC	79w04	35n55	5:16:16
Charleston, SC	79w56	32n46	5:19:44
Charleston, WV	81w38	38n21	5:26:32
Charleston Heights, SC	80w00	32n51	5:20:00
Charlotte, NC	80w51	35n13	5:23:24
Charlottesville, VA	78w30	38n02	5:14:00
Chattanooga, TN	85w19	35n03	5:41:16
Cheektowaga, NY	78w45	42n54	5:15:00
Chelsea, MA	71w02	42n23	4:44:08
Cherry Hill, NJ	75w02	39n56	5:00:08
Chesapeake, VA	76w17	36n50	5:05:08
Chester, PA	75w22	39n51	5:01:28
Cheyenne, WY	104w49	41n08	6:59:16
Chicago, IL	87w38	41n53	5:50:32
Chicago Heights, IL	87w38	41n30	5:50:32
Chicopee, MA	72w37	42n09	4:50:28
Chino, CA	117w41	34n01	7:50:44
Chula Vista, CA	117w05	32n39	7:48:20
Cicero, IL	87w45	41n51	5:51:00
Cincinnati, OH	84w31	39n06	5:38:04
Citrus Heights, CA	121w17	38n42	8:05:08
Claremont, CA	117w43	34n06	7:50:52
Clarksville, TN	87w21	36n32	5:49:24
Clearwater, FL	82w48	27n58	5:31:12
Cleveland, OH	81w42	41n30	5:26:48
Cleveland Heights, OH	81w34	41n30	5:26:16
Clifton, NJ	74w09	40n52	4:56:36
Clinton, IA	90w12	41n51	6:00:48
Clinton Township, MI	83w58	42n04	5:35:52
Clovis, NM	103w12	34n24	6:52:48
College Park, MD	76w56	38n59	5:07:44
Colorado Springs, CO	104w49	38n50	6:59:16
Colton, CA	117w19	34n04	7:49:16
Columbia, MO	92w20	38n57	6:09:20
Columbia, SC	81w03	34n00	5:24:12
Columbus, GA	84w59	32n28	5:39:56
Columbus, IN	85w55	39n13	5:43:40
Columbus, MS	88w25	33n30	5:53:40
Columbus, OH	83w00	39n58	5:32:00
Compton, CA	118w13	33n54	7:52:52
Concord, CA	122w02	37n59	8:08:08
Concord, NH	71w32	43n12	4:46:08
Coon Rapids, MN	93w19	45n09	6:13:16
Coral Gables, FL	80w16	25n45	5:21:04
Corona, CA	117w34	33n53	7:50:16
Corona, NY	73w52	40n45	4:55:28
Coronado, CA	117w10	32n41	7:48:40
Corpus Christi, TX	97w24	27n47	6:29:36
Corvallis, OR	123w16	44n34	8:13:04
Costa Mesa, CA	117w55	33n38	7:51:40
Council Bluffs, IA	95w52	41n16	6:23:28
Covina, CA	117w52	34n05	7:51:28
Covington, KY	84w31	39n05	5:38:04
Cranford, NJ	74w18	40n40	4:57:12
Cranston, RI	71w26	41n47	4:45:44
Crystal, MN	93w22	45n03	6:13:28
Culver City, CA	118w25	34n01	7:53:40
Cumberland, MD	78w46	39n39	5:15:04
Cuyahoga Falls, OH	81w29	41n08	5:25:56
Cypress, CA	118w02	33n50	7:52:08
Dallas, TX	96w49	32n47	6:27:16
Daly City, CA	122w28	37n42	8:09:52
Danbury, CT	73w28	41n24	4:53:52
Danvers, MA	70w56	42n34	4:43:44
Danville, IL	87w37	40n08	5:50:28
Danville, VA	79w23	36n36	5:17:32
Davenport, IA	90w35	41n32	6:02:20
Davis, CA	121w44	38n32	8:06:56
Dayton, OH	84w12	39n45	5:36:48
Daytona Beach, FL	81w01	29n13	5:24:04
Dearborn, MI	83w11	42n19	5:32:44
Dearborn Heights, MI	83w18	42n20	5:33:12
Decatur, AL	86w59	34n36	5:47:56
Decatur, IL	88w57	39n51	5:55:48
Dedham, MA	71w10	42n15	4:44:40
Deer Park, NY	73w20	40n46	4:53:20
De Kalb, IL	88w46	41n56	5:55:04
Del City, OK	97w26	35n26	6:29:44
Denton, TX	97w08	33n13	6:28:32
Denver, CO	104w59	39n44	6:59:56
Des Moines, IA	93w37	41n35	6:14:28
Des Plaines, IL	87w52	42n03	5:51:28
Detroit, MI	83w03	42n20	5:32:12
Dolton, IL	87w36	41n38	5:50:24
Dothan, AL	85w24	31n13	5:41:36
Dover, DE	75w32	39n10	5:02:08
Downers Grove, IL	88w01	41n49	5:52:04
Downey, CA	118w08	33n56	7:52:32
Drexel Hill, PA	75w18	39n57	5:01:12
Dubuque, IA	90w41	42n30	6:02:44
Duluth, MN	92w07	46n47	6:08:28
Dundalk, MD	76w32	39n16	5:06:08
Durham, NC	78w54	36n00	5:15:36
East Brunswick, NJ	74w25	40n26	4:57:40
East Chicago, IN	87w29	41n38	5:49:56
East Cleveland, OH	81w33	41n33	5:26:12
East Detroit, MI	82w57	42n28	5:31:48
East Hartford, CT	72w38	41n46	4:50:32
East Haven, CT	72w52	41n17	4:51:28
East Lansing, MI	84w29	42n44	5:37:56
East Los Angeles, CA	118w09	34n01	7:52:36
East Meadow, NY	73w34	40n43	4:54:16
Easton, PA	75w13	40n41	5:00:52
East Orange, NJ	74w13	40n46	4:56:52
Eastpoint, GA	84w27	33n41	5:37:48
East Providence, RI	71w23	41n49	4:45:32
East Saint Louis, IL	90w09	38n37	6:00:36
Eau Claire, WI	91w30	44n49	6:06:00
Edina, MN	93w21	44n53	6:13:24
Edison, NJ	74w25	40n31	4:57:40
El Cajon, CA	116w58	32n48	7:47:52
El Cerrito, CA	122w19	37n55	8:09:16
El Dorado, AR	92w40	33n12	6:10:40
Elgin, IL	88w17	42n02	5:53:08
Elizabeth, NJ	74w13	40n40	4:56:52
Elkhart, IN	85w58	41n41	5:43:52
Elmhurst, IL	87w56	41n53	5:51:44
Elmira, NY	76w48	42n06	5:07:12
Elmont, NY	73w43	40n43	4:54:52
El Monte, CA	118w01	34n04	7:52:04
Elmwood Park, IL	87w49	41n56	5:51:16
El Paso, TX	106w29	31n45	7:05:56
Elyria, OH	82w07	41n22	5:28:28
Englewood, CO	104w59	39n39	6:59:56
Enid, OK	97w53	36n24	6:31:32
Erie, PA	80w05	42n08	5:20:20
Escondido, CA	117w05	33n07	7:48:20
Essex, MD	76w29	39n19	5:05:56
Euclid, OH	81w32	41n34	5:26:08
Eugene, OR	123w04	44n05	8:12:16
Eureka, CA	124w09	40n47	8:16:36
Evanston, IL	87w41	42n03	5:50:44
Evansville, IN	87w35	37n58	5:50:20
Everett, MA	71w04	42n24	4:44:16
Everett, WA	122w12	47n59	8:08:48
Evergreen Park, IL	87w41	41n43	5:50:44
Fairborn, OH	84w02	39n49	5:36:08
Fairfield, CA	122w03	38n15	8:08:12
Fairfield, CT	73w16	41n09	4:53:04
Fair Lawn, NJ	74w08	40n56	4:56:32
Fairmont, WV	80w09	39n29	5:20:36
Fall River, MA	71w10	41n43	4:44:40
Fargo, ND	96w48	46n53	6:27:12
Farmers Branch, TX	96w54	32n56	6:27:36
Fayetteville, AR	96w10	36n04	6:24:40
Fayetteville, NC	78w53	35n03	5:15:32
Ferguson, MO	90w18	38n45	6:01:12
Ferndale, MI	83w08	42n28	5:32:32
Findlay, OH	83w39	41n02	5:34:36
Fitchburg, MA	71w48	42n35	4:47:12
Flagstaff, AZ	111w39	35n12	7:26:36
Flint, MI	83w41	43n01	5:34:44
Florence, AL	87w41	34n48	5:50:44
Florence, CA	118w15	33n58	7:53:00
Florence, SC	79w46	34n12	5:19:04
Florissant, MO	90w20	38n48	6:01:20
Flushing, NY	73w49	40n45	4:55:16
Fond Du Lac, WI	88w27	43n47	5:53:48
Fontana, CA	117w26	34n06	7:49:44
Forest Hills, NY	73w51	40n42	4:55:24
Fort Collins, CO	105w05	40n35	7:00:20
Fort Dodge, IA	94w11	42n30	6:16:44
Fort Lauderdale, FL	80w08	26n07	5:20:32
Fort Lee, NJ	73w58	40n51	4:55:52
Fort Myers, FL	81w52	26n39	5:27:28
Fort Pierce, FL	80w20	27n27	5:21:20
Fort Smith, AR	94w25	35n23	6:17:40
Fort Wayne, IN	85w09	41n04	5:40:36
Fort Worth, TX	97w18	32n45	6:29:12
Fountain Valley, CA	117w58	33n42	7:51:52
Framingham, MA'	71w25	42n17	4:45:40
Frankfort, KY	84w52	38n12	5:39:28
Franklin Square, NY	73w41	40n43	4:54:44

Freeport, IL	89w36	42N17	5:58:24
Freeport, NY	73w35	40N39	4:54:20
Fremont, CA	121w57	37N32	8:07:48
Fresno, CA	119w47	36N44	7:59:08
Fridley, MN	93w16	45N05	6:13:04
Fullerton, CA	117w56	33N53	7:51:44
Gadsden, AL	86w01	34N01	5:44:04
Gainesville, FL	82w20	29N40	5:29:20
Galesburg, IL	90w22	40N57	6:01:28
Galveston, TX	94w48	29N18	6:19:12
Gardena, CA	118w18	33N53	7:53:12
Garden City, MI	83w21	42N20	5:33:24
Garden City, NY	73w38	40N44	4:54:32
Garden Grove, CA	117w55	33N47	7:51:40
Garfield, NJ	74w06	40N52	4:56:24
Garfield Heights, OH	81w37	41N26	5:26:28
Garland, TX	96w38	32N55	6:26:32
Gary, IN	87w20	41N36	5:49:20
Gastonia, NC	81w11	35N16	5:24:44
Gates, NY	77w41	43N09	5:10:44
Glen Burnie, MD	76w37	39N10	5:06:28
Glen Cove, NY	73w38	40N52	4:54:32
Glendale, AZ	112w11	33N32	7:28:44
Glendale, CA	118w15	34N09	7:53:00
Glendora, CA	117w52	34N08	7:51:28
Gloucester, MA	70w40	42N37	4:42:40
Goldsboro, NC	77w59	35N23	5:11:56
Grand Forks, ND	97w03	47N55	6:28:12
Grand Island, NE	98w21	40N55	6:33:24
Grand Prairie, TX	97w00	32N45	6:28:00
Grand Rapids, MI	85w40	42N58	5:42:40
Granite City, IL	90w09	38N42	6:00:36
Great Falls, MT	111w17	47N30	7:25:08
Greece, NY	77w41	43N13	5:10:44
Greeley, CO	104w42	40N25	6:58:48
Green Bay, WI	88w00	44N31	5:52:00
Greensboro, NC	79w48	36N04	5:19:12
Greenville, MS	91w04	33N24	6:04:16
Greenville, NC	77w23	35N37	5:09:32
Greenville, SC	82w24	34N51	5:29:36
Greenwich, CT	73w38	41N02	4:54:32
Gulfport, MS	89w06	30N22	5:56:24
Hacienda Heights, CA	117w58	33N58	7:51:52
Hackensack, NJ	74w03	40N53	4:56:12
Hagerstown, MD	77w43	39N39	5:10:52
Haltom City, TX	97w16	32N48	6:29:04
Hamden, CT	72w54	41N23	4:51:36
Hamilton, OH	84w34	39N24	5:38:16
Hammond, IN	87w30	41N38	5:50:00
Hampton, VA	76w21	37N02	5:05:24
Hamtramck, MI	83w03	42N24	5:32:12
Harlingen, TX	97w42	26N12	6:30:48
Harrisburg, PA	76w53	40N16	5:07:32
Hartford, CT	72w41	41N46	4:50:44
Harvey, IL	87w50	41N36	5:51:20
Hattiesburg, MS	89w17	31N20	5:57:08
Haverhill, MA	71w05	42N47	4:44:20
Havertown, PA	75w18	39N58	5:01:12
Hawthorne, CA	118w21	33N55	7:53:24
Hayward, CA	122w05	37N40	8:08:20
Hazleton, PA	75w59	40N57	5:03:56
Helena, MT	112w02	46N36	7:28:08
Hempstead, NY	73w38	40N43	4:54:32
Hialeah, FL	80w17	25N50	5:21:08
Hicksville, NY	73w32	40N46	4:54:08
Highland Park, IL	87w48	42N11	5:51:12
Highland Park, MI	83w06	42N24	5:32:24
High Point, NC	80w00	35N57	5:20:00
Hillcrest Center, CA	118w57	35N23	7:55:48
Hilo, HI	155w05	19N44	10:20:20
Hobbs, NM	103w08	32N42	6:52:32
Hoboken, NJ	74w02	40N44	4:56:08
Holland, MI	86w07	42N47	5:44:28
Hollywood, FL	80w09	26N01	5:20:36
Holyoke, MA	72w37	42N12	4:50:28
Honolulu, HI	157w52	21N19	10:31:28
Hot Springs Nat Park, AR	93w03	34N31	6:12:12
Houma, LA	90w43	29N36	6:02:52
Houston, TX	95w22	29N46	6:21:28
Huntington, WV	82w27	38N25	5:29:48
Huntington Beach, CA	118w05	33N40	7:52:20
Huntington Park, CA	118w14	33N59	7:52:56
Huntington Station, NY	73w25	40N51	4:53:40
Huntsville, AL	86w35	34N44	5:46:20
Hurst, TX	97w09	32N49	6:28:36
Hutchinson, KS	97w56	38N05	6:31:44
Idaho Falls, ID	112w02	43N30	7:28:08
Imperial Beach, CA	117w08	32N35	7:48:32
Independence, MO	94w25	39N06	6:17:40
Indianapolis, IN	86w09	39N46	5:44:36
Inglewood, CA	118w21	33N58	7:53:24
Inkster, MI	83w19	42N18	5:33:16
Iowa City, IA	91w32	41N40	6:06:08
Irondequoit, NY	77w35	43N13	5:10:20
Irving, TX	96w56	32N49	6:27:44
Irvington, NJ	74w14	40N44	4:56:56
Ithaca, NY	76w30	42N27	5:06:00
Jackson, MI	84w24	42N15	5:37:36
Jackson, MS	90w12	32N18	6:00:48
Jackson, TN	88w49	35N37	5:55:16
Jacksonville, FL	81w39	30N20	5:26:36
Jamaica, NY	73w47	40N43	4:55:08
Jamestown, NY	79w14	42N06	5:16:56
Janesville, WI	89w01	42N41	5:56:04
Jefferson City, MO	92w10	38N34	6:08:40
Jersey City, NJ	74w04	40N44	4:56:16
Johnson City, TN	82w21	36N19	5:29:24
Johnstown, PA	78w55	40N20	5:15:40
Joliet, IL	88w05	41N32	5:52:20
Jonesboro, AR	90w42	35N50	6:02:48
Joplin, MO	94w31	37N06	6:18:04
Juneau, AK	134w24	58N18	8:57:36
Kailua, HI	157w44	21N24	10:30:56
Kalamazoo, MI	85w35	42N17	5:42:20
Kaneohe, HI	157w48	21N25	10:31:12
Kankakee, IL	87w52	41N07	5:51:28
Kannapolis, NC	80w37	35N30	5:22:28
Kansas City, KS	94w38	39N07	6:18:32
Kansas City, MO	94w35	39N06	6:18:20
Kearny, NJ	74w09	40N46	4:56:36
Kendall, FL	80w19	25N41	5:21:16
Kenner, LA	90w15	29N59	6:01:00
Kenosha, WI	87w49	42N35	5:51:16
Kent, OH	81w22	41N09	5:25:28
Kettering, OH	84w10	39N41	5:36:40
Kew Gardens, NY	73w50	40N42	4:55:20
Key West, FL	81w48	24N33	5:27:12
Killeen, TX	97w44	31N07	6:30:56
Kingsport, TN	82w33	36N33	5:30:12
Kingston, NY	73w59	41N56	4:55:56
Kingsville, TX	97w52	27N31	6:31:28
Kirkwood, MO	90w24	38N35	6:01:36
Knoxville, TN	83w55	35N58	5:35:40
Kokomo, IN	86w08	40N29	5:44:32
Lackawanna, NY	78w50	42N50	5:15:20
La Crosse, WI	91w15	43N48	6:05:00
Lafayette, CA	122w07	37N53	8:08:28
Lafayette, IN	86w54	40N25	5:47:36
Lafayette, LA	92w01	30N14	6:08:04
La Habra, CA	117w57	33N56	7:51:48
Lake Charles, LA	93w13	30N14	6:12:52
Lakeland, FL	81w57	28N03	5:27:48
Lakewood, CA	118w08	33N51	7:52:32
Lakewood, CO	105w05	39N44	7:00:20
Lakewood, NJ	74w13	40N06	4:56:52
Lakewood, OH	81w48	41N29	5:27:12
Lakewood Center, WA	122w32	47N11	8:10:08
La Mesa, CA	117w03	32N46	7:48:12
La Mirada, CA	118w02	33N51	7:52:08
Lancaster, CA	118w08	34N42	7:52:32
Lancaster, OH	82w36	39N43	5:30:24
Lancaster, PA	76w19	40N02	5:05:16
Lansing, IL	87w33	41N34	5:50:12
Lansing, MI	84w33	42N44	5:38:12
La Puente, CA	117w57	34N01	7:51:48
Laredo, TX	99w30	27N30	6:38:00
Las Cruces, NM	106w47	32N19	7:07:08
Las Vegas, NV	115w09	36N10	7:40:36
Lawndale, CA	118w21	33N54	7:53:24
Lawrence, KS	95w14	38N58	6:20:56
Lawrence, MA	71w10	42N43	4:44:40
Lawton, OK	98w25	34N37	6:33:40
Leavenworth, KS	94w55	39N19	6:19:40
Lebanon, PA	76w26	40N20	5:05:44
Lemay, MO	90w16	38N32	6:01:04
Lemon Grove, CA	117w02	32N44	7:48:08
Leominster, MA	71w46	42N32	4:47:04
Levittown, NY	73w31	40N44	4:54:04
Levittown, PA	74w51	40N09	4:59:24
Lewiston, ID	117w01	46N25	7:48:04
Lewiston, ME	70w13	44N06	4:40:52
Lexington, KY	84w30	38N03	5:38:00
Lexington, MA	71w14	42N27	4:44:56
Lima, OH	84w06	40N44	5:36:24
Lincoln, NE	96w41	40N49	6:26:44
Lincoln Park, MI	83w11	42N15	5:32:44
Linden, NJ	74w15	40N38	4:57:00
Lindenhurst, NY	73w23	40N41	4:53:32
Little Rock, AR	92w17	34N45	6:09:08
Littleton, CO	105w00	39N37	7:00:00
Livermore, CA	121w47	37N41	8:07:08
Livingston, NJ	74w19	40N48	4:57:16
Livonia, MI	83w23	42N23	5:33:32
Lockport, NY	78w42	43N10	5:14:48
Lodi, CA	121w16	38N08	8:05:04
Lodi, NJ	74w05	40N53	4:56:20
Lombard, IL	88w01	41N53	5:52:04
Lompoc, CA	120w28	34N38	8:01:52
Long Beach, CA	118w11	33N47	7:52:44
Long Beach, NY	73w39	40N35	4:54:36
Long Branch, NJ	74w00	40N18	4:56:00
Longview, TX	94w44	32N30	6:18:56
Longview, WA	122w57	46N08	8:11:48
Lorain, OH	82w11	41N28	5:28:44
Los Altos, CA	122w07	37N23	8:08:28
Los Angeles, CA	118w15	34N04	7:53:00
Los Gatos, CA	121w59	37N14	8:07:56
Louisville, KY	85w46	38N15	5:43:04
Lowell, MA	71w19	42N38	4:45:16
Lubbock, TX	101w51	33N35	6:47:24
Lynchburg, VA	79w09	37N25	5:16:36
Lynn, MA	70w57	42N28	4:43:48
Lynwood, CA	118w13	33N56	7:52:52
Mcallen, TX	98w14	26N12	6:32:56
Mckeesport, PA	79w52	40N21	5:19:28
Macon, GA	83w38	32N51	5:34:32
Madison, WI	89w24	43N04	5:57:36
Madison Heights, MI	83w06	42N30	5:32:24
Malden, MA	71w04	42N26	4:44:16
Manchester, CT	72w31	41N47	4:50:04
Manchester, NH	71w28	43N00	4:45:52
Manhattan, KS	96w35	39N11	6:26:20
Manhattan Beach, CA	118w25	33N54	7:53:40
Manitowoc, WI	87w40	44N05	5:50:40
Mankato, MN	94w00	44N10	6:16:00
Mansfield, OH	82w31	40N45	5:30:04
Maple Heights, OH	81w34	41N25	5:26:16
Maplewood, MN	93w03	45N00	6:12:12
Marietta, GA	84w33	33N57	5:38:12
Marion, IN	85w40	40N32	5:42:40
Marion, OH	83w08	40N35	5:32:32
Marlboro, MA	71w33	42N21	4:46:12
Marrero, LA	90w06	29N54	6:00:24
Marshalltown, IA	92w55	42N03	6:11:40
Mason City, IA	93w12	43N09	6:12:48
Massapequa, NY	73w29	40N41	4:53:56
Massillon, OH	81w32	40N48	5:26:08
Maywood, IL	87w51	41N53	5:51:24
Medford, MA	71w07	42N25	4:44:28
Medford, OR	122w52	42N19	8:11:28
Melbourne, FL	80w37	28N05	5:22:28
Melrose, MA	71w04	42N27	4:44:16
Memphis, TN	90w03	35N08	6:00:12
Menlo Park, CA	122w12	37N27	8:08:48
Menomonee Falls, WI	88w07	43N11	5:52:28
Mentor, OH	81w21	41N40	5:25:24
Merced, CA	120w29	37N18	8:01:56
Meriden, CT	72w48	41N32	4:51:12
Meridian, MS	88w42	32N22	5:54:48
Merrick, NY	73w33	40N40	4:54:12
Merritt Island, FL	80w42	28N21	5:22:48
Mesa, AZ	111w50	33N25	7:27:20
Mesquite, TX	96w36	32N46	6:26:24
Metairie, LA	90w10	29N58	6:00:40
Methuen, MA	71w11	42N44	4:44:44
Miami, FL	80w11	25N47	5:20:44
Miami Beach, FL	80w08	25N47	5:20:32
Michigan City, IN	86w54	41N43	5:47:36
Middletown, CT	72w39	41N34	4:50:36
Middletown, OH	84w24	39N31	5:37:36
Middletown, RI	71w18	41N33	4:45:12
Midland, MI	84w14	43N37	5:36:56
Midland, TX	102w05	32N00	6:48:20
Midwest City, OK	97w24	35N27	6:29:36
Milford, CT	73w04	41N14	4:52:16
Millbrae, CA	122w24	37N36	8:09:36
Millcreek, UT	111w51	40N43	7:27:24
Milpitas, CA	121w55	37N26	8:07:40
Milton, MA	71w05	42N15	4:44:20
Milwaukee, WI	87w55	43N02	5:51:40
Minneapolis, MN	93w16	44N59	6:13:04
Minnetonka, MN	93w27	44N56	6:13:48
Minot, ND	101w18	48N14	6:45:12
Mishawaka, IN	86w11	41N40	5:44:44
Missoula, MT	114w01	46N52	7:36:04
Mobile, AL	88w03	30N41	5:52:12
Modesto, CA	121w00	37N39	8:04:00
Moline, IL	90w31	41N30	6:02:04
Monroe, LA	92w07	32N30	6:08:28
Monroeville, PA	79w45	40N26	5:19:00
Monrovia, CA	118w00	34N09	7:52:00
Montclair, CA	117w41	34N06	7:50:44
Montclair, NJ	74w13	40N49	4:56:52
Montebello, CA	118w07	34N00	7:52:28
Monterey, CA	121w55	36N37	8:07:40
Monterey Park, CA	118w08	34N04	7:52:32
Montgomery, AL	86w19	32N23	5:45:16
Montpelier, VT	72w35	44N16	4:50:20
Moorhead, MN	96w45	46N53	6:27:00
Morgantown, WV	79w57	39N38	5:19:48
Morton Grove, IL	87w46	42N02	5:51:04
Mountain View, CA	122w05	37N23	8:08:20
Mount Lebanon, PA	80w03	40N23	5:20:12
Mount Prospect, IL	87w56	42N04	5:51:44
Mount Vernon, NY	73w49	40N55	4:55:16
Muncie, IN	85w23	40N12	5:41:32
Murfreesboro, TN	86w24	35N51	5:45:36
Muskegon, MI	86w16	43N14	5:45:04
Muskogee, OK	95w22	35N45	6:21:28
Nansemond, VA	76w40	36N43	5:06:40
Napa, CA	122w17	38N18	8:09:08
Nashua, NH	71w28	42N45	4:45:52
Nashville, TN	86w47	36N10	5:47:08
Natick, MA	71w21	42N17	4:45:24
National City, CA	117w06	32N41	7:48:24
Needham, MA	71w14	42N17	4:44:56
New Albany, IN	85w49	38N18	5:43:16
Newark, CA	122w02	37N32	8:08:08
Newark, NJ	74w10	40N44	4:56:40
Newark, OH	82w24	40N03	5:29:36
New Bedford, MA	70w56	41N38	4:43:44
New Berlin, WI	88w06	42N59	5:52:24
New Britain, CT	72w47	41N40	4:51:08
New Brunswick, NJ	74w27	40N30	4:57:48
Newburgh, NY	74w01	41N30	4:56:04
New Castle, PA	80w21	41N00	5:21:24
New City, NY	73w59	41N09	4:55:56
New Haven, CT	72w55	41N18	4:51:40
New Iberia, LA	91w49	30N01	6:07:16
Newington, CT	72w45	41N43	4:51:00
New London, CT	72w06	41N22	4:48:24
New Orleans, LA	90w04	29N58	6:00:16
Newport, KY	84w30	39N05	5:38:00
Newport, RI	71w19	41N29	4:45:16
Newport Beach, CA	117w56	33N37	7:51:44
Newport News, VA	76w25	36N59	5:05:40
New Rochelle, NY	73w47	40N55	4:55:08
Newton, MA	71w12	42N21	4:44:48
New York, NY	74w00	40N43	4:56:00
Niagara Falls, NY	79w03	43N06	5:16:12
Niles, IL	87w48	42N02	5:51:12
Norfolk, VA	76w17	36N51	5:05:08
Normal, IL	88w59	40N31	5:55:56
Norman, OK	97w26	35N13	6:29:44

Norristown, PA	75w21	40n07	5:01:24
Northampton, MA	72w38	42n19	4:50:32
North Babylon, NY	73w19	40n44	4:53:16
North Bergen, NJ	74w01	40n48	4:56:04
Northbrook, IL	87w50	42n08	5:51:20
North Chicago, IL	87w51	42n19	5:51:24
Northglenn, CO	104w58	39n53	6:59:52
North Highlands, CA	121w23	38n40	8:05:32
North Las Vegas, NV	115w07	36n12	7:40:28
North Little Rock, AR	92w16	34n46	6:09:04
North Miami, FL	80w11	25n54	5:20:44
North Miami Beach, FL	80w10	25n56	5:20:40
North Olmsted, OH	81w56	41n25	5:27:44
North Tonawanda, NY	78w53	43n02	5:15:32
Norwalk, CA	118w05	33n54	7:52:20
Norwalk, CT	73w22	41n07	4:53:28
Norwich, CT	72w05	41n31	4:48:20
Norwood, MA	71w12	42n12	4:44:48
Norwood, OH	84w27	39n10	5:37:48
Novato, CA	122w35	38n06	8:10:20
Nutley, NJ	74w09	40n49	4:56:36
Oakland, CA	122w16	37n49	8:09:04
Oak Lawn, IL	87w44	41n43	5:50:56
Oak Park, IL	87w47	41n53	5:51:08
Oak Park, MI	83w11	42n28	5:32:44
Oak Ridge, TN	84w16	36n01	5:37:04
Oceanside, CA	117w23	33n12	7:49:32
Oceanside, NY	73w38	40n38	4:54:32
Odessa, TX	102w23	31n52	6:49:32
Ogden, UT	111w58	41n13	7:27:52
Oildale, CA	119w01	35n25	7:56:04
Oklahoma City, OK	97w30	35n30	6:30:00
Olympia, WA	122w53	47n03	8:11:32
Omaha, NE	96w01	41n17	6:24:04
Ontario, CA	117w39	34n04	7:50:36
Orange, CA	117w51	33n47	7:51:24
Orange, NJ	74w14	40n46	4:56:56
Orem, UT	111w42	40n19	7:26:48
Orlando, FL	81w23	28n33	5:25:32
Oshkosh, WI	88w33	44n01	5:54:12
Ottumwa, IA	92w25	41n01	6:09:40
Overland Park, KS	94w40	38n58	6:18:40
Owensboro, KY	87w07	37n46	5:48:28
Oxnard, CA	119w11	34n12	7:56:44
Pacifica, CA	122w30	37n36	8:10:00
Paducah, KY	88w37	37n05	5:54:28
Palatine, IL	88w03	42n07	5:52:12
Palm Springs, CA	116w33	33n50	7:46:12
Palo Alto, CA	122w10	37n27	8:08:40
Panama City, FL	85w40	30n10	5:42:40
Paramount, CA	118w10	33n53	7:52:40
Paramus, NJ	74w04	40n55	4:56:16
Parkersburg, WV	81w34	39n16	5:26:16
Park Forest, IL	87w40	41n29	5:50:40
Park Ridge, IL	87w51	42n02	5:51:24
Parkville, MD	76w33	39n23	5:06:12
Parma, OH	81w43	41n23	5:26:52
Parma Heights, OH	81w46	41n23	5:27:04
Pasadena, CA	118w09	34n09	7:52:36
Pasadena, TX	95w13	29n43	6:20:52
Pascagoula, MS	88w33	30n21	5:54:12
Passaic, NJ	74w07	40n51	4:56:28
Paterson, NJ	74w11	40n55	4:56:44
Pawtucket, RI	71w23	41n53	4:45:32
Peabody, MA	70w56	42n31	4:43:44
Pekin, IL	89w40	40n35	5:58:40
Penn Hills, PA	79w52	40n28	5:19:28
Pennsauken, NJ	75w03	39n58	5:00:12
Pensacola, FL	87w13	30n25	5:48:52
Peoria, IL	89w36	40n42	5:58:24
Perth Amboy, NJ	74w16	40n31	4:57:04
Petaluma, CA	122w39	38n14	8:10:36
Petersburg, VA	77w24	37n14	5:09:36
Phenix City, AL	85w00	32n28	5:40:00
Philadelphia, PA	75w10	39n57	5:00:40
Phoenix, AZ	112w04	33n27	7:28:16
Pico Rivera, CA	118w07	33n58	7:52:28
Pierre, SD	100w21	44n22	6:41:24
Pine Bluff, AR	92w01	34n13	6:08:04
Piscataway, NJ	74w27	40n34	4:57:48
Pittsburg, CA	121w53	38n02	8:07:32
Pittsburgh, PA	80w01	40n26	5:20:04
Pittsfield, MA	73w15	42n27	4:53:00
Placentia, CA	117w52	33n52	7:51:28
Plainfield, NJ	74w25	40n37	4:57:40
Plainview, NY	73w29	40n46	4:53:56
Pleasant Hill, CA	122w03	37n57	8:08:12
Pocatello, ID	112w27	42n52	7:29:48
Pomona, CA	117w45	34n04	7:51:00
Pompano Beach, FL	80w08	26n14	5:20:32
Ponca City, OK	97w05	36n42	6:28:20
Pontiac, MI	83w18	42n38	5:33:12
Portage, MI	85w35	42n12	5:42:20
Port Arthur, TX	93w56	29n54	6:15:44
Port Chester, NY	73w40	41n00	4:54:40
Port Huron, MI	82w26	42n58	5:29:44
Portland, ME	70w16	43n39	4:41:04
Portland, OR	122w37	45n32	8:10:28
Portsmouth, NH	70w45	43n05	4:43:00
Portsmouth, OH	83w00	38n44	5:32:00
Portsmouth, VA	76w18	36n50	5:05:12
Pottstown, PA	75w39	40n15	5:02:36
Poughkeepsie, NY	73w56	41n42	4:55:44
Prairie Village, KS	94w38	39n00	6:18:32
Prichard, AL	88w05	30n44	5:52:20
Providence, RI	71w24	41n49	4:45:36
Provo, UT	111w39	40n14	7:26:36
Pueblo, CO	104w36	38n14	6:58:24
Queens, NY	73w52	40n43	4:55:28
Quincy, IL	91w23	39n56	6:05:32
Quincy, MA	71w00	42n15	4:44:00
Racine, WI	87w48	42n44	5:51:12
Rahway, NJ	74w16	40n37	4:57:04
Raleigh, NC	78w38	35n46	5:14:32
Rancho Cordova, CA	121w18	38n36	8:05:12
Randolph, MA	71w02	42n10	4:44:08
Rantoul, IL	88w09	40n19	5:52:36
Rapid City, SD	103w14	44n05	6:52:56
Raytown, MO	94w28	39n01	6:17:52
Reading, PA	75w56	40n20	5:03:44
Redford, MI	83w18	42n23	5:33:12
Redlands, CA	117w11	34n04	7:48:44
Redondo Beach, CA	118w23	33n50	7:53:32
Redwood City, CA	122w15	37n30	8:09:00
Rego Park, NY	73w52	40n44	4:55:28
Reno, NV	119w48	39n31	7:59:12
Renton, WA	122w12	47n29	8:08:48
Revere, MA	71w01	42n25	4:44:04
Rialto, CA	117w22	34n06	7:49:28
Richardson, TX	96w44	32n57	6:26:56
Richfield, MN	93w17	44n53	6:13:08
Richland, WA	119w18	46n17	7:57:12
Richmond, CA	122w21	37n56	8:09:24
Richmond, IN	84w54	39n50	5:39:36
Richmond, VA	77w27	37n33	5:09:48
Ridgewood, NJ	74w07	40n59	4:56:28
Riverside, CA	117w22	33n59	7:49:28
Riverton Heights, WA	122w17	47n28	8:09:08
Roanoke, VA	79w56	37n16	5:19:44
Rochester, MN	92w28	44n01	6:09:52
Rochester, NY	77w37	43n10	5:10:28
Rockford, IL	89w06	42n16	5:56:24
Rock Hill, SC	81w01	34n56	5:24:04
Rock Island, IL	90w34	41n30	6:02:16
Rockville, MD	77w09	39n05	5:08:36
Rockville Centre, NY	73w39	40n40	4:54:36
Rocky Mount, NC	77w48	35n57	5:11:12
Rome, GA	85w10	34n15	5:40:40
Rome, NY	75w27	43n13	5:01:48
Rosemead, CA	118w04	34n05	7:52:16
Roseville, MI	82w56	42n30	5:31:44
Roseville, MN	93w10	45n01	6:12:40
Roswell, NM	104w32	33n24	6:58:08
Rotterdam, NY	74w01	42n48	4:56:04
Royal Oak, MI	83w09	42n30	5:32:36
Sacramento, CA	121w29	38n35	8:05:56
Saginaw, MI	83w56	43n26	5:35:44
Saint Charles, MO	90w29	38n47	6:01:56
Saint Clair Shores, MI	82w53	42n30	5:31:32
Saint Cloud, MN	94w10	45n34	6:16:40
Saint Joseph, MO	94w50	39n46	6:19:20
Saint Louis, MO	90w12	38n37	6:00:48
Saint Louis Park, MN	93w21	44n57	6:13:24
Saint Paul, MN	93w06	44n57	6:12:24
Saint Petersburg, FL	82w39	27n46	5:30:36
Salem, MA	70w53	42n31	4:43:32
Salem, OR	123w02	44n56	8:12:08
Salina, KS	97w37	38n50	6:30:28
Salinas, CA	121w39	36n40	8:06:36
Salt Lake City, UT	111w53	40n45	7:27:32
San Angelo, TX	100w26	31n28	6:41:44
San Antonio, TX	98w30	29n25	6:34:00
San Bernardino, CA	117w19	34n07	7:49:16
San Bruno, CA	122w25	37n38	8:09:40
San Carlos, CA	122w16	37n31	8:09:04
San Diego, CA	117w09	32n43	7:48:36
Sandusky, OH	82w42	41n27	5:30:48
San Francisco, CA	122w25	37n47	8:09:40
San Gabriel, CA	118w06	34n06	7:52:24
San Jose, CA	121w53	37n20	8:07:32
San Leandro, CA	122w09	37n44	8:08:36
San Lorenzo, CA	122w07	37n41	8:08:28
San Luis Obispo, CA	120w40	35n17	8:02:40
San Mateo, CA	122w19	37n34	8:09:16
San Rafael, CA	122w32	37n58	8:10:08
Santa Ana, CA	117w52	33n46	7:51:28
Santa Barbara, CA	119w42	34n25	7:58:48
Santa Clara, CA	121w57	37n21	8:07:48
Santa Cruz, CA	122w01	36n58	8:08:04
Santa Fe, NM	105w57	35n41	7:03:48
Santa Maria, CA	120w26	34n57	8:01:44
Santa Monica, CA	118w29	34n01	7:53:56
Santa Rosa, CA	122w43	38n26	8:10:52
Sarasota, FL	82w32	27n20	5:30:08
Saratoga, CA	122w02	37n16	8:08:08
Saugus, MA	71w01	42n28	4:44:04
Savannah, GA	81w06	32n05	5:24:24
Sayreville, NJ	74w22	40n28	4:57:28
Schenectady, NY	73w57	42n49	4:55:48
Scottsdale, AZ	111w56	33n29	7:27:44
Scranton, PA	75w40	41n25	5:02:40
Seal Beach, CA	118w06	33n44	7:52:24
Seaside, CA	121w50	36n37	8:07:20
Seattle, WA	122w20	47n36	8:09:20
Selma, AL	87w01	32n25	5:48:04
Shaker Heights, OH	81w32	41n29	5:26:08
Shawnee, OK	96w55	35n20	6:27:40
Sheboygan, WI	87w45	43n46	5:51:00
Shelton, CT	73w05	41n19	4:52:20
Sherman, TX	96w36	33n38	6:26:24
Shreveport, LA	98w45	32n31	6:15:00
Silver Spring, MD	77w02	38n59	5:08:08
Simi, CA	118w47	34n16	7:55:08
Sioux City, IA	96w23	42n30	6:25:32
Sioux Falls, SD	96w44	43n33	6:26:56
Skokie, IL	87w45	42n03	5:51:00
Somerville, MA	71w06	42n23	4:44:24
South Bend, IN	86w15	41n41	5:45:00
South Euclid, OH	81w32	41n31	5:26:08
Southfield, MI	83w17	42n29	5:33:08
South Gate, CA	118w12	33n57	7:52:48
Southgate, MI	83w12	42n12	5:32:48
South Lake Tahoe, CA	119w58	38n56	7:59:52
South Pasadena, CA	118w09	34n07	7:52:36
South Saint Paul, MN	93w02	44n53	6:12:08
South San Francisco, CA	122w24	37n39	8:09:36
South Whittier, CA	118w02	33n56	7:52:08
Spartanburg, SC	81w57	34n56	5:27:48
Spokane, WA	117w24	47n40	7:49:36
Springfield, MA	72w35	42n06	4:50:20
Springfield, MO	93w17	37n13	6:13:08
Springfield, OH	83w49	39n55	5:35:16
Springfield, OR	123w01	44n03	8:12:04
Springfield-Delaware, PA	75w24	39n55	5:01:36
Spring Valley, CA	117w00	32n45	7:48:00
Stamford, CT	73w32	41n03	4:54:08
State College, PA	77w52	40n48	5:11:28
Staten Island, NY	74w07	40n35	4:56:28
Sterling Heights, MI	83w02	42n35	5:32:08
Steubenville, OH	80w37	40n22	5:22:28
Stillwater, OK	97w04	36n07	6:28:16
Stockton, CA	121w17	37n58	8:05:08
Stratford, CT	73w08	41n12	4:52:32
Suitland, MD	76w56	38n51	5:07:44
Sunnyvale, CA	122w02	37n23	8:08:08
Superior, WI	92w06	46n44	6:08:24
Syracuse, NY	76w09	43n03	5:04:36
Tacoma, WA	122w26	47n14	8:09:44
Tallahassee, FL	84w17	30n27	5:37:08
Tampa, FL	82w27	27n57	5:29:48
Taunton, MA	71w06	41n54	4:44:24
Taylor, MI	83w16	42n14	5:33:04
Teaneck, NJ	74w01	40n53	4:56:04
Tempe, AZ	111w56	33n25	7:27:44
Temple, TX	97w21	81n06	6:29:24
Temple City, CA	118w01	34n07	7:52:04
Terre Haute, IN	87w25	39n28	5:49:40
Texarkana, TX	94w03	33n26	6:16:12
Texas City, TX	94w54	29n24	6:19:36
Thousand Oaks, CA	118w50	34n10	7:55:20
Titusville, FL	80w49	28n37	5:23:16
Toledo, OH	83w33	41n39	5:34:12
Topeka, KS	95w40	39n03	6:22:40
Torrance, CA	118w19	33n50	7:53:16
Torrington, CT	73w07	41n48	4:52:28
Town Of Tonawanda, NY	78w52	42n59	5:15:28
Towson, MD	76w36	39n24	5:06:24
Trenton, NJ	74w46	40n14	4:59:04
Troy, MI	83w09	42n37	5:32:36
Troy, NY	73w41	42n44	4:54:44
Trumbull, CT	73w12	41n15	4:52:48
Tucson, AZ	110w58	32n13	7:23:52
Tulsa, OK	95w55	36n10	6:23:40
Tuscaloosa, AL	87w34	33n12	5:50:16
Tustin, CA	117w49	33n44	7:51:16
Tyler, TX	95w18	32n21	6:21:12
Union, NJ	74w17	40n42	4:57:08
Union City, NJ	74w02	40n45	4:56:08
University City, MO	90w20	38n40	6:01:20
Upland, CA	117w39	34n06	7:50:36
Upper Arlington, OH	83w04	40n00	5:32:16
Upper Darby, PA	75w16	39n58	5:01:04
Urbana, IL	88w12	40n07	5:52:48
Utica, NY	75w14	43n06	5:00:56
Vacaville, CA	121w59	38n21	8:07:56
Valdosta, GA	83w17	30n50	5:33:08
Vallejo, CA	122w15	38n07	8:09:00
Valley Stream, NY	73w42	40n40	4:54:48
Vancouver, WA	122w40	45n38	8:10:40
Van Nuys, CA	118w26	34n11	7:53:44
Ventura, CA	119w18	34n17	7:57:12
Vernon, CT	72w29	41n49	4:49:56
Vicksburg, MS	90w53	32n21	6:03:32
Victoria, TX	97w00	28n48	6:28:00
Villa Park, IL	87w59	41n53	5:51:56
Vineland, NJ	75w02	39n29	5:00:08
Virginia Beach, VA	75w59	36n51	5:03:56
Visalia, CA	119w18	36n20	7:57:12
Vista, CA	117w14	33n12	7:48:56
Waco, TX	97w09	31n33	6:28:36
Wakefield, MA	71w04	42n30	4:44:16
Wallingford, CT	72w50	41n27	4:51:20
Walnut Creek, CA	122w04	37n54	8:08:16
Waltham, MA	71w14	42n23	4:44:56
Warminster, PA	75w06	40n12	5:00:24
Warner Robins, GA	83w36	32n37	5:34:24
Warren, MI	83w02	42n31	5:32:08
Warren, OH	80w49	41n14	5:23:16
Warwick, RI	71w28	41n42	4:45:52
Washington, DC	77w01	38n53	5:08:04
Waterbury, CT	73w03	41n33	4:52:12

Waterloo, IA	92w21	42N30	6:09:24
Watertown, MA	71w11	42N22	4:44:44
Watertown, NY	75w55	43N59	5:03:40
Waukegan, IL	87w50	42N22	5:51:20
Waukesha, WI	88w14	43N01	5:52:56
Wausau, WI	89w38	44N58	5:58:32
Wauwatosa, WI	88w00	43N03	5:52:00
Wayne, NJ	74w17	40N55	4:57:08
Webster Groves, MO	90w22	38N35	6:01:28
Weirton, WV	80w35	40N24	5:22:20
Wellesley, MA	71w18	42N18	4:45:12
West Allis, WI	88w00	43N01	5:52:00
West Babylon, NY	73w21	40N42	4:53:24
West Covina, CA	117w54	34N04	7:51:36
Westfield, MA	72w45	42N07	4:51:00
Westfield, NJ	74w21	40N39	4:57:24
West Hartford, CT	72w44	41N45	4:50:56
West Haven, CT	72w57	41N17	4:51:48
West Hempstead, NY	73w38	40N42	4:54:32
West Hollywood, CA	118w22	34N05	7:53:28
West Islip, NY	73w18	40N42	4:53:12
Westland, MI	83w23	42N18	5:33:32
West Memphis, AR	90w11	35N09	6:00:44
West Mifflin, PA	79w52	40N22	5:19:28
Westminster, CA	118w00	33N47	7:52:00
West New York, NJ	74w01	40N47	4:56:04
West Orange, NJ	74w14	40N47	4:56:56
West Palm Beach, FL	80w03	26N43	5:20:12
Westport, CT	73w22	41N09	4:53:28
West Seneca, NY	78w48	42N51	5:15:12
West Springfield, MA	72w38	42N06	4:50:32
Wethersfield, CT	72w40	41N42	4:50:40
Weymouth, MA	70w58	42N13	4:43:52
Wheat Ridge, CO	105w05	39N46	7:00:20
Wheaton, IL	88w06	41N52	5:52:24
Wheaton, MD	77w03	39N03	5:08:12
Wheeling, WV	80w43	40N04	5:22:52
Whitehall, OH	82w54	39N58	5:31:36
White Plains, NY	73w46	41N02	4:55:04
Whittier, CA	118w03	33N58	7:52:12
Wichita, KS	97w20	37N42	6:29:20
Wichita Falls, TX	98w30	33N54	6:34:00
Wilkes-Barre, PA	75w53	41N15	5:03:32
Wilkinsburg, PA	79w53	40N26	5:19:32
Williamsport, PA	77w00	41N15	5:08:00
Willingboro, NJ	74w54	40N03	4:59:36
Willow Brook, CA	118w15	33N56	7:53:00
Wilmette, IL	87w42	42N05	5:50:48
Wilmington, DE	75w33	39N45	5:02:12
Wilmington, NC	77w55	34N14	5:11:40
Wilson, NC	77w55	35N44	5:11:40
Winona, MN	91w37	44N02	6:06:28
Winston-Salem, NC	80w15	36N06	5:21:00
Woburn, MA	71w09	42N29	4:44:36
Woodbridge, VA	77w15	38N40	5:09:00
Woodland, CA	121w46	38N41	8:07:04
Woodside, NY	73w55	40N45	4:55:40
Woonsocket, RI	71w31	42N00	4:46:04
Worcester, MA	71w48	42N16	4:47:12
Wyandotte, MI	83w09	42N12	5:32:36
Wyoming, MI	85w42	42N54	5:42:48
Xenia, OH	83w56	39N41	5:35:44
Yakima, WA	120w31	46N36	8:02:04
Yonkers, NY	73w54	40N56	4:55:36
York, PA	76w44	39N58	5:06:56
Youngstown, OH	80w39	41N06	5:22:36
Ypsilanti, MI	83w37	42N14	5:34:28
Yuma, AZ	114w37	32N43	7:38:28
Zanesville, OH	82w01	39N56	5:28:04
Adelaide, Australia	138E36	34S56	-9:14:24
Agra, India	78E00	27N09	-5:12:00
Agram, Yugoslavia	15E58	45N48	-1:03:52
Ahmadabad, India	72E35	23N02	-4:50:20
Aleppo, Syria	37E10	36N14	-2:28:40
Alexandria, Egypt	29E55	31N13	-1:59:40
Algiers, Algeria	3E08	36N42	-0:12:32
Allahabad, India	81E50	25N57	-5:27:20
Amritsar, India	74E56	31N35	-4:59:44
Amsterdam, Netherlands	4E54	52N21	-0:19:36
Ankara, Turkey	32E50	39N55	-2:11:20
Antwerp, Belgium	4E25	51N13	-0:17:40
Athens, Greece	23E44	38N00	-1:34:56
Auckland, New Zealand	174E45	36S53	-11:39:00
Baghdad, Iraq	44E25	33N20	-2:57:40
Baku, USSR	49E53	40N22	-3:19:32
Bangalore, India	77E35	12N58	-5:10:20
Bangkok, Thailand	100E30	13N44	-6:42:00
Barcelona, Spain	2E10	41N25	-0:08:40
Belem, Brazil	48w29	01S27	3:13:56
Belfast, N Ireland	5w55	54N35	0:23:40
Benares, India	83E00	25N20	-5:32:00
Beograd, Yugoslavia	20E30	44N50	-1:22:00
Berlin, Germany	13E25	52N32	-0:53:40
Birmingham, England	1w50	52N30	0:07:20
Bogota, Colombia	74w05	04N40	4:56:20
Bologna, Italy	11E20	44N30	-0:45:20
Bombay, India	72E51	18N56	-4:51:24
Bonn, Germany	7E06	50N44	-0:28:24
Bordeaux, France	0w34	44N50	0:02:16
Bremen, Germany	8E48	53N05	-0:35:12
Breslau, Poland	17E00	51N05	-1:08:00
Brisbane, Australia	153E00	27S30	-10:12:00
Bristol, England	2w35	51N27	0:10:20
Brno, Czechoslovakia	16E37	49N12	-1:06:28
Bruxelles, Belgium	4E21	50N50	-0:17:24
Bucharest, Rumania	26E07	44N25	-1:44:28
Budapest, Hungary	19E03	47N30	-1:16:12
Buenos Aires, Argentina	58w27	34S36	3:53:48
Cairo, Egypt	31E15	30N03	-2:05:00
Calcutta, India	88E21	22N35	-5:53:24
Canton, China	113E16	23N07	-7:33:04
Capetown, S Africa	18E28	33S56	-1:13:52
Casablanca, Morocco	7w35	33N39	0:30:20
Catania, Italy	15E06	37N31	-1:00:24
Cawnpore, India	80E20	26N28	-5:21:20
Changsha, China	113E00	28N10	-7:32:00
Charkov, USSR	36E15	50N00	-2:25:00
Chemnitz, Germany	12E55	50N50	-0:51:40
Chittagong, Pakistan	91E48	22N20	-6:07:12
Chungking, China	106E34	29N39	-7:06:16
Cologne, W Germany	6E59	50N56	-0:27:56
Colombo, Ceylon	79E52	06N55	-5:19:28
Cordoba, Argentina	64w11	31S24	4:16:44
Dacca, Pakistan	90E22	23N42	-6:01:28
Damascus, Syria	36E19	33N30	-2:25:16
Danzig, Poland	18E41	54N22	-1:14:44
Delhi, India	77E14	28N40	-5:08:56
Dnepropetrovsk, USSR	35E01	48N27	-2:20:04
Dortmund, Germany	7E27	51N32	-0:29:48
Dresden, Germany	13E45	51N03	-0:55:00
Dublin, Eire	6w15	53N20	0:25:00
Duisburg, Germany	6E45	51N26	-0:27:00
Durban, S Africa	31E00	29S53	-2:04:00
Dusseldorf, Germany	6E47	51N13	-0:27:08
Edinburgh, Scotland	3w13	55N57	0:12:52
Edmonton, Canada	113w28	53N33	7:33:52
Essen, W Germany	7E01	51N28	-0:28:04
Firenze, Italy	11E15	43N47	-0:45:00
Foochow, China	119E17	26N06	-7:57:08
Frankfurt, Germany	8E41	50N06	-0:34:44
Fukuoka, Japan	130E24	33N35	-8:41:36
Geneva, Switzerland	6E09	46N12	-0:24:36
Genoa, Italy	8E56	44N24	-0:35:44
Glasgow, Scotland	4w15	55N53	0:17:00
Gorki, USSR	44E00	56N20	-2:56:00
Goteborg, Sweden	12E00	57N45	-0:48:00
Greenwich, England	0w00	51N28	0:00:00
Guatemala, Guatemala	90w31	14N38	6:02:04
The Hague, Netherlands	4E16	52N05	-0:17:04
Hamburg, Germany	10E00	53N33	-0:40:00
Hamilton, Canada	79w51	43N15	5:19:24
Hangchow, China	120E07	30N15	-8:00:28
Hannover, Germany	9E44	52N23	-0:38:56
Harbin, China	126E41	45N45	-8:26:44
Havana, Cuba	82w25	23N07	5:29:40
Helsinki, Finland	25E00	60N08	-1:40:00
Hiroshima, Japan	132E27	34N23	-8:49:48
Hong Kong,	114E12	22N16	-7:36:48
Hyderabad, India	78E26	17N22	-5:13:44
Hyderabad, Pakistan	68E24	25N23	-4:33:36
Ibadan, Nigeria	3E56	07N23	-0:15:44
Indore, India	75E54	22N42	-5:03:36
Istanbul, Turkey	28E57	41N02	-1:55:48
Jakarta, Indonesia	106E45	06S08	-7:07:00
Jerusalem, Israel	35E13	31N47	-2:20:52
Johannesburg, S Africa	28E00	26S15	-1:52:00
Karachi, Pakistan	67E02	24N51	-4:28:08
Kazan, USSR	49E08	55N45	-3:16:32
Kiel, Germany	10E08	54N20	-0:40:32
Kiev, USSR	30E32	50N27	-2:02:08
Kjobenhavn, Denmark	12E34	55N43	-0:50:16
Koln, Germany	6E57	50N56	-0:27:48
Konigsberg, USSR	20E30	54N43	-1:22:00
Krakow, Poland	19E58	50N03	-1:19:52
Kuybyshev, USSR	50E09	53N12	-3:20:36
Kyoto, Japan	135E45	35N02	-9:03:00
Lahore, Pakistan	74E22	31N34	-4:57:28
Lanchow, China	103E45	36N01	-6:55:00
La Paz, Bolivia	68w10	16S30	4:32:40
Leeds, England	1w35	53N50	0:06:20
Leipzig, Germany	12E20	51N20	-0:49:20
Leningrad, USSR	30E15	59N55	-2:01:00
Liege, Belgium	5E35	50N38	-0:22:20
Lille, France	3E04	50N38	-0:12:16
Lima, Peru	77w03	12S06	5:08:12
Lisbon, Portugal	9w08	38N44	0:36:32
Liverpool, England	2w55	53N25	0:11:40
Lodz, Poland	19E28	51N49	-1:17:52
London, England	0w10	51N30	0:00:40
Lucknow, India	80E54	26N50	-5:23:36
Lwow, USSR	24E00	49N50	-1:36:00
Lyon, France	4E50	45N46	-0:19:20
Madras, India	80E18	13N05	-5:21:12
Madrid, Spain	3w43	40N25	0:14:52
Madurai, India	78E07	09N55	-5:12:28
Magdeburg, Germany	11E37	52N08	-0:46:28
Manchester, England	2w15	53N29	0:09:00
Manila, Philippines	120E59	14N36	-8:03:56
Mannheim, Germany	8E28	49N30	-0:33:52
Marseille, France	5E22	43N18	-0:21:28
Mecca, Saudi Arabia	39E49	21N26	-2:39:16
Melbourne, Australia	144E58	37S45	-9:39:52
Mexico, Mexico	99w10	19N25	6:36:40
Milano, Italy	9E12	45N28	-0:36:48
Monterrey, Mexico	100w19	25N40	6:41:16
Montevideo, Uruguay	56w10	34S53	3:44:40
Montreal, Canada	73w34	45N31	4:54:16
Moscow, USSR	37E35	55N45	-2:30:20
Mukden, China	123E26	41N50	-8:13:44
Munchen, Germany	11E35	48N08	-0:46:20
Nagoya, Japan	136E53	35N08	-9:07:32
Nagpur, India	79E04	21N08	-5:16:16
Nanking, China	118E47	32N03	-7:55:08
Naples, Italy	14E15	40N50	-0:57:00
Newcastle, England	1w35	54N59	0:06:20
Nice, France	7E16	43N42	-0:29:04
Nottingham, England	1w10	52N58	0:04:40
Novosibirsk, USSR	82E53	55N02	-5:31:32
Nurnberg, Germany	11E05	49N27	-0:44:20
Odessa, USSR	30E46	46N30	-2:03:04
Osaka, Japan	135E30	34N40	-9:02:00
Oslo, Norway	10E45	59N56	-0:43:00
Ottawa, Canada	75w42	45N25	5:02:48
Palermo, Italy	13E23	38N08	-0:53:32
Paris, France	2E20	48N52	-0:09:20
Patna, India	85E06	25N36	-5:40:24
Peking, China	116E25	39N55	-7:45:40
Perth, Australia	115E50	31S56	-7:43:20
Poona, India	73E54	18N31	-4:55:36
Porto, Portugal	8w36	41N11	0:34:24
Porto Alegre, Brazil	51w13	30S02	3:24:52
Portsmouth, England	1w05	50N48	0:04:20
Posen, Poland	16E53	52N25	-1:07:32
Praha, Czechoslovakia	14E25	50N05	-0:57:40
Rangoon, Burma	96E10	16N47	-6:24:40
Recife, Brazil	34w53	08S06	2:19:32
Riga, USSR	24E06	56N57	-1:36:24
Rio De Janeiro, Brazil	43w17	22S53	2:53:08
Rome, Italy	12E30	41N53	-0:50:00
Rosario, Argentina	60w40	33S00	4:02:40
Rostov, USSR	39E42	47N14	-2:38:48
Rotterdam, Netherlands	4E29	51N55	-0:17:56
Saigon, Vietnam	106E41	10N47	-7:06:44
Salvador, Brazil	38w31	12S59	2:34:04
Santiago, Chile	70w40	33S27	4:42:40
Sao Paulo, Brazil	46w39	23S33	3:06:36
Saratov, USSR	45E55	51N30	-3:03:40
Seoul, Korea	127E00	37N30	-8:28:00
Shanghai, China	121E25	31N13	-8:05:40
Sheffield, England	1w30	53N23	0:06:00
Sian, China	108E54	34N16	-7:15:36
Singapore, Singapore	103E50	01N20	-6:55:20
Sofia, Bulgaria	23E18	42N40	-1:33:12
Stalingrad, USSR	44E30	48N45	-2:58:00
Stalino, USSR	37E50	48N00	-2:31:20
Stettin, Poland	14E32	53N25	-0:58:08
Stockholm, Sweden	18E03	59N20	-1:12:12
Stoke On Trent, England	2w10	53N00	0:08:40
Stuttgart, Germany	9E12	48N47	-0:36:48
Surabaya, Indonesia	112E45	07S15	-7:31:00
Sverdlovsk, USSR	60E38	56N50	-4:02:32
Sydney, Australia	151E13	33S52	-10:04:52
Taipei, Taiwan	121E32	25N05	-8:06:08
Talien, China	121E37	38N53	-8:06:28
Tashkent, USSR	69E18	41N20	-4:37:12
Tbilisi, USSR	44E48	41N43	-2:59:12
Teheran, Iran	51E26	35N40	-3:25:44
Tel Aviv-Yafo, Israel	34E46	32N03	-2:19:04
Thessaloniki, Greece	22E58	40N38	-1:31:52
Tientsin, China	117E12	39N08	-7:48:48
Tokyo, Japan	139E45	35N40	-9:19:00
Toronto, Canada	79w25	43N42	5:17:40
Trieste, Italy	13E47	45N39	-0:55:08
Tsinan, China	117E00	36N41	-7:48:00
Tsingtao, China	120E22	36N04	-8:01:28
Turin, Italy	7E40	45N03	-0:30:40
Valencia, Spain	0w24	39N29	0:01:36
Vancouver, Canada	123w06	49N13	8:12:24
Venice, Italy	12E20	45N26	-0:49:20
Vienna, Austria	16E22	48N13	-1:05:28
Voronezh, USSR	39E10	51N40	-2:36:40
Warsaw, Poland	21E00	52N15	-1:24:00
Winnipeg, Canada	97w09	49N53	6:28:36
Wuhan, China	114E19	30N35	-7:37:16
Wuppertal, Germany	7E10	51N15	-0:28:40
Yokohama, Japan	139E39	35N27	-9:18:36
Zurich, Switzerland	8E33	47N23	-0:34:12